A

NEW AND REVISED EDITION

AN ENCYCLOPÆDIA OF FREEMASONRY AND ITS KINDRED SCIENCES

COMPRISING

THE WHOLE RANGE OF ARTS, SCIENCES AND LITERATURE AS CONNECTED WITH THE INSTITUTION

BY

ALBERT G. MACKEY, M.D., 33°

AUTHOR OF "THE HISTORY OF FREEMASONRY," "LEXICON OF FREEMASONRY," "A TEXT-BOOK OF MASONIC JURISPRUDENCE," "SYMBOLISM OF FREEMASONRY," ETC., ETC.

THIS NEW AND REVISED EDITION

PREPARED UNDER THE DIRECTION, AND WITH THE ASSISTANCE, OF THE LATE

WILLIAM J. HUGHAN, 32°

PAST GRAND DEACON (ENGLAND), PAST GRAND WARDEN (EGYPT), PAST GRAND WARDEN (IOWA), PAST ASSISTANT GRAND SOJOURNER (ENGLAND), ONE OF THE FOUNDERS QUATUOR CORONATI LODGE (LONDON); AUTHOR OF "ENGLISH MASONIC RITE," "OLD CHARGES," ETC.

BY

EDWARD L. HAWKINS, M.A., 30°

PROV. S. G. W. (SUSSEX), P. PROV. S. G. W. (OXFORDSHIRE), MEMBER QUATUOR CORONATI LODGE (LONDON), AUTHOR OF "CONCISE CYCLOPÆDIA OF FREEMASONRY"

PROFUSELY ILLUSTRATED

VOLUME II

ISBN: 978-1-63923-237-6

Printed: October 2022

Cover Art By: Amit Paul

Published and Distributed By:
Lushena Books
607 Country Club Drive, Unit E
Bensenville, IL 60106
www.lushenabks.com

ISBN: 978-1-63923-237-6

Yours fraternally

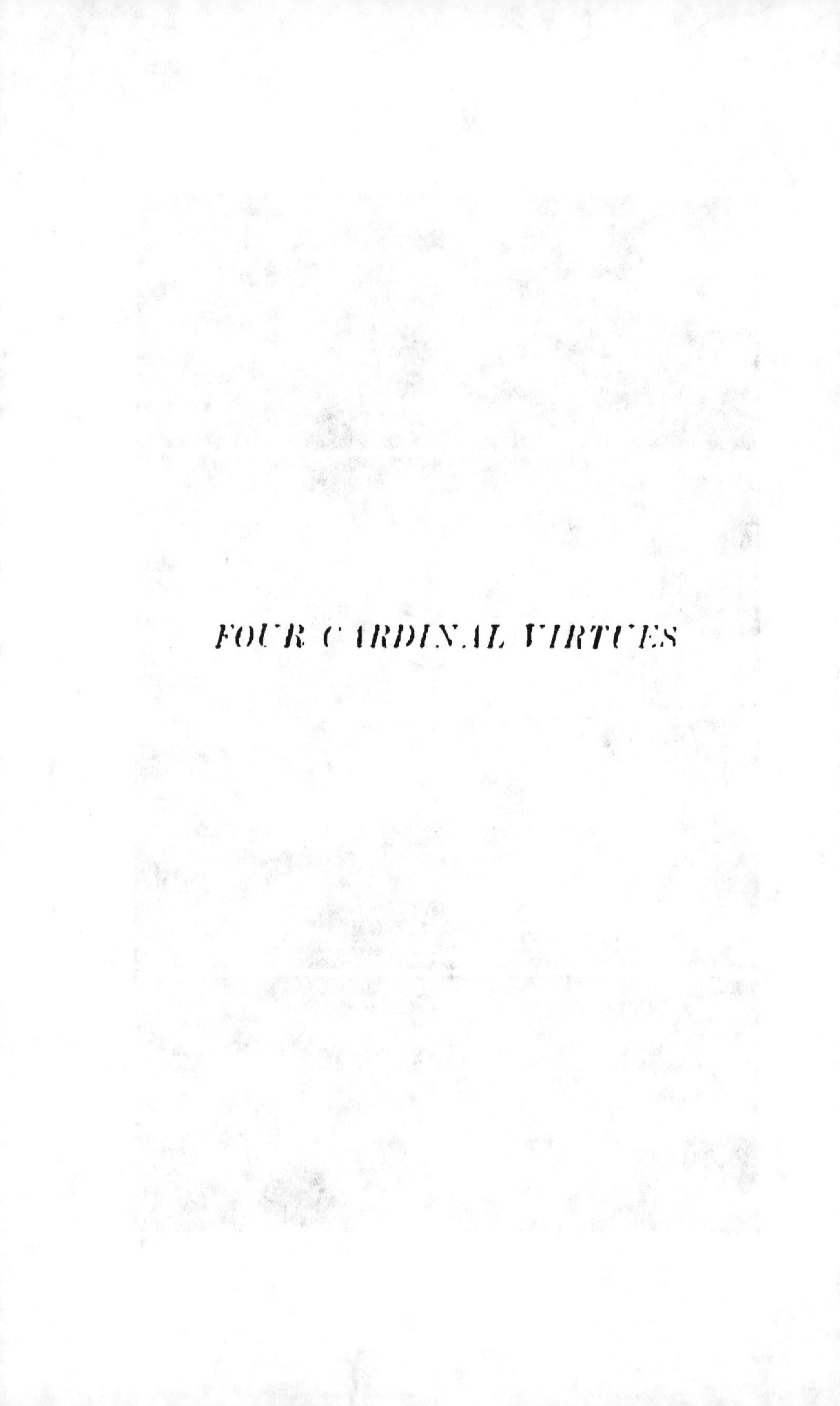

FOUR CARDINAL VIRTUES

A

NEW AND REVISED EDITION

AN ENCYCLOPÆDIA

OF

FREEMASONRY

AND

ITS KINDRED SCIENCES

COMPRISING

THE WHOLE RANGE OF ARTS, SCIENCES AND LITERATURE
AS CONNECTED WITH THE INSTITUTION

BY

ALBERT G. MACKEY, M.D., 33°

AUTHOR OF "THE HISTORY OF FREEMASONRY," "LEXICON OF FREEMASONRY," "A TEXT-BOOK OF MASONIC JURISPRUDENCE," "SYMBOLISM OF FREEMASONRY," ETC., ETC.

THIS NEW AND REVISED EDITION

PREPARED UNDER THE DIRECTION, AND WITH
THE ASSISTANCE, OF THE LATE

WILLIAM J. HUGHAN, 32°

PAST GRAND DEACON (ENGLAND), PAST GRAND WARDEN (EGYPT), PAST GRAND WARDEN (IOWA), PAST ASSISTANT GRAND SOJOURNER (ENGLAND), ONE OF THE FOUNDERS QUATUOR CORONATI LODGE (LONDON); AUTHOR OF "ENGLISH MASONIC RITE," "OLD CHARGES," ETC.

BY

EDWARD L. HAWKINS, M.A., 30°

PROV. S. G. W. (SUSSEX), P. PROV. S. G. W. (OXFORDSHIRE), MEMBER QUATUOR CORONATI LODGE (LONDON), AUTHOR OF "CONCISE CYCLOPÆDIA OF FREEMASONRY"

PROFUSELY ILLUSTRATED

VOLUME II

THE MASONIC HISTORY Co
All Rights Reserved
Manufactured in the United States of America by
R.R. DONNELLEY & SONS COMPANY
at
The Lakeside Press
CHICAGO, ILLINOIS

M

M. (Heb., מ, Mem), which signifies water in motion, having for its hieroglyph a waving line, referring to the surface of the water. As a numeral, M stands for 1000. In Hebrew its numerical value is 40. The sacred name of Deity, applied to this letter, is מברך, Meborach, Benedictus.

Maacha. In the Tenth Degree of the Scottish Rite we are informed that certain traitors fled to "Maacha king of Cheth," by whom they were delivered up to King Solomon on his sending for them. In 1 Kings ii. 39, we find it recorded that two of the servants of Shimei fled from Jerusalem to "Achish, son of Maachah king of Gath." There can be little doubt that the carelessness of the early copyists of the ritual led to the double error of putting *Cheth* for *Gath* and of supposing that Maacha was its king instead of its king's father. The manuscripts of the Ancient and Accepted Scottish Rite, too often copied by unlearned persons, show many such corruptions of Hebrew names, which modern researches must eventually correct. Delaunay, in his *Thuileur*, makes him King of Tyre, and calls him Mahakah.

Mac. Masonic writers have generally given to this word the meaning of "is smitten," deriving it probably from the Hebrew verb נכה, *macha*, to smite. Others, again, think it is the word מק, *mak*, rottenness, and suppose that it means "*he is rotten.*" Both derivations are, I think, incorrect.

Mac is a constituent part of the word *macbenac*, which is the substitute Master's word in the French Rite, and which is interpreted by the French ritualists as meaning "he lives in the son." But such a derivation can find no support in any known Hebrew root. Another interpretation must be sought. I think there is evidence, circumstantial at least, to show that the word was, if not an invention of the Ancient or Dermott Masons, at least adopted by them in distinction from the one used by the Moderns, which latter is the word now in use in this country. I am disposed to attribute the introduction of the word into Masonry to the adherents of the house of Stuart, who sought in every way to make the institution of Freemasonry a political instrument in their schemes for the restoration of their exiled monarch. Thus the old phrase, "the widow's son," was applied by them to James II., who was the son of Henrietta Maria, the widow of Charles I. So, instead of the old Master's word which had hitherto been used, they invented *macbenac* out of the Gaelic, which to them was, on account of their Highland supporters, almost a sacred language in the place of Hebrew. Now, in Gaelic, *Mac* is *son*, and *benach* is *blessed*, from the active verb *beannaich, to bless*. The latest dictionary published by the Highland Society gives this example: "Benach De Righ Albane, Alexander, Mac Alexander," etc., i. e., Bless the King of Scotland, Alexander, son of Alexander, etc. Therefore we find, without any of those distortions to which etymologists so often recur, that *macbenac* means in Gaelic "the *blessed son.*" This word the Stuart Masons applied to their idol, the Pretender, the son of Charles I.

Macbenac. 1. A significant word in the Third Degree according to the French Rite and some other rituals. (See *Mac.*)

2. In the Order of Beneficent Knights of the Holy City, the recipiendary, or novice, is called *Macbenac.*

Maccabees. A heroic family, whose patriotism and valor form bright pictures in the Jewish annals. The name is generally supposed to be derived from the letters מ. כ. ב. י., M. C. B. I.—which were inscribed upon their banners—being the initials of the Hebrew sentence, "Mi Camocha, Baalim, Iehovah," *Who is like unto thee among the gods, O Jehovah.* The Hebrew sentence has been appropriated in some of the high Scottish degrees as a significant word.

Macerio. Du Cange gives this as one of the Middle Age Latin words for *mason*, deriving it from *maceria*, a wall. The word is now never employed.

Macio. Du Cange (*Gloss.*) defines Macio, Mattio, or Machio, on the authority of Isidore, as Maçon, latomus, a mason, a constructor of walls, from *machina*, the machines on which they stood to work on account of the height of the walls. He gives *Maço* also.

Mackenzie, Kenneth R. H. ("Cryptonymus.") Editor of *The Royal Masonic Cyclopædia of History, Rites, Symbolism, and Biography*, published in London in 1877, by Bro. John Hogg, Paternoster Row. He was one of the founders of the present Rosicrucian Society in England.

Macon. The following is extracted from *Kenning's Cyclopædia of Freemasonry*: "The Norman-French word for 'mason'—as the operative mason in early days was called 'le macon,' and this was corrupted into maccon, maccouyn, masoun, masouyn, messouyn, and even mageon. The word seems to come from 'maçonner,' which had both its operative meaning and derivative meaning of conspiring, in 1238, and which again comes from 'mansio,' a word of classic use. Some writers have derived the word 'maçon' from maison; but though 'maisonner' and maçonner appear eventually to be equivalent to 'mansionem facere,' in its first meaning, 'maison' seems to be simply a wooden house, as 'maisonage' is defined by Roquefort to be 'Bois de charpente propre à batir les maisons,' and then he adds, 'C'est aussi l'action de batir.' Roquefort seems to prefer to derive 'maisonner' from the Low Latin verb 'mansionare.' Be this as it may, we have in the word maçon, as it appears to us, a clear evidence of the development of the operative guilds through the Norman-French artificers of the Conquest, who carried the operative guilds, as it were, back to Latin terminology, and to a Roman origin." (See *Mason.*)

Maçon dans la Voie Droite. (*The Mason in the Right Way.*) The second grade of the Hermetic system of Montpellier. (Thory, *Acta Lat.*, i., 321.)

Maçon du Secret. (*The Mason of the Secret.*) The sixth grade of the reformed rite of Baron Tschoudy, and the seventh in the reformed rite of St. Martin. (Thory, *Acta Lat.*, i., 321.)

Maçon, Ecossais, Maître. See *Mason, Scottish Master.*

Maçonetus. Low Latin, signifying a Mason, and found in documents of the fourteenth century.

Maçonne. A French word signifying a female Mason, that is to say, the degrees of the Rite of Adoption. It is a very convenient word. The formation of the Englishlanguage would permit the use of the equivalent word *Masoness*, if custom would sanction it.

Maconne Egyptienne. The Third Degree in Cagliostro's Rite of Adoption.

Maçonne Maîtresse. Third grade of the Maçonnerie d'Adoption.

Maçonner. Du Cange gives citations from documents of the fourteenth century, where this word is used as signifying *to build.*

Maconnerie Rouge. (*Red Freemasonry.*) The designation of the four high grades of the French Rite. Bazot says that the name comes from the color worn in the forth grade.

Maçonnieke Societeiten. Dutch Masonic Clubs, somewhat like unto the English Lodges of Instruction, with more, perhaps, of the character of a club. *Kenning's Cyclopædia* says "there were about nineteen of these associations in the principal towns of Holland in 1860."

"Macoy's Cyclopedia." "A General History, Clycopedia, and Dictionary of Freemasonry," containing some 300 engravings, by Robert Macoy, 33°, published in New York, which has passed through a number of editions. It was originally founded on *A Dictionary of Symbolical Masonry*, by George Oliver, D.D. Bro. Macoy has occupied the prominent position of Deputy G. Master of the G. Lodge of New York, and that of G. Recorder of the State G. Commandery of the Order of the Temple, K. T.

Macrocosm. (*μάκρος κόσμος, the great world.*) The visible system of worlds; the outer world or universe. It is opposed to Microcosm, the little world, as in man. It has been used as the Macric soul in opposition to the Micric animal life, and as the soul of the universe as opposed to the soul of a single world or being. A subject of much note to the Rosicrucians in the study of the Mysterium Magnum.

Maczo. Latin of the Middle Ages for a *mason.* Du Cange quotes a Computum of the year 1324, in which it is said that the work was done "per manum Petri, macsonis de Lagnicio."

Made. A technical word signifying initiated into Masonry. (See *Make.*)

Madman. Madmen are specially designated in the oral law as disqualified for initiation. (See *Qualifications.*)

Magazine. The earliest Masonic magazine was published at Leipsic in 1738 and named *Der Freymaurer.* In 1783 the *Freimaurerzeitung* appeared at Berlin, having only a short existence of six numbers. The *Journal für Freimaurer*, which appeared in 1784 at Vienna, had a longer life of some three years. In England, the first work of this kind was *The Freemasons' Magazine or General and Complete Library*, begun in 1793, and continued until 1798. In Ireland, in 1792, the *Sentimental and Masonic Magazine* appeared and ran to seven volumes (1792–5). In France the *Miroir de la vérité* seems to have been issued from 1800 to 1802, followed by *Hermes* in 1808.

In England the *Freemasons' Quarterly Review* commenced in 1834 and was continued until 1849, followed by the *Freemasons' Quarterly Magazine* in 1853, which lived until 1858. In 1873 a new *Masonic Magazine* was issued, but it had not a very long existence; and the nearest approach to a Masonic magazine now existing is the *Ars Quatuor Coronatorum*, published by the Quatuor Coronati Lodge. Of American Masonic magazines the earliest is the *Freemasons' Magazine and General Miscellany*, published at Philadelphia in 1811. The oldest periodical devoted to Masonry is the *Freemasons' Monthly Magazine*, published by Charles W. Moore, at Boston. It was established in the year 1842.

The *American Freemason* appears monthly, published at Storm Lake, Iowa, and has now reached a third volume; *The American Tyler-Keystone*, published at Ann Arbor, Michigan, twice a month, is in its 26th volume.

In Switzerland the "International Bureau for Masonic Affairs" issues a quarterly magazine, called the *Bulletin*, which is now in its 9th volume. [E. L. H.]

Magi. The ancient Greek historians so term the hereditary priests among the Persians and Medians. The word is derived from *mog* or *mag*, signifying priest in the Pehlevi language. The Illuminati first introduced the word into Masonry, and employed it in the nomenclature of their degrees to signify men of superior wisdom.

Magi, The Three. The "Wise Men of the East" who came to Jerusalem, bringing gifts to the infant Jesus. The traditional names of the three are Melchior, an old man, with a long beard, offering gold; Jasper, a beardless youth, who offers frankincense; Balthasar, a black or Moor, with a large spreading beard, who tenders myrrh. The patron saints of travelers. "Tradition fixed their number at three, probably in allusion to the three races springing from the sons of Noah. The Empress Helena caused their corpses to be transported to Milan from Constantinople. Frederick Barbarossa carried them to Cologne, the place of their special glory as the Three Kings of Cologne."—YONGE. The three principal officers ruling the society of the Rosicrucians are styled Magi.

Magic. The idea that any connection exists between Freemasonry and magic is to be attributed to the French writers, especially to Ragon, who gives many pages of his *Masonic Orthodoxy* to the subject of Masonic magic; and still more to Louis Constance, who has written three large volumes on the *History of Magic*, on the *Ritual and Dogma of the Higher Magic*, and on the *Key of the Grand Mysteries*, in all of which he seeks to trace an intimate connection between the Masonic mysteries and the science of magic. Ragon designates this sort of Masonry by the name of "Occult Masonry." But he loosely confounds magic with the magism of the ancient Persians, the Medieval philosophy and modern magnetism, all of which, as identical sciences, were engaged in the investigation of the nature of man, the mechanism of his thoughts, the faculties of his soul, his power over nature, and the essence of the occult virtues of all things. Magism, he says, is to be found in the sentences of Zoroaster, in the hymns of Orpheus, in the invocations of the Hierophants, and in the symbols of Pythagoras; it is reproduced in the philosophy of Agrippa and of Cardan, and is recognized under the name of *Magic* in the marvelous results of magnetism. Cagliostro, it is well known, mingled with his Spurious Freemasonry the Superstitions of Magic and the Operations of Animal Magnetism. But the writers who have sought to establish a scheme of Magical Masonry refer almost altogether to the supposed power of mystical names or words, which they say is common to both Masonry and magic. It is certain that onomatology, or the science of names, forms a very interesting part of the investigations of the higher Masonry, and it is only in this way that any connection can be created between the two sciences. Much light, it must be confessed, is thrown on many of the mystical names in the higher degrees by the dogmas of magic; and hence magic furnishes a curious and interesting study for the Freemason.

Magicians, Society of the. A society founded at Florence, which became a division of the Brothers of Rose Croix. They wore in their Chapters the habit of members of the Inquisition.

Magic Squares. A magic square is a series of numbers arranged in an equal number of cells constituting a square figure, the enumeration of all of whose columns, vertically, horizontally, and diagonally, will give the same sum. The Oriental philosophers, and especially the Jewish Talmudists, have indulged in many fanciful speculations in reference to these magic squares, many of which were considered as talismans. The following figure of nine squares, containing the nine digits so arranged as to make fifteen when counted in every way, was of peculiar import:

4	9	2
3	5	7
8	1	6

There was no talisman more sacred than this among the Orientalists, when arranged in the following figure:

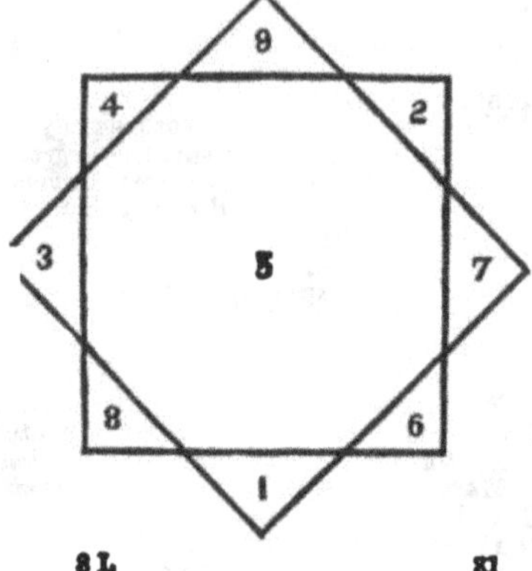

Thus arranged, they called it by the name of the planet Saturn, ZaHaL, because the sum of the 9 digits in the square was equal to 45 (1+2+3+4+5+6+7+8+9), which is the numerical value of the letters in the word ZaHaL, in the Arabic alphabet. The Talmudists also esteemed it as a sacred talisman, because 15 is the numerical value of the letters of the word יה, JaH, which is one of the forms of the Tetragrammaton.

The Hermetic philosophers called these magic squares "tables of the planets," and attributed to them many occult virtues. The table of Saturn consisted of 9 squares, and has just been given. The table of Jupiter consisted of 16 squares of numbers, whose total value is 136, and the sum of them added, horizontally, perpendicularly, and diagonally is always 34; thus:

4	14	15	1
9	7	6	12
5	11	10	8
16	2	3	13

So the table of Mars consists of 25 squares, of the Sun of 36, of Venus of 49, of Mercury of 64, and of the Moon of 81. These magic squares and their values have been used in the symbolism of numbers in some of the high degrees of Masonry.

Magister Cœmentariorum. A title applied in the Middle Ages to one who presided over the building of edifices = Master of the Masons.

Magister Hospitalis. See *Master of the Hospital.*

Magister Lapidum. Du Cange defines this as Master Mason; and he cites the statutes of Marseilles as saying: "Tres Magistros Lapidis bonos et legales," i. e., three good and lawful Master Masons "shall be selected to decide on all questions about water in the city."

Magister Militiæ Christi. See *Master of the Chivalry of Christ.*

Magister Perrerius. A name given in the Middle Ages to a Mason; literally, a Master of Stones, from the French *pierre*, a stone.

Magister Templi. See *Master of the Temple.*

Magistri Comacini. See *Comacine Masters*; also *Como.*

Magna est veritas et prævalebit. (*The truth is great, and will prevail.*) The motto of the Red Cross Degree, or Knights of the Red Cross.

Magnan, B. P. A marshal of France, nominated by Napoleon III., emperor, as Grand Master of the Grand Orient of France, in 1862, and, though not a member of the great Fraternity at the time, was initiated and installed Grand Master, February 8, 1862, and so remained until May 29, 1865.

Magnanimous. The title applied in modern usage to the Order of Knights Templar.

Magnetic Masonry. This is a form of Freemasonry which, although long ago practised by Cagliostro as a species of charlatanism, was first introduced to notice as a philosophic system by Ragon in his treatise on *Maçonnerie Occulte.* "The occult sciences," says this writer, "reveal to man the mysteries of his nature, the secrets of his organization, the means of attaining perfection and happiness; and, in short, the decree of his destiny. Their study was that of the high initiations of the Egyptians; it is time that they should become the study of modern Masons." And again he says: "A Masonic society which should establish in its bosom a *magnetic academy* would soon find the reward of its labors in the good that it would do, and the happiness which it would create." There can be no doubt that the Masonic investigator has a right to search everywhere for the means of moral, intellectual, and religious perfection; and if he can find anything in magnetism which would aid him in the search, it is his duty and wisest policy to avail himself of it. But, nevertheless, *Magnetic Masonry*, as a special *régime*, will hardly ever be adopted by the Fraternity.

Magus. 1. The Fourteenth Degree, and the first of the Greater Mysteries of the system of Illuminism. 2. The Ninth and last degree of the German Rosicrucians. It is the singular of *Magi*, which see.

Mah. The Hebrew interrogative pronoun מָה, signifying *what?* It is a component part of a significant word in Masonry. The combination *mahhah*, literally "what! the," is equivalent, according to the Hebrew method of ellipsis, to the question, "What! is this the ——?"

Mahabharata. A Sanskrit poem, recounting the rivalries of the descendants of King Bharata, and occupying a place among the Shasters of the Hindus. It contains many thousand verses, written at various unknown periods since the completion of the Ramayana.

Mahadeva. ("The great god.") One of the common names by which the Hindu god Siva is called. His consort, Durgà, is similarly styled Mahâdevi (the great goddess). In Buddhistic history, Mahadeva, who lived two hundred years after the death of the Buddha Sakyamuni, or 343, is a renowned teacher who caused a schism in the Buddhistic Church.

Mahakasyapa. The renowned disciple of Buddha Sakyamuni, who arranged the metaphysical portion of the sacred writings called Abhidharma.

Maher-Shalal-Hash-Baz. Hebrew. מהר שלל חש בז. Four Hebrew words which the prophet Isaiah was ordered to write upon a tablet, and which were afterward to be the name of his son. They signify, "make haste to the prey, fall upon the spoil," and were prognostic of the sudden attack of the Assyrians. They may be said, in their Masonic use, to be symbolic of the readiness for action which should distinguish a warrior, and are therefore of significant use in the system of Masonic Templarism.

Maier, Michael. A celebrated Rosicrucian and interpreter and defender of Rosicrucianism. He was born at Resinsburg, in Holstein, in 1568, and died at Magdeburg in 1620. He is said to have been the first to introduce Rosicrucianism into England. He wrote many works on the system, among which the most noted are *Atlanta Fugiens*, 1618; *Septimana Philosophica*, 1620; *De Fraternitate Rosæ Crucis*, 1618; and *Lusus Serius*, 1617. Some of his contemporaries having denied the existence of the Rosicrucian Order, Maier in his writings has refuted the calumny and warmly defended the society, of which, in one of his works, he speaks thus: "Like the Pythagoreans and Egyptians, the Rosicrucians exact vows of silence and secrecy. Ignorant men have treated the whole as a fiction; but this has arisen from the five years' probation to which they subject even well-qualified novices before they are admitted to the higher mysteries, and within this period they are to learn how to govern their own tongues."

Maine. Until the year 1820, the District of Maine composed a part of the political territory of the State of Massachusetts, and its Lodges were under the obedience of the Grand Lodge of Massachusetts. In that year, a political division having taken place, and Maine having been erected into an independent State, the Masons of Maine took the preliminary steps toward an independent Masonic organization, in obedience to the universally recognized law that political territory makes Masonic territory, and that changes of political jurisdiction are followed by corresponding changes of Masonic jurisdiction. A memorial was addressed to the Grand Lodge of Massachusetts praying for its consent to the organization of an independent Grand Lodge and a just division of the charity and other funds. A favorable response having been received, a convention was held at Portland on June 1, 1820, consisting of delegates from twenty-four Lodges, when the Grand Lodge of Maine was organized, and William King elected Grand Master.

The Grand Royal Arch Chapter was organized in 1821, the Grand Council of Royal Arch Masons in 1855, and the Grand Commandery in 1852.

Maitre Maçon. The name of the Third Degree in French.

Maitresse Agissante. Acting Mistress. The title of the presiding officer of a female Lodge in the Egyptian Rite of Cagliostro.

Maîtresse Maçon. The Third Degree of the French Rite of Adoption. We have no equivalent word in English. It signifies a Mistress in Masonry.

Maîtrise. This expressive word wants an equivalent in English. The French use la Maîtrise to designate the Third or Master's Degree.

Major. The Sixth Degree of the German Rose Croix.

Major Illuminate. (*Illuminatus Major.*) The Eighth Degree of the Illuminati of Bavaria.

Majority. Elections in Masonic bodies are as a general rule decided by a majority of the votes cast. A plurality vote is not admissible unless it has been provided for by a special by-law.

Make. "To make Masons" is a very ancient term; used in the oldest charges extant as synonymous with the verb to initiate or receive into the Fraternity. It is found in the Lansdowne MS., whose date is the latter half of the sixteenth century. "These be all the charges . . . read at the making of a Mason."

Malach. מלאך. An angel. A significant word in the high degrees. Lenning gives it as *Melek* or *Melech.*

Malachi or **Malachias.** The last of the prophets. A significant word in the Thirty-second Degree of the Scottish Rite.

Malcolm III. (King of Scotland.) Reported to have chartered the Lodge "St. John of Glasgow" in the year 1051.

Malcolm Canmore Charter. See *Manuscripts, Apocryphal.*

Mallet. One of the working-tools of a Mark Master, having the same emblematic meaning as the common gavel in the Entered Apprentice's Degree. It teaches us to correct the irregularities of temper, and, like enlightened reason, to curb the aspirations of unbridled ambition, to depress the malignity of envy, and to moderate the ebullition of anger. It removes from the mind all the excrescences of vice, and fits it, as a well-wrought stone, for that exalted station in the great temple of nature to which, as an emanation of the Deity, it is entitled.

The mallet or setting maul is also an emblem of the Third Degree, and is said to have been the implement by which the stones were set up at the Temple. It is often improperly confounded with the common gavel.

The French Masons, to whom the word *gavel* is unknown, uniformly use *maillet*, or mallet, in its stead, and confound its symbolic use, as the implement of the presiding officer, with the mallet of the English and American Mark Master.

Malta. Anciently, *Melita.* A small island in the Mediterranean Sea, which, although occupying only about 170 sq. miles, possessed for several centuries a greater degree of celebrity than was attached to any other territory of so little extent. It is now a possession of the British Government, but was occupied from 1530 to 1798 by the Knights Hospitalers, then called Knights of Malta, upon whom it was conferred in the former year by Charles V.

Malta, Cross of. See *Cross, Maltese.*

Malta, Knight of. See *Knight of Malta.*

Maltese Cross. See *Cross, Maltese.*

Man. 1. Man has been called the microcosm, or little world, in contradistinction to the macrocosm, or great world, by some fanciful writers on metaphysics, by reason of a supposed correspondence between the different parts and qualities of his nature and those of the universe. But in Masonic symbolism the idea is borrowed from Christ and the Apostles, who repeatedly refer to man as a symbol of the Temple.

2. A man was inscribed on the standard of the tribe of Reuben, and is borne on the Royal Arch banners as appropriate to the Grand Master of the second veil. It was also the charge in the third quarter of the arms of the Atholl Grand Lodge.

3. Der Mann, or the man, is the Second Degree of the German Union.

4. To be "a man, not a woman," is one of the qualifications for Masonic initiation. It is the first, and therefore the most important, qualification mentioned in the ritual.

Man or **Perfected Creation.** The symbol representing *perfected creation*, which is "very common on ancient Hindu monuments in China," embraces so many of the Masonic emblems, and so directly refers to several of the elementary principles taught in philosophic Masonry, that it is here introduced with its explanations. Forlong, in his *Faiths of Man*, gives this arrangement:

A—is the *Earth*, or foundation on which all build.

Wa—*Water*, as in an egg, or as condensed fire and ether.

Ra—*Fire*, or the elements in motion.

Ka—*Air*, or wind—Juno, or *Io* ni; a condensed element.

Cha—*Ether*, or Heaven, the cosmical *Former*.

This figure is frequently found in India:

As these symbols are readily interpretable by those conversant with Masonic hieroglyphs, it may be seen that the elements, in their ascending scale, show the perfected creation. Forlong remarks that "as it was difficult to show the *All-pervading Ether*, Egypt, for this purpose, surrounded her figures with a powder of stars instead of flame, which on Indra's garments were Yonis. This figure gradually developed, becoming in time a very concrete man, standing on two legs instead of a square base—the horns of the crescent (Air), being outstretched, formed the arms, and the refulgent Flame the head, which, with the Greeks and Romans, represented the Sun, or *Fire*, and gives Light to all. To this being, it was claimed, there were given seven senses; and thus, perfect and erect, stood Man, rising above the animal state."

The seven senses were seeing, hearing, tasting, feeling, smelling, understanding, and speech. See Ecclesiasticus xvii. 5:

"The Lord created man, and they received the use of the five operations of the Lord; and in the sixth place he imparted (to) them *understanding*, and in the seventh *speech*, an interpreter of the cogitations thereof."

The words "seven senses" also occur in the poem of Taliesin, called "Y Bid Mawr, or the Macrocosm" (*Brit. Mag.*, vol. 21, p. 30). See further the "Mysterium Magnum" of Jacob Boehmen, which teaches "how the soul of man, or his inward holy body," was compounded of the *seven properties* under the influence of the seven planets:

"I will adore my Father,
My God, my Supporter,
Who placed, throughout my head,
The soul of my reason,
And made for my perception
My seven faculties
Of Fire, and Earth, and Water, and Air.
And mist, and flowers,
And the southerly wind,
As it were seven senses of reason
For my Father to impel me:
With the first I shall be animated,
With the second I shall touch,
With the third I shall cry out,
With the fourth I shall taste,
With the fifth I shall see,
With the sixth I shall hear,
With the seventh I shall smell."

[C. T. McClenachan.]

Mandate. That which is commanded. The Benedictine editors of Du Cange define *mandatum* as "breve aut edictum regium," i. e., a royal brief or edict, and *mandamentum* as "literæ quibus magistratus aliquid mandat," i. e., letters in which a magistrate commands anything. Hence the orders and decrees of a Grand Master or a Grand Lodge are called mandates, and implicit obedience to them is of Masonic obligation. There is an appeal, yet not a suspensive one, from the mandate of a Grand Master to the Grand Lodge, but there is none from the latter.

Mango. The branches of this tree are a prominent feature in all Eastern religious ceremonies. The mango is the apple-tree of India, with which man, in Indian tale, tempted Eve.

Mangourit, Michel Ange Bernard de. A distinguished member of the Grand Orient of France. He founded in 1776, at Rennes, the Rite of *Sublimes Elus de la Vérité*, or Sublime Elects of Truth, and at Paris the androgynous society of Dames of Mount Thabor. He also created the Masonic Literary Society of Free Thinkers, which existed for three years. He delivered lectures which were subsequently published under the title of *Cours de Philosophie Maçonnique*, in 500 pp., 4to. He also delivered a great many lectures and discourses before different Lodges, several of which were published. He died, after a long and severe illness, February 17, 1829.

Manichæans. (Also termed Gnostics.) A sect taking its rise in the middle of the third century, whose belief was in two eternal principles of good and evil. They derived their name from Manes, a philosopher of Persian birth, sometimes called Manichæus. Of the two principles, Ormudz was the author of the good, while Ahriman was the master spirit of evil. The two classes of neophytes were, the true, *siddi kûn;* the listeners, *samma un.*

Manichéens, Les Frères. A secret Italian society, founded, according to Thory (*Acta Lat.*, i., 325) and Clavel (*Hist. Pitt.*, p. 407), in the eighteenth century, at which the doctrines of Manes were set forth in several grades.

Manitoba. In 1864 a dispensation was issued over the signature of M. W. Bro. A. T. Pierson, then Grand Master of Masons in Minnesota, and "Northern Light" Lodge was organised at Fort Garry (Winnipeg), with Bro. Dr. John Schultz, Worshipful Master, A. G. B. Bannatyne, S. W., and Wm. Inkster, J. W.

In 1867 Bro. Bannatyne was elected W. M and the Lodge went out of existence shortly before the Red River insurrection. At this time, the country was claimed by the "Hon. Hudson Bay Co."; but when the transfer was made to Canada in 1870 and the Red River Settlement, as it was then known, became the Province of Manitoba, the Grand Lodge of Canada assumed jurisdiction and shortly afterward issued Charters to "Prince Rupert's" Lodge, Winnipeg, December, 1870, and Lisgar Lodge, Selkirk.

On May 12, 1875, the three Lodges then existing, viz., "Prince Rupert," "Lisgar," and "Ancient Landmark," held a convention and formed the "Grand Lodge of Manitoba," electing M. W. Bro. the Rev. Dr. W. C. Clarke as Grand Master. [Will H. Whyte.]

Mann, Der. The Man, the second grade of the "Deutsche Union."

Manna, Pot of. Among the articles laid up in the Ark of the Covenant by Aaron was a Pot of Manna. In the substitute ark, commemorated in the Royal Arch Degree, there was, of course, a representation of it. Manna has been considered as a symbol of life; not the transitory, but the enduring one of a future world. Hence the Pot of Manna, Aaron's rod that budded anew, and the Book of the Law, which teaches Divine Truth, all found together, are appropriately considered as the symbols of that eternal life which it is the design of the Royal Arch Degree to teach.

Manningham, Thomas. Dr. Thomas Manningham was a physician, of London, of much repute in the last century. He took an active interest in the concerns of Freemasonry, being Deputy Grand Master of England, 1752–6. According to Oliver (*Revelations of a Square*, p. 86), he was the author of the prayer now so well known to the Fraternity, which was presented by him to the Grand Lodge, and adopted as a form of prayer to be used at the initiation of a candidate. Before that period, no prayer was used on such occasions, and the one composed by Manningham (Oliver says with the assistance of Anderson, which is doubtful, as Anderson died in 1739) is here given as a document of the time. It will be seen that in our day it has been somewhat modified, Preston making the first change; and that, originally used as one prayer, it has since been divided, in this country at least, into two, the first part being used as a prayer at the opening of a Lodge, and the latter at the initiation of a candidate.

"Most Holy and Glorious Lord God, thou Architect of heaven and earth, who art the giver of all good gifts and graces; and hath promised that where two or three are gathered together in thy Name, thou wilt be in the midst of them; in thy Name we assemble and meet together, most humbly beseeching thee to bless us in all our undertakings: to give us thy Holy Spirit, to enlighten our minds with wisdom and understanding; that we may know and serve thee aright, that all our doings may tend to thy glory and the salvation of our souls. And we beseech thee, O Lord God, to bless this our present undertaking, and to grant that this our Brother may dedicate his life to thy service, and be a true and faithful Brother amongst us. Endue him with Divine wisdom, that he may, with the secrets of Masonry, be able to unfold the mysteries of godliness and Christianity. This we humbly beg, in the name and for the sake of Jesus Christ our Lord and Saviour, Amen."

Dr. Manningham rendered other important services to Masonry by his advocacy of healthy reforms and his determined opposition to the schismatic efforts of the "Ancient Masons." He died February 3, 1794. The third edition of the *Book of Constitutions* (1756) speaks of him in exalted terms as "a diligent and active officer" (p. 258.) Two interesting letters written by Dr. Manningham are given at length in Gould's *Concise History of Freemasonry* (pp. 328–334): one dated December 3, 1756, and addressed to what was then the Provincial Grand Lodge of Holland, refusing leave for the holding of Scotch Lodges and pointing out that Freemasonry is the same in all parts of the world; and another dated July 12, 1757, also dealing with the so-called Scotch Masonry, and explaining that its orders of Knighthood were unknown in England, where the only Orders known are those of Masters, Fellow-Crafts, and Apprentices. [E. L. H.]

Mantle. A dress placed over all the others. It is of very ancient date, being a part of the costume of the Hebrews, Greeks, and Romans. Among the Anglo-Saxons it was the decisive mark of military rank, being confined to the cavalry. In the Medieval ages, and on the institution of chivalry, the long, trailing mantle was especially reserved as one of the insignia of knighthood, and was worn by the knight as the most august and noble decoration that he could have, when he was not dressed in his armor. The general color of the mantle, in imitation of that of the Roman soldiers, was scarlet, which was lined with ermine or other precious furs. But some of the Orders wore mantles of other colors. Thus the Knights Templar were clothed with a white mantle having a red cross on the breast, and the Knights Hospitalers a black mantle with a white cross. The mantle is still worn in England and other countries of Europe as a mark of rank on state occasions by peers, and by some magistrates as a token of official rank.

Mantle of Honor. The mantle worn by a knight was called the Mantle of Honor. This mantle was presented to a knight whenever he was made by the king.

Manu. By reference to the *Book of the Dead*, it will be found that this word covers an ideal space corresponding to the word west, in whose bosom is received the setting sun. (See *Truth*.)

Manual. Relating to the hand, from the Latin *manus*, a hand. See the Masonic use of the word in the next two articles.

Manual Point of Entrance. Masons are, in a peculiar manner, reminded, by the hand, of the necessity of a prudent and careful observance of all their pledges and duties, and hence this organ suggests certain symbolic instructions in relation to the virtue of prudence.

Manual Sign. In the early English lectures this term is applied to what is now called the Manual Point of Entrance.

Manuscripts. Anderson tells us, in the second edition of his *Constitutions*, that in the year 1717 Grand Master Payne "desired any brethren to bring to the Grand Lodge any old writings and records concerning Masons and Masonry, in order to show the usages of ancient times, and several old copies of the Gothic Constitutions were produced and collated" (*Constitutions*, 1738, p. 110); but in consequence of a jealous supposition that it would be wrong to commit anything to print which related to Masonry, an act of Masonic vandalism was perpetrated. For Anderson further informs us that in 1720, "at some private Lodges, several very valuable manuscripts (for they had nothing yet in print), concerning the Fraternity, their Lodges, Regulations, Charges, Secrets, and Usages, (particularly one written by Mr. Nicholas Stone, the Warden of Inigo Jones,) were too hastily burnt by some scrupulous Brothers, that those papers might not fall into strange hands." (*Ibid.* p., 111.)

The recent labors of Masonic scholars in England, among whom the late William James Hughan deserves especial notice, have succeeded in rescuing many of the old Masonic manuscripts from oblivion, and we are now actually in possession of more of these heretofore unpublished treasures of the Craft than were probably accessible to Anderson and his contemporaries. (See *Records, Old.*)

Manuscripts, Apocryphal. There are certain documents that at various times have been accepted as genuine, but which are now rejected, and considered to be fabrications, by most, if not by all, critical Masonic writers.

The question of their authenticity has been thoroughly gone into by R. F. Gould in Ch. XI. of his *History of Freemasonry*, and he places them all "within the category of Apocryphal MSS."

The first is the "Leland-Locke MS." (See *Leland MS.*) The second is the "Steinmetz Catechism," given by Krause as one of the three oldest documents belonging to the Craft, but of which Gould says, "there appears to me nothing in the preceding 'examination' (or *catechism*) that is capable of sustaining the claims to antiquity which have been advanced on its behalf." The third is the *Malcolm Canmore Charter*, which came to light in 1806, consequent upon the "claim of the 'Glasgow Freemen Operative St. John's Lodge' to take precedence of the other Lodges in the Masonic procession, at the laying of the foundation-stone of Nelson's monument on 'Glasgow Green,' although at that time it was an independent organization." According to the Charter, the Glasgow St. John's Lodge was given priority over all the other Lodges in Scotland by Malcolm III., King of Scots, in 1051. The controversy as to the document was lively, but finally it was pronounced to be a manufactured parchment, and the Grand Lodge of Scotland declined to recognize it of value. The fourth MS. is that of Krause, known as *Prince Edwin's Constitution of 926.* Upon this unquestioned reliance had for decades been placed, then it came to be doubted, and is now little credited by inquiring Masons. Bro. Gould closes his recital of criticisms with the remark: "The original document, as commonly happens in forgeries of this description, is missing; and how, under all the circumstances of the case Krause could have constituted himself the champion of its authenticity, it is difficult to conjecture. Possibly, however, the explanation may be, that in impostures of this character, credulity, on the one part, is a strong temptation to deceit on the other, especially to deceit of which no personal injury is the consequence, and which flatters the student of old documents with his own ingenuity." These remarks are specially quoted as relating to almost all apocryphal documents. The fifth is the *Charter of Cologne*, a document in cipher, bearing the date June 24, 1535, as to which see *Cologne, Charter of.* The sixth is the *Larmenius Charter*, or *The Charter of Transmission*, upon which rest the claims cf the French Order of the Temple to being the lineal successors of the historic Knights Templar, for which see *Temple, Order of the.* [E. L. H.]

Manuscripts, Old. The following is a list, arranged as far as possible in sequence of age, of the old Masonic MSS., now usually known as the *Old Charges.* They generally consist of three parts—*first*, an opening prayer or invocation; *second*, the legendary history of the Craft; *third*, the peculiar statutes and duties, the regulations and observances, incumbent on Masons. There is no doubt that they were read to candidates on their initiation, and probably each Lodge had a copy which was used for this purpose. The late Bro. W. J. Hughan made a special study of these old MSS., and was instrumental in discovering a great many of them; and his book *The Old Charges of British Freemasons*, published in 1895, is the standard work on the subject.

No.	*Name.*	*Date.*	*Owner.*	*When and Where Published.*
1.	Regius (also Halliwell)	*circa* 1390	British Museum	By Mr. Halliwell in 1840 and 1844; by Mr. Whymper in 1889; by the Quatuor Coronati Lodge in 1889.
2.	Cooke	*circa* 1450	British Museum	By Mr. Cooke in 1861; by the Quatuor Coronati Lodge in 1890.
3.	Grand Lodge, No. 1	1583	Grand Lodge of England	By W. J. Hughan, in *Old Charges*, 1872; by H. Sadler, in *Masonic Facts and Fictions*, 1887; in *Hist. of Freemasonry and Concordant Orders*, 1891; by the Quatuor Coronati Lodge in 1892.

No.	Name.	Date.	Owner.	When and Where Published.
4.	Lansdowne	*circa* 1600	British Museum	In *Freemasons' Quarterly Review*, 1848; in *Freemasons' Magazine*, 1858; in Hughan's *Old Charges*, 1872; by the Quatuor Coronati Lodge in 1890.
	York, No. 1	*circa* 1600	York Lodge, No. 236	In Hughan's *Old Charges*, 1872; in *Masonic Magazine*, 1873; in *Ancient York Masonic Rolls*, 1894.
6.	Wood	1610	Prov. G. Lodge of Worcester	In *Masonic Magazine*, 1881; by the Quatuor Coronati Lodge in 1895.
7.	John T. Thorp	1629	J. T. Thorp, Esq. (Leicester)	In *Ars Quatuor Coronatorum*, vol. ix., 1898; in *Lodge of Research Transactions*, 1898–99.
8.	Sloane, 3848	1646	British Museum	In Hughan's *Old Charges*, 1872; in *Masonic Magazine*, 1873; by the Quatuor Coronati Lodge in 1891.
9.	Sloane, 3323	1659	British Museum	In Hughan's *Masonic Sketches and Reprints*, 1871; by the Quatuor Coronati Lodge in 1891.
10.	Grand Lodge, No. 2	*circa* 1650	Grand Lodge of England	By the Quatuor Coronati Lodge in 1892.
11.	Harleian, 1942	*circa* 1650	British Museum	In *Freemasons' Quarterly Review*, 1836; in Hughan's *Old Charges*, 1872; by the Quatuor Coronati Lodge in 1890.
12.	G. W. Bain	*circa* 1650	R. Wilson, Esq. (Leeds)	In *Ars Quatuor Coronatorum*, vol. xx., 1907.
13.	Harleian, 2054	*circa* 1660	British Museum	In Hughan's *Masonic Sketches and Reprints*, 1871; in *Masonic Magazine*, 1873; by the Quatuor Coronati Lodge in 1891.
14.	Phillipps, No. 1	*circa* 1677	Rev. J. E. A. Fenwick (Cheltenham)	By the Quatuor Coronati Lodge in 1894.
15.	Phillipps, No. 2	*circa* 1677		In *Masonic Magazine*, 1876; in *Archæological Library*, 1878; by the Quatuor Coronati Lodge in 1894.
16.	Lochmore	1650–1700	Prov. G. Lodge of Worcester	In *Masonic Magazine*, 1882.
17.	Buchanan	1650–1700	Grand Lodge of England	In Gould's *Hist. of Freemasonry*, by Quatuor Coronati Lodge in 1892.
18.	Kilwinning	*circa* 1665	Mother Kilwinning Lodge (Scotland)	In Hughan's *Masonic Sketches and Reprints*, 1871; in Lyon's *Hist. of the Lodge of Edinburgh*, 1873.
19.	Ancient Stirling	1650–1700	Ancient Stirling Lodge (Scotland)	By Hughan in 1893.
20.	Taylor	*circa* 1650	Prov. G. Lodge of West Yorkshire	In *Ars Quatuor Coronatorum*, vol. xxi., 1908.
21.	Atcheson Haven	1666	G. Lodge of Scotland	In Lyon's *Hist. of the Lodge of Edinburgh*, 1873.
22.	Aberdeen	1670	Aberdeen Lodge, No. 1 *tris*	In *Voice of Masonry*, Chicago, U. S. A., 1874; in *Freemason*, 1895.
23.	Melrose, No. 2	1674	Melrose St. John Lodge, No. 1 *bis* (Scotland)	In *Masonic Magazine*, 1880; in Vernon's *Hist. of F. M. in Roxburgh, etc.*, 1893.
24.	Henery Heade	1675	Inner Temple Library (London)	In *Ars Quatuor Coronatorum*, vol. xxi., 1908.
25.	Stanley	1677	West Yorkshire Masonic Library	In *West Yorkshire Masonic Reproductions*, 1893.
26.	Carson	1677	E. T. Carson, Esq. (Cincinnati, U. S. A.)	In *Masonic Review* (Cincinnati), 1890; in *Freemasons' Chronicle*, 1890.
27.	Antiquity	1686	Lodge of Antiquity, No. 2 (London)	In Hughan's *Old Charges*, 1872.
28.	Col. Clerke	1686	Grand Lodge of England	In *Freemason*, 1888; in Conder's *Hole Crafte, etc.*, 1894.
29.	William Watson	1687	West Yorkshire Masonic Library	In *Freemason*, 1891; in *West Yorkshire Masonic Reprints*, 1891; by the Quatuor Coronati Lodge in 1891.
30.	T. W. Tew	*circa* 1680	West Yorkshire Masonic Library	In Christmas *Freemason*, 1888; in *West Yorkshire Masonic Reprints*, 1889 and 1892.
31.	Inigo Jones	*circa* 1680	Worcestershire Masonic Library	In *Masonic Magazine*, 1881; by the Quatuor Coronati Lodge in 1895.
32.	Dumfries, No. 1	1675-1700	Dumfries Kilwinning Lodge, No. 53 (Scotland)	In Smith's *Hist. of the Old Lodge of Dumfries*, 1892.
33.	Dumfries, No. 2	1675-1700		In Christmas *Freemason*, 1892; by Hughan, in 1892.
34.	Beaumont	1675-1700	Prov. G. Lodge of West Yorkshire	In *Freemason*, 1894.
35.	Dumfries, No. 3	1675-1700	"	In Smith's *Hist. of the Old Lodge of Dumfries*, 1892.

No.	Name.	Date.	Owner.	When and Where Published.
36.	Hope	1675–1700	Lodge of Hope, No. 302 (Bradford, Yorkshire)	In Hughan's *Old Charges*, 1872; in *West Yorkshire Masonic Reprints*, 1892.
37.	T. W. Embleton	1675–1700	West Yorkshire Masonic Library	In Christmas *Freemason*, 1889; in *West Yorkshire Masonic Reprints*, 1893.
38.	York, No. 5	*circa* 1670	York Lodge, No. 236	In *Masonic Magazine*, 1881; in *Ancient York Masonic Constitutions*, 1894.
39.	York, No. 6	1675–1700	"	In *Masonic Magazine*, 1880; in *Ancient York Masonic Constitutions*, 1894.
40.	Colne, No. 1	1675–1700	Royal Lancashire Lodge, No. 116 (Colne, Lancashire)	In Christmas *Freemason*, 1887.
41.	Clapham	*circa* 1700	West Yorkshire Masonic Library	In *Freemason*, 1890; in *West Yorkshire Masonic Reprints*, 1892.
42.	Hughan	1675–1700		In *West Yorkshire Masonic Reprints*, 1892; in *Freemason*, 1892 and 1911.
43.	Dauntesey	*circa* 1690	R. Dauntesey, Esq. (Manchester)	In *Keystone*, Philadelphia, 1886.
44.	Harris, No. 1		Bedford Lodge, No. 157 (London)	In *Freemasons' Chronicle*, 1882.
45.	David Ramsey		The Library, Hamburg	In *Freemason*, 1906.
46.	Langdale		G. W. Bain, Esq. (Sunderland)	In *Freemason*, 1895.
47.	H. F. Beaumont	1690	West Yorkshire Masonic Library	In *Freemason*, 1894; in *West Yorkshire Masonic Reprints*, 1901.
48.	Waistell	1693	"	In *West Yorkshire Masonic Reprints*, 1892.
49.	York, No. 4	1693	York Lodge, No. 236	In Hughan's *Masonic Sketches and Reprints*, 1871; in *Ancient York Masonic Rolls*, 1894.
50.	Thomas Foxcroft	1699	Grand Lodge of England	In *Freemason*, 1900.
51.	Newcastle College Roll	*circa* 1700	Newcastle College of Rosicrucians	By F. F. Schnitger in 1894.
52.	John Strachan	"	Quatuor Coronati Lodge, No. 2076 (London)	In the *Transactions of the Lodge of Research*, 1899–1900.
53.	Alnwick	1701	Mr. Turnbull (Alnwick)	In Hughan's *Masonic Sketches and Reprints*, 1871, and *Old Charges*, 1872, by the Newcastle College of Rosicrucians in 1895.
54.	York, No. 2	1704	York Lodge, No. 236	In Hughan's *Masonic Sketches and Reprints*, 1871; in *Ancient York Masonic Rolls*, 1894.
55.	Scarborough	1705	G. Lodge of Canada	In *Philadelphia Mirror and Keystone*, 1860; in *Canadian Masonic Record*, 1874; in *Masonic Magazine*, 1879; by the Quatuor Coronati Lodge in 1894; in *Ancient York Masonic Rolls*, 1894.
56.	Colne, No. 2	1700–1725	Royal Lancashire Lodge, No. 116 (Colne, Lancashire)	Has not been reproduced.
57.	Papworth	*circa* 1720	W. Papworth, Esq. (London)	In Hughan's *Old Charges*, 1872.
58.	Macnab	1722	West Yorkshire Masonic Library	In *West Yorkshire Masonic Reprints*, 1896.
59.	Haddon	1723	J. S. Haddon, Esq. (Wellington)	In Hughan's *Old Charges*, 1895.
60.	Phillipps, No. 3	1700–1725	Rev. J. E. A. Fenwick (Cheltenham)	By the Quatuor Coronati Lodge in 1894.
61.	Dumfries, No. 4	1700–1725	Dumfries Kilwinning Lodge, No. 53 (Scotland)	In *Ars Quatuor Coronatorum*, vol. v., 1893.
62.	Cama	1700–1725	Quatuor Coronati Lodge, No. 2076 (London)	By the Quatuor Coronati Lodge in 1891.
63.	Songhurst	*circa* 1725		Has not been reproduced.
64.	Spencer	1726	E. T. Carson, Esq. (Cincinnati, U. S. A.)	In Spencer's *Old Constitutions*, 1871.
65.	Tho. Carmick	1727	P. F. Smith, Esq. (Pennsylvania)	In *Ars Quatuor Coronatorum*, vol. xxii. 1909.
66.	Woodford	1728	Quatuor Coronati Lodge, No. 2076 (London)	A copy of the Cooke MS.
67.	Supreme Council	1728	Supreme Council, 33° (London)	" " " "
68.	Gateshead	*circa* 1730	Lodge of Industry, No. 48 (Gateshead, Durham)	In *Masonic Magazine*, 1875.
69.	Rawlinson	1725–1750	Bodleian Library (Oxford)	In *Freemasons' Monthly Magazine*, 1855; in *Masonic Magazine*, 1876; in *Ars Quatuor Coronatorum*, vol. xi., 1898.
70.	Probity	*circa* 1736	Probity Lodge, No. 61 (Halifax, Yorkshire)	In *Freemason*, 1886; in *West Yorkshire Masonic Reprints*. 1892

No.	Name.	Date.	Owner.	When and Where Published.
71.	Levander-York	*circa* 1740	F. W. Levander, Esq. (London)	In *Ars Quatuor Coronatorum*, vol. xviii., 1905.
72.	Thistle Lodge	1756	Thistle Lodge, No. 62 (Dumfries, Scotland)	Has not been reproduced.
73.	Melrose, No. 2	1768	Melrose St. John, No. 1 *bis* (Scotland)	
74.	Crane, No. 1	1781	Cestrian Lodge, No. 425 (Chester)	In *Freemason*, 1884.
75.	Crane, No. 2	1775–1800	"	" " "
76.	Harris, No. 2	*circa* 1781	British Museum	By the Quatuor Coronati Lodge in 1892.
77.	Tunnah	*circa* 1828	Quatuor Coronati Lodge, No. 2076 (London)	Has not been reproduced.
78.	Wren	1852	Unknown	In *Masonic Magazine*, 1879.

[E. L. H.]

Marcheshvan. מרחשון. The second month of the Jewish civil year. It begins with the new moon in November, and corresponds, therefore, to a part of that month and of December.

Marconis, Gabriel Mathieu, more frequently known as De Negre, from his dark complexion, was the founder and first G. Master and G. Hierophant of the Rite of Memphis, brought by Sam'l Honis, a native of Cairo, from Egypt, in 1814, who with Baron Dumas and the Marquis de la Rogne, founded a Lodge of the Rite at Montauban, France, on April 30, 1815, which was closed March 7, 1816. In a work entitled *The Sanctuary of Memphis*, by Jacques Etienne Marconis, the author—presumptively the son of G. M. Marconis—who styles himself the founder of the Rite of Memphis, thus briefly gives an account of its origin: "The Rite of Memphis, or Oriental Rite, was introduced into Europe by Ormus, a seraphic priest of Alexandria and Egyptian sage, who had been converted by St. Mark, and reformed the doctrines of the Egyptians in accordance with the principles of Christianity. The disciples of Ormus continued until 1118 to be the sole guardians of ancient Egyptian wisdom, as purified by Christianity and Solomonian science. This science they communicated to the Templars. They were then known by the title of Knights of Palestine, or Brethren Rose Croix of the East. In them the Rite of Memphis recognizes its immediate founders."

The above, coming from the G. Hierophant and founder, should satisfy the most scrupulous as to the conversion of Ormus by St. Mark, and his then introducing the Memphis Rite. But Marconis continues as to the object and intention of his Rite: "The Masonic Rite of Memphis is a combination of the ancient mysteries; it taught the first men to render homage to the Deity. Its dogmas are based on the principles of humanity; its mission is the study of that wisdom which serves to discern truth; it is the beneficent dawn of the development of reason and intelligence; it is the worship of the qualities of the human heart and the impression of its vices; in fine, it is the echo of religious toleration, the union of all belief, the bond between all men, the symbol of sweet illusions of hope, preaching the faith in God that saves, and the charity that blesses."

We are further told by the Hierophant founder that "The Rite of Memphis is the sole depository of High Masonry, the true primitive Rite, the Rite par excellence, which has come down to us without any alteration, and is consequently the only Rite that can justify its origin and the combined exercise of its rights by constitutions, the authenticity of which cannot be questioned. The Rite of Memphis, or Oriental Rite, is the veritable Masonic tree, and all systems, whatsoever they be, are but detached branches of this institution, venerable for its great antiquity, and born in Egypt. The real deposit of the principles of Masonry, written in the Chaldee language, is preserved in the sacred ark of the Rite of Memphis, and in part in the Grand Lodge of Scotland, at Edinburgh, and in the Maronite Convent on Mount Lebanon." "Brother Marconis de Negre, the Grand Hierophant, is the sole consecrated depositary of the traditions of this Sublime Order."

The above is enough to reveal the character of the father and reputed son for truth, as also of the institution founded by them, which, like the firefly, is seen now here, now there, but with no steady beneficial light. (See *Memphis, Rite of.*)

Marconis, Jacques Etienne. Born at Montauban, January 3, 1795; died at Paris, November 21, 1868. (See *Memphis, Rite of.*)

Marduk. A victorious warrior-god, described on one of the Assyrian clay tablets of the British Museum, who was said to have engaged the monster Tiamat in a cosmogonic struggle. He was armed with a namzar (grappling-hook), ariktu (lance), shibbu (lasso), qashtu (bow), sizpau (club), and kabab (shield), together with a dirk in each hand.

Maria Theresa. Empress of Austria, who showed great hostility to Freemasonry, presumably from religious leanings and advisers. Her husband was Francis I., elected Emperor of Germany in 1745. He was a zealous Mason, and had been initiated at The Hague in 1731, at a Special Lodge, at which Lord Chesterfield and Dr. Desaguliers were present. He was raised at Houghton Hall, the same year, while on a visit to England. He assisted to found the Lodge "Drei Kanonen," at Vienna, constituted in 1742. During the forty years' reign of Maria Theresa, Freemasonry was tolerated in Vienna doubtless through the intercession of the Emperor. It is stated in the *Pocket Companion* of 1754, one hundred grenadiers were sent to break up the Lodge, taking twelve prisoners, the Emperor escaping by a back staircase. He answered for and freed the twelve prisoners. His son, Emperor Joseph, inherited good-will to Masonry. He was G. Master of the Viennese Masons at the time of his death.

Mark. The appropriate jewel of a Mark Master. It is made of gold or silver, usually of the former metal, and must be in the form of a keystone. On the obverse or front surface, the device or "mark" selected by the owner must be engraved within a circle composed of the following letters: H. T. W. S. S. T. K. S. On the reverse or posterior surface, the name of the owner, the name of his Chapter, and the date of his advancement, may be inscribed, although this is not absolutely necessary. The "mark" consists of the device and surrounding inscription on the obverse. The Mark jewel, as prescribed by the Supreme Grand Chapter of Scotland, is of mother-of-pearl. The circle on one side is inscribed with the Hebrew letters חצבאשאמש, and the circle on the other side with letters containing the same meaning in the vernacular tongue of the country in which the Chapter is situated, and the wearer's mark in the center. The Hebrew letters are the initials of a Hebrew sentence equivalent to the English one familiar to Mark Masons. It is but a translation into Hebrew of the English mystical sentence.

It is not requisite that the device or mark should be of a strictly Masonic character, although Masonic emblems are frequently selected in preference to other subjects. As soon as adopted it should be drawn or described in a book kept by the Chapter for that purpose, and it is then said to be "recorded in the Book of Marks," after which time it can never be changed by the possessor for any other, or altered in the slightest degree, but remains as his "mark" to the day of his death.

This mark is not a mere ornamental appendage of the degree, but is a sacred token of the rites of friendship and brotherly love, and its presentation at any time by the owner to another Mark Master, would claim, from the latter, certain acts of friendship which are of solemn obligation among the Fraternity. A mark thus presented, for the purpose of obtaining a favor, is said to be *pledged;* though remaining in the possession of the owner, it ceases, for any actual purposes of advantage, to be his property; nor can it be again used by him until, either by the return of the favor, or with the consent of the benefactor, it has been redeemed; for it is a positive law of the Order, that no Mark Master shall "pledge his mark a second time until he has redeemed it from its previous pledge." By this wise provision, the unworthy are prevented from making an improper use of this valuable token, or from levying contributions on their hospitable brethren. Marks or pledges of this kind were of frequent use among the ancients, under the name of *tessera hospitalis* and "arrhabo." The nature of the *tessera hospitalis*, or, as the Greeks called it, *σύμβολον*, cannot be better described than in the words of the Scholiast on the *Medea of Euripides*, v. 613, where Jason promises Medea, on her parting from him, to send her the symbols of hospitality which should procure her a kind reception in foreign countries. It was the custom, says the Scholiast, when a guest had been entertained, to break a die in two parts, one of which parts was retained by the guest, so that if, at any future period he required assistance, on exhibiting the broken pieces of the die to each other, the friendship was renewed. Plautus, in one of his comedies, gives us an exemplification of the manner in which these *tesseræ* or pledges of friendship were used at Rome, whence it appears that the privileges of this friendship were extended to the descendants of the contracting parties. Pœnulus is introduced, inquiring for Agorastocles, with whose family he had formerly exchanged the *tessera*.

Ag. Siquidem Antidimarchi quæris adoptatitium,
Ego sum ipsus quem tu quæris.
Pœn. Hem! quid ego audio?
Ag. Antidamæ me gnatum esse.
Pœn. Si ita est, tesseram
Conferre si vis hospitalem, eccam, attuli.
Ag. Agedum huc ostende; est par probe; nam habeo domum.
Pœn. O mi hospes, salve multum; nam mihi tuus pater,
Pater tuus ergo hospes, Antidamas fuit:
Hæc mihi hospitalis tessera cum illo fuit.
Pœnul., act. v., s. c. 2, ser. 85.

Ag. Antidimarchus' adopted son,
If you do seek, I am the very man.
Pœn. How! do I hear aright?
Ag. I am the son
Of old Antidamus.
Pœn. If so, I pray you
Compare with me the hospitable die
I've brought this with me.
Ag. Prithee, let me see it.
It is, indeed, the very counterpart
Of mine at home.
Pœn. All hail, my welcome guest,
Your father was my guest, Antidamus.
Your father was my honored guest, and then
This hospitable die with me he parted.

These *tesseræ*, thus used, like the Mark Master's mark, for the purposes of perpetuating friendship and rendering its union more sacred, were constructed in the following manner: they took a small piece of bone, ivory, or stone, generally of a square or cubical form, and dividing it into equal parts, each wrote his own name, or some other inscription, upon one of the pieces; they then made a mutual exchange, and, lest falling into other hands it should give occasion to imposture, the pledge was preserved with the greatest secrecy, and no one knew the name inscribed upon it except the possessor.

The primitive Christians seem to have adopted a similar practise, and the *tessera* was carried by them in their travels, as a means of introduction to their fellow Christians. A favorite inscription with them were the letters Π. Υ. Α. Π., being the initials of Πατηρ. Υιος, Αγιον Πνευμα, or Father, Son, and Holy Ghost.

The use of these *tesseræ*, in the place of written certificates, continued, says Dr. Harris (*Diss. on the Tess. Hosp.*), until the eleventh century, at which time they are mentioned by Burchardus, Archbishop of Worms, in a visitation charge.

The "arrhabo" was a similar keepsake, formed by breaking a piece of money in two. The etymology of this word shows distinctly that the Romans borrowed the custom of these pledges from the ancient Israelites, for it is derived from the Hebrew *arabon*, a pledge.

With this detail of the customs of the ancients before us, we can easily explain the well-known passage in Revelation ii. 17: "To him that overcometh will I give a white stone, and in it a new name written, which no man knoweth saving he that receiveth it." That is, to borrow the interpretation of Harris, "To him that overcometh will I give a pledge of my affection, which shall constitute him my friend, and entitle him to privileges and honors of which none else can know the value or the extent."

Mark Man. According to Masonic tradition, the Mark Men were the Wardens, as the Mark Masters were the Masters of the Fellow-Craft Lodges, at the building of the Temple. They distributed the marks to the workmen, and made the first inspection of the work, which was afterward to be approved by the overseers. As a degree, the Mark Man is not recognized in the United States. In England it is sometimes, but not generally, worked as preparatory to the degree of Mark Master. In Scotland, in 1778, it was given to Fellow-Crafts, while the Mark Master was restricted to Master Masons. It is not recognized in the present regulations of the Supreme Grand Chapter of Scotland. Much of the esoteric ritual of the Mark Man has been incorporated into the Mark Master of the American System.

Mark Master. The Fourth Degree of the American Rite. The traditions of the degree make it of great historical importance, since by them we are informed that by its influence each Operative Mason at the building of the Temple was known and distinguished, and the disorder and confusion which might otherwise have attended so immense an undertaking was completely prevented. Not less useful is it in its symbolic signification. As illustrative of the Fellow-Craft, the Fourth Degree is particularly directed to the inculcation of order, regularity, and discipline. It teaches us that we should discharge all the duties of our several stations with precision and punctuality; that the work of our hands and the thoughts of our hearts should be good and true—not unfinished and imperfect, not sinful and defective—but such as the Great Overseer and Judge of heaven and earth will see fit to approve as a worthy oblation from his creatures. If the Fellow-Craft's Degree is devoted to the inculcation of learning, that of the Mark Master is intended to instruct us how that learning can most usefully and judiciously be employed for our own honor and the profit of others. And it holds forth to the desponding the encouraging thought that although our motives may sometimes be misinterpreted by our erring fellow mortals, our attainments be underrated, and our reputations be traduced by the envious and malicious, there is one, at least, who sees not with the eyes of man, but may yet make that stone which the builders rejected, the head of the corner. The intimate connection then, between the Second and Fourth degrees of Masonry, is this, that while one inculcates the necessary exercise of all the duties of life, the other teaches the importance of performing them with systematic regularity. The true Mark Master is a type of that man mentioned in the sacred parable, who received from his master this approving language—"Well done, good and faithful servant; thou hast been faithful over a few things, I will make thee ruler over many things: enter thou into the joys of thy Lord."

In America, the Mark Master's is the first degree given in a Royal Arch Chapter. Its officers are a Right Worshipful Master, Senior and Junior Wardens, Secretary, Treasurer, Senior and Junior Deacons, Master, Senior and Junior Overseers. The degree cannot be conferred when less than six are present, who, in that case, must be the first and last three officers above named. The working tools are the *Mallet* and *Indenting Chisel* (which see). The symbolic color is purple. The Mark Master's Degree is now given in England under the authority of the Grand Lodge of Mark Masters, which was established in June, 1856, and is a jurisdiction independent of the Grand Lodge. The officers are the same as in America, with the addition of a Chaplain, Director of Ceremonies, Assistant Director, Registrar of Marks, Inner Guard or Time Keeper, and two Stewards. Master Masons are eligible for initiation. Bro. Hughan says that the degree is virtually the same in England, Scotland, and Ireland. It differs, however, in some respects from the American degree.

Mark of the Craft, Regular. In the Mark Degree there is a certain stone which is said, in the ritual, not to have upon it *the regular mark of the Craft*. This expression is derived from the following tradition of the degree. At the building of the Temple, each workman placed his own mark upon his own materials, so that the workmanship of every Mason might be readily distinguished, and praise or blame be justly awarded. These marks, according to the lectures, consisted of mathematical figures, squares, angles, lines, and perpendiculars, and hence any figure of a different kind, such as a circle, would not be deemed "the regular mark of the Craft." Of the three stones used in the Mark Degree, one is inscribed with a square and another with a plumb or perpendicular, because these were marks familiar to the Craft; but the third, which is inscribed with a circle and certain hieroglyphics, was not known, and was not, therefore, called "regular."

Marks of the Craft. In former times, Operative Masons, the "Steinmetsen" of Germany, were accustomed to place some mark or sign of their own invention, which, like the monogram of the painters, would seem to identify the work of each. They are to be found upon the cathedrals, churches, castles, and other stately buildings erected since the twelfth century, or a little earlier, in Germany, France, England, and Scotland. As Mr. Godwin has observed in his *History in Ruins*, it is curious to see that these marks are of the same character, in form, in all these different countries. They were principally crosses, triangles, and other mathematical figures, and many of them were religious symbols. Specimens taken from different buildings supply such forms as follow.

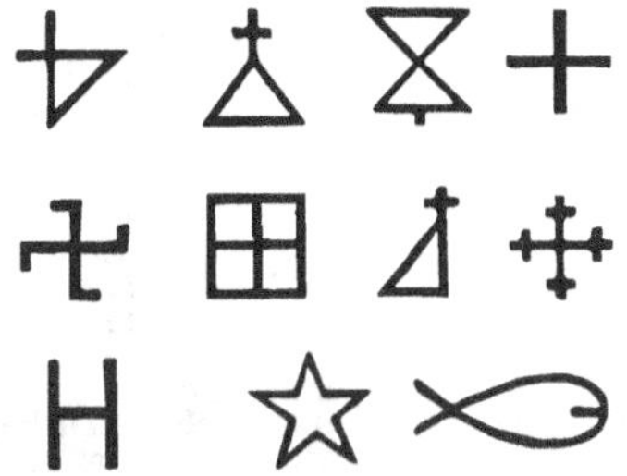

The last of these is the well-known *vesica piscis*, the symbol of Christ among the primitive Christians, and the last but one is the Pythagorean pentalpha. A writer in the *London Times* (August 13, 1835) is incorrect in stating that these marks are confined to Germany, and are to be found only since the twelfth or thirteenth centuries. More recent researches have shown that they existed in many other countries, especially in Scotland, and that they were practised by the builders of ancient times. Thus Ainsworth, in his *Travels* (ii., 107), tells us, in his description of the ruins of Al-Hadhv in Mesopotamia, that "every stone, not only in the chief building, but in the walls and bastions and other public monuments, when not defaced by time, is marked with a character which is for the most part either a Chaldean letter or numeral." M. Didron, who reported a series of observations on the subject of these Masons' marks to the *Comité Historique des Arts et Monumens* of Paris, believes that he can discover in them references to distinct schools or Lodges of Masons. He divides them into two classes: those of the overseers, and those of the men who worked the stones. The marks of the first class consist of monogrammatic characters; those of the second, are of the nature of symbols, such as shoes, trowels, mallets, etc.

A correspondent of the *Freemasons' Quarterly Review* states that similar marks are to be found on the stones which compose the walls of the fortress of Allahabad, which was erected in 1542, in the East Indies. "The walls," says this writer, "are composed of large oblong blocks of red granite, and are almost everywhere covered by Masonic emblems, which evince something more than mere ornament. They are not confined to one particular spot, but are scattered over the walls of the fortress, in many places as high as thirty or forty feet from the ground. It is quite certain that thousands of stones on the walls, bearing these Masonic symbols, were carved, marked, and numbered in the quarry previous to the erection of the building."

In the ancient buildings of England and France, these marks are to be found in great abundance. In a communication, on this subject, to the London Society of Antiquaries, Mr. Godwin states that, "in my opinion, these marks, if collected and compared might assist in connecting the various bands of operatives, who, under the protection of the Church—mystically united—spread themselves over Europe during the Middle Ages, and are known as Freemasons." Mr. Godwin describes these marks as varying in length from two to seven inches, and as formed by a single line, slightly indented, consisting chiefly of crosses, known Masonic symbols, emblems of the Trinity and of eternity, the double triangle, trowel, square, etc.

The same writer observes that, in a conversation, in September, 1844, with a Mason at work on the Canterbury Cathedral, he "found that many Masons (*all* who were Freemasons) had their mystic marks handed down from generation to generation; this man had his mark from his father, and he received it from his grandfather."

Marrow in the Bone. An absurd corruption of a Jewish word, and still more absurdly said to be its translation. It has no appropriate signification in the place to which it is applied, but was once religiously believed in by many Masons, who, being ignorant of the Hebrew language, accepted it as a true interpretation. It is now universally rejected by the intelligent portion of the Craft.

Marseilles, Mother Lodge of. A Lodge was established in 1748, at Marseilles, in France, Thory says, by a traveling Mason, under the name of St. Jean d'Ecosse. It afterward assumed the name of Mother Lodge of Marseilles, and still later the name of Scottish Mother Lodge of France. It granted Warrants of its own authority for Lodges in France and in the colonies; among others for one at New Orleans, in Louisiana.

Marshal. An officer common to several Masonic bodies, whose duty is to regulate processions and other public solemnities. In Grand bodies he is called a Grand Marshal. In the American Royal Arch System, the Captain of the Host acts on public occasions as the Marshal. The Marshal's ensign of office is a baton or short rod. The office of Marshal in State affairs is very ancient. It was found in the court of the Byzantine emperors, and was introduced into England from France at the period of the conquest. His badge of office was at first a rod or verge, which was afterward abbreviated to the baton, for, as an old writer has observed (Thinne), "the verge or rod was the ensign of him who had authority to reform evil in warre and in peace, and to see quiet and order observed among the people."

Martel. Charles Martel, who died in 741, although not actually king, reigned over France under the title of Mayor of the Palace. Rebold (*Hist. Gen.*, p. 69) says that "at the request of the Anglo-Saxon kings, he sent workmen and Masters into England." The Operative Masons of the Middle Ages considered him as one of their patrons, and give the following account of him in their Legend of the Craft. "There was one of the Royal line of France called *Charles Marshall*, and he was a man that loved well the said Craft and took upon him the Rules and Manners, and after that By the Grace of God he was elect to be the *King* of France, and when he was in his Estate, he helped to make those Masons that were now, and sett them on Work and gave them Charges and Manners and good pay as he had learned of other Masons, and confirmed them a Charter from yeare to yeare to hold their Assembly when they would, and Cherished them right well, and thus came this Noble Craft into France." (Lansdowne MS.)

Martha. The Fourth Degree of the Eastern Star; a Rite of American Adoptive Masonry.

Martinism. The Rite of Martinism, called also the Rectified Rite, was instituted at Lyons, by the Marquis de St. Martin, a disciple of Martines Paschalis, of whose Rite it was pretended to be a reform. Martinism was divided into two classes, called Temples, in which were the following degrees:

I. Temple. 1. Apprentice. 2. Fellow-Craft. 3. Master Mason. 4. Past Master. 5. Elect. 6. Grand Architect. 7. Mason of the Secret.

II. Temple. 8. Prince of Jerusalem. 9. Knight of Palestine. 10. Kadosh.

The degrees of Martinism abounded in the reveries of the Mystics. (See *Saint Martin.*)

Martin, Louis Claude de St. See *Saint Martin.*

Martyr. A title bestowed by the Templars on their last Grand Master, James de Molay. If, as Du Cange says, the Church sometimes gives the title of martyr to men of illustrious sanctity, who have suffered death not for the confession of the name of Christ, but for some other cause, being slain by impious men, then De Molay, as the innocent victim of the malignant schemes of an atrocious pope and king, was clearly entitled to the appellation.

Martyrs, Four Crowned. See *Four Crowned Martyrs.*

Maryland. Freemasonry was introduced into Maryland, in 1750, by the Provincial Grand Lodge of Massachusetts, which issued a Charter for the establishment of a Lodge at Annapolis. Five other Lodges were subsequently chartered by the Provincial Grand Lodge of Pennsylvania, and one in 1765, at Joppa, by the Grand Lodge of England. On the 31st of July, 1783, these five Lodges held a convention at Talbot Court-House, and informally organised a Grand Lodge. But as the Lodge at Annapolis had taken no part in this movement, another convention of all the Lodges was held at Baltimore on the 17th of April, 1787, and the Grand Lodge of Maryland was duly organised, John Coates being elected the Grand Master. The Grand Chapter was established in 1812.

Mason Crowned. (*Maçon Couronne.*) A degree in the nomenclature of Fustier.

Mason, Derivation of the Word. The search for the etymology or derivation of the word *Mason* has given rise to numerous theories, some of them ingenious, but many of them very absurd. Thus, a writer in the *European Magazine* for February, 1792, who signs his name as "George Drake," lieutenant of marines, attempts to trace the Masons to the Druids, and derives *Mason* from *May's on*, *May's* being in reference to *May-day*, the great festival of the Druids, and *on* meaning *men*, as in the French *on dit*, for *homme dit*. According to this, *May's on* therefore means the *Men of May*. This idea is not original with Drake, since the same derivation was urged in 1766 by Cleland, in his essays on *The Way to Things in Words*, and on *The Real Secret of Freemasons*.

Hutchinson, in his search for a derivation, seems to have been perplexed with the variety of roots that presented themselves, and, being inclined to believe that the name of *Mason* "has its derivation from a language in which it implies some strong indication or distinction of the nature of the society, and that it has no relation to architects," looks for the root in the Greek tongue. Thus he thinks that *Mason* may come from Μαω Σοον, *Mao Soon*, "I seek salvation," or from Μυστης, *Mystes*, "an initiate"; and that *Masonry* is only a corruption of Μεσουρανεω, *Mesouraneo*, "I am in the midst of heaven"; or from Μαζουρωθ, *Mazourouth*, a constellation mentioned by Job, or from Μυστηριον, *Mysterion*, "a mystery."

Lessing says, in his *Ernst und Falk*, that *Masa* in the Anglo-Saxon signifies a *table*, and that *Masonry*, consequently, is *a society of the table*.

Nicolai thinks he finds the root in the Low Latin word of the Middle Ages *Massonya*, or *Masonia*, which signifies an exclusive society or club, such as that of the round table.

Coming down to later times, we find Bro. C. W. Moore, in his *Boston Magazine*, of May, 1844, deriving *Mason* from Λιθοτομος, *Lithotomos*, "a Stone-cutter." But although fully aware of the elasticity of etymological rules, it surpasses our ingenuity to get *Mason* etymologically out of *Lithotomos*.

Bro. Giles F. Yates sought for the derivation of *Mason* in the Greek word Μαζονες, *Mazones*, a festival of Dionysus, and he thought that this was another proof of the lineal descent of the Masonic order from the Dionysiac Artificers.

The late William S. Rockwell, who was accustomed to find all his Masonry in the Egyptian mysteries, and who was a thorough student of the Egyptian hieroglyphic system, derives the word *Mason* from a combination of two phonetic signs, the one being MAI, and signifying "to love," and the other being SON, which means "a brother." Hence, he says, "this combination, MAISON, expresses exactly in sound our word MASON, and signifies literally *loving brother*, that is, *philadelphus, brother of an association*, and thus corresponds also in sense."

But all of these fanciful etymologies, which would have terrified Bopp, Grimm, or Müller, or any other student of linguistic relations, forcibly remind us of the French epigrammatist, who admitted that *alphina* came from *equus*, but that, in so coming, it had very considerably changed its route.

What, then, is the true derivation of the word *Mason*? Let us see what the orthoepists, who had no Masonic theories, have said upon the subject.

Webster, seeing that in Spanish *masa* means *mortar*, is inclined to derive *Mason*, as denoting one that works in mortar, from the root of *mass*, which of course gave birth to the Spanish word.

In Low or Medieval Latin, *Mason* was *machio* or *macio*, and this Du Cange derives from the Latin *maceria*, "a long wall." Others find a derivation in *machina*, because the builders stood upon machines to raise their walls. But Richardson takes a common-sense view of the subject. He says, "It appears to be obviously the same word as *maison*, a house or *mansion*, applied to the person who builds, instead of the thing built. The French *Maisoner* is to build houses; *Masonner*, to build of stone. The word *Mason* is applied by usage to a builder in stone, and *Masonry* to work in stone."

Carpenter gives *Massom*, used in 1225, for a building of stone, and *Massonus*, used in 1304, for a *Mason;* and the Benedictine editors of Du Cange define *Massoneria* "a building, the French Maçonnerie, and *Massonerius*," as Latomus or a Mason, both words in manuscripts of 1385.

[Dr. Murray, in the *New English Dictionary*, says of the word *Mason:* "the ulterior etymology is obscure, possibly the word is from the root of Latin 'maceria' (a wall)."]

As a practical question, we are compelled to reject all those fanciful derivations which connect the Masons etymologically and historically with the Greeks, the Egyptians, or the Druids, and to take the word *Mason* in its ordinary signification of a worker in stone, and thus indicate the origin of the Order from a society or association of practical and operative builders. We need no better root than the Medieval Latin *Maçonner*, to build, or *Maçonetus*, a builder.

Masoney. Used in the Strassburg Constitutions, and other German works of the Middle Ages, as equivalent to the modern Masonry. Kloss translates it by *Masonhood*. Lessing derives it from *masa*, Anglo-Saxon, a *table*, and says it means a Society of the Table. Nicolai deduces it from the Low Latin *massonya*, which means both a *club* and a *key*, and says it means an exclusive society or club, and so, he thinks, we get our word *Masonry*. Krause traces it to *mas*, *mase*, food or a banquet. It is a pity to attack these speculations, but we are inclined to look at *Masonry* as simply a corruption of the English *Masonrie*.

Mason Hermetic. (*Maçon Hermétique.*) A degree in the Archives of the Mother Lodge of the Eclectic Philosophic Rite.

Masonic Colors. The colors appropriated by the Fraternity are many, and even shades of the same color. The principal ones are *blue*, to the Craft degrees; *purple*, to the Royal Arch; *white* and *black*, to the Order of the Temple; while all colors are used in the respective degrees of the A. A. Scottish Rite: notably, the nine-colored girdle, intertwined with a tenth, worn in the Fourteenth Degree of the last-named system.

Masonic Hall. See *Hall, Masonic.*

Masonic Literature. See *Literature of Masonry.*

Mason, Illustrious and Sublime Grand Master. (*Maçon Illustre et Sublime Grand Maître.*) A degree in the manuscript collection of Peuvret.

Mason of the Secret. (*Maçon du Secret.*) 1. The Sixth Degree of the Rite of Tschoudy. 2. The Seventh Degree of the Rite of Saint Martin.

Mason, Operative. See *Operative Masons.*

Mason, Perfect. (*Maçon Parfait.*) The Twenty-seventh Degree of the collection of the Metropolitan Chapter of France.

Mason Philosopher. (*Maçon Philosophe.*) A degree in the manuscript collection of Peuvret.

Mason, Practical. The French so call an Operative Mason, *Maçon de Pratique.*

Masonry. Although Masonry is of two kinds, Operative and Speculative, yet Masonic writers frequently employ the word *Masonry* as synonymous with *Freemasonry.*

Masonry, Operative. See *Operative Masonry.*

Masonry, Origin of. See *Origin of Freemasonry.*

Masonry, Speculative. See *Speculative Masonry.*

Masons, Company of. One of the ninety-one livery companies of London, but not one of the twelve greater ones. Their arms are azure, on a chevron, between three castles argent, a pair of compasses somewhat extended of the 1st; crest, a castle of the 2d; and motto, "In the Lord is all our trust." These were granted by Clarencieux, King of arms, in 1472, but they were not incorporated until Charles II. gave them a charter in 1677. They are not to be confounded with the Fraternity of Freemasons, but originally there was some connection between the two. At their hall in Basinghall Street, Ashmole says that in 1682 he attended a meeting at which several persons were "admitted into the Fellowship of Freemasons." (See *Ashmole, Elias*, and *Accepted*).

Mason, Scottish Master. (*Maçon Ecossais Maître.*) Also called Perfect Elect, *Elu* *parfait.* A degree in the Archives of the Mother Lodge of the Philosophic Scottish Rite.

Masons, Emperor of all the. (*Maçons, Empereur de tous les.*) A degree cited in the nomenclature of Fustier.

Mason, Speculative. See *Speculative Masonry.*

Mason, Stone. See *Stone Masons.*

Mason Sublime. (*Maçon sublime.*) A degree in the manuscript collection of Peuvret.

Mason, Sublime Operative. (*Maçon Sublime Pratique.*) A degree in the manuscript collection of Peuvret.

Mason's Wife and Daughter. A degree frequently conferred in the United States on the wives, daughters, sisters, and mothers of Masons, to secure to them, by investing them with a peculiar mode of recognition, the aid and assistance of the Fraternity. It may be conferred by any Master Mason, and the requirement is that the recipient shall be the wife, unmarried daughter, unmarried sister, or widowed mother of a Master Mason. It is sometimes called the Holy Virgin, and has been by some deemed of so much importance that a Manual of it, with the title of *The Ladies' Masonry, or Hieroglyphic Monitor,* was published at Louisville, Kentucky, in 1851, by Past Grand Master William Leigh, of Alabama.

Mason, True. (*Maçon Vrai.*) A degree composed by Pernetty. It is the only one of the high Hermetic degrees of the Rite of Avignon, and it became the first degree of the same system after it was transplanted to Montpellier. (See *Academy of True Masons.*)

Masora. A Hebrew work on the Bible, intended to secure it from any alterations or innovations. Those who composed it were termed Masorites, who taught from tradition, and who invented the Hebrew points. They were also known as Melchites.

Masoretic Points. The Hebrew alphabet is without vowels, which were traditionally supplied by the reader from oral instruction, hence the true ancient sounds of the words have been lost. But about the eighth or ninth century a school of Rabbis, called Masorites, invented vowel points, to be placed above or below the consonants, so as to give them a determined pronunciation. These *Masoretic Points* are never used by the Jews in their rolls of the law, and in all investigations into the derivation and meaning of Hebrew names, Masonic scholars and other etymologists always reject them.

Massachusetts. Freemasonry was introduced into Massachusetts, in 1733, by a Deputation granted to Henry Price as Grand Master of North America, dated April 30, 1733. Price, on July 30th of the same year, organized the "St. John's Grand Lodge," which immediately granted a Warrant to "St. John's Lodge" in Boston, which is now the oldest Lodge existing in America. In 1752 some brethren in Boston formed a Lodge, which was afterward known as "St. Andrew's Lodge," and received a Warrant from the Grand Lodge of Scotland; the rivalry between the two Lodges continued for forty years. On December 27, 1769, St. Andrew's Lodge, with the assistance of three traveling Lodges in the British army, organized the Grand Lodge of Massachusetts, and elected Joseph Warren Grand Master. In 1792, the two Grand Lodges united and formed the "Grand Lodge of the Most Ancient and Honorable Society of Free and Accepted Masons for the Commonwealth of Massachusetts," and elected John Cutler Grand Master.

The Grand Chapter of Massachusetts was organized June 12, 1798, and the Grand Council of Royal and Select Masters in 1826. The Grand Commandery, which exercises jurisdiction over both Massachusetts and Rhode Island, was established May 6, 1805. In 1807 it extended its jurisdiction, and called itself "The United States Grand Encampment." In 1816, it united with other Encampments at a convention in Philadelphia, where a General Grand Encampment of the United States was formed; and in 1819, at the meeting of that body, the representatives of the "Grand Encampment of Massachusetts and Rhode Island" are recorded as being present. And from that time it has retained that title, only changing it, in 1859, to "Grand Commandery," in compliance with the new Constitution of the Grand Encampment of the United States.

Massena, Andre. Duke of Rivoli, Prince of Essling, and a Marshal of France, born at Nice in 1758. Early in the French Revolution he joined a battalion of volunteers, and soon rose to high military rank. He was a prominent Grand Officer of the French Grand Orient. He was designated by Napoleon, his master, as the Robber, in consequence of his being so extortionate.

Massonus. Used in the thirteenth and fourteenth centuries, according to Carpenter (*Gloss.*), for Mason.

Master, Absolute Sovereign Grand. (*Souverain Grand Maître absolu.*) The Ninetieth and last degree of the Rite of Misraim.

Master ad Vitam. In the French Masonry of the earlier part of the last century, the Masters of Lodges were not elected annually, but held their office for life. Hence they were called ***Masters ad Vitam,*** or Masters for life.

Master, Ancient. (*Maître Ancien.*) The Fourth Degree of the Rite of Martinism. This would more properly be translated Past Master, for it has the same position in the *régime* of St. Martin that the Past Master has in the English system.

Master Architect, Grand. See *Grand Master Architect.*

Master Architect, Perfect. (*Maître Architecte Parfait.*) A degree in the Archives of the Mother Lodge of the Philosophic Scottish Rite, and in some other collections.

Master Architect, Prussian. (*Maître Architecte Prussien.*) A degree in the Archives of the Mother Lodge of the Philosophic Scottish Rite.

Master, Blue. A name sometimes given, in the Scottish Rite, to Master Masons of the Third Degree, in contradistinction to some of the higher degrees, and in reference to the color of their collar.

Master Builder. Taking the word *master* in the sense of one possessed of the highest degree of skill and knowledge, the epithet "Master Builder" is sometimes used by Masons as an epithet of the Great Architect of the Universe. Urquhart (*Pillars of Hercules*, ii., 67) derives it from the ancient Hebrews, who, he says, "used *algabil*, the Master Builder, as an epithet of God."

Master, Cohen. (*Maître Coën.*) A degree in the collection of the Mother Lodge of the Philosophic Scottish Rite.

Master, Crowned. (*Maître Couronne.*) A degree in the collection of the Lodge of Saint Louis des Amis-Réunis at Calais.

Master, Egyptian. (*Maître Egyptien.*) A degree in the Archives of the Mother Lodge of the Philosophic Scottish Rite.

Master, Elect. See *Elect Master*.

Master, English. (*Maître Anglais.*) The Eighth Degree of the Rite of Misraim.

Master, English Perfect. (*Maître Parfait Anglais.*) A degree in the collection of Le Rouge.

Master, Four Times Venerable. (*Maître quatre fois Vénérable.*) A degree introduced into Berlin by the Marquis de Bernes.

Master, Grand. See *Grand Master*.

Master Hermetic. (*Maître Hermétique.*) A degree in the collection of Lemanceau.

Master, Illustrious. (*Maître Illustre.*) A degree in the collection of Lemanceau.

Master, Illustrious Symbolic. (*Maître Symbolique Illustre.*) A degree in the nomenclature of Fustier.

Master in Israel. See *Intendant of the Building*.

Master in Perfect Architecture. (*Maître en la Parfaite Architecture.*) A degree in the nomenclature of Fustier.

Master in the Chair. (*Meister im Stuhl.*) The name given in Germany to the presiding officer of a Lodge. It is the same as the Worshipful Master in English.

Master, Irish. (*Maître Irlandais.*) The Seventh Degree of the Rite of Misraim. Ramsay gave this name at first to the degree which he subsequently called Maître Ecossais or Scottish Master. It is still the Seventh Degree of the Rite of Misraim.

Master, Kabbalistic. (*Maître Cabalistique.*) A degree in the collection of the Mother Lodge of the Philosophic Scottish Rite.

Master, Little Elect. (*Petit Maître élu.*) A degree in the Archives of the Mother Lodge of the Philosophic Scottish Rite.

Master Mason. In all the Rites of Masonry, no matter how variant may be their organization in the high degrees, the Master Mason constitutes the Third Degree. In form this degree is also everywhere substantially the same, because its legend is an essential part of it; and, as on that legend the degree must be founded, there can nowhere be any important variation, because the tradition has at all times been the same.

The Master Mason's Degree was originally called the summit of Ancient Craft Masonry; and so it must have been before the disseverance from it of the Royal Arch, by which is meant not the ritual, but the symbolism of Arch Masonry. But under its present organization the degree is actually incomplete, because it needs a complement that is only to be supplied in a higher one. Hence its symbolism is necessarily restricted, in its mutilated form, to the first Temple and the present life, although it gives the assurance of a future one.

As the whole system of Craft Masonry is intended to present the symbolic idea of man passing through the pilgrimage of life, each degree is appropriated to a certain portion of that pilgrimage. If, then, the First Degree is a representation of youth, the time to learn, and the Second of manhood or the time to work, the Third is symbolic of old age, with its trials, its sufferings, and its final termination in death. The time for toiling is now over—the opportunity to learn has passed away—the spiritual temple that we all have been striving to erect in our hearts, is now nearly completed, and the wearied workman awaits only the word of the Grand Master of the Universe, to call him from the labors of earth to the eternal refreshments of heaven. Hence, this is, by far, the most solemn and sacred of the degrees of Masonry; and it has, in consequence of the profound truths which it inculcates, been distinguished by the Craft as the sublime degree. As an Entered Apprentice, the Mason was taught those elementary instructions which were to fit him for further advancement in his profession, just as the youth is supplied with that rudimentary education which is to prepare him for entering on the active duties of life; as a Fellow-Craft, he is directed to continue his investigations in the science of the Institution, and to labor diligently in the tasks it prescribes, just as the man is required to enlarge his mind by the acquisition of new ideas, and to extend his usefulness to his fellow-creatures; but, as a Master Mason, he is taught the last, the most important, and the most necessary of truths, that having been faithful to all his trusts, he is at last to die, and to receive the reward of his fidelity.

It was the single object of all the ancient rites and mysteries practised in the very bosom of Pagan darkness, shining as a solitary beacon in all that surrounding gloom, and cheering the philosopher in his weary pilgrimage of life, to teach the immortality of the soul. This is still the great design of the Third Degree of Masonry. This is the scope and aim of its ritual. The Master Mason represents man, when youth, manhood, old age, and life itself, have passed away as fleeting shadows, yet raised from the grave of iniquity, and quickened into another and a better existence. By its legend and all its

ritual, it is implied that we have been redeemed from the death of sin and the sepulcher of pollution. "The ceremonies and the lecture," says Dr. Crucefix, "beautifully illustrate this all-engrossing subject; and the conclusion we arrive at is, that youth, properly directed, leads us to honorable and virtuous maturity, and that the life of man, regulated by morality, faith, and justice, will be rewarded at its closing hour, by the prospect of eternal bliss."

Masonic historians have found much difficulty in settling the question as to the time of the invention and composition of the degree. The theory that at the building of the Temple of Jerusalem the Craft were divided into three or even more degrees, being only a symbolic myth, must be discarded in any historical discussion of the subject. The real question at issue is whether the Master Mason's Degree, as a degree, was in existence among the Operative Freemasons before the eighteenth century, or whether we owe it to the Revivalists of 1717. Bro. Wm. J. Hughan, in a very able article on this subject, published in 1873, in the *Voice of Masonry*, says that "so far the evidence respecting its history goes no farther back than the early part of the last century." The evidence, however, is all of a negative character. There is none that the degree existed in the seventeenth century or earlier, and there is none that it did not. All the old manuscripts speak of Masters and Fellows, but these might have been and probably were only titles of rank. The Sloane MS., No. 3329, speaks, it is true, of modes of recognition peculiar to Masters and Fellows, and also of a Lodge consisting of Masters, Fellows, and Apprentices. But even if we give to this MS. its earliest date, that which is assigned to it by Findel, near the end of the seventeenth century, it will not necessarily follow that these Masters, Fellows, and Apprentices had each a separate and distinct degree. Indeed, it refers only to one Lodge, which was, however, constituted by three different ranks; and it records but one oath, so that it is possible that there was only one common form of initiation.

The first positive historical evidence that we have of the existence of a Master's Degree is to be found in the General Regulations compiled by Payne in 1720. It is there declared that Apprentices must be admitted Masters and Fellow-Crafts only in the Grand Lodge. The degree was then in existence. But this record would not militate against the theory advanced by some that Desaguliers was its author in 1717. Dermott asserts that the degree, as we now have it, was the work of Desaguliers and seven others, who, being Fellow-Crafts, but not knowing the Master's part, boldly invented it, that they might organize a Grand Lodge. He intimates that the true Master's Degree existed before that time, and was in possession of the Ancients. But Dermott's testimony is absolutely worth nothing, because he was a violent partisan, and because his statements are irreconcilable with other facts. If the Ancients were in possession of the degree which had existed before 1717, and the Moderns were not, where did the former get it?

Documentary evidence is yet wanting to settle the precise time of the composition of the Third Degree as we now have it. But it would not be prudent to oppose too positively the theory that it must be traced to the second decade of the eighteenth century. The proofs, as they arise day by day, from the resurrection of old manuscripts, seem to incline that way.

But the legend, perhaps, is of much older date. It may have made a part of the general initiation; but there is no doubt that, like the similar one of the Compagnons de la Tour in France, it existed among the Operative Gilds of the Middle Ages as an esoteric narrative. Such a legend all the histories of the Ancient Mysteries prove to us belongs to the spirit of initiation. There would have been no initiation worth preservation without it.

Master, Most High and Puissant. (*Maître très haut et très puissant.*) The Sixty-second Degree of the Rite of Misraim.

Master, Most Wise. The title of a presiding officer of a Chapter of Rose Croix, usually abbreviated as Most Wise.

Master, Mystic. (*Maître Mystique.*) A degree in the collection of Pyron.

Master of all Symbolic Lodges, Grand. See *Grand Master of all Symbolic Lodges*.

Master of a Lodge. See *Worshipful*.

Master of Cavalry. An officer in a Council of Companions of the Red Cross, whose duties are, in some respects, similar to those of a Junior Deacon in a symbolic Lodge. The two offices of Master of Cavalry and Master of Infantry were first appointed by Constantine the Great.

Master of Ceremonies. An officer found in many American Lodges and at one time in the Lodges of England and the Continent. In English Lodges the office is almost a nominal one, without any duties, but in the continental Lodges he acts as the conductor of the candidate. Oliver says that the title should be, properly, Director of Ceremonies, and he objects to Master of Ceremonies as "unmasonic." In the Constitutions of the Grand Lodge of England, issued in 1884, the title is changed to "Director of Ceremonies."

Master of Dispatches. The Secretary of a Council of Companions of the Red Cross. The *Magister Epistolarum* was the officer under the Empire who conducted the correspondence of the Emperor.

Master of Finances. The Treasurer of a Council of Companions of the Red Cross.

Master of Hamburg, Perfect. (*Maître parfait de Hambourg.*) A degree in the nomenclature of Fustier.

Master of Infantry. The Treasurer of a Council of Companions of the Red Cross. (See *Master of Cavalry*.)

Master of Lodges. (*Maître des Loges.*) The Sixty-first Degree of the Rite of Misraim.

Master of Masters, Grand. (*Grand Maître des Maîtres.*) The Fifty-ninth Degree of the Metropolitan Chapter of France.

Master of Paracelsus. (*Maître de Paracelse.*) A degree in the collection of Pyron.

Master of Secrets, Perfect. (*Maître parfait des Secrets.*) A degree in the manuscript collection of Peuvret.

Master of St. Andrew. The Fifth Degree of the Swedish Rite; the same as the Grand Elu Ecossais of the Clermont system.

Master of the Chivalry of Christ. So St. Bernard addresses Hugh de Payens, Grand Master of the Templars. "Hugoni Militi Christi et Magistro Militiæ Christi, Bernardus Clercevallus," etc.

Master of the Hermetic Secrets, Grand. (*Maître desSecrets Hermétique, Grand.*) A degree in the manuscript collection of Peuvret.

Master of the Hospital. "Sacri Domus Hospitalis Sancto Joannis Hierosolymitani Magister," or Master of the Sacred House of the Hospital of St. John of Jerusalem, was the official title of the chief of the Order of Knights of Malta; more briefly, "Magister Hospitalis," or Master of the Hospital. Late in their history, the more imposing title of "Magnus Magister," or Grand Master, was sometimes assumed; but the humbler designation was still maintained. On the tomb of Zacosta, who died in 1467, we find "Magnus Magister"; but twenty-three years after, D'Aubusson signs himself "Magister Hospitalis Hierosolymitani."

Master of the Key to Masonry, Grand. (*Grand Maître de la Clef de la Maçonnerie.*) The Twenty-first Degree of the Chapter of the Emperors of the East and West.

Master of the Legitimate Lodges, Grand. (*Maître des Loges légitimes.*) A degree in the Archives of the Mother Lodge of the Eclectic Philosophic Rite.

Master of the Palace. An officer in a Council of Companions of the Red Cross, whose duties are peculiar to the degree.

Master of the Sages. The Fourth Degree of the Initiated Knights and Brothers of Asia.

Master of the Seven Kabbalistic Secrets, Illustrious. (*Maître Illustre des sept Secrets Cabalistiques.*) A degree in the manuscript collection of Peuvret.

Master of the Temple. Originally the official title of the Grand Master of the Templars. After the dissolution of the Order in England, the same title was incorrectly given to the *custos* or guardian of the Temple Church at London, and the error is continued to the present day.

Master of the Work. The chief builder or architect of a cathedral or other important edifice in the Middle Ages was called the *Master of the work;* thus, Jost Dotzinger was, in the fifteenth century, called the Master of the work at the cathedral of Strasburg. In the Middle Ages the "Magister operis" was one to whom the public works was entrusted. Such an officer existed in the monasteries. He was also called *operarius* and *magister operarum.* Du Cange says that kings had their *operarii, magistri operarum* or masters of the works. It is these Masters of the works whom Anderson has constantly called Grand Masters. Thus, when he says (*Constitutions,* 1738, p. 69) that "King John made Peter de Cole-Church Grand Master of the Masons in rebuilding London bridge," he should have said that he was appointed *operarius* or Master of the works. The use of the correct title would have made Anderson's history more valuable.

Master, Past. See *Past Master.*

Master, Perfect. See *Perfect Master.*

Master, Perfect Architect. The Twenty-seventh Degree of the Rite of Mizraim.

Master, Perfect Irish. See *Perfect Irish Master.*

Master Philosopher by the Number 3. (*Maître philosophe par le Nombre 3.*) A degree in the manuscript collection of Peuvret.

Master Philosopher by the Number 9. (*Maître philosophe par le Nombre 9.*) A degree in the manuscript collection of Peuvret.

Master Philosopher Hermetic. (*Maître philosophe Hermétique.*) A degree in the collection of Peuvret.

Master, Private. (*Maître Particulier.*) The Nineteenth Degree of the Metropolitan Chapter of France.

Master Provost and Judge. (*Maître Prevôt et Juge.*) The Eighth Degree of the Metropolitan Chapter of France.

Master, Puissant Irish. See *Puissant Irish Master.*

Master, Pythagorean. (*Maître Pythagoricien.*) Thory says that this is the Third and last degree of the Masonic system instituted according to the doctrine of Pythagoras.

Master, Royal. See *Royal Master.*

Master, Secret. See *Secret Master.*

Master, Select. See *Select Master.*

Master, Supreme Elect. (*Maître suprême Elu.*) A degree in the Archives of the Philosophic Scottish Rite.

Master Theosophist. (*Maître Théosophie.*) The Third Degree of the Rite of Swedenborg.

Master through Curiosity. (*Maître par Curiosite.*) 1. The Sixth Degree of the Rite of Mizraim; 2. The Sixth Degree of the collection of the Metropolitan Chapter of France. It is a modification of the Intimate Secretary of the Scottish Rite.

Master to the Number 15. (*Maître au Nombre 15.*) A degree in the manuscript collection of Peuvret.

Master, True. (*Vrai Maître.*) A degree of the Chapter of Clermont.

Master, Worshipful. See *Worshipful.*

Materials of the Temple. Masonic tradition tells us that the trees out of which the timbers were made for the Temple were felled and prepared in the forest of Lebanon, and that the stones were hewn, cut, and squared in the quarries of Tyre. But both the Book of Kings and Josephus concur in the statement that Hiram of Tyre furnished only cedar and fir trees for the Temple. The stones were most probably (and the explorations of modern travelers confirm the opinion) taken from the quarries which abound in and around Jerusalem. The tradition, therefore, which derives these stones from the quarries of Tyre, is incorrect.

Maters. In the Cooke MS. (line 825)—and it is the only Old Constitution in which it occurs—we find the word *maters:* "Hit is seyd in ye art of Masonry y^t^ no man scholde make ende so well of worke begonne bi another to ye profite of his lorde as he began hit for to end hit bi his *maters* or to whom he scheweth his *maters*," where, evidently, *maters* is a corruption of the Latin *matrix*, a mold; this latter being the word used in all the other Old Constitutions in the same connection. (See *Mold*.)

Mathoc. (*Amiability, sweetness.*) The name of the Third Step of the Mystic Ladder of the Kadosh of the A. A. Scottish Rite.

Matriculation Book. In the Rite of Strict Observance, the register which contained the lists of the Provinces, Lodges, and members of the Rite was called the Matriculation Book. The term was borrowed from the usage of the Middle Ages, where *matricula* meant "a catalogue." It was applied by the ecclesiastical writers of that period to lists of the clergy, and also of the poor, who were to be provided for by the churches, whence we have *matricula clericorum* and *matricula pauperum*.

Matter. A subject deemed of important study to the alchemical and hermetical devotees. The subject will not be discussed here. It holds a valued position for instruction in the Society of the Rosicrucians, who hold that matter is subject to change, transformation, and apparent dissolution; but, in obedience to God's great laws of economy, nothing is lost, but is simply transferred.

Mature Age. The Charges of 1722 prescribe that a candidate for initiation must be of "mature and discreet age"; but the usage of the Craft has differed in various countries as to the time when maturity of age is supposed to have arrived. In the Regulations of 1663, it is set down at twenty-one years (*Constitutions*, 1738, p. 102); and this continues to be the construction of maturity in all English Lodges both in Great Britain and this country. France and Switzerland have adopted the same period. At Frankfort-on-the-Main it is fixed at twenty, and in Prussia and Hanover at twenty-five. The Grand Lodge of Hamburg has decreed that the age of Masonic maturity shall be that which is determined by the laws of the land to be the age of legal majority. [Under the Scotch Constitution the age was eighteen until 1891, when it was raised to twenty-one; and under the Irish Constitution it was twenty-one until 1741, when it was raised to twenty-five and so remained until 1817, when it was again lowered to twenty-one.]

Maul or **Setting Maul.** See *Mallet.*

Maurer. German for Mason, as Maurerei is for Masonry, and Freimaurer for Freemason.

Maurer, Gruss. A German Masonic operative expression, divided by some into Gruss Maurer, Wort Maurer, Schrift Maurer, and Briefträger—that is, those who claimed aid and recognition through signs and proving, and those who carried written documents.

Maut. The consort of the god Amon, usually crowned with a pechent or double diadem, emblem of the sovereignty of the two regions. Sometimes a vulture, the symbol of maternity, of heaven, and knowledge of the future, shows its head on the forehead of the goddess, its wings forming the head-dress. Horapollo says the vulture designates *maternal love* because it feeds its young with its own blood; and, according to Pliny, it represents heaven because no one can reach its nest, built on the highest rocks, and, therefore, that it is begotten of the winds. Maut is clothed in a long, close-fitting robe, and holds in her hand the sacred Anch, or sign of life.

Maximilian, Joseph I. King of Bavaria, who, becoming incensed against the Fraternity, issued edicts against Freemasons in 1799 and 1804, which he renewed in 1814.

Mecklenburg. Masonry was introduced here in 1754, but not firmly rooted until 1799. There are two Provincial G. Lodges, with 13 Lodges and 1,250 Brethren.

Medals. A medal is defined to be a piece of metal in the shape of a coin, bearing figures or devices and mottoes, struck and distributed in memory of some person or event. When Freemasonry was in its operative stage, no medals were issued. The medals of the Operative Masons were the monuments which they erected in the form of massive buildings, adorned with all the beauties of architectural art. But it was not long after its transformation into a Speculative Order before it began to issue medals. Medals are now struck every year by Lodges to commemorate some distinguished member or some remarkable event in the annals of the Lodge. Many Lodges in Europe have cabinets of medals, of which the Lodge Minerva of the Three Palms at Leipsic is especially valuable. In America no Lodge has made such a collection except Pythagoras Lodge at New York.

No Masonic medal appears to have been found earlier than that of 1733, commemorative of a Lodge being established at Florence, by Lord Charles Sackville. The Lodge appears not to have been founded by regular authority; but, however that may be, the event was commemorated by a medal, a copy of which exists in the collection in possession of the Lodge "Minerva of the Three Palms," at Leipsic. The *obverse* contains a bust representation of Lord Sackville, with the inscription—"Carolvs Sackville, Magister, Fl." The *reverse* represents Harpocrates in the attitude of silence, leaning upon a broken column, and holding in his left arm the cornucopia filled with rich fruits, also the implements of Masonry, with a thyrsus, staff, and serpent resting upon the fore and back ground.

The minimum of charity found among Ma-

Masters is the Roman penny (*denarius*), weighing 60 grains silver, worth fifteen cents.

THE PENNY OF THE MARK MASTER.

The above was struck at Rome, under Tiberius, A.D. 18. The portrait is "Tiberius"; the reverse the "Goddess Clemency." The inscription reads: "Tiberius Cæsar Augustus, the son of the Deified Augustus, the High Priest."

Two medals, weighing 120 grains each, of silver, about thirty cents, were struck off at

THE JEWISH HALF-SHEKEL OF SILVER.
(TWO SPECIMENS.)

Jerusalem, under Simon Maccabee, the Jewish ruler, B.C. 138, 139. They are the oldest money coined by the Jews. The devices are the brazen laver that stood before the Temple, and three lilies springing from one stem. The inscriptions, translated from the Hebrew of the oldest style, say, "Half-shekel; Jerusalem the Holy."

Bro. Robt. Morris and Bro. Coleman, in their *Calendar*, furnish much valuable information on this subject.

[The earliest work on Masonic Medals is by Ernest Zacharias, entitled *Numotheca Numismatica Latomorum*. It was issued at Dresden in parts, the first appearing on September 13, 1840, the eighth and last on January 29, 1846. It gave 48 medals in all. Then came *Die Denkmünzen der Freimaurerbruderschaft*, by Dr. J. F. L. Theodor Merzdorf, published at Oldenburg in 1851, and describing 334 medals.

The standard work now on the subject is *The Medals of the Masonic Fraternity*, by W. T. R. Marvin, privately printed at Boston in 1880, in which over 700 medals are described.

Mediterranean Pass. A side degree sometimes conferred in America on Royal Arch Masons. It has no lecture or legend, and should not be confounded, as it sometimes is, with the very different degree of Knight of the Mediterranean Pass. It is, however, now nearly obsolete.

Meeting of a Chapter. See *Convocation*.

Meeting of a Lodge. See *Communication*.

Meet on the Level. In the Prestonian lectures as practised in the beginning of the last century, it was said that Masons met on the square and hoped to part on the level. In the American system of Webb a change was made, and we were instructed that they *meet on the level and part on the square*. And in 1842 the Baltimore Convention made a still further change, by adding that *they act by the plumb;* and this formula is now, although quite modern, generally adopted by the Lodges in America.

Megacosm. An intermediate world, great, but not equal to the Macrocosm, and yet greater than the Microcosm, or little world, man.

Mehen. An Egyptian mythological serpent, the winding of whose body represented the tortuous course of the sun in the nocturnal regions. The serpentine course taken when traveling through darkness. The direction metaphorically represented by the initiate in his first symbolic journey as Practicus in the Society of the Rosicrucians.

Mehour. Space, the name given to the feminine principle of the Deity by the Egyptians.

Meister. German for Master; in French, Maître; in Dutch, Meester; in Swedish, Mastar; in Italian, Maestro; in Portuguese, Mestre. The old French word appears to have been Meistrier. In old French operative laws, Le Mestre was frequently used.

Meister im Stuhl. (*Master in the Chair.*) The Germans so call the Master of a Lodge.

Melancthon, Philip. The name of this celebrated reformer is signed to the Charter of Cologne as the representative of Dantzic. The evidence of his connection with Freemasonry depends entirely on the authenticity of that document.

Melchizedek. King of Salem, and a priest of the Most High God, of whom all that we know is to be found in the passages of Scripture read at the conferring of the degree of High Priesthood. Some theologians have supposed him to have been Shem, the son of Noah. The sacrifice of offering bread and wine is first attributed to Melchizedek; and hence, looking to the similar Mithraic sacrifice, Higgins is inclined to believe that he professed the religion of Mithras. He abandoned the sacrifice of slaughtered animals, and, to quote the words of St. Jerome, "offered bread and wine as a type of Christ." Hence, in the New Testament, Christ is represented as a priest after the order of Melchizedek. In Masonry, Melchizedek is connected with the order or degree of High Priesthood, and some of the high degrees.

Melchizedek, Degree of. The Sixth Degree of the Order of Brothers of Asia.

Melech. Properly, *Malach*, a messenger, and hence an angel, because the angels were supposed to be the messengers of God. In the ritual of one of the high degrees we meet with the sentence *hamelech Gebalim*, which has been variously translated. The French ritualists handle Hebrew words with but little attention to Hebrew grammar, and hence they translate this sentence as "Jabulum est un bon Maçon." The former American ritualists gave it as meaning "Guibulum is a good man." Guibulum is undoubtedly used as a proper name, and is a corrupt derivation from the Hebrew Masonic *Giblim*, which means stone-squarers or masons, and *melach* for *malach* means a messenger, one sent to accomplish a certain task. Bros. Pike and Rockwell make the first word *hamalek*, the king or chief. If the words were reversed, we should have the Hebrew vocative, "O! Gibulum the messenger." As it is, Bro. Pike makes it vocative, and interprets it, "Oh! thou glory of the Builders." Probably, however, the inventor of the degree meant simply to say that Gibulum was a messenger, or one who had been sent to make a discovery, but that he did not perfectly express the idea according to the Hebrew idiom, or that his expression has since been corrupted by the copyists.

Melesino, Rite of. This is a Rite scarcely known out of Russia, where it was founded about the year 1765, by Melesino, a very learned man and Mason, a Greek by birth, but high in the military service of Russia. It consisted of seven degrees, viz.: 1. Apprentice. 2. Fellow-Craft. 3. Master Mason. 4. The Mystic Arch. 5. Scottish Master and Knight. 6. The Philosopher. 7. The Priest or High Priest of the Templars. The four higher degrees abounded in novel traditions and myths unknown to any of the other Rites, and undoubtedly invented by the founder. The whole Rite was a mixture of Kabbalism, magic, Gnosticism, and the Hermetic philosophy mixed in almost inextricable confusion. The Seventh or final degree was distinctly Rosicrucian, and the religion of the Rite was Christian, recognizing and teaching the belief in the Messiah and the dogma of the Trinity.

Melita. The ancient name of the island of Malta.

Member, Honorary. See *Honorary Members*.

Member, Life. See *Life Member*.

Member of a Lodge. As soon as permanent Lodges became a part of the Masonic organization, it seems to have been required that every Mason should belong to one, and this is explicitly stated in the charges approved in 1722. (See *Affiliated Mason*.)

Membership, Right of. The first right which a Mason acquires, after the reception of the Third Degree, is that of claiming membership in the Lodge in which he has been initiated. The very fact of his having received that degree makes him at once an inchoate member of the Lodge—that is to say, no further application is necessary, and no new ballot is required; but the candidate, having now become a Master Mason, upon signifying his submission to the regulations of the Society by affixing his signature to the book of by-laws, is constituted, by virtue of that act, a full member of the Lodge, and entitled to all the rights and prerogatives accruing to that position.

[Under the English Constitution (Rule 191), initiation is sufficient for membership.]

Memphis, Rite of. In 1839, two French Masons, named respectively Marconis and Moullet, of whom the former was undoubtedly the leader, instituted, first at Paris, then at Marseilles, and afterward at Brussels, a new Rite which they called the "Rite of Memphis," and which consisted of ninety-one degrees. Subsequently, another degree was added to this already too long list. The Rite, however, has repeatedly undergone modifications. The Rite of Memphis was undoubtedly founded on the extinct Rite of Misraim; for, as Ragon says, the Egyptian Rite seems to have inspired Marconis and Moullet in the organization of their new Rite. It is said by Ragon, who has written copiously on the Rite, that the first series of degrees, extending to the Thirty-fifth Degree, is an assumption of the thirty-three degrees of the Ancient and Accepted Rite, with scarcely a change of name. The remaining degrees of the Rite are borrowed, according to the same authority, from other well-known systems, and some, perhaps, the invention of their founders.

The Rite of Memphis was not at first recognized by the Grand Orient of France, and consequently formed no part of legal French Masonry. So about 1852 its Lodges were closed by the civil authority, and the Rite, to use a French Masonic phrase, "went to sleep."

In the year 1862, Marconis, still faithful to the system which he had invented, applied to the Grand Master of France to give to it a new life. The Grand College of Rites was consulted on the subject, and the Council of the Order having made a favorable decree, the Rite of Memphis was admitted, in November, 1862, among those Masonic systems which acknowledge obedience to the Grand Orient of France, and perform their functions within its bosom. To obtain this position, however, the only one which, in France, preserves a Masonic system from the reputation of being clandestine, it was necessary that Marconis, who was then the Grand Hierophant, should, as a step preliminary to any favorable action on the part of the Grand Orient, take an obligation by which he forever after divested himself of all authority, of any kind whatsoever, over the Rite. It passed entirely out of his hands, and, going into "obedience" to the Grand Orient, that body has taken complete and undivided possession of it, and laid its high degrees upon the shelf, as Masonic curiosities, since the Grand Orient only recognizes, in practise, the thirty-three degrees of the Ancient and Accepted Rite.

This, then, is the present position of the Rite of Memphis in France. Its original possessors have disclaimed all further control or direction of it. It has been admitted by the Grand Orient among the eight systems of

Rites which are placed "under its obedience"; that is to say, it admits its existence, but it does not suffer it to be worked. Like all Masonic Rites that have ever been invented, the organization of the Rite of Memphis is founded on the first three degrees of Ancient Craft Masonry. These three degrees, of course, are given in Symbolic Lodges. In 1862, when Marconis surrendered the Rite into the hands of the ruling powers of French Masonry, many of these Lodges existed in various parts of France, although in a dormant condition, because, as we have already seen, ten years before they had been closed by the civil authority. Had they been in active operation, they would not have been recognized by the French Masons; they would have been looked upon as clandestine, and there would have been no affiliation with them, because the Grand Orient recognizes no Masonic bodies as legal which do not in return recognize it as the head of French Masonry.

But when Marconis surrendered his powers as Grand Hierophant of the Rite of Memphis to the Grand Orient, that body permitted these Lodges to be resuscitated and reopened only on the conditions that they would acknowledge their subordination to the Grand Orient; that they would work only in the first three degrees and never confer any degree higher than that of Master Mason; the members of these Lodges, however high might be their dignities in the Rite of Memphis, were to be recognized only as Master Masons; every Mason of the Rite of Memphis was to deposit his Masonic titles with the Grand Secretary of the Grand Orient; these titles were then to be *visé* or approved and regularized, but only as far as the degree of Master Mason; no Mason of the Rite of Memphis was to be permitted to claim any higher degree, and if he attempted to assume any such title of a higher degree which was not approved by the Grand Master, he was to be considered as irregular, and was not to be affiliated with by the members of any of the regular Lodges.

Such is now the condition of the Rite of Memphis in France. It has been absorbed into the Grand Orient; Marconis, its founder and head, has surrendered all claim to any jurisdiction over it; there are Lodges under the jurisdiction of the Grand Orient which originally belonged to the Rite of Memphis, and they practise its ritual, but only so far as to give the degrees of Apprentice, Fellow-Craft, and Master Mason. Its "Sages of the Pyramids," its "Grand Architects of the Mysterious City," its "Sovereign Princes of the Magi of the Sanctuary of Memphis," with its "Sanctuary," its "Mystical Temple," its "Liturgical College," its "Grand Consistory," and its "Supreme Tribunal," exist no longer except in the diplomas and charters which have been quietly laid away on the shelves of the Secretariat of the Grand Orient. To attempt to propagate the Rite is now in France a high Masonic offense. The Grand Orient alone has the power, and there is no likelihood that it will ever exercise it. Some circumstances which have recently occurred in the Grand Orient of France very clearly show the true condition of the Rite of Memphis. A meeting was held in Paris by the Council of the Order, a body which, something like the Committee of General Purposes of the Grand Lodge of England, does all the preliminary business for the Grand Orient, but which is possessed of rather extensive legislative and administrative powers, as it directs the Order during the recess of the Grand Orient. At that meeting, a communication was received from a Lodge in Moldavia, called "The Disciples of Truth," which Lodge is under the jurisdiction of the Grand Orient of France, having been chartered by that body. This communication stated that certain brethren of that Lodge had been invested by one Carence with the degree of Rose Croix in the Rite of Memphis, and that the diplomas had been dated at the "Grand Orient of Egypt," and signed by Bro. Marconis as Grand Hierophant. The commission of the Council of the Order, to whom the subject was referred, reported that the conferring of these degrees was null and void; that neither Carence nor Marconis had any commission, authority, or power to confer degrees of the Memphis Rite or to organize bodies; and that Marconis had, by oath, solemnly divested himself of all right to claim the title of Grand Hierophant of the Rite; which oath, originally taken in May, 1862, had at several subsequent times, namely, in September, 1863, March, 1864, September, 1865, and March, 1866, been renewed. As a matter of clemency, the Council determined not, for the present at least, to prefer charges against Marconis and Carence before the Grand Orient, but to warn them of the error they committed in making a traffic of Masonic degrees. It also ordered the report to be published and widely diffused, so that the Fraternity might be apprised that there was no power outside of the Grand Orient which could confer the high degrees of any Rite.

An attempt having been made, in 1872, to establish the Rite in England, Bro. Montague, the Secretary-General of the Supreme Council, wrote to Bro. Thevenot, the Grand Secretary of the Grand Orient of France, for information as to its validity. From him he received a letter containing the following statements, from which official authority we gather the fact that the Rite of Memphis is a dead Rite, and that no one has authority in any country to propagate it.

"Neither in 1866, nor at any other period, has the Grand Orient of France recognized 'the Ancient and Primitive Rite of Masonry,' concerning which you inquire, and which has been recently introduced in Lancashire.

"At a particular time, and with the intention of causing the plurality of Rites to disappear, the Grand Orient of France annexed and absorbed the Rite of Memphis, under the express condition that the Lodges of that Rite, which were received under its jurisdiction, should confer only the three symbolic degrees of Apprentice, Fellow-Craft, and Master, adcording to its special rituals, and refused to recognize any other degree, or any other title, belonging to such Rite.

"At the period when this treaty was negotiated with the Supreme Chief of this Rite by Bro. Marconis de Nègre, Bro. H. J. Seymour was at Paris, and seen by us, but no power was conferred on him by the Grand Orient of France concerning this Rite; and, what is more, the Grand Orient of France does not give, and has never given, to any single person the right to make Masons or to create Lodges.

"Afterwards, and in consequence of the bad faith of Bro. Marconis de Nègre, who pretended he had ceded his Rite to the Grand Orient of France for France alone, Bro. Harry J. Seymour assumed the title of Grand Master of the Rite of Memphis in America, and founded in New York a Sovereign Sanctuary of this Rite. A correspondence ensued between this new power and the Grand Orient of France, and even the name of this Sovereign Sanctuary appeared in our Calendar for 1867. But when the Grand Orient of France learned that this power went beyond the three symbolic degrees, and that its confidence had been deceived, the Grand Orient broke off all connection with this power, and personally with Bro. Harry J. Seymour; and, in fact, since that period, neither the name of Bro. Harry J. Seymour, as Grand Master, nor the Masonic power which he founded, have any longer appeared in the Masonic Calendar of the Grand Orient.

"Your letter leads me to believe that Bro. Harry J. Seymour is endeavoring, I do not know with what object, to introduce a new Rite into England, in that country of the primitive and only true Masonry, one of the most respectable that I know of. I consider this event as a misfortune.

"The Grand Orient of France has made the strongest efforts to destroy the Rite of Memphis; it has succeeded. The Lodges of the Rite, which it at first received within its jurisdiction, have all abandoned the Rite of Memphis to work according to the French Rite. I sincerely desire that it may be the same in the United Kingdom, and you will ever find me ready to second your efforts.

"Referring to this letter, I have, very illustrious brother, but one word to add, and that is, that the Constitution of the Grand Orient of France interdicts its founding Lodges in countries where a regular Masonic power already exists; and if it cannot found Lodges *à fortiori*, it cannot grant charters to establish Grand Masonic Powers: in other terms, the Grand Orient of France never has given to Bro. Harry J. Seymour, nor to any other person, powers to constitute a Lodge, or to create a Rite, or to make Masons. Bro. Harry J. Seymour may perfectly well have the signatures of the Grand Master and of the Chief of the Secretary's office of the Grand Orient of France on a diploma, as a fraternal *visé;* but certainly *he has neither a charter nor a power.* I also beg you to make every effort to obtain the textual copy of the documents of which Bro. Harry J. Seymour takes advantage. It is by the inspection of this document it will be necessary to judge the question, and I await new communications on this subject from your fraternal kindness."

Menatzchim. In 2 Chron. ii. 18, it is said that at the building of the Temple there were "three thousand and six hundred overseers to set the people awork." The word translated "overseers" is, in the original, מנצחים, MeNaTZCHIM. Anderson, in his catalogue of workmen at the Temple, calls these Menatzchim "expert Master Masons"; and so they have been considered in all subsequent rituals.

Mental Qualifications. See *Qualifications.*

Menu. In the Indian mythology, Menu is the son of Brahma, and the founder of the Hindu religion. Thirteen other Menus are said to exist, seven of whom have already reigned on earth. But it is the first one whose instructions constitute the whole civil and religious polity of the Hindus. The code attributed to him by the Brahmans has been translated by Sir William Jones, with the title of *The Institutes of Menu.*

Mercy. The point of a Knights Templar's sword is said to be characterized by the quality of "mercy unrestrained"; which reminds us of the Shakespearian expression—"the quality of mercy is not strained." In the days of chivalry, mercy to the conquered foe was an indispensable quality of a knight. An act of cruelty in battle was considered infamous, for whatever was contrary to the laws of generous warfare was also contrary to the laws of chivalry.

Mercy, Prince of. See *Prince of Mercy.*

Mercy-Seat. The lid or cover of the ark of the covenant was called the Mercy-seat or the Propitiatory, because on the day of the atonement the High Priest poured on it the blood of the sacrifice for the sins of the people.

Meridian Sun. The sun in the South is represented in Masonry by the Junior Warden, for this reason: when the sun has arrived at the zenith, at which time he is in the South, the splendor of his beams entitles him to the appellation which he receives in the ritual as "the beauty and glory of the day." Hence, as the Pillar of Beauty which supports the Lodge is referred to the Junior Warden, that officer is said to represent "the sun in the South at High Twelve," at which hour the Craft are called by him to refreshment, and therefore is he also placed in the South that he may the better observe the time and mark the progress of the shadow over the dial-plate as it crosses the meridian line.

Merit. The Old Charges say, "all preferment among Masons is grounded upon real worth and personal merit only; that so the Lords may be well served, the Brethren not put to shame, nor the Royal Craft despised. Therefore no Master or Warden is chosen by seniority, but for his merit." (See *Preferment.*)

Mer-Sker. The space in which the sun moves, as an Egyptian personification, signifying the habitation of Horus.

Merzdorf, J. L. T. A learned German Mason, born in 1812. Initiated in Apollo Lodge, at Leipsic, in 1834. He resuscitated the Lodge "Zum goldenen Hirsch," Oldenburg, and was for years Deputy Master. He published *Die Symbole*, etc., Leipsic, 1836, and later several other works.

Meshia, Meshiane. Corresponding to Adam and Eve, in accordance with Persian cosmogony.

Mesmer, Friedrich Anton. A German physician who was born in Suabia, in 1734, and, after a long life, a part of which was passed in notoriety and the closing years in obscurity, died in 1815. He was the founder of the doctrine of animal magnetism, called after him *Mesmerism*. He visited Paris, and became there in some degree intermixed with the Masonic charlatanism of Cagliostro, who used the magnetic operations of Mesmer's new science in his initiations. (See *Mesmeric Masonry.*)

Mesmeric Masonry. In the year 1782, Mesmer established in Paris a society which he called "the Order of Universal Harmony." It was based on the principles of animal magnetism or mesmerism, and had a form of initiation by which the founder claimed that its adepts were purified and rendered more fit to propagate the doctrines of his science. French writers have dignified this Order by the title of "Mesmeric Masonry."

Mesopolyte. The Fourth Degree of the German Union of XXII.

Mesouraneo. A Greek word, *μεσουρανέω*, signifying, *I am in the center of heaven.* Hutchinson fancifully derives from it the word Masonry, which he says is a corruption of the Greek, and refers to the constellation Magaroth mentioned by Job; but he fails to give a satisfactory reason for his etymology. Nevertheless, Oliver favors it.

Metals. In the divestiture of metals as a preliminary to initiation, we are symbolically taught that Masonry regards no man on account of his wealth. The Talmudical treatise "Beracoth," with a like spirit of symbolism, directs in the Temple service that no man shall go into the mountain of the house, that is, into the Holy Temple, "with money tied up in his purse."

Metal Tools. We are told in Scripture that the Temple was "built of stone made ready before it was brought thither: so that there was neither hammer, nor axe, nor any tool of iron heard in the house while it was in building." (1 Kings vi. 7.) Masonry has adopted this as a symbol of the peace and harmony which should reign in a Lodge, itself a type of the world. But Clarke, in his commentary on the place, suggests that it was intended to teach us that the Temple was a type of the kingdom of God, and that the souls of men are to be prepared *here* for *that* place of blessedness. *There* is no repentance, tears, nor prayers: the stones must be all squared, and fitted *here* for their place in the New Jerusalem; and, being *living stones*, must be built up a holy temple for the habitation of God.

Metropolitan Chapter of France. There existed in France, toward the end of the last century, a body calling itself the Grand Chapter General of France. It was formed out of the *débris* of the Council of Emperors of the East and West, and the Council of Knights of the East, which had been founded by Pirlet. In 1786, it united with the schismatic Grand Orient, and then received the title of the Metropolitan Chapter of France. It possessed in its archives a large collection of manuscript *cahiers* of degrees, most of them being mere Masonic curiosities.

Metusael. The name given to the Hebrew quarryman, who is represented in some legends as one of the assassins, Fanor and Amru being the other two.

Mexico. Masonry was introduced into Mexico, in the Scottish Rite, some time prior to 1810, by the civil and military officers of Spain, but the exact period of its introduction is unknown. The first Work Charters were granted for a Lodge at Vera Cruz in 1816, and one at Campeche in 1817, by the Grand Lodge of Louisiana, followed by a Charter for a Lodge at Vera Cruz in 1823 by the "City" Grand Lodge of New York, and one in the same city in 1824 from the Grand Lodge of Pennsylvania. February 10, 1826, five Charters were granted for Lodges in the City of Mexico by the "Country" Grand Lodge of New York, on the recommendation of Joel R. Poinsett, Past Deputy Grand Master of South Carolina, at that time United States Minister to Mexico, who constituted the Lodges and organized them into a Grand Lodge with Jose Ignacio Esteva as Grand Master.

The Masonic bodies, both York and Scottish Rite, however, soon degenerated into rival political clubs, and the bitter factionalism became so strong that in 1833 the authorities issued an edict suppressing all secret societies. The bodies met, however, secretly, and about 1834 the National Mexican Rite was organized with nine degrees copied after the Scottish Rite. In 1843 a Lodge was chartered at Vera Cruz, and in 1845 at Mexico by the Grand Orient of France. In 1859 a Supreme Council 33°, with jurisdiction over the Symbolic degrees, was organized by authority of Albert Pike, and for a time the Supreme Council dominated all the bodies. In 1865 the Grand Lodge Valle de Mexico was organized as a York Rite Grand Lodge, and worked as such until 1911, when a number of the Lodges, under the leadership of Past Grand Masters Levi and Pro, left the Grand Lodge and organised a rival body, under the obedience of the Supreme Council. [W. J. A.]

Mezuza. The third fundamental principle of Judaism, or the sign upon the door-post. The precept is founded upon the command, "And thou shalt write them upon the posts of thy house, and on thy gates." (Deut. vi. 4-9; xi. 13-21.) The door-posts must be those of a dwelling; synagogues are excluded.

The Karaite Jews affix Mezuzas to synagogues, and not to private houses. The Mezuza is constructed as follows: the two above-mentioned portions of Scripture are written on ruled vellum prepared according to Rabbinical rules, then rolled and fitted into a metallic tube. The word Shaddai (Almighty) is written on the outside of the roll, and can be read, when in the tube, through a slot. The Mezuza is then nailed at each end on the right-hand door-post, while the following prayer is being said: "Blessed art thou, O Lord our God! King of the Universe, who hath sanctified us with His laws, and commanded us to fix the Mezuza." Under the word Shaddai some Jews write the three angelic names Coozu, Bemuchsaz, Coozu. To these some pray for success in business.

The Talmud estimates the virtue of the Talith, the Phylacteries, and the Mezuza in the following terms: "Whosoever has the phylacteries bound to his head and arm, and the fringes thrown over his garments, and the Mezuza fixed on his door-post, is safe from sin; for these are excellent memorials, and the angels secure him from sin; as it is written, 'The angel of the Lord encamped round about them that fear Him, and delivereth them.'" (Ps. xxxiv. 7.) [C. T. McClenachan.]

Michael. מיכאל. *Who is like unto God.* The chief of the seven archangels. He is the leader of the celestial host, as Lucifer is of the infernal spirits, and the especial protector of Israel. He is prominently referred to in the Twenty-eighth Degree of the Ancient and Accepted Scottish Rite, or Knight of the Sun.

Michigan. A Charter was issued by the Prov. Grand Master of New York under date of April 27, 1764, for a Lodge at Detroit, and upon this foundation it has been customary to rest the claim that Michigan Masonry dates from 1764. In fact, there is no evidence that any work was ever done under the Charter of 1764, and if a Lodge ever came into existence thereunder, as is probable, it is certain that it was short-lived, and differed in no respect from several other Lodges known to have been temporarily held at Detroit at various times prior to 1794 by British soldiers and other sojourners.

In 1794 Detroit was still garrisoned by British soldiers and it was British soldiers who were founders of the Lodge of 1794. Afterward, when the British Government had tardily turned the post over to the Americans, and the British soldiers had been removed and the region had become somewhat Americanized, a sentiment arose in favor of building under some American Grand Lodge in preference to a Canadian, and in October, 1803, the members of the Lodge voted to petition the Grand Lodge of New York for a Charter, proposing to surrender their Canadian Charter. Chiefly on account of the slowness of communication in those days, this transaction was not brought to a close until the session of the Grand Lodge of New York, held in September, 1806. Zion Lodge died in 1812, owing to the capture of Detroit by the British, but after the war the Grand Lodge of New York gave the members a new Charter.

Other Lodges were subsequently established, and on July 31, 1826, a Grand Lodge was organized by them, and Lewis Cass elected Grand Master. In consequence of the political pressure of the anti-Masonic party at that time, the Grand Lodge suspended its labors in 1829, and remained in a dormant condition until 1841, when, at a general meeting of the Masons of the State, it was resolved that the old Grand Officers who were still alive should, on the principle that their prerogatives had never ceased, but only been in abeyance, grant dispensations for the revival of the Lodges and the renewal of labor. But this course having been objected to as irregular by most of the Grand Lodges of the United States, delegates of a constitutional number of Lodges met in September, 1844, and organized the Grand Lodge, electing John Mullett Grand Master.

The Grand Chapter was organized in 1848, the Grand Commandery in 1857, and the Grand Council in 1858. [A. G. Pitts.]

Microcosm. See *Man.*

Middle Ages. These are supposed by the best historians to extend from the time Theodoric liberated Rome (493) to the end of the fifteenth century, the important events being the fall of Constantinople in 1453, the discovery of America in 1492, and the doubling of the Cape of Good Hope in 1497. This period of ten centuries is one of great importance to the Masonic student, because it embraces within its scope events intimately connected with the history of the Order, such as the diffusion throughout Europe of the Roman Colleges of Artificers, the establishment of the architectural school of Como, the rise of the gilds, the organization of the building corporations of Germany, and the company of Freemasons of England, as well as many customs and usages which have descended with more or less modification to the modern Institution.

Middle Chamber. There were three stories of side chambers built around the Temple on three sides; what, therefore, is called in the authorized version a *middle chamber* was really the middle story of those three. The Hebrew word is יצע, *yatsang.* They are thus described in 1 Kings vi. 5, 6, 8. "And against the wall of the house he built chambers round about, against the walls of the house round about, both of the temple and of the oracle: and he made chambers round about. The nethermost chamber was five cubits broad, and the middle was six cubits broad, and the third was seven cubits broad: for without in the wall of the house he made narrowed rests round about, that the beams should not be fastened in the walls of the house. The door for the *middle chamber* was in the right side of the house: and they went up with *winding stairs* into the middle chamber, and out of the middle into the third."

These chambers, after the Temple was completed, served for the accommodation of the priests when upon duty; in them they deposited their vestments and the sacred vessels. But the knowledge of the purpose to which the middle chamber was appropriated while the Temple was in the course of construction, is only preserved in Masonic tradition. This tradition is, however, altogether mythical and symbolical in its character, and belongs to the symbolism of the *Winding Stairs*, which see.

Miles. 1. In pure Latin, *miles* means a soldier; but in Medieval Latin the word was used to designate the military knights whose institution began at that period. Thus a Knight Templar was called Miles Templarius, and a Knight Banneret, Miles Bannerettus. The pure Latin word *eques*, which signified a knight in Rome, was never used in that sense in the Middle Ages. (See *Knighthood*.)

2. The Seventh Degree of the Rite of African Architects.

Military Lodges. Lodges established in an army. They are of an early date, having long existed in the British army. In America, the first Lodge of this kind of which we have any record was one the Warrant for which was granted by the Grand Lodge of Massachusetts, in 1738, to Abraham Savage, to be used in the expedition against Canada. A similar one was granted by the same authority, in 1756, to Richard Gridley, for the expedition against Crown Point. In both of these instances the Warrants were of a general character, and might rather be considered as deputations, as they authorized Savage and Gridley to congregate Masons into one or more Lodges. In 1779, the Grand Lodge of Pennsylvania granted a Warrant to Col. Proctor, of the artillery, to open a Military Lodge, which in the Warrant is called a "Movable Lodge." In the Civil War in the United States between 1861 and 1865, many Military Lodges were established on both sides; but it is questionable whether they had a good effect. They met, certainly, with much opposition in many jurisdictions. In England, the system of Military Lodges is regulated by special provisions of the Grand Lodge Constitution. They are strictly limited to the purposes for which the Warrants were granted, and no new Lodge can be established in a regiment without the concurrence of the commanding officer. They cannot make Masons of any but military men who have attained some rank in the army above that of a private soldier, although the latter may by dispensation be admitted as Serving Brethren; and they are strictly enjoined not to interfere with the Masonic jurisdiction of any country in which they may be stationed. Military Lodges also exist on the Continent of Europe. We find one at Berlin, in Prussia, as far back as 1775, under the name of the "Military Lodge of the Blazing Star," of which Wadseck, the Masonic writer, was the orator.

Militia. In Medieval Latin, this word signifies chivalry or the body of knighthood. Hence *Militia Templi*, a title sometimes given to Knights Templar, does not signify, as it has sometimes been improperly translated, the *army of the Temple*, but the *chivalry of the Temple*.

Millin de Grand Maison, A. L. Born, 1759; died, 1818. Founder of the *Magasin Encyclopædique*. He was a Mason under the Rite Ecossais, and also belonged to the "Mère Loge" of the "Rite Ecossais Philosophique."

Minerval. The Third Degree of the Illuminati of Bavaria.

Minister of State. An officer in the Supreme Councils, Grand Consistories, and some of the high degrees of the Ancient and Accepted Scottish Rite.

Minnesota. Masonry was introduced into this State in 1849 by the constitution in the city of St. Paul of a Lodge under a Warrant issued by the Grand Lodge of Ohio. Two other Lodges were subsequently constituted by the Grand Lodges of Wisconsin and Illinois. A convention of delegates from these Lodges was held at St. Paul, and a Grand Lodge organized on February 12, 1853. A. E. Ames was elected Grand Master. The Grand Chapter was organized December 17, 1859, and the Grand Commandery was organized in 1866.

Minor. The Fifth Degree of the German Rose Croix.

Minor Illuminate. (*Illuminatus Minor*.) The Fourth Degree of the Illuminati of Bavaria.

Minute-Book. The records of a Lodge are kept by the Secretary in a journal, which is called the Minute-Book. The French call it *Planche tracée*, and the Minutes a *Morceau d'Architecture*.

Minutes. The records of a Lodge are called its minutes. The minutes of the proceedings of the Lodge should always be read just before closing, that any alterations or amendments may be proposed by the brethren; and again immediately after opening at the next communication, that they may be confirmed. But the minutes of a regular communication are not to be read at a succeeding extra one, because, as the proceedings of a regular communication cannot be discussed at an extra, it would be unnecessary to read them, for, if incorrect, they could not be amended until the next regular communication.

Mischchan, Mischaphereth, Mischtal, משכן העוה, *Tent of Testimony*. משכן זמנא, *Tent of Festival*. (See *Twenty-fourth Degree of the Scottish Rite*.) משט׳ is used in the Thirtieth Degree.

Misconduct. The Constitution of the Grand Lodge of England provides that "if any brother behave in such a manner as to disturb the harmony of the Lodge, he shall be thrice formally admonished by the Master;

and if he persist in his irregular conduct, he shall be punished according to the by-laws of that particular Lodge, or the case may be reported to higher Masonic authority." A similar rule prevails wherever Masonry exists. Every Lodge may exercise instant discipline over any member or visitor who violates the rules of order and propriety, or disturbs the harmony of the Lodge, by extrusion from the room.

Miserable Scald Masons. See *Scald Miserables.*

Mishna. See *Talmud.*

Mississippi. Masonry was introduced into this State at least as far back as 1801, in which year the Grand Lodge of Kentucky chartered a Lodge at Natchez, which became extinct in 1814. The Grand Lodge of Kentucky subsequently granted charters to two other Lodges in 1812 and 1815. Two Lodges were also constituted by the Grand Lodge of Tennessee. The delegates of three of these Lodges met in convention at the city of Natchez in July and August, 1818, and on the 25th of the latter month organized the Grand Lodge of Mississippi, Henry Tooley being elected Grand Master. The Grand Chapter was organized at Vicksburg, May 18, 1846; the Grand Council of R. and S Master, January 19, 1856; and the Grand Commandery, January 22, 1857. Scottish Masonry was introduced into the State in 1815 by the establishment of a Grand Council of Princes of Jerusalem under the obedience of the Southern Supreme Council.

Missouri. Masonry was introduced into this State in 1807 by the constitution of a Lodge in the town of St. Genevieve, under a charter granted by the Grand Lodge of Pennsylvania, which body granted a charter for another Lodge in 1809. Several charters were subsequently granted by the Grand Lodge of Tennessee. In 1821 there appear to have been but three Lodges in the State. Delegates from these organized, April 23, 1821, a Grand Lodge at St. Louis, and elected Thomas F. Riddick Grand Master. The Grand Chapter was organized May 18, 1846, and the Grand Commandery May 22, 1860.

Mistletoe. (*Viscum Album.*) A sacred plant among the Druids. It was to them a symbol of immortality, and hence an analogue of the Masonic Acacia. "The mistletoe," says Vallancey, in his *Grammar of the Irish Language*, "was sacred to the Druids, because not only its berries but its leaves also grow in clusters of three united to one stock. The Christian Irish hold the shamrock (clover, trefoil) sacred, in like manner, because of the three leaves united to one stalk."

In Scandinavian countries it is called Mistel. It is a parasitic evergreen plant bearing a glutinous fruit. It was from a fragment of this plant that the dart was made which cost the life of Balder, according to the Scandinavian Mysteries. (See *Balder*.)

The *Mistletoe*, to the Scandinavian, is the coincident symbol of the *acacia* to the Mason, the *ivy* to those of the Mysteries of Dionysius, the *myrtle* to those of Ceres, the *erica* or *heath* to those of the Osirian, the *lettuce* to those of the Adonisian, and the *lotus* or *water-lily* to those of India and Egypt. The Mistletoe that caused the death of Balder was deemed sacred as the representative of the number three. The berries and leaves of the plant or vine grow in clusters of three united on one stalk. It was profanation to touch it. It was gathered with ceremony, and then consecrated, when it was reputed to possess every sanative virtue, and denominated "All Heal."

Mitchell, James W. S. A Masonic writer and journalist, was born in the State of Kentucky, in the year 1800. He was initiated into Masonry in Owen Lodge, at Port William, now Carrollton, Kentucky, in the year 1821. He subsequently removed to the State of Missouri, where he took a prominent position in the Masonic Fraternity, and held the offices of Grand Master of the Grand Lodge, Grand High Priest of the Grand Chapter, and Grand Commander of the Grand Commandery of Knights Templar. In 1848 he established, in the city of St. Louis, a monthly journal entitled the *Masonic Signet and Literary Mirror*, which he removed to Montgomery, Alabama, in 1852, where it lasted for a short time, and then was discontinued for want of patronage. In 1858 he published *The History of Freemasonry and Masonic Digest*, in two volumes, octavo. Bro. Mitchell was a warm-hearted and devoted Mason, but, unfortunately for his reputation as an author, not an accomplished scholar, hence his style is deficient, not only in elegance, but even in grammatical purity. His natural capacity, however, was good, and his arguments as a controversialist were always trenchant, if the language was not polished. As a Masonic jurist his decisions have been considered generally, but by no means universally, correct. His opinions were sometimes eccentric, and his *History* possesses much less value than such a work should have, in consequence of its numerous inaccuracies, and the adoption by its author of all the extravagant views of earlier writers on the origin of Masonry. He died at Griffin, Georgia November 12, 1873, having been for many years a great sufferer from illness.

Mithras, Mysteries of. There are none of the Ancient Mysteries which afford a more interesting subject of investigation to the Masonic scholar than those of the Persian god Mithras. Instituted, as it is supposed, by Zeradusht or Zoroaster, as an initiation into the principles of the religion which he had founded among the ancient Persians, they in time extended into Europe, and lasted so long that traces of them have been found in the fourth century. "With their penances," says Mr. King (*Gnostics*, p. 47), "and tests of the courage of the candidate for admission, they have been maintained by a constant tradition through the secret societies of the Middle Ages and the Rosicrucians down to the modern faint reflex of the latter—the Freemasons."

Of the identity of Mithras with other deities there have been various opinions. Herodotus says he was the Assyrian Venus and the Arabian Alitta; Porphyry calls him the Demiurgos, and Lord of Generation; the Greeks identified him with Phœbus; and Higgins supposed that he was generally considered the same as Osiris. But to the Persians, who first practised his mysteries, he was a sun god, and worshiped as the God of Light. He was represented as a young man covered with a Phrygian turban, and clothed in a mantle and tunic. He presses with his knee upon a bull, one of whose horns he holds in his left hand, while with the right he plunges a dagger into his neck, while a dog standing near laps up the dripping blood.

This symbol has been thus interpreted: His piercing the throat with his dagger signifies the penetration of the solar rays into the bosom of the earth, by which action all nature is nourished; the last idea being expressed by the dog licking up the blood as it flows from the wound. But it will be seen hereafter that this last symbol admits of another interpretation.

The mysteries of Mithras were always celebrated in caves. They were divided into seven stages or degrees (Suidas says twelve), and consisted of the most rigorous proofs of fortitude and courage. Nonnus the Greek poet says, in his *Dionysiaca*, that these proofs were eighty in number, gradually increasing in severity. No one, says Gregory Nazianzen, could be initiated into the mysteries of Mithras unless he had passed through all the trials, and proved himself passionless and pure. The aspirant at first underwent the purifications by water, by fire, and by fasting; after which he was introduced into a cavern representing the world, on whose walls and roof were inscribed the celestial signs. Here he submitted to a species of baptism, and received a mark on his forehead. He was presented with a crown on the point of a sword, which he was to refuse, declaring at the same time, "Mithras alone is my crown." He was prepared, by anointing him with oil, crowning him with olive, and clothing him in enchanted armor, for the seven stages of initiation through which he was about to pass. These commenced in the following manner: In the first cavern he heard the howling of wild beasts, and was enveloped in total darkness, except when the cave was illuminated by the fitful glare of terrific flashes of lightning. He was hurried to the spot whence the sounds proceeded, and was suddenly thrust by his silent guide through a door into a den of wild beasts, where he was attacked by the initiated in the disguise of lions, tigers, hyenas, and other ravenous beasts. Hurried through this apartment, in the second cavern he was again shrouded in darkness, and for a time in fearful silence, until it was broken by awful peals of thunder, whose repeated reverberations shook the very walls of the cavern, and could not fail to inspire the aspirant with terror. He was conducted through four other caverns, in which the methods of exciting astonishment and fear were ingeniously varied. He was made to swim over a raging flood; was subjected to a rigorous fast; exposed to all the horrors of a dreary desert; and finally, if we may trust the authority of Nicætas, after being severely beaten with rods, was buried for many days up to the neck in snow. In the seventh cavern or Sacellum, the darkness was changed to light, and the candidate was introduced into the presence of the Archimagus, or chief priest, seated on a splendid throne, and surrounded by the assistant dispensers of the mysteries. Here the obligation of secrecy was administered, and he was made acquainted with the sacred words. He received also the appropriate investiture, which, says Maurice (*Ind. Antiq.*, V., ch. i.), consisted of the Kara or conical cap, and *candys* or loose tunic of Mithras, on which was depicted the celestial constellations, the zone, or belt, containing a representation of the figures of the zodiac, the pastoral staff or crosier, alluding to the influence of the sun in the labors of agriculture, and the golden serpent, which was placed in his bosom as an emblem of his having been regenerated and made a disciple of Mithras, because the serpent, by casting its skin annually, was considered in these mysteries as a symbol of regeneration.

He was instructed in the secret doctrines of the rites of Mithras, of which the history of the creation, already recited, formed a part. The mysteries of Mithras passed from Persia into Europe, and were introduced into Rome in the time of Pompey. Here they flourished, with various success, until the year 378, when they were proscribed by a decree of the Senate, and the sacred cave, in which they had been celebrated, was destroyed by the pretorian prefect.

The Mithraic monuments that are still extant in the museums of Europe evidently show that the immortality of the soul was one of the doctrines taught in the Mithraic initiation. The candidate was at one time made to personate a corpse, whose restoration to life dramatically represented the resurrection. Figures of this corpse are found in several of the monuments and talismans. There is circumstantial evidence that there was a Mithraic death in the initiation, just as there was a Carbiric death in the mysteries of Samothrace, and a Dionysiac in those of Eleusis. Commodus, the Roman emperor, had been initiated into the Mithraic mysteries at Rome, and is said to have taken great pleasure in the ceremonies. Lampridius, in his *Lives of the Emperors*, records, as one of the mad freaks of Commodus, that during the Mithraic ceremonies, where "a certain thing was to be done for the sake of inspiring terror, he polluted the rites by a *real murder*"; an expression which evidently shows that a scenic representation of a fictitious murder formed a part of the ceremony of initiation. The dog swallowing the blood of the bull was also considered as a symbol of the resurrection.

It is in the still existing talismans and gems that we find the most interesting memorials of the old Mithraic initiation. One of these is thus described by Mr. C. W. King, in his valuable work on the *Gnostics and their Remains* (London, 1864):

"There is a talisman which, from its frequent repetition, would seem to be a badge of some particular degree amongst the initiated, perhaps of the first admission. A man blindfolded, with hands tied behind his back, is bound to a pillar, on which stands a gryphon holding a wheel; the latter a most ancient emblem of the sun. Probably it was in this manner that the candidate was tested by the appearance of imminent death when the *bandage was suddenly removed from his eyes.*"

As Mithras was considered as synonymous with the sun, a great deal of solar symbolism clustered around his name, his doctrines, and his initiation. Thus, ΜΕΙΘΡΑΣ was found, by the numerical value of the letters in the Greek alphabet, to be equal to 365, the number of days in a solar year; and the decrease of the solar influence in the winter, and its revivification in the summer, was made a symbol of the resurrection from death to life.

Miter. The head-covering of the high priest of the Jews was called מצנפת, *metznephet*, which, coming from the verb NAPHAT, to *roll around*, signified something rolled around the head, a turban; and this was really the form of the Jewish miter. It is described by Leusden, in his *Philologus Hebræo-Mixtus*, as being made of dark linen twisted in many folds around the head. Many writers contend that the miter was peculiar to the high priest; but Josephus and the Mishna assert that it was worn by all the priests, that of the high priest being distinguished from the rest by the golden band, or holy crown, which was attached to its lower rim and fastened around the forehead, and on which was inscribed the words קדש ליהוה, KADOSH L'YEHOVAH, *Holiness to Jehovah*, or, as it is commonly translated, *Holiness to the Lord.* The miter is worn by the High Priest of a Royal Arch Chapter, because he represents the Jewish high priest; but the form is inaccurate. The vestment, as usually made, is a representation rather of the modern Episcopal than of the Jewish miter.

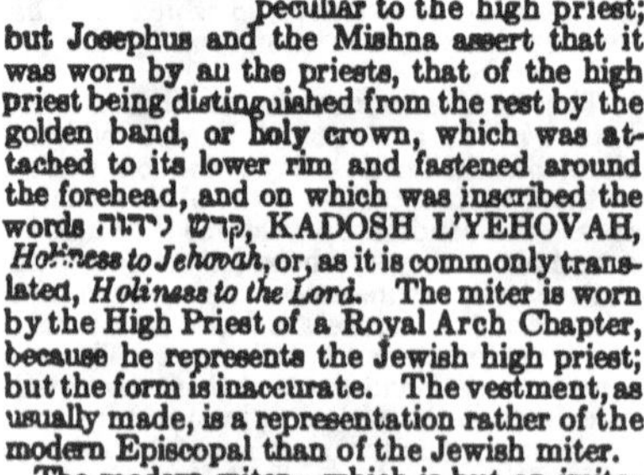

The modern miter—which is but an imitation of the Phrygian cap, and peculiar to bishops of the Christian Church, and which should therefore be worn by the Prelate of a Commandery of Knights Templar, who is supposed to hold Episcopal rank—differs in form from the Jewish vestment. It is a conical cap, divided in the middle so as to come to two points or horns, one in front and one behind, which, Durandus says, are symbolic of the two laws of the Old and New Testament.

Mizraim. Often by Masonic writers improperly spelled *Misraim.* It is the ancient Hebrew name of Egypt, and was adopted as the name of a Rite to indicate the hypothesis that it was derived from the old Egyptian initiation.

Mizraim, Rite of. This Rite originated, says Clavel, at Milan, in the year 1805, in consequence of several brethren having been refused admission into the Supreme Council of the Ancient and Accepted Rite, which had just been established in that city. One Lechangeur has the credit of organizing the Rite and selecting the statutes by which it was to be governed. It consisted at first of only eighty-seven degrees, to which three others were subsequently added. Sixty-six of the ninety degrees thus formed are said to have been taken from the Ancient and Accepted Rite, while the remaining twenty-four were either borrowed from other systems or were the invention of Lechangeur and his colleagues, Joly and Bedarride. The system of Mizraim spread over Italy, and in 1814 was introduced into France. Dissensions in the Rite soon took place, and an attempt was unsuccessfully made to obtain the recognition of the Grand Orient of France. This having been refused, the Supreme Council was dissolved in 1817; but the Lodges of the Rite still continued to confer the degrees, although, according to the constitution of French Masonry, their non-recognition by the Grand Orient had the effect of making them illegal. But eventually the Rite ceased altogether to exist as an active and independent system, and its place in Masonic history seems only to be preserved by two massive volumes on the subject, written by Mark Bedarride, the most intelligent and indefatigable of its founders, who published at Paris, in 1835, a history of the Rite, under the title of *De l'Ordre de Misraim.*

The Rite of Mizraim consisted of 90 degrees, divided into 4 series and 17 classes. Some of these degrees are entirely original, but many of them are borrowed from the Scottish Rite.

For the gratification of the curious inspector, the following list of these degrees is subjoined. The titles are translated as literally as possible from the French.

I. Series—Symbolic.

1st Class: 1, Apprentice; 2, Fellow-Craft; 3, Master. *2d Class:* 4, Secret Master; 5, Perfect Master; 6, Master through Curiosity; 7, Provost and Judge or Irish Master; 8, English Master. *3d Class:* 9, Elect of Nine; 10, Elect of the Unknown; 11, Elect of Fifteen; 12, Perfect Elect; 13, Illustrious Elect. *4th Class:* 14, Scottish Trinitarian; 15, Scottish Fellow-Craft; 16, Scottish Master; 17, Scottish panisière; 18, Master Ecossais; 19, Ecossais of the three J. J. J.; 20, Ecossais of the Sacred Vault of James VI.; 21, Ecossais of St. Andrew. *5th Class:* 22, Little Architect; 23, Grand Architect; 24, Architecture; 25, Apprentice Perfect Architect; 26, Fellow-Craft Perfect Architect; 27, Master Perfect Architect; 28, Perfect Architect; 29, Sublime Ecossais; 30, Sublime Ecossais of Heroden. *6th Class:* 31, Grand Royal Arch; 32, Grand Ax;

33, Sublime Knight of Election, Chief of the First Symbolic Series.

II. SERIES—PHILOSOPHIC.

7th Class: 34, Knight of the Sublime Election; 35, Prussian Knight; 36, Knight of the Temple; 37, Knight of the Eagle; 38, Knight of the Black Eagle; 39, Knight of the Red Eagle; 40, White Knight of the East; 41, Knight of the East. *8th Class:* 42, Commander of the East; 43, Grand Commander of the East; 44, Architecture of the Sovereign Commanders of the Temple; 45, Prince of Jerusalem. *9th Class:* 46, Sovereign Prince Rose Croix of Kilwinning and Heroden; 47, Knight of the West; 48, Sublime Philosopher; 49, Chaos the first, discreet; 50, Chaos the second, wise; 51, Knight of the Sun. *10th Class:* 52, Supreme Commander of the Stars; 53, Sublime Philosopher; 54, First Degree of the Key of Masonry, Minor; 55, Second Degree, Washer; 56, Third Degree, Bellows-blower; 57, Fourth Degree, Caster; 58, True Mason Adept; 59, Sovereign Elect; 60, Sovereign of Sovereigns; 61, Grand Master of Symbolic Lodges; 62, Most High and Most Powerful Grand Priest Sacrificer; 63, Knight of Palestine; 64, Grand Knight of the White and Black Eagle; 65, Grand Elect Knight Kadosh; 66, Grand Inquiring Commander, Chief of the Second Series.

III. SERIES—MYSTICAL.

11th Class: 67, Benevolent Knight; 68, Knight of the Rainbow; 69, Knight Chanuka, called Hynaroth; 70, Most Wise Israelitish Prince. *12th Class:* 71, Sovereign Princes Talmudim; 72, Sovereign Prince Zadkim; 73, Grand Haram. *13th Class:* 74, Sovereign Princes Haram; 75, Sovereign Princes Hasidim; 77, Grand Inspector Intendant, Regulator General of the Order, Chief of the Third Series.

IV. SERIES—KABBALISTIC.

15th and *16th Classes:* 78, 79, 80, 81, 82, 83, 84, 85, 86, degrees whose names are concealed from all but the possessors. *17th Class:* 87, Sovereign Grand Princes, constituted Grand Masters, and legitimate representatives of the order for the First Series; 88, Ditto for the Second Series; 89, Ditto for the Third Series; 90, Absolute Sovereign Grand Master, Supreme Power of the Order, and Chief of the Fourth Series.

The chiefs of this Rite demanded the privilege—which, of course, was never conceded to them—of directing and controlling all the other Rites of Freemasonry, as their common source. Its friends claimed for it an eminently philosophical character. The organization of the Rite is, however, too complicated and diffuse to have ever been practically convenient. Many of its degrees were founded upon, or borrowed from, the Egyptian rites, and its ritual is a very close imitation of the ancient system of initiation.

The legend of the Third Degree in this Rite is abolished. HAB is said to have returned to his family, after the completion of the Temple, and to have passed the remainder of his days in peace and opulence. The legend, substituted by the Rite of Mizraim for that admitted by all the other rites, is carried back to the days of Lamech, whose son Jubal, under the name of Hario-Jubal-Abi, is reported to have been slain by three traitors, Hagava, Hakina, and Heremda.

Lenning calls the Rite of Mizraim "one of the latest of the monstrous visionary schemes introduced into Freemasonry"; and Ragon characterizes it as a "fantastical connection of various rites and degrees."

Moabite Stone. A relic of black basalt, rounded at the top, two by four feet, across it being an inscription of thirty-four lines in the letters of the Hebrew-Phœnician alphabet, discovered in the ruins of ancient Dibon, by Dr. Klein, a German missionary, in 1869. A record of Mesha, King of Moab, who (2 Kings iii. 5), after Ahab's death, "rebelled against the King of Israel." Chemosh was the national god of the Moabites. The covenant name of the God of Israel occurs in the inscription, showing that the name was not then unpronounceable, or unknown to the neighboring nations. The described wars date in the tenth century B.C.

Moabon (מואבן). He whom the Junior Warden represents in the Fourteenth Degree of the A. A. Scottish Rite, as the tried and trusty friend of Hiram the Builder. (See Gen. xix. 36.)

Moabon. This word is found in some of the high degrees according to the French ritual, where it is explained as expressing "Praised be God that the crime and the criminal are punished." (*Les plus secrets des hauts grades*, etc., p. 33.) There is no such word in Hebrew, and the explanation is a fanciful one. The word is undoubtedly a Gallic corruption, first in sound and then in letters, of the Master's Word.

Mock Masons. A name given, says Noorthouck, to the unfaithful brethren and profanes who, in 1747, got up a procession in ridicule of that made at the Grand Feast. (*Constitutions*, 1784, p. 252.) (See *Scald Miserables.*)

Modern Rite. (*Rite Moderne.*) See *French Rite.*

Moderns. The Irish Masons who formed a rival Grand Lodge in London in 1751, called the supporters of the original Grand Lodge established in 1717 *Moderns*, while for themselves they assumed the title of *Ancients.* (See *Ancients.*)

Mohammed. See *Koran.*

Mohrims. Initiates, pilgrims, those entering upon an important undertaking.

Moira, Francis Rawdon, Baron. Born 1754, died 1826. A distinguished statesman and Mason. He was Acting Grand Master of England from 1790 to 1812. Also Grand Master of Scotland in 1806. As a Mason he was always energetic. Dr. Oliver says, "To no person had Masonry for many years been more indebted than to the Earl of Moira, now

Marquess Hastings." He died while Governor of Malta.

Molart, William. Anderson (*Constitutions*, 1738, p. 74) writes: "Nay, even during this King's (Henry VI.) Minority, there was a good Lodge under Grand Master Chicheley held at Canterbury, as appears from the Latin Register of William Molart (entitled *Liberatis generalis Domini Gulielmi Prioris Ecclesiæ Christi Cantuariensis erga Festum Natalis Domini 1429*) Prior of Canterbury, in Manuscript, pap. 88, in which are named Thomas Stapylton the Master, and John Morris Custos de la Lodge Lathomorum or Warden of the Lodge of Masons, with fifteen Fellow Crafts, and three Enter'd Prentices all named there."

What appears to be the register alluded to by Anderson is among the Tanner MSS. (165) in the Bodleian Library, Oxford, and proves to be merely a list kept by William *Molassh* or *Molessh* (the name occurs in both forms, but not as *Molart*), the Prior, of persons connected with the Priory and receiving livery from it. On page 133 there is a list of persons for 1429, which contains "Magr Thom Mapylton Mgr Lathamorum, Morys custos de la loygge Lathamorum" and a list headed "Lathami" with 16 names including Mapylton and below "Apprenticii idem" followed by three names. Similar lists are given for subsequent years, and thus it is plain that there was an organized body of Operative Masons attached to the Priory at that time.

[E. L. H.]

Molay, James de. The twenty-second and last Grand Master of the Templars at the destruction of the Order in the fourteenth century. He was born about the year 1240, at Besançon, in Burgundy, being descended from a noble family. He was received into the Order of Knights Templar in 1265, by Imbert de Peraudo, Preceptor of France, in the Chapel of the Temple at Beaune. He immediately proceeded to Palestine, and greatly distinguished himself in the wars against the infidels, under the Grand Mastership of William de Beaujeu. In 1298, while absent from the Holy Land, he was unanimously elected Grand Master upon the death of Theobald Gaudinius. In 1305, he was summoned to France by Pope Clement V., upon the pretense of a desire, on the part of the Pontiff, to effect a coalition between the Templars and the Hospitalers. He was received by Philip the Fair, the treacherous King of France, with the most distinguished honors, and even selected by him as the godfather of one of his children. In April, 1307, he repaired, accompanied by three of his knights, to Poitiers, where the Pope was then residing, and as he supposed satisfactorily exculpated the Order from the charges which had been preferred against it. But both Pope and King were guilty of the most infamous deceit.

On the 12th of September, 1307, the order was issued for the arrest of the Templars, and De Molay endured an imprisonment for five years and a half, during which period he was subjected to the utmost indignities and sufferings for the purpose of extorting from him a confession of the guilt of his Order. But he was firm and loyal, and on the 11th of March, 1314, he was publicly burnt in front of the Cathedral of Nôtre Dame, in Paris. When about to die, he solemnly affirmed the innocence of the Order, and, it is said, summoned Pope Clement to appear before the judgment-seat of God in forty days and the King of France within a year, and both, it is well known, died within the periods specified. (See *Transactions of the Quatuor Coronati Lodge*, Vol. 20.)

Moloch. (Heb. *Molech, king.*) The chief god of the Phœnicians, and a god of the Ammonites. Human sacrifices were offered at his shrine, and it was chiefly in the valley of Tophet, to the east of Jerusalem, that this brutal idolatry was perpetrated. Solomon built a temple to Moloch upon the Mount of Olives, and Manasseh, long after, imitated his impiety by making his son pass through the fire kindled in honor of this deity. Wierus calls Moloch Prince of the realm of tears.

First Moloch, horrid king, besmeared with blood
Of human sacrifice and parents' tears;
Though for the noise of drums and timbrels loud,
Their children's cries unheard, that passed
through fire
To his grim idol. . . . Nor content with such
Audacious neighborhood, the wisest heart
Of Solomon he led, by fraud, to build
His temple right against the temple of God,
On that opprobrious hill; and made his grove,
The pleasant valley of Hinnom, Tophet thence
And black Gehenna called, the type of Hell.

—*Par. Lost*, B. 1.

Monad. The Monad in the Pythagorean system of numbers was unity or the number one. (See *Numbers* and *One*.)

Monitor. Those manuals published for the convenience of Lodges, and containing the charges, general regulations, emblems, and account of the public ceremonies of the Order, are called Monitors. The amount of ritualistic information contained in these works has gradually increased: thus the monitorial instructions in Preston's *Illustrations*, the earliest Monitor in the English language, are far more scanty than those contained in Monitors of the present day. As a general rule, it may be said that American works of this class give more instruction than English ones, but that the French and German manuals are more communicative than either.

Of the English and American manuals published for monitorial instruction, the first was by Preston, in 1772. This has been succeeded by the works of the following authors: Webb, 1797; Dalcho, 1807; Cole, 1817; Hardie, 1818; Cross, 1819; Tannehill, 1824; Parmele, 1825; Charles W. Moore, 1846; Cornelius Moore, 1846; Dove, 1847; Davis, 1849; Stewart, 1851; Mackey, 1852; Macoy, 1853; Sickels, 1866.

Monitorial Instruction. The instruction contained in Monitors is called *monitorial*, to distinguish it from esoteric instruction, which is not permitted to be written, and can be obtained only in the precincts of the Lodge.

Monitorial Sign. A sign given in the English system, but not recognized in this country. Oliver says of it that it "reminds us of the weakness of human nature, unable of itself to resist the power of Darkness, unless aided by that Light which is from above."

Monitor, Secret. See *Secret Monitor*.

Monogram. An abbreviation of a name by means of a cipher composed of two or more letters intertwined with each other. The Constantinian monogram of Christ is often used by Knights Templar. The Triple Tau, or Royal Arch badge, is also a monogram; although there is a difference of opinion as to its real meaning, some supposing that it is a monogram of Templum Hierosolymæ or the Temple of Jerusalem, others of Hiram of Tyre, and others, again, bestowing on it different significations.

Montana. April 27, 1863, the Grand Lodge of Nebraska granted a Warrant for a Lodge at Bannack, in Montana; but in consequence of the removal of the petitioners, the Lodge was never organized. Three other Lodges were subsequently established by Warrants from the Grand Lodges of Kansas and Colorado. On January 24, 1866, three Lodges met in convention at Virginia City, and organized the Grand Lodge of Montana, John J. Hull being elected Grand Master.

Royal Arch Masonry and Templarism were introduced, the one by the General Grand Chapter, and the other by the Grand Encampment of the United States.

Montfaucon, Prior of. One of the two traitors on whose false accusations was based the persecution of the Templars. (See *Squin de Flexian.*)

Months, Hebrew. Masons of the Ancient and Accepted Scottish Rite use in their documents the Hebrew months of the civil year. Hebrew months commence with the full moon; and as the civil year began about the time of the autumnal equinox, the first Hebrew month must have begun with the new moon in September, which is also used by Scottish Masons as the beginning of their year. Annexed is a table of the Hebrew months, and their correspondence with our own calendar.

תשרי	Tisri,	Sept. and Oct.
חשון	Khesvan,	Oct. and Nov.
כסלו	Kislev,	Nov. and Dec.
טבת	Tebeth,	Dec. and Jan.
שבט	Schebet,	Jan. and Feb.
אדר	Adar,	Feb. and March.
ניסן	Nisan,	March and April.
אייר	Ijar,	April and May.
סיון	Sivan,	May and June.
תמוז	Tamus,	June and July.
אב	Ab,	July and Aug.
אלול	Elul,	August and Sept.

As the Jews computed time by the appearance of the moon, it is evident that there soon would be a confusion as to the keeping of these feasts, if some method had not been taken to correct it; since the lunar year is only 354 days, 8 hours, and 48 minutes, and the solar year is 365 days, 6 hours, 15 minutes, and 20 seconds. Accordingly, they intercalated a month after their 12th month, Adar, whenever they found that the 15th day of the following month, Abib, would fall before the vernal equinox. This intercalated month was named ואדר, Ve-adar, or "the second Adar," and was inserted every second or third year, as they saw occasion; so that the difference between the lunar and solar year could never, in this way, be more than a month.

Months, Masonic. In the French Rite the old calendar is retained, and the year begins with the month of March, the months being designated numerically and not by their usual names. Thus we find in French Masonic documents such dates as this: "Le 10me jour du 3me mois Maçonnique," that is, the 10th day of the 3d Masonic month, or the 10th of May.

Montpellier, Hermetic Rite of. The Hermetic Rite of Pernetty, which had been established at Avignon in 1770, was in 1778 transported to Montpellier, in France, by a Past Master, and some of the members of the Lodge of Persecuted Virtue in the former place, who laid the foundations of the *Academy of True Masons*, which see. Hence the degrees given in that Academy constituted what is known as the Hermetic Rite of Montpellier.

Monument. It is impossible to say exactly at what period the idea of a monument in the Third Degree was first introduced into the symbolism of Freemasonry. The early expositions of the eighteenth century, although they refer to a funeral, make no allusion to a monument. The monument adopted in the American system, and for which we are indebted, it is said, to the inventive genius of Cross, consists of a weeping virgin, holding in one hand a sprig of acacia and in the other an urn; before her is a broken column, on which rests a copy of the *Book of Constitutions*, while Time behind her is attempting to disentangle the ringlets of her hair. The explanation of these symbols will be found in their proper places in this work. Oliver, in his *Landmarks* (ii., 146), cites this monument without any reference to its American origin. Early in the last century the Master's monument was introduced into the French system, but its form was entirely different from the one adopted in this country. It is described as an obelisk, on which is inscribed a golden triangle, in the center of which the Tetragrammaton is engraved. On the top of the obelisk is sometimes seen an urn pierced by a sword. In the Scottish Rite an entire degree has been consecrated to the subject of the Hiramic monument. Altogether, the monument is simply the symbolic expression of the idea that veneration should always be paid to the memory of departed worth.

Moon. The adoption of the moon in the Masonic system as a symbol is analogous to, but could hardly be derived from, the employment of the same symbol in the ancient religions. In Egypt, Osiris was the sun, and Isis the moon; in Syria, Adonis was the sun, and Ashtoroth the moon; the Greeks adored her as Diana, and Hecate; in the mysteries of Ceres, while the hierophant or chief priest represented the Creator, and the torch-bearer the sun, the ἐπιβώμιος, or officer nearest the altar, represented the moon. In short, moon-worship was as widely disseminated as sun-worship. Masons retain her image in their Rites, because the Lodge is a representation of the universe, where, as the sun rules over the day, the moon presides over the night; as the one regulates the year, so does the other the months, and as the former is the king of the starry hosts of heaven, so is the latter their queen; but both deriving their heat, and light, and power from him, who, as the third and the greatest light, the master of heaven and earth, controls them both.

Moore, Charles Whitlock. A distinguished American Masonic journalist, born in Boston, Mass., March 29, 1801. His own account of his initiation into Masonry is in the following words: "In February, 1822, I was proposed for the degrees of Masonry in Massachusetts Lodge, then, as now, one of the three oldest in Boston, and but for the intervention of business engagements, I should have been received into Masonry on the evening of my coming of age. Before that evening arrived, however, I was called temporarily to the State of Maine, where, in May following, I was admitted into Kennebec Lodge, at Hallowell, with the consent and approbation of the Lodge in which I had been originally proposed. I received the third degree on the evening of the 12th of June."

On October 10, 1822, he affiliated with the Lodge St. Andrew. In October, 1872, that Lodge celebrated his semicentennial membership by a festival.

In 1825 he took the Capitular Degrees in St. Andrew's Chapter, and was elected High Priest in 1840, and subsequently Grand High Priest of the Grand Chapter. He was made a Knights Templar in Boston Encampment about the year 1830, and was Eminent Commander in 1837. In 1841 he was elected Grand Master of the Grand Encampment of Massachusetts and Rhode Island, which office he held for three years. In 1832 he received the Royal and Select degrees in Boston Council, over which he presided for twelve years. He was elected General Grand Captain-General of the Grand Encampment of the United States in 1847, and General Grand Generalissimo in 1850. In 1844 he was received into the Ancient Accepted Scottish Rite, and in the same year was elected Secretary-General of the Holy Empire in the Supreme Council for the Northern Jurisdiction of the United States, an office which he held until his resignation in 1862.

"When he was elected R. G. Secretary of the Grand Lodge in 1834," says Bro. John T. Heard, in his *Historical Account of Columbian Lodge* (p. 472), "it was the moment when the anti-Masonic excitement was raging with its greatest violence in this State, and his first official act was to attest the memorial written by him, surrendering to the Legislature the act of incorporation of the Grand Lodge."

The Grand Lodge surrendered its charter and its corporate powers that it might escape the persecution of an anti-Masonic Legislature. The memorial, however, boldly stated that "by divesting itself of its corporate powers, the Grand Lodge bas relinquished none of its Masonic attributes or prerogatives." In Masonic authorship, Bro. Moore is principally distinguished as a journalist. In 1825 he established the *Masonic Mirror*, which was merged in 1834 in the *Bunker Hill Aurora*, a paper with whose Masonic department he was associated. In 1841 he commenced the publication of the *Freemasons' Monthly Magazine*, which he published for thirty-three years; in fact, until his death. In 1828 and 1829 he published the *Amaranth, or Masonic Garland*, and in 1843 the *Masonic Trestle-Board*. Bro. Moore died at Boston, Mass., of pneumonia, on December 12, 1873.

[C. T. McClenachan.]

Moore, James. He was, in 1808, the Senior Grand Warden of the Grand Lodge of Kentucky, and in conjunction with Carey L. Clarke compiled, by order of that body, the *Masonic Constitutions or Illustrations of Masonry*, Lexington, 1808, pp. 191, 12mo. This was the first Masonic work published in the Western States. With the exception of the Constitution of the Grand Lodge, it is little more than a compilation taken from Anderson, Preston, and Webb. It was adopted by the Grand Lodge of Kentucky as its official Book of Constitutions.

Mopses. In 1738 Pope Clement XII. issued a bull, condemning and forbidding the practise of the rites of Freemasonry. Several brethren in the Catholic States of Germany, unwilling to renounce the Order, and yet fearful of offending the ecclesiastical authority, formed at Vienna, September 22, 1738, under the name of *Mopses*, what was pretended to be a new association, but which was in truth nothing else than an imitation of Freemasonry under a less offensive appellation. It was patronized by the most illustrious persons of Germany, and many Princes of the Empire were its Grand Masters; the Duke of Bavaria especially took it under his protection. The title is derived from the German word *mops*, signifying a pug-dog, and was indicative of the mutual fidelity and attachment of the brethren, these virtues being characteristic of that animal. The alarm made for entrance was to imitate the barking of a dog.

The Mopses were an androgynous Order,

and admitted females to all the offices, except that of Grand Master, which was held for life. There was, however, a Grand Mistress, and the male and female heads of the Order alternately assumed, for six months each, the supreme authority. With the revival of the spirit of Masonry, which had been in some degree paralyzed by the attacks of the Church, the society of Mopses ceased to exist.

Morality. In the American system it is one of the three precious jewels of a Master Mason.

Morality of Freemasonry. No one who reads our ancient Charges can fail to see that Freemasonry is a strictly moral Institution, and that the principles which it inculcates inevitably tend to make the brother who obeys their dictates a more virtuous man. Hence the English lectures very properly define Freemasonry to be "a system of morality."

Moral Law. "A Mason," say the old Charges of 1722, "is obliged by his tenure to obey the moral law." Now, this moral law is not to be considered as confined to the decalogue of Moses, within which narrow limits the ecclesiastical writers technically restrain it, but rather as alluding to what is called the *lex naturæ*, or the law of nature. This law of nature has been defined, by an able but not recent writer on this subject, to be "the will of God, relating to human actions, grounded on the moral differences of things; and because discoverable by natural light, obligatory upon all mankind." (Grove, *System of Moral Philosophy*, vol. ii., p. 122. London, 1749.) This is the "moral law," to which the old Charge already cited refers, and which it declares to be the law of Masonry. And this was wisely done, for it is evident that no law less universal could have been appropriately selected for the government of an Institution whose prominent characteristic is its universality.

Morana. The Bohemian goddess of winter and death, Maryana of Scandinavia.

Moravian Brethren. The religious sect of Moravian Brethren, which was founded in Upper Lusatia, about 1722, by Count Zinzendorf, is said at one time to have formed a society of religious Freemasons. For an account of which, see *Mustard Seed, Order of.*

Morgan, William. Born in Culpeper County, in Virginia, in 1775. He published in 1826 a pretended *Exposition of Masonry*, which attracted at the time more attention than it deserved. Morgan soon after disappeared, and the Masons were charged by some enemies of the Order with having removed him by foul means. What was the real fate of Morgan has never been ascertained. There are various myths of his disappearance, and subsequent residence in other countries. They may or may not be true, but it is certain that there is no evidence of his death that would be admitted in a Court of Probate. He was a man of questionable character and dissolute habits, and his enmity to Masonry is said to have originated from the refusal of the Masons of Le Roy to admit him to membership in their Lodge and Chapter.

Moriah, Mount. An eminence situated in the southeastern part of Jerusalem. In the time of David it must have been cultivated, for it is called "the threshing-floor of Ornan the Jebusite," from whom that monarch purchased it for the purpose of placing there an altar. Solomon subsequently erected there his magnificent Temple. Mount Moriah was always profoundly venerated by the Jews, among whom there is an early tradition that on it Abraham was directed to offer up his son. The truth of this tradition has, it is true, been recently denied by some Biblical writers, but it has been as strenuously maintained by others. The Masons, however, have always accepted it, and to them, as the site of the Temple, it is especially sacred, and, combining with this the Abrahamic legend, they have given to Mount Moriah the appellation of the ground floor of the Lodge, and assign it as the place where what are called "the three grand offerings were made."

Morin, Stephen. The founder of the Scottish Rite in America. On the 27th of August, 1761, the "Deputies General of the Royal Art, Grand Wardens, and officers of the Grand Sovereign Lodge of St. John of Jerusalem established at Paris" (so reads the document itself) granted a Patent to Stephen Morin, by which he was empowered "to multiply the sublime degrees of High Perfection, and to create Inspectors in all places where the sublime degrees are not established." This Patent was granted, Thory, Ragon, Clavel, and Lenning say, by the Grand Council of Emperors of the East and West. Others say by the Grand Lodge. Dalcho says by the Grand Consistory of Princes of the Royal Secret at Paris. Bro. Albert Pike, who has very elaborately investigated the question, says that the authority of Morin was "a joint authority" of the two then contending Grand Lodges of France and the Grand Council, which is, I suppose, what Dalcho and the Supreme Council of Charleston call the Grand Consistory. From the Grand Lodge he received the power to establish a Symbolic Lodge, and from the Grand Council or Consistory the power to confer the higher degrees.

Not long after receiving these powers, Morin sailed for America, and established Bodies of the Scottish Rite in St. Domingo and Jamaica. He also appointed M. M. Hayes a Deputy Inspector-General for North America. Hayes, subsequently, appointed Isaac da Costa a Deputy for South Carolina, and through him the Sublime degrees were disseminated among the Masons of the United States. (See *Scottish Rite.*) After appointing several Deputies and establishing some Bodies in the West India Islands, Morin is lost sight of. We know not anything of his subsequent history, or of the time or place of his death. Ragon, Thory, and Clavel say that Morin was a Jew; but as these writers have *judaized* all the founders of the Scottish Rite in America, we have no right to place any confidence in their statements. The name of Morin has been borne by many French Christians of literary reputation, from Peter Morin, a learned ecclesiastical writer of the sixteenth century, to Stephen Morin, an antiquary and Protestant clergyman, who died in 1700, and his son Henry, who became a Catholic, and died in 1728.

Moritz, Carl Philipp. A Privy Councillor, Professor, and Member of the Academy of Sciences in Berlin, was born at Hameln on the 15th of September, 1757, and died the 26th of June, 1793. Gädicke says that he was one of the most celebrated authors of his age, and distinguished by his works on the German language. He was the author of several Masonic works, among which are his *Contributions to the Philosophy of Life and the Diary of a Freemason*, Berlin, 1793, and a *Book of Masonic Songs*.

Mormon Faith. See *Book of Mormon*.

Morphey. The name of one of the twelve Inspectors in the Eleventh Degree of the Ancient and Accepted Scottish Rite. This name, like the others in the same catalogue, bids defiance to any Hebraic derivation. They are all either French corruptions, worse even than *Jakinai* for *Shekinah*, or they have some allusion to names or events connected with the political intrigues of the exiled house of Stuart, which had, it is known, a connection with some of the higher degrees which sprang up at Arras, and other places where Masonry is said to have been patronized by the Pretender. This word Morphey may, for instance, be a corruption of Murray. James Murray, the second son of Lord Stormont, escaped to the court of the Stuarts in 1715. He was a devoted adherent of the exiled family, and became the governor of the young prince and the chief minister of his father, who conferred upon him the empty title of Earl of Dunbar. He died at Avignon in 1770. But almost every etymology of this kind must be entirely conjectural.

Morris, Robert, LL.D. Born August 31, 1818. Was first brought to Masonic light March 5, 1846, in Oxford Lodge, at a place of the same name in Mississippi. The life of Bro. Morris was so active and untiring for the benefit of the Institution of Masonry, that he had the opportunity of filling very many positions in all the departments of Masonry, and was Grand Master of Masons of the Grand Lodge of Kentucky in 1858–59. His writings cover Masonic jurisprudence, rituals and handbooks, Masonic belles-lettres, history and biography, travels, and contributions to *The Review*, *Keystone*, *Advocate*, *N. Y. Dispatch*, and other papers and periodicals. His Masonic songs and poetic effusions stand out in prominent volumes. He was the author of *We Meet upon the Level*, which is sufficient to render his name immortal. A complete biography of Bro. Robert Morris would fill volumes. He died in 1888.

Mortality, Symbol of. The ancient Egyptians introduced a skeleton at their feasts, to impress the idea of the evanescence of all earthly enjoyments; but the skeletons or deaths' heads did not make their appearance in Grecian art, as symbols of mortality, until later times, and on monuments of no artistic importance. In the earliest periods of ancient art, the Greeks and Romans employed more pleasing representations, such as the flower plucked from its stem, or the inverted torch. The moderns have, however, had recourse to more offensive symbolization. In their hatchments or funeral achievements the heralds employ a *death's head and crossed bones*, to denote that the deceased person is the last of his family. The Masons have adopted the same symbol, and in all the degrees where it is necessary to impress the idea of mortality, a skull, or a skull and crossed bones, are used for that purpose.

Mortar, Untempered. See *Untempered Mortar*.

Mosaic Pavement. Mosaic work consists properly of many little stones of different colors united together in patterns to imitate a painting. It was much practised among the Romans, who called it *musivum*, whence the Italians get their *musaico*, the French their *mosaique*, and we our *mosaic*. The idea that the work is derived from the fact that Moses used a pavement of colored stones in the tabernacle has been long since exploded by etymologists. The Masonic tradition is that the floor of the Temple of Solomon was decorated with a mosaic pavement of black and white stones. There is no historical evidence to substantiate this statement. Samuel Lee, however, in his diagram of the Temple, represents not only the floors of the building, but of all the outer courts, as covered with such a pavement. The Masonic idea was perhaps first suggested by this passage in the Gospel of St. John (xix. 13), "when Pilate, therefore, heard that saying, he brought Jesus forth, and sat down in the judgment-seat in a place that is called the Pavement, but in the Hebrew, Gabbatha." The word here translated Pavement is in the original *Lithostroton*, the very word used by Pliny to denote a mosaic pavement. The Greek word, as well as its Latin equivalent, is used to denote a pavement formed of ornamental stones of various colors, precisely what is meant by a mosaic pavement.

There was, therefore, a part of the Temple which was decorated with a mosaic pavement. The Talmud informs us that there was such a pavement in the conclave where the Grand Sanhedrim held its sessions.

By a little torsion of historical accuracy, the Masons have asserted that the ground floor of the Temple was a mosaic pavement, and hence, as the Lodge is a representation of the Temple, that the floor of the Lodge should also be of the same pattern.

The mosaic pavement is an old symbol of the Order. It is met with in the earliest rituals of the last century. It is classed among the ornaments of the Lodge in combination with the indented tessel and the blazing star.

Its party-colored stones of black and white have been readily and appropriately interpreted as symbols of the evil and good of human life.

Mosaic Symbolism. In the religion of Moses, more than in any other which preceded or followed it, is symbolism the predominating idea. From the tabernacle, which may be considered as the central point of the whole system, down to the vestments which clothed the servants at the altar, there will be found an underlying principle of symbolism. Long before the days of Pythagoras the mystical nature of numbers had been inculcated by the Jewish lawgiver, and the very name of God was constructed in a symbolical form, to indicate his eternal nature. Much of the Jewish ritual of worship, delineated in the Pentateuch with so much precision as to its minutest details, would almost seem puerile were it not for the symbolic idea that is conveyed. So the fringes of the garments are patiently described, not as decorations, but that by them the people, in looking upon the fringe, might "remember all the commandments of the Lord and do them." Well, therefore, has a modern writer remarked, that in the symbolism of the Mosaic worship it is only ignorance that can find the details trifling or the prescriptions minute; for if we recognise the worth and beauty of symbolism, we shall in vain seek in the Mosaic symbols for one superfluous enactment or one superstitious idea. To the Mason the Mosaic symbolism is very significant, because from it Freemasonry has derived and transmitted for its own uses many of the most precious treasures of its own symbolical art. Indeed, except in some of the higher, and therefore more modern degrees, the symbolism of Freemasonry is almost entirely deduced from the symbolism of Mosaism. Thus the symbol of the Temple, which persistently pervades the whole of the ancient Masonic system, comes to us directly from the symbolism of the Jewish tabernacle. If Solomon is revered by the Masons as their traditional Grand Master, it is because the Temple constructed by him was the symbol of the Divine life to be cultivated in every heart. And this symbol was borrowed from the Mosaic tabernacle; and the Jewish thought, that every Hebrew was to be a tabernacle of the Lord, has been transmitted to the Masonic system, which teaches that every Mason is to be a temple of the Grand Architect. The Papal Church, from which we get all ecclesiastical symbolism, borrowed its symbology from the ancient Romans. Hence most of the high degrees of Masonry which partake of a Christian character are marked by Roman symbolism transmuted into Christian. But Craft Masonry, more ancient and more universal, finds its symbolic teachings almost exclusively in the Mosaic symbolism instituted in the wilderness.

If we inquire whence the Jewish lawgiver derived the symbolic system which he introduced into his religion, the history of his life will readily answer the question. Philo-Judæus says that "Moses was instructed by the Egyptian priests in the philosophy of symbols and hieroglyphics as well as in the mysteries of the sacred animals." The sacred historian tells us that he was "learned in all the wisdom of the Egyptians"; and Manetho and other traditionary writers tell us that he was educated at Heliopolis as a priest, under his Egyptian name of Osarsiph, and that there he was taught the whole range of literature and science, which it was customary to impart to the priesthood of Egypt. When, then, at the head of his people, he passed away from the servitude of Egyptian taskmasters, and began in the wilderness to establish his new religion, it is not strange that he should have given a holy use to the symbols whose meaning he had learned in his ecclesiastical education on the banks of the Nile.

Thus is it that we find in the Mosaic symbolism so many identities with the Egyptian ritual. Thus the Ark of the Covenant, the Breastplate of the High Priest, the Miter, and many other of the Jewish symbols, will find their analogies in the ritualistic ceremonies of the Egyptians. Reghellini, who has written an elaborate work on *Masonry considered as the result of the Egyptian, Jewish, and Christian Religions*, says on the subject: "Moses, in his mysteries, and after him Solomon, adopted a great part of the Egyptian symbols, which, after them, we Masons have preserved in our own."

Moses, משה, which means *drawn out;* but the true derivation is from two Egyptian words, μο, *mo*, and ουϣε, *oushes*, signifying *saved from the water.* The lawgiver of the Jews, and referred to in some of the higher degrees, especially in the Twenty-fifth Degree, or Knight of the Brazen Serpent in the Scottish Rite, where he is represented as the presiding officer. He plays also an important part in the Royal Arch of the York and American Rites, all of whose ritual is framed on the Mosaic symbolism.

Mossdorf, Friedrich. An eminent German Mason, who was born March 2, 1757, at Eckartsberge, and died about 1830. He resided in Dresden, and took an active part in the affairs of Masonry. He was a warm supporter of Fessler's Masonic reforms, and made several contributions to the Freyberg *Freimaurerischen Taschenbuche* in defense of Fessler's system. He became intimately connected with the learned Krause, the author of *The Three Most Ancient Records of the Masonic Fraternity*, and wrote and published in 1809 a critical review of the work, in consequence of which the Grand Lodge commanded him to absent himself for an indefinite period from the Lodges. Mosdorf then withdrew from any further connection with the Fraternity. His most valuable contributions to Masonic literature are his additions and emendations to Lenning's *Encyclopädie der Freimaurerei.* He is the author also of several other works of great value.

Most Excellent. The title given to a Royal Arch Chapter, and to its presiding officer, the High Priest; also to the presiding officer of a Lodge of Most Excellent Masters.

Most Excellent Master. The Sixth Degree in the York Rite. Its history refers to the dedication of the Temple by King Solomon, who is represented by its presiding officer under the title of Most Excellent. Its officers are the same as those in a Symbolic Lodge. There are, however, some rituals in which the Junior Warden is omitted. This degree is peculiarly American, it being practised in no other country. It was the invention of Webb, who organized the capitular system of Masonry as it exists in America, and established the system of lectures which is the foundation of all subsequent systems taught here.

Most Puissant. The title of the presiding officer of a Grand Council of Royal and Select Masters.

Most Worshipful. The title given to a Grand Lodge and to its presiding officer, the Grand Master. The title of Grand Master of Pennsylvania is Right Worshipful.

Mot de Semestre. Half yearly word. Every six months the Grand Orient of France sends to each of the Lodges of its obedience a password, to be used by its members as an additional means of gaining admission into a Lodge. Each Mason obtains this word only from the Venerable of his own Lodge. It was instituted October 28, 1773, when the Duke of Chartres was elected Grand Master.

Mother Council. The Supreme Council of the Ancient and Accepted Scottish Rite for the Southern Jurisdiction of the United States of America, which was organized in 1801, at Charleston, is called the "Mother Council of the World," because from it have issued directly or indirectly all the other Supreme Councils of the Rite which are now in existence, or have existed since its organization.

Mother Lodge. In the last century certain Lodges in France and Germany assumed an independent position, and issued Charters for the constitution of Daughter Lodges claiming the prerogatives of Grand Lodges. Thus we find the Mother Lodge of Marseilles, in France, which constituted many Lodges. In Scotland the Lodge of Kilwinning took the title of Mother Lodge, and issued Charters until it was merged in the Grand Lodge of Scotland. The system is altogether irregular, and has no sanction in the present laws of the Fraternity.

Motion. A motion when made by a member cannot be brought before the Lodge for deliberation unless it is seconded by another member. Motions are of two kinds, principal and subsidiary; a principal motion is one that presents an independent proposition for discussion. Subsidiary motions are those which are intended to affect the principal motion—such as to amend it, to lay it on the table, to postpone it definitely or indefinitely, or to reconsider it, all of which are governed by the parliamentary law under certain modifications to suit the spirit and genius of the Masonic organization. (See Dr. Mackey's *Treatise on Parliamentary Law as applied to Masonic Bodies.*)

Motto. In imitation of the sentences appended to the coats of arms and seals of the gilds and other societies, the Masons have for the different branches of their Order mottoes, which are placed on their banners or put at the head of their documents, which are expressive of the character and design, either of the whole Order or of the particular branch to which the motto belongs. Thus, in Ancient Craft Masonry, we have as mottoes the sentences, *Ordo ab Chao*, and *Lux e tenebris;* in Capitular Masonry, *Holiness to the Lord;* in Templar Masonry, *In hoc signo vinces;* in Scottish Masonry, *Ne plus ultra* is the motto of the Thirtieth Degree, and *Spes mea in deo est* of the Thirty-second; while the Thirty-third has for its motto *Deus meumque Jus.* All of these will be found with their signification and origin in their appropriate places.

Mold. This word is very common in the Old Constitutions, where it is forbidden that a Freemason should give a mold to a rough Mason, whereby, of course, he would be imparting to him the secrets of the Craft. Thus, in the Harleian MS., No. 2054: "Alsoe that noe Mason make moulds, square or rule to any rough layers. Also, that no Mason set noe layes within a lodge or without to haue Mould Stones with one Mould of his workeing." We find the word in *Piers Ploughman's Vision:*

> "If eny Mason there do makede a molde
> With alle here wyse castes."

Parker (*Gloss. Architect.*, p. 313) thus defines it: "The model or pattern used by workmen, especially by Masons, as a guide in working mouldings and ornaments. It consists of a thin board or plate of metal, cut to represent the exact section of the mouldings to be worked from it." In the Cooke MS. the word *maters* is used, which is evidently a corruption of the Latin *matrix.*

Mold Stone. In the quotation from the Harleian MS. in the preceding article, the expression *mould stones* occurs, as it does in other Constitutions and in many old contracts. It means, probably, large and peaked stones for those parts of the building which were to have moldings cut upon them, as window and door jambs.

Mount Calvary. See *Calvary.*

Mount Caf. In the Mohammedan mythology, a fabulous mountain which encircles the earth. The home of the giants and fairies, and rests upon the sacred stone *Sakhral,* of which a single grain gives miraculous powers. It is of an emerald color, and its reflected light is the cause of the tints of the sky.

Mount Moriah. See *Moriah.*

Mount Sinai. See *Sinai.*

Mourning. The mourning color has been various in different times and countries. Thus, the Chinese mourn in white; the Turks in blue or in violet; the Egyptians in yellow; the Ethiopians in gray. In all the degrees and rites of Masonry, with a single exception black is the symbol of grief, and therefore the mourning color. But in the highest degrees of the Scottish Rite the mourning color, like that used by the former kings of France, is violet.

Mouth to Ear. The Mason is taught by an expressive symbol, to whisper good counsel in his brother's ear, and to warn him of approaching danger. "It is a rare thing," says Bacon, "except it be from a perfect and entire friend, to have counsel given that is not bowed and crooked to some ends which he hath that giveth it." And hence it is an admirable lesson, which Masonry here teaches us, to use the lips and the tongue only in the service of a brother.

Movable Jewels. See *Jewels of a Lodge.*

Mozart, J. C. W. G. Born in 1756 at Salzburg, and died December 5, 1791, at Vienna. One of the greatest and most delightful of musical composers. He first saw the Masonic light about 1780, and was a member of the Lodge "Zur gekrönten Hoffnung." There were many musical compositions and dedications to Masonry by this eminent composer.

Muenter, Friederich. Born in 1761, and died in 1830. He was Professor of Theology in the University of Copenhagen, and afterward Bishop of Seeland. He was the author of a treatise *On the Symbols and Art Representations of the Early Christians.* In 1794 he published his *Statute Book of the Order of Knights Templar*, "Statutenbuch des Ordens der Tempelherren"; a work which is one of the most valuable contributions that we have to the history of Templarism.

Munkhouse, D.D., Rev. Richard. The author of *A Discourse in Praise of Freemasonry*, 8vo, Lond., 1805; *An Exhortation to the Practice of those Specific Virtues which ought to prevail in the Masonic Character, with Historical Notes*, 8vo, Lond., 1805; and *Occasional Discourses on Various Subjects, with Copious Annotations*, 3 vols., 8vo, Lond., 1805. This last work contains many discourses on Masonic subjects. Dr. Munkhouse was an ardent admirer and defender of Freemasonry, into which he was initiated in the Phœnix Lodge of Sunderland. On his removal to Wakefield, where he was rector of St. John the Baptist's Church, he united with the Lodge of Unanimity, under the Mastership of Richard Linnecar, to whose virtues and Masonic knowledge he has paid a high tribute. Dr. Munkhouse died in the early part of this century.

Murat, Joachim. Born in 1771, executed in 1815. The great cavalry general of Napoleon, and titular king of Naples. In 1803 he was appointed S. G. Warden in the Grand Orient of France. When the fifth Supreme Council of the World was established at Naples, on June 11, 1809, by the Supreme Council at Milan, a concordat became necessary, and was executed May 3, 1811, between the Grand Orient which was created June 24, 1809, and the Supreme Council of Naples, whereby the latter should have sole control over the degrees beyond the eighteenth, in like manner as signified in the concordat of France. King Joachim Murat accepted the supreme command of both bodies. The change in his political surroundings allowed him no permanent rest.

Murat, Joachim, Prince. Son of the King of Naples. Was appointed Grand Master of the Grand Orient of France, and initiated February 26, 1825. He resigned the office in 1861.

Murr, Christoph Gottlieb von. A distinguished historical and archeological writer, who was born at Nuremberg, in 1733, and died April 8, 1811. In 1760 he published an *Essay on the History of the Greek Tragic Poets*, in 1777–82, six volumes of *Antiquities of Herculanæum*, and several other historical works. In 1803 he published an essay *On the True Origin of the Orders of Rosicrucianism and Freemasonry, with an Appendix on the History of the Order of Templars.* In this work, Murr attempts to trace Freemasonry to the times of Oliver Cromwell, and maintains that it and Rosicrucianism had an identical origin, and the same history until the year 1633, when they separated.

Muscus Domus. In the early rituals of the last century, the tradition is given, that certain Fellow-Crafts, while pursuing their search, discovered a grave covered with green moss and turf, when they exclaimed, *Muscus Domus, Deo gratias*, which was interpreted, "Thanks be to God, our Master has a mossy house." Whence a Mason's grave came to be called *Muscus Domus.* But both the tradition and its application have become obsolete in the modern rituals.

Music. One of the seven liberal arts and sciences, whose beauties are inculcated in the Fellow-Craft's Degree. Music is recommended to the attention of Masons, because as the "concord of sweet sounds" elevates the generous sentiments of the soul, so should the concord of good feeling reign among the brethren, that by the union of friendship and brotherly love the boisterous passions may be lulled and harmony exist throughout the Craft.

Musical Instruments, Ancient. As in the Fellow-Craft's Degree, music is dilated upon as one of the liberal arts, the sweet and harmonious sounds being the representative of that harmony which should ever exist among the brethren, we are apt to inquire what were the instruments used by the ancients in their mystical service. The oldest ever discovered, we believe, is a small clay pipe not over three inches in length, found by Captain Willock among the presumed ruins of Babylon; if so, it must be 2,600 years old. By the use of the two finger holes, the intervals of the common chord, C, E, and G, are produced, or the harmonic triad. From the ruins of Nineveh we have countless representations of the harp, with strings varying from ten to twenty-six; the lyre, identical in structure with that of the Greeks; a harp-shaped instrument held horizontally, and the six to ten strings struck with a plectrum, which has been termed the Asor, from its resemblance to the Hebrew instrument of that name. There is also the guitar-shaped instrument, and a double pipe with a single mouthpiece and finger-holes on each pipe. The Assyrians used musical bells, trumpets, flutes, drums, cymbals, and tambourines. The Abyssinians call their lyre the Kissar (Greek, *kithara*). There is also the flute, called Monaulos, which is of great antiquity, and named by the Egyptians Photinx, or curved flute. The crooked horn or trumpet, called Buccina, and the Cithara, held sacred in consequence of its shape being that of the Greek delta.

Mustard-Seed, Order of. (*Der Orden vom Senfkorn.*) This association, whose members also called themselves "The Fraternity of Moravian Brothers of the Order of Religious Freemasons," was one of the first innovations introduced into German Freemasonry. It was instituted in the year 1739. Its mysteries were founded on that passage in the fourth chapter of St. Mark's Gospel in which Christ compares the kingdom of heaven to a mustard-seed. The brethren wore a ring, on which was inscribed *Keiner von uns lebt ihm selber*, i. e., "No one of us lives for himself." The jewel of the Order was a cross of gold surmounted by a mustard-plant in full bloom, with the motto, *Quod fuit ante nihil*, i. e., "What was before nothing." It was suspended from a green ribbon. The professed object of the association was, through the instrumentality of Freemasonry, to extend the kingdom of Christ over the world. It has long been obsolete.

Muta. The Roman goddess of silence.

Muttra or **Mathura.** The birthplace of the Hindu Redeemer, Krishna. The capital of a district in the Northwest Provinces of British India.

Myrrh. A resinous gum of a tree growing in Arabia, valued from the most ancient times. (Gen. xxxvii. 25.) It was among the presents Jacob sent to Egypt, and those brought to the infant Jesus by the wise men of the East.

Myrtle. The sacred plant of the Eleusinian mysteries, and analogous in its symbolism to the acacia of the Masons.

Mystagogue. The one who presided at the Ancient Mysteries, and explained the sacred things to the candidate. He was also called the hierophant. The word, which is Greek, signifies literally one who makes or conducts an initiate.

Mysteries, Ancient. Each of the Pagan gods, says Warburton (*Div. Leg.*, I., ii., 4), had, besides the public and open, a secret worship paid to him, to which none were admitted but those who had been selected by preparatory ceremonies called *Initiation.* This secret worship was termed the *Mysteries.* And this is supported by Strabo (lib. x., cap. 3), who says that it was common, both to the Greeks and the Barbarians, to perform their religious ceremonies with the observance of a festival, and that they are sometimes celebrated publicly, and sometimes in mysterious privacy. Noel (*Dict. de la Fable*) thus defines them: Secret ceremonies which were practised in honor of certain gods, and whose secret was known to the initiates alone, who were admitted only after long and painful trials, which it was more than their life was worth to reveal.

As to their origin, Warburton is probably not wrong in his statement that the first of which we have any account are those of Isis and Osiris in Egypt; for although those of Mithras came into Europe from Persia, they were, it is supposed, carried from Egypt by Zoroaster.

The most important of these mysteries were the Osiric in Egypt, the Mithraic in Persia, the Cabiric in Thrace, the Adonisian in Syria, the Dionysiac and Eleusinian in Greece, the Scandinavian among the Gothic nations, and the Druidical among the Celts.

In all these mysteries we find a singular unity of design, clearly indicating a common origin, and a purity of doctrine as evidently proving that this common origin was not to be sought for in the popular theology of the Pagan world. The ceremonies of initiation were all funereal in their character. They celebrated the death and the resurrection of some cherished being, either the object of esteem as a hero, or of devotion as a god. Subordination of degrees was instituted, and the candidate was subjected to probations varying in their character and severity; the rites were practised in the darkness of night, and often amid the gloom of impenetrable forests or subterranean caverns; and the full fruition of knowledge, for which so much labor was endured, and so much danger incurred, was not attained until the aspirant, well tried and thoroughly purified, had reached the place of wisdom and of light.

These mysteries undoubtedly owed their origin to the desire to establish esoteric philosophy, in which should be withheld from popular approach those sublime truths which it was supposed could only be entrusted to those who had been previously prepared for their reception. Whence these doctrines were originally derived it would be impossible to say; but I am disposed to accept Creuzer's hypothesis of an ancient and highly instructed body of priests, having their origin either in Egypt or in the East, from whom was derived religious, physical, and historical knowledge, under the veil of symbols.

By this confinement of these doctrines to a system of secret knowledge, guarded by the most rigid rites, could they only expect to preserve them from the superstitions, innovations, and corruptions of the world as it then existed. "The distinguished few," says Oliver (*Hist. Init.*, p. 2), "who retained their fidelity, uncontaminated by the contagion of evil example, would soon be able to estimate the superior benefits of an isolated institution, which afforded the advantage of a select society, and kept at an unapproachable distance the profane scoffer, whose presence might pollute their pure devotions and social converse, by contumelious language or unholy mirth." And doubtless the prevention of this intrusion, and the preservation of these sublime truths, was the original object of the institution of the ceremonies of initiation, and the adoption of other means by which the initiated could be recognized, and the uninitiated excluded. Such was the opinion of Warburton, who says that "the mysteries were at first the retreats of sense and virtue, till time corrupted them in most of the gods."

The Abbé Robin in a learned work on this subject entitled *Récherches sur les Initiations Anciens et Modernes* (Paris, 1870), places the origin of the initiations at that remote period when crimes first began to appear upon earth. The vicious, he remarks, were urged by the terror of guilt to seek among the virtuous for intercessors with the Deity. The latter, retiring into solitude to avoid the contagion of growing corruption, devoted themselves to a life of contemplation and the cultivation of several of the useful sciences. The periodical return of the seasons, the revolution of the stars, the productions of the earth, and the various phenomena of nature, studied with attention, rendered them useful guides to men, both in their pursuits of industry and in their social duties. These recluse students invented certain signs to recall to the remembrance of the people the times of their festivals and of their rural labors, and hence the origin of the symbols and hieroglyphics that were in use among the priests of all nations. Having now become guides and leaders of the people, these sages, in order to select as associates of their learned labors and sacred functions only such as had sufficient merit and capacity, appointed strict courses of trial and examination, and this, our author thinks, must have been the source of the initiations of antiquity. The Magi, Brahmans, Gymnosophists, Druids, and priests of Egypt, lived thus in sequestered habitations and subterranean caves, and obtained great reputation by their discoveries in astronomy, chemistry, and mechanics, by their purity of morals, and by their knowledge of the science of legislation. It was in these schools, says M. Robin, that the first sages and legislators of antiquity were formed, and in them he supposes the doctrines taught to have been the unity of God and the immortality of the soul; and it was from these mysteries, and their symbols and hieroglyphics, that the exuberant fancy of the Greeks drew much of their mythology.

Warburton deduces from the ancient writers—from Cicero and Porphyry, from Origen and Celsus, and from others—what was the true object of the mysteries. They taught the dogma of the unity of God in opposition to the polytheistic notions of the people, and in connection with this the doctrine of a future life, and that the initiated should be happier in that state than all other mortals; that while the souls of the profane, at their leaving the body, stuck fast in mire and filth and remained in darkness, the souls of the initiated winged their flight directly to the happy islands and the habitations of the gods. "Thrice happy they," says Sophocles, "who descended to the shades below after having beheld these rites; for they alone have life in Hades, while all others suffer there every kind of evil." And Isocrates declares that "those who have been initiated in the mysteries, entertain better hopes both as to the end of life and the whole of futurity."

Others of the ancients have given us the same testimony as to their esoteric character. "All the mysteries," says Plutarch, "refer to a future life and to the state of the soul after death." In another place, addressing his wife, he says, "We have been instructed, in the religious rites of Dionysus, that the soul is immortal, and that there is a future state of existence." Cicero tells us that, in the mysteries of Ceres at Eleusis, the initiated were taught to live happily and to die in the hope of a blessed futurity. And, finally, Plato informs us that the hymns of Musæus, which were sung in the mysteries, celebrated the rewards and pleasures of the virtuous in another life, and the punishments which awaited the wicked.

These sentiments, so different from the debased polytheism which prevailed among the uninitiated, are the most certain evidence that the mysteries arose from a purer source than that which gave birth to the religion of the vulgar.

I must not pass unnoticed Faber's notion of their arkite origin. Finding, as he did, a prototype for every ancient cultus in the ark of Noah, it is not surprising that he should apply his theory to the mysteries. "The initiations," he says (*Orig. Pag. Idol.*, II., iv., 5), "into the mysteries scenically represented the mythic descent into Hades and the return from thence to the light of day, by which was meant the entrance into the ark and the subsequent liberation from its dark enclosure. They all equally related to the allegorical disappearance, or death, or descent of the great father, at their commencement; and his invention, or revival, or return from Hades, at their conclusion."

Döllinger (*Gent. and Jew*, i., 126) says, speaking of the mysteries, "the whole was a drama, the prelude to which consisted in purifications, sacrifices, and injunctions with regard to the behavior to be observed. The adventures of certain deities, their sufferings and joys, their appearance on earth, and relations to mankind, their death, or descent to the nether world, their return, or their rising again—all these, as symbolizing the life of nature, were represented in a connected series of theatrical scenes. These representations, tacked on to a nocturnal solemnity, brilliantly got up, particularly at Athens, with all the resources of art and sensual beauty, and accompanied with dancing and song, were eminently calculated to take a powerful hold on the imagination and the heart, and to excite in the spectators alternately conflicting sentiments of terror, and calm, sorrow, and fear, and hope. They worked upon them, now by agitating, now by soothing, and meanwhile had a strong bearing upon susceptibilities and capacities of individuals, according as their several

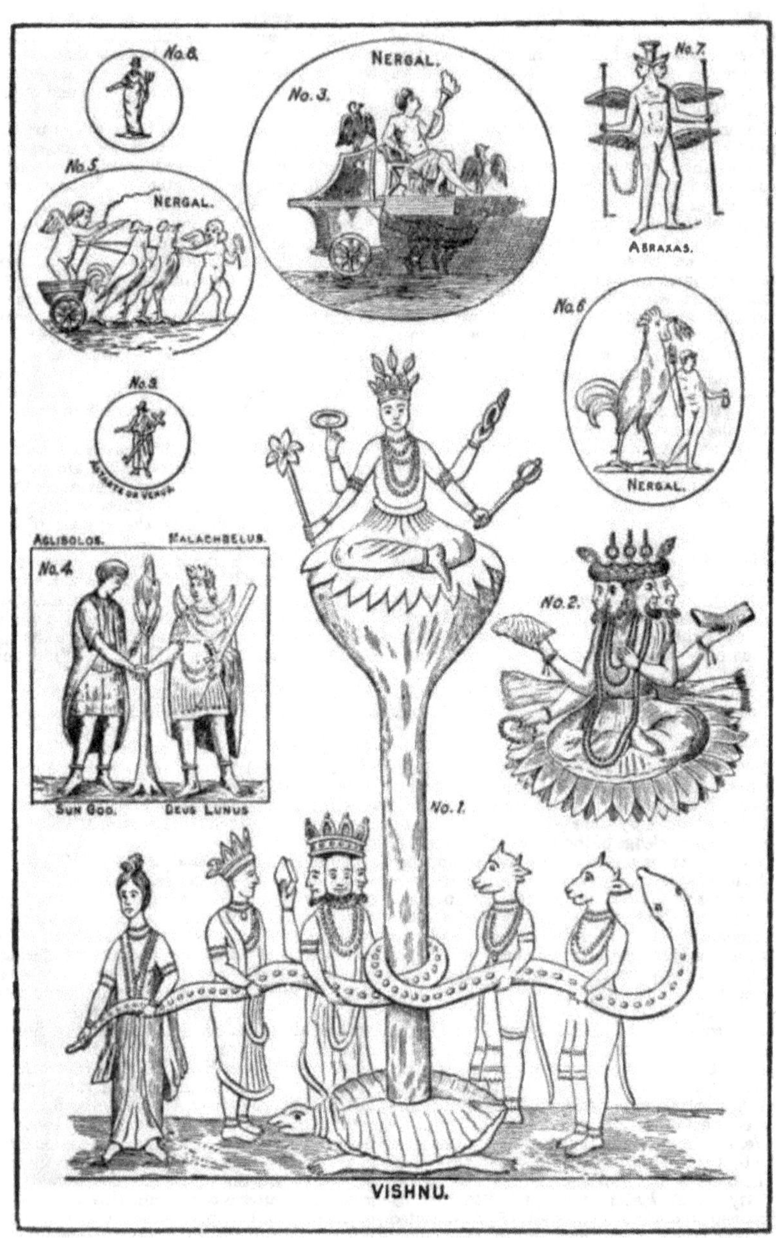
No. 8.
NERGAL.
No. 3.
No. 7.
No. 5.
NERGAL.
ABRAXAS.
No. 6.
No. 9.
NERGAL.
AGLIBOLOS.
MALACHBELUS.
No. 4.
No. 2.
SUN GOD.
DEUS LUNUS.
No. 1.
VISHNU.

dispositions inclined them more to reflection and observation, or to a resigned credulity."

Bunsen (*God in History*, II., b. iv., ch. 6) gives the most recent and the most philosophic idea of the character of the mysteries. They did, he says, "indeed exhibit to the initiated coarse physical symbols of the generative powers of Nature, and of the universal Nature herself, eternally, self-sustaining through all transformations; but the religious element of the mysteries consisted in the relations of the universe to the soul, more especially after death. Thus, even without philosophic proof, we are justified in assuming that the Nature symbolism referring to the Zodiac formed a mere framework for the doctrines relating to the soul and to the ethical theory of the universe. So, likewise, in the Samothracian worship of the Kabiri, the contest waged by the orb of day was represented by the story of the three brothers (the seasons of the year), one of whom is continually slain by the other two, but ever and anon arises to life again. But here, too, the beginning and end of the worship were ethical. A sort of confession was demanded of the candidates before admission, and at the close of the service the victorious God (Dionysus) was displayed as the Lord of the spirit. Still less, however, did theorems of natural philosophy form the subject-matter of the Eleusinian mysteries, of which, on the contrary, psychical conceptions were the beginning and the end. The predominating idea of these conceptions was that of the soul as a Divine, vital force, held captive here on earth and sorely tried; but the initiated were further taught to look forward to a final redemption and blessedness for the good and pious, and eternal torment after death for the wicked and unjust."

The esoteric character of the mysteries was preserved by the most powerful sanctions. An oath of secrecy was administered in the most solemn form to the initiate, and to violate it was considered a sacrilegious crime, the prescribed punishment for which was immediate death, and we have at least one instance in Livy of the infliction of the penalty. The ancient writers were therefore extremely reluctant to approach the subject, and Lobeck gives, in his *Aglaophamus* (vol. i., app. 131, 151; ii., 12, 87), several examples of the cautious manner in which they shrunk from divulging or discussing any explanation of a symbol which had been interpreted to them in the course of initiation. I would forbid, says Horace (L. iii., Od. 2, 26), that man who would divulge the sacred rites of mysterious Ceres from being under the same roof with me, or from setting sail with me in the same precarious bark.

On the subject of their relation to the rites of Freemasonry, to which they bear in many respects so remarkable a resemblance, that some connection seems necessarily implied, there are five principal theories. The first is that embraced and taught by Dr. Oliver, namely, that they are but deviations from that common source, both of them and of Freemasonry, the patriarchal mode of worship established by God himself. With this pure system of truth, he supposes the science of Freemasonry to have been coeval and identified. But the truths thus revealed by divinity came at length to be doubted or rejected through the imperfection of human reason, and though the visible symbols were retained in the mysteries of the Pagan world, their true interpretation was lost.

There is a second theory which, leaving the origin of the mysteries to be sought in the patriarchal doctrines, where Oliver has placed it, finds the connection between them and Freemasonry commencing at the building of King Solomon's Temple. Over the construction of this building, Hiram, the Architect of Tyre, presided. At Tyre the mysteries of Bacchus had been introduced by the Dionysian Artificers, and into their fraternity Hiram, in all probability, had, it is necessarily suggested, been admitted. Freemasonry, whose tenets had always existed in purity among the immediate descendants of the patriarchs, added now to its doctrines the guard of secrecy, which, as Dr. Oliver himself remarks, was necessary to preserve them from perversion or pollution.

A third theory has been advanced by the Abbé Robin, in which he connects Freemasonry indirectly with the mysteries, through the intervention of the Crusaders. In the work already cited, he attempts to deduce, from the ancient initiations, the orders of chivalry, whose branches, he says, produced the Institution of Freemasonry.

A fourth theory, and this has been recently advanced by the Rev. Mr. King in his treatise *On the Gnostics*, is that as some of them, especially those of Mithras, were extended beyond the advent of Christianity, and even to the very commencement of the Middle Ages, they were seized upon by the secret societies of that period as a model for their organization, and that through these latter they are to be traced to Freemasonry.

But perhaps, after all, the truest theory is that which would discard all successive links in a supposed chain of descent from the mysteries to Freemasonry, and would attribute their close resemblance to a natural coincidence of human thought. The legend of the Third Degree, and the legends of the Eleusinian, the Cabiric, the Dionysian, the Adonic, and all the other mysteries, are identical in their object to teach the reality of a future life; and this lesson is taught in all by the use of the same symbolism, and, substantially, the same scenic representation. And this is not because the Masonic rites are a lineal succession from the Ancient Mysteries, but because there has been at all times a proneness of the human heart to nourish this belief in a future life, and the proneness of the human mind to clothe this belief in a symbolic dress. And if there is any other more direct connection between them it must be sought for in the Roman Colleges of Artificers, who did, most probably, exercise some influence over the rising Freemasons of the early ages, and who, as the contemporaries of the mysteries, were, we may well suppose, imbued with something of their organization.

I conclude with a notice of their ultimate fate. They continued to flourish until long after the Christian era; but they at length degenerated. In the fourth century, Christianity had begun to triumph. The Pagans, desirous of making converts, threw open the hitherto inaccessible portals of their mysterious rites. The strict scrutiny of the candidate's past life, and the demand for proofs of irreproachable conduct, were no longer deemed indispensable. The vile and the vicious were indiscriminately, and even with avidity, admitted to participate in privileges which were once granted only to the noble and the virtuous. The sun of Paganism was setting, and its rites had become contemptible and corrupt. Their character was entirely changed, and the initiations were indiscriminately sold by peddling priests, who wandered through the country, to every applicant who was willing to pay a trifling fee for that which had once been refused to the entreaties of a monarch. At length these abominations attracted the attention of the emperors, and Constantine and Gratian forbade their celebration by night, excepting, however, from these edicts, the initiations at Eleusis. But finally Theodosius, by a general edict of proscription, ordered the whole of the Pagan mysteries to be abolished, in the four hundred and thirty-eighth year of the Christian era, and eighteen hundred years after their first establishment in Greece.

Clavel, however, says that they did not entirely cease until the era of the restoration of learning, and that during a part of the Middle Ages the mysteries of Diana, under the name of the "Courses of Diana," and those of Pan, under that of the "Sabbats," were practised in country places. But these were really only certain superstitious rites connected with the belief in witchcraft. The mysteries of Mithras, which, continually attacked by the Fathers of the Church, lived until the beginning of the fifth century, were, I think, the last of the old mysteries which had once exercised so much influence over the Pagan world and the Pagan religions.

Mysteries, Mexican. Instituted among the Mexicans (Aztecs), and were of a sacred nature. The adherents adopted the worship of some special deity, Quetzalcoatl (the Mexican Savior), under secret rites, and rendered themselves seclusive. A similar order was that called Tlamacazajotl, also the order known as Telpochtlistli. It is understood that under the sway of the Aztecs, the Mexican Mysteries had some Masonic affinities. (See *Aztec Writings.*)

Mystery. From the Greek μυστηριον, *a secret*, something to be concealed. The gilds or companies of the Middle Ages, out of which we trace the Masonic organization, were called *mysteries*, because they had trade-secrets, the preservation of which was a primary ordination of these fraternities. "Mystery" and "Craft" came thus to be synonymous words. In this secondary sense we speak of the "Mystery of the Stone-Masons" as equivalent to the "Craft of the Stone-Masons." But the Mystery of Freemasonry refers rather to the primary meaning of the word as immediately derived from the Greek.

Mystes. (From the Greek μύω, *to shut the eyes.*) One who had been initiated into the Lesser Mysteries of Paganism. He was now blind; but when he was initiated into the Greater Mysteries, he was called an Epopt, or one who saw.

The Mystes was permitted to proceed no farther than the vestibule or porch of the temple. To the Epopts only was accorded the privilege of admission to the adytum or sanctuary. A female initiate was called a Mystis.

Mystical. A word applied to any language, symbol, or ritual which is understood only by the initiated. The word was first used by the priests to describe their mysterious rites, and then borrowed by the philosophers to be applied to the inner, esoteric doctrines of their schools. In this sense we speak of the mystical doctrines of Speculative Masonry. Suidas derives the word from the Greek μύω, *to close*, and especially *to close the lips*. Hence the mystical is that about which the mouth should be closed.

Mysticism. A word applied in religious phraseology to any views or tendencies which aspire to more direct communication between God and man by the inward perception of the mind than can be obtained through revelation. "Mysticism," says Vaughan (*Hours with the Mystics*, i., 19), "presents itself in all its phases as more or less the religion of internal as opposed to external revelation—of heated feeling, sickly sentiment, or lawless imagination, as opposed to that reasonable belief in which the intellect and the heart, the inward witness and the outward, are alike engaged." The Pantheism of some of the ancient philosophers and of the modern Spinozaists, the Speculations of the Neoplatonists, the Anabaptism of Munster, the system of Jacob Behmen, the Quietism of Madame Guyon, the doctrines of the Bavarian Illuminati, and the reveries of Swedenborg, all partake more or less of the spirit of mysticism. The Germans have two words, *mystik* and *mysticismus*—the former of which they use in a favorable, the latter in an unfavorable sense. Mysticism is with them only another word for Pantheism, between which and Atheism there is but little difference. Hence a belief in mysticism is with the German Freemasons a disqualification for initiation into the Masonic rites. Thus the second article of the Statutes of the Grand Lodge of Hanover prescribes that "ein Freimaurer muss vom Mysticismus und Atheismus gleich weit entfernt stehen," i. e., "a Freemason must be equally distant from Mysticism and Atheism." Gädicke (*Freimaurer-Lexicon*) thus expresses the German sentiment: "Etwas *mystisch* sollte wohl jeder Mensch seyn, aber man hüte sich vor grobem Mysticismus," i. e.

"Every man ought to be somewhat *mystical*, but should guard against coarse *mysticism*."

Mystic Crown, Knights and Companions of the. A society formed by the adherents of Mesmer, in August, 1787, of a beneficent, non-political, and non-sectarian nature, to which Master Masons only were admitted.

Mystic Tie. That sacred and inviolable bond which unites men of the most discordant opinions into one band of brothers, which gives but one language to men of all nations and one altar to men of all religions, is properly, from the mysterious influence it exerts, denominated the mystic tie; and Freemasons, because they alone are under its influence, or enjoy its benefits, are called "Brethren of the mystic tie."

Myth. The word *myth*, from the Greek μῦθος, *a story*, in its original acceptation, signified simply a statement or narrative of an event, without any necessary implication of truth or falsehood; but, as the word is now used, it conveys the idea of a personal narrative of remote date, which, although not necessarily untrue, is certified only by the internal evidence of the tradition itself. This definition, which is substantially derived from Mr. Grote (*Hist. of Greece*, vol. i., ch. xvi., p. 295), may be applied without modification to the myths of Freemasonry, although intended by the author only for the myths of the ancient Greek religion.

The myth, then, is a narrative of remote date, not necessarily true or false, but whose truth can only be certified by internal evidence. The word was first applied to those fables of the Pagan gods which have descended from the remotest antiquity, and in all of which there prevails a symbolic idea, not always, however, capable of a positive interpretation. As applied to Freemasonry, the words *myth* and *legend* are synonymous.

From this definition it will appear that the myth is really only the interpretation of an idea. But how we are to read these myths will best appear from these noble words of Max Müller (*Science of Lang.*, 2d Ser., p. 578): "Everything is true, natural, significant, if we enter with a reverent spirit into the meaning of ancient art and ancient language. Everything becomes false, miraculous, and unmeaning, if we interpret the deep and mighty words of the seers of old in the shallow and feeble sense of modern chroniclers."

A fertile source of instruction in Masonry is to be found in its traditions and mythical legends; not only those which are incorporated into its ritual and are exemplified in its ceremonies, but those also which, although forming no part of the Lodge lectures, have been orally transmitted as portions of its history, and which, only within a comparatively recent period, have been committed to writing. But for the proper appreciation of these traditions some preparatory knowledge of the general character of Masonic myths is necessary. If all the details of these traditions be considered as asserted historical facts, seeking to convey nothing more nor less than historical information, then the improbabilities and anachronisms, and other violations of historical truth which distinguish many of them, must cause them to be rejected by the scholar as absurd impostures. But there is another and a more advantageous view in which these traditions are to be considered. Freemasonry is a symbolic institution—everything in and about it is symbolic—and nothing more eminently so than its traditions. Although some of them—as, for instance, the legend of the Third Degree—have in all probability a deep substratum of truth lying beneath, over this there is superposed a beautiful structure of symbolism. History has, perhaps, first suggested the tradition; but then the legend, like the myths of the ancient poets, becomes a symbol, which is to enunciate some sublime philosophical or religious truth. Read in this way, and in this way only, the myths or legends and traditions of Freemasonry will become interesting and instructive. (See *Legend*.)

Myth, Historical. An historical myth is a myth that has a known and recognized foundation in historical truth, but with the admixture of a preponderating amount of fiction in the introduction of personages and circumstances. Between the historical myth and the mythical history, the distinction cannot always be preserved, because we are not always able to determine whether there is a preponderance of truth or of fiction in the legend or narrative under examination.

Mythical History. A myth or legend, in which the historical and truthful greatly preponderate over the inventions of fiction, may be called a mythical history. Certain portions of the legend of the Third Degree have such a foundation in fact that they constitute a mythical history, while other portions, added evidently for the purposes of symbolism, are simply an historical myth.

Mythology. Literally, the science of myths; and this is a very appropriate definition, for mythology is the science which treats of the religion of the ancient Pagans, which was almost altogether founded on myths or popular traditions and legendary tales; and hence Keightly (*Mythol. of Ancient Greece and Italy*, p. 2) says that "mythology may be regarded as the repository of the early religion of the people." Its interest to a Masonic student arises from the constant antagonism that existed between its doctrines and those of the Primitive Freemasonry of antiquity and the light that the mythological mysteries throw upon the ancient organization of Speculative Masonry.

Myth, Philosophical. This is a myth or legend that is almost wholly unhistorical, and which has been invented only for the purpose of enunciating and illustrating a particular thought or dogma. The legend of Euclid is clearly a philosophical myth.

N

N. (Heb. נ.) The fourteenth letter in the English and Hebrew alphabets; its numerical value is 50, and its definition, *fish*. As a final, Nun is written ן, and then is of the value of 700. The Hebrew Divine appellation is נורא, or *Formidabilis*.

Naamah. The daughter of Lamech. To her the "Legend of the Craft" attributes the invention of the art of weaving, and she is united with her three brothers, by the same legend, in the task of inscribing the several sciences on two pillars, that the knowledge of them might be preserved after the flood.

Nabaim. See *Schools of the Prophets*.

Naharda, Brotherhood of. After the destruction of the Solomonial Temple, the captives formed an association while slaves at Naharda, on the Euphrates, and are there said to have preserved the secret mysteries.

Naked. In Scriptural symbology, *nakedness* denoted sin, and *clothing*, protection. But the symbolism of Masonry on this subject is different. There, to be "neither naked nor clothed" is to make no claim through worldly wealth or honors to preferment in Masonry, where nothing but internal merit, which is unaffected by the outward appearance of the body, is received as a recommendation for admission.

Name of God. A reverential allusion to the name of God, in some especial and peculiar form, is to be found in the doctrines and ceremonies of almost all nations. This *unutterable name* was respected by the Jews under the sacred form of the word Jehovah. Among the Druids, the three letters I. O. W. constituted the name of Deity. They were never pronounced, says Giraldus Cambrensis, but another and less sacred name was substituted for them. Each letter was a name in itself. The first is the Word, at the utterance of which in the beginning the world burst into existence; the second is the Word, whose sound still continues, and by which all things remain in existence; the third is the Word, by the utterance of which all things will be consummated in happiness, forever approaching to the immediate presence of the Deity. The analogy between this and the past, present, and future significations contained in the Jewish Tetragrammaton will be evident.

Among the Mohammedans there is a science called ISM ALLAH, or the science of the name of God. "They pretend," says Niebuhr, "that God is the lock of this science, and Mohammed the key; that, consequently, none but Mohammedans can attain it; that it discovers what passes in different countries; that it familiarizes the possessors with the genii, who are at the command of the initiated, and who instruct them; that it places the winds and the seasons at their disposal, and heals the bites of serpents, the lame, the maimed, and the blind."

In the chapter of the Koran entitled *Araaf*, it is written: "God has many excellent names. Invoke him by these names, and separate yourselves from them who give him false names." The Mohammedans believe that God has ninety-nine names, which, with that of ALLAH, make one hundred; and, therefore, their chaplets or rosaries are composed of one hundred beads, at each of which they invoke one of these names; and there is a tradition, that whoever frequently makes this invocation will find the gates of Paradise open to him. With them ALLAH is the *Ism al adhem*, the Great Name, and they bestow upon it all the miraculous virtues which the Jews give to the Tetragrammaton. This, they say, is the name that was engraven on the stone which Japheth gave to his children to bring down rain from heaven; and it was by virtue of this name that Noah made the ark float on the waters, and governed it at will, without the aid of oars or rudder.

Among the Hindus there was the same veneration of the name of God, as is evinced in their treatment of the mystical name AUM. The "Institutes of Menu" continually refer to the peculiar efficacy of this word, of which it is said, "All rites ordained in the Veda, oblations to fire, and solemn sacrifices pass away; but that which passes not away is the syllable AUM, thence called *aishara*, since it is a symbol of God, the Lord of created beings."

There was in every ancient nation a sacred name given to the highest god of its religious faith, besides the epithets of the other and subordinate deities. The old Aryans, the founders of our race, called their chief god DYAUS, and in the Vedas we have the invocation to *Dyaus Pitar*, which is the same as the Greek Ζευ πάτηρ, and the Latin, *Jupiter*, all meaning the Heaven-Father, and at once reminding us of the Christian invocation to "Our Father which art in heaven."

There is one incident in the Hindu mythology which shows how much the old Indian heart yearned after this expression of the nature of Deity by a name. There was a nameless god, to whom, as the "source of golden light," there was a worship. This is expressed in one of the Veda hymns, where the invocation in every stanza closes with the exclamation, "Who is the god to whom we shall offer our sacrifice?" Now, says Bunsen (*God in History*, i., 302), "the Brahmanic expositors must needs find in every hymn the name of a god who is invoked in it, and so, in this case, they have actually invented a grammatical divinity, the god *Who*." What more pregnant testimony could we have of the tendency of man to seek a knowledge of the Divine nature in the expression of a name?

The Assyrians worshiped *Assur*, or *Asarac*, as their chief god. On an obelisk, taken from the palace of Nimrod, we find the inscription, "to Asarac, the Great Lord, the King of all the great gods."

Of the veneration of the Egyptians for the name of their supreme god, we have a striking evidence in the writings of Herodotus, the Father of History, as he has been called, who during a visit to Egypt was initiated into the Osirian mysteries. Speaking of these initiations, he says (B. ii., c. 171), "the Egyptians represent by night *his sufferings, whose name I refrain from mentioning.*" It was no more lawful among the Egyptians than it was among the Jews, to give utterance aloud to that Holy Name.

At Byblos the Phœnicians worshiped *Elium*, the Most High God. From him was descended *El*, whom Philo identifies with Saturn, and to whom he traces the Hebrew *Elohim*. Of this EL, Max Müller says that there was undeniably a primitive religion of the whole Semitic race, and that the Strong One in Heaven was invoked under this name by the ancestors of the Semitic races, before there were Babylonians in Babylonia, Phœnicians in Sidon and Tyre, or Jews in Mesopotamia and Jerusalem. If so, then the Mosaic adoption of Jehovah, with its more precise teaching of the Divine essence, was a step in the progress to the knowledge of the Divine Truth.

In China there is an infinite variety of names of elemental powers, and even of ancestral spirits, who are worshiped as subordinate deities; but the ineffable name is TIEN, compounded of the two signs for *great* and *one*, and which the *Imperial Dictionary* tells us signifies "The Great One—He that dwells on high, and regulates all below."

Drummond (*Origines*) says that ABAUR was the name of the Supreme Deity among the ancient Chaldeans. It is evidently the Hebrew אב אור, and signifies "The Father of Light."

The Scandinavians had twelve subordinate gods, but their chief or supreme deity was *Al-Fathr*, or the *All Father*.

Even among the red men of America we find the idea of an invisible deity, whose name was to be venerated. Garcilasso de la Vega tells us that while the Peruvians paid public worship to the sun, it was but as a symbol of the Supreme Being, whom they called *Pachacamac*, a word meaning "the soul of the world," and which was so sacred that it was spoken only with extreme dread.

The Jews had, besides the Tetragrammaton or four-lettered name, two others: one consisting of twelve and the other of forty-two letters. But Maimonides, in his *More Nevochim* (p. i., clxii.), remarks that it is impossible to suppose that either of these constituted a single name, but that each must have been composed of several words, which must, however, have been significant in making man approximate to a knowledge of the true essence of God. The Kabbalistical book called the *Sohar* confirms this when it tells us that there are ten names of God mentioned in the Bible, and that when these ten names are combined into one word, the number of the letters amounts to forty-two. But the Talmudists, although they did not throw around the forty-two-lettered name the sanctity of the Tetragrammaton, prescribed that it should be communicated only to men of middle age and of virtuous habits, and that its knowledge would confirm them as heirs of the future as well as the present life. The twelve-lettered name, although once common, became afterward occult; and when, on the death of Simon I., the priests ceased to use the Tetragrammaton, they were accustomed to bless the people with the name of twelve letters. Maimonides very wisely rejects the idea, that any power was derived from these letters or their pronunciation, and claims that the only virtue of the names consisted in the holy ideas expressed by the words of which they were composed.

The following are the ten Kabbalistic names of God, corresponding to the ten Sephiroth: 1. Eheyeh; 2. Jah; 3. Jehovah; 4. El; 5. Eloab; 6. Elohim; 7. Jehovah Sabaoth; 8. Elohim Sabaoth; 9. Elhi; 10. Adonai.

Lanzi extends his list of Divine names to twenty-six, which, with their signification, are as follows:

1. *At.* The Aleph and Tau, that is, Alpha and Omega. A name figurative of the Tetragrammaton.
2. *Ihoh.* The eternal, absolute principle of creation, and
3. *Hoh.* Destruction, the male and female principle, the author and regulator of time and motion.
4. *Jah.* The Lord and Remunerator.
5. *Oh.* The severe and punisher.
6. *Jao.* The author of life .
7. *Azazel.* The author of death.
8. *Jao-Sabaoth.* God of the coordinations of loves and hatreds. Lord of the solstices and the equinoxes.
9. *Ehie.* The Being; the Ens.
10. *El.* The first cause. The principle or beginning of all things.
11. *Elo-hi.* The good principle.
12. *Elo-ho.* The evil principle.
13. *El-raccum.* The succoring principle.
14. *El-cannum.* The abhorring principle.
15. *Ell.* The most luminous.
16. *Il.* The omnipotent.
17. *Ellohim.* The omnipotent and beneficent.
18. *Elohim.* The most beneficent.
19. *Elo.* The Sovereign, the Excelsus.
20. *Adon.* The Lord, the Dominator.
21. *Eloi.* The illuminator, the most effulgent.
22. *Adonai.* The most firm, the strongest.
23. *Elion.* The most high.
24. *Shaddai.* The most victorious.
25. *Yeshurun.* The most generous.
26. *Noil.* The most sublime.

Like the Mohammedan *Ism Allah*, Freemasonry presents us as its most important feature with this science of the names of God. But here it elevates itself above Talmudical and Rabbinical reveries, and becomes a symbol of Divine Truth. The names of God were undoubtedly intended originally to be a means of communicating the knowledge of God himself. The name was, from its construction and its literal powers, used to give some idea, however scanty, in early times, of the true nature and essence of the Deity. The ineffable name was the symbol of the unutterable sublimity and perfection of truth which emanate from the Supreme God, while the subordinate names were symbols of the subordinate manifestations of truth. Freemasonry has availed itself of this system, and, in its reverence for the Divine Name, indicates its desire to attain to that truth as the ultimate object of all its labor. The significant words of the Masonic system, which describe the names of God wherever they are found, are not intended merely as words of recognition, but as indices, pointing—like the symbolic ladder of Jacob of the First Degree, or the winding stairs of the Second, or the three gates of the Third —the way of progress from darkness to light, from ignorance to knowledge, from the lowest to the highest conceptions of Divine Truth. And this is, after all, the real object of all Masonic science.

Names of Lodges. The precedency of Lodges does not depend on their names, but on their numbers. The rule declaring that "the precedency of Lodges is grounded on the seniority of their Constitution" was adopted on the 27th of December, 1727, (*Constitutions*, 1738, p. 154.) The number of the Lodge, therefore, by which its precedency is established, is always to be given by the Grand Lodge.

In England, Lodges do not appear to have received distinctive names before the latter part of the last century. Up to that period the Lodges were distinguished simply by their numbers. Thus, in the first edition of the *Book of Constitutions*, published in 1723, we find a list of twenty Lodges, registered by their numbers, from "No. 1" to "No. 20," inclusive. Subsequently, they were further designated by the name of the tavern at which they held their meetings. Thus, in the second edition of the same work, published in 1738, we meet with a list of one hundred and six Lodges, designated sometimes, singularly enough, as *Lodge No. 6, at the Rummer Tavern*, in Queen Street; *No. 84, at the Black Dog*, in Castle Street; or *No. 98, at the Bacchus Tavern*, in Little Bush Lane. With such names and localities, we are not to wonder that the "three small glasses of punch," of which Dr. Oliver so feelingly speaks in his *Book of the Lodge*, were duly appreciated; nor, as he admits, that "there were some brethren who displayed an anxiety to have the allowance increased."

In 1766 we read of four Lodges that were erased from the Register, under the similar designations of the *Globe*, Fleet Street; the *Red Cross Inn*, Southwark; *No. 85, at the George*, Ironmongers' Lane; and the *Mercers' Arms*, Mercers' Street. To only one of these, it will be perceived, was a number annexed. The name and locality of the tavern was presumed to be a sufficient distinction. It was not until about the close of the eighteenth century, as has been already observed, that we find distinctive names beginning to be given to the Lodges; for in 1793 we hear of the *Shakspeare Lodge*, at Stratford-on-Avon; the *Royal Brunswick*, at Sheffield; and the *Lodge of Apollo*, at Alcester. From that time it became a usage among our English brethren, from which they have never since departed.

But a better taste began to prevail at a much earlier period in Scotland, as well as in the continental and colonial Lodges. In Scotland, especially, distinctive names appear to have been used from a very early period, for in the very old charter granting the office of Hereditary Grand Masters to the Barons of Rosslyn, of which the date cannot be more recent than 1600, we find among the signatures the names of the officers of the *Lodge of Dunfermline* and the *Lodge of St. Andrew's*. Among the names in the list of the Scotch Lodges, in 1736 are those of *St. Mary's Chapel, Kilwinning, Aberdeen*, etc. These names were undoubtedly borrowed from localities; but in 1763, while the English Lodges were still content with their numerical arrangement only, we find in Edinburgh such designations as *St. Luke's, St. Giles's*, and *St. David's* Lodges.

The Lodges on the Continent, it is true, at first adopted the English method of borrowing a tavern sign for their appellation; whence we find the *Lodge at the Golden Lion*, in Holland, in 1734, and before that the *Lodge at Hure's Tavern*, in Paris, in 1725. But they soon abandoned this inefficient and inelegant mode of nomenclature; and accordingly, in 1739, a Lodge was organized in Switzerland under the appropriate name of *Stranger's Perfect Union*. Tasteful names, more or less significant, began thenceforth to be adopted by the continental Lodges. Among them we may meet with the *Lodge of the Three Globes*, at Berlin, in 1740; the *Minerva Lodge*, at Leipsic, in 1741; *Absalom Lodge*, at Hamburg, in 1742; *St. George's Lodge*, at the same place, in 1743; the *Lodge of the Crowned Column*, at Brunswick, in 1745; and an abundance of others, all with distinctive names, selected sometimes with much and sometimes with but little taste. But the worst of them was undoubtedly better than the *Lodge at the Goose and Gridiron*, which met in London in 1717.

In America, from the very introduction of Masonry into the continent, significant names were selected for the Lodges; and hence we have, in 1734, *St. John's Lodge*, at Boston; a *Solomon's Lodge*, in 1735, at both Charleston and Savannah; and a *Union Kilwinning*, in 1754, at the former place.

This brief historical digression will serve as an examination of the rules which should govern all founders in the choice of Lodge names. The first and most important rule is that the name of a Lodge should be technically significant; that is, it must allude to some Masonic fact or characteristic; in other words, there must be something Masonic about it. Under this rule, all names derived from obscure or unmasonic localities should be rejected as unmeaning and inappropriate. Dr. Oliver, it is true, thinks otherwise, and says that "the name of a hundred, or wahpentake, in which the Lodge is situated, or of a navigable river, which confers wealth and dignity on the town, are proper titles for a Lodge." But a name should always convey an idea, and there can be conceived no idea worth treasuring in a Mason's mind to be deduced from bestowing such names as *New York*, *Philadelphia*, or *Baltimore*, on a Lodge. The selection of such a name shows but little originality in the chooser; and, besides, if there be two Lodges in a town, each is equally entitled to the appellation; and if there be but one, the appropriation of it would seem to indicate an intention to have no competition in the future.

Yet, barren of Masonic meaning as are such geographical names, the adoption of them is one of the most common faults in American Masonic nomenclature. The examination of a very few Registers, taken at random, will readily evince this fact. Thus, eighty-eight, out of one hundred and sixty Lodges in Wisconsin, are named after towns or counties; of four hundred and thirty-seven Lodges in Indiana, two hundred and fifty-one have names derived from the same source; geographical names are found in one hundred and eighty-one out of four hundred and three Lodges in Ohio, and in twenty out of thirty-eight in Oregon. But, to compensate for this, we have seventy-one Lodges in New Hampshire, and only two local geographical appellations in the list.

There are, however, some geographical names which are admissible, and, indeed, highly appropriate. These are the names of places celebrated in Masonic history. Such titles for Lodges as *Jerusalem*, *Tyre*, *Lebanon*, and *Joppa* are unexceptionable. *Patmos*, which is the name of a Lodge in Maryland, seems, as the long residence of one of the patrons of the Order, to be unobjectionable. So, too, *Bethel*, because it signifies "the house of God"; *Mount Moriah*, the site of the ancient Temple; *Calvary*, the small hill on which the sprig of acacia was found; *Mount Ararat*, where the ark of our father Noah rested; *Ophir*, whence Solomon brought the gold and precious stones with which he adorned the Temple; *Tadmor*, because it was a city built by King Solomon; and *Salem* and *Jebus*, because they are synonyms of Jerusalem, and because the latter is especially concerned with Ornan the Jebusite, on whose "threshing-floor" the Temple was subsequently built—are all excellent and appropriate names for Lodges. But all Scriptural names are not equally admissible. *Cabul*, for instance, must be rejected, because it was the subject of contention between Solomon and Hiram of Tyre; and *Babylon*, because it was the place where "language was confounded and Masonry lost," and the scene of the subsequent captivity of our ancient brethren; *Jericho*, because it was under a curse; and *Misgab* and *Tophet*, because they were places of idol worship. In short, it may be adopted as a rule, that no name should be adopted whose antecedents are in opposition to the principles of Masonry.

The ancient patrons and worthies of Freemasonry furnish a very fertile source of Masonic nomenclature, and have been very liberally used in the selection of names of Lodges. Among the most important may be mentioned *St. John*, *Solomon*, *Hiram*, *King David*, *Adoniram*, *Enoch*, *Archimedes*, and *Pythagoras*. *The Widow's Son Lodge*, of which there are several instances in the United States, is an affecting and significant title, which can hardly be too often used.

Recourse is also to be had to the names of modern distinguished men who have honored the Institution by their adherence to it, or who, by their learning in Masonry, and by their services to the Order, have merited some marks of approbation. And hence we meet, in England, as the names of Lodges, with *Sussex*, *Moira*, *Frederick*, *Zetland*, and *Robert Burns;* and in this country with *Washington*, *Lafayette*, *Clinton*, *Franklin*, and *Clay*. Care must, however, be taken that no name be selected except of one who was both a Mason and had distinguished himself, either by services to his country, to the world, or to the Order. Oliver says that "the most appropriate titles are those which are assumed from the name of some ancient benefactor or meritorious individual who was a native of the place where the Lodge is held; as, in a city, the builder of the cathedral church." In this country we are, it is true, precluded from a selection from such a source; but there are to be found some of those old benefactors of Freemasonry, who, like Shakespeare and Milton, or Homer and Virgil, have ceased to belong to any particular country, and have now become the common property of the world-wide Craft. There are, for instance, *Carausius*, the first royal patron of Masonry in England; and *St. Alban*, the first Grand Master; and *Athelstan* and *Prince Edwin*, both active encouragers of the art in the same kingdom. There are *Wykeham*, *Gundulph*, *Giffard*, *Langham*, *Yevele* (called, in the old records, the King's Freemason), and *Chicheley*, *Jermyn*, and *Wren*, all illustrious Grand Masters of England, each of whom would be well entitled to the honor of giving name to a Lodge, and any one of whom would be better, more euphonious, and more spirit-stirring than the unmeaning, and oftentimes crabbed, name of some obscure village or post-office, from which too many of our Lodges derive their titles.

And, then, again, among the great benefactors to Masonic literature and laborers in Masonic science there are such names as

Anderson, *Dunckerley*, *Preston*, *Hutchinson*, *Town*, *Webb*, and a host of others, who, though dead, still live by their writings in our memories.

The virtues and tenets—the inculcation and practise of which constitute an important part of the Masonic system—form very excellent and appropriate names for Lodges, and have always been popular among correct Masonic nomenclators. Thus we everywhere find such names as *Charity*, *Concord*, *Equality*, *Faith*, *Fellowship*, *Harmony*, *Hope*, *Humility*, *Mystic Tie*, *Relief*, *Truth*, *Union*, and *Virtue*. Frequently, by a transposition of the word "Lodge" and the distinctive appellation, with the interposition of the preposition "of," a more sonorous and emphatic name is given by our English and European brethren, although the custom is but rarely followed in this country. Thus we have by this method the *Lodge of Regularity*, the *Lodge of Fidelity*, the *Lodge of Industry*, and the *Lodge of Prudent Brethren*, in England; and in France, the *Lodge of Benevolent Friends*, the *Lodge of Perfect Union*, the *Lodge of the Friends of Peace*, and the celebrated *Lodge of the Nine Sisters*.

As the names of illustrious men will sometimes stimulate the members of the Lodges which bear them to an emulation of their characters, so the names of the Masonic virtues may serve to incite the brethren to their practise, lest the inconsistency of their names and their conduct should excite the ridicule of the world.

Another fertile and appropriate source of names for Lodges is to be found in the symbols and implements of the Order. Hence, we frequently meet with such titles as *Level*, *Trowel*, *Rising Star*, *Rising Sun*, *Olive Branch*, *Evergreen*, *Doric*, *Corinthian*, *Delta*, and *Corner-Stone* Lodges. *Acacia* is one of the most common, and at the same time one of the most beautiful, of these symbolic names; but, unfortunately, through gross ignorance, it is often corrupted into *Cassia*—an insignificant plant, which has no Masonic or symbolic meaning.

An important rule in the nomenclature of Lodges, and one which must at once recommend itself to every person of taste, is that the name should be euphonious. This principle of euphony has been too little attended to in the selection of even geographical names in this country, where names with impracticable sounds, or with ludicrous associations, are often affixed to our towns and rivers. Speaking of a certain island, with the unpronounceable name of "Srh," Lieber says, "If Homer himself were born on such an island, it could not become immortal, for the best-disposed scholar would be unable to remember the name"; and he thinks that it was no trifling obstacle to the fame of many Polish heroes in the revolution of that country, that they had names which left upon the mind of foreigners no effect but that of utter confusion. An error like this must always be avoided in bestowing a name upon a Lodge. The word selected should be soft, vocal—not too long nor too short—and, above all, be accompanied in its sound or meaning by no low, indecorous, or ludicrous association. For this reason such names of Lodges should be rejected as *Sheboygan* and *Oconomowoc* from the registry of Wisconsin, because of the uncouthness of the sound; and *Rough and Ready* and *Indian Diggings* from that of California, on account of the ludicrous associations which these names convey. Again, *Pythagoras* Lodge is preferable to *Pythagorean*, and *Archimedes* is better than *Archimedean*, because the noun is more euphonious and more easily pronounced than the adjective. But this rule is difficult to illustrate or enforce; for, after all, this thing of euphony is a mere matter of taste, and we all know the adage, "de gustibus."

A few negative rules, which are, however, easily deduced from the affirmative ones already given, will complete the topic.

No name of a Lodge should be adopted which is not, in some reputable way, connected with Masonry. Everybody will acknowledge that *Morgan* Lodge would be an anomaly, and that *Cowan* Lodge would, if possible, be worse. But there are some names which, although not quite as bad as these, are on principle equally as objectionable. Why should any of our Lodges, for instance, assume, as many of them have, the names of *Madison*, *Jefferson*, or *Taylor*, since none of these distinguished men were Masons or patrons of the Craft?

The indiscriminate use of the names of saints unconnected with Masonry is for a similar reason objectionable. Beside our patrons St. John the Baptist and St. John the Evangelist, but three other saints can lay any claims to Masonic honors, and these are St. Alban, who introduced, or is said to have introduced, the Order into England, and has been liberally complimented in the nomenclature of Lodges; and St. Swithin, who was at the head of the Craft in the reign of Ethelwolf; and St. Benedict, who was the founder of the Masonic fraternity of Bridge Builders. But St. Mark, St. Luke, St. Andrew, all of whom have given names to numerous Lodges, can have no pretensions to assist as sponsors in these Masonic baptisms, since they were not at all connected with the Craft.

To the Indian names of Lodges there is a radical objection. It is true that their names are often very euphonious and always significant, for the red men of our continent are tasteful and ingenious in their selection of names—much more so, indeed, than the whites, who borrow from them; but their significance has nothing to do with Masonry.

What has been said of Lodges may with equal propriety be said, *mutatis mutandis*, of Chapters, Councils, and Commanderies.

Namur. A city of Belgium, where the Primitive Scottish Rite was first established; hence sometimes called the Rite of Namur.

Naos. The ark of the Egyptian gods. A chest or structure with more height than depth, and thereby unlike the Israelitish Ark of the Covenant. The winged figures embraced the lower part of the Naos, while the cherubim of the Ark of Yahveh were placed above its lid. Yahveh took up his abode above the propitiatory or covering between the wings of the cherubim, exteriorly, while the gods of Egypt were reputed as hidden in the interior of the Naos of the sacred barks, behind hermetically closed doors. (See *Cherubim.*)

Naphtali. The territory of the tribe of Naphtali adjoined, on its western border, to Phœnicia, and there must, therefore, have been frequent and easy communication between the Phœnicians and the Naphtalites, resulting sometimes in intermarriage. This will explain the fact that Hiram the Builder was the son of a widow of Naphtali and a man of Tyre.

Naples. Freemasonry must have been practised in Naples before 1751, for in that year King Charles issued an edict forbidding it in his dominions. The author of *Anti-Saint Nicaise* says that there was a Grand Lodge at Naples, in 1756, which was in correspondence with the Lodges of Germany. But its meetings were suspended by a royal edict in September, 1775. In 1777 this edict was repealed at the instigation of the Queen, and Masonry was again tolerated. This toleration lasted, however, only for a brief period. In 1781 Ferdinand IV. renewed the edict of suppression, and from that time until the end of the century Freemasonry was subjected in Italy to the combined persecutions of the Church and State, and the Masons of Naples met only in secret. In 1793, after the French Revolution, many Lodges were openly organized. A Supreme Council of the Scottish Rite was established on the 11th of June, 1809, of which King Joachim was elected Grand Master, and the Grand Orient of Naples on the 24th of the same month. The fact that the Grand Orient worked according to the French Rite, and the Supreme Council according to the Scottish, caused dissensions between the two bodies, which, however, were finally healed. And on the 23d of May, 1811, a Concordat was established between the Supreme Council and the Grand Orient, by which the latter took the supervision of the degrees up to the Eighteenth, and the former of those from the Eighteenth to the Thirty-third. In October, 1812, King Joachim accepted the presidency of the Supreme Council as its Grand Commander. Both bodies became extinct in 1815, on the accession of the Bourbons.

Napoleon I. It has been claimed, and with much just reason, as shown in his course of life, that Napoleon the Great was a member of the Brotherhood, and it is said was initiated at Malta, between June 12 and July 19, 1798. The *Abeille Maçonnique* of 1829, and Clavel, in 1830, allege that he visited a Lodge incognito in Paris. His life indicated favor to the Fraternity, and in 1804 he appointed Joseph Buonaparte G. Master of the Grand Orient. Lucien and Louis Buonaparte were of the Fraternity, as also Jerome. Louis Napoleon III. was a member of the Supreme Council A. A. Scottish Rite of France.

Napoleonic Masonry. An Order under this name, called also the French Order of Noachites, was established at Paris, in 1816, by some of the adherents of the Emperor Napoleon. It was divided into three degrees: 1. Knight; 2. Commander; 3. Grand Elect. The last degree was subdivided into three points: i. Secret Judge; ii. Perfect Initiate; iii. Knight of the Crown of Oak. The mystical ladder in this Rite consisted of eight steps or stages, whose names were Adam, Eve, Noah, Lamech, Naamah, Peleg, Oubal, and Orient. The initials of these words, properly transposed, compose the word NAPOLEON, and this is enough to show the character of the system. General Bertrand was elected Grand Master, but, as he was then in the island of St. Helena, the Order was directed by a Supreme Commander and two Lieutenants. It was Masonic in form only, and lasted but for a few years.

Narbonne, Rite of. See *Primitive Rite.*

National Grand Lodge of Germany. The Royal Mother Lodge of the Three Globes, which had been established at Berlin in 1740, and recognized as a Grand Lodge by Frederick the Great in 1744, renounced the Rite of Strict Observance in 1771, and, declaring itself free and independent, assumed the title of "The Grand National Mother Lodge of the Three Globes," by which appellation it is still known.

The Grand Orient of France, among its first acts, established, as an integral part of itself, a National Grand Lodge of France, which was to take the place of the old Grand Lodge, which, it declared, had ceased to exist. But the year after, in 1773, the National Grand Lodge was suppressed by the power which had given it birth; and no such power is now recognized in French Masonry.

Naymus Grecus. The Grand Lodge, No. 1., MS. contains the following passage: "Yt befell that their was on' curious Masson that height [was called] Naymus Grecus that had byn at the making of Sallomon's Temple, and he came into ffraunce, and there he taught the science of Massonrey to men of ffraunce." Who was this "Naymus Grecus"? The writers of these old records of Masonry are notorious for the way in which they mangle all names and words that are in a foreign tongue. Hence it is impossible to say who or what is meant by this word. It is differently spelled in the various manuscripts: *Namas Grecious* in the Lansdowne, *Naymus Græcus* in the Sloane, *Grecus* alone in the Edinburgh-Kilwinning, and *Maymus Grecus* in the Dowland.* Anderson, in the second

* For a table of the various spellings see *Ars Quatuor Coronatorum*, iii., 163.

edition of his *Constitutions* (1738, p. 16), calls him *Ninus*. Now, it would not be an altogether wild conjecture to suppose that some confused idea of Magna Græcia was floating in the minds of these unlettered Masons, especially since the Leland Manuscript records that in Magna Græcia Pythagoras established his school, and then sent Masons into France. Between *Magna Græcia* and *Maynus Grecus* the bridge is a short one, not greater than between Tubal-*cain* and *Wackan*, which we find in a German Middle Age document. The one being the name of a place and the other of a person would be no obstacle to these accommodating record writers; nor must we flinch at the anachronism of placing one of the disciples of Pythagoras at the building of the Solomonic Temple, when we remember that the same writers make Euclid and Abraham contemporaries.

Nazareth. A city of Galilee, in which our Savior spent his childhood and much of his life, and whence he is often called, in the New Testament, the Nazarene, or Jesus of Nazareth. *Jesus Nazarenus* was a portion of the inscription on the cross. (See *I. N. R. I.*) In the Rose Croix, Nazareth is a significant word, and Jesus is designated as "our Master of Nazareth," to indicate the origin and nature of the new dogmas on which the Order of the Rosy Cross was instituted.

Nebraska. Masonry was introduced into Nebraska in October, 1855, by a Charter from the Grand Lodge of Illinois to Nebraska Lodge. Two other Lodges were subsequently chartered by the Grand Lodges of Missouri and Iowa. In September, 1857, the Grand Lodge of Nebraska was organized by a convention of delegates from these three Lodges, and R. C. Jordan was elected Grand Master. The Grand Chapter was organized March 19, 1867. The Grand Commandery of Nebraska was instituted at Omaha, December 28, 1871.

Nebuchadnezzar. About 630 years B. C. the empire and city of Babylon were conquered by Nebuchadnezzar, the king of the Chaldeans, a nomadic race, who, descending from their homes in the Caucasian mountains, had overwhelmed the countries of Southern Asia. Nebuchadnezzar was engaged during his whole reign in wars of conquest. Among other nations who fell beneath his victorious arms was Judea, whose king, Jehoiakim, was slain by Nebuchadnezzar, and his son, Jehoiachin, ascended the Jewish throne. After a reign of three years, he was deposed by Nebuchadnezzar, and his kingdom given to his uncle, Zedekiah, a monarch distinguished for his vices. Having repeatedly rebelled against the Babylonian king, Nebuchadnezzar repaired to Jerusalem, and, after a siege of eighteen months, reduced it. The city was leveled with the ground, the Temple pillaged and burned, and the inhabitants carried captive to Babylon. These events are commemorated in the first section of the English and American Royal Arch system.

Nebuzaradan. A captain, or, as we would now call him, a general of Nebuchadnezzar, who commanded the Chaldean army at the siege of Jerusalem, and who executed the orders of his sovereign by the destruction of the city and Temple, and by carrying the inhabitants, except a few husbandmen, as captives to Babylon.

Negro Lodges. The subject of Lodges of colored persons, commonly called "Negro Lodges," was for many years a source of agitation in the United States, not on account, generally, of the color of the members of these Lodges, but on account of the supposed illegality of their Charters. The history of their organization was thoroughly investigated, many years ago, by Bro. Philip S. Tucker, of Vermont, and Charles W. Moore, of Massachusetts, and the result is here given, with the addition of certain facts derived from a statement made by the officers of the Lodge in 1827.

Prince Hall and thirteen other negroes were made Masons in a military Lodge in the British Army then at Boston, on March 6, 1775. When the Army was withdrawn these negroes applied to the Grand Lodge of England for a Charter and on the 20th of September, 1784, a Charter for a Master's Lodge was granted, although not received until 1787, to Prince Hall and others, all colored men, under the authority of the Grand Lodge of England. The Lodge bore the name of "African Lodge, No. 429," and was situated in the city of Boston. This Lodge ceased its connection with the Grand Lodge of England for many years, and about the beginning of the present century its registration was stricken from the rolls of the United Grand Lodge of England, when new lists were made as were many other Lodges in distant parts of the world, its legal existence, in the meantime, never having been recognized by the Grand Lodge of Massachusetts, to which body it had always refused to acknowledge allegiance.

After the death of Hall and his colleagues, to whom the Charter had been granted, the Lodge, for want of some one to conduct its affairs, fell into abeyance, or, to use the technical phrase, became dormant. After some years it was revived, but by whom, or under what process of Masonic law, is not stated, and information of the revival given to the Grand Lodge of England, but no reply or recognition was received from that body. After some hesitation as to what would be the proper course to pursue, they came to the conclusion, as they have themselves stated, "that, with what knowledge they possessed of Masonry, and as people of color by themselves, they were, and ought by rights to be, free and independent of other Lodges." Accordingly, on the 18th of June, 1827, they issued a protocol, in which they said: "We publicly declare ourselves free and independent of any Lodge from this day, and we will not be tributary or governed by any Lodge but that of our own."

They soon after assumed the name of the "Prince Hall Grand Lodge," and issued Charters for the constitution of subordinates, and from it have proceeded all the Lodges of colored persons now existing in the United States.

Admitting even the legality of the English Charter of 1784—it will be seen that there was already a Masonic authority in Massachusetts upon whose prerogatives of jurisdiction such Charter was an invasion—it cannot be denied that the unrecognized self-revival of 1827, and the subsequent assumption of Grand Lodge powers, were illegal, and rendered both the Prince Hall Grand Lodge and all the Lodges which emanated from it clandestine. And this has been the unanimous opinion of all Masonic jurists in America.

[However, Masonry has spread among the negroes until now they have Lodges and Grand Lodges in most of the States and in Canada and Liberia. As they wear emblems of all the other bodies it is presumable they have them as well.]

Neighbor. All the Old Constitutions have the charge that "every Mason shall keep true counsel of Lodge and Chamber." (Sloane MS., No. 3848.) This is enlarged in the Andersonian Charges of 1722 thus: "You are not to let your family, friends, and *neighbours* know the concerns of the Lodge." (*Constitutions*, 1723, p. 55.) However loquacious a Mason may be in the natural confidence of neighborhood intercourse, he must be reserved in all that relates to the esoteric concerns of Masonry.

Neith. The Egyptian synonym of the Greek Athené or Minerva.

Nekam. נקם. But properly according to the Masoretic pointing, NAKAM. A Hebrew word signifying *Vengeance*, and a significant word in the high degrees. (See *Vengeance*.)

Nekamah. נקמה. Hebrew, signifying *Vengeance*, and, like *Nakam*, a significant word in the high degrees.

Nembroth. A corruption of Nimrod, frequently used in the Old Records.

Nemesis. According to Hesiod, the daughter of Night, originally the personification of the moral feeling of right and a just fear of criminal actions; in other words, Conscience. A temple was erected to Nemesis at Attica. She was at times called Adrastea and Rhamnusia, and represented in the earliest days a young virgin like unto Venus; at a later period, as older and holding a helm and wheel. At Rhamnus there was a statue of Nemesis of Parian marble executed by Phidias. The festival in Greece held in her honor was called Nemesia.

Neocorus. A name of the guardian of the Temple.

Neophyte. Greek, *νεόφυτος*, *newly planted.* In the primitive church, it signified one who had recently abandoned Judaism or Paganism and embraced Christianity; and in the Roman Church those recently admitted into its communion are still so called. Hence it has also been applied to the young disciple of any art or science. Thus Ben Jonson calls a young actor, at his first entrance "on the boards," a *neophyte player*. In Freemasonry the newly initiated and uninstructed candidate is sometimes so designated.

Neoplatonism. A philosophical school, founded at Alexandria in Egypt, which added to the theosophic theories of Plato many mystical doctrines borrowed from the East. The principal disciples of this school were Philo-Judæus, Plotinus, Porphyry, Jamblichus, Proclus, and Julian the Apostate. Much of the symbolic teaching of the higher degrees of Masonry has been derived from the school of the Neoplatonists, especially from the writings of Jamblichus and Philo-Judæus.

Nephalia. Festivals, without wine, celebrated in honor of the lesser deities.

Nergal. (Heb. נרגל.) The synonym of misfortune and ill-luck. The Hebrew name for Mars; and in astrology the lesser Malefic. The word in Sanskrit is *Nrigal.*

Ne plus ultra. Latin. *Nothing more beyond.* The motto adopted for the degree of Kadosh by its founders, when it was supposed to be the summit of Masonry, beyond which there was nothing more to be sought. And, although higher degrees have been since added, the motto is still retained.

Netherlands. Speculative Masonry was first introduced in the Netherlands by the opening at The Hague, in 1731, of an occasional Lodge under a Deputation granted by Lord Lovel, G. M. of England, of which Dr. Desaguliers was Master, for the purpose of conferring the First and Second degrees on the Duke of Lorraine, afterward the Emperor Francis I. He received the Third Degree subsequently in England. But it was not until September 30, 1734, that a regular Lodge was opened by Bro. Vincent de la Chapelle, as Grand Master of the United Provinces, who may therefore be regarded as the originator of Masonry in the Netherlands. In 1735, this Lodge received a Patent or Deputation from the Grand Lodge of England, John Cornelius Rademaker being appointed Provincial Grand Master, and several daughter Lodges were established by it. In the same year the States General prohibited all Masonic meetings by an edict issued November 30, 1735. The Roman clergy actively persecuted the Masons, which seems to have produced a reaction, for in 1737 the magistrates repealed the edict of suppression, and forbade the clergy from any interference with the Order, after which Masonry flourished in the United Provinces. The Masonic innovations and controversies that had affected the rest of the continent never successfully obtruded on the Dutch Masons, who practised with great fidelity the simple rite of the Grand Lodge of England, although an attempt had been made in 1757 to introduce them. In 1798, the Grand Lodge adopted a Book of Statutes, by which it accepted the three Symbolic degrees, and referred the four high degrees of the French Rite to a Grand Chapter. In 1816, Prince Frederick attempted a reform in the degrees, which was, however, only partially successful. The Grand Lodge of the Netherlands, whose Orient is at The Hague, tolerates the high degrees without actually recognizing them. Most of the Lodges confine themselves to the Symbolic degrees of St. John's Masonry, while a few practise the reformed system of Prince Frederick.

Network. One of the decorations of the pillars at the porch of the Temple. (See *Pillars of the Porch.*)

Nevada. Nevada was originally a part of California, and when separated from it in 1865, there were eight Lodges in it working under Charters from the Grand Lodge of California. These Lodges in that year held a convention at Virginia, and organized the Grand Lodge of Nevada.

Ne Varietur. Latin. *Lest it should be changed.* These words refer to the Masonic usage of requiring a Brother, when he receives a certificate from a Lodge, to affix his name, in his own handwriting, in the margin, as a precautionary measure, which enables distant brethren, by a comparison of the handwriting, to recognise the true and original owner of the certificate, and to detect any impostor who may surreptitiously have obtained one.

New Brunswick. Freemasonry was introduced into this province about the middle of the last century by both the Grand Lodges of Scotland and England, and afterward by that of Ireland. The former two bodies appointed, at a later period, Provincial Grand Masters, and in 1844 the Provincial Grand Lodge of Nova Scotia and New Brunswick was organized on the registry of Scotland. The province of New Brunswick becoming an independent portion of the Dominion of Canada, a Grand Lodge was established in October, 1867, by a majority of the Lodges of the territory, and B. Lester Peters was elected Grand Master. Capitular, Cryptic, and Templar Masonry each have bodies in the Province.

Newfoundland. The Ancient Colony of Newfoundland still remains without the Confederation of the Canadian Provinces. Masonry in this island dates back to 1746, the first Warrant being granted by the Provincial Grand Lodge at Boston. Bro. J. Lane's list gives six Lodges warranted in the eighteenth century. The Grand Lodge of the Ancients (England) is credited with four—one in 1774 and three in 1788—and the Grand Lodge of England (Moderns) with two—one each in 1784 and 1785. Nine others were chartered by the present Grand Lodge of England up to 1881, a number still remaining active.

New Hampshire. Freemasonry was introduced into New Hampshire in June, 1734, by the constitution of St. John's Lodge at Portsmouth, under a Charter from the Grand Lodge of Massachusetts. Several other Lodges were subsequently constituted by the same authority. In 1789 a convention of these Lodges was held at Dartmouth, and the Grand Lodge of New Hampshire organized, and John Sullivan, the President of the State, was elected Grand Master. A Grand Chapter was organized in 1819, and a Grand Commandery in 1860.

New Jersey. The history of Freemasonry in New Jersey prior to the establishment of the Grand Lodge in A.D. 1786, was involved in such obscurity that only by the diligence and perseverance of the late Grand Secretary Joseph H. Hough, and the cooperation of an intelligent historical committee, has it been possible to ascertain and collate the fragmentary and scanty data into a sequent, albeit incomplete, narrative.

The general upturning due to the Revolutionary War, the unsettled conditions which prevailed for many years, and the infrequency of opportunity for Masonic meetings, must account for the dispersion of such records as were kept, and suggest why it was that the information contained in the earlier works purporting to be Masonic history was so brief and unsatisfactory as to appear to be traditional rather than authentic. The researches of this committee of the Grand Lodge of New Jersey have removed much of the obscurity surrounding the few obtainable facts.

It proved the issue of the first deputation by the Duke of Norfolk, then Grand Master of England, to Daniel Coxe, on June 5, 1730, empowering the latter as "Provincial Grand Master of the Provinces of New York, New Jersey and Pensilvania, in America." Diligent search in the archives of the Grand Lodge of England, and thorough inquiry for the letters and papers bearing upon the subject among the descendants of Bro. Coxe, failed to disclose any testimony whatever of the exercise by him, or by anyone acting under his authority, of the prerogatives contained in that deputation. The chronological fact remains, however, that Daniel Coxe was the first appointed Provincial Grand Master of Masons in the new world.

The establishment of the first Lodges in New Jersey appears to be recorded as follows: The Provincial Grand Master of New York, George Harrison, issued a warrant erecting a Lodge in the city of Newark, dated May 13, 1761, and although the minutes of this Lodge are not continuous, and the meetings were intermitted, once, apparently for sixteen years, yet it survives, venerated and held in high regard for its honorable history, as St. John's Lodge, No. 1, upon the present register.

A year later Provincial Grand Master Jeremy Gridley of Massachusetts procured the issue of a deputation to erect Temple Lodge, No. 1 in Elizabethtown, dated June 24, 1762, and on December 27, 1763, the same Grand Lodge granted a petition for the erection of a Lodge by the name of St. John's, at Princeton. No record of the actual transactions of these two Lodges has been discovered, but the late Recording Grand Secretary of Massachusetts, was the sufficient authority for the averment that both Lodges had been duly organized, and did Masonic work, evidenced by documents regarding them, which were subsequently destroyed in the burning of the Masonic Temple in Boston in 1865. After an interval of three years, Provincial Grand Master Ball of Pennsylvania warranted a

Lodge at Baskingridge, N. J., as No. 10, on the register of Pennsylvania, another was warranted in 1779 at Middletown, and in 1781 Burlington Lodge, No. 32, was given existence.

A word as to the organization of the Grand Lodge of New Jersey. A convention of Free and Accepted Masons was held pursuant to notice in the city of New Brunswick on December 18, 1786, and "being Master Masons, as every one of them find upon strict trial and due examination, and residing in the state of New Jersey, taking into consideration the propriety and necessity of forming a Grand Lodge of F. & A. M. of the state of New Jersey, do hereby unanimously nominate and elect the following Master Masons to the several offices following, to wit."

The civic titles of the respective officers follow: Chief Justice, Vice President of New Jersey, late High Sheriff, Representative in the Assembly, late Colonel in the Army of the U. S., Clerk of the General Assembly and another High Sheriff.

Individual Masons therefore, not Lodges, had the honor of establishing this Grand Lodge, the complete records of which, carefully preserved, are in print and available for information respecting the growth of the Fraternity in New Jersey.

The Grand Chapter was organized at Burlington, December 30, 1856; the Grand Council, November 26, 1860; and the Grand Commandery, February 14, 1860. [R. A. S.]

New Mexico. The Grand Lodge of Missouri issued warrants to the following Lodges in New Mexico, viz.: Aztec Lodge, No. 108; Chapman Lodge, No. 95; and Montezuma Lodge, No. 109.

These Lodges met in convention, August 6, 1877, at Santa Fé, for the purpose of discussing the question of forming a Grand Lodge. Bro. Simon B. Newcomb presided. The committee on credentials found the representatives of the three above-mentioned Lodges to be present.

The next day a Constitution and By-Laws were adopted, the Grand Officers were elected and installed, Bro. Wm. W. Griffin being M. W. Grand Master, and David J. Miller R. W. Grand Secretary.

New Templars. An Order of five degrees instituted in France in the early part of this century. The degrees were termed—Initiati; Intimi Initiati; Adepti; Orientales Adepti; and Magnæ aquilæ nigræ sancti Johannes Apostoli Adepti.

New York. The first Deputation for the American Colonies was that of Daniel Coxe by the Duke of Norfolk, for the Provinces of New York, New Jersey and Pennsylvania, and was for two years. There are no authentic records that he exercised his authority. Richard Riggs was appointed by the Earl of Darnley, November 15, 1737, but, as with his predecessor, there are no records extant except newspaper notices of meetings of "the Lodge." Francis Goelet was appointed by Lord Byron in 1751, and was succeeded by George Harrison, appointed June 9, 1753, by Lord Carysfort. Harrison chartered Lodges in New York, New Jersey, Connecticut, and Michigan. Sir John Johnson was appointed by Lord Blany in 1767, but did not assume office until 1771, and was the last of the "Modern" Provincial Grand Masters. The present Grand Lodge was organized December 15, 1782, under a Provincial Grand Warrant from the "Atholl" Grand Lodge, dated September 5, 1781, declared its independence June 6, 1787, and assumed the title of the "Grand Lodge of Free and Accepted Masons of the State of New York." There have been four schisms, all of which were creditably adjusted. A Grand Chapter was organized in 1783, which had but a short existence and was succeeded by the present Grand Chapter March 4, 1798. The Grand Commandery was organised June 18, 1814, and the Grand Council Royal and Select Masters January 25, 1823. The Supreme Council, Northern Jurisdiction, A. A. S. R. was organized by Emmanuel De La Motta in New York City in 1813, but was preceded by a Lodge of Perfection at Albany. N. Y., in 1767. [W. J. A.]

Nick. (Danish, *Nikken.*) The spirit of the waters, an enemy of man, the devil, or in the vulgate "Old Nick."

Nicolai, Christoph Friedrich. Christopher Frederick Nicolai, author of a very interesting essay on the origin of the Society of Freemasons, was a bookseller of Berlin, and one of the most distinguished of the German savants of that Augustan age of German literature in which he lived. He was born at Berlin on the 18th of March, 1733, and died in the same city on the 8th of January, 1811. He was the editor of, and an industrious contributor to, two German periodicals of high literary character, a learned writer on various subjects of science and philosophy, and the intimate friend of Lessing, whose works he edited, and of the illustrious Mendelssohn.

In 1782–3, he published a work with the following title: *Versuch über die Beschuldigungen welche dem Tempelherrnorden gemacht worden und über dessen Geheimniss; nebst einem Anhange über das Entstehen der Freimaurergesellschaft;* i. e., "An Essay on the accusations made against the Order of Knights Templars and their mystery; with an Appendix on the origin of the Fraternity of Freemasons." In this work Nicolai advanced his peculiar theory on the origin of Freemasonry, which is substantially as follows:

Lord Bacon, taking certain hints from the writings of Andreä, the founder of Rosicrucianism and his English disciple, Fludd, on the subject of the regeneration of the world, proposed to accomplish the same object, but by a different and entirely opposite method. For, whereas, they explained everything esoterically, Bacon's plan was to abolish all distinction between the esoteric and the exoteric, and to demonstrate everything by proofs from nature. This idea he first promulgated in his *Instauratio Magna*, but afterward more fully developed in his *New Atlantis*. In this latter work, he introduced his beautiful apologue, abounding in Masonic ideas, in which he described the unknown island of Bensalem, where a king had built a large edifice, called after himself, Solomon's House. Charles I., it is said, had been much attracted by this idea, and had intended to found something of the kind upon the plan of Solomon's Temple, but the occurrence of the Civil War prevented the execution of the project.

The idea lay for some time dormant, but was subsequently revived, in 1646, by Wallis, Wilkins, and several other learned men, who established the Royal Society for the purpose of carrying out Bacon's plan of communicating to the world scientific and philosophical truths. About the same time another society was formed by other learned men, who sought to arrive at truth by the investigations of alchemy and astrology. To this society such men as Ashmole and Lily were attached, and they resolved to construct a House of Solomon in the island of Bensalem, where they might communicate their instructions by means of secret symbols. To cover their mysterious designs, they got themselves admitted into the Masons' Company, and held their meetings at Masons' Hall, in Masons' Alley, Basinghall Street. As freemen of London, they took the name of Freemasons, and naturally adopted the Masonic implements as symbols. Although this association, like the Royal Society, sought, but by a different method, to inculcate the principles of natural science and philosophy, it subsequently took a political direction. Most of its members were strongly opposed to the puritanism of the dominant party and were in favor of the royal cause, and hence their meetings, ostensibly held for the purpose of scientific investigation, were really used to conceal their secret political efforts to restore the exiled house of Stuart. From this society, which subsequently underwent a decadence, sprang the revival in 1717, which culminated in the establishment of the Grand Lodge of England.

Such was the theory of Nicolai. Few will be found at the present day to concur in all his views, yet none can refuse to award to him the praise of independence of opinion, originality of thought, and an entire avoidance of the beaten paths of hearsay testimony and unsupported tradition. His results may be rejected, but his method of attaining them must be commended.

Nicotiates, Order of. A secret order mentioned by Clavel, teaching the doctrines of Pythagoras.

Night. Lodges, all over the world, meet, except on special occasions, at night. In this selection of the hours of night and darkness for initiation, the usual coincidence will be found between the ceremonies of Freemasonry and those of the Ancient Mysteries, showing their evident derivation from a common origin. Justin says that at Eleusis, Triptolemus invented the art of sowing corn, and that, in honor of this invention, the nights were consecrated to initiation. The application is, however, rather abstruse.

In the *Bacchæ* of Euripides, that author introduces the god Bacchus, the supposed inventor of the Dionysian mysteries, as replying to the question of King Pentheus in the following words:

> ΠΕΝ. Τά δ' ἱερά νύκτωρ, ἤ μεθ' ἡμέραν τελεῖς;
> ΔΙΟ. Νύκτωρ τα πολλά· σεμνότητ' ἔχει σκότος.
>
> *Eurip. Bacch.* Act II., l. 485.

"*Pentheus.*—By night or day, these sacred rites perform'st thou?
Bacchus.—Mostly by night, for venerable is darkness";

and in all the other mysteries the same reason was assigned for nocturnal celebrations, since night and darkness have something solemn and august in them which is disposed to fill the mind with sacred awe. And hence black, as an emblem of darkness and night, was considered as the color appropriate to the mysteries.

In the mysteries of Hindustan, the candidate for initiation, having been duly prepared by previous purifications, was led at the dead of night to the gloomy cavern, in which the mystic rites were performed.

The same period of darkness was adopted for the celebration of the mysteries of Mithras, in Persia. Among the Druids of Britain and Gaul, the principal annual initiation commenced at "low twelve," or midnight of the eve of May-day. In short, it is indisputable that the initiations in all the Ancient Mysteries were nocturnal in their character.

The reason given by the ancients for this selection of night as the time for initiation, is equally applicable to the system of Freemasonry. "Darkness," says Oliver, "was an emblem of death, and death was a prelude to resurrection. It will be at once seen, therefore, in what manner the doctrine of the resurrection was inculcated and exemplified in these remarkable institutions."

Death and the resurrection were the doctrines taught in the Ancient Mysteries; and night and darkness were necessary to add to the sacred awe and reverence which these doctrines ought always to inspire in the rational and contemplative mind. The same doctrines form the very groundwork of Freemasonry; and as the Master Mason, to use the language of Hutchinson, "represents a man saved from the grave of iniquity and raised to the faith of salvation," darkness and night are the appropriate accompaniments to the solemn ceremonies which demonstrate this profession.

Nihongi. ("Chronicles of Nihon.") The companion of the Kojiki; the two works together forming the doctrinal and historic basis of Sintonism. The Japanese adherents of Sinsyn are termed Sintus, or Sintoos, who worship the gods, the chief of which is Ten-sio-dai-yin. The Nihongi was composed about 720 A.D., with the evident design of giving a Chinese coloring to the subject-matter of the Kojiki, upon which it is founded.

Nile. There is a tradition in the old Masonic Records that the inundations of the river

Nile, in Egypt, continually destroying the perishable landmarks by which one man could distinguish his possessions from those of another, Euclid instructed the people in the art of geometry, by which they might measure their lands; and then taught them to bound them with walls and ditches, so that after an inundation each man could identify his own boundaries.

The tradition is given in the Cooke MS. thus: "Euclyde was one of the first founders of Geometry, and he gave hit name, for in his tyme there was a water in that lond of Egypt that is called Nilo, and hit flowid so ferre into the londe that men myght not dwelle therein. Then this worthi clerke Enclide taught hem to make grete wallys and diches to holde owt the watyr, and he by Gemetria mesured the londe and departyd hit in divers partys, and made every man to close his owne parte with walles and diches." (Lines 455–472.) This legend of the origin of the art of geometry was borrowed by the old Operative Masons from the *Origines* of St. Isidore of Seville, where a similar story is told.

Nil nisi clavis deest. Latin. *Nothing but the key is wanting.* A motto or device often attached to the double triangle of Royal Arch Masonry. It is inscribed on the Royal Arch badge or jewel of the Grand Chapter of Scotland, the other devices being a double triangle and a triple tau.

Nimrod. The legend of the Craft in the Old Constitutions refers to Nimrod as one of the founders of Masonry. Thus in the York MS., No. 1, we read: "At ye makeing of ye Toure of Babell there was Masonrie first much esteemed of, and the King of Babilon y^t^ was called Nimrod was A mason himselfe and loved well Masons." And the Cooke MS. thus repeats the story: "And this same Nembroth began the towre of babilon and he taught to his werkemen the craft of Masonrie, and he had with him many Masons more than forty thousand. And he loved and cherished them well." (Line 343.) The idea no doubt sprang out of the Scriptural teaching that Nimrod was the architect of many cities; a statement not so well expressed in the authorized version, as it is in the improved one of Bochart, which says: "From that land Nimrod went forth to Asshur, and builded Nineveh, and Rehoboth city, and Calah, and Resen between Nineveh and Calah, that is the great city."

Nine. If the number three was celebrated among the ancient sages, that of three times three had no less celebrity; because, according to them, each of the three elements which constitute our bodies is ternary: the water containing earth and fire; the earth containing igneous and aqueous particles; and the fire being tempered by globules of water and terrestrial corpuscles which serve to feed it. No one of the three elements being entirely separated from the others, all material beings composed of these three elements, whereof each is triple, may be designated by the figurative number of three times three, which has become the symbol of all formations of bodies. Hence the name of ninth envelop given to matter. Every material extension, every circular line, has for its representative sign the number nine among the Pythagoreans, who had observed the property which this number possesses of reproducing itself incessantly and entire in every multiplication; thus offering to the mind a very striking emblem of matter, which is incessantly composed before our eyes, after having undergone a thousand decompositions.

The number nine was consecrated to the Spheres and the Muses. It is the sign of every circumference; because a circle or 360 degrees is equal to 9, that is to say, 3 + 6 + 0 = 9. Nevertheless, the ancients regarded this number with a sort of terror; they considered it a bad presage; as the symbol of versatility, of change, and the emblem of the frailty of human affairs. Wherefore they avoided all numbers where nine appears, and chiefly 81, the produce of 9 multiplied by itself, and the addition whereof, 8 + 1, again presents the number 9.

As the figure of the number 6 was the symbol of the terrestrial globe, animated by a Divine spirit, the figure of the number 9 symbolized the earth, under the influence of the Evil Principle; and thence the terror it inspired. Nevertheless, according to the Kabbalists, the cipher 9 symbolizes the generative egg, or the image of a little globular being, from whose lower side seems to flow its spirit of life.

The Ennead, signifying an aggregate of nine things or persons, is the first square of unequal numbers.

Everyone is aware of the singular properties of the number 9, which, multiplied by itself or any other number whatever, gives a result whose final sum is always 9, or always divisible by 9.

9, multiplied by each of the ordinary numbers, produces an arithmetical progression, each member whereof, composed of two figures, presents a remarkable fact; for example:

1 . 2 . 3 . 4 . 5 . 6 . 7 . 8 . 9 . 10
9 . 18 . 27 . 36 . 45 . 54 . 63 . 72 . 81 . 90

The first line of figures gives the regular series, from 1 to 10.

The second reproduces this line doubly; first ascending from the first figure of 18, and then returning from the second figure of 81.

In Freemasonry, 9 derives its value from its being the product of 3 multiplied into itself, and consequently in Masonic language the number 9 is always denoted by the expression 3 times 3. For a similar reason, 27, which is 3 times 9, and 81, which is 9 times 9, are esteemed as sacred numbers in the higher degrees.

Nineveh. The capital of the ancient kingdom of Assyria, and built by Nimrod. The traditions of its greatness and the magnificence of its buildings were familiar to the

Arabs, the Greeks, and the Romans. The modern discoveries of Rich, of Botta, and other explorers, have thrown much light upon its ancient condition, and have shown that it was the seat of much architectural splendor and of a profoundly symbolical religion, which had something of the characteristics of the Mithraic worship. In the mythical relations of the Old Constitutions, which make up the legend of the Craft, it is spoken of as the ancient birthplace of Masonry, where Nimrod, who was its builder, and "was a Mason and loved well the Craft," employed 60,000 Masons to build it, and gave them a charge "that they should be true," and this, says the Harleian MS., No. 1942, was the first time that any Mason had any charge of Craft.

Nisan. ניסן. The seventh month of the Hebrew civil year, and corresponding to the months of March and April, commencing with the new moon of the former.

Noachidæ. The descendants of Noah. A term applied to Freemasons on the theory, derived from the "legend of the Craft," that Noah was the father and founder of the Masonic system of theology. And hence the Freemasons claim to be his descendants, because in times past they preserved the pure principles of his religion amid the corruptions of surrounding faiths.

Dr. Anderson first used the word in this sense in the second edition of the *Book of Constitutions:* "A Mason is obliged by his tenure to observe the moral law as a true Noachida." But he was not the inventor of the term, for it occurs in a letter sent by the Grand Lodge of England to the Grand Lodge of Calcutta in 1735, which letter is preserved among the Rawlinson MSS. in the Bodleian Library, Oxford. (See *Ars Quatuor Coronatorum*, xi., 35.)

Noachite, or Prussian Knight. (*Noachite ou Chevalier Prussien.*) 1. The Twenty-first Degree of the Ancient and Accepted Scottish Rite. The history as well as the character of this degree is a very singular one. It is totally unconnected with the series of Masonic degrees which are founded upon the Temple of Solomon, and is traced to the tower of Babel. Hence the Prussian Knights call themselves Noachites, or Disciples of Noah, while they designate all other Masons as Hiramites, or Disciples of Hiram. The early French rituals state that the degree was translated in 1757 from the German by M. de Beraye. Knight of Eloquence in the Lodge of the Count St. Gelaire, Inspector-General of Prussian Lodges in France. Lenning gives no credit to this statement, but admits that the origin of the degree must be attributed to the year above named. The destruction of the tower of Babel constitutes the legend of the degree, whose mythical founder is said to have been Peleg, the chief builder of that edifice. A singular regulation is that there shall be no artificial light in the Lodge room, and that the meetings shall be held on the night of the full moon of each month.

The degree was adopted by the Council of Emperors of the East and West, and in that way became subsequently a part of the system of the Scottish Rite. But it is misplaced in any series of degrees supposed to emanate from the Solomonic Temple. It is, as an unfitting link, an unsightly interruption of the chain of legendary symbolism substituting Noah for Solomon, and Peleg for Hiram Abif. The Supreme Council for the Southern Jurisdiction has abandoned the original ritual and made the degree a representation of the Vehmgericht or Westphalian Franc Judges. But this by no means relieves the degree of the objection of Masonic incompatibility. That it was ever adopted into the Masonic system is only to be attributed to the passion for high degrees which prevailed in France in the middle of the last century.

In the modern ritual the meetings are called Grand Chapters. The officers are a Lieutenant Commander, two Wardens, an Orator, Treasurer, Secretary, Master of Ceremonies, Warder, and Standard-Bearer. The apron is yellow, inscribed with an arm holding a sword and the Egyptian figure of silence. The order is black, and the jewel a full moon or a triangle traversed by an arrow. In the original ritual there is a coat of arms belonging to the degree, which is thus emblazoned: Party per fess; in chief, *azure*, semé of stars, *or* a full moon, *argent;* in base, *sable*, an equilateral triangle, having an arrow suspended from its upper point, barb downward, *or*.

The legend of the degree describes the travels of Peleg from Babel to the north of Europe, and ends with the following narrative: "In trenching the rubbish of the salt-mines of Prussia was found in A. D. 553, at a depth of fifteen cubits, the appearance of a triangular building in which was a column of white marble, on which was written in Hebrew the whole history of the Noachites. At the side of this column was a tomb of freestone on which was a piece of agate inscribed with the following epitaph: Here rest the ashes of Peleg, our Grand Architect of the tower of Babel. The Almighty had pity on him because he became humble."

This legend, although wholly untenable on historic grounds, is not absolutely puerile. The dispersion of the human race in the time of Peleg had always been a topic of discussion among the learned. Long dissertations had been written to show that all the nations of the world, even America, had been peopled by the three sons of Noah and their descendants. The object of the legend seems, then, to have been to impress the idea of the thorough dispersion. The fundamental idea of the degree is, under the symbol of Peleg, to teach the crime of assumption and the virtue of humility.

2. The degree was also adopted into the Rite of Mizraim, where it is the Thirty-fifth.

Noachite, Sovereign. (*Noachite Souverain.*) A degree contained in the nomenclature of Fustier.

Noachites. The same as *Noachidæ*, which see.

Noah. In all the old Masonic manuscript Constitutions that are extant, Noah and the flood play an important part in the "Legend of the Craft." Hence, as the Masonic system became developed, the Patriarch was looked upon as what was called a patron of Masonry. And this connection of Noah with the mythic history of the Order was rendered still closer by the influence of many symbols borrowed from the Arkite worship, one of the most predominant of the ancient faiths. So intimately were incorporated the legends of Noah with the legends of Masonry that Freemasons began, at length, to be called, and are still called, "Noachidæ," or the descendants of Noah, a term first applied by Anderson, and very frequently used at the present day.

It is necessary, therefore, that every scholar who desires to investigate the legendary symbolism of Freemasonry should make himself acquainted with the Noachic myths upon which much of it is founded. Dr. Oliver, it is true, accepted them all with a childlike faith; but it is not likely that the skeptical inquirers of the present day will attribute to them any character of authenticity. Yet they are interesting, because they show us the growth of legends out of symbols, and they are instructive because they are for the most part symbolic.

The "Legend of the Craft" tells us that the three sons of Lamech and his daughter, Naamah, "did know that God would take vengeance for sin, either by fire or water; wherefore they wrote these sciences which they had found in two pillars of stone, that they might be found after the flood." Subsequently, this legend took a different form, and to Enoch was attributed the precaution of burying the stone of foundation in the bosom of Mount Moriah, and of erecting the two pillars above it.

The first Masonic myth referring to Noah that presents itself is one which tells us that, while he was piously engaged in the task of exhorting his contemporaries to repentance, his attention had often been directed to the pillars which Enoch had erected on Mount Moriah. By diligent search he at length detected the entrance to the subterranean vault, and, on pursuing his inquiries, discovered the stone of foundation, although he was unable to comprehend the mystical characters there deposited. Leaving these, therefore, where he had found them, he simply took away the stone of foundation on which they had been deposited, and placed it in the ark as a convenient altar.

Another myth, preserved in one of the ineffable degrees, informs us that the ark was built of cedars which grew upon Mount Lebanon, and that Noah employed the Sidonians to cut them down, under the superintendence of Japheth. The successors of these Sidonians, in after times, according to the same tradition, were employed by King Solomon to fell and prepare cedars on the same mountain for his stupendous Temple.

The record of Genesis lays the foundation for another series of symbolic myths connected with the dove, which has thus been introduced into Masonry.

After forty days, when Noah opened the window of the ark that he might learn if the waters had subsided, he despatched a raven, which, returning, gave him no satisfactory information. He then sent forth a dove three several times, at an interval of seven days between each excursion. The first time, the dove, finding no resting-place, quickly returned; the second time she came back in the evening, bringing in her mouth an olive-leaf, which showed that the waters must have sufficiently abated to have exposed the tops of the trees; but on the third departure, the dry land being entirely uncovered, she returned no more.

In the Arkite rites, which arose after the dispersion of Babel, the dove was always considered as a sacred bird, in commemoration of its having been the first discoverer of land. Its name, which in Hebrew is *ionah*, was given to one of the earliest nations of the earth; and, as the emblem of peace and good fortune, it became the bird of Venus. Modern Masons have commemorated the messenger of Noah in the honorary degree of "Ark and Dove," which is sometimes conferred on Royal Arch Masons.

On the 27th day of the second month, equivalent to the 12th of November, in the year of the world 1657, Noah, with his family, left the ark. It was exactly one year of 365 days, or just one revolution of the sun, that the patriarch was enclosed in the ark. This was not unobserved by the descendants of Noah, and hence, in consequence of Enoch's life of 365 days, and Noah's residence in the ark for the same apparently mystic period, the Noachites confounded the worship of the solar orb with the idolatrous adoration which they paid to the patriarchs who were saved from the deluge. They were led to this, too, from an additional reason, that Noah, as the restorer of the human race, seemed, in some sort, to be a type of the regenerating powers of the sun.

So important an event as the deluge, must have produced a most impressive effect upon the religious dogmas and rites of the nations which succeeded it. Consequently, we shall find some allusion to it in the annals of every people and some memorial of the principal circumstances connected with it, in their religious observances. At first, it is to be supposed that a veneration for the character of the second parent of the human race must have been long preserved by his descendants. Nor would they have been unmindful of the proper reverence due to that sacred vessel—sacred in their eyes—which had preserved their great progenitor from the fury of the waters. "They would long cherish," says Alwood (*Lit. Antiq. of Greece*, p. 182), "the memory of those worthies who were rescued from the common lot of utter ruin; they would call to mind, with an extravagance of admiration, the means adopted for their preservation; they would adore the wisdom which contrived, and the goodness which prompted to, the execution of such a plan." So pious a feeling would exist, and be circumscribed within its proper limits of reverential gratitude, while the legends of the deluge continued to be preserved in their purity, and while the Divine preserver of Noah was remembered as the one god of his posterity. But when, by the confusion and dispersion at Babel, the true teachings of Enoch and Noah were lost, and idolatry or polytheism was substituted for the ancient faith, then Noah became a god, worshiped under different names in different countries, and the ark was transformed into the temple of the Deity. Hence arose those peculiar systems of initiations which, known under the name of the "Arkite rites," formed a part of the worship of the ancient world, and traces of which are to be found in almost all the old systems of religion.

It was in the six hundredth year of his age, that Noah, with his family, was released from the ark. Grateful for his preservation, he erected an altar and prepared a sacrifice of thank-offerings to the Deity. A Masonic tradition says, that for this purpose he made use of that stone of foundation which he had discovered in the subterranean vault of Enoch, and which he had carried with him into the ark. It was at this time that God made his covenant with Noah, and promised him that the earth should never again be destroyed by a flood. Here, too, he received those commandments for the government of himself and his posterity which have been called "the seven precepts of the Noachidæ."

It is to be supposed that Noah and his immediate descendants continued to live for many years in the neighborhood of the mountain upon which the ark had been thrown by the subsidence of the waters. There is indeed no evidence that the patriarch ever removed from it. In the nine hundred and fiftieth year of his age he died, and, according to the tradition of the Orientalists, was buried in the land of Mesopotamia. During that period of his life which was subsequent to the deluge, he continued to instruct his children in the great truths of religion. Hence, Masons are sometimes called Noachidæ, or the sons of Noah, to designate them, in a peculiar manner, as the preservers of the sacred deposit of Masonic truth bequeathed to them by their great ancestor; and circumstances intimately connected with the transactions of the immediate descendants of the patriarch are recorded in a degree which has been adopted by the Ancient and Accepted Scottish Rite under the name of "Patriarch Noachite."

The primitive teachings of the patriarch, which were simple but comprehensive, continued to be preserved in the line of the patriarchs and the prophets to the days of Solomon, but were soon lost to the other descendants of Noah, by a circumstance to which we must now refer. After the death of Noah, his sons removed from the region of Mount Ararat, where, until then, they had resided, and "travelling from the East, found a plain in the land of Shinar, and dwelt there." Here they commenced the building of a lofty tower. This act seems to have been displeasing to God, for in consequence of it, he confounded their language, so that one could not understand what another said; the result of which was that they separated and dispersed over the face of the earth in search of different dwelling-places. With the loss of the original language, the great truths which that language had conveyed, disappeared from their minds. The worship of the one true God was abandoned. A multitude of deities began to be adored. Idolatry took the place of pure theism. And then arose the Arkite rites, or the worship of Noah and the Ark, Sabaism, or the adoration of the stars, and other superstitious observances, in all of which, however, the priesthood, by their mysteries or initiations into a kind of Spurious Freemasonry, preserved, among a multitude of errors, some faint allusions to the truth, and retained just so much light as to make their "darkness visible."

Such are the Noachic traditions of Masonry, which, though if considered as materials of history, would be worth but little, yet have furnished valuable sources of symbolism, and in that way are full of wise instruction.

Noah, Precepts of. The precepts of the patriarch Noah, which were preserved as the Constitutions of our ancient brethren, are seven in number, and are as follows:

1. Renounce all idols.
2. Worship the only true God.
3. Commit no murder.
4. Be not defiled by incest.
5. Do not steal.
6. Be just.
7. Eat no flesh with blood in it.

The "proselytes of the gate," as the Jews termed those who lived among them without undergoing circumcision or observing the ceremonial law, were bound to obey the seven precepts of Noah. The Talmud says that the first six of these precepts were given originally by God to Adam, and the seventh afterward to Noah. These precepts were designed to be obligatory on all the Noachidæ, or descendants of Noah, and consequently, from the time of Moses, the Jews would not suffer a stranger to live among them unless he observed these precepts, and never gave quarter in battle to an enemy who was ignorant of them.

Noffodei. The name of this person is differently spelled by different writers. Villani, and after him Burnes, call him *Noffo Dei*, Reghellini *Neffodei*, and Addison *Nosso de Florentin;* but the more usual spelling is *Noffodei*. He and Squin de Flexian were the first to make those false accusations against the Knights Templars which led to the downfall of the Order. Naffodei, who was a Florentine, is asserted by some writers to have been an apostate Templar, who had been condemned by the Preceptor and Chapter of France to perpetual imprisonment for impiety and crime. But Dupui denies this, and says that he never was a Templar, but that, having been banished from his native country, he had been condemned to rigorous penalties by the Prevost of Paris for his crimes. For a history of his treachery to the Templars, see *Squin de Flexian*.

Nomenclature. There are several Masonic works, printed or in manuscript, which contain lists of the names of degrees in Masonry. Such a list is called by the French writers a nomenclature. The most important of these nomenclatures are those of Peuvret, Fustier, Pyron, and Lemanceau. Ragon has a nomenclature of degrees in his *Tuileur Générale*. And Thory has an exhaustive and descriptive one in his *Acta Latomorum*. Oliver also gives a nomenclature, but an imperfect one, of one hundred and fifty degrees in his *Historical Landmarks*.

Nomination. It is the custom in some Grand Lodges and Lodges to nominate candidates for election to office, and in others this custom is not adopted. But the practise of nomination has the sanction of ancient usage. Thus the records of the Grand Lodge of England, under date of June 24, 1717, tell us that "before dinner the oldest Master Mason . . . in the chair proposed a list of proper candidates, and the brethren, by a majority of hands, elected Mr. Anthony Sayer, Gentleman, Grand Master of Masons." (*Constitutions*, 1738, p. 109.) And the present Constitution of the Grand Lodge of England requires that the Grand Master shall be nominated in December, and the Grand Treasurer in September, but that the election shall not take place until the following March. Nominations appear, therefore, to be the correct Masonic practise; yet, if a member be elected to any office to which he had not previously been nominated, the election will be valid, for a nomination is not essential.

Non-Affiliation. The state of being unconnected by membership with a Lodge. (See *Unaffiliated Mason*.)

Nonesynches. In the Old Constitutions known as the Dowland MS. is found the following passage: "St. Albones loved well Masons and cherished them much. And he made their paie right good, . . . for he gave them ijs-vjd, a weeke, and iijd. to their nonesynches." This word, which cannot, in this precise form, be found in any archaic dictionary, evidently means food or refreshment, for in the parallel passage in other Constitutions the word used is *cheer*, which has the same meaning. The old English word from which we get our *luncheon* is *noonshun*, which is defined to be the refreshment taken at *noon*, when laborers desist from work to *shun* the heat. Of this, *nonesynches* is a corrupt form.

Nonis. A significant word in the Thirty-second Degree of the Scottish Rite. The original old French rituals endeavor to explain it, and say that it and two other words in conjunction are formed out of the initials of the words of a particular aphorism which has reference to the secret arcana and "sacred treasure" of Masonry. Out of several interpretations, no one can be positively asserted as the original, although the intent is apparent to him to whom the same may lawfully belong. (See *Saliz* and *Tengu*.)

Non nobis. It is prescribed that the motto beneath the Passion Cross on the Grand Standard of a Commandery of Knights Templar shall be "Non nobis Domine! non nobis, sed nomini tuo da Gloriam." That is, *Not unto us, O Lord! not unto us, but unto Thy name give Glory*. It is the commencement of the 115th Psalm, which is sung in the Christian church on occasions of thanksgiving. It was the ancient Templar's shout of victory.

Non-Resident. The members of a Lodge who do not reside in the locality of a Lodge, but live at a great distance from it in another State, or, perhaps, country, but still continue members of it, and contribute to its support by the payment of Lodge dues, are called "non-resident members." Many Lodges, in view of the fact that such members enjoy none of the local privileges of their Lodges, require from them a less amount of annual payment than they do from their resident members.

Noorthouck, John. The editor of the fifth, and by far the best, edition of the *Book of Constitutions*, which was published in 1784. He was the son of Herman Noorthouck, a bookseller, and was born in London about the year 1746. Oliver describes him as "a clever and intelligent man, and an expert Mason." His literary pretensions were, however, greater than this modest encomium would indicate. He was patronized by the celebrated printer, William Strahan, and passed nearly the whole of his life in the occupations of an author, an index maker, and a corrector of the press. He was, besides his edition of the *Book of Constitutions*, the writer of a *History of London*, 4to, published in 1773, and an *Historical and Classical Dictionary*, 2 vols., 8vo, published in 1776. To him also, as well as to some others, has been attributed the authorship of a once popular book entitled *The Man after God's own Heart*. In 1852, J. R. Smith, a bookseller of London, advertised for sale "the original autograph manuscript of the life of John Noorthouck." He calls this "a very interesting piece of autobiography, containing many curious literary anecdotes of the last century, and deserving to be printed." Noorthouck died in 1816, aged about seventy years.

Normal. A perpendicular to a curve; and included between the curve and the axis of the abscissas. Sometimes a square, used by Operative Masons, for proving angles.

Nornæ. In the Scandinavian Mysteries these were three maidens, known as Urd, Verdandi, and Skuld, signifying Past, Present, and Future. Their position is seated near the Urdar-wells under the world-tree Yggdrasil, and there they determine the fate of both gods and men. They daily draw water from the spring, and with it and the surrounding clay sprinkle the ash-tree Yggdrasil, that the branches may not wither and decay.

North. The north is Masonically called a place of darkness. The sun in his progress through the ecliptic never reaches farther than 23° 28′ north of the equator. A wall being erected on any part of the earth farther north than that, will therefore, at meridian, receive the rays of the sun only on its south side, while the north will be entirely in shadow at the hour of meridian. The use of the north as a symbol of darkness is found, with the present interpretation, in the early rituals of the last century. It is a portion of the old sun worship, of which we find so many relics in Gnosticism, in Hermetic philosophy, and in Freemasonry. The east was the place of the sun's daily birth, and hence highly revered; the north the place of his annual death, to which he approached only to lose his vivific heat, and to clothe the earth in the darkness of long nights and the dreariness of winter.

However, this point of the compass, or place of Masonic darkness, must not be construed as implying that in the Temple of Solomon no light or ventilation was had from this direction. The Talmud, and as well Josephus, allude to an extensive opening toward the North, framed with costly magnificence, and known as the great "Golden Window." There were as many openings in the outer wall on the north as on the south side. There were three entrances through the "Chel" on the north and six on the south. (See *Temple.*)

While once within the walls and Chel of the Temple all advances were made from east to west, yet the north side was mainly used for stabling, slaughtering, cleansing, etc., and contained the chambers of broken knives, defiled stones, of the house of burning, and of sheep. The Masonic symbolism of the entrance of an initiate from the north, or more practically from the northwest, and advancing toward the position occupied by the corner-stone in the northeast, forcibly calls to mind the triplet of Homer:

> "Two marble doors unfold on either side;
> Sacred the South by which the gods descend;
> But mortals enter on the Northern end."

So in the Mysteries of Dionysos, the gate of entrance for the aspirant was from the north; but when purged from his corruptions, he was termed indifferently new-born or immortal, and the sacred south door was thence accessible to his steps.

In the Middle Ages, below and to the right of the judges stood the accuser, facing north; to the left was the defendant, in the north facing south. Bro. George F. Fort, in his *Antiquities of Freemasonry*, says: "In the centre of the court, directly before the judge, stood an altar piece or shrine, upon which an open Bible was displayed. The south, to the right of the justiciaries, was deemed honorable and worthy for a plaintiff; but the north was typical of a frightful and diabolical sombreness." Thus, when a solemn oath of purgation was taken in grievous criminal accusations, the accused turned toward the north. "The judicial headsman, in executing the extreme penalty of outraged justice, turned the convict's face northward, or towards the place whence emanated the earliest dismal shades of night. When Earl Hakon bowed a tremulous knee before the deadly powers of Paganism, and sacrificed his seven-year-old child, he gazed out upon the far-off, gloomy north.

"In Nastrond, or shores of death, stood a revolting hall, whose portals opened toward the north—the regions of night. North, by the Jutes, was denominated black or sombre; the Frisians called it fear corner. The gallows faced the north, and from these hyperborean shores everything base and terrible proceeded. In consequence of this belief, it was ordered that, in the adjudication of a crime, the accused should be on the north side of the court enclosure. And in harmony with the Scandinavian superstition, no Lodge of Masons illumines the darkened north with a symbolic light, whose brightness would be unable to dissipate the gloom of that cardinal point with which was associated all that was sinstrous and direful." (P. 292.)

North Carolina. The early history of Masonry in no State is more uncertain than in that of North Carolina, in consequence of the carelessness of the authorities who have attempted to write its early annals. Thus, Robert Williams, the Grand Secretary, in a letter written to the Grand Lodge of Kentucky in 1808, said that "the Grand Lodge of North Carolina was constituted by Charter issued from the Grand Lodge of Scotland in the year 1761, signed by Henry Somerset, Duke of Beaufort . . . as Grand Master; and attested by George John Spencer, Earl of Spencer . . . as Grand Secretary." Now this statement contains on its face the evidences of flagrant error. 1. The Duke of Beaufort never was Grand Master of Scotland. 2. The Grand Master of Scotland in 1761 was the Earl of Elgin. 3. The Earl of Spencer never was Grand Secretary either of England or Scotland, but Samuel Spencer was Grand Secretary of the Grand Lodge of England from 1757 to 1767, and died in 1768. 4. The Duke of Beaufort was not Grand Master of England in 1761, but held that office from 1767 to 1771. There is no mention in the printed records of the Grand Lodge of England of a Charter at any time granted for a Provincial Grand Lodge in North Carolina. But in two lists of Lodges chartered by that body, we find that on August 21, 1767, a Warrant was granted for the establishment of "Royal White Hart Lodge," at Halifax, in North Carolina. Probably this is the true date of the introduction of Masonry into that State. A record in the transactions of the St. John's Grand Lodge of Massachusetts says that on October 2, 1767, that body granted a deputation to Thomas Cooper, Master of Pitt County Lodge, as Deputy Grand Master of the province; but there is no evidence that he ever exercised the prerogatives of the office. Judge Martin, in a discourse delivered on June 24, 1789, says that Joseph Montford was appointed, toward the year 1769, as Provincial Grand Master by the Duke of Beaufort, and that in 1771 he constituted St. John's Lodge at Newbern. This was probably the true date of the Provincial Grand Lodge of North Carolina, for in 1787 we find nine Lodges in the territory, five of which, at least, had the provincial numbers 2, 3, 4, 5, and 8, while the Royal Hart Lodge retained its number on the English Register as 403, a number which agrees with that of the English lists in my possession. On December 16, 1787, a convention of Lodges met at Tarborough and organized the "Grand Lodge of the State of North Carolina," electing Hon. Samuel Johnston Grand Master.

There was a Grand Chapter in North Carolina at an early period in the present century, which ceased to exist about the year 1827; but Royal Arch Masonry was cultivated by four Chapters instituted by the General Grand Chapter. On June 28, 1847, the Grand Chapter was reorganized.

The Grand Council was organized in June, 1860, by Councils which had been established by Dr. Mackey, under the authority of the Supreme Council of the Ancient and Accepted Scottish Rite.

North Dakota. As soon as it was determined by the Grand Lodge of Dakota, at its session, held June 11–13, 1889, that there should be a division of the Grand Lodge of Dakota to correspond with the political division of the Territory into North and South Dakota, a convention was held June 12, 1889, at the city of Mitchell, where the Grand Lodge was in session, and the following Lodges of North Dakota were represented, viz.:

Shiloh, No. 8; Pembina, No. 10; Casselton, No. 12; Acacia, No. 15; Bismarck, No. 16; Jamestown, No. 19; Valley City, No. 21; Mandan, No. 23; Cereal, No. 29; Hillsboro, No. 32; Crescent, No. 36; Cheyenne Valley, No. 41; Ellendale, No. 49; Sanborn, No. 51; Wahpeton, No. 58; North Star, No. 59; Minto, No. 60; Mackey, No. 63; Goose River, No. 64; Hiram, No. 74; Minnewaukan, No. 75; Tongue River, No. 78; Bathgate, No. 80; Euclid, No. 84; Anchor, No. 88; Golden Valley, No. 90; Occidental, No. 99.

The convention resolved that it was expedient to organize a Grand Lodge for North Dakota. A constitution and by-laws were adopted.

On June 13th, the first session of the Grand Lodge was held in the city of Mitchell. The elected and appointed officers were present and representatives of the above twenty Lodges.

North Star. This star is frequently used as a Masonic symbol, as are the morning star, the day star, the seven stars. Thus, the morning star is the forerunner of the Great Light that is about to break upon the Lodge; or, as in the grade of G. Master Architect, twelfth of the Scottish system, the initiate is received at the hour "when the day star has risen in the east, and the north star looked down upon the seven stars that circle round him." The symbolism is truth; thus, the North star is the pole star, the Polaris of the mariner, the Cynosura, that guides Masons over the stormy seas of time. The seven stars are the symbol of right and justice to the order and the country.

Northeast Corner. In the "Institutes of Menu," the sacred book of the Brahmans, it is said: "If any one has an incurable disease, let him advance in a straight path towards the invincible *northeast* point, feeding on water and air till his mortal frame totally decays, and his soul becomes united with the supreme."

It is at the same northeast point that those first instructions begin in Masonry which enable the true Mason to commence the erection of that spiritual temple in which, after the decay of his mortal frame, "his soul becomes united with the supreme."

In the important ceremony which refers to the northeast corner of the Lodge, the candidate becomes as one who is, to all outward appearance, *a perfect and upright man and Mason*, the representative of a spiritual corner-stone, on which he is to erect his future moral and Masonic edifice.

This symbolic reference of the corner-stone of a material edifice to a Mason when, at his first initiation, he commences the moral and intellectual task of erecting a spiritual temple in his heart, is beautifully sustained when we look at all the qualities that are required to constitute a "well-tried, true, and trusty" corner-stone. The squareness of its surface, emblematic of morality—its cubical form, emblematic of firmness and stability of character—and the peculiar finish and fineness of the material, emblematic of virtue and holiness—show that the ceremony of the northeast corner of the Lodge was undoubtedly intended to portray, in the consecrated language of symbolism, the necessity of integrity and stability of conduct, of truthfulness and uprightness of character, and of purity and holiness of life, which, just at that time and in that place, the candidate is most impressively charged to maintain.

Notuma. A significant word in some of the high degrees of the Templar system. It is the anagram of AUMONT, who is said to have been the first Grand Master of the Templars in Scotland, and the restorer of the Order after the death of De Molay.

Nova Scotia. The first Lodge established in Nova Scotia was at Annapolis and under authority from Boston by the St. John's

Grand Lodge of Massachusetts. Under date of 1740 the minutes read: "The Rt. Worsh'l Grand Master granted a Deputation at the Petition of sundry Brethren for holding a lodge at Annapolis in Nova Scotia, and appointed the Right Worshipful Erasmus James Phillips, D.G.M., there, who afterward erected a Lodge at Halifax and appointed His Excellency Edward Cornwallis their first Master." For the next hundred years, Lodges were instituted and Provincial Masters appointed by England and Scotland, and Lodges alone without superior provincial authority by Ireland. In June, 1866, an independent Grand Lodge was instituted and recognised by most of the Masonic powers of the United States. But as none of the Lodges holding Warrants from the Grand Lodge of Scotland would recognise it, a subsequent and more satisfactory arrangement took place, and on June 24, 1869, a Grand Lodge was organised by the union of all the subordinate Lodges and Alexander Keith was elected Grand Master.

Novice. 1. The Second Degree of the Illuminati of Bavaria. 2. The Fifth Degree of the Rite of Strict Observance.

Novice, Maçonne. That is to say, a female Mason who is a Novice. It is the First Degree of the Moral Order of the Dames of Mount Tabor.

Novice, Mythological. (*Novice Mythologique.*) The First Degree of the Historical Order of the Dames of Mount Tabor.

Novice, Scottish. (*Novice Ecossaise.*) The First Degree of initiation in the Order of Mount Tabor.

Novitiate. The time of probation, as well as of preparatory training, which, in all religious orders, precedes the solemn profession at least one year. By dispensation only can the period of time be reduced. Novices are immediately subject to a superior called Master of Novices, and their time must be devoted to prayer and to liturgical training.

Nuk-pe-nuk. The Egyptian equivalent for the expression "I am that I am."

Numbers. The symbolism which is derived from numbers was common to the Pythagoreans, the Kabbalists, the Gnostics, and all mystical associations. Of all superstitions, it is the oldest and the most generally diffused. Allusions are to be found to it in all systems of religion; the Jewish Scriptures, for instance, abound in it, and the Christian shows a share of its influence. It is not, therefore, surprising that the most predominant of all symbolism in Freemasonry is that of numbers.

The doctrine of numbers as symbols is most familiar to us because it formed the fundamental idea of the philosophy of Pythagoras. Yet it was not original with him, since he brought his theories from Egypt and the East, where this numerical symbolism had always prevailed. Jamblichus tells us (*Vit. Pyth.*, c. 28) that Pythagoras himself admitted that he had received the doctrine of numbers from Orpheus, who taught that numbers were the most provident beginning of all things in heaven, earth, and the intermediate space, and the root of the perpetuity of Divine beings, of the gods and of demons. From the disciples of Pythagoras we learn (for he himself taught only orally, and left no writings) that his theory was that numbers contain the elements of all things, and even of the sciences. Numbers are the invisible covering of beings as the body is the visible one. They are the primary causes upon which the whole system of the universe rests; and he who knows these numbers knows at the same time the laws through which nature exists. The Pythagoreans, said Aristotle (*Metaph.*, xii., 8), make all things proceed from numbers. Dacier (*Vie de Pyth.*), it is true, denies that this was the doctrine of Pythagoras, and contends that it was only a corruption of his disciples. It is an immaterial point. We know that the symbolism of numbers was the basis of what is called the Pythagorean philosophy. But it would be wrong to suppose that from it the Masons derived their system, since the two are in some points antagonistic; the Masons, for instance, revere the nine as a sacred number of peculiar significance, while the Pythagoreans looked upon it with detestation. In the system of the Pythagoreans, ten was, of all numbers, the most perfect, because it symbolizes the completion of things; but in Masonic symbolism the number ten is unknown. Four is not, in Masonry, a number of much representative importance; but it was sacredly revered by the Pythagoreans as the tetractys, or figure derived from the Jewish Tetragrammaton, by which they swore.

Plato also indulged in a theory of symbolic numbers, and calls him happy who understands spiritual numbers and perceives their mighty influences. Numbers, according to him, are the cause of universal harmony, and of the production of all things. The Neoplatonists extended and developed this theory, and from them it passed over to the Gnostics; from them probably to the Rosicrucians, to the Hermetic philosophers, and to the Freemasons.

Cornelius Agrippa has descanted at great length, in his *Occult Philosophy*, on the subject of numbers. "That there lies," he says, "wonderful efficacy and virtue in numbers, as well for good as for evil, not only the most eminent philosophers teach, but also the Catholic Doctors." And he quotes St. Hilary as saying that the seventy Elders brought the Psalms into order by the efficacy of numbers.

Of the prevalence of what are called representative numbers in the Old and New Testament, there is abundant evidence. "However we may explain it," says Dr. Mahan (*Palmoni*, p. 67), "certain numerals in the Scriptures occur so often in connection with certain classes of ideas, that we are naturally led to associate the one with the other. This is more or less admitted with regard to the numbers *Seven, Twelve, Forty, Seventy*, and it may be a few more. The Fathers were disposed to admit it with regard to many others, *and to see in it the marks of a supernatural design.*"

Among the Greeks and the Romans there was a superstitious veneration for certain numbers. The same practise is found among all the Eastern nations; it entered more or less into all the ancient systems of philosophy; constituted a part of all the old religions; was accepted to a great extent by the early Christian Fathers; constituted an important part of the Kabbala; was adopted by the Gnostics, the Rosicrucians, and all the mystical societies of the Middle Ages; and finally has carried its influence into Freemasonry.

The respect paid by Freemasons to certain numbers, all of which are odd, is founded not on the belief of any magical virtue, but because they are assumed to be the types or representatives of certain ideas. That is to say, a number is in Masonry a symbol, and no more. It is venerated, not because it has any supernatural efficacy, as thought the Pythagoreans and others, but because it has concealed within some allusion to a sacred object or holy thought, which it symbolizes. The number *three*, for instance, like the *triangle*, is a symbol; the number *nine*, like the *triple triangle*, another. The Masonic doctrine of sacred numbers must not, therefore, be confounded with the doctrine of numbers which prevailed in other systems.

The most important symbolic or sacred numbers in Masonry are *three, five, seven, nine, twenty-seven*, and *eighty-one*. Their interpretation will be found under their respective titles.

Numeration by Letters. There is a Kabbalistical process especially used in the Hebrew language, but sometimes applied to other languages, for instance, to the Greek, by which a mystical meaning of a word is deduced from the numerical value of the words of which it is composed, each letter of the alphabet being equivalent to a number. Thus in Hebrew the name of God, יה, JAH, is equivalent to 15, because י=10 and ה=5, and 15 thus becomes a sacred number. In Greek, the Kabbalistic word Abraxas, or ἀβραξας, is made to symbolize the solar year of 365 days, because the sum of the value of the letters of the word is 365; thus, α=1, β=2, ρ=100, α=1, ξ=60, α=1, and ς=200. To facilitate these Kabbalistic operations, which are sometimes used in the high and especially the Hermetical Masonry, the

Hebrew.		Greek.	
א	1	Α, α	1
ב	2	Β, β	2
ג	3	Γ, γ	3
ד	4	Δ, δ	4
ה	5	Ε, ε	5
ו	6	Ζ, ζ	6
ז	7	Η, η	8
ח	8	Θ, θ	9
ט	9	Ι, ι	10
י	10	Κ, κ	20
כ	20	Λ, λ	30
ל	30	Μ, μ	40
מ, ם	40	Ν, ν	50
נ, ן	50	Ξ, ξ	60
ס	60	Ο, ο	70
ע	70	Π, π	80
פ	80	Ρ, ρ	100
צ	90	Σ, σ, ς,	200
ק	100	Τ, τ	300
ר	200	Υ, υ	400
ש	300	Φ, φ	500
ת	400	Χ, χ	600
		Ψ, ψ	700
		Ω, ω	800

numerical value of the Hebrew and Greek letters is here given.

Nun. (Heb. נוּן, a *fish*, in Syriac an *inkhorn*.) The Chaldaic and hieroglyphic form of this Hebrew letter was like Fig. 1, and the Egyptian like Fig. 2, signifying

Fig. 1. Fig. 2.

fishes in any of these forms. Joshua was the son of Nun, or a fish, the deliverer of Israel. As narrated of the Noah in the Hindu account of the deluge, whereby the forewarning of a fish caused the construction of an ark and the salvation of one family of the human race from the flood of waters. (See *Beginnings of History*, by Lenormant.)

Nursery. The first of the three classes into which Weishaupt divided his Order of Illuminati, comprising three degrees. (See *Illuminati*.)

Nyaya. The name of the second of the three great systems of ancient Hindu philosophy.

Nyctazontes. An ancient sect who praised God by day, but rested in quiet and presumed security during the night.

O

O. The fifteenth letter in the English and in most of the Western alphabets. The corresponding letter in the Hebrew and Phœnician alphabets was called *Ayn*, that is, *eye*, the primitive form of the Phœnician letter being the rough picture of an eye, or a circle with a dot in the center. This dot will be observed in ancient MSS., but being dropped the circle forms the letter O. The numerical value is 70, and in Hebrew is formed thus, ע, the hieroglyphic being a plant, as well as at times a circle or an eye.

Oak Apple, Society of the. Instituted about 1658, and lapsed under the disturbances in England during the reign of James II., but it lingered among the Stuart adherents for many years.

Oannes. The earliest instructor of man in letters, sciences, and arts, especially in architecture, geometry, botany, and agriculture, and in all other useful knowledge, was the fish god Oannes (myth). This universal teacher, according to Berossus, appeared in the Persian Gulf, bordering on Babylonia, and, although an animal, was endowed with reason and great knowledge. The usual appearance of the creature was that of a fish, having a human head beneath that of a fish, and feet like unto a man. This personage conversed with men during the day, but never ate with them. At Kouyunjik there was a colossal statue of the fish-god Oannes. The following is from the *Book of Enoch* (vol. ii., p. 154): "The Masons hold their grand festival on the day of St. John, not knowing that therein they merely signify the fish-god Oannes, the first Hermes and the first founder of the Mysteries, the first messenger to whom the Apocalypse was given, and whom they ignorantly confound with the fabulous author of the common Apocalypse. The sun is then (midsummer day) in its greatest altitude. In this the Naros is commemorated."

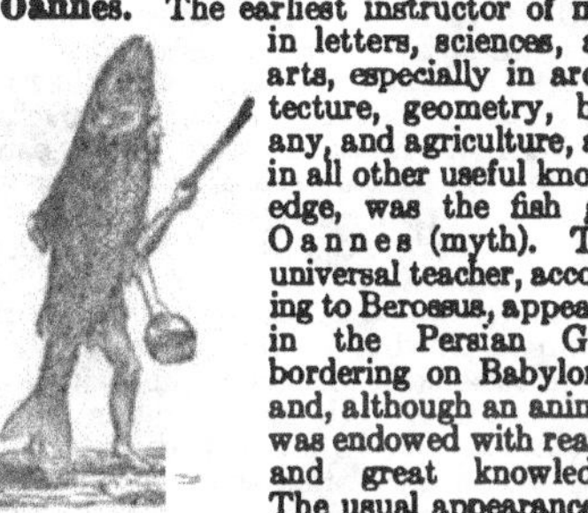

Oath. In the year 1738, Clement XII., at that time Pope of Rome, issued a bull of excommunication against the Freemasons, and assigned, as the reason of his condemnation, that the Institution confederated persons of all religions and sects in a mysterious bond of union, and compelled them to secrecy by an oath taken on the Bible, accompanied by certain ceremonies, and the imprecation of heavy punishments.

This persecution of the Freemasons, on account of their having an obligatory promise of secrecy among their ceremonies, has not been confined to the Papal see. We shall find it existing in a sect which we should suppose, of all others, the least likely to follow in the footsteps of a Roman pontiff. In 1757, the Associate Synod of Seceders of Scotland adopted an act, concerning what they called "the Mason oath," in which it is declared that all persons who shall refuse to make such revelations as the Kirk Sessions may require, and to promise to abstain from all future connection with the Order, "shall be reputed under scandal and incapable of admission to sealing ordinances," or as Pope Clement expressed it, be "ipso facto excommunicated."

In the preamble to the act, the Synod assign the reasons for their objections to this oath, and for their ecclesiastical censure of all who contract it. These reasons are: "That there were very strong presumptions, that, among Masons, an oath of secrecy is administered to entrants into their society, even under a capital penalty, and before any of those things, which they swear to keep secret, be revealed to them; and that they pretend to take some of these secrets from the Bible; besides other things which are ground of scruple in the manner of swearing the said oath."

These have, from that day to this, constituted the sum and substance of the objections to the obligation of Masonic secrecy, and, for the purpose of brief examination, they may be classed under the following heads:

First. It is an oath.

Secondly. It is administered before the secrets are communicated.

Thirdly. It is accompanied by certain superstitious ceremonies.

Fourthly. It is attended by a penalty.

Fifthly. It is considered, by Masons, as paramount to the obligations of the laws of the land.

In replying to these statements, it is evident that the conscientious Freemason labors under great disadvantage. He is at every step restrained by his honor from either the denial or admission of his adversaries in relation to the mysteries of the Craft. But it may be granted, for the sake of argument, that every one of the first four charges is true, and then the inquiry will be in what respect they are offensive or immoral.

First. The oath or promise cannot, in itself, be sinful, unless there is something immoral in the obligation it imposes. Simply to promise secrecy, or the performance of any good action, and to strengthen this promise by the solemnity of an oath, is not, in itself, forbidden by any Divine or human law. Indeed, the infirmity of human nature demands, in many instances, the sacred sanction of such an attestation; and it is continually exacted in the transactions of man with man, without any notion of sinfulness. Where the time, and place, and circumstances are unconnected with levity, or profanity, or crime, the administration of an obligation binding to secrecy, or obedience, or veracity, or any other virtue, and the invocation of Deity to witness, and to strengthen that obligation, or to punish its violation, is incapable, by any perversion of Scripture, of being considered a criminal act.

Secondly. The objection that the oath is administered before the secrets are made known, is sufficiently absurd to provoke a smile. The purposes of such an oath would be completely frustrated, by revealing the thing to be concealed before the promise of concealment was made. In that case, it would be optional with the candidate to give the obligation, or to withhold it, as best suited his inclinations. If it be conceded that the exaction of a solemn promise of secrecy is not, in itself, improper, then certainly the time of exacting it is before and not after the revelation.

Dr. Harris (*Masonic Discourses*, Disc. IX., p. 184) has met this objection in the following language:

"What the ignorant call 'the oath,' is simply an obligation, covenant, and promise, exacted previously to the divulging of the specialties of the Order, and our means of recognizing each other; that they shall be kept from the knowledge of the world, lest their original intent should be thwarted, and their benevolent purport prevented. Now, pray, what harm is there in this? Do you not all, when you have anything of a private nature which you are willing to confide in a particular friend, *before you tell him what it is*, demand a solemn promise of secrecy? And is there not the utmost propriety in knowing whether your friend is determined to conceal your secret, before you presume to reveal it? Your answer confutes your cavil."

Thirdly. The objection that the oath is accompanied by certain superstitious ceremonies does not seem to be entitled to much weight. Oaths, in all countries and at all times, have been accompanied by peculiar rites, intended to increase the solemnity and reverence of the act. The ancient Hebrews, when they took an oath, placed the hand beneath the thigh of the person to whom they swore. Sometimes the ancients took hold of the horns of the altar, and touched the sacrificial fire, as in the league between Latinus and Æneas, where the ceremony is thus described by Virgil:

"Tango aras; medioaque ignes, et numina, testor."

Sometimes they extended the right hand to heaven, and swore by earth, sea, and stars. Sometimes, as among the Romans in private contracts, the person swearing laid his hand upon the hand of the party to whom he swore. In all solemn covenants the oath was accompanied by a sacrifice; and some of the hair being cut from the victim's head, a part of it was given to all present, that each one might take a share in the oath, and be subject to the imputation. Other ceremonies were practised at various times and in different countries, for the purpose of throwing around the act of attestation an increased amount of awe and respect. The oath is equally obligatory without them; but they have their significance, and there can be no reason why the Freemasons should not be allowed to adopt the mode most pleasing to themselves of exacting their promises or confirming their covenants.

Fourthly. It is objected that the oath is attended with a penalty of a serious or capital nature. If this be the case, it does not appear that the expression of a penalty of any nature whatever can affect the purport or augment the solemnity of an oath, which is, in fact, an attestation of God to the truth of a declaration, as a witness and avenger; and hence every oath includes in itself, and as its very essence, the covenant of God's wrath, the heaviest of all penalties, as the necessary consequence of its violation. A writer, in reply to the Synod of Scotland (*Scot's Mag.*, October, 1757), quotes the opinion of an eminent jurist to this effect:

"It seems to be certain that every promissory oath, in whatever form it may be conceived, whether explicitly or implicitly, virtually contains both an attestation and an obsecration; for in an oath the execration supposes an attestation as a precedent, and the attestation infers an execration as a necessary consequence.

"Hence, then, to the believer in a superintending Providence, every oath is an affirmation, negation, or promise, corroborated by the attestation of the Divine Being." This attestation includes an obsecration of Divine punishment in case of a violation, and it is, therefore, a matter of no moment whether this obsecration or penalty be expressed in words or only implied; its presence or absence does not, in any degree, alter the nature of the obligation. If in any promise or vow made by Masons, such a penalty is inserted, it may probably be supposed that it is used only with a metaphorical and paraphrastical signification, and for the purpose of symbolic or historical allusion. Any other interpretation but this would be entirely at variance with the opinions of the most intelligent Masons, who, it is to be presumed, best know the intent and meaning of their own ceremonies.

Fifthly. The last, and, indeed, the most important objection urged is, that these oaths are construed by Masons as being of higher obligation than the law of the land. It is in vain that this charge has been repeatedly and indignantly denied, it is in vain that Masons point to the integrity of character of thousands of eminent men who have been members of the Fraternity; it is in vain that they recapitulate the order-loving and law-fearing regulations of the Institution; the charge is renewed with untiring pertinacity, and believed with a credulity that owes its birth to rancorous prejudice alone. To repeat the denial is but to provoke a repetition of the charge. The answer is, however, made by one who, once a Mason, was afterward an opponent and an avowed enemy of the Institution, W. L. Stone (*Letters on Masonry and Anti-Masonry*, Let. VII., p. 69), who uses the following language:

"Is it, then, to be believed that men of acknowledged talents and worth in public stations, and of virtuous and, frequently, religious habits, in the walks of private life, with the Holy Bible in their hands—which they are solemnly pledged to receive as the rule and guide of their faith and practice—and under the grave and positive charge from the officer administering the obligation, that it is to be taken in strict subordination to the civil laws—can understand that obligation, whatever may be the peculiarities of its phraseology, as requiring them to countenance vice and criminality even by silence? Can it for a moment be supposed that the hundreds of eminent men, whose patriotism is unquestioned, and the exercise of whose talents and virtues has shed a lustre upon the church history of our country, and who, by their walk and conversation, have, in their own lives, illustrated the beauty of holiness? Is it to be credited that the tens of thousands of those persons, ranking among the most intelligent and virtuous citizens of the most moral and enlightened people on earth—is it, I ask, possible that any portion of this community can, on calm reflection, believe that such men have oaths upon their consciences binding them to eternal silence in regard to the guilt of any man because he happens to be a Freemason, no matter what be the grade of offence, whether it be the picking of a pocket or the shedding of blood? It does really seem to me impossible that such an opinion could, at any moment, have prevailed, to any considerable extent, amongst reflecting and intelligent citizens."

Oath, Corporal. The modern form of taking an oath is by placing the hands on the Gospels or on the Bible. The *corporale*, or *corporal cloth*, is the name of the linen cloth on which, in the Roman Catholic Church, the sacred elements consecrated as "the body of our Lord" are placed. Hence the expression *corporal oath* originated in the ancient custom of swearing while touching the corporal cloth. Relics were sometimes made use of. The laws of the Allemanni (cap. 657) direct that he who swears shall place his hand upon the coffer containing the relics. The idea being that something sacred must be touched by the hand of the jurator to give validity to the oath, in time the custom was adopted of substituting the holy Gospels for the corporal cloth or the relics, though the same title was retained. Haydn (*Dict. of Dates*) says that the practise of swearing on the Gospels prevail in England as early as A.D. 528. The laws of the Lombards repeatedly mention the custom of swearing on the Gospels. The sanction of the church was given at an early period to the usage. Thus, in the history of the Council of Constantinople (Anno 381), it is stated that "George, the well-beloved of God, a deacon and keeper of the records, having touched the Holy Gospels of God, swore in this manner," etc. And a similar practise was adopted at the Council of Nice, fifty-six years before. The custom of swearing on the book, thereby meaning the Gospels, was adopted by the Medieval gild of Freemasons, and allusions to it are found in all the Old Constitutions. Thus in the York MS., No. 1, about the year 1600, it is said, "These charges . . . you shall well and truly keep to your power; so help you God and by the contents of that book." And in the Grand Lodge MS., No. 1, in 1583 we find this: "These charges ye shall keepe, so healpe you God, and your haly dome and by this booke in your hande unto your power." The form of the ceremony required that the corporal oath should be taken with both hands on the book, or with one hand, and then always the right hand.

Oath of the Gild. The oath that was administered in the English Freemasons' gild of the Middle Ages is first met with in the Harleian MS., No. 1942, written about the year 1670. The 31st article prescribes: "That noe person shall bee accepted a Free Mason, or know the secrets of the said Society, until hee hath first taken the oath of secrecy hereafter following:

"I, A. B. Doe, in the presence of Almighty God and my Fellowes and Brethren here present, promise and declare that I will not at any time hereafter, by any act or circumstance whatsoever, directly or indirectly, publish, discover, reveale, or make knowne any of the secrets, priviledges or counsells of the Fraternity or fellowship of Free Masonry, which at this time, or any time hereafter, shall be made knowne unto mee; soe helpe mee God and the holy contents of this booke." In the Roberts *Constitutions*, published in 1722, this oath, substantially in the same words, is for the first time printed with the amendment of "privities" for "priviledges."

Oath, Tiler's. Before any strange and unknown visitor can gain admission into a Masonic Lodge, he is required in America to take the following oath:

"I, A. B., do hereby and hereon solemnly and sincerely swear that I have been regularly initiated, passed, and raised to the sublime degree of a Master Mason in a just and legally constituted Lodge of such; that I do not now stand suspended or expelled; and know of no reason why I should not hold Masonic communication with my brethren."

It is called the "Tiler's oath," because it is usually taken in the Tiler's room, and was formerly administered by that officer, whose duty it is to protect the Lodge from the approach of unauthorised visitors. It is now administered by the committee of examination, and not only he to whom it is administered, but he who administers it, and all who are present, must take it at the same time. It is a process of purgation, and each one present, the visitor as well as the members of the Lodge, is entitled to know that all the others are legally qualified to be present at the esoteric examination which is about to take place. [This custom is unknown in English Masonry.]

OB. A Masonic abbreviation of the word *Obligation*, sometimes written O. B.

Obed. (Heb. עוֹבֵד, *serving*.) One of nine favored officials, selected by Solomon after the death of H. Abif.

Obedience. The doctrine of obedience to constituted authority is strongly inculcated in all the Old Constitutions as necessary to the preservation of the association. In them it is directed that "every Mason shall prefer his elder and put him to worship." Thus the Master Mason obeys the order of his Lodge, the Lodge obeys the mandates of the Grand Lodge, and the Grand Lodge submits to the landmarks and the old regulations. The doctrine of passive obedience and non-resistance in politics, however much it may be supposed to be inimical to the progress of free institutions, constitutes undoubtedly the great principle of Masonic government. Such a principle would undoubtedly lead to an unbearable despotism, were it not admirably modified and controlled by the compensating principle of appeal. The first duty of every Mason is to obey the mandate of the Master. But if that mandate should have been unlawful or oppressive, he will find his redress in the Grand Lodge, which will review the case and render justice. This spirit of instant obedience and submission to authority constitutes the great safeguard of the Institution. Freemasonry more resembles a military than a political organization. The order must at once be obeyed; its character and its consequences may be matters of subsequent inquiry. The Masonic rule of obedience is like the nautical, imperative: "Obey orders, even if you break owners."

Obedience of a Grand Body. Obedience, used in the sense of *being under the jurisdiction*, is a technicality borrowed only recently by Masonic authorities from the French, where it has always been regularly used. Thus "the Grand Lodge has addressed a letter to all the Lodges *of its obedience*" means "to all the Lodges under its jurisdiction." In French, "à toutes les Loges de sou obedience." It comes originally from the usage of the Middle Ages, in the Low Latin of which *obedientia* meant the homage which a vassal owed to his lord. In the ecclesiastical language of the same period, the word signified the duty or office of a monk toward his superior.

Obelisk. The obelisk is a quadrangular, monolithic column, diminishing upward, with the sides gently inclined, but not so as to terminate in a pointed apex, but to form at the top a flattish, pyramidal figure, by which the whole is finished off and brought to a point. It was the most common species of monument in ancient Egypt, where they are still to be found in great numbers, the sides being covered with hieroglyphic inscriptions. Obelisks were, it is supposed, originally erected in honor of the sun god. Pliny says (Holland's trans.), "The kings of Egypt in times past made of this stone certain long beams, which they called obelisks, and consecrated them unto the sun, whom they honored as a god; and, indeed, some resemblance they carry of sunbeams." In continental Masonry the monument in the Master's Degree is often made in the form of an obelisk, with the letters M. B. inscribed upon it. And this form is appropriate, because in Masonic, as in Christian, iconography the obelisk is a symbol of the resurrection.

Objections to Freemasonry. The principal objections that have been urged by its opponents to the Institution of Freemasonry may be arranged under six heads: 1. Its *secrecy;* 2. The *exclusiveness* of its charity; 3. Its admission of *unworthy members;* 4. Its claim to be a *religion;* 5. Its administration of unlawful *oaths;* and, 6. Its *puerility* as a system of instruction. Each of these objections is replied to in this work under the respective heads of the words which are italicised above.

Obligated. *To be obligated*, in Masonic language, is to be admitted into the covenant of Masonry. "An obligated Mason" is tautological, because there can be no Mason who is not an obligated one.

Obligation. The solemn promise made by a Mason on his admission into any degree is technically called his obligation. In a legal sense, obligation is synonymous with duty. Its derivation shows its true meaning, for the Latin word *obligatio* literally signifies a *tying* or *binding*. The *obligation* is that which binds a man to do some act, the doing of which thus becomes his duty. By his obligation, a Mason is bound or tied to his Order. Hence the Romans called the military oath which was taken by the soldier his obligation, and, too, it is said that it is the obligation that makes the Mason. Before that ceremony, there is no tie that binds the candidate to the Order so as to make him a part of it; after the ceremony, the tie has been completed, and the candidate becomes at once a Mason, entitled to all the rights and privileges and subject to all the duties and responsibilities that enure in that character. The jurists have divided obligations into imperfect and perfect, or natural and civil. In Masonry there is no such distinction. The Masonic obligation is that moral one which, although it cannot be enforced by the courts of law, is binding on the party who makes it, in conscience and according to moral justice. It varies in each degree, but in each is perfect. Its different clauses, in which different duties are prescribed, are called its *points*, which are either affirmative or negative, a division like that of the precepts of the Jewish law. The *affirmative points* are those which require certain acts to be performed; the *negative points* are those which forbid certain other acts to be done. The whole of them is preceded by a general point of secrecy, common to all the degrees, and this point is called the *tie*.

Oblong Square. A parallelogram, or four-sided figure, all of whose angles are equal, but two of whose sides are longer than the others. [Of course the term "oblong square" is strictly without any meaning, but it is used to denote two squares joined together to form a rectangle.]

This is the symbolic form of a Masonic Lodge, and it finds its prototype in many of the structures of our ancient brethren. The ark of Noah, the camp of the Israelites, the Ark of the Covenant, the Tabernacle, and, lastly, the Temple of Solomon, were all oblong squares. (See *Ground-Floor of the Lodge*.)

Oboth. Ventriloquism. It will be found so denominated in the Septuagint version, Isaiah xxix. 3, also xix. 3.

Obrack, Hibernus. Grand Master of the Order of the Temple in 1392, according to the chronology of the Strict Observance of Germany.

Observance, Clerks of Strict. See *Clerks of Strict Observance*.

Observance, Lax. See *Lax Observance*.

Observance, Relaxed. (*Observance Relachée*.) This is the term by which Ragon translates the *lata observantia* or lax observance applied by the disciples of Von Hund to the other Lodges of Germany. Ragon (*Orth. Maçon.*, p. 236) calls it incorrectly a Rite, and confounds it with the Clerks of Strict Observance. (See *Lax Observance*.)

Observance, Strict. See *Strict Observance, Rite of*.

Obverse. In numismatics that side of a coin or medal which contains the principal figure, generally a face in profile or a full or half-length figure, is called the obverse.

Occasional Lodge. A temporary Lodge convoked by a Grand Master for the purpose of making Masons, after which the Lodge is dissolved. The phrase was first used by Anderson in the second edition of the *Book of Constitutions*, and is repeated by subsequent editors. To make a Mason in an Occasional Lodge is equivalent to making him "at sight." But any Lodge, called temporarily by the Grand Master for a specific purpose and immediately afterward dissolved, is an Occasional Lodge. Its organization as to officers, and its regulations as to ritual, must be the same as in a permanent and properly warranted Lodge. (See *Sight, Making Masons at*.)

Occult Masonry. Ragon, in his *Orthodoxie Maçonnique*, proposes the establishment of a Masonic system, which he calls "Occult Masonry." It consists of three degrees, which are the same as those of Ancient Craft Masonry, only that all the symbols are interpreted after alchemical principles. It is, in fact, the application of Masonic symbolism to Hermetic symbolism—two things that never did, according to Hitchcock, materially differ.

Occult Sciences. This name is given to the sciences of alchemy, magic, and astrology, which existed in the Middle Ages. Many of the speculations of these so-called sciences were in the eighteenth century made use of in the construction of the high degrees. We have even a "Hermetic Rite" which is based on the dogmas of alchemy.

Occupied Territory. A state or kingdom where there is a Grand Lodge organization and subordinate Lodges working under it is said to be occupied territory, and, by the American and English law, all other Grand Lodges are precluded from entering in it and exercising jurisdiction. (See *Jurisdiction of a Grand Lodge*.)

Octagon. The regular octagon is a geometrical figure of eight equal sides and angles. It is a favorite form in Christian ecclesiology, and most of the Chapter-Houses of the cathedrals in England are eight sided. It is sometimes used in rituals of Knights of Malta, and then, like the eight-pointed cross of the same Order, is referred symbolically to the eight beatitudes of our Savior.

Odd Numbers. In the numerical philosophy of the Pythagoreans, odd numbers were male and even numbers female. It is wrong, however, to say, as Oliver and some others after him have, that odd numbers were perfect, and even numbers imperfect. The combination of two odd numbers would make an even number, which was the most perfect. Hence, in the Pythagorean system, 4, made by the combination of 1 and 3, and 10, by the combination of 3 and 7, are the most perfect of all numbers. Herein the Pythagorean differs from the Masonic system of numerals. In this latter all the sacred numbers are odd, such as 3, 5, 7, 9, 27, and 81. Thus it is evident that the Masonic theory of sacred numbers was derived, not, as it has been supposed, from the school of Pythagoras, but from a much older system.

Odem. (Heb. אדם.) The carnelian or agate in the high priest's breastplate. It was of a red color, and claimed to possess medical qualities.

Odin. The chief Scandinavian deity and father of *Balder*, which see. The counterpart of Hermes and Mercury in the Egyptian and Roman mythologies. Odin and his brothers Vili and Ve, the sons of Boer, or the first-born, slew Ymir or Chaos, and from his body created the world. As ruler of heaven, he sends daily his two black ravens, Thought and Memory, to gather tidings of all that is being done throughout the world.

Offenses, Masonic. See *Crimes, Masonic*.

Offerings, The Three Grand. See *Ground Floor of the Lodge*.

Officers. The officers of a Grand Lodge, Grand Chapter, or other Supreme body in Masonry, are divided into Grand and Subordinate; the former, who are the Grand and Deputy Grand Master, the Grand Wardens and Grand Treasurer, Secretary, and Chaplain, are also sometimes called the Dignitaries. The officers of a Lodge or Chapter are divided into the Elected and the Appointed, the former in America being the Master,

Wardens, Treasurer, and Secretary, while in England only the Master and Treasurer are elected.

Officers' Jewels. See *Jewels, Official.*

Office, Tenure of. In Masonry the tenure of every office is not only for the time for which the incumbent was elected or appointed, but extends to the day on which his successor is installed. During the period which elapses from the election of that successor until his installation, the old officer is technically said to "hold over."

Ogmius. The Druidical name for Hercules, who is represented with numberless fine chains proceeding from the mouth to the ears of other people, hence possessing the powers of eloquence and persuasion.

Oheb Eloah. אהב אלוה. *Love of God.* This and Oheb Karobo, *Love of our Neighbor,* are the names of the two supports of the Ladder of Kadosh. Collectively, they allude to that Divine passage, "Thou shalt love the Lord thy God with all thy heart, and with all thy soul, and with all thy mind. This is the first and great commandment. And the second is like unto it, Thou shalt love thy neighbor as thyself. On these two commandments hang all the law and the prophets." Hence the Ladder of Kadosh is supported by these two Christian commandments.

Oheb Karobo. See *Oheb Eloah.*

Ohio. Freemasonry was introduced into Ohio early in the present century. On January 4, 1808, a convention of delegates from the five Lodges then in the State met at Chillicothe, and on January 7th organised a Grand Lodge, electing Rufus Putnam first Grand Master. The Grand Chapter of Ohio was organized in 1816, the Grand Council in 1829, and the Grand Commandery in 1843.

Oklahoma. The Grand Lodge of Oklahoma was organized at a convention of ten Lodges, holding warrants from the Grand Lodge of Indian Territory, held at Oklahoma City, November 10, 1892, when after electing Grand Officers, who were installed at a special communication of the Grand Lodge of Indian Territory, the Grand Lodge was opened and a constitution adopted. The first annual communication was held at El Reno, February 14, 1893. February 10, 1909, the Grand Lodges of Oklahoma and Indian Territory were merged together under the title of "The Grand Lodge of Ancient Free and Accepted Masons of the State of Oklahoma." [W. J. A.]

Oil. The Hebrews anointed their kings, prophets, and high priests with oil mingled with the richest spices. They also anointed themselves with oil on all festive occasions, whence the expression in Psalm xlv. 7, "God hath anointed thee with the oil of gladness." (See *Corn, Wine and Oil.*)

Old Charges. See *Manuscripts, Old.*

Old Man. Old men in their dotage are by the laws of Masonry disqualified for initiation. For the reason of this law, see *Dotage.*

Old Regulations. The regulations for the government of the Craft, which were first compiled by Grand Master Payne in 1720, and approved by the Grand Lodge in 1721 were published by Anderson in 1723, in the first edition of the *Book of Constitutions,* under the name of General Regulations. In 1738 Anderson published a second edition of the *Book of Constitutions,* and inserted these regulations under the name of Old Regulations, placing in an opposite column the alterations which had been made in them by the Grand Lodge at different times between 1723 and 1737, and called these New Regulations. When Dermott published his *Ahiman Rezon,* or Book of Constitutions of the rival Grand Lodge, he adopted Anderson's plan, publishing in two columns the Old and the New Regulations. But he made some important changes in the latter to accommodate the policy of his own Grand Lodge. The Old Regulations, more properly known as the "General Regulations of 1722," are recognized as the better authority in questions of Masonic law.

Olive. In a secondary sense, the olive plant is a symbol of peace and victory; but in its primary sense, like all the other sacred plants of antiquity, it was a symbol of resurrection and immortality. Hence in the Ancient Mysteries it was the analogue of the Acacia of Freemasonry.

Olive-Branch in the East, Brotherhood of the. A new Order, which was proposed at Bombay, in 1845, by Dr. James Burnes, the author of a *History of the Knights Templar,* who was then the Provincial Grand Master of India for Scotland. It was intended to provide a substitute for native Masons for the chivalric degrees, from which, on account of their religious faith, they were excluded. It consisted of three classes, Novice, Companion, and Officer. For the first, it was requisite that the candidate should have been initiated into Masonry; for the second, that he should be a Master Mason; and for the third it was recommended, but not imperatively required, that he should have attained the Royal Arch Degree. The badge of the Order was a dove descending with a green olive-branch in its mouth. The new Order was received with much enthusiasm by the most distinguished Masons of India, but it did not secure a permanent existence.

Oliver, George. The Rev. George Oliver, D.D., one of the most distinguished and learned of English Masons, was descended from an ancient Scottish family of that name, some of whom came into England in the time of James I., and settled at Clipstone Park, Nottinghamshire. He was the eldest son of the Rev. Samuel Oliver, rector of Lambley, Nottinghamshire, and Elizabeth, daughter of George Whitehead, Esq. He was born at Pepplewick, November 5, 1782, and received a liberal education at Nottingham. In 1803, when but twenty-one years of age, he was elected second master of the grammar school at Caiston, Lincoln. In 1809 he was appointed to the head mastership of King Edward's Grammar School at Great Grimsby. In 1813 he entered holy orders in the Church of England, and was ordained a deacon. The subsequent year he was made a priest. In the spring of 1815, Bishop Tomline collated him to the living of Clee, his name being at the time placed on the boards of Trinity College, Cambridge, as a ten-year man by Dr. Bayley, Subdean of Lincoln and examining Chaplain to the Bishop. In the same year he was admitted as Surrogate and a Steward of the Clerical Fund. In 1831, Bishop Kaye gave him the living of Scopwick, which he held to the time of his death. He graduated as Doctor of Divinity in 1836, being then rector of Wolverhampton, and a prebendary of the collegiate church at that place, both of which positions had been presented to him by Dr. Hobart, Dean of Westminster. In 1846 the Lord Chancellor conferred on him the rectory of South Hykeham, which vacated the incumbency of Wolverhampton. At the age of seventy-two Dr. Oliver's physical powers began to fail, and he was obliged to confine the charge of his parishes to the care of curates, and he passed the remaining years of his life in retirement at Lincoln. In 1805 he had married Mary Ann, the youngest daughter of Thomas Beverley, Esq., by whom he left five children. He died March 3, 1867, at Eastgate, Lincoln.

To the literary world Dr. Oliver was well known as a laborious antiquary, and his works on ecclesiastical antiquities during fifty years of his life, from fifty-five, earned for him a high reputation. Of these works the most important were, *History and Antiquities of the Collegiate Church of Beverley, History and Antiquities of the Collegiate Church of Wolverhampton, History of the Conventual Church of Grimsby, Monumental Antiquities of Grimsby, History of the Gild of the Holy Trinity, Sleaford, Letters on the Druidical Remains near Lincoln, Guide to the Druidical Temple at Nottingham* and *Remains of Ancient Britons between Lincoln and Sleaford.*

But it is as the most learned Mason and the most indefatigable and copious Masonic author of his age that Dr. Oliver principally claims our attention. He had inherited a love of Freemasonry from his father, the Rev. Samuel Oliver, who was an expert Master of the work, the Chaplain of his Lodge, and who contributed during a whole year, from 1797 to 1798, an original Masonic song to be sung on every Lodge night. His son has repeatedly acknowledged his indebtedness to him for valuable information in relation to Masonic usages.

Dr. Oliver was initiated by his father, in the year 1801, in St. Peter's Lodge, in the city of Peterborough. He was at that time but nineteen years of age, and was admitted by dispensation during his minority, according to the practise then prevailing, as a lewis, or the son of a Mason.

Under the tuition of his father, he made much progress in the rites and ceremonies then in use among the Lodges. He read with great attention every Masonic book within his reach, and began to collect that store of knowledge which he afterward used with so much advantage to the Craft.

Soon after his appointment as head master of King Edward's Grammar School at Grimsby, he established a Lodge in the borough, the chair of which he occupied for fourteen years. So strenuous were his exertions for the advancement of Masonry, that in 1812 he was enabled to lay the first stone of a Masonic hall in the town, where, three years before, there had been scarcely a Mason residing.

About this time he was exalted as a Royal Arch Mason in the Chapter attached to the Rodney Lodge at Kingston-on-Hull. In Chapters and Consistories connected with the same Lodge he also received the high degrees and those of Masonic Knighthood. In 1813, he was appointed a Provincial Grand Steward; in 1816, Provincial Grand Chaplain; and in 1832, Provincial Deputy Grand Master of the Province of Lincolnshire. These are all the official honors that he received, except that of Past Deputy Grand Master, conferred, as an honorary title, by the Grand Lodge of Massachusetts. In the year 1840, Dr. Crucefix had undeservedly incurred the displeasure of the Grand Master, the Duke of Sussex. Dr. Oliver, between whom and Dr. Crucefix there had always been a warm personal friendship, assisted in a public demonstration of the Fraternity in honor of his friend and brother. This involved him in the odium, and caused the Provincial Grand Master of Lincolnshire, Bro. Charles Tennyson D'Eyncourt, to request the resignation of Dr. Oliver as his Deputy. He complied with the resignation, and after that time withdrew from all active participation in the labors of the Lodge. The transaction was not considered by any means as creditable to the independence of character or sense of justice of the Provincial Grand Master, and the Craft very generally expressed their indignation of the course which he had pursued, and their warm appreciation of the Masonic services of Dr. Oliver. In 1844, this appreciation was marked by the presentation of an offering of plate, which had been very generally subscribed for by the Craft throughout the kingdom.

Dr. Oliver's first contribution to the literature of Freemasonry, except a few Masonic sermons, was a work entitled *The Antiquities of Freemasonry, comprising illustrations of the five Grand Periods of Masonry, from the Creation of the World to the Dedication of King Solomon's Temple*, which was published in 1823. His next production was a little work entitled *The Star in the East*, intended to show, from the testimony of Masonic writers, the connection between Freemasonry and religion. In 1841 he published twelve lectures on the *Signs and Symbols* of Freemasonry, in which he went into a learned detail of the history and signification of all the recognized symbols of the Order. His next important contribution to Freemasonry was *The History of Initiation in twelve lectures; comprising a detailed account of the Rites and Ceremonies, Doctrines and Discipline, of all the Secret and Mysterious*

Institutions of the Ancient World, published in 1840. The professed object of the author was to show the resemblances between these ancient systems of initiation and the Masonic, and to trace them to a common origin; a theory which, under some modification, has been very generally accepted by Masonic scholars.

Following this was *The Theocratic Philosophy of Freemasonry*, a highly interesting work, in which he discusses the speculative character of the Institution. *A History of Freemasonry from 1829 to 1840* has proved a valuable appendix to the work of Preston, an edition of which he had edited in the former year. His next and most important, most interesting, and most learned production was his *Historical Landmarks and other Evidences of Freemasonry Explained*. No work with such an amount of facts in reference to the Masonic system had ever before been published by any author. It will forever remain as a monument of his vast research and his extensive reading. But it would be no brief task to enumerate merely the titles of the many works which he produced for the instruction of the Craft. A few of them must suffice. These are the *Revelations of a Square*, a sort of Masonic romance, detailing, in a fictitious form, many of the usages of the last centuries, with anecdotes of the principal Masons of that period; *The Golden Remains of the Early Masonic Writers*, in 5 volumes, each of which contains an interesting introduction by the editor; *The Book of the Lodge*, a useful manual, intended as a guide to the ceremonies of the Order; *The Symbol of Glory*, intended to show the object and end of Freemasonry; *A Mirror for the Johannite Masons*, in which he discusses the question of the dedication of Lodges to the two Saints John; *The Origin and Insignia of the Royal Arch Degree*, a title which explains itself; *A Dictionary of Symbolic Masonry*, by no means the best of his works. Almost his last contribution to Masonry was his *Institutes of Masonic Jurisprudence*, a book in which he expressed views of law that did not meet with the universal concurrence of his English readers. Besides these elaborate works, Dr. Oliver was a constant contributor to the early volumes of the London *Freemasons' Quarterly Review*, and published a valuable article, "On the Gothic Constitutions," in the *American Quarterly Review of Freemasonry*.

The great error of Dr. Oliver, as a Masonic teacher, was a too easy credulity or a too great warmth of imagination, which led him to accept without hesitation the crude theories of previous writers, and to recognize documents and legends as unquestionably authentic whose truthfulness subsequent researches have led most Masonic scholars to doubt or to deny. His statements, therefore, as to the origin or the history of the Order, have to be received with many grains of allowance. Yet it must be acknowledged that no writer in the English language has ever done so much to elevate the scientific character of Freemasonry.

Dr. Oliver was in fact the founder of what may be called the literary school of Masonry. Bringing to the study of the Institution an amount of archeological learning but seldom surpassed, an inexhaustible fund of multifarious reading, and all the laborious researches of a genuine scholar, he gave to Freemasonry a literary and philosophic character which has induced many succeeding scholars to devote themselves to those studies which he had made so attractive. While his erroneous theories and his fanciful speculations will be rejected, the form and direction that he has given to Masonic speculations will remain, and to him must be accredited the enviable title of the *Father of Anglo-Saxon Masonic Literature*.

In reference to the personal character of Dr. Oliver, a contemporary journalist (*Stanford Mercury*) has said that he was of a kind and genial disposition, charitable in the highest sense of the word, courteous, affable, self-denying, and beneficent; humble, unassuming, and unaffected; ever ready to oblige, easy of approach, and amiable, yet firm in the right.

Dr. Oliver's theory of the system of Freemasonry may be briefly stated in these words: He believed that the Order was to be found in the earliest periods of recorded history. It was taught by Seth to his descendants, and practised by them under the name of Primitive or Pure Freemasonry. It passed over to Noah, and at the dispersion of mankind suffered a division into Pure and Spurious. Pure Freemasonry descended through the Patriarchs to Solomon, and thence on to the present day. The Pagans, although they had slight glimmerings of the Masonic truths which had been taught by Noah, greatly corrupted them, and presented in their mysteries a system of initiation to which he gave the name of the Spurious Freemasonry of Antiquity. These views he had developed and enlarged and adorned out of the similar but less definitely expressed teachings of Hutchinson. Like that writer also, while freely admitting the principle of religious tolerance, he contended for the strictly Christian character of the Institution, and that, too, in the narrowest sectarian view, since he believed that the earliest symbols taught the dogma of the Trinity, and that Christ was meant by the Masonic reference to the Deity under the title of Great Architect of the Universe.

Omega. See *Alpha and Omega*.

Omnific Word. The Tetragrammaton is so called because of the omnific powers attributed by the Kabbalists to its possession and true pronunciation. (See *Tetragrammaton.*) The term is also applied to the most significant word in the Royal Arch system.

On. This is a significant word in Royal Arch Masonry, and has been generally explained as being the name by which Jehovah was worshiped among the Egyptians. As this has been recently denied, and the word asserted to be only the name of a city in Egypt, it is proper that some inquiry should be made into the authorities on the subject.

The first mention of On in the Bible is in the history of Joseph, to whom Pharaoh gave "to wife Asenath, the daughter of Poti-pherah, 'est of On." The city of On was in Lower t, between the Nile and the Red Sea, 'adorned," says Philippson, "by a gorgeous temple of the sun, in which a numerous priesthood officiated."

The investigations of modern Egyptologists have shown that this is an error. On was the name of a city where the sun-god was worshiped, but On was not the name of that god. Champollioin, in his *Dictionnaire Egyptien*, gives the phonetic characters, with the figurative symbols of a serpent and disk, and a seated figure, as the name of the sun-god. Now, of these two characters, the upper one has the power of R, and the lower of A, and hence the name of the god is *Ra*. And this is the concurrent testimony of Bunsen, Lepsius, Gliddon, and all recent authorities.

But although On was really the name of a city, the founders of the Royal Arch had, with the lights then before them, assumed that it was the name of a god, and had so incorporated it with their system. With better light than theirs, we can no longer accept their definition; yet the word may still be retained as a symbol of the Egyptian god. I know not who has power to reject it; and if scholars preserve, outside of the symbolism, the true interpretation, no harm will be done. It is not the only significant word in Masonry whose old and received meaning has been shown to be incorrect, and sometimes even absurd. Higgins (*Celt. Druids*, 171) quotes an Irish commentator as showing that the name AIN or ON was the name of a triad of gods in the Irish language. "All etymologists," Higgins continues, "have supposed the word On to mean the sun; but how the name arose has not before been explained." In another work (*Anacalypsis*, vol. i., p. 109), Higgins makes the following important remarks: "Various definitions are given of the word ON; but they are all unsatisfactory. It is written in the Old Testament in two ways, און, *aun*, and אן, *an*. It is usually rendered in English by the word On. This word is supposed to mean the sun, and the Greeks translated it by the word ἥλιος, or Sol. But I think it only stood for the sun, as the emblem of the procreative power of nature." Bryan says (*Ant. Mythol.*, i., 19), when speaking of this word: "On, Eon or Aon, was another title of the sun among the Amonians. The Seventy, where the word occurs in the Scriptures, interpret it the sun, and call the city of On, Heliopolis; and the Coptic Pentateuch renders the city On by the city of the sun." Plato, in his *Timæus*, says: "Tell me of the god ON, which is, and never knew beginning." And although Plato may have been here thinking of the Greek word ΩN, which means *Being*, it is not improbable that he may have referred to the god worshiped at On, or Heliopolis, as it was thence that the Greeks derived so much of their learning. It would be vain to attempt to make an analogy between the Hindu sacred word AUM and the Egyptian ON. The fact that the M in the former word is the initial of some secret word, renders the conversion of it into N impossible, because it would thereby lose its signification.

The old Masons, misled by the authority of St. Cyril, and by the translation of the name of the city into "City of the Sun" by the Hebrews and the Greeks, very naturally supposed that On was the Egyptian sun-god, their supreme deity, as the sun always was, wherever he was worshiped. Hence, they appropriated that name as a sacred word explanatory of the Jewish Tetragrammaton.

Onech. (Heb. ענך.) The bird Phœnix, named after Enoch or Phenoch. Enoch signifies initiation. The Phœnix, in Egyptian mythological sculptures, as a bird, is placed in the mystical palm-tree. The Phœnix is the representative of eternal and continual regeneration, and is the Holy Spirit which brooded as a dove over the face of the waters, the dove of Noah and of Hasisatra or Xysuthrus (which see), which bore a sprig in its mouth.

Ontario. Lodge No. 156, in the Eighth Regiment of Foot, appears to have been the first Lodge to hold meetings in this Province, at Fort Niagara, about 1755–80. From 1780 to 1792 some ten lodges appear to have worked in what was called "Upper Canada." Some chartered by England, others by the Provincial Grand Lodge at Quebec, among them St. James in the Kings' Rangers, No. 14, at Cataraqui (Kingston), 1781; St. John's, No. 15, at Michilimakinac (Michigan), then part of Canada; St. John's, No. 19, at Niagara and Oswegatchie Lodge, 1786, at Elisabethtown (Brockville).

On March 7, 1792, Bro. William Jarvis was appointed Provincial Grand Master of Upper Canada by the "Ancient" or "Athol" Grand Lodge of England. Bro. Jarvis resided at Newark (Niagara), the then capital of the Province. During his Grand Mastership, 1792 to 1804, twenty warrants for lodges were issued.

In 1797 Bro. Jarvis removed from Newark to York (now Toronto).

The Brethren at Niagara continued to be active and enthusiastic, and urged Bro. Jarvis to assemble Grand Lodge there, but he refused. This refusal caused much dissatisfaction, and the Brethren of Niagara District met in 1803 and elected Bro. Geo. Forsyth as Provincial Grand Master, and trouble and friction ensued.

In 1817, at Kingston, a Grand Convention was called by the Lodges in the Midland District under R. W. Bro. Ziba M. Phillips. All the lodges attended excepting those in the Niagara District. This convention was held annually during the years 1817, 1818, 1820, 1821, 1822.

After repeated entreaty to England during these years, R. W. Bro. Simon McGillivray came to Canada in September, 1822, with authority from the Duke of Sussex to reorganize the Craft in Upper Canada. The Second Provincial Grand Lodge was thus formed at York in 1822, with R. W. Bro. Simon McGillivray as Provincial Grand Master, and met regularly up to 1830, but the Provincial Grand Lodge became dormant and remained so until 1845, when Masonic enthusiasm once more gained the ascendency. An urgent appeal was sent out and a Third Provincial Grand Lodge organised in Hamilton with Bro. Sir Allan MacNab Provincial Grand Master of "Canada West," appointed by the Earl of Zetland. This body continued work until 1858.

In 1853 a number of the lodges holding Irish Warrants organised a Grand Lodge, but it was not very successful. They then endeavored to secure the co-operation of the Provincial Grand Lodge in forming a Grand Lodge for Canada, but the Provincial Grand Body declined. But Home Rule and a self-governing body for Canada was the idea uppermost and would not down, and finally, on October 10, 1855, a convention of all the lodges in the two Provinces was called at Hamilton and the Grand Lodge of Canada was formed. Forty-one lodges were represented, twenty-eight in Canada West (Ontario) and thirteen in Canada East (Quebec), and M. W. Bro. William Mercer Wilson was elected Grand Master.

In September, 1857, the Provincial Grand Lodge under England met and resolved itself into an independent Grand Lodge, under the name of "Ancient Grand Lodge of Canada," but the next year in July, 1858, they united with the Grand Lodge of Canada. In October, 1869, the majority of the lodges in the Province of Quebec held a convention and decided to form a Grand Lodge for that Province. The Grand Lodge of Canada strenuously opposed this new body, and an edict of suspension covering all the lodges and Brethren taking part was issued. The Grand Lodge of Quebec, however, becoming duly recognized by all the leading Grand Lodges of the world, the Grand Lodge of Canada, in 1874, likewise decided to do the same and withdrew from the Province, all the lodges of her obedience joining the Quebec Grand Body. In 1875 a schism occurred and a number of Brethren organised a "Grand Lodge of Ontario." This breach was finally healed and the Brethren and lodges became of allegiance to the Grand Lodge of Canada in 1896.

In 1886 the words "in the Province of Ontario" were added to the title of the "Grand Lodge of Canada."

Onyx, שהם. (*Shohem.*) The second stone in the fourth row of the high priest's breastplate. It is of a bluish-black color, and represented the tribe of Joseph.

Opening of the Lodge. The necessity of some preparatory ceremonies, of a more or less formal character, before proceeding to the despatch of the ordinary business of any association, has always been recognized. Decorum and the dignity of the meeting alike suggest, even in popular assemblies called only for a temporary purpose, that a presiding officer shall, with some formality, be inducted into the chair, and he then, to use the ordinary phrase, "opens" the meeting with the appointment of his necessary assistants, and with the announcement, in an address to the audience, explanatory of the objects that have called them together.

If secular associations have found it expedient, by the adoption of some preparatory forms, to avoid the appearance of an unseeming abruptness in proceeding to business, it may well be supposed that religious societies have been still more observant of the custom, and that, as their pursuits are more elevated, the ceremonies of their preparation for the object of their meeting should be still more impressive.

In the Ancient Mysteries (those sacred rites which have furnished so many models for Masonic symbolism) the opening ceremonies were of the most solemn character. The sacred herald commenced the ceremonies of opening the greater initiations by the solemn formula of "Depart hence, ye profane!" to which was added a proclamation which forbade the use of any language which might be deemed of unfavorable augury to the approaching rites.

In like manner a Lodge of Masons is opened with the employment of certain ceremonies in which, that attention may be given to their symbolic as well as practical importance, every member present is expected to take a part.

These ceremonies, which slightly differ in each of the degrees—but differ so slightly as not to affect their general character—may be considered, in reference to the several purposes which they are designed to effect, to be divided into eight successive steps or parts.

1. The Master having signified his intention to proceed to the labors of the Lodge, every brother is expected to assume his necessary Masonic clothing and, if an officer, the insignia of his office, and silently and decorously to repair to his appropriate station.

2. The next step in the ceremony is, with the usual precautions, to ascertain the right of each one to be present. It is scarcely necessary to say that, in the performance of this duty, the officers who are charged with it should allow no one to remain who is not either well known to themselves or properly vouched for by some discreet and experienced brother.

3. Attention is next directed to the external avenues of the Lodge, and the officers within and without who are entrusted with the performance of this important duty, are expected to execute it with care and fidelity.

4. By a wise provision, it is no sooner intimated to the Master that he may safely proceed, than he directs his attention to an inquiry into the knowledge possessed by his officers of the duties that they will be respectively called upon to perform.

5. Satisfied upon this point, the Master then announces, by formal proclamation, his intention to proceed to business; and, mindful of the peaceful character of our Institution, he strictly forbids all immoral or unmasonic conduct whereby the harmony of the Lodge may be impeded, under no less a penalty than the by-laws may impose, or a majority of the brethren present may see fit to inflict. Nor, after this, is any brother permitted to leave the Lodge during Lodge hours

(that is, from the time of opening to that of closing) without having first obtained the Worshipful Master's permission

6. Certain mystic rites, which can here be only alluded to, are then employed, by which each brother present signifies his concurrence in the ceremonies which have been performed, and his knowledge of the degree in which the Lodge is about to be opened.

7. It is a lesson which every Mason is taught, as one of the earliest points of his initiation, that he should commence no important undertaking without first invoking the blessing of Deity. Hence the next step in the progress of the opening ceremonies is to address a prayer to the Supreme Architect of the Universe. This prayer, although offered by the Master, is to be participated in by every brother, and, at its conclusion, the audible response of "So mote it be: Amen," should be made by all present.

8. The Lodge is then declared, in the name of God and the Holy Saints John, to be opened in due form on the First, Second, or Third Degree of Masonry, as the case may be.

A Lodge is said to be opened *in the name of God and the Holy Saints John*, as a declaration of the sacred and religious purposes of the meeting, of profound reverence for that Divine Being whose name and attributes should be the constant themes of contemplation, and of respect for those ancient patrons whom the traditions of Masonry have so intimately connected with the history of the Institution.

It is said to be opened *in due form*, to intimate that all that is necessary, appropriate, and usual in the ceremonies, all that the law requires or ancient usage renders indispensable, have been observed.

And it is said to be opened *on*, and not *in*, a certain degree (which latter expression is often incorrectly used) in reference rather to the speculative than to the legal character of the meeting, to indicate, not that the members are to be circumscribed *in* the limits of a particular degree, but that they are met together to unite in contemplation *on* the symbolic teachings and divine lessons, to inculcate which is the peculiar object of that degree.

The manner of opening in each degree slightly varies. In the English system, the Lodge is opened in the First Degree "in the name of T. G. A. O. T. U."; in the Second, "on the square, in the name of the Grand Geometrician of the Universe"; and in the Third, "on the center, in the name of the Most High."

It is prescribed as a ritual regulation that the Master shall never open or close his Lodge without a lecture or part of a lecture. Hence, in each of the degrees a portion of a part of the lecture of that degree is incorporated into the opening and closing ceremonies.

There is in every degree of Masonry, from the lowest to the highest, an opening ceremony peculiar to the degree. This ceremony has always more or less reference to the symbolic lesson which it is the design of the degree to teach, and hence the varieties of openings are as many as the degrees themselves.

Operative Art. Masonry is divided by Masonic writers into two branches, an operative art and a speculative science. The operative art is that which was practised by the Stone-Masons of the Middle Ages. The speculative science is that which is practised by the Freemasons of the present day. The technicalities and usages of the former have been incorporated into and modified by the latter. Hence, Freemasonry is sometimes defined as a speculative science founded on an operative art.

Operative Masonry. Freemasonry, in its character as an operative art, is familiar to everyone. As such, it is engaged in the application of the rules and principles of architecture to the construction of edifices for private and public use, houses for the dwelling-place of man, and temples for the worship of the Deity. It abounds, like every other art, in the use of technical terms, and employs, in practise, an abundance of implements and materials which are peculiar to itself.

This operative art has been the foundation on which has been built the speculative science of Freemasonry. (See *Speculative Masonry*.)

Operative Masons. Workers in stone, who construct material edifices, in contra-distinction to Speculative Masons, who construct only spiritual edifices.

Ophites. The Brotherhood of the Serpent, which flourished in the second century, and held that there were two principles of æons and the accompanying theogony. This Egyptian fraternity displayed a living serpent in their ceremonies, which was reverenced as a symbol of wisdom and a type of good.

Option. When a Masonic obligation leaves to the person who assumes it the option to perform or omit any part of it, it is not to be supposed that such option is to be only his arbitrary will or unreasonable choice. On the contrary, in exercising it, he must be governed and restrained by the principles of right and duty, and be controlled by the circumstances which surround the case, so that this option, which at first would seem to be a favor, really involves a great and responsible duty, that of exercising a just judgment in the premises. That which at one time would be proper to perform, at another time and in different circumstances it would be equally proper to omit.

Oral Instruction. Much of the instruction which is communicated in Freemasonry, and, indeed, all that is esoteric, is given orally; and there is a law of the Institution that forbids such instruction to be written. There is in this usage and regulation a striking analogy to what prevailed on the same subject in all the secret institutions of antiquity.

In all the ancient mysteries, the same reluctance to commit the esoteric instructions of the hierophants to writing is apparent; and hence the secret knowledge taught in their initiations was preserved in symbols, the true meaning of which was closely concealed from the profane.

The Druids had a similar regulation; and Cæsar informs us that, although they made use of the letters of the Greek alphabet to record their ordinary or public transactions, yet it was not considered lawful to entrust their sacred verses to writing, but these were always committed to memory by their disciples.

The secret doctrine of the Kabbala, or the mystical philosophy of the Hebrews, was also communicated in an oral form, and could be revealed only through the medium of allegory and similitude. The Kabbalistic knowledge, traditionally received, was, says Maurice (*Ind. Antiq.*, iv., 548), "transmitted verbally down to all the great characters celebrated in Jewish antiquity, among whom both David and Solomon were deeply conversant in its most hidden mysteries. Nobody, however, had ventured to commit anything of this kind to paper."

The Christian church also, in the age immediately succeeding the apostolic, observed the same custom of oral instruction. The early Fathers were eminently cautious not to commit certain of the mysterious dogmas of their religion to writing, lest the surrounding Pagans should be made acquainted with what they could neither understand nor appreciate. St. Basil (*De Spiritu Sancto*), treating of this subject in the fourth century, says: "We receive the dogmas transmitted to us by writing, and those which have descended to us from the apostles, beneath the mystery of oral tradition; for several things have been handed down to us without writing, lest the vulgar, too familiar with our dogmas, should lose a due respect for them." And he further asks, "How should it ever be becoming to write and circulate among the people an account of those things which the uninitiated are not permitted to contemplate?"

A custom, so ancient as this, of keeping the landmarks unwritten, and one so invariably observed by the Masonic Fraternity, it may very naturally be presumed, must have been originally established with the wisest intentions; and, as the usage was adopted by many other institutions whose organization was similar to that of Freemasonry, it may also be supposed that it was connected, in some way, with the character of an esoteric instruction.

Two reasons, it seems to me, may be assigned for the adoption of the usage among Freemasons.

In the first place, by confining our secret doctrines and landmarks to the care of tradition, all danger of controversies and schisms among Masons and in Lodges is effectually avoided. Of these traditions, the Grand Lodge in each jurisdiction is the interpreter, and to its authoritative interpretation every Mason and every Lodge in the jurisdiction is bound to submit. There is no book, to which every brother may refer, whose language each one may interpret according to his own views, and whose expressions—sometimes, perhaps, equivocal and sometimes obscure—might afford ample sources of wordy contest and verbal criticism. The doctrines themselves, as well as their interpretation, are contained in the memories of the Craft; and the Grand Lodges, as the lawful representatives of the Fraternity, are alone competent to decide whether the tradition has been correctly preserved, and what is its true interpretation. And hence it is that there is no institution in which there have been so few and such unimportant controversies with respect to essential and fundamental doctrines.

In illustration of this argument, Dr. Oliver, while speaking of what he calls the antediluvian system of Freemasonry—a part of which must necessarily have been traditional, and transmitted from father to son, and a part entrusted to symbols—makes the following observations:

"Such of the legends as were communicated orally would be entitled to the greatest degree of credence, while those that were committed to the custody of symbols, which, it is probable, many of the collateral legends would be, were in great danger of perversion, because the truth could only be ascertained by those persons who were intrusted with the secret of their interpretation. And if the symbols were of doubtful character, and carried a double meaning, as many of the Egyptian hieroglyphics of a subsequent age actually did, the legends which they embodied might sustain very considerable alteration in sixteen or seventeen hundred years, although passing through very few hands."

Maimonides (*More Nevochim*, c. lxxi.) assigns a similar reason for the unwritten preservation of the Oral Law. "This," he says, "was the perfection of wisdom in our law, that by this means those evils were avoided into which it fell in succeeding times, namely, the variety and perplexity of sentiments and opinions, and the doubts which so commonly arise from written doctrines contained in books, besides the errors which are easily committed by writers and copyists, whence, afterwards, spring up controversies, schisms, and confusion of parties."

A second reason that may be assigned for the unwritten ritual of Masonry is, that by compelling the craftsman who desires to make any progress in his profession, to commit its doctrines to memory, there is a greater probability of their being thoroughly studied and understood. In confirmation of this opinion, it will, I think, be readily acknowledged by anyone whose experience is at all extensive, that, as a general rule, those skilful brethren who are technically called "bright Masons," are better acquainted with the esoteric and unwritten portion of the lectures, which they were compelled to acquire under a competent instructor, and by oral information, than with that which is published in the Monitors, and, therefore, always at hand to be read.

Cæsar (*Bell. Gall.*, vi., 14) thought that this was the cause of the custom among the Druids, for, after mentioning that they did not suffer their doctrines to be committed to writing, he adds: "They seem to me to have adopted this method for two reasons: that their mysteries might be hidden from the common people, and to exercise the memory of their disciples, which would be neglected if they had books on which they might rely, as, we find, is often the case."

A third reason for this unwritten doctrine of Masonry, and one, perhaps, most familiar to the Craft, is also alluded to by Cæsar in the case of the Druids, "because they did not wish their doctrines to be divulged to the common people." Maimonides, in the conclusion of the passage which we have already quoted, makes a similar remark with respect to the oral law of the Jews. "But if," says he, "so much care was exercised that the oral law should not be written in a book and laid open to all persons, lest, peradventure, it should become corrupted and depraved, how much more caution was required that the secret interpretations of that law should not be divulged to every person, and pearls be thus thrown to swine." "Wherefore," he adds, "they were intrusted to certain private persons, and by them were transmitted to other educated men of excellent and extraordinary gifts." And for this regulation he quotes the Rabbis, who say that the secrets of the law are not delivered to any person except a man of prudence and wisdom.

It is, then, for these excellent reasons—to avoid idle controversies and endless disputes; to preserve the secrets of our Order from decay; and, by increasing the difficulties by which they are to be obtained, to diminish the probability of their being forgotten; and, finally, to secure them from the unhallowed gaze of the profane—that the oral instruction of Masonry was first instituted, and still continues to be religiously observed. Its secret doctrines are the precious jewels of the Order, and the memories of Masons are the well-guarded caskets in which those jewels are to be preserved with unsullied purity. And hence it is appropriately said in our ritual, that "the attentive ear receives the sound from the instructive tongue, and the secrets of Freemasonry are safely lodged in the depository of faithful breasts."

Oral Law. The Oral Law is the name given by the Jews to the interpretation of the written code, which is said to have been delivered to Moses at the same time, accompanied by the Divine command: "Thou shalt not divulge the words which I have said to thee out of my mouth." The Oral Law was, therefore, never entrusted to books; but, being preserved in the memories of the judges, prophets, priests, and other wise men, was handed down, from one to the other, through a long succession of ages.

Maimonides has described, according to the Rabbinical traditions, the mode adopted by Moses to impress the principles of this Oral Law upon the people. As an example of perseverance in the acquirement of information by oral instruction, it may be worthy of the consideration and imitation of all those Masons who wish to perfect themselves in the esoteric lessons of their Institution.

When Moses had descended from Mount Sinai, and had spoken to the people, he retired to his tent. Here he was visited by Aaron, to whom, sitting at his feet, he recited the law and its explanation, as he had received it from God. Aaron then rose and seated himself on the right hand of Moses. Eleazar and Ithamar, the sons of Aaron, now entered the tent, and Moses repeated to them all that he had communicated to their father; after which, they seated themselves, one on the left hand of Moses and the other on the right hand of Aaron. Then went in the seventy elders, and Moses taught them, in the same manner as he had taught Aaron and his sons. Afterward, all of the congregation who desired to know the Divine will came in; and to them, also, Moses recited the law and its interpretation, in the same manner as before. The law, thus orally delivered by Moses, had now been heard four times by Aaron, three times by his sons, twice by the seventy elders, and once by the rest of the people. After this, Moses withdrawing, Aaron repeated all that he had heard from Moses, and retired; then Eleazar and Ithamar repeated it, and also withdrew; and, finally, the same thing was done by the seventy elders; so that each of them having heard the law repeated four times, it was thus, finally, fixed in their memories.

The *written* law, divided by the Jewish lawgivers into 613 precepts, is contained in the Pentateuch. But the *oral* law, transmitted by Moses to Joshua, by him to the elders, and from them conveyed by traditionary relation to the time of Judah the Holy, was by him, to preserve it from being forgotten and lost, committed to writing in the work known as the Mishna. And now, no longer an Oral Law, its precepts are to be found in that book, with the subsidiary aid of the Constitutions of the prophets and wise men, the Decrees of the Sanhedrim, the decisions of the Judges, and the Expositions of the Doctors.

Orator. An officer in a Lodge whose duty it is to explain to a candidate after his initiation the mysteries of the degree into which he has just been admitted. The office is therefore, in many respects, similar to that of a lecturer. The office was created in the French Lodges early in the eighteenth century, soon after the introduction of Masonry into France. A writer in the London *Freemasons' Magazine* for 1859 attributes its origin to the constitutional deficiency of the French in readiness of public speaking. From the French it passed to the other continental Lodges, and was adopted by the Scottish Rite. The office is not recognised in the English and American system, where its duties are performed by the Worshipful Master. [Though a few Lodges under the English Constitution do appoint an Orator, e. g., the Lodge of Antiquity, No. 2, the Pilgrim Lodge, No. 238, the Constitutional Lodge, No. 294, and the La Césarée Lodge, No. 590.]

Order. An Order may be defined to be a brotherhood, fellowship, or association of certain persons, united by laws and statutes peculiar to the society, engaged in a common object or design, and distinguished by particular habits, ensigns, badges, or symbols.

Johnson's definition is that an Order is "a regular government, a society of dignified persons distinguished by marks of honor, and a religious fraternity." In all of these senses Freemasonry may be styled an Order.

Its government is of the most regular and systematic character; men the most eminent for dignity and reputation have been its members; and if it does not constitute a religion in itself, it is at least religion's handmaid.

The ecclesiastical writers define an Order to be a congregation or society of religious persons, governed by particular rules, living under the same superior, in the same manner, and wearing the same habit; a definition equally applicable to the society of Freemasons. These ecclesiastical Orders are divided into three classes: 1. Monastic, such as the Benedictines and the Augustinians. 2. The Mendicant, as the Dominicans and the Franciscans. 3. The Military, as the Hospitalers, the Templars, and the Teutonic Knights. Only the first and the third have any connection with Freemasonry; the first because it was by them that architecture was fostered, and the Masonic gilds patronized in the Middle Ages; and the third because it was in the bosom of Freemasonry that the Templars found a refuge after the dissolution of their Order.

Order Book. The book to which all appeals were made, in the Order of Strict Observance, as to matters of history, usage, or ritual. It was invariably bound in red.

Order Name. The name or designation assumed by the Illuminati, the members of the Rite of Strict Observance, and of the Royal Order of Scotland, was called the Order Name, or the Characteristic Name. (See *Eques.*)

The Illuminati selected classical names, of which the following are specimens:

Weishaupt	was	Spartacus.
Knigge	"	Philo.
Bode	"	Amelius.
Nicolai	"	Lucian.
Westenreider	"	Pythagoras.
Constanza	"	Diomedes.
Zwack	"	Cato.
Count Savioli	"	Brutus.
Busche	"	Bayard.
Ecker	"	Saladin.

The members of the Strict Observance formed their Order Names in a different way. Following the custom of the combatants in the old tournaments, each called himself an *eques*, or knight of some particular object; as, Knight of the Sword, Knight of the Star, etc. Where one belonged both to this Rite and to that of Illuminism, his Order Name in each was different. Thus Bode, as an Illuminatus, was, we have seen, called "Amelius," but as a Strict Observant, he was known as "Eques à lilio convallium," or Knight of the Lily-of-the-Valleys. The following examples may suffice. A full list will be found in Thory's *Acta Latomorum.*

Hund was Eques ab ense = Knight of the Sword.

Jacobi was Eques à stellâ = Knight of the Star.

Count Bruhl was Eques à gladio ancipiti = Knight of the Double-edged Sword.

Bode was Eques à lilio convallium = Knight of the Lily-of-the-Valleys.

Beyerle was Eques à fasciâ = Knight of the Girdle.

Berend was Eques à septem stellis = Knight of the Seven Stars.

Decker was Eques à plagula = Knight of the Curtain.

Lavater was Eques ab Æsculapio = Knight of Esculapius.

Seckendorf was Eques à capricorno = Knight of Capricorn.

Prince Charles Edward was Eques à sole aureo = Knight of the Golden Sun.

Zinnendorf was Eques à lapide nigro = Knight of the Black Stone.

Order of Business. In every Masonic body, the by-laws should prescribe an "Order of Business," and in proportion as that order is rigorously observed will be the harmony and celerity with which the business of the Lodge will be despatched.

In Lodges whose by-laws have prescribed no settled order, the arrangement of business is left to the discretion of the presiding officer, who, however, must be governed, to some extent, by certain general rules founded on the principles of parliamentary law, or on the suggestions of common sense.

The order of business may, for convenience of reference, be placed in the following tabular form:

1. Opening of the Lodge.
2. Reading and confirmation of the minutes.
3. Reports on petitions.
4. Balloting for candidates.
5. Reports of special committees.
6. Reports of standing committees.
7. Consideration of motions made at a former meeting, if called up by a member.
8. New business.
9. Initiations.
10. Reading of the minutes for information and correction.
11. Closing of the Lodge.

Order of Christ. See *Christ, Order of.*

Order of the Temple. See *Temple, Order of the.*

Order, Rules of. Every permanent deliberative body adopts a code of rules of order to suit itself; but there are certain rules derived from what may be called the common law of Parliament, the wisdom of which having been proven by long experience, that have been deemed of force at all times and places, and are, with a few necessary exceptions, as applicable to Lodges as to other societies.

The rules of order, sanctioned by uninterrupted usage and approved by all authorities, may be enumerated under the following distinct heads, as applied to a Masonic body:

1. Two independent original propositions cannot be presented at the same time to the meeting.

2. A subsidiary motion cannot be offered out of its rank of precedence.

3. When a brother intends to speak, he is required to stand up in his place, and to address himself always to the presiding officer.

4. When two or more brethren rise nearly at the same time, the presiding officer will

indicate, by mentioning his name, the one who, in his opinion, is entitled to the floor.

5. A brother is not to be interrupted by any other member, except for the purpose of calling him to order.

6. No brother can speak oftener than the rules permit; but this rule may be dispensed with by the Master.

7. No one is to disturb the speaker by hissing, unnecessary coughing, loud whispering, or other unseemly noise, nor should he pass between the speaker and the presiding officer.

8. No personality, abusive remarks, or other improper language should be used by any brother in debate.

9. If the presiding officer rises to speak while a brother is on the floor, that brother should immediately sit down, that the presiding officer may be heard.

10. Everyone who speaks should speak to the question.

11. As a sequence to this, it follows that there can be no speaking unless there be a question before the Lodge. There must always be a motion of some kind to authorize a debate.

Orders of Architecture. An order in architecture is a system or assemblage of parts subject to certain uniform established proportions regulated by the office which such part has to perform, so that the disposition, in a peculiar form, of the members and ornaments, and the proportion of the columns and pilasters, is called an order. There are five orders of architecture, the Doric, Ionic, Corinthian, Tuscan, and Composite—the first three being of Greek and the last two of Italian origin. (See each under its respective title.)

Considering that the orders of architecture must have constituted one of the most important subjects of contemplation to the Operative Masons of the Middle Ages, and that they afforded a fertile source for their symbolism, it is strange that so little allusion is made to them in the primitive lectures and in the earliest catechisms of the last century. In the earliest catechism extant, they are simply enumerated, and said to answer "to the base, perpendicular, diameter, circumference, and square"; but no explanation is given of this reference. Nor are they referred to in the "Legend of the Craft," or in any of the Old Constitutions. Preston, however, introduced them into his system of lectures, and designated the three most ancient orders—the Ionic, Doric, and Corinthian—as symbols of wisdom, strength, and beauty, and referred them to the three original Grand Masters. This symbolism has ever since been retained; and, notwithstanding the reticence of the earlier ritualists, there is abundant evidence, in the architectural remains of the Middle Ages, that it was known to the old Operative Freemasons.

Orders of Architecture, Egyptian. The Egyptians had a system of architecture peculiar to themselves, which, says Barlow (*Essays on Symbolism*, p. 30), "would indicate a people of grand ideas, and of confirmed religious convictions." It was massive, and without the airy proportions of the Greek orders. It was, too, eminently symbolic, and among its ornaments the lotus leaf and plant predominated as a symbol of regeneration. Among the peculiar forms of the Egyptian architecture were the fluted column, which suggested the Ionic order to the Greeks, and the basket capital adorned with the lotus, which afterward became the Corinthian. To the Masonic student, the Egyptian style of architecture becomes interesting, because it was undoubtedly followed by King Solomon in his construction of the Temple. The great similarity between the pillars of the porch and the columns in front of Egyptian temples is very apparent. Our translators have, however, unfortunately substituted the *lily* for the *lotus* in their version.

Orders of Knighthood. An order of knighthood is a confraternity of knights bound by the same rules. Of these there are many in every kingdom of Europe, bestowed by sovereigns on their subjects as marks of honor and rewards of merit. Such, for instance, are in England the Knights of the Garter; in Scotland the Knights of Saint Andrew; and in Ireland the Knights of Saint Patrick. But the only Orders of Knighthood that have had any historical relation to Masonry, except the Order of Charles XII. in Sweden, are the three great religious and military Orders which were established in the Middle Ages. These are the Knights Templar, the Knights Hospitalers or Knights of Malta, and the Teutonic Knights, each of which may be seen under its respective title. Of these three, the Masons can really claim a connection only with the Templars. They alone had a secret initiation, and with them there is at least traditional evidence of a fusion. The Knights of Malta and the Teutonic Knights have always held themselves aloof from the Masonic Order. They never had a secret form of initiation; their reception was open and public; and the former Order, indeed, during the latter part of the eighteenth century, became the willing instruments of the Church in the persecution of the Masons who were at that time in the island of Malta. There is, indeed, a Masonic degree called Knight of Malta, but the existing remnant of the historical order has always repudiated it. With the Teutonic Knights, the Freemasons have no other connection than this, that in some of the high degrees their peculiar cross has been adopted. An attempt has been made, but without reason, to identify the Teutonic Knights with the Prussian Knights, or Noachites.

Orders of the Day. In parliamentary law, propositions which are appointed for consideration at a particular hour and day are called the orders of the day. When the day arrives for their discussion, they take precedence of all other matters, unless passed over by mutual consent or postponed to another day. The same rules in reference to these orders prevail in Masonic as in other assemblies. The parliamentary law is here applicable without modification to Masonic bodies.

Ordinacio. The Old Constitutions known as the Halliwell or Regius MS. (fourteenth century) speak of an *ordinacio* in the sense of a law. "*Alia ordinacio artis gemetriæ.*" (L. 471.) It is borrowed from the Roman law, where *ordinatio* signified an imperial edict. In the Middle Ages, the word was used in the sense of a statute, or the decision of a judge.

Ordination. At the close of the reception of a neophyte into the order of Elect Cohens, the Master, while communicating to him the mysterious words, touched him with the thumb, index, and middle fingers (the other two being closed) on the forehead, heart, and side of the head, thus making the figure of a triangle. This ceremony was called the *ordination*.

Ordo ab Chao. *Order out of Chaos.* A motto of the Thirty-third Degree, and having the same allusion as *lux e tenebris*, which see. The invention of this motto is to be attributed to the Supreme Council of the Ancient and Accepted Scottish Rite at Charleston, and it is first met with in the Patent of Count de Grasse, dated February 1, 1802. When De Grasse afterward carried the Rite over to France and established a Supreme Council there, he changed the motto, and, according to Lenning, *Ordo ab hoc* was used by him and his Council in all the documents issued by them. If so, it was simply a blunder.

Oregon. The first Lodges instituted in Oregon were under Warrants from the Grand Lodge of California, in the year 1849. On August 16, 1851, a convention of three Lodges was held in Oregon City, and the Grand Lodge of Oregon was there organized, Berryman Jennings being elected Grand Master. The Grand Chapter was organized at Salem, September 18, 1860. Templarism was introduced by the organization of Oregon Commandery, No. 1, at Oregon City, on July 24, 1860.

Organist, Grand. An officer in the Grand Lodge of England, Scotland, and Ireland whose duty it is to superintend the musical exercises on private and public occasions. He must be a Master Mason, and is required to attend the Quarterly and other communications of the Grand Lodge. His jewel is an antique lyre. Grand Lodges in this country do not recognize such an officer. But an organist has been recently employed since the introduction of musical services into Lodge ceremonies by some Lodges.

Organization of the Grand Lodges. See *Grand Lodge.*

Orient. The East. The place where a Lodge is situated is sometimes called its "Orient," but more properly its "East." The seat of a Grand Lodge has also sometimes been called its "Grand Orient"; but here "Grand East" would, perhaps, be better. The term "Grand Orient" has been used to designate certain of the Supreme Bodies on the Continent of Europe, and also in South America; as, the Grand Orient of France, the Grand Orient of Portugal, the Grand Orient of Brazil, the Grand Orient of New Grenada, etc. The title always has reference to the East as the place of honor in Masonry. (See *East, Grand.*)

Orient, Grand. See *Grand Orient.*

Orient, Grand Commander of the. (*Grand Commandeur d'Orient.*) The Forty-third Degree of the Rite of Misraim.

Orient, Interior. A name sometimes used in Germany to designate a Grand Chapter or superintending body of the higher degrees.

Orient of France, Grand. See *France.*

Orient, Order of the. (*Ordre d'Orient.*) An Order founded, says Thory (*Act. Lat.*, i., 330), at Paris, in 1806, on the system of the Templars, to whom it traced its origin.

Oriental Chair of Solomon. The seat of the Master in a Symbolic Lodge, and so called because the Master is supposed symbolically to fill the place over the Craft once occupied by King Solomon. For the same reason, the seat of the Grand Master in the Grand Lodge receives the same appellation. In England it is called the *throne*.

Oriental Philosophy. A peculiar system of doctrines concerning the Divine Nature which is said to have originated in Persia, its founder being Zoroaster, whence it passed through Syria, Asia Minor, and Egypt, and was finally introduced among the Greeks, whose philosophical systems it at times modified. Pliny calls it "a magical philosophy," and says that Democritus, having traveled into the East for the purpose of learning it, and returning home, taught it in his mysteries. It gave birth to the sect of Gnostics, and most of it being adopted by the school of Alexandria, it was taught by Philo, Jamblichus, and other disciples of that school. Its essential feature was the theory of emanations (which see). And the Oriental Philosophy permeates, sometimes to a very palpable extent, Ineffable, Philosophic, and Hermetic Masonry, being mixed up and intertwined with the Jewish and Kabbalistic Philosophy. A knowledge of the Oriental Philosophy is therefore essential to the proper understanding of these high degrees.

Oriental Rite. The title first assumed by the Rite of Memphis.

Orientation. The orientation of a Lodge is its situation due east and west. The word is derived from the technical language of architecture, where it is applied, in the expression "orientation of churches," to designate a similar direction in building. Although Masonic Lodges are still, when circumstances will permit, built on an east and west direction, the explanation of the usage, contained in the old lectures of the last century, that it was "because all chapels and churches are, or ought to be so," has become obsolete, and other symbolic reasons are assigned. Yet there can be no doubt that such was really the origin of the usage. The orientation of churches was a principle of ecclesiastical architecture very generally observed by builders, in accordance with ecclesiastical law from the earliest times after the apostolic age. Thus in the Apostolic Constitutions, which, although falsely attributed to St. Clement, are yet of great antiquity, we find the express direction, "sit ædes oblonga ad orientem versus"—*let the church be of an oblong form, directed to the east*—a direction which would be strictly applicable in the building of a Lodge room. St. Charles Borromeo, in his *Instructiones Fabricæ Ecclesiasticæ*, is still more precise, and directs that the rear or altar part of the church shall look directly to the east, "in orientem versus recta spectat," and that it shall be not "ad solstitialem sed ad æquinoctialem orientem" —not to the solstitial east, which varies by the deflection of the sun's rising, but to the equinoctial east, where the sun rises at the equinoxes, that is to say, *due east*. But, as Bingham (*Antiq.*, b. viii., c. iii.) admits, although the usage was very general to erect churches toward the east, yet "it admitted of exceptions, as necessity or expediency"; and the same exception prevails in the construction of Lodges, which, although always erected due east and west, where circumstances will permit, are sometimes from necessity built in a different direction. But whatever may be externally the situation of the Lodge with reference to the points of the compass, it is always considered internally that the Master's seat is in the east, and therefore that the Lodge is "situated due east and west."

As to the original interpretation of the usage, there is no doubt that the Masonic was derived from the ecclesiastical, that is, that Lodges were at first built east and west because churches were; nor can we help believing that the church borrowed and Christianized its symbol from the Pagan reverence for the place of sunrising. The admitted reverence in Masonry for the east as the *place of light*, gives to the usage the modern Masonic interpretation of the symbol of orientation.

Oriflamme. The ancient banner which originally belonged to the Abbey of St. Denis, and was borne by the Counts of Vexin, patrons of that church, but which, after the country of Vexin fell into the hands of the French crown, became the principal banner of the kingdom. It was charged with a saltire wavy Or, with rays issuing from the center crossways; Secoee into five points, each bearing a tassel of green silk.

Original Points. The old lectures of the last century, which are now obsolete, contained the following instruction: "There are in Freemasonry twelve original points, which form the basis of the system and comprehend the whole ceremony of initiation. Without the existence of these points, no man ever was, or can be, legally and essentially received into the Order. Every person who is made a Mason must go through all these twelve forms and ceremonies, not only in the first degree, but in every subsequent one."

Origin of Freemasonry. The origin and source whence first sprang the institution of Freemasonry, such as we now have it, has given rise to more difference of opinion and discussion among Masonic scholars than any other topic in the literature of the Institution. Writers on the history of Freemasonry have, at different times, attributed its origin to the following sources. 1. To the Patriarchal religion. 2. To the Ancient Pagan Mysteries. 3. To the Temple of King Solomon. 4. To the Crusaders. 5. To the Knights Templar. 6. To the Roman Colleges of Artificers. 7. To the Operative Masons of the Middle Ages. 8. To the Rosicrucians of the sixteenth century. 9. To Oliver Cromwell, for the advancement of his political schemes. 10. To the Pretender, for the restoration of the House of Stuart to the British throne. 11. To Sir Christopher Wren at the building of St. Paul's Cathedral. 12. To Dr. Desaguliers and his associates in the year 1717. Each of these twelve theories has been from time to time, and the twelfth within a recent period, sustained with much zeal, if not always with much judgment, by their advocates. A few of them, however, have long since been abandoned, but the others still attract attention and find defenders. Dr. Mackey has his own views of the subject in his book *History of Freemasonry*, to which the reader is referred.*

Orleans, Duke of. Louis Philippe Joseph, Duke of Orleans, better known in history by his revolutionary name of Egalité, was the fifth Grand Master of the Masonic Order in France. As Duke of Chartres, the title which he held during the life of his father, he was elected Grand Master in the year 1771, upon the death of the Count de Clermont. Having appointed the Duke of Luxemburg his Substitute, he did not attend a meeting of the Grand Lodge until 1777, but had in the meantime paid much attention to the interests of Masonry, visiting many of the Lodges, and laying the foundation-stone of a Masonic Hall at Bordeaux.

His abandonment of his family and his adhesion to the Jacobins during the revolution, when he repudiated his hereditary title of Duke of Orleans and assumed the republican one of Egalité, forms a part of the history of the times. On the 22d of February, 1793, he wrote a letter to Milsent, the editor, over the signature of "Citoyen Egalité," which was published in the *Journal de Paris*, and which contains the following passages:

"This is my Masonic history. At one time, when certainly no one could have foreseen our revolution, I was in favor of Freemasonry, which presented to me a sort of *image of equality*, as I was in favor of the parliament, which presented a sort of *image of liberty*. I have since *quitted the phantom for the reality*. In the month of December last, the secretary of the Grand Orient having addressed himself to the person who discharged the functions, near me, of secre-

*See *Antiquity of Masonry; Egyptian Mysteries; Roman College Artificers; Como; Comacine Masters; Traveling Masons; Stone-Masons of Middle Ages; Four Old Lodges; Revival; Speculative Masonry.*

tary of the Grand Master, to obtain my opinion on a question relating to the affairs of that society, I replied to him on the 5th of January as follows: 'As I do not know how the Grand Orient is composed, and as, besides, I think that there should be no mystery nor secret assembly in a republic, especially at the commencement of its establishment, I desire no longer to mingle in the affairs of the Grand Orient, nor in the meetings of the Freemasons.' "

In consequence of the publication of this letter, the Grand Orient on May 13, 1793, declared the Grand Mastership vacant, thus virtually deposing their recreant chief. He soon reaped the reward of his treachery and political debasement. On the 6th of November in the same year he suffered death on the guillotine.

Ormus or **Ormesius.** See *Rose Croix of Gold, Brethren of the.*

Ormuzd and Ahriman. Ormuzd was the principle of good and the symbol of light, and Ahriman the principle of evil and the symbol of darkness, in the old Persian religion. (See *Zoroaster.*)

Ornaments of a Lodge. The lectures describe the ornaments of a Lodge as consisting of the *Mosaic Pavement*, the *Indented Tessel*, and the *Blazing Star*. They are called ornaments because they are really the decorations with which a properly furnished Lodge is adorned. See these respective words.

Ornan the Jebusite. He was an inhabitant of Jerusalem, at the time that that city was called Jebus, from the son of Canaan, whose descendants peopled it. He was the owner of the threshing-floor situated on Mount Moriah, in the same spot on which the Temple was afterward built. This threshing-floor David bought to erect on it an altar to God. (1 Chron. xxi. 18–25.) On the same spot Solomon afterward built the Temple. Hence, in Masonic language, the Temple of Solomon is sometimes spoken of as "the threshing-floor of Ornan the Jebusite." (See *Threshing-Floor.*)

Orphan. The obligation that Masons should care for the children of their deceased brethren has been well observed in the Institution by many Grand Lodges, independent associations of Masons, and of asylums for the support and education of Masonic orphans. Among these, perhaps one of the most noteworthy, is the orphan asylum founded at Stockholm, in 1753, by the contributions of the Swedish Masons, which, by subsequent bequests and endowments, has become one of the richest private institutions of the kind in the world.

Orpheus. There are no less than four persons to whom the ancients gave the name of Orpheus, but of these only one is worthy of notice as the inventor of the mysteries, or, at least, as the introducer of them into Greece. The genuine Orpheus is said to have been a Thracian, and a disciple of Linus, who flourished when the kingdom of the Athenians was dissolved. From him the Thracian or Orphic mysteries derived their name, because he first introduced the sacred rites of initiation and mystical doctrines into Greece. He was, according to fabulous tradition, torn to pieces by Ciconian women, and after his death he was deified by the Greeks. The story, that by the power of his harmony he drew wild beasts and trees to him, has been symbolically interpreted, that by his sacred doctrines he tamed men of rustic and savage disposition. An abundance of fables has clustered around the name of Orpheus; but it is at least generally admitted by the learned, that he was the founder of the system of initiation into the sacred mysteries as practised in Greece. The Grecian theology, says Thomas Taylor—himself the most Grecian of all moderns—originated from Orpheus, and was promulgated by him, by Pythagoras, and by Plato; by the first, mystically and symbolically; by the second, enigmatically and through images; and by the last, scientifically. The mysticism of Orpheus should certainly have given him as high a place in the esteem of the founders of the present system of Speculative Masonry as has been bestowed upon Pythagoras. But it is strange that, while they delighted to call Pythagoras an "ancient friend and brother," they have been utterly silent as to Orpheus.

Orphic Mysteries. These rites were practised in Greece, and were a modification of the mysteries of Bacchus or Dionysus, and they were so called because their institution was falsely attributed to Orpheus. They were, however, established at a much later period than his era. Indeed, M. Freret, who has investigated this subject with much learning in the *Memoires de l'Academie des Inscriptions* (tom. xxiii.), regards the Orphics as a degenerate branch of the school of Pythagoras, formed, after the destruction of that school, by some of its disciples, who, seeking to establish a religious association, devoted themselves to the worship of Bacchus, with which they mingled certain Egyptian practises, and out of this mixture made up a species of life which they called the Orphic life, and the origin of which, to secure greater consideration, they attributed to Orpheus, publishing under his name many apocryphal works.

The Orphic rites differed from the other Pagan rites, in not being connected with the priesthood, but in being practised by a fraternity who did not possess the sacerdotal functions. The initiated commemorated in their ceremonies, which were performed at night, the murder of Bacchus by the Titans, and his final restoration to the supreme government of the universe, under the name of Phanes.

Demosthenes, while reproaching Æschines for having engaged with his mother in these mysteries, gives us some notion of their nature.

In the day, the initiates were crowned with fennel and poplar, and carried serpents in their hands, or twined them around their heads, crying with a loud voice, *enos, sabos*, and danced to the sound of the mystic words, *hyes, attes, attes, hyes*. At night the mystes was bathed in the lustral water, and having been rubbed over with clay and bran, he was clothed in the skin of a fawn, and having risen from the bath, he exclaimed, "I have departed from evil and have found the good."

The Orphic poems made Bacchus identical with Osiris, and celebrated the mutilation and palingenesis of that deity as a symbol teaching the resurrection to eternal life, so that their design was similar to that of the other Pagan mysteries.

The Orphic initiation, because it was not sacerdotal in its character, was not so celebrated among the ancients as the other mysteries. Plato, even, calls its disciples charlatans. It nevertheless existed until the first ages of the Christian religion, being at that time adopted by the philosophers as a means of opposing the progress of the new revelation. It fell, however, at last, with the other rites of Paganism, a victim to the rapid and triumphant progress of the Gospel.

Osiris. He was the chief god of the old Egyptian mythology, the husband of Isis, and the father of Horus. Jabloniski says that Osiris represented the sun only, but Plutarch, whose opportunity of knowing was better, asserts that, while generally considered as a symbol of the solar orb, some of the Egyptian philosophers regarded him as a river god, and called him Nilus. But the truth is, that Osiris represented the male, active or generative, powers of nature; while Isis represented its female, passive or prolific, powers. Thus, when Osiris was the sun, Isis was the earth, to be vivified by his rays; when he was the Nile, Isis was the land of Egypt, fertilized by his overflow. Such is the mythological or mystical sense in which Osiris was received.

Historically, he is said to have been a great and powerful king, who, leaving Egypt, traversed the world, leading a host of fauns or satyrs, and other fabulous beings in his train, actually an army of followers. He civilized the whole earth, and taught mankind to fertilize the soil and to perform the works of agriculture. We see here the idea which was subsequently expressed by the Greeks in their travels of Dionysus, and the wanderings of Ceres; and it is not improbable that the old Masons had some dim perception of this story, which they have incorporated, under the figure of Euclid, in their "Legend of the Craft."

Osiris, Mysteries of. The Osirian mysteries consisted in a scenic representation of the murder of Osiris by Typhon, the subsequent recovery of his mutilated body by Isis, and his deification, or restoration to immortal life. Julius Firmicus, in his treatise *On the Falsity of the Pagan Religions*, thus describes the object of the Osirian Mysteries: "But in those funerals and lamentations which are annually celebrated in honor of Osiris, the defenders of the Pagan rites pretend a physical reason. They call the seeds of fruit, Osiris; the earth, Isis; the natural heat, Typhon; and because the fruits are ripened by the natural heat and collected for the life of man, and are separated from their natural tie to the earth, and are sown again when winter approaches, this they consider is the death of Osiris; but when the fruits, by the genial fostering of the earth, begin again to be generated by a new procreation, this is the finding of Osiris." This explanation does not essentially differ from that already given in the article *Egyptian Mysteries*. The symbolism is indeed precisely the same—that of a restoration or resurrection from death to life. (See *Egyptian Mysteries*.)

Oterfut. The name of the assassin at the west gate in the legend of the Third Degree, according to some of the high degrees. I have vainly sought the true meaning or derivation of this word, which is most probably an anagram of a name. It was, I think, invented by the Stuart Masons, and refers to some person who was inimical to that party.

Otreb. The pseudonym of the celebrated Rosicrucian Michael Maier, under which he wrote his book on *Death and the Resurrection*. (See *Maier*.)

Ouriel. See *Uriel*.

Out of the Lodge. The charges of a Freemason, compiled by Anderson from the Ancient Records, contain the regulations for the behavior of Masons out of the Lodge under several heads; as, behavior after the Lodge is over, when brethren meet without strangers, in the presence of strangers, at home, and toward a strange brother. Gädicke gives the same directions in the following words:

"A brother Freemason shall not only conduct himself in the Lodge, but also out of the Lodge, as a brother towards his brethren; and happy are they who are convinced that they have in this respect ever obeyed the laws of the Order."

Oval Temples. The temple in the Druidical mysteries was often of an oval form. As the oblong temple was a representation of the inhabited world, whence is derived the form of the Lodge, so the oval temple was a representation of the mundane egg, which was also a symbol of the world. The symbolic idea in both was the same.

Overseer. The title of three officers in a Mark Lodge, who are distinguished as the Master, Senior, and Junior Overseer. The jewel of their office is a square. In Mark Lodges attached to Chapters, the duties of these officers are performed by the three Grand Masters of the Veils.

Ox. The ox was the device on the banner of the tribe of Ephraim. The ox on a scarlet field is one of the Royal Arch banners, and is borne by the Grand Master of the Third Veil.

Oyres de Ornellas, Praçao. A Portuguese gentleman, who was arrested as a Freemason, at Lisbon, in 1776, was thrown into a dungeon, where he remained fourteen months. (See *Alincourt*.)

Ozee. Sometimes Osee. The acclamation of the Scottish Rite is so spelled in many French Cahiers. Properly Hoschea, which Delaunay (*Thuileur*, p. 141) derives from the Hebrew הושע, *hosheah*, deliverance, safety, or, as he says, a savior. But see *Hoschea*, where another derivation is suggested

Oziah. (Heb. עזיה; Latin, *Fortitudo domini*.) A prince of Judah, and the name of the Senior Warden in the Fifth Degree of the French Rite of Adoption.

P

P. The sixteenth letter of the English and Greek alphabets, and the seventeenth of the Hebrew, in which last-mentioned language its numerical value is 80, is formed thus פ, signifying a mouth in the Phœnician. The sacred name of God associated with this letter is פודה, *Phodeh* or *Redeemer*.

Pachacamac. The Peruvian name for the Creator of the universe.

Paganis, Hugo de. The Latinized form of the name of Hugh de Payens, the first Grand Master of the Templars. (See *Payens*.)

Paganism. A general appellation for the religious worship of the whole human race, except of that portion which has embraced Christianity, Judaism, or Mohammedanism. Its interest to the Masonic student arises from the fact that its principal development was the ancient mythology, in whose traditions and mysteries are to be found many interesting analogies with the Masonic system. (See *Dispensations of Religion*.)

Paine, Thomas. A political writer of eminence during the Revolutionary War in America. He greatly injured his reputation by his attacks on the Christian religion. He was not a Mason, but wrote *An Essay on the Origin of Freemasonry*, with no other knowledge of the Institution than that derived from the writings of Smith and Dodd, and the very questionable authority of Prichard's *Masonry Dissected*. He sought to trace Freemasonry to the Celtic Druids. For one so little acquainted with his subject, he has treated it with considerable ingenuity. Paine was born in England in 1737, and died in New York, in 1809.

Palestine, called also the *Holy Land* on account of the sacred character of the events that have occurred there, is situated on the coast of the Mediterranean, stretching from Lebanon south to the borders of Egypt, and from the thirty-fourth to the thirty-ninth degrees of longitude. It was conquered from the Canaanites by the Hebrews under Joshua 1450 years B.C. They divided it into twelve confederate states according to the tribes. Saul united it into one kingdom, and David enlarged its territories. In 975 B.C. it was divided into the two kingdoms of Israel and Judea, the latter consisting of the tribes of Judah and Benjamin, and the former of the rest of the tribes. About 740 B.C., both kingdoms were subdued by the Persians and Babylonians, and after the captivity only the two tribes of Judah and Benjamin returned to rebuild the Temple. With Palestine, or the Holy Land, the mythical, if not the authentic, history of Freemasonry has been closely connected. There stood, at one time, the Temple of Solomon, to which some writers have traced the origin of the Masonic Order; there fought the Crusaders, among whom other writers have sought, with equal boldness, to find the cradle of the Fraternity; there certainly the Order of the Templars was instituted, whose subsequent history has been closely mingled with that of Freemasonry; and there occurred nearly all the events of sacred history that, with the places where they were enacted, have been adopted as important Masonic symbols.

Palestine, Explorations in. The desire to obtain an accurate knowledge of the archeology of Palestine, gave rise in 1866 to an association, which was permanently organized in London, as the "Palestine Exploration Fund," with the Queen as the chief patron, and a long list of the nobility and the most distinguished gentlemen in the kingdom, added to which followed the Grand Lodge of England and forty-two subordinate and provincial Grand Lodges and Chapters. Early in the year 1867 the committee began the work of examination, by mining in and about the various points which had been determined upon by a former survey as essential to a proper understanding of the ancient city, which had been covered up by *débris* from age to age, so that the present profiles of the ground, in every direction, were totally different from what they were in the days of David and Solomon, or even the time of Christ.

Lieutenant Charles Warren, R.E. [as he then was, now Lieut.-General Sir Charles Warren, G.C.M.G., K.C.B., F.R.S.], was sent out with authority to act as circumstances might demand, and as the delicacy and the importance of the enterprise required. He arrived in Jerusalem February 17, 1867, and continued his labors of excavating in many parts of the city, with some interruptions, until 1871, when he returned to England. During his operations, he kept the society in London constantly informed of the progress of the work in which he and his associates were so zealously engaged, in a majority of cases at the imminent risk of their lives and always that of their health. The result of these labors has been a vast accumulation of facts in relation to the topography of the holy city which throw much light on its archeology. A branch of the society has been established in this country, and it is still in successful operation.

Palestine, Knight of. See *Knight of Palestine*.

Palestine, Knight of St. John of. See *Knight of St. John of Palestine*.

Palestine, Order of. Mentioned by Baron de Tschoudy, and said to have been the fountain whence the Chevalier Ramsay obtained his information for the regulation of his system.

Palla. An altar-cloth, also a canopy borne over the head of royalty in Oriental lands.

Palladic Masonry. The title given to the Order of the Seven Sages and the Order of the Palladium. (See *Palladium, Order of the*.)

Palladium, Order of the. An androgynous society of Masonic adoption, established, says Ragon, at Paris in 1737. It made great pretensions to high antiquity, claiming that it had its origin in the instructions brought by Pythagoras from Egypt into Greece, and having fallen into decay after the decline of the Roman Emperor, it was revived in 1637 by Fénelon, Archbishop of Canbray; all of which is altogether mythical. Fénelon was not born until 1651. It was a very moral society, consisting of two degrees: 1. Adelph; 2. Companion of Ulysses. When a female took the Second Degree, she was called a Companion of Penelope.

Palmer. From the Latin, *palmifer*, a palm-bearer. A name given in the time of the Crusades to a pilgrim, who, coming back from the holy war after having accomplished his vow of pilgrimage, exhibited upon his return home a branch of palm bound round his staff in token of it.

Palmer, Henry L. Born in New York, October 18, 1819. He was the author of the celebrated report, in October, 1849, which resulted in the union of the two Grand Lodges in New York, the "Herring-Phillips" and the "New York" Grand Lodge. Bro. Palmer occupied almost every known position in Craft Masonry, and was the commanding officer of every one of its departments. He was P. G. Master of the G. Encampment of K. T. of the U. S., and G. Commander of the Supreme Council of the A. A. Scottish Rite, Northern Jurisdiction of the U. S. of America. He died on May 7, 1909.

Pantacle. The pentalpha of Pythagoras is so called in the symbolism of High Magic and the Hermetic Philosophy. (See *Pentalpha*.)

Pantheism. A speculative system, which, spiritually considered, identifies the universe with God, and, in the material form, God with the universe. Material Pantheism is subject to the criticism, if not to the accusation, of being atheistic. Pantheism is as aged as religion, and was the system of worship in India, as it was in Greece. Giordano Bruno was burned for his pantheistic opinions at Rome in 1600.

Pantheistic Brotherhood. Described by John Toland, in his *Pantheisticon*, as having a strong resemblance to Freemasonry. The Socratic Lodge in Germany, based on the Brotherhood, was of short duration.

Papworth Manuscript. A manuscript in the possession of Mr. Wyatt Papworth, of London, who purchased it from a bookseller of that city in 1860. As some of the watermarks of the paper on which it is written bear the initials G. R., with a crown as a watermark, it is evident that the manuscript cannot be older than 1714, that being the year in which the first of the Georges ascended the throne. It is most probably of a still more recent date, perhaps 1720. The Rev. A. F. A. Woodford has thus described its appearance: "The scroll was written originally on pages of foolscap size, which were then joined into a continuous roll, and afterwards, probably for greater convenience, the pages were again separated by cutting them, and it now forms a book, containing twenty-four folios, sewed together in a light-brown paper cover. The text is of a bold character, but written so irregularly that there are few consecutive pages which have the same number of lines, the average being about seventeen to the page." The manuscript is not complete, three or four of the concluding charges being omitted, although some one has written, in a hand different from that of the text, the word *Finis* at the bottom of the last page. The manuscript appears to have been simply a copy, in a little less antiquated language, of some older Constitution. It has been published by Bro. Hughan in his *Old Charges of the British Freemasons*. (1872.)

Papyrus. "The papyrus leaf," says J. W. Simons, in his *Egyptian Symbols*, "is that plant which formed tablets and books, and forms the first letter of the name of the only eternal and all-powerful god of Egypt, *Amon*, who in the beginning of things created the world," whose name signified *occult* or *hidden*. The word עלה, *ole*, which signifies a leaf, and to inscribe on tablets forms עלם, *olm*, the antique origin of things, obscure time, hidden eternity.

The *Turin Funeral Papyrus* is a book published by Dr. Lepsius in original character, but translated by Dr. Birch. This Book of the Dead is invaluable as containing the true philosophic belief of the Egyptians respecting the resurrection and immortality. The manuscript has been gathered from portions which it was obligatory to bury with the dead. The excavations of mummies in Egypt have been fruitful in furnishing the entire work.

Paracelsus. Philippus Aureolus Theophrastus Bombastus Paracelsus de Hohenheim, as he styled himself, was born in Germany in 1493, and died in 1541. He devoted his youth to the study and practise of astrology, alchemy, and magic, and passed many years of his life in traveling over Europe and acquiring information in medicine, of which he proclaimed himself to be the monarch. He was, perhaps, the most distinguished charlatan who ever made a figure in the world. The followers of his school were called Paracelsists, and they continued for more than a century after the death of their master to influence the schools of Germany. Much of the Kabbalistic and mystical science of Paracelsus was incorporated into Hermetic Masonry by the founders of the high degrees.

Paracelsus, Sublime. A degree to be found in the manuscript collections of Peuvret.

Parallel Lines. In every well-regulated Lodge there is found a point within a circle, which circle is imbordered by two perpendicular parallel lines. These lines are representative of St. John the Baptist and St. John the Evangelist, the two great patrons of Masonry to whom our Lodges are dedicated, and who are said to have been "perfect parallels in Christianity as well as Masonry." In those English Lodges which have adopted the "Union System" established by the Grand

Lodge of England in 1813, and where the dedication is "to God and his service," the lines parallel represent Moses and Solomon. As a symbol, the parallel lines are not to be found in the earlier rituals of Masonry. Although Oliver defines the symbol on the authority of what he calls the "Old Lectures," it is not to be found in any anterior to Preston, and even he only refers to the parallelism of the two Sts. John.

Parikchai, Agrouchada. An occult scientific work of the Brahmans. According to a work by Louis Jacolliot, 1884, the Fakirs produced phenomena at will with superior intervention or else with shrewd charlatanism: processes that were known to the Egyptians and Jewish Kabbalists. The doctrines are those known to the Alexandrian school, to the Gauls, and as well to the Christians. In the division of the Kabbala, the first treated of the History of the Genesis or Creation, and taught the science of nature; the second, or Mercaba, of the History of the Chariot, and contained a treatise on theology.

There were three degrees of initiation among the Brahmans:

1st. According to selection, the candidate became a Grihasta, a Pourohita or Fakir, or in twenty years a Guru.

2d. A Sannyassis or Cenobite and Vanaprasthas, and lived in the Temple.

3d. A Sannyassis-Nirvany or Naked Cenobite.

Those of the third degree were visible only once in five years, appearing in a column of light created by themselves, at midnight, and on a stand in the center of a great tank. Strange sounds and terrific shrieks were heard as they were gazed upon as demigods, surrounded by thousands of Hindus.

The government was by a Supreme Council of seventy Brahmans, over seventy years of age, selected from the Nirvany, and chosen to see enforced the *Law of the Lotus*. The Supreme Chief, or Brahmatna, was required to be over eighty years of age, and was looked upon as immortal by the populace. This Pontiff resided in an immense palace surrounded by twenty-one walls.

The primitive holy word composed of the three letters A. U. M., comprises the Vedic trinity, signifying Creation, Preservation, and Transformation, and symbolize all the initiatory secrets of the occult sciences. By some it has been taught that the "*Honover*," or primordial germ, as defined in the Avesta, existed before all else. Also see *Manou*, Book xi., Sloca 265. The following unexplained magical words were always inscribed in two triangles: L'OM. *L'rhom-sh'hrum.* SHO'RIM. *Ramaya-Nahama.*

He who possessed the word greater than the A. U. M. was deemed next to Brahma. The word was transmitted in a sealed box.

The Hindu triad, of which in later times OM is the mystic name, represents the union of the three gods, viz., *a* (Vishnu), *u* (Siva), *m* (Brahma). It may also be typical of the three Vedas. *Om* appears first in the Upanishads as a mystical monosyllable, and is thus set forth as the object of profound meditation. It is usually called *pranava*, more rarely *aksharam*. The Buddhists use *Om* at the beginning of their Vidyâ Shad-akshari or mystical formulary in six syllables (viz., Om mâni pad me hûm). (See *Pitris Indische Mysterien* and *Aum*.) [C. T. McClenachan.]

Paris, Congresses of. Three important Masonic Congresses have been held in the city of Paris. The first was convened by the Rite of Philalethes in 1785, that by a concourse of intelligent Masons of all rites and countries, and by a comparison of oral and written traditions, light might be educed on the most essential subjects of Masonic science, and on the nature, origin, and historic application as well as the actual state of the Institution. Savalette de Lauges was elected President. It closed after a protracted session of three months, without producing any practical result. The second was called in 1787, as a continuation of the former, and closed with precisely the same negative result. The third was assembled in 1855, by Prince Murat, for the purpose of effecting various reforms in the Masonic system. At this Congress, ten propositions, some of them highly important, were introduced, and their adoption recommended to the Grand Lodges of the world. But the influence of this Congress has not been more successful than that of its predecessors.

Paris Constitutions. A copy of these Constitutions, said to have been adopted in the thirteenth century, will be found in G. P. Depping's *Collection de Documents inedits sur l'Histoire de France*. (Paris, 1837.) A part of this work contains the *Reglemens sur les arts et métiers de Paris, rédigés au 13me siecle et connus sous le nom de livre des métiers d'Etienne Boileau*. This treats of the masons, stonecutters, plasterers, and mortar-makers, and, as Steinbrenner (*Or. and Hist. of Mas.*, p. 104) says, "is interesting, not only as exhibiting the peculiar usages and customs of the Craft at that early period, but as showing the connection which existed between the laws and regulations of the French Masons and those of the Steinmetzen of Germany and the Masons of England." A translation of the Paris Constitutions was published in the *Freemasons' Magazine*, Boston, 1863, p. 201. In the year 1743, the "English Grand Lodge of France" published, in Paris, a series of statutes, taken principally from Anderson's work of the editions of 1723 and 1738. It consisted of twenty articles, and bore the title of *General Regulations taken from the Minutes of the Lodges, for the use of the French Lodges, together with the alterations adopted at the General Assembly of the Grand Lodge, December 11, 1743, to serve as a rule of action for the said kingdom.* A copy of this document, says Findel, was translated into German, with annotations, and published in 1856 in the *Zeitschrift für Freimaurer* of Altenberg.

Parliamentary Law. Parliamentary Law, or the *Lex Parliamentaria*, is that code originally framed for the government of the Parliament of Great Britain in the transaction of its business, and subsequently adopted, with necessary modifications, by the Congress of the United States.

But what was found requisite for the regulation of public bodies, that order might be secured and the rights of all be respected, has been found equally necessary in private societies. Indeed, no association of men could meet together for the discussion of any subject, with the slightest probability of ever coming to a conclusion, unless its debates were regulated by certain and acknowledged rules.

The rules thus adopted for its government are called its parliamentary law, and they are selected from the parliamentary law of the national assembly, because that code has been instituted by the wisdom of past ages, and modified and perfected by the experience of subsequent ones, so that it is now universally acknowledged that there is no better system of government for deliberative societies than the code which has so long been in operation under the name of parliamentary law.

Not only, then, is a thorough knowledge of parliamentary law necessary for the presiding officer of a Masonic body, if he would discharge the duties of the chair with credit to himself and comfort to the members, but he must be possessed of the additional information as to what parts of that law are applicable to Masonry, and what parts are not; as to where and when he must refer to it for the decision of a question, and where and when he must lay it aside, and rely for his government upon the organic law and the ancient usages of the Institution.

Parlirer. In the Lodges of Stone-Masons of the Middle Ages, there was a rank or class of workmen called Parlirers, literally, spokesmen. They were an intermediate class of officers between the Masters of the Lodges and the Fellows, and were probably about the same as our modern Wardens. Thus, in the *Strasbourg Constitutions of 1459*, it is said: "No Craftsman or Mason shall promote one of his apprentices as a parlirer whom he has taken as an apprentice from his rough state, or who is still in the years of apprenticeship," which may be compared with the old English charge that "no Brother can be a Warden until he has passed the part of a Fellow-Craft." (*Constitutions*, 1723, p. 52.) They were called Partirers, properly, says Heldmann, *Parlierers*, or Spokesmen, because, in the absence of the Masters, they spoke for the Lodge, to traveling Fellows seeking employment, and made the examination. There are various forms of the word. Kloss, citing the *Strasbourg Constitutions*, has *Parlirer;* Krause has, from the same document, *Parlierer*, but says it is usually *Polier;* Heldmann uses *Parlierer*, which has been now generally adopted.

Parole. A *Mot de sémestre* (*q. v.*), communicated by the Grand Orient of France, and in addition an annual word in November, which tends to show at once whether a member is in good standing.

Parrot Masons. One who commits to memory the questions and answers of the catechetical lectures, and the formulas of the ritual, but pays no attention to the history and philosophy of the Institution, is commonly called a *Parrot Mason*, because he is supposed to repeat what he has learned without any conception of its true meaning. In former times, such superficial Masons were held by many in high repute, because of the facility with which they passed through the ceremonies of a reception, and they were generally designated as "Bright Masons." But the progress of Masonry as a science now requires something more than a mere knowledge of the lectures to constitute a Masonic scholar.

Parsees. The descendants of the original fire-worshipers of Persia, or the disciples of Zoroaster, who emigrated to India about the end of the eighth century. There they now constitute a body very little short of a million of industrious and moral citizens, adhering with great tenacity to the principles and practises of their ancient religion. Many of the higher classes have become worthy members of the Masonic fraternity, and it was for their sake principally that Dr. Burnes attempted some years ago to institute his new Order, entitled the Brotherhood of the Olive-Branch, as a substitute for the Christian degrees of Knighthood, from which, by reason of their religion, they were excluded. (See *Olive-Branch in the East, Brotherhood of the*, and *Zendavesta*.)

Particular Lodges. In the Regulations of 1721, it is said that the Grand Lodge consists of the representatives of all the *particular* Lodges on record. (*Constitutions*, 1723, p. 61.) In the modern Constitutions of England, the term used is *private* Lodges. In America, they are called *subordinate* Lodges.

Parts. In the old obligations, which may be still used in some portions of the country, there was a provision which forbade the revelation of any of the *arts, parts, or points of Masonry*. Oliver explains the meaning of the word parts by telling us that it was "an old word for degrees or lectures." (See *Points*.)

Parvin, Theodore S. Born January 15, 1817, in Cumberland County, New Jersey. His journey in life gradually tending westward, he located in Ohio, and graduated in 1837 at the Cincinnati Law School. He was appointed private secretary by Robert Lucas, first Governor of Iowa, in which state he became Judge of the Probate Court and afterward Curator and Librarian of the State University at Iowa City. Bro. Parvin was initiated in Nova Cesarea Lodge, No. 2, Cincinnati, Ohio, March 14, 1838, and raised the 9th of the May following, and the same year demitted and removed to Iowa. He participated in the organization of the first Lodge, Des Moines, No. 1, and also of the second, Iowa Lodge, No. 2, at Muscatine. He was elected Grand Secretary of the Grand Lodge at its organization (1844), and held the office continuously to the time of his death, with the exception of the year 1852–3, when he served as Grand Master. He founded and organized the Grand Lodge Library and held the office of Grand Librarian until his death. His official signature is on every charter of the Grand Lodge of Iowa from 1844 to 1900.

He was exalted in Iowa City Chapter, No. 2, January 7, 1845, and held the offices of Grand High Priest of the Grand Chapter, 1854, and Grand Secretary of the Grand Chapter, 1855–56, and represented the Grand Chapter in the General Grand Chapter for many years.

He was created a Royal Select Master in Dubuque Council, No. 3, September 27, 1847, and presided over the Convention organizing the Grand Council of Iowa, 1857.

Knighted January 18, 1855, in Apollo Encampment, No. 1, Chicago, Ill., he was a member of the Convention organizing the Grand Commandery of Iowa, 1864, being the first Grand Commander. He was Grand Recorder of the Grand Encampment K. T. of the U. S. for fifteen years, 1871–86.

In 1859 he received the degrees of the Scottish Rite and was crowned in that year an Inspector-General, Thirty-third Degree.

In addition to this record, our brother also organized the Grand Bodies of Dakota, and the Grand Commandery of Nebraska, and his contributions to Masonic literature placed him among the leading writers and thinkers of the Craft.

He died at Cedar Rapids, Iowa, June 28, 1901.

Parvis. In the French system, the room immediately preceding a Masonic Lodge is so called. It is equivalent to the Preparation Room of the American and English systems.

Paschal Feast. Celebrated by the Jews in commemoration of the Passover, by the Christians in commemoration of the resurrection of our Lord. The Paschal Feast, called also the Mystic Banquet, is kept by all Princes of the Rose Croix Where two are together on Maundy Thursday, it is of obligation that they should partake of a portion of roasted lamb. This banquet is symbolic of the doctrine of the resurrection.

Paschalis, Martinez. The founder of a new Rite or modification of Masonry, called by him *the Rite of Elected Cohens or Priests*. It was divided into two classes, in the first of which was represented the fall of man from virtue and happiness, and in the second, his final restoration. It consisted of nine degrees, namely: 1. Apprentice; 2. Fellow-Craft; 3. Master; 4. Grand Elect; 5. Apprentice Cohen; 6. Fellow-Craft Cohen; 7. Master Cohen; 8. Grand Architect; 9. Knight Commander. Paschalis first introduced this Rite into some of the Lodges of Marseilles, Toulouse, and Bordeaux, and afterward, in 1767, he extended it to Paris, where, for a short time, it was rather popular, ranking some of the Parisian literati among its disciples. It has now ceased to exist.

Paschalis was a German, born about the year 1700, of poor but respectable parentage. At the age of sixteen he acquired a knowledge of Greek and Latin. He then traveled through Turkey, Arabia, and Palestine, where he made himself acquainted with the Kabbalistic learning of the Jews. He subsequently repaired to Paris, where he established his Rite.

Paschalis was the Master of St. Martin, who afterward reformed his Rite. After living for some years at Paris, he went to St. Domingo, where he died in 1779. Thory, in his *Histoire de la Fondation du Grand Orient de France* (pp. 239–253), has given very full details of this Rite and of its receptions.

Paschal Lamb. See *Lamb, Paschal.*

Pas perdus. The French call the room appropriated to visitors the *Salle des pas perdus*. It is the same as the Tiler's Room in the English and American Lodges.

Passage. The Fourth Degree of the Fessler Rite, of which Patria forms the Fifth.

Passages of the Jordan. See *Fords of the Jordan.*

Passed. A candidate, on receiving the Second Degree, is said to be "passed as a Fellow-Craft." It alludes to his having passed through the porch to the middle chamber of the Temple, the place in which Fellow-Crafts received their wages. In America "crafted" is often improperly used in its stead.

Passing of Conyng. That is, *surpassing in skill*. The expression occurs in the Cooke MS. (line 676), "The forsayde Maister Euglet ordeynet thei were passing of conyng schold be passing honoured"; i. e., The aforesaid Master, Euclid, ordained that they that were surpassing in skill should be exceedingly honored. It is a fundamental principle of Masonry to pay all honor to knowledge.

"Passing the River." A mystical alphabet said to have been used by the Kabbalists. These characters, with certain explanations, become the subject of consideration with brethren of the Fifteenth Degree, A. A. Scottish Rite. The following are the characters:

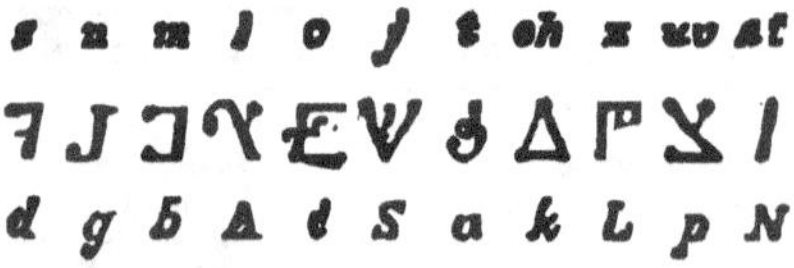

s n m l o j t ch x uv st

d g b A e S a k L p N

Password. A word intended, like the military countersign, to prove the friendly nature of him who gives it, and is a test of his right to pass or be admitted into a certain place. Between a *Word* and a *Password* there seems to be this difference: the former is given for instruction, as it always contains a symbolic meaning; the latter, for recognition only. Thus, the author of the life of the celebrated Elias Ashmole says, "Freemasons are known to one another all over the world by certain passwords known to them alone; they have Lodges in different countries, where they are relieved by the brotherhood if they are in distress." (See *Sign.*)

Past. An epithet applied in Masonry to an officer who has held an office for the prescribed period for which he was elected, and has then retired. Thus, a Past Master is one who has presided for twelve months over a Lodge, and the Past High Priest one who, for the same period, has presided over a Chapter. The French use the word *passé* in the same sense, but they have also the word *ancien*, with a similar meaning. Thus, while they would employ *Maître passé* to designate the degree of Past Master, they would call the official Past Master, who had retired from the chair at the expiration of his term of service, an *Ancien Vénérable*, or *Ancien Maître*.

Past Master. An honorary degree conferred on the Master of a Lodge at his installation into office. In this degree the necessary instructions are conferred respecting the various ceremonies of the Order, such as installations, processions, the laying of corner-stones, etc.

When a brother, who has never before presided, has been elected the Master of a Lodge, an emergent Lodge of Past Masters, consisting of not less than three, is convened, and all but Past Masters retiring, the degree is conferred upon the newly elected officer.

Some form of ceremony at the installation of a new Master seems to have been adopted at an early period after the revival. In the "manner of constituting a new Lodge," as practised by the Duke of Wharton, who was Grand Master in 1723, the language used by the Grand Master when placing the candidate in the chair is given, and he is said to use "some other expressions that are proper and usual on that occasion, *but not proper to be written*." (*Constitutions*, 1738, p. 150.) Whence we conclude that there was an esoteric ceremony. Often the rituals tell us that this ceremony consisted only in the outgoing Master communicating certain modes of recognition to his successor. And this actually, even at this day, constitutes the essential ingredient of the Past Master's Degree.

The degree is also conferred in Royal Arch Chapters, where it succeeds the Mark Master's Degree. The conferring of this degree, which has no historical connection with the rest of the degrees, in a Chapter, arises from the following circumstance: Originally, when Chapters of Royal Arch Masonry were under the government of Lodges in which the degree was then always conferred, it was a part of the regulations that no one could receive the Royal Arch Degree unless he had previously presided in the Lodge as Master. When the Chapters became independent, the regulation could not be abolished, for that would have been an innovation; the difficulty has, therefore, been obviated, by making every candidate for the degree of Royal Arch a Past Virtual Master before his exaltation.

[Under the English Constitution this practise was forbidden in 1826, but seems to have lingered on in some parts until 1850.]

Some extraneous ceremonies, by no means creditable to their inventor, were at an early period introduced into America. In 1856, the General Grand Chapter, by a unanimous vote, ordered these ceremonies to be discontinued, and the simpler mode of investiture to be used; but the order has only been partially obeyed, and many Chapters still continue what one can scarcely help calling the indecorous form of initiation into the degree.

For several years past the question has been agitated in some of the Grand Lodges of the United States, whether this degree is within the jurisdiction of Symbolic or of Royal Arch Masonry. The explanation of its introduction into Chapters, just given, manifestly demonstrates that the jurisdiction over it by Chapters is altogether an assumed one. The Past Master of a Chapter is only a *quasi* Past Master; the true and legitimate Past Master is the one who has presided over a Symbolic Lodge.

Past Masters are admitted to membership in many Grand Lodges, and by some the inherent right has been claimed to sit in those bodies. But the most eminent Masonic authorities have made a contrary decision, and the general, and, indeed, almost universal opinion now is that Past Masters obtain their seats in Grand Lodges by courtesy, and in consequence of local regulations, and not by inherent right.

The jewel of a Past Master in the United States is a pair of compasses extended to sixty degrees on the fourth part of a circle, with a sun in the center. In England it was formerly the square on a quadrant, but is at present the square with the forty-seventh problem of Euclid engraved on a silver plate suspended within it.

The French have two titles to express this degree. They apply *Maître passé* to the Past Master of the English and American system, and they call in their own system one who has formerly presided over a Lodge an *Ancien Maître*. The indiscriminate use of these titles sometimes leads to confusion in the translation of their rituals and treatises.

Pastophori. Couch or shrine bearers. The company of Pastophori constituted a sacred college of priests in Egypt, whose duty it was to carry in processions the image of the god. Their chief, according to Apuleius (*Met.* xi.), was called a Scribe. Besides acting as mendicants in soliciting charitable donations from the populace, they took an important part in the mysteries.

Pastos. (Greek, παστος, *a couch.*) The pastos was a chest or close cell, in the Pagan mysteries (among the Druids, an excavated stone), in which the aspirant was for some time placed, to commemorate the mystical death of the god. This constituted the symbolic death which was common to all the mysteries. In the Arkite rites, the pastos represented the ark in which Noah was confined. It is represented among Masonic symbols by the coffin.

Patents. Diplomas or certificates of the higher degrees in the Scottish Rite are called Patents. The term is also sometimes applied to commissions granted for the exercise of high

Masonic authority. *Literæ patentes* or *apertæ*, that is, letters patent or open letters, was a term used in the Middle Ages in contradistinction to *literæ clausæ*, or closed letters, to designate those documents which were spread out on the whole length of the parchment, and sealed with the public seal of the sovereign; while the secret or private seal only was attached to the closed patents. The former were sealed with green wax, the latter with white. There was also a difference in their heading; letters patent were directed "universis tum præsentibus quam futuris," i. e., *to all present or to come;* while closed letters were directed "universis præsentibus literas inspecturis," i. e., *to all present who shall inspect these letters.* Masonic diplomas are therefore properly called letters patent, or, more briefly, patents.

Patience. In the ritual of the Third Degree according to the American Rite, it is said that "time, patience, and perseverance will enable us to accomplish all things, and perhaps at last to find the true Master's Word." The idea is similar to one expressed by the Hermetic philosophers. Thus Pernetty tells us (*Dict. Mythol. Herm.*) that the alchemists said: "The work of the philosopher's stone is a work of patience, on account of the length of time and of labor that is required to conduct it to perfection; and Geber says that many adepts have abandoned it in weariness, and others, wishing to precipitate it, have never succeeded." With the alchemists, in their esoteric teaching, the philosopher's stone had the same symbolism as the WORD has in Freemasonry.

Patriarchal Masonry. The theory of Dr. Oliver on this subject has, we think, been misinterpreted. He does not maintain, as has been falsely supposed, that the Freemasonry of the present day is but a continuation of that which was practised by the patriarchs, but simply that, in the simplicity of the patriarchal worship, unencumbered as it was with dogmatic creeds, we may find the true model after which the religious system of Speculative Masonry has been constructed. Thus he says: "Nor does it (Freemasonry) exclude a survey of the patriarchal mode of devotion, which indeed forms the primitive model of Freemasonry. The events that occurred in these ages of simplicity of manners and purity of faith, when it pleased God to communicate with his favoured creature, necessarily, therefore, form subjects of interesting illustration in our Lodges, and constitute legitimate topics on which the Master in the chair may expatiate and exemplify, for the edification of the brethren and their improvement in morality and the love and fear of God." (*Hist. Landm.*) i., 207.) There is here no attempt to trace an historical connection, but simply to claim an identity of purpose and character in the two religious systems, the Patriarchal and the Masonic.

Patriarch, Grand. The Twentieth Degree of the Council of Emperors of the East and West. The same as the Twentieth Degree, or Noachite, of the Ancient and Accepted Rite.

Patriarch of the Crusades. One of the names formerly given to the degree of Grand Scottish Knight of St. Andrew, the Twenty-ninth of the Ancient and Accepted Scottish Rite. The legend of that degree connects it with the Crusades, and hence the name; which, however, is never used officially, and is retained by regular Supreme Councils only as a synonym.

Patriarch of the Grand Luminary. A degree contained in the nomenclature of Le Page.

Patron. In the year 1812, the Prince of Wales, becoming Regent of the kingdom, was constrained by reasons of state to resign the Grand Mastership of England, but immediately afterward accepted the title of Grand Patron of the Order in England, and this was the first time that the title was officially recognized. George IV. held it during his life, and on his death, William IV., in 1830, officially accepted the title of "Patron of the United Grand Lodge." On the accession of Victoria, the title fell into abeyance, because it was understood that it could only be assumed by a sovereign who was a member of the Craft, but King Edward VII. became "Protector of English Freemasons" on his accession to the throne in 1901. The office is not known in other countries.

Patrons of Masonry. St. John the Baptist and St. John the Evangelist. At an early period we find that the Christian church adopted the usage of selecting for every trade and occupation its own patron saint, who is supposed to have taken it under his especial charge. And the selection was generally made in reference to some circumstance in the life of the saint, which traditionally connected him with the profession of which he was appointed the patron. Thus St. Crispin, because he was a shoemaker, is the patron saint of the "gentle craft," and St. Dunstan, who was a blacksmith, is the patron of blacksmiths. The reason why the two Saints John were selected as the patron saints of Freemasonry will be seen under the head of *Dedication of Lodges.*

Paul, Confraternity of Saint. In the time of the Emperor Charles V. there was a secret community at Trapani, in Sicily, which called itself *La Confraternità di San Paolo.* These people, when assembled, passed sentence on their fellow-citizens; and if anyone was condemned, the waylaying and putting him to death was allotted to one of the members, which office he was obliged, without murmuring, to execute. (*Stolberg's Travels,* vol. iii., p. 472.) In the travels of Brocquire to and from Palestine in 1432 (p. 328), an instance is given of the power of the association over its members. In the German romance of *Hermann of Unna,* of which there are an English and French translation, this tribunal plays an important part.

Paul I. This emperor of Russia was induced by the machinations of the Jesuits, whom he had recalled from banishment, to prohibit in his domains all secret societies, and especially the Freemasons. This prohibition lasted from 1797 to 1803, when it was repealed by his successor. Paul had always expressed himself an enthusiastic admirer of the Knights of Malta; in 1797 he had assumed the title of Protector of the Order, and in 1798 accepted the Grand Mastership. This is another evidence, if one was needed, that there was no sympathy between the Order of Malta and the Freemasons.

Pavement, Mosaic. See *Mosaic Pavement.*

Pax Vobiscum. ("Peace be with you!") Used in the Eighteenth Degree, A.A. Scottish Rite.

Payens, Hugh de. In Latin, Hugo de Paganis. The founder and the first Grand Master of the Order of Knights Templar. He was born at Troyes, in the kingdom of Naples. Having, with eight others, established the Order at Jerusalem, in 1118 he visited Europe, where, through his representations, its reputation and wealth and the number of its followers were greatly increased. In 1129 he returned to Jerusalem, where he was received with great distinction, but shortly afterward died, and was succeeded in the Grand Mastership by Robert de Craon, surnamed the Burgundian.

P. D. E. P. Letters placed on the ring of profession of the Order of the Temple, being the initials of the Latin sentence, *Pro Deo et Patria,* i. e., For God and my country.

Peace. The spirit of Freemasonry is antagonistic to war. Its tendency is to unite all men in one brotherhood, whose ties must necessarily be weakened by all dissension. Hence, as Bro. Albert Pike says, "Masonry is the great peace society of the world. Wherever it exists, it struggles to prevent international difficulties and disputes, and to bind republics, kingdoms, and empires together in one great band of peace and amity."

Pectoral. Belonging to the breast; from the Latin *pectus,* the breast. The heart has always been considered the seat of fortitude and courage, and hence by this word is suggested to the Mason certain symbolic instructions in relation to the virtue of fortitude. In the earliest lectures of the last century it was called one of the "principal signs," and had this hieroglyphic, X; but in the modern rituals the hieroglyphic has become obsolete, and the word is appropriated to one of the perfect points of entrance.

Pectoral of the High Priest. The breastplate worn by the high priest of the Jews was so called from *pectus,* the breast, upon which it rested. (See *Breastplate.*)

Pedal. Belonging to the feet, from the Latin *pedes,* the feet. The just man is he who, firmly planting his feet on the principles of right, is as immovable as a rock, and can be thrust from his upright position neither by the allurements of flattery, nor the frowns of arbitrary power. And hence by this word is suggested to the Mason certain symbolic instructions in relation to the virtue of justice. Like "Pectoral," this word was assigned, in the oldest rituals, to the principal signs of a Mason, having < for its hieroglyphic; but in the modern lectures it is one of the perfect points of entrance, and the hieroglyphic is no longer used.

Pedestal. The pedestal is the lowest part or base of a column on which the shaft is placed. In a Lodge, there are supposed to be three columns, the column of Wisdom in the east, the column of Strength in the west, and the column of Beauty in the south. These columns are not generally erected in the Lodge, but their pedestals always are, and at each pedestal sits one of the three superior officers of the Lodge. Hence we often hear such expressions as these, *advancing to the pedestal,* or *standing before the pedestal,* to signify advancing to or standing before the seat of the Worshipful Master. The custom in some Lodges of placing tables or desks before the three principal officers is, of course, incorrect. They should, for the reason above assigned, be representations of the pedestals of columns, and should be painted to represent marble or stone.

Pedum. Literally, a shepherd's crook, and hence sometimes used in ecclesiology for the bishop's crozier. In the statutes of the Order of the Temple at Paris, it is prescribed that the Grand Master shall carry a "pedum magistrale seu patriarchale." But the better word for the staff of the Grand Master of the Templars is *baculus,* which see.

Peetash. The demon of calumny in the religious system of Zoroaster, Persia.

Pelasgian Religion. The Pelasgians were the oldest, if not the aboriginal, inhabitants of Greece. Their religion differed from that of the Hellenes, who succeeded them, in being less poetical, less mythical, and more abstract. We know little of their religious worship except by conjecture; but we may suppose it resembled in some respects the doctrines of what Dr. Oliver calls the Primitive Freemasonry. Creuzer thinks that the Pelasgians were either a nation of priests or a nation ruled by priests.

Peleg. פלג, *Division.* A son of Eber. In his day the world was divided. A significant word in the high degrees. In the Noachite, or Twentieth Degree of the Scottish Rite, there is a singular legend of Peleg, which of course is altogether mythical, in which he is represented as the architect of the Tower of Babel.

Pelican. The pelican feeding her young with her blood is a prominent symbol of the Eighteenth or Rose Croix Degree of the Ancient and Accepted Scottish Rite, and was adopted as such from the fact that the pelican, in ancient Christian art, was considered as an emblem of the Savior. Now this symbolism of the pelican, as a representative of the Savior, is almost universally supposed to be derived from the common belief that the pelican feeds her young with her blood, as the Savior shed his blood for

mankind; and hence the bird is always represented as sitting on her nest, and surrounded by her brood of young ones, who are dipping their bills into a wound in their mother's breast. But this is not the exact idea of the symbolism, which really refers to the resurrection, and is, in this point of view, more applicable to our Lord, as well as to the Masonic degree of which the resurrection is a doctrine.

In an ancient *Bestiarium*, or Natural History, in the Royal Library at Brussels, cited by Larwood and Hotten in a recent work on *The History of Sign-Boards*, this statement is made: "The pelican is very fond of his young ones, and when they are born and begin to grow, they rebel in their nest against their parent, and strike him with their wings, flying about him, and beat him so much till they wound him in his eyes. Then the father strikes and kills them. And the mother is of such a nature that she comes back to the nest on the third day, and sits down upon her dead young ones, and opens her side with her bill and pours her blood over them, and so resuscitates them from death; for the young ones, by their instinct, receive the blood as soon as it comes out of the mother, and drink it."

The *Ortus Vocabulorum*, compiled early in the fifteenth century, gives the fable more briefly: "It is said, if it be true, that the pelican kills its young, and grieves for them for three days. Then she wounds herself, and with the aspersione of her blood resuscitates her children." And the writer cites, in explanation, the verses

"Ut pelicanu. fit matris sanguine sanus,
Sic Sancti sumus nos omnes sanguine nati."

i. e., "As the Pelican is restored by the blood of its mother, so are we all born by the blood of the Holy One," that is, of Christ.

St. Jerome gives the same story, as an illustration of the destruction of man by the old serpent, and his salvation by the blood of Christ. And Shelton, in an old work entitled the *Armorie of Birds*, expresses the same sentiment in the following words:

"Then said the pelican,
When my birds be slain,
With my blood I them revive;
Scripture doth record
The same did our Lord,
And rose from death to life."

This romantic story was religiously believed as a fact of natural history in the earliest ages of the church. Hence the pelican was very naturally adopted as a symbol of the resurrection and, by consequence, of him whose resurrection is, as Cruden terms it, "the cause, pattern, and argument of ours."

But in the course of time the original legend was, to some extent, corrupted, and a simpler one was adopted, namely, that the pelican fed her young with her own blood merely as a means of sustenance, and the act of maternal love was then referred to Christ as shedding his blood for the sins of the world. In this view of the symbolism, Pugin has said that the pelican is "an emblem of our Blessed Lord shedding his blood for mankind, and therefore a most appropriate symbol to be introduced on all vessels or ornaments connected with the Blessed Sacrament." And in the *Antiquities of Durham Abbey*, we learn that "over the high altar of Durham Abbey hung a rich and most sumptuous canopy for the Blessed Sacrament to hang within it, whereon stood a pelican, all of silver, upon the height of the said canopy, very finely gilt, giving her blood to her young ones, in token that Christ gave his blood for the sins of the world."

But I think the true theory of the pelican is, that by restoring her young ones to life by her blood, she symbolizes the resurrection. The old symbologists said, after Jerome, that the male pelican, who destroyed his young, represents the serpent, or evil principle, which brought death into the world; while the mother, who resuscitates them, is the representative of that Son of Man of whom it is declared, "except ye drink of his blood, ye have no life in you."

And hence the pelican is very appropriately assumed as a symbol in Masonry, whose great object is to teach by symbolism the doctrine of the resurrection, and especially in that sublime degree of the Scottish Rite wherein, the old Temple being destroyed and the old Word being lost, a new temple and a new word spring forth—all of which is but the great allegory of the destruction by death and the resurrection to eternal life.

Pellegrini, Marquis of. One of the pseudonyms assumed by Joseph Balsamo, better known as Count Cagliostro (*q. v.*).

Penal Sign. That which refers to a penalty.

Penalty. The adversaries of Freemasonry have found, or rather invented, abundant reasons for denouncing the Institution; but on nothing have they more strenuously and fondly lingered than on the accusation that it makes, by horrid and impious ceremonies, all its members the willing or unwilling executioners of those who prove recreant to their vows and violate the laws which they are stringently bound to observe. Even a few timid and uninstructed Masons have been found who were disposed to believe that there was some weight in this objection. The fate of Morgan, apocryphal as it undoubtedly was, has been quoted as an instance of Masonic punishment inflicted by the regulations of the Order; and, notwithstanding the solemn asseverations of the most intelligent Masons to the contrary, men have been found, and still are to be found, who seriously entertain the opinion that every member of the Fraternity becomes, by the ceremonies of his initiation and by the nature of the vows which he has taken, an active Nemesis of the Order, bound by some unholy promise to avenge the Institution upon any treacherous or unfaithful brother. All of this arises from a total misapprehension, in the minds of those who are thus led astray, of the true character and design of vows or oaths which are accompanied by an imprecation. It is well, therefore, for the information both of our adversaries—who may thus be deprived of any further excuse for slander, and of our friends—who will be relieved of any continued burden on their consciences, that we should show that, however solemn may be the promises of secrecy, of obedience, and of charity which are required from our initiates, and however they may be guarded by the sanctions of punishment upon their offenders, they never were intended to impose upon any brother the painful and—so far as the laws of the country are concerned—the illegal task of vindicating the outrage committed by the violator. The only Masonic penalty inflicted by the Order upon a traitor, is the scorn and detestation of the Craft whom he has sought to betray.

But that this subject may be thoroughly understood, it is necessary that some consideration should be given to oaths generally, and to the character of the imprecations by which they are accompanied.

The obsecration, or imprecation, is that part of every oath which constitutes its sanction, and which consists in calling some superior power to witness the declaration or promise made, and invoking his protection for or anger against the person making it, according as the said declaration or promise is observed or violated. This obsecration has, from the earliest times, constituted a part of the oath—and an important part, too—among every people, varying, of course, according to the varieties of religious beliefs and modes of adoration. Thus, among the Jews, we find such obsecrations as these: *Co yagnashsh li Elohim*, "So may God do to me." A very common obsecration among the Greeks was, *isto Zeus* or *theon marturomai*, "May Jove stand by me," or "I call God to witness." And the Romans, among an abundance of other obsecrations, often said, *dii me perdant*, "May the gods destroy me," or *ne vivam*, "May I die."

These modes of obsecration were accompanied, to make them more solemn and sacred, by certain symbolic forms. Thus the Jews caused the person who swore to hold up his right hand toward heaven, by which action he was supposed to signify that he appealed to God to witness the truth of what he had averred or the sincerity of his intention to fulfil the promise that he had made. So Abraham said to the King of Sodom, "I have lift up my hand unto the Lord, . . . that I will not take anything that is thine." Sometimes, in taking an oath of fealty, the inferior placed his hand under the thigh of his lord, as in the case of Eliezer and Abraham, related in the 24th chapter of Genesis. Among the Greeks and Romans, the person swearing placed his hands, or sometimes only the right hand, upon the altar, or upon the victims when, as was not unusual, the oath was accompanied by a sacrifice, or upon some other sacred thing. In the military oath, for instance, the soldiers placed their hands upon the *signa*, or standards.

The obsecration, with an accompanying form of solemnity, was indeed essential to the oath among the ancients, because the crime of perjury was not generally looked upon by them in the same light in which it is viewed by the moderns. It was, it is true, considered as a heinous crime, but a crime not so much against society as against the gods, and its punishment was supposed to be left to the deity whose sanctity had been violated by the adjuration of his name to a false oath or broken vow. Hence, Cicero says that "death was the divine punishment of perjury, but only dishonor was its human penalty." And therefore the crime of giving false testimony under oath was not punished in any higher degree than it would have been had it been given without the solemnity of an oath. Swearing was entirely a matter of conscience, and the person who was guilty of false swearing, where his testimony did not affect the rights or interests of others, was considered as responsible to the deity alone for his perjury.

The explicit invocation of God as a witness to the truth of the thing said, or, in promissory oaths, to the faithful observance of the act promised, the obsecration of Divine punishment upon the jurator if what he swore to be true should prove to be false, or if the vow made should be thereafter violated, and the solemn form of lifting up the hand to heaven or placing it upon the altar or the sacred victims, must necessarily have given confidence to the truth of the attestation, and must have been required by the hearers as some sort of safeguard or security for the confidence they were called upon to exercise. This seems to have been the true reason for the ancient practise of solemn obsecration in the administration of oaths.

Among modern nations, the practise has been continued, and from the ancient usage of invoking the names of the gods and of placing the hands of the person swearing upon their altars, we derive the present method of sanctifying every oath by the attestation contained in the phrase "So help me God," and the concluding form of kissing the Holy Scriptures.

And now the question naturally occurs as to what is the true intent of this obsecration, and what practical operation is expected to result from it. In other words, what is the nature of a penalty attached to an oath, and how is it to be enforced? When the ancient Roman, in attesting with the solemnity of an oath to the truth of what he had just said or was about to say, concluded with the formula, "May the gods destroy me," it is evident that he simply meant to say that he was so convinced of the truth of what he had said that he was entirely willing that his destruction by the gods whom he had invoked should be the condition consequent upon his falsehood. He had no notion that he was to become outlawed among his fellow-creatures, and that it should be not only the right, but the duty, of any man to destroy him. His crime would have been one against the Divine law, and subject only to a Divine punishment.

In modern times, perjury is made a penal offense against human laws, and its punishment is inflicted by human tribunals. But here the punishment of the crime is entirely different from that inferred by the obsecration which terminates the oath. The words "So help me God," refer exclusively to the withdrawal of Divine aid and assistance from the jurator in the case of his proving false, and not to the human punishment which society would inflict.

In like manner, we may say of what are called Masonic penalties, that they refer in no case to any kind of human punishment; that is to say, to any kind of punishment which is to be inflicted by human hand or instrumentality. The true punishments of Masonry affect neither life nor limb. They are expulsion and suspension only. But those persons are wrong, be they mistaken friends or malignant enemies, who suppose or assert that there is any other sort of penalty which a Mason recreant to his vows is subjected to by the laws of the Order, or that it is either the right or duty of any Mason to inflict such penalty on an offending brother. The obsecration of a Mason simply means that if he violates his vows or betrays his trust he is worthy of such penalty, and that if such penalty were inflicted on him it would be but just and proper. "May I die," said the ancient, "if this be not true, or if I keep not this vow." Not may any man put me to death, nor is any man required to put me to death, but only, if I so act, then would I be worthy of death. The ritual penalties of Masonry, supposing such to be, are in the hands not of man, but of God, and are to be inflicted by God, and not by man.

Bro. Fort says, in the 29th chapter of his *Early History and Antiquities of Freemasonry*, that "Penalties inflicted upon convicts of certain grades during the Middle Ages, were terrible and inhuman.

"The most cruel punishment awaited him who broke into and robbed a Pagan temple. According to a law of the Frisians, such desecration was redressed by dragging the criminal to the seashore and burying the body at a point in the sands where the tide daily ebbed and flowed." (*Lex Frision.*, Add. Sap., Tit. 12.)

"A creditor was privileged to subject his delinquent debtor to the awful penalty of having the flesh torn from his breast and fed to birds of prey. Convicts were frequently adjudged by the ancient Norse code to have their hearts torn out." (Grimm, *Deutsche Rechts-Alterthümer*, p. 690. And for the following, see pp. 693 and 700.) "The oldest death penalties of the Scandinavians prescribed that the body should be exposed to fowls of the air to feed upon. Sometimes it was decreed that the victim be disemboweled, his body burnt to ashes and scattered as dust to the winds. Judges of the secret Vehmgericht passed sentences of death as follows: 'Your body and flesh to the beasts of the field, to the birds of the air, and to the fishes in the stream.' The judicial executioner, in carrying into effect this decree, severed the body in twain, so that, to use the literal text, 'the air might strike together between the two parts.' The tongue was oftentimes torn out as a punishment. A law of the early Roman Empire, known as *ex Jure Orientis Cæsareo*, enacted that any person, suitor at law or witness, having sworn upon the evangelists, and proving to be a perjurer, should have the tongue cut from its roots. A cord about the neck was used symbolically, in criminal courts, to denote that the accused was worthy of the extreme penalty of law by hanging or decapitation. When used upon the person of a freeman, it signified a slight degree of subjection or servitude." (Pp. 318–320.)

Some eminent brethren of the Fraternity insist that the penalty had its origin in the manner in which the lamb was sacrificed under the charge of the Captain of the Temple, who directed the priests: and said, "Come and cast lots." "Who is to slaughter?" "Who is to sprinkle?" "Go and see if the time for slaughter approaches?" "Is it light in the whole East, even to Hebron?" and when the priest said "Yes," he was directed to "go and bring the lamb from the lamb-chamber"; this was in the northwest corner of the court. The lamb was brought to the north of the altar, its head southward and its face northward. The lamb was then slaughtered; a hole was made in its side, and thus it was hung up. The priest skinned it downward until he came to the breast, then he cut off the head, and finished the skinning; he tore out the heart; subsequently he cleft the body, and it became all open before him; he took out the intestines, etc.; and the various portions were divided as they had cast lots. (*The Talmud*, Joseph Barclay, LL.D.)

Pencil. In the English system this is one of the working-tools of a Master Mason, and is intended symbolically to remind us that our words and actions are observed and recorded by the Almighty Architect, to whom we must give an account of our conduct through life. In the American system the pencil is not specifically recognized. The other English working-tools of a Master Mason are the skirrit and compasses.

In the French Rite "to hold the pencil," *tenir le crayon*, is to discharge the functions of a secretary during the communication of a lodge.

Penitential Sign. Called also the Supplicatory Sign. It is the third sign in the

English Royal Arch system. It denotes that frame of heart and mind without which our prayers and oblations will not obtain acceptance; in other words, it is a symbol of humility.

Pennsylvania. [The early history of Freemasonry in this State is wrapped in obscurity; the first mention of it as yet discovered is in the *Pennsylvania Gazette* for December 5–8, 1730, which contains the following: "As there are several Lodges of Freemasons erected in this Province, and People have lately been much amus'd with Conjectures concerning them; we think the following account of Freemasonry from London will not be unacceptable to our readers," and then follows a Masonic catechism. Benjamin Franklin, the editor of the paper, was not then a Mason, but became one in the following year, and makes frequent references to the Craft in the *Gazette*, from which we learn that he was appointed J. G. W. by Grand Master Allen in June, 1732, and elected Grand Master of this Grand Lodge of Pennsylvania in 1734.

From this it is quite plain that there were Masonic Lodges in Pennsylvania in 1730 and a Provincial Grand Lodge there in 1732, and it seems fairly certain that these early Lodges were formed by brethren from the Mother Country acting on their own authority.

In 1743 Thomas Oxnard of Boston was appointed by the Grand Master of England to be Provincial Grand Master of all North America, and in 1749 he appointed Benjamin Franklin to be Provincial Grand Master of Pennsylvania.

In 1755 there were three Lodges in Philadelphia, and in 1758 a Lodge was warranted there by the "Ancients," followed by another in 1761, and in 1764 authority was granted by the "Ancients" for forming a Provincial Grand Lodge in Philadelphia, which in 1786 became the Grand Lodge of Pennsylvania.—E. L. H.]

The Grand Chapter of Pennsylvania was established in 1795. The Grand Chapter was at first only an integral part of the Grand Lodge, but in 1824 it became an independent body, except so far as that members of the Grand Lodge, who were Royal Arch Masons, were declared to be members of the Grand Chapter.

The Royal and Select degrees were formerly conferred in Pennsylvania by the Chapters, but on October 16, 1847, a Grand Council was organized.

A Grand Encampment, independent of the General Grand Encampment of the United States, was organized on February 16, 1814. On April 14, 1854, a Grand Commandery was organized under the authority of the Grand Encampment of the United States, and in February, 1857, both of these bodies united to form the present Grand Commandery of Pennsylvania.

Pennsylvania Work. The method of Entering, Passing, and Raising candidates in the Lodges of Pennsylvania differs so materially from that practised in the other States of the Union, that it cannot be considered as a part of the American Rite as first taught by Webb, but rather as an independent, Pennsylvania modification of the York Rite of England. Indeed, the Pennsylvania system of work much more resembles the English than the American. Its ritual is simple and didactic, like the former, and is almost entirely without the impressive dramatization of the latter. Bro. Vaux, a Past Grand Master of Pennsylvania, thus speaks of the Masonic work of his State with pardonable, although not with impartial, commendations: "The Pennsylvania work is sublime from its simplicity. That it is the ancient work is best shown conclusively, however, from this single fact, it is so simple, so free from those displays of modern inventions to attract the attention, without enlightening, improving, or cultivating the mind. In this work every word has its significance. Its types and symbols are but the language in which truth is conveyed. These are to be studied to be understood. In the spoken language no synonyms are permitted. In the ceremonial no innovations are tolerated. In the ritual no modern verbiage is allowed."

Penny. In the parable read in the Mark Degree a penny is the amount given to each of the laborers in the vineyard for his day's labor. Hence, in the ritual, a penny a day is said to be the wages of a Mark Master. In several passages of the authorized version of the New Testament, *penny* occurs as a translation of the Greek, *δηνάριον*, which was intended as the equivalent of the Roman *denarius*. This was the chief silver coin of the Romans from the beginning of the coinage of the city to the early part of the third century. Indeed, the name continued to be employed in the coinage of the continental States, which imitated that of the Byzantine empire, and was adopted by the Anglo-Saxons. The specific value of each of so many coins, going under the same name, cannot be ascertained with any precision. In its Masonic use, the penny is simply a symbol of the reward of faithful labor. The smallness of the sum, whatever may have been its exact value, to our modern impressions is apt to give a false idea of the liberality of the owner. Dr. Lightfoot, in his essay on a *Fresh Revision of the New Testament*, remarks: "It is unnecessary to ask what impression the mention of this sum will leave on the minds of an uneducated peasant or shopkeeper of the present day. Even at the time when our version was made, and when wages were lower, it must have seemed wholly inadequate." However improper the translation is, it can have no importance in the Masonic application of the parable, where the "penny" is, as has already been said, only a symbol, meaning any reward or compensation.

Pentacle, The. The "*pentaculum Salomonis*," or magical pentalpha, not to be confounded with Solomon's seal. The pentacle is frequently referred to in Hermetic formulæ.

Pentagon. A geometrical figure of five sides and five angles. It is the third figure from the exterior, in the camp of the Sublime Princes of the Royal Secret, or Thirty-second Degree of the Scottish Rite. In the Egyptian Rite of Cagliostro, he constructed, with much formality, an implement called the "sacred pentagon," and which, being distributed to his disciples, gave, as he affirmed, to each one the power of holding spiritual intercourse.

Pentagram. From the Greek *pente*, five, and *gramma*, a letter. In the science of magic the pentalpha is called the holy and mysterious pentagram. Eliphas Levi says (*Dog. et Rituel de la Haute Magie*, ii., 55) that the pentagram is the star of the Magians; it is the sign of the word made flesh; and according to the direction of its rays, that is, as it points upward with one point or with two, it represents the good or the evil principle, order or disorder; the blessed lamb of Ormuzd and of St. John, or the accursed god of Mendes; initiation or profanation; Lucifer or Vesper; the morning or the evening star; Mary or Lilith; victory or death; light or darkness. (See *Pentalpha*.)

Pentalpha. The triple triangle, or the pentalpha of Pythagoras, is so called from the Greek πεντε, *pente*, five, and αλφα, *alpha*, the letter A, because in its configuration it presents the form of that letter in five different positions. It was a doctrine of Pythagoras, that all things proceeded from numbers, and the number five, as being formed by the union of the first odd and the first even, was deemed of peculiar value; and hence Cornelius Agrippa says (*Philos. Occult.*) of this figure, that, "by virtue of the number five, it has great command over evil spirits because of its five double triangles and its five acute angles within and its five obtuse angles without, so that this interior pentangle contains in it many great mysteries." The disciples of Pythagoras, who were indeed its real inventors, placed within each of its interior angles one of the letters of the Greek word ΥΓΙΕΙΑ, or the Latin one SALUS, both of which signify *health*; and thus it was made the talisman of health. They placed it at the beginning of their epistles as a greeting to invoke secure health to their correspondent. But its use was not confined to the disciples of Pythagoras. As a talisman, it was employed all over the East as a charm to resist evil spirits. Moné says that it has been found in Egypt on the statue of the god Anubis. Lord Brougham says, in his *Italy*, that it was used by Antiochus Epiphanes, and a writer in *Notes and Queries* (3 Ser., ix., 511) says that he has found it on the coins of Lysimmachus. On old British and Gaulish coins it is often seen beneath the feet of the sacred and mythical horse, which was the ensign of the ancient Saxons. The Druids wore it on their sandals as a symbol of Deity, and hence the Germans call the figure "Druttenfuss," a word originally signifying *Druid's foot*, but which, in the gradual corruptions of language, is now made to mean *Witchs's foot*. Even at the present day it retains its hold upon the minds of the common people of Germany, and is drawn on or affixed to cradles, thresholds of houses, and stable-doors, to keep off witches and elves.

The early Christians referred it to the five wounds of the Savior, because, when properly inscribed upon the representation of a human body, the five points will respectively extend to and touch the side, the two hands, and the two feet.

The Medieval Masons considered it a symbol of deep wisdom, and it is found among the architectural ornaments of most of the ecclesiastical edifices of the Middle Ages.

But as a Masonic symbol it peculiarly claims attention from the fact that it forms the outlines of the *five-pointed star*, which is typical of the bond of brotherly love that unites the whole Fraternity. It is in this view that the pentalpha or triple triangle is referred to in Masonic symbolism as representing the intimate union which existed between our three ancient Grand Masters, and which is commemorated by the living pentalpha at the closing of every Royal Arch Chapter.

Many writers have confounded the pentalpha with the seal of Solomon, or shield of David. This error is almost inexcusable in Oliver, who constantly commits it, because his Masonic and archeological researches should have taught him the difference, Solomon's seal being a double, interlaced triangle, whose form gives the outline of a star of six points.

Perau, Gabriel Louis Calabre. A man of letters, an Abbé, and a member of the Society of the Sorbonne. He was born at Semur, in Auxois, in 1700, and died at Paris, March 31, 1767. De Feller (*Biog. Univ.*) speaks of his uprightness and probity, his frankness, and sweetness of disposition which endeared him to many friends. Certainly, the only work which gives him a place in Masonic history indicates a gentleness and moderation of character with which we can find no fault. In general literature, he was distinguished as the continuator of d'Avrigny's *Vies des Hommes illustres de la France;* which, however, a loss of sight prevented him from completing. In 1742, he published at Geneva a work entitled *Le Secret des Franc-Maçons*. This work at its first appearance attracted much attention and went through many editions, the title being sometimes changed to a more attractive one by booksellers. The Abbé Larudan attempted to palm off his libelous and malignant work on the Abbé Perau, but without success; for while the work of Larudan is marked with the bitterest malignity to the Order of Freemasonry, that of Perau is simply a detail of the ceremonies and ritual of Masonry as then practised, under the guise of friendship.

Perfect Ashlar. See *Ashlar.*

Perfect Initiates, Rite of. A name given to the Egyptian Rite when first established at Lyons by Cagliostro.

Perfect Irish Master. (*Parfait Maître Irlandais.*) One of the degrees given in the Irish Colleges instituted by Ramsay.

Perfect Lodge. See *Just Lodge.*

Perfect Master. (*Maître Parfait.*) The Fifth Degree in the Ancient and Accepted Scottish Rite. The ceremonies of this degree were originally established as a grateful tribute of respect to a worthy departed brother. The officers of the Lodge are a Master, who represents Adoniram, the Inspector of the Works at Mount Lebanon, and one Warden. The symbolic color of the degree is green, to remind the Perfect Master that, being dead in vice, he must hope to revive in virtue. His jewel is a compass extended sixty degrees, to teach him that he should act within measure, and ever pay due regard to justice and equity.

The apron is white, with a green flap; and in the middle of the apron must be embroidered or painted, within three circles, a cubical stone, in the center of which the letter J is inscribed, according to the old rituals; but the Samaritan *yod* and *he*, according to the ritual of the Southern Jurisdiction.

Delaunay, in his *Thuileur de l'Ecossisme*, gives the Tetragrammaton in this degree, and says the degree should more properly be called Past Master, *Ancien Maître*, because the Tetragrammaton makes it in some sort the complement of the Master's Degree. But the Tetragrammaton is not found in any of the approved rituals, and Delaunay's theory falls therefore to the ground. But besides, to complete the Master's with this degree would be to confuse all the symbolism of the Ineffable degrees, which really conclude with the Fourteenth.

Perfect Prussian. (*Parfait Prussien.*) A degree invented at Geneva, in 1770, as a second part of the Order of Noachites.

Perfect Stone. A name frequently given to the cubic stone discovered in the Thirteenth Degree of Perfection, the tenth of the Ineffable Series. It denotes justice and firmness, with all the moral lessons and duties in which the mystic cube is calculated to instruct us.

Perfect Union, Lodge of. A Lodge at Rennes, in France, where the Rite of Elect of Truth was instituted. (See *Elect of Truth, Rite of.*)

Perfection. The Ninth and last degree of Fessler's Rite. (See *Fessler, Rite of.*)

Perfectionists. The name by which Weishaupt first designated the Order which he founded in Bavaria, and which he subsequently changed for that of the Illuminati.

Perfection, Lodge of. The Lodge in which the Fourteenth Degree of the Ancient and Accepted Scottish Rite is conferred. In England and America this degree is called Grand Elect Perfect and Sublime Mason, but the French designate it Grand Scottish Mason of the Sacred Vault of James VI., or *Grand écossais de la Voûte Sacrée du Jacques VI.* This is one of the evidences—and a very pregnant one—of the influence exercised by the exiled Stuarts and their adherents on the Masonry of that time in making it an instrument for the restoration of James II., and then of his son, to the throne of England.

This degree, as concluding all reference to the first Temple, has been called the ultimate degree of ancient Masonry. It is the last of what is technically styled the Ineffable degrees, because their instructions relate to the Ineffable word.

Its place of meeting is called the Sacred Vault. Its principal officers are a Thrice Puissant Grand Master, two Grand Wardens, a Grand Treasurer, and Grand Secretary. In the first organization of the Rite in this country, the Lodges of Perfection were called "Sublime Grand Lodges," and, hence, the word "Grand" is still affixed to the title of the officers.

The following mythical history is connected with and related in this degree.

When the Temple was finished, the Masons who had been employed in constructing it acquired immortal honor. Their Order became more uniformly established and regulated than it had been before. Their caution and reserve in admitting new members produced respect, and merit alone was required of the candidate. With these principles instilled into their minds, many of the Grand Elect left the Temple after its dedication, and, dispersing themselves among the neighboring nations, instructed all who applied and were found worthy in the sublime degrees of Ancient Craft Masonry.

The Temple was completed in the year of the world 3000. Thus far, the wise King of Israel had behaved worthy of himself, and gained universal admiration; but in process of time, when he had advanced in years, his understanding became impaired; he grew deaf to the voice of the Lord, and was strangely irregular in his conduct. Proud of having erected an edifice to his Maker, and intoxicated with his great power, he plunged into all manner of licentiousness and debauchery, and profaned the Temple, by offering to the idol Moloch that incense which should have been offered only to the living God.

The Grand Elect and Perfect Masons

saw this, and were sorely grieved, afraid that his apostasy would end in some dreadful consequences, and bring upon them those enemies whom Solomon had vaingloriously and wantonly defied. The people, copying the vices and follies of their King, became proud and idolatrous, and neglected the worship of the true God for that of idols.

As an adequate punishment for this defection, God inspired the heart of Nebuchadnezzar, King of Babylon, to take vengeance on the kingdom of Israel. This prince sent an army with Nebuzaradan, Captain of the Guards, who entered Judah with fire and sword, took and sacked the city of Jerusalem, razed its walls, and destroyed the Temple. The people were carried captive to Babylon, and the conquerors took with them all the vessels of silver and gold. This happened four hundred and seventy years, six months, and ten days after its dedication.

When, in after times, the princes of Christendom entered into a league to free the Holy Land from the oppression of the infidels, the good and virtuous Masons, anxious for the success of so pious an undertaking, voluntarily offered their services to the confederates, on condition that they should be permitted a chief of their own election, which was granted; they accordingly rallied under their standard and departed.

The valor and fortitude of these elected knights was such that they were admired by, and took the lead of, all the princes of Jerusalem, who, believing that their mysteries inspired them with courage and fidelity in the cause of virtue and religion, became desirous of being initiated. Upon being found worthy, their desires were complied with; and thus the royal art, meeting the approbation of great and good men, became popular and honorable, was diffused through their various dominions, and has continued to spread through a succession of ages to the present day.

The symbolic color of this degree is red—emblematic of fervor, constancy, and assiduity. Hence, the Masonry of this degree was formerly called Red Masonry on the Continent of Europe.

The jewel of the degree is a pair of compasses extended on an arc of ninety degrees, surmounted by a crown, and with a sun in the center. In the Southern Jurisdiction the sun is on one side and a five-pointed star on the other.

The apron is white with red flames, bordered with blue, and having the jewel painted on the center and the stone of foundation on the flap.

Perfection, Rite of. In 1754, the Chevalier de Bonneville established a Chapter of the high degrees at Paris, in the College of Jesuits of Clermont, hence called the Chapter of Clermont. The system of Masonry he there practised received the name of the Rite of Perfection, or Rite of Heredom. The College of Clermont was, says Rebold (*Hist. de 3 G. L.*, 46), the asylum of the adherents of the house of Stuart, and hence the Rite is to some extent tinctured with Stuart Masonry. It consisted of twenty-five degrees, as follows: 1. Apprentice; 2. Fellow-Craft; 3. Master; 4. Secret Master; 5. Perfect Master; 6. Intimate Secretary; 7. Intendant of the Building; 8. Provost and Judge; 9. Elect of Nine; 10. Elect of Fifteen; 11. Illustrious Elect, Chief of the Twelve Tribes; 12. Grand Master Architect; 13. Royal Arch; 14. Grand, Elect, Ancient, Perfect Master; 15. Knight of the Sword; 16. Prince of Jerusalem; 17. Knight of the East and West; 18. Rose Croix Knight; 19. Grand Pontiff; 20. Grand Patriarch; 21. Grand Master of the Key of Masonry; 22. Prince of Libanus; 23. Sovereign Prince Adept Chief of the Grand Consistory; 24. Illustrious Knight, Commander of the Black and White Eagle; 25. Most Illustrious Sovereign Prince of Masonry, Grand Knight, Sublime Commander of the Royal Secret. It will be seen that the degrees of this Rite are the same as those of the Council of Emperors of the East and West, which was established four years later, and to which the Chapter of Clermont gave way. Of course, they are the same, so far as they go, as those of the Ancient and Accepted Scottish Rite which succeeded the Council of Emperors.

The distinguishing principle of this Rite is, that Freemasonry was derived from Templarism, and that consequently every Freemason was a Knight Templar. It was there that the Baron von Hund was initiated, and from it, through him, proceeded the Rite of Strict Observance; although he discarded the degrees and retained only the Templar theory.

Perignan. When the Elu degrees were first invented, the legend referred to an unknown person, a tiller of the soil, to whom King Solomon was indebted for the information which led to the discovery of the craftsmen who had committed the crime recorded in the Third Degree. This unknown person, at first designated as "l'inconnu," afterward received the name of Perignan, and a degree between the *elu of nine* and the *elu of fifteen* was instituted, which was called the "Elu of Perignan," and which became the Sixth Degree of the Adonhiramite Rite. The derivation or radical meaning of the word is unknown, but it may contain, as do many other words in the high degrees, a reference to the adherents, or to the enemies, of the exiled house of Stuart, for whose sake several of these degrees were established. (See *Elect of Perignan*.)

Periods of the Grand Architect. See *Six Periods*.

Perjury. In the municipal law perjury is defined to be a wilful false swearing to a material matter, when an oath has been administered by lawful authority. The violation of vows or promissory oaths taken before one who is not legally authorized to administer them, that is to say, one who is not a magistrate, does not in law involve the crime of perjury. Such is the technical definition of the law; but the moral sense of mankind does not assent to such a doctrine, and considers perjury, as the root of the word indicates, the doing of that which one has sworn not to do, or the omitting to do that which he has sworn to do. The old Romans seem to have taken a sensible view of the crime of perjury. Among them oaths were not often administered, and, in general, a promise made under oath had no more binding power in a court of justice than it would have had without the oath. False swearing was with them a matter of conscience, and the person who was guilty of it was responsible to the Deity alone. The violation of a promise under oath and of one not under such a form was considered alike, and neither was more liable to human punishment than the other. But perjury was not deemed to be without any kind of punishment. Cicero expressed the Roman sentiment when he said "perjurii pœna divina exitium; humana dedecus—*the divine punishment of perjury is destruction; the human, infamy*." Hence every oath was accompanied by an execration, or an appeal to God to punish the swearer should he falsify his oath. "In the case of other sins," says Archbishop Sharp, "there may be an appeal made to God's mercy, yet in the case of perjury there is none; for he that is perjured hath precluded himself of this benefit, because he hath braved God Almighty, and hath in effect told him to his face that if he was foresworn he should desire no mercy."

It is not right thus to seek to restrict God's mercy, but there can be no doubt that the settlement of the crime lies more with him than with man. Freemasons look in this light on what is called the *penalty*; it is an invocation of God's vengeance on him who takes the vow, should he ever violate it; men's vengeance is confined to the contempt and infamy which the foreswearer incurs.

Pernetti or **Pernety, Antoine Joseph.** Born at Roanne, in France, in 1716. At an early age he joined the Benedictines, but in 1765 applied, with twenty-eight others, for a dispensation of his vows. A short time after, becoming disgusted with the Order, he repaired to Berlin, where Frederick the Great made him his librarian. In a short time he returned to Paris, where the archbishop strove in vain to induce him to reenter his monastery. The parliament supported him in his refusal, and Pernetti continued in the world. Not long after, Pernetti became infected with the mystical theories of Swedenborg, and published a translation of his *Wonders of Heaven and Hell*. He then repaired to Avignon, where, under the influence of his Swedenborgian views, he established an academy of Illuminati, based on the three primitive grades of Masonry, to which he added a mystical one, which he called the *True Mason*. This Rite was subsequently transferred to Montpellier by some of his disciples, and modified in form under the name of the "Academy of True Masons." Pernetti, besides his Masonic labors at Avignon, invented several other Masonic degrees, and to him is attributed the authorship of the degree of Knight of the Sun, now occupying the twenty-eighth place in the Ancient and Accepted Scottish Rite. He was a very learned man and a voluminous writer of versatile talents, and published numerous works on mythology, the fine arts, theology, geography, philosophy, and the mathematical sciences, besides some translations from the Latin. He died at Valence, in Dauphiny, in the year 1800.

Perpendicular. In a geometrical sense, that which is upright and erect, leaning neither one way nor another. In a figurative and symbolic sense, it conveys the signification of Justice, Fortitude, Prudence, and Temperance. Justice, that leans to no side but that of Truth; Fortitude, that yields to no adverse attack; Prudence, that ever pursues the straight path of integrity; and Temperance, that swerves not for appetite nor passion.

Persecutions. Freemasonry, like every other good and true thing, has been subjected at times to suspicion, to misinterpretation, and to actual persecution. Like the church, it has had its martyrs, who, by their devotion and their sufferings, have vindicated its truth and its purity.

With the exception of the United States, where the attacks on the Institution can hardly be called persecutions—not because there was not the will, but because the power to persecute was wanting—all the persecutions of Freemasonry have, for the most part, originated with the Roman Church. "Notwithstanding," says a writer in the *Freemasons' Quarterly Magazine* (1851, p. 141), "the greatest architectural monuments of antiquity were reared by the labors of Masonic gilds, and the Church of Rome owes the structure of her magnificent cathedrals, her exquisite shrines, and her most splendid palaces, to the skill of the wise master-builders of former ages, she has been for four centuries in antagonism to the principles inculcated by the Craft."

Leaving unnoticed the struggles of the corporations of Freemasons in the fifteenth, sixteenth, and seventeenth centuries, we may begin the record with the persecutions to which the Order has been subjected since the revival in 1717.

One of the first persecutions to which Masonry, in its present organization, was subjected, occurred in the year 1735, in Holland. On the 16th of October of that year, a crowd of ignorant fanatics, whose zeal had been enkindled by the denunciations of some of the clergy, broke into a house in Amsterdam, where a Lodge was accustomed to be held, and destroyed all the furniture and ornaments of the Lodge. The States General, yielding to the popular excitement, or rather desirous of giving no occasion for its action, prohibited the future meetings of the Lodges. One, however, continuing, regardless of the edict, to meet at a private house, the members were arrested and brought before the Court of Justice. Here, in the presence of the whole city, the Masters and Wardens defended themselves with great dexterity; and while acknowledging their inability to prove the innocence of their Institution by a public exposure of their secret doctrines, they freely offered to receive and initiate any person in the confidence of the magistrates, and who could then give them information upon which they might depend, relative to the true designs of the Institution. The proposal was acceded to, and the town clerk was chosen. He was immediately initiated, and his report so pleased his superiors, that all the magistrates and principal persons of the city became members and zealous patrons of the Order.

In France, the fear of the authorities that the Freemasons concealed, within the recesses of their Lodges, designs hostile to the government, gave occasion to an attempt, in 1737, on the part of the police, to prohibit the meeting of the Lodges. But this unfavorable disposition did not long continue, and the last instance of the interference of the government with the proceedings of the Masonic body was in June, 1745, when the members of a Lodge, meeting at the Hotel de Soissons, were dispersed, their furniture and jewels seized, and the landlord amerced in a penalty of three thousand livres.

The persecutions in Germany were owing to a singular cause. The malice of a few females had been excited by their disappointed curiosity. A portion of this disposition they succeeded in communicating to the Empress, Maria Theresa, who issued an order for apprehending all the Masons in Vienna, when assembled in their Lodges. The measure was, however, frustrated by the good sense of the Emperor, Joseph I., who was himself a Mason, and exerted his power in protecting his brethren.

The persecutions of the church in Italy, and other Catholic countries, have been the most extensive and most permanent. On the 28th of April, 1738, Pope Clement XII. issued the famous bull against Freemasons whose authority is still in existence. In this bull, the Roman Pontiff says, "We have learned, and public rumor does not permit us to doubt the truth of the report, that a certain society has been formed, under the name of Freemasons, into which persons of all religions and all sects are indiscriminately admitted, and whose members have established certain laws which bind themselves to each other, and which, in particular, compel their members, under the severest penalties, by virtue of an oath taken on the Holy Scriptures, to preserve an inviolable secrecy in relation to every thing that passes in their meetings." The bull goes on to declare, that these societies have become suspected by the faithful, and that they are hurtful to the tranquillity of the state and to the safety of the soul; and after making use of the now threadbare argument, that if the actions of Freemasons were irreproachable, they would not so carefully conceal them from the light, it proceeds to enjoin all bishops, superiors, and ordinaries to punish the Freemasons "with the penalties which they deserve, as people greatly suspected of heresy, having recourse, if necessary, to the secular arm."

What this delivery to the secular arm means, we are at no loss to discover, from the interpretation given to the bull by Cardinal Firrao in his edict of publication in the beginning of the following year, namely, "that no person shall dare to assemble at any Lodge of the said society, nor be present at any of their meetings, under *pain of death* and confiscation of goods, the said penalty to be without hope of pardon."

The bull of Clement met in France with no congenial spirits to obey it. On the contrary, it was the subject of universal condemnation as arbitrary and unjust, and the parliament of Paris positively refused to enroll it. But in other Catholic countries it was better respected. In Tuscany the persecutions were unremitting. A man named Crudeli was arrested at Florence, thrown into the dungeons of the Inquisition, subjected to torture, and finally sentenced to a long imprisonment, on the charge of having furnished an asylum to a Masonic Lodge. The Grand Lodge of England, upon learning the circumstances, obtained his enlargement, and sent him pecuniary assistance. Francis de Lorraine, who had been initiated at The Hague in 1731, soon after ascended the grand ducal throne, and one of the first acts of his reign was to liberate all the Masons who had been incarcerated by the Inquisition; and still further to evince his respect for the Order, he personally assisted in the constitution of several Lodges at Florence, and in other cities of his dominions.

The other sovereigns of Italy were, however, more obedient to the behests of the holy father, and persecutions continued to rage throughout the peninsula. Nevertheless, Masonry continued to flourish, and in 1751, thirteen years after the emission of the bull of prohibition, Lodges were openly in existence in Tuscany, at Naples, and even in the "eternal city" itself.

The priesthood, whose vigilance had abated under the influence of time, became once more alarmed, and an edict was issued in 1751 by Benedict XIV., who then occupied the papal chair, renewing and enforcing the bull which had been fulminated by Clement.

This, of course, renewed the spirit of persecution. In Spain, one Tournon, a Frenchman, was convicted of practising the rites of Masonry, and after a tedious confinement in the dungeons of the Inquisition, he was finally banished from the kingdom.

In Portugal, at Lisbon, John Coustos, a native of Switzerland, was still more severely treated. He was subjected to the torture, and suffered so much that he was unable to move his limbs for three months. Coustos, with two companions of his reputed crime, was sentenced to the galleys, but was finally released by the interposition of the English ambassador.

In 1745, the Council of Berne, in Switzerland, issued a decree prohibiting, under the severest penalties, the assemblages of Freemasons. In 1757, in Scotland, the Synod of Sterling adopted a resolution debarring all adhering Freemasons from the ordinances of religion. And, as if to prove that fanaticism is everywhere the same, in 1748 the Divan at Constantinople caused a Masonic Lodge to be demolished, its jewels and furniture seized, and its members arrested. They were discharged upon the interposition of the English minister; but the government prohibited the introduction of the Order into Turkey.

America has not been free from the blighting influence of this demon of fanaticism. But the exciting scenes of anti-Masonry are too recent to be treated by the historian with coolness or impartiality. The political party to which this spirit of persecution gave birth was the most abject in its principles, and the most unsuccessful in its efforts, of any that our times have seen. It has passed away; the clouds of anti-Masonry have been, we trust, forever dispersed, and the bright sun of Masonry, once more emerging from its temporary eclipse, is beginning to bless our land with the invigorating heat and light of its meridian rays.

Perseverance. A virtue inculcated, by a peculiar symbol in the Third Degree, in reference to the acquisition of knowledge, and especially the knowledge of the True Word. (See *Patience.*)

Perseverance, Order of. An Adoptive Order established at Paris, in 1771, by several nobles and ladies. It had but little of the Masonic character about it; and, although at the time of its creation it excited considerable sensation, it existed but for a brief period. It was instituted for the purpose of rendering services to humanity. Ragon says (*Tuileur Gen.*, p. 92) that there was kept in the archives of the Order a quarto volume of four hundred leaves, in which was registered all the good deeds of the brethren and sisters. This volume is entitled *Livre d'Honneur de l'Ordre de la Perseverance.* Ragon intimates that this document is still in existence. Thory (*Fondation G. O.*, p. 383) says that there was much mystification about the establishment of the Order in Paris. Its institutors contended that it originated from time immemorial in Poland, a pretension to which the King of Poland lent his sanction. Many persons of distinction, and among them Madame de Genlis, were deceived and became its members.

Persia. Neither the Grand Lodge of England, nor any other of the European Powers, seem ever to have organized Lodges in the kingdom of Persia; yet very strange and somewhat incomprehensible stories are told by credible authorities of the existence either of the Masonic institution, or something very much like it, in that country. In 1808, on November 24th, Askeri Khan, the Ambassador of Persia near the court of France, was received into the Order at Paris by the Mother Lodge of the Philosophic Scottish Rite, on which occasion the distinguished neophyte presented his sword, a pure Damascus blade, to the Lodge, with these remarks: "I promise you, gentlemen, friendship, fidelity, and esteem. I have been told, and I cannot doubt it, that Freemasons were virtuous, charitable, and full of love and attachment for their sovereigns. Permit me to make you a present worthy of true Frenchmen. Receive this sabre, which has served me in twenty-seven battles. May this act of homage convince you of the sentiments with which you have inspired me, and of the gratification that I feel in belonging to your Order." The Ambassador subsequently seems to have taken a great interest in Freemasonry while he remained in France, and consulted with the Venerable of the Lodge on the subject of establishing a Lodge at Ispahan. This is the first account that we have of the connection of any inhabitant of Persia with the Order. Thory, who gives this account (*Act. Lat.*, i., 237), does not tell us whether the project of an Ispahan Lodge was ever executed. But it is probable that on his return home the Ambassador introduced among his friends some knowledge of the Institution, and impressed them with a favorable opinion of it. At all events, the Persians in later times do not seem to have been ignorant of its existence.

Mr. Holmes, in his *Sketches on the Shores of the Caspian*, gives the following as the Persian idea of Freemasonry:

"In the morning we received a visit from the Governor, who seemed rather a dull person, though very polite and civil. He asked a great many questions regarding the *Feramoosh Khoneh*, as they called the Freemasons' Hall in London; which is a complete mystery to all the Persians who have heard of it. Very often, the first question we have been asked is, 'What do they do at the Feramoosh Khoneh? What is it?' They generally believe it to be a most wonderful place, where a man may acquire in one day the wisdom of a thousand years of study; but every one has his own peculiar conjectures concerning it. Some of the Persians who went to England became Freemasons; and their friends complain that they will not tell what they saw at the Hall, and cannot conceive why they should all be so uncommunicative."

And now we have, from the *London Freemason* (June 28, 1873), this further account; but the conjecture as to the time of the introduction of the Order unfortunately wants confirmation:

"Of the Persian officers who are present in Berlin pursuing military studies and making themselves acquainted with Prussian military organization and arrangements, one belongs to the Masonic Order. He is a Mussulman. He seems to have spontaneously sought recognition as a member of the Craft at a Berlin

Lodge, and his claim was allowed only after such an examination as satisfied the brethren that he was one of the brethren. From the statement of this Persian Mason it appears that nearly all the members of the Persian Court belong to the mystic Order, even as German Masonry enjoys the honor of counting the emperor and crown prince among its adherents. The appearance of this Mohammedan Mason in Berlin seems to have excited a little surprise among some of the brethren there, and the surprise would be natural enough to persons not aware of the extent to which Masonry has been diffused over the earth. Account for it as one may, the truth is certain that the mysterious Order was established in the Orient many ages ago. Nearly all of the old Mohammedan buildings in India, such as tombs, mosques, etc., are marked with the Masonic symbols, and many of these structures, still perfect, were built in the time of the Mogul Emperor Akbar, who died in 1605. Thus Masonry must have been introduced into India from Middle Asia by the Mohammedans hundreds of years ago."

Since then there was an initiation of a Persian in the Lodge Clémente Amitié at Paris. There is a Lodge at Teheran, of which many native Persians are members.

Persian Philosophical Rite. A Rite which its founders asserted was established in 1818, at Erzerum, in Persia, and which was introduced into France in the year 1819. It consisted of seven degrees, as follows: 1. Listening Apprentice; 2. Fellow-Craft, Adept, Esquire of Benevolence; 3. Master, Knight of the Sun; 4. Architect of all Rites, Knight of the Philosophy of the Heart; 5. Knight of Eclecticism and of Truth; 6. Master Good Shepherd; 7. Venerable Grand Elect. This Rite never contained many members, and has been long extinct.

Personal Merit. "All preferment among Masons is grounded upon real worth and *personal merit* only, that so the Lords may be well served, the Brethren not put to shame, nor the Royal Craft despised. Therefore no Master or Warden is chosen by seniority, but for his *merit*." *Charges of* 1723. (*Constitutions*, 1723, p. 51.)

Peru. Freemasonry was first introduced into Peru about the year 1807, during the French invasion, and several Lodges worked until the resumption of the Spanish authority and the Papal influence, in 1813, when their existence terminated. In 1825, when the independence of the republic, declared some years before, was completely achieved, several Scottish Rite Lodges were established, first at Lima and then at other points, by the Grand Orient of Colombia. A Supreme Council of the Ancient and Accepted Rite was instituted in 1830. In 1831 an independent Grand Lodge, afterward styled the Grand Orient of Peru, was organised by the Symbolic Lodges in the republic. Political agitations have, from time to time, occasioned a cessation of Masonic labor, but both the Supreme Council and the Grand Orient are now in successful operation. The Royal Arch Degree was introduced in 1852 by the establishment of a Royal Arch Chapter at Callao, under a Warrant granted by the Supreme Chapter of Scotland.

Petition for a Charter. The next step in the process of organizing a Lodge, after the Dispensation has been granted by the Grand Master, is an application for a Charter or Warrant of Constitution. The application may be, but not necessarily, in the form of a petition. On the report of the Grand Master, that he had granted a Dispensation, the Grand Lodge, if the new Lodge is recommended by some other, generally the nearest Lodge, will confirm the Grand Master's action and grant a Charter; although it may refuse to do so, and then the Lodge will cease to exist. Charters or Warrants for Lodges are granted only by the Grand Lodge in America, Ireland and Scotland. In England this great power is vested in the Grand Master. The Constitutions of the Grand Lodge of England say that "every application for a Warrant to hold a new Lodge must be, by petition to the Grand Master, signed by at least seven regularly registered Masons." Although, in the United States, it is the general usage that a Warrant must be preceded by a Dispensation, yet there is no general law which would forbid the Grand Lodge to issue a Charter in the first place, no Dispensation having been previously granted.

The rule for issuing Charters to Lodges prevails, with no modification in relation to granting them by Grand Chapters, Grand Councils, or Grand Commanderies for the bodies subordinate to them.

Petition for a Dispensation. When it is desired to establish a new Lodge, application by petition must be made to the Grand Master. This petition ought to be signed by at least seven Master Masons, and be recommended by the nearest Lodge; and it should contain the proposed name of the Lodge and the names of the three principal officers. This is the usage of America; but it must be remembered that the Grand Master's prerogative of granting Dispensations cannot be rightfully restricted by any law. Only, should the Grand Master grant a Dispensation for a Lodge which, in its petition, had not complied with these prerequisites, it is not probable that, on subsequent application to the Grand Lodge, a Warrant of Constitution would be issued.

Petition for Initiation. According to American usage any person who is desirous of initiation into the mysteries of Masonry must apply to the Lodge nearest to his place of residence, by means of a petition signed by himself, and recommended by at least two members of the Lodge to which he applies. The application of a Mason to a Chapter, Council, or Commandery for advancement to higher degrees, or of an unaffiliated Mason for membership in a Lodge, is also called a petition. For the rules that govern the disposition of these petitions, see Dr.

Mackey's *Text Book of Masonic Jurisprudence*, Book I., ch. ii.

Peuvret, Jean Eustache. An usher of the parliament of Paris, and Past Master of the Lodge of St. Pierre in Martinico, and afterward a dignitary of the Grand Orient at France. Peuvret was devoted to Hermetic Masonry, and acquired some reputation by numerous compilations on Masonic subjects. During his life he amassed a valuable library of mystical, alchemical, and Masonic books, and a manuscript collection of eighty-one degrees of Hermetic Masonry in six quarto volumes. He asserts in this work that the degrees were brought from England and Scotland; but this Thory (*Act. Lat.*, i., 205) denies, and says that they were manufactured in Paris. Peuvret's exceeding zeal without knowledge made him the victim of every charlatan who approached him. He died at Paris in 1800.

Phainoteletian Society. (*Société Phainotéléte.*) A society founded at Paris, in 1840, by Louis Theodore Juge, the editor of the *Globe*, composed of members of all rites and degrees, for the investigation of all non-political secret associations of ancient and modern times. The title is taken from the Greek, and signifies literally the society of the explainers of the mysteries of initiation.

Phallic Worship. The Phallus was a sculptured representation of the *membrum virile*, or male organ of generation; and the worship of it is said to have originated in Egypt, where, after the murder of Osiris by Typhon, which is symbolically to be explained as the destruction or deprivation of the sun's light by night, Isis, his wife, or the symbol of nature, in the search for his mutilated body, is said to have found all the parts except the organs of generation, which myth is simply symbolic of the fact that the sun having set, its fecundating and invigorating power had ceased. The Phallus, therefore, as the symbol of the male generative principle, was very universally venerated among the ancients, and that too as a religious rite, without the slightest reference to any impure or lascivious application.

As a symbol of the generative principle of nature, the worship of the Phallus appears to have been very nearly universal. In the mysteries it was carried in solemn procession. The Jews, in their numerous deflections into idolatry, fell readily into that of this symbol. And they did this at a very early period of their history, for we are told that even in the time of the Judges (Jud. iii. 7) they "served Baalim and the groves." Now the word translated, here and elsewhere, as *groves*, is in the original *Asherah*, and is by all modern interpreters supposed to mean a species of Phallus. Thus Movers (*Phöniz.*, p. 56) says that Asherah is a sort of Phallus erected to the telluric goddess Baaltes, and the learned Holloway (*Originals*, i., 18) had long before come to the same conclusion.

But the Phallus, or, as it was called among the Orientalists, the Lingam, was a representation of the male principle only. To perfect the circle of generation, it is necessary to advance one step farther. Accordingly we find in the *Cteis* of the Greeks, and the *Yoni* of the Indians, a symbol of the female generative principle of coextensive prevalence with the Phallus. The *Cteis* was a circular and concave pedestal, or receptacle, on which the Phallus or column rested, and from the center of which it sprang.

The union of these two, as the generative and the producing principles of nature, in one compound figure, was the most usual mode of representation. And here, I think, we undoubtedly find the remote origin of the *point within a circle*, an ancient symbol which was first adopted by the old sun-worshipers, and then by the ancient astronomers, as a symbol of the sun surrounded by the earth or the universe—the sun as the generator and the earth as the producer—and afterward modified in its signification and incorporated into the symbolism of Freemasonry. (See *Point within a Circle.*)

Phallus. Donegan says from an Egyptian or Indian root. (See *Phallic Worship.*)

Pharaxal. A significant word in the high degrees, and there said, in the old rituals, to signify "we shall all be united." Delaunay gives it as *pharas kol*, and says it means "all is explained." If it is derived from פרש, and the adverbial קל, *kol*, "altogether," it certainly means not to be united, but to be separated, and has the same meaning as its cognate *polkal*. This incongruity in the words and their accepted explanation has led Bro. Pike to reject them both from the degree in which they are originally found. And it is certain that the radical *pal* and *phar* both have everywhere in Hebrew the idea of separation. But my reading of the old rituals compels me to believe that the degree in which these words are found always contained an idea of separation and subsequent reunion. It is evident that there was either a blunder in the original adoption of the word *pharaxal*, or more probably a corruption by subsequent copyists. I am satisfied that the ideas of division, disunion, or separation, and of subsequent reunion, are correct; but I am equally satisfied that the Hebrew form of this word is wrong.

Pharisees. A school among the Jews at the time of Christ, so called from the Aramaic *Perushim*, Separated, because they held themselves apart from the rest of the nation. They claimed to have a mysterious knowledge unknown to the mass of the people, and pretended to the exclusive possession of the true meaning of the Scriptures, by virtue of the oral law and the secret traditions which, having been received by Moses on Mount Sinai, had been transmitted to successive generations of initiates. They are supposed to have been essentially the same as the Assideans or Chasidim. The character of their organization is interesting to the Masonic student. They held a secret doctrine, of which the dogma of the resurrection was an important feature; they met in sodalities or societies, the members of which called themselves *chabirim*, fellows or associates; and they styled all who were outside of their mystical association, *yom haharetz*, or people of the land.

Phœnicia. The Latinized form of the Greek *Phoinikia*, from φοῖνιξ, a palm, because of the number of palms anciently, but not now, found in the country. A tract of country on the north of Palestine, along the shores of the Mediterranean, of which Tyre and Sidon were the principal cities. The researches of Gesenius and other modern philologers have confirmed the assertions of Jerome and Augustine, that the language spoken by the Jews and the Phœnicians was almost identical; a statement interesting to the Masonic student as giving another reason for the bond which existed between Solomon and Hiram, and between the Jewish workmen and their fellow-laborers of Tyre, in the construction of the Temple. (See *Tyre*.)

Philadelphia. Placed on the imprint of some Masonic works of the last century as a pseudonym of Paris.

Philadelphians, Rite of the. See *Primitive Rite.*

Philadelphes, Lodge of the. The name of a Lodge at Narbonne, in France, in which the Primitive Rite was first instituted; whence it is sometimes called the "Rite of the Philadelphians." (See *Primitive Rite.*)

Philalethes, Rite of the. Called also the *Seekers of Truth*, although the word literally means *Friends of Truth*. It was a Rite founded in 1773 at Paris, in the Lodge of Amis Réunis, by Savalette de Langes, keeper of the Royal Treasury, with whom were associated the Vicomte de Tavannes, Court de Gebelin, M. de Sainte-James, the President d'Hericourt, and the Prince of Hesse. The Rite, which was principally founded on the system of Martinism, did not confine itself to any particular mode of instruction, but in its reunions, called "convents," the members devoted themselves to the study of all kinds of knowledge that were connected with the occult sciences, and thus they welcomed to their association all who had made themselves remarkable by the singularity or the novelty of their opinions, such as Cagliostro, Mesmer, and Saint Martin. It was divided into twelve classes or chambers of instruction. The names of these classes or degrees were as follows: 1. Apprentice; 2. Fellow-Craft; 3. Master; 4. Elect; 5. Scottish Master; 6. Knight of the East; 7. Rose Croix; 8. Knight of the Temple; 9. Unknown Philosopher; 10. Sublime Philosopher; 11. Initiate; 12. Philalethes, or Searcher after Truth. The first six degrees were called Petty, and the last six High Masonry. The Rite did not increase very rapidly; nine years after its institution, it counted only twenty Lodges in France and in foreign countries which were of its obedience. In 1785 it attempted a radical reform in Masonry, and for this purpose invited the most dstinguished Masons of all countries to a congress at Paris. But the project failed, and Savalette de Langes dying in 1788, the Rite, of which he alone was the soul, ceased to exist, and the Lodge of Amis Réunis was dissolved.

Philip, IV. Surnamed "le Bel," or "the Fair," who ascended the throne of France in 1285. He is principally distinguished in history on account of his persecution of the Knights Templar. With the aid of his willing instrument, Pope Clement V., he succeeded in accomplishing the overthrow of the Order. He died in 1314, execrated by his subjects, whose hearts he had alienated by the cruelty, avarice, and despotism of his administration.

Philippian Order. Finch gives this as the name of a secret Order instituted by King Philip "for the use only of his first nobility and principal officers, who thus formed a select and secret council in which he could implicitly confide." It has attracted the attention of no other Masonic writer, and was probably no more than a coinage of a charlatan's brain.

Philocoreites, Order of. An androgynous secret society established in the French army in Spain, in 1808. The members were called Knights and Ladies Philocoreites, or Lovers of Pleasure. It was not Masonic in character. But Thory has thought it worth a long description in his *History of the Foundation of the Grand Orient of France.*

Philo Judæus. A Jewish philosopher of the school of Alexandria, who was born about thirty years before Christ. Philo adopted to their full extent the mystical doctrines of his school, and taught that the Hebrew Scriptures contained, in a system of allegories, the real source of all religious and philosophical knowledge, the true meaning of which was to be excluded from the vulgar, to whom the literal signification alone was to be made known. Whoever, says he, has meditated on philosophy, has purified himself by virtue, and elevated himself by a contemplative life to God and the intellectual world, receiving their inspiration, thus pierces the gross envelop of the letter, and is initiated into mysteries of which the literal instruction is but a faint image. A fact, a figure, a word, a rite or custom, veils the profoundest truths, to be interpreted only by him who has the true key of science. Such symbolic views were eagerly seized by the early inventors of the high, philosophical degrees of Masonry, who have made frequent use of the esoteric philosophy of Philo in the construction of their Masonic system.

Philosopher, Christian. (*Philosophe Chrétien.*) The Fourth Degree of the Order of African Architects.

Philosopher, Grand and Sublime Hermetic. (*Grand et Sublime Philosophe Hermétique.*) A degree in the manuscript collection of Peuvret. Twelve other degrees of Philosopher were contained in the same collection, namely, Grand Neapolitan Philosopher, Grand Practical Philosopher, Kabbalistic Philosopher, Kabbalistic Philosopher to the Number 5, Perfect Mason Philosopher, Perfect Master Philosopher, Petty Neapolitan Philosopher, Petty Practical Philosopher, Sublime Philosopher, Sublime Philosopher to the Number 9, and Sublime Practical Philosopher. They are probably all Kabbalistic or Hermetic degrees.

Philosopher of Hermes. (*Philosophe d'Hermes.*) A degree contained in the Archives of the Lodge of St. Louis des Amis Réunis at Calais.

Philosopher, Sublime. (*Sublime Philosophe.*) 1. The Fifty-third Degree of the Rite of Mizraim. 2. The tenth class of the Rite of the Philalethes.

Philosopher, Sublime Unknown. (*Sublime Philosophe Inconnu.*) The Seventy-ninth Degree of the Metropolitan Chapter of France.

Philosopher, The Little. (*Le petit Philosophe.*) A degree in the collection of Pyron.

Philosopher, Unknown. (*Philosophe Inconnu.*) The ninth class of the Rite of the Philalethes. It was so called in reference to St. Martin, who had adopted that title as his pseudonym, and was universally known by it among his disciples.

Philosopher's Stone. It was the doctrine of the alchemists, that there was a certain mineral, the discovery of which was the object of their art, because, being mixed with the baser metals, it would transmute these into gold. This mineral, known only to the adepts, they called *lapis philosophorum*, or the philosopher's stone. Hitchcock, who wrote a book in 1857 (*Alchemy and the Alchemists*), to maintain the proposition that alchemy was a symbolic science, that its subject was *Man*, and its object the perfection of men, asserts that the philosopher's stone was a symbol of man. He quotes the old Hermetic philosopher, Isaac Holland, as saying that "though a man be poor, yet may he very well attain unto it [the work of perfection], and may be employed in making the philosopher's stone." And Hitchcock (p. 76), in commenting on this, says: "That is, every man, no matter how humble his vocation, may do the best he can in his place—may 'love mercy, do justly, and walk humbly with God'; and what more doth God require of any man?"

If this interpretation be correct, then the philosopher's stone of the alchemists, and the spiritual temple of the Freemasons are identical symbols.

Philosophic Degrees. All the degrees of the Ancient and Accepted Scottish Rite above the Eighteenth and below the Thirty-third are called philosophic degrees, because, abandoning the symbolism based on the Temple, they seek to develop a system of pure theosophy. Some writers have contended that the Seventeenth and Eighteenth degrees should be classed with the philosophic degrees. But this is not correct, since both of those degrees have preserved the idea of the Temple system. They ought rather to be called apocalyptic degrees, the Seventeenth especially, because they do not teach the ancient philosophies, but are connected in their symbolism with the spiritual temple of the New Jerusalem.

Philosophic Scottish Rite. This Rite consists of twelve degrees, as follows: 1. 2. 3. Knight of the Black Eagle or Rose Croix of Heredom, divided into three parts; 4. Knight of the Phenix; 5. Knight of the Sun; 6. Knight of the Rainbow; 7. True Mason; 8. Knight of the Argonaut; 9. Knight of the Golden Fleece; 10. Perfectly Initiated Grand Inspector; 11. Grand Scottish Inspector; 12. Sublime Master of the Luminous Ring.

The three degrees of Ancient Craft Masonry form the necessary basis of this system, although they do not constitute a part of the Rite. In its formation it expressly renounced the power to constitute Symbolic Lodges, but reserved the faculty of affiliating regularly constituted Lodges into its high degrees. Thory (*Fond. du G. O.*, p. 162) seems desirous of tracing the origin of the Rite to the Rosicrucians of the fourteenth century. But the reasons which he assigns for this belief are by no means satisfactory. The truth is, that the Rite was founded in 1775, in the celebrated Lodge of the Social Contract (*Contrat Social*), and that its principal founder was M. Boileau, a physician of Paris, who had been a disciple of Pernetti, the originator of the Hermetic Rite at Avignon, whose Hermetic principles he introduced into the Philosophic Scottish Rite. Some notion may be formed of the nature of the system which was taught in this Rite, from the name of the degree which is at its summit. The Luminous Ring is a Pythagorean degree. In 1780, an Academy of the Sublime Masters of the Luminous Ring was established in France, in which the doctrine was taught that Freemasonry was originally founded by Pythagoras, and in which the most important portion of the lectures was engaged in an explanation of the peculiar dogmas of the sage of Samos.

The chief seat of the Rite had always been in the Lodge of Social Contract until 1792, when, in common with all the other Masonic bodies of France, it suspended its labors. It was resuscitated at the termination of the Revolution, and in 1805 the Lodge of the Social Contract, and that of St. Alexander of Scotland, assumed the title of the "Mother Lodge of the Philosophic Scottish Rite in France." This body was eminently literary in its character, and in 1811 and 1812 possessed a mass of valuable archives, among which were a number of old charters, manuscript rituals, and Masonic works of great interest, in all languages.

Philosophus. The fourth grade of the First Order of the Society of Rosicrucians, as practised in Europe and America.

Philosophy Sublime. (*Philosophie Sublime.*) The Forty-eighth Degree of the Rite of Mizraim.

Phœnix. The old mythological legend of the phœnix is a familiar one. The bird was described as of the size of an eagle, with a head finely crested, a body covered with beautiful plumage, and eyes sparkling like stars. She was said to live six hundred years in the wilderness, when she built for herself a funereal pile of aromatic woods, which she ignited with the fanning of her wings, and emerged from the flames with a new life. Hence the phœnix has been adopted universally as a symbol of immortality. Higgins (*Anacalypsis*, ii., 441) says that the phœnix is the symbol of an ever-revolving solar cycle of six hundred and eight years, and refers to the Phœnician word *phen*, which signifies a cycle. Aumont, the first Grand Master of the Templars after the martyrdom of De Molay, and called the "Restorer of the Order," took, it is said, for his seal, a phœnix brooding on the flames, with the motto, "Ardet ut vivat"—*She burns that she may live*. The phœnix was adopted at a very early period as a Christian symbol, and several representations of it have been found in the catacombs. Its ancient legend, doubtless, caused it to be accepted as a symbol of the resurrection.

Phylacteries. The second fundamental principle of Judaism is the wearing of phylacteries; termed by some writers Tataphoth, "ornaments," and refer to the law and commandments, as "Bind them about thy neck; write them upon the table of thine head." (Prov. iii. 3; vi. 21; viii. 3.) The phylacteries are worn on the forehead and arm, and are called in Hebrew *Tephillin*, from *Palal*, to pray. These consist of two leathern boxes. One contains four compartments, in which are enclosed four portions of the law written on parchment and carefully folded. The box is made of leather pressed upon blocks of wood specially prepared, the leather being well soaked in water. The following passages of the law are sewn into it: Ex. xiii. 1–10, 11–16; Deut. vi. 4–9; xi. 13–21. On this box is the letter ש (*shin*), with three strokes for the right side, and the same letter with four strokes for the left side of the wearer. The second box has but one compartment, into which the same passages of Scripture are sewed with the sinews of animals, specially prepared for this object. The phylacteries are bound on the forehead and arm by long leathern straps. The straps on the head must be tied in a knot shaped like the letter ד (*daleth*). The straps on the arm must go round it seven times, and three times round the middle finger, with a small surplus over in the form of the letter י (*yod*). Thus we have the שדי, Shaddai, or Almighty. The phylacteries are kept in special bags, with greatest reverence, and the Rabbis assert "that the single precept of the phylacteries is equal to all the commandments."

Physical Qualifications. The physical qualifications of a candidate for initiation into Masonry may be considered under the three heads of Sex, Age, and Bodily Conformation. 1. *As to Sex.* It is a landmark that the candidate shall be a man. This, of course, prohibits the initiation of a woman. 2. *As to Age.* The candidate must, say the Old Regulations, be of "mature and discreet age." The ritual forbids the initiation of an "old man in his dotage, or a young man under age." The man who has lost his faculties by an accumulation of years, or not yet acquired them in their full extent by immaturity of age, is equally incapable of initiation. (See *Dotage* and *Mature Age.*) 3. *As to Bodily Conformation.* The Gothic Constitutions of 926, or what is said to be that document, prescribe that the candidate "must be without blemish, and have the full and proper use of his limbs"; and the Charges of 1722 say "that he must have no maim or defect in his body that may render him incapable of learning the art, of serving his Master's lord, and of being made a brother." (*Constitutions*, 1723, p. 51.) And although a few jurists have been disposed to interpret this law with unauthorized laxity, the general spirit of the Institution, and of all its authorities, is to observe it rigidly. (See the subject fully dicussed in Dr. Mackey's *Text Book of Masonic Jurisprudence*, pp. 100–113.)

Picart's Ceremonies. Bernard Picart was a celebrated engraver of Amsterdam, and the author of a voluminous work, which was begun in 1723, and continued after his death, until 1737, by J. F. Bernard, entitled *Cérémonies Religieuses de tous les peuple du monde*. A second edition was published at Paris, in 1741, by the Abbés Banier and Le Mascrier, who entirely remodeled the work; and a third in 1783 by a set of free-thinkers, who disfigured, and still further altered the text to suit their own views. Editions, professing to be reprints of the original one, have been subsequently published in 1807–9 and 1816. The book has been recently deemed of some importance by the investigators of the Masonic history of the last century, because it contains an engraved list in two pages of the English Lodges which were in existence in 1735. The plate is, however, of no value as an original authority, since it is merely a copy of the *Engraved List of Lodges*, published by J. Pine in 1735.

Pickax. An instrument used to loosen the soil and prepare it for digging. It is one of the working-tools of a Royal Arch Mason, and symbolically teaches him to loosen from his heart the hold of evil habits.

Piece of Architecture. (*Morçeau d'Architecture.*) The French so call a discourse, poem, or other production on the subject of Freemasonry. The definition previously given in this work under the title *Architecture*, in being confined to the minutes of the Lodge, is not sufficiently comprehensive.

Pike, Albert. Born at Boston, Mass., December 29, 1809, and died April 2, 1891. After a sojourn in early life in Mexico, he returned to the United States and settled in Little Rock, Arkansas, as an editor and lawyer. Subsequent to the War of the Rebellion, in which he had cast his fortunes with the South, he located in Washington, D. C., uniting with ex-Senator Robert Johnson in the profession of the law, making his home, however, in Alexandria. His library, in extent and selections, was a marvel, especially in all that pertains to the wonders in ancient literature. Bro. Pike was the Sov. G. Commander of the Southern Supreme Council, A. A. Scottish Rite, having been elected in 1859. He was Prov. G. Master of the G. Lodge of the Royal Order of Scotland in the U. S., and an honorary member of almost every Supreme Council in the world. His standing as a Masonic author and historian, and withal as a poet, was most distinguished, and his untiring zeal was without a parallel.

Pilgrim. A pilgrim (from the Italian *pelegrino*, and that from the Latin *peregrinus*, signifying a traveler) denotes one who visits holy places from a principle of devotion. Dante (*Vita Nuova*) distinguishes pilgrims from palmers thus: palmers were those who went beyond the sea to the East, and often brought back staves of palm-wood; while pilgrims went only to the shrine of St. Jago, in Spain. But Sir Walter Scott says that the palmers were in the habit of passing from shrine to shrine, living on charity; but pilgrims made the journey to any shrine only once; and this is the more usually accepted distinction of the two classes.

In the Middle Ages, Europe was filled with pilgrims repairing to Palestine to pay their veneration to the numerous spots consecrated in the annals of Holy Writ, more especially to the sepulcher of our Lord.

"It is natural," says Robertson (*Hist.*, ch. v., i., 19), "to the human mind, to view those places which have been distinguished by being the residence of any illustrious personage, or the scene of any great transaction, with some degree of delight and veneration. From this principle flowed the superstitious devotion with which Christians, from the earliest ages of the church, were accustomed to visit that country which the Almighty had selected as the inheritance of his favorite people, and in which the Son of God had accomplished the redemption of mankind. As this distant pilgrimage could not be performed without considerable expense, fatigue, and danger, it appeared the more meritorious, and came to be considered as an expiation for almost every crime."

Hence, by a pilgrimage to the Holy Land or to the shrine of some blessed martyr, the thunders of the church, and the more quiet, but not less alarming, reproaches of conscience were often averted. And as this was an act of penance, sometimes voluntarily assumed, but oftener imposed by the command of a religious superior, the person performing it was called a "*Pilgrim Penitent.*"

While the Califs of the East, a race of monarchs equally tolerant and sagacious, retained the sovereignty of Palestine, the penitents were undisturbed in the performance of their pious pilgrimages. In fact, their visits to Jerusalem were rather encouraged by these sovereigns as a commerce which, in the language of the author already quoted, "brought into their dominions gold and silver, and carried nothing out of them but relics and consecrated trinkets."

But in the eleventh century, the Turks, whose bigoted devotion to their own creed was only equaled by their hatred of every other form of faith, but more especially of Christianity, having obtained possession of Syria, the pilgrim no longer found safety or protection in his pious journey. He who would then visit the sepulcher of his Lord must be prepared to encounter the hostile attacks of ferocious Saracens, and the "*Pilgrim Penitent,*" laying aside his peaceful garb, his staff and russet cloak, was compelled to assume the sword and coat of mail and become a "*Pilgrim Warrior.*"

Having at length, through all the perils of a distant journey, accomplished the great object of his pilgrimage, and partly begged his way amid poor or inhospitable regions, where *a crust of bread and a draft of water* were often the only alms that he received, and partly fought it amid the gleaming scimitars of warlike Turks, the Pilgrim Penitent and Pilgrim Warrior was enabled to kneel at the sepulcher of Christ, and offer up his devotions on that sacred spot consecrated in his pious mind by so many religious associations.

But the experience which he had so dearly bought was productive of a noble and a generous result. The Order of Knights Templar was established by some of those devoted heroes, who were determined to protect the pilgrims who followed them from the dangers and difficulties through which they themselves had passed, at times with such remote prospects of success. Many of the pilgrims having performed their vow of visiting the holy shrine, returned home, to live upon the capital of piety which their penitential pilgrimage had gained for them; but others, imitating the example of the defenders of the sepulcher, doffed their pilgrim's garb and united themselves with the knights who were contending with their infidel foes, and thus the *Pilgrim Penitent*, having by force of necessity become a *Pilgrim Warrior*, ended his warlike pilgrimage by assuming the vows of a *Knights Templar.*

In this brief synopsis, the modern and Masonic Knights Templar will find a rational explanation of the ceremonies of that degree.

Pilgrim Penitent. A term in the ritual of Masonic Templarism. It refers to the pilgrimage, made as a penance for sin, to the sepulcher of the Lord; for the church promised the remission of sins and various spiritual advantages as the reward of the pious and faithful pilgrim. (See *Pilgrim.*)

Pilgrim's Shell. See *Scallop Shell.*

Pilgrim's Weeds. The costume of a pilgrim was thus called. It may be described as follows: In the first place, he wore a *sclavina*, or long gown, made of the darkest colors and the coarsest materials, bound by a leathern girdle, as an emblem of his humility and an evidence of his poverty; a *bourdon*, or staff, in the form of a long walking stick, with two knobs at the top, supported his weary steps; the *rosary* and *cross*, suspended from his neck, denoted the religious character he had assumed; a *scrip*, or bag, held his scanty supply of provisions; a pair of sandals on his feet, and a coarse round hat turned before, in the front of which was fastened a scallop shell, completed the rude toilet of the pilgrim of the Middle Ages. Spenser's description, in the *Fairie Queen* (B. I., c. vi., st. 35), of a pilgrim's weeds, does not much differ from this:

"A silly man in simple weeds forewom,
 And soiled with dust of the long dried way;
His sandals were with toilsome travel torne,
 And face all tann'd with scorching sunny ray;
As he had travell'd many a summer's day,
 Through boiling sands of Araby and Inde;
And in his hand a Jacob's staff to stay
 His weary limbs upon; and eke behind
 His scrip did hang, in which his needments he did bind."

Pilgrim Templar. The part of the pilgrim represented in the ritual of the Masonic Knights Templar Degree is a symbolic reference to the career of the pilgrim of the Middle Ages in his journey to the sepulcher in the Holy Land. (See *Pilgrim*.)

Pilgrim Warrior. A term in the ritual of Masonic Templarism. It refers to the pilgrimage of the knights to secure possession of the holy places. This was considered a pious duty. "Whoever goes to Jerusalem," says one of the canons of the Council of Clermont, "for the liberation of the Church of God, in a spirit of devotion only, and not for the sake of glory or of gain, that journey shall be esteemed a substitute for every kind of penance." The difference between the pilgrim penitent and the pilgrim warrior was this: that the former bore only his staff, but the latter wielded his sword.

Piller. The title given to each of the conventual bailiffs or heads of the eight languages of the Order of Malta, and by which they were designated in all official records. It signifies a pillar or support of an edifice, and was metaphorically applied to these dignitaries as if they were the supports of the Order.

Pillar. In the earliest times it was customary to perpetuate remarkable events, or exhibit gratitude for providential favors, by the erection of pillars, which by the idolatrous races were dedicated to their spurious gods. Thus Sanconiatho tells us that Hypsourianos and Ousous, who lived before the flood, dedicated two pillars to the elements fire and air. Among the Egyptians the pillars were, in general, in the form of obelisks from fifty to one hundred feet high, and exceedingly slender in proportion. Upon their four sides hieroglyphics were often engraved. According to Herodotus, they were first raised in honor of the sun, and their pointed form was intended to represent his rays. Many of these monuments still remain.

In the antediluvian ages, the posterity of Seth erected pillars; "for," says the Jewish historian, "that their inventions might not be lost before they were sufficiently known, upon Adam's prediction, that the world was to be destroyed at one time by the force of fire, and at another time by the violence of water, they made two pillars, the one of brick, the other of stone; they inscribed their discoveries on them both, that in case the pillar of brick should be destroyed by the flood, the pillar of stone might remain, and exhibit those discoveries to mankind, and also inform them that there was another pillar of brick erected by them." Jacob erected a pillar at Bethel, to commemorate his remarkable vision of the latter, and afterward another one at Galeed as a memorial of his alliance with Laban. Joshua erected one at Gilgal to perpetuate the remembrance of his miraculous crossing of the Jordan. Samuel set up a pillar between Mizpeh and Shen, on account of a defeat of the Philistines, and Absalom erected another in honor of himself.

The doctrine of gravitation was unknown to the people of the primitive ages, and they were unable to refer the support of the earth in its place to this principle. Hence they looked to some other cause, and none appeared to their simple and unphilosophic minds more plausible than that it was sustained by pillars. The Old Testament abounds with reference to this idea. Hannah, in her song of thanksgiving, exclaims: "The pillars of the earth are the Lord's, and he hath set the world upon them." (1 Sam. ii. 8.) The Psalmist signifies the same doctrine in the following text: "The earth and all the inhabitants thereof are dissolved; I bear up the pillars of it." (Ps. lxxv. 3.) And Job says: "He shaketh the earth out of her places, and the pillars thereof tremble." (xxvi. 7.) All the old religions taught the same doctrine; and hence pillars being regarded as the supporters of the earth, they were adopted as the symbol of strength and firmness. To this, Dudley (*Naology*, 123) attributes the origin of pillar worship, which prevailed so extensively among the idolatrous nations of antiquity. "The reverence," says he, "shown to columns, as symbols of the power of the Deity, was readily converted into worship paid to them as idols of the real presence." But here he seems to have fallen into a mistake. The double pillars or columns, acting as an architectural support, were, it is true, symbols derived from a natural cause of strength and permanent firmness. But there was another more prevailing symbology. The monolith, or circular pillar, standing alone, was, to the ancient mind, a representation of the Phallus, the symbol of the creative and generative energy of Deity, and it is in these Phallic pillars that we are to find the true origin of pillar worship, which was only one form of Phallic worship, the most predominant of all the cults to which the ancients were addicted.

Pillars of Cloud and Fire. The pillar of cloud that went before the Israelites by day, and the pillar of fire that preceded them by night, in their journey through the wilderness, are supposed to be alluded to by the pillars of Jachin and Boaz at the porch of Solomon's Temple. We find this symbolism at a very early period in the last century, having been incorporated into the lecture of the Second Degree, where it still remains. "The pillar on the right hand," says Calcott (*Cand. Disq.*, 66), "represented the pillar of the cloud, and that on the left the pillar of fire." If this symbolism be correct, the pillars of the porch, like those of the wilderness, would refer to the superintending and protecting power of Deity.

Pillars of Enoch. Two pillars which were erected by Enoch, for the preservation of the antediluvian inventions, and which are repeatedly referred to in the "Legend of the Craft," contained in the *Old Constitutions*, and in the high degrees of modern times. (See *Enoch*.)

Pillars of the Porch. The pillars most remarkable in Scripture history were the two erected by Solomon at the porch of the Temple, and which Josephus (*Antiq.*, lib. i., cap. ii.) thus describes: "Moreover, this Hiram made two hollow pillars, whose outsides were of brass, and the thickness of the brass was four fingers' breadth, and the height of the pillars was eighteen cubits, (27 feet,) and the circumference twelve cubits, (18 feet;) but there was cast with each of their chapiters lily-work, that stood upon the pillar, and it was elevated five cubits, (7½ feet,) round about which there was net-work interwoven with small palms made of brass, and covered the lily-work. To this also were hung two hundred pomegranates, in two rows. The one of these pillars he set at the entrance of the porch on the right hand, (*or south*,) and called it Jachin, and the other at the left hand, (*or north*,) and called it Boaz."

It has been supposed that Solomon, in erecting these pillars, had reference to the pillar of cloud and the pillar of fire which went before the Israelites in the wilderness, and that the right hand or south pillar represented the pillar of cloud, and the left hand or north pillar represented that of fire. Solomon did not simply erect them as ornaments to the Temple, but as memorials of God's repeated promises of support to his people of Israel. For the pillar יכין (*Jachin*), derived from the words יה (*Jah*), "Jehovah," and הכין (*achin*), "to establish," signifies that "God will establish his house of Israel"; while the pillar בעז (*Boaz*), compounded of ב (*b*), "in" and עז (*oaz*), "strength," signifies that "in strength shall it be established." And thus were the Jews, in passing through the porch to the Temple, daily reminded of the abundant promises of God, and inspired with confidence in his protection and gratitude for his many acts of kindness to his chosen people.

The construction of these pillars.—There is no part of the architecture of the ancient Temple which is so difficult to be understood in its details as the Scriptural account of these memorable pillars. Freemasons, in general, intimately as their symbolical signification is connected with some of the most beautiful portions of their ritual, appear to have but a confused notion of their construction and of the true disposition of the various parts of which they are composed. Mr. Ferguson says (Smith, *Dict. Bib.*) that there are no features connected with the Temple which have given rise to so much controversy, or been so difficult to explain, as the form of these two pillars.

Their situation, according to Lightfoot, was *within* the porch, at its very entrance, and on each side of the gate. They were therefore seen, one on the right and the other on the left, as soon as the visitor stepped within the porch. And this, it will be remembered, in confirmation, is the very spot in which Ezekiel (xi. 49) places the pillars that he saw in his vision of the Temple. "The length of the porch was twenty cubits, and the breadth eleven cubits; and he brought me by the steps whereby they went up to it, and there were pillars by the posts, one on this side, and another on that side." The assertion made by some writers, that they were not columns intended to support the roof, but simply obelisks for ornament, is not sustained by sufficient authority; and as Ferguson very justly says, not only would the high roof look painfully weak, but it would have been impossible to construct it, with the imperfect science of those days, without some such support.

These pillars, we are told, were of brass, as well as the chapiters that surmounted them, and were cast hollow. The thickness of the brass of each pillar was "four fingers, or a hand's breadth," which is equal to three inches. According to the accounts in 1 Kings viii. 15, and in Jeremiah lii. 21, the circumference of each pillar was twelve cubits. Now, according to the Jewish computation, the cubit used in the measurement of the Temple buildings was six hands' breadth, or eighteen inches. According to the tables of Bishop Cumberland, the cubit was rather more, he making it about twenty-two inches; but I adhere to the measure laid down by the Jewish writers as probably more correct, and certainly more simple for calculation. The circumference of each pillar, reduced by this scale to English measure, would be eighteen feet, and its diameter about six.

The reader of the Scriptural accounts of these pillars will be not a little puzzled with the apparent discrepancies that are found in the estimates of their height as given in the Books of Kings and Chronicles. In the former book, it is said that their height was eighteen cubits, and in the latter it was thirty-five, which latter height Whiston observes would be contrary to all the rules of architecture. But the discrepancy is easily reconciled by supposing—which, indeed, must have been the case—that in the Book of Kings the pillars are spoken of separately, and that in

Chronicles their aggregate height is calculated; and the reason why, in this latter book, their united height is placed at thirty-five cubits instead of thirty-six, which would be the double of eighteen, is because they are there measured as they appeared with the chapiters upon them. Now half a cubit of each pillar was concealed in what Lightfoot calls "the whole of the chapiter," that is, half a cubit's depth of the lower edge of the chapiter covered the top of the pillar, making each pillar, apparently, only seventeen and a half cubits' high, or the two thirty-five cubits as laid down in the Book of Chronicles.

This is a much better method of reconciling the discrepancy than that adopted by Calcott, who supposes that the pedestals of the pillars were seventeen cubits high—a violation of every rule of architectural proportion with which we would be reluctant to charge the memory of so "cunning a workman" as Hiram the Builder. The account in Jeremiah agrees with that in the Book of Kings. The height, therefore, of each of these pillars was, in English measure, twenty-seven feet. The chapiter or pommel was five cubits, or seven and a half feet more; but as half a cubit, or nine inches, was common to both pillar and chapiter, the whole height from the ground to the top of the chapiter was twenty-two cubits and a half, or thirty-three feet and nine inches.

Mr. Ferguson has come to a different conclusion. He says in the article *Temple*, in Smith's *Dictionary of the Bible*, that "according to 1 Kings vii. 15, the pillars were eighteen cubits high and twelve in circumference, with capitals five cubits in height. Above this was (ver. 19) another member, called also chapiter of lily-work, four cubits in height, but which, from the second mention of it in ver. 22, seems more probably to have been an entablature, which is necessary to complete the order. As these members make out twenty-seven cubits, leaving three cubits, or 4½ feet, for the slope of the roof, the whole design seems reasonable and proper." He calculates, of course, on the authority of the Book of Kings, that the height of the roof of the porch was thirty cubits, and assumes that these pillars were columns by which it was supported, and connected with it by an entablature.

Each of these pillars was surmounted by a chapiter, which was five cubits, or seven and a half feet in height. The shape and construction of this chapiter require some consideration. The Hebrew word which is used in this place is כותרת (*koteret*). Its root is to be found in the word כתר (*keter*), which signified "a crown," and is so used in Esther vi. 8, to designate the royal diadem of the King of Persia. The Chaldaic version expressly calls the chapiter "a crown"; but Rabbi Solomon, in his commentary, uses the word פומל (*pomel*), signifying "a globe or spherical body," and Rabbi Gershom describes it as "like two crowns joined together." Lightfoot says, "it was a huge, great oval, five cubits high, and did not only sit upon the head of the pillars, but also flowered or spread them, being larger about, a great deal, than the pillars themselves." The Jewish commentators say that the two lower cubits of its surface were entirely plain, but that the three upper were richly ornamented. To this ornamental part we now come.

In the 1st Book of Kings, ch. vii., verses 17, 20, 22, the ornaments of the chapiters are thus described:

"And nets of checker-work and wreaths of chain-work, for the chapiters which were upon the tops of the pillars; seven for the one chapiter, and seven for the other chapiter.

"And he made the pillars, and two rows round about upon the one net-work, to cover the chapiters that were upon the top, with pomegranates; and so did he for the other chapiter.

"And the chapiters that were upon the top of the pillars were of lily-work in the porch, four cubits.

"And the chapiters upon the two pillars had pomegranates also above, over against the belly, which was by the net-work; and the pomegranates were two hundred in rows, round about upon the other chapiter.

"And upon the top of the pillars was lily-work; so was the work of the pillars finished."

Let us endeavor to render this description, which appears somewhat confused and unintelligible, plainer and more comprehensible.

The "nets of checker-work" is the first ornament mentioned. The words thus translated are in the original מעשה שבכה שבכים, which Lightfoot prefers rendering "thickets of branch work"; and he thinks that the true meaning of the passage is, that "the chapiters were curiously wrought with branch work, seven goodly branches standing up from the belly of the oval, and their boughs and leaves curiously and lovelily intermingled and interwoven one with another." He derives his reason for this version from the fact that the same word, שבכה, is translated "thicket" in the passage in Genesis (xxii. 13), where the ram is described as being "caught in a thicket by his horns"; and in various other passages the word is to be similarly translated. But, on the other hand, we find it used in the Book of Job, where it evidently signifies a net made of meshes: "For he is cast into a *net* by his own feet and he walketh upon a snare." (Job xvii. 8.) In 2 Kings i. 2, the same word is used, where our translators have rendered it a *lattice;* "Ahaziah fell down through a lattice in his upper chamber." I am, therefore, not inclined to adopt the emendation of Lightfoot, but rather coincide with the received version, as well as the Masonic tradition, that this ornament was a simple network or fabric consisting of reticulated lines—in other words, a lattice-work.

The "wreaths of chain-work" that are next spoken of are less difficult to be understood. The word here translated "wreath" is גדלים, and is to be found in Deuteronomy xxii. 12, where it distinctly means *fringes:* "Thou shalt make thee fringes upon the four quarters of thy vesture." *Fringes* it should also be translated here. "The fringes of chain-work," I suppose, were therefore attached to, and hung down from, the network spoken of above, and were probably in this case, as when used upon the garments of the Jewish high priest, intended as a "memorial of the law."

The "lily-work" is the last ornament that demands our attention. And here the description of Lightfoot is so clear and evidently correct, that I shall not hesitate to quote it at length. "At the head of the pillar, even at the setting on of the chapiter, there was a curious and a large border or circle of lily-work, which stood out four cubits under the chapiter, and then turned down, every lily or long tongue of brass, with a neat bending, and so seemed as a flowered crown to the head of the pillar, and as a curious garland whereon the chapiter had its seat."

There is a very common error among Masons, which has been fostered by the plates in our Monitors, that there were on the pillars chapiters, and that these chapiters were again surmounted by globes. The truth, however, is that the chapiters themselves were "the pomels or globes," to which our lecture, in the Fellow-Craft's Degree, alludes. This is evident from what has already been said in the first part of the preceding description. The lily here spoken of is not at all related, as might be supposed, to the common lily—that one spoken of in the New Testament. It was a species of the lotus, the Nymphæa lotus, or lotus of the Nile. This was among the Egyptians a sacred plant, found everywhere on their monuments, and used in their architectural decorations. It is evident, from their description in Kings, that the pillars of the porch of King Solomon's Temple were copied from the pillars of the Egyptian temples. The maps of the earth and the charts of the celestial constellations which are sometimes said to have been engraved upon these globes, must be referred to the pillars, where, according to Oliver, a Masonic tradition places them—an ancient custom, instances of which we find in profane history. This is, however, by no means of any importance, as the symbolic allusion is perfectly well preserved in the shapes of the chapiters, without the necessity of any such geographical or astronomical engraving upon them. For being globular, or nearly so, they may be justly said to have represented the celestial and terrestrial spheres.

The true description, then, of these memorable pillars, is simply this. Immediately within the porch of the Temple, and on each side of the door, were placed two hollow brazen pillars. The height of each was twenty-seven feet, the diameter about six feet, and the thickness of the brass three inches. Above the pillar, and covering its upper part to the depth of nine inches, was an oval body or chapiter seven feet and a half in height. Springing out from the pillar, at the junction of the chapiter with it, was a row of lotus petals, which, first spreading around the chapiter, afterward gently curved downward toward the pillar, something like the Acanthus leaves on the capital of a Corinthian column. About two-fifths of the distance from the bottom of the chapiter, or just below its most bulging part, a tissue of network was carved, which extended over its whole upper surface. To the bottom of this network was suspended a series of fringes, and on these again were carved two rows of pomegranates, one hundred being in each row.

This description, it seems to me, is the only one that can be reconciled with the various passages in the Books of Kings, Chronicles, and Josephus, which relate to these pillars, and the only one that can give the Masonic student a correct conception of the architecture of these important symbols.

And now as to the Masonic symbolism of these two pillars. As symbols they have been very universally diffused and are to be found in all rites. Nor are they of a very recent date, for they are depicted on the earliest tracing-boards, and are alluded to in the catechisms before the middle of the last century. Nor is this surprising; for as the symbolism of Freemasonry is founded on the Temple of Solomon, it was to be expected that these important parts of the Temple would be naturally included in the system. But at first the pillars appear to have been introduced into the lectures rather as parts of an historical detail than as significant symbols—an idea which seems gradually to have grown up. The catechism of 1731 describes their name, their size, and their material, but says nothing of their symbolic import. Yet this had been alluded to in the Scriptural account of them, which says that the names bestowed upon them were significant.

What was the original or Scriptural symbolism of the pillars has been very well explained by Dudley, in his *Naology*. He says (p. 121) that "the pillars represented the sustaining power of the great God. The flower of the lotus or water-lily rises from a root growing at the bottom of the water, and maintains its position on the surface by its columnar stalk, which becomes more or less straight as occasion requires; it is therefore aptly symbolical of the power of the Almighty constantly employed to secure the safety of all the world. The chapiter is the body or mass of the earth; the pomegranates, fruits remarkable for the number of their seeds, are symbols of fertility; the wreaths, drawn variously over the surface of the chapiter or globe, indicate the courses of the heavenly bodies in the heavens around the earth, and the variety of the seasons. The pillars were properly placed in the porch or portico of the Temple, for they suggested just ideas of the power of the Almighty, of the entire dependence of man upon him, the Creator; and doing this, they exhorted all to fear, to love, and obey him."

It was, however, Hutchinson who first introduced the symbolic idea of the pillars into the Masonic system. He says: "The pillars erected at the porch of the Temple were not only ornamental, but also carried with them an emblematical import in their names: Boaz being, in its literal translation, *in thee is strength;* and Jachin, *it shall be established,* which, by a very natural transposition, may be put thus: O Lord, thou art mighty, and thy power is established from everlasting to everlasting."

Preston subsequently introduced the symbolism, considerably enlarged, into his system of lectures. He adopted the reference to the pillars of fire and cloud, which is still retained.

The Masonic symbolism of the two pillars may be considered, without going into minute details, as being twofold. First, in reference to the names of the pillars, they are symbols of the *strength* and *stability* of the Institution; and then in reference to the ancient pillars of fire and cloud, they are symbolic of our dependence on the superintending guidance of the Great Architect of the Universe, by which alone that strength and stability are secured.

Pinceau. French, a *pencil;* but in the technical language of French Masonry it is a *pen.* Hence, in the minutes of French Lodges, *tenir le pinceau* means *to act as Secretary.*

Pine-Cone. The tops or points of the rods of deacons are often surmounted by a pine-cone or pineapple. This is in imitation of the *Thyrsus,* or sacred staff of Bacchus, which was a lance or rod enveloped in leaves of ivy, and having on the top a cone or apple of the pine. To it surprising virtues were attributed, and it was introduced into the Dionysiac mysteries as a sacred symbol.

Pinnacles. Generally ornamented terminations much used in Gothic architecture. They are prominently referred to in the Eleventh Degree of the A. A. Scottish Rite, where the pinnacles over the three gates support the warning to all evil-doers, and give evidence of the certainty of punishment following crime.

Pirlet. The name of a tailor of Paris, who, in 1762, organized a body called "Council of Knights of the East," in opposition to the Council of Emperors of the East and West.

Pitaka. ("Basket.") The Bible of Buddhism, containing 116 volumes, divided into three classes, collectively known as the Tripitaka or Pitakattayan, that is, the "Triple Basket"; the Soutras, or discourses of Buddha; the Vinaga, or Discipline; and the Abhadharma, or Metaphysics. The canon was fixed about 240 B.C., and commands a following of more than one-third of the human race—the estimates vary from 340,000,000 to 500,000,000. Masonically considered, this indeed must be a great Light or Trestle-Board, if it is the guide of the conduct and practise of so vast a number of our brethren; for are not all men our brethren?

Pitdah. (Heb. פטדה.) One of the twelve stones in the breastplate of the high priest, of a yellow color. The Sanskrit for yellow is *pita.*

Pitris. Spirits. Among the Hindus, Pitris were spirits; so mentioned in the *Agrouchada Parikchai,* the philosophical compendium of the Hindu spiritists, a scientific work giving an account of the creation and the Mercaba, and finally the Zohar; the three principal parts of which treat "of the attributes of God," "of the world," and "of the human soul." A fourth part sets forth the relevancy of souls to each other, and the evocation of Pitris. The adepts of the occult sciences were said by the votaries of the Pitris of India to have "entered the garden of delights." (See *Parikchai, Agrouchada;* also, *Indische Mysterien.*)

Pius VII. On the 13th of August, 1814, Pope Pius VII. issued an edict forbidding the meetings of all secret societies, and especially the Freemasons and Carbonari, under heavy corporal penalties, to which were to be added, according to the malignity of the cases, partial or entire confiscation of goods, or a pecuniary fine. The edict also renewed the bull of Clement XII., by which the punishment of death was incurred by those who obstinately persisted in attending the meetings of Freemasons.

Place. In strict Masonic ritualism the positions occupied by the Master and Wardens are called *stations;* those of the other officers, *places.* This distinction is not observed in the higher degrees. (See *Stations.*)

Planche Tracee. The name by which the minutes are designated in French Lodges. Literally, *planche* is a board, and *tracée,* delineated. The *planche tracée* is therefore the board on which the plans of the Lodge have been delineated.

Plans and Designs. The plans and designs on the Trestle-Board of the Master, by which the building is erected, are, in Speculative Masonry, symbolically referred to the moral plans and designs of life by which we are to construct our spiritual temple, and in the direction of which we are to be instructed by some recognized Divine authority. (See *Trestle-Board.*)

Platonic Academy. See *Academy, Platonic.*

Plenty. The ear of corn, or sheaf of wheat, is, in the Masonic system, the symbol of plenty. In ancient iconography, the goddess Plenty was represented by a young nymph crowned with flowers, and holding in the right hand the horn of Amalthea, the goat that suckled Jupiter, and in her left a bundle of sheaves of wheat, from which the ripe grain is falling profusely to the ground. There have been some differences in the representation of the goddess on various medals; but, as Montfauçon shows, the ears of corn are an indispensable part of the symbolism. (See *Shibboleth.*)

Plot Manuscript. Dr. Plot, in his *Natural History of Staffordshire,* published in 1686, speaks of "a scrole or parchment volume," in the possession of the Masons of the seventeenth century, in which it is stated that the "charges and manners were after perused and approved by King Henry VI." Dr. Oliver (*Golden Remains,* iii., 35) thinks that Plot here referred to what is known as the Leland MS., which, if true, would be a proof of the authenticity of that document. But Oliver gives no evidence of the correctness of his assumption. It is more probable that the manuscript which Dr. Plot loosely quotes has not yet been recovered.

Plot, Robert, M.D. Born in 1651, and died in 1696. He was a Professor of Chemistry at Oxford, and Keeper of the Ashmolean Museum, to which position he had been appointed by Elias Ashmole, to whom, however, he showed but little gratitude. Dr. Plot published, in 1686, *The Natural History of Staffordshire*, a work in which he went out of his way to attack the Masonic institution. An able defense against this attack will be found in the third volume of Oliver's *Golden Remains of the Early Masonic Writers.* The work of Dr. Plot is both interesting and valuable to the Masonic student, as it exhibits the condition of Freemasonry in the latter part of the seventeenth century, certainly, if not at a somewhat earlier period, and is an anticipated answer to the assertions of the iconoclasts who would give Freemasonry its birth in 1717. For this purpose, I insert so much of his account as refers to the customs of the society in 1686.

"They have a custom in Staffordshire, of admitting men into the Society of Freemasons, that in the moorelands of this county seems to be of greater request than anywhere else, though I find the custom spread more or less all over the nation; for here I found persons of the most eminent quality that did not disdain to be of this fellowship. Nor, indeed, need they, were it of that antiquity and honor, that is pretended in a large parchment volum they have amongst them, containing the history and rules of the Craft of Masonry. Which is there deduced not only from sacred writ, but profane story; particularly that it was brought into England by St. Amphibal, and first communicated to St. Alban, who set down the charges of Masonry, and was made paymaster and governor of the king's works, and gave them charges and manners as St. Amphibal had taught him. Which were after confirmed by King Athelstan, whose youngest son Edwyn loved well Masonry, took upon him the charges, and learned the manners, and obtained for them of his father a free charter. Whereupon he caused them to assemble at York, and to bring all the old books of their Craft, and out of them ordained such charges and manners as they then thought fit; which charges in the said Schrole, or parchment volum, are in part declared; and thus was the Craft of Masonry grounded and confirmed in England. It is also there declared that these charges and manners were after perused and approved by King Henry VI. and his council, both as to Masters and fellows of this Right Worshipful Craft.

"Into which Society, when they are admitted, they call a meeting (or Lodg, as they term it in some places),which must consist at lest of five or six of the ancients of the Order, whom the candidates present with gloves, and so likewise to their wives, and entertain with a collation, according to the custom of the place: this ended, they proceed to the admission of them, which chiefly consists in the communication of certain secret signes, whereby they are known to one another all over the nation, by which means they have maintenance whither ever they travel, for if any man appear, though altogether unknown, that can show any of these signs to a fellow of the Society, whom they otherwise call an Accepted Mason, he is obliged presently to come to him, from what company or place soever he be in; nay, though from the top of a steeple (what hazard or inconvenience soever he run), to know his pleasure and assist him; viz., if he want work, he is bound to find him some; or if he cannot do that, to give him mony, or otherwise support him till work can be had, which is one of their articles; and it is another, that they advise the masters they work for according to the best of their skill, acquainting them with the goodness or badness of their materials, and if they be any way out in the contrivance of the buildings, modestly to rectify them in it, that Masonry be not dishonored; and many such like that are commonly known; but some others they have (to which they are sworn after their fashion) that none know but themselves." (*Nat. Hist. of Staffordshire*, ch. viii., p. 316.)

Plumb. An instrument used by Operative Masons to erect perpendicular lines, and adopted in Speculative Masonry as one of the working-tools of a Fellow-Craft. It is a symbol of rectitude of conduct, and inculcates that integrity of life and undeviating course of moral uprightness which can alone distinguish the good and just man. As the operative workman erects his temporal building with strict observance of that plumb-line, which will not permit him to deviate a hair's breadth to the right or to the left, so the Speculative Mason, guided by the unerring principles of right and truth inculcated in the symbolic teachings of the same implement, is steadfast in the pursuit of truth, neither bending beneath the frowns of adversity nor yielding to the seductions of prosperity.

To the man thus just and upright, the Scriptures attribute, as necessary parts of his character, kindness and liberality, temperance and moderation, truth and wisdom; and the Pagan poet Horace (lib. iii., od. 3) pays, in one of his most admired odes, an eloquent tribute to the stern immutability of the man who is upright and tenacious of purpose.

It is worthy of notice that, in most languages, the word which is used in a direct sense to indicate straightness of course or perpendicularity of position, is also employed in a figurative sense to express uprightness of conduct. Such are the Latin "*rectum,*" which signifies at the same time a *right line* and *honesty* or *integrity;* the Greek, *ὀρθός*, which means *straight, standing upright,* and also *equitable, just, true;* and the Hebrew *tsedek,* which in a physical sense denotes *right-*

ness, straightness, and in a moral, *what is right and just*. Our own word RIGHT partakes of this peculiarity, *right* being *not wrong*, as well as *not crooked*.

As to the name, it may be remarked that *plumb* is the word used in Speculative Masonry. Webster says that as a noun the word is seldom used except in composition. Its constant use, therefore, in Masonry, is a peculiarity.

Plumb-Line. A line to which a piece of lead is attached so as to make it hang perpendicularly. The plumb-line, sometimes called simply the *line*, is one of the working-tools of the Past Master. According to Preston, it was one of the instruments of Masonry which was presented to the Master of a Lodge at his installation, and he defines its symbolism as follows: "The line teaches the criterion of rectitude, to avoid dissimulation in conversation and action, and to direct our steps in the path which leads to immortality." This idea of the immortal life was always connected in symbology with that of the perpendicular—something that rose directly upward. Thus in the primitive church, the worshiping Christians stood up at prayer on Sunday, as a reference to the Lord's resurrection on that day. This symbolism is not, however, preserved in the verse of the prophet Amos (vii. 7), which is read in this country as the Scripture passage of the Second Degree, where it seems rather to refer to the strict justice which God will apply to the people of Israel. It there coincides with the first Masonic definition that the line teaches the criterion of moral rectitude.

Plumb-Rule. A narrow board, having a plumb-line suspended from its top and a perpendicular mark through its middle. It is one of the working-tools of a Fellow-Craft, but in Masonic language is called the *Plumb*, which see.

Plurality of Votes. See *Majority*.

Poetry of Masonry. Although Freemasonry has been distinguished more than any other single institution for the number of verses to which it has given birth, it has not produced any poetry of a very high order, except a few lyrical effusions. Rime, although not always of transcendent merit, has been a favorite form of conveying its instructions. The oldest of the Constitutions, that known as the Halliwell or Regius MS., is written in verse; and almost all the early catechisms of the degrees were in the form of rime, which, although often doggerel in character, served as a convenient method of assisting the memory. But the imagination, which might have been occupied in the higher walks of poetry, seems in Freemasonry to have been expended in the construction of its symbolism, which may, however, be considered often as the results of true poetic genius. There are, besides the songs, of which the number in all languages is very great, an abundance of prologues and epilogues, of odes and anthems, some of which are not discreditable to their authors or to the Institution. But there are very few poems on Masonic subjects of any length. The French have indulged more than any other nation in this sort of composition, and the earliest Masonic poem known is one published at Frankfort, 1756, with the title of *Noblesse des Franc-Maçons ou Institution de leur Société avant le deluge universel et de son renouvellement après le Deluge*.

It was printed anonymously, but the authorship of it is attributed to M. Jartigue. It is a transfer to verse of all the Masonic myths contained in the "Legend of the Craft" and the traditional history of Anderson. Neither the material nor the execution exempt the author from Horace's denunciation of poetic mediocrity.

Pointed Cubical Stone. The "Broached Thurnel" (*q. v.*) mentioned by Dr. Oliver and others in the Tracing-Board of an Entered Apprentice, and known to the French Mason as the *pierre cubique*, has an ax inserted in the apex. Bro. William S. Rockwell considered this feature in the Tracing-Board remarkable and suggestive of curious reflections, and thus reasoned: "The cubic stone pointed with an axe driven into it, is strikingly similar to a peculiar hieroglyphic of the Egyptians.

The name of one of their gods is written with a determinative sign affixed to it, consisting of a smooth rectangular stone with a knife over it; but the most singular portion of the circumstance is, that this hieroglyphic, which is read by Egyptologists, *Seth*, is the symbol of falsehood and error, in contradistinction to the rough (Brute) stone, which is the symbol of faith and truth. The symbol of error was the soft stone, which could be cut; the symbol of truth, the hard stone, on which no tool could be used."

Seth is the true Egyptian name of the god known afterward by the name of Typhon, at one time devoutly worshiped and profoundly venerated in the culminating epoch of the Pharaonic empire, as the monuments of Karnac and Medinet-Abou testify. But in time his worship was overthrown, his shrines desecrated, his name and titles chiseled from the monumental granite, and he himself, from being venerated as the giver of life and blessings to the rulers of Egypt, degraded from his position, treated as a destroying demon, and shunned as the personification of evil. This was not long before the exode of the children of Israel. Seth was the father of Judæus and Palestinus, is the god of the Semitic tribes who rested on the seventh day, and bears the swarthy complexion of the hated race. Seth is also known by other names in the hieroglyphic legends, among the most striking of which is Bar, that is Bal, known to us in sacred history as the fatal stumbling-block of idolatry to the Jewish people. (See *Triangle and Square.*) [C. T. McClenachan.]

Points. In the *Old Constitutions* known as the Halliwell or Regius MS., there are fifteen regulations which are called *points.* The fifteen articles which precede are said to have been in existence before the meeting at York, and then only collected after search, while the fifteen points were then enacted. Thus we are told—

'Fifteen artyculus they there sougton, (*sought, found out,*)
And fifteen poyntys there they wrogton, (*wrought, enacted.*)'

The *points* referred to in the ritualistic phrase, "arts, parts, and points of the hidden mysteries of Masonry," are the rules and regulations of the Institution. Phillips's *New World of Words* (edit. 1706) defines *point* as "an head or chief matter." It is in this sense that we speak of the "points of Masonry."

Points of Entrance, Perfect. In the earliest lectures of the last century these were called "Principal Points." The designation of them as "Perfect Points of Entrance" was of a later date. They are described both in the English and the American systems. Their specific names, and their allusion to the four cardinal virtues, are the same in both; but the verbal explanations differ, although not substantially. They are so called because they refer to four important points of the initiation. The Guttural refers to the entrance upon the penal responsibilities; the Pectoral, to the entrance into the Lodge; the Manual, to the entrance on the covenant; and the Pedal, to the entrance on the instructions in the northeast.

Points of Fellowship, Five. There are duties owing by every Mason to his brethren, which, from their symbolic allusion to certain points of the body, and from the lesson of brotherly love which they teach, are called the "Five Points of Fellowship." They are symbolically illustrated in the Third Degree, and have been summed up by Oliver as "assisting a brother in his distress, supporting him in his virtuous undertakings, praying for his welfare, keeping inviolate his secrets, and vindicating his reputation as well in his absence as in his presence." (*Landm.*, i., 185.)

Cole, in the *Freemasons' Library* (p. 190), gives the same ideas in diffuser language, as follows:

"First. When the necessities of a brother call for my aid and support, I will be ever ready to lend him such assistance, to save him from sinking, as may not be detrimental to myself or connections, if I find him worthy thereof.

"Second. Indolence shall not cause my footsteps to halt, nor wrath turn them aside; but forgetting every selfish consideration, I will be ever swift of foot to serve, help, and execute benevolence to a fellow-creature in distress, and more particularly to a brother Mason.

"Third. When I offer up my ejaculations to Almighty God, a brother's welfare I will remember as my own; for as the voices of babes and sucklings ascend to the Throne of Grace, so most assuredly will the breathings of a fervent heart arise to the mansions of bliss, as our prayers are certainly required of each other.

"Fourth. A brother's secrets, delivered to me as such, I will keep as I would my own; as betraying that trust might be doing him the greatest injury he could sustain in this mortal life; nay, it would be like the villany of an assassin, who lurks in darkness to stab his adversary, when unarmed and least prepared to meet an enemy.

"Fifth. A brother's character I will support in his absence as I would in his presence: I will not wrongfully revile him myself, nor will I suffer it to be done by others, if in my power to prevent it."

The enumeration of these Points by some other more recent authorities differs from Cole's, apparently, only in the order in which the Points are placed. The latter order is given as follows in Mackey's *Lexicon of Freemasonry:*

"First. Indolence should not cause our footsteps to halt, or wrath turn them aside; but with eager alacrity and swiftness of foot, we should press forward in the exercise of charity and kindness to a distressed fellow-creature.

"Secondly. In our devotions to Almighty God, we should remember a brother's welfare as our own; for the prayers of a fervent and sincere heart will find no less favor in the sight of Heaven, because the petition for self is mingled with aspirations of benevolence for a friend.

"Thirdly. When a brother intrusts to our keeping the secret thoughts of his bosom, prudence and fidelity should place a sacred seal upon our lips, lest, in an unguarded moment, we betray the solemn trust confided to our honor.

"Fourthly. When adversity has visited our brother, and his calamities call for our aid, we should cheerfully and liberally stretch forth the hand of kindness, to save him from sinking, and to relieve his necessities.

"Fifthly. While with candor and kindness we should admonish a brother of his faults, we should never revile his character behind his back, but rather, when attacked by others, support and defend it."

The difference here is apparently only in the order of enumeration, but really there is an important difference in the symbols on which the instructions are founded. In the old system, the symbols are the hand, the foot, the knee, the breast, and the back. In the new system, the first symbol or the hand is omitted, and the mouth and the ear substituted. There is no doubt that this omission of the first and insertion of the last are innovations, which sprung up in 1842 at the Baltimore Convention, and the enumeration given by Cole is the old and genuine one, which was originally taught in England by Preston, and in this country by Webb.

Points, The Five. See *Chromatic Calendar.*

Points, Twelve Grand. See *Twelve Original Points of Masonry.*

Point within a Circle. This is a symbol of great interest and importance, and brings us into close connection with the early symbolism of the solar orb and the universe, which was predominant in the ancient sun-worship. The lectures of Freemasonry give what modern Monitors have made an exoteric explanation of the symbol, in telling us that the point represents an individual brother, the circle the boundary line of his duty to God and man, and the two perpendicular parallel lines the patron saints of the Order—St. John the Baptist and St. John the Evangelist.

But that this was not always its symbolic signification, we may collect from the true history of its connection with the phallus of the Ancient Mysteries. The phallus, as I have already shown under the word, was among the Egyptians the symbol of fecundity, expressed by the male generative principle. It was communicated from the rites of Osiris to the religious festivals of Greece. Among the Asiatics the same emblem, under the name of lingam, was, in connection with the female principle, worshiped as the symbols of the Great Father and Mother, or producing causes of the human race, after their destruction by the deluge. On this subject, Captain Wilford (*Asiat. Res.*) remarks "that it was believed in India, that, at the general deluge, everything was involved in the common destruction except the male and female principles, or organs of generation, which were destined to produce a new race, and to repeople the earth when the waters had subsided from its surface. The female principle, symbolized by the moon, assumed the form of a lunette or crescent; while the male principle, symbolized by the sun, assuming the form of the lingam, placed himself erect in the center of the lunette, like the mast of a ship. The two principles, in this united form, floated on the surface of the waters during the period of their prevalence on the earth; and thus became the progenitors of a new race of men." Here, then, was the first outline of the point within a circle, representing the principle of fecundity, and doubtless the symbol, connected with a different history, that, namely, of Osiris, was transmitted by the Indian philosophers to Egypt, and to the other nations, who derived, as I have elsewhere shown, all their rites from the East.

It was in deference to this symbolism that, as Higgins remarks (*Anacal.*, ii., 306), circular temples were in the very earliest ages universally erected in cyclar numbers to do honor to the Deity.

In India stone circles, or rather their ruins, are everywhere found; among the oldest of which, according to Moore (*Panth.*, 242), is that of Dipaldiana, and whose execution will compete with that of the Greeks. In the oldest monuments of the Druids we find, as at Stonehenge and Abury, the circle of stones. In fact, all the temples of the Druids were circular, with a single stone erected in the center. A Druidical monument in Pembrokeshire, called Y Cromlech, is described as consisting of several rude stones pitched on end in a circular order, and in the midst of the circle a vast stone placed on several pillars. Near Keswick, in Cumberland, says Oliver (*Signs and Symbols*, 174), is another specimen of this Druidical symbol. On a hill stands a circle of forty stones placed perpendicularly, of about five feet and a half in height, and one stone in the center of greater altitude.

Among the Scandinavians, the hall of Odin contained twelve seats, disposed in the form of a circle, for the principal gods, with an elevated seat in the center for Odin. Scandinavian monuments of this form are still to be found in Scania, Zealand, and Jutland.

But it is useless to multiply examples of the prevalence of this symbol among the ancients. And now let us apply this knowledge to the Masonic symbol.

We have seen that the phallus and the point within a circle come from the same source, and must have been identical in signification. But the phallus was the symbol of fecundity, or the male generative principle, which by the ancients was supposed to be the sun (they looking to the creature and not to the Creator), because by the sun's heat and light the earth is made prolific, and its productions are brought to maturity. The point within the circle was then originally the symbol of the sun; and as the lingam of India stood in the center of the lunette, so it stands within the center of the Universe, typified by the circle, impregnating and vivifying it with its heat. And thus the astronomers have been led to adopt the same figure as their symbol of the sun.

Now it is admitted that the Lodge represents the world or the universe, and the Master and Wardens within it represent the sun in three positions. Thus we arrive at the true interpretation of the Masonic symbolism of the point within the circle. It is the same thing, but under a different form, as the Master and Wardens of a Lodge. The Master and Wardens are symbols of the sun, the Lodge of the universe, or world, just as the point is the symbol of the same sun, and the surrounding circle of the universe.

*An addition to the above may be given, by referring to one of the oldest symbols among the Egyptians, and found upon their monuments, which was a circle centered by an A U M, supported by two erect parallel serpents; the circle being expressive of the collective people of the world, protected by the parallel attributes, the Power and Wisdom of

* From this point the article is by C. T. McClenachan.

the Creator. The Alpha and Omega, or the W.ee representing the Egyptian omnipotent God, surrounded by His creation, having for a boundary no other limit than what may come within his boundless scope, his Wisdom and Power. At times this circle is represented

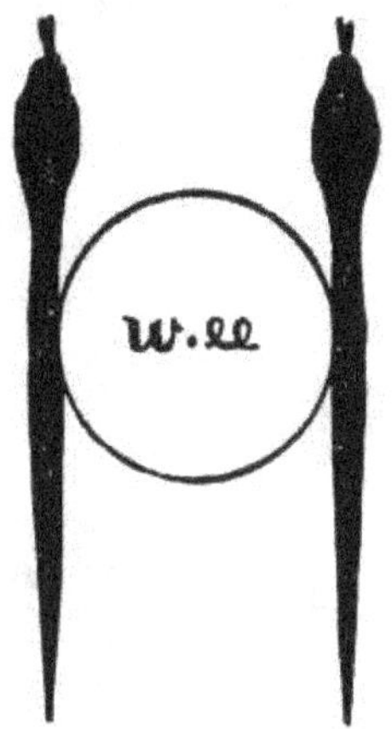

by the Ananta (Sanskrit, *eternity*), a serpent with its tail in its mouth. The parallel serpents were of the cobra species.

It has been suggestively said that the Masonic symbol refers to the circuits or circumambulation of the initiate about the sacred Altar, which supports the three Great Lights as a central point, while the brethren stand in two parallel lines.

Poland. Freemasonry was introduced into Poland, in 1736, by the Grand Lodge of England; but in 1739 the Lodges were closed in consequence of the edict of King Augustus II., who enforced the bull of Pope Clement XII. From 1742 to 1749 Masonry was revived and several Lodges erected, which flourished for a time, but afterward fell into decay. In 1766 Count Moszynski sought to put it on a better footing, and in 1769 a Grand Lodge was formed, of which he was chosen Grand Master. The Grand Lodge of England recognized this body as a Provincial Grand Lodge. On the first division of Poland, the labors of the Grand Lodge were suspended; but they were revived in 1773 by Count Bruhl, who introduced the ritual of the Strict Observance, established several new Lodges, and acknowledged the supremacy of the United Lodges of Germany. There was a Lodge in Warsaw, working in the French Rite, under the authority of the Grand Orient of France, and another under the English system. These differences of Rites created many dissensions, but in August, 1781, the Lodge Catherine of the North Star received a Warrant as a Provincial Grand Lodge, and on December 27th of the same year the body was organised, and Ignatius Pococki elected Grand Master of all Polish and Lithuanian Lodges, the English system being provisionally adopted. In 1794, with the dissolution of the kingdom, the Lodges in the Russian and Austrian portions of the partition were suppressed, and those only in Prussian Poland continued their existence. Upon the creation, by Napoleon, of the Grand Duchy of Warsaw, a Grand Orient of Poland was immediately established. This body continued in operation until 1823, with more than forty Lodges under its obedience. In November of that year the Order was interdicted in consequence of the ukase of the Emperor Alexander prohibiting all secret societies, and all the Lodges were thereon closed. During the revolt of 1830 a few Lodges arose, but they lasted only until the insurrection was suppressed.

Politics. There is no charge more frequently made against Freemasonry than that of its tendency to revolution, and conspiracy, and to political organizations which may affect the peace of society or interfere with the rights of governments. It was the substance of all Barruel's and Robison's accusations, that the Jacobinism of France and Germany was nurtured in the Lodges of those countries; it was the theme of all the denunciations of the anti-Masons of America, that the Order was seeking a political ascendancy and an undue influence over the government; it has been the unjust accusation of every enemy of the Institution in all times past, that its object and aim is the possession of power and control in the affairs of state. It is in vain that history records no instance of this unlawful connection between Freemasonry and politics; it is in vain that the libeler is directed to the Ancient Constitutions of the Order, which expressly forbid such connection; the libel is still written, and Masonry is again and again condemned as a political club.

Polkal. A significant word in the high degrees, which means *allogether separated*, in allusion to the disunited condition of the Masonic Order at the time, divided as it was into various and conflicting rites. The word is corrupted from *palcol*, and is derived from the radical פל, *pal*, which, as Gesenius says, everywhere implies separation, and the adverbial כל, *kol*, wholly, altogether.

Polychronicon. Ranulf Higden, a monk of Chester, wrote, about 1350, under this title a Latin chronicle, which was translated into English in 1387 by John Trevisa, and published by William Caxton, in 1482, as *The Polychronicon;* "conteynyng the Berynges and Dedes of many Tymes." Another edition was published (though, perhaps, it was the same book with a new title) by Wynkyn de Woorde, in 1485, as *Policronicon, in which booke ben comprysed bryefly many wonderful hystoryes, Englished by one Trevisa, vicarye of Barkley*, etc., a copy of which sold in 1857 for £37. There was another translation in the same century by an unknown author. The two translations made the book familiar to the English public, with whom it was at one time a favorite work. It was much used by the compiler or compilers of the *Old Consti-*

tutions now known as the Cooke Manuscript. Indeed, there is very little doubt that the writers of the old Masonic records borrowed from the *Polychronicon* many of their early legends of Masonry. In 1865 there was published at London, under the authority of the Master of the Rolls, an edition of the original Latin chronicle, with both the English translations, that of Trevisa and that of the unknown writer.

Pomegranate. The pomegranate, as a symbol, was known to and highly esteemed by the nations of antiquity. In the description of the pillars which stood at the porch of the Temple (see 1 Kings vii. 15), it is said that the artificer "made two chapiters of molten brass to set upon the tops of the pillars." Now the Hebrew word *caphtorim*, which has been translated "chapiters," and for which, in Amos ix. 1, the word "lintel" has been incorrectly substituted (though the marginal reading corrects the error), signifies an *artificial large pomegranate*, or *globe*. The original meaning is not preserved in the Septuagint, which has σφαιρωτήρ, nor in the Vulgate, which uses "sphærula," both meaning simply "a round ball." But Josephus, in his *Antiquities*, has kept to the literal Hebrew. It was customary to place such ornaments upon the tops or heads of columns, and in other situations. The skirt of Aaron's robe was ordered to be decorated with golden bells and pomegranates, and they were among the ornaments fixed upon the golden candelabra. There seems, therefore, to have been attached to this fruit some mystic signification, to which it is indebted for the veneration thus paid to it. If so, this mystic meaning should be traced into Spurious Freemasonry; for there, after all, if there be any antiquity in our Order, we shall find the parallel of all its rites and ceremonies.

The Syrians at Damascus worshiped an idol which they called Rimmon. This was the same idol that was worshiped by Naaman before his conversion, as recorded in the Second Book of Kings. The learned have not been able to agree as to the nature of this idol, whether he was a representation of Helios or the Sun, the god of the Phœnicians, or of Venus, or according to Grotius, in his commentary on the passage in Kings, of Saturn, or what, according to Statius, seems more probable, of Jupiter Cassius. But it is sufficient for the present purpose to know that *Rimmon* is the Hebrew and Syriac for *pomegranate*.

Cumberland, the learned Bishop of Peterborough (*Orig. Gent. Ant.*, p. 60), quotes Achilles Statius, a converted Pagan, and Bishop of Alexandria, as saying that on Mount Cassius (which Bochart places between Canaan and Egypt) there was a temple wherein Jupiter's image held a pomegranate in his hand, which Statius goes on to say, "had a mystical meaning." Sanconiathon thinks this temple was built by the descendants of the Cabiri. Cumberland attempts to explain this mystery thus: "Agreeably hereunto I guess that the pomegranate in the hand of Jupiter or Juno, (because, when it is opened, it discloses a great number of seeds,) signified only, that those deities were, being long-lived, the parents of a great many children, and families that soon grew into nations, which they planted in large possessions, when the world was newly begun to be peopled, by giving them laws and other useful inventions to make their lives comfortable."

Pausanias (*Corinthiaca*, p. 59) says he saw, not far from the ruins of Mycenæ, an image of Juno holding in one hand a scepter, and in the other a pomegranate; but he likewise declines assigning any explanation of the emblem, merely declaring that it was ἀπορρητότεροι λόγοι—"a forbidden mystery." That is, one which was forbidden by the Cabiri to be divulged.

In the festival of the Thesmophoria, observed in honor of the goddess Ceres, it was held unlawful for the celebrants (who were women) to eat the pomegranate. Clemens Alexandrinus assigns as a reason, that it was supposed that this fruit sprang from the blood of Bacchus.

Bryant (*Anc. Myth.*, iii., 237) says that the Ark was looked upon as the mother of mankind, and on this account it was figured under the semblance of a pomegranate; for as this fruit abounds with seeds, it was thought no improper emblem of the Ark, which contained the rudiments of the future world. In fact, few plants had among the ancients a more mythical history than the pomegranate.

From the Hebrews, who used it mystically at the Temple, it passed over to the Masons, who adopted it as the symbol of plenty, for which it is well adapted by its swelling and seed-abounding fruit.

Pomme Verte (Green Apple), **Order of the.** An androgynous Order, instituted in Germany in 1780, and afterward introduced into France. (Thory, *Acta Lat.*, i., 333.)

Pommel. A round knob; a term applied to the globes or balls on the top of the pillars which stood at the porch of Solomon's Temple. It was introduced into the Masonic lectures from Scriptural language. *The two pommels of the chapiters* is in 2 Chron. iv. 13. It is, however, an architectural term, thus defined by Parker (*Gloss. Arch.*, p. 365): "Pommel denotes generally any ornament of a globular form."

Pontifes Frères. See *Bridge Builders*.

Pontifex. See *Bridge Builders*.

Pontiff. In addition to what has been said of this word in the article on the "Bridge Builders of the Middle Ages," the following from Athanase Coquerel, fils, in a recent essay entitled *The Rise and Decline of the Romish Church*, will be interesting.

"What is the meaning of 'pontiff'? 'Pontiff' means bridge maker, bridge builder. Why are they called in that way? Here is the explanation of the fact: In the very first years of the existence of Rome, at a time of which we have a very fabulous history and but few existing monuments, the little town of Rome, not built on seven hills, as is generally supposed—there are eleven of them now; then there were within the town less than seven, even—that little town had a great deal to fear from an enemy which should take one of the hills that were out of town—the Janiculum—because the Janiculum is higher than the others, and from that hill an enemy could very easily throw stones, fire, or any means of destruction into the town. The Janiculum was separated from the town by the Tiber. Then the first necessity for the defense of that little town of Rome was to have a bridge. They had built a wooden bridge over the Tiber, and a great point of interest to the town was, that this bridge should be kept always in good order, so that at any moment troops could pass over. Then, with the special genius of the Romans, of which we have other instances, they ordained, curiously enough, that the men, who were a corporation, to take care of that bridge should be sacred; that their function, necessary to the defense of the town, should be considered holy; that they should be priests; and the highest of them was called 'the high bridge maker.' So it happened that there was in Rome a corporation of bridge makers—*pontifices*—of whom the head was the most sacred of all Romans; because in those days his life and the life of his companions was deemed necessary to the safety of the town."

And thus it is that the title of Pontifex Maximus, assumed by the Pope of Rome, literally means the Grand Bridge Builder.

Pontiff, Grand. See *Grand Pontiff*.

Poor Fellow-Soldiers of Jesus Christ. (*Pauperes commilitones Jesu Christi.*) This was the title first assumed by the Knights Templars.

Pooroosh. The spirit or essence of Brahm in the Indian religious system.

Poppy. In the mysteries of the ancients, the poppy was the symbol of regeneration. The somniferous qualities of the plant expressed the idea of quiescence; but the seeds of a new existence which it contained were thought to show that nature, though her powers were suspended, yet possessed the capability of being called into a renewed existence. Thus the poppy planted near a grave symbolized the idea of a resurrection. Hence, it conveyed the same symbolism as the evergreen or sprig of acacia does in the Masonic mysteries.

Porch of the Temple. See *Temple of Solomon*.

Porta, Gambattista. A physicist of Naples, who was born in 1545 and died in 1615. He was the founder of the *Segreti*, or "Academy of Secrets," which see. He devoted himself to the study of the occult sciences, was the inventor of the camera obscura, and the author of several treatises on Magic, Physiognomy, and Secret Writing. De Feller (*Biog. Univ.*) classes him with Cornelius Agrippa, Cardan, Paracelsus, and other disciples of occult philosophy.

Portiforium. A banner like unto the *gonfalon*, used as an ensign in cathedrals, and borne at the head of religious processions.

Portugal. Freemasonry was introduced into Portugal in 1736, when a Lodge was instituted at Lisbon, under a Deputation to George Gordon from Lord Weymouth, Grand Master of England. An attempt was made by John Coustos to establish a second in 1743, but he and his companions were arrested by the Inquisition, and the Lodge suppressed. Freemasonry must, however, have continued to exist, although secretly practised, for in 1776 other arrests of Freemasons were made by the Holy Office. But through the whole of the eighteenth century the history of Masonry in Portugal was the history of an uninterrupted persecution by the Church and the State. In 1805 a Grand Lodge was established at Lisbon, and Egaz-Moritz was elected Grand Master. John VI., during his exile, issued from Santa Cruz, in 1818, a decree against the Masons, which declared that every Mason who should be arrested should suffer death, and his property be confiscated to the State; and this law was extended to foreigners residing in Portugal, as well as to natives. This bigoted sovereign, on his restoration to the throne, promulgated in 1823 another decree against the Order, and Freemasonry fell into abeyance; but in 1834 the Lodges were again revived. But dissensions in reference to Masonic authority unfortunately arose among the Fraternity of Portugal, which involved the history of the Order in that country in much confusion. There were in a few years no less than four bodies claiming Masonic jurisdiction, namely, a Grande Oriente Lusitano, which had existed for more than a quarter of a century, and which, in 1846, received Letters-Patent from the Supreme Council of Brazil for the establishment of a Supreme Council; a Provincial Grand Lodge, under the jurisdiction of the Grand Lodge of Ireland, with a Chapter of Rose Croix working under the authority of the Grand Council of Rites of Ireland; and two Grand Orients working under contending Grand Masters. Many attempts were made to reconcile these opposing bodies, but without success; and, to add to the difficulty, we find, about 1862, another body calling itself the Orient of the Masonic Confederation. But all embarrassments were at length removed by the alliance, in 1871, of the United Grand Orient with the Supreme Council, and the Masonic interests of Portugal are now prosperously conducted by the "Grande Oriente Lusitano Unido, Supremo Conselho de Maçonaria Portugueza."

Postulant. The title given to the candidate in the degree of Knight Kadosh. From the Latin *postulans*, asking for, wishing to have.

Pot of Incense. As a symbol of the sacrifice which should be offered up to Deity, it has been adopted in the Third Degree. (See *Incense*.)

Pot of Manna. See *Manna, Pot of*.

Poursuivant. More correctly, *Pursuivant*, which see.

Practicus. The Third Degree of the German Rose Croix.

Praxoeans. The followers of Praxeas in the second century, who proclaimed a unity in God, and that He had suffered upon the cross.

Prayer. Freemasonry is a religious institution, and hence its regulations inculcate the use of prayer "as a proper tribute of gratitude," to borrow the language of Preston, "to the beneficent Author of Life." Hence it is of indispensable obligation that a Lodge, a Chapter, or any other Masonic body, should be both opened and closed with prayer; and in the Lodges working in the English and American systems the obligation is strictly observed. The prayers used at opening and closing in America differ in language from the early formulas found in the second edition of Preston, and for the alterations we are probably indebted to Webb. The prayers used in the middle and perhaps the beginning of the eighteenth century are to be found in Preston (ed. 1775), and are as follows:

At Opening.—"May the favor of Heaven be upon this our happy meeting; may it be begun, carried on, and ended in order, harmony, and brotherly love: Amen."

At Closing.—"May the blessing of Heaven be with us and all regular Masons, to beautify and cement us with every moral and social virtue: Amen."

There is also a prayer at the initiation of a candidate, which has, at the present day, been very slightly varied from the original form. This prayer, but in a very different form, is much older than Preston, who changed and altered the much longer formula which had been used previous to his day. It was asserted by Dermott that the prayer at initiation was a ceremony only in use among the "Ancients" or Atholl Masons, and that it was omitted by the "Moderns." But this cannot be so, as is proved by the insertion of it in the earliest editions of Preston. We have moreover a form of prayer "to be used at the admission of a brother," contained in the *Pocket Companion*, published in 1754, by John Scott, an adherent of the "Moderns," which proves that they as well as the "Ancients" observed the usage of prayer at an initiation. There is a still more ancient formula of "Prayer to be used of Christian Masons at the empointing of a brother," said to have been used in the reign of Edward IV., from 1461 to 1483, which is as follows:

"The might of God, the Father of Heaven, with the wisdom of his glorious Son through the goodness of the Holy Ghost, that hath been three persons in one Godhead, be with us at our beginning, give us grace to govern in our living here, that we may only come to his bliss that shall never have an end."

The custom of commencing and ending labor with prayer was adopted at an early period by the Operative Freemasons of England. Findel says (*Hist.*, p. 78), that "their Lodges were opened at sunrise, the Master taking his station in the East and the brethren forming a half circle around him. After prayer, each craftaman had his daily work pointed out to him, and received his instructions. At sunset they again assembled after labor, prayer was offered, and their wages paid to them." We cannot doubt that the German Stone-Masons, who were even more religiously demonstrative than their English brethren, must have observed the same custom.

As to the posture to be observed in Masonic prayer, it may be remarked that in the lower degrees the usual posture is standing. At an initiation the candidate kneels, but the brethren stand. In the higher degrees the usual posture is to kneel on the right knee. These are at least the usages which are generally practised in America.

Preadamite. A degree contained in the Archives of the Mother Lodge of the Philosophic Scottish Rite.

Precaution. In opening and closing the Lodge, in the admission of visitors, in conversation with or in the presence of strangers, the Mason is charged to use the necessary precaution, lest that should be communicated to the profane which should only be known to the initiated.

Precedency of Lodges. The precedency of Lodges is always derived from the date of their Warrants of Constitution, the oldest Lodge ranking as No. 1. As this precedency confers certain privileges, the number of the Lodge is always determined by the Grand Lodge, while the name is left to the selection of the members.

Preceptor. Grand Preceptor, or Grand Prior, or Preceptor, or Prior, was the title indifferently given by the Knights Templar to the officer who presided over a province or kingdom, as the Grand Prior or Grand Preceptor of England, who was called in the East the Prior or Preceptor of England. The principal of these Grand Preceptors were those of Jerusalem, Tripolis, and Antioch.

Preceptory. The houses or residences of the Knights Templar were called Preceptories, and the superior of such a residence was called the Preceptor. Some of the residences were also called Commanderies. The latter name has been adopted by the Masonic Templars of America. An attempt was made in 1856, at the adoption of a new Constitution by the Grand Encampment of the United States, which met at Hartford, to abolish the title "Commanderies," and adopt that of "Preceptories," for the Templar organizations; a change which would undoubtedly have been more in accordance with history, but unfortunately the effort to effect the change was not successful.

Precious Jewels. See *Jewels, Precious.*

Preferment. In all the Old Constitutions we find a reference made to ability and skill as the only claims for preferment or promotion. Thus in one of them, the Lansdowne Manuscript, whose date is about 1560, it is said that Nimrod gave a charge to the Masons that "they should ordaine the most wise and cunninge man to be Master of the King or Lord's worke that was amongst them, and neither for love, riches, nor favour, to sett another that had little cunninge to be Master of that worke, whereby the Lord should bee ill served and the science ill defamed." And again, in another part of the same Manuscript, it is ordered, "that noe Mason take on him noe Lord's worke nor other man's but if he know himselfe well able to performe the worke, so that the Craft have noe slander." Charges to the same effect, almost, indeed, in the same words, are to be found in all the Old Constitutions. So Anderson, when he compiled *The Charges of a Freemason*, which he says were "extracted from the ancient records," and which he published in 1723, in the first edition of the *Book of Constitutions*, lays down the rule of preferment in the same spirit, and in these words:

"All preferment among Masons is grounded upon real worth and personal merit only; that so the Lords may be well served, the brethren not put to shame, nor the royal Craft despised; therefore no Master or Warden is chosen by seniority, but for his merit."

And then he goes on to show how the skilful and qualified Apprentice may in due time become a Fellow-Craft, and, "when otherwise qualified, arrive to the Honour of being the Warden, and then the Master of the Lodge, the Grand Warden, and at length the Grand Master of all the Lodges, according to his merit." (*Constitutions*, 1723, p. 51.) This ought to be now, as it has always been, the true law of Masonry; and when ambitious men are seen grasping for offices, and seeking for positions whose duties they are not qualified to discharge, one is inclined to regret that the Old Charges are not more strictly obeyed.

Prelate. The fourth officer in a Commandery of Knights Templar and in a Council of Companions of the Red Cross. His duties are to conduct the religious ceremonies of the organization. His jewel is a triple triangle, the symbol of Deity, and within each of the triangles is suspended a cross, in allusion to the Christian character of the chivalric institution of which he is an officer. The corresponding officer in a Grand Commandery and in the Grand Encampment is called a Grand Prelate.

Prelate of Lebanon. (*Prélat du Liban.*) A mystical degree in the collection of Pyron.

Prentice. An archaism, or rather a vulgarism for *Apprentice*, constantly found in the Old Records. It is now never used.

Prentice Pillar. In the southeast part of the Chapel of Roslyn Castle, in Scotland, is the celebrated column which goes by this name, and with which a Masonic legend is connected. The pillar is a plain fluted shaft, having a floral garland twined around it, all carved out of the solid stone. The legend is, that when the plans of the chapel were sent from Rome, the master builder did not clearly understand about this pillar, or, as another account states, had lost this particular portion of the plans, and, in consequence, had to go to Rome for further instructions or to procure a fresh copy. During his absence, a clever apprentice, the only son of a widow, either from memory or from his own invention, carved and completed the beautiful pillar. When the master returned and found the work completed, furious with jealous rage, he killed the apprentice, by striking him a frightful blow on the forehead with a heavy setting-maul. In testimony of the truth of the legend, the visitor is shown three heads in the west part of the chapel—the master's, the apprentice's (with the gash on his forehead), and the widow's. There can be but little doubt that this legend referred to that of the Third Degree, which is thus shown to have existed, at least substantially, at that early period.

Preparation of the Candidate. Great care was taken of the personal condition of every Israelite who entered the Temple for Divine worship. The Talmudic treatise entitled *Baracoth*, which contains instructions as to the ritual worship among the Jews, lays down the following rules for the preparation of all who visit the Temple: "No man shall go into the Temple with his staff, nor with shoes on his feet, nor with his outer garment, nor with money tied up in his purse." There are certain ceremonial usages in Freemasonry which furnish what may be called at least very remarkable coincidences with this old Jewish custom.

The preparation of the candidate for initiation in Masonry is entirely symbolic. It varies in the different degrees, and therefore the symbolism varies with it. Not being arbitrary and unmeaning, but, on the contrary, conventional and full of signification, it cannot be altered, abridged, or added to in any of its details, without affecting its esoteric design. To it, in its fullest extent, every candidate must, without exception, submit.

The preparation of a candidate is one of the most delicate duties we have to perform and care should be taken in appointing the officer, who should bear in mind that "that which is not permittible among gentlemen should be impossible among Masons." [E. E. C.]

Preparing Brother. The brother who prepares the candidate for initiation. In English, he has no distinctive title. In French Lodges he is called "Frère terrible," and in German he is called "Vorbereitender Bruder," or "Fürchterlicher Bruder." His duties require him to have a competent knowledge of the ritual of reception, and therefore an experienced member of the Lodge is generally selected to discharge the functions of this office. In most jurisdictions in America this is performed by the Master of Ceremonies.

President. The presiding officer in a convention of High Priests, according to the American system, is so called. The second officer is styled Vice-President. On September 6, 1871, the Grand Orient of France, in violation of the landmarks, abolished the office of Grand Master, and conferred his powers on a Council of the Order. The President of the Council is now the official representative of the Grand Orient and the Craft, and exercises several of the prerogatives hitherto administered by the Grand Master.

Presiding Officer. Whoever acts, although temporarily and *pro hac vice*, as the presiding officer of a Masonic body, assumes for the time all the powers and functions of the officer whom he represents. Thus, in the absence of the Worshipful Master, the Senior Warden presides over the Lodge, and for the time is invested with all the prerogatives that pertain to the Master of a Lodge, and can, while he is in the chair, perform any act that it would be competent for the Master to perform were he present.

Press, Masonic. The number of the Masonic press throughout the world is small, but the literary ability commands attention. In every nation Masonry has its advocate and newsbearer, in the form of a weekly or semi-monthly chronicle of events, or the more sedate magazine or periodical, sustaining the literature of the Fraternity.

Preston, William. This distinguished Mason was born at Edinburgh on the 7th of August, 1742. The usual statement, that he was born on the 28th of July, refers to old style, and requires therefore to be amended. He was the son of William Preston, Esq., a writer to the Signet, and Helena Cumming. The elder Preston was a man of much intellectual culture and abilities, and in easy circumstances, and took, therefore, pains to bestow upon his son an adequate education. He was sent to school at a very early age, and having completed his preliminary education in English under the tuition of Mr. Stirling, a celebrated teacher in Edinburgh, he entered the High School before he was six years old, and made considerable progress in the Latin tongue. From the High School he went to college, where he acquired a knowledge of the rudiments of Greek.

After the death of his father he retired from college, and became the amanuensis of that celebrated linguist, Thomas Ruddiman, to whose friendship his father had consigned him. Mr. Ruddiman having greatly impaired and finally lost his sight by his intense application to his classical studies, Preston remained with him as his secretary until his decease. His patron had, however, previously bound young Preston to his brother, Walter Ruddiman, a printer, but on the increasing failure of his sight, Mr. Thomas Ruddiman withdrew Preston from the printing-office, and occupied him in reading to him and translating such of his works as were not completed, and in correcting the proofs of those that were in the press. Subsequently Preston compiled a catalogue of Ruddiman's books, under the title of *Bibliotheca Ruddimana*, which is said to have exhibited much literary ability.

After the death of Mr. Ruddiman, Preston returned to the printing-office, where he remained for about a year; but his inclinations leading him to literary pursuits, he, with the consent of his master, repaired to London in 1760, having been furnished with several letters of introduction by his friends in Scotland. Among them was one to William Strahan, the king's printer, in whose service, and that of his son and successor, he remained for the best years of his life as a corrector of the press, devoting himself, at the same time, to other literary vocations, editing for many years the *London Chronicle*, and furnishing materials for various periodical publications.

Mr. Preston's critical skill as a corrector of the press led the literary men of that day to submit to his suggestions as to style and language; and many of the most distinguished authors who were contemporary with him honored him with their friendship. As an evidence of this, there were found in his library, at his death, presentation copies of their works, with their autographs, from Gibbon, Hume, Robertson, Blair, and many others.

It is, however, as a distinguished teacher of the Masonic ritual, and as the founder of a system of lectures which still retain their influence, that William Preston more especially claims our attention.

Stephen Jones, the disciple and intimate friend of Preston, published in 1795, in the *Freemasons' Magazine*, a sketch of Preston's life and labors; and as there can be no doubt, from the relations of the author and the subject, of the authenticity of the facts related, I shall not hesitate to use the language of this contemporary sketch, interpolating such explanatory remarks as I may deem necessary.

Soon after Preston's arrival in London, a number of brethren from Edinburgh resolved to institute a Freemasons' Lodge in that city, under the sanction of a Constitution from Scotland; but not having succeeded in their application, they were recommended by the Grand Lodge of Scotland to the ancient Lodge in London, which immediately granted them a Dispensation to form a Lodge and to make Masons. They accordingly met at the White Hart in the Strand, and Mr. Preston was the second person initiated under that Dispensation. This was in 1762. Lawrie records the application as having been in that year to the Grand Lodge of Scotland. It thus appears that Preston was made a Mason under the Dermott system. It will be seen, however, that he subsequently went over to the legitimate Grand Lodge.

The Lodge was soon after regularly constituted by the officers of the ancient Grand Lodge in person. Having increased considerably in numbers, it was found necessary to remove to the Horn Tavern in Fleet Street, where it continued some time, till, that house being unable to furnish proper accommodations, it was removed to Scots' Hall, Blackfriars. Here it continued to flourish about two years, when the decayed state of that building obliged it to remove to the Half Moon Tavern, Cheapside, where it continued to meet for a considerable time.

At length Mr. Preston and some others of the members having joined the Lodge, under the regular English Constitution, at the Talbot Inn, in the Strand, they prevailed on the rest of the Lodge at the Half Moon Tavern to petition for a Constitution. Lord Blaney, at that time Grand Master, readily acquiesced with the desire of the brethren, and the Lodge was soon after constituted a second time, in ample form, by the name of "The Caledonian Lodge." The ceremonies observed, and the numerous assembly of respectable brethren who attended the Grand Officers on that occasion, were long remembered to the honor of the Lodge.

This circumstance, added to the absence of a very skilful Mason, to whom Mr. Preston was attached, and who had departed for Scotland on account of his health, induced him to turn his attention to the Masonic lectures; and to arrive at the depths of the science, short of which he did not mean to stop, he spared neither pains nor expense.

Preston's own remarks on this subject, in the introduction to his *Illustrations of Masonry*, are well worth the perusal of every brother who intends to take office. "When," says he, "I first had the honor to be elected Master of a Lodge, I thought it proper to inform myself fully of the general rules of the society, that I might be able to fulfil my own duty, and officially enforce obedience in others. The methods which I adopted, with this view, excited in some of superficial knowledge an absolute dislike of what they considered as innovations; and in others, who were better informed, a jealousy of pre-eminence, which the principles of Masonry ought to have checked. Notwithstanding these discouragements, however, I persevered in my intention of supporting the dignity of the society, and of discharging with fidelity the trust reposed in me." Masonry has not changed. We still too often find the same mistaking of research for innovation, and the same ungenerous jealousy of preeminence of which Preston complains.

Wherever instruction could be acquired, thither Preston directed his course; and with the advantage of a retentive memory, and an extensive Masonic connection, added to a diligent literary research, he so far succeeded in his purpose as to become a competent master of the subject. To increase the knowledge he had acquired, he solicited the company and conversation of the most experienced Masons from foreign countries; and, in the course of a literary correspondence with the Fraternity at home and abroad, made such progress in the mysteries of the art as to become very useful in the connections he had formed. He was frequently heard to say, that in the ardor of his inquiries he had explored the abodes of poverty and wretchedness, and, where it might have been least expected, acquired very valuable scraps of information. The poor brother in return, we are assured, had no cause to think his time or talents ill bestowed. He was also accustomed to convene his friends once or twice a week, in order to illustrate the lectures; on which occasion objections were started, and explanations given, for the purpose of mutual improvement. At last, with the assistance of some zealous friends, he was enabled to arrange and digest the whole of the first lecture. To establish its validity, he resolved to submit to the society at large the progress he had made; and for that purpose he instituted, at a very considerable expense, a grand gala at the Crown and Anchor Tavern, in the Strand, on Thursday, May 21, 1772, which was honored with the presence of the then Grand Officers, and many other eminent and respectable brethren. On this occasion he delivered an oration on the Institution, which, having met with general approbation, was afterward printed in the first edition of the *Illustrations of Masonry*, published by him the same year.

Having thus far succeeded in his design, Mr. Preston determined to prosecute the plan he had formed, and to complete the lectures. He employed, therefore, a number of skilful brethren, at his own expense, to visit different town and country Lodges, for the purpose of gaining information; and these brethren communicated the result of their visits at a weekly meeting.

When by study and application he had arranged his system, he issued proposals for a regular course of lectures on all the degrees of Masonry, and these were publicly delivered by him at the Miter Tavern, in Fleet Street, in 1774.

For some years afterward, Mr. Preston indulged his friends by attending several schools of instruction, and other stated meetings, to propagate the knowledge of the science, which had spread far beyond his expectations, and considerably enhanced the reputation of the society. Having obtained the sanction of the Grand Lodge, he continued to be a zealous encourager and supporter of all the measures of that assembly which tended to add dignity to the Craft, and in all the Lodges in which his name was enrolled, which were very numerous, he enforced a due obedience to the laws and regulations of that body. By these means the subscriptions to the charity became much more considerable; and daily acquisitions to the society were made of some of the most eminent and distinguished characters. At last he was invited by his friends to visit the Lodge of Antiquity, No. 1, then held at the Miter Tavern, in Fleet Street, when on June 15, 1774, the brethren of that Lodge were pleased to admit him a member, and, what was very unusual, elected him Master at the same meeting.

He had been Master of the Philanthropic Lodge at the Queen's Head, Gray's-inn-gate, Holborn, for over six years, and of several other Lodges before that time. But he was now taught to consider the importance of the first Master under the English Constitution; and he seemed to regret that some eminent character in the walks of life had not been selected to support so distinguished a station. Indeed, this too small consideration of his own importance pervaded his conduct on all occasions; and he was frequently seen voluntarily to assume the subordinate offices of an assembly, over which he had long presided, on occasions where, from the absence of the proper persons, he had conceived that his services would promote the purposes of the meeting.

To the Lodge of Antiquity he now began chiefly to confine his attention, and during his Mastership, which continued for some years, the Lodge increased in numbers and improved in its finances.

That he might obtain a complete knowledge of the state of the society under the English Constitution, he became an active member of the Grand Lodge, was admitted a member of the hall committee, and during the secretaryship of Mr. Thomas French, under the auspices of the Duke of Beaufort, then Grand Master, had become a useful assistant in arranging the general regulations of the society, and reviving the foreign and country correspondence. Having been appointed to the office of Deputy Grand Secretary under James Heseltine, Esq., he compiled, for the benefit of the charity, the *History of Remarkable Occurrences*, inserted in the first two publications of the *Freemasons' Calendar;* prepared for the press an *Appendix to the Book of Constitutions*, and attended so much to the correspondence with the different Lodges as to merit the approbation of his patron. This enabled him, from the various memoranda he had made, to form the History of Masonry, which was afterward printed in his *Illustrations*. The office of Deputy Grand Secretary he afterward resigned.

An unfortunate dispute having arisen in the society in 1777, between the Grand Lodge and the Lodge of Antiquity, in which Mr Preston took the part of the Lodge and his private friends, his name was ordered to be erased from the hall committee; and he was afterward, with a number of gentlemen, members of that Lodge, expelled.

The treatment he and his friends received at that time was circumstantially narrated in a well-written pamphlet, printed by Mr. Preston at his own expense, and circulated among his friends, but never published, and the leading circumstances were recorded in some of the later editions of the *Illustrations of Masonry*. Ten years afterward, however, on a reinvestigation of the subject in dispute, the Grand Lodge was pleased to reinstate Mr. Preston, with all the other members of the Lodge of Antiquity, and that in the most handsome manner, at the grand feast in 1790, to the general satisfaction of the Fraternity.

During Mr. Preston's exclusion, he seldom or ever attended any of the Lodges, though he was actually an enrolled member of a great many Lodges at home and abroad, all of which he politely resigned at the time of his suspension, and directed his attention to his other literary pursuits, which may fairly be supposed to have contributed more to the advantage of his fortune.

So much of the life of Preston we get from the interesting sketch of Stephen Jones. To other sources we must look for a further elucidation of some of the circumstances which he has so concisely related.

The expulsion of such a man as Preston from the Order was a disgrace to the Grand Lodge which inflicted it. It was, to use the language of Oliver, who himself, in aftertimes, had undergone a similar act of injustice, "a very ungrateful and inadequate return for his services."

The story was briefly this: It had been determined by the brethren of the Lodge of Antiquity, held on December 17, 1777, that at the annual festival on St. John's day, a procession should be formed to St. Dunstan's Church, a few steps only from the tavern where the Lodge was held; a protest of a few of the members was entered against it on the day of the festival. In consequence of this only ten members attended, who, having clothed themselves as Masons in the vestry room, sat in the same pew and heard a sermon, after which they crossed the street in their gloves and aprons to return to the Lodge room. At the next meeting of the Lodge, a motion was made to repudiate this act; and while speaking against it, Mr. Preston asserted the inherent privileges of the Lodge of Antiquity, which, not working under a Warrant of the Grand Lodge, was, in his opinion, not subject in the matter of processions to the regulations of the Grand Lodge. It was for maintaining this opinion, which, whether right or wrong, was after all only an opinion, Preston was, under circumstances which exhibited neither magnanimity nor dignity on the part of the Grand Lodge, expelled from the Order. One of the unhappy results of this act of oppression was that the Lodge of Antiquity severed itself from the Grand Lodge, and formed a rival body under the style of the "Grand Lodge of England South of the River Trent," acting under authority from the Lodge of All England at York.

But ten years afterward, in 1787, the Grand Lodge saw the error it had committed, and Preston was restored with all his honors and dignities and the new Grand Lodge collapsed. And now, while the name of Preston is known and revered by all who value Masonic learning, the names of all his bitter enemies, with the exception of Noorthouck, have sunk into a well-deserved oblivion.

Preston had no sooner been restored to his Masonic rights than he resumed his labors for the advancement of the Order. In 1787 he organized the Order of Harodim, a society in which it was intended to thoroughly teach the lectures which he had prepared. Of this Order some of the most distinguished Masons of the day became members, and it is said to have produced great benefits by its well-devised plan of Masonic instruction.

But William Preston is best known to us by his invaluable work entitled *Illustrations of Masonry*. The first edition of this work was published in 1772. Although it is spoken of in some resolutions of a Lodge, published in the second edition, as "a very ingenious and elegant pamphlet," it was really a work of some size, consisting, in its introduction and text, of 288 pages. It contained an account of the "grand gala," or banquet, given by the author to the Fraternity in May, 1772, when he first proposed his system of lectures. This account was omitted in the second and all subsequent editions "to make room for more useful matter." The second edition, enlarged to 324 pages, was published in 1775, and this was followed by others in 1776, 1781, 1788, 1792, 1799, 1801, and 1812. There must have been three other editions, of which I can find no account in the bibliographies, for Wilkie calls his 1801 edition the tenth, and the edition of 1812, the last published by the author, is called the twelfth. The thirteenth and fourteenth editions were published after the author's death, with additions—the former by Stephen Jones in 1821, and the latter by Dr. Oliver in 1829. Other English editions have been subsequently published. [The last being edited by Dr. Oliver in 1861.] The work was translated into German, and two editions published, one in 1776 and the other in 1780. In America, two editions were published in 1804, one at Alexandria, in Virginia, and the other, with numerous important additions, by George Richards, at Portsmouth, New Hampshire. Both claim, on the title-page, to be the "first American edition"; and it is probable that both works were published by their respective editors about the same time, and while neither had any knowledge of the existence of a rival copy.

Preston died, after a long illness, in Dean Street, Fetter Lane, London, on April 1, 1818, at the age of seventy-six, and was buried in St. Paul's Cathedral. In the latter years of his life he seems to have taken no active public part in Masonry, for in the very full account of the proceedings at the union in 1813 of the two Grand Lodges, his name does not appear as one of the actors, and his system was then ruthlessly surrendered to the newer but not better one of Dr. Hemming. But he had not lost his interest in the Institution which he had served so well and so long, and by which he had been so illy requited. For he bequeathed at his death £300 in Consols, the interest of which was to provide for the annual delivery of a lecture according to his system. He also left £500 to the Royal Freemasons' Charity, for female children, and a like sum to the General Charity Fund of the Grand Lodge. He was never married, and left behind him only his name as a great Masonic teacher and the memory of his services to the Craft. Jones's edition of his *Illustrations* contains an excellently engraved likeness of him by Ridley, from an original portrait said to be by S. Drummond, Royal Academician. There is an earlier engraved likeness of him in the *Freemasons' Magazine* for 1795, from a painting known to be by Drummond, and taken in 1794. They present the differences of features which may naturally be ascribed to a lapse of twenty-six years. The latter print is said, by those who personally knew him, to be an excellent likeness.

Prestonian Lecture. In 1818, Bro. Preston, the author of the *Illustrations of Masonry*, bequeathed £300 in Consols, the interest of which was to provide for the annual delivery of a lecture according to the system which he had elaborated. The appointment of the Lecturer was left to the Grand Master for the time being. Stephen Jones, a Past Master of the Lodge of Antiquity, and an intimate friend of Preston, received the first appointment; and it was subsequently given to Bro. Laurence Thompson, the only surviving pupil of Preston. He held it until his death, after which no appointment of a Lecturer was made until 1857, when the W. M. of the Royal York Lodge was requested by Lord Zetland, Grand Master, to deliver the lecture, which he did in January, 1858; twice again in the same year the lecture was delivered, and again, in subsequent years until 1862, since which time the lecture seems to have been abandoned.

Prestonian Lectures. About the year 1772, Preston submitted his course of lectures on the first three degrees to the Craft of England. These lectures were a revision of those which had been practised, with various modifications, since the revival of 1717, and were intended to confer a higher literary character on the Masonic ritual. Preston had devoted much time and labor to the compilation of these lectures, a syllabus of which will be found in his *Illustrations*. They were adopted eagerly by the English Fraternity, and continued to be the authoritative system of the Grand Lodge of England until the union in 1813, when, for the sake of securing uniformity, the new and inferior system of Dr. Hemming was adopted. But the Prestonian lectures and ritual are still used by many Lodges in England. In America they were greatly altered by Webb, and are no longer practised there.

Pretender. James Stuart, the son of James II., who abdicated the throne of Great Britain, and Charles Edward, his son, are known in history as the Old and the Young Pretender. Their intrigues with Masonry, which they are accused of attempting to use as an instrument to aid in a restoration to the throne, constitute a very interesting episode in the history of the Order. (See *Stuart Masonry*.)

Previous Question. A parliamentary motion intended to suppress debate. It is utterly unknown in the parliamentary law of Masonry, and it would be always out of order to move it in a Masonic body.

Prichard, Samuel. "An unprincipled and needy brother," as Oliver calls him, who published at London, in 1730, a book with the following title: *Masonry Dissected; being a Universal and Genuine Description of all its Branches, from the Original to this Present Time: as it is delivered in the constituted, regular Lodges, both in City and Country, according to the several Degrees of Admission; giving an impartial account of their regular Proceedings in initiating their New Members in the whole Three Degrees of Masonry, viz., I. Entered Prentice; II. Fellow Craft; III. Master. To which is added, The Author's Vindication of Himself, by Samuel Prichard, Late Member of a constituted Lodge.* This work, which contained a great deal of plausible matter, mingled with some truth as well as falsehood, passed through a great many editions, was translated into the French, German, and Dutch languages, and became the basis or model on which all the subsequent so-called expositions, such as Tubal-Cain, Jachin and Boaz, etc., were framed. In the same year of the appearance of Prichard's book, a *Defence of Masonry*, as a reply to the *Masonry Dissected* was anonymously published, and has often been erroneously attributed to Dr. Anderson, but it has been discovered that its author was Bro. Martin Clare (*q. v.*). No copy is now known to exist of this *Defence*, but it will be found at the end of the 1738 edition of the *Constitutions*. It is not, however, a reply to Prichard, but rather an attempt to interpret the ceremonies which are described in the *Masonry Dissected* in their symbolic import, and this it is that gives to the *Defence* a value which ought to have made it a more popular work among the Fraternity than it is. Prichard died in obscurity; but the Abbé Larudan, in his *Franc-Maçons ecrasés* (p. 135), has manufactured a wild tale about his death; stating that he was carried by force at night into the Grand Lodge at London, put to death, his body burned to ashes, and all the Lodges in the world informed of the execution. The Abbé is satisfied of the truth of this wondrous narrative because he had heard it told in Holland and in Germany, all of which only proves that the French calumniator of Masonry abounded either in an inventive faculty or in a trusting faith.

Price, Henry. He received a Deputation as Provincial Grand Master of New England, which was issued on April 30, 1733, by Viscount Montague, Grand Master of England. On the 30th of the following July, Price organised a Provincial Grand Lodge; and he may thus be considered as the founder of Masonry in New England. He was born in England about the year 1697, and died in Massachusetts in 1780. A very able memoir of Price, by Bro. William Sewell Gardner, will be found in the Proceedings of the Grand Lodge of Massachusetts for the year 1871.

Priest. In the primitive ages of the world every father was the priest of his family, and offered prayer and sacrifice for his household. So, too, the patriarchs exercised the same function. Melchisedek is called "the priest of the most high God"; and everywhere in Scripture we find the patriarchs perform ng the duties of prayer and sacrifice. But when political society was organized, a necessity was found, in the religious wants of the people, for a separate class, who should become, as they have been described, the mediators between men and God, and the interpreters of the will of the gods to men. Hence arose the sacerdotal class—the *cohen* among the Hebrews, the *hiereus* among the Greeks, and the *sacerdos* among the Romans. Thereafter prayer and sacrifice were entrusted to these, and the people paid them reverence for the sake of the deities whom they served. Ever since, in all countries, the distinction has existed between the priest and the layman, as representatives of two distinct classes.

But Masonry has preserved in its religious ceremonies, as in many of its other usages, the patriarchal spirit. Hence the Master of the Lodge, like the father of a primitive family, on all occasions offers up prayer and serves at the altar. A chaplain is sometimes, through courtesy, invited to perform the former duty, but the Master is really the priest of the Lodge.

Having then such solemn duties to discharge, and sometimes, as on funereal occasions, in public, it becomes every Master so to conduct his life and conversation as not, by contrast, to make his ministration of a sacred office repulsive to those who see and hear him, and especially to profanes. It is not absolutely required that he should be a religious man, resembling the clergyman in seriousness of deportment; but in his behavior he should be an example of respect for religion. He who at one time drinks to intoxication, or indulges in profane swearing, or obscene and vulgar language, is unfit at any other time to conduct the religious services of a society. Such a Master could inspire the members of his Lodge with no respect for the ceremonies he was conducting; and if the occasion was a public one, as at the burial of a brother, the circumstance would subject the Order which could tolerate such an incongruous exhibition to contempt and ridicule.

Priest, Grand High. See *Grand High Priest.*

Priest, High. See *High Priest.*

Priesthood, Order of High. See *High Priesthood, Order of.*

Priestly Order. A Rite which Bro. John Yarker, of Manchester, says (*Myst. of*

Antiq., p. 126) was formerly practised in Ireland, and formed the system of the York Grand Lodge. It consisted of seven degrees, as follows: 1. 2. 3. Symbolic degrees; 4. Past Master; 5. Royal Arch; 6. Knight Templar; 7. Knight Templar Priest, or Holy Wisdom. The last degree was called a Tabernacle, and was governed by seven "Pillars." Bro. Hughan (*Hist. of Freem. in York*, p. 32) doubts the York origin of the Priestly Order, as well as the claim it made to have been revived in 1786. It is now obsolete.

Priest, Royal. The Fifth Degree of the Initiated Brothers of Asia.

Priest Theosophist. Thory says that it is the Sixth Degree of the Kabbalistic Rite.

Priestly Vestments. The high priest ministered in eight vestments, and the ordinary priest in four—the tunic, drawers, bonnet, and girdle. To these the high priest added the breastplate, ephod, robe and golden plate, and when occasion required the Urim and Thummim.

Primitive Freemasonry. The Primitive Freemasonry of the antediluvians is a term for which we are indebted to Oliver, although the theory was broached by earlier writers, and among them by the Chevalier Ramsay. The theory is, that the principles and doctrines of Freemasonry existed in the earliest ages of the world, and were believed and practised by a primitive people, or priesthood, under the name of Pure or Primitive Freemasonry; and that this Freemasonry, that is to say, the religious doctrine inculcated by it, was, after the flood, corrupted by the Pagan philosophers and priests, and, receiving the title of *Spurious Freemasonry*, was exhibited in the Ancient Mysteries. The Noachidæ, however, preserved the principles of the Primitive Freemasonry, and transmitted them to succeeding ages, when at length they assumed the name of *Speculative Masonry*. The Primitive Freemasonry was probably without ritual or symbolism, and consisted only of a series of abstract propositions derived from antediluvian traditions. Its dogmas were the unity of God and the immortality of the soul. Dr. Oliver, who gave this system its name, describes it (*Hist. Landm.*, i., p. 61) in the following language: "It included a code of simple morals. It assured men that they who did well would be approved of God; and if they followed evil courses, sin would be imputed to them, and they would thus become subject to punishment. It detailed the reasons why the seventh day was consecrated and set apart as a Sabbath, or day of rest; and showed why the bitter consequences of sin were visited upon our first parents, as a practical lesson that it ought to be avoided. But the great object of this Primitive Freemasonry was to preserve and cherish the promise of a Redeemer, who should provide a remedy for the evil that their transgression had introduced into the world, when the appointed time should come."

In his *History of Initiation* he makes the supposition that the ceremonies of this Primitive Freemasonry would be few and unostentatious, and consist, perhaps, like that of admission into Christianity, of a simple lustration, conferred alike on all, in the hope that they would practise the social duties of benevolence and good-will to man, and unsophisticated devotion to God.

He does not, however, admit that the system of Primitive Freemasonry consisted only of those tenets which are to be found in the first chapters of Genesis, or that he intends, in his definition of this science, to embrace so general and indefinite a scope of all the principles of truth and light, as Preston has done in his declaration, that "from the commencement of the world, we may trace the foundation of Masonry." On the contrary, Oliver supposes that this Primitive Freemasonry included a particular and definite system, made up of legends and symbols, and confined to those who were initiated into its mysteries. The knowledge of these mysteries was of course communicated by God himself to Adam, and from him traditionally received by his descendants, throughout the patriarchal line.

This view of Oliver is substantiated by the remarks of Rosenberg, a learned French Mason, in an article in the *Freemasons' Quarterly Review*, on the Book of Raziel, an ancient Kabbalistic work, whose subject is these Divine mysteries. "This book," says Rosenberg, "informs us that Adam was the first to receive these mysteries. Afterward, when driven out of Paradise, he communicated them to his son Seth; Seth communicated them to Enoch; Enoch to Methuselah; Methuselah to Lamech; Lamech to Noah; Noah to Shem; Shem to Abraham; Abraham to Isaac; Isaac to Jacob; Jacob to Levi; Levi to Kelhoth; Kelhoth to Amram; Amram to Moses; Moses to Joshua; Joshua to the Elders; the Elders to the Prophets; the Prophets to the Wise Men; and then from one to another down to Solomon."

Such, then, was the Pure or Primitive Freemasonry, the first system of mysteries which, according to modern Masonic writers of the school of Oliver, has descended, of course with various modifications, from age to age, in a direct and uninterrupted line, to the Freemasons of the present day.

The theory is an attractive one, and may be qualifiedly adopted, if we may accept what appears to have been the doctrine of Anderson, of Hutchinson, of Preston, and of Oliver, that the purer theosophic tenets of "the chosen people of God" were similar to those subsequently inculcated in Masonry, and distinguished from the corrupted teaching of the Pagan religions as developed in the mysteries. But if we attempt to contend that there was among the Patriarchs any esoteric organization at all resembling the modern system of Freemasonry, we shall find no historical data on which we may rely for support.

Primitive Rite. This Rite was founded at Narbonne, in France, on April 19, 1780, by the pretended "Superiors of the Order of Free and Accepted Masons." It was attached to the Lodge of the *Philadelphes*, under the title of the "First Lodge of St. John united to the Primitive Rite for the country of France." Hence it is sometimes called the Primitive Rite of Narbonne, and sometimes the Rite of the Philadelphes. It was divided into three classes, which comprised ten degrees of instruction. These were not, in the usual sense, degrees, but rather collections of grades, out of which it was sought to develop all the instructions of which they were capable. These classes and degrees were as follows:

First Class. 1. Apprentice. 2. Fellow-Craft. 3. Master Mason. These were conformable to the same degrees in all the other Rites.

Second Class. Fourth Degree, comprising Perfect Master, Elu, and Architect. Fifth Degree, comprising the Sublime Ecossais. Sixth Degree, comprising the Knight of the Sword, Knight of the East, and Prince of Jerusalem.

Third Class. 7. The First Chapter of Rose Croix, comprising ritual instructions. 8. The Second Chapter of Rose Croix. It is the depository of historical documents of rare value. 9. The Third Chapter of Rose Croix, comprising physical and philosophical instructions. 10. The Fourth and last Chapter of Rose Croix, or Rose Croix Brethren of the Grand Rosary, engaged in researches into the occult sciences, the object being the rehabilitation and reintegration of man in his primitive rank and prerogatives. The Primitive Rite was united to the Grand Orient in 1786, although some of its Lodges, objecting to the union, maintained their independence. It secured, at one time, a high consideration among French Masons, not only on account of the objects in which it was engaged, but on account also of the talents and position of many of its members. But it is no longer practised.

Primitive Scottish Rite. This Rite claims to have been established in 1770, at Namur, in Belgium, by a body called the Metropolitan Grand Lodge of Edinburgh. But the truth, according to Clavel (*Hist. Pitt.*, p. 220), is that it was the invention of one Marchot, an advocate of Nivelles, who organized it in 1818, at Namur, beyond which city, and the Lodge of "Bonne Amitié," it scarcely ever extended. It consists of thirty-three degrees, as follows: 1. Apprentice; 2. Fellow-Craft; 3. Master; 4. Perfect Master; 5. Irish Master; 6. Elect of Nine; 7. Elect of the Unknown; 8. Elect of Fifteen; 9. Illustrious Master; 10. Perfect Elect; 11. Minor Architect; 12. Grand Architect; 13. Sublime Architect; 14. Master in Perfect Architecture; 15. Royal Arch; 16. Prussian Knight; 17. Knight of the East; 18. Prince of Jerusalem; 19. Master of All Lodges; 20. Knight of the West; 21. Knight of Palestine; 22. Sovereign Prince of Rose Croix; 23. Sublime Scottish Mason; 24. Knight of the Sun; 25. Grand Scottish Mason of St. Andrew; 26. Master of the Secret; 27. Knight of the Black Eagle; 28. Knight of K——H; 29. Grand Elect of Truth; 30. Novice of the Interior; 31. Knight of the Interior; 32. Prefect of the Interior; 33. Commander of the Interior. The Primitive Scottish Rite appears to have been founded upon the Rite of Perfection, with an intermixture of the Strict Observance of Hund, the Adonhiramite, and some other Rites.

Prince. The word Prince is not attached as a title to any Masonic office, but is prefixed as a part of the name to several degrees, as Prince of the Royal Secret, Prince of Rose Croix, and Prince of Jerusalem. In all of these instances it seems to convey some idea of sovereignty inherent in the character of the degree. Thus the Prince of the Royal Secret was the ultimate, and, of course, controlling degree of the Rite of Perfection, whence, shorn, however, of its sovereignty, it has been transferred to the Ancient and Accepted Scottish Rite. The Prince of Rose Croix, although holding in some Rites a subordinate position, was originally an independent degree, and the representative of Rosicrucian Masonry. It is still at the head of the French Rite. The Princes of Jerusalem, according to the Old Constitutions of the Rite of Perfection, were invested with power of jurisdiction over all degrees below the Sixteenth, a prerogative which they exercised long after the promulgation of the *Constitutions of 1786*; and even now they are called, in the ritual of the Ancient and Accepted Rite, "Chiefs in Masonry," a term borrowed from the *Constitutions of 1762*. But there are several other Prince degrees which do not seem, at least now, to claim any character of sovereignty—such are the Prince of Lebanon, Prince of the Tabernacle, and Prince of Mercy, all of which are now subordinate degrees in the Scottish Rite.

Prince Adept. See *Adept, Prince*.

Prince Depositor, Grand. (*Grand Prince Dépositaire.*) A degree in the collection of Pyron.

Prince Edward Island. Previous to November, 1798, Prince Edward Island was called St. John's Island, the name being changed by Imperial Act on that date.

On the 9th of October, 1797, St. John's Lodge, now No. 1 on the Registry of that Province, was established by Warrant at Charlottetown by the Grand Lodge of England. The then Lieutenant-Governor, General Edward Fanning, was one of the Charter members. In 1857, Victoria Lodge at Charlottetown was chartered by Scotland. In 1875 there were seven lodges in this Province working under English Warrants, viz., St. John's, King Hiram, St. George, Alexandra, Mount Lebanon, and True Brothers, and one under the Scottish Register, "Victoria."

On the 23d day of June, 1875, these eight Lodges met and formed the Grand Lodge of Prince Edward Island. The Hon. John Yeo was elected Grand Master and was installed, together with his officers, the following day by M. Wor. Bro. John V. Ellis, Grand Master of New Brunswick.

Prince Mason. A term applied in the old Scottish Rite Constitutions to the possessors of the high degrees above the Fourteenth. It was first assumed by the Council of the Emperors of the East and West. Rose Croix Masons in Ireland are still known by this name.

Prince of Jerusalem. (*Prince de Jerusalem.*) This was the Sixteenth Degree of the Rite of Perfection, whence it was transferred to the Ancient and Accepted Scottish Rite, where it occupies the same numerical position. Its legend is founded on certain incidents which took place during the rebuilding of the second Temple, when the Jews were so much incommoded by the attacks of the Samaritans and other neighboring nations, that an embassy was sent to King Darius to implore his favor and protection, which was accordingly obtained. This legend, as developed in the degree, is contained neither in Ezra nor in the apocryphal books of Esdras. It is found only in the *Antiquities* of Josephus (lib. xi., cap. iv., sec. 9), and thence there is the strongest internal evidence to show that it was derived by the inventor of the degree. Who that inventor was we can only conjecture. But as we have the statements of both Ragon and Kloss that the Baron de Tschoudy composed the degree of Knight of the East, and as that degree is the first section of the system of which the Prince of Jerusalem is the second, we may reasonably suppose that the latter was also composed by him. The degree being one of those adopted by the Emperors of the East and West in their system, which Stephen Morin was authorized to propagate in America, it was introduced into America long before the establishment of the Supreme Council of the Scottish Rite. A Council was established by Henry A. Francken, about 1767, at Albany, in the State of New York, and a Grand Council organized by Myers, in 1788, in Charleston, South Carolina. This body exercised sovereign powers even after the establishment of the Supreme Council, May 31, 1801, for, in 1802, it granted a Warrant for the establishment of a Mark Lodge in Charleston, and another in the same year, for a Lodge of Perfection, in Savannah, Georgia. But under the present regulations of the Ancient and Accepted Scottish Rite, this prerogative has been abolished, and Grand Councils of Princes of Jerusalem no longer exist. The old regulation, that the Master of a Lodge of Perfection must be at least a Prince of Jerusalem, which was contained in the Constitution of the Grand Council, has also been repealed, together with most of the privileges which formerly appertained to the degree. A decision of the Supreme Council, in 1870, has even obliterated Councils of the Princes of Jerusalem as a separate organization, authorized to confer the preliminary degree of Knights of the East, and placed such Councils within the bosom of Rose Croix Chapters, a provision of which, as a manifest innovation on the ancient system, the expediency, or at least the propriety, may be greatly doubted.

Bodies of this degree are called Councils. According to the old rituals, the officers were a Most Equitable, a Senior and Junior Most Enlightened, a Grand Treasurer, and Grand Secretary. The more recent ritual of the Southern Jurisdiction of the United States has substituted for these a Most Illustrious Tarshatha, a Most Venerable High Priest, a Most Excellent Scribe, two Most Enlightened Wardens, and other officers. Yellow is the symbolic color of the degree, and the apron is crimson (formerly white), lined and bordered with yellow. The jewel is a medal of gold, on one side of which is inscribed a hand holding an equally poised balance, and on the other a double-edged, cross-hilted sword erect, between three stars around the point, and the letters D and Z on each side.

The Prince of Jerusalem is also the Fifty-third Degree of the Metropolitan Chapter of France, and the Forty-fifth of the Rite of Mizraim.

Prince of Jerusalem, Jewel of. Should be a gold incrustation on a lozenge-shaped piece of mother-of-pearl. Equipoise scales held by hand, sword, five stars, one larger than

the other four, and the letters D and Z in Hebrew, one on either side of the scales. The five-pointed crown, within a triangle of gold, has also been used as a jewel of this Sixteenth Degree.

Prince of Lebanon. See *Knight of the Royal Ax.*

Prince of Libanus. Another title for *Prince of Lebanon.*

Prince of Mercy. (*Prince du Merci.*) The Twenty-sixth Degree of the Ancient and Accepted Scottish Rite, called also *Scottish Trinitarian* or *Ecossais Trinitaire.* It is one of the eight degrees which were added on the organization of the Scottish Rite to the original twenty-five of the Rite of Perfection.

It is a Christian degree in its construction, and treats of the triple covenant of mercy which God made with man; first with Abraham by circumcision; next, with the Israelites in the wilderness, by the intermediation of Moses; and lastly, with all mankind, by the death and sufferings of Jesus Christ. It is in allusion to these three acts of mercy, that the degree derives its two names of Scottish Trinitarian and Prince of Mercy, and not, as

Ragon supposes, from any reference to the Fathers of Mercy, a religious society formerly engaged in the ransoming of Christian captives at Algiers. Chemin Dupontès (*Mem. Sur l'Ecoss*, p. 373) says that the Scottish rituals of the degree are too full of the Hermetic philosophy, an error from which the French Cahiers are exempt; and he condemns much of its doctrines as "hyperbolique plaisanterie." But the modern rituals as now practised are obnoxious to no such objection. The symbolic development of the number three of course constitutes a large part of its lecture; but the real dogma of the degree is the *importance of Truth*, and to this all its ceremonies are directed.

Bodies of the degree are called Chapters. The presiding officer is called Most Excellent Chief Prince, the Wardens are styled Excellent. In the old rituals these officers represented Moses, Aaron, and Eleazar; but the abandonment of these personations in the modern rituals is, I think, an improvement. The apron is red bordered with white, and the jewel is an equilateral triangle, within which is a heart. This was formerly inscribed with the Hebrew letter *tau*, now with the letters I. H. S.; and, to add to the Christianization which these letters give to the degree, the American Councils have adopted a tessera in the form of a small fish of ivory or mother-of-pearl, in allusion to the well-known usage of the primitive Christians.

Prince of Rose Croix. See *Rose Croix, Prince of*.

Prince of the Captivity. According to the Talmudists, the Jews, while in captivity at Babylon, kept a genealogical table of the line of their kings, and he who was the rightful heir of the throne of Israel was called the Head or Prince of the Captivity. At the time of the restoration, Zerubbabel, being the lineal descendant of Solomon, was the Prince of the Captivity.

Prince of the East, Grand. (*Grand Prince d'Orient.*) A degree in the collection of Le Page.

Prince of the Levites. (*Prince des Lévites.*) A degree in the collection of the Lodge of Saint Louis des Amis Réunis at Calais.

Prince of the Royal Secret. See *Sublime Prince of the Royal Secret.*

Prince of the Seven Planets, Illustrious Grand. (*Illustre Grand Prince des sept Planètes.*) A degree in the manuscript collection of Peuvret.

Prince of the Tabernacle. (*Prince du Tabernacle.*) The Twenty-fourth Degree of the Ancient and Accepted Scottish Rite. In the old rituals the degree was intended to illustrate the directions given for the building of the tabernacle, the particulars of which are recorded in the twenty-fifth chapter of Exodus. The Lodge is called a Hierarchy, and its officers are a Most Powerful Chief Prince, representing Moses, and three Wardens, whose style is Powerful, and who respectively represent Aaron, Besaleel, and Aholiab. In the modern rituals of the United States, the three principal officers are called the Leader, the High Priest, and the Priest, and respectively represent Moses, Aaron, and Ithamar, his son. The ritual is greatly enlarged; and while the main idea of the degree is retained, the ceremonies represent the initiation into the mysteries of the Mosaic tabernacle.

The jewel is the letter A, in gold, suspended from a broad crimson ribbon. The apron is white, lined with scarlet and bordered with green. The flap is sky-blue. On the apron is depicted a representation of the tabernacle.

This degree appears to be peculiar to the Scottish Rite and its modifications. I have not met with it in any of the other Rites.

Prince of Wales' Grand Lodge. About the time of the reconciliation of the two contending Grand Lodges in England, in 1813, they were called, by way of distinction, after their Grand Masters. That of the "Moderns" was called the "Prince of Wales' Grand Lodge," and that of the "Ancients" the "Duke of Kent's Grand Lodge." The titles were used colloquially, and not officially.

Princess of the Crown. (*Princesse de la Couronne.*) The Tenth and last degree of the Masonry of Adoption according to the French *régime*. The degree, which is said to have been composed in Saxony, in 1770, represents the reception of the Queen of Sheba by King Solomon. The Grand Master and Grand Mistress personate Solomon and his wife (which one, the Cahier does not say), and the recipiendary plays the part of the Queen of Sheba. The degree, says Ragon (*Tuil. Gen.*, p. 78), is not initiatory, but simply honorary.

Principal Officers. The number *three*, as a sacred number in the Masonic system, is, among many other ways, developed in the fact that in all Masonic bodies there are three principal officers.

Principals. The three presiding officers in a Chapter of Royal Arch Masons, according to the system practised in England, are called the Three Principals, or King, Prophet, and Priest, and, under the titles of Z, H, and J, represent Zerubbabel, Haggai, and Joshua. No person is eligible to the First Principal's chair unless he has served twelve months in each of the others; and he must also be the Master or Past Master of a Lodge, and have served in the Chapter the office of Scribe, Sojourner, or Assistant Sojourner. At his installation, each of the Principals receives an installing degree like that of the Master of a Blue Lodge. There is, however, no resemblance between any of these degrees and the order of High Priesthood which is conferred in this country.

The presiding officers of the Grand Chapter are called Grand Principals, and represent the same personages.

The official jewel of Z, is a crown; of H, an All-seeing eye; and of J, a book, each surrounded by a nimbus, or rays of glory, and placed within an equilateral triangle.

Principal Sojourner. The Hebrew word גר, *ger*, which we translate "a sojourner," signifies a man living out of his own country, and is used in this sense throughout the Old Testament. The children of Israel were, therefore, during the captivity, sojourners in Babylon, and the person who is represented by this officer, performed, as the incidents of the degree relate, an important part in the restoration of the Israelites to Jerusalem. He was the spokesman and leader of a party of three sojourners, and is, therefore, emphatically called the chief, or principal sojourner.

In the English Royal Arch system there are three officers called Sojourners. But in the American system the three Historical Sojourners are represented by the candidates, while only the supposed chief of them is represented by an officer called the Principal Sojourner. His duties are those of a conductor, and resemble, in some respects, those of a Senior Deacon in a Symbolic Lodge; which office, indeed, he occupies when the Chapter is open on any of the preliminary degrees.

Printed Proceedings. In 1741, the Grand Lodge of England adopted a regulation, which Entick (*Constitutions*, 1756, p. 236) is careful to tell us, "was unanimously agreed to," forbidding any brother "to print, or cause to be printed, the proceedings of any Lodge or any part thereof, or the names of the persons present at such Lodge, but by the direction of the Grand Master or his deputy, under pain of being disowned for a brother, and not to be admitted into any Quarterly Communication or Grand Lodge, or any Lodge whatsoever, and of being rendered incapable of bearing any office in the Craft." The law has never been repealed, but the Grand Lodge of England issues reports of its meetings, as also do most of the Grand Lodges of the world. Bulletins are published at stated intervals by the Grand Orients of France, Italy, and Portugal, and by nearly all those of South America. In the United States, every Grand Lodge publishes annually the journal of its proceedings, and many subordinate Lodges print the account of any special meeting held on an important or interesting occasion.

Prior. 1. The superiors of the different nations or provinces into which the Order of the Templar was divided, were at first called Priors or Grand Priors, and afterward Preceptors or Grand Preceptors.

2. Each of the languages of the Order of Malta was divided into Grand Priories, of which there were twenty-six, over which a Grand Prior presided. Under him were several Commanderies.

3. The second officer in a Council of Kadosh, under the Supreme Council for the Southern Jurisdiction of the United States.

4. The Grand Prior is the third officer in the Supreme Council of the Ancient and Accepted Scottish Rite for the Southern Jurisdiction of the United States.

Prior, Grand. See *Grand Prior*.

Priory. The jurisdiction of a Grand Prior in the Order of Malta or St. John of Jerusalem.

Priory, Great. See *Great Priory*.

Prison. A Lodge having been held in 1782, in the King's Bench prison, London, the Grand Lodge of England passed a resolution declaring that "it is inconsistent with the principles of Masonry for any Freemason's Lodge to be held for the purposes of making, passing, or raising Masons in any prison or place of confinement." (*Constitutions*, 1784, p. 349.) The resolution is founded on the principle that there must be perfect freedom of action in all that relates to the admission of candidates, and that this freedom is not consistent with the necessary restraints of a prison.

Private Committee. See *Committee, Private*.

Privileged Questions. In parliamentary law, privileged questions are defined to be those to which precedence is given over all other questions. They are of four kinds: 1. Those which relate to the rights and privileges of the assembly or any of its members. 2. Motions for adjournment. 3. Motions for reconsideration. 4. Special orders of the day. The first, third, and fourth only are applicable to Masonic parliamentary law.

Privilege, Questions of. In all parliamentary or legislative bodies, there occur certain questions which relate to matters affecting the dignity of the assembly or the rights and privileges of some of its members, and these are hence called "questions of privilege"; such, for instance, are motions arising out of or having relation to a quarrel between two of the members, an assault upon any member, charges affecting the integrity of the assembly or any of its members, or any other matters of a similar character. Questions referring to any of these matters take precedence of all other business, and hence are always in order. These questions of privilege are not to be confounded with privileged questions; for, although all questions of privilege are privileged questions, all privileged questions are not questions of privilege. Strictly speaking, questions of privilege relate to the house or its members, and privileged questions relate to matters of business. (See Dr. Mackey's *Parliamentary Law, as applied to the Government of Masonic Bodies*, ch. xxiv., xxv.)

Probation. The interval between the reception of one degree and the succeeding one is called the probation of the candidate, because it is during this period that he is to prove his qualification for advancement. In England and in this country the time of probation between the reception of degrees is four weeks, to which is generally added the further safeguard of an open examination in the preceding degree. In France and Germany the probation is extended to one year. The time is greatly extended in the Ancient and Accepted Scottish Rite. The statutes of the Southern Supreme Council require an interval of two years to be passed between the reception of the Fourteenth and the Thirty-second degrees. An extraordinary rule prevailed in the Constitutions of 1762, by which the Rite of Perfection was governed. According to this rule, a candidate was required to pass a probation, from the time of his application as an Entered Apprentice until his reception of the Twenty-fifth or ultimate degree of the Rite, of no less than six years and nine months. But as all the separate times of probation depended on symbolic numbers, it is not to be presumed that this regulation was ever practically enforced.

Problem, Forty-Seventh. See *Forty-Seventh Problem*.

Processions. Public processions of the Order, although not as popular as they were some years ago, still have the warrant of early and long usage. The first procession, after the revival, of which we have a record, took place June 24, 1721, when, as Anderson tells us (*Constitutions*, 1738, p. 112), "Payne, Grand Master, with his Wardens, the former Grand officers, and the Masters and Wardens of twelve Lodges, met the Grand Master elect in a Grand Lodge at the King's Arms Tavern, St. Paul's Churchyard, in the morning, . . . and from thence they marched on foot to the Hall in proper clothing and due form." Anderson and Entick continue to record the annual processions of the Grand Lodge and the Craft on the feast day, with a few exceptions, for the next twenty-five years; but after this first pedestrian procession all the subsequent ones were made in carriages, the record being, "the procession of March was made in coaches and chariots." (*Constitutions*, 1756, p. 227.) But ridicule being thrown by the enemies of the Order upon these processions, by a mock one in 1741 (see *Scald Miserables*), and in subsequent years, in 1747 the Grand Lodge unanimously resolved to discontinue them, nor have they since been renewed. (*Ibid.*, p. 248.) *

In America, public processions of the Craft were some years ago very common, nor have they yet been altogether abandoned; although now practised with greater discretion and less frequently, being in general restricted to special occasions of importance, such as funerals, the laying of corner-stones, or the dedication of public edifices.

The question has been often mooted, whether public processions, with the open exhibition of its regalia and furniture, are or are not of advantage to the Order. In 1747 it was thought not to be so, at least in London, but the custom was continued, to a great extent, in the provinces. Dr. Oliver was in favor of what he calls (*Symb. of Glory*) "the good old custom, so strongly recommended and assiduously practised by the Masonic worthies of the last century, and imitated by many other public bodies of men, of assembling the brethren of a province annually under their own banner, and marching in solemn procession to the house of God, to offer up their thanksgiving in the public congregation for the blessings of the preceding year; to pray for mercies in prospect, and to hear from the pulpit a disquisition on the moral and religious purposes of the Order."

Processions are not peculiar to the Masonic Fraternity. The custom comes to us from remote antiquity. In the initiations at Eleusis, the celebration of the Mysteries was accompanied each day by a solemn procession of the initiates from Athens to the temple of initiation. Apuleius describes the same custom as prevailing in the celebration of the Mysteries of Isis. Among the early Romans, it was the custom, in times of public triumph or distress, to have solemn processions to the temples, either to thank the gods for their favor or to invoke their protection. The Jews also went in procession to the Temple to offer up their prayers. So, too, the primitive Christians walked in procession to the tombs of the martyrs. Ecclesiastical processions were first introduced in the fourth century. They are now used in the Catholic Church on various occasions, and the *Pontificale Romanum* supplies the necessary ritual for their observance. In the Middle Ages these processions were often carried to an absurd extent. Polydore describes them as consisting of "ridiculous contrivances, of a figure with a great gaping mouth, and other pieces of merriment." But these displays were abandoned with the increasing refinement of the age. At this day, processions are common in all countries, not only of religious confraternities, but of political and social societies.

There are processions also in Masonry which are confined to the internal concerns of the Order, and are not therefore of a public nature. The procession "round the Hall," at the installation of the Grand Master, is first mentioned in 1721. Previous to that year there is no allusion to any such ceremony. From 1717 to 1720 we are simply told that the new Grand Master "was saluted," and that he was "homaged," or that "his health was drunk in due form." But in 1721 a processional ceremony seems to have been composed, for in that year we are informed (*Const.*, 1738, p. 113) that "Brother Payne, the old Grand Master, made the first procession round the Hall, and when returned, he proclaimed aloud the most noble prince and our brother." This procession was not abolished with the public processions in 1747, but continued for many years afterward. In America it gave rise to the procession at the installation of Masters, which, although provided for by the ritual, and practised by most Lodges until very recently, has been too often neglected by

* On the subject of these mock processions, see an article by Dr. W. J. Chetwode Crawley in *Ars Quatuor Coronatorum*, vol. 18.

many. The form of the procession, as adopted in 1724, is given by Anderson (*Constitutions*, 1738, p. 117), and is almost precisely the same as that used in all Masonic processions at the present day, except funeral ones. The rule was then adopted, which has ever since prevailed, that in all processions the juniors in degree and in office shall go first, so that the place of honor shall be the rear.

Proclamation. At the installation of the officers of a Lodge, or any other Masonic body, and especially a Grand Lodge or Grand Chapter, proclamation is made in a Lodge or Chapter by the installing officer, and in a Grand Lodge or Grand Chapter by the Grand Marshal. Proclamation is also made on some other occasions, and on such occasions the Grand Marshal performs the duty.

Proclamation of Cyrus. A ceremony in the American Royal Arch. We learn from Scripture that in the first year of Cyrus, the King of Persia, the captivity of the Jews was terminated. Cyrus, from his conversations with Daniel and the other Jewish captives of learning and piety, as well as from his perusal of their sacred books, more especially the prophecies of Isaiah, had become imbued with a knowledge of true religion, and hence had even publicly announced to his subjects his belief in the God "which the nation of the Israelites worshipped." He was consequently impressed with an earnest desire to fulfil the prophetic declarations of which he was the subject, and to rebuild the Temple of Jerusalem. Accordingly, he issued a proclamation, which we find in Ezra, as follows:

"Thus saith Cyrus, King of Persia, The Lord God of heaven hath given me all the kingdoms of the earth; and he hath charged me to build him a house at Jerusalem, which is in Judea. Who is there among you of all his people? his God be with him, and let him go up to Jerusalem, which is in Judea, and build the house of the Lord God of Israel (he is the God) which is in Jerusalem."

With the publication of this proclamation of Cyrus commences what may be called the second part of the Royal Arch Degree.

Proclus. Known as the successor of Syrianus as the head of the Athenian school. Born in Constantinople, 412, died at Athens, 485. Proclus was a Neo-Platonist, and waged war against the new religion of Christianity, which caused him to be banished from the city; but was subsequently readmitted. His works were chiefly mystical, such as devoting hymns to the sun, Venus, or the poetic muses, and so far were harmless.

Profane. There is no word whose technical and proper meaning differs more than this. In its ordinary use *profane* signifies one who is irreligious and irreverent, but in its technical adaptation it is applied to one who is ignorant of sacred rites. The word is compounded of the two Latin words *pro* and *fanum*, and literally means *before* or *outside of the temple;* and hence a *profanus* among the ancients was one who was not allowed to enter the temple and behold the mysteries. "Those," says Vossius, "were called profane who were not initiated in the sacred rites, but to whom it was allowed only to stand before the temple—*pro fano*—not to enter it and take part in the solemnities." The Greek equivalent, Βέβηλος, had a similar reference; for its root is found in Βηλὸς, a *threshold*, as if it denoted one who was not permitted to pass the threshold of the temple. In the celebrated hymn of Orpheus, which it is said was sung at the Mysteries of Eleusis, we meet with this phrase, Φθέγξομαι οἷς θέμις ἐστὶ θύρας δ' ἐπίθεσθε βεβήλοις. "I speak to those to whom it is lawful, but close the doors against the profane." When the mysteries were about to begin, the Greeks used the solemn formula, ἑκὰς, ἑκὰς, ἔστε βέβηλοι; and the Romans, "Procul, O procul este profani," both meaning, "Depart, depart, ye profane!" Hence the original and inoffensive signification of *profane* is that of being uninitiated; and it is in this sense that it is used in Masonry, simply to designate one who has not been initiated as a Mason. The word *profane* is not recognized as a noun substantive in the general usage of the language, but it has been adopted as a technical term in the dialect of Freemasonry, in the same relative sense in which the word *layman* is used in the professions of law and divinity.

Proficiency. The necessity that anyone who devotes himself to the acquisition of a science should become a proficient in its elementary instructions before he can expect to grasp and comprehend its higher branches, is so almost self-evident as to need no argument. But as Speculative Masonry is a science, it is equally necessary that a requisite qualification for admission to a higher degree should be a suitable proficiency in the preceding one. It is true, that we do not find in express words in the Old Constitutions any regulations requiring proficiency as preliminary to advancement, but their whole spirit is evidently to that effect; and hence we find it prescribed in the Old Constitutions, that no Master shall take an apprentice for less than seven years, because it was expected that he should acquire a competent knowledge of the *mystery* before he could be admitted as a Fellow. The modern Constitution of the Grand Lodge of England provides that no Lodge shall confer a higher degree on any brother until he has passed an examination in open Lodge on the preceding degrees (Rule 195), and many, perhaps most, of the Grand Lodges of this country have adopted a similar regulation. The ritual of all the Symbolic degrees, and, indeed, of the higher degrees, and that too in all rites, makes the imperative demand of every candidate whether he has made suitable proficiency in the preceding degree, an affirmative answer to which is required before the rites of initiation can be proceeded with. This answer is, according to the ritual, that "he has"; but some Masons have sought to evade the consequence of an acknowledgment of ignorance and want of proficiency by a change of the language of the ritual into "such as time and circumstances would permit." But this is an innovation, unsanctioned by any authority, and should be repudiated. If the candidate has not made proper proficiency, the ritual, outside of all statutory regulations, refuses him advancement.

Anderson, in the second edition of his *Constitutions* (p. 71), cites what he calls "an old record," which says that in the reign of Edward III. of England it was ordained "that Master Masons, or Masters of work, shall be examined whether they be able of cunning to serve their respective Lords, as well the Highest as the Lowest, to the Honour and Worship of the aforesaid Art, and to the Profit of their Lords."

Here, then, we may see the origin of that usage, which is still practised in every well-governed Lodge, not only of demanding a proper degree of proficiency in the candidate, but also of testing that proficiency by an examination.

This cautious and honest fear of the Fraternity lest any brother should assume the duties of a position which he could not faithfully discharge, and which is, in our time, tantamount to a candidate's advancing to a degree for which he is not prepared, is again exhibited in all the Old Constitutions. Thus in the Lansdowne Manuscript, whose date is referred to the middle of the sixteenth century, it is charged "that no Mason take on him no Lord's work, nor other man's, but if [unless] he know himself well able to perform the work, so that the Craft have no slander." The same regulation, and almost in the same language, is to be found in all the subsequent manuscripts.

In the Charges of 1722, it is directed that "a younger brother shall be instructed in working, to prevent spoiling the materials for want of judgment, and for encreasing and continuing of brotherly love." (*Constitutions*, 1723, p. 53.) It was, with the same view, that all of the Old Constitutions made it imperative that no Master should take an apprentice for less than seven years, because it was expected that he should acquire a competent knowledge of the mystery of the Craft before he could be admitted as a Fellow.

Notwithstanding these charges had a more particular reference to the operative part of the art, they clearly show the great stress that was placed by our ancient brethren upon the necessity of skill and proficiency; and they have furnished the precedents upon which are based all the similar regulations that have been subsequently applied to Speculative Masonry.

Pro Grand Master. An officer known only to the English system, and adopted for the first time in 1782, when, on the election of the Duke of Cambridge to the office of Grand Master, a regulation was adopted by the Grand Lodge of England, that whenever a prince of the blood accepted the office of Grand Master, he should be at liberty to nominate any peer of the realm to be the Acting Grand Master, and to this officer is now given the title of Pro Grand Master. His collar, jewel, and authority are the same as those of a Grand Master, and in the case of a vacancy he actually assumes the office until the next annual election.

The following have been Pro Grand Masters:

1782–9, Earl of Effingham.
1790–1813, Earl of Moira.
1834–8, Lord Dundas.
1839–40, Earl of Durham.
1841–3, Earl of Zetland.
1874–90, Earl of Carnarvon.
1891–8, Earl of Lathom.
1898–1908, Earl Amherst.
1908, Lord Ampthill.

Progressive Masonry. Freemasonry is undoubtedly a progressive science, and yet the fundamental principles of Freemasonry are the same now as they were at the very beginning of the Institution. Its landmarks are unchangeable. In these there can be no alteration, no diminution, no addition. When, therefore, we say that Freemasonry is progressive in its character, we of course do not mean to allude to this unalterable part of its constitution. But there is a progress which every science must undergo, and which many of them have already undergone, to which the science of Freemasonry is subject. Thus we say of chemistry that it is a progressive science. Two hundred years ago, all its principles, so far as they were known, were directed to such futile inquiries as the philosopher's stone and the elixir of immortality. Now these principles have become more thoroughly understood, and more definitely established, and the object of their application is more noble and philosophic. The writings of the chemists of the former and the present period sufficiently indicate this progress of the science. And yet the elementary principles of chemistry are unchangeable. Its truths were the same then as they are now. Some of them were at that time unknown, because no mind of sufficient research had discovered them; but they existed as truths, from the very creation of matter; and now they have only been developed, not invented.

So it is with Freemasonry. It too has had its progress. Masons are now expected to be more learned than formerly in all that relates to the science of the Order. Its origin, its history, its objects, are now considered worthy of the attentive consideration of its disciples. The rational explanation of its ceremonies and symbols, and their connection with ancient systems of religion and philosophy, are now considered as necessary topics of inquiry for all who desire to distinguish themselves as proficients in Masonic science.

In all these things we see a great difference between the Masons of the present and of former days. In Europe, a century ago, such inquiries were considered as legitimate subjects of Masonic study. Hutchinson published in 1760, in England, his admirable work entitled *The Spirit of Freemasonry*, in which the deep philosophy of the Institution was fairly developed with much learning and ingenuity. Preston's *Illustrations of Masonry*, printed at a not much later period, also exhibits the system treated, in many places, in a philosophical manner. Lawrie's *History of Freemasonry*, published in Scotland in 1804, is a work containing much profound historical and antiquarian research. And in the present century, the works of Oliver alone would be sufficient to demonstrate to the most cursory observer that Freemasonry has a claim to be ranked among the learned institutions of the day. In Germany and France, the press has been borne down with the weight of abstruse works on our Order, written by men of the highest literary pretensions.

In America, notwithstanding the really excellent work of Salem Town on *Speculative Masonry*, published in 1818, and the learned *Discourses* of Dr. T. M. Harris, published in 1801, it is only within a few years that Masonry has begun to assume the exalted position of a literary institution.

Promise. In entering into the covenant of Masonry, the candidate makes a promise to the Order; for his covenant is simply a promise where he voluntarily places himself under a moral obligation to act within certain conditions in a particular way. The law of promise is, therefore, strictly applicable to this covenant, and by that law the validity and obligation of the promises of every candidate must be determined. In every promise there are two things to be considered: the intention and the obligation. As to the intention: of all casuists, the Jesuits alone have contended that the intention may be concealed within the bosom of the promiser. All Christian and Pagan writers agree on the principle that the words expressed must convey their ordinary meaning to the promisee. If I promise to do a certain thing to-morrow, I cannot, when the morrow comes, refuse to do it on the ground that I only promised to do it if it suited me when the time of performance had arrived. The obligation of every promiser is, then, to fulfil the promise that he has made, not in any way that he may have secretly intended, but in the way in which he supposes that the one to whom he made it understood it at the time that it was made. Hence all Masonic promises are accompanied by the declaration that they are given without equivocation or mental reservation of any kind whatsoever.

All voluntary promises are binding, unless there be some paramount consideration which will release the obligation of performance. It is worth while, then, to inquire if there be any such considerations which can impair the validity of Masonic promises. Dr. Wayland (*Elem. of Mor. Science*, p. 285) lays down five conditions in which promises are not binding: 1. Where the performance is impossible; 2. Where the promise is unlawful; 3. Where no expectation is voluntarily excited by the promiser; 4. Where they proceed upon a condition which the promiser subsequently finds does not exist; and, 5. Where either of the parties is not a moral agent.

It is evident that no one of these conditions will apply to Masonic promises, for, 1. Every promise made at the altar of Masonry is possible to be performed; 2. No promise is exacted that is unlawful in its nature; for the candidate is expressly told that no promise exacted from him will interfere with the duty which he owes to God and to his country; 3. An expectation is voluntarily excited by the promiser, and that expectation is that he will faithfully fulfil his part of the covenant; 4. No false condition of things is placed before the candidate, either as to the character of the Institution or the nature of the duties which would be required of him; and, 5. Both parties to the promise, the candidate who makes it and the Craft to whom it is made, are moral agents, fully capable of entering into a contract or covenant.

This, then, is the proper answer to those adversaries of Freemasonry who contend for the invalidity of Masonic promises on the very grounds of Wayland and other moralists. Their conclusions would be correct, were it not that every one of their premises is false.

Promotion. Promotion in Masonry should not be governed, as in other societies, by succession of office. The fact that one has filled a lower office gives him no claim to a higher, unless he is fitted, by skill and capacity, to discharge its duties faithfully. This alone should be the true basis of promotion. (See *Preferment.*)

Proofs. What the German Masons call "proben und prüfungen," *trials and proofs*, and the French, "épreuves Maçonniques," or *Masonic proofs*, are defined by Bazot (*Manuel*, p. 141) to be "mysterious methods of discovering the character and disposition of a recipiendary." They are, in fact, those ritualistic ceremonies of initiation which are intended to test the fortitude and fidelity of the candidate. They seem to be confined to continental Masonry, for they are not known to any extent in the English or American systems, where all the ceremonies are purely symbolic. Krause (*Kunsturkund.* i., 152, n. 37) admits that no trace of them, at least in the perilous and fearful forms which they assume in the continental rituals, are to be found in the oldest English catechisms; and he admits that, as appealing to the sentiments of fear and hope, and adopting a dramatic form, they are contrary to the spirit of Masonry, and greatly interfere with its symbolism and with the pure and peaceful sentiments which it is intended to impress upon the mind of the neophyte.

Property of a Lodge. As a Lodge owes its existence, and all the rights and prerogatives that it exercises, to the Grand Lodge from which it derives its Charter or Warrant of Constitution, it has been decided, as a principle of Masonic law, that when such Lodge ceases to exist, either by a withdrawal or a surrender of its Warrant, all the property which it possessed at the time of its dissolution reverts to the Grand Lodge. But should the Lodge be restored by a revival of its Warrant, its property should be restored, because the Grand Lodge held it only as the general trustee or guardian of the Craft.

Prophet. Haggai, who in the American system of the Royal Arch is called the scribe, in the English system receives the title of *prophet*, and hence in the order of precedence he is placed above the high priest.

Prophets, Schools of the. See *Schools of the Prophets*.

Proponenda. The matters contained in the "notices of motions," which are required by the Grand Lodge of England to be submitted to the members previous to the Quarterly Communication when they are to be discussed, are sometimes called the *proponenda*, or subjects to be proposed.

Proposing Candidates. The only method recognized in America of proposing candidates for initiation or membership is by the written petition of the applicant, who must at the same time be recommended by two members of the Lodge. In England, the applicant for initiation must previously sign the declaration, which in America is only made after his election. He is then posed by one brother, and, the proposition seconded by another, he is balloted for a e next regular Lodge. Applicants for membership are also proposed without petition, but the certificate of the former Lodge must be produced, as in the United States the demit is required. Nor can any candidate for affiliation be balloted for unless previous notice of the application be given to all the members of the Lodge.

Propylæum (also *Propylon*). The court or vestibule in front of an edifice.

Proscription. The German Masons employ this word in the same sense in which we do *expulsion*, as the highest Masonic punishment that can be inflicted. They also use the word *verbannung*, banishment, for the same purpose.

Proselyte of Jerusalem. (*Prosélyte de Jerusalem*). The Sixty-eighth Degree of the Metropolitan Chapter of France.

Proselytism. Brahmanism is, perhaps, the only religion which is opposed to proselytism. The Brahman seeks no convert to his faith, but is content with that extension of his worship which is derived from the natural increase only of its members. The Jewish Church, perhaps one of the most exclusive, and which has always seemed indifferent to progress, yet provided a special form of baptism for the initiation of its proselytes into the Mosaic rites. Buddhism, the great religion of the Eastern world, which, notwithstanding the opposition of the leading Brahmans, spread with amazing rapidity over the Oriental nations, so that now it seems the most popular religion of the world, owes its extraordinary growth to the energetic propagandism of Sakya-muni, its founder, and to the same proselyting spirit which he inculcated upon his disciples.

The Christian church, mindful of the precept of its Divine founder, "Go ye into all the world, and preach the Gospel to every creature," has always considered the work of missions as one of the most important duties of the Church, and owes its rapid increase, in its earlier years, to the proselyting spirit of Paul, and Thomas, and the other apostles.

Mohammedanism, springing up and lingering for a long time in a single family, at length acquired rapid growth among the Oriental nations, through the energetic proselytism of the Prophet and his adherents. But the proselytism of the religion of the New Testament and that of the Koran differed much in character. The Christian made his converts by persuasive accents and eloquent appeals; the Mussulman converted his penitents by the sharp power of the sword. Christianity was a religion of peace, Mohammedanism of war; yet each, though pursuing a different method, was equally energetic in securing converts.

In respect to this doctrine of proselytism, Freemasonry resembles more the exclusive faith of Brahma than the inviting one of Moses, of Buddha, of Christ, or of Mohammed.

In plain words, Freemasonry is rigorously opposed to all proselytism. While its members do not hesitate, at all proper times and on all fitting occasions, to defend the Institution from all attacks of its enemies, it never seeks, by voluntary laudation of its virtues, to make new accessions of friends, or to add to the number of its disciples.

Nay, it boasts, as a peculiar beauty of its system, that it is a voluntary Institution. Not only does it forbid its members to use any efforts to obtain initiates, but actually requires every candidate for admission into its sacred rites to seriously declare, as a preparatory step, that in this voluntary offer of himself he has been unbiased by the improper solicitations of friends. Without this declaration, the candidate would be unsuccessful in his application. Although it is required that he shoud be prompted to solicit the privilege by the favorable opinion which he had conceived of the Institution, yet no provision is made by which that opinion can be inculcated in the minds of the profane; for were a Mason, by any praises of the Order, or any exhibitions of its advantages, to induce anyone under such representations to seek admission, he would not only himself commit a grievous fault, but would subject the candidate to serious embarrassment at the very entrance of the Lodge.

This Brahmanical spirit of anti-proselytism, in which Masonry differs from every other association, has imprinted upon the Institution certain peculiar features. In the first place, Freemasonry thus becomes, in the most positive form, a voluntary association. Whoever comes within its mystic circle, comes there of his "own free will and accord, and unbiased by the influence of friends." These are the terms on which he is received, and to all the legitimate consequences of this voluntary connection he must submit. Hence comes the axiom, "Once a Mason, always a Mason"; that is to say, no man, having once been initiated into its sacred rites, can, at his own pleasure or caprice, divest himself of the obligations and duties which, as a Mason, he has assumed. Coming to us freely and willingly, he can urge no claim for retirement on the plea that he was unduly persuaded, or that the character of the Institution had been falsely represented. To do so, would be to convict himself of fraud and falsehood, in the declarations made by him preliminary to his admission. And if these declarations were indeed false, he at least cannot, under the legal maxim, take advantage of his own wrong. The knot which binds him to the Fraternity has been tied by himself, and is indissoluble. The renouncing Mason may, indeed, withdraw from his connection with a Lodge, but he cannot release himself from his obligations to the regulation, which requires every Mason to be a member of one. He may abstain from all communication with his brethren, and cease to take any interest in the concerns of the Fraternity; but he is not thus absolved from the performance of any of the duties imposed upon him by his original admission into the brotherhood. A proselyte, persuaded against his will, might claim his right to withdraw; but the voluntary seeker must take and hold what he finds.

Another result of this anti-proselyting spirit of the Institution is, to relieve its members from all undue anxiety to increase its membership. It is not to be supposed that Masons have not the very natural desire to see the growth of their Order. Toward this end, they are ever ready to defend its character when attacked, to extol its virtues, and to maintain its claims to the confidence and approval of the wise and good. But the growth they wish is not that abnormal one, derived from sudden revivals or ephemeral enthusiasm, where passion too often takes the place of judgment; but that slow and steady, and therefore healthy, growth which comes from the adhesion of wise and virtuous and thoughtful men, who are willing to join the brotherhood, that they may the better labor for the good of their fellow-men.

Thus it is that we find the addresses of our Grand Masters, the reports of our committees on foreign correspondence, and the speeches of our anniversary orators, annually denouncing the too rapid increase of the Order, as something calculated to affect its stability and usefulness.

And hence, too, the black ball, that antagonist of proselytism, has been long and familiarly called the bulwark of Masonry. Its faithful use is ever being inculcated by the fathers of the Order upon its younger members; and the unanimous ballot is universally admitted to be the most effectual means of preserving the purity of the Institution.

And so, this spirit of anti-proselytism, impressed upon every Mason from his earliest initiation, although not itself a landmark, has come to be invested with all the sacredness of such a law, and Freemasonry stands out alone, distinct from every other human association, and proudly proclaims, "Our portals are open to all the good and true, but we ask no man to enter."

Protector of English Freemasons. A title assumed by King Edward VII. on his accession to the throne of England in 1901.

Protector of Innocence. (*Protecteur de l'Innocence.*) A degree in the nomenclature of Fustier, cited by him from the collection of Viany.

Protocol. In French, the formulæ or technical words of legal instruments; in Germany, the rough draft of an instrument or transaction; in diplomacy, the original copy of a treaty. Gädicke says that, in Masonic language, the protocol is the rough minutes of a Lodge. The word is used in this sense in Germany only.

Prototype. The same as *Archetype*, which see.

Provincial Grand Lodge. In each of the counties of England is a Grand Lodge composed of the various Lodges within that district, with the Provincial Grand Master at their head, and this body is called a Provincial Grand Lodge. It derives its existence, not from a Warrant, but from the Patent granted to the Provincial Grand Master by the Grand Master, and at his death, resignation, or removal, it becomes extinct, unless the Provincial Grand Registrar keeps up its existence by presiding over the province until the appointment of another Provincial Grand Master. Its authority is confined to the framing of by-laws, making regulations, hearing disputes, etc., but no absolute sentence can be promulgated by its authority without a reference to the Grand Lodge. Hence Oliver (*Jurisprud.*, 272) says that a Provincial Grand Lodge "has a shadow of power, but very little substance. It may talk, but it cannot act." The system does not exist in the United States. In England and Ireland the Provincial Grand Master is appointed by the Grand Master, but in Scotland his commission emanates from the Grand Lodge.

Provincial Grand Master. The presiding officer of a Provincial Grand Lodge. He is appointed by the Grand Master, during whose pleasure he holds his office. An appeal lies from his decisions to the Grand Lodge.

Provincial Grand Officers. The officers of a Provincial Grand Lodge correspond in title to those of the Grand Lodge. The Provincial Grand Treasurer is elected, but the other officers are nominated by the Provincial Grand Master. They are not by such appointment members of the Grand Lodge, nor do they take any rank out of their province. They must all be residents of the province and subscribing members to some Lodge therein. Provincial Grand Wardens must be Masters or Past Masters of a Lodge, and Provincial Grand Deacons, Wardens, or Past Wardens.

Provincial Master of the Red Cross. The Sixth Degree of the Rite of Clerks of Strict Observance.

Provost and Judge. (*Prévôt et Juge.*) The Seventh Degree of the Ancient and Accepted Scottish Rite. The history of the degree relates that it was founded by Solomon, King of Israel, for the purpose of strengthening his means of preserving order among the vast number of craftsmen engaged in the construction of the Temple. Tito, Prince Harodim, Adoniram, and Abda his father, were first created Provosts and Judges, who were afterward directed by Solomon to initiate his favorite and intimate secretary, Joabert, and to give him the keys of all the building. In the old rituals, the Master of a Lodge of Provosts and Judges represents Tito, Prince Harodim, the first Grand Warden and Inspector of the three hundred architects. The number of lights is six, and the symbolic color is red. In the more recent ritual of the Southern Jurisdiction of the United States there has been a slight change. The legend is substantially preserved, but the presiding officer represents Azarias, the son of Nathan.

The jewel is a golden key, having the letter A within a triangle engraved on the ward. The collar is red. The apron is white, lined with red, and is furnished with a pocket.

This was one of Ramsay's degrees, and was originally called *Maître Irlandais*, or Irish Master.

Proxy Installation. The Regulations of 1721 provide that, if the new Grand Master be absent from the Grand Feast, he may be proclaimed if proper assurance be given that he will serve, in which case the old Grand Master shall act as his proxy and receive the usual homage. This has led to a custom, once very common in America, but now getting into disuse, of installing an absent officer by proxy. Such installations are called proxy installations. Their propriety is very questionable.

Proxy Master. In the Grand Lodge of Scotland, a Lodge is permitted to elect any Master Mason who holds a diploma of the Grand Lodge, although he may not be a member of the Lodge, as its Proxy Master. He nominates two Proxy Wardens, and the three then become members of the Grand Lodge and representatives of the Lodge. Great opposition has recently been made to this system, because by it a Lodge is often represented by brethren who are in no way connected with it, who never were present at any of its meetings, and who are personally unknown to any of its members. A similar system prevailed in the Grand Lodge of South Carolina, but was, after a hard struggle, abolished in 1860, at the adoption of a new Constitution.

Prudence. This is one of the four cardinal virtues, the practise of which is inculcated upon the Entered Apprentice. Preston first introduced it into the degree as referring to what was then, and long before had been called the four principal signs, but which are now known as the perfect points of entrance. Preston's eulogium on prudence differs from that used in the lectures of this country, which was composed by Webb. It is in these words: "Prudence is the true guide to human understanding, and consists in judging and determining with propriety what is to be said or done upon all our occasions, what dangers we should endeavor to avoid, and how to act in all our difficulties." Webb's definition, which is much better, may be found in all the Monitors. The Masonic reference of prudence to the manual point reminds us of the classic method of representing her statutes with a rule or measure in her hand.

Prussia. Frederick William I. of Prussia was so great an enemy of the Masonic Institution, that until his death it was scarcely known in his dominions, and the initiation, in 1738, of his son, the Crown Prince, was necessarily kept a secret from his father. But in 1740 Frederick II. ascended the throne, and Masonry soon felt the advantages of a royal patron. The Baron de Bielefeld says (*Lettres*, i.. 157) that in that year the king himself opened a Lodge at Charlottenburg, and initiated his brother, Prince William, the Margrave of Brandenburg, and the Duke of Holstein-Beck. Bielefeld and the Counselor Jordan, in 1740, established the Lodge of the Three Globes at Berlin, which soon afterward assumed the rank of a Grand Lodge. There are now in Prussia three Grand Lodges, the seats of all of them being at Berlin. These are the Grand Lodge of the Three Globes, established in 1740, the Grand Lodge Royal York of Friendship, established in 1760, and the National Grand Lodge of Germany, established in 1770. There is no country in the world where Freemasonry is more profoundly studied as a science than in Prussia, and much of the abstruse learning of the Order, for which Germany has been distinguished, is to be found among the members of the Prussian Lodges. Unfortunately, they have, for a long time, been marked with an intolerant spirit toward the Jews, whose initiation was strictly forbidden until very recently, when that stain was removed, and the tolerant principles of the Order were recognized by the abrogation of the offensive laws.

Prussian Knight. See *Noachite*.

Psaterians. A sect of Arians who maintained, at the Council of Antioch, A.D. 360, that the Son was dissimilar to the Father in will; that He was made from nothing; and that in God, creation and generation were synonymous terms.

Pseudonym. A false or fictitious name. Continental writers on Freemasonry in the last century often assumed fictitious names, sometimes from affectation, and sometimes because the subjects they treated were unpopular with the government or the church. Thus, Carl Rösler wrote under the pseudonym of Acerrellas, Arthuseus under that of Irenæus Agnostus, Guillemain de St. Victor under that of De Gaminville or Querard, Louis Travenol under that of Leonard Gabanon, etc.

The Illuminati also introduced the custom of giving pseudonyms to the kingdoms and cities of Europe; thus, with them, Austria was Achaia; Munich, Athens; Vienna, Rome; Ingolstadt, Eleusis, etc. But this practise was not confined to the Illuminati, for we find many books published at Paris, Berlin, etc., with the fictitious imprint of Jerusalem, Cosmopolis, Latomopolis, Philadelphia, Edessa, etc. This practise has long since been abandoned.

Publications, Masonic. The fact that, within the past few years, Freemasonry has taken its place—and an imposing one, too—in the literature of the times; that men of genius and learning have devoted themselves to its investigation; that its principles and its system have become matters of study and research; and that the results of this labor of inquiry have been given, and still continue to be given, to the world at large, in the form of treatises on Masonic science, have at length introduced the new question among the Fraternity, whether Masonic books are of good or of evil tendency to the Institution. Many well-meaning but timid members of the Fraternity object to the freedom with which Masonic topics are discussed in printed works. They think that the veil is too much withdrawn by modern Masonic writers, and that all doctrine and instruction should be confined to oral teaching, within the limits of the Lodge room. Hence, to them, the art of printing becomes useless for the diffusion of Masonic knowledge; and thus, whatever may be the attainments of a Masonic scholar, the fruits of his study and experience would be confined to the narrow limits of his personal presence. Such objectors draw no distinction between the ritual and the philosophy of Masonry. Like the old priests of Egypt, they would have everything concealed under hieroglyphics, and would as soon think of opening a Lodge in public as they would of discussing, in a printed book, the principles and design of the Institution.

The Grand Lodge of England, some years ago, adopted a regulation which declared it penal to print or publish any part of the proceedings of a Lodge, or the names of the persons present at such a Lodge, without the permission of the Grand Master. The rule, however, evidently referred to local proceedings only, and had no relation whatever to the publication of Masonic authors and editors; for the English Masonic press, since the days of Hutchinson, in the Middle of the last century, has been distinguished for the freedom, as well as learning, with which the most abstruse principles of our Order have been discussed.

Fourteen years ago the Committee of Foreign Correspondence of a prominent Grand Lodge affirmed that Masonic literature was doing more "harm than good to the Institution." About the same time the committee of another equally prominent Grand Lodge were not ashamed to express their regret that so much prominence of notice is, "in several Grand Lodge proceedings, given to Masonic publications. Masonry existed and flourished, was harmonious and happy, in their absence."

When one reads such diatribes against Masonic literature and Masonic progress—such blind efforts to hide under the bushel the light that should be on the hill-top—he is incontinently reminded of a similar iconoclast, who, more than four centuries ago, made a like onslaught on the pernicious effects of learning.

The immortal Jack Cade, in condemning Lord Say to death as a patron of learning, gave vent to words of which the language of these enemies of Masonic literature seems to be but the echo:

"Thou hast most traitorously corrupted the youth of the realm, in erecting a grammar-school; and whereas, before, our forefathers had no other books but the score and the tally, thou hast caused printing to be used; and contrary to the king, his crown, and dignity, thou hast built a paper-mill. It will be proved to thy face that thou hast men about thee that usually talk of a noun and a verb, and such abominable words as no Christian ear can endure to hear."

I belong to no such school. On the contrary, I believe that too much cannot be written and printed and read about the philosophy and history, the science and symbolism of Freemasonry; provided always the writing is confided to those who rightly understand their art. In Masonry, as in astronomy, in geology, or in any other of the arts and sciences, a new book by an expert must always be esteemed a valuable contribution. The production of silly and untutored minds will fall of themselves into oblivion without the aid of official persecution; but that which is really valuable—which presents new facts, or furnishes suggestive thoughts—will, in spite of the denunciations of the Jack Cades of Masonry, live to instruct the brethren, and to elevate the tone and standing of the Institution.

Dr. Oliver, who has written more on Masonry than any other author, says on this subject: "I conceive it to be an error in judgment to discountenance the publication

Yours fraternally
E. L. Hawkins

of philosophical disquisitions on the subject of Freemasonry, because such a proceeding would not only induce the world to think that our pretensions are incapable of enduring the test of inquiry, but would also have a tendency to restore the dark ages of superstition, when even the sacred writings were prohibited, under an apprehension that their contents might be misunderstood or perverted to the propagation of unsound doctrines and pernicious practices; and thus would ignorance be transmitted, as a legacy, from one generation to another."

Still further pursuing this theme, and passing from the unfavorable influence which must be exerted upon the world by our silence, to the injury that must accrue to the Craft, the same learned writer goes on to say, that "no hypotheses can be more untenable than that which forebodes evil to the Masonic Institution from the publication of Masonic treatises illustrative of its philosophical and moral tendency." And in view of the meager and unsatisfactory nature of the lectures, in the form in which they are delivered in the Lodges, he wisely suggests that "if strictures on the science and philosophy of the Order were placed within every brother's reach, a system of examination and research would soon be substituted for the dull and uninteresting routine which, in so many instances, characterizes our private meetings. The brethren would become excited by the inquiry, and a rich series of new beauties and excellences would be their reward."

Of such a result I have no doubt. In consequence of the increase of Masonic publications in this country within a few years, Masonry has already been elevated to a high position. If there be any who still deem it a merely social institution, without a philosophy or literature; if there be any who speak of it with less admiration than it justly deserves, we may be assured that such men have read as little as they have thought on the subject of its science and its history. A few moments of conversation with a Mason will show whether he is one of those contracted craftsmen who suppose that Masonic "*brightness*" consists merely in a knowledge of the correct mode of working one's way into a Lodge, or whether he is one who has read and properly appreciated the various treatises on the "royal art," in which men of genius and learning have developed the true spirit and design of the Order.

Such is the effect of Masonic publications upon the Fraternity; and the result of all my experience is, that *enough has not been published*. Cheap books on all Masonic subjects, easily accessible to the masses of the Order, are necessaries essential to the elevation and extension of the Institution. Too many of them confine their acquirements to a knowledge of the signs and the ceremonies of initiation. There they cease their researches. They make no study of the philosophy and the antiquities of the Order. They do not seem to know that the modes of recognition are simply intended as means of security against imposition, and that the ceremonial rites are worth nothing without the symbolism of which they are only the external exponents. Masonry for them is nerveless—senseless—lifeless; it is an empty voice without meaning—a tree of splendid foliage, but without a single fruit.

The monitorial instructions of the Order, as they are technically called, contain many things which probably, at one time, it would have been deemed improper to print; and there are some Masons, even at this day, who think that Webb and Cross were too free in their publications. And yet we have never heard of any evil effects arising from the reading of our Monitors, even upon those who have not been initiated. On the contrary, meager as are the explanations given in those works, and unsatisfactory as they must be to one seeking for the full light of Masonry, they have been the means, in many instances, of inducing the profane, who have read them, to admire our Institution, and to knock at the "door of Masonry" for admission—while we regret to say that they sometimes comprise the whole instruction that a candidate gets from an ignorant Master. Without these published Monitors, even that little beam of light would be wanting to illuminate his path.

But if the publication and general diffusion of our elementary text-books have been of acknowledged advantage to the character of the Institution, and have, by the information, little as it is, which they communicate, been of essential benefit to the Fraternity, we cannot see why a more extensive system of instruction on the legends, traditions, and symbols of the Order should not be productive of still greater good.

Years ago, we uttered on this subject sentiments which we now take occasion to repeat.

Without an adequate course of reading, no Mason can now take a position of any distinction in the ranks of the Fraternity. Without extending his studies beyond what is taught in the brief lectures of the Lodge, he can never properly appreciate the end and nature of Freemasonry as a speculative science. The lectures constitute but the skeleton of Masonic science. The muscles and nerves and blood-vessels, which are to give vitality, and beauty, and health, and vigor to that lifeless skeleton, must be found in the commentaries on them which the learning and research of Masonic writers have given to the Masonic student.

The objections to treatises and disquisitions on Masonic subjects, that there is danger, through them, of giving too much light to the world without, has not the slightest support from experience. In England, in France, and in Germany, scarcely any restriction has been observed by Masonic writers, except as to what is emphatically esoteric; and yet we do not believe that the profane world is wiser in those countries than in our own in respect to the secrets of Freemasonry. In the face of these publications, the world without has remained as ignorant of the aporrheta of our art, as if no work had ever been written on the subject; while the world within—the Craft themselves—have been enlightened and instructed, and their views of Masonry (not as a social or charitable society, but as a philosophy, a science, a religion) have been elevated and enlarged.

The truth is, that men who are not Masons never read authentic Masonic works. They have no interest in the topics discussed, and could not understand them, from a want of the preparatory education which the Lodge alone can supply. Therefore, were a writer even to trench a little on what may be considered as being really the *arcana* of Masonry, there is no danger of his thus making an improper revelation to improper persons.

Public Ceremonies. Most of the ceremonies of Masonry are strictly private, and can be conducted only in the presence of the initiated. But some of them, from their nature, are necessarily performed in public. Such are the burials of deceased brethren, the laying of corner-stones of public edifices, and the dedications of Masonic halls. The installation of the officers of a Lodge, or Grand Lodge, are also sometimes conducted in public in America. But the ceremonies in this case differ slightly from those of a private installation in the Lodge room, portions of the ceremony having to be omitted. The reputation of the Order requires that these ceremonies should be conducted with the utmost propriety, and the Manuals and Monitors furnish the fullest details of the order of exercises. Preston, in his *Illustrations*, was the first writer who gave a printed account of the mode of conducting these public ceremonies, and to him we are most probably indebted for their ritual. Anderson, however, gave in the first edition of the *Constitutions* the prescribed form for constituting new Lodges, and installing their officers, which is the model upon which Preston, and other writers, have subsequently framed their more enlarged formulæ.

Puerility of Freemasonry. "The absurdities and puerilities of Freemasonry are fit only for children, and are unworthy of the time or attention of wise men." Such is the language of its adversaries, and the apothegm is delivered with all that self-sufficiency which shows that the speaker is well satisfied with his own wisdom, and is very ready to place himself in the category of those wise men whose opinion he invokes. This charge of a puerility of design and object of Freemasonry is worth examination.

Is it then possible, that those scholars of unquestioned strength of intellect and depth of science, who have devoted themselves to the study of Masonry, and who have in thousands of volumes given the result of their researches, have been altogether mistaken in the direction of their labors, and have been seeking to develop, not the principles of a philosophy, but the mechanism of a toy? Or is the assertion that such is the fact a mere sophism, such as ignorance is every day uttering, and a conclusion to which men are most likely to arrive when they talk of that of which they know nothing, like the critic who reviews a book that he has never read, or the skeptic who attacks a creed that he does not comprehend? Such claims to an inspired infallibility are not uncommon among men of unsound judgment. Thus, when Gall and Spurzheim first gave to the world their wonderful discoveries in reference to the organization and the functions of the brain—discoveries which have since wrought a marked revolution in the sciences of anatomy, physiology, and ethics—the Edinburgh reviewers attempted to demolish these philosophers and their new system, but succeeded only in exposing their own ignorance of the science they were discussing. Time, which is continually evolving truth out of every intellectual conflict, has long since shown that the German philosophers were right and that their Scottish critics were wrong. How common is it, even at this day, to hear men deriding Alchemy as a system of folly and imposture, cultivated only by madmen and knaves, when the researches of those who have investigated the subject without prejudice, but with patient learning, have shown, without any possibility of doubt, that these old alchemists, so long the objects of derision to the ignorant, were religious philosophers, and that their science had really nothing to do with the discovery of an elixir of life or the transmutation of the baser metals into gold, but that they, like the Freemasons, with whom they have a strong affinity, concealed under profound symbols, intelligible only to themselves, the search after Divine Truth and the doctrine of immortal life. Truth was the gold which they eliminated from all mundane things, and the immortality of the soul was the elixir of everlasting life which perpetually renewed youth, and took away the power of death.

So it is with Freemasonry. Those who abuse it know nothing of its inner spirit, of its profound philosophy, of the pure religious life that it inculcates.

To one who is at all acquainted with its organization, Freemasonry presents itself under two different aspects:

First, as a secret society distinguished by a peculiar ritual;

And secondly, as a society having a philosophy on which it is founded, and which it proposes to teach to its disciples.

These by way of distinction may be called

the *ritualistic* and the *philosophical* elements of Freemasonry.

The *ritualistic* element of Freemasonry is that which relates to the due performance of the rites and ceremonies of the Order. Like the rubrics of the church, which indicate when the priest and congregation shall kneel and when they shall stand, it refers to questions such as these: What words shall be used in such a place, and what ceremony shall be observed on such an occasion? It belongs entirely to the inner organization of the Institution, or to the manner in which its services shall be conducted, and is interesting or important only to its own members. The language of its ritual or the form of its ceremonies has nothing more to do with the philosophic designs of Freemasonry than the rubrics of a church have to do with the religious creed professed by that church. It might at any time be changed in its most material points, without in the slightest degree affecting the essential character of the Institution.

Of course, this ritualistic element is in one sense important to the members of the society, because, by a due observance of the ritual, a general uniformity is preserved. But beyond this, the Masonic ritual makes no claim to the consideration of scholars, and never has been made, and, indeed, from the very nature of its secret character, never can be made, a topic of discussion with those who are outside of the Fraternity.

But the other, the *philosophical* element of Freemasonry, is one of much importance. For it, and through it, I do make the plea that the Institution is entitled to the respect, and even veneration, of all good men, and is well worth the careful consideration of scholars.

A great many theories have been advanced by Masonic writers as to the real origin of the Institution, as to the time when and the place where it first had its birth. It has been traced to the mysteries of the ancient Pagan world, to the Temple of King Solomon, to the Roman Colleges of Artificers, to the Crusades for the recovery of the Holy Land, to the Gilds of the Middle Ages, to the Stone-Masons of Strasburg and Cologne and even to the revolutionary struggle in England in the time of the commonwealth, and to the secret efforts of the adherents of the house of Stuart to recover the throne. But whatever theory may be selected, and wheresoever and whensoever it may be supposed to have received its birth, one thing is certain, namely, that for generations past, and yet within the records of history, it has, unlike other mundane things, presented to the world an unchanged organization. Take, for instance, the theory which traces it back to one of the most recent periods, that, namely, which places the organization of the Order of Freemasons at the building of the Cathedral of Strasburg, in the year 1275. During all the time that has since elapsed, full six hundred years, how has Freemasonry presented itself? Why, as a brotherhood organized and controlled by a secret discipline, engaged in important architectural labors, and combining with its operative tasks speculations of great religious import. If we see any change, it is simply this, that when the necessity no longer existed, the operative element was laid aside, and the speculative only was retained, but with a scrupulous preservation (as if it were for purposes of identification) of the technical language, the rules and regulations, the working-tools, and the discipline of the operative art. The material only on which they wrought was changed. The disciples and followers of Erwin of Steinbach, the Master Builder of Strasburg, were engaged, under the influence of a profoundly religious sentiment, in the construction of a material edifice to the glory of God. The more modern workers in Freemasonry are under the same religious influence, engaged in the construction of a spiritual temple. Does not this long continuance of a brotherhood employed in the same pursuit, or changing it only from a material to a spiritual character, but retaining its identity of organization, demand for itself some respect, and, if for nothing else, at least for its antiquity, some share of veneration?

But this is not all. This society or brotherhood, or confraternity as it might more appropriately be called, is distinguished from all other associations by the possession of certain symbols, myths, and, above all else, a *Golden Legend*, all of which are directed to the purification of the heart, to the elevation of the mind, to the development of the great doctrine of immortality.

Now the question where and when these symbols, myths, and legends arose is one that is well worth the investigation of scholars, because it is intimately connected with the history of the human intellect. Did the Stone-Masons and building corporations of the Middle Ages invent them? Certainly not, for they are found in organizations that existed ages previously. The Greeks at Eleusis taught the same dogma of immortal life in the same symbolic mode, and their legend, if it differed from the Masonic in its accidents, was precisely identical in its substance. For Hiram there was Dionysus, for the acacia the myrtle, but there were the same mourning, the same discovery, the same rejoicing, because what had been lost was found, and then the same ineffable light, and the same sacred teaching of the name of God and the soul's immortality. And so an ancient orator, who had passed through one of these old Greek Lodges—for such, without much violence of language, they may well be called—declared that those who have endured the initiation into the mysteries entertain better hopes both of the end of life and of the eternal future. Is not this the very object and design of the legend of the Master's Degree? And this same peculiar form of symbolic initiation is to be found among the old Egyptians and in the island of Samothracia, thousands of years before the light of Christianity dawned upon the world to give the seal of its Master and Founder to the Divine truth of the resurrection.

This will not, it is true, prove the descent of Freemasonry, as now organised, from the religious mysteries of antiquity; although this is one of the theories of its origin entertained and defended by scholars of no mean pretension. But it will prove an identity of design in the moral and intellectual organisation of all these institutions, and it will give the Masonic student subjects for profound study when he asks the interesting questions—Whence came these symbols, myths, and legends? Who invented them? How and why have they been preserved? Looking back into the remotest days of recorded history, we find a priesthood in an island of Greece and another on the banks of the Nile, teaching the existence of a future life by symbols and legends, which convey the lesson in a peculiar mode. And now, after thousands of years have elapsed, we find the same symbolic and legendary method of instruction, for the same purpose, preserved in the depository of what is comparatively a modern institution. And between these two extremes of the long past and the present now, we find the intervening period occupied by similar associations, succeeding each other from time to time, and spreading over different countries, but all engaged in the same symbolic instruction, with substantially the same symbols and the same mythical history.

Does not all this present a problem in moral and intellectual philosophy, and in the archeology of ethics, which is well worthy of an attempted solution? How unutterably puerile seem the objections and the objurgations of a few contracted minds, guided only by prejudice, when we consider the vast questions of deep interest that are connected with Freemasonry as a part of those great brotherhoods that have filled the world for so many ages, so far back, indeed, that some philosophic historians have supposed that they must have derived their knowledge of the doctrines which they taught in their mystic assemblies from direct revelation through an ancient priesthood that gives no other evidence of its former existence but the results which it produced.

Man needs something more than the gratification of his animal wants. The mind requires food as well as the body, and nothing can better give that mental nutriment than the investigation of subjects which relate to the progress of the intellect and the growth of the religious sentiment.

Again, man was not made for himself alone. The old Stoic lived only for and within himself. But modern philosophy and modern religion teach no such selfish doctrine. Man is but part of the great brotherhood of man, and each one must be ready to exclaim with the old poet, "Homo sum; humani nihil à me alienum puto," *I am a man, and I deem nothing relating to mankind to be foreign to my feelings.* Men study ancient history simply that they may learn what their brother men have done in former times, and they read the philosophers and poets of Greece and Rome that they may know what were the speculations of those old thinkers, and they strive to measure the intellect of man as it was then and as it is now, because the study of the growth of intellectual philosophy and the investigation of the mental and moral powers come home to us all as subjects of common interest.

Looking, then, upon Freemasonry as one of those associations which furnish the evidence and the example of the progress of man in intellectual, moral, and religious development, it may be well claimed for it that its design, its history, and its philosophy, so far from being puerile, are well entitled to the respect of the world, and are worth the careful research of scholars.

Puissant. A title given to the presiding officer in several of the high degrees.

Puissant Irish Master. The Eighth Degree of Ramsay's Irish Colleges.

Pullen, William Hyde. An eminent and accomplished craftsman of England, who was renowned among English and American "workmen" for his excellence in the conduct of the forms and varied ceremonies of Masonry.

Pulsanti Operietur. Latin. *To him who knocks it shall be opened.* An inscription sometimes placed over the front door of Masonic temples or Lodge rooms.

Punishments, Masonic. Punishment in Masonry is inflicted that the character of the Institution may remain unsullied, and that the unpunished crimes of its members may not injuriously reflect upon the reputation of the whole society. The nature of the punishment to be inflicted is restricted by the peculiar character of the Institution, which is averse to some forms of penalty, and by the laws of the land, which do not give to private corporations the right to impose certain species of punishment.

The infliction of fines or pecuniary penalties has, in modern times at least, been considered as contrary to the genius of Masonry, because the sanctions of Masonic law are of a higher nature than any that could be furnished by a pecuniary penalty.

Imprisonment and corporal punishment are equally adverse to the spirit of the Institution, and are also prohibited by the laws of the land, which reserve the infliction of such penalties for their own tribunals.

Masonic punishments are therefore restricted to an expression of disapprobation or the deprivation of Masonic rights, and are: 1. Censure; 2. Reprimand; 3. Exclusion; 4. Suspension, Definite or Indefinite; and 5. Expulsion—all of which see under their respective titles.

Punjaub. Freemasonry was founded in Punjaub, India, in 1872, by an ardent Mason, W. Bro. Major Henry Basevi, whose failing health caused him to forsake his post shortly thereafter, leaving as his successor Major M. Ramsay, who became R. W. D. Grand Master. By last returns received there were 26 Lodges in the District. It is reported authoritatively that in 1879 the Institution maintained, clothed, and educated twenty-one children.

Puranas. ("Knowledge.") The text-books of the worshipers of Vishnu and of Siva, forming, with the Tantras, the basis of the popular creed of the Brahmanical Hindus. There are about 18 Puranas, and as many more minor works, called Upapuranas, all written in Sanskrit, and founded to some extent upon the Mahabharata and Ramâyana. Otherwise their date is very uncertain. The followers of Brahmanism number about 175,000,000.

Purchase. In the Cooke MS. (line 630) it is said that the son of Athelstan "purchased a free patent of the kyng that they [the Masons] shulde make a sembly." This does not mean that he bought the patent, but that he obtained or procured it. Such was the use of purchase in old English. The booty of a thief was called his purchase, because he bad acquired it. Colloquially, the word is still used to designate the getting a hold on anything.

Pure Freemasonry. See *Primitive Freemasonry.*

Purification. As the aspirant in the Ancient Mysteries was not permitted to pass through any of the forms of initiation, or to enter the sacred vestibule of the temple, until, by water or fire, he had been symbolically purified from the corruptions of the world which he was about to leave behind, so in Masonry there is in the First Degree a symbolical purification by the presentation to the candidate of the common gavel, an implement whose emblematic use teaches a purification of the heart. (See *Lustration.*)

Purity. In the Ancient Mysteries purity of heart and life was an essential prerequisite to initiation, because by initiation the aspirant was brought to a knowledge of God, to know whom was not permitted to the impure. For, says Origen (*Cont. Cel.*, vi.), "a defiled heart cannot see God, but he must be pure who desires to obtain a proper view of a pure Being." And in the same spirit the Divine Master says: "Blessed are the pure in heart, for they shall see God." But "to see God" is a Hebraism, signifying to possess him, to be spiritually in communion with him, to know his true character. Now to acquire this knowledge of God, symbolized by the knowledge of his Name, is the great object of Masonic, as it was of all ancient initiation; and hence the candidate in Masonry is required to be pure, for "he only can stand in the holy place who hath clean hands and a pure heart." (See *White.*)

Purity, Brothers of. An association of Arabic philosophers, founded at Bosra, in Syria, in the tenth century. Many of their writings, which were much studied by the Jews of Spain in the twelfth century, were mystical. Steinschneider (*Jew. Lit.*, 174, 295) calls them "the Freemasons of Bosra," and says that they were "a celebrated society of a kind of Freemasons."

Purple. Purple is the appropriate color of those degrees which, in the American Rite, have been interpolated between the Royal Arch and Ancient Craft Masonry, namely, the Mark, Past, and Most Excellent Masters. It is in Masonry a symbol of fraternal union, because, being compounded of blue, the color of the Ancient Craft, and red, which is that of the Royal Arch, it is intended to signify the close connection and harmony which should ever exist between those two portions of the Masonic system. It may be observed that this allusion to the union and harmony between blue and red Masonry is singularly carried out in the Hebrew word which signifies purple. This word, which is ארגמן, *argaman*, is derived from רגם, *ragam* or *regem*, one of whose significations is "a friend." But Portal (*Coul. Symb.*, 230) says that purple, in the profane language of colors, signifies constancy in spiritual combats, because blue denotes fidelity, and red, war.

In the religious services of the Jews we find purple employed on various occasions. It was one of the colors of the curtains of the tabernacle, where, Josephus says, it was symbolic of the element of water, of the veils, and of the curtain over the great entrance; it was also used in the construction of the ephod and girdle of the high priest, and the cloths for Divine service.

Among the Gentile nations of antiquity purple was considered rather as a color of dignity than of veneration, and was deemed an emblem of exalted office. Hence Homer mentions it as peculiarly appropriated to royalty, and Virgil speaks of *purpura regum*, or "the purple of kings." Pliny says it was the color of the vestments worn by the early kings of Rome; and it has ever since, even to the present time, been considered as the becoming insignia of regal or supreme authority.

In American Masonry, the purple color seems to be confined to the intermediate degrees between the Master and the Royal Arch, except that it is sometimes employed in the vestments of officers representing either kings or men of eminent authority—such, for instance, as the Scribe in a Chapter of Royal Arch Masons.

In the Grand Lodge of England, Grand Officers and Provincial Grand Officers wear purple collars and aprons. As the symbolic color of the Past Master's Degree, to which all Grand Officers should have attained, it is also considered in this country as the appropriate color for the collars of officers of a Grand Lodge.

Purple Brethren. In English Masonry, the Grand Officers of the Grand Lodge and the Past Grand and Deputy Grand Masters and Past and Present Provincial Grand Masters are called "purple brethren," because of the color of their decorations, and at meetings of the Grand Lodge are privileged to sit on the dais.

Purple Lodges. Grand and Provincial Grand Lodges are thus designated by Dr. Oliver in his *Institutes of Masonic Jurisprudence.* The term is not used in this country.

Purrah, The. A society of Susu negroes exercising similar powers to, and for a somewhat similar purpose as, the Vehmgericht.

Pursuivant. The third and lowest order of heraldic officers. In Masonry the lowest officer in rank except the Tiler, if he may be termed an officer.

Pyron, Jean Baptiste Pierre Julien. A distinguished French Mason of the latter part of the last and beginning of the present century, who died at Paris in September, 1821. He was the author of many Masonic discourses, but his most important work was a profound and exhaustive *History of the Organization of the Ancient and Accepted Rite in France*, published in 1814. He was one of the founders of the Grand Orient, and having received the Thirty-third Degree from the Count de Grasse Tilly, he afterward assisted in the organization of the Supreme Council of Italy, at Milan, and the Supreme Council of France. In 1805, his name was struck from the register of the Grand Orient in consequence of his opposition to that body, but he remained the Secretary-General of the Supreme Council until his death. Ragon calls him an intriguer and bold innovator, but Thory speaks more highly of his Masonic character. He was undoubtedly a man of talent, learning, and Masonic research. He made a manuscript collection of many curious degrees, which Thory has liberally used in his *Nomenclature of Rites and Degrees.*

Pythagoras. One of the most celebrated of the Grecian philosophers, and the founder of what has been called the Italic school, was born at Samos about 586 B.C. Educated as an athlete, he subsequently abandoned that profession and devoted himself to the study of philosophy. He traveled through Egypt, Chaldea, and Asia Minor, and is said to have submitted to the initiations in those countries for the purpose of acquiring knowledge. On his return to Europe, he established his celebrated school at Crotona, much resembling that subsequently adopted by the Freemasons. His school soon acquired such a reputation that disciples flocked to him from all parts of Greece and Italy. Pythagoras taught as the principal dogma of his philosophy the system of metempsychosis, or the transmigration of souls. He taught the mystical power of numbers, and much of the symbolism on that subject which we now possess is derived from what has been left to us by his disciples, for of his own writings there is nothing extant. He was also a geometrician, and is regarded as having been the inventor of several problems, the most important of which is that now known as the forty-seventh problem of Euclid. He was also a proficient in music, and is said to have demonstrated the mathematical relations of musical intervals, and to have invented a number of musical instruments. Disdaining the vanity and dogmatism of the ancient sages, he contented himself with proclaiming that he was simply a seeker after knowledge, not its possessor, and to him is attributed the introduction of the word *philosopher*, or *lover of wisdom*, as the only title which he would assume. After the lawless destruction of his school at Crotona, he fled to the Locrians, who refused to receive him, when he repaired to Metapontum, and sought an asylum from his enemies in the temple of the Muses, where tradition says that he died of starvation 506 B.C., when eighty years old.

Pythagoras, School of. The schools established by Pythagoras at Crotona and other cities, have been considered by many writers as the models after which Masonic Lodges were subsequently constructed. They undoubtedly served the Christian ascetics of the first century as a pattern for their monastic institutions, with which institutions the Freemasonry of the Middle Ages, in its operative character, was intimately connected. A brief description of the school of Crotona will not therefore be inappropriate. The disciples of this school wore the simplest kind of clothing, and having on their entrance surrendered all their possessions to the common fund, they submitted for three years to voluntary poverty, during which time they were also compelled to a rigorous silence. The doctrines of Pythagoras were always delivered as infallible propositions which admitted of no argument, and hence the expression *αὐτὸς ἔφη, he said it*, was considered as a sufficient answer to anyone who demanded a reason. The scholars were divided into *Exoterics* and *Esoterics*. This distinction was borrowed by Pythagoras from the Egyptian priests, who practised a similar mode of instruction. The exoteric scholars were those who attended the public assemblies, where general ethical instructions were delivered by the sage. But only the esoterics constituted the true school, and these alone Pythagoras called, says Jamblichus, his companions and friends. Before admission to the privileges of this school, the previous life and character of the candidate were rigidly scrutinised, and in the preparatory initiation secrecy was enjoined by an oath, and he was made to submit to the severest trials of his fortitude and self-command. He who after his admission was alarmed at the obstacles he had to encounter, was permitted to return to the world, and the disciples, considering him as dead, performed his funeral obsequies, and erected a monument to his memory.

The mode of living in the school of Crotona was like that of the modern communists. The brethren, about six hundred in number, with their wives and children, resided in one large building. Every morning the business and duties of the day were arranged, and at night an account was rendered of the day's transactions. They arose before day to pay their devotions to the sun, and recited verses from Homer, Hesiod, or some other poet. Several hours were spent in study, after which there was an interval before dinner, which was occupied in walking and in gymnastic exercises. The meals consisted principally of bread, honey, and water, for though the table was often covered with delicacies, no one was permitted to partake of them. It was in this secret school that Pythagoras gave his instructions on his interior doctrine, and explained the hidden meaning of his symbols. There were three degrees: the first, or Mathematici, being engaged in the study of the exact sciences; and the second, or Theoretici, in the knowledge of God and the future state of man; but the third, or highest degree, was communicated only to a few whose intellects were capable of grasping the full fruition of the Pythagorean philosophy. This school, after existing for thirty years, was finally dissolved through the machinations of Kylo, a wealthy inhabitant of Crotona, who, having been refused admission, in revenge excited the citizens against it, when a lawless mob attacked the scholars while assembled in the house of Milo, set fire to the building and dispersed the disciples, forty of them being burned to death. The school was never resumed, but after the death of the philosopher summaries of his doctrines were made by some of his disciples. Still many of his symbols and his esoteric teachings have to this day remained uninterpreted and unexplained.

After this account of the Pythagorean school, the Mason will find no difficulty in understanding that part of the so-called Leland Manuscript which is said to have so much puzzled the great metaphysician John Locke.

This manuscript—the question of its authenticity is not here entered upon—has the following paragraphs:

"How comede ytt [Freemasonry] yn Engelonde?

"Peter Gower, a Grecian, journeyeded for kunnynge yn Egypte and in Syria, and yn everyche londe whereat the Venetians hadde plauntedde Maconrye, and wynnynge entraunce yn al Lodges of Maconnes, he lerned muche, and retournedde and worked yn Grecia Magna wachsynge and becommynge a myghtye wysacre and gratelyche renowned, and here he framed a grate Lodge at Groton, and maked many Maconnes, some whereoffe dyd journeye yn Fraunce, and maked manye Maconnes wherefromme, yn process of tyme, the arte passed yn Engelonde."

Locke confesses that he was at first puzzled with those strange names, *Peter Gower*, *Groton*, and the *Venetians;* but a little thinking taught him that they were only corruptions of *Pythagoras*, *Crotona*, and the *Phœnicians*.

It is not singular that the old Masons should have called Pythagoras their "ancient friend and brother," and should have dedicated to him one of their geometrical symbols, the forty-seventh problem of Euclid; an epithet and a custom that have, by the force of habit, been retained in all the modern rituals.

Q

Q. (Heb. ק, Q or K, *Koph.*) The seventeenth letter in the English and modern Latin alphabets. In the Phœnician or Ancient Hebrew its form was one circle within another. Its numerical value is 100. The Canaanite signification is ear.

Quadrivium. In classical Latin the word *quadrivium* meant a place where four roads met, and *trivium*, a place where three roads met. The scholastics of the Middle Ages, looking to the metaphorical meaning of the phrase *the paths of learning*, divided what were called the seven liberal arts and sciences, but which comprised the whole cycle of instruction in those days, into two classes, calling grammar, rhetoric, and logic the *trivium*, and arithmetic, geometry, music, and astronomy the *quadrivium*. These two roads to the temple of wisdom, including seven distinct sciences, were, in the Middle Ages, supposed to include universal knowledge. (See *Liberal Arts and Sciences.*)

Quadrivium and Trivium. The seven liberal arts and sciences. The Quadrivium, in the language of the schools, were the four lesser arts, arithmetic, music, geometry, and astronomy; while the Trivium were the triple way to eloquence by the study of grammar, logic, and rhetoric.

Quakers. The question of the admissibility of a Quaker's affirmation in Masonry is discussed under the word *Affirmation*, which see.

Qualifications of Candidates. Every candidate for initiation into the mysteries of Freemasonry must be qualified by certain essential conditions. These qualifications are of two kinds, *Internal* and *External*. The internal qualifications are those which lie within his own bosom, the external are those which refer to his outward and apparent fitness. The external qualifications are again divided into *Moral*, *Religious*, *Physical*, *Mental*, and *Political*.

I. The Internal Qualifications are:

1. That the applicant must come of his own free will and accord. His application must be purely voluntary, to which he has not been induced by persuasion of friends.

2. That he must not be influenced by mercenary motives.

3. That he must be prompted to make the

application in consequence of a favorable opinion that he entertains of the Institution.

4. That he must be resolved to conform with cheerfulness to the established usages and customs of the Fraternity.

II. The External Qualifications are, as has already been said, divided into four kinds:

1. The *Moral.* That candidate only is qualified for initiation who faithfully observes the precepts of the moral law, and leads a virtuous life, so conducting himself as to receive the reward of his own conscience as well as the respect and approbation of the world.

2. The *Religious.* Freemasonry is exceedingly tolerant in respect to creeds, but it does require that every candidate for initiation shall believe in the existence of God as a superintending and protecting power, and in a future life. No inquiry will be made into modifications of religious belief, provided it includes these two tenets.

3. The *Physical.* These refer to sex, age, and bodily conformation. The candidate must be a man, not a woman; of mature age, that is, having arrived at his majority, and not so old as to have sunk into dotage; and he must be in possession of all his limbs, not maimed or dismembered, but, to use the language of one of the old Charges, "have his right limbs as a man ought to have."

4. The *Mental.* This division excludes all men who are not intellectually qualified to comprehend the character of the Institution, and to partake of its responsibilities. Hence fools or idiots and madmen are excluded. Although the landmarks do not make illiteracy a disqualification, and although it is undeniable that a large portion of the Craft in olden times was uneducated, yet there seems to be a general opinion that an incapacity to read and write will, in this day, disqualify a candidate.

5. The *Political.* These relate to the condition of the candidate in society. The old rule required that none but those who were free born could be initiated, which, of course, excluded slaves and those born in servitude; and although the Grand Lodge of England substituted *free man* for *free born*, it is undeniable that that action was a violation of a landmark; and the old rule still exists, at least in America.

Quarrels. Contention or quarreling in the Lodge, as well as without, is discountenanced by the spirit of all the Old Constitutions of Masonry. In the Charges compiled from them, approved by the Grand Lodge of England in 1722, and published by Dr. Anderson, it is said, "No private piques or quarrels must be brought within the door of the Lodge, far less any quarrels about religion, or nations, or State policy." (*Constitutions*, 1723, p. 54.)

Quarries. It is an error to speak, as Oliver does, misguided by some Masonic traditions, of the quarries of Tyre in connection with the Temple of Solomon. Modern researches have shown without question that the stones used in the construction of the Temple were taken out of quarries in the immediate vicinity; and the best traditions, as well as Scripture, claim only that the wood from the forests of Lebanon was supplied by King Hiram. The great quarries of Jerusalem are situated in the northeast portion of the city, near the Damascus gate. The entrance to them was first discovered by Barclay. A writer, quoted by Barclay, thus describes them (*City of the Great King*, p. 466): "Here were blocks of stones but half quarried, and still attached by one side to the rock. The work of quarrying was apparently effected by an instrument resembling a pickaxe, with a broad chisel-shaped end, as the spaces between the blocks were not more than four inches wide, in which it would be impossible for a man to work with a chisel and mallet. The spaces were, many of them, four feet deep and ten feet in height, and the distance between them was about four feet. After being cut away at each side and at the bottom, a lever was inserted, and the combined force of three or four men could easily pry the block away from the rock behind. The stone was extremely soft and friable, nearly white, and very easily worked, but, like the stone of Malta and Paris, hardening by exposure. The marks of the cutting instrument were as plain and well-defined as if the workman had just ceased from his labor. The heaps of chippings which were found in these quarries showed that the stone had been dressed there, and confirm the Bible statement that the stone of which the Temple was built was made ready before it was brought thither." Barclay remarks (*ib.*, p. 118) that "those extra cyclopean stones in the south-east and south-west corners of the Temple wall were doubtless taken from this great quarry, and carried to their present position down the gently inclined plain on rollers—a conjecture which at once solves the mystery that has greatly puzzled travellers in relation to the difficulty of transporting and *handling* such immense masses of rock, and enables us to understand why they were called 'stones of rolling' by Ezra." Mr. Prime also visited these quarries, and in his *Tent Life in the Holy Land* (p. 114) speaks of them thus: "One thing to me is very manifest: there has been solid stone taken from the excavation sufficient to build the walls of Jerusalem and the Temple of Solomon. The size of many of the stones taken from here appears to be very great. I know of no place to which the stone can have been carried but to these works, and I know no other quarries in the neighborhood from which the great stone of the walls would seem to have come. These two connected ideas compelled me strongly toward the belief that this was the ancient quarry whence the city was built; and when the magnitude of the excavation between the two opposing hills and of this cavern is considered, it is, to say the least of it, a difficult question to answer, what has become of the stone once here, on any other theory than that I have suggested." And he adds: "Who can say that the cavern which we explored was not the place where the hammers rang on the stone which were forbidden to sound in the silent growth of the great Temple of Solomon?"

The researches of subsequent travelers, and especially the labors of the "Palestine Exploration Fund," have substantiated these statements, and confirmed the fact that the quarries where the workmen labored at the building of the Solomonic Temple were not in the dominions of the King of Tyre, but in the immediate vicinity of the Temple. In 1868, Rob. Morris held what he calls a "Moot Lodge" in these quarries, which event he describes in his *Freemasonry in the Holy Land*, a work of great interest to Masonic scholars.

Quarterly Communication. The Old Records of the Institution state that the Fraternity met annually in their General Assembly. The Halliwell or Regius Manuscript says it is true that the Assembly may be held triennially, "Eche year or third year it should be hold" (line 475); but wherever spoken of in subsequent records, it is always as an Annual Meeting. It is not until 1717 that we find anything said of quarterly communications; and the first allusion to these subordinate meetings in any printed work to which we now have access is in 1738, in the edition of the *Constitutions* published in that year. The expression there used is that the quarterly communications were "forthwith revived." This of course implies that they had previously existed; but as no mention is made of them in the Regulations of 1663, which, on the contrary, speak expressly only of an "Annual General Assembly," we may infer that quarterly communications must have been first introduced into the Masonic system after the middle of the seventeenth century. They have not the authority of antiquity, and have been very wisely discarded by nearly all the Grand Lodges in this country. They are still retained by the Grand Lodges of England, Scotland, and Ireland, but in the United States only by those of Massachusetts and Pennsylvania.

Quaternion. From the Latin *quater*, the number *Four*, which see. Oliver calls it the *quaternary*, but *quaternion* is the better usage.

Quatuor Coronati. See *Four Crowned Martyrs*.

Quatuor Coronati Lodge. This Lodge, No. 2076 on the roll of the Grand Lodge of England, was established in 1886, for the purpose of studying the History, Symbols, and Legends of Freemasonry, and it is in fact a Masonic Literary and Archeological Society, meeting as a tiled Lodge. Attached to the Lodge proper, which is limited to 40 full members, is a Correspondence Circle established in 1887, and now numbering over 3,000 members drawn from all parts of the world. The transactions of the Lodge are published under the title of *Ars Quatuor Coronatorum*. The Lodge is named after the "Four Crowned Martyrs" (*q. v.*). All Master Masons in good standing are eligible to membership in the Correspondence Circle. The dues are $2.50 a year, for which the valuable Transactions of the Lodge are sent to each member. [E. L. H.]

Quebec. From 1855 to 1869 the Grand Lodge of Canada was the controlling Masonic power in the Province of Quebec, but with the birth of the Dominion came also the agitation for separate Grand Lodges. Several meetings were held, and finally, on the 20th of October, 1869, the Grand Lodge of Quebec was formed by twenty-eight of the Warranted Lodges then in the Province, with M. W. Bro. John Hamilton Graham, LL.D., as Grand Master. [W. H. W.]

Questions of Henry VI. Questions said to have been proposed by King Henry VI. of England to the Masons of the kingdom, which, with their answers, are contained in the manuscript known as the *Leland Manuscript*, which see.

Quetzalcoatl. The Mexican idea of the Deity of Enlightenment. The spirit-man from whom they received their civilization, and for whose second coming they wait. Him for whom they mistook Cortez, and therefore welcomed him with joy.

Quorum. The parliamentary law provides that a deliberative body shall not proceed to business until a quorum of its members is present. And this law is applicable to Masonry, except that, in constituting a quorum for opening and working a Lodge, it is not necessary that the quorum shall be made up of actual members of the Lodge; for the proper officers of the Lodge being present, the quorum may be completed by any brethren of the Craft. As to the number of brethren necessary to make a quorum for the transaction of business, the Old Constitutions and Regulations are silent, and the authorities consequently differ. In reply to an inquiry directed to him in 1857, the editor of the London *Freemasons' Magazine* affirmed that *five* Masons are sufficient to open a Lodge and carry on business other than initiation; for which latter purpose *seven* are necessary. This opinion appears to be the general English one, and is acquiesced in by Dr. Oliver; but there is no authority of law for it. And when, in the year 1818, the suggestion was made that some regulation was necessary relative to the number of brethren requisite to constitute a legal Lodge, with competent powers to perform the rite of initiation, and transact all other business, the Board of General Purposes of the Grand Lodge of England, to whom the suggestion had been referred, replied, with something like Dogberrian astuteness, "that it is a matter of so much delicacy and difficulty, that it is thought advisable not to depart from the silence on the subject which had been observed in all the Books of Constitutions."

In the absence, then, of all written laws upon the subject, and without any constitutional provision to guide us, we are compelled to recur to the ritual for authority. There the answer to the question in each degree, "How many compose a Lodge?" will supply us with the rule by which we are to establish the quorum in that degree. For whatever number composes a Lodge, that is the number which will authorize the Lodge to proceed to business. The ritual has thus established the number which constitutes a "perfect Lodge," and without which number a Lodge could not be legally opened, and therefore, necessarily, could not proceed to work or business; for there is no distinction, in respect to a quorum, between a Lodge when at work or when engaged in business.

According to the ritualistic rule referred to, seven constitute a quorum, for work or business, in an Entered Apprentice's Lodge, five in a Fellow-Craft's, and three in a Master Mason's. Without this requisite number no Lodge can be opened in either of these degrees. In a Chapter of Royal Arch Masons nine Companions constitute a quorum, and in a Commandery of Knights Templar eleven Knights; although, under certain circumstances well known to the Order, three Knights are competent to transact business.

R

R. (Heb. ר, *Resh.*) The eighteenth letter in the English and other Western alphabets. The word Resh signifies *forehead*, and in the Phœnician and hieroglyphic character is thus represented. Its numerical value is 200, and the equivalent as a name of God is רחום, *Rahum*, signifying clemency.

Rabbanaim. רב־בנאים, Rabbinical Hebrew, and signifying "the chief of the architects." A significant word in the high degrees.

Rabbinism. The system of philosophy taught by the Jewish Rabbis subsequent to the dispersion, which is engaged in mystical explanations of the oral law. With the reveries of the Jewish teachers was mingled the Egyptian, the Arabic, and the Grecian doctrines. From the Egyptians, especially, Rabbinism derived its allegorical and symbolic mode of instruction. Out of it sprang the Therapeutists and the Essenians; and it gave rise to the composition of the Talmud, many of whose legends have been incorporated into the mythical philosophy of Speculative Masonry. And this it is that makes Rabbinism an interesting subject of research to the Masonic student.

Rabboni. רבוני. Literally, *my Master*, equivalent to the pure Hebrew, *Adoni*. As a significant word in the higher degrees, it has been translated "*a most excellent Master*," and its usage by the later Jews will justify that interpretation. Buxtorf (*Lex. Talmud.*) tells us that about the time of Christ this title arose in the school of Hillel, and was given to only seven of their wise men who were preeminent for their learning. Jahn (*Arch. Bib.*, § 106) says that Gamaliel, the preceptor of St. Paul, was one of these. They styled themselves the children of wisdom, which is an expression very nearly corresponding to the Greek φιλοσοφοι. The word occurs once, as applied to Christ, in the New Testament (John xx. 16), "Jesus said unto her, Mary. She turned herself, and saith unto him, Rabboni, which is to say, Master." The Masonic myth in the "Most Excellent Master's Degree," that it was the title addressed by the Queen of Sheba to King Solomon on beholding the magnificence and splendor of the Temple, wants the element of plausibility, inasmuch as the word was not in use in the time of Solomon.

Ragon, J. M. One of the most distinguished Masonic writers of France. His contemporaries did not hesitate to call him "the most learned Mason of the nineteenth century." He was born in the last quarter of the eighteenth century, most probably at Bruges, in Belgium, where in 1803 he was initiated in the Lodge Réunion des Amis du Nord, and subsequently assisted in the foundation of the Lodge and Chapter of Vrais Amis in the same city. On his removal to Paris he continued his devotion to Freemasonry, and was the founder in 1805 of the celebrated Lodge of Les Trinosophes. In that Lodge he delivered, in 1818, a course of lectures on ancient and modern initiations, which twenty years afterward were repeated at the request of the Lodge, and published in 1841, under the title of *Cours Philosophique et Interpratif des Initiations Anciennes et Modernes*. This work was printed with the express permission of the Grand Orient of France, but three years after that body denounced its second edition for containing some additional matter. Rebold charges this act to the petty passions of the day, and twenty-five years after the Grand Orient made ample reparation in the honor that it paid to the memory of Ragon. In 1818 and 1819, he was editor in chief of the periodical published during those years under the title of *Hermès, ou Archives Maçonniques*. In 1853, he published *Orthodoxie Maçonnique*, a work abounding in historical information, although some of his statements are inaccurate. In 1861, he published the *Tuileur Général de la Franc-Maçonnerie, ou Manuel de l'Initié;* a book not merely confined to the details of degrees, but which is enriched with many valuable and interesting notes. Ragon died at Paris about the year 1866. In the preface to his *Orthodoxie*, he had announced his intention to crown his Masonic labors by writing a work to be entitled *Les Fastes Initiatiques*, in which he proposed to give an exhaustive view of the Ancient Mysteries, of the Roman Colleges of Architects and their successors, the building corporations of the Middle Ages, and of the institution of Modern or Philosophic Masonry at the beginning of the eighteenth century. This was to constitute the first volume. The three following volumes were to embrace a history of the Order and of all its Rites in every country. The fifth volume was to be appropriated to the investigation of other secret associations, more or less connected with Freemasonry; and the sixth and last volume was to contain a General Tiler or manual of all the known rites and degrees. Such a work would have been an inestimable boon to the Masonic student, but Ragon unfortunately began it too late in life. He did not live to complete it, and in 1868 the unfinished manuscript was purchased, by the Grand Orient of France, from his heirs for a thousand francs. It was destined to be quietly deposited in the archives of that body, because, as it was confessed, no Mason could be found in France who had ability enough to supply its lacunæ and prepare it for the press.

Ragon's theory of the origin of Masonry was that its primitive idea is to be found in the initiations of the Ancient Mysteries, but that for its present form it is indebted to Elias Ashmole, who fabricated it in the seventeenth century.

Ragotzky, Carl August. A German who was distinguished for his labors in Masonry, and for the production of several works of high character, the principal of which were *Der Freidenker in der Maurerei oder Freimüthige Briefe über wichtige Gegenstände in der Frei-Maurerei*, i. e., The Freethinker in Masonry, or Candid Letters on important subjects in Freemasonry, published at Berlin, in 1793, in an octavo volume of three hundred and eleven pages, of which a second edition appeared in 1811; and a smaller work entitled *Ueber Maurerische Freiheit, für eingeweihte und uneingeweihte*, i. e., An Essay on Masonic Liberty, for initiated and uninitiated readers, published in 1792. He died January 5, 1823.

Rainbow, The Most Ancient Order of the. A secret association existing in Moorfields in 1760.

Rains. It was a custom among the English Masons of the middle of the last century, when conversing together on Masonry, to announce the appearance of a profane by the warning expression "it rains." The custom was adopted by the German and French Masons, with the equivalent expression, *es regnet* and *il pluie*. Baron Tschoudy, who condemns the usage, says that the latter refined upon it by designating the approach of a female by *il neige*, it snows. Dr. Oliver says (*Rev. Sq.*, 142) that the phrase "it rains," to indicate that a cowan is present and the proceedings must be suspended, is derived from the ancient punishment of an eavesdropper, which was to place him under the eaves of a house in rainy weather, and to retain him there till the droppings of water ran in at the collar of his coat and out at his shoes.

Raised. When a candidate has received the Third Degree, he is said to have been "raised" to the sublime degree of a Master Mason. The expression refers, *materially*, to a portion of the ceremony of initiation, but *symbolically*, to the resurrection, which it is the object of the degree to exemplify.

Raising Sheet. A term sometimes given to one of the common properties known to Master Masons.

Ramayana. The great epic of ancient India, deemed a sacred writing by its people, narrating the history of Rama, or Vishnu incarnate, and his wife Siva. It contains about 24,000 verses, in seven books, written in Sanskrit, and is ascribed to Valmîki, who lived about the beginning of the Christian era.

Ramsay, Andrew Michael. Commonly called the Chevalier Ramsay. He was born at Ayr, in Scotland. [There is some uncertainty about the date of his birth, but according to his own account he must have been born in 1680 or 81, because in 1741 he told Herr von Gensau that he was 60 years old.] His father was a baker, but being the possessor of considerable property was enabled to give his son a liberal education. He was accordingly sent to school in his native burgh, and afterward to the University of Edinburgh, where he was distinguished for his abilities and diligence. In 1709 he was entrusted with the education of the two sons of the Earl of Wemyss. Subsequently, becoming unsettled in his religious opinions, he resigned that employment and went to Holland, residing for some time at Leyden. There he became acquainted with Pierre Poiret, one of the most celebrated teachers of the mystic theology which then prevailed on the Continent. From him Ramsay learned the principal tenets of that system; and it is not unreasonable to suppose that he was thus indoctrinated with that love of mystical speculation which he subsequently developed as the inventor of Masonic degrees, and as the founder of a Masonic Rite. In 1710, he visited the celebrated Fénelon, Archbishop of Cambrai, of whose mystical tendencies he had heard, and met with a cordial reception. The archbishop invited Ramsay to become his guest, and in six months he was converted to the Catholic faith. Fénelon procured for him the preceptorship of the Duc de Chateau-Thierry and the Prince de Turenne. As a reward for his services in that capacity, he was made a Knight of the Order of St. Lazarus, whence he received the title of "Chevalier" by which he was usually known. He was subsequently selected by James III., the Pretender, as the tutor of his two sons,

Charles Edward and Henry, the former of whom became afterward the Young Pretender, and the latter the Cardinal York. For this purpose he repaired, in 1724, to Rome. But the political and religious intrigues of that court became distasteful to him, and in a short time he obtained permission to return to France. In 1728, he visited England, and became an inmate of the family of the Duke of Argyle. Chambers says (*Biog. Dict.*) that while there he wrote his *Principles of Natural and Revealed Religion*, and his *Travels of Cyrus*. This statement is evidently incorrect. The former did not appear until after his death, and was probably one of the last productions of his pen. The latter had already been published at Paris in 1727. But he had already acquired so great a literary reputation, that the University of Oxford conferred on him the degree of Doctor of Civil Law. He then returned to France, and resided for many years at Pointoise, a seat of the Prince of Turenne, where he wrote his *Life of Fénelon*, and a *History of the Viscount Turenne*. During the remainder of his life he resided as Intendant in the Prince's family, and died May 6, 1743, in the sixty-second year of his age.

[He was a Freemason and Grand Chancellor of the Grand Lodge of Paris, but it is not known where and when he became a Mason; it was probably during his visit to England about 1730.]

Ramsay, although born of humble parentage, was by subsequent association an aristocrat in disposition. Hence, in proposing his theory of the origin of Freemasonry, he repudiated its connection with an operative art, and sought to find its birthplace in Palestine, among those kings and knights who had gone forth to battle as Crusaders for the conquest of Jerusalem. In 1737, Ramsay, as Grand Orator, pronounced a discourse before the Grand Lodge of France, in which he set forth his theory in explicit terms. The following is a translation of part of the speech:

"During the time of the holy wars in Palestine, several principal lords and citizens associated themselves together, and entered into a vow to re-establish the temples of the Christians in the Holy Land; and engaged themselves by an oath to employ their talents and their fortunes in restoring architecture to its primitive institution. They adopted several ancient signs and symbolic words drawn from religion, by which they might distinguish themselves from the infidels and recognize each other in the midst of the Saracens. They communicated these signs and words only to those who had solemnly sworn, often at the foot of the altar, never to reveal them. This was not an oath of execration, but a bond uniting men of all nations into the same confraternity. Some time after our Order was united with the Knights of St. John of Jerusalem. Hence our Lodges are in all countries called Lodges of St. John. This union was made in imitation of the Israelites when they rebuilt the second Temple, during which time with one hand they managed the trowel and mortar, and in the other held the sword and buckler.

"Our Order must not, therefore, be regarded as a renewal of the Bacchanals and a source of senseless dissipation, of unbridled libertinism and of scandalous intemperance, but as a moral Order, instituted by our ancestors in the Holy Land to recall the recollection of the most sublime truths in the midst of the innocent pleasures of society.

"The kings, princes, and nobles, when they returned from Palestine into their native dominions, established Lodges there. At the time of the last Crusade several Lodges had already been erected in Germany, Italy, Spain, France, and, from the last, in Scotland, on account of the intimate alliance which then existed between those two nations.

"James, Lord Steward of Scotland, was the Grand Master of a Lodge established at Kilwinning, in the west of Scotland, in the year 1236, a short time after the death of Alexander III., King of Scotland, and a year before John Baliol ascended the throne. This Scottish lord received the Earls of Gloucester and Ulster, English and Irish noblemen, as Masons in his Lodge.

"By degrees our Lodges, our festivals, and our solemnities were neglected in most of the countries where they had been established. Hence the silence of the historians of all nations, except Great Britain, on the subject of the Order. It was preserved, however, in all its splendor by the Scotch, to whom for several centuries the kings of France had intrusted the guardianship of their sacred persons.

"After the lamentable reverses of the Crusades, the destruction of the Christian armies, and the triumph of Bendocdar, Sultan of Egypt, in 1263, during the eighth and ninth Crusades, the great Prince Edward, son of Henry III., King of England, seeing that there would be no security for the brethren in the Holy Land when the Christian troops should retire, led them away, and thus this colony of the Fraternity was established in England. As this prince was endowed with all the qualities of mind and heart which constitute the hero, he loved the fine arts, and declared himself the protector of our Order. He granted it several privileges and franchises, and ever since the members of the confraternity have assumed the name of *Freemasons*. From this time Great Britain became the seat of our sciences, the conservatrix of our laws, and the depository of our secrets. The religious dissensions which so fatally pervaded and rent all Europe during the sixteenth century, caused our Order to degenerate from the grandeur and nobility of its origin. Several of our rites and usages, which were opposed to the prejudices of the times, were changed, disguised, or retrenched. Thus it is that several of our brethren have, like the ancient Jews, forgotten the spirit of our laws, and preserved only the letter and the outer covering. But from the British isles the ancient science is now beginning to pass again into France."

Such was the peculiar theory of Ramsay. Rejecting all reference to the Traveling Architects from Como, to the Stone Masons of Germany, and the Operative Freemasons of England, he had sought a noble and chivalric origin for Freemasonry, which with him was not a confraternity founded on a system of architecture, but solely on the military prowess and religious enthusiasm of knighthood. The theory was as clearly the result of his own inventive genius as was his fable of the travels of Cyrus. He offered no documentary or historical authority to support his assertions, but gave them as if they were already admitted facts. The theory was, however, readily accepted by the rich, the fashionable, and the noble, because it elevated the origin and the social position of the Order, and to it we are to attribute the sudden rise of so many high degrees, which speedily overshadowed the humbler pretensions of primitive Craft Masonry. [After the delivery of this speech a number of Chivalric Degrees were invented in France and styled Scottish Masonry, and they have been attributed to Ramsay, acting as has been supposed in the interests of the exiled Stuarts; and he has also been considered the inventor of the Royal Arch Degree; but R. F. Gould in his *History of Freemasonry* has shown that there is no foundation for either of these theories; and that Ramsay's influence on Freemasonry was due to his speech alone.]

All writers concur in giving the most favorable opinions of Ramsay's character. Chambers asserts that he was generous and kind to his relatives, and that on his temporary return to Great Britain, although he did not visit them in Scotland, he sent them liberal offers of money, which, however, incensed at his apostasy from the national religion, they indignantly refused to accept. Clavel (*Hist. Pittor.*, p. 165) describes him as "a man endowed with an ardent imagination, and a large amount of learning, wit, and urbanity." And Robison (*Proofs of a Consp.*, p. 39) says he was "as eminent for his piety as he was for his enthusiasm," and speaks of his "eminent learning, his elegant talents, and his amiable character."

His general literary reputation is secured by his *Life of Fénelon*, his *Travels of Cyrus*, and the elaborate work, published after his death, entitled *The Philosophical Principles of Natural and Revealed Religion, Unfolded in a Geometrical Order*. He is said to have been the author of an *Apologetic and Historical Relation of the Society of Freemasonry*, which was published in 1738, and had the honor to be burnt the next year at Rome by the public executioner, on the sentence of the Sacred Congregation of the Inquisition.

Raphael. (Hebrew interpretation, "The healing of God.") The title of an officer in a Rose Croix Chapter. The name of the angel, under the Kabbalistical system, that governed the planet Mercury. A messenger.

Ratisbon. A city of Bavaria, in which two Masonic Congresses have been held. The first was convoked in 1459, by Jost Dotzinger, the master of the works of the Strasburg cathedral. It established some new laws for the government of the Fraternity in Germany. The second was called in 1464, by the Grand Lodge of Strasburg, principally to define the relative rights of, and to settle existing difficulties between, the Grand Lodges of Strasburg, Cologne, Vienna, and Bern. (See *Stone Masons of the Middle Ages*.)

Rawlinson Manuscript. In 1855, the Rev. J. S. Sidebotham, of New College, Oxford, published in the *Freemasons' Monthly Magazine* a series of interesting extracts from a manuscript volume which he stated was in the Bodleian Library, and which he described as seeming "to be a kind of Masonic album, or commonplace book, belonging to Brother Richard Rawlinson, LL.D. and F. R. S., of the following Lodges: Sash and Cocoa-tree, Moorfields, 37; St. Paul's Head, Ludgate Street, 40; Rose Tavern, Cheapside, and Oxford Arms, Ludgate Street, 94; in which he inserted anything that struck him either as useful or particularly amusing. It is partly in manuscript, partly in print, and comprises some ancient Masonic Charges, Constitutions, forms of summons, a list of all the Lodges of his time under the Grand Lodge of England, whether in London, the country, or abroad; together with some extracts from the *Grub Street Journal*, the *General Evening Post*, and other journals of the day. The dates range from 1724 to 1740." (*F. M. Monthly Mag.*, 1855, p. 81.)

Among the materials thus collected is one which bears the following title: *The Freemasons' Constitutions, Copied from an Old MS. in the possession of Dr. Rawlinson*. This copy of the Old Constitutions does not differ materially in its contents from the other old manuscripts, but its more modern spelling and phraseology would seem to give it a later date, which may be from 1725 to 1750. In a note to the statement that King Athelstan "caused a roll or book to be made, which declared how this science was first invented, afterwards preserved and augmented, with the utility and true intent thereof, which roll or book he commanded to be read and plainly recited when a man was to be made a Freemason," Dr. Rawlinson says: "One of these rolls I have seen in the possession of Mr. Baker, a carpenter in Moorfields." The title of the manuscript in the scrap-book of Rawlinson is *The Freemasons' Constitution, Copied from an Old MS. in the possession of Dr. Rawlinson*. The original MS. has not yet been traced, but possibly if found would be of about the end of the seventeenth century.

Richard Rawlinson, LL.D., was a celebrated antiquary, who was born in London about 1690, and died April 6, 1755. He was the author of a *Life of Anthony Wood*, published in 1711, and of *The English Topographer*, published in 1720. Dr. Rawlinson was consecrated a bishop of the nonjuring communion of the Church of England, March 25, 1728. He was an assiduous collector of old manuscripts, invariably purchasing, sometimes at high prices, all that were offered him for sale. In his will, dated June 2, 1752, he bequeathed the whole collection to the University of Oxford. The manuscripts were placed in the Bodleian Library, and still remain there. In 1898, Dr. W. J. Chetwode Crawley published in the *Ars Quatuor Coronatorum*, vol. xi., a full account of the Rawlinson MSS., in which he shows that the collection was not really made by Dr. Rawlinson, but by one Thomas Towl. (P. 15.)

Received and Acknowledged. A term applied to the initiation of a candidate into the Sixth or Most Excellent Master's Degree of the American Rite. (See *Acknowledged*.)

Reception. The ceremony of initiation into a degree of Masonry is called a reception.

Recipient. The French call the candidate in any degree of Masonry the *Récipiendaire*, or Recipient.

Recognition, Modes of. Smith says (*Use and Abuse*, p. 46) that at the institution of the Order, to each of the degrees "a particular distinguished *test* was adapted, which *test*, together with the explication, was accordingly settled and communicated to the Fraternity previous to their dispersion, under a necessary and solemn injunction to secrecy; and they have been most cautiously preserved and transmitted down to posterity by faithful brethren ever since their emigration."

Hence, of all the landmarks, the modes of recognition are the most legitimate and unquestioned. They should admit of no variation, for in their universality consist their excellence and advantage. And yet such variations have unfortunately been admitted, the principal of which originated about the middle of the eighteenth century, and were intimately connected with the division of the Fraternity in England into the two conflicting societies of the "Ancients" and the "Moderns"; and although by the reconciliation in 1813 uniformity was restored in the United Grand Lodge which was then formed, that uniformity did not extend to the subordinate bodies in other countries which had derived their existence and their different modes of recognition from the two separated Grand Lodges; and this was, of course, equally applicable to the high degrees which sprang out of them. Thus, while the modes of recognition in the York and Scottish Rites are substantially the same, those of the French or Modern Rite differ in almost everything. In this there is a P. W. in the First Degree unrecognised by the two other Rites, and all afterward are different.

Again, there are important differences in the York and American Rites, although there is sufficient similarity to relieve American and English Masons from any embarrassment in mutual recognition. Although nearly all the Lodges in the United States, before the Revolution of 1776, derived their existence from the Grand Lodges of England, the American Masons do not use the multitude of signs that prevail in the English system, while they have introduced, I think, through the teachings of Webb, the D. G., which is totally unknown to English Masonry. Looking to these differences, the Masonic Congress of Paris, held in 1856, recommended, in the seventh proposition, that "Masters of Lodges, in conferring the degree of Master Mason, should invest the candidate with the words, signs, and grips of the Scottish and Modern Rites." This proposition, if it had been adopted, would have mitigated, if it did not abolish, the evil; but, unfortunately, it did not receive the general concurrence of the Craft.

As to the antiquity of modes of recognition in general, it may be said that, from the very nature of things, there was always a necessity for the members of every secret society to have some means for recognizing a brother that should escape the detection of the uninitiated. We find evidence in several of the classic writings showing that such a custom prevailed among the initiated in the Pagan mysteries. Livy tells us (xxxi., 14) of two Acarnanian youths who accidentally entered the temple of Ceres during the celebration of the mysteries, and, not having been initiated, were speedily detected as intruders, and put to death by the managers of the temple. They must, of course, have owed their detection to the fact that they were not in possession of those modes of recognition which were known only to the initiated.

That they existed in the Dionysiac rites of Bacchus we learn from Plautus, who, in his *Miles Gloriosus* (Act IV., Sc. ii.), makes Misphidippa say to Pyrgopolonices, "Cedo signum si harunc Baccharum es," *Give the sign, if you are one of these Bacchæ.*

Jamblichus (*Vit. Pyth.*) tells the story of a disciple of Pythagoras, who, having been taken sick, on a long journey, at an inn, and having exhausted his funds, gave, before he died, to the landlord, who had been very kind to him, a paper, on which he had written the account of his distress, and signed it with a symbol of Pythagoras. This the landlord affixed to the gate of a neighboring temple. Months afterward another Pythagorean, passing that way, recognised the secret symbol, and, inquiring into the tale, reimbursed the landlord for all his trouble and expense.

Apuleius, who was initiated into the Osirian and Isiac mysteries, says, in his

Defensio, "if any one is present who has been initiated into the same secret rites as myself, if he will give me the sign, he shall then be at liberty to hear what it is that I keep with such care." But in another place he is less cautious, and even gives an inkling of what was one of the signs of the Osirian initiation. For in his *Golden Ass* (lib. xi.) he says that in a dream he beheld one of the disciples of Osiris, "who walked gently, with a hesitating step, the ankle of his left foot being slightly bent, in order, no doubt, that he might afford me some sign by which I could recognize him." The Osirian initiates had then, it seems, like the Freemasons, mystical steps.

That the Gnostics had modes of recognition we learn from St. Epiphanius, himself at one time in early life a Gnostic, who says in his *Panarium*, written against the Gnostics and other heretics, that "on the arrival of any stranger belonging to the same belief, they have a sign given by one to another. In holding out the hand, under pretence of saluting each other, they feel and tickle it in a peculiar manner underneath the palm, and so discover if the new-comer belongs to the same sect. Thereupon, however poor they may be, they serve up to him a sumptuous feast, with abundance of meats and wine."

I do not refer to the fanciful theories of Dr. Oliver—the first one most probably a joke, and therefore out of place in his *Symbolical Dictionary*—founded on passages of Homer and Quintus Curtius, that Achilles and Alexander of Macedon recognized the one Priam and the other the High Priest by a sign. But there are abundant evidences of an authentic nature that a system of recognition by signs, and words, and grips has existed in the earliest times, and, therefore, that they were not invented by the Masons, who borrowed them, as they did much more of their mystical system, from antiquity.

Recommendation. The petition of a candidate for initiation must be recommended by at least two members of the Lodge. Preston requires the signature to be witnessed by one person (he does not say whether he must be a member of the Lodge or not), and that the candidate must be proposed in open Lodge by a member. Webb says that "the candidate must be proposed in form, by a member of the Lodge, and the proposition seconded by another member." Cross says that the recommendation "is to be signed by two members of the Lodge," and he dispenses with the formal proposition. These gradual changes, none of them, however, substantially affecting the principle, have at last resulted in the present simpler usage, which is, for two members of the Lodge to affix their names to the petition, as recommenders of the applicant.

The petition for a Dispensation for a new Lodge, as preliminary to the application for a Warrant of Constitution, must be recommended by the nearest Lodge. Preston says that it must be recommended "by the Masters of three regular Lodges adjacent to the place where the new Lodge is to be held." This is also the language of the Constitution of the Grand Lodge of Ireland. The Grand Lodge of Scotland requires the recommendation to be signed "by the Masters and officers of two of the nearest Lodges." The modern Constitution of the Grand Lodge of England requires a recommendation "by the officers of some regular Lodge," without saying anything of its vicinity to the new Lodge. The rule now universally adopted is, that it must be recommended by the nearest Lodge.

Reconciliation, Lodge of. When the two contending Grand Lodges of England, known as the "Ancients" and the "Moderns," resolved, in 1813, under the respective Grand Masterships of the Dukes of Kent and Sussex, to put an end to all differences, and to form a United Grand Lodge, it was provided, in the fifth article of union, that each of the two Grand Masters should appoint nine Master Masons to meet at some convenient place; and each party having opened a just and perfect Lodge in a separate apartment, they should give and receive mutually and reciprocally the obligations of both Fraternities; and being thus duly and equally enlightened in both forms, they should be empowered and directed to hold a Lodge, under the Warrant or Dispensation to be entrusted to them, and to be entitled "The Lodge of Reconciliation." The duty of this Lodge was to visit the several Lodges under both Grand Lodges, and to instruct the officers and members of the same in the forms of initiation, obligation, etc., in both, so that uniformity of working might be established. The Lodge of Reconciliation was constituted on the 27th of December, 1813, the day on which the union was perfected. This Lodge was only a temporary one, and the duties for which it had been organised having been performed, it ceased to exist by its own limitation in 1816. [For a full account of this Lodge and its proceedings, see *Ars Quatuor Coronatorum*, vol. xxiii., for 1910.]

Reconsideration, Motion for. A motion for reconsideration can only be made in a Grand Lodge, Grand Chapter, or other Grand Body, on the same day or the day after the adoption of the motion which it is proposed to reconsider. In a Lodge or other subordinate body, it can only be made at the same meeting. It cannot be moved by one who has voted in the minority. It cannot be made when the matter to be reconsidered has passed out of the control of the body, as when the original motion was for an appropriation which has been expended since the motion for it was passed. A motion for reconsideration is not debatable if the question proposed to be reconsidered is not. It cannot always be adopted by a simple majority vote. It may be postponed or laid upon the table.

If postponed to a time definite, and when that time arrives is not acted upon, it cannot be renewed. If laid upon the table, it cannot be taken up out of its order, and no second motion for reconsideration can be offered while it lies upon the table, hence to lay a motion for reconsideration on the table is considered as equivalent to rejecting it. When a motion for reconsideration is adopted, the original motion comes up immediately for consideration, as if it had been for the first time brought before the body, in the form which it presented when it was adopted.

Reconsideration of the Ballot. When the petition of a candidate for initiation has been rejected, it is not permissible for any member to move for a reconsideration of the ballot. The following four principles set forth in a summary way the doctrine of Masonic parliamentary law on this subject:

1. It is never in order for a member to move for the reconsideration of a ballot on the petition of a candidate, nor for a presiding officer to entertain such a motion. 2. The Master or presiding officer alone can, for reasons satisfactory to himself, order such a reconsideration. 3. The presiding officer cannot order a reconsideration on any subsequent night, nor on the same night, after any member who was present and voted has departed. 4. The Grand Master cannot grant a Dispensation for a reconsideration, nor in any other way interfere with the ballot. The same restriction applies to the Grand Lodge.

Recorder. In some of the high degrees, as in a Council of Select Masters and a Commandery of Knights Templar, the title of Recorder is given to the Secretary. The recording officer of the Grand Encampment of Knights Templar of the United States, of State Grand Commanderies, and of Grand Councils of Royal and Select Masters, is styled a Grand Recorder.

Records, Old. The early history of Masonry, as written by Anderson, Preston, Smith, Calcott, and writers of that generation, was little more than a collection of fables, so absurd as to excite the smile of every reader, or bare statements of incidents, without any authority to substantiate their genuineness.

The recent writers on the same subject have treated it in a very different manner, and one that gives to the investigation of the early annals of Freemasonry a respectable position in the circle of historic studies. Much of the increased value that is given in the present day to Masonic history is derivable from the fact that, ceasing to repeat the gratuitous statements of the older writers, some of whom have not hesitated to make Adam a Grand Master, and Eden the site of a Lodge, our students of this day are drawing their conclusions from, and establishing their theories on, the old records, which Masonic archeology is in this generation bringing to light. Hence, one of these students (Bro. Woodford, of England) has said that, when we begin to investigate the real facts of Masonic history, "not only have we to discard at once much that we have held tenaciously and taught habitually, simply resting on the reiterated assertions of others, but we shall also find that we have to get rid of what, I fear, we must call 'accumulated rubbish,' before we can see clearly how the great edifice of Masonic history, raised at last on sure and good foundations, stands out clearer to the sight, and even more honorable to the builders, from those needful, if preparatory, labors."

Anderson tells us that in the year 1719, at some of the private Lodges, "several very valuable manuscripts concerning the Fraternity, their Lodges, Regulations, Charges, Secrets, and Usages, were too hastily burnt by some scrupulous brothers, that those papers might not fall into strange hands." (*Constitutions*, 1738, p. 111.)

In the last quarter of a century the archeologists of Masonry have labored very diligently and successfully to disinter from the old Lodges, libraries, and museums many of these ancient manuscripts, and much light has thus been thrown upon the early history of Freemasonry.

The following is a list of the most important of these old records which the industry of Masonic antiquaries has brought to light. They are generally called "Manuscripts," because their originals, for the most part, exist in manuscript rolls, or there is competent evidence that the original manuscripts, although now lost, once existed. There are, however, a few instances in which this evidence is wanting, and the authenticity of the manuscript rests only on probability. Each of them is noted in this work under its respective title.

1. Halliwell or Regius Manuscript.
2. Book of the Fraternity of Stone Masons.
3. Paris Regulations.
4. Strasburg Constitutions.
5. Cooke's Manuscript.
6. Lansdowne Manuscript.
7. Schaw Manuscript.
8. St. Clair Charters.
9. Eglinton Manuscript.
10. York Manuscripts (six in number).
11. Grand Lodge Manuscript.
12. Sloane Manuscripts (two in number).
13. Aitcheson-Haven Manuscript.
14. Kilwinning Manuscript.
15. Harleian Manuscript.
16. Hope Manuscript.
17. Alnwick Manuscript.
18. Papworth Manuscript.
19. Roberts' Manuscript.
20. Edward III. Manuscript.
21. St. Albans' Regulations.
22. Anderson Manuscript.
23. Stone Manuscripts.
24. Constitutions of Strasburg.
25. Constitutions of Torgau.
26. Dowland Manuscript.
27. Wilson Manuscript.

28. Spencer Manuscript.
29. Cole Manuscript.
30. Plot Manuscript.
31. Inigo Jones Manuscript.
32. Rawlinson Manuscript.
33. Woodford Manuscript.
34. Krause Manuscript.
35. Antiquity Manuscript.
36. Leland Manuscript, sometimes called the Locke Manuscript.
37. Charter of Cologne.

There may be some other manuscript records, especially in France and Germany, not here noticed, but the list above contains the most important of those now known to the Fraternity. Many of them have never yet been published, and the collection forms a mass of material absolutely necessary for the proper investigation of Masonic history. Every Mason who desires to know the true condition of the Fraternity during the last three or four centuries, and who would learn the connection between the Stone-Masons of the Middle Ages and the Free and Accepted Masons of the present day, so as perfectly to understand the process by which the Institution became changed from an operative art to a speculative science, should attentively read and thoroughly digest these ancient records of the Brotherhood. (See also *Manuscripts, Old.*)

Rectification. The German Masons use this word to designate that process of removing an irregularity of initiation which, in American Masonry, is called *healing*, which see.

Rectified Rite. (*Rite Rectifié.*) See *Martinism.*

Rectified Rose Croix, Rite of. See *Rose Croix, Rectified.*

Recusant. A term applied in English history to one who refused to acknowledge the supremacy of the king as head of the church. In Masonic law, the word is sometimes used to designate a Lodge or a Mason that refuses to obey an edict of the Grand Lodge. The arrest of the Charter, or the suspension or expulsion of the offender, would be the necessary punishment of such an offense.

Red. Red, scarlet, or crimson, for it is indifferently called by each of these names, is the appropriate color of the Royal Arch Degree, and is said symbolically to represent the ardor and zeal which should actuate all who are in possession of that sublime portion of Masonry. Portal (*Couleurs Symb.*, p. 116) refers the color red to fire, which was the symbol of the regeneration and purification of souls. Hence there seems to be a congruity in adopting it as the color of the Royal Arch, which refers historically to the regeneration or rebuilding of the Temple, and symbolically to the regeneration of life.

In the religious services of the Hebrews, red, or scarlet, was used as one of the colors of the veils of the tabernacle, in which, according to Josephus, it was an emblem of the element of fire; it was also used in the ephod of the high priest, in the girdle, and in the breastplate. Red was, among the Jews, a color of dignity, appropriated to the most opulent or honorable, and hence the prophet Jeremiah, in describing the rich men of his country, speaks of them as those who "were brought up in scarlet."

In the Middle Ages, those knights who engaged in the wars of the Crusades, and especially the Templars, wore a red cross, as a symbol of their willingness to undergo martyrdom for the sake of religion; and the priests of the Roman Church still wear red vestments when they officiate on the festivals of those saints who were martyred.

Red is in the higher degrees of Masonry as predominating a color as blue is in the lower. Its symbolic significations differ, but they may generally be considered as alluding either to the virtue of fervency when the symbolism is moral, or to the shedding of blood when it is historical. Thus in the degree of Provost and Judge, it is historically emblematic of the violent death of one of the founders of the Institution; while in the degree of Perfection it is said to be a moral symbol of zeal for the glory of God, and for our own advancement toward perfection in Masonry and virtue.

In the degree of Rose Croix, red is the predominating color, and symbolizes the ardent zeal which should inspire all who are in search of that which is lost.

Where red is not used historically, and adopted as a memento of certain tragical circumstances in the history of Masonry, it is always, under some modification, a symbol of zeal and fervency.

These three colors, blue, purple, and red, were called in the former English lectures "the old colors of Masonry," and were said to have been selected "because they are royal, and such as the ancient kings and princes used to wear; and sacred history informs us that the veil of the Temple was composed of these colors."

Red Brother. The Sixth and last degree of the Swedenborgian system.

Red Cross Knight. When, in the tenth century, Pope Urban II., won by the enthusiasm of Peter the Hermit, addressed the people who had assembled at the city of Clermont during the sitting of the Council, and exhorted them to join in the expedition to conquer the Holy Land, he said, in reply to their cry that God wills it, *Dieux el volt*, "it is indeed the will of God; let this memorable word, the inspiration, surely, of our Holy Spirit, be forever adopted as your cry of battle, to animate the devotion and courage of the champions of Christ. His cross is the symbol of your salvation; wear it, a red, a bloody cross, as an external mark on your breasts or shoulders, as a pledge of your sacred and irrevocable engagement." The proposal was eagerly accepted, and the Bishop of Puy was the first who solicited the Pope to affix the cross in red cloth on his shoulder. The example was at once followed, and thenceforth the red cross on the breast was recognized as the sign of him who was engaged in the Holy Wars, and Crusader and Red Cross Knight became convertible terms. Spenser, in the *Fairie Queen* (Cant. I.), thus describes one of these knights:

"And on his breast a bloody cross he bore,
The dear remembrance of his dying Lord,
For whose sweet sake that glorious badge he wore,
And dead, as living, ever him ador'd:
Upon his shield the like was also scor'd."

The application of this title, as is sometimes done in the ritual of the degree, to a Masonic degree of Knight of the Red Cross, is altogether wrong, and it is now called Companion of the Red Cross. A Red Cross Knight and a Knight of the Red Cross are two entirely different things.

Red Cross Legend. The embassy of Zerubbabel to the court of Darius constitutes what has been called the Legend of the Red Cross Degree. (See *Embassy*, and *Companion of the Red Cross.*)

Red Cross of Babylon. See *Babylonish Pass.*

Red Cross of Rome and Constantine. A degree founded on the circumstance of the vision of a cross, with the inscription ΕΝ ΤΟΥΤΩ ΝΙΚΑ, which appeared in the heavens to the Emperor Constantine. It formed originally a part of the Rosaic Rite, and is now practised in England, Ireland, Scotland, and some of the English colonies, as a distinct Order; the meetings being called "Conclaves," and the presiding officer of the Grand Imperial Council of the whole Order, "Grand Sovereign." Its existence in England as a Masonic degree has been traced, according to Bro. R. W. Little (*Freemas. Mag.*), to the year 1780, when it was given by Bro. Charles Shirreff. It was reorganized in 1804 by Walter Rodwell Wright, who supplied its present ritual. The ritual of the Order contains the following legend:

"After the memorable battle fought at Saxa Rubra, on the 28th October, A.D. 312, the emperor sent for the chiefs of the Christian legion, and—we now quote the words of an old ritual—'in presence of his other officers constituted them into an Order of Knighthood, and appointed them to wear the form of the Cross he had seen in the heavens upon their shields, with the motto *In hoc signo vinces* round it, surrounded with clouds; and peace being soon after made, he became the Sovereign Patron of the Christian Order of the Red Cross.' It is also said that this Cross, together with a device called the *Labarum*, was ordered to be embroidered upon all the imperial standards. The Christian warriors were selected to compose the body-guard of Constantine, and the command of these privileged soldiers was confided to Eusebius, Bishop of Nicomedia, who was thus considered the second officer of the Order."

Red Cross Sword of Babylon. A degree worked in the Royal Arch Chapters of Scotland, and also in some parts of England. It is very similar to the Knight of the Red Cross conferred in the United States, which is now called the Companion of the Red Cross.

Red Letters. In the Ancient and Accepted Scottish Rite, edicts, summonses or other documents, written or printed in red letters, are supposed to be of more binding obligation, and to require more implicit obedience, than any others. Hence, in the same Rite, to publish the name of one who has been expelled in red letters is considered an especial mark of disgrace. It is derived from the custom of the Middle Ages, when, as Muratori shows (*Antiq. Ital. Med.*), red letters were used to give greater weight to documents; and he quotes an old Charter of 1020, which is said to be confirmed "per literas rubeas," or by red letters.

Reflection, Chamber of. See *Chamber of Reflection.*

Reformed Helvetic Rite. The Reformed Rite of Wilhelmsbad was introduced into Poland, in 1784, by Bro. Glayre, of Lausanne, the minister of King Stanislaus, and who was also the Provincial Grand Master of this Rite in the French part of Switzerland. But, in introducing it into Poland, he subjected it to several modifications, and called it the Reformed Helvetic Rite. The system was adopted by the Grand Orient of Poland.

Reformed Rite. This Rite was established, in 1872, by a Congress of Freemasons assembled at Wilhelmsbad, in Germany, over whose deliberations Ferdinand, Duke of Brunswick, presided as Grand Master. It was at this Convention that the Reformed Rite was first established, its members assuming the title of the "Beneficent Knights of the Holy City," because they derived their system from the French Rite of that name. It was called the Reformed Rite, because it professed to be a reformation of a Rite which had been established in Germany about a quarter of a century before under the name of the "Rite of Strict Observance." This latter Rite had advanced an hypothesis in relation to the connection between Freemasonry and the Order of Knights Templar, tracing the origin of our Institution to those Knights at the Crusades. This hypothesis the Convention at Wilhelmsbad rejected as unfounded in history or correct tradition. By the adoption of this Rite, the Congress gave a death-blow to the Rite of Strict Observance.

The Reformed Rite is exceedingly simple in its organization, consisting only of five degrees, namely:

1. Entered Apprentice; 2. Fellow-Craft; 3. Master Mason; 4. Scottish Master; 5. Knight of the Holy City.

The last degree is, however, divided into three sections, those of Novice, Professed Brother, and Knight, which really gives seven degrees to the Rite.

Refreshment. In Masonic language, *refreshment* is opposed in a peculiar sense to *labor*. While a Lodge is in activity it must be either at labor or at refreshment. If a Lodge is permanently closed until its next communication, the intervening period is one of abeyance, its activity for Masonic duty having for the time been suspended; although its powers and privileges as a Lodge still exist, and may be at any time resumed. But where it is only temporarily closed, with the intention of soon again resuming labor, the intermediate period is called a time of refreshment, and the Lodge is said not to be closed, but to be called from labor to refreshment. The phrase is an old one, and is found in the earliest rituals of the last century. *Calling from labor to refreshment* differs from closing in this, that the ceremony is a very brief one, and that the Junior Warden then assumes the control of the Craft, in token of which he erects his column on his stand or pedestal, while the Senior Warden lays his down. This is reversed in *calling on*, in which the ceremony is equally brief.

The word *refreshment* no longer bears the meaning among Masons that it formerly did. It signifies not necessarily eating and drinking, but simply cessation from labor. A Lodge at refreshment may thus be compared to any other society when in a recess. During the whole of the last century, and a part of the present, a different meaning was given to the word, arising from a now obsolete usage, which Dr. Oliver (*Mas. Juris.*, p. 210) thus describes:

"The Lodges in ancient times were not arranged according to the practice in use amongst ourselves at the present day. The Worshipful Master, indeed, stood in the east, but both the Wardens were placed in the west. The south was occupied by the senior Entered Apprentice, whose business it was to obey the instructions of the Master, and to welcome the visiting brethren, after having duly ascertained that they were Masons. The junior Entered Apprentice was placed in the north to prevent the intrusion of cowans and eavesdroppers; and a long table, and sometimes two, where the Lodge was numerous, were extended in parallel lines from the pedestal to the place where the Wardens sat, on which appeared not only the emblems of Masonry, but also materials for refreshment;—for in those days every section of the lecture had its peculiar toast or sentiment;—and at its conclusion the Lodge was called from labour to refreshment by certain ceremonies, and a toast, technically called 'the charge,' was drunk in a bumper, with the honours, and not unfrequently accompanied by an appropriate song. After which the Lodge was called from refreshment to labour, and another section was delivered with the like result."

At the present day, the banquets of Lodges, when they take place, are always held after the Lodge is closed; although they are still supposed to be under the charge of the Junior Warden. When modern Lodges are called to refreshment, it is either as a part of the ceremony of the Third Degree, or for a brief period; sometimes extending to more than a day, when labor, which had not been finished, is to be resumed and concluded.

The mythical history of Masonry tells us that high twelve or noon was the hour at Solomon's Temple when the Craft were permitted to suspend their labor, which was resumed an hour after. In reference to this myth, a Lodge is at all times supposed to be called from labor to refreshment at "high twelve," and to be called on again "one hour after high twelve."

Regalia. Strictly speaking, the word regalia, from the Latin, *regalia*, royal things, signifies the ornaments of a king or queen, and is applied to the apparatus used at a coronation, such as the crown, scepter, cross, mound, etc. But it has in modern times been loosely employed to signify almost any kind of ornaments. Hence the collar and jewel, and sometimes even the apron, are called by many Masons the regalia. The word has the early authority of Preston. In the second edition of his *Illustrations* (1775), when on the subject of funerals, he uses the expression, "the body, with the regalia placed thereon, and two swords crossed." And at the end of the service he directs that "the *regalia* and ornaments of the deceased, if an officer of a Lodge, are returned to the Master in due form, and with the usual ceremonies." *Regalia* cannot here mean the Bible and *Book of Constitutions*, for there is a place in another part of the procession appropriated to them. It might have been supposed that, by regalia, Preston referred to some particular decorations of the Lodge, had not his subsequent editors, Jones and Oliver, both interpolated the word "other" before ornaments, so as to make the sentence read "regalia and *other* ornaments," thus clearly indicating that they deemed the regalia a part of the ornaments of the deceased. The word is thus used in one of the headings of the modern Constitutions of the Grand Lodge of England. But in the text the more correct words "clothing and insignia" (Rule 282) are employed. There is, however, so great an error in the use of the word *regalia* to denote Masonic clothing, that it would be better to avoid it.

Regeneration. In the Ancient Mysteries the doctrine of regeneration was taught by symbols: not the theological dogma of regeneration peculiar to the Christian church, but the philosophical dogma as a change from death to life—a new birth to immortal existence. Hence the last day of the Eleusinian mysteries, when the initiation was completed, was called, says Court de Gebelin (*M. P.*, iv., 322), *the day of regeneration.* This is the doctrine in the Masonic mysteries, and more especially in the symbolism of the Third Degree. We must not say that the Mason is regenerated when he is initiated, but that he has been indoctrinated into the philosophy of the regeneration, or the new birth of all things—of light out of darkness, or life out of death, of eternal life out of temporal death.

Regent. The Fourth Degree of the Lesser Mysteries of the Illuminati.

Reghellini, M. A learned Masonic writer, who was born of Venetian parents on the island of Scio, whence he was usually styled Reghellini de Scio. The date of 1750, at which his birth has been placed, is certainly an error. Michaud supposes that it is twenty or thirty years too soon. The date of the publication of his earliest works would indicate that he could not have been born much before 1780. After receiving a good education, and becoming especially proficient in mathematics and chemistry, he settled at Brussels, where he appears to have spent the remaining years of his life, and wrote various works, which indicate extensive research and a lively and, perhaps, a rather ill-directed imagination. In 1834 he published a work entitled *Examen du Mosaisme et du Christianisme*, whose bold opinions were not considered as very orthodox. He had previously become attached to the study of Masonic antiquities, and in 1826 published a work in one volume, entitled *Esprit du dogme de la Franc-Maçonnerie: recherches sur son origine et celle de ses differents rites.* He subsequently still further developed his ideas on this subject, and published at Paris, in 1833, a much larger work, in three volumes, entitled, *La Maçonnerie, considerée comme le resultat des Religions Egyptienne, Juive et Chrétienne.* In this work he seeks to trace both Freemasonry and the Mosaic religion to the worship that was practised on the banks of the Nile in the time of the Pharaohs. Whatever may be thought of his theory, it must be confessed that he has collected a mass of learned and interesting facts that must be attractive to the Masonic scholar. From 1822 to 1829 Reghellini devoted his labors to editing the *Annales Chronologiques, Litteraires et Historiques de la Maçonnerie des Pays-Bas*, a work that contains much valuable information.

Outside of Masonry, the life of Reghellini is not well known. It is said that in 1848 he became implicated with the political troubles which broke out that year in Vienna, and, in consequence, experienced some trouble. His great age at the time precluded the likelihood that the statement is true. In his latter days he was reduced to great penury, and in August, 1855, was compelled to take refuge in the House of Mendicity at Brussels, where he shortly afterward died.

Regimental Lodge. An expression used by Dr. Oliver, in his *Jurisprudence*, to designate a Lodge attached to a regiment in the British army. The title is not recognized in the English Constitutions, where such a Lodge is always styled a *Military Lodge*, which see.

Register. A list of the officers and members of a Grand or Subordinate Lodge. The registers of Grand Lodges are generally published in this country annually, attached to their Proceedings. The custom of publishing annual registers of subordinate Lodges is almost exclusively confined to the Masonry of the Continent of Europe. Sometimes it is called a *Registry*.

Registrar, Grand. 1. An officer of the Grand Lodge of England, whose principal duty it is to take charge of the seal, and attach it, or cause it to be attached by the Grand Secretary, to documents issued by the Grand Lodge or Grand Master. Also to superintend the records of the Grand Lodge, and to take care that the several documents issued be in due form. (*Constitutions*, Rules 31, 32.) 2. An officer in a Grand Consistory of the Scottish Rite, whose duties are those of Grand Secretary.

Registration. The modern Constitutions of the Grand Lodge of England require that every Lodge must be particularly careful in registering the names of the brethren initiated therein, and also in making the returns of its members; as no person is entitled to partake of the general charity, unless his name be duly registered, and he shall have been at least five years a contributing member of a Lodge, except in the following cases, to which the limitation of five years is not meant to extend, viz., shipwreck, or capture at sea, loss by fire, or blindness or serious accident fully attested and proved. (Rule 234.) To prevent injury to individuals, by their being excluded the privileges of Masonry through the neglect of their Lodges in not registering their names, any brother so circumstanced, on producing sufficient proof that he has paid the full fees to his Lodge, including the register fee, shall be capable of enjoying the privileges of the Craft. But the offending Lodge shall be reported to the Board of General Purposes, and rigorously proceeded against for withholding moneys which are the property of the Grand Lodge. (Rule 237.)

An unregistered member in England is therefore equivalent, so far as the exercise of his rights is concerned, to an unaffiliated Mason. In America the same rule exists of registration in the Lodge books and an annual return of the same to the Grand Lodge, but the penalties for neglect or disobedience are neither so severe nor so well defined.

Registry. The roll or list of Lodges and their members under the obedience of a Grand Lodge. Such registries are in general published annually by the Grand Lodges of the United States at the end of their printed Proceedings.

Regius MS. See *Halliwell Manuscript.*

Regular. A Lodge working under the legal authority of a Warrant of Constitution is said to be regular. The word was first used in 1723, in the first edition of Anderson's *Constitutions*. In the eighth General Regulation published in that work it is said: "If any set or number of Masons shall take upon themselves to form a Lodge without the Grand Master's Warrant, the *regular Lodges* are not to countenance them." Ragon says (*Orthod. Maç.*, 72) that the word was first heard of in French Masonry in 1773, when an edict of the Grand Orient thus defined it: "A regular Lodge is a Lodge attached to the Grand Orient, and a regular Mason is a member of a regular Lodge."

Regulations. See *Old Regulations.*

Rehum. Called by Ezra the chancellor. He was probably a lieutenant-governor of the province of Judea, who, with Shimshai the scribe, wrote to Artaxerxes to prevail upon him to stop the building of the second Temple. His name is introduced into some of the high degrees that are connected in their ritual with the second Temple.

Reinhold, Karl Leonhard. A German philosopher, who was born at Vienna in 1758, and died in 1823. He was associated with Wieland, whose daughter he married, in the editorship of the *Deutschen Mercur*. He afterward became a professor of philosophy at Kiel, and published *Letters on the Philosophy of Kant.* He was much interested in the study of Freemasonry, and published, under the pseudonym of Decius, at Leipsic, in 1788, two lectures entitled *Die Hebraischen Mysterien oder die älteste religiöse Freimaurerei*, i. e., The Hebrew Mysteries, or the Oldest Religious Freemasonry. The fundamental idea of this work is, that Moses derived his system from the Egyptian priesthood. Eichhorn attacked his theory in his *Universal Repository of Biblical Literature.* Reinhold delivered and published, in 1809, *An Address on the Design of Freemasonry*, and another in 1820, on the occasion of the reopening of a Lodge at Kiel. This was probably his last Masonic labor, as he died in 1823, at the age of sixty-five years. In 1828, a *Life* of him was published by his son, a professor of philosophy at Jena.

Reinstatement. See *Restoration.*

Rejection. Under the English Constitutions three black balls must exclude a candidate; but the by-laws of a Lodge may enact that one or two shall do so. (Rule 190.) In America one black ball will reject a candidate for initiation. If a candidate be rejected, he can apply in no other Lodge for admission. If admitted at all, it must be in the Lodge where he first applied. But the time when a new application may be made never having been determined by the general or common law of Masonry, the rule has been left to the special enactment of Grand Lodges, some of which have placed it at six months, and some at from one to two years. Where the Constitution of a Grand Lodge is silent on the subject, it is held that a new application has never been specified, so that it is held that a rejected candidate may apply for a reconsideration of his case at any time. The unfavorable report of the committee to whom the letter was referred, or the withdrawal of the letter by the candidate or his friends, is considered equivalent to a rejection. (See *Unanimous Consent.*)

Rejoicing. The initiation of the Ancient Mysteries, like that of the Third Degree of Masonry, began in sorrow and terminated in rejoicing. The sorrow was for the death of the hero-god, which was represented in the sacred rites, and the rejoicing was for his resuscitation to eternal life. "Thrice happy," says Sophocles, "are those who descend to the shades below when they have beheld these rites of initiation." The lesson there taught was, says Pindar, the Divine origin of life, and hence the rejoicing at the discovery of this eternal truth.

Relief. One of the three principal tenets of a Mason's profession, and thus defined in the lecture of the First Degree.

To relieve the distressed is a duty incumbent on all men, but particularly on Masons, who are linked together by an indissoluble chain of sincere affection. To soothe the unhappy, to sympathize with their misfortunes, to compassionate their miseries, and to restore peace to their troubled minds, is the great aim we have in view. On this basis we form our friendships and establish our connections.

Of the three tenets of a Mason's profession, which are Brotherly Love, Relief, and Truth, it may be said that *Truth* is the column of wisdom, whose rays penetrate and enlighten the inmost recesses of our Lodge; *Brotherly Love*, the column of strength, which binds us as one family in the indissoluble bond of fraternal affection; and *Relief*, the column of beauty, whose ornaments, more precious than the lilies and pomegranates that adorned the pillars of the porch, are the widow's tear of joy and the orphan's prayer of gratitude.

Relief, Board of. The liability to imposition on the charity of the Order, by the applications of impostors, has led to the establishment in the larger cities of America of Boards of Relief. These consist of representatives of all the Lodges, to whom all applications for temporary relief are referred. The members of the Board, by frequent consultations, are better enabled to distinguish the worthy from the unworthy, and to detect attempts at imposition. A similar organization, but under a different name, was long ago established by the Grand Lodge of England, for the distribution of the fund of benevolence. (See *Fund of Benevolence.*) In New Orleans, Louisiana, the Board of Relief, after twenty-five years of successful operation, was chartered in July, 1854, by the Grand Lodge as "Relief Lodge, No. 1," to be composed of the Masters and Wardens of all the Lodges who were united in the objects of the Board.

Religion of Masonry. There has been a needless expenditure of ingenuity and talent, by a large number of Masonic orators and essayists, in the endeavor to prove that Masonry is not religion. This has undoubtedly arisen from a well-intended but erroneous view that has been taken of the connection between religion and Masonry, and from a fear that if the complete disseverance of the two was not made manifest, the opponents of Masonry would be enabled successfully to establish a theory which they have been fond of advancing, that the Masons were disposed to substitute the teachings of their Order for the truths of Christianity. Now I have never for a moment believed that any such unwarrantable assumption, as that Masonry is intended to be a substitute for Christianity, could ever obtain admission into any well-regulated mind, and, therefore, I am not disposed to yield, on the subject of the religious character of Masonry, quite so much as has been yielded by more timid brethren. On the contrary, I contend, without any sort of hesitation, that Masonry is, in every sense of the word, except one, and that its least philosophical, an eminently religious institution—that it is indebted solely to the religious element which it contains for its origin and for its continued existence, and that without this religious element it would scarcely be worthy of cultivation by the wise and good. But, that I may be truly understood, it will be well first to agree upon the true definition of religion. There is nothing more illogical than to reason upon undefined terms. Webster has given four distinct definitions of religion:

1. Religion, in a comprehensive sense, includes, he says, a belief in the being and perfections of God—in the revelation of his will to man—in man's obligation to obey his commands—in a state of reward and punishment, and in man's accountableness to God; and also true godliness or piety of life, with the practise of all moral duties.

2. His second definition is, that religion, as distinct from theology, is godliness or real piety in practise, consisting in the performance of all known duties to God and our fellow-men, in obedience to Divine command, or from love to God and his law.

3. Again, he says that religion, as distinct from virtue or morality, consists in the performance of the duties we owe directly to God, from a principle of obedience to his will.

4. And lastly, he defines religion to be any system of faith or worship; and in this sense, he says, religion comprehends the belief and worship of Pagans and Mohammedans as well as of Christians—any religion consisting in the belief of a superior power, or powers, governing the world, and in the worship of such power or powers. And it is in this sense that we speak of the Turkish religion, or the Jewish religion, as well as of the Christian.

Now, it is plain that, in either of the first three senses in which we may take the word religion (and they do not very materially differ from each other), Masonry may rightfully claim to be called a religious institution. Closely and accurately examined, it will be found to answer to any one of the requirements of either of these three definitions. So much does it "include a belief in the being and perfections of God," that the public profession of such a faith is essentially necessary to gain admission into the Order. No disbeliever in the existence of a God can be made a Mason. The "revelation of his will to man" is technically called the "spiritual, moral, and Masonic trestle-board" of every Mason, according to the rules and designs of which he is to erect the spiritual edifice of his eternal life. A "state of reward and punishment" is necessarily included in the very idea of an obligation, which, without the belief in such a state, could be of no binding force or efficacy. And "true godliness or piety of life" is inculcated as the invariable duty of every Mason, from the inception of the first to the end of the very last degree that he takes. So, again, in reference to the second and third definitions, all this practical piety and performance of the duties we owe to God and to our fellow men arise from and are founded on a principle of obedience to the Divine will. Else whence, or from what other will, could they have arisen? It is the voice of the G. A. O. T. U. symbolised to us in every ceremony of our ritual and from every portion of the furniture of our Lodge, that speaks to the true Mason, commanding him to fear God and to love the brethren. It is idle to say that the Mason does good simply in obedience to the statutes of the Order. These very statutes owe their sanction to the Masonic idea of the nature and perfections of God, which idea has come down to us from the earliest history of the Institution, and the promulgation of which idea was the very object and design of its origin.

But it must be confessed that the fourth definition does not appear to be strictly applicable to Masonry. It has no pretension to assume a place among the religions of the world as a sectarian "system of faith and worship," in the sense in which we distinguish Christianity from Judaism, or Judaism from Mohammedanism In this meaning of the word we do not and can not speak of the Masonic religion, nor say of a man that he is not a Christian, but a Mason. Here it is that the opponents of Freemasonry have assumed mistaken ground, in confounding the idea of a religious institution with that of the Christian religion as a peculiar form of worship, and in supposing, because Masonry teaches religious truth, that it is offered as a substitute for Christian truth and Christian obligation. Its warmest and most enlightened friends have never advanced nor supported such a claim. Freemasonry is not Christianity, nor a substitute for it. It is not intended to supersede it nor any other form of worship or system of faith. It does not meddle with sectarian creeds or doctrines, but teaches fundamental religious truth—not enough to do away with the necessity of the Christian scheme of salvation, but more than enough to show, to demonstrate, that it is, in every philosophical sense of the word, a religious institution, and one, too, in which the true Christian Mason will find, if he earnestly seeks for them, abundant types and shadows of his own exalted and divinely inspired faith.

The tendency of all true Masonry is toward religion. If it make any progress, its progress is to that holy end. Look at its ancient landmarks, its sublime ceremonies, its profound symbols and allegories—all inculcating religious doctrine, commanding religious observance, and teaching religious truth, and who can deny that it is eminently a religious institution?

But, besides, Masonry is, in all its forms, thoroughly tinctured with a true devotional spirit. We open and close our Lodges with prayer; we invoke the blessing of the Most

High upon all our labors; we demand of our neophytes a profession of trusting belief in the existence and the superintending care of God; and we teach them to bow with humility and reverence at his awful name, while his holy law is widely opened upon our altars. Freemasonry is thus identified with religion; and although a man may be eminently religious without being a Mason, it is impossible that a Mason can be "true and trusty" to his Order unless he is a respecter of religion and an observer of religious principle.

But the religion of Masonry is not sectarian. It admits men of every creed within its hospitable bosom, rejecting none and approving none for his peculiar faith. It is not Judaism, though there is nothing in it to offend a Jew; it is not Christianity, but there is nothing in it repugnant to the faith of a Christian. Its religion is that general one of nature and primitive revelation—handed down to us from some ancient and patriarchal priesthood—in which all men may agree and in which no men can differ. It inculcates the practise of virtue, but it supplies no scheme of redemption for sin. It points its disciples to the path of righteousness, but it does not claim to be "the way, the truth, and the life." In so far, therefore, it cannot become a substitute for Christianity, but its tendency is thitherward; and, as the handmaid of religion, it may, and often does, act as the porch that introduces its votaries into the temple of Divine truth.

Masonry, then, is, indeed, a religious institution; and on this ground mainly, if not alone, should the religious Mason defend it.

Religious Qualifications. See *Qualifications.*

Removal of Lodges. On January 25, 1738, the Grand Lodge of England adopted a regulation that no Lodge should be removed without the Master's knowledge; that no motion for removing it should be made in his absence; and that if he was opposed to the removal, it should not be removed unless two-thirds of the members present voted in the affirmative. (*Constitutions*, 1738, p. 157.) But as this rule was adopted subsequent to the General Regulations of 1722, it is not obligatory as a law of Masonry at present. The Grand Lodges of England and of New York have substantially the same rule. But unless there be a local regulation in the Constitution of any particular Grand Lodge to that effect, there would seem to be no principle of Masonic law set forth in the Ancient Landmarks or Regulations which forbids a Lodge, upon the mere vote of the majority, from removing from one house to another in the same town or city; and unless the Grand Lodge of any particular jurisdiction has adopted a regulation forbidding the removal of a Lodge from one house to another without its consent, there is no law in Masonry of universal force which would prohibit such a removal at the mere option of the Lodge.

This refers, of course, only to the removal from one house to another; but as the town or village in which the Lodge is situated is designated in its Warrant of Constitution, no such removal can be made except with the consent of the Grand Lodge, or, during the recess of that body, by the Dispensation of the Grand Master, to be subsequently confirmed by the Grand Lodge.

Renouncing Masons. During the anti-Masonic excitement in the United States, which began in 1828, and lasted for a few years, many Masons left the Order, actuated by various motives (seldom good ones), and attached themselves to the anti-Masonic party. It is not singular that these deserters, who called themselves "Renouncing Masons," were the bitterest in their hatred and the loudest in their vituperations of the Order. But, as may be seen in the article *Indelibility*, a renunciation of the name cannot absolve any-one from the obligations of a Mason.

Repeal. As a Lodge cannot enact a new by-law without the consent of the Grand Lodge, neither can it repeal an old one without the same consent; nor can anything done at a stated meeting be repealed at a subsequent extra or emergent one.

Report of a Committee. When a committee, to which a subject had been referred, has completed its investigation and come to an opinion, it directs its chairman, or some other member, to prepare an expression of its views, to be submitted to the Lodge. The paper containing this expression of views is called its report, which may be framed in three different forms: It may contain only an expression of opinion on the subject which had been referred; or it may contain, in addition to this, an express resolution or series of resolutions, the adoption of which by the assembly is recommended; or, lastly, it may contain one or more resolutions, without any preliminary expression of opinion.

The report, when prepared, is read to the members of the committee, and, if it meets with their final sanction, the chairman, or one of the members, is directed to present it to the Lodge.

The reading of the report is its reception, and the next question will be on its adoption. If it contains a recommendation of resolutions, the adoption of the report will be equivalent to an adoption of the resolutions, but the report may, on the question of adoption, be otherwise disposed of by being laid on the table, postponed, or recommitted. (See the subject fully discussed in Dr. Mackey's treatise on *Parliamentary Law as applied to the Government of Masonic Bodies*, ch. xxxi.)

Reportorial Corps. A name recently given in the United States to that useful and intelligent body of Masons who write, in their respective Grand Lodges, the reports on Foreign Correspondence. Through the exertions of Dr. Corson, the chairman of the Committee of Foreign Correspondence of New Jersey, a convention of this body was held at Baltimore in 1871, during the session of the General Grand Chapter, and measures were then taken to establish a triennial convention. Such a convention would assume no legislative powers, but would simply meet for the intercommunication of ideas and the interchange of fraternal greetings.

Representative of a Grand Lodge. A brother appointed by one Grand Lodge to represent its interest in another. The representative is generally, although not necessarily, a member of the Grand Lodge to whom he is accredited, and receives his appointment on its nomination, but he wears the clothing of the Grand Lodge which he represents. He is required to attend the meetings of the Grand Lodge to which he is accredited, and to communicate to his constituents an abstract of the proceedings, and other matters of Masonic interest. But it is doubtful whether these duties are generally performed. The office of representative appears to be rather one of honor than of service. In the French system, a representative is called a "gage d'amitié."

Representatives of Lodges. In the General Regulations of 1721 it was enacted that "The Grand Lodge consists of and is formed by the Masters and Wardens of all the regular particular Lodges upon record"; and also that "The majority of every particular Lodge, when congregated, shall have the privilege of giving instructions to their Master and Wardens before the assembling of the Grand Chapter or Lodge, at the three quarterly communications hereafter mentioned and of the Annual Grand Lodge too; because their Master and Wardens are their Representatives and are supposed to speak their mind." (*Constitutions*, 1723, p. 61.) A few modern Grand Lodges have disfranchised the Wardens also, and confined the representation to the Masters only. But this is evidently an innovation, having no color of authority in the Old Regulations. [E. L. H.]

Representative System. The system of appointing representatives of Grand Lodges originated some years ago with the Grand Lodge of New York. It at first met with much opposition, but has gradually gained favor, and there are now but few Grand Lodges in Europe or America that have not adopted it. Although the original plan intended by the founders of the system does not appear to have been effectually carried out in all its details, it has at least been successful as a means of more closely cementing the bonds of union between the bodies mutually represented.

Reprimand. A reproof formally communicated to the offender for some fault committed, and the lowest grade, above censure, of Masonic punishment. It can be inflicted only on charges made, and by a majority vote of the Lodge. It may be private or public. Private reprimand is generally communicated to the offender by a letter from the Master. Public reprimand is given orally in the Lodge and in the presence of the brethren. A reprimand does not affect the Masonic standing of the person reprimanded.

Reputation. In the technical language of Masonry, a man of good reputation is said to be one who is "under the tongue of good report"; and this constitutes one of the indispensable qualifications of a candidate for initiation.

Residence. It is the general usage in America, and may be considered as the Masonic law of custom, that the application of a candidate for initiation must be made to the Lodge nearest his place of residence. There is, however, no express law upon this subject either in the ancient landmarks or the Old Constitutions, and its positive sanction as a law in any jurisdiction must be found in the local enactments of the Grand Lodge of that jurisdiction. Still there can be no doubt that expediency and justice to the Order make such a regulation necessary, and accordingly many Grand Lodges have incorporated such a regulation in their Constitutions; and of course, whenever this has been done, it becomes a positive law in that jurisdiction.

It has also been contended by some American Masonic jurists that a non-resident of a State is not entitled, on a temporary visit to that State, to apply for initiation. There is, however, no landmark nor written law in the ancient Constitutions which forbids the initiation of non-residents. Still, as there can be no question that the conferring of the degrees of Masonry on a stranger is always inexpedient, and frequently productive of injury and injustice, by foisting on the Lodges near the candidate's residence unworthy and unacceptable persons, there has been a very general disposition among the Grand Lodges of this country to discountenance the initiation of non-residents. Many of them have adopted a specific regulation to this effect, and in all jurisdictions where this has been done, the law becomes imperative; for, as the landmarks are entirely silent on the subject, the local regulation is left to the discretion of each jurisdiction. But no such rule has ever existed among European Lodges.

Resignation of Membership. The spirit of the law of Masonry does not recognize the right of any member of a Lodge to resign his membership, unless it be for the purpose of uniting with another Lodge. This mode of resignation is called a demission. (See *Demit.*)

Resignation of Office. Every officer of a Lodge, or rather Masonic organization, being required at the time of his installation into office to enter into an obligation that he will perform the duties of that office for a specified time and until his successor is installed, it has been repeatedly held by the Masonic jurists of this country that an officer once elected and installed cannot resign his office; and this may be considered as a well-established law of American Masonry.

Resolution. In parliamentary law, a proposition, when first presented, is called a motion; if adopted, it becomes a resolution. Many Grand Lodges adopt, from time to time, in addition to the provisions of their Constitution, certain resolutions on important subjects, which, giving them an apparently greater weight of authority than ordinary enactments, are frequently appended to their Constitution, or their transaction, under the imposing title of "Standing Regulations." But this weight of authority is only apparent. These standing resolutions having been adopted, like all other resolutions, by a mere majority vote, are subject, like them, to be repealed or rescinded by the same vote.

Respectable. A title given by the French, as *Worshipful* is by the English, to a Lodge. Thus, *La Respectable Loge de la Candeur* is equivalent to "The Worshipful Lodge of Candor." It is generally abbreviated as R∴ L∴ or R∴ □∴

Response. In the liturgical services of the church an answer made by the people speaking alternately with the clergyman. In the ceremonial observances of Freemasonry there are many responses, the Master and the brethren taking alternate parts, especially in the funeral service as laid down first by Preston, and now very generally adopted. In all Masonic prayers the proper response, never to be omitted, is, "So mote it be."

Restoration. The restoration, or, as it is also called, the reinstatement of a Mason who had been excluded, suspended, or expelled, may be the voluntary act of the Lodge, or that of the Grand Lodge on appeal, when the sentence of the Lodge has been reversed on account of illegality in the trial, or injustice, or undue severity in the sentence. It may also, as in the instance of definite suspension, be the result of the termination of the period of suspension, when the suspended member is, *ipso facto*, restored without any further action of the Lodge.

The restoration from indefinite suspension must be equivalent to a reinstatement in membership, because the suspension being removed, the offender is at once invested with the rights and privileges of which he had never been divested, but only temporarily deprived.

But restoration from expulsion may be either to membership in the Lodge or simply to the privileges of the Order.

It may also be *ex gratia*, or an act of mercy, the past offense being condoned; or *ex debito justitiæ*, by a reversal of the sentence for illegality of trial or injustice in the verdict.

The restoration *ex gratia* may be either by the Lodge or the Grand Lodge on appeal. If by the Lodge, it may be to membership, or only to good standing in the Order. But if by the Grand Lodge, the restoration can only be to the rights and privileges of the Order. The Mason having been justly and legally expelled from the Lodge, the Grand Lodge possesses no prerogative by which it could enforce a Lodge to admit one legally expelled any more than it could a profane who had never been initiated.

But if the restoration be *ex debito justitiæ*, as an act of justice, because the trial or verdict had been illegal, then the brother, never having been lawfully expelled from the Lodge or the Order, but being at the very time of his appeal a member of the Lodge, unjustly or illegally deprived of his rights, the restoration in this case by the Grand Lodge must be to membership in the Lodge. Any other course, such as to restore him to the Order but not to membership, would be manifestly unjust. The Grand Lodge having reversed the trial and sentence of the subordinate Lodge, that trial and sentence become null and void, and the Mason who had been unjustly expelled is at once restored to his original status. (See this subject fully discussed in Dr. Mackey's *TextBook of Masonic Jurisprudence*, Book VI., chap. iii.)

Resurrection. The doctrine of a resurrection to a future and eternal life constitutes an indispensable portion of the religious faith of Masonry. It is not authoritatively inculcated as a point of dogmatic creed, but is impressively taught by the symbolism of the Third Degree. This dogma has existed among almost all nations from a very early period. The Egyptians, in their mysteries, taught a final resurrection of the soul. Although the Jews, in escaping from their Egyptian thraldom, did not carry this doctrine with them into the desert—for it formed no part of the Mosaic theology—yet they subsequently, after the captivity, borrowed it from the Zoroastrians. The Brahmans and Buddhists of the East, the Etruscans of the South, and the Druids and the Scandinavian Skalds of the West, nursed the faith of a resurrection to future life. The Greeks and the Romans subscribed to it; and it was one of the great objects of their mysteries to teach it. It is, as we all know, an essential part of the Christian faith, and was exemplified, in his own resurrection, by Christ to his followers. In Freemasonry, a particular degree, the Master's, has been appropriated to teach it by an impressive symbolism. "Thus," says Hutchinson (*Spirit of Masonry*, p. 164), "our Order is a positive contradiction to Judaic blindness and infidelity, and testifies our faith concerning the resurrection of the body."

We may deny that there has been a regular descent of Freemasonry, as a secret organization, from the mystical association of the Eleusinians, the Samothracians, or the Dionysians. No one, however, who carefully examines the mode in which the resurrection or restoration to life was taught by a symbol and a ceremony in the Ancient Mysteries, and how the same dogma is now taught in the Masonic initiation, can, without absolutely rejecting the evident concatenation of circumstances which lies patent before him, refuse his assent to the proposition that the latter was derived from the former. The resemblance between the Dionysiac legend, for instance, and the Hiramic, cannot have been purely accidental. The chain that connects them is easily found in the fact that the Pagan mysteries lasted until the fourth century of the Christian era, and, as the fathers of the church lamented, exercised an influence over the secret societies of the Middle Ages.

Returns of Lodges. Every subordinate Lodge is required to make annually to the

Grand Lodge a statement of the names of its members, and the number of admissions, demissions, and expulsions or rejections that have taken place within the year. This statement is called a *return*. A neglect to make the annual return causes a forfeiture of the right of representation in the Grand Lodge. The sum due by the Lodge is based on the return, as a tax is levied for each member and each initiation. The Grand Lodge is also, by this means, made acquainted with the state of its subordinates and the condition of the Order in its jurisdiction.

Reuben. The eldest son of Jacob. Among the Royal Arch banners, that of Reuben is purple, and bears a man as the device. It is appropriated to the Grand Master of the Second Veil.

Revelation. The following is an extract from Mackenzie's *Royal Masonic Cyclopædia* upon this subject: "With infinite learning and patience the author of *The Book of God*, who preserves strict anonymity, has endeavoured to show that the work (Apocalypse) was originally revealed to a primæval John, otherwise Oannes, and identical with the first messenger of God to man. This theory is sufficiently remarkable to be mentioned here. The messengers, twelve in number, are supposed by the author to appear at intervals of 600 years. Thus: 1, Adam, A. M. 3000; 2, Enoch, A. M. 3600; 3, Fohi, A. M. 4200; 4, Brigoo, A. M. 4800; 5, Zaratusht, A. M. 5400; 6, Thoth, A. M. 6000; 7, Amosis or Moses, A. M. 6600; 8, Laotseu, A. M. 7200; 9, Jesus, A. M. 7800; 10, Mohammed, A. M. 8400; 11, Chengis-Khan, A. M. 9000; and, 12, the twelfth messenger yet to be revealed, A. M. 9600. With the aid of this theory, the whole history of the world, down to our own days, is shown to be foretold in the Apocalypse, and although it is difficult to agree with the accomplished writer's conclusions, supported by him with an array of learning and a sincere belief in what is stated, no one with any taste for these studies should be without this wonderful series of books. The same author has published, in two volumes, a revised edition of the *Book of Enoch*, with a commentary, and he promises to continue, and, if possible, complete his design."

Revelations of Masonry. See *Expositions*.

Revels, Master of the. An officer attached to the royal or other eminent household, whose function it was to preside when the members and guests were at refreshment, physical and intellectual, to have charge of the amusements of the court or of the nobleman to whose house he was attached during the twelve Christmas holidays. In Masonic language, the Junior Warden.

Reverend. A title sometimes given to the chaplain of a Masonic body.

Reverential Sign. The second sign in the English Royal Arch system, and thus explained. We are taught by the reverential sign to bend with submission and resignation beneath the chastening hand of the Almighty, and at the same time to engraft his law in our hearts. This expressive form, in which the Father of the human race first presented himself before the face of the Most High, to receive the denunciation and terrible judgment, was adopted by our Grand Master Moses, who, when the Lord appeared to him in the burning bush on Mount Horeb, covered his face from the brightness of the Divine presence.

Revestiary. The wardrobe, or place for keeping sacred vestments. Distinctive costumes in public worship formed a part not only of the Jewish, but of almost all the ancient religions. The revestiary was common to them all. The Master of the Wardrobe became a necessity.

Revival. The occurrences which took place in the city of London, in the year 1717, when that important body, which has since been known as the Grand Lodge of England, was organized, have been always known in Masonic history as the "Revival of Masonry." Anderson, in the first edition of the *Constitutions*, published in 1723 (p. 47), speaks of the freeborn British nations having revived the drooping Lodges of London; but he makes no other reference to the transaction. In his second edition, published in 1738, he is more diffuse, and the account there given is the only authority we possess of the organization made in 1717: Preston and all subsequent writers have of course derived their authority from Anderson. The transactions are thus detailed by Preston (*Illust.*, ed. 1792, p. 246), whose account is preferred, as containing in a more succinct form all that Anderson has more profusely detailed.

"On the accession of George I., the Masons in London and its environs, finding themselves deprived of Sir Christopher Wren and their annual meetings discontinued, resolved to cement themselves under a new Grand Master, and to revive the communications and annual festivals of the Society. With this view, the Lodges at the Goose and Gridiron, in St. Paul's Church-Yard; the Crown, in Parker's Lane, near Drury Lane; the Apple-Tree Tavern, in Charles Street, Covent Garden; and the Rummer and Grapes Tavern, in Channel Row, Westminster, the only four Lodges in being in the South of England at that time, with some other old brethren, met at the Apple-Tree Tavern, above mentioned, in February, 1717; and, having voted the oldest Master Mason then present into the chair, constituted themselves a Grand Lodge, *pro tempore*, in due form. At this meeting it was resolved to revive the Quarterly Communications of the Fraternity, and to hold the next annual assembly and feast on the 24th of June at the Goose and Gridiron, in St. Paul's Church-Yard, (in compliment to the oldest Lodge, which then met there,) for the purpose of electing a Grand Master among themselves, till they should have the honor of a noble brother at their head. Accordingly, on St. John the Baptist's day, 1717, in the third year of the reign of King George I., the assembly and feast were held at the said house; when the oldest Master Mason and the Master of a Lodge having taken the chair, a list of proper candidates for the office of Grand Master was produced; and the names being separately proposed, the brethren, by a great majority of hands, elected Mr. Anthony Sayer Grand Master of Masons for the ensuing year; who was forthwith invested by the said oldest Master, installed by the Master of the oldest Lodge, and duly congratulated by the assembly, who paid him homage. The Grand Master then entered on the duties of his office, appointed his Wardens, and commanded the brethren of the four Lodges to meet him and his Wardens quarterly in communication; enjoining them at the same time to recommend to all the Fraternity a punctual attendance on the next annual assembly and feast."

Recently, this claim, that Masonry was not for the first time organised, but only revived in 1717, has been attacked by some of those modern iconoclasts who refuse credence to anything traditional, or even to any record which is not supported by other contemporary authority. Chief among these is Bro. W. P. Buchan, of England, who, in his numerous articles in the *London Freemason* (1871 and 1872), has attacked the antiquity of Freemasonry, and refuses to give it an existence anterior to the year 1717. His exact theory is that "our system of degrees, words, grips, signs, etc., was not in existence until about A. D. 1717." He admits, however, that certain of the "elements or groundwork" of the degrees existed before that year, but not confined to the Masons, being common to all the gilds. He thinks that the present system was indebted to the inventive genius of Anderson and Desaguliers. And he supposes that it was simply "a reconstruction of an ancient society, viz., of some form of old Pagan philosophy." Hence, he contends that it was not a "revival," but only a "renaissance," and he explains his meaning in the following language:

"Before the eighteenth century we had a renaissance of Pagan architecture; then, to follow suit, in the eighteenth century we had a renaissance in a new dress of Pagan mysticism; but for neither are we indebted to the Operative Masons, although the Operative Masons were made use of in both cases." (*London Freemason*, September 23, 1871.)

Buchan's theory has been attacked by Bros. William J. Hughan and Chalmers I. Paton. That he is right in his theory, that the three degrees of Master, Fellow-Craft, and Apprentice were unknown to the Masons of the seventeenth century, and that these classes existed only as gradations of rank, will be very generally admitted. But there is unquestionable evidence that the modes of recognition, the method of government, the legends, and much of the ceremonial of initiation, were in existence among the Operative Masons of the Middle Ages, and were transmitted to the Speculative Masons of the eighteenth century. The work of Anderson, of Desaguliers, and their contemporaries, was to improve and to enlarge, but not to invent. The Masonic system of the present day has been the result of a slow but steady growth. Just as the lectures of Anderson, known to us from their publication in 1725, were subsequently modified and enlarged by the successive labors of Clare, of Dunckerley, of Preston, and of Hemming, did he and Desaguliers submit the simple ceremonial, which they found at the reorganisation of the Grand Lodge in 1717, to a similar modification and enlargement.

Revoke. When a Dispensation is issued by a Grand Master for the organization of a Lodge, it is granted "to continue of force until the Grand Lodge shall grant a Warrant, or until the Dispensation is revoked by the Grand Master or the Grand Lodge." A Dispensation may therefore be revoked at any time by the authority which issued it, or by a higher authority. Charters are *arrested*, *forfeited*, or *declared null and void;* Dispensations are revoked.

Rhetoric. The art of embellishing language with the ornaments of construction, so as to enable the speaker to persuade or affect his hearers. It supposes and requires a proper acquaintance with the rest of the liberal arts; for the first step toward adorning a discourse is for the speaker to become thoroughly acquainted with its subject, and hence the ancient rule that the orator should be acquainted with all the arts and sciences. Its importance as a branch of liberal education is recommended to the Mason in the Fellow-Craft's Degree. It is one of the seven liberal arts and sciences, the second in order, and is described in the ancient Constitutions as "retoricke that teacheth a man to speake faire and in subtill termes." (*Harleian MS.*, No. 1942.)

Rhode Island. Masonry was introduced into Rhode Island in 1750 by the establishment of a Lodge at Newport, the Charter for which had been granted by the St. John's Grand Lodge of Boston on December 27, 1749. The same Grand Lodge established a second Lodge at Providence on January 18, 1757. On April 6, 1791, these two Lodges organised a Grand Lodge at Providence, Christopher Champlin being elected the first Grand Master. This is the first instance known in Masonic history of the organisation of a Grand Lodge by only two subordinates. The act was irregular, and the precedent has never subsequently been followed. It was not until 1799 that the new Grand Lodge granted its first Charter for the establishment of a third Lodge at Warren. The Grand Chapter was organised in March, 1798, and the Grand Council in October, 1860. The Grand Commandery forms a part of a common body known as the Grand Commandery of Massachusetts and Rhode Island. It was formed in 1805, and the celebrated Thomas Smith Webb was its first presiding officer.

Rhodes. An island in the Mediterranean Sea, which, although nominally under the government of the Emperor of Constantinople, was in 1308 in the possession of Saracen pirates. In that year, Fulke de Villaret, Grand Master of the Knights Hospitalers, having landed with a large force, drove out the Saracens and took possession of the island, which became the seat of the Order, who removed to it from Cyprus and continued to occupy it until it was retaken by the Saracens in 1522, when the knights were transferred to the island of Malta. Their residence for over two hundred years at Rhodes caused them sometimes to receive the title of the Knights of Rhodes.

Rhodes, Knight of. See *Knight of Rhodes.*

Ribbon. The use of a ribbon, with the official jewel suspended and attached to a buttonhole instead of the collar, recently adopted by a few American Lodges, is a violation of the ancient customs of the Order. The collar cut in a triangular shape, with the jewel suspended from the apex, dates from the earliest time of the revival, and is perhaps as old as the apron itself. (See *Collar.*)

Ridel, Cornelius Johann Rudolph. Born at Hamburg, May 25, 1759, and died at Weimar, January 16, 1821. He was an active and learned Mason, and for many years the Master of the Lodge Amalia at Weimar. In 1817, he published in four volumes an elaborate and valuable work entitled *Versuch eines Alphabetischen Verzeichnisses, u. s. w.*, i. e., "An essay toward an Alphabetical Catalogue of important events, for the knowledge and history of Freemasonry, and especially for a critical examination of the origin and growth of the various rituals and systems from 1717 to 1817."

Right Angle. A right angle is the meeting of two lines in an angle of ninety degrees, or the fourth part of a circle. Each of its lines is perpendicular to the other; and as the perpendicular line is a symbol of uprightness of conduct, the right angle has been adopted by Masons as an emblem of virtue. Such was also its signification among the Pythagoreans. The right angle is represented in the Lodges by the square, as the horizontal is by the level, and the perpendicular by the plumb.

Right Eminent. An epithet prefixed to the title of the Deputy Grand Master of the Grand Encampment of Knights Templar of the United States, and to that of the Grand Commander of a State Grand Commandery.

Right Excellent. The epithet prefixed to the title of all superior officers of a Grand Chapter of Royal Arch Masonry below the dignity of a Grand High Priest.

Right Hand. The right hand has in all ages been deemed an important symbol to represent the virtue of fidelity. Among the ancients, the right hand and fidelity to an obligation were almost deemed synonymous terms. Thus, among the Romans, the expression "fallere dextram," *to betray the right hand*, also signified *to violate faith;* and "jungere dextras," *to join right hands*, meant *to give a mutual pledge.* Among the Hebrews, יָמִין, *iamin*, the right hand, was derived from אָמַן, *aman*, to be faithful.

The practise of the ancients was conformable to these peculiarities of idiom. Among the Jews, to give the right hand was considered as a mark of friendship and fidelity. Thus St. Paul says, "when James, Cephas, and John, who seemed to be pillars, perceived the grace that was given unto me, they gave to me and Barnabas the *right hands of fellowship*, that we should go unto the heathen, and they unto the circumcision." (Gal. ii. 9.) The same expression, also, occurs in Maccabees. We meet, indeed, continually in the Scriptures with allusions to the right hand as an emblem of truth and fidelity. Thus in Psalm cxliv. it is said, "their right hand is a right hand of falsehood," that is to say, they lift up their right hand to swear to what is not true. This lifting up of the right hand was, in fact, the universal mode adopted among both Jews and Pagans in taking an oath. The custom is certainly as old as the days of Abraham, who said to the King of Salem, "I have lifted up my hand unto the Lord, the most high God, the possessor of heaven and earth, that I will not take anything that is thine." Sometimes among the Gentile nations, the right hand, in taking an oath, was laid upon the horns of the altar, and sometimes upon the hand of the person administering the obligation. But in all cases it was deemed necessary, to the validity and solemnity of the attestation, that the right hand should be employed.

Since the introduction of Christianity, the use of the right hand in contracting an oath has been continued, but instead of extending it to heaven, or seizing with it a horn of the altar, it is now directed to be placed upon the Holy Scriptures, which is the universal mode at this day in all Christian countries. The antiquity of this usage may be learned from the fact, that in the code of the Emperor Theodosius, adopted about the year 438, the placing of the right hand on the Gospels is alluded to; and in the code of Justinian (lib. ii., tit. 53, lex. i.), whose date is the year 529, the ceremony is distinctly laid down as a necessary part of the formality of the oath, in the words "tactis sacrosanctis Evangeliis"—the Holy Gospels being touched.

This constant use of the right hand in the most sacred attestations and solemn compacts, was either the cause or the consequence of its being deemed an emblem of fidelity. Dr. Potter (*Arch. Græc.*, p. 229) thinks it was the cause, and he supposes that the right hand was naturally used instead of the left, because it was more honorable, as being the instrument by which superiors give commands to those below them. Be this as it may, it is well known that the custom existed universally, and that there are abundant allusions in the most ancient writers to the junction of right hands in making compacts.

The Romans had a goddess whose name was *Fides*, or Fidelity, whose temple was first consecrated by Numa. Her symbol was two right hands joined, or sometimes two human figures holding each other by the right hands, whence, in all agreements among the Greeks and Romans, it was usual for the parties to take each other by the right hand, in token of their intention to adhere to the compact.

By a strange error for so learned a man, Oliver mistakes the name of this goddess, and calls her Faith. "The spurious Freemasonry," he remarks, "had a goddess called Faith." No such thing. *Fides*, or, as Horace calls her, "incorrupta Fides," incorruptible Fidelity, is very different from the theological virtue of Faith.

The joining of the right hands was esteemed among the Persians and Parthians as conveying a most inviolable obligation of fidelity. Hence, when King Artabanus desired to hold a conference with his revolted subject, Asineus, who was in arms against him, he despatched a messenger to him with the request, who said to Asineus, "the king hath sent me to give you his right hand and security," that is, a promise of safety in going and coming. And when Asineus sent his brother Asileus to the proposed conference, the king met him and gave him his right hand, upon which Josephus (*Ant. Jud.*, lib. xviii., cap. ix.) remarks: "This is of the greatest force there with all these barbarians, and affords a firm security to those who hold intercourse with them; for none of them will deceive, when once they have given you their right hands, nor will any one doubt of their fidelity, when that is once given, even though they were before suspected of injustice."

Stephens (*Travels in Yucatan*, vol. ii., p. 474) gives the following account of the use of the right hand as a symbol among the Indian tribes:

"In the course of many years' residence on the frontiers including various journeyings among the tribes, I have had frequent occasion to remark the use of the right hand as a symbol; and it is frequently applied to the naked body after its preparation and decoration for sacred or festive dances. And the fact deserves further consideration from these preparations being generally made in the arcanum of the secret Lodge, or some other private place, and with all the skill of the adept's art. The mode of applying it in these cases is by smearing the hand of the operator with white or colored clay, and impressing it on the breast, the shoulder, or other part of the body. The idea is thus conveyed that a secret influence, a charm, a mystical power is given, arising from his sanctity, or his proficiency in the occult arts. This use of the hand is not confined to a single tribe or people. I have noticed it alike among the Dacotahs, the Winnebagoes, and other Western tribes, as among the numerous branches of the red race still located east of the Mississippi River, above the latitude of 42 degrees, who speak dialects of the Algonquin language."

It is thus apparent that the use of the right hand as a token of sincerity and a pledge of fidelity, is as ancient as it is universal; a fact which will account for the important station which it occupies among the symbols of Freemasonry.

Right Side. Among the Hebrews, as well as the Greeks and Romans, the right side was considered superior to the left; and as the right was the side of good, so was the left of bad omen. *Dexter*, or right, signified also propitious, and *sinister*, or left, unlucky. In the Scriptures we find frequent allusions to this superiority of the right. Jacob, for instance, called his youngest and favorite child, *Ben-jamin*, the son of his right hand, and Bathsheba, as the king's mother, was placed at the right hand of Solomon. (See *Left Side.*)

Right Worshipful. An epithet applied in most jurisdictions of the United States to all Grand Officers below the dignity of a Grand Master.

Ring, Luminous. See *Academy of Sublime Masters of the Luminous Ring.*

Ring, Masonic. The ring, as a symbol of the covenant entered into with the Order, as the wedding ring is the symbol of the covenant of marriage, is worn in some of the high degrees of Masonry. It is not used in Ancient Craft Masonry. In the Order of the Temple the "ring of profession," as it is called, is of gold, having on it the cross of the Order and the letters P. D. E. P., being the initials of "*Pro Deo et Patria.*" It is worn on the index finger of the right hand. The Inspectors-General of the Thirty-third Degree of the Ancient and Accepted Rite wear a ring on the little finger of the right hand. Inside is the motto of the Order, "DEUS MEUM QUE JUS." In the Fourteenth Degree of the same Rite a ring is worn, which is described as "a plain gold ring," having inside the motto, "*Virtus junxit, mors non separabit.*" It is worn in the Northern Jurisdiction on the fourth or ring finger of the left hand. In the Southern Jurisdiction it is worn on the same finger of the right hand.

The use of the ring as a symbol of a covenant may be traced very far back into antiquity. The Romans had a marriage ring, but according to Swinburne, the great canonist, it was of iron, with a jewel of adamant, "to signify the durance and perpetuity of the contract."

In reference to the rings worn in the high degrees of Masonry, it may be said that they partake of the double symbolism of power and affection. The ring, as a symbol of power and dignity, was worn in ancient times by kings and men of elevated rank and office. Thus Pharaoh bestowed a ring upon Joseph as a mark or token of the power he had conferred upon him, for which reason the people bowed the knee to him. It is in this light that the ring is worn by the Inspectors of Scottish Masonry as representing the sovereigns of the Rite. But those who receive only the Fourteenth Degree, in the same Rite, wear the ring as a symbol of the covenant of affection and fidelity into which they have entered.

While on the subject of the ring as a symbol of Masonic meaning, it will not be irrelevant to refer to the magic ring of King Solomon, of which both the Jews and the Mohammedans have abundant traditions. The latter, indeed, have a book on magic rings, entitled *Scalcuthal*, in which they trace the ring of Solomon from Jared, the father of Enoch. It was by means of this ring, as a talisman of wisdom and power, that Solomon was, they say, enabled to perform those wonderful acts and accomplish those vast enterprises that have made his name so celebrated as the wisest monarch of the earth.

Rising Sun. The rising sun is represented by the Master, because as the sun by his rising opens and governs the day, so the Master is taught to open and govern his Lodge with equal regularity and precision.

Rite. The Latin word *ritus*, whence we get the English *rite*, signifies an approved usage or custom, or an external observance. Vossius derives it by metathesis from the Greek τρίβειν, whence literally it signifies a trodden path, and, metaphorically, a long-followed custom. As a Masonic term its application is therefore apparent. It signifies a method of conferring Masonic light by a collection and distribution of degrees. It is, in other words, the method and order observed in the government of a Masonic system.

The original system of Speculative Masonry consisted of only the three Symbolic degrees, called, therefore, Ancient Craft Masonry. Such was the condition of Freemasonry at the time of what is called the revival in 1717. Hence, this was the original Rite or approved usage, and so it continued in England until the year 1813, when at the union of the two Grand Lodges the "Holy Royal Arch" was declared to be a part of the system; and thus the English Rite was made legitimately to consist of four degrees.

But on the Continent of Europe, the organization of new systems began at a much earlier period, and by the invention of what are known as the high degrees a multitude of Rites was established. All of these agreed in one important essential. They were built upon the three Symbolic degrees, which, in every instance, constituted the fundamental basis upon which they were erected. They were intended as an expansion and development of the Masonic ideas contained in these degrees. The Apprentice, Fellow-Craft, and Master's degrees were the porch through which every initiate was required to pass before he could gain entrance into the inner temple which had been erected by the founders of the Rite. They were the text, and the high degrees the commentary.

Hence arises the law, that whatever may be the constitution and teachings of any Rite as to the higher degrees peculiar to it, the three Symbolic degrees being common to all the Rites, a Master Mason, in any one of the Rites, may visit and labor in a Master's Lodge of every other Rite. It is only after that degree is passed that the exclusiveness of each Rite begins to operate.

There has been a multitude of these Rites. Some of them have lived only with their authors, and died when their parental energy in fostering them ceased to exert itself. Others have had a more permanent existence, and still continue to divide the Masonic family, furnishing, however, only diverse methods of attaining to the same great end, the acquisition of Divine Truth by Masonic light. Ragon, in his *Tuilier Général*, supplies us with the names of a hundred and eight, under the different titles of Rites, Orders, and Academies. But many of these are unmasonic, being merely of a political, social, or literary character. The following catalogue embraces the most important of those which have hitherto or still continue to arrest the attention of the Masonic student.

1. York Rite.
2. Ancient and Accepted Scottish Rite.
3. French or Modern Rite.
4. American Rite.
5. Philosophic Scottish Rite.
6. Primitive Scottish Rite.
7. Reformed Rite.
8. Reformed Helvetic Rite.
9. Fessler's Rite.
10. Schröder's Rite.
11. Rite of the Grand Lodge of the Three Globes.
12. Rite of the Elect of Truth.
13. Rite of the Vielle Bru.
14. Rite of the Chapter of Clermont.
15. Pernetty's Rite.
16. Rite of the Blazing Star.
17. Chastanier's Rite.
18. Rite of the Philalethes.
19. Primitive Rite of the Philadelphians
20. Rite of Martinism.
21. Rite of Brother Henoch.
22. Rite of Misraim.
23. Rite of Memphis.
24. Rite of Strict Observance.
25. Rite of Lax Observance.
26. Rite of African Architects.
27. Rite of Brothers of Asia.
28. Rite of Perfection.
29. Rite of Elected Cohens.
30. Rite of the Emperors of the East and West.
31. Primitive Rite of Narbonne.
32. Rite of the Order of the Temple.
33. Swedish Rite.
34. Rite of Swedenborg.
35. Rite of Zinnendorf.
36. Egyptian Rite of Cagliostro.
37. Rite of the Beneficent Knights of the Holy City.

These Rites are not here given in either the order of date or of importance. The distinct history of each will be found under its appropriate title.

Rite des Elus Coens, ou Prêtres. A system adopted in 1750, but which did not attain its full vigor until twenty-five years thereafter, when Lodges were opened in Paris, Marseilles, Bordeaux, and Toulouse. The devotees of Martines Pasqualis, the founder, were called Martinistes, and were partly Hermetic and partly Swedenborgian in their teachings. Martines was a religious man, and based his teachings partly on the Jewish Kabbala and partly on Hermetic supernaturalism. The grades were as follows: 1. Apprenti; 2. Compagnon; 3. Maître; 4. Grand Elu; 5. Apprenti Coen; 6. Compagnon Coen; 7. Maître Coen; 8. Grand Architecte; 9. Grand Commandeur.

Ritter. German for *knight*, as "Der Preussische Ritter," the Prussian Knight. The word is not, however, applied to a Knight Templar, who is more usually called "Tempelherr"; although, when spoken of as a *Knight of the Temple*, he would be styled *Ritter vom Tempel*.

Ritual. The mode of opening and closing a Lodge, of conferring the degrees, of installation, and other duties, constitute a system of ceremonies which are called the Ritual. Much of this ritual is esoteric, and, not being permitted to be committed to writing, is communicated only by oral instruction. In each Masonic jurisdiction it is required, by the superintending authority, that the ritual shall be the same; but it more or less differs in the different Rites and jurisdictions. But this does not affect the universality of Masonry. The ritual is only the external and extrinsic form. The doctrine of Freemasonry is everywhere the same. It is the body which is unchangeable—remaining always and everywhere the same. The ritual is but the outer garment which covers this body, which is subject to continual variation. It is right and desirable that the ritual should be made perfect, and everywhere alike. But if this be impossible, as it is, this at least will console us, that while the ceremonies, or ritual, have varied at different periods, and still vary in different countries, the science and philosophy, the symbolism and the religion, of Freemasonry continue, and will continue, to be the same wherever true Masonry is practised.

Robelot. Formerly an advocate of the parliament of Dijon, a distinguished French Mason, and the author of several Masonic discourses, especially of one delivered before the Mother Lodge of the Philosophic Scottish Rite, of which he was Grand Orator, December 8, 1808, at the reception of Askeri Khan, the Persian Ambassador, as a Master Mason. This address gave so much satisfaction to the Lodge, that it decreed a medal to M. Robelot, on one side of which was a bust of the Grand Master, and on the other an inscription which recounted the valuable services rendered to the society by M. Robelot as its Orator, and as a Masonic author. Robelot held the theory that Freemasonry owed its origin to the East, and was the invention of Zoroaster.

Robert I. Commonly called Robert Bruce. He was crowned King of Scotland in 1306, and died in 1329. After the turbulence of the early years of his reign had ceased, and peace had been restored, he devoted himself to the encouragement of architecture in his kingdom. His connection with Masonry, and especially with the high degrees, is thus given by Dr. Oliver (*Landm.*, ii., 12): "The only high degree to which an early date can be safely assigned is the Royal Order of H. R. D. M., founded by Robert Bruce in 1314. Its history in brief refers to the dissolution of the Order of the Temple. Some of those persecuted individuals took refuge in Scotland, and placed themselves under the protection of Robert Bruce, and assisted him at the battle of Bannockburn, which was fought on St. John's day, 1314. After this battle the Royal Order was founded; and from the fact of the Templars having contributed to the victory, and the subsequent grants to their Order by King Robert, for which they were formally excommunicated by the church, it has, by some persons, been identified with that ancient military Order. But there are sound reasons for believing that the two systems were unconnected with each other." Thory (*Act. Lat.*, i., 6), quoting from a manuscript ritual in the library of the Mother Lodge of the Philosophic Rite, gives the following statement: "Robert Bruce, King of Scotland, under the name of Robert I., created on the 24th June, after the battle of Bannockburn, the Order of St. Andrew of the Thistle, to which he afterwards united that of H. R. D., for the sake of the Scottish Masons who made a part of the thirty thousand men with whom he had fought an army of one hundred thousand English. He reserved forever to himself and his successors the title of Grand Master. He founded the Grand Lodge of the Royal Order of H. R. D. at Kilwinning, and died, covered with glory and honor, on the 9th July, 1329." Both of these statements or legends require for all their details authentication. (See *Royal Order of Scotland*.)

Roberts Manuscript. This is the first of those manuscripts the originals of which have not yet been recovered, and which are known to us only in a printed copy. The Roberts Manuscript, so called from the name of the printer, J. Roberts, was published by him at London, in 1722, under the title of *The Old Constitutions belonging to the Ancient and Honorable Society of Free and Accepted Masons. Taken from a Manuscript wrote above five hundred years since.* Of this work, which had passed out of the notice and knowledge of the Masonic world, Richard Spencer, of London, being in possession of a copy, published a second edition in 1871. On a collation of this work with the Harleian MS., it is evident that either both were derived from one and the same older manuscript, or that one of them has been copied from the other; although, if this be the case, there has been much carelessness on the part of the transcriber. If the one was transcribed from the other, there is internal evidence that the Harleian is the older exemplar. The statement on the title-page of Roberts's book, that it was "taken from a manuscript wrote over five hundred years since," is contradicted by the simple fact that, like the Harleian MS., it contains the regulations adopted at the General Assembly held in 1663.

Robes. A proposition was made in the Grand Lodge of England, on April 8, 1778, that the Grand Master and his officers should be distinguished in future at all public meetings by robes. This measure, Preston says (*Illustrations*, ed. 1792, p. 332), was at first favorably received; but it was, on investigation, found to be so diametrically opposed to the original plan of the Institution, that it was very properly laid aside. In no jurisdiction are robes used in Symbolic Masonry. In many of the high degrees, however, they are employed. In the United States and in England they constitute an important part of the paraphernalia of a Royal Arch Chapter. (See *Royal Arch Robes.*)

Robin, Abbé Claude. A French littérateur, and curate of St. Pierre d'Angers. In 1776 he advanced his views on the origin of Freemasonry in a lecture before the Lodge of Nine Sisters at Paris. This he subsequently enlarged, and his interesting work was published at Paris and Amsterdam, in 1779, under the title of *Recherches sur les Initiations Anciennes et Modernes.* A German translation of it appeared in 1782, and an exhaustive review, or, rather, an extensive synopsis of it, was made by Chemin des Pontès in the first volume of his *Encyclopédie Maçonnique.* In this work the Abbé deduces from the ancient initiations in the Pagan Mysteries the orders of chivalry, whose branches, he says, produced the initiation of Freemasonry.

Robison, John. He was Professor of Natural Philosophy in the University of Edinburgh, and Secretary of the Royal Society in that city. He was born at Boghall, in Scotland, in 1739, and died in 1805. He was the author of a *Treatise on Mechanical Philosophy*, which possessed some merit; but he is better known in Masonic literature by his anti-Masonic labors. He published in 1797, at Edinburgh and London, a work entitled *Proofs of a Conspiracy against all the Religions and Governments of Europe, carried on in the Secret Meetings of the Freemasons, Illuminati, and Reading Societies, collected from Good Authorities.* In consequence of the anti-Jacobin sentiment of the people of Great Britain at that time, the work on its first appearance produced a great sensation. It was not, however, popular with all readers. A contemporary critic (*Month. Rev.*, xxv., 315) said of it, in a very unfavorable review: "On the present occasion, we acknowledge that we have felt something like regret that a lecturer on natural philosophy, of whom his country is so justly proud, should produce any work of literature by which his high character for knowledge and for judgment is liable to be at all depreciated." It was intended for a heavy blow against Masonry; the more heavy because the author himself was a Mason, having been initiated at Liege in early life, and for some time a working Mason. The work is chiefly devoted to a history of the introduction of Masonry on the Continent, and of its corruptions, and chiefly to a violent attack on the Illuminati. But while recommending that the Lodges in England should be suspended, he makes no charge of corruption against them, but admits the charities of the Order, and its respectability of character. There is much in the work on the history of Masonry on the Continent that is interesting, but many of his statements are untrue and his arguments illogical, nor was his crusade against the Institution followed by any practical results. The *Encyclopædia Britannica*, to which Robison had contributed many valuable articles on science, says of his *Proofs of a Conspiracy*, that "it betrays a degree of credulity extremely remarkable in a person used to calm reasoning and philosophical demonstration," giving as an example his belief in the story of an anonymous German writer, that the minister Turgot was the protector of a society that met at Baron d'Holbach's for the purpose of examining living children in order to discover the principle of vitality. What Robison has said of Masonry in the 531 pages of his book may be summed up in the following lines (p. 522) near its close: "While the Freemasonry of the continent was tricked up with all the frippery of stars and ribands, or was perverted to the most profligate and impious purposes, and the Lodges became seminaries of foppery, of sedition, and impiety, it has retained in Britain its original form, simple and unadorned, and the Lodges have remained the scenes of innocent merriment or meetings of charity and beneficence." So that, after all, his charges are not against Freemasonry in its original constitution, but against its corruption in a time of great political excitement.

Rockwell, William Spencer. A distinguished Mason of the United States, who was born at Albany, in New York, in 1804, and died in Maryland in 1865. He had been Grand Master of the Grand Lodge of Georgia, and at the time of his death was Lieutenant Grand Commander of the Supreme Council of the Ancient and Accepted Rite for the Southern Jurisdiction of the United States. He was a man of great learning, having a familiar acquaintance with many languages, both ancient and modern, and was well versed in the sciences. He was an able lawyer, and occupied a high position at the bar of Georgia, his adopted State. Archeology was his favorite study. In 1848, he was induced by the great Egyptologist, George R. Gliddon, to direct his attention particularly to the study of Egyptian antiquities. Already well acquainted with the philosophy and science of Masonry, he applied his Egyptian studies to the interpretation of the Masonic symbols to an extent that led him to the formation of erroneous views. His investigations, however, and their results, were often interesting, if not always correct. Mr. Rockwell was the author of an *Ahiman Rezon* for the Grand Lodge of Georgia, published in 1859, which displays abundant evidences of his learning and research. He also contributed many valuable articles to various Masonic periodicals, and was one of the collaborators of Mackey's *Quarterly Review of Freemasonry*. Before his death he had translated Portal's *Treatise on Hebrew and Egyptian Symbols*, and had written an *Exposition of the Pillars of the Porch*, and an *Essay on the Fellow-Craft's Degree*. The manuscripts of these works, in a completed form, are in the hands of his friends, but have never been published.

Rod. The rod or staff is an emblem of power either inherent, as with a king, where it is called a scepter, or with an inferior officer, where it becomes a rod, verge, or staff. The Deacons, Stewards, and Marshal of a Lodge carry rods. The rods of the Deacons, who are the messengers of the Master and Wardens, as Mercury was of the gods, may be supposed to be derived from the caduceus, which was the insignia of that deity, and hence the Deacon's rod is often surmounted by a pine-cone. The Steward's rod is in imitation of the white staff borne by the Lord High Steward of the king's household. The Grand Treasurer also formerly bore a white staff like that of the Lord High Treasurer. The Marshal's baton is only an abbreviated or short rod. It is in matters of state the ensign of a Marshal of the army. The Duke of Norfolk, as hereditary Earl Marshal of England, bears two batons crossed in his arms. Mr. Thynne, the antiquary, says (*Antiq. Disc.*, ii., 113) that the rod "did in all ages, and yet doth amongst all nations and amongst all officers, signify correction and peace; for by correction follows peace, wherefore the verge or rod was the ensign of him which had authority to reform evil in war and in peace, and to see quiet and order observed amongst the people; for therefore beareth the king his sceptre. The church hath her pastoral staff; and other magistrates which have the administration of justice or correction, as have the judges of the law and the great officers of the prince's house, have also a verge or staff assigned to them." We thus readily see the origin of the official rods or staves used in Masonry.

Rod, Deacon's. The proper badge or ensign of office of a Deacon, which he should always carry when in the discharge of the duties of his office, is a blue rod surmounted by a pine-cone, in imitation of the caduceus, or rod of Mercury, who was the messenger of the gods as is the Deacon of the superior officers of the Lodge. In the beginning of this century *columns* were prescribed as the proper badges of these officers, and we find the fact so stated in Webb's *Monitor*, which was published in 1797, and in an edition of Preston's *Illustrations*, published at Portsmouth, New Hampshire, in the year 1804. In the installation of the Deacons, it is said "these columns, as badges of your office, I intrust to your care." A short time afterward, however, the columns were transferred to the Wardens as their appropriate badges, and then we find that in the hands of the Deacon they were replaced by the rods. Thus in Dalcho's *Ahiman Rezon*, the first edition of which was printed in 1807, the words of the charge are altered to "those *staves* the badges of your office." In the *Masons' Manual*, published in 1822, by the Lodge at Easton, Pennsylvania, the badges are said to be "wands," and in Cole's *Library* they are said to carry "rods." All the subsequent Monitors agree in assigning the *rods* to the Deacons as insignia of their office, while the *columns* are appropriated to the Wardens.

In Pennsylvania, however, as far back as 1778, "the proper pillars" were carried in procession by the Wardens, and "wands tipped with gold" were borne by the Deacons. This appears from the account of a procession in that year, which is appended to Smith's edition of the *Ahiman Rezon* of Pennsylvania. The rod or wand is now universally recognized in America and in England as the Deacon's badge of office.

Rod, Marshal's. See *Baton*.

Rod of Iron. The Master is charged in the ritual not to rule his Lodge with "a rod of iron," that is to say, not with cruelty or oppression. The expression is Scriptural. Thus in Psalm ii. 9, "Thou shalt break them with a rod of iron," and in Revelation ii. 27, "He shall rule them with a rod of iron."

Rod, Steward's. The badge or ensign of office of the Stewards of a Lodge, or of the Grand Stewards of a Grand Lodge, is a white rod or staff. It is an old custom. In the first formal account of a procession in the *Book of Constitutions*, on June 24, 1724, the Stewards are described as walking "two and two abreast with white rods." (*Constitutions*, 1738, p. 117.) This use of a white rod comes from the political usages of England, where the Steward of the king's household was appointed by the delivery of a staff, the breaking of which dissolved the office. Thus an old book quoted by Thynne says that in the reign of Edward IV., the creation of the Steward of the household "only consisteth by the king's delivering to him the household staffe, with these words, *Seneschall, tenez le bastone de notre Maison*." When the Lord High Steward presides over the House of Lords at the trial of a Peer, at the conclusion of the trial he breaks the white staff which thus terminates his office.

Rod, Treasurer's. See *Staff*.

Roessler, Carl. A German Masonic writer, who translated from French into German the work of Reghellini on Masonry in its relations to the Egyptian, Jewish, and Christian religions, and published it at Leipsic in 1834 and 1835, under the assumed name of R. S. Acerrellos. He was the author of some other less important Masonic works.

Roll. In the Prestonian ritual of the funeral service, it is directed that the Master, while the brethren are standing around the coffin, shall take "the sacred roll" in his hand, and, after an invocation, shall "put the ROLL into the chest." (*Illustrations*, ed. 1792, p. 123.) In the subsequent part of the ceremony, a procession being formed, consisting of the members of visiting Lodges and of the Lodge to which the deceased belonged, it is stated that all the Secretaries of the former Lodges carry rolls, while the Secretary of the latter has none, because, of course, it had been deposited by the Master in the coffin. From the use of the words "sacred roll," we presume that the rolls borne by the Secretaries in funeral processions are intended to represent the roll of the law, that being the form still used by the Jews for inscribing the Sacred Books.

Roman Colleges of Artificers. It was the German writers on the history of the Institution, such as Krause, Heldmann, and some others of less repute, who first discovered, or at least first announced to the world, the connection that existed between the Roman Colleges of Architects and the Society of Freemasons.

The theory of Krause on this subject is to be found principally in his well-known work entitled *Die drei ältesten Kunsterkunden*. He there advances the doctrine that Freemasonry as it now exists is indebted for all its characteristics, religious and social, political and professional, its interior organization, its modes of thought and action, and its very design and object, to the *Collegia Artificum* of the Romans, passing with but little characteristic changes through the *Corporationen von Baukünstlern*, or "Architectural Gilds," of the Middle Ages up to the English organization of the year 1717; so that he claims an almost absolute identity between the Roman Colleges of Numa, seven hundred years before Christ, and the Lodges of the nineteenth century. We need not, according to his view, go any farther back in history, nor look to any other series of events, nor trouble ourselves with any other influences for the origin and the character of Freemasonry.

This theory, which is perhaps the most popular one on the subject, requires careful examination; and in the prosecution of such an inquiry the first thing to be done will be to investigate, so far as authentic history affords us the means, the true character and condition of these Roman Colleges.

It is to Numa, the second king of Rome, that historians, following after Plutarch, ascribe the first organization of the Roman Colleges; although, as Newman reasonably conjectures, it is probable that similar organizations previously existed among the Alban population, and embraced the resident Tuscan artificers. But it is admitted that Numa gave to them that form which they always subsequently maintained.

Numa, on ascending the throne, found the citizens divided into various nationalities, derived from the Romans, the Sabines, and the inhabitants of neighboring smaller and weaker towns, who, by choice or by compulsion, had removed their residence to the banks of the Tiber. Hence resulted a disseverance of sentiment and feeling, and a constant tendency to disunion. Now the object of Numa was to obliterate these contending elements and to establish a perfect identity of national feeling, so that, to use the language of Plutarch, "the distribution of the people might become a harmonious mingling of all with all."

For this purpose he established one common religion, and divided the citizens into curiæ and tribes, each curia and tribe being composed of an admixture indifferently of Romans, Sabines, and the other denizens of Rome.

Directed by the same political sagacity, he distributed the artisans into various gilds or corporations, under the name of *Collegia*, or "Colleges." To each collegium was assigned the artisans of a particular profession, and each had its own regulations, both secular and religious. These colleges grew with the growth of the republic; and although Numa had originally established but nine, namely, the College of Musicians, of Goldsmiths, of Carpenters, of Dyers, of Shoemakers, of Tanners, of Smiths, of Potters, and a ninth composed of all artisans not embraced under either of the preceding heads, they were subsequently greatly increased in number. Eighty years before the Christian era they were, it is true, abolished, or sought to be abolished, by a decree of the Senate, who looked with jealousy on their political influence, but twenty years afterward they were revived, and new ones established by a law of the tribune Clodius, which repealed the Senatus Consultum. They continued to exist under the empire, were extended into the provinces, and even outlasted the decline and fall of the Roman power.

And now let us inquire into the form and organization of these Colleges, and, in so doing, trace the analogy between them and the Masonic Lodges, if any such analogy exists.

The first regulation, which was an indispensable one, was that no College could consist of less than three members. So indispensable was this rule that the expression *tres faciunt collegium*, "three make a college," became a maxim of the civil law. So rigid too was the application of this rule, that the body of Consuls, although calling each other "colleagues," and possessing and exercising all collegiate rights, were, because they consisted only of two members, never legally recognized as a College. The reader will very readily be struck with the identity of this regulation of the Colleges and that of Freemasonry, which with equal rigor requires three Masons to constitute a Lodge. The College and the Lodge each demanded three members to make it legal. A greater number might give it more efficiency, but it could not render it more legitimate. This, then, is the first analogy between the Lodges of Freemasons and the Roman Colleges.

These Colleges had their appropriate officers, who very singularly were assimilated in stations and duties to the officers of a Masonic Lodge. Each College was presided over by a chief or president, whose title of *Magister* is exactly translated by the English word "Master." The next officers were the *Decuriones*. They were analogous to the Masonic "Wardens," for each *Decurio* presided over a section or division of the College, just as in the most ancient English and in the present continental ritual we find the Lodge divided into two sections or "columns," over each of which one of the Wardens presided, through whom the commands of the Master were extended to "the brethren of his column." There was also in the Colleges a *Scriba*, or "secretary," who recorded its proceedings; a *Thesaurensis*, or "treasurer," who had charge of the common chest; a *Tabularius*, or keeper of the archives, equivalent to the modern "Archivist"; and lastly, as these Colleges combined a peculiar religious worship with their operative labors, there was in each of them a *sacerdos*, or priest, who conducted the religious ceremonies, and was thus exactly equivalent to the "chaplain" of a Masonic Lodge. In all this we find another analogy between these ancient institutions and our Masonic bodies.

Another analogy will be found in the distribution or division of classes in the Roman Colleges. As the Masonic Lodges have their Master Masons, their Fellow-Crafts, and their Apprentices, so the Colleges had their *Seniores*, "Elders," or chief men of the trade, and their journeymen and apprentices. The members did not, it is true, like the Freemasons, call themselves "Brothers," because this term, first adopted in the gilds or corporations of the Middle Ages, is the offspring of a Christian sentiment; but, as Krause remarks, these Colleges were, in general, conducted after the pattern or model of a family; and hence the appellation of *brother* would now and then be found among the family appellations.

The partly religious character of the Roman Colleges of Artificers constitutes a very peculiar analogy between them and the Masonic Lodges. The history of these Colleges shows that an ecclesiastical character was bestowed upon them at the very time of their organization by Numa. Many of the workshops of these artificers were erected in the vicinity of temples, and their *curia*, or place of meeting, was generally in some way connected with a temple. The deity to whom such temple was consecrated was peculiarly worshiped by the members of the adjacent College, and became the patron god of their trade or art. In time, when the Pagan religion was abolished and the religious character of these Colleges was changed, the Pagan gods gave way, through the influences of the new religion, to Christian saints, one of whom was always adopted as the patron of the modern gilds, which, in the Middle Ages, took the place of the Roman Colleges; and hence the Freemasons derive the dedication of their Lodges to Saint John from a similar custom among the Corporations of Builders.

These Colleges held secret meetings, in which the business transacted consisted of the initiations of neophytes into their fraternity, and of mystical and esoteric instructions to their apprentices and journeymen. They were, in this respect, secret societies like the Masonic Lodges.

There were monthly or other periodical contributions by the members for the support of the College, by which means a common fund was accumulated for the maintenance of indigent members or the relief of destitute strangers belonging to the same society.

They were permitted by the government to frame a constitution and to enact laws and regulations for their own government. These privileges were gradually enlarged and their provisions extended, so that in the latter days of the empire the Colleges of Architects especially were invested with extraordinary powers in reference to the control of builders. Even the distinction so well known in Masonic jurisprudence between "legally constituted" and "clandestine" Lodges, seems to find a similitude or analogy here; for the Colleges which had been established by lawful authority, and were, therefore, entitled to the enjoyment of the privileges accorded to those institutions, were said to be *collegia licita*, or "lawful colleges," while those which were voluntary associations, not authorized by the express decree of the senate or the emperor, were called *collegia illicita*, or "unlawful colleges." The terms *licita* and *illicita* were exactly equivalent in their import to the *legally constituted* and the *clandestine* Lodges of Freemasonry.

In the Colleges the candidates for admission were elected, as in the Masonic Lodges, by the voice of the members. In connection with this subject, the Latin word which was used to express the art of admission or reception is worthy of consideration. When a person was admitted into the fraternity of a College, he was said to be *cooptatus in collegium*. Now, the verb *cooptare*, almost exclusively employed by the Romans to signify an election into a College, comes from the root "op" which also occurs in the Greek ὄψομαι, "to see, to behold." This same word gives origin, in Greek, to *epoptes*, a spectator or beholder, *one who has attained to the last degree in the Eleusinian mysteries;* in other words, *an initiate*. So that, without much stretch of etymological ingenuity, we might say that *cooptatus in collegium* meant "to be initiated into a College." This is, at least, singular. But the more general interpretation of *cooptatus* is "admitted or accepted in a fraternity," and so "made free of all the privileges of the gild or corporation." And hence the idea is the same as that conveyed among the Masons by the title "Free and Accepted."

Finally, it is said by Krause that these Colleges of workmen made a symbolic use of the implements of their art or profession, in other words, that they cultivated the science of symbolism; and in this respect, therefore, more than in any other, is there a striking analogy between the Collegiate and the Masonic institutions. The statement cannot be doubted; for as the organization of the Colleges partook, as has already been shown, of a religious character, and, as it is admitted, that all the religion of Paganism was eminently and almost entirely symbolic, it must follow that any association which was based upon or cultivated the religious or mythological sentiment, must cultivate also the principle of symbolism.

I have thus briefly but succinctly shown that in the form, the organization, the mode of government, and the usages of the Roman Colleges, there is an analogy between them and the modern Masonic Lodges which is evidently more than accidental. It may be that long after the dissolution of the Colleges, Freemasonry, in the establishment of its Lodges, designedly adopted the collegiate organization as a model after which to frame its own system, or it may be that the resemblance has been the result of a slow but inevitable growth of a succession of associations arising out of each other, at the head of which stands the Roman Colleges.

This problem can only be determined by an investigation of the history of these Colleges, and of the other similar institutions which finally succeeded them in the progress of architecture in Europe. We shall then be prepared to investigate with understanding the theory of Krause, and to determine whether the Lodges are indebted to the Colleges for their form alone, or for both form and substance.

We have already seen that in the time of Numa the Roman Colleges amounted to only nine. In the subsequent years of the Republic the number was gradually augmented, so that almost every trade or profession had its peculiar College. With the advance of the empire, their numbers were still further increased and their privileges greatly extended, so that they became an important element in the body politic. Leaving untouched the other Colleges, I shall confine myself to the *Collegia Artificum*, "the Colleges of Architects," as the only one whose condition and history are relevant to the subject under consideration.

The Romans were early distinguished for a spirit of colonization. Their victorious arms had scarcely subdued a people, before a portion of the army was deputed to form a colony. Here the barbarism and ignorance of the native population were replaced by the civilization and the refinement of their Roman conquerors.

The Colleges of Architects, occupied in the construction of secular and religious edifices, spread from the great city to municipalities and the provinces. Whenever a new city, a temple, or a palace was to be built, the members of these corporations were convoked by the Emperor from the most distant points, that with a community of labor they might engage in the construction. Laborers might be employed, like the "bearers of burdens" of the Jewish Temple, in the humbler and coarser tasks, but the conduct and the direction of the works were entrusted only to the "accepted members"—the *cooptati*—of the Colleges.

The colonizations of the Roman Empire were conducted through the legionary soldiers of the army. Now, to each legion there was attached a College or corporation of artificers, which was organized with the legion at Rome, and passed with it through all its campaigns, encamped with it where it encamped, marched with it where it marched, and when it colonized, remained in the colony to plant the seeds of Roman civilization, and to teach the principles of Roman art. The members of the College erected fortifications for the legion in times of war, and in times of peace, or when the legion became stationary, constructed temples and dwelling houses.

When England was subdued by the Roman arms, the legions which went there to secure and to extend the conquest, carried with them, of course, their Colleges of Architects. One of these legions, for instance, under Julius Cæsar, advancing into the northern limits of the country, established a colony, which, under the name of Eboracum, gave birth to the city of York, afterward so celebrated in the history of Masonry. Existing inscriptions and architectural remains attest how much was done in the island of Britain by these associations of builders.

Druidism was at that time the prevailing religion of the ancient Britons. But the toleration of Paganism soon led to an harmonious admixture of the religious ideas of the Roman builders with those of the Druid priests. Long anterior to this Christianity had dawned upon the British islands; for, to use the emphatic language of Tertullian, "Britain, inaccessible to the Romans, was subdued by Christ." The influences of the new faith were not long in being felt by the Colleges, and the next phase in their history is the record of their assumption of the Christian life and doctrine.

But the incursions of the northern barbarians into Italy demanded the entire force of the Roman armies to defend the integrity of the Empire at home. Britain was abandoned, and the natives, with the Roman colonists who had settled among them, were left to defend themselves. These were soon driven, first by the Picts, their savage neighbors, and then by the Saxon sea-robbers, whom the English had incautiously summoned to their aid, into the mountains of Wales and the islands of the Irish Sea. The architects who were converted to Christianity, and who had remained when the legions left the country, went with them, and having lost their connection with the mother institution, they became thenceforth simply corporations or societies of builders, the organization which had always worked so well being still retained.

Subsequently, when the whole of England was taken possession of by the Saxon invaders, the Britons, headed by the monks and priests, and accompanied by their architects, fled into Ireland and Scotland, which countries they civilized and converted, and whose inhabitants were instructed in the art of building by the corporations of architects.

Whenever we read of the extension in barbarous or Pagan countries of Christianity, and the conversion of their inhabitants to the true faith, we also hear of the propagation of the art of building in the same places by the corporations of architects, the immediate successors of the legionary Colleges, for the new religion required churches, and in time cathedrals and monasteries, and the ecclesiastical architecture speedily suggested improvements in the civil.

In time all the religious knowledge and all the architectural skill of the northern part of Europe were concentrated in the remote regions of Ireland and Scotland, whence missionaries were sent back to England to convert the Pagan Saxons. Thus the Venerable Bede tells us (*Eccl. Hist.*, lib. iii., cap. 4, 7) that West Saxony was converted by Agilbert, an Irish bishop, and East Anglia, by Fursey, a Scotch missionary. From England these energetic missionaries, accompanied by their pious architects, passed over into Europe, and effectually labored for the conversion of the Scandinavian nations, introducing into Germany, Sweden, Norway, and even Ireland, the blessings of Christianity and the refinements of civilized life.

It is worthy of note that in all the early records the word *Scotland* is very generally used as a generic term to indicate both Scotland and Ireland. This error arose most probably from the very intimate geographical and social connections of the Scotch and the northern Irish, and perhaps, also, from the general inaccuracy of the historians of that period. Thus has arisen the very common opinion, that Scotland was the germ whence sprang all the Christianity of the northern nations, and that the same country was the cradle of ecclesiastical architecture and Operative Masonry.

This historical error, by which the glory of Ireland has been merged in that of her sister country, Scotland, has been preserved in much of the language and many of the traditions of modern Freemasonry. Hence the story of the Abbey of Kilwinning as the birthplace of Masonry, a story which is still the favorite of the Freemasons of Scotland. Hence the tradition of the apocryphal mountain of Heroden, situated in the northwest of Scotland, where the first or metropolitan Lodge of Europe was held; hence the high degrees of Ecossais, or Scottish Master, which play so important a part in modern philosophical Masonry; and hence the title of "Scottish Masonry," applied to one of the leading Rites of Freemasonry, which has, however, no other connection with Scotland than that historical one, through the corporations of builders, which is common to the whole Institution.

It is not worth while to trace the religious contests between the original Christians of Britain and the Papal power, which after years of controversy terminated in the submission of the British Bishops to the Pope. As soon as the Papal authority was firmly established over Europe, the Roman Catholic hierarchy secured the services of the builders' corporations, and these, under the patronage of the Pope and the Bishops, were everywhere engaged as "travelling freemasons," in the construction of ecclesiastical and regal edifices.

Henceforth we find these corporations of builders exercising their art in all countries, everywhere proving, as Mr. Hope says, by the identity of their designs, that they were controlled by universally accepted principles, and showing in every other way the characteristics of a corporation or gild. So far the chain of connection between them and the *Collegia Artificum* at Rome has not been broken.

In the year 926 a general assembly of these builders was held at the city of York, in England.

Four years after, in 930, according to Rebold, Henry the Fowler brought these builders, now called Masons, from England into Germany, and employed them in the construction of various edifices, such as the cathedrals of Magdeburg, Meissen, and Merseburg. But Krause, who is better and more accurate as a historian than Rebold, says that, as respects Germany, the first account that we find of these corporations of builders is at the epoch when, under the direction of Edwin of Steinbach, the most distinguished architects had congregated from all parts at Strasburg for the construction of the cathedral of that city. There they held their general assembly, like that of their English brethren at York, enacted Constitutions, and established, at length, a Grand Lodge, to whose decisions numerous Lodges or *hütten*, subsequently organized in Germany, Bohemia, Hungary, France, and other countries, yielded obedience. George Kloss, in his exhaustive work entitled *Die Freimaurerei in ihrer wahren Bedeutung*, has supplied us with a full collation of the statutes and regulations adopted by these Strasburg Masons. (See *Stone-Masons of Germany*.)

We have now reached recent historical ground, and can readily trace these associations of builders to the establishment of the Grand Lodge of England at London, in 1717, when the Lodges abandoned their operative charters and became exclusively speculative. The record of the continued existence of Lodges of Free and Accepted Masons from that day to this, in every civilized country of the world, is in the hands of every Masonic student. To repeat it would be a tedious work of supererogation.

Such is the history, and now what is the necessary deduction? It cannot be doubted that Krause is correct in his theory that the incunabula—the cradle or birthplace—of the modern Masonic Lodges is to be found in the Roman Colleges of Architects. That theory is correct, if we look only to the outward form and mode of working of the Lodges. To the Colleges are they indebted for everything that distinguished them as a gild or corporation, and especially are they indebted to the architectural character of these Colleges for the fact, so singular in Freemasonry, that its religious symbolism—that by which it is distinguished from all other institutions—is founded on the elements, the working-tools, and the technical language of the stone-masons' art.

But when we view Freemasonry in a higher aspect, when we look at it as a science of symbolism, the whole of which symbolism is directed to but one point, namely, the elucidation of the great doctrine of the immortality of the soul, and the teaching of the two lives, the present and the future, we must go beyond the Colleges of Rome, which were only operative associations, the speculative Craft has borrowed from the older type to be found in the Ancient Mysteries, where the same doctrine was taught in a similar manner. Krause does not, it is true, altogether omit a reference to the priests of Greece, who, he thinks, were in some way the original whence the Roman Colleges derived their existence; but he has not pressed the point. He gives in his theory a preeminence to the Colleges to which they are not in truth entitled.

Romvel. In the Hiramic legend of some of the high degrees, this is the name given to one of the assassins of the Third Degree. This seems to be an instance of the working of Stuart Masonry, in giving names of infamy in the legends of the Order to the enemies of the house of Stuart. For we cannot doubt the correctness of Bro. Albert Pike's suggestion, that this is a manifest corruption of *Cromwell*. If with them Hiram was but a symbol of Charles I., then the assassin of Hiram was properly symbolized by Cromwell.

Rosaic System. The system of Masonry taught by Rosa in the Lodges which he established in Germany and Holland, and which were hence sometimes called "Rosaic Lodges." Although he professed that it was the system of the Clermont Chapter, for the propagation of which he had been appointed by the Baron Von Printzen, he had mixed with that system many alchemical and theosophic notions of his own. The system was at first popular, but it finally succumbed to the greater attractions of the Rite of Strict Observance, which had been introduced into Germany by the Baron von Hund.

Rosa, Philipp Samuel. Born at Yeenberg; at one time a Lutheran clergyman, and in 1757 rector of the Cathedral of St. James at Berlin. He was initiated into Masonry in the Lodge of the Three Globes, and Von Printzen having established a Chapter of the high degrees at Berlin on the system of the French Chapter of Clermont, Rosa was appointed his deputy, and sent by him to propagate the system. He visited various places in Germany, Holland, Denmark, and Sweden. In Denmark and Sweden, although well received personally on account of his pleasing manners, he made no progress in the establishment of the Rite; but his success was far better in Germany and Holland, where he organized many Lodges of the high degrees, engrafting them on the English system, which alone had been theretofore known in those countries. Rosa was a mystic and a pretended alchemist, and as a Masonic charlatan accumulated large sums of money by the sale of degrees and decorations. Lenning does not speak well of his moral conduct, but some contemporary writers describe him as a man of very attractive manners, to which indeed may be ascribed his popularity as a Masonic leader. While residing at Halle, he, in 1765, issued a protestation against the proceedings of the Congress of Jena, which had been convoked in that year by the impostor Johnson. But it met with no success, and thenceforth Rosa faded away from the knowledge of the Masonic world. We can learn nothing of his subsequent life, nor of the time or place of his death.

Rose. The symbolism of the rose among the ancients was twofold. First, as it was dedicated to Venus as the goddess of love, it became the symbol of secrecy, and hence came the expression "under the rose," to indicate that which was spoken in confidence. Again, as it was dedicated to Venus as the personification of the generative energy of nature, it became the symbol of immortality. In this latter and more recondite sense it was, in Christian symbology, transferred to Christ, through whom "life and immortality were brought to light." The "rose of Sharon" of the Book of Canticles is always applied to Christ, and hence Fuller (*Pisgah Sight of Palestine*) calls him "that prime rose and lily." Thus we see the significance of the rose on the cross as a part of the jewel of the Rose Croix Degree. Reghellini (vol. i., p. 358), after showing that anciently the rose was the symbol of secrecy, and the cross of immortality, says that the two united symbols of a rose resting on a cross always indicate the *secret*

of immortality. Ragon agreeswith him in this opinion, and says that it is the simplest mode of writing that dogma. But he subsequently gives a different explanation, namely, that as the rose was the emblem of the female principle, and the cross or triple phallus of the male, the two together, like the Indian lingam, symbolized universal generation. But Ragon, who has adopted the theory of the astronomical origin of Freemasonry, like all theorists, often carries his speculations on this subject to an extreme point. A simpler allusion will better suit the character and teachings of the degree in its modern organization. The rose is the symbol of Christ, and the cross, the symbol of his death—the two united, the rose suspended on the cross—signify his death on the cross, whereby the secret of immortality was taught to the world. In a word, the rose on the cross is Christ crucified.

Rose and Triple Cross. A degree contained in the Archives of the Lodge of Saint Louis des Amis Réunis at Calais.

Rose Croix. French. Literally, *Rose Cross*. 1. The Seventh Degree of the French Rite; 2. The Seventh Degree of the Philalethes; 3. The Eighth Degree of the Mother Lodge of the Philosophic Scottish Rite; 4. The Twelfth Degree of the Elect of Truth; 5. The Eighteenth Degree of the Mother Scottish Lodge of Marseilles; 6. The Eighteenth Degree of the Rite of Heredom, or of Perfection.

Rose Croix, Brethren of the. Thory says (*Fondat. du G. Or.*, p. 163) that the Archives of the Mother Lodge of the Philosophic Scottish Rite at Paris contain the manuscripts and books of a secret society which existed at The Hague in 1622, where it was known under the title of the *Frères de la Rose Croix*, which pretended to have emanated from the original Rosicrucian organization of Christian Rosenkruz. Hence Thory thinks that the Philosophic Rite was only a continuation of this society of the Brethren of the Rose Croix.

Rose Croix, Jacobite. The original Rose Croix conferred in the Chapter of Arras, whose Charter was said to have been granted by the Pretender, was so called with a political allusion to King James III., whose adherents were known as Jacobites.

Rose Croix, Jewel of the. Although there are six well-known Rose Croix degrees, belonging to as many systems, the jewel has invariably remained the same, while the interpretation has somewhat differed. The usual jewel of a Rose Croix Knight and also that of the M. Wise Sov. of an English Chapter are presented in opposite column.

Rose Croix, Knight. (*Chevalier Rose Croix.*) The Eighteenth Degree of the Rite of Perfection. It is the same as the Prince of Rose Croix of the Ancient and Accepted Rite.

Rose Croix, Magnetic. The Thirty-eighth Degree of the Rite of Mizraim.

Rose Croix of Germany. A Hermetic degree, which Ragon says belongs rather to the class of Elus than to that of Rose Croix.

Rose Croix of Gold, Brethren of the. (*Frères de la Rose Croix d'Or.*) An alchemical and Hermetic society, which was founded in Germany in 1777. It promised to its disciples the secret of the transmutation of metals, and the panacea or art of prolonging life. The Baron Gleichen, who was Secretary for the German language of the Philalethan Congress at Paris in 1785, gives the following history of the organization of this society:

"The members of the Rose Croix affirm that they are the legitimate authors and superiors of Freemasonry, to all of whose symbols they give a hermetical interpretation. The Masons, they say, came into England under King Arthur. Raymond Lully initiated Henry IV. The Grand Masters were formerly designated, as now, by the titles of John I., II., III., IV., etc.

"Their jewel is a golden compass attached to a blue ribbon, the symbol of purity and wisdom. The principal emblems on the ancient tracing-board were the sun, the moon, and the double triangle, having in its centre the first letter of the Hebrew alphabet. The brethren wore a silver ring on which were the letters I. A. A. T., the initials of *Ignis, Aer, Aqua, Terra*.

"The Ancient Rose Croix recognized only three degrees; the third degree, as we now know it, has been substituted for another more significant one."

The Baron de Westerode, in a letter dated 1784, and quoted by Thory (*Act.Lat.*, i., 336), gives another mythical account. He says:

"The disciples of the Rose Croix came, in 1188, from the East into Europe, for the propagation of Christianity after the troubles in Palestine. Three of them founded in Scotland the Order of the Masons of the East (Knights of the East,) to serve as a seminary for instruction in the most sublime sciences. This Order was in existence in 1196. Edward, the son of Henry III., was received into the society of the Rose Croix by Raymond Lully. At that time only learned men and persons of high rank were admitted.

"Their founder was a seraphic priest of Alexandria, a magus of Egypt named Ormesius, or Ormus, who with six of his companions was converted in the year 96 by St. Mark. He purified the doctrine of the Egyptians according to the precepts of Christianity, and founded the society of Ormus, that is to say, the Sages of Light, to the members of which he gave a red cross as a decoration. About the same time the Essenes and other Jews founded a school of Solomonic wisdom, to which the disciples of Ormus united themselves. Then the society was divided into various Orders known as the Conservators of Mosaic Secrets, of Hermetic Secrets, etc.

"Several members of the association having yielded to the temptations of pride, seven Masters united, effected a reform, adopted a modern constitution, and collected together on their tracing-board all the allegories of the hermetic work."

In this almost altogether fabulous narrative we find an inextricable confusion of the Rose Croix Masons and the Rosicrucian philosophers.

Rose Croix of Heredom. The First Degree of the Royal Order of Scotland, the Eighteenth of the Ancient and Accepted Rite, the Eighteenth of the Rite of Perfection, the Ninetieth of the Rite of Mizraim, and some others affix to the title of Rose Croix that of *Heredom*, for the signification of which see the word.

Rose Croix of the Dames. (*Rose Croix des Dames.*) This degree, called also the Ladies of Beneficence (*Chevalieres de la Bienfaisance*), is the Sixth Capitular or Ninth Degree of the French Rite of Adoption. It is not only Christian, but Roman Catholic in its character, and is derived from the ancient Jesuitical system as first promulgated in the Rose Croix Chapter of Arras.

Rose Croix of the Grand Rosary. (*Rose Croix du Grand Rosaire.*) The Fourth and highest Rose Croix Chapter of the Primitive Rite.

Rose Croix, Philosophic. A German Hermetic degree found in the collection of M. Pyron, and in the Archives of the Philosophic Scottish Rite. It is probably the same as the Brethren of the Rose Croix, of whom Thory thinks that that Rite is only a continuation.

Rose Croix, Prince of. French, *Souverain Prince Rose Croix.* German, *Prinz vom Rosenkreuz.* This important degree is, of all the high grades, the most widely diffused, being found in numerous Rites. It is the Eighteenth of the Ancient and Accepted Scottish Rite, the Seventh of the French or Modern, the Eighteenth of the Council of Emperors of the East and West, the Third of the Royal Order of Scotland, the Twelfth of the Elect of Truth, and the Seventh of the Philalethes. It was also given, formerly, in some Encampments of Knights Templars, and was the Sixth of the degrees conferred by the Encampment of Baldwyn at Bristol, in England. It must not, however, be confounded with the Rosicrucians, who, however, similar in name, were only a Hermetic and mystical Order.

The degree is known by various names: sometimes its possessors are called "Sovereign Princes of Rose Croix," sometimes "Princes of Rose Croix de Heroden," and sometimes "Knights of the Eagle and Pelican." In relation to its origin, Masonic writers have made many conflicting statements, some giving it a much higher antiquity than others; but all agreeing in supposing it to be one of the earliest of the higher degrees. The name has, undoubtedly, been the cause of much of this confusion in relation to its history; and the Masonic Degree of Rose Croix has, perhaps, often been confounded with the Kabbalistical and alchemical sect of "Rosicrucians," or "Brothers of the Rosy Cross," among whose adepts the names of such men as Roger Bacon, Paracelsus, and Elias Ashmole, the celebrated antiquary, are to be found. Notwithstanding the invidious attempts of Barruel and other foes of Masonry to confound the two Orders, there is a great distinction between them. Even their names, although somewhat similar in sound, are totally different in signification. The Rosicrucians, who were alchemists, did not derive their name, like the Rose Croix Masons, from the emblems of the rose and cross—for they had nothing to do with the rose—but from the Latin *ros*, signifying *dew*, which was supposed to be of all natural bodies the most powerful solvent of gold, and *crux*, the cross, a chemical hieroglyphic of light.

Baron de Westerode, who wrote in 1784, in the *Acta Latomorum* (i., 336), gives the earliest origin of any Masonic writer to the degree of Rose Croix. He supposes that it was instituted among the Knights Templars in Palestine, in the year 1188, and he adds that Prince Edward, the son of Henry III. of England, was admitted into the Order by Raymond Lully in 1196. De Westerode names Ormesius, an Egyptian priest, who had been converted to Christianity, as its founder.

Some have sought to find its origin in the labors of Valentine Andreä, the reputed founder of the Rosicrucian fraternity. But the Rose Croix of Masonry and the Hermetic Rosicrucianism of Andreä were two entirely different things; and it would be difficult to trace any connection between them, at least any such connection as would make one the legitimate successor of the other. J. G. Buhle, in a work, published in Göttingen in 1804, under the title of *Ueber den Ursprung und die vornehmsten Schicksale der Orden der Rosenkreutzer und Freimaurer*, reverses this theory, and supposes the Rosicrucians to be a branch of the Freemasons; and Higgins, in his *Anacalypsis* (ii., 388), thinks that the "modern Templars, the Rosicrucians, and the Masons are little more than different Lodges of one Order," all of which is only a confusion of history in consequence of a confounding of names. It is thus that Inge has written an elaborate essay on the *Origine de la Rose Croix* (*Globe*, vol. iii.); but as he has, with true Gallic *insouciance* of names, spoken indifferently of the Rose Croix Masons and the Rosicrucian Adepts, his statements supply no facts available for history.

The Baron de Gleichen, who was, in 1785, the German secretary of the Philalethan Congress at Paris, says that the Rose Croix and the Masons were united in England under King Arthur. (*Acta Lat.*, i., 336.) But he has, undoubtedly, mixed up Rosicrucianism with the Masonic legends of the Knights of the Round Table, and his assertions must go for nothing.

Others, again, have looked for the origin of the Rose Croix Degree, or, at least, of its emblems, in the *Symbola divina et humana pontificum, imperatorum, regum* of James Typot, or Typotius, the historiographer of the Emperor Rudolph II., a work which was published in 1601; and it is particularly in that part of it which is devoted to the "symbol of the holy cross" that the allusions are supposed to be found which would seem to indicate the author's knowledge of this degree. But Ragon refutes the idea of any connection between the symbols of Typotius and those of the Rose Croix. Robison (*Proofs*, p. 72) also charges Von Hund with borrowing his symbols from the same work, in which, however, he declares "there is not the least trace of Masonry or Templars."

Clavel, with his usual boldness of assertion, which is too often independent of facts, declares that the degree was invented by the Jesuits for the purpose of countermining the insidious attacks of the freethinkers upon the Roman Catholic religion, but that the philosophers parried the attempt by seizing upon the degree and giving to all its symbols an astronomical signification. Clavel's opinion is probably derived from one of those sweeping charges of Professor Robison, in which that systematic enemy of our Institution declares that, about the beginning of the eighteenth century, the Jesuits interfered considerably with Masonry, "insinuating themselves into the Lodges, and contributing to increase that religious mysticism that is to be observed in all the ceremonies of the Order." But there is no better evidence than these mere vague assertions of the connection of the Jesuits with the Rose Croix Degree.

Oliver (*Landm.*, ii., 81) says that the earliest notice that he finds of this degree is in a publication of 1613, entitled *La Réformation universelle du monde entier avec la fama fraternitatis de l'Ordre respectable de la Rose Croix.* But he adds, that "it was known much sooner, although not probably as a degree in Masonry; for it existed as a cabalistic science from the earliest times in Egypt, Greece, and Rome, as well as amongst the Jews and Moors in times more recent."

Oliver, however, undoubtedly, in the latter part of this paragraph, confounds the Masonic Rose Croix with the alchemical Rosicrucians; and the former is singularly inconsistent with the details that he gives in reference to the Rosy Cross of the Royal Order of Scotland.

There is a tradition, into whose authenticity I shall not stop to inquire, that after the dissolution of the Order, many of the Knights repaired to Scotland and placed themselves under the protection of Robert Bruce; and that after the battle of Bannockburn, which took place on St. John the Baptist's Day, in the year 1314, this monarch instituted the Royal Order of Heredom and Knight of the Rosy Cross, and established the chief seat of the Order at Kilwinning. From that Order, it seems to us by no means improbable that the present degree of Rose Croix de Heroden may have taken its origin. In two respects, at least, there seems to be a very close connection between the two systems: they both claim the kingdom of Scotland and the Abbey of Kilwinning as having been at one time their chief seat of government, and they both seem to have been instituted to give a Christian explanation to Ancient Craft Masonry. There is, besides, a similarity in the names of the degrees of "Rose Croix de Heroden," and "Heredom and Rosy Cross," amounting almost to an identity, which appears to indicate a very intimate relation of one to the other.

The subject, however, is in a state of inextricable confusion, and I confess that, after all my researches, I am still unable distinctly to point to the period when, and to the place where, the present degree of Rose Croix received its organization as a Masonic grade.

We have this much of history to guide us. In the year 1747, the Pretender, Prince Charles Edward, is said to have established a Chapter in the town of Arras, in France, with the title of the "Chapitre Primordial de Rose Croix." The Charter of this body is now extant in an authenticated copy deposited in the departmental archives of Arras. In it the Pretender styles himself "King of England, France, Scotland, and Ireland, and, by virtue of this, Sovereign Grand Master of the Chapter of H. known under the title of the Eagle and Pelican, and, since our sorrows and misfortunes, under that of Rose Croix." From this we may infer that the title of "Rose Croix" was first known in 1747; and that the degree had been formerly known as "Knight of the Eagle and Pelican," a title which it still retains. Hence it is probable that the Rose Croix Degree has been borrowed from the Rosy Cross of the Scottish Royal Order of Heredom, but in passing from Scotland to France it greatly changed its form and organization, as it resembles in no respect its archetype, except that both are eminently Christian in their design. But in its adoption by the Ancient and Accepted Rite, its organization has been so changed that, by a more liberal interpretation of its symbolism, it has been rendered less sectarian and more tolerant in its design. For while the Christian reference is preserved, no peculiar theological dogma is retained, and the degree is made cosmopolite in its character.

It was, indeed, on its first inception, an attempt to Christianize Freemasonry; to apply the rites, and symbols, and traditions of Ancient Craft Masonry to the last and greatest dispensation; to add to the first Temple of Solomon and the second of Zerubbabel a third, that to which Christ alluded when he said, "Destroy this temple. and in three days will I raise it up." The great discovery which was made in the Royal Arch ceases to be of value in this degree; for it another is substituted of more Christian application; the Wisdom, Strength, and Beauty which supported the ancient Temple are replaced by the Christian pillars of Faith, Hope and Charity; the great lights, of course, remain, because they are of the very essence of Masonry; but the three lesser give way to the thirty-three, which allude to the years of the Messiah's sojourning on earth. Everything, in short, about the degree, is Christian; but, as I have already said, the Christian teachings of the degree have been applied to the sublime principles of a universal system, and an interpretation and illustration of the doctrines of the "Master of Nazareth," so adapted to the Masonic dogma of tolerance, that men of every faith may embrace and respect them. It thus performs a noble mission. It obliterates, alike, the intolerance of those Christians who sought to erect an impassable barrier around the sheepfold, and the equal intolerance of those of other religions who would be ready to exclaim, "Can any good thing come out of Nazareth?"

In the Ancient and Accepted Scottish Rite, whence the Rose Croix Masons of the United States have received the degree, it is placed as the eighteenth on the list. It is conferred in a body called a "Chapter," which derives its authority immediately from the Supreme Council of the Thirty-third, and which confers with it only one other and inferior degree, that of "Knights of the East and West." Its principal officers are a Most Wise Master and two Wardens. Maundy Thursday and Easter Sunday are two obligatory days of meeting.

The aspirant for the degree makes the usual application duly recommended; and if accepted, is required, before initiation, to make certain declarations which shall show his competency for the honor which he seeks, and at the same time prove the high estimation entertained of the degree by those who already possess it.

The jewel of the Rose Croix is a golden compass, extended on an arc to the sixteenth part of a circle, or twenty-two and a half degrees. The head of the compass is surmounted by a triple crown, consisting of three series of points arranged by three, five, and seven. Between the legs of the compass is a cross resting on the arc; its center is occupied by a full-blown rose, whose stem twines around the lower limb of the cross; at the foot of the cross, on the same side on which the rose is exhibited, is the figure of a pelican wounding its breast to feed its young which are in a nest surrounding it, while on the other side of the jewel is the figure of an eagle with wings displayed. On the arc of the circle, the P.·. W.·. of the degree is engraved in the cipher of the Order.

In this jewel are included the most important symbols of the degree. The *Cross*, the *Rose*, the *Pelican*, and the *Eagle* are all important symbols, the explanations of which will go far to a comprehension of what is the true design of the Rose Croix Order. They may be seen in this work under their respective titles.

Rose Croix, Rectified. The name given by F. J. W. Schröder to his Rite of seven magical, theosophical, and alchemical degrees. (See *Schroeder, Friedrich Joseph Wilhelm.*)

Rose Croix, Sovereign Prince of. Because of its great importance in the Masonic system, and of the many privileges possessed by its possessors, the epithet of "Sovereign" has been almost universally bestowed upon the degree of Prince of Rose Croix. Recently, however, the Mother Council of the Ancient and Accepted Scottish Rite at Charleston has discarded this title, and directed that the word "Sovereign" shall only be applied to the Thirty-third Degree of the Rite; and this is now the usage in the Southern Jurisdiction of the United States.

Rose, Knights and Ladies of the. See *Knight of the Rose.*

Rose, Order of the. A Masonic adventurer, Franz Rudolph Van Grossing, but whose proper name, Wadzeck says, was Franz Matthäus Grossinger, established, as a financial speculation, at Berlin, in 1778, an androgynous society, which he called *Rosen-Order*, or the Order of the Rose. It consisted of two degrees: 1. Female Friends, and 2. Confidants; and the meetings of the society were designated as "holding the rose." The society had but a brief duration, and the life and adventures of the founder and the secrets of the Order were published in 1789, by Friederich Wadzeck, in a work entitled *Leben und Schicksale des berüchtigten F. R. Von Grossing*.

Rosenkreuz, Christian. An assumed name, invented, it is supposed, by John Valentine Andreä, by which he designated a fictitious person, to whom he has attributed the invention of *Rosicrucianism*, which see.

Rosicrucianism. Many writers have sought to discover a close connection between the Rosicrucians and the Freemasons, and some, indeed, have advanced the theory that the latter are only the successors of the former. Whether this opinion be correct or not, there are sufficient coincidences of character between the two to render the history of Rosicrucianism highly interesting to the Masonic student.

There appeared at Cassel, in the year 1614, a work bearing the title of *Allgemeine und General-Reformation der ganzen weiten Welt. Beneben der Fama Fraternitatis des Löblichen Ordens des Rosencreuzes an alle Gelehrte und Häupter Europä geschrieben*. A second edition appeared in 1615, and several subsequent ones; and in 1652 it was introduced to the English public in a translation by the celebrated adept, Thomas Vaughan, under the title of *Fame and Confession of Rosie-Cross*.

This work has been attributed, although not without question, to the philosopher and theologian, John Valentine Andreä, who is reported, on the authority of the preacher, M. C. Hirschen, to have confessed that he, with thirty others in Wurtemberg, had sent forth the *Fama Fraternitatis*; that under this veil they might discover who were the true lovers of wisdom, and induce them to come forward.

In this work Andreä gives an account of the life and adventures of Christian Rosenkreuz, a fictitious personage, whom he makes the founder of the pretended Society of Rosicrucians.

According to Andreä's tale, Rosenkreuz was of good birth, but, being poor, was compelled to enter a monastery at a very early period of his life. At the age of 100 years, he started with one of the monks on a pilgrimage to the Holy Sepulcher. On their arrival at the island of Cyprus, the monk was taken sick and died, but Rosenkreuz proceeded on his journey. At Damascus he remained for three years, devoting himself to the study of the occult sciences, taught by the sages of that city. He then sailed for Egypt, where he continued his studies; and, having traversed the Mediterranean, he at length arrived at Fez, in Morocco, as he had been directed by his masters of Damascus. He passed two years in acquiring further information from the philosophers of Africa, and then crossed over into Spain. There, however, he met with an unfavorable reception, and then determined to return to Germany, and give to his own countrymen the benefit of his studies and researches, and to establish there a society for the cultivation of the sciences which he had acquired during his travels. Accordingly, he selected three of the monks of the old convent in which he was educated. To them he imparted his knowledge, under a solemn vow of secrecy. He imposed on them the duty of committing his instructions to writing, and forming a magic vocabulary for the benefit of future students. They were also taught the science of medicine, and prescribed gratuitously for all the sick who applied to them. But the number of their patients soon materially interfering with their other labors, and the new edifice, the House of the Holy Spirit, being now finished, Father Christian, as he was called, resolved to enlarge his society by the initiation of four new members.

The eight brethren being now thoroughly instructed in the mysteries, they agreed to separate—two to remain with Father Christian, and the others to travel, but to return at the end of each year, and mutually to communicate the results of their experience. The two who had remained at home were then relieved by two of the others, and they again separated for another year.

The society thus formed was governed by a code of laws, by which they agreed that they would devote themselves to no occupation except that of physic, which they were to practise without pecuniary reward; that they would not distinguish themselves from the rest of the world by any peculiar costume; that each one should annually present himself at the House of the Holy Spirit, or send an excuse for his absence; that each one should, during his life, appoint somebody to succeed him at his death; that the letters R. C. were to be their title and watchword; and that the brotherhood should be kept a secret for one hundred years.

At the age of 106 years Father Christian Rosenkreus died, and was buried by the two brethren who had remained with him; but the place of his burial remained a secret to all of the rest—the two carrying the mystery with them to the grave. The society, however, continued, notwithstanding the death of the founder, to exist, but unknown to the world, always consisting of eight members. There was a tradition among them, that at the end of one hundred and twenty years the grave of Father Rosenkreus was to be discovered, and the brotherhood no longer remain a secret. About that time the brethren began to make some alterations in their building, and attempted to remove to a more fitting situation the memorial table on which was inscribed the names of those who had been members of the fraternity. The plate was of brass, and was affixed to the wall by a nail driven through its center; but so firmly was it attached, that in tearing it away, a portion of the plaster came off and exposed a secret door. Upon removing the incrustation on the door, there appeared written in large letters, "POST CXX ANNOS PATEBO"—*after one hundred and twenty years I will open*. Returning the next morning to renew their researches, they opened the door and discovered a heptagonal vault, each of its seven sides being five feet wide, and in height eight feet. The light was received from an artificial sun in the roof, and in the middle of the floor there stood, instead of a tomb, a circular altar, on which was an inscription, importing that this apartment, as a compendium of the universe, had been erected by Christian Rosenkreuz. Other later inscriptions about the apartment—such as *Jesus mihi omnia; Legis jugum; Libertas Evangelii:* Jesus is my all; the yoke of the law; the liberty of the Gospel—indicated the Christian character of the builder. In each of the sides was a door opening into a closet, and in these closets they found many rare and valuable articles, such as the life of the founder, the vocabulary of Paracelsus, and the secrets of the Order, together with bells, mirrors, burning lamps, and other curious articles. On removing the altar and a brass plate beneath it, they came upon the body of Rosenkreuz in a perfect state of preservation.

Such is the sketch of the history of the Rosicrucians given by Andreä in his *Fama Fraternitatis*. It is evidently a romance; and scholars now generally assent to the theory advanced by Nicolai, that Andreä, who, at the time of the appearance of his book, was a young man full of excitement, seeing the defects of the sciences, the theology, and the manners of his time, sought to purify them; and, to accomplish this design, imagined the union into one body of all those who, like himself, were the admirers of true virtue; in other words, that he wrote this account of the rise and progress of Rosicrucianism for the purpose of advancing, by a poetical fiction, his peculiar views of morals and religion.

But the fiction was readily accepted as a truth by most people, and the invisible society of Rosenkreuz was sought for with avidity by many who wished to unite with it. The sensation produced in Germany by the appearance of Andreä's book was great; letters poured in on all sides from those who desired to become members of the Order, and who, as proofs of their qualifications, presented their claims to skill in Alchemy and Kabbalism. No answers, of course, having been received to these petitions for initiation, most of the applicants were discouraged and retired; but some were bold, became impostors, and proclaimed that they had been admitted into the society, and exercised their fraud upon those who were credulous enough to believe them. There are records that some of these charlatans, who extorted money from their dupes, were punished for their offense by the magistrates of Nuremberg, Augsburg, and some other German cities. There was, too, in Holland, in the year 1722, a Society of Alchemists, who called themselves Rosicrucians, and who claimed that Christian Rosenkreuz was their founder, and that they had affiliated societies in many of the German cities. But it is not to be doubted that this was a self-created society, and that it had nothing in common, except the name, with the imaginary brotherhood invented by Andreä. Des Cartes, indeed, says that he sought in vain for a Rosicrucian Lodge in Germany.

But although the brotherhood of Rosenkreuz, as described by Andreä in his *Fama Fraternitatis*, his *Chemical Nuptuals*, and other works, never had a real tangible existence as an organized society, the opinions advanced by Andreä took root, and gave rise to the philosophic sect of the Rosicrucians, many of whom were to be found, during the seventeenth century, in Germany, in France, and in England. Among these were such men as Michael Maier, Richard Fludd, and Elias Ashmole. Nicolai even thinks that he has found some evidence that the *Fama Fraternitatis* suggested to Lord Bacon the notion of his *Instauratio Magna*. But, as Vaughan says (*Hours with the Mystics*, ii., 104), the name Rosicrucian became by degrees a generic term, embracing every species of doubt, pretension, arcana, elixirs, the philosopher's stone, theurgic ritual, symbols, or initiations.

Higgins, Sloane, Vaughan, and several other writers have asserted that Freemasonry sprang out of Rosicrucianism. But this is a great error. Between the two there is no similarity of origin, of design, or of organization. The symbolism of Rosicrucianism is derived from a Hermetic philosophy; that of Freemasonry from an operative art. The latter had its cradle in the Stone-Masons of Strasburg and the Masters of Como long before the former had its birth in the inventive brain of John Valentine Andreä.

It is true, that about the middle of the eighteenth century, a period fertile in the invention of high degrees, a Masonic Rite was established which assumed the name of Rose Croix Masonry, and adopted the symbol of the Rose and Cross. But this was a coincidence, and not a consequence. There was nothing in common between them and the Rosicrucians, except the name, the symbol, and the Christian character. Doubtless the symbol was suggested to the Masonic Order from the use of it by the philosophic sect; but the Masons modified the interpretation, and the symbol, of course, gave rise to the name. But here the connection ends. A Rose Croix Mason and a Rosicrucian are two entirely different persons.

The Rosicrucians had a large number of symbols, some of which were in common with those of the Freemasons, and some peculiar to themselves. The principal of these were the globe, the circle, the compasses, the square (both the working-tool and the geometrical figure), the triangle, the level, and the plummet. These are, however, interpreted, not like the Masonic, as symbols of the moral virtues, but of the properties of the philosopher's stone. Thus, the twenty-first emblem of Michael Maier's *Atlanta Fugiens* gives the following collection of the most important symbols: A philosopher is measuring with a pair of compasses a circle which surmounts a triangle. The triangle encloses a square, within which is another circle, and inside of the circle a nude man and woman, representing, it may be supposed, the first step of the experiment. Over all is this epigraph: "Fac ex mare et femina circulum, inde quadrangulum, hinc triangulum, fac circulum et habebis lapidem Philosophorum." That is, "Make of man and woman a circle; thence a square; thence a triangle; form a circle, and you will have the Philosopher's stone." But it must be remembered that Hitchcock, and some other recent writers, have very satisfactorily proved that the labors of the real Hermetic philosophers (outside of the charlatans) were rather of a spiritual than a material character; and that their "great work" symbolized not the acquisition of inexhaustible wealth and the infinite prolongation of life, but the regeneration of man and the immortality of the soul.

As to the etymology of the word *Rosicrucian*, several derivations have been given. Peter Gassendi (*Exam. Phil. Fludd*, sect. 15), first, and then Mosheim (*Hist. Eccles.*, iv., i.) deduce it from the two words *ros*, dew, and *crux*, a cross, and thus define it: Dew, according to the Alchemists, was the most powerful of all substances to dissolve gold; and the cross, in the language of the same philosophers, was identical with light, or LVX, because the figure of a cross exhibits the three letters of that word. But the word *lux* was referred to the seed or menstruum of the Red Dragon, which was that crude and material light which, being properly concocted and digested, produces gold. Hence, says Mosheim, a Rosicrucian is a philosopher, who by means of *dew* seeks for *light*, that is, for the substance of the philosopher's stone. But notwithstanding the high authority for this etymology, I think it untenable, and altogether at variance with the history of the origin of the Order, as will be presently seen.

Another and more reasonable derivation is from *rose* and *cross*. This was undoubtedly in accordance with the notions of Andreä, who was the founder of the Order, and gave it its name, for in his writings he constantly calls it the "Fraternitas Roseæ Crucis," or "the Fraternity of the Rosy Cross." If the idea of *dew* had been in the mind of Andreä in giving a name to the society, he would have called it the "Fraternity of the Dewy Cross," not that of the "Rosy Cross." "Fraternitas Roscidæ Crucis," not "Roseæ Crucis." This ought to settle the question. The man who invents a thing has the best right to give it a name.

The origin and interpretation of the symbol have been variously given. Some have supposed that it was derived from the Christian symbolism of the rose and the cross. This is the interpretation that has been assumed by the Rose Croix Order of the Masonic system; but it does not thence follow that the same interpretation was adopted by the Rosicrucians. Others say that the rose meant the generative principle of nature, a symbolism borrowed from the Pagan mythologers, and not likely to have been appropriated by Andreä. Others, again, contend that he derived the symbol from his own arms, which were a St. Andrew's cross between four roses, and that he alluded to Luther's well-known lines:

"Des Christen Herz auf Rosen geht,
Wenn's mitten unter'n Kreutze steht,"

i. e., "The heart of the Christian goes upon roses when it stands close beneath the cross." But whatever may have been the effect of Luther's lines in begetting an idea, the suggestion of Andreä's arms must be rejected. The symbol of the Rosicrucians was a single rose upon a passion cross, very different from four roses surrounding a St. Andrew's cross.

Another derivation may be suggested, namely: That, the rose being a symbol of secrecy, and the cross of light, the rose and cross were intended to symbolize the secret of the true light, or the true knowledge, which the Rosicrucian brotherhood were to give to the world at the end of the hundred years of their silence, and for which purpose of moral and religious reform Andreä wrote his books and sought to establish his sect. But the whole subject of Rosicrucian etymology is involved in confusion.

*The Rosicrucian Society, instituted in the fourteenth century, was an extraordinary Brotherhood, exciting curiosity and commanding attention and scrutiny. The members delved in abstruse studies; many became Anchorites, and were engrossed in mystic philosophy and theosophy. This strange Fraternity, asserted by some authorities to have been instituted by Roger Bacon near the close of the thirteenth century, filled the world with renown as to their incomprehensible doctrines and presumed abilities. They claimed to be the exponents of the true Kabbala, as embracing theosophy as well as the science of numbers. They were said to delve in strange things and deep mysteries; to be enwrapt in the occult sciences, sometimes vulgarly termed the "Black Art"; and in the secrets of magic and sorcery, which are looked upon by the critical eyes of the world as tending to the supernatural, and a class of studies to be avoided.

These mystics, for whom great philanthropy is claimed, and not without reason, are heard of as early as the commencement of the fourteenth century, in the person of Raymond Lully, the renowned scholiast and metaphysical chemist, who proved to be an adept in the doctrines taught at the German seat of Hermetic learning in 1302, and who died in 1315. Fidelity and secrecy were the first care of the Brotherhood. They claimed a kinship to the ancient philosophies of Egypt, the Chaldeans, the Magi of Persia, and even the Gymnosophists of India. They were unobtrusive and retiring in the extreme. They were learned in the principles and sciences of chemistry, hermeticism, magnetism, astrology, astronomy, and theosophy, by which they obtained great powers through their discoveries, and

*From this point the article is by C. T. McClenachan.

aimed at the universal solvent—the Philosopher's Stone—thereby striving to acquire the power of transmuting baser metals into silver and gold, and of indefinitely prolonging human life. As a Fraternity they were distinct from the Kabbalists, Illuminati, and Carbonari, and in this relation they have been largely and unpleasantly misrepresented. Ignorance and prejudice on the part of the learned as to the real purposes of the Rosicrucians, and as to the beneficence of that Fraternity, has wrought them great injustice. Science is infinitely indebted to this Order. The renowned reviver of Oriental literature, John Reuchlin, who died in 1522; the famous philosopher and classic scholar, John Picus di Mirandola, who died in 1494; the celebrated divine and distinguished philosopher, Cornelius Henry Agrippa, who died in 1535; the remarkable chemist and physician, John Baptist Von Helmont, who died in 1644; and the famous physician and philosopher, Robert Fludd, who died in 1637, all attest the power and unquestioned prominence of the famous Brotherhood. It is not the part of wisdom to disdain the Astrological and Hermetic Association of Elias Ashmole, author of the *Way to Bliss.* All Europe was permeated by this secret organization, and the renown of the Brotherhood was preeminent about the year 1615. Wessel's *Fama Fraternitatis*, the curious work *Secretioris Philosophiæ Consideratis*, and *Cum Confessione Fraternitatis*, by P. A. Gabella, with Fludd's *Apologia*, the *Chemische Hochzeit of Christian Rosenkreuz*, by Valentine Andreä; and the endless number of volumes, such as the *Fama Ramissa*, establish the high rank in which the Brotherhood was held. Its curious, unique, and attractive Rosaic doctrines interested the masses of scholars of the sixteenth and seventeenth centuries. With the Rosicrucians worldly grandeur faded before intellectual elevation. They were simple in their attire, and passed individually through the world unnoticed and unremarked, save by deeds of benevolence and humanity.

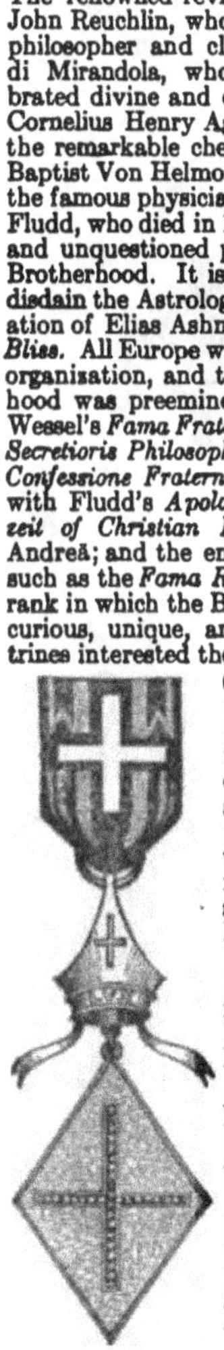

The *Modern Society* of Rosicrucians was given its present definite form by Robert Wentworth Little, of England, in 1866; it is founded upon the remains or the embers of an old German association which had come under his observation during some of his researches. Bro. Little Anglicised it, giving it more perfect system. The purpose of Robert Wentworth Little was to create a literary organization, having in view a base for the collection and deposit of archeological and historical subjects pertaining to Freemasonry, secret societies in general, and interesting provincial matter; to inspire a greater disposition to obtain historical truth and to displace error; to bring to light much in relation to a certain class of scientists and scholars, and the results of their life-labors, that were gradually dying away in the memories of men. To accomplish this end he called about him some of his most prominent English and Scottish Masonic friends inclined to literary pursuits, and they awarded their approval and hearty cooperation.

Rosicruciana in Anglia, Societas. A society whose objects are of a purely literary character, and connected with the sect of the Rosicrucians of the Middle Ages. It is secret, but not Masonic, in its organization; although many of the most distinguished Masons of England take great interest in it, and are active members of the society. (See the preceding article.)

Rosy Cross. One of the degrees conferred in the *Royal Order of Scotland*, which see.

Rough Ashlar. See *Ashlar*.

Round Table, King Arthur's. The old English legends, derived from the celebrated chronicle of the twelfth century known as the *Brut of England*, say that the mythical King Arthur, who died in 542, of a wound received in battle, instituted a company of twenty-four (or, according to some, twelve) of his principal knights, bound to appear at his court on certain solemn days, and meet around a circular table, whence they were called "Knights of the Round Table." Arthur is said to have been the institutor of those military and religious orders of chivalry which afterward became so common in the Middle Ages. Into the Order which he established none were admitted but those who had given proofs of their valor; and the knights were bound to defend widows, maidens, and children; to relieve the distressed, maintain the Christian religion, contribute to the support of the church, protect pilgrims, advance honor, and suppress vice. They were to administer to the care of soldiers wounded in the service of their country, and bury those who died, to ransom captives, deliver prisoners, and record all noble enterprises for the honor and renown of the noble Order. King Arthur and his knights have been very generally considered by scholars as mythical; notwithstanding that, many years ago Whittaker, in his *History of Manchester*, attempted to establish the fact of his existence, and to separate the true from the fabulous in his history. The legend has been used by some of the fabricators of irregular degrees in Masonry.

Round Towers of Ireland. Edifices, sixty-two in number, varying in height from 80 to 120 feet, which are found in various parts of Ireland. They are cylindrical in shape, with a single door eight or ten feet from the ground, and a small aperture near the top. The question of their origin and design has been a source of much perplexity to antiquaries. They have been supposed by Mont-

morency to have been intended as beacons; by Vallancey, as receptacles of the sacred fire; by O'Brien, as temples for the worship of the sun and moon; and more recently, by Petrie, simply as bell-towers, and of very modern date. This last theory has been adopted by many; while the more probable supposition is still maintained by others, that, whatever was their later appropriation, they were, in their origin, of a phallic character, in common with the towers of similar construction in the East. O'Brien's work *On the Round Towers of Ireland*, which was somewhat extravagant in its arguments and hypotheses, led some Masons to adopt, forty years ago, the opinion that they were originally the places of a primitive Masonic initiation. But this theory is no longer maintained as tenable.

Rowers. See *Knight Rower*.

Royal and Select Masters. See *Council of Royal and Select Masters*.

Royal Arch, Ancient. See *Knight of the Ninth Arch*.

Royal Arch Apron. At the triennial meeting of the General Grand Chapter of the United States at Chicago, in 1859, a Royal Arch apron was prescribed, consisting of a

lambskin (silk or satin being strictly prohibited), to be lined and bound with scarlet, on the flap of which should be placed a triple tau cross within a triangle, and all within a circle.

Royal Arch Badge. The triple tau, consisting of three tau crosses conjoined at their feet, constitutes the Royal Arch badge. The English Masons call it the "emblem of all emblems," and the "grand emblem of Royal Arch Masonry." The English Royal Arch lecture thus defines it: "The triple tau forms two right angles on each of the exterior lines, and another at the centre, by their union; for the three angles of each triangle are equal to two right angles. This, being triplified, illustrates the jewel worn by the companions of the Royal Arch, which, by its intersection, forms a given number of angles that may be taken in five several combinations." It is used in the Royal Arch Masonry of Scotland, and has, for the last ten or fifteen years, been adopted officially in the United States.

Royal Arch Banners. See *Banners, Royal Arch*.

Royal Arch Captain. The sixth officer in a Royal Arch Chapter according to the American system. He represents the *sar habahim*, or Captain of the King's Guards. He sits in front of the Council and at the entrance to the fourth veil, to guard the approaches to which is his duty. He wears a white robe and cap, is armed with a sword, and bears a white banner on which is inscribed a lion, the emblem of the tribe of Judah. His jewel is a triangular plate of gold inscribed with a sword. In the preliminary Lodges of the Chapter he acts as Junior Deacon.

Royal Arch Clothing. The clothing or regalia of a Royal Arch Mason in the American system consists of an apron (already described), a scarf of scarlet velvet or silk, on which is embroidered or painted, on a blue ground, the words, "Holiness to the Lord"; and if an officer, a scarlet collar, to which is attached the jewel of his office. The scarf, once universally used, has, within a few years past, been very much abandoned. Every Royal Arch Mason should also wear at his buttonhole, attached by a scarlet ribbon, the jewel of the Order.

Royal Arch Colors. The peculiar color of the Royal Arch Degree is red or scarlet, which is symbolic of fervency and zeal, the characteristics of the degree. The colors also used symbolically in the decorations of a Chapter are blue, purple, scarlet, and white, each of which has a symbolic meaning. (See *Veils, Symbolism of the*.)

Royal Arch Degree. The early history of this degree is involved in obscurity, but in the opinion of the late Bro. W. J. Hughan its origin may be ascribed to the fourth decade of the eighteenth century. The earliest known mention of it occurs in a contemporary account of the meeting of a Lodge (No. 21) at Youghal, in Ireland, in 1743, when the members walked in procession and the Master was preceded by "the Royal Arch carried by two Excellent Masons." (See *Excellent Master*.)

The next mention of it is in Dr. Dassigny's *A Serious and Impartial Enquiry into the cause of the present Decay of Freemasonry in the Kingdom of Ireland*, published in 1744, in which the writer says that he is informed that in York "is held an assembly of Master Masons under the title of Royal Arch Masons, who, as their qualifications and excellencies are superior to others, receive a larger pay than working Masons." He also speaks of "a certain propagator of a false system, some few years ago, in this city (Dublin), who imposed upon several very worthy men, under a pretence of being Master of the Royal Arch, which he asserted he had brought with him from the city of York, and that the beauties of the Craft did principally consist in the knowledge of this valuable piece of Masonry. However, he carried on his scheme for several months, and many of the learned and wise were his followers, till, at length, his fallacious art was discovered by a Brother of probity and wisdom, who had some small space before attained that excellent part of Masonry in London, and plainly proved that his doctrine was false: whereupon the Brethren justly despised him, and ordered him to be excluded from all benefits of the Craft, and although some of the fraternity have expressed an uneasiness at this matter being kept a secret from them (since they had already passed through the usual degrees of probation), I cannot help being of opinion that they have no right to any such benefit until they make a proper application, and are received with due ormality, and as it is an organis'd body of men who have passed the chair, and given undeniable proofs of their skill in architecture, it cannot be treated with too much reverence, and more especially since the character of the present members of that particular Lodge are untainted, and their behaviour judicious and unexceptionable, so that there cannot be the least hinge to hang a doubt on, but that they are most excellent Masons."

This passage makes it plain that the Royal Arch Degree was conferred in London before 1744 (say about 1740), and would suggest that York was considered to be its place of origin. Also as Laurence Dermott became a Royal Arch Mason in 1746 it is clear that he could not have been, as is sometimes asserted, the inventor of the Rite.

The next mention of the degree occurs in the minutes of the "Ancients" Grand Lodge for March 4, 1752, when "A formal complaint was made by several brethren against Thos. Phealon and John Macky, better known as 'leg of mutton Masons' for clandestinely making Masons for the mean consideration of a leg of mutton for dinner or supper. Upon examining some brothers whom they pretended to have made Royal Arch men, the parties had not the least idea of that secret. The Grand Secretary had examined Macky, and stated that he had not the least idea or knowledge of Royal Arch Masonry, but instead thereof he had told the people he had deceived, a long story about twelve white marble stones, &c., &c., and that the rainbow was the Royal Arch, with many other absurdities equally foreign and ridiculous."

The earliest known record of the degree being actually conferred is a minute of the Fredericksburg Lodge, Virginia, U. S. A., stating that on December 22, 1753, three brethren were raised to the degree of Royal Arch Mason (for a facsimile of this entry see *Ars Quatuor Coronatorum*, iv., p. 222); while the earliest records traced in England are of the year 1758, during which year several brethren were "raised to the degree of Royal Arch" in a Lodge meeting at The Crown at Bristol. This Lodge was a "Modern" one and its records therefore make it abundantly clear that the Royal Arch Degree was not by any means confined to the "Ancients," though it was not officially recognized by the Grand Lodge of the "Moderns," whose Secretary wrote in 1759, "Our Society is neither Arch, Royal Arch or Ancient."

However, at the Union of "Ancients" and "Moderns," in 1813, it was declared that "pure Ancient Masonry consists of three degrees, and no more, *viz.*, those of the Entered Apprentice, the Fellow Craft, and the Master Mason, including the Supreme Order of the Holy Royal Arch."

And this lends color to the idea that at some time or other the Royal Arch had formed part of the Master Mason's Degree, though when and by whom it was separated from it no one has yet discovered, for we may dismiss as utterly uncorroborated by any proof the assertion that Ramsay was the fabricator of the Royal Arch Degree, and equally unsupported is the often made assertion that Dunckerley invented it, though he undoubtedly played a very active part in extending it.

The late Bro. W. J. Hughan, in his *Origin of the English Rite of Free Masonry* (ed. 1909, p. 90), favors "the theory that a *word* was placed in the Royal Arch *prominently* which was previously given in the *sections* of the Third Degree and known 'as the ancient word of a Master Mason,'" and considers that "according to this idea, that *which was once lost, and then found*, in the Third Degree (in one of the sections), was subsequently under the new regime discovered in the 'Royal Arch,' only *much extended, and under most exalted and dignified surroundings.*"

In England, Scotland, and the United States, the legend of the degree is the same, though varying in some of the details, but the ceremony in Ireland differs much, for it has nothing to do with the rebuilding of the Temple as narrated by Ezra, but with the repairing of the Temple by Josiah, the three chief Officers, or Principals, being the King (Josiah), the Priest (Hilkiah), and the Scribe (Shaphan), not as in England Zerubbabel, Haggai, and Jeshua, or as in America, High Priest, King, and Scribe.

At one time in England only Past Masters were eligible for the degree, and this led to a system called "passing the chair," by which a sort of degree of Past Master was conferred upon brethren who had never really served in the chair of a Lodge; now a Master Mason who has been so for four weeks is eligible for exaltation.

In Scotland, Royal Arch Masonry is not officially recognized by the Grand Lodge, though the Grand Chapter of Royal Arch Masons for Scotland was formed in 1817.

Dr. W. J. Chetwode Crawley, in his *Cæmentaria Hibernica, Fasciculus I.*, says, "It (the Royal Arch Degree) is not a separate entity, but the completing part of a Masonic legend, a constituent ever present in the compound body, even before it developed into a Degree . . . if the Royal Arch fell into desuetude, the cope-stone would be removed, and the building left obviously incomplete."

[E. L. H.]

Royal Arch, Grand. The Thirty-first Degree of the Rite of Mizraim. It is nearly the same as the Thirteenth Degree of the Ancient and Accepted Scottish Rite.

Royal Arch Grand Bodies in America. The first meeting of delegates out of which arose the General Grand Chapter was at Boston, October 24, 1797. The convention adjourned to assemble at Hartford, in January,

1798, and it was there the Grand Chapter of the Northern States of America was organised. Again, on the 9th of January, 1799, an adjourned meeting was held, whereat it was resolved to change its name to that of "General Grand Royal Arch Chapter of the Northern States of America." On January 9, 1806, the present designation was adopted, to wit: "The General Grand Chapter of Royal Arch Masonry for the U. S. of America." New York was determined upon as the place for the first convocation, September, 1812, and the sessions to be made septennial. It failed to meet at the appointed time, but an important convocation was held in New York City, on June 6, 1816.

Joseph K. Wheeler, G. Secretary, in his introduction to the *Records of Capitular Masonry in the State of Connecticut*, says, after mentioning the names of the Chapters represented at the organization of the Grand Chapter in 1798: "In tracing their history it will be observed that all of these Chapters obtained their authority from a Washington Chapter in the city of New York, with the exception of Vanderbroeck, No. 5," chartered at an early date, by the G. Chapter of New York, after which no more Chapters were established by any authority outside the jurisdiction of Connecticut except Lynch Chapter, No. 8, located at Reading and Weston, which was chartered by the Grand Chapter of New York, August 23, 1801, which charter was signed by Francis Lynch, H. P. Grand Chapter of R. A. Masons; James Woods, King; and Samuel Clark, Scribe; which was admitted to membership in G. Chapter of Connecticut, May 19, 1808.

It is of interest here to note that the oldest Chapter in New York State is Ancient, No. 1, whose date of origin is lost, its records up to 1804 having been destroyed by fire, but tradition fixes the year 1763. For years it wielded the powers of a Grand Chapter, and until 1799 was known as the Old Grand Chapter. It granted charters for Chapters in New York, New Jersey, and Connecticut. In this last named State it issued a charter to Lynch Chapter (see above), which was received into full fellowship by the G. Chapter of Connecticut, although the G. Chapter of New York had been in existence some time before the charter was issued.

On the formation of the Grand Chapter of the State of New York, the numbers 1 and 2 were left vacant for the acceptance of Old and Washington Chapters (which latter was an offspring of the former), who at that time refused to place themselves under its jurisdiction. In 1806, Old Chapter enrolled itself as "Ancient" under the State Grand Body, accepted the number *one*, and was further honored by having its H. Priest, James Woods, elected Dep. G. H. Priest. (See *Pennsylvania*.) [C. T. McClenachan.]

Royal Arch Jewel. The jewel which every Royal Arch Mason is permitted to wear as a token of his connection with the Order. In America it is usually suspended by a scarlet ribbon to the button. In England it is to be worn pendant from a narrow ribbon on the left breast, the color of the ribbon varying with the rank of the wearer. It is of gold, and consists of a triple tau cross within a triangle, the whole circumscribed by a circle. This jewel is eminently symbolic, the *tau* being the mark mentioned by Ezekiel (ix. 4), by which those were distinguished who were to be saved from the wicked who were to be slain; the *triple tau* is symbolic of the peculiar and more eminent separation of Royal Arch Masons from the profane; the *triangle*, or *delta*, is a symbol of the sacred name of God, known

only to those who are thus separated; and the *circle* is a symbol of the eternal life, which is the great dogma taught by Royal Arch Masonry. Hence, by this jewel, the Royal Arch Mason makes the profession of his separation from the unholy and profane, his reverence for God, and his belief in the future and eternal life.

In America, the emblem worn by Royal Arch Masons without the Chapter is a Keystone, on which are the letters H. T. W. S. S. T. K. S. arranged in a circle and within the circle may or should be his mark.

Royal Arch Masonry. That division of Speculative Masonry which is engaged in the investigation of the mysteries connected with the Royal Arch, no matter under what name or in what Rite. Thus the mysteries of the Knight of the Ninth Arch constitute the Royal Arch Masonry of the Ancient and Accepted Scottish Rite just as much as those of the Royal Arch of Zerubbabel do the Royal Arch of the American Rite.

Royal Arch Masonry, Massachusetts. A statement of the origin and record of St. Andrew's Chapter in Boston is to trace early Royal Arch Masonry in Massachusetts. The following is extracted from Comp. Thomas Waterman's admirable history of St. Andrew's Royal Arch Chapter, the result of much earnest research: "The first meeting recorded of this Chapter was held on the 28th of August, 1769, and was then styled the Royal Arch Lodge, of which R. W. James Brown was Master." It is presumable this Lodge derived its authority from the Grand Lodge (Ancients) of England, as did that of the same name in Philadelphia, whereby it was authorized to confer the Holy Royal Arch Degree, as also did Independent Royal Arch, No. 2, of New York, but surrendered the right to confer the Royal Arch Degree when it joined the Grand Lodge of New York.

Comp. Waterman adds: "It appears by the record that the Degrees of 'Excellent, Super-Excellent, and Royal Arch' were conferred in the Royal Arch Lodge." Winthrop Gray, on April 17, 1770, was elected Master. On the succeeding May 14th, "Most Worshipful Joseph Warren, Esq.," was made a Royal Arch Mason. No record appears between March 26, 1773, and March 20, 1789. In an old register-book, dated April 1, 1789, is found "Original members, April 1, 1789, M. E. William McKeen, H. P." The next recorded election, October 21, 1790, gives William McKeen, R. A. Master. "On November 28, 1793, the Degree of Mark Masterwas connected with the other Degrees conferred in the Chapter." "January 30, 1794, the words 'Royal Arch Chapter' are used for the first time in recording the proceedings of the Chapter."

"The Grand Royal Arch Chapter of Massachusetts was organized by delegates from St. Andrew's Chapter, Boston, and King Cyrus' Chapter, Newburyport, who assembled at Masons' Hall, in the Green Dragon Tavern, Boston, on Tuesday, the 13th of March, A. D. 1798."

Royal Arch of Enoch. The Royal Arch system which is founded upon the legend of Enoch. (See *Enoch.*)

Royal Arch of Solomon. One of the names of the degree of Knight of the Ninth Arch, or Thirteenth Degree of the Ancient and Accepted Scottish Rite.

Royal Arch of Zerubbabel. The Royal Arch Degree of the American Rite is so called to distinguish it from the Royal Arch of Solomon in the Ancient and Accepted Scottish Rite.

Royal Arch Robes. In the working of a Royal Arch Chapter in the United States, great attention is paid to the robes of the several officers. The High Priest wears, in imitation of the high priest of the Jews, a robe of blue, purple, scarlet, and white linen, and is decorated with the breastplate and miter. The King wears a scarlet robe, and has a crown and scepter. The Scribe wears a purple robe and turban. The Captain of the Host wears a white robe and cap, and is armed with a sword. The Principal Sojourner wears a dark robe, with tessellated border, a slouched hat, and pilgrim's staff. The Royal Arch Captain wears a white robe and cap, and is armed with a sword. The three Grand Masters of the Veils wear, respectively, the Grand Master of the third veil a scarlet robe and cap, of the second veil a purple robe and cap, of the first veil a blue robe and cap. Each is armed with a sword. The Treasurer, Secretary, and Sentinel wear no robes nor peculiar dress. All of these robes have either an historical or symbolical allusion.

Royal Arch Tracing-Board. The oldest Royal Arch tracing-board extant is one which was formerly the property of a Chapter in the city of Chester, and which Dr. Oliver thinks was "used only a very few years after the degree was admitted into the system of constitutional Masonry." He has given a copy of it in his work *On the Origin of the English Royal Arch.* The symbols which it displays are, in the center of the top an arch scroll, with the words in Greek, ΕΝ ΑΡΧΗ ΗΝ Ο ΛΟΓΟΣ, i. e., *In the beginning was the Word;* beneath, the word JEHOVAH written in Kabbalistic letters; on the right side an arch and keystone, a rope falling in it, and a sun darting its rays obliquely; on the left a pot of incense beneath a rainbow; in the center of the tracing-board, two interlaced triangles and a sun in the center, all surrounded by a circle; on the right and left of this the seven-branched candlestick and the table of shew-bread. Beneath all, on three scrolls, are the words, "Solomon, King of Israel; Hiram, King of Tyre; Hiram, the Widow's Son," in Hebrew and Latin. Dr. Oliver finds in these emblems a proof that the Royal Arch was originally taken from the Master's Degree, because they properly belong to that degree, according to the English lecture, and were afterward restored to it. But the American Mason will find in this board how little his system has varied from the primitive one practised at Chester, since all the emblems, with the exception of the last three, are still recognized as Royal Arch symbols according to the American system.

Royal Arch Word. See *Tetragrammaton.*

Royal Arch Working-Tools. See *Working-Tools.*

Royal Ark Mariners. A side degree in England which is conferred on Mark Master Masons, and worked under the authority of the Grand Master of Mark Masons, assisted by a Royal Ark Council. The language of the Order is peculiar. The Supreme body is called a "Grand Ark"; subordinate Lodges are "vessels"; organizing a Lodge is "launching a vessel"; to open a Lodge is "to float an ark"; to close the Lodge is "to moor." All its references are nautical, and allude to the deluge and the ark of Noah. The degree is useless for any light that it sheds on Masonry. The degree seems to have been invented in England about the end of the last century. A correspondent of the London *Monthly Magazine* for December, 1798 (vol. vi., p. 424), calls it "one of the new degrees in Freemasonry," and thus describes the organization:

"They profess to be followers of Noah, and therefore call themselves Noachidæ, or Sons of Noah. Hence their President, who at present is Thomas Boothby Parkins, Lord Rancliffe, is dignified with the venerable title of GRAND NOAH, and the Lodge where they assemble is called the ROYAL ARK VESSEL.

"These brother mariners wear in Lodge time a broad sash ribbon, representing a rainbow, with an apron fancifully embellished with an ark, dove, etc.

"Among other rules of this society is one that no brother shall be permitted to enter as a mariner on board a Royal Ark vessel for any less sum than ten shillings and sixpence, of which sum sixpence shall be paid to the Grand and Royal Ark vessel for his registry, and the residue be disposed of at the discretion of the officers of the vessel."

Their principal place of meeting in London was at the Surry Tavern, Surry Street, in the Strand.

The writer gives the following verse from one of their songs written by Dr. Ebenezer Sibley, which does not speak much for the poetical taste of the Mariners or their laureate:

"They entered safe—lo! the deluge came
And none were protected but Masons and wives;
The crafty and knavish came floating along,
The rich and the beggar of profligate lives:
It was now in woe,
For mercy they call
To old Father Noah,
And loudly did bawl,
But Heaven shut the door and the ark was afloat,
To perish they must, for they were found out."

Royal Art. The earliest writers speak of Freemasonry as a "Royal Art." Anderson used the expression in 1723, and in such a way as to show that it was even then no new epithet. (*Constitutions*, 1723, p. 5.) The term has become common in all languages as an appellative of the Institution, and yet but few perhaps have taken occasion to examine into its real signification or have asked what would seem to be questions readily suggested, "Why is Freemasonry called an *art?*" and next, "Why is it said to be a *Royal Art?*"

The answer which is generally supposed to be a sufficient one for the latter inquiry, is that it is so called because many monarchs have been its disciples and its patrons, and some writers have gone so far as to particularize, and to say that Freemasonry was first called a "Royal Art" in 1693, when William III., of England, was initiated into its rites; and Gädicke, in his *Freimaurer Lexicon*, states that some have derived the title from the fact that in the times of the English Commonwealth, the members of the English Lodges had joined the party of the exiled Stuarts, and labored for the restoration of Charles II. to the throne. He himself, however, seems to think that Freemasonry is called a Royal Art because its object is to erect stately edifices, and especially palaces, the residences of kings.

Such an answer may serve for the profane, who can have no appreciation of a better reason, but it will hardly meet the demands of the intelligent initiate, who wants some more philosophic explanation—something more consistent with the moral and intellectual character of the Institution.

Let us endeavor to solve the problem, and to determine why Freemasonry is called an art at all; and why, above all others, it is dignified with the appellation of a Royal Art. Our first business will be to find a reply to the former question.

An art is distinguished from a handicraft in this, that the former consists of and supplies the principles which govern and direct the latter. The stone-mason, for instance, is guided in his construction of the building on which he is engaged by the principles which are furnished to him by the architect. Hence stone-masonry is a trade, a handicraft, or, as the German significantly expresses it, a *handwerk*, something which only requires the skill and labor of the hands to accomplish. But architecture is an art, because it is engaged in the establishment of principles and scientific tenets which the "handwork" of the Mason is to carry into practical effect.

The handicraftsman, the handworker, of course, is employed in manual labor. It is the work of his hands that accomplishes the purpose of his trade. But the artist uses no such means. He deals only in principles, and his work is of the head. He prepares his designs according to the principles of his art, and the workman obeys and executes them, often without understanding their ulterior object.

Now, let us apply this distinction to Freemasonry. Eighteen hundred years ago many thousand men were engaged in the construction of a Temple in the city of Jerusalem. They felled and prepared the timbers in the forests of Lebanon, and they hewed and cut and squared the stones in the quarries of Judea; and then they put them together under the direction of a skilful architect, and formed a goodly edifice, worthy to be called, as the Rabbis named it, "the chosen house of the Lord." For there, according to the Jewish ritual, in preference to all other places, was the God of Hosts to be worshiped in Oriental splendor. Something like this has been done thousands of times since. But the men who wrought with the stone-hammer and trowel at the Temple of Solomon, and the men who afterward wrought at the temples and cathedrals of Europe and Asia, were no artists. They were simply handicraftsmen—men raising an edifice by the labor of their hands—men who, in doing their work, were instructed by others skilful in art, but which art looked only to the totality, and had nothing to do with the operative details. The Giblemites, or stone-squarers, gave form to the stones and laid them in their proper places. But in what form they should be cut, and in what spots they should be laid so that the building might assume a proposed appearance, were matters left entirely to the superintending architect, the artist, who, in giving his instructions, was guided by the principles of his art.

Hence Operative Masonry is not an art. But after these handicraftsmen came other men, who, simulating, or, rather, symbolizing, their labors, converted the operative pursuit into a speculative system, and thus made of a handicraft an art. And it was in this wise that the change was accomplished.

The building of a temple is the result of a religious sentiment. Now, the Freemasons intended to organize a religious institution. I am not going into any discussion, at this time, of its history. When Freemasonry was founded is immaterial to the theory, provided that the foundation is made posterior to the time of the building of King Solomon's Temple. It is sufficient that it be admitted that in its foundation as an esoteric institution the religious idea prevailed, and that the development of this idea was the predominating object of its first organizers.

Borrowing, then, the name of their Institution from the operative masons who constructed the Temple at Jerusalem, by a very natural process they borrowed also the technical language and implements of the same handicraftsmen. But these they did not use for any manual purpose. They did not erect with them temples of stone, but were occupied solely in developing the religious idea which the construction of the material temple had first suggested; they symbolized this language and these implements, and thus established an art whose province and object it was to elicit religious thought, and to teach religious truth by a system of symbolism. And this symbolism—just as peculiar to Freemasonry as the doctrine of lines and surfaces is to geometry, or of numbers is to arithmetic—constitutes the art of Freemasonry.

If I were to define Freemasonry as an art, I should say that it was an art which taught the construction of a spiritual temple, just as the art of architecture teaches the construction of a material temple. And I should illustrate the train of ideas by which the Freemasons were led to symbolize the Temple of Solomon as a spiritual temple of man's nature, by borrowing the language of St. Peter, who says to his Christian initiates: "Ye also, as lively stones, are built up a spiritual house." And with greater emphasis, and as still more illustrative, would I cite the language of the Apostle of the Gentiles—that Apostle who, of all others, most delighted in symbolism, and who says: "Know ye not that ye are the temple of God, and that the spirit of God dwelleth in you?"

And this is the reason why Freemasonry is called an art.

Having thus determined the conditions under which Freemasonry becomes an art, the next inquiry will be why it has been distinguished from all other arts in being designated, *par excellence*, the *Royal Art*. And here we must abandon all thought that this title comes in any way from the connection of Freemasonry with earthly monarchs—from the patronage or the membership of kings. Freemasonry obtains no addition to its intrinsic value from a connection with the political heads of states. Kings, when they enter within its sacred portals, are no longer kings, but brethren. In the Lodge all men are on an equality, and there can be no distinction or preference, except that which is derived from virtue and intelligence. Although a great king once said that Freemasons made the best and truest subjects, yet in the Lodge is there no subjection save to the law of love—that law which, for its excellence above all other laws, has been called by an Apostle the "royal law," just as Freemasonry, for its excellence above all other arts, has been called the "Royal Art."

St. James says, in his general Epistle: "If ye fulfil the *royal law* according to the Scripture, Thou shalt love thy neighbor as thyself, ye do well." Dr. Adam Clarke, in his commentary on this passage—which is so appropriate to the subject we are investigating, and so thoroughly explanatory of this expression in its application to Freemasonry, that it is well worth a citation—uses the following language:

Speaking of the expression of St. James, *nomon basilicon*, "the royal law," he says: "This epithet, of all the New Testament writers, is peculiar to James; but it is frequent among the Greek writers in the sense in which it appears St. James uses it. Basilikos, *royal*, is used to signify anything that is of general concern, is suitable to all, and necessary for all, as brotherly love is. This commandment, *Thou shalt love thy neighbor as thyself*, is a *royal law;* not only because it is ordained of God, proceeds from his *kingly* authority over men, but because it is so useful, suitable, and necessary to the present state of man; and as it was given us particularly by Christ himself, who is our *king*, as well as prophet and priest, it should ever put us in mind of his authority over us, and our subjection to him. As the *regal state* is the most excellent for secular dignity and civil utility that exists among men, hence we give the epithet *royal* to whatever is excellent, noble, grand, or useful."

How beautifully and appropriately does all this definition apply to Freemasonry as a Royal Art. It has already been shown how the art of Freemasonry consisted in a symbolization of the technical language and implements and labors of an operative society to a moral and spiritual purpose. The Temple which was constructed by the builders at Jerusalem was taken as the groundwork. Out of this the Freemasons have developed an admirable science of symbolism, which on account of its design, and on account of the means by which that design is accomplished, is well entitled, for its "excellence, nobility, grandeur, and utility," to be called the "Royal Art."

The stone-masons at Jerusalem were engaged in the construction of a material temple. But the Freemasons who succeeded them are occupied in the construction of a moral and spiritual temple, man being considered, through the process of the act of symbolism, that holy house. And in this symbolism the Freemasons have only developed the same idea that was present to St. Paul when he said to the Corinthians that they were "God's building," of which building he, "as a wise master-builder, had laid the foundation"; and when, still further extending the metaphor, he told the Ephesians that they were "built upon the foundation of the apostles and prophets, Jesus Christ himself being the chief cornerstone, in whom all the building fitly framed together, groweth unto a holy temple in the Lord; in whom also ye are builded together for a habitation of God through the spirit."

This, then, is the true art of Freemasonry. It is an art which teaches the right method of symbolising the technical language and the material labors of a handicraft, so as to build up in man a holy house for the habitation of God's spirit; to give perfection to man's nature; to give purity to humanity, and to unite mankind in one common bond.

It is singular, and well worthy of notice, how this symbolism of building up man's body into a holy temple, so common with the New Testament writers, and even with Christ himself—for he speaks of man as a temple which, being destroyed, he could raise up in three days; in which, as St. John says, "he spake of the temple of his body"—gave rise to a new word or to a word with a new meaning in all the languages over which Christianity exercises any influence. The old Greeks had from the two words *oikos*, "a house," and *domein*, "to build," constructed the word *oikodomein*, which of course signified "to build a house." In this plain and exclusive sense it is used by the Attic writers. In like manner. the Romans, out of the two words *ædes*, "a house," and *facere*, "to make," constructed their word *ædificare*, which always meant simply "to build a house," and in this plain sense it is used by Horace, Cicero, and all the old writers. But when the New Testament writers began to symbolize man as a temple or holy house for the habitation of the Lord, and when they spoke of building up this symbolic house, although it was a moral and spiritual growth to which they alluded, they used the Greek word *oikodomein*, and their first translators, the Latin word *ædificare* in a new sense, meaning "to build up morally," that is, to educate, to instruct. And as modern nations learned the faith of Christianity, they imbibed this symbolic idea of a moral building, and adapted for its expression a new word or gave to an old word a new meaning, so that it has come to pass that in French *edifier*, in Italian *edificare*, in Spanish *edificar*, in German *erbauen*, and in English *edify*, each of which literally and etymologically means "to build a house," has also the other signification, "to instruct, to improve, to educate." And thus we speak of a marble building as a magnificent edifice, and of a wholesome doctrine as something that will edify its hearers. There are but few who, when using the word in this latter sense, think of that grand science of symbolism which gave birth to this new meaning, and which constitutes the very essence of the Royal Art of Freemasonry.

For when this temple is built up, it is to be held together only by the cement of love. Brotherly love, the love of our neighbor as ourself—that love which suffereth long and is kind, which is not easily provoked, and thinketh no evil—that love pervades the whole system of Freemasonry, not only binding all the moral parts of man's nature into one harmonious whole, the building being thus, in the language of St. Paul, "fitly framed together," but binding man to man, and man to God.

And hence Freemasonry is called a "Royal Art," because it is of all arts the most noble; the art which teaches man how to perfect his temple of virtue by pursuing the "royal law" of universal love, and not because kings have been its patrons and encouragers.

A similar idea is advanced in a Catechism published by the celebrated Lodge "Wahreit und Einigkeit," at Prague, in the year 1800, where the following questions and answers occur:

Q. "What do Freemasons build?

A. "An invisible temple, of which King Solomon's Temple is the symbol.

Q. "By what name is the instruction how to erect this mystic building called?

A. "*The Royal Art;* because it teaches man how to govern himself."

Appositely may these thoughts be closed with a fine expression of Ludwig Bechstein, a German writer, in the *Astræa*.

"Every king will be a Freemason, even though he wears no Mason's apron, if he shall be God-fearing, sincere, good, and kind; if he shall be true and fearless, obedient to the law, his heart abounding in reverence for religion and full of love for mankind; if he shall be a ruler of himself, and if his kingdom be founded on justice. And every Freemason is a king, in whatsoever condition God may have placed him here, with rank equal to that of a king and with sentiments that become a king, for his kingdom is LOVE, the love of his fellow-man, a love which is long-suffering and kind, which beareth all things, believeth all things, hopeth all things, endureth all things."

And this is why Freemasonry is an art, and of all arts, being the most noble, is well called the "Royal Art."

Royal Ax. See *Knight of the Royal Ax.*

Royal Lodge. The Royal Arch lectures in the English system say that the Royal Lodge was held in the city of Jerusalem, on the return of the Babylonish captives, in the first year in the reign of Cyrus; over it presided Zerubbabel the prince of the Jews, Haggai the prophet, and Joshua the high priest.

Royal Master. The Eighth Degree of the American Rite, and the first of the degrees conferred in a Council of Royal and Select Masters. Its officers are a Thrice Illustrious Grand Master, representing King Solomon; Illustrious Hiram of Tyre, Principal Conductor of the Works, representing Hiram Abif; Master of the Exchequer, Master of Finances, Captain of the Guards, Conductor of the Council and Steward. The place of meeting is called the "Council Chamber," and represents the private apartment of King Solomon, in which he is said to have met for consultation with his two colleagues during the construction of the Temple. Candidates who receive this degree are said to be "honored with the degree of Royal Master." Its symbolic colors are black and red—the former significant of grief, and the latter of martyrdom, and both referring to the chief builder of the Temple.

The events recorded in this degree, looking at them in a legendary point of view, must have occurred at the building of the first Temple, and during that brief period of time after the death of the builder which is embraced between the discovery of his body and its "Masonic interment." In all the initiations into the mysteries of the ancient world, there was, as it is well known to scholars, a legend of the violent death of some distinguished personage, to whose memory the particular mystery was consecrated, of the concealment of the body, and of its subsequent discovery. That part of the initiation which referred to the concealment of the body was called the *Aphanism*, from a Greek verb which signifies "to conceal," and that part which referred to the subsequent finding was called the *euresis*, from another Greek verb which signifies "to discover." It is impossible to avoid seeing the coincidences between the system of initiation and that practised in the Masonry of the Third Degree. But the ancient initiation was not terminated by the *euresis* or discovery. Up to that point, the ceremonies had been funereal and lugubrious in their character. But now they were changed from wailing to rejoicing. Other ceremonies were performed by which the restoration of the personage to life, or his apotheosis or change to immortality, was represented, and then came the *autopsy* or illumination of the neophyte, when he was invested with a full knowledge of all the religious doctrines which it was the object of the ancient mysteries to teach—when, in a word, he was instructed in Divine truth.

Now, a similar course is pursued in Masonry. Here also there is an illumination, a symbolic teaching, or, as we call it, an *investiture* with that which is the representative of Divine truth. The communication to the candidate, in the Master's Degree, of that which is admitted to be merely a representation of or a substitution for that symbol of Divine truth (the search for which, under the name of the *true word*, makes so important a part of the degree), how imperfect it may be in comparison with that more thorough knowledge which only future researches can enable the Master Mason to attain, constitutes the *autopsy* of the Third Degree. Now, the principal event recorded in the legend of the Royal Master, the interview between Adoniram and his two Royal Masters, is to be placed precisely at that juncture of time which is between the *euresis* or discovery in the Master Mason's Degree and the autopsy, or investiture with the great secret. It occurred between the discovery by means of the sprig of acacia and the final interment. It was at the time when Solomon and his colleague, Hiram of Tyre, were in profound consultation as to the mode of repairing the loss which they then supposed had befallen them.

We must come to this conclusion, because there is abundant reference, both in the organised form of the Council and in the ritual of the degree, to the death as an event that had already occurred; and, on the other hand, while it is evident that Solomon had been made acquainted with the failure to recover, on the person of the builder, that which had been lost, there is no reference whatever to the well-known *substitution* which was made at the time of the interment.

If, therefore, as is admitted by all Masonic ritualists, the *substitution* was precedent and preliminary to the establishment of the Master Mason's Degree, it is evident that at the time that the degree of Royal Master is said to have been founded in the ancient Temple, by our "first Most Excellent Grand Master," all persons present, except the first and second officers, must have been merely Fellow-Craft Masons. In compliance with this tradition, therefore, a Royal Master is, at this day, supposed to represent a Fellow-Craft in the search, and making his demand for that reward which was to elevate him to the rank of a Master Mason.

If from the legendary history we proceed to the symbolism of the degree, we shall find that, brief and simple as are the ceremonies, they present the great Masonic idea of the laborer seeking for his reward. Throughout all the symbolism of Masonry, from the first to the last degree, the search for the WORD has been considered but as a symbolic expression for the search after TRUTH. The attainment of this truth has always been acknowledged to be the great object and design of all Masonic labor. Divine truth—the knowledge of God—concealed in the old Kabbalistic doctrine, under the symbol of his ineffable name—and typified in the Masonic system under the mystical expression of the True Word, is the reward proposed to every Mason who has faithfully wrought his task. It is, in short, the "Master's wages."

Now, all this is beautifully symbolised

in the degree of Royal Master. The reward has been promised, and the time had now come, as Adoniram thought, when the promise was to be redeemed, and the true word—Divine truth—was to be imparted. Hence, in the person of Adoniram, or the Royal Master, we see symbolized the Speculative Mason, who, having labored to complete his spiritual temple, comes to the Divine Master that he may receive his reward, and that his labor may be consummated by the acquisition of truth. But the temple that he had been building is the temple of this life; that first temple which must be destroyed by death that the second temple of the future life may be built on its foundations. And in this first temple the truth cannot be found. We must be contented with its substitute.

Royal Order of Scotland. This is an Order of Freemasonry confined exclusively to the kingdom of Scotland, and which, formerly conferred on Master Masons, is now restricted to those who have been exalted to the Royal Arch Degree. It consists of two degrees, namely, that of H. R. D. M. and R. S. Y. C. S., or, in full, *Heredom* and *Rosy Cross*. The first may be briefly described as a Christianized form of the Third Degree, purified from the dross of Paganism, and even of Judaism, by the Culdees, who introduced Christianity into Scotland in the early centuries of the church. The Second Degree is an Order of civil knighthood, supposed to have been founded by Robert Bruce after the battle of Bannockburn, and conferred by him upon certain Masons who had assisted him on that memorable occasion. He, so the tradition goes, gave power to the Grand Master of the Order for the time being to confer this honor, which is not inherent in the general body itself, but is specially given by the Grand Master and his Deputy, and can be conferred only by them, or Provincial Grand Masters appointed by them. The number of knights is limited, and formerly only sixty-three could be appointed, and they Scotchmen; now, however, that number has been much increased, and distinguished Masons of all countries are admitted to its ranks. In 1747, Prince Charles Edward Stuart, in his celebrated Charter to Arras is said to have claimed to be the Sovereign Grand Master of the Royal Order, "Nous Charles Edouard Stewart, Roi d'Angleterre, de France, de l'Ecosse, et d'Irlande, et en cette qualité, S. G. M. du Chapitre de H." Prince Charles goes on to say that H. O. or H. R. M. is known as the "Pelican and Eagle." "Connu sous le titre de Chevalier de l'Aigle et de Pelican, et depuis nos malheurs et nos infortunes, sous celui de Rose Croix." Now, there is not the shadow of a proof that the Rose Croix, says Bro. Reitam, was ever known in England till twenty years after 1747; and in Ireland it was introduced by a French chevalier, M. L'Aurent, about 1782 or 1783. The Chapter at Arras was the first constituted in France—"Chapitre primordial de Rose Croix"; and from other circumstances (the very name Rose Croix being a translation of R. S. Y. C. S.) some writers have been led to the conclusion that the degree chartered by Prince Charles Edward Stuart was, if not the actual Royal Order in both points, a Masonic ceremony founded on and pirated from that most ancient and venerable Order.

This, however, is an error; because, except in name, there does not appear to be the slightest connection between the Rose Croix and the Royal Order of Scotland. In the first place, the whole ceremonial is different, and different in essentials. Most of the language used in the Royal Order is couched in quaint old rime, modernized, no doubt, to make it "understanded of the vulgar," but still retaining sufficient about it to stamp its genuine antiquity. The Rose Croix Degree is most probably the genuine descendant of the old Rosicrucians, and no doubt it has always had a more or less close connection with the Templars.

Clavel says that the Royal Order of Heredom of Kilwinning is a Rosicrucian degree, having many different gradations in the ceremony of consecration. The kings of England are *de jure*, if not *de facto*, Grand Masters; each member has a name given him, denoting some moral attribute. In the initiation the sacrifice of the Messiah is had in remembrance, who shed his blood for the sins of the world, and the neophyte is in a figure sent forth to seek the lost word. The ritual states that the Order was first established at Icomkill, and afterward at Kilwinning, where the King of Scotland, Robert Bruce, took the chair in person; and oral tradition affirms that, in 1314, this monarch again reinstated the Order, admitting into it the Knights Templar who were still left. The Royal Order, according to this ritual, which is written in Anglo-Saxon verse, boasts of great antiquity.

Findel disbelieves in the Royal Order, as he does in all the Christian degrees. He remarks that the Grand Lodge of Scotland formerly knew nothing at all about the existence of this Order of Heredom, as a proof of which he adduces the fact that Laurie, in the first edition of his *History of the Grand Lodge of Scotland*, has not mentioned it. Oliver, however, as it will be seen, had a high opinion of the Order, and expressed no doubt of its antiquity.

As to the origin of the Order, we have abundant authority both mythical and historical.

Thory (*Act. Lat.*, i., 6) thus traces its establishment:

"On the 24th of June, 1314, Robert Bruce, king of Scotland, instituted, after the battle of Bannockburn, the Order of St. Andrew of the Thistle, to which was afterward united that of H. D. M., for the sake of the Scottish Masons who had composed a part of the thirty thousand men with whom he had fought the English army, consisting of one hundred thousand. He formed the Royal Grand Lodge of the Order of H. D. M. at Kilwinning, reserving to himself and his successors forever the title of Grand Masters."

Oliver, in his *Historical Landmarks* (ii., 15), defines the Order more precisely, thus:

"The Royal Order of H. R. D. M. had formerly its chief seat at Kilwinning, and there is every reason to think that it and St. John's Masonry were then governed by the same Grand Lodge. But during the sixteenth and seventeenth centuries Masonry was at a very low ebb in Scotland, and it was with the greatest difficulty that St. John's Masonry was preserved. The Grand Chapter of H. R. D. M. resumed its functions about the middle of the last century at Edinburgh; and, in order to preserve a marked distinction between the Royal Order and Craft Masonry,—which had formed a Grand Lodge there in 1736,—the former confined itself solely to the two degrees of H. R. D. M. and R. S. Y. C. S."

Again, in the history of the Royal Order, officially printed in Scotland, the following details are found:

"It is composed of two parts, H. R. M. and R. S. Y. C. S. The former took its rise in the reign of David I., king of Scotland, and the latter in that of King Robert the Bruce. The last is believed to have been originally the same as the most ancient Order of the Thistle, and to contain the ceremonial of admission formerly practised in it.

"The Order of H. R. M. had formerly its seat at Kilwinning, and there is reason to suppose that it and the Grand Lodge of St. John's Masonry were governed by the same Grand Master. The introduction of this Order into Kilwinning appears to have taken place about the same time, or nearly the same period, as the introduction of Freemasonry into Scotland. The Chaldees, as is well known, introduced Christianity into Scotland; and, from their known habits, there are good grounds for believing that they preserved among them a knowledge of the ceremonies and precautions adopted for their protection in Judea. In establishing the degree in Scotland, it is more than probable that it was done with the view to explain, in a correct Christian manner, the symbols and rites employed by the Christian architects and builders; and this will also explain how the Royal Order is purely catholic,—not Roman Catholic,—but adapted to all who acknowledge the great truths of Christianity, in the same way that Craft or Symbolic Masonry is intended for all, whether Jew or Gentile, who acknowledge a supreme God. The second part, or R. S. Y. C. S., is an Order of Knighthood, and, perhaps, the only genuine one in connection with Masonry, there being in it an intimate connection between the trowel and the sword, which others try to show. The lecture consists of a figurative description of the ceremonial, both of H. R. M. and R. S. Y. C. S., in simple rhyme, modernized, of course, by oral tradition, and breathing the purest spirit of Christianity. Those two degrees constitute, as has already been said, the Royal Order of Scotland, the Grand Lodge of Scotland. Lodges or Chapters cannot legally meet elsewhere, unless possessed of a Charter from it or the Grand Master, or his deputy. The office of Grand Master is vested in the person of the king of Scotland, (now of Great Britain,) and one seat is invariably kept vacant for him in whatever country a Chapter is opened, and cannot be occupied by any other member. Those who are in possession of this degree, and the so-called higher degrees, cannot fail to perceive that the greater part of them have been concocted from the Royal Order, to satisfy the morbid craving for distinction which was so characteristic of the continent during the latter half of the last century.

"There is a tradition among the Masons of Scotland that, after the dissolution of the Templars, many of the Knights repaired to Scotland and placed themselves under the protection of Robert Bruce, and that, after the battle of Bannockburn, which took place on St. John the Baptist's day, 1314, this monarch instituted the Royal Order of H. R. M. and Knights of the R. S. Y. C. S., and established the chief seat at Kilwinning. From that Order it seems by no means improbable that the present degree of Rose Croix de Heredom may have taken its origin. In two respects, at least, there seems to be a very close connection between the two systems. They both claim the kingdom of Scotland and the Abbey of Kilwinning as having been at one time the chief seat of government, and they both seem to have been instituted to give a Christian explanation to Ancient Craft Masonry. There is, besides, a similarity in the name of the degrees of Rose Croix de Heredom and H. R. M. and R. S. Y. C. S. amounting almost to an identity, which appears to indicate a very intimate relation of one to the other."

And now recently there comes Bro. Randolph Hay, of Glasgow, who, in the London *Freemason*, gives us this legend, which he is pleased to call "the real history of the Royal Order," and which he, at least, religiously believes to be true:

"Among the many precious things which were carefully preserved in a sacred vault of King Solomon's Temple was a portrait of the monarch, painted by Adoniram, the son of Elkanah, priest of the second court. This vault remained undiscovered till the time of Herod, although the secret of its existence and a description of its locality were retained by the descendants of Elkanah. During the war of the Maccabees, certain Jews, fleeing from their native country, took refuge, first in Spain and afterward in Britain, and amongst them was one Aholiab, the then possessor of the document necessary to find the hidden treasure. As is well known, buildings were then in progress in Edinburgh, or Dun

Edwin, as the city was then called, and thither Aholiab wended his way to find employment. His skill in architecture speedily raised him to a prominent position in the Craft, but his premature death prevented his realizing the dream of his life, which was to fetch the portrait from Jerusalem and place it in the custody of the Craft. However, prior to his dissolution, he confided the secret to certain of the Fraternity under the bond of secrecy, and these formed a class known as 'The Order of the King,' or 'The Royal Order.' Time sped on; the Romans invaded Britain; and, previous to the crucifixion, certain members of the old town guard of Edinburgh, among whom were several of the Royal Order, proceeded to Rome to enter into negotiations with the sovereign. From thence they proceeded to Jerusalem, and were present at the dreadful scene of the crucifixion. They succeeded in obtaining the portrait, and also the blue veil of the Temple rent upon the terrible occasion. I may dismiss these two venerable relics in a few words. Wilson, in his *Memorials of Edinburgh*, (2 vols., published by Hugh Patton,) in a note to Masonic Lodges, writes that this portrait was then in the possession of the brethren of the Lodge St. David. This is an error, and arose from the fact of the Royal Order then meeting in the Lodge St. David's room in Hindford's Close. The blue veil was converted into a standard for the trades of Edinburgh, and became celebrated on many a battle-field, notably in the First Crusade as 'The Blue Blanket.' From the presence of certain of their number in Jerusalem on the occasion in question, the Edinburgh City Guard were often called Pontius Pilate's Prætorians. Now, these are facts well known to many Edinburghers still alive. Let 'X. Y. Z.' go to Edinburgh and inquire for himself.

"The brethren, in addition, brought with them the teachings of the Christians, and in their meetings they celebrated the death of the Captain and Builder of our Salvation. The oath of the Order seals my lips further as to the peculiar mysteries of the brethren. I may, however, state that the Ritual, in verse, as in present use, was composed by the venerable Abbot of Inchaffray, the same who, with a crucifix in his hand, passed along the Scots' line, blessing the soldiers and the cause in which they were engaged, previous to the battle of Bannockburn. Thus the Order states justly that it was revived, that is, a profounder spirit of devotion infused into it, by King Robert, by whose directions the Abbot reorganized it."

In this account, it is scarcely necessary to say that there is far more of myth than of legitimate history.

The King of Scotland is hereditary Grand Master of the Order, and at all assemblies a chair is kept vacant for him.

Provincial Grand Lodges are held at Glasgow, Rouen in France, in Sardinia, Spain, the Netherlands, Calcutta, Bombay, China, and New Brunswick. The Provincial Grand Lodge of London was established in July, 1872, and there the membership is confined to those who have previously taken the Rose Croix, or Eighteenth Degree of the Ancient and Accepted Scottish Rite.

Royal Priest. The Fifth Degree of the Initiated Brothers of Asia, also called the True Rose Croix.

Royal Secret, Sublime Prince of the. See *Sublime Prince of the Royal Secret.*

R. S. Y. C. S. An abbreviation of *Rosy Cross* in the Royal Order of Scotland.

Ruchiel. In the old Jewish Angelology, the name of the angel who ruled the air and the winds. The angel in charge of one of the four tests in Philosophic Masonry.

Ruffians. The traitors of the Third Degree are called *Assassins* in continental Masonry and in the high degrees. The English and American Masons have adopted in their ritual the more homely appellation of *Ruffians*. The fabricators of the high degrees adopted a variety of names for these Assassins (see *Assassins of the Third Degree*), but the original names are preserved in the rituals of the York and American Rites. There is no question that has so much perplexed Masonic antiquaries as the true derivation and meaning of these three names. In their present form, they are confessedly uncouth and without apparent signification. Yet it is certain that we can trace them in that form to the earliest appearance of the legend of the Third Degree, and it is equally certain that at the time of their adoption some meaning must have been attached to them. I am convinced that this must have been a very simple one, and one that would have been easily comprehended by the whole of the Craft, who were in the constant use of them. Attempts, it is true, have been made to find the root of these three names in some recondite reference to the Hebrew names of God. But there is, I think, no valid authority for any such derivation. In the first place, the character and conduct of the supposed possessors of these names preclude the idea of any congruity and appropriateness between them and any of the Divine names. And again, the literary condition of the Craft at the time of the invention of the names equally precludes the probability that any names would have been fabricated of a recondite signification, and which could not have been readily understood and appreciated by the ordinary class of Masons who were to use them. The names must naturally have been of a construction that would convey a familiar idea, would be suitable to the incidents in which they were to be employed, and would be congruous with the character of the individuals upon whom they were to be bestowed. Now all these requisites meet in a word which was entirely familiar to the Craft at the time when these names were probably invented. The *Ghiblim* are spoken of by Anderson, meaning *Giblim*, as stone-cutters or Masons; and the early rituals show us very clearly that the Fraternity in that day considered *Giblim* as the name of a Mason; not only of a Mason generally, but especially of that class of Masons who, as Drummond says, "put the finishing hand to King Solomon's Temple"—that is to say, the Fellow-Crafts. Anderson also places the *Ghiblim* among the Fellow-Crafts; and so, very naturally, the early Freemasons, not imbued with any amount of Hebrew learning, and not making a distinction between the singular and plural forms of that language, soon got to calling a Fellow-Craft a *Giblim*. The steps of corruption between *Giblim* and *Jubelum* were not very gradual; nor can anyone doubt that such corruptions of spelling and pronunciation were common among these illiterate Masons, when he reads the Old Manuscripts, and finds such verbal distortions as *Nembroch* for *Nimrod*, *Euglet* for *Euclid*, and *Aymon* for *Hiram*. Thus, the first corruption was from *Giblim* to *Gibalim*, which brought the word to three syllables, making it thus nearer to its eventual change. Then we find in the early rituals another transformation into *Chibbelum*. The French Masons also took the work of corruption in hand, and from *Giblim* they manufactured *Jiblime* and *Jibulum* and *Jabulum*. Some of these French corruptions came back to English Masonry about the time of the fabrication of the high degrees, and even the French words were distorted. Thus in the Leland Manuscript, the English Masons made out of *Pytagore*, the French for *Pythagoras*, the unknown name *Peter Gower*, which is said so much to have puzzled Mr. Locke. And so we may through these mingled English and French corruptions trace the genealogy of the word Jubelum; thus, Ghiblim, Giblim, Gibalim, Chibbelum, Jiblime, Jibelum, Jabelum, and, finally, Jubelum. It meant simply a Fellow-Craft, and was appropriately given as a common name to a particular Fellow-Craft who was distinguished for his treachery. In other words, he was designated, not by a special and distinctive name, but by the title of his condition and rank at the Temple. He was *the Fellow-Craft*, who was at the head of a conspiracy. As for the names of the other two Ruffians, they were readily constructed out of that of the greatest one by a simple change of the termination of the word from *um* to *a* in one, and from *um* to *o* in the other, thus preserving, by a similarity of names, the idea of their relationship, for the old rituals said that they were brothers who had come together out of Tyre. This derivation seems to me to be easy, natural, and comprehensible. The change from *Giblim*, or rather from *Gibalim* to *Jubelum*, is one that is far less extraordinary than that which one-half of the Masonic words have undergone in their transformation from their original to their present form.

Rule. An instrument with which straight lines are drawn, and therefore used in the Past Master's Degree as an emblem admonishing the Master punctually to observe his duty, to press forward in the path of virtue, and, neither inclining to the right nor the left, in all his actions to have eternity in view. The twenty-four-inch gage is often used in giving the instruction as a substitute for this working-tool. But they are entirely different; the twenty-four-inch gage is one of the working-tools of an Entered Apprentice, and requires to have the twenty-four inches marked upon its surface; the rule is one of the working-tools of a Past Master, and is without the twenty-four divisions. The rule is appropriated to the Past or Present Master, because, by its assistance, he is enabled to lay down on the trestle-board the designs for the Craft to work by.

Rule of the Templars. The code of regulations for the government of the Knights Templars, called their "Rule," was drawn up by St. Bernard, and by him submitted to Pope Honorius II. and the Council of Troyes, by both of whom it was approved. It is still in existence, and consists of seventy-two articles, partly monastic and partly military in character, the former being formed upon the Rule of the Benedictines. The first articles of the Rule are ecclesiastical in design, and require from the Knights a strict adherence to their religious duties. Article twenty defines the costume to be worn by the brotherhood. The professed soldiers were to wear a white costume, and the serving brethren were prohibited from wearing anything but a black or brown cassock. The Rule is very particular in reference to the fit and shape of the dress of the Knights, so as to secure uniformity. The brethren are forbidden to receive and open letters from their friends without first submitting them to the inspection of their superiors. The pastime of hawking is prohibited, but the nobler sport of lion-hunting is permitted, because the lion, like the devil, goes about continually roaring, seeking whom he may devour. Article fifty-five relates to the reception of married members, who are required to bequeath the greater portion of their property to the Order. The fifty-eighth article regulates the reception of aspirants, or secular persons, who are not to be received immediately on their application into the society, but are required first to submit to an examination as to sincerity and fitness. The seventy-second and concluding article refers to the intercourse of the Knights with females. No brother was allowed to kiss a woman, though she were his mother or sister. "Let the soldier of the cross," says St. Bernard, "shun all ladies' lips." At first this rule was rigidly enforced, but in time it was greatly relaxed, and the picture of the interior of a house of the Temple, as portrayed by the Abbot of Clairvaux, would scarcely have been appropriate a century or two later.

Rulers. Obedience to constituted authority has always been inculcated by the laws of Masonry. Thus, in the installation charges as prefixed to the Constitutions of the

Grand Lodge of England, the incoming Master is required to promise "to hold in veneration the original *rulers* and patrons of the Order of Freemasonry, and their regular successors, supreme and subordinate, according to their stations."

Russia. In 1731 Capt. John Philips was appointed to be Provincial Grand Master of Russia by Lord Lovel, Grand Master of England (*Constitutions*, 1738, p. 194), but it does not follow that there were any Lodges in Russia at that time. It is said that there was a Lodge in St. Petersburg as early as 1732; but its meetings must have been private, as the first notice that we have of a Lodge openly assembling in the empire is that of "Silence," established at St. Petersburg, and the "North Star" at Riga, both in the year 1750. Thory says that Masonry made but little progress in Russia until 1763, when the Empress Catherine II. declared herself the Protectress of the Order.

In 1765 the Rite of Melesino, a Rite unknown in any other country, was introduced by a Greek of that name; and there were at the same time the York, Swedish, and Strict Observance Rites practised by other Lodges. In 1783 twelve of these Lodges united and formed the National Grand Lodge, which, rejecting the other Rites, adopted the Swedish system. For a time Masonry flourished with unalloyed prosperity and popularity. But about the year 1794, the Empress, becoming alarmed at the political condition of France, and being persuaded that the members of some of the Lodges were in opposition to the government, withdrew her protection from the Order. She did not, however, direct the Lodges to be closed, but most of them, in deference to the wishes of the sovereign, ceased to meet. The few that continued to work were placed under the surveillance of the police, and soon languished, holding their communications only at distant intervals. In 1797, Paul I., instigated by the Jesuits, whom he had recalled, interdicted the meetings of all secret societies, and especially the Masonic Lodges. Alexander succeeded Paul in 1801, and renewed the interdict of his predecessor. In 1803, M. Boeber, counselor of state and director of the school of cadets at St. Petersburg, obtained an audience of the Emperor, and succeeded in removing his prejudices against Freemasonry. In that year, the edict was revoked, the Emperor himself was initiated in one of the revived Lodges, and the Grand Orient of all the Russias was established, of which M. Boeber was deservedly elected Grand Master. (*Acta Latomorum*, i., 218.) Freemasonry now again flourished, although in 1817 there were two Grand Lodges, that of Astrea, which worked on the system of tolerating all Rites, and a Provincial Lodge, which practised the Swedish system.

But suddenly, on the 12th of August, 1822, the Emperor Alexander, instigated, it is said, by the political condition of Poland, issued a decree ordering all the Lodges to be closed, and forbidding the erection of any new ones. The order was quietly obeyed by the Freemasons of Russia, and is still in force.

Russia, Secret Societies of. First, the Skopzis, founded about 1740, by Seliwanoff, on the ruins of an anterior sect, the Chlysty, which was originated by a peasant named Philippoff, in the seventeenth century. The Skopzis practise self-mutilation and other horrors. They are rich, and abound throughout Russia and in Bulgaria. Second, the Montainists, who declare that they have a "living Christ," a "living Mother of God," a "living Holy Spirit," and twelve "living Apostles." Their ceremonies are peculiar and but little resembling those of Masonry.

S

S. (Heb. ס, *Samech.*) The nineteenth letter in the English alphabet. Its numerical value is 60. The sacred application to the Deity is in the name Somech, סומך, *Fulcieus* or *Firmas*. The Hebrew letter Shin (a tooth, from its formation, ש) is of the numerical value of 300.

Saadh. One of a certain Indian sect, who have embraced Christianity, and who in some respects resemble the Quakers in their doctrine and mode of life. Sometimes written *saud*.

Sabaism. The worship of the sun, moon, and stars, the צבא השמים, Tsaba *Hashmaim*, "the host of heaven." It was practised in Persia, Chaldea, India, and other Oriental countries, at an early period of the world's history. (See *Blazing Star* and *Sun Worship*.)

Sabaoth. יהוה צבאות, *Jehovah Tsabaoth*, Jehovah of Hosts, a very usual appellation for the Most High in the prophetical books, especially in Isaiah, Jeremiah, Zechariah, and Malachi, but not found in the Pentateuch.

Sabbal. ("The Burthen.") The name of the sixth step of the mystic ladder of Kadosh of the A. A. Scottish Rite.

Sabbath. In the lecture of the Second or Fellow-Craft's Degree, it is said, In six days God created the heavens and the earth, and rested upon the seventh day;

the seventh, therefore, our ancient brethren consecrated as a day of rest from their labors, thereby enjoying frequent opportunities to contemplate the glorious works of creation, and to adore their great Creator.

Sabianism. See *Sabaism.*

Sacellum. A walled enclosure without roof. An ornamental chapel within a church.

Sackcloth. In the Rose Croix ritual, sackcloth is a symbol of grief and humiliation for the loss of that which it is the object of the degree to recover.

Sacred Asylum of High Masonry. In the *Institutes, Statutes, and Regulations,* signed by Adington, Chancellor, which are given in the *Recueil des Actes du Suprème Conseil du France,* as a sequence to the Constitutions of 1762, this title is given to any subordinate body of the Scottish Rite. Thus in Article XVI.: "At the time of the installation of a Sacred Asylum of High Masonry, the members composing it shall all make and sign their pledge of obedience to the Institutes, Statutes, and General Regulations of High Masonry." In this document the Rite is always called "High Masonry," and any body, whether a Lodge of Perfection, a Chapter of Rose Croix, or a Council of Kadosh, is styled a "Sacred Asylum."

Sacred Law. The first Tables of Stone, or Commandments, which were delivered to Moses on Mount Sinai, are referred to in a preface to the *Mishna,* bearing this tradition: "God not only delivered the Law to Moses on Mount Sinai, but the explanation of it likewise. When Moses came down from the Mount and entered into his tent, Aaron went to visit him, and Moses acquainted Aaron with the Laws he had received from God, together with the explanation of them. After this Aaron placed himself at the right hand of Moses, and Eleazar and Ithamar (the sons of Aaron) were admitted, to whom Moses repeated what he had just before told to Aaron. These being seated, the one on the right hand, the other on the left hand of Moses, the seventy elders of Israel, who compose the Sanhedrim, came in, and Moses again declared the same laws to them, as he had done before to Aaron and his sons. Lastly, all who pleased of the common people were invited to enter, and Moses instructed them likewise in the same manner as the rest. So that Aaron heard four times what Moses had been taught by God upon Mount Sinai, Eleazar and Ithamar three times, the seventy elders twice, and the people once. Moses afterward reduced the laws which he had received into writing, but not the explanation of them. These he thought it sufficient to trust to the memories of the above-mentioned persons, who, being perfectly instructed in them, delivered them to their children, and these again to theirs, from age to age."

The Sacred Law is repeated in the ritual of the Fourteenth Degree A. A. Scottish Rite.

Sacred Lodge. In the lectures according to the English system, we find this definition of the "Sacred Lodge." The symbol has not been preserved in the American ritual. Over the Sacred Lodge presided Solomon, the greatest of kings, and the wisest of men; Hiram, the great and learned King of Tyre; and Hiram Abif, the widow's son, of the tribe of Naphtali. It was held in the bowels of the sacred Mount Moriah, under the part whereon was erected the Holy of Holies. On this mount it was where Abraham confirmed his faith by his readiness to offer up his only son, Isaac. Here it was where David offered that acceptable sacrifice on the threshing-floor of Araunah by which the anger of the Lord was appeased, and the plague stayed from his people. Here it was where the Lord delivered to David, in a dream, the plan of the glorious Temple, afterward erected by our noble Grand Master, King Solomon. And lastly, here it was where he declared he would establish his sacred name and word, which should never pass away; and for these reasons this was justly styled the Sacred Lodge.

Sacrificant. (*Sacrifiant.*) A degree in the Archives of the Lodge of Saint Louis des Amis Réunis at Calais.

Sacrifice, Altar of. See *Altar.*

Sacrificer. (*Sacrificateur.*) 1. A degree in the Archives of the Lodge of Saint Louis des Amis Réunis at Calais. 2. A degree in the collection of Pyron.

Sadda. (Persian *Saddar,* the hundred gates.) A work in the Persian tongue, being a summary of the Avesta, or sacred books.

Sadducees. (*Zedukim.*) A sect called from its founder *Sadoc,* who lived about 250 years B.C. They denied the resurrection, a future state, and the existence of angels. The Sadducees are often mentioned in the New Testament, the Talmud, and the Midrash. The tenets of the Sadducees are noticed as contrasted with those of the Pharisees. While Jesus condemned the Sadducees and Pharisees, he is nowhere found criticizing the acts, words, or doctrines of the third sect of the Jews, the Essenes; wherefore, it has been strongly favored that Jesus was himself one of the last-named sect, who in many excellent qualities resembled Freemasons.

Sadler, Henry. (Born 1840, died 1911.) One of the most painstaking, patient, and persevering of Masonic students. He was initiated in 1862 in the Lodge of Justice, No. 147, being at the time an A. B. in the mercantile marine. He became W. M. of this Lodge in 1872. In 1882 he was a founder of the Southgate Lodge, No. 1950, and in 1886 he was a founder and first Master of the Walsingham Lodge, No. 2148; in 1869 he was exalted to the Royal Arch Degree in the Royal York Chapter, No. 7; in 1872 he joined the Temperance Chapter, No. 169, and became its First Principal in 1880. In 1879 he was appointed Grand Tiler of the Grand Lodge of England, and held the post until 1910, when he retired on a pension. In 1887 he was appointed Sub-

Librarian to the Grand Lodge of England and was promoted to be its Librarian in 1910. His position in the Grand Lodge Library gave him access to all the old records of the Grand Lodge of England, and enabled him to write most valuable books on various points in connection with the history of English Freemasonry. In 1887 appeared his principal work, *Masonic Facts and Fictions*, in which he proved that the Grand Lodge of the "Ancients" was formed in London by some Irish Freemasons, who had not seceded (as had been supposed) from the Regular Grand Lodge. In 1889 he published *Notes on the Ceremony of Installation;* in 1891, the *Life of Thomas Dunckerley;* in 1898, *Masonic Reprints and Historical Revelations;* in 1904, *Some Memorials of the Globe Lodge, No. 23*, also the *Illustrated History of Emulation Lodge of Improvement, No. 256;* and in 1906, the *History and Records of the Lodge of Emulation, No. 21.* [E. L. H.]

Sagitta. The keystone of an arch. The abscissa of a curve.

Saint Adhabell. Introduced into the Cooke MS. (l. 603), where the allusion evidently is to *St. Amphibalus*, which see.

Saint Alban. St. Alban, or Albanus, the proto-martyr of England, was born in the third century, at Verulam, now St. Albans, in Hertfordshire. In his youth he visited Rome, and served seven years as a soldier under the Emperor Diocletian. On his return to Britain he embraced Christianity, and was the first who suffered martyrdom in the great persecution which raged during the reign of that emperor. The Freemasons of England have claimed St. Alban as being intimately connected with the early history of the Fraternity in that island. Anderson (*Constitutions*, 1738, p. 57) says, "This is asserted by all the old copies of the Constitutions, and the old English Masons firmly believed it," and he quotes from the Old Constitutions:

"St. Alban loved Masons well and cherished them much, and he made their pay right good; *viz.*, two shillings per week and three pence to their cheer; whereas before that time, through all the land, a Mason had but a penny a day and his meat, until St. Alban amended it. He also obtained of the King a Charter for the Free Masons, for to hold a general council, and gave it the name of Assembly, and was thereat himself as Grand Master and helped to make Masons and gave them good charges."

We have another tradition on the same subject; for in a little work published about 1764, at London, under the title of *The Complete Free Mason or Multa Paucis for the Lovers of Secrets*, we find the following statement in reference to the Masonic character and position of St. Alban (p. 47):

"In the following (the third) century, Gordian sent many architects over [into England], who constituted themselves into Lodges, and instructed the Craftsmen in the true principles of Freemasonry; and a few years later, Carausius was made emperor of the British Isles, and, being a great lover of art and science, appointed Albanus Grand Master of Masons, who employed the Fraternity in building the palace of Verulam, or St. Albans."

Both of these statements are simply legends, or traditions of the not unusual character, in which historical facts are destroyed by legendary additions. The fact that St. Alban lived at Verulam may be true—most probably is so. It is another fact that a splendid Episcopal palace was built there, whether in the time of St. Alban or not is not so certain; but the affirmative has been assumed; and hence it easily followed that, if built in his time, he must have superintended the building of the edifice. He would, of course, employ the workmen, give them his patronage, and, to some extent, by his superior abilities, direct their labors. Nothing was easier, then, than to make him, after all this, a Grand Master. The assumption that St. Alban built the palace at Verulam was very natural, because when the true builder's name was lost—supposing it to have been so—St. Alban was there ready to take his place, Verulam having been his birthplace.

The increase of pay for labor and the annual congregation of the Masons in a General Assembly, having been subsequent events, the exact date of whose first occurrence had been lost, by a process common in the development of traditions, they were readily transferred to the same era as the building of the palace at Verulam. It is not even necessary to suppose, by way of explanation, as Preston does, that St. Alban was a celebrated architect, and a real encourager of able workmen. The whole of the tradition is worked out of these simple facts: that architecture began to be encouraged in England about the third century; that St. Alban lived at that time at Verulam; that a palace was erected then, or at some subsequent period, in the same place; and in the lapse of time, Verulam, St. Alban, and the Freemasons became mingled together in one tradition. The inquiring student of history will neither assert nor deny that St. Alban built the palace of Verulam. He will be content with taking him as the representative of that builder, if he was not the builder himself; and he will thus recognize the proto-martyr as the type of what is supposed to have been the Masonry of his age, or, perhaps, only of the age in which the tradition received its form.

Saint Albans, Earl of. Anderson (*Constitutions*, 1738, p. 101) says, and, after him, Preston, that a General Assembly of the Craft was held on December 27, 1663, by Henry Jermyn, Earl of St. Albans, Grand Master, who appointed Sir John Denham his Deputy, and Sir Christopher Wren and John Web his Wardens. Several useful regulations were made at this assembly, known as the "Regulations of 1663." These regulations are given by Anderson and by Preston, and also in the Roberts MS., with the addition of the oath of secrecy. The Roberts MS. says that the assembly was held on the 8th of December.

Saint Amphibalus. The ecclesiastical legend is that St. Amphibalus came to England, and converted St. Alban, who was the great patron of Masonry. The Old Constitutions do not speak of him, except the Cooke MS., which has the following passage (l. 602): "And sone after that came Seynt Adhabell into Englond, and he convertyd Seynt Albon to Cristendome"; where, evidently, St. Adhabell is meant for St. Amphibalus. But *amphibalus* is the Latin name of a cloak worn by priests over their other garments; and Higgins (*Celtic Druids*, p. 201) has shown that there was no such saint, but that the "Sanctus Amphibalus" was merely the holy cloak brought by St. Augustine to England. His connection with the history of the origin of Masonry in England is, therefore, altogether apocryphal.

Saint Andrew. Brother of St. Peter and one of the twelve Apostles. He is held in high reverence by the Scotch, Swedes, and Russians. Tradition says he was crucified on a cross thus shaped, X. Orders of knighthood have been established in his name. (See *Knight of St. Andrew*.)

Saint Andrew, Knight of. See *Knight of St. Andrew*.

Saint Andrew's Day. The 30th of November, adopted by the Grand Lodge of Scotland as the day of its Annual Communication.

Saint Augustine. St. Augustine, or St. Austin, was sent with forty monks into England, about the end of the sixth century, to evangelize the country. Lenning says that, according to a tradition, he placed himself at the head of the corporations of builders, and was recognized as their Grand Master. No such tradition, nor, indeed, even the name of St. Augustine, is to be found in any of the Old Constitutions which contain the "Legend of the Craft."

Saint Bernard. Saint Bernard of Clairvaux was one of the most eminent names of the church in the Middle Ages. In 1128 he was present at the Council of Troyes, where, through his influence, the Order of Knights Templar was confirmed; and he himself is said to have composed the Rule or constitution by which they were afterward governed. Throughout his life he was distinguished for his warm attachment to the Templars, and "rarely," says Burnes (*Sketch of K. T.*, p. 12), "wrote a letter to the Holy Land, in which he did not praise them, and recommend them to the favor and protection of the great." To his influence, untiringly exerted in their behalf, has always been attributed the rapid increase of the Order in wealth and popularity.

Saint Constantine, Order of. Presumed to have been founded by the Emperor Isaac Angelus Comnenus, in 1190.

Saint Domingo. One of the principal islands of the West Indies. Freemasonry was introduced there at an early period in the last century. Rebold (*Hist. des Trois G. L.*, p. 687) says in 1746. It must certainly have been in an active condition there at a time not long after, for in 1761 Stephen Morin, who had been deputed by the Council of Emperors of the East and West to propagate the high degrees, selected St. Domingo for the seat of his Grand East, and thence disseminated the system, which resulted in the establishment of the Supreme Council of the Ancient and Accepted Scottish Rite at Charleston, South Carolina. The French Revolution, and the insurrection of the slaves at about the same period, was for a time fatal to the progress of Masonry in St. Domingo. Subsequently, the island was divided into two independent governments—that of Dominica, inhabited by whites, and that of Hayti, inhabited by blacks. In each of these a Masonic obedience has been organized. The Grand Lodge of Hayti has been charged with irregularity in its formation, and has not been recognised by the Grand Lodges of the United States. It has been, however, by those of Europe generally, and a representative from it was accredited at the Congress of Paris, held in 1855. Masonry was revived in Dominica, Rebold says (*ibid.*), in 1822; other authorities say in 1855. A Grand Lodge was organized at the city of St. Domingo, December 11, 1858. At the present time Dominican Masonry is established under the Ancient and Accepted Scottish Rite, and the National Grand Orient of the Dominican Republic is divided into four sections, namely, a Grand Lodge, Grand Chapter General, Grand Consistory General, and Supreme Council. The last body has not been recognized by the Mother Council at Charleston, since its establishment is in violation of the Scottish Constitutions, which prescribe one Supreme Council only for all the West India Islands.

Sainte Croix, Emanuel Joseph Guilhem de Clermont-Lodeve de. A French antiquary, and member of the Institute, who was born at Mormoiron, in 1746, and died in 1809. His work, published in two volumes in 1784, and entitled *Recherches Historiques et Critiques sur les Mystères du Paganisme*, is one of the most valuable and instructive essays that we have in any language on the ancient mysteries—those religious associations whose history and design so closely connect them with Freemasonry. The later editions were enriched by the valuable notes of Silvestre de Tracy.

Saint George's Day. The twenty-third of April. Being the patron saint of England, his festival is celebrated by the Grand Lodge. The Constitution requires that "there shall be a Grand Masonic festival annually on the Wednesday next following St. George's Day."

Saint Germain. A town in France, about ten miles from Paris, where James II. established his court after his expulsion from England, and where he died. Oliver says (*Landm.*, ii., 28), and the statement has been repeatedly made by others, that the followers of the dethroned monarch who accompanied him in his exile, carried Freemasonry into France, and laid the foundation of that system of innovation which subsequently threw the Order into confusion by the establishment of a new degree, which they called the Chevalier Maçon Ecossais, and which they worked in the Lodge of St. Germain. But Oliver has here antedated history. James II. died in 1701, and Freemasonry was not introduced into France from England until 1725. The exiled house of Stuart undoubtedly made use of Masonry as an instrument to aid in their attempted restoration; but their connection with the Institution must have been after the time of James II., and most probably under the auspices of his grandson, the Young Pretender, Charles Edward.

Saint John, Favorite Brother of. The Eighth Degree of the Swedish Rite.

Saint John, Lodge of. See *Lodge of St. John.*

St. John of Jerusalem, Knight of. See *Knight of St. John of Jerusalem.*

Saint John's Masonry. The Constitutions of the Grand Lodge of Scotland (ed. 1848, chap. ii.) declare that that body "practises and recognizes no degrees of Masonry but those of Apprentice, Fellow Craft, and Master Mason, denominated *St. John's Masonry.*"

Saint John's Order. In a system of Masonry which Oliver says (*Mirror for the Johannites*, p. 58) was "used, as it is confidently affirmed, in the fourteenth century" (but it is doubtful if it could be traced farther back than the early part of the seventeenth), this appellation occurs in the obligation:

"That you will always keep, guard, and conceal,
And from this time you never will reveal,
Either to M. M., F. C., or Apprentice,
Of *St. John's* ORDER, what our grand intent is."

The same title of "Joannis Ordo" is given in the document of uncertain date known as the "Charter of Cologne."

St. John the Almoner. The son of the King of Cyprus, and born in that island in the sixth century. He was elected Patriarch of Alexandria, and has been canonized by both the Greek and Roman churches, his festival among the former occurring on the 11th of November, and among the latter on the 23d of January. Bazot (*Man. du Franc-Maçon.*, p. 144) thinks that it is this saint, and not St. John the Evangelist or St. John the Baptist, who is meant as the true patron of our Order. "He quitted his country and the hope of a throne," says this author, "to go to Jerusalem, that he might generously aid and assist the knights and pilgrims. He founded a hospital and organized a fraternity to attend upon sick and wounded Christians, and to bestow pecuniary aid upon the pilgrims who visited the Holy Sepulcher. St. John, who was worthy to become the patron of a society whose only object is charity, exposed his life a thousand times in the cause of virtue. Neither war, nor pestilence, nor the fury of the infidels, could deter him from pursuits of benevolence. But death, at length, arrested him in the midst of his labors. Yet he left the example of his virtues to the brethren, who have made it their duty to endeavor to imitate them. Rome canonized him under the name of St. John the Almoner, or St. John of Jerusalem; and the Masons—whose temples, overthrown by the barbarians, he had caused to be rebuilt—selected him with one accord as their patron." Oliver, however (*Mirror for the Johannite Masons*, p. 39), very properly shows the error of appropriating the patronage of Masonry to this saint, since the festivals of the Order are June 24th and December 27th, while those of St. John the Almoner are January 23d and November 11th. He has, however, been selected as the patron of the Masonic Order of the Templars, and their Commanderies are dedicated to his honor on account of his charity to the poor, whom he called his "Masters," because he owed them all service, and on account of his establishment of hospitals for the succor of pilgrims in the East.

Saint John the Baptist. One of the patron saints of Freemasonry, and at one time, indeed, the only one, the name of St. John the Evangelist having been introduced subsequent to the sixteenth century. His festival occurs on the 24th of June, and is very generally celebrated by the Masonic Fraternity. Dalcho (*Ahim. Rez.*, p. 150) says that "the stern integrity of St. John the Baptist, which induced him to forego every minor consideration in discharging the obligations he owed to God; the unshaken firmness with which he met martyrdom rather than betray his duty to his Master; his steady reproval of vice, and continued preaching of repentance and virtue, make him a fit patron of the Masonic institution."

The Charter of Cologne says: "We celebrate, annually, the memory of St. John, the Forerunner of Christ and the Patron of our Community." The Knights Hospitalers also dedicated their Order to him; and the ancient expression of our ritual, which speaks of a "Lodge of the Holy St. John of Jerusalem," probably refers to the same saint.

Krause, in his *Kunsturkunden* (p. 295–305), gives abundant historical proofs that the earliest Masons adopted St. John the Baptist, and not St. John the Evangelist as their patron. It is worthy of note that the Grand Lodge of England was revived on St. John the Baptist's Day, 1717 (*Constitutions*, 1738, p 109), and that the annual feast was kept on that day until 1725, when it was held for the first time on the festival of the Evangelist. (*Ibid.*, p. 119.) Lawrie says that the Scottish Masons always kept the festival of the Baptist until 1737, when the Grand Lodge changed the time of the annual election to St. Andrew's Day. (*Hist. of F. M.*, p. 152.)

Saint John the Evangelist. One of the patron saints of Freemasonry, whose festival is celebrated on the 27th of December. His constant admonition, in his Epistles, to the cultivation of brotherly love. and the mystical nature of his Apocalyptic visions, have been, perhaps, the principal reasons for the veneration paid to him by the Craft. Notwithstanding a well-known tradition, all documentary evidence shows that the connection of the name of the Evangelist with the Masonic Order is to be dated long after the sixteenth century, before which time St. John the Baptist was exclusively the patron saint of Masonry. The two are, however, now always united, for reasons set forth in the article on the *Dedication of Lodges*, which see.

Saint Leger. See *Aldworth, Mrs.*

Saint Martin, Louis Claude. A mystical writer and Masonic leader of considerable reputation in the last century, and the founder of the Rite of Martinism. He was born at Amboise, in France, on January 18, 1743, being descended from a family distinguished in the military service of the kingdom. Saint Martin when a youth made great progress in his studies, and became the master of several ancient and modern languages. After leaving school, he entered the army, in accordance with the custom of his family, becoming a member of the regiment of Foix. But after six years of service, he retired from a profession which he found uncongenial with his fondness for metaphysical pursuits. He then traveled in Switzerland, Germany, England, and Italy, and finally retired to Lyons, where he remained for three years in a state of almost absolute seclusion, known to but few persons, and pursuing his philosophic studies. He then repaired to Paris, where, notwithstanding the tumultuous scenes of the revolution which was working around, he remained unmoved by the terrible events of the day, and intent only on the prosecution of his theosophic studies. Attracted by the mystical systems of Boehme and Swedenborg, he became himself a mystic of no mean pretensions, and attracted around him a crowd of disciples, who were content, as they said, to hear, without understanding, the teachings of their leader. In 1775 appeared his first and most important work, entitled *Des Erreurs et de la Vérité, ou les Hommes rappelés au principe universal de la Science*. This work, which contained an exposition of the ideology of Saint Martin, acquired for its author, by its unintelligible transcendentalism, the title of the "Kant of Germany." Saint Martin had published this work under the pseudonym of the "Unknown Philosopher" (*le Philosophe inconnu*); whence he was subsequently known by this name, which was also assumed by some of his Masonic adherents; and even a degree bearing that title was invented and inserted in the Rite of Philalethes. The treatise *Des Erreurs et de la Vérité* was in fact made a sort of text-book by the Philalethans, and highly recommended by the Order of the Initiated Knights and Brothers of Asia, whose system was in fact a compound of theosophy and mysticism. It was so popular, that between 1775 and 1784 it had been through five editions.

Saint Martin, in the commencement of his Masonic career, attached himself to Martines Paschalis, of whom he was one of the most prominent disciples. But he subsequently attempted a reform of the system of Paschalis, and established what he called a Rectified Rite, but which is better known as the Rite or system of Martinism, which consisted of ten degrees. It was itself subsequently reformed, and, being reduced to seven degrees, was introduced into some of the Lodges of Germany under the name of the Reformed Ecossism of Saint Martin.

The theosophic doctrines of Saint Martin were introduced into the Masonic Lodges of Russia by Count Gabrianko and Admiral Pleshcheyeff, and soon became popular. Under them the Martinist Lodges of Russia became distinguished not only for their Masonic and religious spirit—although too much tinged with the mysticism of Jacob Boehme and their founder—but for an active zeal in practical works of charity of both a private and public character.

The character of Saint Martin has been much mistaken, especially by Masonic writers. Those who, like Voltaire, have derided his metaphysical theories, seem to have forgotten the excellence of his private character, his kindness of heart, his amiable manners, and his varied and extensive erudition. Nor should it be forgotten that the true object of all his Masonic labors was to introduce into the Lodges of France a spirit of pure religion. His theory of the origin of Freemasonry was not, however, based on any historical research, and is of no value, for he believed that it was an emanation of the Divinity, and was to be traced to the very beginning of the world.

Saint Nicaise. A considerable sensation was produced in Masonic circles by the appearance at Frankfort, in 1755, of a work entitled *Saint Nicaise, oder eine Sammlung merkwürdiger Maürerischer Briefe, für Freimaürer und die es nicht*. A second edition was issued in 1786. Its title-page asserts it to be a translation from the French, but it was really written by Dr. Starck. It professes to contain the letters of a French Freemason who was traveling on account of Freemasonry, and having learned the mode of work in England and Germany, had become dissatisfied with both, and had retired into a cloister in France. It was really intended, although Starck had abandoned Masonry, to defend his system of Spiritual Templarism, in opposition to that of the Baron Von Hund. Accordingly, it was answered in 1786 by Von Sprengseisen, who was an ardent friend and admirer of Von Hund, in a work entitled *Anti Saint Nicaise*, which was immediately followed by two other essays by the same author, entitled *Archimedes*, and *Scala Algebraica Œconomica*. These three works have become exceedingly rare.

Saint Paul's Church. As St. Paul's, the Cathedral Church of London, was rebuilt by

Sir Christopher Wren—who is called, in the *Book of Constitutions* (1738, p. 107), the Grand Master of Masons—and some writers have advanced the theory that Freemasonry took its origin at the construction of that edifice. In the Fourth Degree of Fessler's Rite—which is occupied in the critical examination of the various theories on the origin of Freemasonry—among the seven sources that are considered, the building of St. Paul's Church is one. Nicolai does not positively assert the theory; but he thinks it not an improbable one, and believes that a new system of symbols was at that time invented. It is said that there was, before the revival in 1717, an old Lodge of St. Paul's; and it is reasonable to suppose that the Operative Masons engaged upon the building were united with the architects and men of other professions in the formation of a Lodge, under the regulation which no longer restricted the Institution to Operative Masonry. But there is no authentic historical evidence that Freemasonry first took its rise at the building of St. Paul's Church.

Saints John. The "Holy Saints John," so frequently mentioned in the ritual of Symbolic Masonry, are *St. John the Baptist* and *St. John the Evangelist*, which see. The original dedication of Lodges was to the "Holy St. John," meaning the Baptist.

Saints John, Festivals of. See *Festivals.*

Saint Victor, Louis Guillemain de. A French Masonic writer, who published, in 1781, a work in Adonhiramite Masonry, entitled *Receuil Précieux de la Maçonnerie Adonhiramite.* This volume contained the ritual of the first four degrees, and was followed, in 1787, by another, which contained the higher degrees of the Rite. If St. Victor was not the inventor of this Rite, he at least modified and established it as a working system, and, by his writings and his labors, gave to it whatever popularity it at one time possessed. Subsequent to the publication of his *Receuil Précieux,* he wrote his *Origine de la Maçonnerie Adonhiramite,* a learned and interesting work, in which he seeks to trace the source of the Masonic initiation to the mysteries of the Egyptian priesthood.

Sakinat. The Divine presence. The *Shekinah,* which see.

Sakti. The female energy of Brahma, of Vishnu, or especially of Siva. This lascivious worship was inculcated in the TANTRA ("Instrument of Faith"), a Sanskrit work, found under various forms, and regarded by its numerous Brahmanical and other followers as a "fifth Veda."

Salaam. The name of the Arabic form of salutation, which is by bowing the head and bringing the extended arms from the sides until the thumbs touch, the palms being down.

Saladin. More properly Salah-ed-din, Yusuf ibn Ayub, the Sultan of Egypt and Syria, in the time of Richard Cœur-de-Lion, and the founder of the Ayubite dynasty. As the great Moslem hero of the third Crusade, and the beau-ideal of Moslem chivalry, he is one of the most imposing characters presented to us by the history of that period. Born at Takreit, 1137; died at Damascus, 1193. In his manhood he had entered the service of Noureddin. He became Grand Vizier of the Fatimite Calif, and received the title of "the Victorious Prince." At Noureddin's death, Salah-ed-din combated the succession and became the Sultan of Syria and Egypt. For ten succeeding years he was in petty warfare with the Christians, until at Tiberias, in 1187, the Christians were terribly punished for plundering a wealthy caravan on its way to Mecca. The King of Jerusalem, two Grand Masters, and many warriors were taken captive, Jerusalem stormed, and many fortifications reduced. This roused Western Europe; the Kings of France and England, with a mighty host, soon made their appearance; they captured Acre in 1191, and Richard Cœur-de-Lion, with an invading force, twice defeated the Sultan, and obtained a treaty in 1192, by which the coast from Jaffa to Tyre was yielded to the Christians.

Salah-ed-din becomes a prominent character in two of the Consistorial degrees of the A. A. Scottish Rite, mainly exemplifying the universality of Masonry.

Salfi, Francesco. An Italian philosopher and litterateur, who was born at Cozenza, in Calabria, January 1, 1759, and died at Passy, near Paris, September, 1832. He was at one time professor of history and philosophy at Milan. He was a prolific writer, and the author of many works on history and political economy. He published, also, several poems and dramas, and received, in 1811, the prize given by the Lodge at Leghorn for a Masonic essay entitled *Della utilità della Franca-Massoneria sotto il rapporto filantropico è morale.*

Salix. A significant word in the high degrees, invented, most probably, at first for the system of the Council of Emperors of the East and West, and transferred to the Ancient and Accepted Scottish Rite. It is derived, say the old French rituals, from the initials of a part of a sentence, and has, therefore, no other meaning.

Salle des Pas Perdus. (*The Hall of the Lost Steps.*) The French thus call the anteroom in which visitors are placed before their admission into the Lodge. The Germans call it the fore-court (*Vorhof*), and sometimes, like the French, *der Saal der verlornen Schritte.* Lenning says that it derives its name from the fact that evcry step taken before entrance into the Fraternity, or not made in accordance with the precepts of the Order, is considered as lost.

Salomonis Sanctificatus Illuminatus, Magnus Jehova. The title of the reigning Master or third class of the Illuminated Chapter according to the Swedish system.

Salsette. An island in the Bay of Bombay, celebrated for stupendous caverns excavated artificially out of the solid rock, with a labor which must, says Mr. Grose, have been equal to that of erecting the Pyramids, and which were appropriated to the initiations in the Ancient Mysteries of India.

Salt. In the Helvetian ritual salt is added to corn, wine, and oil as one of the elements of consecration, because it is a symbol of the wisdom and learning which should characterize a Mason's Lodge. When the foundation-stone of a Lodge is laid, the Helvetian ritual directs that it shall be sprinkled with salt, and this formula be used: "May this undertaking, contrived by wisdom, be executed in strength and adorned with beauty, so that it may be a house where peace, harmony, and brotherly love shall perpetually reign."

Salutation. Lenning says, that in accordance with the usage of the Operative Masons, it was formerly the custom for a strange brother, when he visited a Lodge, to bring to it such a salutation as this: "From the Right Worshipful Brethren and Fellows of a Right Worshipful and Holy Lodge of St. John." The English salutation, at the middle of the last century, was: "From the Right Worshipful Brothers and Fellows of the Right Worshipful and Holy Lodge of St. John, from whence I come and greet you thrice heartily well." The custom has become obsolete, although there is an allusion to it in the answer to the question, "Whence come you?" in the modern catechism of the Entered Apprentice's Degree. But Lenning is incorrect in saying that the salutation went out of use after the introduction of certificates. The salutation was, as has been seen, in use in the eighteenth century, and certificates were required as far back at least as the year 1683.

Salutem. (*Lat.* Health.) When the Romans wrote friendly letters, they prefixed the letter S as the initial of Salutem, or health, and thus the writer expressed a wish for the health of his correspondent. At the head of Masonic documents we often find this initial letter thrice repeated, thus: S.·. S.·. S.·., with the same signification of Health, Health, Health. It is equivalent to the English expression, "Thrice Greeting."

Salute Mason. Among the Stone-Masons of Germany, in the Middle Ages, a distinction was made between the *Grussmaurer* or *Wortmaurer*, the *Salute Mason* or *Word Mason*, and the *Schriftmaurer* or *Letter Mason.* The Salute Masons had signs, words, and other modes of recognition by which they could make themselves known to each other; while the Letter Masons, who were also called *Briefträger* or *Letter Bearers*, had no mode, when they visited strange Lodges, of proving themselves, except by the certificates or written testimonials which they brought with them. Thus, in the "examination of a German Stone-Mason," which has been published in Fallou's *Mysterien der Freimaurerei* (p. 25), and copied thence by Findel, we find these questions proposed to a visiting brother, and the answers thereto:

"*Warden.* Stranger, are you a Letter Mason or a Salute Mason?

"*Stranger.* I am a Salute Mason.

"*Warden.* How shall I know you to be such?

"*Stranger.* By my salute and words of my mouth." (*Hist. of F. M.*, p. 659.)

Samaria. A city situated near the center of Palestine, and built by Omri, King of Israel, about 925 B.C. It was the metropolis of the kingdom of Israel, or of the ten tribes, and was, during the exile, peopled by many Pagan foreigners sent to supply the place of the deported inhabitants. Hence it became a seat of idolatry, and was frequently denounced by the prophets. (See *Samaritans.*)

Samaritan, Good. See *Good Samaritan.*

Samaritans. The Samaritans were originally the descendants of the ten revolted tribes who had chosen Samaria for their metropolis. Subsequently, the Samaritans were conquered by the Assyrians under Shalmaneser, who carried the greater part of the inhabitants into captivity, and introduced colonies in their place from Babylon, Cultah, Ava, Hamath, and Sepharvaim. These colonists, who assumed the name of Samaritans, brought with them of course the idolatrous creed and practises of the region from which they emigrated. The Samaritans, therefore, at the time of the rebuilding of the second Temple, were an idolatrous race, and as such abhorrent to the Jews. Hence, when they asked permission to assist in the pious work of rebuilding the Temple, Zerubbabel, with the rest of the leaders, replied, "Ye have nothing to do with us to build a house unto our God; but we ourselves together will build unto the Lord God of Israel, as King Cyrus, the king of Persia, has commanded us."

Hence it was that, to avoid the possibility of these idolatrous Samaritans polluting the holy work by their cooperation, Zerubbabel found it necessary to demand of every one who offered himself as an assistant in the undertaking that he should give an accurate account of his lineage, and prove himself to have been a descendant (which no Samaritan could be) of those faithful Giblemites who worked at the building of the first Temple.

There were many points of religious difference between the Jews and the Samaritans. One was, that they denied the authority of any of the Scriptures except the Pentateuch; another was that they asserted that it was on Mount Gerizim, and not on Mount Moriah, that Melchizedek met Abraham when returning from the slaughter of the kings, and that here also he came to sacrifice Isaac, whence they paid no reverence to Moriah as the site of the "Holy House of the Lord." A few of the sect still remain at Nabulus. They do not exceed one hundred and fifty. They have a high priest, and observe all the feasts of the ancient Jews, and especially that of the Passover, which they keep on Mount Gerizim with all the formalities of the ancient rites.

Samothracian Mysteries. The Mysteries of the Cabiri are sometimes so called because the principal seat of their celebration was in the island of Samothrace. "I ask," says Voltaire (*Dict. Phil.*), "who were these Hierophants, these sacred Freemasons, who celebrated their Ancient Mysteries of Samothracia, and whence came they and their gods Cabiri?" (See *Cabiric Mysteries.*)

Sanctuary. The Holy of Holies in the Temple of Solomon. (See *Holy of Holies.*)

Sanctum Sanctorum. Latin for *Holy of Holies*, which see.

Sandalphon. In the Rabbinical system of Angelology, one of the three angels who receive the prayers of the Israelites and weave crowns from them. Longfellow availed himself of this idea in one of his most beautiful poems.

Sandwich Islands. Freemasonry was first introduced into those far islands of the Pacific by the Grand Orient of France, which issued a Dispensation for the establishment of a Lodge about 1848, or perhaps earlier; but it was not prosperous, and soon became dormant. In 1852, the Grand Lodge of California granted a Warrant to Hawaiian Lodge, No. 21, on its register at Honolulu. Royal Arch and Templar Masonry have both been since introduced. Honolulu Chapter was established in 1859, and Honolulu Commandery in 1871.

San Graal. Derived, probably, from the old French, *sang real*, the true blood; although other etymologies have been proposed. The San Graal is represented, in legendary history, as being an emerald dish in which our Lord had partaken of the last supper. Joseph of Arimathea, having further sanctified it by receiving into it the blood issuing from the five wounds, afterward carried it to England. Subsequently it disappeared in consequence of the sins of the land, and was long lost sight of. When Merlin established the Knights of the Round Table, he told them that the San Graal should be discovered by one of them, but that he only could see it who was without sin. One day, when Arthur was holding a high feast with his Knights of the Round Table, the San Graal suddenly appeared to him and to all his chivalry, and then as suddenly disappeared. The consequence was that all the knights took upon them a solemn vow to seek the Holy Dish. "The quest of the San Graal" became one of the most prominent myths of what has been called the Arthuric cycle. The old French romance of the *Morte d'Arthur*, which was published by Caxton in 1485, contains the adventures of Sir Galahad in search of the San Graal. There are several other romances of which this wonderful vessel, invested with the most marvelous properties, is the subject. *The quest of the San Graal* very forcibly reminds us of *the search for the Lost Word.* The symbolism is precisely the same—the loss and the recovery being but the lesson of death and eternal life—so that the San Graal in the Arthurian myth, and the Lost Word in the Masonic legend, seem to be identical in object and design. Hence it is not surprising that a French writer, M. de Caumont, should have said (*Bulletin Monument*, p. 129) that "the poets of the twelfth and fourteenth centuries, who composed the romances of the Round Table, made Joseph of Arimathea the chief of a military and religious Freemasonry."

Sanhedrim. The highest judicial tribunal among the Jews. It consisted of seventy-two persons besides the high priest. It is supposed to have originated with Moses, who instituted a council of seventy on the occasion of a rebellion of the Israelites in the wilderness The room in which the Sanhedrim met was a rotunda, half of which was built without the Temple and half within, the latter part being that in which the judges sat. The Nasi, or prince, who was generally the high priest, sat on a throne at the end of the hall; his deputy, called Ab-beth-din, at his right hand; and the subdeputy, or Chacan, at his left; the other senators being ranged in order on each side. Most of the members of this council were priests or Levites, though men in private stations of life were not excluded.

According to the English system of the Royal Arch, a Chapter of Royal Arch Masons represents the Sanhedrim, and therefore it is a rule that it shall never consist of more than seventy-two members, although a smaller number is competent to transact any business. This theory is an erroneous one, for in the time of Zerubbabel there was no Sanhedrim, that tribunal having been first established after the Macedonian conquest. The place in the Temple where the Sanhedrim met was called "Gabbatha," or the "Pavement"; it was a room whose floor was formed of ornamental square stones, and it is from this that the Masonic idea has probably arisen that the floor of the Lodge is a tessellated or mosaic pavement.

Sapicole, The. Thory (*Acta Lat.*, i., 339) says that a degree by this name is cited in the nomenclature of Fustier, and is also found in the collection of Viany.

Sapphire. Hebrew, ספיר. The second stone in the second row of the high priest's breastplate, and was appropriated to the tribe of Naphtali. The chief priest of the Egyptians wore round his neck an image of truth and justice made of sapphire.

Saracens. Although originally only an Arab tribe, the word Saracens was afterward applied to all the Arabs who embraced the tenets of Mohammed. The Crusaders especially designated as Saracens those Mohammedans who had invaded Europe, and whose possession of the Holy Land gave rise not only to the Crusades, but to the organization of the military and religious orders of Templars and Hospitalers, whose continual wars with the Saracens constitute the most important chapters of the history of those times.

Sardinia. Freemasonry was introduced into this kingdom in 1737. (Rebold, *Hist. des Trois Grandes Loges*, p. 686.)

Sardius. Hebrew, אדם, *Odem*. The first stone in the first row of the high priest's breastplate. It is a species of carnelian of a blood-red color, and was appropriated to the tribe of Reuben.

Sarsena. A pretended exposition of Freemasonry, published at Baumberg, Germany, in 1816, under the title of "Sarsena, or the Perfect Architect," created a great sensation at the time among the initiated and the profane.

It professed to contain the history of the origin of the Order, and the various opinions upon what it should be, "faithfully described by a true and perfect brother, and extracted from the papers which he left behind him." Like all other expositions, it contained, as Gädicke remarks, very little that was true, and of that which was true nothing that had not been said before.

Sash. The old regulation on the subject of wearing sashes in a procession is in the following words: "None but officers, who must always be Master Masons, are permitted to wear sashes; and this decoration is only for particular officers." In this country the wearing of the sash appears, very properly, to be confined to the W.·. Master, as a distinctive badge of his office.

The sash is worn by all the companions of the Royal Arch Degree, and is of a scarlet color, with the words "Holiness to the Lord" inscribed upon it. These were the words placed upon the miter of the high priest of the Jews.

In the Ancient and Accepted Scottish Rite, the white sash is a decoration of the Thirty-third Degree. A recent decree of the Supreme Council of the Southern Jurisdiction confines its use to honorary members, while active members only wear the collar.

The sash, or scarf, is analogous to the Zennar, or sacred cord, which was placed upon the candidate in the initiation into the mysteries of India, and which every Brahman was compelled to wear. This cord was woven with great solemnity, and being put upon the left shoulder, passed over to the right side and hung down as low as the fingers could reach.

Saskatchewan. The Brethren of the Province of Saskatchewan assembled at Regina on the 10th day of August, 1906, and formally resolved themselves into the "Grand Lodge of Saskatchewan." Twenty-five lodges out of twenty-eight located in the Province were represented. M. W. Bro. H. H. Campkin was elected Grand Master and was installed by M. W. Bro. McKenzie, Grand Master of Manitoba.

Sastra. One of the sacred books of the Hindu law.

Sat B'hai, Royal Oriental Order of the. Said to have originated in India, and so named after a bird held sacred by the Hindus, whose flight, invariably in sevens, has obtained for the Society the appellation of the "Seven Brethren," hence the name. It embosoms seven degrees—Arch Censor, Arch Courier, Arch Minister, Arch Herald, Arch Scribe, Arch Auditor, and Arch Mute. It promises overmuch.

The figure in opposite column is termed the Mystery of the Apex.

Satrap. The title given by the Greek writers to the Persian governors of provinces before Alexander's conquest. It is from the Persian word *satrab*. The authorized version calls them the "kings lieutenants"; the Hebrew, *achashdarpenim*, which is doubtless a Persian word Hebraized. It was these satraps who gave the Jews so much trouble in the rebuilding of the Temple. They are alluded to in the congeneric degrees of Companion of the Red Cross and Prince of Jerusalem.

Savalette de Langes. Founder of the Rite of Philalethes at Paris, in 1773. He was also the President and moving spirit of the Masonic Congress at Paris, which met in 1785 and 1787 for the purpose of discussing many important points in reference to Freemasonry. The zeal and energy of Savalette de Langes had succeeded in collecting for the Lodge of the Philalethes a valuable cabinet of natural history and a library containing many manuscripts and documents of great importance. His death, which occurred soon

after the beginning of the French Revolution, and the political troubles that ensued, caused the dispersion of the members and the loss of a great part of the collection. The remnant subsequently came into the possession of the Lodges of St. Alexander of Scotland, and of the Social Contrat, which constituted the Philosophic Scottish Rite.

Saxony. The first Masonic Lodge in Saxony appeared at Dresden, in 1738; within four years thereafter two others had been established in Leipzig and Altenburg. The Grand Lodge was formed in 1811.

Sayer, Anthony. At the revival in 1717, "Mr. Antony Sayer, gentleman," was elected Grand Master. (*Constitutions*, 1738, p. 110.) He was succeeded in the next year by George Payne, Esq. In 1719, he was appointed Senior Grand Warden by Grand Master Desaguliers. Afterward he fell into bad circumstances and in 1730 a sum of £15 was granted to him by Grand Lodge, followed by a further grant of £2.2.0 in 1741. In December, 1730, a complaint was made to Grand Lodge of some irregular conduct on his part, and he was acquitted of the charge, whatever it was, but told to do nothing so irregular for the future. When he died, either late in 1741 or early in 1742, he was Tiler of what is now the Old King's Arms Lodge, No. 28. A portrait of him by Highmore, the celebrated painter, is in existence, mezzotinto copies of which are not uncommon. [E. L. H.]

Scald Miserables. A name given to a set of persons who, in 1741, formed a mock procession in derision of the Freemasons. Sir John Hawkins, speaking, in his *Life of*

Johnson (p. 336), of Paul Whitehead, says: "In concert with one Carey, a surgeon, he planned and exhibited a procession along the Strand of persons on foot and on horseback, dressed for the occasion, carrying mock ensigns and the symbols of Freemasonry; the design of which was to expose to laughter the insignia and ceremonies of that mysterious institution; and it was not until thirty years afterward that the Fraternity recovered from the disgrace which so ludicrous a representation had brought on it." The incorrectness of this last statement will be evident to all who are acquainted with the successful progress made by Freemasonry between the years 1741 and 1771, during which time Sir John Hawkins thinks that it was languishing under the blow dealt by the mock procession of the Scald Miserables.

A better and fuller account is contained in the *London Daily Post* of March 20, 1741. "Yesterday, some mock Freemasons marched through Pall Mall and the Strand as far as Temple Bar in procession; first went fellows on jackasses, with cows' horns in their hands; then a kettle-drummer on a jackass, having two butter firkins for kettle-drums; then followed two carts drawn by jackasses, having in them the stewards with several badges of their order; then came a mourning-coach drawn by six horses, each of a different color and size, in which were the Grand Master and Wardens; the whole attended by a vast mob. They stayed without Temple Bar till the Masons came by, and paid their compliments to them, who returned the same with an agreeable humor that possibly disappointed the witty contriver of this mock scene, whose misfortune is that, though he has some wit, his subjects are generally so ill chosen that he loses by it as many friends as other people of more judgment gain."

April 27th, being the day of the annual feast, "a number of shoe-cleaners, chimney-sweepers, etc., on foot and in carts, with ridiculous pageants carried before them, went in procession to Temple Bar, by way of jest on the Freemasons." A few days afterward, says the same journal, "several of the Mock Masons were taken up by the constable empowered to impress men for his Majesty's service, and confined until they can be examined by the justices."

It was, as Hone remarks (*Anc. Myst.*, p. 242), very common to indulge in satirical pageants, which were accommodated to the amusement of the vulgar, and he mentions this procession as one of the kind. A plate of the mock procession was engraved by A. Benoist, a drawing-master, under the title of "A Geometrical View of the Grand Procession of the Scald Miserable Masons, designed as they were drawn up over against Somerset House in the Strand, on the 27th day of April, Anno 1742." Of this plate there is a copy in Clavel's *Histoire Pittoresque*. With the original plate Benoist published a key, as follows, which perfectly agrees with the copy of the plate in Clavel:

"No. 1. The grand Sword-Bearer, or Tyler, carrying the Swoard of State, (a present of Ishmael Abiff to old Hyram, King of the Saracens,) to his Grace of Wattin, Grand Master of the Holy Lodge of St. John of Jerusalem in Clerkenwell. 2. Tylers or Guarders. 3. Grand Chorus of Instruments. 4. The Stewards, in three Guttcarts drawn by Asses. 5. Two famous Pillars. 6. Three great Lights: the Sun, Hieroglyphical, to rule the Day; the Moon, Emblematical, to rule the Night; a Master Mason, Political, to rule his Lodge. 7. The Entered Prentice's Token. 8. The letter G, famous in Masonry for differencing the Fellow Craft's Lodge from that of Prentices. 9. The Funeral of a Grand Master according to the Rites of the Order, with the Fifteen loving Brethren. 10. A Master Mason's Lodge. 11. Grand Band of Musick. 12. Two Trophies; one being that of a Black-shoe Boy and a Sink Boy, the other that of a Chimney-Sweeper. 13. The Equipage of the Grand Master, all the Attendants wearing Mystical Jewells."

The *historical* mock procession of the Scald Miserables was, it thus appears, that which occurred on April 27th, and not the preceding one of March 20th, which may have been only a feeler, and having been well received by the populace there might have been an encouragement for its repetition. But it was not so popular with the higher classes, who felt a respect for Freemasonry, and were unwilling to see an indignity put upon it. A writer in the London *Freemasons' Magazine* (1858, I., 875) says: "The contrivers of the mock procession were at that time said to be Paul Whitehead, Esq., and his intimate friend (whose real Christian name was *Esquire*) Carey, of Pall Mall, surgeon to Frederick, Prince of Wales. The city officers did not suffer this procession to go through Temple Bar, the common report then being that its real interest was to affront the annual procession of the Freemasons. The Prince was so much offended at this piece of ridicule, that he immediately removed Carey from the office he held under him."

Smith (*Use and Abuse of Freemas.*, p. 78) says that "about this time (1742) an order was issued to discontinue all public processions on feast days, on account of a mock procession which had been planned, at a considerable expense, by some prejudiced persons, with a view to ridicule these public cavalcades." Smith is not altogether accurate. There is no doubt that the ultimate effect of the mock procession was to put an end to what was called "the march of procession" on the feast day, but that effect did not show itself until 1747, in which year it was resolved that it should in future be discontinued. (*Constitutions*, 1756, p. 248.)*

---

* On the subject of these mock processions there is an article by Dr. W. J. Chetwode Crawley in *Ars Quatuor Coronatorum*, vol. 18.

Scales, Pair of. "Let me be weighed in an even balance," said Job, "that God may know mine integrity"; and Solomon says that "a false balance *is* abomination to the Lord, but a just weight is his delight." So we find that among the ancients a balance, or pair of scales, was a well-known recognized symbol of a strict observation of justice and fair dealing. This symbolism is also recognized in Masonry, and hence in the degree of Princes of Jerusalem, the duty of which is to administer justice in the inferior degrees, a pair of scales is the most important symbol.

Scallop-Shell. The scallop-shell, the staff, and sandals form a part of the costume of a Masonic Knights Templar in his character as a Pilgrim Penitent. Shakespeare makes Ophelia sing—

> "And how shall I my true love know
> From any other one?
> O, by his scallop-shell and staff,
> And by his sandal shoon!"

The scallop-shell was in the Middle Ages the recognized badge of a pilgrim; so much so, that Dr. Clarke (*Travels*, ii., 538) has been led to say: "It is not easy to account for the origin of the shell as a badge worn by the pilgrims, but it decidedly refers to much earlier Oriental customs than the journeys of Christians to the Holy Land, and its history will probably be found in the mythology of eastern nations." He is right as to the question of antiquity, for the shell was an ancient symbol of the Syrian goddess Astarte, Venus Pelagia, or Venus rising from the sea. But it is doubtful whether its use by pilgrims is to be traced to so old or so Pagan an authority. Strictly, the scallop-shell was the badge of pilgrims visiting the shrine of St. James of Compostella, and hence it is called by naturalists the *pecten Jacobœus*—the comb shell of St. James. Fuller (*Ch. Hist.*, ii., 228) says: "All pilgrims that visit St. James of Compostella in Spain returned thence *obsiti conchis*, 'all beshelled about' on their clothes, as a religious donative there bestowed upon them." Pilgrims were, in fact, in Medieval times distinguished by the peculiar badge which they wore, as designating the shrine which they had visited. Thus pilgrims from Rome wore the keys, those from St. James the scallop-shell, and those from the Holy Land palm branches, whence such a pilgrim was sometimes called a *palmer*. But this distinction was not always rigidly adhered to, and pilgrims from Palestine frequently wore the shell. At first the shell was sewn on the cloak, but afterward transferred to the hat; and while, in the beginning, the badge was not assumed until the pilgrimage was accomplished, eventually pilgrims began to wear it as soon as they had taken their vow of pilgrimage, and before they had commenced their journey.

Both of these changes have been adopted in the Templar ritual. The pilgrim, although symbolically making his pilgrimage to the Holy Sepulcher in Palestine, adopts the shell more properly belonging to the pilgrimage to Compostella; and adopts it, too, not after his visit to the shrine, but as soon as he has assumed the character of a pilgrim, which, it will be seen from what has been said, is historically correct, and in accordance with the later practise of Medieval pilgrims.

Scarlet. See *Red*.

Scenic Representations. In the Ancient Mysteries scenic representations were employed to illustrate the doctrines of the resurrection, which it was their object to inculcate. Thus the allegory of the initiation was more deeply impressed, by being brought vividly to the sight as well as to the mind of the aspirant. Thus, too, in the religious mysteries of the Middle Ages, the moral lessons of Scripture were dramatized for the benefit of the people who beheld them. The Christian virtues and graces often assumed the form of personages in these religious plays, and fortitude, prudence, temperance, and justice appeared before the spectators as living and acting beings, inculcating by their actions and by the plot of the drama those lessons which would not have been so well received or so thoroughly understood, if given merely in a didactic form. The advantage of these scenic representations, consecrated by antiquity and tested by long experience, is well exemplified in the ritual of the Third Degree of Masonry, where the dramatization of the great legend gives to the initiation a singular force and beauty. It is surprising, therefore, that the English system never adopted, or, if adopted, speedily discarded, the drama of the Third Degree, but gives only in the form of a narrative what the American system more wisely and more usefully presents by living action. Throughout America, in every State excepting Pennsylvania, the initiation into the Third Degree constitutes a scenic representation. The latter State alone preserves the less impressive didactic method of the English system. The rituals of the Continent of Europe pursue the same scenic form of initiation, and it is therefore most probable that this was the ancient usage, and that the present English ritual is of comparatively recent date.

Scepter. An ensign of sovereign authority, and hence carried in several of the high degrees by officers who represent kings.

Schaw Manuscript. This is a code of laws for the government of the Operative Masons of Scotland, drawn up by William Schaw, the Master of the Work to James VI. It bears the following title: "The Statutis and Ordinanceis to be obseruit be all the Maister-Maissounis within this realme sett down be Williame Schaw, Maister of Wark to his Maieste and generall Wardene of the said Craft, with the consent of the Maisteris efter specifeit." As will be perceived by this title, it is in the Scottish dialect. It is written on paper, and dated XXVIII December, 1598. Although containing substantially the general regulations which are to be found in the English manuscripts, it differs materially from them in many particulars. Masters, Fellow-Crafts, and Apprentices are spoken of, but simply as gradations of rank, not as degrees, and the word "Ludge" or Lodge is constantly used to define the place of meeting. The government of the Lodge was vested in the Warden, Deacons, and Masters, and these the Fellow-Crafts and Apprentices were to obey. The highest officer of the Craft is called the General Warden. The Manuscript is in possession of the Lodge of Edinburgh, but has several times been published—first in the *Laws and Constitutions of the Grand Lodge of Scotland*, in 1848; then in the American edition of that work, published by Dr. Robert Morris, in the ninth volume of the *Universal Masonic Library;* afterward by W. A. Laurie, in 1859, in his *History of Freemasonry and the Grand Lodge of Scotland;* D. Murray Lyon in *Hist. of the Lodge of Edinburgh* gives a transcript and the last part in facsimile; and lastly, by W. J. Hughan, in his *Unpublished Records of the Craft.*

Schaw, William. A name which is intimately connected with the history of Freemasonry in Scotland. For the particulars of his life, we are principally indebted to the writer (said to have been Sir David Brewster, *Lyon's Hist. of Lodge of Edinburgh,* p. 55) of "Appendix Q. 2," in the *Constitutions of the Grand Lodge of Scotland* (1848).

William Schaw was born in the year 1550, and was probably a son of Schaw of Sauchie, in the shire of Clackmannon. He appears from an early period of life to have been connected with the royal household. In proof of this we may refer to his signature attached to the original parchment deed of the National Covenant, which was signed by King James VI. and his household at the Palace of Holyrood, 28th January, 1580-1. In 1584, Schaw became successor to Sir Robert Drummond, of Carnock, as Master of Works. This high official appointment placed under his superintendence all the royal buildings and palaces in Scotland; and in the Treasurer's accounts of a subsequent period various sums are entered as having been paid to him in connection with these buildings for improvements, repairs, and additions. Thus, in September, 1585, the sum of £315 was paid "to *William Schaw, his Majestie's Maister of Wark,* for the reparation and mending of the Castell of Striueling," and in May, 1590, £400, by his Majesty's precept, was "delyverit to William Schaw, the Maister of Wark, for reparation of the hous of Dumfermling, befoir the Queen's Majestie passing thairto."

Sir James Melville, in his *Memoirs,* mentions that, being appointed to receive the three Danish Ambassadors who came to Scotland in 1585 (with overtures for an alliance with one of the daughters of Frederick II.), he requested the king that two other persons might be joined with him, and for this purpose he named Schaw and James Meldrum, of Seggie, one of the Lords of Session. It further appears that Schaw had been employed in various missions to France. He accompanied James VI. to Denmark in the winter of 1589, previous to the king's marriage with the Princess Anna of Denmark, which was celebrated at Upslo, in Norway, on the 23d of November. The king and his attendants remained during the winter season in Denmark, but Schaw returned to Scotland on the 16th of March, 1589-90, for the purpose of making the necessary arrangements for the reception of the wedding-party. Schaw brought with him a paper subscribed by the king, containing the "Ordour set down be his Majestie to be effectuat be his Hienes Secreit Counsall, and preparit agane his Majestie's returne in Scotland," dated in February, 1589-90. The king and his royal bride arrived in Leith on the 1st of May, and remained there six days, in a building called "The King's Work," until the Palace of Holyrood was prepared for their reception. Extensive alterations had evidently been made at this time at Holyrood, as a warrant was issued by the Provost and Council of Edinburgh to deliver to William Schaw, Maister of Wark, the sum of £1000, "restand of the last taxation of £20,000" granted by the Royal Buroughs in Scotland, the sum to be expended "in biggin and repairing of his Hienes Palice of Halyrud-house," 14th March, 1589-90. Subsequent payments to Schaw occur in the Treasurer's accounts for broad scarlet cloth and other stuff for "burde claythes and coverings to forms and windows bayth in the Kirk and Palace of Halyrud-house." On this occasion various sums were also paid by a precept from the king for dresses, etc., to the ministers and others connected with the royal household. On this occasion William Schaw, Maister of Wark, received £133 6*s.* 8*d.* The queen was crowned on the 17th of May, and two days following she made her first public entrance into Edinburgh. The inscription on Schaw's monument states that he was, in addition to his office of Master of the Works, "Sacris ceremoniis præpositus" and "Reginæ Quæstor," which Monteith has translated "Sacrist and Queen's Chamberlain." This appointment of Chamberlain evinces the high regard in which the queen held him; but there can be no doubt that the former words relate to his holding the office of General Warden of the ceremonies of the Masonic Craft, an office analogous to that of Substitute Grand Master as now existing in the Grand Lodge of Scotland.

William Schaw died April 18, 1602, and was buried in the Abbey Church of Dunfermline, where a monument was erected to his memory by his grateful mistress, the queen. On this monument is his name and monogram cut in a marble slab, which, tradition says, was executed by his own hand, and containing his Mason's mark, and an inscription in Latin, in which he is described as one imbued with every liberal art and science, most skilful in architecture, and in labors and business not only unwearied and indefatigable, but ever assiduous and energetic. No man appears, from the records, to have lived with more of the commendation, or died with more of the regret of others, than this old Scottish Mason.

Schismatic. Thory (*Hist. de la Fond. du G. O.*) thus calls the brethren who, expelled by the Grand Lodge of France, had formed, in the year 1772, a rival body under the name of the National Assembly. Any body of Masons separating from the legal obedience, and establishing a new one not authorized by the laws of Masonry—such, for instance, as the Saint John's Grand Lodge in New York—is properly schismatic.

Schisms. This, which was originally an ecclesiastical term, and signifies, as Milton defines it, "a rent or division in the church when it comes to the separating of congregations," is unfortunately not unknown in Masonic history. It is in Masonic, as in canon law, a withdrawing from recognized authority, and setting up some other authority in its place. The first schism recorded after the revival of 1717, was that of the Duke of Wharton, who, in 1722, caused himself to be irregularly nominated and elected Grand Master. His ambition is assigned in the *Book of Constitutions* as the cause, and his authority was disowned "by all those," says Anderson, "that would not countenance irregularities." But the breach was healed by Grand Master Montague, who, resigning his claim to the chair, caused Wharton to be regularly elected and installed. (*Constitutions*, 1738, p. 114.) [The second schism in England was when Preston and others in 1779 formed the "Grand Lodge of England South of the River Trent" owing to a dispute with the Grand Lodge of the "Moderns," which continued for ten years. (See *Preston.*)] In France, although irregular Lodges began to be instituted as early as 1756, the first active schism is to be dated from 1761, when the dancing-master Lacorne, whom the respectable Masons refused to recognise as the substitute of De Clermont the Grand Master, formed, with his adherents, an independent and rival Grand Lodge; the members of which, however, became reconciled to the legal Grand Lodge the next year, and again became schismatic in 1765. In fact, from 1761 until the organization of the Grand Orient in 1772, the history of Masonry in France is but a history of schisms.

In Germany, in consequence of the Germanic principle of Masonic law that two or more controlling bodies may exist at the same time and in the same place with concurrent and coextensive jurisdiction, it is legally impossible that there ever should be a schism. A Lodge or any number of Lodges may withdraw from the parent stock and assume the standing and prerogatives of a mother Lodge with powers of constitution or an independent Grand Lodge, and its regularity would be indisputable, according to the German interpretation of the law of territorial jurisdiction. Such an act of withdrawal would be a secession, but not a schism.

In America there have been several instances of Masonic schism. Thus, in Massachusetts, by the establishment in 1752 of the St. Andrew's Grand Lodge; in South Carolina, by the formation of the Grand Lodge of York Masons in 1787; in Louisiana, in 1848, by the institution of the Grand Lodge of Ancient York Masons; and in New York, by the establishment in 1823 of the city and country Grand Lodges; and in 1849 by the formation of the body known as the Philip's Grand Lodge. In all of these instances a reconciliation eventually took place; nor is it probable that schisms will often occur, because the principle of exclusive territorial jurisdiction has been now so well settled and so universally recognized, that no seceding or schismatic body can expect to receive the countenance or support of any of the Grand Lodges of the Union.

There are these essential points of difference between ecclesiastical and Masonic schism; the former, once occurring, most generally remains perpetual. Reconciliation with a parent church is seldom effected. The schisms of Calvin and Luther at the time of the Reformation led to the formation of the Protestant Churches, who can never be expected to unite with the Roman Church, from which they separated. The Quakers, the Baptists, the Methodists, and other sects which seceded from the Church of England, have formed permanent religious organizations, between whom and the parent body from which they separated there is a breach which will probably never be healed. But all Masonic schisms, as experience has shown, have been temporary in their duration, and sometimes very short-lived. The spirit of Masonic brotherhood which continues to pervade both parties, always leads, sooner or later, to a reconciliation and a reunion; concessions are mutually made, and compromises effected, by which the schismatic body is again merged in the parent association from which it had seceded. Another difference is this, a religious schismatic body is not necessarily an illegal one, nor does it always profess a system of false doctrine. "A schism," says Milton, "may happen to a true church, as well as to a false." But a Masonic schism is always illegal; it violates the law of exclusive jurisdiction; and a schismatic body cannot be recognized as possessing any of the rights or prerogatives which belong alone to the supreme dogmatic Masonic power of the State.

Schneider, Johann August. A zealous and learned Mason of Altenburg, in Germany, where he was born May 22, 1755, and died August 13, 1816. Besides contributing many valuable articles to various Masonic journals, he was the compiler of the *Constitutions-Buch* of the Lodge "Archimedes zu den drei Reissbretten" at Altenburg, in which he had been initiated, and of which he was a member; an important but scarce work, containing a history of Masonry, and other valuable essays.

Schools. None of the charities of Freemasonry have been more important or more worthy of approbation than those which have been directed to the establishment of schools for the education of the orphan children of Masons; and it is a very proud feature of the Order, that institutions of this kind are to be found in every country where Freemasonry has made a lodgment as an organized society. In England, the Royal Freemasons' Girls' School was established in 1788. In 1798, a similar one for boys was founded. At a very early period charity schools were erected by the Lodges in Germany, Denmark, and Sweden. The Masons of Holland instituted a school for the blind in 1808. In the United States much attention has been paid to this subject. In 1842, the Grand Lodge of Missouri instituted a Masonic college, and the example was followed by several other Grand Lodges. But colleges have been found too unwieldly and complicated in their management for a successful experiment, and the scheme has generally been abandoned. But there are numerous schools in the United States which are supported in whole or m part by Masonic Lodges.

Schools of the Prophets. Oliver (*Landm.*, ii., 374) speaks of "the secret institution of the Nabiim" as existing in the time of Solomon, and says they were established by Samuel "to counteract the progress of the Spurious Freemasonry which was introduced into Palestine before his time." This claim of a Masonic character for these institutions has been gratuitously assumed by the venerable author. He referred to the well-known Schools of the Prophets, which were first organized by Samuel, which lasted from his time to the closing of the canon of the Old Testament. They were scattered all over Palestine, and consisted of scholars who devoted themselves to the study of both the written and the oral law, to the religious rites, and to the interpretation of Scripture. Their teaching of what they had learned was public, not secret, nor did they in any way resemble, as Oliver suggests, the Masonic Lodges of the present day. They were, in their organization, rather like our modern theological colleges, though their range of studies was very different.

Schor-Laban. ("White Ox," or morally, "Innocence.") The name of the second step of the Mystic Ladder of Kadosh of the A. A. Scottish Rite.

Schrepfer, Johann Georg. The keeper of a coffee-house in Leipsic, where, having obtained a quantity of Masonic, Rosicrucian, and magical books, he opened, in 1768, what he called a Scottish Lodge, and pretended that he had been commissioned by Masonic superiors to destroy the system of Strict Observance, whose adherents he abused and openly insulted. He boasted that he alone possessed the great secret of Freemasonry, and that nearly all the German Masons were utterly ignorant of anything about it except its external forms. He declared that he was an anointed priest, having power over spirits, who were compelled to appear at his will and obey his commands, by which means he became acquainted not only with the past and the present, but even with the future. It was in thus pretending to evoke spirits that his Masonry principally consisted. Many persons became his dupes; and although they soon discovered the imposture, shame at being themselves deceived prevented them from revealing the truth to others, and thus his initiations continued for a considerable period, and he was enabled to make some money, the only real object of his system. He has himself asserted, in a letter to a Prussian clergyman, that he was an emissary of the Jesuits; but of the truth of this we have only his own unreliable testimony. He left Leipsic at one time and traveled abroad, leaving his Deputy to act for him during his absence. On his return he asserted that he was the natural son of one of the French princes, and assumed the title of Baron Von Steinbach. But at length there was an end to his practises of jugglery. Seeing that he was beginning to be detected, fearing exposure, and embarrassed by debt, he invited some of his disciples to accompany him to a wood near Leipsic called the Rosenthal, where, on the morning of October 8, 1774, having retired to a little distance from the crowd, he blew out his brains with a pistol. Clavel has thought it worth while to preserve the memory of this incident by inserting an engraving representing the scene in his *Histoire Pittoresque de la Franc-Maçonnerie* (p. 183). Schrepfer had much low cunning, but was devoid of education. Lenning sums up his character in saying that he was one of the coarsest and most impudent swindlers who ever chose the Masonic brotherhood for his stage of action.

Schroeder, Friedrich Joseph Wilhelm. A doctor and professor of pharmacology in Marburg; was born at Bielefeld, in Prussia, March 19, 1733, and died October 27, 1778. Of an infirm constitution from his youth, he still further impaired his bodily health and his mental faculties by his devotion to chemical, alchemical, and theosophic pursuits. He established at Marburg, in 1766, a Chapter of True and Ancient Rose Croix Masons, and in 1779 he organized in a Lodge of Sarreburg a school or Rite, founded on magic, theosophy, and alchemy, which consisted of seven degrees, four high degrees founded on these occult sciences being superadded to the original three Symbolic degrees. This Rite, called the "Rectified Rose Croix," was only practised by two Lodges under the Constitution of the Grand Lodge of Hamburg. Clavel (*Histoire Pittoresque*, p. 183) calls him the Cagliostro of Germany, because it was in his school that the Italian charlatan learned his first lessons of magic and theosophy. Oliver, misunderstanding Clavel, styles him an adventurer. (*Landmarks*, ii., 710.) But it is perhaps more just that we should attribute to him a diseased imagination and misdirected studies than a bad heart or impure practises. He must not be confounded with Fried. Ludwig Schroeder, who was a man of a very different character.

Schroeder, Friedrich Ludwig. An actor and a dramatic and Masonic writer, born at Schwerin, November 3, 1744, and died near Hamburg, September 3, 1816. He commenced life as an actor at Vienna, and was so distinguished in his profession that Hoffmann says "he was incontestably the greatest actor that Germany ever had, and equally eminent in tragedy and comedy." As an active, zealous Mason, he acquired a high character. Bode himself, a well-known Mason, was his intimate friend. Through his influence, he was initiated into Freemasonry, in 1774, in the Lodge Emanuel zur Maienblume. He soon after, himself, established a new Lodge working in the system of Zinnendorf, but which did not long remain in existence. Schroeder then went to Vienna, where he remained until 1785, when he returned to Hamburg. On his return, he was elected by his old friends the Master of the Lodge Emanuel, which office he retained until 1799. In 1794 he was elected Deputy Grand Master of the English Provincial Grand Lodge of Lower Saxony, and in 1814, in the seventieth year of his life, he was induced to accept the Grand Mastership. It was after his election, in 1787, as Master of the Lodge Emanuel at Hamburg, that he first resolved to devote himself to a thorough reformation of the Masonic system, which had been much corrupted on the continent by the invention of almost innumerable high degrees, many of which found their origin in the fantasies of Alchemy, Rosicrucianism, and Hermetic Philosophy. It is to this resolution, thoroughly executed, that we owe the Masonic scheme known as Schroeder's Rite, which, whatever may be its defects in the estimation of others, has become very popular among many German Masons. He started out with the theory that, as Freemasonry had proceeded from England to the Continent, in the English Book of Constitutions and the Primitive English Ritual we must look for the pure unadulterated fountain of Freemasonry.

He accordingly selected the well-known English Exposition entitled "Jachin and Boaz" as presenting, in his opinion, the best formula of the old initiation. He therefore translated it into the German language, and, remodeling it, presented it to the Provincial Grand Lodge in 1801, by whom it was accepted and established. It was soon after accepted by many other German Lodges on account of its simplicity. The system of Schroeder thus adopted consisted of the three degrees of Ancient Craft Masonry, all the higher degrees being rejected. But Schroeder found it necessary to enlarge his system, so as to give to brethren who desired it an opportunity of farther investigation into the philosophy of Masonry. He, therefore, established an *Engbund*, or Select Historical Union, which should be composed entirely of Master Masons, who were to be engaged in the study of the different systems and degrees of Freemasonry. The Hamburg Lodges constituted the *Mutterbund*, or central body, to which all the other Lodges were to be united by correspondence.

Of this system, the error seems to be that, by going back to a primitive ritual which recognizes nothing higher than the Master's Degree, it rejects all the developments that have resulted from the labors of the philosophic minds of a century. Doubtless in the high degrees of the eighteenth century there was an abundance of chaff, but there was also much nourishing wheat. Schroeder, with the former, has thrown away the latter. He has committed the logical blunder of arguing from the abuse against the use. His system, however, has some merit, and is still practised by the Grand Lodge of Hamburg.

Schroeder's Rite. See *Schroeder, Friedrich Joseph Wilhelm.*

Schroeder's System. See *Schroeder, Friedrich Ludwig.*

Sciences, Liberal. See *Liberal Arts and Sciences.*

Scientific Masonic Association. (*Scientifischer Freimaurer Bund.*) A society founded in 1803 by Fessler, Mossdorf, Fischer, and other distinguished Masons, the object being, by the united efforts of its members, to draw up, with the greatest accuracy and care, and from the most authentic sources, a full and complete history of Freemasonry, of its origin and objects, from its first formation to the present day, and also of the various systems or methods of working that have been introduced into the Craft; such history, together with the evidence upon which it was founded, was to be communicated to worthy and zealous brethren. The members had no peculiar ritual, clothing, or ceremonies; neither were they subjected to any fresh obligation; every just and upright Freemason who had received a liberal education, who was capable of feeling the truth, and desirous of investigating the mysteries of the Order, could become a member of this society, provided the ballot was unanimous, let him belong to what Grand Lodge he might. But those whose education had not been sufficiently liberal to enable them to assist in those researches were only permitted to attend the meetings as trusty brethren to receive instruction.

Scorpion. A genus of *Arachnida*, of numerous species, with an elongated body, but no marked division between the thorax

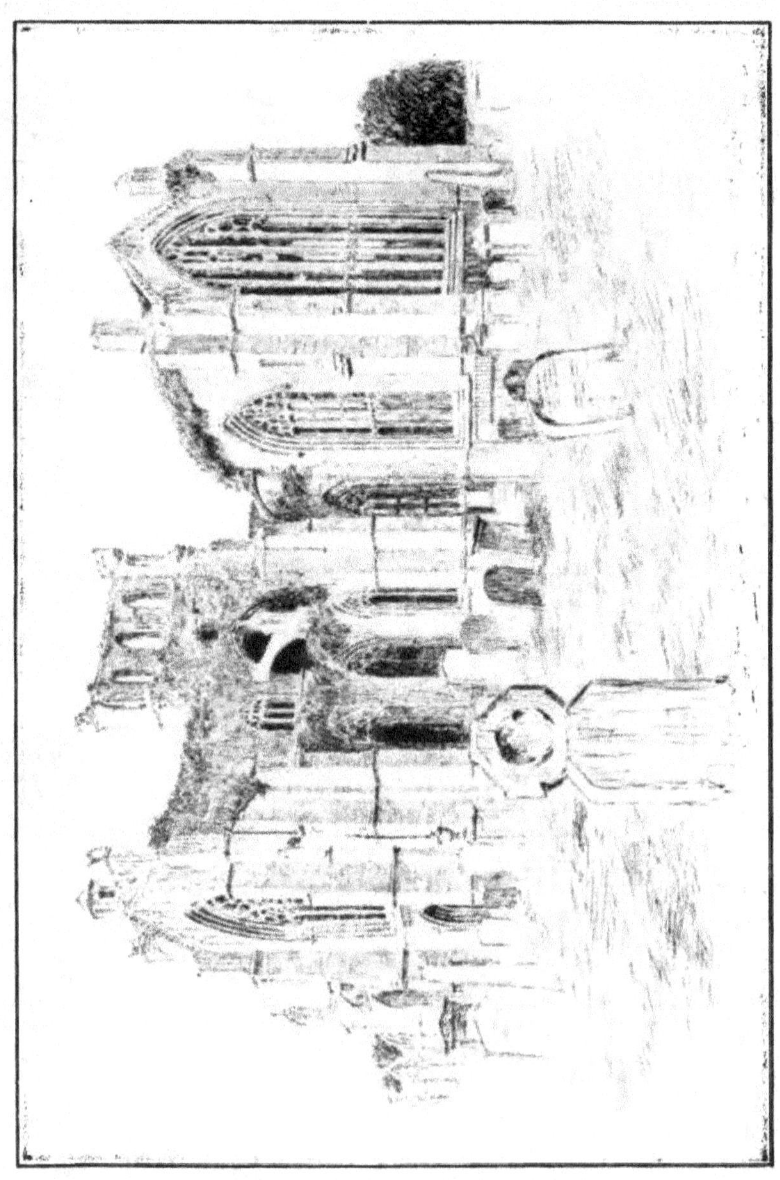

and abdomen. Those of the south of Europe and on the borders of the Mediterranean have six eyes. This reptile, dreaded by the Egyptian, was sacred to the goddess Selk, and was solemnly cursed in all temples once a year.

Scotland. The tradition of the Scotch Masons is that Freemasonry was introduced into Scotland by the architects who built the Abbey of Kilwinning; and the village of that name bears, therefore, the same relation to Scotch Masonry that the city of York does to English. "That Freemasonry was introduced into Scotland," says Laurie (*Hist.*, p. 89), "by those architects who built the Abbey of Kilwinning, is manifest not only from those authentic documents by which the Kilwinning Lodge has been traced back as far as the end of the fifteenth century, but by other collateral arguments which amount almost to a demonstration." In Sir John Sinclair's *Statistical Account of Scotland*, the same statement is made in the following words: "A number of Freemasons came from the continent to build a monastery there, and with them an architect or Master Mason to superintend and carry on the work. This architect resided at Kilwinning, and being a good and true Mason, intimately acquainted with all the arts and parts of Masonry known on the continent, was chosen Master of the meetings of the brethren all over Scotland. He gave rules for the conduct of the brethren at these meetings, and decided finally in appeals from all the other meetings or Lodges in Scotland." Which statement amounts to about this: that the brethren assembled at Kilwinning elected a Grand Master (as we should now call him) for Scotland, and that the Lodge of Kilwinning became the Mother Lodge, a title which it has always assumed. Manuscripts preserved in the Advocates' Library of Edinburgh, which were first published by Laurie, furnish further records of the early progress of Masonry in Scotland.

It is said that in the reign of James II., the office of Grand Patron of Scotland was granted to William St. Clair, Earl of Orkney and Caithness and Baron of Roslin, "his heirs and successors," by the king's charter. But, in 1736, the St. Clair who then exercised the Grand Mastership, "taking into consideration that his holding or claiming any such jurisdiction, right, or privilege might be prejudicial to the Craft and vocation of Masonry," renounced his claims, and empowered the Freemasons to choose their Grand Master. The consequence of this act of resignation was the immediate organization of the Grand Lodge of Scotland, over whom, for obvious reasons, the late hereditary Grand Master or Patron was unanimously called to preside.

Scotland, Royal Order of. See *Royal Order of Scotland*.

Scottish. We use indiscriminately the word *Scotch* or *Scottish* to signify something relating to Scotland. Thus we say the Scotch Rite or the Scottish Rite; the latter is, however, more frequently used by Masonic writers. This has been objected to by some purists because the final syllable *ish* has in general the signification of diminution or approximation, as in *brackish*, *saltish*, and similar words. But *ish* in Scottish is not a sign of diminution, but is derived, as in English, Danish, Swedish, etc., from the German termination *ische*. The word is used by the best writers.

Scottish Degrees. The high degrees adopted by Ramsay, under the name of Irish degrees, were subsequently called by him Scottish degrees in reference to his theory of the promulgation of Masonry from Scotland. (See *Irish Chapters*.)

Scottish Master. See *Ecossais*.

Scottish Rite. French writers call this the "Ancient and Accepted Rite," but as the Latin Constitutions of the Order designate it as the "Antiquus Scoticus Ritus Acceptus," or the "Ancient and Accepted Scottish Rite," that title has now been very generally adopted as the correct name of the Rite. Although one of the youngest of the Masonic Rites, having been established not earlier than the year 1801, it is at this day the most popular and the most extensively diffused. Supreme Councils or governing bodies of the Rite are to be found in almost every civilized country of the world, and in many of them it is the only Masonic obedience. The history of its organisation is briefly this: In 1758, a body was organised at Paris called the "Council of Emperors of the East and West." This Council organized a Rite called the "Rite of Perfection," which consisted of twenty-five degrees, the highest of which was "Sublime Prince of the Royal Secret." In 1761, this Council granted a Patent or Deputation to Stephen Morin, authorizing him to propagate the Rite in the Western continent, whither he was about to repair. In the same year, Morin arrived at the city of St. Domingo, where he commenced the dissemination of the Rite, and appointed many Inspectors, both for the West Indies and for the United States. Among others, he conferred the degrees on M. Hayes, with a power of appointing others when necessary. Hayes accordingly appointed Isaac Da Costa Deputy Inspector-General for South Carolina, who in 1783 introduced the Rite into that State by the establishment of a Grand Lodge of Perfection in Charleston. Other Inspectors were subsequently appointed, and in 1801 a Supreme Council was opened in Charleston by John Mitchell and Frederick Dalcho. There is abundant evidence in the Archives of the Supreme Council that up to that time the twenty-five degrees of the Rite of Perfection were alone recognized. But suddenly, with the organization of the Supreme Council, there arose a new Rite, fabricated by the adoption of eight more of the continental high degrees, so as to make the Thirty-third and not the Twenty-fifth Degree the summit of the Rite.

The Rite consists of thirty-three degrees, which are divided into seven sections, each section being under an appropriate jurisdiction, and are as follows:

I.

SYMBOLIC LODGE.

1. Entered Apprentice.
2. Fellow-Craft.
3. Master Mason.

These are called blue or Symbolic degrees. They are not conferred in England, Scotland, Ireland, or in the United States, because the Supreme Councils of the Rite have refrained from exercising jurisdiction through respect to the older authority in those countries of the York and American Rite.

II.

LODGE OF PERFECTION.

4. Secret Master.
5. Perfect Master.
6. Intimate Secretary.
7. Provost and Judge.
8. Intendant of the Building.
9. Elected Knight of the Nine.
10. Illustrious Elect of the Fifteen.
11. Sublime Knights Elect of the Twelve.
12. Grand Master Architect.
13. Knight of the Ninth Arch, or Royal Arch of Solomon.
14. Grand Elect, Perfect and Sublime Mason.

III.

COUNCIL OF PRINCES OF JERUSALEM.

15. Knight of the East.
16. Prince of Jerusalem.

IV.

CHAPTER OF ROSE CROIX.

17. Knight of the East and West.
18. Prince Rose Croix.

V.

COUNCIL OF KADOSH.

19. Grand Pontiff.
20. Grand Master of Symbolic Lodges.
21. Noachite, or Prussian Knight.
22. Knight of the Royal Ax, or Prince of Libanus.
23. Chief of the Tabernacle.
24. Prince of the Tabernacle.
25. Knight of the Brazen Serpent.
26. Prince of Mercy.
27. Knight Commander of the Temple.
28. Knight of the Sun, or Prince Adept.
29. Grand Scottish Knight of St. Andrew.
30. Knight Kadosh.

VI.

CONSISTORY OF SUBLIME PRINCES OF THE ROYAL SECRET.

31. Inspector Inquisitor Commander.
32. Sublime Prince of the Royal Secret.

VII.

SUPREME COUNCIL.

33. Sovereign Grand Inspector-General.

Scottish Templars. See *Templars of Scotland.*

Scottish Trinitarians. See *Prince of Mercy.*

Scribe. The Scribe is the third officer in a Royal Arch Chapter, according to the American ritual, and is the representative of Haggai. The *Sofer*, or Scribe in the earlier Scriptures, was a kind of military secretary; but in the latter he was a learned man, and doctor of the laws, who expounded them to the people. Thus Artaxerxes calls Ezra the priest, "a Scribe of the law of the God of heaven." Horne says that the Scribe was the King's Secretary of State, who registered all acts and decrees. It is in this sense that Haggai is called the Scribe in Royal Arch Masonry. In the English system of Royal Arch Masonry there are two Scribes, who represent Ezra and Nehemiah, and whose position and duties are those of Secretaries. The American Scribe is the Third Principal. The Scribes, according to the English system, appear to be analogous to the Soferim or Scribes of the later Hebrews from the time of Ezra. These were members of the Great Synod, and were literary men, who occupied themselves in the preservation of the letter of the Scriptures and the development of its spirit.

Scriptures, Belief in the. In 1820, the Grand Lodge of Ohio resolved that "in the first degrees of Masonry religious tests shall not be a barrier to the admission or advancement of applicants, provided they profess a belief in God and his holy word"; and in 1854 the same body adopted a resolution declaring that "Masonry, as we have received it from our fathers, teaches the divine authenticity of the Holy Scriptures." In 1845, the Grand Lodge of Illinois declared a belief in the authenticity of the Scriptures a necessary qualification for initiation. Although in Christendom very few Masons deny the Divine authority of the Scriptures of the Old and New Testaments, yet to require, as a preliminary to initiation, the declaration of such a belief, is directly in opposition to the express regulations of the Order, which demand a belief in God and, by implication, in the immortality of the soul as the only religious tests.

Scriptures, Reading of the. By an ancient usage of the Craft, the Book of the Law is always spread open in the Lodge. There is in this, as in everything else that is Masonic, an appropriate symbolism. The Book of the Law is the Great Light of Masonry. To close it would be to intercept the rays of Divine light which emanate from it, and hence it is spread open, to indicate that the Lodge is not in darkness, but under the influence of its illuminating power. Masons in this respect obey the suggestion of the

Divine Founder of the Christian religion, "Neither do men light a candle and put it under a bushel, but on a candlestick; and it giveth light unto all that are in the house." A closed book, a sealed book, indicates that its contents are secret; and a book or roll folded up was the symbol, says Wemyss, of a law abrogated, or of a thing of no further use. Hence, as the reverse of all this, the Book of the Law is opened in our Lodges, to teach us that its contents are to be studied, that the law which it inculcates is still in force, and is to be "the rule and guide of our conduct."

But the Book of the Law is not opened at random. In each degree there are appropriate passages, whose allusion to the design of the degree, or to some part of its ritual, makes it expedient that the book should be opened upon those passages.

Masonic usage has not always been constant, nor is it now universal in relation to what particular passages shall be unfolded in each degree. The custom in America, at least since the publication of Webb's *Monitor*, has been very uniform, and is as follows:

In the First Degree the Bible is opened at Psalm cxxxiii., an eloquent description of the beauty of brotherly love, and hence most appropriate as the illustration of a society whose existence is dependent on that noble principle. In the Second Degree the passage adopted is Amos vii. 7, 8, in which the allusion is evidently to the plumb-line, an important emblem of that degree. In the Third Degree the Bible is opened at Ecclesiastes xii. 1-7, in which the description of old age and death is appropriately applied to the sacred object of this degree.

But, as has been said, the choice of these passages has not always been the same. At different periods various passages have been selected, but always with great appropriateness, as may be seen from the following brief sketch.

Formerly, the Book of the Law was opened in the First Degree at the 22d chapter of Genesis, which gives an account of Abraham's intended sacrifice of Isaac. As this event constituted the *first grand offering*, commemorated by our ancient brethren, by which the ground floor of the Apprentice's Lodge was consecrated, it seems to have been very appropriately selected as the passage for this degree. That part of the 28th chapter of Genesis which records the vision of Jacob's ladder was also, with equal appositeness, selected as the passage for the First Degree.

The following passage from 1 Kings vi. 8, was, during one part of the last century, used in the Second Degree:

"The door of the middle chamber was in the right side of the house, and they went up with winding stairs into the middle chamber, and out of the middle into the third."

The appositeness of this passage to the Fellow-Craft's Degree will hardly be disputed.

At another time the following passage from 2 Chronicles iii. 17, was selected for the Second Degree; its appropriateness will be equally evident:

"And he reared up the pillars before the Temple, one on the right hand, and the other on the left; and he called the name of that on the right hand Jachin, and the name of that on the left Boaz."

The words of Amos v. 25, 26, were sometimes adopted as the passage for the Third Degree:

"Have ye offered unto me sacrifices and offerings in the wilderness forty years, O house of Israel? But ye have borne the tabernacle of your Moloch and Chiun your images, the star of your god, which ye made to yourselves."

The allusions in this paragraph are not so evident as the others. They refer to historical matters, which were once embodied in the ancient lectures of Freemasonry. In them the sacrifices of the Israelites to Moloch were fully described, and a tradition, belonging to the Third Degree, informs us that Hiram Abif did much to extirpate this idolatrous worship from the religious system of Tyre.

The 6th chapter of 2 Chronicles, which contains the prayer of King Solomon at the dedication of the Temple, was also used at one time for the Third Degree. Perhaps, however, this was with less fitness than any other of the passages quoted, since the events commemorated in the Third Degree took place at a somewhat earlier period than the dedication. Such a passage might more appropriately be annexed to the ceremonies of the Most Excellent Master as practised in this country.

At present the usage in England differs in respect to the choice of passages from that adopted in this country.

There the Bible is opened, in the First Degree, at Ruth iv. 7:

"Now this was the manner in former time in Israel concerning redeeming and concerning changing, for to confirm all things; a man plucked off his shoe, and gave it to his neighbor: and this was a testimony in Israel."

In the Second Degree the passage is opened at Judges xii. 6:

"Then said they unto him, Say now Shibboleth: and he said Sibboleth; for he could not frame to pronounce it right. Then they took him, and slew him at the passages of Jordan. And there fell at that time of the Ephraimites forty and two thousand."

In the Third Degree the passage is opened at 1 Kings vii. 13, 14:

"And king Solomon sent and fetched Hiram out of Tyre. He was a widow's son of the tribe of Naphtali, and his father was a man of Tyre, a worker in brass: and he was filled with wisdom, and understanding, and cunning to work all works in brass. And he came to king Solomon, and wrought all his work."

While from the force of habit, as well as from the extrinsic excellence of the passages themselves, the American Mason will, perhaps, prefer the selections made in our own

Lodges, especially for the First and Third Degrees, he at the same time will not fail to admire the taste and ingenuity of our English brethren in the selections that they have made. In the Second Degree the passage from Judges is undoubtedly preferable to our own.

In conclusion it may be observed, that to give these passages their due Masonic importance it is essential that they should be covered by the square and compasses. The *Bible*, *square*, and *compasses* are significant symbols of Freemasonry. They are said to allude to the peculiar characteristics of our ancient Grand Masters. The Bible is emblematic of the wisdom of King Solomon; the square, of the power of Hiram; and the compasses, of the skill of the Chief Builder. Some Masonic writers have still further spiritualised these symbols by supposing them to symbolise the wisdom, truth, and justice of the Great Architect of the Universe. In any view they become instructive and inseparably connected portions of the true Masonic ritual, which, to be understood, must be studied together.

Scroll. The written portion of the Jewish law, read at stated periods before the congregation, and preserved in the synagogue with great security.

Scythe. In the classic mythology, the scythe was one of the attributes of Saturn, the god of time, because that deity is said to have taught men the use of the implement in agriculture. But Saturn was also the god of time; and in modern iconography Time is allegorised under the figure of an old man, with white hair and beard, two large wings at his back, an hour-glass in one hand and a scythe in the other. It is in its cutting and destructive quality that the scythe is here referred to. Time is thus the great mower who reaps his harvest of men. Masonry has adopted this symbolism, and in the Third Degree the scythe is described as an emblem of time, which cuts the brittle thread of life and makes havoc among the human race.

Seal. A stamp on which letters and a device are carved for the purpose of making an impression, and also the wax or paper on which the impression is made. Lord Coke defines a seal to be an impression on wax, "sigillum est cera impressa," and wax was originally the legal material of a seal. Many old Masonic diplomas and charters are still in existence, where the seal consists of a circular tin box filled with wax, on which the seal is impressed, the box being attached by a ribbon to the parchment. But now the seal is placed generally on a piece of circular paper. The form of a seal is circular; oval seals were formerly appropriated to ecclesiastical dignitaries and religious houses, and the shape alluded to the old Christian symbol of the Vesica Piscis.

No Masonic document is valid unless it has appended to it the seal of the Lodge or Grand Lodge. Foreign Grand Lodges never recognise the transactions of subordinate Lodges out of their jurisdictions, if the standing of the Lodges is not guaranteed by the seal of the Grand Lodge and the signatures of the proper officers.

Seal of Solomon. The Seal of Solomon or the Shield of David, for under both names the same thing was denoted, is a hexagonal figure consisting of two interlaced triangles, thus forming the outlines of a six-pointed star. Upon it was inscribed one of the sacred names of God, from which inscription it was supposed principally to derive its talismanic powers. These powers were very extensive, for it was believed that it would extinguish fire, prevent wounds in a conflict, and perform many other wonders. The Jews called it the Shield of David in reference to the protection which it gave to its possessors. But to the other Orientalists it was more familiarly known as the Seal of Solomon. Among these imaginative people, there was a very prevalent belief in the magical character of the King of Israel. He was esteemed rather as a great magician than as a great monarch, and by the signet which he wore, on which this talismanic seal was engraved, he is supposed to have accomplished the most extraordinary actions, and by it to have enlisted in his service the labors of the genii for the construction of his celebrated Temple.

Robinson Crusoe and the *Thousand and One Nights* are two books which every child has read, and which no man or woman ever forgets. In the latter are many allusions to Solomon's seal. Especially is there a story of an unlucky fisherman who fished up in his net a bottle secured by a leaden stopper, on which this seal was impressed. On opening it, a fierce Afrite, or evil genius, came forth, who gave this account of the cause of his imprisonment. "Solomon," said he, "the son of David, exhorted me to embrace the faith and submit to his authority; but I refused; upon which he called for this bottle, and confined me in it, and closed it upon me with the leaden stopper and stamped upon it his seal, with the great name of God engraved upon it. Then he gave the vessel to one of the genii, who submitted to him, with orders to cast me into the sea."

Of all talismans, there is none, except, perhaps, the cross, which was so generally prevalent among the ancients as this Seal of Solomon or Shield of David. It has been found in the cave of Elephanta, in India, accompanying the image of the Deity, and many other places celebrated in the Brahmanical and the Buddhist religions. Mr. Hay, in an exploration into western Barbary, found it in the harem of a Moor, and in a Jewish synagogue, where it was suspended in front of the recess in which the sacred rolls were deposited. In fact, the interlaced triangles or Seal of Solomon may be considered as *par excellence* the great Oriental talisman.

In time, with the progress of the new religion, it ceased to be invested with a magical reputation, although the Hermetic philosophers of the Middle Ages did employ it as one of their mystical symbols; but true to the theory that superstitions may be repudiated, but never will be forgotten, it was adopted by the Christians as one of the emblems of their faith, but with varying interpretations. The two triangles were said sometimes to be symbols of fire and water, sometimes of prayer and remission, sometimes of creation and redemption, or of life and death, or of resurrection and judgment. But at length the ecclesiologists seem to have settled on the idea that the figure should be considered as representing the two natures of our Lord—his Divine and his human. And thus we find it dispersed all over Europe, in medallions, made at a very early period, on the breasts of the recumbent effigies of the dead as they lie in their tombs, and more especially in churches, where it is presented to us either carved on the walls or painted in the windows. Everywhere in Europe, and now in this country, where ecclesiastical architecture is beginning at length to find a development of taste, is this old Eastern talisman to be found doing its work as a Christian emblem. The spirit of the old talismanic faith is gone, but the form remains, to be nourished by us as the natural homage of the present to the past.

Among the old Kabbalistic Hebrews, the Seal of Solomon was, as a talisman, of course deemed to be a sure preventive against the danger of fire. The more modern Jews, still believing in its talismanic virtues, placed it as a safeguard on their houses and on their breweries, because they were especially liable to the danger of fire. The common people, seeing this figure affixed always to Jewish brew-houses, mistook it for a sign, and in time, in Upper Germany, the hexagon, or Seal of Solomon, was adopted by German innkeepers as the sign of a beer-house, just as the chequers have been adopted in England, though with a different history, as the sign of a tavern.

Seals, Book of the Seven. "And I saw," says St. John in the Apocalypse (v. 1), "in the right hand of him that sat on the throne a book written within and on the back side, sealed with seven seals." The seal denotes that which is secret, and seven is the number of perfection; hence the Book of the Seven Seals is a symbol of that knowledge which is profoundly secured from all unhallowed search. In reference to the passage quoted, the Book of the Seven Seals is adopted as a symbol in the Apocalyptic Degree of the Knights of the East and West, the seventeenth of the Ancient and Accepted Rite.

Seals, Keeper of the. An officer who has charge of the seal or seals of the Lodge. It is found in some of the high degrees and in continental Lodges, but not recognized in the York or American Rites. In German Lodges he is called *Siegelbewahrer*, and in French, *Garde des Sceaux*.

Search for Truth. This is the object of all Freemasonry and it is pursued from the first to the last step of initiation. The Apprentice begins it seeking for the light which is symbolised by the WORD, itself only a symbol of Truth. As a Fellow-Craft he continues the search, still asking for more light. And the Master Mason, thinking that he has reached it, obtains only its substitute; for the True Word, Divine Truth, dwells not in the first temple of our earthly life, but can be found only in the second temple of the eternal life.

There is a beautiful allegory of the great Milton, who thus describes the search after truth: "Truth came into the world with her Divine Master, and was a perfect shape and glorious to look upon. But when he ascended, and his apostles after him were laid asleep, there straight arose a wicked race of deceivers, who, as the story goes of the Egyptian Typhon, with his conspirators, how they dealt with the good Osiris, took the virgin Truth, hewed her lovely frame into a thousand pieces, and scattered them to the four winds of heaven. Ever since that time the friends of Truth, such as durst appear, imitating the careful search that Isis made for the mangled body of Osiris, went up and down, gathering up limb by limb still as they could find them."

Seceders. During the anti-Masonic excitement in America, which gave rise to the anti-Masonic party, many Masons, fearing the loss of popularity, or governed by an erroneous view of the character of Freemasonry, withdrew from the Order, and took a part in the political and religious opposition to it. These men called themselves, and were recognized by the title of, "seceders" or "seceding Masons."

Second Temple. See *Temple of Zerubbabel.*

Secrecy and Silence. These virtues constitute the very essence of all Masonic character; they are the safeguard of the Institution, giving to it all its security and perpetuity, and are enforced by frequent admonitions in all the degrees, from the lowest to the highest. The Entered Apprentice begins his Masonic career by learning the duty of secrecy and silence. Hence it is appropriate that in that degree which is the consummation of initiation, in which the whole cycle of Masonic science is completed, the abstruse machinery of symbolism should be employed to impress the same important virtues on the mind of the neophyte.

The same principles of secrecy and silence existed in all the ancient mysteries and systems of worship. When Aristotle was asked what thing appeared to him to be most difficult of performance, he replied, "To be secret and silent."

"If we turn our eyes back to antiquity," says Calcott, "we shall find that the old Egyptians had so great a regard for silence and secrecy in the mysteries of their religion, that they set up the god Harpocrates, to whom they paid peculiar honour and veneration, who was represented with the right hand placed near the heart, and the left down by his side, covered with a skin before, full of eyes and ears, to signify, that of many things to be seen and heard, few are to be published." (*Candid Disquisition*, p. 50.)

Apuleius, who was an initiate in the mysteries of Isis, says: "By no peril will I ever be compelled to disclose to the uninitiated the things that I have had intrusted to me on condition of silence."

Lobeck, in his *Aglaophamus*, has collected several examples of the reluctance with which the ancients approached a mystical subject, and the manner in which they shrank from divulgingany explanation or fable which had been related to them at the mysteries, under the seal of secrecy and silence.

And, lastly, in the school of Pythagoras, these lessons were taught by the sage to his disciples. A novitiate of five years was imposed upon each pupil, which period was to be passed in total silence, and in religious and philosophical contemplation. And at length, when he was admitted to full fellowship in the society, an oath of secrecy was administered to him on the sacred tetractys, which was equivalent to the Jewish Tetragrammaton.

Silence and secrecy are called "the cardinal virtues of a Select Master," in the Ninth or Select Master's Degree of the American Rite.

Among the Egyptians the sign of silence was made by pressing the index finger of the right hand on the lips. It was thus that they represented Harpocrates, the god of silence, whose statue was placed at the entrance of all temples of Isis and Serapis, to indicate that silence and secrecy were to be preserved as to all that occurred within.

Secretary. The recording and corresponding officer of a Lodge. It is his duty to keep a just and true record of all things proper to be written, to receive all moneys that are due the Lodge, and to pay them over to the Treasurer. The jewel of his office is a pen, and his position in the Lodge is on the left of the Worshipful Master in front.

Secretary-General of the Holy Empire. The title given to the Secretary of the Supreme Council of the Ancient and Accepted Rite.

Secretary, Grand. See *Grand Secretary*.

Secret Doctrine. The secret doctrine of the Jews was, according to Steinschneider, nothing else than a system of metaphysics founded on the commentaries on the law and the legends of the Talmudists. Of this secret doctrine, Maimonides says: "Beware that you take not these words of the wise men in their literal signification, for this would be to degrade and sometimes to contradict the sacred doctrine. Search rather for the hidden sense; and if you cannot find the kernel, let the shell alone, and confess that you cannot understand it." All mystical societies, and even liberal philosophers, were, to a comparatively recent period, accustomed to veil the true meaning of their instructions in intentional obscurity, lest the unlearned and uninitiated should be offended. The Ancient Mysteries had their secret doctrine; so had the school of Pythagoras, and the sect of the Gnostics. The Alchemists, as Hitchcock has clearly shown, gave a secret and spiritual meaning to their jargon about the transmutation of metals, the elixir of life, and the philosopher's stone. Freemasonry alone has no secret doctrine. Its philosophy is open to the world. Its modes of recognition by which it secures identification, and its rites and ceremonies which are its method of instruction, alone are secret. All men may know the tenets of the Masonic creed.

Secret Master. The Fourth Degree in the Ancient and Accepted Scottish Rite, and the first of what are called the "Ineffable Degrees." It refers to those circumstances which occurred at the Temple when Solomon repaired to the building for the purpose of supplying the loss of its illustrious builder by the appointment of seven experts, among whom were to be divided the labors which heretofore had been entrusted to one gigantic mind. The lecture elaborately explains the mystic meaning of the sacred things which were contained in the Sanctum Sanctorum, or Holy of Holies.

The Lodge is hung with black curtains strewed with tears, symbolic of grief. There should be eighty-one lights, distributed by nine times nine; but this number is often dispensed with, and three times three substituted. Later rituals reduce them to eight.

There are but two presiding officers—a Master, styled "Puissant," and representing King Solomon, and an Inspector, representing Adoniram, the son of Abda, who had the inspection of the workmen on Mount Lebanon, and who is said to have been the first Secret Master.

Solomon is seated in the east, clothed in mourning robes lined with ermine, holding a scepter in his hand, and decorated with a blue sash from the right shoulder to the left hip, from which is suspended a triangle of gold. Before him is placed a triangular altar, on which is deposited a wreath of laurel and olive leaves.

Adoniram, called "Venerable Inspector," is seated in the west, but without any implement of office, in commemoration of the fact that the works were suspended at the time of the institution of this degree. He is decorated with a triangular white collar, bordered with black, from which is suspended an ivory key, with the letter Z engraved thereon, which constitute the collar, and jewel of the degree. These decorations are worn by all the brethren.

The apron is white edged with black and with black strings; the flap blue, with an open eye thereon embroidered in gold. The modern ritual prescribes that two branches of olive and laurel crossing each other shall be on the middle of the apron.

Secret Monitor. An honorary or side degree very commonly conferred in the United States. The communication of it is not accompanied, it is true, with any impressive ceremonies, but it inculcates a lesson of unfaltering friendship which the prospect of danger could not appal, and the hour of adversity could not betray. It is, in fact, devoted to the practical elucidation of the Masonic virtue of Brotherly Love. In conferring it, those passages of Scripture which are contained in the twentieth chapter of the 1st Book of Samuel, from the sixteenth to the twenty-third, and from the thirty-fifth to the forty-second verses inclusive, are usually considered as appropriate. It may be conferred on a *worthy* Master Mason by any brother who is in possession of its ritual. There was in Holland, in 1778, a secret Masonic society called the Order of Jonathan and David, which was probably much the same as this American degree. Kloss in his *Catalogue* (1910[b]) gives the title of a book published in that year at Amsterdam which gives its statutes and formulary of reception.

Secret of the Secrets, The. A degree cited in the nomenclature of Fustier.

Secret Societies. Secret societies may be divided into two classes: First, those whose secrecy consists in nothing more than methods by which the members are enabled to recognise each other; and in certain doctrines, symbols, or instructions which can be obtained only after a process of initiation, and under the promise that they shall be made known to none who have not submitted to the same initiation; but which, with the exception of these particulars, have no reservations from the public. And secondly, of those societies which, in addition to their secret modes of recognition and secret doctrine, add an entire secrecy as to the object of their association, the times and places of their meeting, and even the very names of their members. To the first of these classes belong all those moral or religious secret associations which have existed from the earliest times. Such were the Ancient Mysteries, whose object was, by their initiations, to cultivate a purer worship than the popular one; such, too, the schools of the old philosophers, like Pythagoras and Plato, who in their esoteric instructions taught a higher doctrine than that which they communicated to their exoteric scholars. Such, too, are the modern secret societies which have adopted an exclusive form only that they may restrict the social enjoyment which it is their object to cultivate, or the system of benevolence for which they are organised, to the persons who are united with them by the tie of a common covenant, and the possession of a common knowledge; such, lastly, is Freemasonry, which is a secret society only as respects its signs, a few of its legends and traditions, and its method of inculcating its mystical philosophy, but which, as to everything else—its design, its object, its moral and religious tenets, and the great doctrine which it teaches—is as open a society as if it met on the highways beneath the sun of day, and not within the well-guarded portals of a Lodge. To the second class of secret societies belong those which sprung up first in the Middle Ages, like the *Vehm Gericht* of Westphalia, formed for the secret but certain punishment of criminals; and in the eighteenth century those political societies like the Carbonari, which have been organised at revolutionary periods to resist the oppression or overthrow the despotism of tyrannical governments. It is evident that these two classes of secret societies are entirely different in character; but it has been the great error of writers like Barruel and Robison, who have attacked Freemasonry on the ground of its being a secret association that they utterly confounded the two classes.

An interesting discussion on this subject took place in 1848, in the National Assembly of France, during the consideration of those articles of the law by which secret societies were prohibited. A part of this discussion is worth preserving, and is in the following words:

M. Volette: I should like to have one define what is meant by a secret society.

M. Coquerel: Those are secret societies which have made none of the declarations prescribed by law.

M. Paulin Gillon: I would ask if *Freemasonry* is also to be suppressed?

M. Floçon: I begin by declaring that, under a republican government, every secret society having for its object a change of the form of such government ought to be severely dealt with. Secret societies may be directed against the sovereignty of the people; and this is the reason why I ask for their suppression; but, from the want of a precise definition, *I would not desire to strike, as secret societies, assemblies that are perfectly innocent.* All my life, until the 24th of February, have I lived in secret societies. Now I desire them no more. Yes, we have spent our life in conspiracies, and we had the right to do so; for we lived under a government which did not derive its sanctions from the people. To-day I declare that under a republican government, and with universal suffrage, it is a crime to belong to such an association.

M. Coquerel: As to Freemasonry, your committee has decided that it *is not a secret society.* A society may have a secret, and yet not be a secret society. I have not the honor of being a Freemason.

The President: The thirteenth article has been amended, and decided that a *secret society is one which seeks to conceal its existence and its objects.*

Secret Vault. See *Vault, Secret.*

Sectarianism. Masonry repudiates all sectarianism, and recognises the tenets of no sect as preferable to those of any other, requiring in its followers assent only to those dogmas of the universal religion which teach the existence of God and the resurrection to eternal life. (See *Toleration.*)

Secular Lodges. The epithet *secular* has sometimes, but very incorrectly, been applied to subordinate Lodges to distinguish them from Grand Lodges. In such a connection the word is unmeaning, or, what is worse, is a term bearing a meaning entirely different from that which was intended by the writer. "Secular," says Richardson, "is used as distinguished from eternal, and equivalent to temporal; pertaining to temporal things,

things of this world; worldly; also opposed to spiritual, to holy." And every other orthoepist gives substantially the same definition. It is then evident, from this definition, that the word *secular* may be applied to all Masonic bodies, but not to one class of them in contradistinction to another. All Masonic Lodges are secular, because they are worldly, and not spiritual or holy institutions. But a subordinate Lodge is no more secular than a Grand Lodge.

Sedition Act. On July 12, 1799, the British Parliament, alarmed at the progress of revolutionary principles, enacted a law, commonly known as the Sedition Act, for the suppression of secret societies; but the true principles of Freemasonry were so well understood by the legislators of Great Britain, many of whom were members of the Order, that the following clause was inserted in the Act:

"And whereas, certain societies have been long accustomed to be holden in this kingdom, under the denomination of Lodges of Freemasons, the meetings whereof have been in a great measure directed to charitable purposes, be it therefore enacted, that nothing in this Act shall extend to the meetings of any such society or Lodge which shall, before the passing of this Act, have been usually holden under the said denomination, and in conformity to the rules prevailing among the said societies of Freemasons."

Seeing. One of the five human senses, whose importance is treated of in the Fellow-Craft's Degree. By sight, things at a distance are, as it were, brought near, and obstacles of space overcome. So in Freemasonry, by a judicious use of this sense, in modes which none but Masons comprehend, men distant from each other in language, in religion, and in politics, are brought near, and the impediments of birth and prejudice are overthrown. But, in the natural world, sight cannot be exercised without the necessary assistance of light, for in darkness we are unable to see. So in Masonry, the peculiar advantages of *Masonic sight* require, for their enjoyment, the blessing of *Masonic light*. Illuminated by its Divine rays, the Mason sees where others are blind; and that which to the profane is but the darkness of ignorance, is to the initiated filled with the light of knowledge and understanding.

Seekers. (*Chercheurs.*) The First Degree of the Order of Initiated Knights and Brothers of Asia.

Sefidd Schamagan. A secret Moslem Society, called also the Candidati, from being clothed in white. They taught that the wicked would be transformed, after death, into beasts, while the good would be reabsorbed into the Divine Creator. The chief was known as the Veiled Prophet.

Sejjin. The Arabic register of all the wicked, also the title of the residence of Eblis.

Selamu Aleikum, Es. The Arabic salutation of "Peace be with you"; which meets with the response "*Aleikum es Selaam.*" These expressions are prominently in use by ancient Arabic associations.

Select Master. The Ninth Degree in the American Rite, and the last of the two conferred in a Council of Royal and Select Masters. Its officers are a Thrice Illustrious Grand Master, Illustrious Hiram of Tyre, Principal Conductor of the Works, Treasurer, Recorder, Captain of the Guards, Conductor of the Council, and Steward. The first three represent the three Grand Masters at the building of Solomon's Temple. The symbolic colors are black and red, the former significant of secrecy, silence, and darkness; the latter of fervency and zeal. A Council is supposed to consist of neither more nor less than twenty-seven; but a smaller number, if not less than nine, is competent to proceed to work or business. The candidate, when initiated, is said to be "chosen as a Select Master." The historical object of the degree is to commemorate the deposit of an important secret or treasure which, after the preliminary preparations, is said to have been made by Hiram Abif. The place of meeting represents a secret vault beneath the Temple.

A controversy has sometimes arisen among ritualists as to whether the degree of Select Master should precede or follow that of Royal Master in the order of conferring. But the arrangement now existing, by which the Royal Master is made the First and the Select Master the Second Degree of Cryptic Masonry, has been very generally accepted, and this for the best of reasons. It is true that the circumstances referred to in the degree of Royal Master occurred during a period of time which lies between the death of the Chief Builder of the Temple and the completion of the edifice, while those referred to in the degree of Select Master occurred anterior to the builder's death. Hence, in the order of time, the events commemorated in the Select Master's Degree took place anterior to those which are related in the degree of Royal Master; although in Masonic sequence the latter degree is conferred before the former. This apparent anachronism is, however, reconciled by the explanation that the secrets of the Select Master's Degree were not brought to light until long after the existence of the Royal Master's Degree had been known and recognized.

In other words, to speak only from the traditional point of view, Select Masters had been designated, had performed the task for which they had been selected, and had closed their labors, without ever being openly recognized as a class in the Temple of Solomon. The business in which they were engaged was a secret one. Their occupation and their very existence, according to the legend, were unknown to the great body of the Craft in the first Temple. The Royal Master's Degree, on the contrary, as there was no reason for concealment, was publicly conferred and acknowledged during the latter part of the construction of the Temple of Solomon; whereas the degree of

Select Master, and the important incidents on which it was founded, are not supposed to have been revealed to the Craft until the building of the temple of Zerubbabel. Hence the Royal Master's Degree should always be conferred anterior to that of the Select Master.

The proper jurisdiction under which these degrees should be placed, whether under Chapters and to be conferred preparatory to the Royal Arch Degree or under Councils and to be conferred after it, has excited discussion. The former usage prevails in Maryland and Virginia, but the latter in all the other States. There is no doubt that these degrees belonged originally to the Ancient and Accepted Rite, and were conferred as honorary degrees by the Inspectors of that Rite. This authority and jurisdiction the Supreme Council for the Southern Jurisdiction of the Rite continued to claim until the year 1870; although, through negligence, the Councils of Royal and Select Masters in some of the States had been placed under the control of independent jurisdictions called Grand Councils. Like all usurped authority, however, this claim of the State Grand Councils does not seem to have ever been universally admitted or to have been very firmly established. Repeated attempts have been made to take the degrees out of the hands of the Councils and to place them in the Chapters, there to be conferred as preparatory to the Royal Arch. The General Grand Chapter, in the triennial session of 1847, adopted a resolution granting this permission to all Chapters in States where no Grand Councils exist. But, seeing the manifest injustice and inexpediency of such a measure, at the following session of 1850 it refused to take any action on the subject of these degrees. In 1853 it disclaimed all control over them, and forbade the Chapters under its jurisdiction to confer them. As far as regards the interference of the Ancient and Accepted Scottish Rite, that question was set at rest in 1870 by the Mother Council, which, at its session at Baltimore, formally relinquished all further control over them.

Semelius. An officer in the Sixth Degree of the Modern French Rite, known as the Grand Master of Despatches.

Semester. The *mot de semestre*, or semi-annual word, is used only in France. Every six months a secret word is communicated by the Grand Orient to all the Lodges under its jurisdiction. This custom was introduced October 28, 1773, during the Grand Mastership of the Duke of Chartres, to enable him the better to control the Lodges, and to afford the members a means whereby they could recognize the members who were not constant in their attendance, and also those Masons who either belonged to an unrecognised Rite, or who were not affiliated with any Lodge. The Chapters of the higher degrees receive a word annually from the Grand Orient for the same purpose. This, with the password, is given to the Tiler on entering the Temple.

Senatorial Chamber. When the Supreme Council of the Ancient and Accepted Rite meets in the Thirty-third Degree, it is said to meet in its senatorial chamber.

Seneschal. An officer found in some of the high degrees, as in the Thirty-second of the Ancient and Accepted Rite, where his duties are similar to those of a Warden of a Lodge, he acting as the deputy of the presiding officer. The title is derived from the old German *senne*, house, and *schalk*, servant. The seneschals in the Middle Ages were the lieutenants of the dukes and other great feudatories, and took charge of the castles of their masters during their absence.

Senior Deacon. See *Deacon*.

Senior Entered Apprentice. In the ritual of the early part of the last century the Senior and Junior Entered Apprentices acted in the place of the Deacons, which offices were then unknown. The Senior Entered Apprentice was placed in the south, and his duty was "to hear and receive instructions, and to welcome strange Brethren." (See *Junior Entered Apprentice*.)

Senior Warden. The second officer in a Symbolic Lodge. He presides over the Craft during the hours of labor, as the Junior does during the hours of refreshment, and in the absence of the Master he performs his duty. (See *Wardens*.)

Senses, Five. See *Five Senses*.

Senses, Seven. See *Man*.

Sentinel. An officer in a Royal Arch Chapter, in a council of Knights of the Red Cross, and in a Commandery of Knights Templar, whose duties are similar to those of a Tiler in a Symbolic Lodge. In some bodies the word *Janitor* has been substituted for *Sentinel*, but the change is hardly a good one. Janitor has been more generally appropriated to the porter of a collegiate institution, and has no old Masonic authority for its use.

Sephiroth. (Hebrew, ספירות.) It is a plural noun, the singular being *Sephira*. Buxtorf (*Lex. Talm.*) says the word means *numerations*, from SAPHAR, *to number;* but the Kabbalistic writers generally give it the signification of *splendors*, from SAPHIRI, *splendid*. The account of the creation and arrangement of the Sephiroth forms the most important portion of the secret doctrine of the Kabbalists, and has been adopted and referred to in many of the high philosophic degrees of Masonry. Some acquaintance with it, therefore, seems to be necessary to the Mason who desires to penetrate into the more abstruse arcana of his Order. (See *Kabbala*.)

Sephora. Wife of Moses, and daughter of Raguel or Jethro, Priest of Midian. Mentioned in the Fourth Degree of the French Rite of Adoption.

Septenary. The number *Seven*, which see.

Sepulcher. The spirit of gratitude has from the earliest period led men to venerate the tombs in which have been deposited the remains of their benefactors. In all of the ancient religions there were sacred tombs to which worship was paid. The tombs of the prophets, preserved by the Israelites, gave testimony to their reverence for the memory of these holy personages. After the advent of Christianity, the same sentiment of devotion led the pilgrims to visit the Holy Land, that they might kneel at what was believed to be the sepulcher of their Lord. In many of the churches of the Middle Ages there was a particular place near the altar called the sepulcher, whch was used at Easter for the performance of solemn rites commemorative of the Savior's resurrection. This custom still prevails in some of the churches on the Continent. In Templar Masonry, which is professedly a Christian system, the sepulcher forms a part of the arrangements of a Commandery. In England, the sepulcher is within the Asylum, and in front of the Eminent Commander. In America it is placed without; and the scenic representation observed in every well-regulated and properly arranged Commandery furnishes a most impressive and pathetic ceremony.

Sepulcher, Knight of the Holy. See *Knight of the Holy Sepulcher.*

Seraphim. (Heb., שרפים.) Singular *Seraph*, signifying "burning, fiery." Celestial beings in attendance upon Jehovah, mentioned by Isaiah. Similar to the Cherubim, having the human form, face, voice, two hands, and two feet, but six wings, with four of which they cover their faces and feet —as a sign of reverence—while with two they fly. Their specific office is to sing the praises of the Holy One, and convey messages from heaven to earth.

Seraphim, Order of. A Swedish Rite, instituted in 1334, revived in 1748. The number of knights, exclusive of the royal family, was twenty-four.

Serapis, Mysteries of. See *Egyptian Mysteries.*

Sermons, Masonic. Sermons on Masonic subjects, and delivered in churches before Masonic bodies or on Masonic festivals, are peculiar to the British and American Freemasons. Neither the French nor German, nor, indeed, any continental literature of Masonry, supplies us with any examples. The first Masonic sermon of which we have any knowledge, from its publication, was "A General Charge to Masons, delivered at Christ Church, in Boston, [Massachusetts], on the 27th of December, 1749, by the Rev. Charles Brockwell, A. M., published at the request of the Grand Officers and Brethren there." It was, however, not printed at Boston, but was first published in the *Freemasons' Pocket Companion* for 1754. Brockwell was chaplain of the English troops stationed at Boston. But in America, at least, the custom of delivering sermons on St. John's day prevailed many years before. In Dr. Mackey's *History of Freemasonry in South Carolina* (pp. 15–20) will be found the authentic evidence that the Lodges in Charleston attended Divine service on December 27, 1738, and for several years after, on each of which occasions it is to be presumed that a sermon was preached. In 1742 it is distinctly stated, from a contemporary gazette, that "both Lodges proceeded regularly, with the ensigns of their Order and music before them, to church, where they heard a very learned sermon from their brother, the Rev. Mr. Durand." Brockwell's, however, is the first of these early sermons which has had the good fortune to be embalmed in type. But though first delivered, it was not the first printed. In 1750, John Entick, afterward the editor of an edition of Anderson's *Constitutions*, delivered a sermon at Walbrook, England, entitled "The Free and Accepted Mason Described." The text on this occasion was from Acts xxviii. 22, and had some significance in reference to the popular character of the Order. "But we desire to hear of thee what thou thinkest; for as concerning this sect, we know that everywhere it is spoken against." Entick preached several other sermons, which were printed. From that time, both in England and America, the sermon became a very usual part of the public celebration of a Masonic festival. One preached at Newcastle-upon-Tyne, in 1775, is in its very title a sermon of itself: "The Basis of Freemasonry displayed; or, an Attempt to show that the general Principles of true Religion, genuine Virtue, and sound Morality are the noble Foundations on which this renowned Society is established: Being a Sermon preached in Newcastle, on the Festival of St. John the Evangelist, 1775, by Bro. Robert Green."

In 1799, the Rev. Jethro Inwood published a volume of *Sermons, in which are expressed and enforced the religious, moral, and political virtues of Freemasonry, preached upon several occasions before the Provincial Grand Officers and other Brethren in the Counties of Kent and Essex.* In 1849 Spencer published an edition of this work, enriched by the valuable notes of Dr. Oliver. In 1801 the Rev. Thaddeus Mason Harris, Grand Chaplain of the Grand Lodge and Grand Chapter of Massachusetts, published at Charlestown, Massachusetts, a volume of *Discourses delivered on Public Occasions, illustrating the Principles, displaying the Tendency, and vindicating the Design of Freemasonry.* This work has also been annotated in a new edition by Dr. Oliver, and republished in his *Golden Remains of Early Masonic Writers.* During this century there has been an abundance of single sermons preached and published, but no other collected volume of any by one and the same author has been given to the public since those of Dr. Harris. Yet the fact that annually in Great Britain and America hundreds of sermons in praise or in defense of Freemasonry are delivered from Christian pulpits, is a valuable testimony given by the clergy to the purity of the Institution.

Serpent. As a symbol, the serpent obtained a prominent place in all the ancient

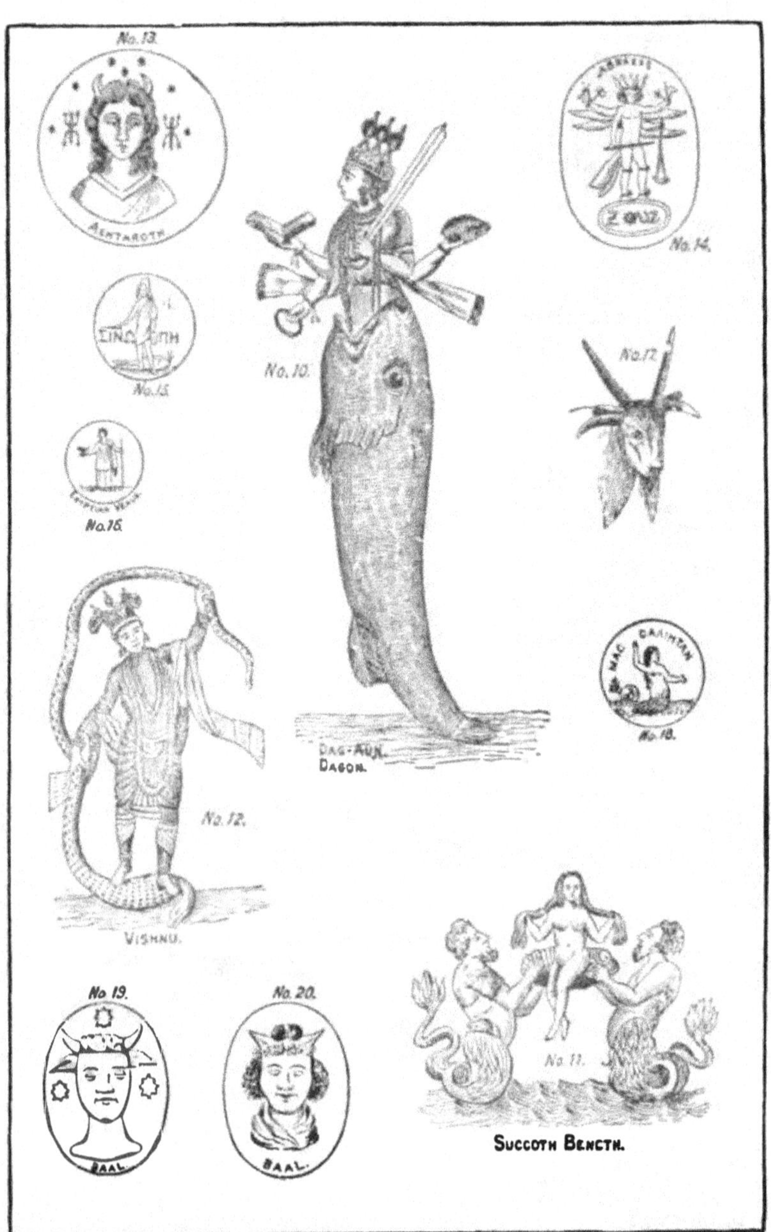
No. 13.
ASHTAROTH
No. 14.
No. 15.
No. 16.
No. 10.
No. 17.
DAG-AUN.
DAGON.
No. 18.
No. 12.
VISHNU.
No. 19.
BAAL.
No. 20.
BAAL.
No. 11.
SUCCOTH BENCTH.

initiations and religions. Among the Egyptians it was the symbol of Divine Wisdom when extended at length, and the serpent with his tail in his mouth was an emblem of eternity. The winged globe and serpent symbolized their triune deity. In the ritual of Zoroaster, the serpent was a symbol of the universe. In China, the ring between two serpents was the symbol of the world governed by the power and wisdom of the Creator. The same device is several times repeated on the Isiac table. Higgins (*Anacol.*, i., 521) says that, from the faculty which the serpent possessed of renewing itself, without the process of generation as to outward appearance, by annually casting its skin, it became, like the Phœnix, the emblem of eternity; but he denies that it ever represented, even in Genesis, the evil principle. Faber's theory of the symbolism of the serpent, as set forth in his work on the *Origin of Pagan Idolatry,* is ingenious. He says that the ancients in part derived their idea of the serpent from the first tempter, and hence it was a hieroglyphic of the evil principle. But as the deluge was thought to have emanated from the evil principle, the serpent became a symbol of the deluge. He also represented the good principle; the idea being borrowed from the winged Seraphim which was blended with the Cherubim who guarded the tree of life—the Seraphim and Cherubim being sometimes considered as identical; and besides, in Hebrew, שרף means both a *seraph* and a *serpent*. But as the good principle was always male and female, the male serpent represented the Great Father, Adam or Noah, and the female serpent represented the ark or world, the microcosm and the macrocosm. Hence the serpent represented the perpetually renovated world, and as such was used in all the mysteries. Dr. Oliver brings his peculiar views to the interpretation, and says that in Christian Masonry the serpent is an emblem of the fall and the subsequent redemption of man. In Ancient Craft Masonry, however, the serpent does not occur as a symbol. In the Templar and in the Philosophic degrees—such as the Knight of the Brazen Serpent, where the serpent is combined with the cross—it is evidently a symbol of Christ; and thus the symbolism of these degrees is closely connected with that of the Rose Croix.

Serpent and Cross. A symbol used in the degrees of Knights Templar and Knight of the Brazen Serpent. The cross is a tau cross T, and the serpent is twined around. Its origin is found in Numbers xxi. 9, where it is said, "Moses made a serpent of brass, and put it upon a pole." The word נס, *Nes*, here translated "a pole," literally means a standard, or something elevated on high as a signal, and may be represented by a cross as well as by a pole. Indeed, Justin Martyr calls it a cross.

Serpent, Knight of the Brazen. See *Knight of the Brazen Serpent.*

Serpent Worship. In ancient times, the serpent was an object of adoration in almost all nations. It was, in fact, one of the earliest deviations from the true system, and in almost all the ancient rites we find some allusion to the serpent. It was worshiped in India, Egypt, Phœnicia, Babylonia, Greece, and Italy. Indeed, so widely was this worship distributed, presenting everywhere so many similar features, that it is not surprising that it has been regarded by some writers as the primitive religion of man. And so long did it continue, that in the sect of Ophites it became one of the earliest heresies of the church. In some nations, as the Egyptians, the serpent was the representative of the good principle; but in most of them it was the emblem of the evil principle.

Serving Brethren. Masons whose duty it is to serve the Lodge as Tilers, waiters at the Lodge table, and to perform other menial services, are called in European Lodges "serving brethren." They are not known in America, but were long recognized as a distinct class in England and on the Continent. In 1753 the Grand Lodge of England adopted a regulation for their initiation, which, slightly modified, is still in force. By it every Lodge is empowered to initiate without charge "serving brethren," who cannot, however, become members of the Lodge, although they may join another. In military Lodges private soldiers may be received as serving brethren. On the Continent, at one time, a separate and preliminary form of reception, with peculiar signs, etc., was appropriated to those who were initiated as serving brethren, and they were not permitted to advance beyond the first degree; which, however, worked no inconvenience, as all the business and refreshment of the Lodges were done at that time in the Entered Apprentice's Degree. The regulation for admitting serving brethren arose from the custom of Lodges meeting at taverns; and as at that period labor and refreshment were intermixed, the waiters for the tavern were sometimes required to enter the room while the Lodge was in session, and hence it became necessary to qualify them for such service by making them Masons. In France they are called *Frères Servants;* in Germany, *Dienenden Brüder.*

The Knights Templar had a class called serving brothers, who were not, however, introduced into the Order until it had greatly increased in wealth and numbers. The form of their reception varied very slightly from that of the Knights; but their habit was different, being black. They were designated for the performance of various services inside or outside of the Order. Many rich and well-born men belonged to this class. They were permitted to take part in the election of a Grand Master. The treasurer of the Order was always a serving brother. Of these serving brothers there were two kinds: *servants at arms* and *artificers*. The former were the most highly esteemed; the latter being considered a very inferior class, except the *armorers*, who were held, on account of the importance of their occupation, in higher estimation.

Seth. It is a theory of some Masonic writers that the principles of the Pure or Primitive Freemasonry were preserved in the race of Seth, which had always kept separate from that of Cain, but that after the flood they became corrupted by a secession of a portion of the Sethites, who established the Spurious Freemasonry of the Gentiles. This theory has been very extensively advanced by Dr. Oliver in all his works. The pillars erected by Seth to preserve the principles of the arts and sciences are mentioned by Josephus. But although the Old Constitutions speak of Seth, they ascribe the erection of these pillars to the children of Lamech. But in the high degrees of Masonry the erection is attributed to Enoch. (See *Enoch*.)

Sethos. In 1731, the Abbé Terrasson published at Paris a work entitled *Sethos histoire ou vie tirée des monumens anecdotes de l'ancienne Egypte*. It has passed through a great many editions and has been translated into German and English. Under the form of fiction it contains an admirable description of the initiation into the ancient Egyptian mysteries. The labors and researches of Terrasson have been very freely used by Lenoir, Clavel, Oliver, and other writers on the ancient initiations.

Setting-Maul. A wooden hammer used by Operative Masons to "set" the stones in their proper positions. It is in Speculative Masonry a symbol, in the Third Degree, reminding us of the death of the builder of the Temple, which is said to have been effected by this instrument. In some Lodges it is very improperly used by the Master as his gavel, from which it totally differs in form and in symbolic signification. The gavel is a symbol of order and decorum; the setting-maul, of death by violence.

Setting Sun. It was the duty of the Senior Wardens to pay and dismiss the Craft at the close of day, when the sun sinks in the West; so now the Senior Warden is said in the Lodge to represent the setting sun.

Seven. In every system of antiquity there is a frequent reference to this number, showing that the veneration for it proceeded from some common cause. It is equally a sacred number in the Gentile as in the Christian religion. Oliver says that this can scarcely be ascribed to any event, except it be the institution of the Sabbath. Higgins thinks that the peculiar circumstance, perhaps accidental, of the number of the days of the week coinciding exactly with the number of the planetary bodies probably procured for it its character of sanctity. The Pythagoreans called it a perfect number, because it was made up of 3 and 4, the triangle and the square, which are the two perfect figures. They called it also a virgin number, and without mother, comparing it to Minerva, who was a motherless virgin, because it cannot by multiplication produce any number within ten, as twice two does four, and three times three does nine; nor can any two numbers, by their multiplication, produce it.

It is singular to observe the important part occupied by the number seven in all the ancient systems. There were, for instance, *seven* ancient planets, *seven* Pleiades, and *seven* Hyades; *seven* altars burned continually before the god Mithras; the Arabians had *seven* holy temples; the Hindus supposed the world to be enclosed within the compass of *seven* peninsulas; the Goths had *seven* deities, viz., the Sun, the Moon, Tuisco, Woden, Thor, Friga, and Seatur, from whose names are derived our days of the week; in the Persian mysteries were *seven* spacious caverns, through which the aspirant had to pass; in the Gothic mysteries, the candidate met with *seven* obstructions, which were called the "road of the seven stages"; and, finally, sacrifices were always considered as most efficacious when the victims were *seven* in number.

Much of the Jewish ritual was governed by this number, and the etymology of the word shows its sacred import, for the radical meaning of שבע, *shabang*, is, says Parkhurst, *sufficiency* or *fulness*. The Hebrew idea, therefore, like the Pythagorean, is that of *perfection*. To both the seven was a perfect number. Again: שבע, means *to swear*, because oaths were confirmed either by seven witnesses, or by seven victims offered in sacrifice, as we read in the covenant of Abraham and Abimelech. (Gen. xxi. 28.) Hence, there is a frequent recurrence to this number in the Scriptural history. The Sabbath was the *seventh* day; Noah received *seven* days' notice of the commencement of the deluge, and was commanded to select clean beasts and fowls by *sevens; seven* persons accompanied him into the ark; the ark rested on Mount Ararat in the *seventh* month; the intervals between despatching the dove were, each time, *seven* days; the walls of Jericho were encompassed *seven* days by *seven* priests, bearing *seven* rams' horns; Solomon was *seven* years building the Temple, which was dedicated in the *seventh* month, and the festival lasted *seven* days; the candlestick in the tabernacle consisted of *seven* branches; and, finally, the tower of Babel was said to have been elevated *seven* stories before the dispersion.

Seven is a sacred number in Masonic symbolism. It has always been so. In the earliest rituals of the last century it was said that a Lodge required seven to make it perfect; but the only explanation to be found in any of those rituals of the sacredness of the number is the seven liberal arts and sciences, which, according to the old "Legend of the Craft," were the foundation of Masonry. In modern ritualism the symbolism of seven has been transferred from the First to the Second Degree, and there it is made to refer only to the seven steps of the Winding Stairs; but the symbolic seven is to be found diffused in a hundred ways over the whole Masonic system.

*The sun was naturally the great central planet of the ancient seven, and is ever represented as the central light of the seven in the branched candlestick. Of the days of the week one was known as Sol's day, or Sunday, and as the Sun was the son of Saturn, he was ushered in by his father Saturn (or Saturday), whom he superseded. The Jews got their Sabbath from the Babylonians about 700 B.C. (*Anc. Faiths*, p. 863; also see *Philo Judæus*, *Josephus*, and *Clement of Alexandria*), while Sol's day dates from time immemorial, and was always a sacred one. In a phallic sense, when the sun has been in conjunction with the moon, he only leaves Luna after impregnation, and as Forlong, in his *Rivers of Life*, expresses it, "the young sun is that faint globe we so often see in the arms of the new moon," which is in gestation with the sun. The occult meaning of the word *Mi-mi* perhaps is

here revealed, as mentioned in 2 Kings xviii. 27, being defined *Firewater*. *Mi* is the name of the sun, and as well signifies gold. It is designated in the musical scale, and is also the name of *fire* in Burmese, Siamese, and cognate tongues, as mentioned by Forlong in treating of the *Early Faiths of Western Asia* (vol. ii., p. 65).

Next to the sun in beauty and splendor the moon leads all the hosts of heaven. And the Occidental, as well as the Oriental, nations were strongly moved in their imaginations by the awful majesty, the solemn silence, and the grandeur of that brilliant body progressing nightly through the starry vault: from the distant plains of India to ancient Egypt, and even those far-off lands where the Incas ruled, altars were erected to the worship of the Moon. On every seventh day the moon assumed a new phase, which gave rise to festivals to Luna being correspondingly celebrated; the day so set apart was known as *Moon*-day, or the second day of the week, that following *Sun*-day. "The Moon, whose phases marked and appointed their holy days." (Cicero, *Tusculan Disputations*, Book I., ch. 28.) In the Hebrew, Syrian, Persian, Phœnician, Chaldean, and Saxon, the word Seven signifies *full* or *complete*, and every seventh day after the first quarter the moon is complete in its change. In all countries the moon is best known under the beautiful figure of the *unveiling Queen of Heaven*.

The relative values of Seven in the musical scale and in the ancient planetary formula are as follows:

Si .	. Moon . . .	Silver.
Ut .	. Mercury . .	Quicksilver.
Re .	. Venus . . .	Copper.
Mi	Sun . .	. Gold.
Fa .	. Mars .	Iron.
Sol	. Jupiter	Tin.
La .	. Saturn	Lead.

The eminent professor of music, Carl Bergstein, in connection herewith, furnishes the information that Guido Aretinus, Monk, in the eleventh century, the great reformer of music, invented the staff, several keys, and the names *ut*, *re*, *mi*, *fa*, *sol*, *la*, *si*; they being taken from a prayer to St. John to protect the voice, running thus:

Ut queant laxis *Re*sonare fibris
*Mi*ra gestorum *Fa*muli tuorum
*Sol*ve polluti *La*bii reatum, Sancte Johannes.

The literal translation of which would be rendered:

"For that (or to enable) with expanded breast Thy servants are able to sing the praise of Thy Deeds, forgive the polluted lips the sins uttered."

The syllable *ut* has since been changed for the more satisfactory *do*.

In the year 1562 there was printed at Leipzig a work entitled *Heptalogium Virgilii Salsburgensis*, in honor of the number Seven. It consists of seven parts, each embracing seven divisions. In 1624 appeared in London a curious work on the subject of numbers, bearing the following title: "*The Secret of Numbers according to Theological, Arithmetical, Geometrical, and Harmonical Computation; drawn, for the better part, out of those Ancients, as well as Neoteriques.* Pleasing to read, profitable to understand, opening

*From this point the article is by C. T. McClenachan.

themselves to the capacities of both learned and unlearned; being no other than a key to lead men to any doctrinal knowledge whatsoever." In the ninth chapter the author has given many notable opinions from learned men, to prove the excellency of the number Seven. "First, it neither begets nor is begotten, according to the saying of Philo. Some numbers, indeed, within the compass of ten, beget, but are not begotten; and that is the unarie. Others are begotten, but beget not, as the octonarie. Only the septenaries have a prerogative above them all, they neither beget nor are begotten. This is its first divinity or perfection. Secondly, this is a harmonical number, and the well and fountain of that fair and lovely Sigamma, because it includeth within itself all manner of harmony. Thirdly, it is a theological number, consisting of perfection. Fourthly, because of its compositure; for it is compounded of the first two perfect numbers equal and unequal, three and four; for the number two, consisting of repeated unity, which is no number, is not perfect. Now every one of these being excellent of themselves (as hath been demonstrated), how can this number be but far more excellent, consisting of them all, and participating, as it were, of all their excellent virtues?"

Hippocrates says that the septenary number, by its occult virtue, tends to the accomplishment of all things, is the dispenser of life and fountain of all its changes; and, like Shakespeare, he divides the life of man into seven ages. In seven months a child may be born and live, and not before. Anciently a child was not named before seven days, not being accounted fully to have life before that periodical day. The teeth spring out in the seventh month, and are renewed in the seventh year, when infancy is changed into childhood. At thrice seven years the faculties are developed, manhood commences, and we become legally competent to all civil acts; at four times seven man is in full possession of his strength; at five times seven he is fit for the business of the world; at six times seven he becomes grave and wise, or never; at seven times seven he is in his apogee, and from that time he decays; at eight times seven he is in his first climacteric; at nine times seven, or sixty-three, he is in his grand climacteric, or years of danger; and ten times seven, or threescore years and ten, has, by the Royal Prophet, been pronounced the natural period of human life.

Seven Stars. In the Tracing-Board of the Seventeenth Degree, or Knight of the East and West, is the representation of a man clothed in a white robe, with a golden girdle round his waist, his right hand extended, and surrounded with seven stars. The Seventeenth is an apocalyptic degree, and this symbol is taken from the passage in Revelation i. 16, "and he had in his right hand seven stars." It is a symbol of the seven churches of Asia.

Seventy Years of Captivity. This period must be computed from the defeat of the Egyptians at Carchemish, in the same year that the prophecy was given, when Nebuchadnezzar reduced the neighboring nations of Syria and Palestine, as well as Jerusalem, under his subjection. At the end of seventy years, on the accession of Cyrus, an end was put to the Babylonish monarchy.

Shaddai. One of the names of God. In Exodus vi. 3, the word translated God Almighty is, in the original, *Shaddai*, שדי; it is therefore the name by which he was known to the Israelites before he communicated to Moses the Tetragrammaton. The word is a *pluralis majestatis*, and signifies all-powerful, omnipotent.

Shalal Shalom Abi. (Hebrew, שלום אבי שלל, *Diripuit pacem patri.*) A covered word in the Fifteenth Degree of the A. A. Scottish Rite.

Shalash Esrim. (Heb. שלש עשרים.) "Twenty-three," and refers to a day in the month Adar, noted in the Sixteenth Degree of the A. A. Scottish Rite.

Shamir. King Solomon is said, in a Rabbinical legend, to have used the worm *Shamir* as an instrument for building the Temple. The legend is that Moses engraved the names of the twelve tribes on the stones of the breastplate by means of the blood of the worm *Shamir*, whose solvent power was so great that it could corrode the hardest substances. When Solomon was about to build the Temple of stones without the use of any metallic implement, he was desirous of obtaining this potent blood; but the knowledge of the source whence Moses had derived it had been lost by the lapse of time. Solomon enclosed the chick of a bird, either an ostrich or a hoopoe, in a crystal vessel, and placed a sentinel to watch it. The parent bird, finding it impossible to break the vessel with her bill so as to gain access to the young one, flew to the desert, and returned with the miraculous worm, which, by means of its blood, soon penetrated the prison of glass, and liberated the chick. By a repetition of the process, the King of Israel at length acquired a sufficiency of the dissolving blood to enable him to work upon the stones of the Temple.

It is supposed that the legend is based on a corruption of the word *Smiris*, the Greek for emery, which was used by the antique engravers in their works and medallions, and that the name *Shamir* is merely the Hebrew form of the Greek word.

Sharp Instrument. The emblematic use of a "sharp instrument," as indicated in the ritual of the First Degree, is intended to be represented by a warlike weapon (the old rituals call it "a warlike instrument"), such as a dagger or sword. The use of the point of a pair of compasses, as is sometimes improperly done, is an erroneous application of the symbol, which should not be tolerated in a properly conducted Lodge. The compasses are, besides, a symbol peculiar to the Third Degree.

Shaster. ("Instruction.") Any book held more or less sacred among the Hindus, whether included in the Sruti or not. The Great Shasters comprise the Vedas, the Upavedas, and the Vedangas, with their appended works of learning, including the Puranas, the Ramayâna, and the Mahabharata.

Shastras. The sacred book of the Hindus, which contains the dogmas of their religion and the ceremonies of their worship. It is a commentary on the Vedas, and consists of three parts: the moral law, the rites and ceremonies of the religion, and the distribution of the people into tribes. To the Hindu Mason it would be the Greater Light and his Book of the Law, as the Bible is to his Christian brother.

Sheba, Queen of. In the Books of Kings and Chronicles, we are told that "when the Queen of Sheba heard of the fame of Solomon concerning the name of the Lord, she came to prove him with hard questions." Sheba, or Saba, is supposed to have been a province of Arabia Felix, situated to the south of Jerusalem. The queen, whose visit is thus described, is spoken of nowhere else in Scripture. But the Jews and the Arabs, who gave her the name of Balkis, recite many traditions concerning her. The Masonic one will be found under the words *Admiration, Sign of,* which see.

Shebat. (שבת.) The fifth month of the Hebrew civil year, and corresponding with the months January and February, beginning with the new moon of the former.

Shekel. In the Fourth or Mark Master's Degree, it is said that the value of a mark is "a Jewish half-shekel of silver, or twenty-five cents in the currency of this country." The shekel of silver was a weight of great antiquity among the Jews, its value being

about a half-dollar. In the time of Solomon, as well as long before and long after, until the Babylonish exile, the Hebrews had no regularly stamped money, but generally used in traffic a currency which consisted of uncoined shekels, which they weighed out to one another. The earliest specimens of the coined shekel which we know are of the coinage of Simon Maccabeus, issued about the year 144 B.C. Of these, we generally find on the obverse the sacred pot of manna, with the inscription, "Shekel Israel," in the old Samaritan character; on the reverse, the rod of Aaron, having three buds, with the inscription, "Ierushalem Kadoshah," or Jerusalem the Holy, in a similar character.

Shekinah Heb., שכינה, derived from SHAKAN, to dwell. A term applied by the Jews, especially in the Targums, to the Divine glory which dwelt in the tabernacle and the Temple, and which was manifested by a visible cloud resting over the mercy-seat in the Holy of Holies. It first appeared over the ark when Moses consecrated the tabernacle; and was afterward, upon the consecration of the Temple by Solomon, translated thither, where it remained until the destruction of that building.

The Shekinah disappeared after the destruction of the first Temple, and was not present in the second. Mr. Christie, in his learned treatise on the *Worship of the Elements*, says that "the loss of the Shekinah, that visible sign of the presence of the Deity, induced an early respect for solar light as its substitute." Now there is much that is significative of Masonic history in this brief sentence. The sun still remains as a prominent symbol in the Masonic system. It has been derived by the Masons from those old sun-worshipers. But the idea of Masonic light is very different from their idea of solar light. The Shekinah was the symbol of the Divine glory; but the true glory of divinity is *Truth*, and Divine Truth is therefore the Shekinah of Masonry. This is symbolized by light, which is no longer used by us as a "substitute" for the Shekinah, or the Divine glory, but as its symbol—the physical expression of its essence.

Shelum lecka. The password of the Order of Felicity. It is of Arabic root, signifying, "Peace be with you!"

Shem. שם. *The Name.* The Jews in their sacred rites often designated God by the word *Name*, but they applied it only to him in his most exalted character as expressed by the Tetragrammaton, JEHOVAH. To none of the other titles of God, such as *El*, *Eheyeh*, or *Adonai*, do they apply the word. Thus, *Shemchah Kadosh*, Thy name is holy, means Thy name Jehovah is holy. To the *Name* thus exalted, in its reference to the Tetragrammaton, they applied many epithets, among which are the following used by the Talmudists, שם של ארבע, *Shem shal arbang*, the name of four, i. e., four letters; שם המיוחד, *Shem hamjukad*, the appropriated name, i. e., appropriated solely to God. שם הגדול, *Shem haggadol*, the great name, and שם הקדוש, *Shem hakkadosh*, the holy name. To the Jew, as to the Mason, this great and holy name was the symbol of all Divine truth. The *Name* was the true name, and therefore it symbolized and represented the true God.

Shem, Ham, Japheth. The three sons of Noah, who assisted him in the construction of the ark of safety, and hence they became significant words in the Royal Arch Degree according to the American system. The interpolation of *Adoniram* in the place of one of these names, which is sometimes met with, is a blunder of some modern, ignorant ritual maker.

Shem Hamphorasch. שם המפורש, *the separated name.* The Tetragrammaton is so called because, as Maimonides (*More Nevoch.*) says, all the names of God are derived from his works except the Tetragrammaton, which is called the *separated name*, because it is derived from the substance of the Creator, in which there is no participation of any other thing. That is to say, this name indicates the self-existent essence of God, which is something altogether within himself, and separate from his works.

Shemitic. One of the three historical divisions of religion—the other two being the Turanian and the Aryan—and embraces Mosaism, Christianity, the Eddaic Code, and Moslemism.

Sheriff. According to Preston, the sheriff of a county possessed, before the revival of 1717, a power now confined to Grand Masters. He says (*Illust.*, p. 182) that "A sufficient number of Masons met together within a certain district, with the consent of the Sheriff or chief magistrate of the place, were empowered, at this time, to make Masons, and practise the rites of Masonry without a Warrant of Constitution." This is confirmed by the following passage in the Cooke MS. (lines 901–912): "When the masters and fellows be forewarned, and are come to such congregations, if need be, the Sheriff of the Country, or the Mayor of the City, or Aldermen of the Town in which such Congregation is holden, shall be fellow and sociate to the master of the congregation in help of him against rebels and [for the] upbearing the right of the realm."

Shermah, Insect. See *Insect Shermah.*

Shesha. The seven-headed serpent floating in the cosmical ocean, upon which the throne of Brahma rested.

Shetharboznai. See *Tatnai.*

Shewbread. The twelve loaves which were placed upon a table in the sanctuary of the Temple, and which were called the shewbread or bread of the presence, are represented among the paraphernalia of a Lodge of Perfection in the Ancient and Accepted Rite. Bähr (*Symbolik*) says that the shewbread was a symbol of the bread of life—of the eternal life by which we are brought into the presence of God and know him; an interpretation that is equally applicable to the Masonic symbolism.

Shibboleth. (Heb. שבלת.) The word which the Gileadites under Jephthah made use of as a test at the passages of the river Jordan after a victory over the Ephraimites. The word has two meanings in Hebrew: First, an ear of corn; and, secondly, a stream of water. As the Ephraimites were desirous of crossing the river, it is probable that this second meaning suggested it to the Gileadites as an appropriate test word on the occasion. The proper sound of the first letter of this word is *sh*, a harsh breathing which is exceedingly difficult to be pronounced by persons whose vocal organs have not been accustomed to it. Such was the case with the Ephraimites, who substituted for the aspiration the hissing sound of *s*. Their organs of voice were incapable of the aspiration, and therefore, as the record has it, they "could not frame to pronounce it right." The learned Burder remarks (*Orient. Cust.*, ii., 782) that in Arabia the difference of pronunciation among persons of various districts is much greater than in most other places, and such as easily accounts for the circumstance mentioned in the passage of Judges. Hutchinson (*Sp. of Mas.*, p. 182), speaking of this word, rather fancifully derives it from the Greek σιβω, *I revere*, and λιθος, *a stone*, and, therefore, he says "Σιβολιθον, Sibbolithon, *Colo Lapidem*, implies that they (the Masons) retain and keep inviolate their obligations, as the *Juramentum per Jovem Lapidem*, the most obligatory oath held among the heathen."

It may be remarked that in the ritual of the Fellow-Craft's Degree, where the story of the Ephraimites is introduced, and where Shibboleth is symbolically interpreted as meaning *plenty*, the word *water-ford* is sometimes used incorrectly, instead of *waterfall*. Shibboleth means a *flood of water*, a rapid stream, not a *ford*. In Psalm lxix. 3, the word is used in this exact sense. שטפתני שבלת, *Shibboleth shetafatni*, the flood has overwhelmed me. And, besides, a *waterfall* is an emblem of plenty, because it indicates an abundance of water; while a *water-ford*, for the converse reason, is, if any symbol at all, a symbol of scarcity.

Shield. The shape of the shield worn by the knight in the Middle Ages varied according to the caprice of the wearer, but generally it was large at the top and gradually diminished to a point, being made of wood and covered with leather, and on the outside was seen the escutcheon or representation of the armorial bearings of the owner. The shield, with all the other parts of the armor worn by the knights except the gauntlets, has been discontinued by the modern Masonic Knights. Oliver thinks that in some of the military initiations, as in those of the Scandinavian mysteries, the shield was substituted for the apron. An old heraldic writer, quoted by Sloane-Evans (*Gram. Brit. Her.*, 153), thus gives the symbolic import of the shield: "Like as the shield served in the battle for a safeguard of the body of soldiers against wounds, even so in time of peace, the same being hanged up, did defend the owner against the malevolent detractions of the envious."

Shield of David. Two interlaced triangles, more commonly known as the Seal of Solomon, and considered by the ancient Jews as a talisman of great efficacy. (See *Seal of Solomon.*) Because the shield was, in battle, a protection, like a talisman, to the person, the Hebrews used the same word, מגן, *Magen*, to signify both a *shield* and a *talisman*. Gaffarel says, in his *Curiositates Inauditæ* (*Lond. Trans.*, 1650, p. 133), "The

Hebrew word *Maghen* signifies a scutcheon, or any other thing noted with Hebrew characters, the virtue whereof is like to that of a scutcheon." After showing that the shield was never an image, because the Mosaic law forbade the making of graven images, he adds: "*Maghen*, therefore, signifies properly any piece of paper or other like matter marked or noted with certain characters drawn from the Tetragrammaton, or Great Name of four letters, or from any

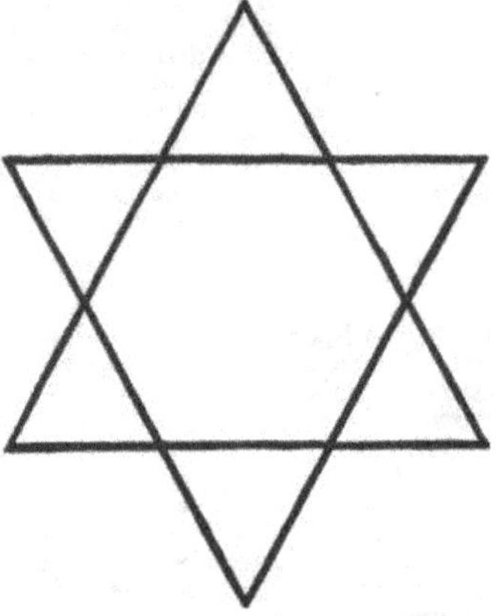

other." The most usual form of the Shield of David was to place in the center of the two triangles, and at the intersecting points, the Hebrew word אגלא, AGLA, which was compounded of the initials of the words of the sentence, אתה גבר לעלם ארני, *Atah Gibor Lolam Adonai*, "Thou art strong in the eternal God." Thus constructed, the Shield of David was supposed to be a preservative against all sorts of dangers.

Shinto. The national worship of the Japanese, and signifies the "path of the gods." It is presumed to be more ancient than the days of King Solomon, and is analogous to sun-worship.

Shintoism. The ancient religion of Japan, and founded on the worship of ancestors. It acknowledges a Supreme Creator and many subordinate gods called *Kami*, many of whom are the apotheoses of emperors and great men. It believes in the immortality of the soul, and in its ritual uses symbols, such as the mirror—which is the symbol of an unsoiled life—and lustrations symbolic of moral purification. Like the early Grecian mythology, Shintoism has deified natural objects, such as the sun, the air, earth, fire, water, lightning, thunder, etc. It is a system much mixed up with the philosophy of Confucius and with myths and legends.

Shock. A striking of hands and feet, so as to produce a sudden noise. There is a ceremony called "the shock," which was in use in the reception of an Apprentice in the beginning of this century, and is still used by some Lodges in what is called "the Shock of Entrance," and by all in "the Shock of Enlightenment." Of the first shock as well as of the second, there are evident traces in some of the earlier rituals of the last century, and there is no doubt that it was an ancient ceremony, the gradual disuse of which is an innovation.

Shock of Enlightenment. A ceremony used in all the degrees of Symbolic Masonry. By it we seek to symbolize the idea of the birth of material light, by the representation of the circumstances that accompanied it, and their reference to the birth of intellectual or Masonic light. The one is the type of the other; and hence the illumination of the candidate is attended with a ceremony that may be supposed to imitate the primal illumination of the universe—most feebly, it is true, and yet not altogether without impressiveness.

The *Shock of Enlightenment* is, then, a symbol of the change which is now taking place in the intellectual condition of the candidate. *It is the symbol of the birth of intellectual light and the dispersion of intellectual darkness.*

Shock of Entrance. A ceremony formerly used on the admission of an Entered Apprentice, but now partly becoming obsolete. In the old initiations, the same word signified *to die* and *to be initiated*, because, in the initiation, the lesson of death and the resurrection to eternal life was the dogma inculcated. In the initiation of an Apprentice in Masonry the same lesson is begun to be taught, and the initiate, entering upon a new life and new duties, disrupting old ties and forming new ones, passes into a new birth. This is, or ought to be, necessarily accompanied by some ceremony which should symbolically represent this great moral change. Hence the impression of this idea is made by the symbolism of the shock at the entrance of the candidate.

The shock or entrance is then the symbol of the disruption of the candidate from the ties of the world, and his introduction into the life of Masonry. *It is the symbol of the agonies of the first death and of the throes of the new birth.*

Shoe. Among the ancient Israelites, the shoe was made use of in several significant ways. *To put off the shoes*, imported reverence, and was done in the presence of God, or on entering the dwelling of a superior. *To unloose one's shoe and give it to another* was the way of confirming a contract. Thus we read in the Book of Ruth, that Boaz having proposed to the nearest kinsman of Ruth to exercise his legal right by redeeming the land of Naomi, which was offered for sale, and marrying her daughter-in-law, the kinsman, being unable to do so, resigned his right of purchase to Boaz; and the narrative goes on to say (Ruth iv. 7, 8), "Now this was the manner in former time in Israel concerning redeeming and concerning changing, for to confirm all things; a man plucked off his shoe, and gave it to his neighbor: and this was a testimony in Israel. Therefore the kinsman said unto Boaz, Buy it for thee. So he drew off his shoe." The reference to the shoe in the First Degree is therefore really as a symbol of a covenant to be entered into. In the Third Degree the symbolism is altogether different. For an explanation of it, see *Discalceation*.

Shoulkain. (Heb. שׁוּל־קִין, *Fimbria possessionis.*) Stolkin, mentioned in the Ninth and other degrees of the A. A. Scottish Rite.

Shovel. An instrument used to remove rubbish. It is one of the working-tools of a Royal Arch Mason, and symbolically teaches him to remove the rubbish of passions and prejudices, that he may be fitted, when he thus escapes from the captivity of sin, for the search and the reception of Eternal Truth and Wisdom.

Shrine. Oliver says that the shrine is the place where the secrets of the Royal Arch are deposited. The word is not so used in America, nor does it seem properly applicable according to the legend of the degree.

Side Degrees. There are certain Masonic degrees, which, not being placed in the regular routine of the acknowledged degrees, are not recognized as a part of Ancient Masonry, but receive the name of "Honorary or Side Degrees." They constitute no part of the regular ritual, and are not under the control of either Grand Lodges, Grand Chapters, or any other of the legal, administrative bodies of the Institution. Although a few of them are very old, the greater number are of a comparatively modern origin, and are generally supposed to have been indebted for their invention to the ingenuity of either Grand Lecturers, or other distinguished Masons. Their history and ceremonies are often interesting, and so far as we have been made acquainted with them, their tendency, when they are properly conferred, is always moral. They are not given in Lodges or Chapters, but at private meetings of the brethren or companions possessing them, informally and temporarily called for the sole purpose of conferring them. These temporary assemblies owe no allegiance to any supreme, controlling body, except so far as they are composed of Master or Royal Arch Masons, and when the business of conferring the degrees is accomplished, they are dissolved at once, not to meet again, except under similar circumstances and for a similar purpose.

Some of them are conferred on Master Masons, some on Royal Arch Masons, and some only on Knights Templar. There is another class which females, connected by certain ties of relationship with the Fraternity, are permitted to receive; and this fact, in some measure, assimilates these degrees to the Masonry of Adoption, or Female Masonry, which is practised in France and some other European countries, although there are important points of difference between them. These female side degrees have received the name of "androgynous degrees," from two Greek words signifying *man* and *woman*, and are thus called to indicate the participation in them by both sexes.

The principal side degrees practised in America are as follows:

1. Secret Monitor.
2. Knight of the Three Kings.
3. Knight of Constantinople.
4. Mason's Wife and Daughter.
5. Ark and Dove.
6. Mediterranean Pass.
7. Knight and Heroine of Jericho.
8. Good Samaritan.
9. Knight of the Mediterranean Pass.

Sight, Making Masons at. The prerogative of the Grand Master to make Masons at sight is described as the eighth landmark of the Order. It is a technical term, which may be defined to be the power to initiate, pass, and raise candidates, by the Grand Master, in a Lodge of emergency, or, as it is called in the *Book of Constitutions*, "an occasional Lodge," specially convened by him, and consisting of such Master Masons as he may call together for that purpose only; the Lodge ceasing to exist as soon as the initiation, passing, or raising has been accomplished, and the brethren have been dismissed by the Grand Master.

It is but right to say that this doctrine is not universally received as established law by the Craft. I do not think, however, that it was ever disputed until within a comparatively recent period. It is true that Cole (*Freemas.*, lib. 51), as far back as 1817, remarked that it was "a great stretch of power, not recognized, or at least, he believed, not practised in this country." But the qualifying phrases in this sentence, clearly show that he was by no means certain that he was correct in denying the recognition of the right. Cole, however, would hardly be considered as competent authority on a question of Masonic law, as he was evidently unacquainted with the *Book of Constitutions*, and does not quote or refer to it throughout his voluminous work.

In that *Book of Constitutions*, however, several instances are furnished of the exercise of this right by various Grand Masters.

In 1731, Lord Lovell being Grand Master, he "formed an occasional Lodge at Houghton Hall, Sir Robert Walpole's House in Norfolk," and there made the Duke of Lorraine, afterward Emperor of Germany, and the Duke of Newcastle, Master Masons.

I do not quote the case of the initiation, passing, and raising of Frederick, Prince of Wales, in 1737, which was done in "an occasional Lodge," over which Dr. Desaguliers presided, because, as Desaguliers was not the Grand Master, nor even, as has been incorrectly stated by the New York Committee of Correspondence, Deputy Grand Master, but only a Past Grand Master, it cannot be called *a making at sight.* He most probably acted under the Dispensation of the Grand Master, who at that time was the Earl of Darnley.

But in 1766, Lord Blaney, who was then Grand Master, convened "an occasional Lodge," and initiated, passed, and raised the Duke of Gloucester.

Again in 1767, John Salter, the Deputy, then acting as Grand Master, convened "an occasional Lodge," and conferred the three degrees on the Duke of Cumberland.

In 1787, the Prince of Wales was made a Mason "at an occasional Lodge convened," says Preston, "for the purpose at the Star and Garter, Pall Mall, over which the Duke of Cumberland (Grand Master) presided in person."

It has been said, however, by those who deny the existence of this prerogative, that these "occasional Lodges" were only special communications of the Grand Lodge, and the "makings" are thus supposed to have taken place under the authority of that body, and not of the Grand Master. The facts, however, do not sustain this position. Throughout the *Book of Constitutions*, other meetings, whether regular or special, are distinctly recorded as meetings of the Grand Lodge; while these "occasional Lodges" appear only to have been convened by the Grand Master for the purpose of making Masons. Besides, in many instances the Lodge was held at a different place from that of the Grand Lodge, and the officers were not, with the exception of the Grand Master, the officers of the Grand Lodge. Thus the occasional Lodge which initiated the Duke of Lorraine was held at the residence of Sir Robert Walpole, in Norfolk, while the Grand Lodge always met in London. In 1766, the Grand Lodge held its communications at the Crown and Anchor, but the occasional Lodge, which in the same year conferred the degrees on the Duke of Gloucester, was convened at the Horn Tavern. In the following year, the Lodge which initiated the Duke of Cumberland was convened at the Thatched House Tavern, the Grand Lodge continuing to meet at the Crown and Anchor.

But I think that a conclusive argument *à fortiori* may be drawn from the dispensing power of the Grand Master, which has never been denied. No one ever has doubted, or can doubt, the inherent right of the Grand Master to constitute Lodges by Dispensation, and in these Lodges, so constituted, Masons may be legally entered, passed, and raised. This is done every day. Seven Master Masons applying to the Grand Master, he grants them a Dispensation, under authority of which they proceed to open and hold a Lodge, and to make Masons. This Lodge is, however, admitted to be the mere creature of the Grand Master, for it is in his power at any time to revoke the Dispensation he had granted, and thus to dissolve the Lodge.

But if the Grand Master has the power thus to enable others to confer the degrees and make Masons, by his individual authority out of his presence, are we not permitted to argue *à fortiori* that he has also the right of congregating seven brethren and causing a Mason to be made in his sight? Can he delegate a power to others which he does not himself possess? And is his calling together an "occasional Lodge," and making, with the assistance of the brethren thus assembled, a Mason "at sight," that is to say, in his presence, any thing more or less than the exercise of his dispensing power for the establishment of a Lodge under Dispensation, for a temporary period and for a special purpose. The purpose having been effected, and the Mason having been made, he revokes his Dispensation, and the Lodge is dismissed. If we assumed any other ground than this, we should be compelled to say that though the Grand Master might authorize others to make Masons when he was absent, he could not do it himself when present. The form of the expression "making Masons at sight" is borrowed from Laurence Dermott, the Grand Secretary of the Atholl or Schismatic Grand Lodge; "making Masons in an occasional Lodge" is the phrase used by Anderson and his subsequent editors. Dermott (*True Ahim. Rez.*), commenting on the thirteenth of the old regulations, which prescribes that Fellow-Crafts and Master Masons cannot be made in a private Lodge except by the Dispensation of the Grand Master, says: "This is a very ancient regulation, but seldom put in practice, new Masons being generally made at private Lodges; however, the Right Worshipful Grand Master has full power and authority to make, or cause to be made, in his worship's presence, Free and Accepted Masons at sight, and such making is good. But they cannot be made out of his worship's presence without a written Dispensation for that purpose. Nor can his worship oblige any warranted Lodge to receive the person so made, if the members should declare against him or them; but in such case the Right Worshipful Grand Master may grant them a Warrant and form them into a new Lodge."

But the fact that Dermott uses the phrase does not militate against the existence of the prerogative, nor weaken the argument in its favor. For, in the first place, he is not quoted as authority; and secondly, it is very possible that he did not invent the expression, but found it already existing as a technical phrase generally used by the Craft, although not to be found in the Book of Constitutions. The form there used is "making Masons in an occasional Lodge," which, as I have already said, is of the same signification.

The mode of exercising the prerogative is this: The Grand Master summons to his assistance not less than six other Masons, convenes a Lodge, and without any previous probation, but *on sight* of the candidate, confers the degrees upon him, after which he dissolves the Lodge and dismisses the brethren.*

Sign. Signs constitute that universal language of which the commentator on the Leland MS. says that "it is a thing rather to be wished than hoped for." It is evident, however, that such a substitute for a universal language has always existed among mankiud. There are certain expressions of ideas which, by an implied common consent, are familiar even to the most barbarous tribes. An extension forward of the open hands will be understood at once by an Australian savage or an American Indian as a gesture betokening peace, while the idea of war or dislike would be as readily conveyed to either of them by a repulsive gesture of the same hands. These are not, however, what constitute the signs of Masonry.

It is evident that every secret society must have some conventional mode of distinguishing strangers from those who are its members, and Masonry, in this respect, must have followed the universal custom of adopting such modes of recognition.

The Abbé Grandidier (*Essais Historiques et Topographiques*, p. 422) says that when Josse Dotzinger, as architect of the Cathedral of Strasburg, formed, in 1452, all the Master Masons in Germany into one body, "he gave them a word and a particular sign by which they might recognize those who were of their Confraternity." Martene, who wrote a treatise on the ancient rites of the monks (*De Antiquis Monachorum ritibus*), says that, at the Monastery of Hirschau, where many Masons were incorporated as lay brethren, one of the officers of the monastery was called the Master of the Works; and the Masons under him had a sign which he describes as "pugnam super pugnam pone vicissim quasi simules constructores marum"; that is, they placed alternately fist upon fist, as if imitating the builders of walls. He also says, and other writers confirm the statement, that in the Middle Ages the monks had a system of signs by which they were enabled to recognize the members of their different orders.

Krause (*Kunsturkunden*, iv., 420) thinks that the Masons derived their custom of having signs of recognition from this rule of the old monks. But we can trace the existence of signs to remote antiquity. In the Ancient Mysteries, the initiates were always instructed in a sign.

*This custom of making Masons at sight has been practised by many Grand Lodges in America, but is becoming less usual, and some Grand Lodges have prohibited it by a constitutional enactment. A few noted cases may be mentioned: John Wanamaker, at Philadelphia; former Vice-President Charles W. Fairbanks, at Indianapolis, Indiana; the late Rear-Admiral Winfield Scott Schley, at Washington, D. C.; and when William Howard Taft was President-Elect, he was made a Mason "at-sight" on February 18, 1909, at Cincinnati, by the Grand Master of Ohio.

Thus, when a wreath was presented to an initiate of the mysteries of Mithras by another, instead of receiving it, he cast it upon the ground, and this gesture of casting down was accepted as a sign of recognition.

So, too, Apuleius (*Metamorph.*) describes the action of one of the devotees of the mysteries of Isis, and says: "He walked gently, with a hesitating step, the ankle of the left foot being slightly bent, in order, no doubt, that he might afford me some *sign* by which I might recognize him." And in another work (*Apologia*) he says: "If any one happens to be present who has been initiated into the same rites as myself, if he will *give me the sign*, he shall then be at liberty to hear what it is that I keep with so much care."

Plautus, too, alludes to this custom in one of his plays (*Miles Gloriosus*, iv., 2), when he says:

"*Cedo signum*, si harunc Baccharum est,"

i. e., "*Give me the sign*, if you are one of these Bacchantes."

Signs, in fact, belong to all secret associations, and are no more peculiar to Masonry than is a system of initiation. The forms differ, but the principle has always existed.

Signature. Every Mason who receives a certificate or diploma from a Grand Lodge is required to affix his signature in the margin, for a reason which is given under the words *Ne Varietur*, which see.

Signet. A ring on which there is an impression of a device is called a signet. They were far more common among the ancients than they are among the moderns, although they are still used by many persons. Formerly, as is the custom at this day in the East, letters were never signed by the persons who sent them; and their authenticity depended solely on the impression of the signets which were attached to them. So common was their use among the ancients, that Clement of Alexandria, while forbidding the Christians of the second century to deck their fingers with rings, which would have been a mark of vanity, makes an exception in favor of signet rings. "We must wear," he says, "but one ring, for the use of a signet; all other rings we must cast aside." Signets were originally engraved altogether upon stone; and Pliny says that metal ones did not come into use until the time of Claudius Cæsar.

Signets are constantly alluded to in Scripture. The Hebrews called them סבעות, *Sabaoth*, and they appear to have been used among them from an early period, for we find that when Judah asks Tamar what pledge he shall give her, she replies, "Thy signet, and thy bracelets, and thy staff that is in thine hand." (Gen. xxxviii. 18.) They were worn on the finger, generally the index finger, and always on the right hand, as being the most honorable; thus in Jeremiah xxii. 24, we read: "As I live, saith the Lord, though Coniah, the son of

Jehoiakim, king of Judah, were the signet upon my right hand, yet would I pluck thee thence." The signets of the ancients were generally sculptured with religious symbols or the heads of their deities. The sphinx and the sacred beetle were favorite signets among the Egyptians. The former was adopted from that people by the Roman Emperor Augustus. The Babylonians followed the same custom, and many of their signets, remaining to this day, exhibit beautifully sculptured images of Baal-Berith and other Chaldean deities.

The impression from the signet-ring of a king gave the authority of a royal decree to any document to which it was affixed; and hence the delivery or transfer of the signet to anyone made him, for the time, the representative of the king, and gave him the power of using the royal name.

Signet of Truth. The signet of Zerubbabel, used in the ritual of the Royal Arch Degree, is also there called the *Signet of Truth*, to indicate that the neophyte who brings it to the Grand Council is in search of Divine Truth, and to give to him the promise that he will by its power speedily obtain his reward in the possession of that for which he is seeking. The Signet of Truth is presented to the aspirant to assure him that he is advancing in his progress to the attainment of truth, and that he is thus invested with the power to pursue the search.

Signet of Zerubbabel. This is used in the American ritual of the Royal Arch Degree. It refers to a passage of Haggai (ii. 23), where God has promised that he will make Zerubbabel his signet. It has the same symbolic meaning as is given to its synonym the "Signet of Truth," because Zerubbabel, as the head of the second Temple, was the symbol of the searcher after truth. But something may be said of the incorrect form in which it is found in many Chapters. At least from the time when Cross presented an engraving of this signet in his *Hieroglyphic Chart*, and perhaps from a much earlier period, for he may possibly have only perpetuated the blunder, it has been represented in most Chapters by a triangular plate of metal. Now, an unattached plate of metal, in any shape whatsoever, is about as correct a representation of a signet as a walking-cane is of a piece of money. The signet is and always has been a finger-ring, and so it should be represented in the ceremonies of the Chapter. What the peculiar device of this signet was—for every signet must have a device—we are unable to show, but we may suppose that it was the Tetragrammaton, perhaps in its well-known abbreviated form of a *yod within a triangle*. Whether this was so or not, such a device would be most appropriate to the symbolism of the Royal Arch ritual.

Significant Word. Significant is making a sign. A significant word is a sign-making word, or a word that is equivalent to a sign; so the secret words used in the different degrees of Masonry, and the knowledge of which becomes a sign of the possession of the degree, are called significant words. Such a word Lenning calls "ein bedeutendes Wort," which has the same meaning.

Sign of Distress. This is probably one of the original modes of recognition adopted at the revival period, if not before. It is to be found in the earliest rituals extant of the last century, and its connection with the legend of the Third Degree makes it evident that it probably belongs to that degree. The Craft in the last century called it sometimes "the Master's Clap," and sometimes "the Grand Sign," which latter name has been adopted by the Masons of the present century, who call it the "Grand Hailing Sign," to indicate its use in *hailing* or calling a brother whose assistance may be needed. The true form of the sign has unfortunately been changed by carelessness or ignorance from the ancient one, which is still preserved in Great Britain and on the Continent of Europe. It is impossible to be explicit; but it may be remarked, that looking to its traditional origin, the sign is a defensive one, first made in an hour of attack, to give protection to the person. This is perfectly represented by the European and English form, but utterly misrepresented by the American. The German Rite of Schroeder attempted some years ago to induce the Craft to transfer this sign from the Third to the First Degree. As this would have been an evident innovation, and would have contradicted the ritual history of its origin and meaning, the attempt was not successful.

Sijel, Al. The recording angel in Islam.

Silence. See *Secrecy and Silence*.

Silent Brotherhood. Dwellers in the priories of Clugny and Hirsan in the eleventh century were placed under rigid discipline as to speech. Those of Clugny were the first to adopt the system of signs for daily intercommunication, which system, by consent or permissal, granted after application through three special messengers from the priory of Hirsan, was adopted by that priory in all its elaborateness, and indeed enlarged and perfected by the well-known Abbot William. The doctrine of a perfect silence in such extensive communities became noteworthy in history. These earnest and devoted men, under strong discipline, as "*Conversi* or *barbati fratres*," were encouraged by the abbeys of the Middle Ages. Their labors were conducted in companies of ten each, under deans of the monastery, who were in turn instructed by wardens and superiors.

Siloam Inscription. An inscription accidently discovered in 1880 by a native pupil of Mr. Schick, a German architect, who had long settled in Jerusalem. It is chiseled in the rock that forms the southern wall of the channel which opens out upon the ancient Pool of Siloam, and is partly concealed by the water. The present modern pool includes the older reservoir, supplied with water by an excavated tunnel, 1708 yards long, communicating with the Spring of the Virgin, which is cut through the ridge that forms the southern part of the Temple Hill. The pool is on the opposite side of the ridge, at the mouth of the Tyropœon (Cheesemakers) valley, which is now filled with rubbish, and largely built over.

The inscription is on an artificial tablet in the rock, about nineteen feet from the opening upon the pool. The first intelligible copy was made by Prof. A. H. Sayce, whose admirable little work, called *Fresh Light from the Ancient Monuments*, gives full details. Dr. Guthe, in March, 1881, made a complete *facsimile* of the six lines, which read thus:

"(Behold) the excavation! now this is the history of the excavation. While the excavators were still lifting up the pick, each towards his neighbor, and while there were yet three cubits to (excavate, there was heard) the voice of one man calling to his neighbor, for there was an excess in the rock on the right hand (and on the left). And after that on the day of excavating, the excavators had struck pick against pick, one against the other, the waters flowed from the spring to the pool for a distance of 1200 cubits. And (part) of a cubit was the height of the rock over the head of the excavators."

The engineering skill must have been considerable, as the work was tortuous, and yet the excavators met at the middle. There is no date, but the form of the letters show the age to be nearly that of the Moabite stone. Scholars place the date during the reign of Hezekiah. "He made the pool and the aqueduct, and brought the water into the city." (2 Kings xx. 20, Heb. B.). The discovery was an important one. Prof. Sayce deduces the following: "That the modern city of Jerusalem occupies very little of the same ground as the ancient one; the latter stood entirely on the rising ground to the east of the Tyropœon valley, the northern portion of which is at present occupied by the Mosque of Omar, while the southern portion is uninhabited. The Tyropœon valley itself must be the Valley of the Sons of Hinnom, where the idolaters of Jerusalem burnt their children in the fire to Moloch. It must be in the southern cliff of this valley that the tombs of the kings are situated," they being buried under the rubbish with which the valley is filled; and "among this rubbish must be the remains of the city and temple destroyed by Nebuchadnezzar. Here, as well as in the now obliterated Valley of the Cheesemakers, probably lie the relics of the dynasty of David."

Hebrew inscriptions of an early date have hitherto long been sought for in vain. Seals and fragmentary inscriptions have heretofore been discovered. Several of these seals have been found in Babylonia and Mesopotamia, and are regarded as memorials of the Jewish exiles; but the Schick discovery gives us a writing certainly as old as the time of Isaiah.

Silver and Gold. When St. Peter healed the lame man whom he met at the gate Beautiful of the Temple, he said to him, "Silver and gold have I none; but such as I have give I thee" (Acts iii. 6); and he bestowed on him the gift of health. When the pious pilgrim begged his way, through all the perils of a distant journey, to kneel at the Holy Sepulcher, in his passage through poor and inhospitable regions, a crust of bread and a draft of water were often the only alms that he received. This has been symbolized in the ritual of reception of a Knights Templar, and in it the words of St. Peter have been preserved, to be applied to the allegorical pilgrimage there represented.

Silver Cord. In the beautiful and affecting description of the body of man suffering under the infirmities of old age given in the twelfth chapter of Ecclesiastes, we find the expression "or ever the silver cord be loosed, or the golden bowl be broken, or the pitcher be broken at the fountain, or the wheel broken at the cistern: then shall the dust return to the earth as it was, and the spirit shall return to God who gave it." Dr. Clarke thus explains these beautiful metaphors. The silver cord is the spinal marrow; its loosening is the cessation of all nervous sensibility; the golden bowl is the brain, which is rendered unfit to perform its functions by the approach of death; the pitcher means the great vein which carries the blood to the right ventricle of the heart, here called the fountain; by the wheel is meant the great artery which receives the blood from the left ventricle of the heart, here designated as the cistern. This collection of metaphors is a part of the Scripture reading in the Third Degree, and forms an appropriate introduction to those sublime ceremonies whose object is to teach symbolically the resurrection and life eternal.

Simorgh. A monstrous griffin, guardian of the Persian mysteries.

Sinai. A mountain of Arabia between the horns of the Red Sea. It is the place where Moses received the Law from Jehovah, and where he was directed to construct the tabernacle. Hence, says Lenning, the Scottish Masons make Mt. Sinai a symbol of truth. Of the high degrees, the Twenty-third and Twenty-fourth of the Ancient and Accepted Rite, or the Chief and the Prince of the Tabernacle, refer in their rituals to this mountain and the Tabernacle there constructed.

Sir. This is the distinctive title given to the possessors of the degrees of Masonic knighthood, and is borrowed from the heraldic usage. The word "knight" is sometimes interposed between the title and the personal name, as, for example, "Sir Knight John Smith." English knights are in the habit of using the word *frater*, or *brother*, a usage which to some extent is being adopted in America. English Knights Templar have been led to the abandonment of the title *Sir* because legal enactments made the use of titles not granted by the crowu unlawful. But there is no such law in America. The addition of *Sir* to the names of all Knights is accounted, says Ashmole, "parcel of their style." The use of it is as old, certainly, as the time of Edward I., and it is supposed to be a contraction of the old French *Sire*, meaning *Seigneur*, or *Lord*.

Sirat, As or Al. See *Al-Sirat*.

Siroc. שרוך. A significant word, formerly used in the Order of High Priesthood in America. It signifies a shoe-latchet, and refers to the declaration of Abraham to Melchizedek, that of the goods which had been captured he would "not take from a thread even to a shoe-latchet" (Genesis xiv. 23), that is, nothing even of the slightest value. The introduction of this word into some of the lower capitular degrees is a recent error of ignorant ritualists.

Sister Lodges. Lodges are so called which are in the same Masonic jurisdiction, and owe obedience to the same Grand Lodge.

Sisters by Adoption. In the Lodges of the French Adoptive Rite this is the title by which the female members are designated. The female members of all androgynous degrees are sisters, as the male members are brethren.

Sisters of the Gild. The attempt of a few writers to maintain that women were admitted into the Medieval confraternities of Masons fails to be substantiated for want of sufficient proof. The entire spirit of the Old Constitutions indicates that none but men, under the titles of "brethren" and "fellows," were admitted into these Masonic gilds; and the first code of charges adopted at the revival in 1717, declares that "the persons admitted members of a Lodge must be good and true men . . . no women, etc." The opinion that women were originally admitted into the Masonic gild, as it is asserted that they were into some of the others, is based upon the fact that, in what is called the "York MS., No. 4," whose date as affixed to the roll is 1693, we find the following words: "The one of the elders takeing the Booke, and that hee or shee that is to be made mason shall lay their hands theron, and the charge shall be given." But in the "Alnwick MS.," which is inserted as a Preface to the Records of the Lodge at Alnwick, beginning September 29, 1701, and which manuscript was therefore probably at least contemporary with that of York, we find the corresponding passage in the following words: "Then shall one of the most ancient of them all hold a book that he or they may lay his or their hands upon the said Book," etc. Again, in the "Grand Lodge, No. 1, MS.," whose date is 1583, we meet with the regulation in Latin thus: "Tunc unus ex senioribus teneat librum et ille vel illi apposuerunt manus sub librum et tunc præcepta deberent legi." This was no doubt the original form of which the writer of the York MS. gives a translation, and either through ignorance or clerical carelessness, the "ille vel illi," instead of *he or they*, has been translated *he or she*. Besides, the whole tenor of the charges in the York MS. clearly shows that they were intended for men only. A woman could scarcely have been required to swear that she "would not take her fellow's wife in villainy," nor make anyone a Mason unless "he has his right limbs as a man ought to have." It cannot be admitted on the authority of a mistranslation of a single letter, by which an *a* was taken for an *e*, thus changing *ille* into *illa*, or *he* into *she*, that the Masonic gild admitted women into a craft whose labors were to hew heavy stones and to ascend tall scaffolds. Such never could have been the case in Operative Masonry.

There is, however, abundant evidence that in the other gilds, or livery companies of England, women or sisters were admitted to the freedom of the company. Herbert (*Hist. Liv. Comp.*, xi., 83) thinks that the custom was borrowed, on the constitution of the Companies, by Edward III. from the ecclesiastical or religious gilds, which were often composed of both sexes. But there does not seem to be any evidence that the usage was extended to the building corporations or Freemasons' gilds. A woman might be a female grocer or haberdasher, but she could hardly perform the duties of a female builder.

"Sit Lux et Lux Fuit." A motto frequently used in Masonry, although sometimes written, "Lux Fiat et Lux Fit," signifying, "Let there be light, and there was light"; the strict translation from the Hebrew continues, "And the Lord took care of the light, that it was useful, and he divided the light from the darkness."

Situation of the Lodge. A Lodge is, or ought to be, always situated due east and west, for reasons which are detailed in the articles *East* and *Orientation*, which see.

Sivan. (סיון.) The ninth month of the Hebrew civil year, corresponding with the months May and June, beginning with the new moon of the former.

Six Lights. The six lights of Symbolic Masonry are divided into the *Greater* and *Lesser Lights*, which see. In the American system of the Royal Arch there is no symbol of the kind, but in the English system there are six lights—three lesser and three greater—placed in the form of two interlaced triangles. The three lesser represent the Patriarchal, Mosaic, and Christian dispensations; the three greater the Creative, Preservative, and Destructive power of God. The four lesser triangles, formed by the intersection of the two great triangles, are emblematic of the four degrees of Ancient Craft Masonry.

Six Periods. The Great Architect's Six Periods constituted a part of the old Prestonian lecture in the Fellow-Craft's Degree. It referred to the six days of creation, the six periods being the six days. It no longer forms a part of the lecture as modified by Hemming in England, although Oliver devotes a chapter in his *Historical Landmarks* to this subject. It was most probably at one time taught in America before Webb modified and abridged the Prestonian lectures, for Hardie gives the "Six Periods" in full in his *Monitor*, which was published in 1818. The Webb lecture, now practised in this country, comprehends the whole subject of the Six Periods, which make a closely printed page in Browne's *Master Key*, in these few words: "In six days God created the heavens and the earth, and rested upon the seventh day; the seventh, therefore, our ancient brethren consecrated as a day of rest from their labors; thereby enjoying frequent opportunities to contemplate the glorious works of creation, and to adore their great Creator."

Skeleton. A symbol of death. The ancient Egyptians often introduced a skeleton in their feasts to remind the revelers of the transitory nature of their enjoyments, and to teach them that in the midst of life we are in death. As such an admonitory symbol it is used in some of the high degrees.

Skirret. In the English system the skirret is one of the working-tools of a Master Mason. It is an implement which acts on a center-pin, whence a line is drawn, chalked, and struck to mark out the ground for the foundation of the intended structure. Symbolically, it points to us that straight and undeviating line of conduct laid down for our pursuits in the volume of the Sacred Law. The skirret is not used in the American system.

Skull. The skull as a symbol is not used in Masonry except in Masonic Templarism, where it is a symbol of mortality. Among the articles of accusation sent by the Pope to the bishops and papal commissaries upon which to examine the Knights Templar, those from the forty-second to the fifty-seventh refer to the human skull, "cranium humanum," which the Templars were accused of using in their reception, and worshiping as an idol. It is possible that the Old Templars made use of the skull in their ceremony of reception; but Modern Templars will readily acquit their predecessors of the crime of idolatry, and find in their use of a skull a symbolic design. (See *Baphomet*.)

Skull and Cross-bones. They are a symbol of mortality and death, and are so used by heralds in funeral achievements. As the means ef inciting the mind to the contemplation of the most solemn subjects, the skull and cross-bones are used in the Chamber of Reflection in the French and Scottish Rites, and in all those degrees where that Chamber constitutes a part of the preliminary ceremonies of initiation.

Slander. Inwood, in his sermon on "Union Amongst Masons," says: "To defame our brother, or suffer him to be defamed, without interesting ourselves for the preservation of his name and character, there is scarcely the shadow of an excuse to be formed. Defamation is always wicked. Slander and evil speaking are the pests of civil society, are the disgrace of every degree of religious profession, are the poisonous bane of all brotherly love."

Slave. See *Free Born*.

Slip. This technical expression in American Masonry, but mostly confined to the Western States, and not generally used, is of very recent origin; and both the action and the word most probably sprang up, with a few other innovations, intended as especial methods of precaution, about the time of the anti-Masonic excitement.

Sloane Manuscripts. There are three copies of the Old Constitutions which bear this name. All of them were found in the British Museum among the heterogeneous collection of papers which were once the property of Sir Hans Sloane. The first, which is known in the Museum as No. 3848, is one of the most complete of the copies extant of the Old Constitutions. At the end of it, the date is certified by the following subscription: "Finis p.me Eduardu Sankey decimo sexto die Octobris Anno Domini 1646." It was published for the first time, from an exact transcript of the original, by Bro. Hughan in his *Old Charges of the British Freemasons*. The second Sloane MS. is known in the British Museum as No. 3323. It is in a large folio volume of three hundred and twenty-eight leaves, on the fly-leaf of which Sir Hans Sloane has written, "Loose papers of mine Concerning Curiosities." There are many Manuscripts by different hands. The Masonic one is subscribed "Hæc scripta fuerunt p. me Thomam Martin, 1659," and this fixes the date. It consists of three leaves of paper six inches by seven and a half, is written in a small, neat hand, and endorsed "Free Masonry." It was first published, in 1871, by Bro. Hughan in his *Masonic Sketches and Reprints*. The Rev. Bro. A. F. A. Woodford thinks this an "indifferent copy of the former one." But this seems unlikely. The entire omission of the "Legend of the Craft" from the time of Lamech to the building of the Temple, including the important "Legend of Euclid," all of which is given in full in the MS. No. 3848, together with a great many verbal discrepancies, and a total difference in the eighteenth charge, would lead one to suppose that the former MS. never was seen, or at least copied, by the writer of the latter. On the whole, it is, from this very omission, one of the least valuable of the copies of the Old Constitutions.

The third Sloane MS. is really one of the most interesting and valuable of those that have been heretofore discovered. A portion of it, a small portion, was inserted by Findel in his *History of Freemasonry*; but the whole has been since published in the *Voice of Masonry*, a periodical printed at Chicago in 1872. The number of the MS. in the British Museum is 3329, and Mr. Hughan places its date at from 1640 to 1700; but he says that Messrs. Bond and Sims, of the British Museum, agree in stating that it is "probably of the beginning of the eighteenth century." But the Rev. Mr. Woodford mentions a *great authority* on MSS., who declares it to be "previous to the middle of the seventeenth century." Findel thinks it originated at the end of the seventeenth century, and "that it was found among the papers which Dr. Plot left behind him on his death, and was one of the sources whence his communications on Freemasonry were derived." It is not a copy of the Old Constitutions, in which respect it differs from all the other Manuscripts, but is a description of the ritual of the society of Free Operative Masons at the period when it was written. This it is that makes it so valuable a contribution to the history of Freemasonry, and renders it so important that its precise date should be fixed.

Smaragdine, Tablet of Hermes. The foundation of Hermetic knowledge, with an unknown author. Translated in the *Œdipus Ægyptiacus.*

Smith, George. Captain George Smith was a Mason of some distinction during the latter part of the eighteenth century. Although born in England, he at an early age entered the military service of Prussia, being connected with noble families of that kingdom. During his residence on the Continent it appears that he was initiated in one of the German Lodges. On his return to England he was appointed Inspector of the Royal Military Academy at Woolwich, and published, in 1779, a *Universal Military Dictionary*, and, in 1783, a *Bibliotheca Militaris.*

He devoted much attention to Masonic studies, and is said to have been a good workman in the Royal Military Lodge at Woolwich, of which he was for four years the Master. During his Mastership the Lodge had, on one occasion, been opened in the King's Bench prison, and some persons who were confined there were initiated. For this the Master and brethren were censured, and the Grand Lodge declared that "it is inconsistent with the principles of Masonry for any Freemason's Lodge to be held, for the purpose of making, passing, or raising Masons, in any prison or place of confinement." (*Constitutions*, 1784, p. 349.) Smith was appointed by the Duke of Manchester, in 1778, Provincial Grand Master of Kent, and on that occasion delivered his *Inaugural Charge* before the Lodge of Friendship at Dover. He also drew up a code of laws for the government of the province, which was published in 1781. In 1780 he was appointed Junior Grand Warden of the Grand Lodge; but objections having been made by Heseltine, the Grand Secretary, between whom and himself there was no very kind feeling, on the ground that no one could hold two offices in the Grand Lodge, Smith resigned at the next quarterly communication. As at the time of his appointment there was really no law forbidding the holding of two offices, its impropriety was so manifest, that the Grand Lodge adopted a regulation that "it is incompatible with the laws of this society for any brother to hold more than one office in the Grand Lodge at the same time." (*Constitutions*, 1784, p 336.) Captain Smith, in 1783, published a work entitled *The Use and Abuse of Freemasonry: a work of the greatest utility to the Brethren of the Society, to Mankind in general, and to the Ladies in particular.* The interest to the ladies consists in some twenty pages, in which he gives the "Ancient and Modern reasons why the ladies have never been admitted into the Society of Freemasons," a section the omission of which would scarcely have diminished the value of the work or the reputation of the author.

The work of Smith would not at the present day, in the advanced progress of Masonic knowledge, enhance the reputation of its writer. But at the time when it appeared, there was a great dearth of Masonic literature —Anderson, Calcott, Hutchinson, and Preston being the only authors of any repute that had as yet written on the subject of Masonry. There was much historical information contained within its pages, and some few suggestive thoughts on the symbolism and philosophy of the Order. To the Craft of that day the book was therefore necessary and useful. Nothing, indeed, proves the necessity of such a work more than the fact that the Grand Lodge refused its sanction to the publication on the general ground of opposition to Masonic literature. Noorthouck (*Constitutions*, 1784, p. 347), in commenting on the refusal of a sanction, says:

"No particular objection being stated against the above-mentioned work, the natural conclusion is, that a sanction was refused on the general principle that, considering the flourishing state of our Lodges, where *regular* instruction and suitable exercises are ever ready for all brethren who zealously aspire to improve in masonical knowledge, new publications are unnecessary on a subject which books cannot teach. Indeed, the temptations to authorship have effected a strange revolution of sentiments since the year 1720, when even *antient* manuscripts were destroyed, to prevent their appearance in a *printed* Book of Constitutions! for the principal materials in this very work, then so much dreaded, have since been retailed in a variety of forms, to give consequence to fanciful productions that might have been safely withheld, without sensible injury, either to the Fraternity or to the literary reputation of the writers."

To dispel such darkness almost any sort of book should have been acceptable. The work was published without the sanction, and the Craft being wiser than their representatives in the Grand Lodge, the edition was speedily exhausted.

In 1785 Captain Smith was expelled from the Society for "uttering an instrument purporting to be a certificate of the Grand Lodge recommending two distressed Brethren."

Dr. Oliver (*Rev. of a Sq.*, p. 215) describes Captain Smith as a man "plain in speech and manners, but honourable and upright in his dealings, and an active and zealous Mason." It is probable that he died about the end of the last or the beginning of the present century.

Smitten Builder. The old lectures used to say: "The veil of the Temple is rent, *the builder is smitten*, and we are raised from the tomb of transgression." Hutchinson, and after him Oliver, apply the expression, "The smitten builder," to the crucified Savior, and define it as a symbol of his Divine mediation; but the general interpretation of the symbol is, that it refers to death as the necessary precursor of immortality. In this sense, the *smitten builder* presents, like every other part of the Third Degree, the symbolic instruction of Eternal Life.

Snow, John. A distinguished lecturer on Masonry, who was principally instrumental in introducing the system of Webb, of whom he was a pupil, into the Lodges of the Western States. He was also a Grand Master of the Grand Lodge of Ohio, and was the founder and first Grand Commander of the first Grand Encampment of Knights Templar in the same State. He was born in Providence, Rhode Island, February 25, 1780; was initiated into Freemasonry in Mount Vernon Lodge, of Providence, in 1809, and died May 16, 1852, at Worthington, Ohio.

Snows. See *Rains*.

Social Character of Freemasonry. Freemasonry attracts our attention as a great SOCIAL Institution. Laying aside for the time those artificial distinctions of rank and wealth, which, however, are necessary in the world to the regular progression of society, its members meet in their Lodges on one common level of brotherhood and equality. There virtue and talent alone claim and receive preeminence, and the great object of all is to see who can best work and best agree. There friendship and fraternal affection are strenuously inculcated and assiduously cultivated, and that great mystic tie is established which peculiarly distinguishes the society. Hence is it that Washington has declared that the benevolent purpose of the Masonic Institution is to enlarge the sphere of social happiness, and its grand object to promote the happiness of the human race.

Socius. The Sixth Degree of the Order of Strict Observance.

Sodalities. Societies or companies of friends or companions assembled together for a special purpose. Such confraternities, under the name of *Sodalitia*, were established in Rome, by Cato the Censor, for the mutual protection of the members. As their proceedings were secret, they gave offense to the government, and were suppressed, 80 B.C., by a decree of the Senate, but were afterward restored by a law of Clodius.

Sofism. The Sofis were a mystical sect which greatly prevailed in Eastern countries, and especially in Persia, whose religious faith was supposed by most writers to embody the secret doctrine of Mohammedanism. Sir John Malcolm (*Hist. Pers.*, ch. xx.) says that they have among them great numbers of the wisest and ablest men of Persia and the East, and since his time the sect has greatly increased.

The name is most probably derived from the Greek σοφία, *wisdom;* and Malcolm states that they also bore the name of *philosaufs*, in which we may readily detect the word *philosophers*. He says also: "The Mohammedan Sofis have endeavored to connect their mystic faith with the doctrine of their prophet, who, they assert, was himself an accomplished *Sofi*." The principal Sofi writers are familiar with the opinions of Aristotle and Plato, and their most important works abound with quotations from the latter. Sir John Malcolm compares the school of Sofism with that of Pythagoras. It is evident that there is a great similarity between Sofism and Gnosticism, and all the features of the Sofic initiation remind us very forcibly of those of the Masonic. The object of the system is the attainment of *Truth*, and the novice is invited "to embark on the sea of doubt," that is, to commence his investigations, which are to end in its discovery.

There are four stages or degrees of initiation: the first is merely preliminary, and the initiate is required to observe the ordinary rites and ceremonies of religion for the sake of the vulgar, who do not understand their esoteric meaning. In the Second Degree he is said to enter the pale of Sofism, and exchanges these external rites for a spiritual worship. The Third Degree is that of *Wisdom*, and he who reaches it is supposed to have attained supernatural knowledge, and to be equal to the angels. The Fourth and last degree is called *Truth*, for he has now reached it, and has become completely united with Deity. They have, says Malcolm, secrets and mysteries in every stage or degree which are never revealed to the profane, and to reveal which would be a crime of the deepest turpitude. The tenets of the sect, so far as they are made known to the world, are, according to Sir William Jones (*Asiat. Researches*, ii., 62), "that nothing exists absolutely but God; that the human soul is an emanation of his essence, and, though divided for a time from its heavenly source, will be finally reunited with it; that the highest possible happiness will arise from its reunion; and that the chief good of mankind in this transitory world consists in as perfect a union with the Eternal Spirit as the incumbrances of a mortal frame will allow." It is evident that an investigation of the true system of these Eastern mysteries must be an interesting subject of inquiry to the student of Freemasonry; for Higgins is hardly too enthusiastic in supposing them to be the ancient Freemasons of Mohammedanism. His views are thus expressed in the second volume of his *Anacalypsis*, p. 301: a wonderful work—wonderful for the vast and varied learning that it exhibits; but still more so for the bold and strange theories which, however untenable, are defended with all the powers of a more than ordinary intellect.

"The circumstances," he says, "of the gradation of ranks, the initiation, and the head of the Order in Persia being called Grand Master, raise a presumption that the, Sofis were, in reality, the Order of Masons."

Without subscribing at once to the theory of Higgins, we may well be surprised at the coincidences existing between the customs and the dogmas of the Sofis and those of the Freemasons, and we would naturally be curious to investigate the causes of the close communication which existed at various times during the Crusades between this Mohammedan sect of philosophers and the Christian Order of Templars.

Mr. C. W. King, in his learned treatise on the Gnostics, seems to entertain a similar idea of this connection between the Templars and the Sofis. He says that, "inasmuch as these *Sofis* were composed exclusively of the learned amongst the Persians and Syrians, and learning at that time meant little more than a proficiency in medicine and astrology, the two points that brought the Eastern sages into amicable contact with their barbarous invaders from the West, it is easy to see how the latter may have imbibed the secret doctrines simultaneously with the science of those who were their instructors in all matters pertaining to science and art. The Sofi doctrine involved the grand idea of one universal creed, which could be secretly held under any profession of an outward faith: and in fact took virtually the same view of religious systems as that in which the ancient philosophers had regarded such matters."

Softas. Students in the universities of Islam.

So Help Me God. The usual obsecration or imprecation affixed in modern times to oaths, and meaning, "May God so help me as I keep this vow."

Sojourner. See *Principal Sojourner*.

Soldiers of Christ. *Milites Christi* is the title by which St. Bernard addressed his exhortations to the Knights Templar. They are also called in some of the old documents, "*Militia Templi Salomonis*," The Chivalry of the Temple of Solomon; but their ancient statutes were entitled "*Regula pauperum commilitonum Templi Salomonis*," The Rule of the poor fellow-soldiers of the Temple of Solomon; and this is the title by which they are now most generally designated.

Soli Sanctissimo Sacrum. ("Sacred to the most holy Sun.") Mentioned in the Twenty-eighth Degree, A. A. Scottish Rite.

Solomon. In writing the life of King Solomon from a Masonic point of view, it is impossible to omit a reference to the legends which have been preserved in the Masonic system. But the writer, who, with this preliminary notice, embodies them in his sketch of the career of the wise King of Israel, is by no means to be held responsible for a belief in their authenticity. It is the business of the Masonic biographer to relate all that has been handed down by tradition in connection with the life of Solomon; it will be the duty of the severer critic to seek to separate out of all these materials that which is historical from that which is merely mythical, and to assign to the former all that is valuable as fact, and to the latter all that is equally valuable as symbolism.

Solomon, the King of Israel, the son of David and Bathsheba, ascended the throne of his kingdom 2989 years after the creation of the world, and 1015 years before the Christian era. He was then only twenty years of age, but the youthful monarch is said to have commenced his reign with the decision of a legal question of some difficulty, in which he exhibited the first promise of that wise judgment for which he was ever afterward distinguished.

One of the great objects of Solomon's life, and the one which most intimately connects him with the history of the Masonic institution, was the erection of a temple to Jehovah. This, too, had been a favorite design of his father David. For this purpose, that monarch, long before his death, had numbered the workmen whom he found in his kingdom; had appointed the overseers of the work, the hewers of stones, and the bearers of burdens; had prepared a great quantity of brass, iron, and cedar; and had amassed an immense treasure with which to support the enterprise. But on consulting with the prophet Nathan, he learned from that holy man, that although the pious intention was pleasing to God, yet that he would not be permitted to carry it into execution, and the Divine prohibition was proclaimed in these emphatic words: "Thou hast shed blood abundantly, and hast made great wars; thou shalt not build a house unto my name, because thou hast shed much blood upon the earth in my sight." The task was, therefore, reserved for the more peaceful Solomon, his son and successor.

Hence, when David was about to die, he charged Solomon to build the Temple of God as soon as he should have received the kingdom. He also gave him directions in relation to the construction of the edifice, and put into his possession the money, amounting to ten thousand talents of gold and ten times that amount of silver, which he had collected and laid aside for defraying the expense.

Solomon had scarcely ascended the throne of Israel, when he prepared to carry into execution the pious designs of his predecessor. For this purpose, however, he found it necessary to seek the assistance of Hiram, King of Tyre, the ancient friend and ally of his father. The Tyrians and Sidonians, the subjects of Hiram, had long been distinguished for their great architectural skill; and, in fact, many of them, as the members of a mystic operative society, the fraternity of Dionysian artificers, had long monopolized the profession of building in Asia Minor. The Jews, on the contrary, were rather more eminent for their military valor than for their knowledge of the arts of peace, and hence King Solomon at once conceived the necessity of invoking the aid of these foreign architects, if he expected to complete the edifice he was about to erect, either in a reasonable time or with the splendor and magnificence appropriate to the sacred object for which it was intended. For this purpose he addressed the following letter to King Hiram:

"Know thou that my father would have built a temple to God, but was hindered by wars and continual expeditions, for he did not leave off to overthrow his enemies till he made them all subject to tribute. But I give thanks to God for the peace I, at present, enjoy, and on that account I am at leisure, and design to build a house to God, for God foretold to my father, that such a house should be built by me; wherefore I desire thee to send some of thy subjects with mine to Mount Lebanon, to cut down timber, for the Sidonians are more skilful than our people in cutting of wood. As for wages to the hewers of wood, I will pay whatever price thou shalt determine."

Hiram, mindful of the former amity and alliance that had existed between himself and David, was disposed to extend the friendship he had felt for the father to the son, and replied, therefore, to the letter of Solomon in the following epistle:

"It is fit to bless God that he hath committed thy father's government to thee, who art a wise man endowed with all virtues. As for myself, I rejoice at the condition thou art in, and will be subservient to thee in all that thou sendest to me about; for when, by my subjects, I have cut down many and large trees of cedar and cypress wood, I will send them to sea, and will order my subjects to make floats of them, and to sail to what places soever of thy country thou shalt desire, and leave them there, after which thy subjects may carry them to Jerusalem. But do thou take care to procure us corn for this timber, which we stand in need of, because we inhabit in an island."

Hiram lost no time in fulfilling the promise of assistance which he had thus given; and accordingly we are informed that Solomon received thirty-three thousand six hundred workmen from Tyre, besides a sufficient quantity of timber and stone to construct the edifice which he was about to erect. Hiram sent him, also, a far more important gift than either men or materials, in the person of an able architect, "a curious and cunning workman," whose skill and experience were to be exercised in superintending the labors of the craft, and in adorning and beautifying the building. Of this personage, whose name was also Hiram, and who plays so important a part in the history of Freemasonry, an account will be found in the article *Hiram Abif*, to which the reader is referred.

King Solomon commenced the erection of the Temple on Monday, the second day of the Hebrew month Zif, which answers to the twenty-first of April, in the year of the world 2992, and 1012 years before the Christian era. Advised in all the details, as Masonic tradition informs us, by the wise and prudent counsels of Hiram, King of Tyre, and Hiram Abif, who, with himself, constituted at that time the three Grand Masters of the Craft, Solomon made every arrangement in the disposition and government of the workmen, in the payment of their wages, and in the maintenance of concord and harmony which should insure despatch in the execution and success in the result.

To Hiram Abif was entrusted the general superintendence of the building, while subordinate stations were assigned to other eminent artists, whose names and offices have been handed down in the traditions of the Order.

In short, the utmost perfection of human wisdom was displayed by this enlightened monarch in the disposition of everything that related to the construction of the stupendous edifice. Men of the most comprehensive minds, imbued with the greatest share of zeal and fervency, and inspired with the strongest fidelity to his interests, were employed as masters to instruct and superintend the workmen; while those who labored in inferior stations were excited to enthusiasm by the promise of promotion and reward.

The Temple was at length finished in the month Bul, answering to our November, in the year of the world 3000, being a little more than seven years from its commencement.

As soon as the magnificent edifice was completed, and fit for the sacred purposes for which it was intended, King Solomon determined to celebrate the consummation of his labors in the most solemn manner. For this purpose he directed the ark to be brought from the king's house, where it had been placed by King David, and to be deposited with impressive ceremonies in the holy of holies, beneath the expanded wings of the cherubim. This important event is commemorated in the beautiful ritual of the Most Excellent Master's Degree.

Our traditions inform us, that when the Temple was completed, Solomon assembled all the heads of the tribes, the elders and chiefs of Israel to bring the ark up out of Zion, where King David had deposited it in a tabernacle until a more fitting place should have been built for its reception. This duty, therefore, the Levites now performed, and delivered the ark of the covenant into the hands of the priests, who fixed it in its place in the center of the holy of holies.

Here the immediate and personal connection of King Solomon with the Craft begins to draw to a conclusion. It is true, that he subsequently employed those worthy Masons, whom the traditions say, at the completion and dedication of the Temple, he had received and acknowledged as Most Excellent Masters, in the erection of a magnificent palace and other edifices, but in process of time he fell into the most grievous errors; abandoned the path of truth; encouraged the idolatrous rites of Spurious Masonry; and, induced by the persuasions of those foreign wives and concubines whom he had espoused in his later days, he erected a fane for the celebration of these heathen mysteries, on one of the hills that overlooked the very spot where, in his youth, he had consecrated a temple to the one true God. It is however believed that before his death he deeply repented of this temporary aberration from virtue, and in the emphatic expression, "Vanity of vanities! all is vanity," he is supposed to have acknowledged that in his own experience he had discovered that falsehood and sensuality, however they may give pleasure for a season, will, in the end, produce the bitter fruits of remorse and sorrow.

That King Solomon was the wisest monarch that swayed the scepter of Israel, has been the unanimous opinion of posterity. So much was he beyond the age in which he flourished, in the attainments of science, that the Jewish and Arabic writers have attributed to him a thorough knowledge of the secrets of magic, by whose incantations they suppose him to have been capable of calling spirits and demons to his assistance; and the Talmudists and Mohammedan doctors record many fanciful legends of his exploits in controlling these ministers of darkness. As a naturalist, he is said to have written a work on animals of no ordinary character, which has however perished; while his qualifications as a poet were demonstrated by more than a thousand poems which he composed, of which his epithalamium on his marriage with an Egyptian princess and the Book of Ecclesiastes alone remain. He has given us in his Proverbs an opportunity of forming a favorable opinion of his pretensions to the character of a deep and right-thinking philosopher; while the long peace and prosperous condition of his empire for the greater portion of his reign, the increase of his kingdom in wealth and refinement, and the encouragement which he gave to architecture, the mechanic arts, and commerce, testify his profound abilities as a sovereign and statesman.

After a reign of forty years he died, and with him expired forever the glory and the power of the Hebrew empire.

Solomon, House of. Lord Bacon composed, in his *New Atlantis*, an apologue, in which he describes the island of Bensalem—that is, island of the Sons of Peace—and on it an edifice called the House of Solomon, where there was to be a confraternity of philosophers devoted to the acquisition of knowledge. Nicolai thought that out of this subsequently arose the society of Freemasons, which was, be supposes, established by Elias Ashmole and his friends. (See *Nicolai*.)

Solomon, Temple of. See *Temple of Solomon*.

Solstices. The days on which the sun reaches his greatest northern and southern declination, which are the 21st of June and the 22d of December. Near these days are those in which the Christian church commemorates St. John the Baptist and St. John the Evangelist, who have been selected as the patron saints of Freemasonry for reasons which are explained in the article on the *Dedication of a Lodge*, which see.

Son of Hiram. A mixed tradition states that Aynon was a son of Hiram Abif, and was appointed master of the workmen who hewed the cedars and shaped the timber for the temple, and was recognized for his geometrical knowledge and skill as an engraver. (See *Aynon*.)

Songs of Masonry. The song formed in early times a very striking feature in what may be called the domestic manners of the Masonic Institution. Nor has the custom of festive entertainments been yet abandoned. In the beginning of the eighteenth century songs were deemed of so much importance that they were added to the Books of Constitutions in Great Britain and on the Continent, a custom which was followed in America, where all the early Monitors contain an abundant supply of lyrical poetry. In the *Constitutions* published in 1723 we find the well-known Entered Apprentice's song, written by Matthew Birkhead, which still retains its popularity among Masons, and has attained an elevation to which its intrinsic merits as a lyrical composition would hardly entitle it. Songs appear to have been incorporated into the ceremonies of the Order at the revival of Masonry in 1717. At that time, to use the language of the venerable Oliver, "Labor and refreshment relieved each other like two loving brothers, and the gravity of the former was rendered more engaging by the characteristic cheerfulness and jocund gayety of the latter." In those days the word "refreshment" had a practical meaning, and the Lodge was often called from labor that the brethren might indulge in innocent gaiety, of which the song formed an essential part. This was called harmony, and the brethren who were blessed with talents for vocal music were often invited "to contribute to the harmony of the Lodge." Thus, in the minute-book of a Lodge at Lincoln, in England, in the year 1732, which is quoted by Dr. Oliver, the records show that the Master usually "gave an elegant charge, also went through an examination, and the Lodge was closed with song and decent merriment." In this custom of singing there was an established system. Each officer was furnished with a song appropriate to his office, and each degree had a song for itself.

Thus, in the first edition of the *Book of Constitutions*, we have the "Master's Song," which, says Dr. Anderson, the author, is "to be sung with a chorus—when the Master shall give leave—either one part only or all together, as he pleases"; the "Warden's song," which was "to be sung and played at the Quarterly Communication"; the "Fellow-Craft's song," which was to be sung and played at the grand feast; and, lastly, the "Entered 'Prentiss' song," which was "to be sung when all grave business is over, and with the Master's leave."

In the second edition the number was greatly increased, and songs were appropriated to the Deputy Grand Master, the Secretary, the Treasurer, and other officers. For all this provision was made in the *Old Charges* so that there should be no confusion between the hours of labor and refreshment; for while the brethren were forbidden to behave "ludicrously or jestingly while the Lodge is engaged in what is serious or solemn," they were permitted, when work was over, "to enjoy themselves with innocent mirth."

The custom of singing songs peculiarly appropriate to the Craft at their Lodge meetings, when the grave business was over, was speedily introduced into France and Germany, in which countries a large number of Masonic songs were written and adopted, to be sung by the German and French Masons at their "Table Lodges," which corresponded to the "refreshment" of their English brethren. The lyrical literature of Masonry has, in consequence of this custom, assumed no inconsiderable magnitude; as an evidence of which it may be stated that Kloss, in his *Bibliography of Freemasonry*, gives a catalogue—by no means a perfect one—of two hundred and thirteen Masonic song-books published between the years 1734 and 1837, in the English, German, French, Danish, and Polish languages.

The Masons of the present day have not abandoned the usage of singing at their festive meetings after the Lodge is closed; but the old songs of Masonry are passing into oblivion, and we seldom hear any of them, except sometimes the never-to-be-forgotten Apprentice's song of Matthew Birkhead. Modern taste and culture reject the rude but hearty stanzas of the old song-makers, and the more artistic and pathetic productions of Mackay, and Cooke, and Morris, and Dibdin, and Wesley, and other writers of that class, are taking their place.

Some of these songs cannot be strictly called Masonic, yet the covert allusions here and there of their authors, whether intentional or accidental, have caused them to be adopted by the Craft and placed among their minstrelsy. Thus the well-known ballad of "Tubal Cain," by Charles Mackay, always has an inspiring effect when sung at a Lodge banquet, because of the reference to this old worker in metals, whom the Masons fondly consider as one of the mythical founders of their Order; although the song itself has in its words or its ideas no connection whatever with Freemasonry. Burns's "Auld Lang Syne" is another production not strictly Masonic, which has met with the universal favor of the Craft, because the warm fraternal spirit that it breathes is in every way Masonic, and hence it has almost become a rule of obligation that every festive party of Freemasons should close with the great Scotchman's invocation to part in love and kindness.

But Robert Burns has also supplied the Craft with several purely Masonic songs, and his farewell to the brethren of Tarbolton Lodge, beginning,

> "Adieu! a heart-warm, fond adieu,
> Dear brothers of the mystic tie,"

is often sung with pathetic effect at the Table Lodges of the Order.

As already observed, we have many productions of our Masonic poets which are taking the place of the older and coarser songs of our predecessors. It would be tedious to name all who have successfully invoked the Masonic muse. Masonic songs—that is to say, songs whose themes are Masonic incidents, whose language refers to the technical language of Freemasonry, and whose spirit breathes its spirit and its teachings—are now a well-settled part of the literary curriculum of the Institution. At first they were all festive in character and often coarse in style, with little or no pretension to poetic excellence. Now they are festive, but refined; or sacred, and used on occasions of public solemnity; or mythical, and constituting a part of the ceremonies of the different degrees. But they all have a character of poetic art which is far above the mediocrity so emphatically condemned by Horace.

Son of a Mason. The son of a Mason is called a Louveteau, and is entitled to certain privileges, for which see *Louveteau* and *Lewis*.

Sons of Light. The science of Freemasonry often has received the title of "Lux," or "Light," to indicate that mental and moral illumination is the object of the Institution. Hence Freemasons are often called "Sons of Light."

Sons of the Prophets. We repeatedly meet in the Old Testament with references to the *Beni Hanabiim*, or sons of the prophets. These were the disciples of the prophets, or wise men of Israel, who underwent a course of esoteric instruction in the secret institutions of the Nabiim, or prophets, just as the disciples of the Magi did in Persia, or of Pythagoras in Greece. "These sons of the prophets," says Stehelin (*Rabbinical Literature*, i., 16), "were their disciples, brought up under their tuition and care, and therefore their masters or instructors were called their fathers."

Sons of the Widow. This is a title often given to Freemasons in allusion to Hiram the Builder, who was "a widow's son, of the tribe of Naphtali." By the advocates of the theory that Freemasonry originated with the exiled house of Stuart, and was organized as a secret institution for the purpose of reestablishing that house on the throne of Great Britain, the phrase has been applied as if referring to the adherents of Queen Henrietta, the widow of Charles I.

Sorbonne. A college of theological professors in Paris, who exercised a great influence over religious opinion in France during the sixteenth, seventeenth, and greater part of the eighteenth centuries. The bigotry and intolerance for which they were remarkable made them the untiring persecutors of Freemasonry. In the year 1748 they published a *Letter and Consultation on the Society of Freemasons*, in which they declared that it was an illegal association, and that the meetings of its members should be prohibited. This was republished in 1764, at Paris, by the Freemasons, with a reply, in the form of an appendix, by De la Tierce, and again in 1766, at Berlin, with another reply by a writer under the assumed name of Jarhetti.

Sorrow Lodge. It is the custom among Masons on the Continent of Europe to hold special Lodges at stated periods, for the purpose of commemorating the virtues and deploring the loss of their departed members, and other distinguished worthies of the Fraternity who have died. These are called Funeral or Sorrow Lodges. In Germany they are held annually; in France at longer intervals. In America the custom has been introduced by the Ancient and Accepted Rite, whose Sorrow Lodge ritual is peculiarly beautiful and impressive, and the usage has been adopted by many Lodges of the American Rite. On these occasions the Lodge is clothed in the habiliments of mourning and decorated with the emblems of death, solemn music is played, funereal dirges are chanted, and eulogies on the life, character, and Masonic virtues of the dead are delivered.

Soter. A Greek appellation implying "Savior."

Soul of Nature. A platonic expression, more properly the *anima mundi*, that has been adopted into the English Royal Arch system to designate the Sacred Delta, or Triangle, which Dunckerley, in his lecture, considered as the symbol of the Trinity. "So highly," says the modern lecture, "indeed did the ancients esteem the figure, that it became among them an object of worship as the great principle of animated existence, to which they gave the name of God because it represented the animal, mineral, and vegetable creation. They also distinguished it by an appellation which, in the Egyptian language, signifies the *Soul of Nature*." Dr. Oliver (*Juris.*, p. 446) warmly protests against the introduction of this expression as an unwarrantable innovation, borrowed most probably from the Rite of the Philalethes. It has not been introduced into the American system.

South. When the sun is at his meridian height, his invigorating rays are darted from the south. When he rises in the east, we are called to labor; when he sets in the west, our daily toil is over; but when he reaches the south, the hour is high twelve, and we are summoned to refreshment. In Masonry, the south is represented by the Junior Warden and by the Corinthian column, because it is said to be the place of beauty.

South Carolina. Freemasonry was introduced into South Carolina by the organization of Solomon's Lodge, in the city of Charleston, on October 28, 1736, the Warrant for which had been granted in the previous year by Lord Weymouth, Grand Master of England. John Hammerton was, in 1736, appointed Provincial Grand Master by the Earl of Loudoun. In 1738 a Lodge was established in Charleston by the St. John's Grand Lodge of Boston; but it does not appear to have long existed. The Provincial Lodge appears after some time to have suspended operations, for a second Provincial Grand Lodge was established by the Deputation of the Marquis of Carnarvon to Chief Justice Leigh in 1754. In 1787 this body assumed independence, and became the "Grand Lodge of Free and Accepted Masons of South Carolina," Barnard Elliott being the first Grand Master. As early as 1783 the Atholl or Ancient Masons invaded the jurisdiction of South Carolina, and in 1787, there being then five Lodges of the Ancients in the State, they held a Convention, and on the 24th of March organized the "Grand Lodge of Ancient York Masons of South Carolina." Between the Modern and the Ancient Grand Lodge there was always a very hostile feeling until the year 1808, when a union was effected; which was, however, but temporary, for a disruption took place in the following year. However, the union was permanently established in 1817, when the two Grand Lodges were merged into one, under the name of the "Grand Lodge of Ancient Freemasons of South Carolina."

The Grand Royal Arch Chapter was organized on May 29, 1812.

The Grand Council of Royal and Select Masters was established February, 1860, by eight Councils, who had received their Charters under the authority of the Supreme Council of the Scottish Rite.

The Grand Encampment of Knights Templar was instituted in 1826 by three subordinate Encampments, but it enjoyed only an ephemeral existence, and is not heard of after the year 1830. There is now but one Commandery in the State, which derives its Warrant from the Grand Encampment of the United States, the date of which is May 17, 1843.

The Supreme Council of the Ancient and Accepted Rite was opened on May 31, 1801. This body is now recognized as the Mother Council of the World.

Sovereign. An epithet applied to certain degrees which were invested with supreme power over inferior ones; as, *Sovereign Prince of Rose Croix*, which is the highest degree of the French Rite and of some other Rites, and *Sovereign Inspector-General*, which is the controlling degree of the Ancient and Accepted Rite. Some degrees, originally Sovereign in the Rites in which they were first established, in being transferred to other Rites, have lost their sovereign character, but still improperly retain the name. Thus the Rose Croix Degree of the Scottish Rite, which is there only the Eighteenth, and subordinate to the Thirty-third or Supreme Council, still retains everywhere, except in the Southern Jurisdiction of the United States, the title of Sovereign Prince of Rose Croix.

Sovereign Commander of the Temple. (*Souverain Commandeur du Temple.*) Styled in the more recent rituals of the Southern Supreme Council "Knight Commander of the Temple." This is the Twenty-seventh Degree of the Ancient and Accepted Scottish Rite. The presiding officer is styled "Most Illustrious and Most Valiant," the Wardens are called "Most Sovereign Commanders,' and the Knights "Sovereign Commanders." The place of meeting is called a "Court." The apron is flesh-colored, lined and edged with black, with a Teutonic cross encircled by a wreath of laurel and a key beneath, all inscribed in black upon the flap. The scarf is red bordered with black, hanging from the right shoulder to the left hip, and suspending a Teutonic cross in enameled gold. The jewel is a triangle of gold, on which is engraved the Ineffable Name in Hebrew. It is suspended from a white collar bound with red and embroidered with four Teutonic crosses.

Vassal, Ragon, and Clavel are all wrong in connecting this degree with the Knights Templar, with which Order its own ritual declares that it is not to be confounded. It is without a lecture. Vassal expresses the following opinion of this degree:

"The twenty-seventh degree does not deserve to be classed in the Scottish Rite as a degree, since it contains neither symbols nor allegories that connect it with initiation. It deserves still less to be ranked among the philosophic degrees. I imagine that it has been intercalated only to supply an hiatus, and as a memorial of an Order once justly celebrated."

It is also the Forty-fourth Degree of the Rite of Misraim.

Sovereign Grand Inspector-General. The Thirty-third and last degree of the Ancient and Accepted Scottish Rite. The Latin Constitutions of 1786 call it "Tertius et trigesimus et sublimissimus gradus," i. e., "the Thirty-third and Most Sublime Degree"; and it is styled "the Protector and Conservator of the Order." The same Constitutions, in Articles I. and II., say:

"The thirty-third degree confers on those Masons who are legitimately invested with it, the quality, title, privilege, and authority of Sovereign [Supremorum] Grand Inspectors-General of the Order.

"The peculiar duty of their mission is to teach and enlighten the brethren; to preserve charity, union, and fraternal love among them; to maintain regularity in the works of each degree, and to take care that it is preserved by others; to cause the dogmas, doctrines, institutes, constitutions, statutes, and regulations of the Order to be reverently regarded, and to preserve and defend them on every occasion; and, finally, everywhere to occupy themselves in works of peace and mercy."

The body in which the members of this degree assemble is called a Supreme Council.

The symbolic color of the degree is white, denoting purity.

The distinctive insignia are a sash, collar, jewel, Teutonic cross, decoration, and ring.

The sash is a broad, white watered ribbon, bordered with gold, bearing on the front a triangle of gold glittering with rays of gold, which has in the center the numerals 33, with a sword of silver, directed from above, on each side of the triangle, pointing to its center. The sash, worn from the right shoulder to the left hip, ends in a point, and is fringed with gold, having at the junction a circular band of scarlet and green containing the jewel of the Order.

The collar is of white watered ribbon fringed with gold, having the rayed triangle at its point and the swords at the sides. By a regulation of the Southern Supreme Council of the United States, the collar is worn by the active, and the sash by the honorary, members of the Council.

The jewel is a black double-headed eagle, with golden beaks and talons, holding in the latter a sword of gold, and crowned with the golden crown of Prussia.

The red Teutonic cross is affixed to the left side of the breast.

The decoration rests upon a Teutonic cross. It is a nine-pointed star, namely, one formed by three triangles of gold one upon the other, and interlaced from the lower part of the left side to the upper part of the right a sword extends, and in the opposite direction is a hand of (as it is called) *Justice*. In the center is the shield of The Order, *azure* charged with an eagle like that on the banner, having on the dexter side a Balance *or*, and on the sinister side a Compass of the second, united with a

Square of the second. Around the whole shield runs a band of the first, with the Latin inscription, of the second, Ordo Ab Chao, which band is enclosed by two circles, formed by two Serpents of the second, each biting his own tail. Of the smaller triangles that are formed by the intersection of the greater ones, those nine that are nearest the band are of crimson color, and each of them has one of the letters that compose the word S. A. P. I. E. N. T. I. A.

The ring is a triple one, like three small rings, each one-eighth of an inch wide, side by side, and having on the inside a delta surrounding the figures 33, and inscribed with the wearer's name, the letters S.·. G.·. I.·. G.·., and the motto of the Order, "Deus meumque Jus." It is worn on the fourth finger of the left hand in the Southern Jurisdiction and on the third in the Northern Jurisdiction of America.

Until the year 1801, the Thirty-third Degree was unknown. Until then the highest degree of the Rite, introduced into America by Stephen Morin, was the Sublime Prince of the Royal Secret, or the Twenty-fifth of the Rite established by the Emperors of the East and West. The administrative heads of the Order were styled Grand Inspectors-General and Deputy Inspectors-General; but these were titles of official rank and not of degree. Even as late as May 24, 1801, John Mitchell signs himself as "Kadosh, Prince of the Royal Secret and Deputy Inspector-General." The document thus signed is a Patent which certifies that Frederick Dalcho is a Kadosh, and Prince of the Royal Secret, and which creates him a Deputy Inspector-General. But on May 31, 1801, the Supreme Council was created at Charleston, and from that time we hear of a Rite of thirty-three degrees, eight having been added to the twenty-five introduced by Morin, and the last being called Sovereign Grand Inspector-General. The degree being thus legitimately established by a body which, in creating a Rite, possessed the prerogative of establishing its classes, its degrees and its nomenclature were accepted unhesitatingly by all subsequently created Supreme Councils; and it continues to be recognised as the administrative head of the Ancient and Accepted Scottish Rite.

Sovereign Master. 1. The presiding officer in a Council of Companions of the Red Cross. He represents Darius, King of Persia. 2. The Sixtieth Degree of the Rite of Mizraim.

Sovereign Prince Mason. A title first conferred on its members by the Council of Emperors of the East and West.

Sovereign Prince of Rose Croix. See *Rose Croix*.

Spain. Anderson says (*Constit.*, 2d ed., p. 194) that a Deputation was granted by Lord Coleraine, Grand Master, in 1728, for constituting a Lodge at Madrid; another in 1731, by Lord Lovell, to Capt. James Cummerford, to be Provincial Grand Master of Andalusia; and a third in 1732, by Lord Montagu, for establishing a Lodge at Valenciennes. Smith, writing in 1783, says (*Use and Abuse*, p. 203): "The first, and, I believe, the only Lodge established in Spain was by a Deputation sent to Madrid to constitute a Lodge in that city, under the auspices of Lord Coleraine, A. D. 1727, which continued under English jurisdiction till the year 1776, when it refused that subordination, but still continues to meet under its own authority." From these two differing authorities we derive only this fact, in which they concur: that Masonry was introduced into Spain in 1727, more probably 1728, by the Grand Lodge of England. Smith's statement that there never was a second Lodge at Madrid is opposed by that of Gädicke, who says that in 1751 there were two Lodges in Madrid.

Llorente says (*Hist. Inquis.*, p. 525) that in 1741 Philip V. issued a royal ordinance against the Masons, and, in consequence, many were arrested and sent to the galleys. The members of the Lodge at Madrid were especially treated by the Inquisition with great severity. All the members were arrested, and eight of them sent to the galleys. In 1751, Ferdinand VI., instigated by the Inquisitor Joseph Torrubia, published a decree forbidding the assemblies of Freemasons, and declaring that all violators of it should be treated as persons guilty of high treason. In that year, Pope Benedict XIV. had renewed the bull of Clement XII. In 1793, the Cardinal Vicar caused a decree of death to be promulgated against all Freemasons. Notwithstanding these persecutions of the Church and the State, Freemasonry continued to be cultivated in Spain; but the meetings of the Lodges were held with great caution and secrecy.

On the accession of Joseph Napoleon to the throne in 1807, the liberal sentiments that characterized the Napoleonic dynasty prevailed, and all restrictions against the Freemasons were removed. In October, 1809, a National Grand Lodge of Spain was established, and, as if to make the victory of tolerance over bigotry complete, its meetings were held in the edifice formerly occupied by the Inquisition, which body had been recently abolished by an imperial decree.

But the York Rite, which had been formerly practised, appears now to have been abandoned, and the National Grand Lodge just alluded to was constituted by three Lodges of the Scottish Rite which, during that year, had been established at Madrid. From that time the Masonry of Spain has been that of the Ancient and Accepted Scottish Rite.

Clavel says (*Hist. Pittoresque*, p. 252) that "in 1810, the Marquis de Clermont-Tonnere, member of the Supreme Council of France, created, near the National Grand Lodge, (of the Scottish Rite in Spain,) a Grand Consistory of the thirty-second degree; and, in 1811, the Count de Grasse added to this a Supreme Council of the thirty-third degree, which immediately organized the National Grand Lodge under the title of Grand Orient of Spain and the Indies. The overthrow of French domination dispersed, in 1813, most of the Spanish Masons, and caused the suspension of Masonic work in that country."

In 1814, Ferdinand VII., having succeeded to the throne, restored the Inquisition with all its oppressive prerogatives, proscribed Freemasonry, and forbade the meetings of the Lodges. It was not until 1820 that the Grand Orient of Spain recovered its activity, and in

1821 we find a Supreme Council in actual existence, the history of whose organization was thus given, in 1870, to Bro. A. G. Goodall, the Representative of the Supreme Council of the Northern Jurisdiction of the United States:

"The parties now claiming to be a Supreme Council assert that the Count de Tilly, by authority from his cousin, De Grasse Tilly, constituted a Supreme Council, Ancient Accepted Rite, at Seville, in 1807; but in consequence of a revolution, in which Tilly was a prominent actor, the Grand Body was removed to Aranjuez, where, on the 21st of September, 1808, the officers were duly installed; Saavedra as Sov.·. Gr.·. Commander, ad vitam; Count de Tilly, Lieutenant Grand Commander; Carlos de Rosas, Grand Treasurer; Jovellanos, Grand Chancellor; Quintana, Grand Secretary; Pelajos, Captain of Guard. On the death of Tilly and Saavedra, Badilla became Sovereign Grand Commander; and under his administration the Supreme Council was united with the Grand Orient of Spain at Granada, in 1817, under the title of Supreme Council, Grand Orient National of Spain."

On the death of Ferdinand VII. in 1853, the persecutions against the Freemasons ceased, because, in the civil war that ensued, the priests lost much of their power. Between 1845 and 1849, according to Findel (*Hist.*, p. 584), several Lodges were founded and a Grand Orient established, which appears to have exercised powers up to at least 1848. But subsequently, during the reign of Queen Isabella, Masonry again fell into decadence. It has now, however, revived, and many Lodges are in existence who, three years ago, were under the jurisdiction of the Grand Orient of Portugal. There is now a Grand Orient of Spain at Madrid with 14 Chapters and 87 Lodges under its jurisdiction.

Spartacus. The characteristic name assumed by Weishaupt, the founder of the Order of the Illuminati.

Speculative Masonry. The lectures of the Symbolic degrees instruct the neophyte in the difference between the Operative and the Speculative divisions of Masonry. They tell him that "we work in Speculative Masonry, but our ancient brethren wrought in both Operative and Speculative." The distinction between an Operative art and a Speculative science is, therefore, familiar to all Masons from their early instructions.

To the Freemason, this Operative art has been symbolized in that intellectual deduction from it which has been correctly called Speculative Masonry. At one time each was an integral part of one undivided system. Not that the period ever existed when every Operative Mason was acquainted with, or initiated into, the Speculative science. Even now, there are thousands of skilful artisans who know as little of that as they do of the Hebrew language which was spoken by its founder. But Operative Masonry was, in the inception of our history, and is, in some measure, even now, the skeleton upon which was strung the living muscles and tendons and nerves of the Speculative system. It was the block of marble, rude and unpolished it may have been, from which was sculptured the life-breathing statue.

Speculative Masonry (which is but another name for Freemasonry in its modern acceptation) may be briefly defined as the scientific application and the religious consecration of the rules and principles, the language, the implements, and materials of Operative Masonry to the veneration of God, the purification of the heart, and the inculcation of the dogmas of a religious philosophy.

Speculative Masonry, or Freemasonry, is then a system of ethics, and must therefore, like all other ethical systems, have its distinctive doctrines. These may be divided into three classes, viz., the Moral, the Religious, and the Philosophical.

1. *The Moral Doctrines.* These are dependent on, and spring out of, its character as a social institution. Hence among its numerous definitions is one that declares it to be "a science of morality," and morality is said to be, symbolically, one of the precious jewels of a Master Mason. Freemasonry is, in its most patent and prominent sense, that which most readily and forcibly attracts the attention of the uninitiated; a fraternity, an association of men bound together by a peculiar tie; and therefore it is essential, to its successful existence, that it should, as it does, inculcate, at the very threshold of its teachings, obligation of kindness, man's duty to his neighbor. "There are three great duties," says the Charge given to an Entered Apprentice, "which, as a Mason, you are charged to inculcate—to God, your neighbor, and yourself." And the duty to our neighbor is said to be that we should act upon the square, and do unto him as we wish that he should do unto ourselves.

The object, then, of Freemasonry, in this moral point of view, is to carry out to their fullest practical extent those lessons of mutual love and mutual aid that are essential to the very idea of a brotherhood. There is a socialism in Freemasonry from which spring all Masonic virtues—not that modern socialism exhibited in a community of goods, which, although it may have been practised by the primitive Christians, is found to be uncongenial with the independent spirit of the present age—but a community of sentiment, of principle, of design, which gives to Masonry all its social, and hence its moral, character. As the old song tells us:

"That virtue has not left mankind,
Her social maxims prove,
For stamp'd upon the Mason's mind
Are unity and love."

Thus the moral design of Freemasonry, based upon its social character, is to make men better to each other; to cultivate brotherly love, and to inculcate the practise of all those virtues which are essential to the perpetuation of a brotherhood. A Mason is bound, say the Old Charges, to obey the moral law, and of this law the very keystone is the Divine precept—the "Golden Rule' of our Lord—to do unto others as we would that they should do unto us. To relieve the distressed, to give good counsel to the erring, to speak well of the absent, to observe temperance in the indulgence of appetite, to bear evil with fortitude, to be prudent in life and conversation, and to dispense justice to all men, are duties that are inculcated on every Mason by the moral doctrines of his Order.

These doctrines of morality are not of recent origin. They are taught in all the Old Constitutions of the Craft, as the parchment records of the fifteenth, sixteenth, and seventeenth centuries show, even when the Institution was operative in its organisation, and long before the speculative element was made its predominating characteristic. Thus these Old Charges tell us, almost all of them in the same words, that Masons "shal be true, each one to other, (that is to say,) to every Mason of the science of Masonrye that are Masons allowed, ye shal doe to them as ye would that they should doe unto you."

2. *The Religious Doctrines* of Freemasonry are very simple and self-evident. They are darkened by no perplexities of sectarian theology, but stand out in the broad light, intelligible and acceptable by all minds, for they ask only for a belief in God and in the immortality of the soul. He who denies these tenets can be no Mason, for the religious doctrines of the Institution significantly impress them in every part of its ritual. The neophyte no sooner crosses the threshold of the Lodge, but he is called upon to recognise, as his first duty, an entire trust in the superintending care and love of the Supreme Being, and the series of initiations into Symbolic Masonry terminate by revealing the awful symbol of a life after death and an entrance upon immortality.

Now this and the former class of doctrines are intimately connected and mutually dependent. For we must first know and feel the universal fatherhood of God before we can rightly appreciate the universal brotherhood of man. Hence the Old Records already alluded to, which show us what was the condition of the Craft in the Middle Ages, exhibit an eminently religious spirit. These ancient Constitutions always begin with a pious invocation to the Trinity, and sometimes to the saints, and they tell us that "the first charge is that a Mason shall be true to God and holy Church, and use no error nor heresy." And the Charges published in 1723, which professes to be a compilation made from those older records, prescribe that a Mason, while left to his particular opinions, must be of that "religion in which all men agree," that is to say, the religion which teaches the existence of God and an eternal life.

3. *The Philosophical Doctrines* of Freemasonry are scarcely less important, although they are less generally understood than either of the preceding classes. The object of these philosophical doctrines is very different from that of either the moral or the religious. For the moral and religious doctrines of the Order are intended to make men virtuous, while its philosophical doctrines are designed to make them zealous Masons. He who knows nothing of the philosophy of Freemasonry will be apt to become in time lukewarm and indifferent, but he who devotes himself to its contemplation will feel an ever-increasing ardor in the study. Now these philosophical doctrines are developed in that symbolism which is the especial characteristic of Masonic teaching, and relate altogether to the lost and recovered word, the search after Divine truth, the manner and time of its discovery, and the reward that awaits the faithful and successful searcher. Such a philosophy far surpasses the abstract quiddities of metaphysicians. It brings us into close relation to the profound thought of the ancient world, and makes us familiar with every subject of mental science that lies within the grasp of the human intellect. So that, in conclusion, we find that the moral, religious, and philosophical doctrines of Freemasonry respectively relate to the social, the eternal, and the intellectual progress of man.

Finally, it must be observed that while the old Operative institution, which was the cradle and forerunner of the Speculative, as we now have it, abundantly taught in its Constitutions the moral and religious doctrines of which we have been treating, it makes no reference to the philosophical doctrines. That our Operative predecessors were well acquainted with the science of symbolism is evident from the architectural ornaments of the buildings which they erected; but they do not seem to have applied its principles to any great extent to the elucidation of their moral and religious teachings; at least, we find nothing said of this symbolic philosophy in the Old Records that are extant. And whether the Operative Masons were reticent on this subject from choice or from ignorance, we may lay it down as an axiom, not easily to be controverted, that the philosophic doctrines of the Order are altogether a development of the system for which we are indebted solely to Speculative Freemasonry.

Spencer Manuscript. A MS. copy of the "Old Charges" of the date of 1726, which belonged to the late Mr. Richard Spencer and was sold in 1875 to Mr. E. T. Carson, of Cincinnati, U. S. A. It was reproduced in Spencer's *Old Constitutions* in 1871.

Spes mea in Deo est. (*My hope is in God.*) The motto of the Thirty-second Degree of the Ancient and Accepted Scottish Rite.

Spire, Congress of. Spire is a city in Bavaria, on the banks of the Rhine, and the seat of a cathedral which was erected in the eleventh century. A Masonic Congress was convoked there in 1469 by the Grand Lodge of Strasburg, principally to take into consideration the condition of the Fraternity and of the edifices in the course of construction by them, as well as to discuss the rights of the Craft.

Spiritualizing. In the early lectures of the last century, this word was used to express the method of symbolic instruction applied to the implements of Operative Masonry. In a ritual of 1725, it is said: "As we are not all working Masons, we apply the working-tools to our morals, which we call spiritualizing." Thus, too, about the same time, Bunyan wrote his symbolic book which he called *Solomon's Temple Spiritualized.* Phillips, in his *New World of Words,* 1706, thus defines to spiritualize: "to explain a passage of an author in a spiritual manner, to give it a godly or mystical sense."

Spiritual Lodge. Hutchinson (*Sp. of Masonry,* p. 94) says: "We place the spiritual Lodge in the vale of *Jehosophat,* implying thereby, that the principles of Masonry are derived from the knowledge of God, and are established in the *Judgment of the Lord;* the literal translation of the word *Jehosophat,* from the Hebrew tongue, being no other than those express words." This refers to the Lodge, which is thus described in the old lectures at the beginning of the last century, which were in vogue at the time of Hutchinson.

"*Q.* Where does the Lodge stand?

"*A.* Upon the Holy ground, on the highest hill or lowest vale, or in the vale of Jehoshaphat, or any other sacred place."

The spiritual Lodge is the imaginary or Symbolic Lodge, whose form, magnitude, covering, supports, and other attributes are described in the lectures.

Spiritual Temple. The French Masons say: "We erect temples for virtue and dungeons for vice"; thus referring to the great Masonic doctrine of a spiritual temple. There is no symbolism of the Order more sublime than that in which the Speculative Mason is supposed to be engaged in the construction of a spiritual temple, in allusion to that material one which was erected by his operative predecessors at Jerusalem. Indeed, the difference, in this point of view, between Operative and Speculative Masonry is simply this: that while the former was engaged in the construction, on Mount Moriah, of a material temple of stones and cedar, and gold and precious stones, the latter is occupied, from his first to his last initiation, in the construction, the adornment, and the completion of the spiritual temple of his body. The idea of making the temple a symbol of the body is not, it is true, exclusively Masonic. It had occurred to the first teachers of Christianity. Christ himself alluded to it when he said, "Destroy this temple, and in three days I will raise it up"; and St. Paul extends the idea, in the first of his Epistles to the Corinthians, in the following language: "Know ye not that ye are the temple of God, and that the spirit of God dwelleth in you?" (iii. 16.) And again, in a subsequent passage of the same Epistle, he reiterates the idea in a more positive form: "What, know ye not that your body is the temple of the Holy Ghost which is in you, which ye have of God, and ye are not your own?" (vi. 19.)

But the mode of treating this symbolism by a reference to the particular Temple of Solomon, and to the operative art engaged in its construction, is an application of the idea peculiar to Freemasonry. Hitchcock, in his *Essay on Swedenborg,* thinks that the same idea was also shared by the Hermetic philosophers. He says: "With perhaps the majority of readers, the Temple of Solomon, and also the tabernacle, were mere buildings—very magnificent, indeed, but still mere buildings—for the worship of God. But some are struck with many portions of the account of their erection admitting a moral interpretation; and while the buildings are allowed to stand (or to have stood, once,) visible objects, these interpreters are delighted to meet with indications that Moses and Solomon, in building the Temples, were wise in the knowledge of God and of man; from which point it is not difficult to pass on to the moral meaning altogether, and affirm that the building, which was erected without the noise of a 'hammer, nor ax, nor any tool of iron' (1 Kings vi. 7,) was altogether a moral building—a building of God, not made with hands. In short, many see in the story of Solomon's Temple, a symbolical representation of MAN as the temple of God, with its HOLY OF HOLIES deep seated in the centre of the human heart."

Spoulée, John de. He appears to have presided over the Masons of England in 1350, in the reign of Edward III. Anderson says he was called Master of the "Ghiblim." (*Constitutions,* 1738, p. 70.)

Spreading the Ballot. Taking the vote on the application of a candidate for initiation or admission. It is an Americanism, principally used in the Western States. Thus: "The ballot may be *spread* a second time in almost any case if the harmony of the Lodge seems to require it."—*Swigert, G.·. M.·. of Kentucky.* "It is legal to *spread* the ballot the third time, if for the correction of mistakes, not otherwise."—*Rob. Morris.* It is a technicality, and scarcely English.

Sprengseisen, Christian Friedrich Kessler Von. An ardent adherent of Von Hund and admirer of his Templar system, in defense of which, and against the Spiritual Templarism of Starck, he wrote, in 1786, the book, now very rare, entitled *Anti Saint Nicaise,* and other works. He was born at Saalsfield, in 1731, and died January 11, 1809. (See *Saint Nicaise.*)

Sprig of Acacia. See *Acacia.*

Spurious Freemasonry. For this term, and for the theory connected with it, we are indebted to Dr. Oliver, whose speculations led him to the conclusion that in the earliest ages of the world there were two systems of Freemasonry, the one of which, preserved by the patriarchs and their descendants, he called Primitive or Pure Freemasonry. (See *Primitive Freemasonry.*) The other, which was a schism from this system, he designated as the Spurious Freemasonry of Antiquity. To comprehend this system of Oliver, and to understand his doctrine of the declension of the Spurious from the Primitive Freemasonry, we must remember that there were two races of men descended from the loins of Adam, whose history is as different as their characters were dissimilar. There was the virtuous race of Seth and his descendants, and the wicked one of Cain. Seth and his children, down to Noah, preserved the dogmas and instructions, the legends and symbols, which had been received from their common progenitor, Adam; but Cain and his descendants, whose vices at length brought on the destruction of the earth, either totally forgot or greatly corrupted them. Their Freemasonry was not the same as that of the Sethites. They distorted the truth, and varied the landmarks to suit their own profane purposes. At length the two races became blended together. The descendants of Seth, becoming corrupted by their frequent communications with those of Cain, adopted their manners, and soon lost the principles of the Primitive Freemasonry, which at length were confined to Noah and his three sons, who alone, in the destruction of a wicked world, were thought worthy of receiving mercy.

Noah consequently preserved this system, and was the medium of communicating it to the post-diluvian world. Hence, immediately after the deluge, Primitive Freemasonry was the only system extant.

But this happy state of affairs was not to last. Ham, the son of Noah, who had been accursed by his father for his wickedness, had been long familiar with the corruptions of the system of Cain, and with the gradual deviations from truth which, through the influence of evil example, had crept into the system of Seth. After the deluge, he propagated the worst features of both systems among his immediate descendants. Two sets or parties, so to speak, now arose in the world—one which preserved the great truths of religion, and consequently of Masonry, which had been handed down from Adam, Enoch, and Noah—and another which deviated more and more from this pure, original source. On the dispersion at the tower of Babel, the schism became still wider and more irreconcilable. The legends of Primitive Freemasonry were altered, and its symbols perverted to a false worship; the mysteries were dedicated to the worship of false gods and the practise of idolatrous rites, and in the place of the Pure or Primitive Freemasonry which continued to be cultivated among the patriarchal descendants of Noah, was established those mysteries of Paganism to which Dr. Oliver has given the name of the "Spurious Freemasonry."

It is not to Dr. Oliver, nor to any very modern writer, that we are indebted for the idea of a Masonic schism in this early age of the world. The doctrine that Masonry was lost, that is to say, lost in its purity, to the larger portion of mankind, at the tower of Babel, is still preserved in the ritual of Ancient Craft Masonry. And in the degree of Noachites, a degree which is attached to the Scottish Rite, the fact is plainly adverted to as, indeed, the very foundation of the degree. Two races of Masons are there distinctly named, the *Noachites* and the *Hiramites;* the former were the conservators of the Primitive Freemasonry as the descendants of Noah; the latter were the descendants of Hiram, who was himself of the race which had fallen into Spurious Freemasonry, but had reunited himself to the true sect at the building of King Solomon's Temple, as we shall hereafter see. But the inventors of the degree do not seem to have had any very precise notions in relation to this latter part of the history.

The mysteries, which constituted what has been thus called Spurious Freemasonry, were all more or less identical in character. Varying in a few unimportant particulars, attributable to the influence of local causes, their great similarity in all important points showed their derivation from a common origin.

In the first place, they were communicated through a system of initiation, by which the aspirant was gradually prepared for the reception of their final doctrines; the rites were performed at night, and in the most retired situations, in caverns or amid the deep recesses of groves and forests; and the secrets were only communicated to the initiated after the administration of an obligation. Thus, Firmicus (*Astrol.*, lib. vii.) tells us that "when Orpheus explained the ceremonies of his mysteries to candidates, he demanded of them, at the very entrance, an oath, under the solemn sanction of religion, that they would not betray the rites to profane ears." And hence, as Warburton says from Horus Apollo, the Egyptian hieroglyphic for the mysteries was a grasshopper, because that insect was supposed to have no mouth.

The ceremonies were all of a funereal character. Commencing in representations of a lugubrious description, they celebrated the legend of the death and burial of some mythical being who was the especial object of their love and adoration. But these rites, thus beginning in lamentation, and typical of death, always ended in joy. The object of their sorrow was restored to life and immortality, and the latter part of the ceremonial was descriptive of his resurrection. Hence, the great doctrines of the mysteries were the immortality of the soul and the existence of a God.

Such, then, is the theory on the subject

of what is called "Spurious Freemasonry," as taught by Oliver and the disciples of his school. Primitive Freemasonry consisted of that traditional knowledge and symbolic instruction which had been handed down from Adam, through Enoch, Noah, and the rest of the patriarchs, to the time of Solomon. Spurious Freemasonry consisted of the doctrines and initiations practised at first by the antediluvian descendants of Cain, and, after the dispersion at Babel, by the Pagan priests and philosophers in their "Mysteries."

Spurs. In the Orders of Chivalry, the spurs had a symbolic meaning as important as their practical use was necessary. "To win one's spurs" was a phrase which meant "to win one's right to the dignity of knighthood." Hence, in the investiture of a knight, he was told that the spurs were a symbol of promptitude in military service; and in the degradation of an unfaithful knight, his spurs were hacked off by the cook, to show his utter unworthiness to wear them. Stowe says (*Annals*, 902), in describing the ceremony of investing knights: "Evening prayer being ended, there stood at the chapel-door the king's master-cook, with his white apron and sleeves, and chopping-knife in his hand, gilded about the edge, and challenged their spurs, which they redeemed with a noble a piece; and he said to every knight, as they passed by him: 'Sir Knight, look that you be true and loyal to the king, my master, or else I must hew these spurs from your heels.'" In the Masonic Orders of Chivalry, the symbolism of the spurs has unfortunately been omitted.

Square. This is one of the most important and significant symbols in Freemasonry. As such, it is proper that its true form should be preserved. The French Masons have almost universally given it with one leg longer than the other, thus making it a carpenter's square. The American Masons, following the incorrect delineations of Jeremy L. Cross, have, while generally preserving the equality of length in the legs, unnecessarily marked its surface with inches; thus making it an instrument for measuring length and breadth, which it is not. It is simply the *trying square* of a stone-mason, and has a plain surface; the sides or legs embracing an angle of ninety degrees, and is intended only to test the accuracy of the sides of a stone, and to see that its edges subtend the same angle.

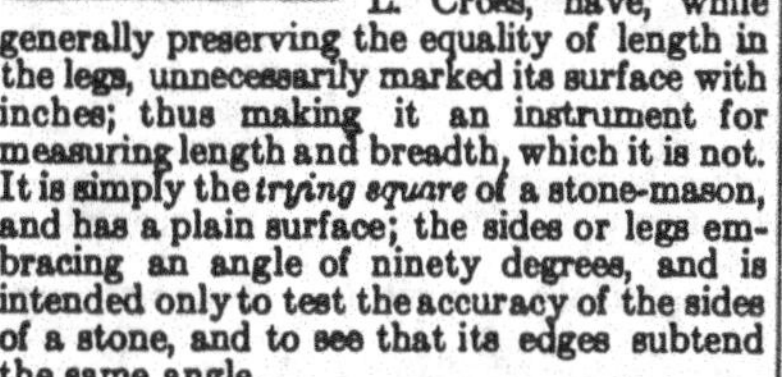

In Freemasonry, it is a symbol of morality. This is its general signification, and is applied in various ways: 1. It presents itself to the neophyte as one of the three great lights; 2. To the Fellow-Craft as one of his working-tools; 3. To the Master Mason as the official emblem of the Master of the Lodge. Everywhere, however, it inculcates the same lesson of morality, of truthfulness, of honesty. So universally accepted is this symbolism, that it has gone outside of the Order, and has been found in colloquial language communicating the same idea. Square, says Halliwell (*Dict. Archaisms*), means honest, equitable, as in "square dealing." To *play upon the square* is proverbial for *to play honestly*. In this sense the word is found in the old writers.

As a Masonic symbol, it is of very ancient date, and was familiar to the Operative Masons. In the year 1830, the architect, in rebuilding a very ancient bridge called Baal Bridge, near Limerick, in Ireland, found under the foundation-stone an old brass square, much eaten away, containing on its two surfaces the following inscription: I. WILL. STRIUE. TO. LIUE.—WITH. LOUE. & CARE.—UPON. THE. LEUL.—BY. THE. SQUARE., and the date 1517. The modern Speculative Mason will recognize the idea of *living on the level and by the square*. This discovery proves, if proof were necessary, that the familiar idea was borrowed from our Operative brethren of former days.

The square, as a symbol in Speculative Masonry, has therefore presented itself from the very beginning of the revival period. In the very earliest catechism of the last century, of the date of 1725, we find the answer to the question, "How many make a Lodge?" is "God and the Square, with five or seven right or perfect Masons." God and the Square, religion and morality, must be present in every Lodge as governing principles. Signs at that early period were to be made by squares, and the furniture of the Lodge was declared to be the Bible, Compasses, and Square.

In all rites and in all languages where Masonry has penetrated, the square has preserved its primitive signification as a symbol of morality.

Square and Compasses. These two symbols have been so long and so universally combined—to teach us, as says an early ritual, "to square our actions and to keep them within due bounds," they are so seldom seen apart, but are so kept together, either as two great lights, or as a jewel worn once by the Master of the Lodge, now by the Past Master—that they have come at last to be recognized as the proper badge of a Master Mason, just as the triple tau is of a Royal Arch Mason or the passion cross of a Knights Templar.

So universally has this symbol been recognized, even by the profane world, as the peculiar characteristic of Freemasonry, that it has recently been made in the United States the subject of a legal decision. A manufacturer of flour having made, in 1873, an application to the Patent Office for permission to adopt the square and compasses as a trade-mark, the Commissioner of Patents refused the permission on the ground that the mark was a Masonic symbol.

"If this emblem," said Mr. J. M. Thacher, the Commissioner, "were something other than precisely what it is—either less known, less significant, or fully and universally understood—all this might readily be admitted. But, considering its peculiar character and relation to the public, an anomalous question is presented. There can be no doubt that this device, so commonly worn and employed by Masons, has an established mystic significance, universally recognized as existing; whether comprehended by all or not, is not material to this issue. In view of the magnitude and extent of the Masonic organization, it is impossible to divest its symbols, or at least this particular symbol —perhaps the best known of all—of its ordinary signification, wherever displayed, either as an arbitrary character or otherwise. It will be universally understood, or misunderstood, as having a Masonic significance; and, therefore, as a trade-mark, must constantly work deception. Nothing could be more mischievous than to create as a monopoly, and uphold by the power of law, anything so calculated, as applied to purposes of trade, to be misinterpreted, to mislead all classes, and to constantly foster suggestions of mystery in affairs of business."

In a religious work by John Davies, entitled *Summa Totalis*, or *All in All and the Same Forever*, printed in 1607, we find an allusion to the square and compasses by a profane in a really Masonic sense. The author, who proposes to describe mystically the form of the Deity, says in his dedication:

"Yet I this forme of formelesse Deity,
Drewe by the Squire and Compasse of our Creed."

In Masonic symbolism the Square and Compasses refer to the Mason's duty to the Craft and to himself; hence it is properly a symbol of brotherhood, and there significantly adopted as the badge or token of the Fraternity.

Berage, in his work on the high degrees (*Les plus secrets Mystères des Hauts Grades*), gives a new interpretation to the symbol. He says: "The square and the compasses represent the union of the Old and New Testaments. None of the high degrees recognize this interpretation, although their symbolism of the two implements differs somewhat from that of symbolic Masonry. The square is with them peculiarly appropriated to the lower degrees, as founded on the operative art; while the compasses, as an implement of higher character and uses, is attributed to the degrees, which claim to have a more elevated and philosophical foundation. Thus they speak of the initiate, when he passes from the blue Lodge to the Lodge of Perfection, as 'passing from the square to the compasses,' to indicate a progressive elevation in his studies. Yet even in the high degrees, the square and compasses combined retain their primitive signification as a symbol of brotherhood and as a badge of the Order."

Squaremen. The companies of wrights, slaters, etc., in Scotland, in the seventeenth century, were called "Squaremen." They had ceremonies of initiation, and a word, sign, and grip, like the Masons. Lyon (*Hist. of the L. at Edinb.*, p. 23) says: "The 'Squaremen Word' was given in conclaves of journeymen and apprentices, wrights, slaters, etc., in a ceremony in which the aspirant was blindfolded and otherwise 'prepared'; he was sworn to secrecy, had word, grip, and sign communicated to him, and was afterward invested with a leather apron. The entrance to the apartment, usually a public house, in which the 'brithering' was performed, was guarded, and all who passed had to give the grip. The fees were spent in the entertainment of the brethren present. Like the Masons, the Squaremen admitted non-operatives." In the St. Clair charter of 1628, among the representatives of the Masonic Lodges, we find the signature of "George Liddell, deakin of squarmen and nov quartermaistir." (*Ibid.*, p. 62.) This would show that there must have been an intimate connection between the two societies or crafts.

Squin de Flexian. A recreant Templar, to whom, with Noffodei and, as some say, another unknown person, is attributed the invention of the false accusations upon which were based the persecutions and the downfall of the Order of Knights Templar. He was a native of the city of Beziers, in the south of France, and having been received as a Knights Templar, had made so much proficiency in the Order as to have been appointed to the head of the Priory of Montfaucon. Reghellini states that both Squin de Flexian and Noffodei were Templars, and held the rank of Commanders; but Dupuy (*Condemnation des Templiers*) denies that the latter was a Templar. He says: "All historians agree that the origin of the ruin of the Templars was the work of the Prior of Montfaucon and of Noffodei, a Florentine, banished from his country, and whom nobody believes to have been a Templar. This Prior, by the sentence of the Grand Master, had been condemned, for heresy and for having led an infamous life, to pass the remainder of his days in a prison. The other is reported to have been condemned to rigorous penalties by the provost of Paris."

Reghellini's account (*La Maçonnerie considerée, etc.*, i., p. 451) is more circumstantial. He says: "In 1506, two Knights Templar, Noffodei and Florian, were punished for crimes, and lost their Commanderies, that of the latter being Montfaucon. They petitioned the Provincial Grand Master of Mount Carmel for a restoration to their offices, but met with a refusal. They then obtained an entrance into the Provincial

Grand Master's country-house, near Milan, and having assassinated him, concealed the body in the woods under some thick shrubbery; after which they fled to Paris. There they obtained access to the king, and thus furnished Philip with an occasion for executing his projects, by denouncing the Order and exposing to him the immense wealth which it possessed.

"They proposed the abolition of the Order, and promised the king, for a reward, to be its denouncers. The king accepted their proposition, and, assuring them of his protection, pointed out to them the course which they were to pursue.

"They associated with themselves a third individual, called by historians 'the Unknown' (*l'Inconnu*); and Noffodei and Florian sent a memorial to Enguerand de Marigni, Superintendent of the Finances, in which they proposed, if he would guarantee them against the attacks of the Order of Templars, and grant them civil existence and rights, to discover to the king secrets which they deemed of more value than the conquest of an empire.

"As a sequel to this first declaration, they addressed to the king an accusation, which was the same as he had himself dictated to them for the purpose of the turn which he desired to the affair. This accusation contained the following charges:

"1. That the Order of Templars was the foe of all kings and all sovereign authority; that it communicated secrets to its initiates under horrible oaths, with the criminal condition of the penalty of death if they divulged them; and that the secret practices of their initiations were the consequences of irreligion, atheism, and rebellion.

"2. That the Order had betrayed the religion of Christ, by communicating to the Sultan of Babylon all the plans and operations of the Emperor Frederick the Second, whereby the designs of the Crusaders for the recovery of the Holy Land were frustrated.

"3. That the Order prostituted the mysteries most venerated by Christians, by making a Knight, when he was received, trample upon the Cross, the sign of redemption; and abjured the Christian religion by making the neophyte declare that the true God had never died, and never could die; that they carried about them and worshipped a little idol called *Bafomet;* and that after his initiation the neophyte was compelled to undergo certain obscene practices.

"4. That when a Knight was received, the Order bound him by an oath to a complete and blind obedience to the Grand Master, which was a proof of rebellion against the legitimate authority.

"5. That Good Friday was the day selected for the grand orgies of the Order.

"6. That they were guilty of unnatural crimes.

"7. That they burned the children of their concubines, so as to destroy all traces of their debauchery."

These calumnies formed the basis of the longer catalogue of accusations, afterward presented by the Pope, upon which the Templars were finally tried and condemned.

In the preliminary examinations of the accused, Squin de Flexian took an active part as one of the Commissioners. In the pleadings for their defense presented by the Knights, they declare that "Knights were tortured by Flexian de Beziers, prior of Montfaucon, and by the monk, William Robert, and that already thirty-six had died of the tortures inflicted at Paris, and several others in other places."

Of the ultimate fate of these traitors nothing is really known. When the infamous work which they had inaugurated had been consummated by the king and the Pope, as their services were no longer needed, they sank into merited oblivion. The author of the *Secret Societies of the Middle Ages* (p. 268) says: "Squin was afterwards hanged, and Noffodei beheaded, as was said, with little probability, by the Templars."

Hardly had the Templars in their prostrate condition, the power, even if they had the will, to inflict such punishment. It was not Squin, but Marigni, his abettor, who was hanged at Montfaucon, by order of Louis X., the successor of Philip, two years after his persecution of the Templars. The revenge they took was of a symbolic character. In the change of the legend of the Third Degree into that of the Templar system, when the martyred James de Molay was substituted for Hiram Abif, the three assassins were represented by Squin de Flexian, Noffodei, and the Unknown. As there is really no reference in the historical records of the persecution to this third accuser, it is most probable that he is altogether a mythical personage, invented merely to complete the triad of assassins, and to preserve the congruity of the Templar with the Masonic legend.

The name of Squin de Flexian, as well as that of Noffodei, have been differently spelled by various writers, to say nothing of the incomprehensible error found in some of the oldest French Cahiers of the Kadosh, such as that of De la Hogue, where the two traitors are named Gerard Tabé and Benoit Mehui. The *Processus contra Templarios* calls him *Esquius de Flexian de Biteriis;* and Raynouard always names him *Squin de Florian,* in which he is blindly followed by Reghellini, Ragon, and Thory. But the weight of authority is in favor of *Squin de Flexian*, which appears to be the true name of this Judas of the Templars.

Sruti. ("Revelation.") A collective name of those Sanskrit writings supposed by the Hindus to have been revealed by a deity, and applied at first only to the Vedic Mantras and Brahmanas, but afterward extended to the older Upanishads.

Staff. A white staff is the proper insignia of a Treasurer. In the order of Procession for laying a foundation-stone as given by Preston (*Illustrations*, ed. 1792, p. 111), we find "Grand Treasurer with his staff." In America the use of the staff by the Treasurer of a Lodge has been discontinued. It was derived from the old custom for the Treasurer of the king's household to carry a staff as the ensign of authority. In the old "Customary Books" we are told that the Steward or Treasurer of the household—for the offices were formerly identical—received the office from the king himself by the presentation of a staff in these words: *Tennez le baston de nostre maison*, "Receive the staff of our house." Hence the Grand Lodge of England decreed, June 24, 1741, that "in the procession in the hall" the Grand Treasurer should appear "with the staff." (*Constitutions*, 1756, p. 236.)

Stairs, Winding. See *Winding Stairs*.

St. Alban's Regulations. The regulations said to have been made by St. Alban for the government of the Craft are referred to by Anderson, in his second edition (p. 57), and afterward by Preston. (See *St. Alban*.)

Standard. An ensign in war, being that under which the soldiers stand or to which they rally in the fight. It is sometimes used in the higher degrees, in connection with the word *Bearer*, to denote a particular officer. But the term mostly used to indicate any one of the ensigns of the different degrees of Masonry is *Banner*.

The Grand Standard of the Order of Knights Templar in the United States is described in the regulations as being "of white woollen or silk stuff, six feet in height and five feet in width, made tripartite at the bottom, fastened at the top to the cross-bar by nine rings; in the centre of the field a blood-red passion cross, over which the motto, *In hoc signo vinces*, and under, *Non Nobis, Domine! non Nobis sed Nomini tuo da Gloriam!* The cross to be four feet high, and the upright and bar to be seven inches wide. On the top of the staff a gilded globe or ball four inches in diameter, surmounted by the patriarchal cross, twelve inches in height. The cross to be crimson, edged with gold."

The standard of the Order in the Ancient and Accepted Scottish Rite is thus described in the *Fundamental Statutes*. It is white with a gold fringe, bearing in the center a black double-headed eagle with wings displayed; the beaks and thighs are of gold; it holds in one talon the golden hilt and in the other the silver blade of an antique sword, placed horizontally from right to left; to the sword is suspended the Latin device, in letters of gold, *Deus meumque Jus*. The eagle is crowned with a triangle of gold, and holds a purple band fringed with gold and strewn with golden stars.

There is really no standard of the Order properly belonging to Symbolic or Royal Arch Masonry. Many Grand Chapters, however, and some Grand Lodges in this country, have adopted for a standard the blazonment of the arms of Masonry first made by Dermott for the Atholl Grand Lodge of Masons. In the present condition of the ritual, occasioned by the disseverance of the Royal Arch Degree from the Master's, and its organization as a distinct system, this standard, if adopted at all, would be most appropriate to the Grand Chapters, since its charges consist of symbols no longer referred to in the ritual of Symbolic Masonry.

Standard-Bearer. An officer in a Commandery of Knights Templar, whose duty it is to carry and protect the standard of the Order. A similar officer exists in several of the high degrees.

Stand to and Abide by. The covenant of Masonry requires every Mason "to stand to and abide by" the laws and regulations of the Order, whether expressed in the edicts of the Grand Lodge, the by-laws of his Lodge, or the landmarks of the Institution. The terms are not precisely synonymous, although generally considered to be so. *To stand to* has a somewhat active meaning, and signifies to maintain and defend the laws; while *to abide by* is more passive in meaning, and signifies to submit to the award made by such laws.

St. Anthony. An order taking its rise from the life and habits of St. Anthony, the hermit, who died about 357. His disciples, called Anchorites, near Ethiopia, lived in austerity and solitariness in the desert, until John, Emperor of Ethiopia, in 370, created them a religious order of knighthood, and bestowed privileges upon them under the title of St. Anthony, who was made patron of the empire. They established monasteries, adopted a black habit, and wore a blue cross in the shape of a Tau.

The vow embraced chastity, defense of the Christian faith, to guard the empire, obey their superiors, and go to war when and wheresoever commanded. Marriage required a license. There were two classes—combatants and non-combatants—the second class being composed of those too old for military duty. Yet ere they retired they were required to serve three years against Arabian pirates, three against the Turks, and three against the Moors.

The ancient monastery is in the deserts of Thebais, surrounded by an oval wall 500 paces in circumference and 40 feet in height. It is entered by ropes let down from the watch-house, the crane being turned by monks. By age, the cells, which are four by five by seven feet, have been reduced from 300 to 40. Advantage had been taken of one of nature's curiosities in obtaining abundant water from a riven rock, which is reached through a subterraneous passage of 50 paces, extending beyond the walls. In France, Italy, and Spain there are ecclesiastical and military organizations styled Knights of St. Anthony, who wear a plain cross, the principals a double cross. The chief seat is at Vienna. In the abbey rest the remains of St. Anthony.

Star. In the French and Scottish Rites lighted candles or torches are called stars when used in some of the ceremonies, especially in the reception of distinguished visitors, where the number of lights or stars with which the visitor is received is proportioned to his rank; but the number is always odd, being 3, 5, 7, 9, or 11.

Star, Blazing. See *Blazing Star.*

Star, Eastern. See *Eastern Star, Order of the.*

Star, Five-Pointed. See *Five-Pointed Star.*

Star in the East. The Blazing Star is thus called by those who entertain the theory that there is "an intimate and necessary connection between Masonry and Christianity." This doctrine, which Dr. Oliver thinks is "the fairest gem that Masonry can boast," is defended by him in his early work entitled *The Star in the East.* The whole subject is discussed in the article *Blazing Star,* which see.

Star of Jerusalem. A degree cited in the nomenclature of Fustier.

Star of the Syrian Knights. (*Etoile des Chevaliers Syriens.*) The Order of Syrian Knights of the Star is contained in the collection of Pyron. It is divided into three degrees—Novice, Professed, and Grand Patriarch.

Starck, Johann August von. Von Starck, whose life is closely connected with the history of German Freemasonry, and especially with that of the Rite of Strict Observance, was born at Schwerin, October 29, 1741. He studied at the University of Göttingen, and was made in 1761 a Freemason in a French Military Lodge. In 1763 he went to St. Petersburg, where he received the appointment of teacher in one of the public schools. There, too, it is supposed that he was adopted into the Rite of Melesino, then flourishing in the Russian capital, and became first acquainted with the Rite of Strict Observance, in which he afterward played so important a part. After two years' residence at St. Petersburg, he went for a short time to England, and was in August, 1766, in Paris. In 1767 he was director of the schools at Wismar, where he was Junior Warden of the Lodge of the Three Lions. In 1770 he was called to Königsberg, to occupy the chair of theology, and to fill the post of court chaplain. The following year he resigned both offices, and retired to Mettau, to devote himself to literary and philosophical pursuits. But in 1781 the Court at Darmstadt conferred upon him the posts of chief preacher and the first place in the consistory, and there he remained until his death, which occurred March 3, 1816.

The knowledge that Starck acquired of the Rite of Strict Observance convinced him of its innate weakness, and of the necessity of some reformation. He therefore was led to the idea of reviving the spiritual branch of the Order, a project which he sought to carry into effect, at first quietly and secretly, by gaining over influential Masons to his views. In this he so far succeeded as to be enabled to establish, in 1767, the new system of clerical Knights Templar, as a schism from the Strict Observance, and to which he gave the name of Clerks of Relaxed Observance. It consisted of seven degrees, as follows: 1. Apprentice; 2. Fellow; 3. Master; 4. Young Scottish Master; 5. Old Scottish Master, or Knight of St. Andrew; 6. Provincial Chapter of the Red Cross; 7. Magus, or Knight of Brightness and Light; which last degree was divided into five classes, of Novice, Levite, and Priest—the summit of the Order being Knight Priest. Thus he embodied the idea that Templarism was a hierarchy, and that not only was every Mason a Templar, but every true Templar was both a Knight and a Priest. Starck, who was originally a Protestant, had been secretly connected with Romanism while in Paris; and he attempted surreptitiously to introduce Roman Catholicism into his new system. He professed that the Rite which he was propagating was in possession of secrets not known to the chivalric branch of the Order; and he demanded, as a prerequisite to admission, that the candidate should be a Roman Catholic, and have previously received the degrees of Strict Observance.

Starck entered into a correspondence with Von Hund, the head of the Rite of Strict Observance, for the purpose of effecting a fusion of the two branches—the chivalric and the spiritual. But, notwithstanding the willingness of Von Hund to accept any league which promised to give renewed strength to his own decaying system, the fusion was never effected. It is true that in 1768 there was a formal union of the two branches at Wismar, but it was neither sincere nor permanent. At the Congress of Brunswick, in 1775, the clerical branch seceded and formed an independent Order; and, after the death of Von Hund, the Lodges of the Strict Observance abandoned their name, and called themselves the United German Lodges. The spiritual branch, too, soon began to lose favor with the German Freemasons, partly because the Swedish system was getting to be popular in Germany, and partly because Starck was suspected of being in league with the Catholics, for whose sake he had invented his system. Documentary evidence has since proved that this suspicion was well founded. Ragon says that the Order continued in successful existence until the year 1800; but I doubt if it lasted so long.

The German writers have not hesitated to accuse Starck of having been an emissary of the Jesuits, and of having instituted his Rite in the interests of Jesuitism. This, of course, rendered both him and the Rite unpopular, and gave an impetus to its decay and fall. Starck himself, even before his appointment as court chaplain at Darmstadt, in 1781, had, by his own confession, not only abandoned the Rite, but all interest in Freemasonry. In 1785 he wrote his *Saint Nicaise*, which was really anti-Masonic in principle, and in 1787 he published his work *Ueber Kripto-Catholicesmus, etc.*, or *A Treatise on Secret Catholicism, on Proselyte Making, on Jesuitism, and on Secret Societies*, which was a controversial work directed against Nicolai, Gädicke, and Biester. In this book he says: "It is true that in my youthful days I was a Freemason. It is also true that when the so-called Strict Observance was introduced into Masonry I belonged to it, and was, like others, an Eques, Socius, Armiger, Commendator, Prefect, and Sub-Prior; and, having taken some formal cloister-like profession, I have been a Clericus. But I have withdrawn from all that, and all that is called Freemasonry, for more than nine years."

While an active member of the Masonic Order, whatever may have been his secret motives, he wrote many valuable Masonic works, which produced at the time of their appearance a great sensation in Germany. Such were his *Apology for the Order of Freemasonry*, Berlin, 1778, which went through many editions; *On the Design of the Order of Freemasonry*, Berlin, 1781; and *On the Ancient and Modern Mysteries*, 1782. He was distinguished as a man of letters and as a learned theologian, and has left numerous works on general literature and on religion, the latter class showing an evident leaning toward the Roman Catholic faith, of which he was evidently a partisan. "There is," says Feller (*Biog. Univ.*), "in the life of Starck something singular, that has never been made public." I think the verdict is now well established. that in his labors for the apparent reformation of Freemasonry there was a deplorable want of honesty and sincerity, and that he abandoned the Order finally because his schemes of ambition failed, and the Jesuitical designs with which he entered it were frustrated.

Stare Super Vias Antiquas. (*To stand on the old paths.*) A Latin adage, appropriately applied as a Masonic motto to inculcate the duty of adhering to the ancient landmarks.

State. The political divisions of the United States are called States and Territories. In every State and in every populous Territory there is a Grand Lodge and a Grand Chapter, each of which exercises exclusive jurisdiction over all the Lodges and Chapters within its political boundaries; nor does it permit the introduction of any other Grand Lodge or Grand Chapter within its limits; so that there is, and can be, but one Grand Lodge and one Grand Chapter in each State. In most of the States there are also a Grand Council of Royal and Select Masters, and a Grand Commandery of Knights Templar, which claim the same right of exclusive jurisdiction. (See *Jurisdiction of a Grand Lodge.*)

Stations. The positions occupied by the subordinate officers of a Lodge are called *places*, as "the Junior Deacon's place in the Lodge." But the positions occupied by the Master and Wardens are called *stations*, as "the Senior Warden's station in the Lodge." This is because these three officers, representing the sun in his three prominent points of rising, culminating, and setting, are supposed to be stationary, and therefore remain in the spot appropriated to them by the ritual, while the Deacon and other officers are required to move about from place to place in the Lodge.

Statistics of Freemasonry. The assertion that "in every land a Mason may find a home, and in every clime a brother," is well sustained by the statistics of the Order, which show that, wherever civilized men have left their footprints, its temples have been established. It is impossible to venture on anything more than a mere approximation to the number of Freemasons scattered over the world. The following is a table of the countries in which Freemasonry is openly practised with the permission of the public authorities, omitting the States, now, by the increasing spirit of tolerance, very few, indeed, where the suspicions of the government compel the Masons, if they meet at all, to meet in private:

I. Europe.

Anhalt-Bernburg,
Anhalt-Dessau,
Bavaria,
Belgium,
Bremen,
Brunswick,
Denmark,
England,
France,
Germany,
Greece,
Hamburg,
Hanover,
Hesse-Darmstadt,
Holland,
Holstein-Oldenburg,
Hungary,
Ionian Islands,
Ireland,
Italy,
Malta,
Mecklenburg-Schwerin,
Netherlands.
Norway,
Portugal,
Posen, Duchy of,
Prussia,
Prussian Poland,
Saxe,
Saxe-Coburg,
Saxe-Gotha,
Saxe-Hildburghausen,
Saxe-Meiningen,
Saxe-Weimar,
Saxony,
Schwarzburg-Rudolstadt,
Scotland,
Spain,
Sweden,
Switzerland,
Wurtemberg.

II. Asia.

Ceylon,
China,
India,
Japan,
Persia,
Pondicherry,
Turkey.

III. OCEANICA.

Java,
New South Wales,
New Zealand,
Sumatra,
Sandwich Islands.

IV. AFRICA.

Algeria,
Bourbon, Isle of,
Canary Islands,
Cape of Good Hope,
Egypt,
Goa,
Guinea,
Mauritius,
Mozambique,
Senegambia,
St. Helena.

V. AMERICA.

Antigua,
Argentine Republic,
Barbadoes,
Bermudas,
Brazil,
Canada,
Carthagena,
Chili,
Colombia,
Curaçoa,
Dominica,
Dutch Guiana,
English Guiana,
French Guiana,
Guadeloupe,
Hayti,
Jamaica,
Martinico,
Mexico,
New Brunswick,
New Granada,
Nova Scotia,
Panama,
Peru,
Rio de la Plata,
St. Bartholomew's,
St. Christopher's,
St. Croix,
St. Eustatia,
St. Martin,
St. Thomas,
St. Vincent,
Trinidad,
United States,
Uruguay,
Venezuela.

Statistics of Craft Masonry in the United States of America for 1915:

Alabama	27,548
Arizona	2,324
Arkansas	20,962
California	53,179
Colorado	16,955
Connecticut	24,815
Delaware	3,436
District of Columbia	9,924
Florida	12,051
Georgia	40,458
Idaho	4,413
Illinois	130,778
Indiana	66,192
Iowa	49,550
Kansas	42,412
Kentucky	42,139
Louisiana	15,883
Maine	30,294
Maryland	16,464
Massachusetts	65,697
Michigan	74,964
Minnesota	28,735
Mississippi	19,690
Missouri	61,522
Montana	7,500
Nebraska	21,122
Nevada	1,939
New Hampshire	10,728
New Jersey	38,694
New Mexico	3,361
New York	192,463
North Carolina	22,879
North Dakota	9,130
Ohio	96,075
Oklahoma	25,382
Oregon	13,260
Pennsylvania	115,505
Rhode Island	8,833
South Carolina	15,155
South Dakota	10,730
Tennessee	27,091
Texas	63,394
Utah	2,201
Vermont	13,874
Virginia	24,146
Washington	19,542
West Virginia	16,710
Wisconsin	29,242
Wyoming	9,190
Total	1,656,061

Statistics of Capitular Masonry—Royal Arch—in the United States of America, to 1915:

Grand Chapters.	Subordinates.	Members.
Alabama	67	4,149
Arizona	9	763
Arkansas	85	4,351
California	108	13,466
Colorado	42	5,327
Connecticut	40	9,479
Delaware	4	1,169
District of Columbia	12	3,580
Florida	32	2,425
Georgia	32	8,471
Idaho	13	1,339
Illinois	199	39,260
Indiana	114	17,469
Iowa	128	14,080
Kansas	92	10,144
Kentucky	106	9,620
Louisiana	32	3,733
Maine	62	10,536
Maryland	23	4,021
Massachusetts	81	24,754
Michigan	149	24,026
Minnesota	71	9,213
Mississippi	72	4,447
Missouri	107	14,703
Montana	17	2,198
Nebraska	56	4,939
Nevada	9	429
New Hampshire	26	4,552
New Jersey	38	7,642
New Mexico	14	1,137
New York	208	40,368
North Carolina	40	23,724
North Dakota	19	2,816
Ohio	170	37,184
Oklahoma	66	5,271
Oregon	31	4,052
Pennsylvania	133	35,118
Rhode Island	10	4,641
South Carolina	31	3,170
South Dakota	31	3,571
Tennessee	85	5,685
Texas	239	20,302
Utah	5	694
Vermont	30	4,486
Virginia	64	7,058
Washington	30	4,500
West Virginia	35	6,343
Wisconsin	81	11,678
Wyoming	12	950
	3,142	483,033

Statistics of the Order of the Temple in all countries wherein it has been established, 1915:

Grand Commandery.	Subordinates.	Members.
Alabama	23	1,808
Arizona	5	495
Arkansas	21	1,395
California	50	7,446
Colorado	30	3,224
Connecticut	11	4,171
District of Columbia	5	1,643
Florida	19	1,315
Georgia	29	3,446
Idaho	10	734
Illinois	80	18,413
Indiana	57	7,984
Iowa	62	7,016
Kansas	55	6,404
Kentucky	33	4,987
Louisiana	12	1,108
Maine	23	5,609
Maryland	13	2,234
Massachusetts and Rhode Island	47	18,165
Michigan	50	9,132
Minnesota	31	4,599
Mississippi	28	2,054
Missouri	61	7,137
Montana	14	1,307
Nebraska	29	2,828
New Hampshire	11	2,783
New Jersey	19	3,451
New Mexico	12	708
New York	64	23,114
North Carolina	20	1,598
North Dakota	15	1,614
Ohio	65	17,330
Oklahoma	38	2,474
Oregon	17	1,813
Pennsylvania	86	22,974
South Carolina	9	1,660
South Dakota	19	1,829
Tennessee	18	1,906
Texas	61	6,553
Utah	3	435
Vermont	13	2,797
Virginia	25	3,450
Washington	15	2,256
West Virginia	29	3,925
Wisconsin	36	5,219
Wyoming	10	685
Grand Encampment	9	674
Total in the U. S.	1,392	233,892
Canada	61	7,905
England and Wales	145	3,140
Ireland	14	1,300
Scotland	16	1,828
Total in the World	1,628	248,065

Statute of Henry VI. See *Laborers, Statutes of.*

Statutes. The permanent rules by which a subordinate Lodge is governed are called its *By-Laws;* the regulations of a Grand Lodge are called its *Constitution:* but the laws enacted for the government of a Supreme Council of the Scottish Rite are denominated *Statutes.*

St. Clair Charters. In the Advocates' Library, of Edinburgh, is a manuscript entitled "Hay's Memoirs," which is, says Lawrie, "a collection of several things relating to the historical account of the most famed families of Scotland. Done by Richard Augustine Hay, Canon Regular of Sainte Genevefs of Paris, Prior of Sainte Pierremont, etc., *Anno Domini* 1700." Among this collection are two manuscripts, supposed to have been copied from the originals by Canon Hay, and which are known to Masonic scholars as the "St. Clair Charters." These copies, which it seems were alone known in the last century, were first published by Lawrie, in his *History of Freemasonry,* where they constitute Appendices I. and II. But it appears that the originals have since been discovered, and they have been republished by Bro. W. J. Hughan, in his *Unpublished Records of the Craft,* with the following introductory account of them by Bro. D. Murray Lyon:

"These MSS. were several years ago accidentally discovered by David Lang, Esq., of the Signet Library, who gave them to the late Bro. Aytoun, Professor of Belles-Lettres in the University of Edinburgh, in exchange for some antique documents he had. The Professor presented them to the Grand Lodge of Scotland, in whose repositories they now are. There can be no doubt of their identity as originals. We have compared several of the signatures with autographs in other MSS. of the time. The charters are in scrolls of paper, —the one 15 by 11½ inches, the other 26 by 11½ inches,—and for their better preservation have been affixed to cloth. The caligraphy is beautiful; and though the edges of the paper have been frayed, and holes worn in one or two places where the sheets had been folded, there is no difficulty in supplying the few words that have been obliterated, and making out the whole of the text. About three inches in depth at the bottom of No. 1, in the right-hand corner, is entirely wanting, which may have contained some signatures in addition to those given. The left hand bottom corner of No. 2 has been similarly torn away, and the same remark with regard to signatures may apply to it. The first document is a letter of jurisdiction, granted by the Freemen Masons of Scotland to William St. Clair of Roslin, (probable date 1600–1). The second purports to have been granted by the Freemen Masons and Hammermen of Scotland to Sir William St. Clair of Roslin, (probable date May 1, 1628)." Facsimiles and transcripts of these MSS. are given by D. M. Lyon in his *History of the Lodge of Edinburgh.*

However difficult it may be to decide as to the precise date of these charters, there are no Masonic manuscripts whose claim to authenticity is more indisputable; for the statements which they contain tally not only with the uniformly accepted traditions of Scotch Masonry, but with the written records of the Grand Lodge of Scotland, both of which show the intimate connection that existed between the Freemasonry of that kingdom and the once powerful but now extinct family of St. Clair.

St. Clair, William. The St. Clairs of Roslin, or, as it is often spelled, of Rosslyn, held for more than three hundred years an intimate connection with the history of Masonry in Scotland. William St. Clair, Earl of Orkney and Caithness, was, in 1441, appointed by King James II. the Patron and Protector of the Masons of Scotland, and the office was made hereditary in his family. Charles Mackie says of him (*Lond. Freem.*, May, 1851, p. 166) that "he was considered one of the best and greatest Masons of the age." He planned the construction of a most magnificent collegiate church at his palace of Roslin, of which, however, only the chancel and part of the transept were completed. To take part in this design, he invited the most skilful Masons from foreign countries; and in order that they might be conveniently lodged and carry on the work with ease and despatch, he ordered them to erect the neighboring town of Roslin, and gave to each of the most worthy a house and lands. After his death, which occurred about 1480, the office of hereditary Patron was transmitted to his descendants, who, says Lawrie (*Hist.*, p. 100), "held their principal annual meetings at Kilwinning."

The prerogative of nominating the office-bearers of the Craft, which had always been exercised by the kings of Scotland, appears to have been neglected by James VI. after his accession to the throne of England. Hence the Masons, finding themselves embarrassed for want of a Protector, about the year 1600 (if that be the real date of the first of the St. Clair Manuscripts), appointed William St. Clair of Roslin, for himself and his heirs, their "patrons and judges." After presiding over the Order for many years, says Lawrie, William St. Clair went to Ireland, and in 1630 a second Charter was issued, granting to his son, Sir William St. Clair, the same power with which his father had been invested. This Charter having been signed by the Masters and Wardens of the principal Lodges of Scotland, Sir William St. Clair assumed the active administration of the affairs of the Craft, and appointed his Deputies and Wardens, as had been customary with his ancestors. For more than a century after this renewal of the compact between the Lairds of Roslin and the Masons of Scotland, the Craft continued to flourish under the successive heads of the family.

But in the year 1736, William St. Clair, Esq., to whom the Hereditary Protectorship had descended in due course of succession, having no children of his own, became anxious that the office of Grand Master should not become vacant at his death. Accordingly, he assembled the members of the Lodges of Edinburgh and its vicinity, and represented to them the good effects that would accrue to them if they should in future have at their head a Grand Master of their own choice, and declared his intention to resign into the hands of the Craft his hereditary right to the office. It was agreed by the assembly that all the Lodges of Scotland should be summoned to appear by themselves, or proxies, on the approaching St. Andrew's Day, at Edinburgh to take the necessary steps for the election of a Grand Master.

In compliance with the call, the representatives of thirty-two Lodges met at Edinburgh on the 30th of November, 1736, when William St. Clair tendered the following resignation of his hereditary office:

"I, William St. Clair, of Roslin, Esq., taking into my consideration that the Masons in Scotland did, by several deeds, constitute and appoint William and Sir William St. Clairs of Roslin, my ancestors and their heirs, to be their patrons, protectors, judges, or masters, and that my holding or claiming any such jurisdiction, right, or privilege might be prejudicial to the Craft and vocation of Masonry, whereof I am a member; and I, being desirous to advance and promote the good and utility of the said Craft of Masonry to the utmost of my power, do therefore hereby, for me and my heirs, renounce, quit, claim, overgive, and discharge all right, claim, or pretence that I, or my heirs, had, have, or any ways may have, pretend to, or claim to be, patron, protector, judge, or master of the Masons in Scotland, in virtue of any deed or deeds made and granted by the said Masons, or of any grant or charter made by any of the kings of Scotland to and in favor of the said William and Sir William St. Clairs of Roslin, my predecessors, or any other manner or way whatsoever, for now and ever; and I bind and oblige me and my heirs to warrant this present renunciation and discharge at all hands. And I consent to the registration hereof in the books of council and session, or any other judges' books competent, therein to remain for preservation." And then follows the usual formal and technical termination of a deed. (Lawrie's *Hist. of F. M.*, p. 148.)

The deed of resignation having been accepted, the Grand Lodge proceeded to the election of its office-bearers, when William St. Clair, as was to be expected, was unanimously chosen as Grand Master; an office which, however, he held but for one year, being succeeded in 1737 by the Earl of Cromarty. He lived, however, for more than half a century afterward, and died in January, 1778, in the seventy-eighth year of his age.

The Grand Lodge of Scotland was not unmindful of his services to the Craft, and on the announcement of his death a funeral Lodge was convened, when four hundred brethren, dressed in deep mourning, being present, Sir William Forbes, who was then the Grand Master, delivered an impressive address, in the course of which he paid the following tribute to the character of St. Clair. After alluding to his voluntary resignation of his high office for the good of the Order, he added: "His zeal, however, to promote the welfare of our society was not confined to this single instance; for he continued almost to the very close of life, on all occasions where his influence or his example could prevail, to extend the spirit of Masonry and to increase the number of the brethren. . . . To these more conspicuous and public parts of his character I am happy to be able to add, that he possessed in an eminent degree the virtues of a benevolent and good heart—virtues which ought ever to be the distinguishing marks of a true brother." (*Ibid.*, p. 224.)

Bro. Charles Mackie, in the London *Freemasons' Quarterly Review* (1831, p. 167), thus describes the last days of this venerable patron of the Order: "William St. Clair of Roslin, the last of that noble family, was one of the most remarkable personages of his time; although stripped of his paternal title and possessions, he walked abroad respected and reverenced. He moved in the first society; and if he did not carry the purse, he was stamped with the impress of nobility. He did not require a cubit to be added to his stature, for he was considered the stateliest man of his age."

[The preceding account of the connection of the St. Clairs with Scotch Freemasonry is based almost entirely on Lawrie's *History of Freemasonry* (1804), but a later and more critical writer—D. Murray Lyon, in his *History of the Lodge of Edinburgh* (1873)—considers the statement that James II. invested the Earl of Orkney and Caithness with the dignity of Grand Master and subsequently made the office hereditary to be "altogether apocryphal" (p. 3). The real fact appears to be that the Operative Masons of Scotland by the St. Clair Charters did confer upon the St. Clair family the office of Patron and Protector of the Craft, and that William St. Clair was made a Mason in 1735 in order to resign this office, and in return for such apparent magnanimity to be elected in 1736 the first Grand Master of Scotland.—E. L. H.]

Steinbach, Erwin von. See *Erwin von Steinbach.*

Steinmetz. German. A stone-mason. For an account of the German fraternity of Steinmetzen, see *Stone-Masons of the Middle Ages.*

"Stellato Sedet Solo." ("He sits on his starry throne.") A symbolic expression in the Twenty-eighth Degree of the A. A. Scottish Rite.

Step. The *step* can hardly be called a mode of recognition, although Apuleius informs us that there was a peculiar step in the Osiriac initiation which was deemed a sign. It is in Freemasonry rather an esoteric usage of the ritual. The *steps* can be traced back as far as to at least the middle of the last century, in the rituals of which they are fully described. The custom of advancing in a peculiar manner and form, to some sacred place or elevated personage, has been preserved in the customs of all countries, especially among the Orientalists, who resort even to prostrations of the body when approaching the throne of the sovereign or the holy part of a religious edifice. The steps of Masonry are symbolic of respect and veneration for the altar, whence Masonic light is to emanate.

In former times, and in some of the high degrees, a bier or coffin was placed in front of the altar, as a well-known symbol, and in passing over this to reach the altar, those various positions of the feet were necessarily taken which constitute the proper mode of advancing. Respect was thus necessarily paid to the memory of a worthy artist as well as to the holy altar. Lenning says of the steps—which the German Masons call *die Schritte der Aufzunehmenden*, the steps of the recipients, and the French, *les pas Mystérieux*, the mysterious steps—that "every degree has a different number, which are made in a different way, and have an allegorical meaning." Of the "allegorical meaning" of those in the Third Degree, I have spoken above as explicitly as would be proper. Gädicke says: "The three grand steps symbolically lead from this life to the source of all knowledge."

It must be evident to every Master Mason, without further explanation, that the three steps are taken from the place of darkness to the place of light, either figuratively or really over a coffin, the symbol of death, to teach symbolically that the passage from the darkness and ignorance of this life is through death to the light and knowledge of the eternal life. And this, from the earliest times, was the true symbolism of the step.

Steps on the Master's Carpet. The three steps delineated on the Master's carpet, as one of the symbols of the Third Degree, refer to the three steps or stages of human life—youth, manhood, and old age. This symbol is one of the simplest forms or modifications of the mystical ladder, which pervades all the systems of initiation ancient and modern. (See *Carpet.*)

Sterkin. One of the three Assassins, according to the Hiramic legend of some of the high degrees. Lenning says the word means *vengeance*, but does not state his authority. STR are the letters of the Chaldaic verb *to strike a blow*, and it may be that the root of the name will be there found; but the Masonic corruptions of Hebrew words often defy the rules of etymology. Perhaps this and some kindred words are mere anagrams, or corruptions introduced into the high degrees by the adherents of the Pretender, who sought in this way to do honor to the friends of the house of Stuart, or to cast infamy on its enemies. (See *Romvel.*)

Stewards. Officers in a Symbolic Lodge, whose duties are, to assist in the collection of dues and subscriptions; to provide the necessary refreshments, and make a regular report to the Treasurer; and generally to aid the Deacons and other officers in the performance of their duties. They usually carry white rods, and the jewel of their office is a cornucopia, which is a symbol of plenty.

Stewards, Grand. See *Grand Stewards.*

Stewards' Lodge. See *Grand Stewards' Lodge.*

Stirling. A city in Scotland which was the seat of a Lodge called the "Stirling Ancient Lodge," which the author of the introduction to the *General Regulations of the Supreme Grand Chapter of Scotland* says conferred the degrees of Royal Arch, Red Cross or Ark, the Sepulcher, Knight of Malta, and Knights Templar until about the beginning of the last century, when two Lodges were formed—one for the cultivation of St. John's Masonry, which was the old one, and a new one called the "Royal Arch," for the high degrees; although it, too, soon began to confer the first three degrees. The "Ancient Lodge" joined the Grand Lodge of Scotland at its formation in 1736, but the new Lodge remained independent until 1759.

The same authority tells us that "in the Stirling Ancient Lodge are still preserved two old, rudely-engraved brass plates: one of these relates to the first two degrees of Masonry; the other contains on the one side certain emblems belonging to a Master's Lodge, and on the reverse five figures; the one at the top is called the 'Redd Cross or Ark.' At the bottom is a series of concentric arches, which might be mistaken for a rainbow, were there not a keystone on the summit, indicative of an arch. The three other figures are enclosed within a border; the upper is called the 'Sepulcher'; the second, 'Knight of Malta'; and the third, 'Knights Templar.' The age of these plates is unknown, but they can scarcely be more modern than the beginning or middle of the seventeenth century."

So circumstantial a description, inserted, too, in a book of official authority, would naturally lead to the conclusion that these plates must have been in existence in 1845, when the description was written. If they ever existed, they have now disappeared, nor have any traces of them been discovered. Bro. W. James Hughan, whose indefatigable labors have been rewarded with so many valuable discoveries, has failed, in this search, to find success. He says (*Lond. Freemason*), "I spent some weeks, in odd hours, looking up the question a few years ago, and wrote officials in Edinburgh and at Stirling, and also made special inquiries at Stirling by kind co-operation of Masonic students who also investigated the matter; but all our many attempts only resulted in confirming what I was told at the outset, viz., that 'No one knows aught about them, either in Stirling or elsewhere. The friends at Stirling say the plates were sent to Edinburgh, and *never* returned, and the Fraternity at Edinburgh declared they *were* returned, and have since been lost.'"

St. Leger. See *Aldworth*.

Stockings. In the last century, when knee-breeches constituted a portion of the costume of gentlemen, Masons were required, by a ritual regulation, to wear white stockings. The fashion having expired, the regulation is no longer in force.

Stolkin. In the *elu* degrees this is the name of one of those appointed to search for the criminals commemorated in the legend of the Third Degree. It is impossible to trace its derivation to any Hebrew root. It may be an anagram of a name, perhaps that of one of the friends of the house of Stuart.

Stone. The stone, on account of its hardness, has been from the most ancient times a symbol of strength, fortitude, and a firm foundation. The Hebrew word אבן, EBEN, which signifies a stone, is derived, by Gesenius, from an obsolete root, ABAN, to build, whence *aban*, an architect; and he refers it to AMANAH, which means a column, a covenant, and truth. The stone, therefore, says Portal (*Symb. des Egypt.*), may be considered as the symbol of faith and truth: whence Christ taught the very principle of symbology, when he called Peter, who represented *faith*, the rock or stone on which he would build his Church. But in Hebrew as well as in Egyptian symbology the stone was also sometimes the symbol of *falsehood*. Thus the name of Typhon, the principle of evil in the Egyptian theogony, was always written in the hieroglyphic characters with the determinative sign for a stone. But the stone of Typhon was a *hewn stone*, which had the same evil signification in Hebrew. Hence Jehovah says in Exodus, "Thou shalt not build me an altar of hewn stone"; and Joshua built, in Mount Ebal, "an altar of *whole stones*, over which no man hath lift up any iron." The *hewn stone* was therefore a symbol of evil and falsehood; the *unhewn stone* of good and truth. This must satisfy us that the Masonic symbolism of the stone, which is the converse of this, has not been derived from either the Hebrew or the Egyptian symbology, but sprang from the architectural ideas of the Operative Masons; for in Masonry the *rough ashlar*, or *unhewn stone*, is the symbol of man's evil and corrupt condition; while the *perfect ashlar*, or the *hewn stone*, is the symbol of his improved and perfected nature.

Stone, Corner. See *Corner-Stone.*

Stone, Cubical. See *Cubical Stone.*

Stone Manuscript. This Manuscript is no longer in existence, having been one of those which was destroyed, in 1720, by some too scrupulous brethren. Preston (ed. 1792, p. 167) describes it as "an old manuscript, which was destroyed with many others in 1720, said to have been in the possession of Nicholas Stone, a curious sculptor under Inigo Jones." Preston gives, however, an extract from it, which details the affection borne by St. Alban for the Masons, the wages he gave them, and the charter which he obtained from the king to hold a general assembly. (See *St. Alban.*) Anderson (*Constitutions*, 1738, p. 99), who calls Stone the Warden of Inigo Jones, intimates that he wrote the Manuscript, and gives it as authority for a statement that in 1607 Jones held the Quarterly Communications. The extract made by Preston, and the brief reference by Anderson, are all that is left of the Stone Manuscript.

Stone-Masons of the Middle Ages. The history of the origin and progress of the

GRAND LODGE OF ENGLAND
GRAND
ELECTED
DEDICATED TO HIS ROYAL HIGHNESS
THE DUKE OF CUMBERLAND
GRAND MASTER
GRAND MAITRE

Brotherhood of Stone-Masons in Europe, during the Middle Ages, is of great importance, as a study, to the Masonic scholar, because of the intimate connection that existed between that Brotherhood and the Fraternity of Freemasons. Indeed, the history of the one is but the introduction to the history of the other. In an historical excursus, we are compelled to take up the speculative science where we find it left by the operative art. Hence, whoever shall undertake to write a history of Freemasonry, must give, for the completion of his labor, a very full consideration to the Brotherhood of Stone-Masons.

In the year 1820, there issued from the press of Leipsic, in Germany, a work, by Dr. Christian Ludwig Steiglitz, under the title of *Von Altdeutscher Baukunst*, that is, "An Essay on the Old German Architecture," published in 1820. In this work the author traces, with great exactness, the rise and the progress of the fraternities of Stone-Masons from the earliest times, through the Middle Ages, until their final absorption into the associations of Freemasons. From the labors of Dr. Steiglitz, collated with some other authorities in respect to matters upon which he is either silent or erroneous, I have compiled the following sketch.

It is universally admitted that, in the early ages of Christianity, the clergy were the most important patrons of the arts and sciences. This was because all learning was then almost exclusively confined to ecclesiastics. Very few of the laity could read or write, and even kings affixed the sign of the cross, in the place of their signatures, to the charters and other documents which they issued, because, as they frankly confessed, of their inability to write their names; and hence comes the modern expression of *signing* a paper, as equivalent to subscribing the name.

From the time of Charlemagne, in the eighth century, to the middle of the twelfth, all knowledge and practise of architecture, painting, and sculpture were exclusively confined to the monks; and bishops personally superintended the erection of the churches and cathedrals in their dioceses, because not only the principles, but the practise of the art of building were secrets scrupulously maintained within the walls of cloisters, and utterly unknown to laymen.*

Many of the founders of the Monastic Orders, and especially among these St. Benedict, made it a peculiar duty for the brethren to devote themselves to architecture and church building. The English monk Winfrid, better known in ecclesiastical history as St. Boniface, and who, for his labors in Christianizing that country, has been styled the Apostle of Germany, followed the example of his predecessors in the erection of German monasteries. In the eighth century he organized an especial class of monks for the practise of building, under the name of *Operarii*, or Craftsmen, and *Magistri Operum*, or Masters of the Works. The labors and duties of these monks were divided. Some of them designed the plan of the building; others were painters and sculptors; others were occupied in working in gold and silver and embroidery; and others again, who were called *Cæmentarii*, or Stone-Masons, undertook the practical labors of construction. Sometimes, especially in extensive buildings, where many workmen were required, laymen were also employed, under the direction of the monks. So extensive did these labors become, that bishops and abbots often derived a large portion of their revenues from the earnings of the workmen in the monasteries.

Among the laymen who were employed in the monasteries as assistants and laborers, many were of course possessed of superior intelligence. The constant and intimate association of these with the monks in the prosecution of the same design led to this result, that in process of time, gradually and almost unconsciously, the monks imparted to them their art secrets and the esoteric principles of architecture. Then, by degrees, the knowledge of the arts and sciences went from these monkish builders out into the world, and the laymen architects, withdrawing from the ecclesiastical fraternities, organized brotherhoods of their own. Such was the beginning of the Stone-Masons in Germany, and the same thing occurred in other countries. These brotherhoods of Masons now began to be called upon, as the monks formerly had been, when an important building, and especially a church or a cathedral, was to be erected. Eventually they entirely superseded their monkish teachers in the prosecution of the art of building about the beginning of the twelfth century. To their knowledge of architecture they added that of the other sciences, which they had learned from the monks. Like these, too, they devoted themselves to the higher principles of the art, and employed other laymen to assist their labors as stone-masons. And thus the union of these architects and stone-masons presented, in the midst of an uneducated people, a more elevated and intelligent class, engaged as an exclusive association in building important and especially religious edifices.

But now a new classification took place. As formerly, the monks, who were the sole depositaries of the secrets of high art, separated themselves from the laymen, who were entrusted with only the manual labor of building; so now the more intelligent of the laymen, who had received these secrets from the monks, were distinguished as architects from the ordinary laborers, or common masons. The latter knew only the use of the trowel and mortar, while the former were occupied in devising plans for building and the construction of ornaments by sculpture and skilful stone-cutting.

These brotherhoods of high artists soon won

* This view was long held, but is by no means correct, for we now know that there were many scholarly architects during this period of supposed darkness. [E. E. C.]

great esteem, and many privileges and franchises were conceded to them by the municipal authorities among whom they practised their profession. Their places of assembly were called *Hutten*, *Logen*, or *Lodges*, and the members took the name of *Steinmetzen*. Their patron saint was St. John the Baptist, who was honored by them as the mediator between the Old and the New Covenants, and the first martyr of the Christian religion. To what condition of art these Freemasons of the Middle Ages had attained, we may judge from what Hallam says of the edifices they erected —that they "united sublimity in general composition with the beauties of variety and form, skilful or at least fortunate effects of shadow and light, and in some instances extraordinary mechanical science." (*Mid. Ages*, iv., 280.) And he subsequently adds, as an involuntary confirmation of the truth of the sketch of their origin just given, that the mechanical execution of the buildings was "so far beyond the apparent intellectual powers of those times, that some have ascribed the principal ecclesiastical structures to the Fraternity of Freemasons, depositaries of a concealed and traditionary science. There is probably some ground for this opinion, and the earlier archives of that mysterious association, if they existed, might illustrate the progress of Gothic architecture, and perhaps reveal its origin." (*Ib.*, 284.) These archives do exist, or many of them; and although unknown to Mr. Hallam, because they were out of the course of his usual reading, they have been thoroughly sifted by recent Masonic scholars, especially by our German and English brethren; and that which the historian of the Middle Ages had only assumed as a plausible conjecture has, by their researches, been proved to be a fact.

The prevalence of Gnostic symbols—such as lions, serpents, and the like—in the decorations of churches of the Middle Ages, have led some writers to conclude that the Knights Templar exercised an influence over the architects, and that by them the Gnostic and Ophite symbols were introduced into Europe. But Dr. Steiglitz denies the correctness of this conclusion. He ascribes the existence of Gnostic symbols in the church architecture to the fact that, at an early period in ecclesiastical history, many of the Gnostic dogmas passed over into Christendom with the Oriental and Platonic philosophy, and he attributes their adoption in architecture to the natural compliance of the architects or Masons with the predominant taste in the earlier periods of the Middle Ages for mysticism, and the favor given to grotesque decorations, which were admired without any knowledge of their actual import.

Steiglitz also denies any deduction of the Builders' Fraternities, or Masonic Lodges, of the Middle Ages from the Mysteries of the old Indians, Egyptians, and Greeks; although he acknowledges that there is a resemblance between the organizations. This, however, he attributes to the fact that the Indians and Egyptians preserved all the sciences, as well as the principles of architecture, among their secrets, and because, among the Greeks, the artists were initiated into their mysteries, so that, in the old as well as in the new brotherhoods, there was a purer knowledge of religious truth, which elevated them as distinct associations above the people. In like manner, he denies the descent of the Masonic fraternities from the sect of Pythagoreans, which they resembled only in this: that the Samian sage established schools which were secret, and were based upon the principles of geometry.

But he thinks that those are not mistaken who trace the associations of Masons of the Middle Ages to the Roman Colleges, the *Collegia Cæmentariorum*, because these colleges appear in every country that was conquered and established as a province or a colony by the Romans, where they erected temples and other public buildings, and promoted the civilization of the inhabitants. They continued until a late period. But when Rome began to be convulsed by the wars of its decline, and by the incursions of hordes of barbarians, they found a welcome reception at Byzantium, or Constantinople, whence they subsequently spread into the west of Europe, and were everywhere held in great estimation for their skill in the construction of buildings.

In Italy the associations of architects never entirely ceased, as we may conclude from the many buildings erected there during the domination of the Ostrogoths and the Longobards. Subsequently, when civil order was restored, the Masons of Italy were encouraged and supported by popes, princes, and nobles. And Muratori tells us, in his *Historia d'Italia*, that under the Lombard kings the inhabitants of Como were so superior as masons and bricklayers, that the appellation of Magistri Comacini, or Masters from Como, became generic to all those of the profession. (See *Comacine Masters*.)

In England, when the Romans took possession of it, the corporations, or colleges of builders, also appeared, who were subsequently continued in the Fraternity of Freemasons, probably established, as Steiglitz thinks, about the middle of the fifth century, after the Romans had left the island. The English Masons were subjected to many adverse difficulties, from the repeated incursions of Scots, Picts, Danes, and Saxons, which impeded their active labors; yet were they enabled to maintain their existence, until, in the year 926, they held that General Assembly at the city of York which framed the Constitutions that governed the English Craft for eight hundred years, and which is claimed to be the oldest Masonic record now extant. It is but fair to say that the recent researches of Bro. Hughan and other English writers have thrown a doubt upon the authenticity of these Constitutions, and that the very existence of this York assembly has been denied and practically confirmed.

In France, as in Germany, the Fraternities

of Architects originally sprang out of the connection of lay builders with the monks in the era of Charlemagne. The French Masons continued their fraternities throughout the Middle Ages, and erected many cathedrals and public buildings.

We have now arrived at the middle of the eleventh century, tracing the progress of the fraternities of Stone-Masons from the time of Charlemagne to that period. At that time all the architecture of Europe was in their hands. Under the distinctive name of *Traveling Freemasons* they passed from nation to nation, constructing churches and cathedrals wherever they were needed. Of their organization and customs, Sir Christopher Wren, in his *Parentalia*, gives the following account:

"Their government was regular, and where they fixed near the building in hand, they made a camp of huts. A surveyor governed in chief; every tenth man was called a warden, and overlooked each nine."

Mr. Hope, who, from his peculiar course of studies, was better acquainted than Mr. Hallam with the history of these Traveling Freemasons, thus speaks, in his *Essay on Architecture*, of their organization at this time, by which they effected an identity of architectural science throughout all Europe:

"The architects of all the sacred edifices of the Latin Church, wherever such arose,—north, south, east, or west—thus derived their science from the same central school; obeyed in their designs the dictates of the same hierarchy; were directed in their constructions by the same principles of propriety and taste; kept up with each other, in the most distant parts to which they might be sent, the most constant correspondence; and rendered every minute improvement the property of the whole body, and a new conquest of the art."

Working in this way, the Stone-Masons, as corporations of builders, daily increased in numbers and in power. In the thirteenth century they assumed a new organization, which allied them more closely than ever with that Brotherhood of Speculative Freemasons into which they were finally merged in the eighteenth century, in England, but not in Germany, France, or Italy.

These fraternities or associations became at once very popular. Many of the potentates of Europe, and among them the Emperor Rudolph I., conceded to them considerable powers of jurisdiction, such as would enable them to preserve the most rigid system in matters pertaining to building, and would facilitate them in bringing master builders and stone-masons together at any required point. Pope Nicholas III. granted the Brotherhood, in 1278, letters of indulgence, which were renewed by his successors, and finally, in the next century, by Pope Benedict XII.

The Steinmetzen, as a fraternity of Operative Masons, distinguished from the ordinary masons and laborers of the craft, acquired at this time great prominence, and were firmly established as an association. In 1452 a general assembly was convened at Strasburg, and a new constitution framed, which embraced many improvements and modifications of the former one. But seven years afterward, in 1459,* Jost Dotzinger, then holding the position of architect of the Cathedral of Strasburg, and, by virtue of his office, presiding over the Craft of Germany, convened a general assembly of the Masters of all the Lodges at the city of Ratisbon. There the code of laws which had been adopted at Strasburg in 1452, under the title of "Statutes and Regulations of the Fraternity of Stone-Masons of Strasburg," was fully discussed and sanctioned. It was then also resolved that there should be established four Grand Lodges—at Strasburg, at Vienna, at Cologne, and at Zurich; and they also determined that the master workman, for the time being, of the Cathedral of Strasburg should be the Grand Master of the Masons of Germany. These constitutions or statutes are still extant, and are older than any other existing Masonic record of undoubted authenticity, except the manuscript of Halliwell. They were "kindly and affably agreed upon," according to their preamble, "for the benefit and requirements of the Masters and Fellows of the whole Craft of Masonry and Masons in Germany."

General assemblies, at which important business was transacted, were held in 1464 at Ratisbon, and in 1469 at Spire, while provincial assemblies in each of the Grand Lodge jurisdictions were annually convened.

In consequence of a deficiency of employment, from political disturbances and other causes, the Fraternity now for a brief period declined in its activity. But it was speedily revived when, in October, 1498, the Emperor Maximilian I. confirmed its statutes, as they had been adopted at Strasburg, and recognized its former rights and privileges. This act of confirmation was renewed by the succeeding emperors, Charles V. and Ferdinand I. In 1563 a general assembly of the Masons of Germany and Switzerland was convened at the city of Basle by the Grand Lodge of Strasburg. The Strasburg constitutions were again renewed with amendments, and what was called the Stone-Masons' Law (*das Steinwerkrecht*) was established. The Grand Lodge of Strasburg continued to be recognized as possessing supreme appellate jurisdiction in all matters relating to the Craft. Even the Senate of that city had acknowledged its prerogatives, and had conceded to it the privilege of settling all controversies in relation to matters connected with building; a concession which was, however, revoked in 1620, on the charge that the privilege had been misused.

Thus the Operative Freemasons of Germany continued to work and to cultivate the high principles of a religious architectural art. But on March 16, 1707, up to which time

*Besides the Strasburg Constitution of 1459 there are two other very important documents of the Steinmetzen of Germany: The Torgau Ordinances of 1462 and the Brothers' Book of 1563. [E. E. C.]

the Fraternity had uninterruptedly existed, a decree of the Imperial Diet at Ratisbon dissolved the connection of the Lodges of Germany with the Grand Lodge of Strasburg, because that city had passed into the power of the French. The head being now lost, the subordinate bodies began rapidly to decline. In several of the German cities the Lodges undertook to assume the name and exercise the functions of Grand Lodges; but these were all abolished by an imperial edict in 1731, which at the same time forbade the administration of any oath of secrecy, and transferred to the government alone the adjudication of all disputes among the Craft. From this time we lose sight of any national organization of the Freemasons in Germany until the restoration of the Order, in the eighteenth century, through the English Fraternity.* But in many cities—as in Basle, Zurich, Hamburg, Dantzic, and Strasburg—they preserved an independent existence under the statutes of 1559, although they lost much of the profound symbolical knowledge of architecture which had been possessed by their predecessors.

Before leaving these German Stone-Masons, it is worth while to say something of the symbolism which they preserved in their secret teachings. They made much use, in their architectural plans, of mystical numbers, and among these five, seven, and nine were especially prominent. Among colors, gold and blue and white possessed symbolic meanings. The foot rule, the compasses, the square, and the gavel, with some other implements of their art, were consecrated with a spiritual signification. The east was considered as a sacred point; and many allusions were made to Solomon's Temple, especially to the pillars of the porch, representations of which are to be found in several of the cathedrals.

In France the history of the Free Stone-Masons was similar to that of their German brethren. Originating, like them, from the cloisters, and from the employment of laymen by the monkish architects, they associated themselves together as a brotherhood superior to the ordinary stone-masons. The connection between the Masons of France and the Roman Colleges of Builders was more intimate and direct than that of the Germans, because of the early and very general occupation of Gaul by the Roman legions: but the French organization did not materially differ from the German. Protected by popes and princes, the Masons were engaged, under ecclesiastical patronage, in the construction of religious edifices. In France there was also a peculiar association, the *Pontifices*, or *Bridge Builders*, closely connected in design and character with the Masonic Fraternity, and the memory of which is still preserved in the name of one of thedegrees of the Scottish Rite, that of "Grand Pontiff." The principal seat of the French Stone-Masonry was in Lombardy, whence the Lodges were disseminated over the kingdom, a fact which is thus accounted for by Mr. Hope: "Among the arts exercised and improved in Lombardy," he says, "that of building held a pre-eminent rank, and was the more important because the want of those ancient edifices to which they might recur for materials already wrought, and which Rome afforded in such abundance, made the architects of these more remote regions dependent on their own skill and free to follow their own conceptions." But in the beginning of the sixteenth century, the necessity for their employment in the further construction of religious edifices having ceased, the Fraternity began to decline, and the Masonic corporations were all finally dissolved, with those of other workmen, by Francis I., in 1539. Then originated that system which the French call *Compagnonage*, a system of independent gilds or brotherhoods, retaining a principle of community as to the art which they practised, and with, to some extent, a secret bond, but without elevated notions or general systematic organizations. The societies of *Compagnons* were, indeed, but the *débris* of the Building Masons. Masonry ceased to exist in France as a recognised system until its revival in the eighteenth century.

We see, then, in conclusion, that the Stone-Masons—coming partly from the Roman Colleges of Architects, as in England, in Italy, and in France, but principally, as in Germany, from the cloistered brotherhoods of monks—devoted themselves to the construction of religious edifices. They consisted mainly of architects and skilful operatives; but—as they were controlled by the highest principles of their art, were in possession of important professional secrets, were actuated by deep sentiments of religious devotion, and had united with themselves in their labors men of learning, wealth, and influence—to serve as a proud distinction between themselves and the ordinary laborers and uneducated workmen, many of whom were of servile condition.

Subsequently, in the beginning of the eighteenth century, they threw off the operative element of their institution, and, adopting an entirely speculative character, they became the Freemasons of the present day, and established on an imperishable foundation that sublime Institution which presents over all the habitable earth the most wonderful system of religious and moral symbolism that the world ever saw.

Stone, Nicholas. See *Stone Manuscript*.

Stone of Foundation. The Stone of Foundation constitutes one of the most important and abstruse of all the symbols of Freemasonry. It is referred to in numerous legends and traditions not only of the Freemasons, but also of the Jewish Rabbis, the Talmudic writers, and even the Mussulman doctors. Many of these, it must be confessed, are apparently puerile and absurd; but most

*Thus we see that the great order of the Steinmetsen of Germany took no part in the formation of the Speculative Freemasons. [E. E. C.]

of them, and especially the Masonic ones, are deeply interesting in their allegorical signification.

The Stone of Foundation is, properly speaking, a symbol of the higher degrees. It makes its first appearance in the Royal Arch, and forms indeed the most important symbol of that degree. But it is so intimately connected, in its legendary history, with the construction of the Solomonic Temple, that it must be considered as a part of Ancient Craft Masonry, although he who confines the range of his investigations to the first three degrees will have no means, within that narrow limit, of properly appreciating the symbolism of the Stone of Foundation.

As preliminary to the inquiry, it is necessary to distinguish the Stone of Foundation, both in its symbolism and its legendary history, from other stones which play an important part in the Masonic ritual, but which are entirely distinct from it. Such are the *corner-stone*, which was always placed in the north-east corner of the building about to be erected, and to which such a beautiful reference is made in the ceremonies of the First Degree; or the *keystone*, which constitutes an interesting part of the Mark Master's Degree; or, lastly, the *cape-stone*, upon which all the ritual of the Most Excellent Master's Degree is founded. There are all, in their proper places, highly interesting and instructive symbols, but have no connection whatever with the Stone of Foundation, whose symbolism it is our present object to discuss. Nor, although the Stone of Foundation is said, for peculiar reasons, to have been of a cubical form, must it be confounded with that stone called by the continental Masons the *cubical stone*—the *pierre cubique* of the French and the *cubik stein* of the German Masons but which in the English system is known as the *perfect ashlar*.

The Stone of Foundation has a legendary history and a symbolic signification which are peculiar to itself, and which differ from the history and meaning which belong to these other stones. I propose first to define this Masonic Stone of Foundation, then to collate the legends which refer to it, and afterward to investigate its significance as a symbol. To the Mason who takes a pleasure in the study of the mysteries of his Institution, the investigation cannot fail to be interesting, if it is conducted with any ability.

But in the very beginning, as a necessary preliminary to any investigation of this kind, it must be distinctly understood that all that is said of this Stone of Foundation in Masonry is to be strictly taken in a mythical or allegorical sense. Dr. Oliver, while undoubtedly himself knowing that it was simply a symbol, has written loosely of it as though it were a substantial reality; and hence, if the passages in his *Historical Landmarks*, and in his other works which refer to this celebrated stone, are accepted by his readers in a literal sense, they will present absurdities and puerilities which would not occur if the Stone of Foundation was received, as it really is, as a myth conveying a most profound and beautiful symbolism. It is as such that it is to be treated here; and, therefore, if a legend is recited or a tradition related, the reader is requested on every occasion to suppose that such legend or tradition is not intended as the recital or relation of what is deemed a fact in Masonic history, but to wait with patience for the development of the symbolism which it conveys. Read in this spirit, as all the legends of Masonry should be read, the legend of the Stone of Foundation becomes one of the most important and interesting of all the Masonic symbols.

The Stone of Foundation is supposed, by the theory which establishes it, to have been a stone placed at one time within the foundations of the Temple of Solomon, and afterward, during the building of the second Temple, transported to the Holy of Holies. It was in form a perfect cube, and had inscribed upon its upper face, within a delta or triangle, the sacred Tetragrammaton, or ineffable name of God. Oliver, speaking with the solemnity of an historian, says that Solomon thought that he had rendered the house of God worthy, so far as human adornment could effect, for the dwelling of God, "when he had placed the celebrated Stone of Foundation, on which the sacred name was mystically engraven, with solemn ceremonies, in that sacred depository on Mount Moriah, along with the foundations of Dan and Asher, the centre of the Most Holy Place, where the ark was overshadowed by the shekinah of God." The Hebrew Talmudists, who thought as much of this stone, and had as many legends concerning it, as the Masonic Talmudists, called it *eben shatijah*, or "Stone of Foundation," because, as they said, it had been laid by Jehovah as the foundation of the world, and hence the apocryphal Book of Enoch speaks of the "stone which supports the corners of the earth."

This idea of a foundation-stone of the world was most probably derived from that magnificent passage of the Book of Job (ch. xxxviii. v. 4-7) in which the Almighty demands of Job,

"Where wast thou, when I laid the foundation of the earth?
Declare, since thou hast such knowledge!
Who fixed its dimensions, since thou knowest!
Or who stretched out the line upon it?
Upon what were its foundations fixed?
And who laid its corner-stone,
When the morning stars sang together,
And all the sons of God shouted for joy?"

Noyes, whose translation I have adopted as not materially differing from the common version, but far more poetical and more in the strain of the original, thus explains the allusions to the foundation-stone: "It was the custom to celebrate the laying of the corner-stone of an important building with music, songs, shouting, etc. Hence the morning stars are represented as celebrating the laying of the corner-stone of the earth."

Upon this meager statement has been accumulated more traditions than appertain to any other Masonic symbol. The Rabbis, as has already been intimated, divide the glory of these apocryphal histories with the Masons; indeed, there is good reason for a suspicion that nearly all the Masonic legends owe their first existence to the imaginative genius of the writers of the Jewish Talmud. But there is this difference between the Hebrew and the Masonic traditions: that the Talmudic scholar recited them as truthful histories, and swallowed, in one gulp of faith, all their impossibilities and anachronisms; while the Masonic scholar has received them as allegories, whose value is not in the facts, but in the sentiments which they convey.

With this understanding of their meaning, let us proceed to a collation of these legends.

In that blasphemous work, the *Toldoth Jeshu*, or *Life of Jesus*, written, it is supposed, in the thirteenth or fourteenth century, we find the following account of this wonderful stone:

"At that time [the time of Jesus] there was in the House of the Sanctuary [that is, the Temple] a stone of foundation, which is the very stone that our father Jacob anointed with oil, as it is described in the twenty-eighth chapter of the Book of Genesis. On that stone the letters of the Tetragrammaton were inscribed, and whosoever of the Israelites should learn that name would be able to master the world. To prevent, therefore, any one from learning these letters, two iron dogs were placed upon two columns in front of the Sanctuary. If any person, having acquired the knowledge of these letters, desired to depart from the Sanctuary, the barking of the dogs, by magical power, inspired so much fear that he suddenly forgot what he had acquired."

This passage is cited by the learned Buxtorf in his *Lexicon Talmudicum;* but in my copy of the *Toldoth Jeshu*, I find another passage, which gives some additional particulars, in the following words:

"At that time there was in the Temple the ineffable name of God, inscribed upon the Stone of Foundation. For when King David was digging the foundation for the Temple, he found in the depths of the excavation a certain stone on which the name of God was inscribed. This stone he removed and deposited it in the Holy of Holies."

The same puerile story of the barking dogs is repeated still more at length. It is not pertinent to the present inquiry, but it may be stated, as a mere matter of curious information, that this scandalous book, which is throughout a blasphemous defamation of our Savior, proceeds to say, that he cunningly obtained a knowledge of the Tetragrammaton from the Stone of Foundation, and by its mystical influence was enabled to perform his miracles.

The Masonic legends of the Stone of Foundation, based on these and other rabbinical reveries, are of the most extraordinary character, if they are to be viewed as histories, but readily reconcilable with sound sense, if looked at only in the light of allegories. They present an uninterrupted succession of events in which the Stone of Foundation takes a prominent part, from Adam to Solomon, and from Solomon to Zerubbabel.

Thus, the first of these legends, in order of time, relates that the Stone of Foundation was possessed by Adam while in the Garden of Eden; that he used it as an altar, and so reverenced it that, on his expulsion from Paradise, he carried it with him into the world in which he and his descendants were afterward to earn their bread by the sweat of their brow.

Another legend informs us that from Adam the Stone of Foundation descended to Seth. From Seth it passed by regular succession to Noah, who took it with him into the ark, and after the subsidence of the deluge made on it his first thank-offering. Noah left it on Mount Ararat, where it was subsequently found by Abraham, who removed it, and constantly used it as an altar of sacrifice. His grandson Jacob took it with him when he fled to his uncle Laban in Mesopotamia, and used it as a pillow when, in the vicinity of Luz, he had his celebrated vision.

Here there is a sudden interruption in the legendary history of the stone, and we have no means of conjecturing how it passed from the possession of Jacob into that of Solomon. Moses, it is true, is said to have taken it with him out of Egypt at the time of the exodus, and thus it may have finally reached Jerusalem. Dr. Adam Clarke repeats, what he very properly calls "a foolish tradition," that the stone on which Jacob rested his head was afterward brought to Jerusalem, thence carried after a long lapse of time to Spain, from Spain to Ireland, and from Ireland to Scotland, where it was used as a seat on which the kings of Scotland sat to be crowned. Edward I., we know, brought a stone to which this legend is attached from Scotland to Westminster Abbey, where, under the name of Jacob's Pillow, it still remains, and is always placed under the chair upon which the British sovereign sits to be crowned; because there is an old distich which declares that wherever this stone is found the Scottish kings shall reign.

But this Scottish tradition would take the Stone of Foundation away from all its Masonic connections, and therefore it is rejected as a Masonic legend.

The legends just related are in many respects contradictory and unsatisfactory, and another series, equally as old, is now very generally adopted by Masonic scholars as much better suited to the symbolism by which all these legends are explained.

This series of legends commences with the patriarch Enoch, who is supposed to have been the first consecrator of the Stone of Foundation. The legend of Enoch is so interesting and important in this connection as to excuse its repetition in the present work.

The legend in full is as follows: Enoch, under the inspiration of the Most High, and in obedience to the instructions which he had received in a vision, built a temple underground on Mount Moriah, and dedicated it to God. His son, Methuselah, constructed the building, although he was not acquainted with his father's motives for the erection. This temple consisted of nine vaults, situated perpendicularly beneath each other, and communicating by apertures left in each vault.

Enoch then caused a triangular plate of gold to be made, each side of which was a cubit long; he enriched it with the most precious stones, and encrusted the plate upon a stone of agate of the same form. On the plate he engraved the true name of God, or the Tetragrammaton, and placing it on a cubical stone, known thereafter as the Stone of Foundation, he deposited the whole within the lowest arch.

When this subterranean building was completed, he made a door of stone, and attaching to it a ring of iron, by which it might be occasionally raised, he placed it over the opening of the uppermost arch, and so covered it that the aperture could not be discovered. Enoch, himself, was permitted to enter it but once a year; and on the deaths of Enoch, Methuselah, and Lamech, and the destruction of the world by the deluge, all knowledge of the vault or subterranean temple and of the Stone of Foundation, with the sacred and ineffable name inscribed upon it, was lost for ages to the world.

At the building of the first Temple of Jerusalem, the Stone of Foundation again makes its appearance. Reference has already been made to the Jewish tradition that David, when digging the foundations of the Temple, found in the excavation which he was making a certain stone, on which the ineffable name of God was inscribed, and which stone he is said to have removed and deposited in the Holy of Holies. That King David laid the foundations of the Temple upon which the superstructure was subsequently erected by Solomon, is a favorite theory of the legend-mongers of the Talmud.

The Masonic tradition is substantially the same as the Jewish, but it substitutes Solomon for David, thereby giving a greater air of probability to the narrative, and it supposes that the stone thus discovered by Solomon was the identical one that had been deposited in his secret vault by Enoch. This Stone of Foundation, the tradition states, was subsequently removed by King Solomon and, for wise purposes, deposited in a secret and safer place.

In this the Masonic tradition again agrees with the Jewish, for we find in the third chapter of the *Treatise on the Temple*, the following narrative:

"There was a stone in the Holy of Holies, on its west side, on which was placed the ark of the covenant, and before the pot of manna and Aaron's rod. But when Solomon had built the Temple, and foresaw that it was at some future time to be destroyed, he constructed a deep and winding vault under ground, for the purpose of concealing the ark, wherein Josiah afterwards, as we learn in the Second Book of Chronicles, xxxv. 3, deposited it with the pot of manna, the rod of Aaron, and the oil of anointing."

The Talmudical book *Yoma* gives the same tradition, and says that "the ark of the covenant was placed in the centre of the Holy of Holies, upon a stone rising three fingers' breadth above the floor, to be as it were a pedestal for it." This stone, says Prideaux, in his *Old and New Testament Connected* (vol. i., p. 148), "the Rabbins call the Stone of Foundation, and give us a great deal of trash about it."

There is much controversy as to the question of the existence of any ark in the second Temple. Some of the Jewish writers assert that a new one was made; others that the old one was found where it had been concealed by Solomon; and others again contend that there was no ark at all in the temple of Zerubbabel, but that its place was supplied by the Stone of Foundation on which it had originally rested.

Royal Arch Masons well know how all these traditions are sought to be reconciled by the Masonic legend, in which the substitute ark and the Stone of Foundation play so important a part.

In the Thirteenth Degree of the Ancient and Accepted Rite, the Stone of Foundation is conspicuous as the resting-place of the sacred delta.

In the Royal Arch and Select Master's degrees of the American Rite, the Stone of Foundation constitutes the most important part of the ritual. In both of these it is the receptacle of the ark, on which the ineffable name is inscribed.

Lee, in his *Temple of Solomon*, has devoted a chapter to this Stone of Foundation, and thus recapitulates the Talmudic and Rabbinical traditions on the subject:

"Vain and futilous are the feverish dreams of the ancient Rabbins concerning the Foundation-Stone of the Temple. Some assert that God placed this stone in the centre of the world, for a future basis and settled consistency for the earth to rest upon. Others held this stone to be the first matter out of which all the beautiful visible beings of the world have been hewn forth and produced to light. Others relate that this was the very same stone laid by Jacob for a pillow under his head, in that night when he dreamed of an angelic vision at Bethel, and afterwards anointed and consecrated it to God. Which when Solomon had found (no doubt by forged revelation or some tedious search like another Rabbi Selemoh) he durst not but lay it sure, as the principal Foundation-Stone of the Temple. Nay, they say further, he caused to be engraved upon it the Tetragrammaton, or the ineffable name of Jehovah."

It will be seen that the Masonic traditions on the subject of the Stone of Foundation do not differ very materially from these Rabbinical ones, although they add a few additional circumstances.

In the Masonic legend, the Foundation-Stone first makes its appearance, as we have already said, in the days of Enoch, who placed it in the bowels of Mount Moriah.

There it was subsequently discovered by King Solomon, who deposited it in a crypt of the first Temple, where it remained concealed until the foundations of the second Temple were laid, when it was discovered and removed to the Holy of Holies. But the most important point of the legend of the Stone of Foundation is its intimate and constant connection with the Tetragrammaton or ineffable name. It is this name, inscribed upon it within the sacred and symbolic delta, that gives to the stone all its Masonic value and significance. It is upon this fact, that it was so inscribed, that its whole symbolism depends.

Looking at these traditions in anything like the light of historical narratives, we are compelled to consider them, to use the plain language of Lee, "but as so many idle and absurd conceits." We must go behind the legend, which we acknowledge at once to be only an allegory, and study its symbolism.

The following facts can, I think, be readily established from history. First, that there was a very general prevalence among the earliest nations of antiquity of the worship of stones as the representatives of Deity; secondly, that in almost every ancient temple there was a legend of a sacred or mystical stone; thirdly, that this legend is found in the Masonic system; and lastly, that the mystical stone there has received the name of the "Stone of Foundation."

Now, as in all the other systems the stone is admitted to be symbolic, and the traditions connected with it mystical, we are compelled to assume the same predicates of the Masonic stone. It, too, is symbolic, and its legend a myth or an allegory.

Of the fable, myth, or allegory, Bailly has said that, "subordinate to history and philosophy, it only deceives that it may the better instruct us. Faithful in preserving the realities which are confided to it, it covers with its seductive envelop the lessons of the one and the truths of the other." It is from this standpoint that we are to view the allegory of the Stone of Foundation, as developed in one of the most interesting and important symbols of Masonry.

The fact that the mystical stone in all the ancient religions was a symbol of the Deity, leads us necessarily to the conclusion that the Stone of Foundation was also a symbol of Deity. And this symbolic idea is strengthened by the Tetragrammaton, or sacred name of God, that was inscribed upon it. This ineffable name sanctifies the stone upon which it is engraved as the symbol of the Grand Architect. It takes from it its heathen signification as an idol, and consecrates it to the worship of the true God.

The predominant idea of the Deity, in the Masonic system, connects him with his creative and formative power. God is to the Freemason *Al Gabil*, as the Arabians called him, that is, *The Builder;* or, as expressed in his Masonic title, the *Grand Architect of the Universe*, by common consent abbreviated in the formula G A O T U. Now, it is evident that no symbol could so appropriately suit him in this character as the Stone of Foundation, upon which he is allegorically supposed to have erected his world. Such a symbol closely connects the creative work of God, as a pattern and exemplar, with the workman's erection of his temporal building on a similar foundation-stone.

But this Masonic idea is still further to be extended. The great object of all Masonic labor is *Divine truth.* The search for the *lost word* is the search for truth. But Divine truth is a term synonymous with God. The ineffable name is a symbol of truth, because God, and God alone, is truth. It is properly a Scriptural idea. The Book of Psalms abounds with this sentiment. Thus it is said that the truth of the Lord "reacheth unto the clouds," and that "his truth endureth unto all generations." If, then, God is truth, and the Stone of Foundation is the Masonic symbol of God, it follows that it must also be the symbol of Divine truth.

When we have arrived at this point in our speculations, we are ready to show how all the myths and legends of the Stone of Foundation may be rationally explained as parts of that beautiful "science of morality, veiled in allegory and illustrated by symbols," which is the acknowledged definition of Freemasonry.

In the Masonic system there are two temples: the first temple, in which the degrees of Ancient Craft Masonry are concerned, and the second temple, with which the higher degrees, and especially the Royal Arch, are related. The first temple is symbolic of the present life; the second temple is symbolic of the life to come. The first temple, the present life, must be destroyed; on its foundations the second temple, the life eternal, must be built.

But the mystical stone was placed by King Solomon in the foundations of the first Temple. That is to say, the first temple of our present life must be built on the sure foundation of Divine truth, "for other foundation can no man lay."

But although the present life is necessarily built upon the foundation of truth, yet we never thoroughly attain it in this sublunary sphere. The Foundation-Stone is concealed in the first temple, and the Master Mason knows it not. He has not the true word. He receives only a substitute.

But in the second temple of the future life, we have passed from the grave which had been the end of our labors in the first. We have removed the rubbish, and have found that Stone of Foundation which had been hitherto concealed from our eyes. We now throw aside the substitute for truth which had contented us in the former temple, and the brilliant effulgence of the Tetragrammaton and the Stone of Foundation are discovered, and thenceforth we are the possessors of the true word—of Divine truth. And in this way, the Stone of Foundation, or Divine truth, concealed in the first temple, but discovered and brought to light in the second, will explain that passage of the Apostle: "For now we see through a glass darkly; but then, face to face: now I know in part; but then I shall know face to face."

And so the result of this inquiry is, that the Masonic Stone of Foundation is a symbol of Divine truth, upon which all speculative Masonry is built, and the legends and traditions which refer to it are intended to describe, in an allegorical way, the progress of truth in the soul, the search for which is a Mason's labor, and the discovery of which is his reward.

Stone Pavement. Oliver says that, in the English system, "the stone pavement is a figurative appendage to a Master Masons' Lodge, and, like that of the Most Holy Place in the Temple, is for the High Priest to walk on." This is not recognized in the American system, where the stone or mosaic pavement is appropriated to the Entered Apprentice's Degree.

Stone, Rejected. St. Matthew records (xxi. 42) that our Lord said to the chief priests and elders, "Did ye never read in the Scriptures, The stone which the builders rejected, the same is become the head of the corner?" Commenting on this, Dr. Adam Clarke says: "It is an expression borrowed from masons, who, finding a stone which, being tried in a particular place, and appearing improper for it, is thrown aside and another taken; however, at last, it may happen that the *very stone* which had been before *rejected* may be found the most suitable as *the head stone of the corner*." This is precisely the symbolism of the Mark Master or Fourth Degree of the American Rite, where the *rejected stone* is suggested to the neophyte "as a consolation under all the frowns of fortune, and as an encouragement to hope for better prospects." Bro. G. F. Yates says that the symbolism of the rejected stone in the present Mark Degree is not in the original Master Mark Mason's Degree, out of which Webb manufactured his ritual, but was introduced by him from some other unknown source.

Stone-Squarers. See *Giblim*.

Stone, White. Among the ancient Greeks and Romans, sentence was given in courts of judicature by white and black stones or pebbles. Those who were in favor of acquittal cast a white stone, and those who were for condemning, a black one. So, too, in popular elections a white stone was deposited by those who were favorable to the candidate, and a black one by those who wished to reject him. In this ancient practise we find the origin of white and black balls in the Masonic ballot. Hence, too, the white stone has become the symbol of absolution in judgment, and of the conferring of honors and rewards. The white stone with the new name, mentioned in the Mark Master's Degree, refers to the keystone.

Stone, William Leete. An American journalist and writer, who was born in the State of New York in 1792, and died in 1844. He was the author of several literary works, generally of a biographical character. But his largest work was *Letters on Masonry and anti-Masonry, addressed to the Hon. John Quincy Adams*, New York, 1832, 8vo, pp. 566. This was one of the productions which were indebted for their appearance to the anti-Masonic excitement that prevailed at that time in this country. Although free from the bitterness of tone and abusive language which characterized most of the contemporaneous writings of the anti-Masons, it is, as an argumentative work, discreditable to the critical acumen of the author. It abounds in statements made without authority and unsustained by proofs, while its premises being in most instances false, its deductions are necessarily illogical.

Stone-Worship. This was, perhaps, the earliest form of fetishism. Before the discovery of metals, men were accustomed to worship unhewn stones. From Chna, whom Sanchoniathan calls "the first Phœnician," the Canaanites learned the practise, the influence of which we may trace in the stone pillar erected and consecrated by Jacob. The account in Genesis xxviii. 18, 22, is that "Jacob took the stone that he had put for his pillows and set it up for a pillar, and poured oil upon the top of it; and he called the name of that place Bethel, saying, This stone which I have set for a pillar shall be God's house." The Israelites were repeatedly commanded to destroy the stone idols of the Canaanites, and Moses corrects his own people when falling into this species of idolatry.

Various theories have been suggested as to the origin of stone-worship. Lord Kames' theory was that stones erected as monuments of the dead became the place where posterity paid their veneration to the memory of the deceased, and that the monumental stones at length became objects of worship, the people having lost sight of the emblematical signification, which was not readily understood.

Others have sought to find the origin of stone-worship in the stone that was set up and anointed by Jacob at Bethel, and the tradition of which had extended into the heathen nations and become corrupted. It is certain that the Phœnicians worshiped sacred stones under the name of *Bætylia*, which word is evidently derived from the Hebrew *Bethel*, and this undoubtedly gives some appearance of probability to the theory.

But a third theory supposes that the worship of stones was derived from the unskilfulness of the primitive sculptors, who, unable to frame, by their meager principles of plastic art, a true image of the God whom they adored, were content to substitute in its place a rude or scarcely polished stone. Hence the Greeks, according to Pausanias, originally used unhewn stones to represent their deities, thirty of which, that historian says, he saw in the city of Pharæ. These stones were of a cubical form, and, as the greater number of them were dedicated to the god Hermes, or Mercury, they received the generic name of *Hermæ*. Subsequently, with the improvement of the plastic art, the head was added.

So difficult, indeed, was it, in even the most refined era of Grecian civilization, for the people to divest themselves of the influences of this superstition, that Theophrastus characterizes "the superstitious man" as one who could not resist the impulse to bow to those mysterious stones which served to mark the confluence of the highways.

One of these consecrated stones was placed before the door of almost every house in Athens. They were also placed in front of the temples, in the gymnasia or schools, in libraries, and at the corners of streets, and in the roads. When dedicated to the god Terminus they were used as landmarks, and placed as such upon the concurrent lines of neighboring possessions.

The Thebans worshiped Bacchus under the form of a rude, square stone.

Arnobius says that Cybele was represented by a small stone of a black color. Eusebius cites Porphyry as saying that the ancients represented the Deity by a black stone, because his nature is obscure and inscrutable. The reader will here be reminded of the black stone, *Hadsjar el Aswad*, placed in the southwest corner of the Kaaba at Mecca, which was worshiped by the ancient Arabians, and is still treated with religious veneration by the modern Mohammedans. The Mussulman priests, however, say that it was originally white, and of such surprising splendor that it could be seen at the distance of four days' journey, but that it has been blackened by the tears of pilgrims.

The Druids, it is well known, had no other images of their gods but cubical or sometimes columnar stones, of which Toland gives several instances.

The Chaldeans had a sacred stone, which they held in great veneration, under the name of *Mnizuris*, and to which they sacrificed for the purpose of evoking the Good Demon.

Stone-worship existed among the early American races. Squier quotes Skinner as asserting that the Peruvians used to set up rough stones in their fields and plantations, which were worshiped as protectors of their crops. And Gama says that in Mexico the presiding god of the spring was often represented without a human body, and in place thereof a pilaster or square column, whose pedestal was covered with various sculptures.

Indeed, so universal was this stone-worship, that Higgins, in his *Celtic Druids*, says that "throughout the world the first object of idolatry seems to have been a plain, unwrought stone, placed in the ground, as an emblem of the generative or procreative powers of nature." And Bryant, in his *Analysis of Ancient Mythology*, asserts that "there is in every oracular temple some legend about a stone."

Without further citations of examples from the religious usages of antiquity, it will, I think, be conceded that the cubical stone formed an important part of the religious worship of primitive nations. But Cudworth, Bryant, Faber, and all other distinguished writers who have treated the subject, have long since established the theory that the Pagan religions were eminently symbolic. Thus, to use the language of Dudley, the pillar or stone "was adopted as a symbol of strength and firmness—a symbol, also, of the Divine power, and, by a ready inference, a symbol or idol of the Deity himself." And this symbolism is confirmed by Phurnutus, whom Toland quotes as saying that the god Hermes was represented without hands or feet, being a cubical stone, because the cubical figure betokened his solidity and stability.

The influence of this old stone worship, but of course divested of its idolatrous spirit, and developed into the system of symbolic instruction, is to be found in Masonry, where the reference to sacred stones is made in the Foundation-Stone, the Cubical Stone, the Corner-Stone, and some other symbols of a similar character. Indeed, the stone supplies Masonic science with a very important and diversified symbolism.

As stone-worship was one of the oldest of the deflections from the pure religion, so it was one of the last to be abandoned. A decree of the Council of Arles, which was held in the year 452, declares that "if, in any diocese, any infidel either lighted torches or worshipped trees, fountains, or *stones*, or neglected to destroy them, he should be found guilty of sacrilege." A similar decree was subsequently issued by the Council of Tours in 567, that of Nantes in 658, and that of Toledo in 681. Charlemagne, of France, in the eighth century, and Canute, of England, in the eleventh, found it necessary to execrate and forbid the worship of stones.

Even in the present day, the worship has not been altogether abandoned, but still exists in some remote districts of Christendom. Scheffer, in his *Description of Lapland* (cited by Mr. Tennent, in *Notes and Queries*, 1st ser., v. 122), says that in 1673 the Laplanders worshiped an unhewn stone found upon the banks of lakes and rivers, and which they called "*kied kie jubmal*, that is, the stone god." Martin, in his *Description of the Western Islands* (p. 88), says: "There is a stone set up near a mile to the south of St. Columbus's church, about eight feet high and two broad. It is called by the natives the *bowing stone;* for when the inhabitants had the first sight of the church, they set up this, and then bowed, and said the Lord's Prayer." He also describes several other stones in different parts of the islands which were objects of veneration. Finally, in a work published about twenty years ago by the Earl of Roden, entitled *Progress of the Reformation in Ireland*, he says (p. 51), that at Inniskea, an island off the coast of Mayo, "a stone carefully wrapped up in flannel is brought out at certain periods to be adored; and when a storm arises, this god is supplicated to send a wreck on their coasts."

Tennent, to whom I am indebted for these citations, adds another from Borlase, who, in his *Antiquities of Cornwall*, says (b. iii., c. ii., p. 162), that "after Christianity took place, many [in Cornwall] continued to worship these stones; coming thither with lighted torches, and praying for safety and success."

It is more than probable that in many remote regions of Europe, where the sun of Christianity has only darted its dimmest rays, this old worship of sacred stones still remains.

Strasburg, Cathedral of. This has always been considered as one of the finest Gothic buildings in Europe. The original cathedral was founded in 504, but in 1007 it was almost completely destroyed by lightning. The present edifice was begun in 1015 and completed in 1439. The cathedral of Strasburg is very closely connected with the history of Masonry. The most important association of master builders, says Stieglitz (*Von Altdeusch. Bauk.*), for the culture and extension of German art, was that which took place at Strasburg under Erwin von Steinbach. As soon as this architect had undertaken the direction of the works at the Strasburg cathedral, he summoned Masons out of Germany and Italy, and formed with them a brotherhood. Thence *hütten*, or Lodges, were scattered over Europe. In 1459, on April 25th, says the Abbé Grandidier, the Masters of many of these Lodges assembled at Ratisbon and drew up an Act of Fraternity, which made the master of the works at Strasburg, and his successors, the perpetual Grand Masters of the Fraternity of German Masons. This was confirmed by the Emperor Maximilian in 1498. By the statutes of this association, the *Haupt-Hütte*, Grand or Mother Lodge of Strasburg, was invested with a judicature, without appeal, over all the Lodges of Germany. Strasburg thus takes in German Masonry a position equivalent to that of legendary Lodge York in the Masonry of England, or Kilwinning in that of Scotland. And although the Haupt-Hütte of Strasburg with all other Haupt-Hütten were abolished by an imperial edict on August 16, 1731, the Mother Lodge never lost its prestige. "This," says Findel (*Hist.*, 72), "is the case even now in many places in Germany; the Saxon Stone-Masons still regarding the Strasburg Lodge as their chief Lodge." (See *Stone-Masons of the Middle Ages*.)

Strasburg, Congress of. Two important Masonic Congresses have been held at Strasburg.

The First Congress of Strasburg. This was convoked in 1275 by Erwin von Steinbach. The object was the establishment of a brotherhood for the continuation of the labors on the cathedral. It was attended by a large concourse of Masons from Germany and Italy. It was at this Congress that the German builders and architects, in imitation of their English brethren, assumed the name of *Freemasons*, and established a system of regulations for the government of the Craft. (See *Combinations of Masons*.)

The Second Congress of Strasburg. This was convoked by the Grand Lodge, or Haupte-Hütte of Strasburg, in 1564, as a continuation of one which had been held in the same year at Basle. Here several statutes were adopted, by which the *Steinwerksrecht*, or Stone-Masons' law, was brought into a better condition.

Strasburg, Constitutions of. On April 25, 1459, nineteen Bauhütten, or Lodges, in Southern and Central Germany met at Ratisbon, and adopted regulations for the government of the German stone-masons. Another meeting was held shortly afterward at Strasburg, where these statutes were definitively adopted and promulgated, under the title of *Ordenunge der Steinmetzen Strasburg*, or "Constitutions of the Stone-Masons of Strasburg." They from time to time underwent many alterations, and were confirmed by Maximilian I. in 1498, and subsequently by many succeeding emperors. This old document has several times been printed; in 1810, by Krause, in his *drei ältesten Kunsterkunden der Freimaurerbrüderschaft;* in 1819, by Heldmann, in *die drei ältesten geschichtlichen Denkmale der deutschen Freimaurerbrüderschaft;* in 1844, by Heideloff, in his *Bauhütte des Mittelalters in ihrer wahren Bedeutung;* Findel also, in 1866, inserted portions of it in his *Geschichte der Freimaurerei*, of which work there is a good English translation.*

The invocation with which these Constitutions commence is different from that of the English Constitutions. The latter begin thus: "The might of the Father of Heaven, with the wisdom of the blessed Son, through the grace of God and goodness of the Holy Ghost, that be three persons in one Godhead, be with us," etc. The Strasburg Constitutions begin: "In the name of the Father, and of the Son, and of the Holy Ghost, and of our gracious Mother Mary, and also her blessed servants, the holy four crowned martyrs of everlasting memory"; etc. The reference to the Virgin

*Findel says the Strasburg *Constitution* was first printed, from a well-authenticated manuscript, by Heldmann. Others also confirm this. [E. E. C.]

Mary and to the four crowned martyrs is found in none of the English Constitutions except the oldest of them, the Halliwell or Regius MS. (line 498). But Kloss has compared the Strasburg and the English statutes, and shown the great similarity in many of the regulations of both.

Strength. This is said to be one of the three principal supports of a Lodge, as the representative of the whole Institution, because it is necessary that there should be Strength to support and maintain every great and important undertaking, not less than there should be Wisdom to contrive it, and Beauty to adorn it. Hence, Strength is symbolized in Masonry by the Doric column, because, of all the orders of architecture, it is the most massive; by the Senior Warden, because it is his duty to strengthen and support the authority of the Master; and by Hiram of Tyre, because of the material assistance that he gave in men and materials for the construction of the Temple.

Strict Observance, Rite of. The Rite of Strict Observance was a modification of Masonry, based on the Order of Knights Templar, and introduced into Germany in 1754 by its founder, the Baron von Hund. It was divided into the following seven degrees: 1. Apprentice; 2. Fellow-Craft; 3. Master; 4. Scottish Master; 5. Novice; 6. Templar; 7. Professed Knight.

According to the system of the founder of this Rite, upon the death of Jacques de Molay, the Grand Master of the Templars, Pierre d'Aumont, the Provincial Grand Master of Auvergne, with two Commanders and five Knights, retired for purposes of safety into Scotland, which place they reached disguised as Operative Masons, and there finding the Grand Commander, George Harris, and several Knights, they determined to continue the Order. Aumont was nominated Grand Master, at a Chapter held on St. John's Day, 1313. To avoid persecution, the Knights became Freemasons. In 1361, the Grand Master of the Temple removed his seat to Old Aberdeen, and from that time the Order, under the veil of Masonry, spread rapidly through France, Germany, Spain, Portugal, and elsewhere. These events constituted the principal subject of many of the degrees of the Rite of Strict Observance. The others were connected with alchemy, magic, and other superstitious practises. The great doctrine contended for by the followers of the Rite was, "that every true Mason is a Knights Templar." For an account of the rise, the progress, the decay, and the final extinction of this once important Rite, see *Hund, Baron von*.

Strict Trial. See *Vouching*.

Striking Off. Striking off a Lodge from the registry of the Grand Lodge is a phrase of English Masonry, equivalent to what in America is called a forfeiture of charter. It is more commonly called "erasing from the list of Lodges."

Stuart Masonry. This title is given by Masonic historians to that system of Freemasonry which is supposed to have been invented by the adherents of the exiled house of Stuart for the purpose of being used as a political means of restoring, first, James II., and afterward his son and grandson, James and Charles Edward, respectively known in history as the Chevalier St. George and the Young Pretender. Most of the conclusions to which Masonic writers have arrived on the subject of this connection of the Stuarts with the high degrees of Masonry are based on conjecture; but there is sufficient internal evidence in the character of some of these degrees, as well as in the known history of their organization, to establish the fact that such a connection did actually exist.

The first efforts to create a Masonic influence in behalf of his family is attributed to James II., who had abdicated the throne of England in 1688. Of him, Noorthouck says (*Constitutions*, 1784, p. 192), that he was not "a Brother Mason," and sneeringly adds, in his index, that "he might have been a better king had he been a Mason." But Lenning says that after his flight to France, and during his residence at the Jesuit College of Clermont, where he remained for some time, his adherents, among whom were the Jesuits, fabricated certain degrees with the ulterior design of carrying out their political views. At a later period these degrees were, he says, incorporated into French Masonry under the name of the Clermont system, in reference to their original construction at that place. Gädicke had also said that many Scotchmen followed him, and thus introduced Freemasonry into France. But this opinion is only worthy of citation because it proves that such an opinion was current among the German scholars of the last century.

On his death, which took place at the palace of St. Germain en Laye in 1701, he was succeeded in his claims to the British throne by his son, who was recognized by Louis XIV., of France, under the title of James III., but who is better known as the Chevalier St. George, or the Old Pretender. He also sought, says Lenning, to find in the high degrees of Masonry a support for his political views, but, as he remarks, with no better results than those which had attended the attempts of his father.

His son, Prince Charles Edward, who was commonly called by the English the Young Pretender, took a more active part than either his father or grandfather in the pursuits of Masonry; and there is abundant historical evidence that he was not only a Mason, but that he held high office in the Order, and was for a time zealously engaged in its propagation; always, however, it is supposed, with political views.

In 1745 he invaded Scotland, with a view to regain the lost throne of his ancestors, and met for some time with more than partial success. On September 24, 1745, he was admitted into the Order of Knights Templar, and was elected Grand Master, an office which it is said that he held until his death. On his return to France after his ill-fated expedition, the Prince is said to have established at the city of Arras, on April 15, 1747, a Rose Croix Chapter under the title of Scottish Jacobite Chapter. In the Patent for this Chapter he styles himself "King of England, France, Scotland, and Ireland, and, as such, Substitute Grand Master of the Chapter of Herodem, known under the title of Knight of the Eagle and Pelican, and since our misfortunes and disasters under that of Rose Croix."

In 1748, the Rite of the *Veille-Bru*, or Faithful Scottish Masons, was created at Toulouse in grateful remembrance of the reception given by the Masons of that Orient to Sir Samuel Lockhart, the aide-de-camp of the Pretender. Ragon says (*Orth. Maçon.*, p. 122), in a note to this statement, the "favorites who accompanied this prince into France were in the habit of selling to speculators Charters for Mother Lodges, Patents for Chapters, etc. These titles were their property, and they did not fail to make use of them as a means of livelihood."

Ragon says (*Thuil. Gen.*, p. 367), that the degrees of Irish Master, Perfect Irish Master, and Puissant Irish Master were invented in France, in 1747, by the favorites of Charles Edward Stuart, and sold to the partisans of that prince. One degree was openly called the "Scottish Master of the Sacred Vault of James VI.," as if to indicate its Stuart character. The degree still exists as the Thirteenth of the Ancient and Accepted Scottish Rite, but it has been shorn of its political pretensions and its title changed.

Findel has given in his *History of Freemasonry* (English translation, p. 209) a very calm and impartial account of the rise of this Stuart Masonry. He says:

"Ever since the banishment of the Stuarts from England in 1688, secret alliances had been kept up between Rome and Scotland; for to the former place the Pretender James Stuart had retired in 1719, and his son Charles Edward was born there in 1720; and these communications became the more intimate, the higher the hopes of the Pretender rose. The Jesuits played a very important part in these conferences. Regarding the reinstatement of the Stuarts and the extension of the power of the Roman church as identical, they sought at that time to make the society of Freemasons subservient to their ends. But to make use of the Fraternity to restore the exiled family to the throne could not possibly have been contemplated, as Freemasonry could hardly be said to exist in Scotland then. Perhaps in 1724, when Ramsay was a year in Rome, or in 1728, when the Pretender in Parma kept up an intercourse with the restless Duke of Wharton, a Past Grand Master, this idea was first entertained; and then, when it was apparent how difficult it would be to corrupt the loyalty and fealty of Freemasonry in the Grand Lodge of Scotland, founded in 1736, this scheme was set on foot, of assembling the faithful adherents of the banished royal family in the high degrees! The soil which was best adapted for this innovation was France, where the low ebb to which Masonry had sunk had paved the way for all kinds of new-fangled notions, and where the Lodges were composed of Scotch conspirators and accomplices of the Jesuits. When the path had thus been smoothed by the agency of these secret propagandists, Ramsay, at that time Grand Orator (an office unknown in England), by his speech completed the preliminaries necessary for the introduction of the high degrees; their further development was left to the instrumentality of others, whose influence produced a result somewhat different from that originally intended. Their course we can now pursue, assisted by authentic historical information. In 1752, Scottish Masonry, as it was denominated, penetrated into Germany (Berlin) prepared from a ritual very similar to one used in Lille in 1749 and 1750. In 1743, Thory tells us, the Masons in Lyons, under the name of the 'Petit Elu,' invented the degree of Kadosh, which represents the revenge of the Templars. The Order of Knights Templar had been abolished in 1311, and to that epoch they were obliged to have recourse when, after the banishment of several Knights from Malta in 1720 because they were Freemasons, it was not longer possible to keep up a connection with the Order of St. John or Knights of Malta, then in the plenitude of their power under the sovereignty of the Pope. A pamphlet entitled *Freemasonry Divested of all its Secrets*, published in Strasburg in 1745, contains the first glimpse of the Strict Observance, and demonstrates how much they expected the brotherhood to contribute towards the expedition in favor of the Pretender."

From what has been said, it is evident that the exiled house of Stuart exercised an important part in the invention and extension of what has been called the High Masonry. The traces of the political system are seen at the present day in the internal organization of some of the high degrees—especially in the derivation and meaning of certain significant words. There is, indeed, abundant reason for believing that the substitute word of the Third Degree was changed by Ramsay, or some other fabricator of degrees, to give it a reference to James II. as the "son of the widow," Queen Henrietta Maria.

Further researches are needed to enable any author to satisfactorily write all the details of this interesting episode in the history of continental Masonry. Documents are still wanting to elucidate certain intricate and, at present, apparently contradictory points.

Stukely, Dr. In accordance with the Doctor's diary, he "was made a Mason,

January 6, 1721, at the Salutation Tavern, Tavistock street, London, with Mr. Collins and Captain Rowe, who made the famous diving engine." The Doctor adds: "I was the first person in London made a Freemason in that city for many years. We had great difficulty to find members enough to perform the ceremony. Immediately upon that it took a run, and ran itself out of breath through the folly of its members." The Stukely papers containing the Doctor's diary are of continuous interest; and according to Rev. W. C. Lukis, P.M., F.S.A., "Pain (or Payne) had been re-elected Grand Master in 1720, and Dr. Desaguliers was the Immediate Past Grand Master." The last mentioned Brother pronouncing the Oration on June 24, 1721, at Stationers' Hall; on the following St. John's Day (Evangelist), December 27, 1721, "We met at the Fountain Tavern, Strand, and by consent of the Grand Master present, Dr. Beal constituted a new Lodge, where I was chosen Master." A trite remark of Dr. Stukely as to symbolism, was: "The first learning of the world consisted chiefly of symbols, the wisdom of the Chaldeans, Phœnicians, Egyptians, Jews, of Zoroaster, Sanchoniathon, Pherecydes, Syrus, Pythagoras, Socrates, Plato, of all the ancients that have come to our hand, is symbolic."

Sublime. The Third Degree is called "the Sublime Degree of a Master Mason," in reference to the exalted lessons that it teaches of God and of a future life. The epithet is, however, comparatively modern. It is not to be found in any of the rituals of the last century. Neither Hutchinson, nor Smith, nor Preston use it; and it was not, probably, in the original Prestonian lecture. Hutchinson speaks of "the most sacred and solemn Order" and of "the exalted," but not of "the sublime" degree. Webb, who based his lectures on the Prestonian system, applies no epithet to the Master's Degree. In an edition of the *Constitutions*, published at Dublin in 1769, the Master's Degree is spoken of as "the most respectable"; and forty years ago the epithet "high and honorable" was used in some of the rituals of this country. The first book in which we meet with the adjective "*sublime*" applied to the Third Degree, is the *Masonic Discourses* of Dr. T. M. Harris, published at Boston in 1801. Cole also used it in 1817, in his *Freemasons' Library;* and about the same time Jeremy Cross, the well-known lecturer, introduced it into his teachings, and used it in his *Hieroglyphic Chart,* which was, for many years, the text-book of American Lodges. The word is now, however, to be found in the modern English lectures, and is of universal use in the rituals of the United States, where the Third Degree is always called "the sublime degree of a Master Mason."

The word *sublime* was the password of the Master's Degree in the Adonhiramite Rite, because it was said to have been the surname of Hiram, or Adonhiram. On this subject, Guillemain, in his *Recueil Précieux* (i., 91), makes the following singular remarks:

"For a long time a great number of Masons were unacquainted with this word, and they erroneously made use of another in its stead which they did not understand, and to which they gave a meaning that was doubtful and improbable. This is proved by the fact that the first knights adopted for the Master's password the Latin word *Sublimis,* which the French, as soon as they received Masonry, pronounced *Sublime,* which was so far very well. But some profanes, who were desirous of divulging our secrets, but who did not perfectly understand this word, wrote it *Jiblime,* which they said signified *excellence.* Others, who followed, surpassed the error of the first by printing it *Giblos,* and were bold enough to say that it was the name of the place where the body of Adonhiram was found. As in those days the number of uneducated was considerable, these ridiculous assertions were readily received, and the truth was generally forgotten."

The whole of this narrative is a mere visionary invention of the founder of the Adonhiramite system; but it is barely possible that there is some remote connection between the use of the word *sublime* in that Rite, as a significant word of the Third Degree, and its modern employment as an epithet of the same degree. However, the ordinary signification of the word, as referring to things of an exalted character, would alone sufficiently account for the use of the epithet.

Sublime Degrees. The eleven degrees of the Ancient and Accepted Scottish Rite, from the Fourth to the Fourteenth inclusive, are so called. Thus Dalcho (*Report of Com.,* 1802) says: "Although many of the *Sublime degrees* are in fact a continuation of the Blue degrees, yet there is no interference between the two bodies."

Sublime Grand Lodge. A title formerly given in the Ancient and Accepted Rite to what is now simply called a Lodge of Perfection. Thus, in 1801, Dr. Dalcho delivered in Charleston, South Carolina, an address which bears the title of "An oration delivered in the Sublime Grand Lodge."

Sublime Knight Elected. (*Sublime Chevalier élu.*) Called also Sublime Knight Elected of the Twelve. The Eleventh Degree of the Ancient and Accepted Scottish Rite. Its legend is that it was instituted by King Solomon after punishment had been inflicted on certain traitors at the Temple, both as a recompense for the zeal and constancy of the Illustrious Elect of Fifteen, who had discovered them, and also to enable him to elevate other deserving brethren from the lower degrees to that which had been vacated by their promotion. Twelve of these fifteen he elected Sublime Knights, and made the selection by ballot, that he might give none offense, putting the names of the whole in an urn. The first twelve that were drawn he formed into a Chapter, and gave them command over the twelve tribes, bestowing on them a name which in Hebrew signifies a true man.

The meeting of a body of Sublime Knights is called a Chapter.

The room is hung with black strewed with tears.

The presiding officer represents King Solomon, and in the old rituals is styled "Most Puissant," but in recent ones "Thrice Illustrious."

The apron is white, lined and bordered with black, with black strings; on the flap a flaming heart.

The sash is black, with a flaming heart on the breast, suspended from the right shoulder to the left hip.

The jewel is a sword of justice.

This is the last of the three Elus which are found in the Ancient and Accepted Scottish Rite. In the French Rite they have been condensed into one, and make the Fourth Degree of that ritual, but not, as Ragon admits, with the happiest effect.

The names of the Twelve Illustrious Knights selected to preside over the twelve tribes, as they have been transmitted to us in the ritual of this degree, have undoubtedly assumed a very corrupted form. The restoration of their correct orthography, and with it their true signification, is worthy the attention of the Masonic student.

Sublime Masons. The initiates into the Fourteenth degree of the Ancient and Accepted Rite are so called. Thus Dalcho (Orat., p. 27) says: "The Sublime Masons view the symbolic system with reverence, as forming a test of the character and capacity of the initiated." This abbreviated form is now seldom used, the fuller one of "Grand, Elect, Perfect, and Sublime Masons" being more generally employed.

Sublime Prince of the Royal Secret. This is the Thirty-second Degree of the Ancient and Accepted Rite. There is abundant internal evidence, derived from the ritual and from some historical facts, that the degree of Sublime Prince of the Royal Secret was instituted by the founders of the Council of Emperors of the East and West, which body was established in the year 1758. It is certain that before that period we hear nothing of such a degree in any of the Rites. The Rite of Heredom or of Perfection, which was that instituted by the Council of Emperors, consisted of twenty-five degrees. Of these the Twenty-fifth, and highest, was the Prince of the Royal Secret. It was brought to America by Morin, as the summit of the High Masonry which he introduced, and for the propagation of which he had received his Patent. In the subsequent extension of the Scottish Rite about the beginning of the present century, by the addition of eight new degrees to the original twenty-five, the Sublime Prince of the Royal Secret became the Thirty-second.

Bodies of the Thirty-second Degree are called Consistories, and where there is a superintending body erected by the Supreme Council for the government of the inferior degrees in a State or Province, it is called a Grand Consistory.

The clothing of a Sublime Prince consists of a collar, jewel, and apron. The collar is black edged with white.

The jewel is a Teutonic cross of gold.

The apron is white edged with black. On the flap are embroidered six flags, three on each side the staffs in saltier, and the flags blue, red, and yellow. On the center of the flap, over these, is a Teutonic cross surmounted by an All-seeing Eye, and on the cross a double-headed eagle not crowned. On the body of the apron is the tracing-board of the degree. The most important

part of the symbolism of the degree is the tracing-board, which is technically called "The Camp." This is a symbol of deep import, and in its true interpretation is found that "royal secret" from which the degree derives its name. This Camp constitutes an essential part of the furniture of a Consistory during an initiation, but its explanations are altogether esoteric. It is a singular fact, that notwithstanding the changes which the degree must have undergone in being transferred from the Twenty-fifth of one Rite to the Thirty-second of another, no alteration was ever made in the Camp, which retains at the present day the same form and signification that were originally given to it.

The motto of the degree is "Spes mea in Deo est," i. e., My hope is in God.

Sublime Solomon. (*Salomon Sublime.*) A degree in the manuscript collection of Peuvret.

Sublimes, The. (*Les Sublimes.*) One of the degrees of the Ancient Chapter of Clermont.

Submission. Submission to the mediatorial offices of his brethren in the case of a dispute is a virtue recommended to the Mason, but not necessarily to be enforced. In the "Charges of a Freemason" (*Constitutions*, 1723, p. 56) it is said (vi., 6): "With respect to Brothers or Fellows at law, the Master and Brethren should kindly offer their mediation; which ought to be thankfully *submitted* to by the contending Brethren; and if that *submission* is impracticable, they must, however, carry on their process or lawsuit without wrath or rancor."

Subordinate Lodge. So called to indicate its subordination to the Grand Lodge as a supreme, superintending power. (See *Lodge*.)

Subordinate Officers. In a Grand Lodge, all the officers below the Grand Master, and in a Lodge, all those below the Worshipful Master, are styled *Subordinate Officers*. So, too, in all the other branches of the Order, the presiding officer is supreme, the rest subordinate.

Subordination. Although it is the theory of Freemasonry that all the brethren are on a level of equality, yet in the practical working of the Institution a subordination of rank has been always rigorously observed. So the Charges approved in 1722, which had been collected by Anderson from the Old Constitutions, say: "These rulers and governors, supreme and subordinate, of the ancient Lodge, are to be obeyed in their respective stations by all the Brethren, according to the Old Charges and Regulations, with all humility, reverence, love, and alacrity." (*Constitutions*, 1723, p. 52.)

Substitute Ark. See *Ark, Substitute*.

Substitute Candidate. An arrangement resorted to in the Royal Arch Degree of the American system, so as to comply *pro forma* with the requisitions of the ritual. In the English, Scotch, and Irish systems, there is no regulation requiring the presence of three candidates, and, therefore, the practise of employing substitutes is unknown in those countries. In the United States the usage has prevailed from a very early period, although opposed at various times by conscientious Companions, who thought that it was an improper evasion of the law. Finally, the question as to the employment of substitutes came before the General Grand Chapter in September, 1872, when it was decided, by a vote of ninety-one to thirty, that the use of substitutes is not in violation of the ritual of Royal Arch Masonry or the installation charges delivered to a High Priest. The use of them was therefore authorized, but the Chapters were exhorted not to have recourse to them except in cases of emergency; an unnecessary exhortation, it would seem, since it was only in such cases that they had been employed.

Substitute Grand Master. The third officer in the Grand Lodge of Scotland. He presides over the Craft in the absence of the Grand and Deputy Grand Masters. The office was created in the year 1738. He is appointed by the Grand Master annually.

Substitute Word. This is an expression of very significant suggestion to the thoughtful Master Mason. If the *Word* is, in Masonry, a symbol of Divine Truth; if the search for the Word is a symbol of the search for that Truth; if the *Lost Word* symbolizes the idea that Divine Truth has not been found, then the *Substitute Word* is a symbol of the unsuccessful search after Divine Truth and the attainment in this life, of which the first Temple is a type, of what is only an approximation to it. The idea of a substitute word and its history is to be found in the oldest rituals of the last century; but the phrase itself is of more recent date, being the result of the fuller development of Masonic science and philosophy.

The history of the substitute word has been an unfortunate one. Subjected from a very early period to a mutilation of form, it underwent an entire change in some Rites, after the introduction of the high degrees; most probably through the influence of the Stuart Masons, who sought by an entirely new word to give a reference to the unfortunate representative of that house as the similitude of the stricken builder. (See *Macbenac*.) And so it has come to pass that there are now two substitutes in use, of entirely different form and meaning; one used on the Continent of Europe, and one in England and this country.

It is difficult in this case, where almost all the knowledge that we can have of the subject is so scanty, to determine the exact time when or the way in which the new word was introduced. But there is, I think, abundant internal evidence in the words themselves as to their appropriateness and the languages whence they came (the one being pure Hebrew, and the other, I think, Gaelic), as well as from the testimony of old rituals, to show that the word in use in the United States is the true word, and was the one in use before the revival.

Both of these words have, however, unfortunately been translated by persons ignorant of the languages whence they are derived, so that the most incorrect and even absurd interpretations of their significations have been given. The word in universal use in this country has been translated as "rottenness in the bone," or "the builder is dead," or by several other phrases equally as far from the true meaning.

The correct word has been mutilated. Properly, it consists of four syllables, for the last syllable, as it is now pronounced, should be divided into two. These four syllables compose three Hebrew words, which constitute a perfect and grammatical phrase, appropriate to the occasion of their utterance. But to understand them, the scholar must seek the meaning in each syllable, and combine the whole. In the language of Apuleius, I must forbear to enlarge upon these holy mysteries.

Succession to the Chair. The regulations adopted in 1721 by the Grand Lodge of England have been generally esteemed as setting forth the ancient landmarks of the Order. But certain regulations, which were adopted on the 25th of November, 1723, as amendments to or explanatory of these, being enacted under the same authority, and almost by the same persons, can scarcely be less binding upon the Order than the original regulations. Both these compilations of Masonic law refer expressly to the subject of the succession to the chair on the death or removal of the Master.

The old regulation of 1721, in the second of the thirty-nine articles adopted in that year, is in the following words:

"In case of death or sickness, or necessary absence of the Master, the Senior Warden shall act as Master *pro tempore*, if no brother is present who has been Master of that Lodge before. For the absent Master's authority reverts to the last Master present, *though he cannot act till the Senior Warden has congregated the Lodge*." (*Constitutions*, 1738, p. 153.)

The words in italics indicate that even at that time the power of calling the brethren together and "setting them to work," which is technically called "congregating the Lodge," was supposed to be vested in the Senior Warden alone during the absence of the Master; although, perhaps, from a supposition that he had greater experience, the difficult duty of presiding over the communication was entrusted to a Past Master. The regulation is, however, contradictory in its provisions. For if the "last Master present" could not act, that is, could not exercise the authority of the Master until the Senior Warden had congregated the Lodge, then it is evident that the authority of the Master did not revert to him in an unqualified sense, for that officer required no such concert nor consent on the part of the Warden, but could congregate the Lodge himself.

This evident contradiction in the language of the regulation probably caused, in a brief period, a further examination of the ancient usage, and accordingly on the 25th of November, 1723, a very little more than two years after, the following regulation was adopted:

"If a Master of a particular Lodge is deposed or demits, the Senior Warden shall forthwith fill the Master's chair till the next time of choosing; and ever since, in the Master's absence, he fills the chair, even though a former Master be present." (*Ibid.*)

The present Constitution of the Grand Lodge of England appears, however, to have been formed rather in reference to the regulation of 1721 than to that of 1723. It prescribes that on the death, removal, or incapacity of the Master, the Senior Warden, or in his absence, the Junior Warden, or in his absence, the immediate Past Master, or in his absence, the Senior Past Master, "shall act as Master in summoning the Lodge, until the next installation of Master." (Rule 141.) But the English Constitution goes on to direct that, "in the Master's absence, the immediate Past Master, or if he be absent, the Senior Past Master of the Lodge present shall take the chair. And if no Past Master of the Lodge be present, then the Senior Warden, or in his absence the Junior Warden, shall rule the Lodge."

Here again we find ourselves involved in the intricacies of a divided sovereignty. The Senior Warden congregates the Lodge, but a Past Master rules it. And if the Warden refuses to perform his part of the duty, then the Past Master will have no Lodge to rule. So that, after all, it appears that of the two the authority of the Senior Warden is the greater.

But in this country the usage has always conformed to the regulation of 1723, as is apparent from a glance at our rituals and monitorial works.

Webb, in his *Freemasons' Monitor* (edition of 1808), lays down the rule, that "in the absence of the Master, the Senior Warden is to govern the Lodge"; and that officer receives annually, in every Lodge in the United States, on the night of his installation, a charge to that effect. It must be remembered, too, that we are not indebted to Webb himself for this charge, but that he borrowed it, word for word, from Preston, who wrote long before, and who, in his turn, extracted it from the rituals which were in force at the time of his writing.

In the United States, accordingly, it has been held, that on the death or removal of the Master, his authority descends to the Senior Warden, who may, however, by courtesy, offer the chair to a Past Master present, after the Lodge has been congregated.

There is some confusion in relation to the question of who is to be the successor of the Master, which arises partly from the contradiction between the regulations of 1721 and 1723, and partly from the contradiction in different clauses of the regulation of 1723 itself. But whether the Senior Warden or a Past Master is to succeed, the regulation of 1721 makes no provision for an election, but implies that the vacancy shall be temporarily supplied during the official term, while that of 1723 expressly states that such temporary succession shall continue "till the next time of choosing," or, in the words of the present English Constitution, "until the next installation of Master."

But, in addition to the authority of the ancient regulation and general and uniform usage, reason and justice seem to require that the vacancy shall not be supplied permanently until the regular time of election. By holding the election at an earlier period, the Senior Warden is deprived of his right, as a member, to become a candidate for the vacant office. For the Senior Warden having been regularly installed, has of course been duly obligated to serve in the office to which he had been elected during the full term. If then an election takes place before the expiration of that term, he must be excluded from the list of candidates, because, if elected, he could not vacate his present office without a violation of his obligation. The same disability would affect the Junior Warden, who by a similar obligation is bound to the faithful discharge of his duties in the South. So that by anticipating the election, the two most prominent officers of the Lodge, and the two most likely to succeed the Master in due course of rotation, would be excluded from the chance of promotion. A grievous wrong would thus be done to these officers, which no Dispensation of a Grand Master should be permitted to inflict.

But even if the Wardens were not ambitious of office, or were not likely, under any circumstances, to be elected to the vacant office, another objection arises to the anticipation of an election for Master which is worthy of consideration.

The Wardens, having been installed under the solemnity of an obligation to discharge the duties of their respective offices to the best of their ability, and the Senior Warden having been expressly charged that "in the absence of the Master he is to rule the Lodge," a conscientious Senior Warden might very naturally feel that he was neglecting these duties and violating this obligation, by permitting the office which he has sworn to temporarily occupy in the absence of his Master to be permanently filled by any other person.

On the whole, then, the old regulations, as well as ancient, uninterrupted, and uniform usage and the principles of reason and justice, seem imperatively to require that, on the death or removal of the Master, the chair shall be occupied temporarily until the regular time of election; and although the law is not equally explicit in relation to the person who shall fill that temporary position, the weight of law and precedent seems to incline toward the principle that the authority of the absent Master shall be placed in the hands of the Senior Warden.

Succoth. An ancient city of Palestine, about forty-five miles northeast of Jerusalem, and the site of which is now occupied by the village of Seikoot. It is the place near which Hiram Abif cast the sacred vessels for the Temple. (See *Clay Ground.*)

Sufferer. (*Souffrant.*) The Second Degree of the Order of Initiated Knights and Brothers of Asia.

Summons. A warning to appear at the meeting of a Lodge or other Masonic body. The custom of summoning the members of a Lodge to every communication, although now often neglected, is of very ancient date, and was generally observed up to a very recent period. In the Anderson Charges of 1722, it is said: "In ancient times, no Master or Fellow could be absent from the Lodge, especially when warned to appear at it, without incurring a severe censure." (*Constitutions*, 1723, p. 51.) In the Constitutions of the Cooke MS., about 1450, we are told that the Masters and Fellows were to be *forewarned* to come to the congregations. (L 902.) All the old records, and the testimony of writers since the revival, show that it was always the usage to summon the members to attend the meetings of the General Assembly or the particular Lodges. A summons of a Lodge is often improperly or illegally worded and care should be taken when issued.

Sun. Hardly any of the symbols of Masonry are more important in their signification or more extensive in their application than the sun. As the source of material light, it reminds the Mason of that intellectual light of which he is in constant search. But it is especially as the ruler of the day, giving to it a beginning and end, and a regular course of hours, that the sun is presented as a Masonic symbol. Hence, of the three lesser lights, we are told that one represents or symbolizes the sun, one the moon. and one the Master of the Lodge, because, as the sun rules the day and the moon governs the night, so should the Worshipful Master rule and govern his Lodge with equal regularity and precision. And this is in strict analogy with other Masonic symbolisms. For if the Lodge is a symbol of the world, which is thus governed in its changes of times and seasons by the sun, it is evident that the Master who governs the Lodge, controlling its time of opening and closing, and the work which it should do, must be symbolized by the sun. The heraldic definition of the sun as a bearing fits most appositely to the symbolism of the sovereignty of the Master. Thus Gwillim says: "The sun is the symbol of sovereignty, the hieroglyphic of royalty; it doth signify absolute authority." This representation of the sun as a symbol of authority, while it explains the reference to the Master, enables us to amplify its meaning, and apply it to the three sources of authority in the Lodge, and accounts for the respective positions of the officers wielding this authority. The Master, therefore, in the East is a symbol of the rising sun; the Junior Warden in the South, of the Meridian Sun; and the Senior Warden in the West, of the Setting Sun. So in the mysteries of India, the chief officers were placed in the east, the west, and the south, respectively, to represent Brahma, or the rising; Vishnu, or the setting; and Siva, or the meridian sun. And in the Druidical rites, the Arch-druid, seated in the east, was assisted by two other officers—the one in the west representing the moon, and the other in the south representing the meridian sun.

This triple division of the government of a Lodge by three officers, representatives of the sun in his three manifestations in the east, south, and west, will remind us of similar ideas in the symbolism of antiquity. In the Orphic mysteries, it was taught that the sun generated from an egg, burst forth with power to triplicate himself by his own unassisted energy. Supreme power seems always to have been associated in the ancient mind with a threefold division. Thus the sign of authority was indicated by the three-forked lightning of Jove, the trident of Neptune, and the three-headed Cerberus of Pluto. The government of the Universe was divided between these three sons of Saturn. The chaste goddess ruled the earth as Diana, the heavens as Luna, and the infernal regions as Hecate, whence her rites were only performed in a place where three roads met.

The sun is then presented to us in Masonry first as a symbol of light, but then more emphatically as a symbol of sovereign authority.

But, says Wemyss (*Symb. Lang.*), speaking of Scriptural symbolism, "the sun may be considered to be an emblem of Divine Truth," because the sun or light, of which it is the source, "is not only manifest in itself, but makes other things; so one truth detects, reveals, and manifests another, as all truths are dependent on, and connected with, each other more or less." And this again is applicable to the Masonic doctrine which makes the Master the symbol of the sun; for as the sun discloses and makes manifest, by the opening of day, what had been hidden in the darkness of night, so the Master of the Lodge, as the analogue of the ancient hierophant or explainer of the mysteries, makes Divine truth manifest to the neophyte, who had been hitherto in intellectual darkness, and reveals the hidden or esoteric lessons of initiation.

Sun of Mercy, Society of the. Of this Society little is known, but Antoine Joseph Pernetty, the presumed author of the Twenty-eighth Degree, A. A. Scottish Rite, became a devotee to it, and induced Swedenborg to become a member. Its central point appears to have been Avignon and Montpellier; and its nature Hermetic.

Sun, Knight of the. See *Knight of the Sun.*

Sun, Moon, and Stars. The plates prefixed to the *Hieroglyphic Chart* of Jeremy Cross contain a page on which are delineated a sun, moon, seven stars, and a comet, which has been copied into the later illustrated editions of Webb's *Monitor*, and is now to be found in all the modern Masters' carpets. In the connection in which they are there placed they have no symbolic meaning, although many have erroneously considered that they have. The sun and moon are not symbols in the Third, but only in the First Degree; the stars are a symbol in the high degrees, and the comet is no symbol at all. They are simply mnemonic in character, and intended to impress on the memory, by a pictured representation of the object, a passage in the Webb lectures taken from the Prestonian, which is in these words: "The All-seeing Eye, whom the sun, moon, and stars obey, and under whose watchful care even comets perform their stupendous revolutions, pervades the inmost recesses of the human heart, and will reward us according to our merits." It would have been more creditable to the symbolic learning of Cross, if he had omitted these plates from his collection of Masonic symbols. At least the too common error of mistaking them for symbols in the Third Degree would have been avoided.

Sun-Worship. Sir William Jones has remarked that two of the principal sources of mythology were a wild admiration of the heavenly bodies, particularly the sun, and an inordinate respect paid to the memory of powerful, wise, and virtuous ancestors, especially the founders of kingdoms, legislators, and warriors. To the latter cause we may attribute the euhemerism of the Greeks and the shintoism of the Chinese. But in the former we shall find the origin of sun-worship the oldest and by far the most prevalent of all the ancient religions.

Eusebius says that the Phœnicians and the Egyptians were the first who ascribed divinity to the sun. But long—very long—before these ancient peoples the primeval race of Aryans worshiped the solar orb in his various manifestations as the producer of light. "In the Veda," says a native commentator, "there are only three deities: Surya in heaven, Indra in the sky, and Agni on the earth." But Surya, Indra, Agni are but manifestations of God in the sun, the bright sky, and the fire derived from the solar light. In the profoundly poetic ideas of the Vedic hymns we find perpetual allusion to the sun with his life-bestowing rays. Everywhere in the East, amidst its brilliant skies, the sun claimed, as the glorious manifestation of Deity, the adoration of those primitive peoples. The Persians, the Assyrians, the Chaldeans—all worshiped the sun. The Greeks, a more intellectual people, gave a poetic form to the grosser idea, and adored Apollo or Dionysius as the sun-god.

Sun-worship was introduced into the mysteries not as a material idolatry, but as the means of expressing an idea of restoration to life from death, drawn from the daily reappearance in the east of the solar orb after its nightly disappearance in the west. To the sun, too, as the regenerator or revivifier of all things, is the Phallic worship, which made a prominent part of the mysteries, to be attributed. From the Mithraic initiations, in which sun-worship played so important a part, the Gnostics derived many of their symbols. These, again, exercised their influence upon the Medieval Freemasons. Thus it is that the sun has become so prominent in the Masonic system; not, of course, as an object of worship, but purely as a symbol, the interpretation of which presents itself in many different ways. (See *Sun.*)

Superexcellent Masons. Dr. Oliver devotes the fifteenth lecture of his *Historical Landmarks* (vol. i., pp. 401–438) to an essay "On the number and classification of the Workmen at the building of King Solomon's Temple." His statement, based entirely on old lectures and legends, is that there were nine Masons of supereminent ability who were called Superexcellent Masons, and who presided over as many Lodges of Excellent Masons, while the nine Superexcellent Masons formed also a Lodge over which Tito Zadok, Prince of Harodim, presided. In a note on p. 423, he refers to these Superexcellent Masons as being the same as the Most Excellent Masters who constitute the Sixth Degree of the American Rite. The theory advanced by Dr. Oliver is not only entirely unauthenticated by historical evidence of any kind, but also inconsistent with the ritual of that degree. It is, in fact, merely a myth, and not a well-constructed one.

Superexcellent Master. A degree which was originally an honorary or side degree conferred by the Inspectors-General of the Ancient and Accepted Scottish Rite at Charleston. It has since been introduced into some of the Royal and Select Councils of the United States, and there conferred as an additional degree. This innovation on the regular series of Cryptic degrees, with which it actually has no historical connection, met with great opposition; so that the convention of Royal and Select Masters, which met at New York in June, 1873, resolved to place it in the category of an honorary degree, which might or might not be conferred at the option of a Council, but not as an integral part of the Rite. Although this body had no dogmatic authority, its decision will doubtless have some influence in settling the question. The degree is simply an enlargement of that part of the ceremonies of the Royal Arch which refer to the Temple destruction. To that place it belongs, if it belongs anywhere, but has no more to do with the ideas inculcated in Cryptic Masonry, than have any of the degrees lately invented for modern secret societies.

Whence the degree originally sprang, it is impossible to tell. It could hardly have had its birth on the Continent of Europe; at least, it does not appear to have been known to European writers. Neither Gädicke nor Lenning mention it in their *Encyclopedias;* nor is it found in the catalogue of more than seven hundred degrees given by Thory in his *Acta Latomorum;* nor does Ragon allude to it in his *Tuileur Général*, although he has there given a list of one hundred and fifty-three degrees or modifications of the *Master*. Oliver, it is true, speaks of it, but he evidently derived his knowledge from an American source. It may have been manufactured in America, and possibly by some of those engaged in founding the Scottish Rite. The only Cahier that I ever saw of the original ritual, which is still in my possession, is in the handwriting of Alexander McDonald, a very intelligent and enthusiastic Mason, who was at one time the Grand Commander of the Supreme Council for the Southern Jurisdiction.

The Masonic legend of the degree of Superexcellent Master refers to circumstances which occurred on the last day of the siege of Jerusalem by Nebuzaradan, the captain of the Chaldean army, who had been sent by Nebuchadnezzar to destroy the city and Temple, as a just punishment of the Jewish king Zedekiah for his perfidy and rebellion. It occupies, therefore, precisely that point of time which is embraced in that part of the Royal Arch Degree which represents the destruction of the Temple, and the carrying of the Jews in captivity to Babylon. It is, in fact, an exemplification and extension of that part of the Royal Arch Degree.

As to the symbolic design of the degree, it is very evident that its legend and ceremonies are intended to inculcate that important Masonic virtue—fidelity to vows. Zedekiah, the wicked King of Judah, is, by the modern ritualists who have symbolized the degree, adopted very appropriately as the symbol of perfidy; and the severe but well-deserved punishment which was inflicted on him by the King of Babylon is set forth in the lecture as a great moral lesson, whose object is to warn the recipient of the fatal effects that will ensue from a violation of his sacred obligations.

Superintendent of Works, Grand. An officer of the Grand Lodge of England, who is appointed annually by the Grand Master. He should be well skilled in geometry and architecture. His duty is to advise with the Board of General Purposes on all plans of building or edifices undertaken by the Grand Lodge, and furnish plans and estimates for the same; to superintend their construction, and see that they are conformable to the plans approved by the Grand Master, the Grand Lodge, and the Board of General Purposes; to suggest improvements, and make an annual report on the condition of all the Grand Lodge edifices. The office is not known in the Grand Lodges of this country, but where there is a temple or hall belonging to a Grand Lodge, the duty of attending to it is referred to a hall committee, which, when necessary, engages the services of a professional architect.

Superior. The Sixth and last degree of the German Union of the Twenty-two.

Superiors, Unknown. See *Unknown Superiors*.

Super-Masonic. Ragon (*Orth. Maçon.*, p. 73) calls the high degrees, as being beyond Ancient Craft Masonry, "Grades super Maçonniques."

Supplanting. All the Old Constitutions, without exception, contain a charge against one Fellow supplanting another in his work. Thus, for instance, the third charge in the Harleian MS., No. 2054, says: "Alsoe that noe maister nor fellowe shall subplant others of their worke, that is to say, if they haue taken a worke or stand maister of a Lord's worke, y[e] shall not put him out of it if he be able of cuning to end the worke." From this we derive the modern doctrine that one Lodge cannot interfere with the work of another, and that a candidate beginning his initiation in a Lodge must finish it in the same Lodge.

Supports of the Lodge. The symbolism connected with the supports of the Lodge is one of the earliest and most extensively prevalent in the Order. The oldest Catechism of the eighteenth century gives it in these words:

"*Q*. What supports your Lodge?

"*A*. Three great Pillars.

"*Q*. What are their names?

"*A*. Wisdom, Strength, and Beauty.

"*Q*. Who doth the Pillar of Wisdom represent?

"*A*. The Master in the East.

"*Q*. Who doth the Pillar of Strength represent?

"*A*. The Senior Warden in the West.

"*Q*. Who doth the Pillar of Beauty represent?

"*A*. The Junior Warden in the South.

"*Q*. Why should the Master represent the Pillar of Wisdom?

"*A*. Because he gives instructions to the Crafts to carry on their work in a proper manner, with good harmony.

"*Q*. Why should the Senior Warden represent the Pillar of Strength?

"*A.* As the Sun sets to finish the day, so the Senior Warden stands in the West to pay the hirelings their wages, which is the strength and support of all business.

"*Q.* Why should the Junior Warden represent the Pillar of Beauty?

"*A.* Because he stands in the South at high twelve at noon, which is the beauty of the day, to call the men off from work to refreshment, and to see that they come on again in due time, that the Master may have pleasure and profit therein.

"*Q.* Why is it said that your Lodge is supported by these three great Pillars—Wisdom, Strength, and Beauty?

"*A.* Because Wisdom, Strength, and Beauty is the finisher of all works, and nothing can be carried on without them.

"*Q.* Why so, Brother?

"*A.* Because there is Wisdom to contrive, Strength to support, and Beauty to adorn."

Preston repeats substantially (but, of course, with an improvement of the language) this lecture; and he adds to it the symbolism of the three orders of architecture of which these pillars are said to be composed. These, he says, are the Tuscan, Doric, and Corinthian. The mistake of enumerating the Tuscan among the ancient orders was corrected by subsequent ritualists. Preston also referred the supports symbolically to the three Ancient Grand Masters. This symbolism was afterward transferred by Webb from the First to the Third Degree.

Webb, in modifying the lecture of Preston, attributed the supports not to the Lodge, but to the Institution; an unnecessary alteration, since the Lodge is but the type of the Institution. His language is: "Our Institution is said to be supported by wisdom, strength, and beauty; because it is necessary that there should be wisdom to contrive, strength to support, and beauty to adorn all great and important undertakings." He follows the ancient reference of the pillars to the three officers, and adopts Preston's symbolism of the three orders of architecture, but he very wisely substitutes the Ionic for the Tuscan. Hemming, in his lectures adopted by the Grand Lodge of England in 1813, retained the symbolism of the pillars, but gave a change in the language. He said: "A Mason's Lodge is supported by three grand pillars. They are called Wisdom, Strength, and Beauty. Wisdom to contrive, Strength to support, and Beauty to adorn. Wisdom to direct us in all our undertakings, Strength to support us in all our difficulties, and Beauty to adorn the inward man."

The French Masons preserve the same symbolism. Bazot (*Manuel*, p. 225) says: "Three great pillars sustain the Lodge. The first, the emblem of wisdom, is represented by the Master who sits in the east, whence light and his commands emanate. The second, the emblem of strength, is represented by the Senior Warden, who sits in the west, where the workmen are paid, whose strength and existence are preserved by the wages which they receive. The third and last pillar is the emblem of beauty; it is represented by the Junior Warden, who sits in the south, because that part typifies the middle of the day, whose beauty is perfect; during this time the workmen repose from work; and it is thence that the Junior Warden sees them return to the Lodge and resume their labors."

The German Masons have also maintained these three pillars in their various rituals. Schröder, the author of the most philosophical one, says: "The universal Lodge, as well as every particular one, is supported by three great invisible columns—Wisdom, Strength, and Beauty; for as every building is planned and fashioned by Wisdom, owes its durability and solidity to Strength, and is made symmetrical and harmonious by Beauty, so ought our spiritual building to be designed by Wisdom, which gives it the firm foundation of Truth, on which the Strength of conviction may build, and self-knowledge complete the structure, and give it permanence and continuance by means of right, justice, and resolute perseverance; and Beauty will finally adorn the edifice with all the social virtues, with brotherly love and union, with benevolence, kindness, and a comprehensive philanthropy."

Stieglitz, in his work *On the Old German Architecture*(i.,239), after complaining that the building principles of the old German artists were lost to us, because, considering them as secrets of the brotherhood, they deemed it unlawful to commit them to writing, yet thinks that enough may be found in the old documents of the Fraternity to sustain the conjecture that these three supports were familiar to the Operative Masons. He says:

"Wisdom, Strength, and Beauty were honored by them as supporting pillars for the perfect accomplishment of the works; and thence they considered them symbolically as essential pillars for the support of the Lodge. Wisdom, which, established on science, gives invention to the artist, and the right arrangement and appropriate disposition of the whole and of all its parts; Strength, which, proceeding from the harmonious balance of all the forces, promotes the secure erection of the building; and Beauty, which, manifested in God's creation of the world, adorns the work and makes it perfect."

I can hardly doubt, from the early appearance of this symbol of the three supports, and from its unchanged form in all countries, that it dates its origin from a period earlier than the revival in 1717, and that it may be traced to the Operative Masons of the Middle Ages, where Stieglitz says it existed.

One thing is clear, that the symbol is not found among those of the Gnostics, and was not familiar to the Rosicrucians; and, therefore, out of the three sources of our symbolism—Gnosticism, Rosicrucianism, and Operative Masonry—it is most probable that it has been derived from the last.

When the high degrees were fabricated, and Christianity began to furnish its symbols and doctrine to the new Masonry, the old Temple of Solomon was by some of them abandoned, and that other temple adopted to which Christ had referred when he said, "Destroy this temple, and in three days I will raise it up." The old supports of wisdom, strength, and beauty, which had sufficed for the Gothic builders, and which they, borrowing them from the results of their labors on the cathedrals, had applied symbolically to their Lodges, were discarded, and more spiritual supports for a more spiritual temple were to be selected. There had been a new dispensation, and there was to be a new temple. The great doctrine of that new dispensation was to furnish the supporting pillars for the new temple. In these high Christianized degrees we therefore no longer find the columns of Wisdom, Strength, and Beauty, but the spiritual ones of Faith, Hope, and Charity.

But the form of the symbolism is unchanged. The East, the West, and the South are still the spots where we find the new, as we did the old, pillars. Thus the triangle is preserved; for the triangle is the Masonic symbol of God, who is, after all, the true support of the Lodge.

Supreme Authority. The supreme authority in Masonry is that dogmatic power from whose decisions there is no appeal. At the head of every Rite there is a supreme authority which controls and directs the acts of all subordinate bodies of the Rite. In the United States, and in the American Rite which is there practised, it would, at the first glance, appear that the supreme authority is divided. That of symbolic Lodges is vested in Grand Lodges, of Royal Arch Chapters in Grand Chapters, of Royal and Select Councils in Grand Councils, and of Commanderies of Knights Templar in the Grand Encampment. And so far as ritualistic questions and matters of internal arrangement are concerned, the supreme authority is so divided. But the supreme authority of Masonry in each State is actually vested in the Grand Lodge of that State. It is universally recognized as Masonic law that a Mason expelled or suspended by the Grand Lodge, or by a subordinate Lodge with the approval and confirmation of the Grand Lodge, thereby stands expelled or suspended from Royal Arch, from Cryptic, and from Templar Masonry. The same rules apply to the A. and A. S. Rite. Nor can he be permitted to visit any of the bodies in either of these divisions of the Rite so long as he remains under the ban of expulsion of the Grand Lodge. So the status or condition of every Mason in the jurisdiction is controlled by the Grand Lodge, from whose action on that subject there is no appeal. The Masonic life and death of every member of the Craft, in every class of the Order, is in its hands, and thus the Grand Lodge becomes the real supreme authority of the jurisdiction.

Supreme Commander of the Stars. (*Suprême Commandeur des Astres.*) A degree said to have been invented at Geneva in 1779, and found in the collection of M. A. Viany.

Supreme Consistory. (*Suprême Consistoire.*) The title of some of the highest bodies in the Rite of Mizraim. In the original construction of the Rite at Naples the members of the Ninetieth Degree met in a Supreme Consistory. When the Bederides took charge of the Rite they changed the title of the governing body to Supreme Council.

Supreme Council. The Supreme Masonic authority of the Ancient and Accepted Scottish Rite is called a Supreme Council. A Supreme Council claims to derive the authority for its existence from the Constitutions of 1786.* I have no intention here of entering into the question of the authenticity of that document. The question is open to the historian, and has been amply discussed, with the natural result of contradictory conclusions. But he who accepts the Ancient and Accepted Scottish Rite as genuine Freemasonry, and owes his obedience as a Mason to its constituted authorities, is compelled to recognize those Constitutions wherever or whenever they may have been enacted as the fundamental law—the constitutional rule of his Rite. To their authority all the Supreme Councils owe their legitimate existence.

Dr. Frederick Dalcho, who, I think, may very properly be considered as the founder in the United States, and therefore in the world, of the Ancient and Accepted Scottish Rite in its present form as the legitimate successor of the Rite of Perfection or of Herodem, has given in the *Circular* written by him, and published December 4, 1802, by the Supreme Council at Charleston, the following account of the establishment of Supreme Councils:

"On the 1st of May, 1786, the Grand Constitution of the thirty-third degree, called the Supreme Council of Sovereign Grand Inspectors General, was finally ratified by his Majesty the King of Prussia, who, as Grand Commander of the Order of Prince of the Royal Secret, possessed the Sovereign Masonic power over all the Craft. In the new Constitution, this high power was conferred on a Supreme Council of nine brethren in each nation, who possess all the Masonic prerogatives, in their own district, that his Majesty individually possessed, and are *Sovereigns of Masonry.*"

The law for the establishment of a Supreme Council is found in the following words in the Latin Constitutions of 1786: "The first degree will be subordinated to the second, that to the third, and so in order to the sublime, Thirty-third, and last, which will watch over all the others, will correct their errors and will govern them, and whose congregation or convention will be a dogmatic *Supreme Grand Council*, the Defender and Conservator of the Order, which it will govern and administer according to the present Constitutions and those which may hereafter be enacted."

But the Supreme Council at Charleston derived its authority and its information from what are called the French Constitutions; and it is in them that we find the statement

*See *Constitutions of 1786.*

that Frederick invested the Supreme Council with the same prerogatives that he himself possessed, a provision not contained in the Latin Constitutions. The twelfth article says: "The Supreme Council will exercise all the Masonic sovereign powers of which his Majesty Frederick II., King of Prussia, was possessed."*

These Constitutions further declare (Art. 5) that "every Supreme Council is composed of nine Inspectors-General, five of whom should profess the Christian religion." In the same article it is provided that "there shall be only one Council of this degree in each nation or kingdom in Europe, two in the United States of America as far removed as possible the one from the other, one in the English islands of America, and one likewise in the French islands."

It was in compliance with these Constitutions that the Supreme Council at Charleston, South Carolina, was instituted. In the *Circular*, already cited, Dalcho gives this account of its establishment:

"On the 31st of May, 1801, the Supreme Council of the thirty-third degree for the United States of America was opened, with the high honors of Masonry, by Brothers John Mitchell and Frederick Dalcho, Sovereign Grand Inspectors-General; and in the course of the present year, [1802,] the whole number of Grand Inspectors-General was completed, agreeably to the Grand Constitutions."

This was the first Supreme Council of the Ancient and Accepted Scottish Rite ever formed; from it has emanated either directly or indirectly all the other Councils which have been since established in America or Europe; and although it now exercises jurisdiction only over a part of the United States under the title of the Supreme Council for the Southern Jurisdiction of the United States, it claims to be and is recognized as "the Mother Council of the World."

Under its authority a Supreme Council, the second in date, was established by Count de Grasse in the French West Indies, in 1802; a third in France, by the same authority, in 1804; and a fourth in Italy in 1805. In 1813 the Masonic jurisdiction of the United States was divided; the Mother Council establishing at the city of New York a Supreme Council for the Northern Jurisdiction, and over the States north of the Ohio and east of the Mississippi, reserving to itself all the remainder of the territory of the United States. The seat of the Northern Council is now at Boston; and although the offices of the Grand Commander and Secretary-General of the Southern Council are now in the city of Washington, whence its documents emanate, its seat is still constructively at Charleston.

On their first organization, the Supreme Councils were limited to nine members in each. That rule continued to be enforced in the Mother Council until the year 1859, when the number was increased to thirty-three. Similar enlargements have been made in all the other Supreme Councils except that of Scotland, which still retains the original number.

The officers of the original Supreme Council at Charleston were: a Most Puissant Sovereign Grand Commander, Most Illustrious Lieutenant Grand Commander, Illustrious Treasurer-General of the Holy Empire, Illustrious Secretary-General of the Holy Empire, Illustrious Grand Master of Ceremonies, and Illustrious Captain of the Guards.

In 1859, with the change of numbers in the membership, there was also made a change in the number and titles of the officers. These now in the Mother Council, according to its present Constitution, are: 1. Sovereign Grand Commander; 2. Lieutenant Grand Commander; 3. Secretary-General of the Holy Empire; 4. Grand Prior; 5. Grand Chancellor; 6. Grand Minister of State; 7. Treasurer-General of the Holy Empire; 8. Grand Auditor; 9. Grand Almoner; 10. Grand Constable; 11. Grand Chamberlain; 12. First Grand Equerry; 13. Second Grand Equerry; 14. Grand Standard-Bearer; 15. Grand Sword-Bearer; 16. Grand Herald. The Secretary-General is properly the seventh officer, but by a decree of the Supreme Council he is made the third officer in rank "while the office continues to be filled by Bro. Albert G. Mackey, the present incumbent, who is the Dean of the Supreme Council." Dr. Mackey held this position until his death.

The officers somewhat vary in other Supreme Councils, but the presiding and recording officers are everywhere a Sovereign Grand Commander and a Secretary-General of the Holy Empire.

Supreme Councils, A. A. Scottish Rite. These Councils are organised in almost every country of the world, a number being under royal patronage, and in many nations are the governing power over all existing Masonry. A synoptical history of all the Supreme Councils that have ever existed, with the manner of their formation in chronological order, is published in the *Proceedings of the Supreme Council for the Northern Masonic Jurisdiction for 1908*. From this article is taken the following list (on p. 742), giving the Supreme Councils which have received general recognition.

The following Supreme Councils have been formed, but have not received formal recognition and the courtesy of an exchange of representation: Florence, Hungary, Luxembourg, Naples, Palermo, Rome, and Turkey. The number of these Supreme Bodies accomplishes 33.

On the 22d of September, 1875, a congress of the various Supreme Councils was convened at Lausanne, Switzerland, to consider such matters as might then and there be submitted for consideration and united action, and be deemed for the general benefit of the Rite.

*This shows the difference in the sources of authority between the A. and A. S. Rite and Symbolic Masonry. The former is monarchical, while the latter is supposed to be democratic. [E. E. C.]

Supreme Council.	Grand Commander.	Orient.	Constituted.
America, N. J. United States	Hon. Barton Smith, 33°	Boston	Aug. 5, 1813
America, S. J. United States	Hon. George F. Moore, 33°	Washington	May 31, 1801
Argentine Republic	Emilio Gouchon, 33°	Buenos Ayres	Sept. 13, 1858
Belgium	Comte Goblet d'Alviella, 33°	Bruxelles	Mar. 11, 1817
Brasil	Dr. Lauro Sodré, 33°	Lavradio	1829
Canada	Hon. J. Morison Gibson, 33°	Hamilton	Oct. 16, 1874
Central America (Guatemala)	Dr. Juan Padilla, 33°	San José	Nov. 27, 1870
Chili	Victor G.mo. Ewing, 33°	Santiago	May 11, 1870
Colombia, U. S. of	Dr. Simon Bossa, 33°	Cartagena	
Colon, for Cuba	Dr. Manuel S. Castellanos, 33°	Havana	Mar. 25, 1859
Dominican Republic	C. Rafael Alardo, 33°		
England, Wales, etc	Rt. Hon. the Earl of Dartrey, 33°	London	Oct. 26, 1845
Egypt	Idris Bey Ragheb, 33°	Cairo	1878
France	Jean M. Raymond, 33°	Paris	Sept. 22, 1804
Greece	Dr. Prof. E. M. Galani, 33°	Athens	July 24, 1872
Ireland	Col. A. Vesey Davoren, 33°	Dublin	June 11, 1826
Italy	Cav. Saverio Fera, 33°	Rome	1858
Mexico	Hon. José Castellot, 33°	Mexico	April 28, 1868
Paraguay	Christian G. Heisecke, 33°		
Peru	Col. Alejanro Rivera, 33°	Lima	Nov. 2, 1830
Portugal	Sebastio de Megalhaes Lima, 33°	Lisbon	Oct. 30, 1869
Scotland	Rt. Hon. the Earl of Kintore, 33°	Edinburgh	1846
Spain	Dead	Madrid	July 4, 1811
Switzerland	Paul Etier, 33°	Lausanne	Mar. 30, 1873
Turkey	S. A. Prince Aziz Hassan Pasha	Constantinople	1908
Uruguay	Hon. Ricardo J. Areco, 33°	Montevideo	1856
Venezuela	Dr. Emilio Conde Flores, 33°		

Much speculation and lack of confidence was the result among many of the invited participants lest they might be committed by uniting in the conference. The Congress, however, was held, and a declaration of principles set forth. There was also stipulated and agreed upon a treaty, involving highly important measures, embraced within twenty-three articles, which was concluded September 22, 1875. "The intimate alliance and confederation of the contracting Masonic powers extended and extends under their auspices to all the subordinates and to all true and faithful Masons of their respective jurisdictions." "Whoever may have illegitimately and irregularly received any Degree of the A. A. Scottish Rite can nowhere enjoy the prerogatives of a Freemason until he has been lawfully healed by the regular Supreme Council of his own country." The confederated powers again recognized and proclaimed as Grand Constitutions of the A. A. Scottish Rite, the constitutions and statutes adopted May 1, 1876, with the modifications and "Tiler" adopted by the Congress of Lausanne, the 22d of September, 1875.

The declaration and articles were signed by representatives of eighteen Supreme Councils, who recognised the territorial jurisdictions of the following Supreme Councils, to wit:

Northern Jur., U. S.	Southern Jur., U. S.
Central America,	England,
Belgium,	Canada,
Chili,	Colon,
Scotland,	U. S. of Colombia,
France,	Greece,
Hungary,	Ireland,
Italy,	Mexico,
Peru,	Portugal,
Argentine Republic,	Switzerland,
Uruguay.	Venezuela.

The same delegates, by virtue of the plenary powers they held, and by which they were justified, promised, for their principals, to maintain and defend with all their power, to preserve, and cause to be observed and respected, not only the territorial jurisdiction of the Confederated Supreme Councils represented in the said Congress at Lausanne, and the parties therein contracting, but also the territorial jurisdiction of the other Supreme Councils named in the foregoing table.

It is not possible to give statistics as to the number of the A. A. Scottish Rite Masons in the world, but calculating those, of whatever degree, who are governed by Supreme Councils in the different nations, it is but reasonable to presume one-half of the entire Fraternity is of that Rite, and as a matter of extensiveness, it is *par excellence* the Universal Rite. In many nations there is no other Rite known, and therein it confers all the degrees of its system, including the first three. Among the English-speaking Masons, it builds its structure upon the York or the American system of three degrees.

In the United States the number of this Rite, enrolled and unenrolled, will approximate one hundred and fifty thousand in the two Jurisdictions. Its organizations are to be found in every prominent city and many towns, and in numerous instances possessing and occupying temples built specially to accommodate its own peculiar forms, elegant of structure and in appointments, and of great financial value.

The progress of this Rite in the last half century has been most remarkable, and its future appears without a cloud.

[C. T. McClenachan.]

Suspension. This is a Masonic punishment, which consists of a temporary deprivation of the rights and privileges of Masonry. It is of two kinds, *definite* and *indefinite;* but the effect of the penalty, for the time that it lasts, is the same in both kinds. The mode in which restoration is effected differs in each.

1. *Definite Suspension.*—By definite suspension is meant a deprivation of the rights and privileges of Masonry for a fixed period of time, which period is always named in the sentence. By the operation of this penalty, a Mason is for the time prohibited from the exercise of all his Masonic privileges. His rights are placed in abeyance, and he can neither visit Lodges, hold Masonic communication, nor receive Masonic relief, during the period for which he has been suspended. Yet his Masonic citizenship is not lost. In this respect suspension may be compared to the Roman punishment of "relegatio," or banishment, which Ovid, who had endured it, describes (*Tristia*, v. 11), with technical correctness, as a penalty which "takes away neither life nor property nor rights of citizens, but only drives away from the country." So by suspension the rights and duties of the Mason are not obliterated, but their exercise only interdicted for the period limited by the sentence, and as soon as this has terminated he at once resumes his former position in the Order, and is reinvested with all his Masonic rights, whether those rights be of a private or of an official nature.

Thus, if an officer of a Lodge has been suspended for three months from all the rights and privileges of Masonry, a suspension of his official functions also takes place. But a suspension from the discharge of the functions of an office is not a deprivation of the office; and therefore, as soon as the three months to which the suspension had been limited have expired, the brother resumes all his rights in the Order and the Lodge, and with them, of course, the office which he had held at the time that the sentence of suspension had been inflicted.

2. *Indefinite Suspension.*—This is a suspension for a period not determined and fixed by the sentence, but to continue during the pleasure of the Lodge. In this respect only does it differ from the preceding punishment. The position of a Mason, under definite or indefinite suspension, is precisely the same as to the exercise of all his rights and privileges, which in both cases remain in abeyance, and restoration in each brings with it a resumption of all the rights and functions, the exercise of which had been interrupted by the sentence of suspension.

Neither definite nor indefinite suspension can be inflicted except after due notification and trial, and then only by a vote of two-thirds of the members present.

Restoration to Masonic rights differs, as I have said, in these two kinds. Restoration from definite suspension may take place either by a vote of the Lodge abridging the time, when two-thirds of the members must concur, or it will terminate by the natural expiration of the period fixed by the sentence, and that without any vote of the Lodge. Thus, if a member is suspended for three months, at the end of the third month his suspension terminates, and he is *ipso facto* restored to all his rights and privileges.

In the case of indefinite suspension, the only method of restoration is by a vote of the Lodge at a regular meeting, two-thirds of those present concurring.

Lastly, it may be observed that, as the suspension of a member suspends his prerogatives, it also suspends his dues. He cannot be expected, in justice, to pay for that which he does not receive, and Lodge dues are simply a compensation made by a member for the enjoyment of the privileges of membership.

Sussex, Duke of. The Duke of Sussex is entitled to a place in Masonic biography, not only because, of all the Grand Masters on record, he held the office the longest—the Duke of Leinster, of Ireland, alone excepted—but also because of his devotion to the Institution, and the zeal with which he cultivated and protected its interests. Augustus Frederick, ninth child and sixth son of George III., King of England, was born January 27, 1773. He was initiated in 1798 at a Lodge in Berlin. In 1805, the honorary rank of a Past Grand Master was conferred on him by the Grand Lodge of England. May 13, 1812, he was appointed Deputy Grand Master; and April 13, 1813, the Prince Regent, afterward George IV., having declined a reelection as Grand Master, the Duke of Sussex was unanimously elected; and in the same year the two rival Grand Lodges of England were united. The Duke was Most Excellent Zerubbabel of the Grand Chapter, and Grand Superintendent of the Grand Conclave of Knights Templars. He never, however, took any interest in the orders of knighthood, to which, indeed, he appears to have had some antipathy. During his long career the Grand Conclave met but once. By annual elections, he retained the office of Grand Master until his death, which took place April 21, 1843, in the seventy-first year of his age, having completed a Masonic administration as head of the English Craft of upward of thirty years.

During that long period, it was impossible that some errors should not have been committed. The Grand Master's conduct in reference to two distinguished Masons, Drs. Crucefix and Oliver, was by no means creditable to his reputation for justice or forbearance. But the general tenor of his life as an upright man and Mason, and his great attachment to the Order, tended to compensate for the few mistakes of his administration. One who had been most bitterly opposed to his course in reference to Brothers Crucefix and Oliver, and had not been sparing of his condemnation, paid, after his death, this tribute to his Masonic virtues and abilities:

"As a Freemason," said the *Freemasons' Quarterly Review* (1843, p. 120), "the Duke of Sussex was the most accomplished craftsman of his day. His knowledge of the mysteries was, as it were, intuitive; his reading on the subject was extensive; his correspondence equally so; and his desire to be introduced to any brother from whose experience he could derive any information had in it a craving that marked his great devotion to the Order."

On the occasion of the presentation of an offering by the Fraternity in 1838, the Duke gave the following account of his Masonic life, which embodies sentiments that are highly honorable to him:

"My duty as your Grand Master is to take care that no political or religious question intrudes itself; and had I thought that, in presenting this tribute, any political feeling had influenced the brethren, I can only say that then the Grand Master would not have been gratified. Our object is unanimity, and we can find a centre of unanimity unknown elsewhere. I recollect twenty-five years ago, at a meeting in many respects similar to the present, a magnificent jewel (by voluntary vote) was presented to the Earl Moira previous to his journey to India. I had the honor to preside, and I remember the powerful and beautiful appeal which that excellent brother made on the occasion. I am now sixty-six years of age—I say this without regret—the true Mason ought to think that the first day of his birth is but a step on his way to the final close of life. When I tell you that I have completed forty years of a Masonic life—there may be older Masons—but that is a pretty good specimen of my attachment to the Order.

"In 1798, I entered Masonry in a Lodge at Berlin, and there I served several offices, and as Warden was a representative of the Lodge in the Grand Lodge of England. I afterwards was acknowledged and received with the usual compliment paid to a member of the Royal Family, by being appointed a Past Grand Warden. I again went abroad for three years, and on my return joined various Lodges, and upon the retirement of the Prince Regent, who became Patron of the Order, I was elected Grand Master. An epoch of considerable interest intervened, and I became charged, in 1813–14, with a most important mission—the union of the two London societies. My most excellent brother, the Duke of Kent, accepted the title of Grand Master of the Atholl Masons, as they were denominated; I was the Grand Master of those called the Prince of Wales's. In three months we carried the union of the two societies, and I had the happiness of presiding over the united Fraternity. This I consider to have been the happiest event of my life. It brought all Masons upon the Level and the Square, and showed the world at large that the differences of common life did not exist in Masonry, and it showed to Masons that by a long pull, a strong pull, and a pull all together, what great good might be effected."

Sweden. Freemasonry was introduced into Sweden in the year 1735, when Count Sparre, who had been initiated in Paris, established a Lodge at Stockholm. Of this Lodge scarcely anything is known, and it probably soon fell into decay. In 1738, King Frederick I. promulgated a decree which interdicted all Masonic meetings under the penalty of death. At the end of seven years the edict was removed, and Masonry became popular. Lodges were publicly recognized, and in 1746 the Masons of Stockholm struck a medal on the occasion of the birth of the Prince Royal, afterward Gustavus III. In 1753, the Swedish Masons laid the foundation of an orphan asylum at Stockholm which was built by the voluntary contributions of the Fraternity, without any assistance from the State. In 1762, King Adolphus Frederick, in a letter to the Grand Master, declared himself the Protector of the Swedish Lodges, and expressed his readiness to become the Chief of Freemasonry in his dominions, and to assist in defraying the expenses of the Order. In 1765, Lord Blayney, Grand Master of England, granted a Deputation to Charles Fullmann, Secretary of the English embassy at Stockholm, as Provincial Grand Master, with the authority to constitute Lodges in Sweden. At the same time, Schubarb, a member of the Rite of Strict Observance, appeared at Stockholm, and endeavored to establish that Rite. He had but little success, as the high degrees had been previously introduced from France.

But this admixture of English, French, and German Masonry occasioned great dissatisfaction, and gave rise, about this time, to the establishment of an independent system known as the Swedish Rite. In 1770, the Illuminated Grand Chapter was established, and the Duke of Sudermania appointed the Vicarius Salomonis. In 1780, the Grand Lodge of Sweden, which for some years had been in abeyance, was revived, and the same Prince elected Grand Master. This act gave an independent and responsible position to Swedish Masonry, and the progress of the Institution in that kingdom has been ever since regular and uninterrupted. On March 22, 1793, Gustavus IV., the King of Sweden, was initiated into Masonry in a Lodge at Stockholm, the Duke of Sudermania, then acting as Regent of the kingdom, presiding as the Grand Master of the Order.

In 1799, on the application of the Duke of Sudermania, a fraternal alliance was consummated between the Grand Lodges of England and Sweden, and mutual representatives appointed.

In 1809, the Duke of Sudermania ascended the throne under the title of Charles XIII. He continued his attachment to the Order, and retained the Grand Mastership. As a singular mark of his esteem for Freemasonry, the king instituted, May 27, 1811, a new order of knighthood, known as the Order of Charles XIII., the members of which were to be selected from Freemasons only. In the Patent of institution the king declared that, in founding the Order, his intention "was not only to excite his subjects to the practice of charity, and to perpetuate the memory of the devotion of the Masonic Order to his person while it was under his protection, but also to give further proofs of his royal benevolence to those whom he had so long embraced and cherished under the name of Freemasons." The Order, besides the princes of the royal family, was to consist of twenty-seven lay, and three ecclesiastical knights, all of whom were to hold equal rank.

The Grand Lodge of Sweden practises the Swedish Rite, and exercises its jurisdiction under the title of the National Grand Lodge of Sweden. It has now 13 St. Andrew's and 27 St. John's Lodges under its jurisdiction. (See *Swedish Rite.*)

Swedenborg. Emanuel Swedenborg, a distinguished theologian of his age, and the founder of a sect which still exists, has been always mythically connected with Freemasonry. The eagerness is indeed extraordinary with which all Masonic writers, German, French, English, and American, have sought to connect the name and labors of the Swedish sage with the Masonic institution, and that, too, without the slightest foundation for such a theory either in his writings, or in any credible memorials of his life.

Findel (*Hist. of F. M.*, p. 329), speaking of the reforms in Swedish Masonry, says: "Most likely Swedenborg, the mystic and visionary, used his influence in bringing about the new system; at all events, he smoothed the way for it." Lenning speaks of the influence of his teachings upon the Swedish system of Freemasonry, although he does not absolutely claim him as a Mason.

Reghellini, in his *Esprit du Dogme de la Franche-Maçonnerie*, writes thus: "Swedenborg made many very learned researches on the subject of the Masonic mysteries. He thought that their doctrines were of the highest antiquity, having emanated from the Egyptians, the Persians, the Magi, the Jews, and the Greeks. He also became the head of a new religion in his effort to reform that of Rome. For this purpose he wrote his *Celestial Jerusalem*, or his Spiritual World:* he mingled with his reform, ideas which were purely Masonic. In this celestial Jerusalem the Word formerly communicated by God to Moses is found; this word is *Jehovah*, lost on earth, but which he invites us to find in Great Tartary, a country still governed, even in our days, by the patriarchs, by which he means allegorically to say that this people most nearly approach to the primitive condition of the perfection of innocence." The same writer, in his *Maçonnerie considerée comme le resultat des religions Egyptienne, Jeuve et Chrétienne* (ii., 454), repeatedly speaks of Swedenborg as a Masonic reformer, and sometimes as a Masonic impostor. Ragon also cites Reghellini in his *Orthodoxie Maçonnique* (p. 255), and recognises Swedenborg as the founder of a Masonic system. Thory, in his *Acta Latomorum*, cites "the system of Swedenborg"; and in fact al' the French writers on Masonic ritualism appear to have borrowed their idea of the Swedish theosophist from the statement of Reghellini, and have not hesitiated to rank him among the principal Masonic teachers of his time.

*There is no work written by Swedenborg which bears either of those titles. It is possible that Reghellini alludes either to the *Arcana Cælestia*, published in 1749–1753, or to the *De Nova Hierosolyma*, published in 1758.

Oliver is the earliest of the English Masonic writers of eminence who has referred to Swedenborg. He, too often careless of the weight of his expressions and facile in the acceptance of authority, speaks of the degrees, the system, and the Masonry of Swedenborg just in the same tone as he would of those of Cagliostro, of Hund, or of Tschoudy.

And, lastly, in America we have a recent writer, Bro. Samuel Beswick, who is evidently a man of ability and of considerable research. He has culminated to the zenith in his assumpt ons of the Masonic character of Swedenborg. He published at New York, in 1870, a volume entitled, *The Swedenborg Rite and the Great Masonic Leaders of the Eighteen h Century*. In this work, which, outside of its Swedenborgian fancies, contains much interesting matter, he traces the Masonic life of Swedenborg from his initiation, the time and place of which he makes in 1706, in a Scottish Lodge in the town of Lund, in Sweden, which is a fair specimen of the value of his historical statements. But after treating the great Swede as a Masonic reformer, as the founder of a Rite, and as evincing during his whole life a deep interest in Freemasonry, he appears to me to surrender the whole question in the following closing words of his work:

"From the very moment of his initiation, Swedenborg appears to have resolved never to allude to his membership or to his knowledge of Freemasonry, either publicly or privately. He appears to have made up his mind to keep it a profound secret, and to regard it as something which had no relation to his public life.

"We have searched his *Itinerary*, which contains brief references to everything he saw, heard, and read during his travels, for something having relation to his Masonic knowledge, intercourse, correspondence, visits to Lodges, places, or persons; but there is a studied silence, a systematic avoidance of all allusion to it. In his theological works, his *Memorable Relations* speak of almost every sect in Christendom, and of all sorts of organizations, or of individuals belonging thereto. But Masonry is an exception: there is a systematic silence in relation to it."

It is true that he finds in this reticence of Swedenborg the evidence that he was a Mason and interested in Masonry, but others will most probably form a different conclusion. The fact is that Swedenborg never was a Freemason. The reputation of being one, that has been so continuously attributed to him by Masonic writers, is based first upon the assumptions of Reghellini, whose statements in his *Esprit du Dogme* were never questioned nor their truth investigated, as they should have been, but were blindly followed by succeeding writers. Neither Wilkinson, nor Burk, nor White, who wrote his biography—the last the most exhaustively—nor anything in his own voluminous writings, lead us to any such conclusion.

But the second and more important basis on which the theory of a Swedenborgian Masonry has been built is the conduct of some of his own disciples, who, imbued with his religious views, being Masons, carried the spirit of the New Jerusalem doctrines into their Masonic speculations. There was, it is true, a Masonic Rite or System of Swedenborg, but its true history is this:

About that period we find Pernetty working out his schemes of Masonic reform. Pernetty was a theosophist, a Hermetic philosopher, a disciple, to some extent, of Jacob Böhme, that prince of mystics. To such a man, the reveries, the visions, and the spiritual speculations of Swedenborg were peculiarly attractive. He accepted them as an addition to the theosophic views which he already had received. About the year 1760 he established at Avignon his Rite of the Illuminati, in which the reveries of both Böhme and Swedenborg were introduced. In 1783 this system was reformed by the Marquis de Thomé, another Swedenborgian, and out of that reform arose what was called the "Rite of Swedenborg," not because Swedenborg had established it, or had anything directly to do with its establishment, but because it was based on his peculiar theological views, and because its symbolism was borrowed from the ideas he had advanced in the highly symbolical works that he had written. A portion of these degrees, or other degrees much like them, have been called apocalyptic; not because St. John had, any more than Swedenborg, a connection with them, but because their system of initiation is based on the mystical teachings of the Apocalypse; a work which, not less than the theories of the Swede, furnishes abundant food for a system of Masonico-religious symbolism. Benedict Chastanier, also another disciple of Swedenborg, and who was one of the founders of the Avignon Society, carried these views into England, and founded at London a similar Rite, which afterward was changed into a purely religious association under the name of "The Theosophical Society, instituted for the purpose of promoting the Heavenly Doctrines of the New Jerusalem."

In one of his visions, Swedenborg thus describes a palace in the spiritual world which he had visited. From passages such as these which abound in his various treatises, the theosophic Masons concocted those degrees which have been called the Masonry of Swedenborg. To no reader of the passage annexed can its appropriateness as the basis of a system of symbolism fail to be apparent.

"I accordingly entered the temple, which was magnificent, and in the midst of which a woman was represented clothed in purple, holding in her right hand a golden crown piece, and in her left a chain of pearls. The statue and the representation were only *fantastic representations*; for these *infernal spirits*, by closing the interior degree and opening the exterior only, are able at the pleasure of their imagination to represent magnificent objects. Perceiving that they were illusions, I prayed to the Lord. Immediately the interior of my spirit was opened, and I saw, instead of the superb temple, a tottering house, open to the weather from the top to the bottom. In the place of the woman-statue, an image was suspended, having the head of a dragon, the body of a leopard, the feet of a bear, and the mouth of a lion: in short, it was the beast rising out of the sea, as described in the Apocalypse xiii. 2. In the place of a park, *there was a marsh full of frogs*, and I was informed that under this marsh there was a great HEWN STONE, beneath which the WORD was entirely hidden. Afterwards I said to the prelate, *who was the fabricator of these illusions*, 'Is that your temple?' 'Yes,' replied he, 'it is.' Immediately his interior sight was opened like mine, and he saw what I did. 'How now, what do I see?' cried he. I told him that it was the effect of *the celestial light, which discovers the interior quality of everything*, and which taught him at that very moment what faith separated from good works was. While I was speaking, a wind blowing from the *east* destroyed the temple and the image, dried up the marsh, and *discovered the stone under which the Sacred Word was concealed*. A genial warmth, like that of the spring, descended from heaven; and in the place of that temple we saw a tent, the exterior of which was very plain. I looked into the interior of it, and there I saw *the foundation-stone beneath which the Sacred Word was concealed*, ornamented with precious stones, the splendor of which, diffusing itself over the walls of the temple, diversified the colors of the paintings, which represented cherubims. The angels, perceiving me to be filled with admiration, told me that I should see still greater wonders than these. They were then permitted to *open* the *third heaven*, inhabited by the celestial angels, who dwelt in *love*. All on a sudden the splendor of a *light of fire* caused the temple to disappear, and left nothing to be seen but the Lord himself, standing upon the *foundation-stone*—the Lord, who was the Word, such as he showed Himself. (Apocal. i. 13–16.) Holiness immediately filled all the interior of the spirit of the angels, upon which they *made an effort* to prostrate themselves, but the Lord *shut the passage to the light* from the *third* heaven, *opening* the passage to the light of the *second*, which caused the temple to reappear, with the tent in the midst."

Such passages as these might lead one to suppose that Swedenborg was familiar with the system of Masonic ritualism. His complete reticence upon the subject, however, and the whole tenor of his life, his studies, and his habits, assure us that such was not the case; and that if there was really a borrowing of one from the other, and not an accidental coincidence, it was the Freemasons of the high degrees who borrowed from Swedenborg, and not Swedenborg from them. And if so, we cannot deny that he has unwittingly exercised a powerful influence on Masonry.

Swedenborg, Rite of. The so-called Rite of Swedenborg, the history of whose foundation has been given in the preceding article, consists of six degrees: 1. Apprentice. 2. Fellow-Craft. 3. Master Neophyte. 4. Illuminated Theosophite. 5. Blue Brother. 6. Red Brother. It is said to be still practised by some of the Swedish Lodges, but is elsewhere extinct. Reghellini, in his *Esprit du Dogme*, gives it as consisting of eight degrees; but he has evidently confounded it with the Rite of Martinism, also a theosophic Rite, and the ritualism of which also partakes of a Swedenborgian character.

Swedish Rite. The Swedish Rite was established about the year 1777, and is indebted for its existence to the exertions and influence of King Gustavus III. It is a mixture of the pure Rite of York, the high degrees of the French, the Templarism of the former Strict Observance, and the system of Rosicrucianism. Zinnendorf also had something to do with the formation of the Rite, although his authority was subsequently repudiated by the Swedish Masons. It is a Rite confined exclusively to the kingdom of Sweden, and was really established as a reform or compromise to reconcile the conflicting elements of English, German, and French Masonry that about the middle of the last century convulsed the Masonic atmosphere of Sweden. It consists of twelve degrees, as follows:

1, 2, 3. The three Symbolic degrees, constituting the St. John's Lodge.

4, 5. The Scottish Fellow-Craft and the Scottish Master of St. Andrew. These constitute the Scottish Lodge. The Fifth Degree entitles its members to civil rank in the kingdom.

6. Knight of the East. In this degree, which is apocalyptic, the New Jerusalem and its twelve gates are represented.

7. Knight of the West, or True Templar, Master of the Key. The jewel of this degree, which is a triangle with five red rosettes, refers to the five wounds of the Savior.

8. Knight of the South, or Favorite Brother of St. John. This is a Rosicrucian degree, the ceremony of initiation being derived from that of the Medieval Alchemists.

9. Favorite Brother of St. Andrew. This degree is evidently derived from the Masonry of the Scottish Rite.

10. Member of the Chapter.

11. Dignitary of the Chapter.

12. Vicar of Solomon.

The first nine degrees are under the obedience of the National Grand Lodge of Sweden and Norway, and essentially compose the Rite. The members of the last three are called "Brethren of the Red Cross," and constitute another Masonic authority, styled the "Illuminated Chapter." The Twelfth Degree is simply one of office, and is only held by the king, who is perpetual Grand Master of the Order. No one is admitted to the Eleventh Degree unless he can show four quarterings of nobility.

Switzerland. In 1737 Lord Darnley, Grand Master of England, granted a Deputation for Geneva, in Switzerland, to George Hamilton, Esq., who, in the same year, established a Provincial Grand Lodge at Geneva. Warrants were granted by this body to several Lodges in and around the city of Geneva. Two years afterward, a Lodge, composed principally of Englishmen, was established at Lausanne, under the name of "La Parfaite Union des Etrangers." Findel, on the authority of Mossdorf's edition of Lenning, says that the Warrant for this Lodge was granted by the Duke of Montagu; a statement also made by Thory. This is an error. The Duke of Montagu was Grand Master of the Grand Lodge of England in 1721, and could not, therefore, have granted a Warrant in 1739. The Warrant must have been issued by the Marquis of Carnarvon, who was Grand Master from April, 1738, to May, 1739. In an old list of the Regular Lodges on the registry of England, this Lodge is thus described: "Private Room, Lausanne, in the Canton of Bern, Switzerland, February 2, 1739." Soon after, this Lodge assumed a superintending authority with the title of "Helvetic Roman Directory," and instituted many other Lodges in the Pays de Vaud.

But in Switzerland, as elsewhere, Masonry was at an early period exposed to persecution. In 1738, almost immediately after their institution, the Lodges at Geneva were suppressed by the magistrates. In 1740, so many calumnies had been circulated in the Swiss Cantons against the Order, that the Freemasons published an *Apology for the Order* in *Der Brachmann*, a Zurich journal. It had, however, but little effect, for in 1743 the magistrates of Bern ordered the closing of all the Lodges. This edict was not obeyed; and therefore, on March 3, 1745, another, still more severe, was issued, by which a penalty of one hundred thalers, and forfeiture of his situation, was to be inflicted on every officer of the government who should continue his connection with the Freemasons. To this the Masons replied in a pamphlet entitled *Le Franc-Maçon dans la République*, published simultaneously, in 1746, at Frankfort and Leipsic. In this work they ably defended themselves from all the unjust charges that had been made against them. Notwithstanding that the result of this defense was that the magistrates pushed their opposition no farther, the Lodges in the Pays de Vaud remained suspended for nineteen years. But in 1764 the primitive Lodge at Lausanne was revived, and the revival was gradually followed by the other Lodges. This resumption of labor was, however, but of brief duration. In 1770 the magistrates again interdicted the meetings.

During all this period the Masons of Geneva, under a more liberal government, were uninterrupted in their labors, and extended their operations into German Switzerland. In 1771 Lodges had been erected in Vevay and Zurich, which, working at first according to the French system, soon afterward adopted the German ritual.

In 1775 the Lodges of the Pays de Vaud were permitted to resume their labors. Formerly, they had worked according to the system of the Grand Lodge of England, whence they had originally derived their Masonry; but this they now abandoned, and adopted the Rite of Strict Observance. In the same year the high degrees of France were introduced into the Lodge at Basle. Both it and the Lodge at Lausanne now assumed higher rank, and took the title of Scottish Directories.

In 1777 a Congress was held at the city of Basle, in which there were representatives from the Strict Observance Lodges of the Pays de Vaud and the English Lodge of Zurich. It was then determined that the Masonry of Switzerland should be divided under two distinct authorities: the one to be called the German Helvetic Directory, with its seat at Zurich; and the other to be called the Scottish Helvetic Roman Directory, whose seat was at Lausanne. This word *Roman*, or more properly Romansh, is the name of one of the four languages spoken in Switzerland. It is a corruption of the Latin, and supposed to have been the colloquial dialect of a large part of the Grisons.

Still there were great dissensions in the Masonry of Switzerland. A clandestine Lodge had been established in 1777, at Lausanne, by one Sidrac, whose influence it was found difficult to check. The Helvetic Roman Directory found it necessary, for this purpose, to enter, in 1779, into a treaty of alliance with the Grand Lodge at Geneva, and the Lodge of Sidrac was then at length dissolved and its members dispersed.

In 1778, the Helvetic Roman Directory published its Constitutions. The Rite it practised was purely philosophic, every Hermetic element having been eliminated. The appointment of the Masters of Lodges, who held office for three years, was vested in the Directory, and, in consequence, men of ability and learning were chosen, and the Craft were skilfully governed.

In November, 1782, the Council of Bern interdicted the meetings of the Lodges and the exercise of Freemasonry. The Helvetic Roman Directory, to give an example of obedience to law, however unjust and oppressive, dissolved its Lodges and discontinued its own meetings. But it provided for a maintenance of its foreign relations, by the appointment of a committee invested with the power of conducting its correspondence and of controlling the foreign Lodges under its obedience.

In the year 1785 there was a conference of the Swiss Lodges at Zurich to take into consideration certain propositions which had been made by the Congress of Paris, held by the Philalethes; but the desire that a similar Congress should be convened at Lausanne met with no favor from the Directorial Committee. The Grand Orient of France began to exert an influence, and many Lodges of Switzerland, among others ten in Geneva, gave their adhesion to that body. The seven other Genevan Lodges which were faithful to the English system organized a Grand Orient of Geneva, and in 1789 formed an alliance with the Grand Lodge of England. About the same time, the Lodges of the Pays de Vaud, which had been suppressed in 1782 by the government of Bern, resumed their vitality.

But the political disturbances consequent on the French Revolution began to exercise their influences in the Cantons. In 1792, the Helvetic Roman Directory suspended work; and its example was followed in 1793 by the Scottish Directory. From 1793 to 1803, Freemasonry was dead in Switzerland, although a few Lodges in Geneva and a German one in Nuremberg continued a sickly existence.

In 1803 Masonry revived, with the restoration of a better order in the political world. A Lodge, *Zur Hoffnung* or *Hope Lodge*, allusive in its name to the opening prospect, was established at Bern under a French Constitution.

With the cession of the Republic of Geneva to France, the Grand Lodge ceased to exist, and all the Lodges were united with the Grand Orient of France. Several Lodges, however, in the Pays de Vaud, whose Constitution had been irregular, united together to form an independent body under the title of the "Grand National Helvetic Orient." Peter Maurice Glaire introduced his modified Scottish Rite of seven degrees, and was at the age of eighty-seven elected its Grand Master for life. Glaire was possessed of great abilities, and had been the friend of Stanislaus, King of Poland, in whose interests he had performed several important missions to Russia, Prussia, Austria, and France. He was much attached to Masonry, and while in Poland had elaborated on the Scottish system the Rite which he subsequently bestowed upon the Helvetic Orient.

It would be tedious and painful to recapitulate all the dissensions and schisms with which the Masonry of Switzerland continued for years to be harassed. In 1820 there were nineteen Lodges, which worked under four different obediences, the Scottish Directory, the Grand Helvetic Roman Orient, the English Provincial Grand Lodge, and the Grand Orient of France. Besides, there were two Lodges of the Rite of Mizraim, which had been introduced by the Brothers Bedarride.

The Masons of Switzerland, weary of these divisions, had been long anxious to build a firm foundation of Masonic unity, and to obliterate forever this state of isolation, where Lodges were proximate in locality but widely asunder in their Masonic relations.

Many attempts were made, but the rivalries of petty authorities and the intolerance of opinion caused them always to be failures. At length a movement, which was finally crowned with success, was inaugurated by the Lodge *Modestia cum Libertate*, of Zurich. Being about to celebrate the twenty-fifth anniversary of its existence in 1836, it invited the Swiss Lodges of all Rites to be present at the festival. There a proposition for a National Masonic union was made, which met with a favorable response from all who were present. The reunion at this festival had given so much satisfaction that similar meetings were held in 1838 at Bern, in 1840 at Basle, and in 1842 at Locle. The preliminary means for establishing a Confederacy were discussed at these various biennial conventions, and progress slowly but steadily was made toward the accomplishment of that object. In 1842 the task of preparing a draft of a Constitution for a United Grand Lodge was entrusted to Bro. Gysi-Schinz, of Zurich, who so successfully completed it that it gave almost universal satisfaction. Finally, on June 22, 1844, the new Grand Lodge was inaugurated with the title of the "Grand Lodge Alpina," and Bro. J. J. Hottinger was elected the Grand Master. Masonry has since then been in great activity in Switzerland.

Sword. The sword is in chivalry the ensign or symbol of knighthood. Thus Monstrelet says: "The sons of the kings of France are knights at the font of baptism, being regarded as the chiefs of knighthood, and they receive, from the cradle, the sword which is the sign thereof." St. Palaye calls the sword "the most honorable badge of chivalry, and a symbol of the labor the knight was to encounter." No man was considered a knight until the ceremony of presenting him the sword had been performed; and when this weapon was presented, it was accompanied with the declaration that the person receiving it was thereby made a knight. "The lord or knight," says St. Palaye, "on the girding on of the sword, pronounced these or similar words: In the name of God, of St. Michael, and St. George, I make thee a knight."

So important an ensign of knighthood as the sword must have been accompanied with some symbolic meaning, for in the Middle Ages symbolism was referred to on all occasions.

Francisco Redi, an Italian poet of the seventeenth century, gives, in his *Bacco in Toscano*, an account, from a Latin MS., of an investiture with knighthood in the year 1260, which describes the symbolic meaning of all the insignia used on that occasion. Of the sword it says: "Let him be girded with the sword as a sign of security against the devil; and the two edges of the blade signify right and law, that the poor are to be defended from the rich and the weak from the strong."

But there is a still better definition of the symbolism of the sword of knighthood in an old MS. in the library of the London College of Arms to the following effect:

"Unto a knight, which is the most honorable office above all other, is given a sword, which is made like unto a crosse for the redemption of mankynde in signifying that like as our Lord God died uppon the crosse for the redemption of mankynde, even so a knight ought to defend the crosse and to overcome and destroie the enemies of the same; and it hath two edges in tokening that with the sword he ought to mayntayne knighthood and justice."

Hence in Masonic Templarism we find that this symbolism has been preserved, and that the sword with which the modern knight is created is said to be endowed with the qualities of justice, fortitude, and mercy.

The charge to a Knights Templar, that he should never draw his sword unless convinced of the justice of the cause in which he is engaged, nor to sheathe it until his enemies were subdued, finds also its origin in the custom of the Middle Ages. Swords were generally manufactured with a legend on the blade. Among the most common of these legends was that used on swords made in Spain, many examples of which are still to be found in modern collections. That legend is: "No me saques sin rason. No me embaines sin honor"; i. e., *Do not draw me without justice. Do not sheathe me without honor.*

So highly was the sword esteemed in the Middle Ages as a part of a knight's equipment, that special names were given to those of the most celebrated heroes, which have been transmitted to us in the ballads and romances of that period. Thus we have among the warriors of Scandinavia,

Foot-breaath,	the sword of	Thoralf Skolinson,
Quern-biter,	"	King Hako,
Balmung,	"	Siegfried,
Angurvardal,	"	Frithiof.

To the first two, Longfellow alludes in the following lines:

"Quern-biter of Hakom the Good,
Wherewith at a stroke he hewed
The millstone through and through,
And Foot-breaath of Thoralf the Strong,
Were neither so broad nor so long
Nor so true."

And among the knights of chivalry we have

Durandal,	the sword of	Orlando,
Balisardo,	"	Ruggiero,
Colado,	"	the Cid,
Aroun-dight,	"	Lancelot du Sac,
Joyeuse,	"	Charlemagne,
Excalibur,	"	King Arthur.

Of the last of these, the well-known legend is, that it was found embedded in a stone as its sheath, on which was an inscription that it could be drawn only by him who was the rightful heir to the throne of Britain. After two hundred and one of the strongest knights had essayed in vain, it was at once drawn forth by Arthur, who was then proclaimed king by acclamation. On his death-bed, he ordered it to be thrown into a neighboring lake; but as it fell, an arm issued from the waters, and, seizing it by the hilt, waved it thrice, and then it sank never again to appear. There are many other famous swords in these old romances, for the knight invariably gave to his sword, as he did to his horse, a name expressive of its qualities or of the deeds which he expected to accomplish with it.

In Masonry, the use of the sword as a part of the Masonic clothing is confined to the high degrees and the degrees of chivalry, when, of course, it is worn as a part of the insignia of knighthood. In the symbolic degrees its appearance in the Lodge, except as a symbol, is strictly prohibited. The Masonic prints engraved in the last century, when the sword, at least as late as 1780, constituted a part of the dress of every gentleman, show that it was discarded by the members when they entered the Lodge. The official swords of the Tiler and the Pursuivant or Sword-Bearer are the only exceptions. This rule is carried so far, that military men, when visiting a Lodge, are required to divest themselves of their swords, which are to be left in the Tiler's room.

Sword and Trowel. See *Trowel and Sword.*

Sword-Bearer. An officer in a Commandery of Knights Templar. His station is in the west, on the right of the Standard-Bearer, and when the knights are in line, on the right of the second division. His duty is to receive all orders and signals from the Eminent Commander, and see them promptly obeyed. He is, also, to assist in the protection of the banners of the order. His jewel is a triangle and cross swords.

Sword-Bearer, Grand. A subordinate officer, who is found in most Grand Lodges. Anderson says, in the second edition of the *Constitutions* (p. 127), that in 1731 the Duke of Norfolk, being then Grand Master, presented to the Grand Lodge of England "the old trusty sword of Gustavus Adolphus, king of Sweden, that was wore next by his successor in war the brave Bernard, Duke of Sax-Weimar, with both their names on the blade; which the Grand Master had ordered Brother George Moody (the king's sword cutler) to adorn richly with the arms of Norfolk in silver on the scabbard, in order to be the Grand Master's sword of state in future." At the following feast, Bro. Moody was appointed Sword-Bearer; and the office has ever since existed, and is to be found in almost all the Grand Lodges of this country. Anderson further says that, previous to this donation, the Grand Lodge had no sword of state, but used one belonging to a private Lodge. It was borne before the Grand Master by the Master of the Lodge to which it belonged, as appears from the account of the procession in 1730.

The Grand Sword-Bearer should be appointed by the Grand Master, and it is his duty to carry the sword of state immediately in front of that officer in all processions of the Grand Lodge. In Grand Lodges which have not provided for a Grand Sword-Bearer, the duties of the office are usually performed by the Grand Pursuivant.

Sword of State. Among the ancient Romans, on all public occasions, a lictor carried a bundle of rods, sometimes with an ax inserted among them, before the consul or other magistrate as a token of his authority and his power to punish criminals. Hence, most probably, arose the custom in the Middle Ages of carrying a naked sword before kings or chief magistrates. Thus at the election of the Emperor of Germany, the Elector of Saxony, as Arch-Marshal of the Empire, carried a naked sword before the newly elected Emperor. We find the same practise prevailing in England as early certainly as the reign of Henry III., at whose coronation, in 1236, a sword was carried by the Earl of Chester. It was named Curtana, and, being without a point, was said to be emblematic of the spirit of mercy that should actuate a sovereign. This sword is known as the "Sword of State," and the practise prevailing to the present day, it has always been borne in England in public processions before all chief magistrates, from the monarch of the realm to the mayor of the city. The custom was adopted by the Masons; and we learn from Anderson that, from the time of the revival, a sword of state, the property of a private Lodge, was borne by the Master of that Lodge before the Grand Master, until the Grand Lodge acquired one by the liberality of the Duke of Norfolk, which has ever since been borne by the Grand Sword-Bearer.

Sword Pointing to the Naked Heart. Webb says that "the sword pointing to the naked heart demonstrates that justice will, sooner or later, overtake us." The symbol is a modern one; but its adoption was probably suggested by the old ceremony, both in English and in continental Lodges, and which is still preserved in some places, in which the candidate found himself surrounded by swords pointing at his heart, to indicate that punishment would duly follow his violation of his obligations.

Sword, Revolving. With the Cherubim, Yahveh stationed at the gate of Eden, "to keep the way of the tree of Life," the *lahat ha'hereb hammithhappeketh*, "The revolving phenomenon of the curved sword," or "the flaming blade of the sword which turns." There were two Cherubim, one at each side of the gate. These angels, or winged bulls, did not hold the weapon in their hands, but it was apart, separate from them. The *lahat ha'hereb* was endowed with proper motion, or turned upon itself. There was but one, and presumably it was between the Cherubim, suspended at a certain height in the air. Prof. Lenormant, in speaking of this terrible weapon, states, that "the circumference, which was turned fully upon the spectator, could have been full of eyes all around, and that when the prophet says 'that they had a circumference and a height that were dreadful,' the second dimension refers to the breadth of their rims," and when advancing with the Cherubim against the irreverent intruder at the forbidden gate, it would strike and cut him in pieces as soon as it should graze him. The symbolism of this instrument has been fixed by Obry as the tchakra of India, which is a disk with sharp edges, hollow at the center, which is flung horizontally, after having been whirled around the fingers. "A weapon for slinging, shaped like a disk, moving horizontally with a gyratory motion, like that of a waterspout, having a hollow centre, that the tips of the fingers can pass through, whence seven divergent rays issue toward a circumference, about which are studded fifty sharp points." (See *Cherubim.*)

Sword, Templar's. According to the regulations of the Grand Encampment of the United States, the sword to be worn by the Knights Templar must have a helmet head or pommel, a cross handle, and a metal scabbard. The length from the top of the hilt to the end of the scabbard must be from thirty-four to forty inches.

Sword, Tiler's. In modern times the implement used by the Tiler is a sword of the ordinary form. This is incorrect. Formerly, and indeed up to a comparatively recent period, the Tiler's sword was wavy in shape, and so made in allusion to the "flaming sword which was placed at the east of the garden of Eden, which turned every way to keep the way of the tree of life." It was, of course, without a scabbard, because the Tiler's sword should ever be drawn and ready for the defense of his post.

Sworn Brothers. (*Fratres jurati.*) It was the custom in the Middle Ages for soldiers, and especially knights, when going into battle, to engage each other by reciprocal oaths to share the rewards of victory and to defend each other in the fight. Thus Kennet tells us (*Paroch. Antiq.*) that in the commencement of the expedition of William of Normandy into England, Robert de Oiley and Roger de Iverio, "fratres jurati, et per fidem et sacramentum confederati, venerunt ad conquestum Angliæ," i. e., *they came to the conquest of England, as sworn brothers, bound by their faith and an oath.* Consequently, when William allotted them an estate as the reward of their military service, they divided it into equal portions, each taking one.

Syllable. To pronounce the syllables, or only one of the syllables, of a Sacred Word, such as a name of God, was among the Orientalists considered far more reverent than to give to it in all its syllables a full and continuous utterance. Thus the Hebrews reduced the holy name JEHOVAH to the syllable JAH; and the Brahmans, taking the initial letters of the three words which expressed the three attributes of the Supreme Brahma, as Creator, Preserver, and Destroyer, made of it the syllable AUM, which, on account of its awful and sacred meaning, they hesitated to pronounce aloud. To divide a word into syllables, and thus to interrupt the sound, either by pausing or by the alternate pronunciation by two persons, was deemed a mark of reverence.

Symbol. A symbol is defined to be a visible sign with which a spiritual feeling, emotion, or idea is connected. It was in this sense that the early Christians gave the name of symbols to all rites, ceremonies, and outward forms which bore a religious meaning; such, for instance, as the cross, and other pictures and images, and even the sacraments and the sacramental elements. At a still earlier period, the Egyptians communicated the knowledge of their esoteric philosophy in mystic symbols. In fact, man's earliest instruction was by means of symbols. "The first learning of the world," says Stukely, "consisted chiefly of symbols. The wisdom of the Chaldeans, Phœnicians, Egyptians, Jews, of Zoroaster, Sanchoniathon, Pherecydes, Syrus, Pythagoras, Socrates, Plato, of all the ancients that is come to our hand, is symbolic." And the learned Faber remarks that "allegory and personification were peculiarly agreeable to the genius of antiquity, and the simplicity of truth was continually sacrificed at the shrine of poetical decoration."

The word "symbol" is derived from a Greek verb which signifies "to compare one thing with another"; and hence a symbol or emblem, for the two words are often used synonymously in Masonry, is the expression of an idea which is derived from the comparison or contrast of some object with a moral conception or attribute. Thus the plumb is a symbol of rectitude; the level, of equality; the beehive, of industry. The physical qualities of the plumb are compared or contrasted with the moral conception of virtue or rectitude of conduct. The plumb becomes to the Mason, after he has once been taught its symbolic meaning, forever afterward the visible expression of the idea of rectitude, or uprightness of conduct. To study and compare these visible objects—to elicit from them the moral ideas which they are intended to express—is to make oneself acquainted with the Symbolism of Masonry.

The objective character of a symbol, which presents something material to the sight and touch, as explanatory of an internal idea, is best calculated to be grasped by the infant mind, whether the infancy of that mind be considered *nationally* or *individually*. And hence, in the first ages of the world, in its infancy, all propositions, theological, political, or scientific, were expressed in the form of symbols. Thus the first religions were eminently symbolical, because, as that great philosophical historian, Grote, has remarked, "At a time when language was yet in its infancy, visible symbols were the most vivid means of acting upon the minds of ignorant hearers."

To the man of mature intellect, each letter of the alphabet is the symbol of a certain sound. When we instruct the child in the form and value of these letters, we make the picture of some familiar object the representation of the letter which aids the infantile memory. Thus, when the teacher says, "A was an Archer," the Archer becomes a symbol of the letter A, just as in after-life the letter becomes the symbol of a sound.

"Symbolical representations of things sacred," says Dr. Barlow (*Essays on Symbolism*, i., p. 1), "were coeval with religion itself as a system of doctrine appealing to sense, and have accompanied its transmission to ourselves from the earliest known period of monumental history.

"Egyptian tombs and stiles exhibit religious symbols still in use among Christians. Similar forms, with corresponding meanings, though under different names, are found among the Indians, and are seen on the monuments of the Assyrians, the Etruscans, and the Greeks.

"The Hebrews borrowed much of their early religious symbolism from the Egyptians, their later from the Babylonians, and through them this symbolical imagery, both verbal and objective, has descended to ourselves.

"The Egyptian priests were great proficients in symbolism, and so were the Chaldeans, and so were Moses and the Prophets, and the Jewish doctors generally —and so were many of the early fathers of the Church, especially the Greek fathers.

"Philo of Alexandria was very learned in symbolism, and the Evangelist St. John has made much use of it.

"The early Christian architects, sculptors, and painters drank deep of symbolical lore, and reproduced it in their works."

Squier gives in his *Serpent Symbolism in America* (p. 19) a similar view of the antiquity and the subsequent growth of the use of symbols. He says: "In the absence of a written language or forms of expression capable of conveying abstract ideas, we can readily comprehend the necessity, among a primitive people, of a symbolic system. That symbolism in a great degree resulted from this necessity is very obvious; and that, associated with man's primitive religious systems, it was afterwards continued, when in the advanced stage of the human mind the previous necessity no longer existed, is equally undoubted. It thus came to constitute a kind of sacred language, and became invested with an esoteric significance understood only by the few."

In Freemasonry, all the instructions in its mysteries are communicated in the form of symbols. Founded, as a speculative science, on an operative art, it has taken the working-tools of the profession which it spiritualizes, the terms of architecture, the Temple of Solomon, and everything that is connected with its traditional history, and adopting them as symbols, it teaches its great moral and philosophical lessons by this system of symbolism. But its symbols are not confined to material objects as were the hieroglyphics of the Egyptians. Its myths and legends are also, for the most part, symbolic. Often a legend, unauthenticated by history, distorted by anachronisms, and possibly absurd in its pretensions if viewed historically or as a narrative of actual occurrences, when interpreted as a symbol, is found to impress the mind with some great spiritual and philosophical truth. The legends of Masonry are parables, and a parable is only a spoken symbol. By its utterance, says Adam Clarke, "spiritual things are better understood, and make a deeper impression on the attentive mind."

Symbol, Compound. In Dr. Mackey's work on the *Symbolism of Freemasonry*, he has given this name to a species of symbol that is not unusual in Freemasonry, where the symbol is to be taken in a double sense, meaning in its general application one thing, and then in a special application another. An example of this is seen in the symbolism of Solomon's Temple, where, in a general sense, the Temple is viewed as a symbol of that spiritual temple formed by the aggregation of the whole Order, and in which each Mason is considered as a stone; and, in an individual or special sense, the same Temple is considered as a type of that spiritual temple which each Mason is directed to erect in his heart.

Symbolic Degrees. The first three degrees of Freemasonry, namely, those of Entered Apprentice, Fellow-Craft, and Master Mason, are known, by way of distinction, as the "symbolic degrees." This term is never applied to the degrees of Mark, Past, and Most Excellent Master, and the Royal Arch, which, as being conferred in a body called a Chapter, are generally designated as "capitular degrees"; nor to those of Royal and Select Master, which, conferred in a Council, are, by an excellent modern usage, styled "cryptic degrees," from the crypt or vault which plays so important a part in their ritual. But the term "symbolic" is exclusively confined to the degrees conferred in a Lodge of the three primitive degrees, which Lodge, therefore, whether opened on the First, the Second or the Third Degree, is always referred to as a "symbolic Lodge." As this distinctive term is of constant and universal use, it may be considered not al-

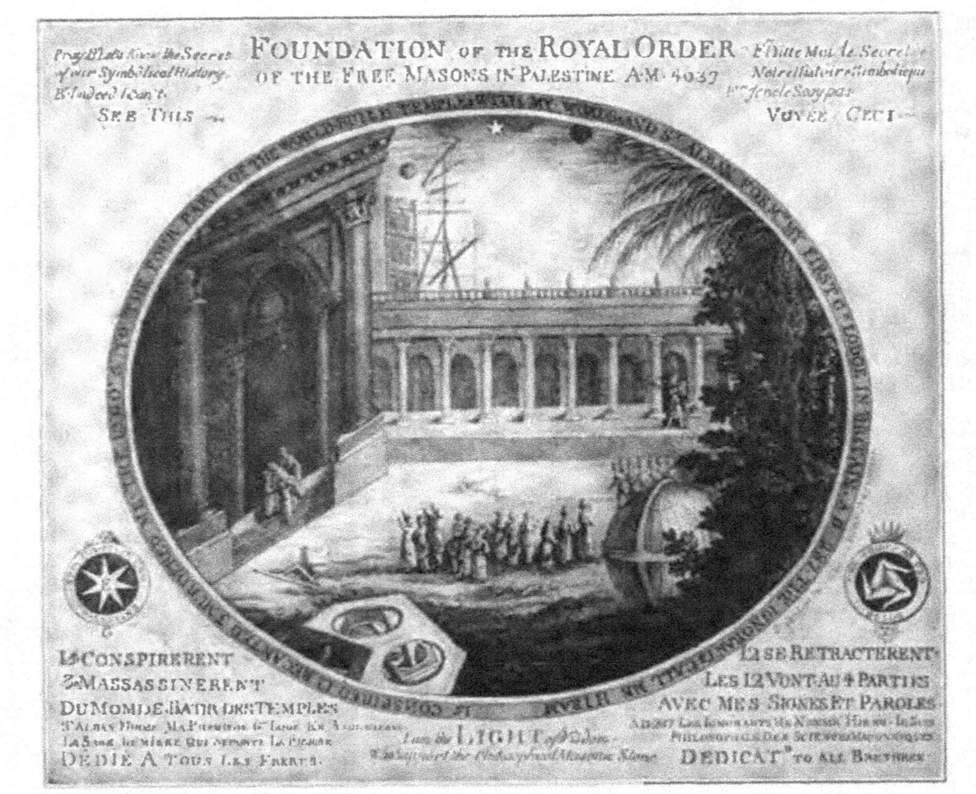
FOUNDATION OF THE ROYAL ORDER
OF THE FREE MASONS IN PALESTINE A.M. 4037
SEE THIS
VOYEZ CECI
LES CONSPIRERENT
MASSASSINERENT
DU MONDE BATIR DES TEMPLES
DEDIE A TOUS LES FRERES
LIGHT
LES RETRACTERENT
LES 12 VONT AU 4 PARTIES
AVEC MES SIGNES ET PAROLES
DEDICAT TO ALL BRETHREN

together useless to inquire into its origin and signification.

The germ and nucleus of all Freemasonry is to be found in the three primitive degrees —the Apprentice, the Fellow-Craft, and the Master Mason. They were at one time (under a modification, however, which included the Royal Arch) the only degrees known to or practised by the Craft, and hence they are often called "Ancient Craft Masonry," to distinguish them from those comparatively modern additions which constitute what are designated as the "high degrees," or, by the French, "*les hautes grades*." The striking peculiarity of these primitive degrees is that their prominent mode of instruction is by symbols. Not that they are without legends. On the contrary, they have each an abundance of legends; such, for instance, as the details of the building of the Temple; of the payment of wages in the middle chamber, or of the construction of the pillars of the porch. But these legends do not perform any very important part in the constitution of the degree. The lessons which are communicated to the candidate in these primitive degrees are conveyed, principally, through the medium of symbols, while there is (at least in the working of the degrees) but little tradition or legendary teaching, with the exception of the great legend of Masonry, the "GOLDEN LEGEND" of the Order, to be found in the Master's Degree, and which is, itself, a symbol of the most abstruse and solemn signification. But even in this instance, interesting as are the details of the legend, they are only subordinate to the symbol. Hiram the Builder is the profound symbol of manhood laboring for immortality, and all the different points of the legend are simply clustered around it, only to throw out the symbol in bolder relief. The legend is of itself inert— it is the symbol of the Master Workman that gives it life and true meaning.

Symbolism is, therefore, the prevailing characteristic of these primitive degrees; and it is because all the science and philosophy and religion of Ancient Craft Masonry is thus concealed from the profane but unfolded to the initiates in symbols, that the first three degrees which comprise it are said to be symbolic.

Now, nothing of this kind is to be found in the degrees above and beyond the third, if we except the Royal Arch, which, however, as I have already intimated, was originally a part of Ancient Craft Masonry, and was unnaturally torn from the Master's Degree, of which it, as every Masonic student knows, constituted the complement and consummation. Take, for example, the intermediate degrees of the American Chapter, such, for instance, as the Mark and Most Excellent Master. Here we find the symbolic feature ceasing to predominate, and the traditional or legendary taking its place. It is true that in these capitular degrees the use of symbols is not altogether abandoned. This could not well be, for the symbol constitutes the very essence of Freemasonry. The symbolic element is still to be discovered in these degrees, but only in a position subordinate to legendary instruction. As an illustration, let us consider the keystone in the Mark Master's Degree. Now, no one will deny that this is, strictly speaking, a symbol, and a very important and beautiful one, too. It is a symbol of a fraternal covenant between those who are engaged in the common search after Divine truth. But, in the *rôle* which it plays in the ritual of this degree, the symbol, however beautiful and appropriate it may be, is in a manner lost sight of, and the keystone derives almost all its importance and interest from the traditional history of its construction, its architectural design, and its fate. It is as the subject of a legend, and not as a symbol, that it attracts attention. Now, in the Third or Master's Degree we find the trowel, which is a symbol of almost precisely the same import as the keystone. They both refer to a Masonic covenant. But no legend, no tradition, no history, is connected with the trowel. It presents itself simply and exclusively as a symbol. Hence we learn that symbols do not in the capitular, as in the primitive, degrees of Masonry strike the eye, and inform the mind, and teach the heart, in every part of the Lodge, and in every part of the ceremonial initiation. On the contrary, the capitular degrees are almost altogether founded on and composed of a series of events in Masonic history. Each of them has attached to it some tradition or legend which it is the design of the degree to illustrate, and the memory of which is preserved in its ceremonies and instructions. That most of these legends are themselves of symbolic signification is not denied. But this is their interior sense. In their outward and ostensible meaning, they appear before us simply as legends. To retain these legends in the memory of Masons appears to have been the primary design of the establishment of the higher degrees, and as the information intended to be communicated in these degrees is of an historical character, there can of course be but little room for symbols or for symbolic instruction, the profuse use of which would rather tend to an injury than to a benefit, by complicating the purposes of the ritual and confusing the mind of the aspirant.

The celebrated French writer, Ragon, objects to this exclusive application of the term "symbolic" to the first three degrees as a sort of unfavorable criticism on the higher degrees, and as if implying that the latter are entirely devoid of the element of symbolism. But he has mistaken the true import and meaning of the application. It is not because the higher or capitular and cryptic degrees are altogether without symbols—for such is not the case—that the term symbolic is withheld from them, but because symbolic instruction does not constitute their predominating characteristic, as it does of the first three degrees.

And hence the Masonry taught in these

three primitive degrees is very properly called *Symbolic Masonry*, and the Lodge in which this Masonry is taught is known as a *Symbolic Lodge*.

Symbolic Lectures. The lectures appropriated to the First, Second, and Third degrees are sometimes called Symbolic lectures; but the term is more properly applied to any lecture which treats of the meaning of Masonic symbols, in contradistinction to one which discusses only the history of the Order, and which would, therefore, be called an Historical Lecture. But the English Masons have a lecture called "the symbolical lecture," in which is explained the forms, symbols, and ornaments of Royal Arch Masonry, as well as its rites and ceremonies.*

Symbolic Lodge. A Lodge of Master Masons, with the Fellow-Craft and Apprentice Lodge worked under its Constitution, is called a Symbolic Lodge, because in it the Symbolic degrees are conferred. (See *Symbolic Degrees*.)

Symbolic Machinery. Machinery is a term employed in epic and dramatic poetry to denote some agency introduced by the poet to serve some purpose or accomplish some event. Faber, in treating of the Apocalypse, speaks of "a patriarchal scheme of symbolical machinery derived most plainly from the events of the deluge, and borrowed, with the usual perverse misapplication, by the contrivers of paganism, but which has since been reclaimed by Christianity to its proper use." Dr. Oliver thinks that this "scheme of symbolical machinery" was "the primitive Freemasonry, veiled in allegory and illustrated by symbols." Without adopting this questionable hypothesis, it must be admitted that Freemasonry, in the scenic representations sometimes used in its initiations, has, like the epic poets, and dramatists, and the old hierophants, availed itself of the use of symbolic machinery.

Symbolic Masonry. The Masonry that is concerned with the first three degrees in all the Rites. This is the technical meaning. But in a more general sense, Symbolic Masonry is that Masonry, wherever it may be found, whether in the primary or in the high degrees, in which the lessons are communicated by symbols. (See *Symbolic Degrees*.)

Symbolism, The Science of. The science which is engaged in the investigation of the meaning of symbols, and the application of their interpretation to moral, religious, and philosophical instruction. In this sense, Freemasonry is essentially a science of symbolism. The English lectures define Freemasonry to be "a peculiar system of morality veiled in allegory and illustrated by symbols." The definition would be more correct were it in these words: *Freemasonry is a system of morality developed and inculcated by the science of symbolism*. It is this peculiar character as a symbolic institution, this entire adoption of the method of instruction by symbolism, which gives its whole identity to Freemasonry and has caused it to differ from every other association that the ingenuity of man has devised. It is this that has bestowed upon it that attractive form which has always secured the attachment of its disciples and its own perpetuity.

The Roman Catholic Church is, perhaps, the only contemporaneous institution which continues to cultivate, in any degree, the beautiful system of symbolism. But that which, in the Catholic Church, is, in a great measure, incidental, and the fruit of development, is, in Freemasonry, the very life-blood and soul of the Institution, born with it at its birth, or, rather, the germ from which the tree has sprung, and still giving it support, nourishment, and even existence. Withdraw from Freemasonry its Symbolism, and you take from the body its soul, leaving behind nothing but a lifeless mass of effete matter, fitted only for a rapid decay.

Since, then, the science of symbolism forms so important a part of the system of Freemasonry, it will be well to commence any discussion of that subject by an investigation of the nature of symbols in general.

There is no science so ancient as that of symbolism, and no mode of instruction has ever been so general as was the symbolic in former ages. "The first learning in the world," says the great antiquary, Dr. Stukely, "consisted chiefly of symbols. The wisdom of the Chaldeans, Phœnicians, Egyptians, Jews, of Zoroaster, Sanchoniathon, Pherecydes, Syrus, Pythagoras, Socrates, Plato, of all the ancients that is come to our hand, is symbolic." And the learned Faber remarks, that "allegory and personification were peculiarly agreeable to the genius of antiquity, and the simplicity of truth was continually sacrificed at the shrine of poetical decoration."

In fact, man's earliest instruction was by symbols. The objective character of a symbol is best calculated to be grasped by the infant mind, whether the infancy of that mind be considered *nationally* or *individually*. And hence, in the first ages of the world in its infancy, all propositions, theological, political, or scientific, were expressed in the form of symbols. Thus the first religions were eminently symbolical, because, as that great philosophical historian, Grote, has remarked, "At a time when language was yet in its infancy, visible symbols were the most vivid means of acting upon the minds of ignorant hearers."

Even in the very formation of language, the medium of communication between man and man, and which must hence have been an elementary step in the progress of human improvement, it was found necessary to have

*It is unfortunate that the Historical Lecture usually given in the Master's Degree is often absurd from any known historical or Masonic basis. This is misleading to those who have every reason to expect a different treatment at our hands, and efforts should be made to correct this error. [E. E. C.]

recourse to symbols, for words are only and truly certain arbitrary symbols by which and through which we give an utterance to our ideas. The construction of language was, therefore, one of the first products of the science of symbolism.

We must constantly bear in mind this fact of the primary existence and predominance of symbolism in the earliest times, when we are investigating the nature of the ancient religions, with which the history of Freemasonry is so intimately connected. The older the religion, the more the symbolism abounds. Modern religions may convey their dogmas in abstract propositions; ancient religions always conveyed them in symbols. Thus there is more symbolism in the Egyptian religion than in the Jewish, more in the Jewish than in the Christian, more in the Christian than in the Mohammedan, and, lastly, more in the Roman than in the Protestant.

But symbolism is not only the most ancient and general, but it is also the most practically useful, of sciences. We have already seen how actively it operates in the early stages of life and of society. We have seen how the first ideas of men and of nations are impressed upon their minds by means of symbols. It was thus that the ancient peoples were almost wholly educated.

"In the simpler stages of society," says one writer on this subject, "mankind can be instructed in the abstract knowledge of truths only by symbols and parables. Hence we find most heathen religions becoming mythic, or explaining their mysteries by allegories, or instructive incidents. Nay, God himself, knowing the nature of the creatures formed by him, has condescended, in the earlier revelations that he made of himself, to teach by symbols; and the greatest of all teachers instructed the multitudes by parables. The great exemplar of the ancient philosophy and the grand archetype of modern philosophy were alike distinguished by their possessing this faculty in a high degree, and have told us that man was best instructed by similitudes."

Such is the system adopted in Freemasonry for the development and inculcation of the great religious and philosophical truths, of which it was, for so many years, the sole conservator. And it is for this reason that I have already remarked, that any inquiry into the symbolic character of Freemasonry, must be preceded by an investigation of the nature of symbolism in general, if we would properly appreciate its particular use in the organization of the Masonic Institution.

Symbol of Glory. In the old lectures of the last century, the Blazing Star was called "the glory in the centre"; because it was placed in the centre of the floor-cloth or tracing-board, and represented hieroglyphically the glorious name of God. Hence Dr. Oliver has given to one of his most interesting works, which treats of the symbolism of the Blazing Star, the title of *The Symbol of Glory*.

Syndication of Lodges. A term used in France, in 1773, by the Schismatic Grand Orient during its contests with the Grand Lodge, to denote the fusion of several Lodges into one. The word was never introduced into English Masonry, and has become obsolete in France.

Synod of Scotland. In 1757, the Associate Synod of Seceders of Scotland adopted an act, concerning what they called "the Mason oath," in which it is declared, that all persons who shall refuse to make such revelations as the Kirk Sessions may require, and to promise to abstain from all future connection with the Order, "shall be reputed under scandal, and incapable of admission to sealing ordinances." In consequence of this act, passed more than a century ago, the sect of Seceders, of which there are a few in America, continue to be at the present day inveterate enemies of the Masonic Institution.

Syria. A country of Asia Minor lying on the western shores of the Mediterranean. To the Freemason, it is associated with the legendary history of his Order in several interesting points, especially in reference to Mount Lebanon, from whose forests was derived the timber for the construction of the Temple. The modern Templar will view it as the scene of the contests waged during the Crusades by the Christian knights with their Saracen adversaries. In modern Syria, Freemasonry has been slow to find a home. The only Lodges existing in the country are at the city of Beyrout, which contains two—Palestine Lodge, No. 415, which was instituted by the Grand Lodge of Scotland, May 6, 1861, and the Lodge Le Liban, by the Grand Orient of France, January 4, 1869. Morris says (*Freemasonry in the Holy Land*, p. 216) that "the Order of Freemasonry is not in a condition satisfactory to the members thereof, nor creditable to the great cause in which the Fraternity are engaged."

Syrian Rite. A religious sect which had its origin in Syria, and which was anciently comprehended in the patriarchates of Antioch and of Jerusalem. It was an exceedingly flourishing system. Before the end of the fourth century it numbered 119 distinct sees, with a population of several millions. The liturgy is known as the Liturgy of St. James.

System. Lenning defines a system of Freemasonry to be the doctrine of Freemasonry as exhibited in the Lodge government and Lodge work or ritual. The definition is not, perhaps, satisfactory. In Freemasonry, a system is a plan or scheme of doctrines intended to develop a particular view as to the origin, the design, and the character of the Institution. The word is often used as synonymous with Rite, but the two words do not always express the same meaning. A system is not always developed into a Rite, or the same system may give birth to two or more different Rites. Dr. Oliver established a system founded on the literal acceptance of almost all the legendary traditions, but he never invented a Rite. Ramsay and Hund both held the same system as to the Templar origin of Masonry; but the Rite of Ramsay and the Rite of Strict Observance are very different. The system of Schröder and that of the Grand Lodge of England do not essentially vary, but there is no similarity between the York Rite and the Rite of Schröder. Whoever in Masonry sets forth a connected series of doctrines peculiar to himself invents a system. He may or be may not afterward fabricate a Rite. But the Rite would be only a consequence, and not a necessary one, of the system.

Systyle. An arrangement of columns in which the intercolumniation is equal to the diameter of the column.

T

T. The twentieth letter of the English alphabet, and the twenty-second and last of the Hebrew. As a symbol, it is conspicuous in Masonry. Its numerical value as ט, *Teth*, is 9, but as ת, *Thau*, it is 400. (See *Tau*.)

Tabaor. Toffet. Edom. Three obsolete names which are sometimes given to the three Elect in the Eleventh Degree in the A. A. Scottish Rite.

Tabernacle. Many Masonic students have greatly erred in the way in which they have referred to the Sinaitic tabernacle, as if it were represented by the tabernacle said in the legends to have been erected by Zerubbabel at Jerusalem at the time of the building of the second Temple. The belief that the tabernacle of Zerubbabel was an exact representation of that erected by Moses, arose from the numerous allusions to it in the writings of Oliver, but in this country principally from the teachings of Webb and Cross. It is, however, true, that although the symbols of the ark, the golden candlestick, the altar of incense, and some others were taken, not from the tabernacle, but from the Temple, the symbolism of the veils was derived from the latter, but in a form by no means similar to the original disposition. It is therefore necessary that some notice should be taken of the real tabernacle, that we may be enabled to know how far the Masonic is connected with the Sinaitic edifice.

The word *tabernacle* means a tent. It is the diminutive of *taberna*, and was used by the Romans to denote a soldier's tent. It was constructed of planks and covered with skins, and its outward appearance presented the precise form of the Jewish tabernacle. The Jews called it sometimes *mishcan*, which, like the Latin *taberna*, meant a dwelling-place, but more commonly *ohel*, which meant, like *tabernaculum*, a tent. In shape it resembled a tent, and is supposed to have derived its form from the tents used by the patriarchs during their nomadic life.

There are three tabernacles mentioned in Scripture history—the Anti-Sinaitic, the Sinaitic, and the Davidic.

1. The Anti-Sinaitic tabernacle was the tent used, perhaps from the beginning of the exodus, for the transaction of business, and was situated at some distance from the camp. It was used only provisionally, and was superseded by the tabernacle proper.

2. The Sinaitic tabernacle. This was constructed by Aholiab and Bezaleel under the immediate direction of Moses. The costliness and splendor of this edifice exceeded, says Kitto, in proportion to the means of the people who constructed it, the magnificence of any cathedral of the present day. It was situated in the very center of the camp, with its door or entrance facing the east, and was placed toward the western part of an enclosure or outward court, which was one hundred and fifty feet long and fifty feet wide, and surrounded by canvas screens seven and a half feet high, so as to prevent any one on the outside from overlooking the court.

The tabernacle itself was, according to Josephus, forty-five feet long by fifteen wide; its greater length being from east to west. The sides were fifteen feet high, and there was a sloping roof. There was no aperture or place of entrance except at the eastern end, which was covered by curtains. Internally, the tabernacle was divided into two apartments by a richly decorated curtain. The one at the western end was fifteen feet long, making, therefore, a perfect cube. This was the Holy of Holies, into which no one entered, not even the high priest, except on extraordinary occasions. In it was placed the Ark of the Covenant, against the western wall. The Holy of Holies was separated from the Sanctuary by a curtain embroidered with figures of Cherubim, and supported by four golden pillars. The Sanctuary, or eastern apartment, was in the form of a double cube, being fifteen feet high, fifteen feet wide, and thirty feet long. In it were placed the table of shewbread on the northern side, the golden candlestick on the southern, and the altar of incense between them. The tabernacle thus constructed was decorated with rich curtains. These were of four colors—white or fine-twined linen, blue, purple, and red. They were so suspended as to cover the sides and top of the tabernacle, not being distributed as veils separating it into apartments, as in the Masonic tabernacle. Josephus, in describing the symbolic signification of the tabernacle, says that it was an imitation of the system of the world; the Holy of Holies, into which not even the priests were admitted, was as it were a heaven peculiar to God; but the Sanctuary, where the people were allowed to assemble for worship, represented the sea and land on which men live. But the symbolism of the tabernacle was far more complex than anything that Josephus has said upon the subject would lead us to suppose. Its connection would, however, lead us to an inquiry into the religious life of the ancient Hebrews, and into an investigation of the question how much Moses was, in the appointment of ceremonies, influenced by his previous Egyptian life; topics whose consideration would throw no light on the subject of the Masonic symbolism of the tabernacle.

3. The Davidic tabernacle in time took the place of that which had been constructed by Moses. The old or Sinaitic tabernacle accompanied the Israelites in all their wanderings, and was their old temple until David obtained possession of Jerusalem. From that time it remained at Gibeon, and we have no account of its removal thence. But when David removed the ark to Jerusalem, he erected a tabernacle for its reception. Here the priests performed their daily service, until Solomon erected the Temple, when the ark was deposited in the Holy of Holies, and the Davidic tabernacle put away as a relic. At the subsequent destruction of the Temple it was most probably burned. From the time of Solomon we altogether lose sight of the Sinaitic tabernacle, which perhaps became a victim to carelessness and the corroding influence of time.

The three tabernacles just described are the only ones mentioned in Scripture or in Josephus. Masonic tradition, however, enumerates a fourth—the tabernacle erected by Zerubbabel on his arrival at Jerusalem with his countrymen, who had been restored from captivity by Cyrus for the purpose of rebuilding the Temple. Ezra tells us that on their arrival they built the altar of burnt-offerings and offered sacrifice. This would not, however, necessitate the building of a house, because the altar of sacrifices had always been erected in the open court, both of the old tabernacle and Temple. Yet as the priests and Levites were there, and it is said that the religious ordinances of Moses were observed, it is not unlikely that some sort of temporary shelter was erected for the performance of Divine worship. But of the form and character of such a building we have no account.

A Masonic legend has, however, for symbolical purposes, supplied the deficiency. This legend is, however, peculiar to the American modification of the Royal Arch Degree. In the English system a Royal Arch Chapter represents the "ancient Sanhedrim," where Zerubbabel, Haggai, and Joshua administer the law. In the American system a Chapter is said to represent "the tabernacle erected by our ancient brethren near the ruins of King Solomon's Temple."

Of the erection of this tabernacle, I have said that there is no historical evidence. It is simply a myth, but a myth constructed, of course, for a symbolical purpose. In its legendary description, it bears no resemblance whatsoever, except in the colors of its curtains or veils, to the Sinaitic tabernacle. In the latter the Holy of Holies was in the western extremity, in the former it was in the eastern; in that was contained the Ark of the Covenant with the overshadowing Cherubim and the Shekinah; in this there are no such articles; in that the most holy was inaccessible to all persons, even to the priests; in this it is the seat of the three presiding officers, and is readily accessible by proper means. In that the curtains were attached to the sides of the tent; in this they are suspended across, dividing it into four apartments. The Masonic tabernacle used in the American Royal Arch Degree is not, therefore, a representation of the ancient tabernacle erected by Moses in the wilderness, but must be supposed to be simply a temporary construction for purposes of shelter, of consultation, and of worship. It was, in the strictest sense of the word, a tabernacle, a tent. As a myth, with no historical foundation, it would be valueless, were it not that it is used, and was undoubtedly fabricated, for the purpose of developing a symbolism. And this symbolism is found in its veils. There is no harm in calling it a tabernacle any more than there is in calling it a Sanhedrim, provided we do not fall into the error of supposing that either was actually its character. As a myth, and only as a myth, must it be viewed, and there its symbolic meaning presents, as in all other Masonic myths, a fund of useful instruction. For an interpretation of that symbolism, see *Veils, Symbolism of the.*

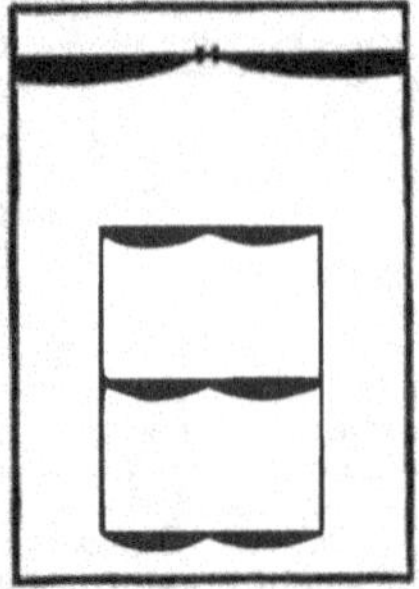

In some Chapters a part of the furniture is called the tabernacle; in other words, a piece of framework is erected inside of the room, and is called the tabernacle. This is incorrect. According to the ritual, the whole Chapter room represents the tabernacle, and the veils should be suspended from wall to wall. Indeed, I have reasons for believing that this interior tabernacle is an innovation of little more than twenty years' standing. The oldest Chapter rooms that I have seen are constructed on the correct principle.

Tabernacle, Chief of the. See *Chief of the Tabernacle.*

Tabernacle, Prince of the. See *Prince of the Tabernacle.*

Table Lodge. After the labors of the Lodge have been completed, Masons frequently meet at tables to enjoy a repast in common. In England and America, this repast is generally called a banquet, and the Lodge is said to be, during its continuance, at refreshment. The Master, of course, presides, assisted by the Wardens, and it is considered most proper that no profanes should be present. But with these exceptions, there are no rules specially laid down for the government of Masonic banquets. It will be seen, by an inspection of the article *Refreshment* in this work, that during the last century, and even at the commencement of the present, refreshments in English Lodges were taken during the sessions of the Lodge and in the Lodge room, and then, of course, rigid rules were in existence for the government of the Fraternity, and for the regulation of the forms in which the refreshments should be partaken. But this system has long grown obsolete, and the Masonic banquets of the present day differ very little from those of other societies, except, perhaps, in a more strict observance of the rules of order, and in the exclusion of all non-Masonic visitors.

But French Masons have prescribed a very formal system of rules for what they call a "Loge de Table," or *Table Lodge.* The room in which the banquet takes place is as much protected by its isolation from observation as the Lodge room itself. Table Lodges are always held in the Apprentice's Degree, and none but Masons are permitted to be present. Even the attendants are taken from the class known as "Serving Brethren," that is to say, waiters who have received the First Degree for the special purpose of entitling them to be present on such occasions.

The table is in the form of a horseshoe or elongated semicircle. The Master sits at the head, the Senior Warden at the northwest extremity, and the Junior Warden at the southwest. The Deacons or equivalent officers sit between the two Wardens. The brethren are placed around the exterior margin of the table, facing each other; and the void space between the sides is occupied by the serving brethren or attendants. It is probable that the form of the table was really adopted at first from motives of convenience. But M. Hermitte (*Bull. G. O.*, 1869, p. 83) assigns for it a symbolism. He says that as the entire circle represents the year, or the complete revolution of the earth around the sun, the semicircle represents the half of that revolution, or a period of six months, and therefore refers to each the two solstitial points of summer and winter, or the two great festivals of the Order in June and December, when the most important Table Lodges are held.

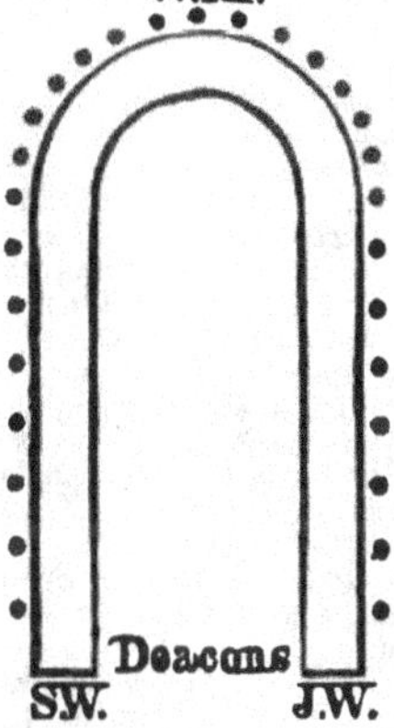

W.M.

Deacons

S.W. J.W.

The Table Lodge is formally opened with an invocation to the Grand Architect. During the banquet, seven toasts are given. These are called "santés d'obligation," or *obligatory toasts.* They are drunk with certain ceremonies which are prescribed by the ritual, and from which no departure is permitted. These toasts are: 1. The health of the Sovereign or Chief Magistrate of the State. 2. That of the Grand Master and the Supreme power of the Order, that is, the Grand Orient or the Grand Lodge. 3. That of the Master of the Lodge; this is offered by the Senior Warden. 4. That of the two Wardens. 5. That of the Visiting Brethren. 6. That of the other officers of the Lodge, and the new initiates or affiliates if there be any. 7. That of all Masons wheresoever spread over the face of the globe. (See *Toasts.*)

Ragon (*Tuill. Gen.*, p. 17) refers these seven toasts of obligation to the seven libations made by the ancients in their banquets in honor of the seven planets, the Sun, Moon, Mars, Mercury, Jupiter, Venus, and Saturn, and the seven days of the week which are named after them; and he assigns some striking reasons for the reference. But this symbolism, although very beautiful, is evidently very modern.

The Table Lodge is then closed with the fraternal kiss, which is passed from the Master around the table, and with the usual forms.

One of the most curious things about these Table Lodges is the vocabulary used. The instant that the Lodge is opened, a change takes place in the names of things, and no person is permitted to call a plate a *plate*, or a knife a *knife*, or anything else by the appellation by which it is known in ordinary conversation. Such a custom formerly prevailed in England, if we may judge from a passage in Dr. Oliver's *Revelations of a Square* (p. 215), where an instance is given of its use in 1780, when the French vocabulary was employed. It would seem, from the same authority, that the custom was introduced into England from France by Capt. George Smith, the author of the *Use and Abuse of Freemasonry*, who was initiated in a continental Lodge.

The vocabulary of the Table Lodge as used at French Masonic banquets is as follows:

Table-cloth	they call	standard.
Napkins	"	flags.
Table	"	tracing-board.
Dishes	"	great plates.
Plates	"	tiles.
Spoons	"	trowels.
Knives	"	swords.
Forks	"	pickaxes.
Bottles	"	casks.
Glasses	"	cannons.
Lights	"	stars.

Snuffers	they call	pincers.
Chairs	"	stalls.
Meals	"	materials.
Bread		rough ashlar.
Red wine		strong red powder.
White wine		strong white powder.
Water		weak powder.
Beer		yellow powder.
Brandy, or liqueurs		fulminating powder.
Coffee		black powder.
Salt		white sand.
Pepper		cement.
To eat		to masticate.
To drink		to fire.
To carve		to hew.

Tablets, Engraved. A designation frequently used in the A. A. Scottish Rite for the book of minutes or record; as in the Rose Croix Chapter is used the term "engraved columns."

Tablets of Hiram Abif. Among the traditions of the Order there is a legend referring to the tablets used by Hiram Abif as a Trestle-Board on which to lay down his designs. This legend, of course, can lay no claim to authenticity, but is intended simply as a symbol inculcating the duty of every man to work in the daily labor of life after a design that will construct in his body a spiritual temple. (See *Hiram Abif*.)

Taciturnity. In the earliest catechisms of the last century it is said that "the three particular points that pertain to a Mason are Fraternity, Fidelity, and Taciturnity," and that they "represent Love, Relief, and Truth among all Right Masons." The symbol is now obsolete.

Tactics. The importance that has in the last few years been given to the military element in the Order of Masonic Knights Templar in America has made it necessary that special Manuals should be prepared for the instruction of Knights in the elementary principles of military movements. The most popular works of this kind are: 1. *Knights' Templar, Tactics and Drill for the use of Commanderies, and the Burial Service of the Orders of Masonic Knighthood. Prepared by Sir Orrin Welsh, Past Grand Commander, State of New York;* 2. *Knights' Templar, Tactics and Drill, with the Working, Text, and Burial Service of the Orders of Knighthood, as adopted by the Grand Commandery of the State of Michigan. By Ellery Irving Garfield, E. G. C. G. Grand Commandery of Michigan;* and 3. *Tactics for Knights Templar, and Appendant Orders. Prepared by E. Sir Knight George Wingate Chase, of Massachusetts.* These works contain the necessary instructions in the "school of the knight," or the proper method of marching, halting, saluting, handling the sword, etc., and the "school of the commandery," or directions for properly performing the evolutions on a public parade. Books of this kind have now become as necessary and as common to the Knights Templar as *Monitors* are to the Master Mason.

Talisman. From the Hebrew *tselem* and the Chaldaic *tsalma*, an image or idol. A talisman signifies an implement or instrument, either of wood, or metal, or some precious stone, or even parchment, of various forms, such as a triangle, a cross, a circle, and sometimes a human head or human figure, generally inscribed with characters and constructed with mystical rites and ceremonies. The talisman thus constructed was supposed by the ancients, and even in the Middle Ages, to be invested with supernatural powers and a capacity for protecting its wearer or possessor from evil influences, and for securing to him good fortune and success in his undertakings.

The word *amulet*, from the Latin "amuletum," which comes from the Arabic "hamalet," anything worn, though sometimes confounded with the talisman, has a less general signification. For while the talisman served both to procure good and to avert evil, the powers of the amulet were entirely of a protective nature. Frequently, however, the two words are indifferently used.

The use of talismans was introduced in the Middle Ages from the Gnostics. Of the

*ELOHIM * ELOHI*

ADONAI (left side) — *ZEBOATH* (right side)

4 .	14 .	15 .	1 .
9 .	7 .	6 .	12 .
5 .	11 .	10 .	8 .
16 .	2 .	3 .	13 .

*BOOYEL * IOSIPHIEL*

Gnostic talismans none were more frequent than those which were inscribed with Divine names. Of these the most common were IAO and SABAO, although we find also the Tetragrammaton, and *Elohim, Elohi, Adonai*, and other Hebrew appellations of the Deity. Sometimes the talisman contained, not one of the names of God, but that of some mystical person, or the expression of some mystical idea. Thus, on some of the Gnostic talismanic gems, we find the names of the three mythical kings of Cologne, or the sacred *Abraxas*. The orthodox Christians of the early days of the church were necessarily influenced, by the popular belief in talismans, to adopt many of them; although, of course, they sought to divest them of their magical signification, and to use them simply as symbols. Hence we find among these Christians the Constantinian monogram, composed of the letters X and P, or the *vesica piscis*, as a symbol of Christ, and the image of a little fish as a token of Christian recognition, and the anchor as a mark of Christian hope.

Many of the symbols and symbolic expressions which were in use by the alchemists, the astrologers, and by the Rosicrucians, are to be traced to the Gnostic talismans. The talisman was, it is true, converted from an instrument of incantation into a symbol; but the symbol was accompanied with a mystical signification which gave it a sacred character.

It has been said that in the Gnostic talismans the most important element was some one or more of the sacred names of God, derived either from the Hebrews, the Arabians,

or from their own abstruse philosophy; sometimes even in the same talisman from all these sources combined. Thus there is a Gnostic talisman, said by Mr. King to be still current in Germany as an amulet against plague. It consists of a silver plate, on which are inscribed various names of God surrounding a magic square, whose figures computed every way make the number 34.

In this Gnostic talisman, we will observe the presence not only of sacred names, but also of mystical. And it is to the influence of these talismanic forms, developed in the symbols of the secret societies of the Middle Ages, and even in the architectural decorations of the builders of the same period, such as the triangle, the pentalpha, the double triangle, etc., that we are to attribute the prevalence of sacred names and sacred numbers in the symbolic system of Freemasonry.

We do not need a better instance of this transmutation of Gnostic talismans into Masonic symbols, by a gradual transmission through alchemy, Rosicrucianism, and Medieval architecture, than a plate to be found in the *Azoth Philosophorum* of Basil Valentine, the Hermetic philosopher, who flourished in the seventeenth century.

This plate, which is Hermetic in its design, but is full of Masonic symbolism, represents a winged globe inscribed with a triangle within a square, and on it reposes a dragon. On the latter stands a human figure with two hands and two heads, surrounded by the sun, the moon, and five stars representing the seven planets. One of the heads is that of a male, the other of a female. The hand attached to the male part of the figure holds a compass, that to the female, a square. The square and compass thus distributed seem to indicate that originally a phallic meaning was attached to these symbols as there was to the point within the circle, which in this plate also appears in the center of the globe. The compass held by the male figure would represent the male generative principle, and the square held by the female, the female productive principle. The subsequent interpretation given to the combined square and compass was the transmutation from the Hermetic talisman to the Masonic symbol.

Talith. An oblong shawl worn over the head or shoulders, named, from its having four corners, the arba canphoth. It is also called tsitsith, from the fringes on which its holiness depends. The talith is made of wool or camel's hair. The wool fringe is carefully shorn and specially spun. Four threads, one of which must be blue, are passed through eyelet holes made in the four corners. The threads being double make eight. Seven are of equal length; the eighth must twist five times round the rest and be tied into five knots, and yet remain equal in length to the other seven. The five knots and eight threads make thirteen, which, with the value of the Hebrew word tsitsith, 600, accomplishes 613, the number of precepts of the moral law, and which is the number of letters in Hebrew composing the Decalogue. 613 represents 248 positive precepts, or members of the human body, and 365 negative pre-

cepts, or number of human veins. Jesus of Nazareth wore the tsitsith: "And behold a woman . . . came behind him and touched the *hem* of his garment" (Matt. ix. 20); and he rebuked the Pharisees for their ostentation in enlarging the "borders" (κράσπεδα, fringes) of their garments. (Matt. xxiii. 5.)

Taljahad. Rendered in Hebrew thus: טל וידר, "Angel of Water," and found in the Twenty-ninth Degree of the A. A. Scottish Rite ritual.

Talmud. Hebrew, תלמוד, signifying *doctrine*. The Jews say that Moses received on Mount Sinai not only the written law which is contained in the Pentateuch but an oral law, which was first communicated by him to Aaron, then by them to the seventy elders, and finally by these to the people, and thus transmitted, by memory, from generation to generation. This oral law was never committed to writing until about the beginning of the third century, when Rabbi Jehuda the Holy, finding that there was a possibility of its being lost, from the decrease of students of the law, collected all the traditionary laws into one book, which is called the *Mishna*, a word signifying *repetition*, because it is, as it were, a repetition of the written law.

The Mishna was at once received with great veneration and many wise men among the Jews devoted themselves to its study.

Toward the end of the fourth century, these opinions were collected into a book of commentaries, called the *Gemara*, by the school at Tiberias. This work has been falsely attributed to Rabbi Jochanan; but he died in 279, a hundred years before its composition. The Mishna and its commentary, the Gemara, are, in their collected form, called the *Talmud*.

The Jews in Chaldea, not being satisfied with the interpretations in this work, composed others, which were collected together by Rabbi Ashe into another Gemara. The former work has since been known as the *Jerusalem Talmud*, and that of R. Ashe as the *Babylonian Talmud*, from the places in which they were respectively compiled. In both works the Mishna or law is the same; it is only the Gemara or commentary that is different.

The Jewish scholars place so high a value on the Talmud as to compare the Bible to water, the Mishna to wine, and the Gemara to spiced wine; or the first to salt, the second to pepper, and the third to spices. For a long time after its composition it seemed to absorb all the powers of the Jewish intellect, and the labors of Hebrew writers were confined to treatises and speculations on Talmudical opinions.

The Mishna is divided into six divisions called *Sederim*, whose subjects are: 1. The productions of the earth; 2. Festivals; 3. The rights and duties of women; 4. Damages and injuries; 5. Sacrifices; 6. Purifications. Each of these *Sederim* is again divided into *Massicoth*, or treatises, of which there are altogether sixty-three.

The *Gemara*, which differs in the Jerusalem and Babylonian redactions, consists of commentaries on these *Massicoth*, or treatises.

Of the Talmud, Lightfoot has said that the matters it contains "do everywhere abound with trifles in that manner, as though they had no mind to be read; with obscurities and difficulties, as though they had no mind to be understood; so that the reader has need of patience all along to enable him to bear both trifling in sense and roughness in expression." Stehelin concurs in a similar opinion; but Steinschneider, as learned a Hebraist as either, has expressed a more favorable judgment.

Although the Talmud does indeed contain many passages whose conceits are puerile, it is, nevertheless, extremely serviceable as an elaborate compendium of Jewish customs, and has therefore been much used in the criticism of the Old and New Testaments. It furnishes also many curious illustrations of the Masonic system; and several of the traditions and legends, especially of the higher degrees, are either found in or corroborated by the Talmud. The treatise entitled *Middoth*, for instance, gives us the best description extant of the Temple of Solomon.

Tamarisk. The sacred tree of the Osirian mysteries, classically called the *Erica*, which see.

Tammus. תמוז. The tenth month of the Hebrew civil year, and corresponding to the months June and July, beginning with the new moon of the former.

Tanga-Tango. A Peruvian triune symbol, signifying "one in three and three in one."

Tannehill, Wilkins. Born in Tennessee, in 1787. He was one of the founders, in 1813, of the Grand Lodge of Tennessee, and was for seven years Grand Master of that body. He was also a contributor to the literature of Masonry, having published in 1845 a *Master Mason's Manual*; which was, however, little more than a compilation from the preceding labors of Preston and Webb. In 1847, he commenced the publication of a Masonic periodical under the title of the *Portfolio*. This was a work of considerable merit, but he was compelled to discontinue it in 1850, in consequence of an attack of amaurosis. One who knew him well, has paid this just tribute to his character: "Simple in feeling as a child, with a heart warm and tender to the infirmities of his brethren, generous even to a fault, he passed through the temptations and trying scenes of an eventful life without a soil upon the purity of his garments." He died June 2, 1858, aged seventy-one years.

Tapis. The name given in German Lodges to the carpet or floor-cloth on which formerly the emblems of Masonry were drawn in chalk. It is also sometimes called the Teppich.

Tarsel. In the earliest catechisms of the eighteenth century, it is said that the furniture of a Lodge consists of a "Mosaic Pavement, Blazing Star, and Indented Tarsel." In more modern catechisms, the expression is "indented tassel," which is incorrectly defined to mean a "tessellated border." *Indented Tarsel* is evidently a corruption of *indented tassel;* for a definition of which see *Tessellated Border*.

Tarsel-Board. We meet with this expression in some of the old catechisms as a corruption of *Trestle-Board*.

Tarshatha. Used in the degree of Knight of the East in the Ancient and Accepted Scottish Rite, according to the modern ritual of the Southern Jurisdiction of the United States, for Tirshatha, and applied to the presiding officer of a Council of Princes of Jerusalem. (See *Tirshatha.*)

Tassels. In the English and French tracing-boards of the First Degree, there are four tassels, one at each angle, which are attached to a cord that surrounds a tracing-board, and which constitutes the true *tessellated border.* These four cords are described as referring to the four principal points, the guttural, pectoral, manual, and pedal, and through them to the four cardinal virtues, temperance, fortitude, prudence, and justice. (See *Tessellated Border.*)

Tasting and Smelling. Of the five senses, hearing, seeing, and feeling only are deemed essential to Masons. Tasting and smelling are therefore not referred to in the ritual, except as making up the sacred number five. Preston says: "Smelling and Tasting are inseparably connected; and it is by the unnatural kind of life which men commonly lead in society that these senses are rendered less fit to perform their natural duties."

Tatnai and Shethar-Boznai. Tatnai was a Persian satrap of the province west of the Euphrates in the time of Darius and Zerubbabel; Shethar-Boznai was an officer under his command. The two united with the Apharsachites in trying to obstruct the building of the second Temple, and in writing a letter to Darius, of which a copy is preserved in Ezra (ch. v.). In this letter they reported that "the house of the great God" in Judea was being builded with great stones, and that the work was going on fast, on the alleged authority of a decree from Cyrus. They requested that search might be made in the rolls' court whether such a decree was ever given, and asked for the king's pleasure in the matter. The decree was found at Ecbatana, and a letter was sent to Tatnai and Shethar-Boznai from Darius, ordering them no more to obstruct, but, on the contrary, to aid the elders of the Jews in rebuilding the Temple by supplying them both with money and with beasts, corn, salt, wine, and oil for the sacrifices. Shethar-Boznai, after the receipt of this decree, offered no further obstruction to the Jews. Their names have been hence introduced into some of the high degrees in Masonry.

Tau. The last letter of the Hebrew alphabet is called *tau,* and it has the power of the Roman T. In its present form ת, in the square character now in use, it has no resemblance to a cross; but in the ancient Hebrew alphabet, its figure ×, or +, was that of a cross. Hence, when it is said, in the vision of Ezekiel (ix. 4), "Go through the midst of the city, and set a mark (in the original, תו, *tau*) upon the foreheads of the men that sigh and that cry for all the abominations that be done in the midst thereof"—which mark was to distinguish them as persons to be saved, on account of their sorrow for sin, from those who, as idolators, were to be slain—the evident allusion is to a cross. The form of this cross was × or +, a form familiar to the people of that day. But as the Greek letter *tau* subsequently assumed the form which is still preserved in the Roman T, the tau or tau cross was made also to assume the same form; so that the mark tau is now universally recognized in this form, T. This *tau, tau cross,* or *tau mark,* was of very universal use as a sacred symbol among the ancients. From the passage of Ezekiel just cited, it is evident that the Hebrews recognized it as a sign of salvation; according to the Talmudists, the symbol was much older than the time of Ezekiel, for they say that when Moses anointed Aaron as the high priest, he marked his forehead with this sign. Speaking of the use of the tau cross in the Old Testament, Didron says (*Christ. Iconog.,* p. 370) that "it saved the youthful Isaac from death, redeemed from destruction an entire people whose houses were marked with that symbol, healed the envenomed bites of those who looked at the serpent raised in the form of a 'tau' upon a pole, and called back the soul into the dead body of the son of that poor widow who had given bread to the prophet."

Hence, in Christian iconography, the tau cross, or cross of the Old Testament, is called the anticipatory cross, because it anticipated the four-limbed cross of the passion, and the typical cross because it was its type. It is also called the cross of St. Anthony, because on it that saint is supposed to have suffered martyrdom.

Maurice, in his *Indian Antiquities,* refers to it the *tiluk,* or mark worn by the devotees of Brahma.

Davies, in his *Celtic Researches,* says that the "Gallicum tau," or the tau of the ancient Gauls, was among the Druids a symbol of their supreme god, or Jupiter.

Among the Egyptians, the tau, with an oval ring or handle, became the *crux ansata,* and was used by them as the constant symbol of life. Dr. Clarke says (*Travels,* v., 311) that the tau cross was a monogram of Thoth, "the symbolical or mystical name of hidden wisdom among the ancient Egyptians."

Dupuy, in his *History of the Templars,* says that the tau was a Templar emblem. Von Hammer, who lets no opportunity of maligning the Order escape him, adduces this as a proof of the idolatrous tendencies of the Knights. He explains the tau, which, he says, was inscribed on the forehead of the Baphomet or Templar idol, as a figure of the phallus; whence he comes to the conclusion that the Knights Templar were addicted to the obscene worship of that symbol. It is, however, entirely doubtful, notwithstanding the authority of Dupuy, whether the tau was a symbol of the Templars. But if it was, its origin is rather to be looked for in the supposed Hebrew idea as a symbol of preservation.

It is in this sense, as a symbol of salvation from death and of eternal life, that it has been adopted into the Masonic system, and presents itself, especially under its triple combination, as a badge of Royal Arch Masonry. (See *Triple Tau.*)

Tau Cross. A cross of three limbs, so called because it presents the figure of the Greek letter T. (See *Tau.*)

Tchandalas. Mentioned in the *Institutes* of Manu as a class of pariahs, or the lowest in society, but are referred to as the inventors of brick for building purposes, as is attested by Vina-Snati and Veda Vyasa. In the course of time they were banished from the towns, the rites of burial, and the use of rice, water, and fire. They finally emigrated, and became the progenitors of great nations.

Team. Royal Arch Masons in America apply this word rather inelegantly to designate the three candidates upon whom the degree is conferred at the same time.

Tears. In the Master's Degree in some of the continental Rites, and in all the high degrees where the legend of the degree and the ceremony of reception are intended to express grief, the hangings of the Lodge are black strewn with tears. The figures representing tears are in the form depicted in the annexed cut. The symbolism is borrowed from the science of heraldry, where these figures are called *guttes*, and are defined to be "drops of anything that is by nature liquid or liquefied by art." The heralds have six of these charges, viz., *yellow*, or drops of liquid gold; *white*, or drops of liquid silver; *red*, or drops of blood; *blue*, or drops of tears; *black*, or drops of pitch; and *green*, or drops of oil. In funeral hatchments, a black velvet cloth, sprinkled with these "drops of tears," is placed in front of the house of a deceased nobleman and thrown over his bier; but there, as in Masonry, the *guttes de larmes*, or drops of tears, are not painted blue, but white.

Tebeth. טבת. The fourth month of the Hebrew civil year, corresponding to the months December and January, beginning with the new moon of the former.

Telamones. See *Caryatides.*

Tempelorden or **Tempelherrenorden.** The title in German of the Order of Knights Templar.

Temperance. One of the four cardinal virtues, the practise of which is inculcated in the First Degree. The Mason who properly appreciates the secrets which he has solemnly promised never to reveal, will not, by yielding to the unrestrained call of appetite, permit reason and judgment to lose their seats, and subject himself, by the indulgence in habits of excess, to discover that which should be concealed, and thus merit and receive the scorn and detestation of his brethren. And lest any brother should forget the danger to which he is exposed in the unguarded hours of dissipation, the virtue of temperance is wisely impressed upon his memory, by its reference to one of the most solemn portions of the ceremony of initiation. Some Masons, very properly condemning the vice of intemperance and abhorring its effects, have been unwisely led to confound temperance with total abstinence in a Masonic application, and resolutions have sometimes been proposed in Grand Lodges which declare the use of stimulating liquors in any quantity a Masonic offense. But the law of Masonry authorizes no such regulation. It leaves to every man the indulgence of his own tastes within due limits, and demands not abstinence, but only moderation and temperance, in anything not actually wrong.

Templar. See *Knights Templar.*

Templarius. The Latin title of a Knights Templar. Constantly used in the Middle Ages.

Templar Land. The Order of Knights Templar was dissolved in England, by an act of Parliament, in the seventeenth year of the reign of Edward II., and their possessions transferred to the Order of St. John of Jerusalem, or Knights Hospitalers. Subsequently, in the thirty-second year of the reign of Henry VIII., their possessions were transferred to the king. One of the privileges possessed by the English Templars was that their lands should be free of tithes; and these privileges still adhere to these lands, so that a farm being what is termed "Templar land," is still exempt from the imposition of tithes, if it is occupied by the owner; an exemption which ceases when the farm is worked under a lease.

Templar Origin of Masonry. The theory that Masonry originated in the Holy Land during the Crusades, and was instituted by the Knights Templar, was first advanced by the Chevalier Ramsay, for the purpose, it is supposed, of giving an aristocratic character to the association. It was subsequently adopted by the College of Clermont, and was accepted by the Baron von Hund as the basis upon which he erected his Rite of Strict Observance. The legend of the Clermont College is thus detailed by M. Berage in his work entitled *Les Plus Secrets Mystères des Hauts Grades* (iii., 194). "The Order of Masonry was instituted by Godfrey de Bouillon, in Palestine in 1330, after the defeat of the Christian armies, and was communicated only to a few of the French Masons, sometime afterwards, as a reward for the services which they had rendered to the English and Scottish Knights. From these latter true Masonry is derived. Their Mother Lodge is situated on the mountain of Heredom, where the first Lodge in Europe was held, which still exists in all its splendor. The Council General is always held there, and it is the seat of the Sovereign Grand Master for the time being. This mountain is situated between the west and the north of Scotland, sixty miles from Edinburgh.

"There are other secrets in Masonry which were never known among the French, and which have no relation to the Apprentice, Fellow Craft, and Master degrees which were constructed for the general class of Masons. The high degrees, which developed the true design of Masonry and its true secrets, have never been known to them.

"The Saracens having obtained possession of the holy places in Palestine, where all the mysteries of the Order were practised, made use of them for the most profane purposes. The Christians then leagued together to conquer this beautiful country, and to drive these barbarians from the land. They succeeded in obtaining a footing on these shores under the protection of the numerous armies of Crusaders which had been sent there by the Christian princes. The losses which they subsequently experienced put an end to the Christian power, and the Crusaders who remained were subjected to the persecutions of the Saracens, who massacred all who publicly proclaimed the Christian faith. This induced Godfrey de Bouillon, towards the end of the third century, to conceal the mysteries of religion under the veil of figures, emblems, and allegories.

"Hence the Christians selected the Temple of Solomon because it has so close a relation to the Christian Church, of which its holiness and its magnificence make it the true symbol. So the Christians concealed the mystery of the building up of the Church under that of the construction of the Temple, and gave themselves the title of Masons, Architects, or Builders, because they were occupied in building the faith. They assembled under the pretext of making plans of architecture to practise the rites of their religion, with all the emblems and allegories that Masonry could furnish, and thus protect themselves from the cruelty of the Saracens.

"As the mysteries of Masonry were in their principles, and still are only those of the Christian religion, they were extremely scrupulous to confide this important secret only to those whose discretion had been tried, and who had been found worthy. For this purpose they fabricated degrees as a test of those to whom they wished to confide it, and they gave them at first only the symbolic secret of Hiram, on which all the mystery of Blue Masonry is founded, and which is, in fact, the only secret of that Order which has no relation to true Masonry. They explained nothing else to them as they were afraid of being betrayed, and they conferred these degrees as a proper means of recognizing each other, surrounded as they were by barbarians. To succeed more effectually in this, they made use of different signs and words for each degree, so as not only to distinguish themselves from the profane Saracens, but to designate the different degrees. These they fixed at the number of seven, in imitation of the Grand Architect, who built the Universe in six days and rested on the seventh; and also because Solomon was seven years in constructing the Temple, which they had selected as the figurative basis of Masonry. Under the name of Hiram they gave a false application to the Masters, and developed the true secret of Masonry only to the higher degrees."

Such is the theory of the Templar origin of Masonry, which, mythical as it is, and wholly unsupported by the authority of history, has exercised a vast influence in the fabrication of high degrees and the invention of continental Rites. Indeed, of all the systems propounded during the eighteenth century, so fertile in the construction of extravagant systems, none has played so important a part as this in the history of Masonry. Although the theory is no longer maintained, its effects are everywhere seen and felt.

Templars of England. An important change in the organization of Templarism in England and Ireland took place in 1873. By it a union took place of the Grand Conclave of Masonic Knights Templar of England and the Grand Conclave of High Knights Templar of Ireland into one body, under the title of the "Convent General of the United Religious and Military Orders of the Temple and of St. John of Jerusalem, Palestine, Rhodes, and Malta." The following is a summary of the statutes by which the new Order is to be governed, as given by Sir Knight W. J. B. McLeod Moore, Grand Prior, in his circular to the Preceptors of Canada:

"1. The existing Grand Masters in the Empire are to be termed Great Priors, and Grand Conclaves or Encampments, Great Priories, under and subordinate to one Grand Master, as in the early days of the Order, and one Supreme Governing Body, the Convent General.

"2. The term Great is adopted instead of Grand, the latter being a French word; and grand in English is not grand in French. Great is the proper translation of 'Magnus' and 'Magnus Supremus.'

"3. The Great Priories of each nationality—England, Scotland, and Ireland, with their dependencies in the Colonies—retain their internal government and legislation, and appoint their Provincial Priors, doing nothing inconsistent with the supreme statutes of the Convent General.

"4. The title Masonic is not continued; the Order being purely Christian, none but Christians can be admitted; consequently it cannot be considered strictly as a Masonic body: Masonry, while inculcating the highest reverence for the Supreme Being, and the doctrine of the immortality of the soul, does not teach a belief in one particular creed, or unbelief in any. The connection with Masonry is, however, strengthened still more, as a candidate must now be two years a Master Mason, in addition to his qualification as a Royal Arch Mason.

"5. The titles Eminent 'Commander' and 'Encampment' have been discontinued, and the original name 'Preceptor' and 'Preceptory' substituted, as also the titles 'Constable' and 'Marshal' for 'First' and 'Second Captains.' 'Encampment' is a modern term, adopted probably when, as our traditions inform us, 'at the suppression of the ancient Military Order of the Temple, some of their number sought refuge and held conclaves in the Masonic Society, being independent small bodies, without any governing head.' 'Prior' is the correct and original title for the head of a langue or nationality, and 'Preceptor' for the subordinate bodies. The Preceptories were the ancient 'Houses' of the Templar Order; 'Commander' and 'Commanderies' was the title used by the Order of St. John, commonly known as Knights of Malta.

"6. The title by which the Order is now known is that of 'The United Religious and Military Orders of the Temple and of St. John of Jerusalem, Palestine, Rhodes, and Malta.' The Order of the Temple originally had no connection with that of Malta or Order of St. John; but the combined title appears to have been adopted in commemoration of the union which took place in Scotland with 'The Temple and Hospital of St. John,' when their lands were in common, at the time of the Reformation. But our Order of 'St. John of Jerusalem, Palestine, Rhodes, and Malta,' has no connection with the present Knights of Malta in the Papal States, or of the Protestant branches of the Order, the lineal successors of the ancient Knights of St. John, the sixth or English langue of which is still in existence, and presided over, in London, by His Grace the Duke of Manchester. The Order, when it occupied the Island of Malta as a sovereign body, was totally unconnected with Freemasonry.

"7. Honorary past rank is abolished, substituting the chivalric dignities of 'Grand Crosses' and 'Commanders,' limited in number, and confined to Preceptors. These honors to be conferred by His Royal Highness the Grand Master, the Fountain of Grace and Dignity; and it is contemplated to create an Order of Merit, to be conferred in like manner, as a reward to Knights who have served the Order.

"8. A Preceptor holds a degree as well as rank, and will always retain his rank and privileges as long as he belongs to a Preceptory.

"9. The abolition of honorary past rank is not retrospective, as their rank and privileges are reserved to all those who now enjoy them.

"10. The number of officers entitled to precedence has been reduced to seven; but others may be appointed at discretion, who do not, however, enjoy any precedence.

"11. Equerries, or serving brethren, are not to receive the accolade, or use any but a brown habit, and shall not wear any insignia or jewel: they are to be addressed as 'Frater,' not Sir Knight. In the early days of the Order they were not entitled to the accolade, and, with the esquires and men-at-arms, wore a dark habit, to distinguish them from the Knights, who wore white, to signify that they were bound by their vows to cast away the works of darkness and lead a new life.

"12. The apron is altogether discontinued, and a few immaterial alterations in the insignia will be duly regulated and promulgated: they do not, however, affect the present, but only apply to future, members of the Order. The apron was of recent introduction, to accord with Masonic usage: but reflection will at once show that, as an emblem of care and toil, it is entirely inappropriate to a Military Order, whose badge is the sword. A proposition to confine the wearing of the star to the Preceptors was negatived; the star and ribbon being in fact as much a part of the ritual as of the insignia of the Order.

"13. From the number of instances of persons totally unfitted having obtained admission into the Order, the qualification of candidates has been increased. A declaration is now required, to be signed by every candidate, that he is of the full age of twenty-one years, and in addition to being a Royal Arch Mason, that he is a Master Mason of two years' standing, professing the doctrines of the Holy and Undivided Trinity, and willing to submit to the statutes and ordinances, present and future, of the Order."

Templars of Scotland. The *Statutes of the Grand Priory of the Temple* of Scotland prescribe for the Order of Knights Templar in that kingdom an organization very different from that which prevails in other countries.

"The Religious and Military Order of the Temple" in Scotland consists of two classes: 1. Novice and Esquire; 2. Knight Templar. The Knights are again divided into four classes: 1. Knights created by Priories; 2. Knights elected from the companions on memorial to the Grand Master and Council, supported by the recommendation of the Priories to which they belong; 3. Knights Commanders; 4. Knights Grand Crosses, to be nominated by the Grand Master.

The supreme legislative authority of the Order is the Chapter General, which consists of the Grand Officers, the Knights Grand Crosses, and the Knights Commanders. One Chapter is held annually, at which the Grand Master, if present, acts as President. The anniversary of the death of James de Molay, March 11th, is selected as the time of this meeting, at which the Grand Officers are elected.

During the intervals of the meetings of the Chapter General, the affairs of the Order, with the exception of altering the Statutes, is entrusted to the Grand Master's Council, which consists of the Grand Officers, the Grand Priors of Foreign Langues, and the Knights Grand Crosses.

The Grand Officers, with the exception of the Past Grand Masters, who remain so for life, the Grand Master, who is elected triennially, and the Grand Aides-de-Camp, who are appointed by him and removed at his pleasure, are elected annually. They are as follows:

Grand Master,
Past Grand Masters,
Grand Seneschal,
Preceptor and Grand Prior of Scotland,
Grand Constable and Mareschal,
Grand Admiral,
Grand Almoner or Hospitaler,
Grand Chancellor,
Grand Treasurer,
Grand Registrar,
Primate or Grand Prelate,
Grand Provost or Governor-General,
Grand Standard-Bearer or Beaucennifer,
Grand Bearer of the Vexillum Belli,
Grand Chamberlain,
Grand Steward,
Two Grand Aides-de-Camp.

A Grand Priory may be instituted by the Chapter General in any nation, colony, or langue, to be placed under the authority of a Grand Prior, who is elected for life, unless superseded by the Chapter General.

A Priory, which is equivalent to our Commanderies, consists of the following officers:

Prior,
Subprior,
Mareschal or Master of Ceremonies,
Hospitaler or Almoner,
Chancellor,
Treasurer,
Secretary,
Chaplain and Instructor,
Beaucennifer, or Bearer of the Beauseant,
Bearer of the Red Cross Banner, or Vexillum Belli,
Chamberlain,
Two Aides-de-Camp.

The Chapter General or Grand Priory may unite two or more Priories into a Commandery, to be governed by a Provincial Commander, who is elected by the Chapter General.

The costume of the Knights, with the exception of a few slight variations to designate difference of rank, is the same as the ancient costume.

Templar Statistics. See *Statistics of the Order of the Temple.*

Temple. The symbolism of Speculative Masonry is so intimately connected with temple building and temple worship, that some notice of these edifices seems necessary. The Hebrews called a temple *beth*, which literally signifies a house or dwelling, and finds its root in a word which signifies "to remain or pass the night," or *hecal*, which means a palace, and comes from an obsolete word signifying "magnificent." So that they seem to have had two ideas in reference to a temple. When they called it *beth Jehovah*, or the "house of Jehovah" they referred to the continued presence of God in it; and when they called it *hecal Jevohah*, or the "palace of Jehovah," they referred to the splendor of the edifice which was selected as his residence. The Hebrew idea was undoubtedly borrowed from the Egyptian, where the same hieroglyphic ▭ I signified both a house and a temple. Thus, from an inscription at Philæ, Champollion (*Dict. Egyptienne*) cites the sentence, "He has made his devotions in the house of his mother Isis."

The classical idea was more abstract and philosophical. The Latin word *templum* comes from a root which signifies "to cut off," thus referring to any space, whether open or occupied by a building, which was cut off, or separated for a sacred purpose, from the surrounding profane ground. The word properly denoted a sacred enclosure where the omens were observed by the augurs. Hence Varro (*De Ling. Lat.*, vi., 81) defines a temple to be "a place for auguries and auspices." As the same practise of worshiping under the sky in open places prevailed among the northern nations, we might deduce from these facts that the temple of the sky was the Aryan idea, and the temple of the house the Semitic. It is true, that afterward, the augurs having for their own convenience erected a tent within the enclosure where they made their observations, or, literally, their *contemplations*, this in time gave rise among the Greeks and the Romans to permanent edifices like those of the Egyptians and the Hebrews.

Masonry has derived its temple symbolism, as it has almost all its symbolic ideas, from the Hebrew type, and thus makes the temple the symbol of a Lodge. But of the Roman temple worship it has not been neglectful, and has borrowed from it one of the most significant and important words in its vocabulary. The Latin word *specular* means to observe, to look around. When the augur, standing within the sacred precincts of his open temple on the Capitoline hill, watched the flight of birds, that from it he might deduce his auspices of good or bad fortune, he was said, *speculari*, to speculate. Hence the word came at length to denote, like *contemplate* from *templum*, an investigation of sacred things, and thus we got into our technical language the title of "Speculative Masonry," as distinguished by its religious design from Operative or Practical Masonry, which is devoted to more material objects. The EGYPTIAN TEMPLE was the real archetype of the Mosaic tabernacle, as that was of the temple of Jerusalem. The direction of an Egyptian temple was usually from east to west, the entrance being at the east. It was a quadrangular building, much longer than its width, and was situated in the western part of a sacred enclosure. The approach through this enclosure to the temple proper was frequently by a double row of sphinxes. In front of the entrance were a pair of tall obelisks, which will remind the reader of the two pillars at the porch of Solomon's Temple. The temple was divided into a spacious hall, the sanctuary where the great body of the worshipers assembled. Beyond it, in the western extremity, was the cell or sekos, equivalent to the Jewish Holy of Holies, into which the priests only entered; and in the remotest part, behind a curtain, appeared the image of the god seated on his shrine, or the sacred animal which represented him.

Grecian Temples, like the Egyptian and the Hebrew, were placed within an enclosure, which was separated from the profane land around it, in early times, by ropes, but afterward by a wall. The temple was usually quadrangular, although some were circular in form. It was divided into two parts, the πρόναος, porch or vestibule, and the ναός, or cell. In this latter part the statue of the god was placed, surrounded by a balustrade. In temples connected with the mysteries, the cell was called the ἄδυτον (Lat. *adytum*), and to it only the priests and the initiates had access; and we learn from Pausanias that various stories were related of calamities that had befallen persons who had unlawfully ventured to cross the threshold. Vitruvius says that the entrance of Greek temples was always toward the west; but this statement is contradicted by the appearance of the temples still partly existing in Attica, Ionia, and Sicily.

Roman Temples, after they emerged from their primitive simplicity, were constructed much upon the model of the Grecian. There were the same vestibule and cells, or adytum, borrowed, as with the Greeks, from the holy and the most holy place of the Egyptians. Vitruvius says that the entrance of a Roman temple was, if possible, to the west, so that the worshipers, when they offered prayers or sacrifices, might look toward the east; but this rule was not always observed.

It thus appears, notwithstanding what Montfaucon (*Antiq.*, ii., l. ii., ch. 2) says to the contrary, that the Egyptian form of a temple was the type from which other nations borrowed their idea.

This Egyptian form of a temple was borrowed by the Jews, and with some modifications adopted by the Greeks and Romans, whence it passed over into modern Europe. The idea of a separation into a holy and a most holy place has everywhere been preserved. The same idea is maintained in the construction of Masonic Lodges, which are but imitations, in spirit, of the ancient temples. But there has been a transposition of parts, the most holy place, which with the Egyptians and the Jews was in the west, being placed in Lodges in the east.

Temple, Grand Commander of the. (*Grand Commandeur du Temple.*) The Fifty-eighth Degree of the collection of the Metropolitan Chapter of France. It is the name of the Knight Commander of the Temple of the Scottish Rite.

Temple of Ezekiel. An ideal temple seen by the prophet Ezekiel, in the twenty-fifth year of the captivity, while residing in Babylon. It is supposed by Calmet, that the description given by the prophet was that of the Temple of Solomon, which he must have seen before its destruction. But an examination of its admeasurements will show that this could not have been the fact, and that the whole area of Jerusalem would not have been sufficient to contain a building of its magnitude. Yet, as Mr. Ferguson observes (*Smith Dict.*), the description, notwithstanding its ideal character, is curious, as showing what were the aspirations of the Jews in that direction, and how different they were from those of other nations; and also because it influenced Herod to some extent in his restoration of the temple of Zerubbabel. Between the visionary temple of Ezekiel and the symbolic city of the New Jerusalem, as described by the Evangelist, there is a striking resemblance, and hence it finds a place among the symbols in the Apocalyptic degrees. But with Symbolic or with Royal Arch Masonry it has no connection.

Temple of Herod. This was not the construction of a third temple, but only a restoration and extensive enlargement of the second, which had been built by Zerubbabel. To the Christian Mason it is interesting, even more than that of Solomon, because it was the scene of our Lord's ministrations, and was the temple from which the Knights Templar derived their name. It was begun by Herod 7 B.C., finished A.D. 4, and destroyed by the Romans in A.D. 70, having subsisted only seventy-seven years.

Temple of Solomon. The first Temple of the Jews was called *hecal Jehovah* or *beth Jehovah*, the palace or the house of Jehovah, to indicate its splendor and magnificence, and that it was intended to be the perpetual dwelling-place of the Lord. It was King David who first proposed to substitute for the nomadic tabernacle a permanent place of worship for his people; but although he had made the necessary arrangements, and even collected many of the materials, he was not permitted to commence the undertaking, and the execution of the task was left to his son and successor, Solomon.

Accordingly, that monarch laid the foundations of the edifice in the fourth year of his reign, 1012 B.C., and, with the assistance of his friend and ally, Hiram, King of Tyre, completed it in about seven years and a half, dedicating it to the service of the Most High in 1004 B.C. This was the year of the world 3000, according to the Hebrew chronology; and although there has been much difference among chronologists in relation to the precise date, this is the one that has been generally accepted, and it is therefore adopted by Masons in their calculations of different epochs.

The Temple stood on Mount Moriah, one of the eminences of the ridge which was known as Mount Zion, and which was originally the property of Ornan the Jebusite, who used it as a threshing-floor, and from whom it was purchased by David for the purpose of erecting an altar on it.

The Temple retained its original splendor for only thirty-three years. In the year of the world 3033, Shishak, King of Egypt, having made war upon Rehoboam, King of Judah, took Jerusalem, and carried away the choicest treasures. From that time to the period of its final destruction, the history of the Temple is but a history of alternate spoliations and repairs, of profanations to idolatry and subsequent restorations to the purity of worship. One hundred and thirteen years after the conquest of Shishak, Joash, King of Judah, collected silver for the repairs of the Temple, and restored it to its former condition in the year of the world 3148. In the year 3264, Ahaz, King of Judah, robbed the Temple of its riches, and gave them to Tiglath-Pileser, King of Assyria, who had united with him in a war against the Kings of Israel and Damascus. Ahaz also profaned the Temple by the worship of idols. In 3276, Hezekiah, the son and successor of Ahaz, repaired the portions of the Temple which his father had destroyed, and restored the pure worship. But fifteen years after he was compelled to give the treasures of the Temple as a ransom to Sennacherib, King of Assyria, who had invaded the land of Judah. But Hezekiah is supposed, after his enemy had retired, to have restored the Temple.

Manasseh, the son and successor of Hezekiah, fell away to the worship of Sabianism, and desecrated the Temple in 3306 by setting up altars to the host of heaven. Manasseh was then conquered by the King of Babylon, who in 3328 carried him beyond the Euphrates. But subsequently repenting of his sins he was released from captivity, and having returned to Jerusalem he destroyed the idols, and restored the altar of burnt-offerings. In 3380, Josiah, who was then King of Judah, devoted his efforts to the repairs of the Temple, portions of which had been demolished or neglected by his predecessors, and replaced the ark in the sanctuary. In 3398, in the reign of Jehoiakim, Nebuchadnezzar, King of Chaldea, carried a part of the sacred vessels to Babylon. Seven years afterward, in the reign of Jechoniah, he took away another portion; and finally, in 3416, in the eleventh year of the reign of Zedekiah, he took the city of Jerusalem, and entirely destroyed the Temple, and carried many of the inhabitants captives to Babylon.

The Temple was originally built on a very hard rock, encompassed with frightful precipices. The foundations were laid very deep, with immense labor and expense. It was surrounded with a wall of great height, exceeding in the lowest part four hundred and fifty feet, constructed entirely of white marble.

The body of the Temple was in size much less than many a modern parish church, for its length was but ninety feet, or, including the porch, one hundred and five, and its width but thirty. It was its outer court, its numerous terraces, and the magnificence of its external and internal decorations, together with its elevated position above the surrounding dwellings which produced that splendor of appearance that attracted the admiration of all who beheld it, and gives a color of probability to the legend that tells us how the Queen of Sheba, when it first broke upon her view, exclaimed in admiration, "A most excellent master must have done this!"

HOLY OF HOLIES.

HOLY PLACE.

PORCH.

The Temple itself, which consisted of the porch, the sanctuary, and the Holy of Holies, was but a small part of the edifice on Mount Moriah. It was surrounded with spacious courts, and the whole structure occupied at least half a mile in circumference. Upon passing through the outer wall, you came to the first court, called the court of the Gentiles, because the Gentiles were admitted into it, but were prohibited from passing farther. It was surrounded by a range of porticoes or cloisters, above which were galleries or apartments, supported by pillars of white marble.

Passing through the court of the Gentiles, you entered the court of the children of Israel, which was separated by a low stone wall, and an ascent of fifteen steps, into two divisions, the outer one being occupied by the women, and the inner by the men. Here the Jews were in the habit of resorting daily for the purposes of prayer.

Within the court of the Israelites, and separated from it by a wall one cubit in height, was the court of the priests. In the center of this court was the altar of burnt-offerings, to which the people brought their oblations and sacrifices, but none but the priests were permitted to enter it.

From this court, twelve steps ascended to the Temple, strictly so called, which, as I have already said, was divided into three parts, the porch, the sanctuary, and the Holy of Holies.

The PORCH of the Temple was twenty cubits in length, and the same in breadth. At its entrance was a gate made entirely of Corinthian brass, the most precious metal known to the ancients. Beside this gate there were the two pillars Jachin and Boaz, which had been constructed by Hiram Abif, the architect whom the King of Tyre had sent to Solomon.

From the porch you entered the SANCTUARY by a portal, which, instead of folding doors, was furnished with a magnificent veil of many colors, which mystically represented the universe. The breadth of the sanctuary was twenty cubits, and its length forty, or just twice that of the porch and Holy of Holies. It occupied, therefore, one-half of the body of the Temple. In the sanctuary were placed the various utensils necessary for the daily worship of the Temple, such as the altar of incense, on which incense was daily burnt by the officiating priest; the ten golden candlesticks; and the ten tables on which the offerings were laid previous to the sacrifice.

THE HOLY OF HOLIES, or innermost chamber, was separated from the sanctuary by doors of olive, richly sculptured and inlaid with gold, and covered with veils of blue, purple, scarlet, and the finest linen. The size of the Holy of Holies was the same as that of the porch, namely, twenty cubits square. It contained the Ark of the covenant, which had been transferred into it from the tabernacle, with its overshadowing Cherubim and its mercy-seat. Into the most sacred place, the high priest alone could enter, and that only once a year, on the day of atonement.

The Temple, thus constructed, must have been one of the most magnificent structures of the ancient world. For its erection, David had collected more than four thousand millions of dollars, and one hundred and eighty-four thousand six hundred men were engaged in building it for more than seven years; and after its completion it was dedicated by Solomon with solemn prayer and seven days of feasting; during which a peace-offering of twenty thousand oxen and six times that number of sheep was made, to consume which the holy fire came down from heaven.

In Masonry, the Temple of Solomon has played a most important part. Time was when every Masonic writer subscribed with unhesitating faith to the theory that Masonry was there first organized; that there Solomon, Hiram of Tyre, and Hiram Abif presided as Grand Masters over the Lodges which they had established; that there the Symbolic degrees were instituted and systems of initiation were invented; and that from that period to the present Masonry has passed down the stream of Time in unbroken succession and unaltered form. But the modern method of reading Masonic history has swept away this edifice of imagination with as unsparing a hand, and as effectual a power, as those with which the Babylonian king demolished the structure upon which they are founded. No writer who values his reputation as a critical historian would now attempt to defend this theory. Yet it has done its work. During the long period in which the hypothesis was accepted as a fact, its influence was being exerted in molding the Masonic organizations into a form closely connected with all the events and characteristics of the Solomonic Temple. So that now almost all the Symbolism of Freemasonry rests upon or is derived from the "House of the Lord" at Jerusalem. So closely are the two connected, that to attempt to separate the one from the other would be fatal to the further existence of Masonry. Each Lodge is and must be a symbol of the Jewish Temple; each Master in the chair a representative of the Jewish king; and every Mason a personation of the Jewish workman.

Thus must it ever be while Masonry endures. We must receive the myths and legends that connect it with the Temple, not indeed as historic facts, but as allegories; not as events that have really transpired, but as symbols; and must accept these allegories and these symbols for what their inventors really meant that they should be —the foundations of a science of morality.

Temple of Zerubbabel. For the fifty-two years that succeeded the destruction of Jerusalem by Nebuchadnezzar that city saw nothing but the ruins of its ancient Temple. But in the year of the world 3468 and 536 B.C., Cyrus gave permission to the Jews to return to Jerusalem, and there to rebuild the Temple of the Lord. Forty-two thousand three hundred and sixty of the liberated captives returned under the guidance of Joshua, the High Priest, Zerubbabel, the Prince or Governor, and Haggai, the Scribe, and one year after they laid the foundations of the second Temple. They were, however, much disturbed in their labors by the Samaritans, whose offer to unite with them in the building they had rejected. Artaxerxes, known in profane history as Cambyses, having succeeded Cyrus on the throne of Persia, forbade the Jews to proceed with the work, and the Temple remained in an unfinished state until the death of Artaxerxes and the succession of Darius to the throne. As in early life there had been a great intimacy between this sovereign and Zerubbabel, the latter proceeded to Babylon, and obtained permission from the monarch to resume the labor. Zerubbabel returned to Jerusalem, and notwithstanding some further delays, consequent upon the enmity of the neighboring nations, the second Temple, or, as it may be called by way of distinction from the first, the Temple of Zerubbabel, was completed in the sixth year of the reign of Darius, 515 B.C., and just twenty years after its commencement. It was then dedicated with all the solemnities that accompanied the dedication of the first.

The general plan of this second Temple was similar to that of the first. But it exceeded it in almost every dimension by one-third. The decorations of gold and other ornaments in the first Temple must have far surpassed those bestowed upon the second, for we are told by Josephus (*Antiq.*, xi., 4) that "the Priests and Levites and Elders of families were disconsolate at seeing how much more sumptuous the old Temple was than the one which, on account of their poverty, they had just been able to erect."

The Jews also say that there were five things wanting in the second Temple which had been in the first, namely, the Ark, the Urim and Thummim, the fire from heaven, the Divine presence or cloud of glory, and the spirit of prophecy and power of miracles.

Such are the most important events that relate to the construction of this second Temple. But there is a Masonic legend connected with it which, though it may have no historical foundation, is yet so closely interwoven with the Temple system of Masonry, that it is necessary it should be recounted. It was, says the legend, while the workmen were engaged in making the necessary excavations for laying the foundation, and while numbers continued to arrive at Jerusalem from Babylon, that three worn and weary sojourners, after plodding on foot over the rough and devious roads between the two cities, offered themselves to the Grand Council as willing participants in the labor of erection. Who these sojourners were, we have no historical means of discovering; but there is a Masonic tradition (entitled, perhaps, to but little weight) that they were Hananiah, Mishael, and Azariah, three holy men, who are better known to general readers by their Chaldaic names of Shadrach, Meshach, and Abed-nego, as having been miraculously preserved from the fiery furnace of Nebuchadnezzar.

Their services were accepted, and from their diligent labors resulted that important discovery, the perpetuation and preservation of which constitute the great end and design of the Royal Arch Degree.

As the symbolism of the first or Solomonic Temple is connected with and refers entirely to the Symbolic degrees, so that of the second, or Temple of Zerubbabel, forms the basis of the Royal Arch in the York and American Rites, and of several high degrees in other Rites.

Temple, Order of the. When the Knights Templar had, on account of their power and wealth, excited the fears and the cupidity of Pope Clement V., and King Philip the Fair, of France, the Order was soon compelled to succumb to the combined animosity of a spiritual and a temporal sovereign, neither of whom was capable of being controlled by a spirit of honor or a dictate of conscience. The melancholy story of the sufferings of the Knights, and of the dissolution of their Order, forms a disgraceful record, with which the history of the fourteenth century begins.

On the 13th of March, in the year 1314, and in the refined city of Paris, James de Molay, the last of a long and illustrious line of Grand Masters of the Order of Knights Templar, testified at the stake his fidelity to his vows; and eleven years of service in the cause of religion were terminated, not by the sword of a Saracen, but by the iniquitous sentence of a Catholic pope and a Christian king.

The manufacturers of Masonic legends have found in the death of de Molay and the dissolution of the Order of Templars a fertile source from which to draw materials for their fanciful theories and surreptitious documents. Among these legends there was, for instance, one which maintained that during his captivity in the Bastile the Grand Master of the Templars established four Chiefs of the Order in the north, the south, the east, and the west of Europe, whose seats of government were respectively at Stockholm, Naples, Paris, and Edinburgh. Another invention of these Masonic speculators was the forgery of that document so well known as the Charter of Larmenius, of which I shall presently take notice. Previously, however, to any consideration of this document, I must advert to the condition of the Templar Order in Portugal, because there is an intimate connection between the society there organized and the ORDER OF THE TEMPLE in France, which is more particularly the subject of the present article.

Surprising as it may appear, it is nevertheless true, that the Templars did not receive that check in Portugal to which they were subjected in France, in England, and some other countries of Europe. On the contrary, they were there maintained by King Denis in all their rights and privileges; and although compelled, by a bull of Clement V., to change their names to that of the Knights of Christ, they continued to be governed by the same rules and to wear the same costume as their predecessors, excepting the slight addition of placing a white Latin cross in the center of the usual red one of the ancient Order; and in the decree of establishment it was expressly declared that the king, in creating this new Order, intended only to effect a reform in that of the Templars. In 1420, John I., of Portugal, gave the Knights of Christ the control of the possessions of Portugal in the Indies, and succeeding monarchs granted them the proprietorship of all countries which they might discover, reserving, of course, the royal prerogative of sovereignty. In process of time the wealth and the power of the Order became so great, that the kings of Portugal found it expedient to reduce their rights to a considerable extent; but the Order itself was permitted to continue in existence, the Grand Mastership, however, being for the future vested in the sovereign.

We are now prepared to investigate understandingly the history of the Charter of Larmenius, and of the Order of the Temple at Paris, which was founded on the assumed authenticity of that document. The writings of Thory, of Ragon, and of Clavel, with the passing remarks of a few other Masonic writers, will furnish us with abundant materials for this narrative, interesting to all Freemasons, but more especially so to Masonic Knights Templar.

In the year 1682, and in the reign of Louis XIV., a licentious society was established by several young noblemen, which took the name of "La Petite Resurrection des Templiers," or "*The Little Resurrection of the Templars.*" The members wore concealed upon their shirts a decoration in the form of a cross, on which was embossed the figure of a man trampling on a woman, who lay prostrate at his feet. The emblematic signification of this symbol was, it is apparent, as unworthy of the character of man as it was derogatory to the condition and claims of woman; and the king, having been informed of the infamous proceedings which took place at the meetings, dissolved the society (which it was said was on the eve of initiating the dauphin); caused its leader, a prince of the blood, to be ignominiously punished, and banished the members from the court; the heaviest penalty that, in those days of servile submission to the throne, could be inflicted on a courtier.

In 1705, Philip of Orleans, who was subsequently the regent of France during the minority of Louis XV., collected together the remnants of this society, which still secretly existed, but had changed its object from a licentious to one of a political character. He caused new statutes to be constructed; and an Italian Jesuit, by name Father Bonani, who was a learned antiquary and an excellent designer, fabricated the document now known as the Charter of Larmenius, and thus pretended to attach the new society to the ancient Order of the Templars.

As this charter is not the least interesting of those forged documents with which the history of Freemasonry unfortunately abounds, a full description of it here will not be out of place.

The theory of the Duke of Orleans and his accomplice Bonani was (and the theory is still maintained by the Order of the Temple at Paris) that when James de Molay was about to suffer at the stake, he sent for Larmenius, and in prison, with the consent and approbation of such of his knights as were present, appointed him his successor, with the right of making a similar appointment before his death. On the demise of de Molay, Larmenius accordingly assumed the office of Grand Master, and ten years after issued this charter, transmitting his authority to Theobaldus Alexandrinus, by whom it was in like manner transmitted through a long line of Grand Masters, until in 1705 it reached Philip, Duke of Orleans. It will be seen hereafter that the list was subsequently continued to a later period.

The signatures of all these Grand Masters are affixed to the charter, which is beautifully executed on parchment, illuminated in the choicest style of Medieval chirography, and composed in the Latin language, but written in the Templar cipher. From the copy of the document given by Thory in his *Acta Latomorum* (ii., 145), I make the following translation:

"I, Brother John Mark Larmenius, of Jerusalem, by the grace of God and the secret decree of the most venerable and holy martyr, the Grand Master of the Soldiery of the Temple, (to whom be honor and glory,) confirmed by the common council of the brethren, being endowed with the Supreme Grand Mastership of the whole Order of the Temple, to every one who shall see these letters decretal thrice greeting:

"Be it known to all, both present and to come, that the failure of my strength, on account of extreme age, my poverty, and the weight of government being well considered, I, the aforesaid humble Master of the Soldiery of the Temple, have determined, for the greater glory of God and the protection and safety of the Order, the brethren, and the statutes, to resign the Grand Mastership into stronger hands.

"On which account, God helping, and with the consent of a Supreme Convention of Knights, I have conferred, and by this present decree do confer, for life, the authority and prerogatives of Grand Master of the Order of the Temple upon the Eminent Commander and very dear brother, Francis Thomas Theobald Alexandrinus, with the power, according to time and circumstances, of conferring the Grand Mastership of the Order of the Temple and the supreme authority upon another brother, most eminent for the nobility of his education and talent and decorum of his manners: which is done for the purpose of maintaining a perpetual succession of Grand Masters, an uninterrupted series of successors, and the integrity of the statutes. Nevertheless, I command that the Grand Mastership shall not be transmitted without the consent of a general convention of the fellow-soldiers of the Temple, as often as that Supreme Convention desires to be convened; and, matters being thus conducted, the successor shall be elected at the pleasure of the knights.

"But, lest the powers of the supreme office should fall into decay, now and for ever let there be four Vicars of the Grand Master, possessing supreme power, eminence, and authority over the whole Order, with the reservation of the rights of the Grand Master; which Vicars of the Grand Masters shall be chosen from among the elders, according to the order of their profession. Which is decreed in accordance with the above-mentioned wish, commended to me and to the brethren by our most venerable and most blessed Master, the martyr, to whom be honor and glory. Amen.

"Finally, in consequence of a decree of a Supreme Convention of the brethren, and by the supreme authority to me committed, I will, declare, and command that the Scottish Templars, as deserters from the Order, are to be accursed, and that they and the brethren of St. John of Jerusalem, (upon whom may God have mercy,) as spoliators of the domains of our soldiery, are now and hereafter to be considered as beyond the pale of the Temple.

"I have therefore established signs, unknown to our false brethren, and not to be known by them, to be orally communicated to our fellow-soldiers, and in which way I have already been pleased to communicate them in the Supreme Convention.

"But these signs are only to be made known after due profession and knightly consecration, according to the statutes, rites, and usages of the fellow-soldiery of the Temple, transmitted by me to the above-named Eminent Commander as they were delivered into my hands by the venerable and most holy martyr, our Grand Master, to whom be honor and glory. Let it be done as I have said. So mote it be. Amen.

"I, John Mark Larmenius, have done this on the thirteenth day of February, 1324.

"I, Francis Thomas Theobaldus Alexandrinus, God helping, have accepted the Grand Mastership, 1324."

And then follow the acceptances and signatures of twenty-two succeeding Grand Masters—the last, Bernard Raymund Fabré, under the date of 1804.*

The society, thus organized by the Duke of Orleans in 1705, under this Charter, which purported to contain the signatures *manu propria* of eighteen Grand Masters in regular succession, commencing with Larmenius and ending with himself, attempted to obtain a recognition by the Order of Christ, which we have already said was established in Portugal as the legitimate successor of the old Templars, and of which King John V. was at that time the Grand Master. For this purpose the Duke of Orleans ordered two of his members to proceed to Lisbon, and there to open negotiations with the Order of Christ. The king caused inquiries to be made of Don Luis de Cunha, his ambassador at Paris, upon whose report he gave orders for the arrest of the two French Templars. One of them escaped to Gibraltar; but the other, less fortunate, after an imprisonment of two years, was banished to Angola, in Africa, where he died.

The society, however, continued secretly to exist for many years in France, and is supposed by some to have been the same which, in 1789, was known by the name of the *Société d'Aloyau*, a title which might be translated into English as the "Society of the Sirloin"—a name much more appropriate to a club of *bons vivants* than to an association of knights. The members of this society were dispersed at the time of the French Revolution, the Duke of Casse Brissac, who was massacred at Versailles in 1792, being its Grand Master at the period of its dispersion. Thory says that the members of this association claimed to be the successors of the Templars, and to be in possession of their charters.

A certain Bro. Ledru, one of the sons of the learned Nicholas Philip Ledru, was the physician of Casse Brissac. On the death of that nobleman and the sale of his property, Ledru purchased a piece of furniture, probably an escritoire, in which was concealed the celebrated Charter of Larmenius, the manuscript statutes of 1705, and the journal of proceedings of the Order of the Temple. Clavel says that about the year 1804, Ledru showed these articles to two of his friends—de Saintot and Fabré Palaprat; the latter of whom had formerly been an ecclesiastic. The sight of these documents suggested to them the idea of reviving the Order of the Temple. They proposed to constitute Ledru the Grand Master, but he refused the offer, and nominated Claudius Matheus Radix de Chevillon for the office, who would accept it only under the title of Vicar; and he is inscribed as such on the list attached to the Charter of Larmenius, his name immediately following that of Casse Brissac, who is recorded as the last Grand Master.

These four restorers of the Order were of opinion that it would be most expedient to place it under the patronage of some distinguished personage; and while making the effort to carry this design into execution, Chevillon, excusing himself from further official labor on account of his advanced age, proposed that Fabré Palaprat should be elected Grand Master, but for one year only, and with the understanding that he would resign the dignity as soon as some notable person could be found who would be willing to accept it. But Fabré, having once been invested with the Grand Mastership, ever afterward refused to surrender the dignity.

Among the persons who were soon after admitted into the Order were Decourchant, a notary's clerk; Leblond, an official of the imperial library; and Arnal, an ironmonger, all of whom were entrusted with the secret of the fraud, and at once engaged in the construction of what have since been designated the "Relics of the Order." Of these relics, which are preserved in the treasury of the Order of the Temple at Paris, an inventory was made on the 18th day of May, 1810, being, it is probable, soon after their construction. Dr. Burnes, who was a firm believer in the legitimacy of the Parisian Order and in the authenticity of its archives, has given in his *Sketch of the History of the Knights Templars* (App., p. xii.) a copy of this inventory in the original French. Thory gives it also in his *Acta Latomorum* (ii., 143). A brief synopsis of it may not be uninteresting. The *relics* consist of twelve pieces—"a round dozen"—and are as follows:

1. The Charter of Larmenius, already described. But to the eighteen signatures of Grand Masters in the Charter, which was in 1705 in possession of Philip, Duke of Orleans, are added six more, carrying the succession on from the last-named to Fabré Palaprat, who attests as Grand Master in 1804.

2. A volume of twenty-seven paper sheets, in folio, bound in crimson velvet, satin, and gold, containing the statutes of the Order in manuscript, and signed "Philip."

3. A small copper reliquary, in the shape of a Gothic church, containing four fragments of burnt bones, wrapped in a piece

*After having disappeared for many years, the original of this Charter was rediscovered and purchased by Bro. F. J. W. Crowe, of Chichester, England, who thought it too important and valuable to remain in private hands, and it is now in the possession of the Great Priory of England. A transcript of the document, differing slightly from that given above, has been published by Bro. Crowe in *Ars Quatuor Coronatorum*, vol. 24. [E. L. H.]

of linen. These are said to have been taken from the funeral pile of the martyred Templars.

4. A sword, said to be one which belonged to James de Molay.

5. A helmet, supposed to have been that of Guy, Dauphin of Auvergne.

6. An old gilt spur.

7. A bronze patina, in the interior of which is engraved an extended hand, having rhe ring and little fingers bent in upon the palm, which is the form of the episcopal benediction in the Roman Church.

8. A pax in gilt bronze, containing a representation of St. John, under a Gothic arch. The pax is a small plate of gold, silver, or other rich material, carried round by the priest to communicate the "kiss of peace."

9. Three Gothic seals.

10. A tall ivory cross and three miters, richly ornamented.

11. The beauseant, in white linen, with the cross of the Order.

12. The war standard in white linen, with four black rays.

Of these "relics," Clavel, who, as being on the spot, may be supposed to know something of the truth, tells us that the copper reliquary, the sword, the ivory cross, and the three miters were bought by Leblond from an old iron shop in the market of St. Jean, and from a maker of church vestments in the suburbs of Paris, while the helmet was taken by Arnal from one of the government armories.

Francisco Alvaro da Sylva Freyre de Porto, a knight of the Order of Christ, and a secret agent of John VI., King of Portugal, was admitted into the Order in 1805, and continued a member until 1815. He was one of the few, Clavel says, whom Fabré and the other founders admitted into their full confidence, and in 1812 he held the office of Grand Master's Secretary. Fabré having signified to him his desire to be recognized as the successor of James de Molay by the Grand Master of the Order of Christ, Da Sylva sent a copy of the Charter of Larmenius to John VI., who was then in Brazil; but the request for recognition was refused.

The Order of the Temple, which had thus been ingeniously organized by Fabré Palaprat and his colleagues, began now to assume high prerogatives as the only representative of Ancient Templarism. The Grand Master was distinguished by the sounding titles of "Most Eminent Highness, Very Great, Powerful, and Excellent Prince, and Most Serene Lord." The whole world was divided into different jurisdictions, under the names of provinces, bailiwicks, priories, and commanderies, all of which were distributed among the members; and proofs of nobility were demanded of all candidates; but if they were not able to give these proofs, they were furnished by the Grand Master with the necessary patents.

The ceremonies of initiation were divided into three houses, again subdivided into eight degrees, and were as follows:

I. House of Initiation.

1. *Initiate.* This is the Entered Apprentice's Degree of Freemasonry.

2. *Initiate of the Interior.* This is the Fellow-Craft.

3. *Adept.* This is the Master Mason.

4. *Adept of the East.* The Elu of Fifteen of the Scottish Rite.

5. *Grand Adept of the Black Eagle of St. John.* The Elu of Nine of the Scottish Rite.

II. House of Postulance.

6. *Postulant of the Order.* The Rose Croix Degree.

III. Council.

7. *Esquire.* Merely a preparation for the Eighth Degree.

8. *Knight*, or *Levite of the Interior Guard.* The Philosophical Kadosh.

At first the members of the Order professed the Roman Catholic religion, and hence, on various occasions, Protestants and Jews were denied admission. But about the year 1814, the Grand Master having obtained possession of a manuscript copy of a spurious Gospel of St. John, which is supposed to have been forged in the fifteenth century, and which contradicted in many particulars the canonical Gospel, he caused it to be adopted as the doctrine of the Order; and thus, as Clavel says, at once transformed an Order which had always been perfectly orthodox into a schismatic sect. Out of this spurious Gospel and an introduction and commentary called the "Levitikon," said to have been written by Nicephorus, a Greek monk of Athens, Fabré and his colleagues composed a liturgy, and established a religious sect to which they gave the name of "Johannism."

The consequence of this change of religious views was a schism in the Order. The orthodox party, however, appears to have been the stronger; and after the others had for a short time exhibited themselves as *soi-disant* priests in a Johannite church which they erected, and in which they publicly chanted the liturgy which they had composed, the church and the liturgy were given up, and they retired once more into the secrecy of the Order.

Such is the brief history of the rise and progress of the celebrated Order of the Temple, which still exists at Paris, with, however, a much abridged exercise, if not with less assumption of prerogative. It still claims to be the only true depository of the powers and privileges of the ancient Order of Knights Templar, denouncing all other Templars as spurious, and its Grand Master proclaims himself the legal successor of James de Molay; with how much truth the narrative already given will enable every reader to decide.

The question of the legality of the "Order of the Temple," as the only true body of Knights Templar in modern days, is to be settled only after three other points have been determined: First, was the Charter of Larmenius, which was brought for the first time to light in 1705 by the Duke of Orleans, an authentic or a forged document? Next, even if authentic, was the story that Larmenius was invested with the Grand Mastership and the power of transmission by de Molay a fact or a fable? And, lastly, was the power exercised by Ledru, in reorganizing the Order in 1804, assumed by himself or actually derived from Casse Brissac, the previous Grand Master? There are many other questions of subordinate but necessary importance to be examined and settled before we can consent to give the Order of the Temple the high and, as regards Templarism, the exclusive position that it claims.

Temple, Second. The Temple built by Zerubbabel is so called. See *Temple of Zerubbabel.*

Temple, Sovereign Commander of the. See *Sovereign Commander of the Temple.*

Temple, Sovereign of the Sovereigns Grand Commander of the. (*Souverain des Souverain Grands Commandeur du Temple.*) A degree in the collection of Lemanceau and Le Page. It is said to be a part of the Order of Christ or Portuguese Templarism.

Temple, Spiritual. See *Spiritual Temple.*

Temple, Symbolism of the. Of all the objects which constitute the Masonic science of symbolism, the most important, the most cherished by Masons, and by far the most significant, is the Temple of Jerusalem. The spiritualizing of the Temple is the first, the most prominent, and the most pervading of all symbols of Freemasonry. It is that which most emphatically gives it its religious character. Take from Freemasonry its dependence on the Temple; leave out of its ritual all reference to that sacred edifice, and to the legends and traditions connected with it, and the system itself would at once decay and die, or at best remain only as some fossilized bone, serving merely to show the nature of the once living body to which it had belonged.

Temple worship is in itself an ancient type of the religious sentiment in its progress toward spiritual elevation. As soon as a nation emerged out of Fetishism, or the worship of visible objects, which is the most degraded form of idolatry, its people began to establish a priesthood, and to erect temples. The Goths, the Celts, the Egyptians, and the Greeks, however much they may have differed in the ritual, and in the objects of their polytheistic worship, were all in the possession of priests and of temples. The Jews, complying with this law of our religious nature, first constructed their tabernacle, or portable temple, and then, when time and opportunity permitted, transferred their monotheistic worship to that more permanent edifice which towered in all its magnificence above the pinnacle of Mount Moriah. The mosque of the Mohammedan and the church or chapel of the Christian is but an embodiment of the same idea of temple worship in a simpler form.

The adaptation, therefore, of the Temple of Jerusalem to a science of symbolism, would be an easy task to the mind of those Jews and Tyrians who were engaged in its construction. Doubtless, at its original conception, the idea of this temple symbolism was rude and unembellished. It was to be perfected and polished only by future aggregations of succeeding intellects. And yet no Biblical nor Masonic scholar will venture to deny that there was, in the mode of building and in all the circumstances connected with the construction of King Solomon's Temple, an apparent design to establish a foundation for symbolism.

The Freemasons have, at all events, seized with avidity the idea of representing in their symbolic language the interior and spiritual man by a material temple. They have the doctrine of the great Apostle of the Gentiles, who has said, "Know ye are the temple of God, and that the spirit of God dwelleth in you." The great body of the Masonic Craft, looking only to this first Temple erected by the wisdom of King Solomon, make it the symbol of life; and as the great object of Masonry is the search after truth, they are directed to build up this temple as a fitting receptacle for truth when found, a place where it may dwell, just as the ancient Jews built up their great Temple as a dwelling-place for Him who is the author of all truth.

To the Master Mason, this Temple of Solomon is truly the symbol of human life; for, like life, it was to have its end. For four centuries it glittered on the hills of Jerusalem in all its gorgeous magnificence; now, under some pious descendant of the wise King of Israel, the spot from whose altars arose the burnt-offerings to a living God, and now polluted by some recreant monarch of Judah to the service of Baal; until at length it received the Divine punishment through the mighty King of Babylon, and, having been despoiled of all its treasures, was burnt to the ground, so that nothing was left of all its splendor but a smoldering heap of ashes. Variable in its purposes, evanescent in its existence, now a gorgeous pile of architectural beauty, and anon a ruin over which the resistless power of fire has passed, it becomes a fit symbol of human life occupied in the search after Divine truth, which is nowhere to be found; now sinning and now repentant; now vigorous with health and strength, and anon a senseless and decaying corpse.

Such is the symbolism of the first Temple, that of Solomon, as familiar to the class of Master Masons. But there is a second and higher class of the Fraternity, the Masons of the Royal Arch, by whom this temple symbolism is still further developed.

This second class, leaving their early symbolism and looking beyond this Temple of Solomon, find in Scriptural history another Temple, which, years after the destruction of the first one, was erected upon its ruins; and they have selected the second Temple, the Temple of Zerubbabel, as their prominent

symbol. And as the first class of Masons find in their Temple the symbol of mortal life, limited and perishable, they, on the contrary, see in this second Temple, built upon the foundations of the first, a symbol of life eternal, where the lost truth shall be found, where new incense shall arise from a new altar, and whose perpetuity their great Master had promised when, in the very spirit of symbolism, he exclaimed, "Destroy this temple, and in three days I will raise it up."

And so to these two classes or Orders of Masons the symbolism of the Temple presents itself in a connected and continuous form. To the Master Mason, the Temple of Solomon is the symbol of this life; to the Royal Arch Mason, the Temple of Zerubbabel is the symbol of the future life. To the former, his Temple is the symbol of the search for truth; to the latter, his is the symbol of the discovery of truth; and thus the circle is completed and the system made perfect.

Temple, Workmen at the. See *Workmen at the Temple.*

Templier. The title of a Knights Templar in French. The expression "Chevalier Templier" is scarcely ever used by French writers.

Templum Hierosolymæ. Latin for the Temple of Jerusalem. It is supposed by some to be a phrase concealed under the monogram of the *Triple Tau*, which see.

Ten. Ten cannot be considered as a sacred number in Masonry. But by the Pythagoreans it was honored as a symbol of the perfection and consummation of all things. It was constituted of the monad and duad, the active and passive principles, the triad or their result, and the quaternior or first square, and hence they referred it to their sacred tetractys. They said that ten contained all the relations of numbers and harmony. (See *Tetractys.*)

Ten Expressions. Using, as do the Rabbis, the expression, "In the beginning God created the heaven and the earth," as one, we find nine other expressions in the first chapter of Genesis in which "God said"; thus making ten expressions by which the world was created. There were ten generations from Adam to Noah, to show that God was long-suffering before he deluged the earth. For a similar reason, says the *Talmud*, there were ten generations from Noah to Abraham, until the latter "took the reward of them all." Abraham was proved with ten trials. Ten miracles were wrought for the children of Israel in Egypt, and ten at the Red Sea. Ten plagues afflicted the Egyptians in Egypt, and ten at the Red Sea. And ten miracles were wrought in the Holy Temple. (See *Ten.*)

Tengu. A significant word in the high degrees of the Scottish Rite. The original old French rituals explain it, and say that it and the two other words that accompany are formed out of the initials of the words of a particular sentence which has reference to the "Sacred treasure" of Masonry.

Tennessee. Until the end of the year 1813, the State of Tennessee constituted a part of the Masonic jurisdiction of North Carolina, and the Lodges were held under warrants issuing from the Grand Lodge of "North Carolina and Tennessee," with the exception of one Lodge in Davidson County, which derived its Charter from the Grand Lodge of Kentucky. In December, 1811, a convention was held at Knoxville, when an address was directed to the Grand Lodge of North Carolina, soliciting its assent to the severance of the Masonic jurisdiction and the establishment of an independent Grand Lodge. In October, 1813, this consent was granted, and a convention of the Lodges was ordered by the Grand Master to assemble at Knoxville on December 27, 1813, that the Grand Lodge of Tennessee might be legally constituted. Delegates from eight Lodges accordingly assembled on that day at Knoxville, and a convention was duly organized. A deed of relinquishment from the Grand Lodge of North Carolina was read. By this instrument the Grand Lodge of North Carolina relinquished all authority and jurisdiction over the several Lodges in the State of Tennessee, and assented to the erection of an independent Grand Lodge. A Constitution was accordingly adopted and the Grand Lodge of Tennessee organized, Thomas Claiborne being elected Grand Master.

The first Royal Arch Chapters in Tennessee were instituted by the General Grand Chapter, and the Grand Chapter of Tennessee was organized in 1826.

The Grand Council of Royal and Select Masters was established October 13, 1847.

The Grand Commandery of Tennessee was organized October 12, 1859.

There are in the State a few bodies of the Ancient and Accepted Scottish Rite, which derive their Charters from the Supreme Council for the Southern Jurisdiction.

Tensio-Dai-Sin. A deity held in adoration by the Japanese; the zodiacal sun, with its twelve constellations, as the representative of the god and his twelve apostles. This omnific being, like the zodiacal light, of triangular form, seen only in the evening after twilight and in the morning before dawn, and whose nature is unknown, is possessed of ineffable attributes, inexpressible and unutterable, with a supreme power to overcome eruptions of nature and the elements. Like unto Masonry, there are four periods of festival, to wit, in the third, fifth, seventh, and ninth of the third, fifth, seventh, and ninth months. The initiates are called Jammabos, and wear aurora-colored robes, like unto the light of the dawn of day.

Tent. The tent, which constitutes a part of the paraphernalia or furniture of a Commandery of Knights Templar, is not only intended for a practical use, but also has a symbolic meaning. The Order of the Templars was instituted for the protection of Christian pilgrims who were visiting the sepulcher of their Lord. The Hospitalers might remain in the city and fulfil their vows by attendance on the sick, but the Templar must away to the plains, the hills, and the desert, there, in his lonely tent, to watch the wily Saracen, and to await the toilsome pilgrim, to whom he might offer the crust of bread and the draft of water, and instruct him in his way, and warn him of danger, and give him words of good cheer. Often in the early history of the Order, before luxury and wealth and vice had impaired its purity, must these meetings of the toilsome pilgrim, on his way to the holy shrine, with the valiant Knight who stood by his tent door on the roadside, have occurred. And it is just such events as these that are commemorated in the tent scenes of the Templar ritual.

Tenure of Office. All offices in the bodies of the York and American Rites are held by annual election or appointment. But the holder of an office does not become *functus officii* by the election of his successor; he retains the office until that successor has been installed. This is technically called "holding over." It is not election only, but election and installation that give possession of an office in Masonry. If a new Master, having been elected, should, after the election and installation of the other officers of the Lodge, refuse to be installed, the old Master would "hold over," or retain the office until the next annual election. The oath of office of every officer is that he will perform the duties of the office for twelve months, and *until his successor shall have been installed*. In France, in the last century, Warrants of Constitution were granted to certain Masters who held the office for life, and were thence called "Maîtres inamovibles," or immovable Masters. They considered the Lodges committed to their care as their personal property, and governed them despotically, according to their own caprices. But in 1772 this class of Masters had become so unpopular, that the Grand Lodge removed them, and made the tenure of office the same as it was in England.

In the Ancient and Accepted Scottish Rite the officers of a Supreme Council hold their offices, under the Constitutions of 1786, for life. In the subordinate bodies of the Rite, the elections are held annually or triennially. This is also the rule in the Supreme Council of the Northern Jurisdiction, which has abandoned the law of perpetual tenure. The Supreme Council elects its members independently of the Consistories and is thereby self-perpetuating.

Tercy. One of the nine Elus recorded in the high degrees as having been sent out by Solomon to make the search which is referred to in the Master's legend. The name was invented, with some allusion, not now explicable, to the political incidents of Stuart Masons. The name is probably an anagram or corruption of some friend of the house of Stuart. (See *Anagram*.)

Terminus. The god of landmarks, whose worship was introduced among the Romans by Numa. The god was represented by a *cubical stone*. Of all the gods, Terminus was the only one who, when the new Capitol was building, refused to remove his altar. Hence Ovid (*Fasti*, ii., 673) addressed him thus: "O Terminus, no inconstancy was permitted thee; in whatever situation thou hast been placed, there abide, and do not yield one jot to any neighbor asking thee." The Masons pay the same reverence to their landmarks that the Romans did to their god Terminus.

Ternary Allusions. Some of the well-considered and beautiful thoughts of Rev. George Oliver on Ternary Allusions as applicable to the construction of the Temple services of Solomon are the three principal religious festivals—the Feast of Passover, of Pentecost, and of Tabernacles. The Camp was threefold. The Tabernacle, with its precinct, was called "The Camp of the Divine Majesty"; the next, "The Camp of Levi, or little host of the Lord"; and the largest, "The Camp of Israel, or the great host." The tribes were marshaled in subdivisions of three, each being designated by a banner containing one of the cherubic forms of the Deity. The Temple, in like manner, had three divisions and three symbolical references—historical, mystical, and moral. The golden candlestick had twice three branches, each containing three bowls, knobs, and flowers. In the Sanctuary were three sacred utensils—the candlestick, the table of shewbread, and the altar of incense; and three hallowed articles were deposited in the Ark of the Covenant—the tables of the law, the rod of Aaron, and the pot of manna. There were three orders of priests and Levites, and the High Priest was distinguished by a triple crown.

Three allusions may be observed through the whole of Jewish history. Thus, Elijah raised the widow's son by stretching himself upon the child three times. Samaria sustained a siege of three years. Some of the kings of Israel and Judah reigned three years, some three months, some three days. Rehoboam served God three years before he apostated. The Jews fasted three days and three nights, by command of Esther, before their triumph over Haman. Their sacred writings had three grand divisions—the law, the prophets, and the psalms.

In the Masonic system there were three Temples—those of Solomon, Zerubbabel, and Herod. The Jews speak of two that have been, and believe in one, as described by Ezekiel the Prophet, yet to come. The Rabbis say: "The third Temple we hope and look for." (See *Three*.)

[C. T. McClenachan.]

Terrasson, the Abbé Jean. The Abbé Terrasson was born at Lyons, in France, in 1670. He was educated by the congregation of the Oratory, of which his brother André was a priest, but eventually abandoned it, which gave so much offense to his father, that he left him by his will only a very moderate income. The Abbé obtained a chair in the Academy of Sciences in 1707, and a professorship in the Royal College in 1724, which position he occupied until his death in 1750. He was the author of a *Critical Dissertation on the Iliad of Homer*, a translation of *Diodorus Siculus*, and several other classical and philosophical works. But the work most interesting to the Masonic scholar is his *Séthos, histoire ou vie tirée des monumens anecdotes de l'ancienne Egypt*, published at Paris in 1731. This work excited on its appearance so much attention in the literary world, that it was translated into the German and English languages under the respective titles of: 1. *Abris der wahren Helden-Tugend, oder Lebensgeschichte des Sethos;* translated by Chro. Gli. Wendt, Hamburg, 1732. 2. *Geschichte des Konigs Sethos;* translated by Matth. Claudius, Breslau, 1777; and 3. *The Life of Sethos, taken from private Memoirs of the ancient Egyptians; translated from a Greek MS. into French, and now done into English*, by M. Lediard, London, 1732.

In this romance he has given an account of the initiation of his hero, Sethos, an Egyptian prince, into the Egyptian mysteries. We must not, however, be led into the error, into which Kloss says that the Masonic Fraternity fell on its first appearance, that this account is a well-proved, historical narrative. Much as we know of the Egyptian mysteries, compared with our knowledge of the Grecian or the Asiatic, we have no sufficient documents from which to obtain the consecutive and minute detail which the Abbé Terrasson has constructed. It is like Ramsay's *Travels of Cyrus*, to which it has been compared—a romance rather than a history; but it still contains so many scintillations of truth, so much of the substantials of fact amid the ornaments of fiction, that it cannot but prove instructive as well as amusing. We have in it the outlines of an initiation into the Egyptian mysteries such as the learned Abbé could derive from the documents and monuments to which he was able to apply, with many *lacunæ* which he has filled up from his own inventive and poetic genius.

Terrible Brother. French, *Frère terrible*. An officer in the French Rite, who in an initiation conducts the candidate, and in this respect performs the duty of a Senior Deacon in the York Rite.

Territorial Jurisdiction. It has now become the settled principle of, at least, American Masonic law, that Masonic and political jurisdiction should be coterminous, that is, that the boundaries which circumscribe the territorial jurisdiction of a Grand Lodge should be the same as those which define the political limits of the State in which it exists. And so it follows that if a State should change its political boundaries, the Masonic boundaries of the Grand Lodge should change with it. Thus, if a State should diminish its extent by the cession of any part of its territory to an adjoining State, the Lodges situated within the ceded territory would pass over to the jurisdiction of the Grand Lodge of the State to which that territory had been ceded.

Tessellated. From the Latin *tessella*, a little square stone. Checkered, formed in little squares of Mosaic work. Applied in Masonry to the Mosaic pavement of the Temple, and to the border which surrounds the tracing-board, probably incorrectly in the latter instance. (See *Tessellated Border*.)

Tessellated Border. Browne says in his *Master Key*, which is supposed to present the general form of the Prestonian lectures, that the ornaments of a Lodge are the Mosaic Pavement, the Blazing Star, and the Tessellated Border; and he defines the Tessellated Border to be "the skirt-work round the Lodge." Webb, in his lectures, teaches that the ornaments of a Lodge are the Mosaic pavement, the indented tessel, and the blazing star; and he defines the indented tessel to be that "beautifully tessellated border or skirting which surrounded the ground-floor of King Solomon's Temple." The French call it "la houpe dentelée," which is literally the *indented tessel;* and they describe it as "a cord forming true-lovers' knots, which surrounds the tracing-board." The Germans call it "die Schnur von starken Faden," or the *cord of strong threads*, and define it as a border surrounding the tracing-board of an Entered Apprentice, consisting of a cord tied in lovers' knots, with two tassels attached to the ends.

The idea prevalent in America, and derived from a misapprehension of the plate in the *Monitor* of Cross, that the tessellated border was a decorated part of the Mosaic pavement, and made like it of little square stones, does not seem to be supported by these definitions. They all indicate that the *tessellated border* was a cord. The interpretation of its symbolic meaning still further sustains this idea. Browne says "it alludes to that kind care of Providence which so cheerfully surrounds and keeps us within its protection whilst we justly and uprightly govern our lives and actions by the four cardinal virtues in divinity, namely, temperance, fortitude, prudence, and justice." This last allusion is to the four tassels attached to the cord. (See *Tassels*.)

Webb\ says that it is "emblematic of those blessings and comforts which surround us, and which we hope to obtain by a faithful reliance on Divine Providence."

The French ritual says that it is intended "to teach the Mason that the society of which he constitutes a part surrounds the earth, and that distance, so far from relaxing the bonds which unite the members to each other, ought to draw them closer."

Lenning says that it symbolizes the fraternal bond by which all Masons are united.

But Gädicke is more precise. He defines it as "the universal bond by which every Mason ought to be united to his brethren," and he says that "it should consist of sixty threads or yarns, because, according to the ancient statutes, no Lodge was allowed to have above sixty members."

Oliver (*Landm.*, i., 174) says "the Tracing-Board is surrounded by an indented or tessellated border . . . at the four angles appear as many tassels." But in the old English tracing-boards the two lower tassels are often omitted. They are, however, generally found in the French. Lenning, speaking, I suppose, for the German, assigns to them but two. Four tassels are, however, necessary to complete the symbolism, which is said to be that of the four cardinal virtues. The tessellated, more properly, therefore, the tassellated, border consists of a cord intertwined with knots, to each end of which is appended a tassel. It surrounds the border of the tracing-board, and appears at the top in the following form:

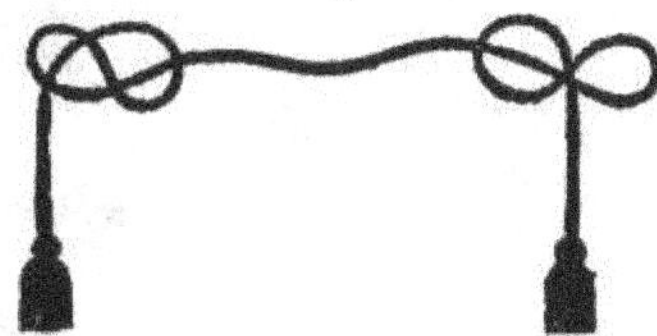

There is, however, in these old tracing-boards another border, which surrounds the entire picture with lines, as in the following figure:

This indented border, which was made to represent a cord of black and white threads, was, I think, in time mistaken for *tessellæ*, or little stones; an error probably originating in confounding it with the tessellated pavement, which was another one of the ornaments of the Lodge.

We find that we have for this symbol five different names: in English, the indented tarsel, the indented tassel, the indented tessel, the tassellated border, and the tessellated border; in French, the houpe dentelée, or indented tessel; and in German, the Schnur von starken Faden, or the cord of strong threads.

The question what is the true tessellated border would not be a difficult one to answer, if it were not for the variety of names given to it in the English rituals. We know by tradition, and by engravings that have been preserved, that during the ceremonies of initiation in the early part of the last century the symbols of the Order were marked out in chalk on the floor, and that this picture was encircled by a waving cord. This cord was ornamented with tassels, and formerly a border to the tracing on the floor was called the indented tassel, the cord and the tufts attached to it being the tassel, which, being by its wavy direction partly in and partly outside of the picture, was said to be indented. This *indented tassel* was subsequently corrupted by illiterate Masons into *indented tarsel*, the appellation met with in some of the early catechisms.

Afterward, looking to its decoration with tassels and to its position as a border to the tracing-board, it was called the *tassellated border*. In time the picture on the floor was transferred to a permanent tracing-board, and then the tassels were preserved at the top, and the rest of the cord was represented around the board in the form of white and black angular spaces. These were mistaken for little stones, and the *tassellated border* was called, by a natural corruption, the *tessellated* border. Many years ago, when I first met with the idea of this corruption from *tassellated* to *tessellated*, which was suggested to Dr. Oliver by "a learned Scottish Mason," whose name he does not give, I was inclined to doubt its correctness. Subsequent investigations have led me to change that opinion. I think that I can readily trace the gradual steps of corruption and change from the original name *indented tassel*, which the early French Masons had literally translated by *houpe dentelée*, to *indented tarsel*, and sometimes, according to Oliver, to *indented trasel;* then to *tassellated border*, and, finally, to *tessellated border*, the name which it now bears.

The form and the meaning of the symbol are now apparent. The *tessellated border*, as it is called, is a cord, decorated with tassels, which surrounds the tracing-board of an Entered Apprentice, the said tracing-board being a representation of the Lodge, and it symbolizes the bond of love—the mystic tie—which binds the Craft wheresoever dispersed into one band of brotherhood.

Tessel, Indented. See *Tessellated Border*.

Tessera Hospitalis. Latin. Literally, "the token of the guest," or "the hospitable die." It was a custom among the ancients, that when two persons formed an alliance of friendship, they took a small piece of bone, ivory, stone, or even wood, which they divided into two parts, each one inscribing his name upon his half. They then made an exchange of the pieces, each promising to retain the part entrusted to him as a perpetual token of the covenant into which they had entered, of which its production at any future time would be a proof and a reminder. (See the subject more fully treated in the article *Mark.*)

Testimony. In Masonic trials the testimony of witnesses is taken in two ways—that of profanes by affidavit, and that of Masons on their Masonic obligation.

Tests. Test questions, to which the conventional answers would prove the Masonic character of the person interrogated, were in very common use in the last century in England. They were not, it is true, enjoined by authority, but were conventionally used to such an extent that every Mason was supposed to be acquainted with them. They are now obsolete; but not very long ago such "catch questions" as "Where does the

Master hang his hat?" and a few others, equally trivial, were in use.

Oliver gives (*Golden Remains*, iv., 14) the following as the tests in use in the early part of the last century. They were introduced by Desaguliers and Anderson at the revival in 1717. Some of them, however, were of a higher character, being taken from the catechism or lecture then in use as a part of the instructions of the Entered Apprentice.

What is the place of the Senior Entered Apprentice?

What are the fixed lights?

How ought the Master to be served?

What is the punishment of a cowan?

What is the bone box?

How is it said to be opened only with ivory keys?

By what is the key suspended?

What is the clothing of a Mason?

What is the brand?

How high was the door of the middle chamber?

What does this stone smell of?

The name of an Entered Apprentice?

The name of a Fellow-Craft?

The name of Master Mason?

In the year 1730, Martin Clare having, by order of the Grand Lodge, remodeled the lectures, he abolished the old tests and introduced the following new ones:

Whence came you?

Who brought you here?

What recommendation do you bring?

Do you know the secrets of Masonry?

Where do you keep them?

Have you the key?

Where is it deposited?

When you were made a Mason, what did you consider most desirable?

What is the name of your Lodge?

Where is it situated?

What is its foundation?

How did you enter the Temple of Solomon?

How many windows did you see there?

What is the duty of the youngest apprentice?

Have you ever worked as a Mason?

What did you work with?

Salute me as a Mason.

Ten years afterward Clare's tests were superseded by a new series of "examination questions," which were promulgated by Dr. Manningham, and very generally adopted. They are as follows:

Where were you made a Mason?

What did you learn there?

How do you hope to be rewarded?

What access have you to that Grand Lodge?

How many steps?

What are their names?

How many qualifications are required in a Mason?

What is the standard of a Mason's faith?

What is the standard of his actions?

Can you name the peculiar characteristics of a Mason's Lodge?

What is the interior composed of?

Why are we termed brethren?

By what badge is a Mason distinguished?

To what do the reports refer?

How many principal points are there in Masonry?

To what do they refer?

Their names?

The allusion?

Thomas Dunckerley subsequently made a new arrangement of the lectures, and with them the tests. For the eighteen which composed the series of Manningham, he invented ten, but which were more significant and important in their bearing. They were as follows:

How ought a Mason to be clothed?

When were you born?

Where were you born?

How were you born?

Did you endure the brand with fortitude and patience?

The situation of the Lodge?

What is its name?

With what have you worked as a Mason?

Explain the sprig of Cassia.

How old are you?

Preston subsequent y, as his first contribution to Masonic literature, presented the following system of tests, which were at a later period adopted:

Whither are you bound?

Are you a Mason?

How do you know that?

How will you prove it to me?

Where were you made a Mason?

When were you made a Mason?

By whom were you made a Mason?

From whence come you?

What recommendation do you bring?

Any other recommendation?

Where are the secrets of Masonry kept?

To whom do you deliver them?

How do you deliver them?

In what manner do you serve your Master?

What is your name?

What is the name of your son?

If a Brother were lost, where should you hope to find him?

How should you expect him to be clothed?

How blows a Mason's wind?

Why does it thus blow?

What time is it?

These Prestonian tests continued in use until the close of the last century, and Dr. Oliver says that at his initiation, in 1801, he was fully instructed in them.

Tests of this kind appear to have existed at an early period. The "examination of a Steinmetz," given by Findel in his *History of Freemasonry*, presents all the characteristics of the English "tests."

The French Masons have one, "Comment êtes vous entré dans le Temple de Salomon?" and in America, besides the one already mentioned, there are a few others which are sometimes used, but without legal authority. A review of these tests will lead to the conclusion adopted by Oliver, that "they are doubtless of great utility, but in their selection a pure and discriminating taste has not always been used."

Test Word. In the year 1829, during the anti-Masonic excitement in America, the Grand Lodge of New York proposed, as a safeguard against "the introduction of impostors among the workmen," a test word to be used in all examinations in addition to the legitimate tests. But as this was deemed an innovation on the landmarks, and as it was impossible that it could ever become universal, the Grand Lodges of the United States very properly rejected it, and it was never used.

Tetractys. The Greek word τετρακτὺς signifies, literally, the number four, and is therefore synonymous with the *quaternion;* but it has been peculiarly applied to a symbol of the Pythagoreans, which is composed of ten dots arranged in a triangular form of four rows.

This figure was in itself, as a whole, emblematic of the Tetragrammaton, or sacred name of four letters (for *tetractys*, in Greek, means *four*), and was undoubtedly learned by Pythagoras during his visit to Babylon. But the parts of which it is composed were also pregnant symbols. Thus the one point was a symbol of the active principle or creator, the two points of the passive principle or matter, the three of the world proceeding from their union, and the four of the liberal arts and sciences, which may be said to complete and perfect that world.

This arrangement of the ten points in a triangular form was called the *tetractys* or number four, because each of the sides of the triangle consisted of four points, and the whole number of ten was made up by the summation of the first four figures, $1 + 2 + 3 + 4 = 10$.

Hierocles says, in his *Commentaries on the Golden Verses* (v., p. 47): "But how comes God to be the Tetractys? This thou mayst learn in the sacred book ascribed to Pythagoras, in which God is celebrated as the number of numbers. For if all things exist by His eternal decrees, it is evident that in each species of things the number depends on the cause that produces them. . . . Now the power of ten is four; for before we come to a complete and perfect decade, we discover all the virtue and perfection of the ten in the four. Thus, in assembling all numbers from one to four inclusive, the whole composition makes ten," etc.

And Dacier, in his Notes on these Commentaries and on this particular passage, remarks that "Pythagoras, having learned in Egypt the name of the true God, the mysterious and ineffable name Jehovah, and finding that in the original tongue it was composed of four letters, translated it into his own language by the word tetractys, and gave the true explanation of it, saying that it properly signified the source of nature that perpetually rolls along."

So much did the disciples of Pythagoras venerate the tetractys, that it is said that they took their most solemn oaths, especially that of initiation, upon it. The exact words of the oath are given in the *Golden Verses*, and are referred to by Jamblichus in his *Life of Pythagoras:*

Ναὶ μὰ τὸν ἁμετέρᾳ ψυχᾷ παραδόντα τετρακτὺν
Παγὰν ἀενάου φύσεως, ἀλλ' ἔρχευ ἐπ' ἔργον.

i. e.,

"I swear it by him who has transmitted into our soul the sacred tetractys,
The source of nature, whose course is eternal."

Jamblichus gives a different phraseology of the oath, but with substantially the same meaning. In the symbols of Masonry, we will find the sacred delta bearing the nearest analogy to the tetractys of the Pythagoreans.

The outline of these points form, it will be perceived, a triangle; and if we draw short lines from point to point, we will have within this great triangle nine smaller ones. Dr. Hemming, in his revision of the English lectures, adopted in 1813, thus explains this symbol:

"The great triangle is generally denominated Pythagorean, because it served as a principal illustration of that philosopher's system. This emblem powerfully elucidates the mystical relation between the numerical and geometrical symbols. It is composed of ten points, so arranged as to form one great equilateral triangle, and at the same time to divide it into nine similar triangles of smaller dimensions. The first of these, representing unity, is called a *monad*, and answers to what is denominated a point in geometry, each being the principle by the multiplication of which all combinations of form and number are respectively generated. The next two points are denominated a *duad*, representing the number two, and answers to the geometrical line which, consisting of length without breadth, is bounded by two extreme points. The three following points are called the *triad*, representing the number three, and may be considered as having an indissoluble relation to all superficies, which consist of length and breadth, when contemplated as abstracted from thickness."

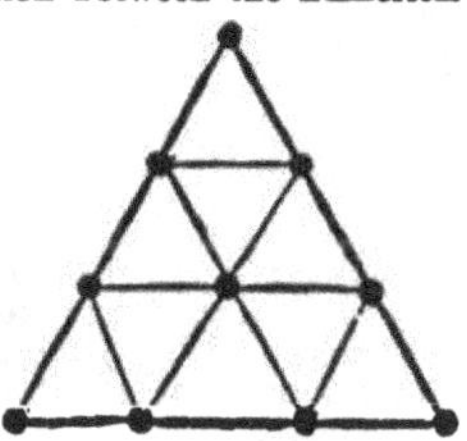

Dr. Hemming does not appear to have improved on the Pythagorean symbolisation.

Tetradites. Believers in the occult powers of the numeral four, and in a Godhead of four persons in lieu of three. In this connection, the following figure is worthy of examination, it being a star of five points

enclosing the three letters of the Ineffable Name, but forming the Tetragrammaton, the *Shem Hamphorash*. This figure has been claimed to represent the Godhead.

Tetragrammaton. In Greek, it signifies a word of four letters. It is the title given by the Talmudists to the name of God Jehovah, which in the original Hebrew consists of four letters, יהוה. (See *Jehovah*.)

Teutonic Knights. The origin of this Order was a humble but a pious one. During the Crusades, a wealthy gentleman of Germany, who resided at Jerusalem, commiserating the condition of his countrymen who came there as pilgrims, made his house their receptacle, and afterward built a hospital, to which, by the permission of the Patriarch of Jerusalem, he added an oratory dedicated to the Virgin Mary. Other Germans coming from Lubeck and Bremen contributed to the extension of this charity, and erected at Acre, during the third Crusade, a sumptuous hospital, and assumed the title of Teutonic Knights, or Brethren of the Hospital of our Lady of the Germans of Jerusalem. They elected Henry Walpott their first Master, and adopted for their government a Rule closely approximating to that both of the Templars and the Hospitalers, with an additional one that none but Germans should be admitted into the Order. Their dress consisted of a white mantle, with a black cross embroidered in gold. Clark says (*Hist. of Knighthood*, ii., 30) that the original badge, which was assigned to them by the Emperor Henry VI., was a black cross potent; and that form of cross has ever since been known as a Teutonic Cross. John, King of Jerusalem, added the cross double potent gold, that is, a cross potent of gold on the black cross. The Emperor Frederick II. gave them the black double-headed eagle, to be borne in an inescutcheon in the center of the cross; and St. Louis, of France, added to it, as an augmentation, a blue chief strewn with fleur-de-lis.

During the siege of Acre they did good service to the Christian cause; but on the fall of that city, the main body returned to Europe with Frederick II. For many years they were engaged in crusades against the pagan inhabitants of Prussia and Poland. Ashmole says that in 1340 they built the city of Maryburg, and there established the residence of their Grand Master. They were for a long time engaged in contests with the kings of Poland on account of their invasion of their territory. They were excommunicated by Pope John XXII., but relying on their great strength, and the remoteness of their province, they bid defiance to ecclesiastical censures, and the contest ended in their receiving Prussia proper as a brief of the kings of Poland.

In 1511, Albert, Margrave of Brandenburg, was elected their Grand Master. In 1525 he abandoned the vows of his Order; became a Protestant, and exchanged his title of Grand Master for that of Duke of Eastern Prussia; and thus the dominion of the Knights was brought to an end, and the foundation laid of the future kingdom of Prussia.

The Order, however, still continued its existence, the seat of the Grand Master being at Mergentheim, in Swabia. By the peace of Presburg, in 1805, the Emperor Francis II. obtained the Grand Mastership, with all its rights and privileges. In 1809 Napoleon abolished the Order, but it still has a titular existence in Austria.

Attempts have been made to incorporate the Teutonic Knights into Masonry, and their cross has been adopted in some of the high degrees. But we fail to find in history the slightest traces of any actual connection between the two Orders.

Texas. Freemasonry was introduced in Texas by the formation of a Lodge at Brasoria, which met for the first time, December 27, 1835. The Dispensation for this Lodge was granted by J. H. Holland, Grand Master of Louisiana, and in his honor the Lodge was called Holland Lodge, No. 36. It continued to meet until February, 1836, when the war with Mexico put an end to its labors for the time. In October, 1837, it was reopened at Houston, a Charter having in the interval been issued for it by the Grand Lodge of Louisiana. In the meantime two other Lodges had been chartered by the Grand Lodge of Louisiana, Milam, No. 40, at Nacogdoches, and McFarlane, No. 41, at San Augustine. Delegates from these Lodges met at Houston, December 20, 1837, and organized the Grand Lodge of the Republic of Texas, Anson Jones being elected Grand Master.

The introduction of Royal Arch Masonry into Texas was accompanied with some difficulties. In 1838, the General Grand Chapter of the United States granted a

Charter for a Chapter at San Felipe de Austin. The members, finding it impracticable to meet at that place, assumed the responsibility of opening it at Galveston, which was done June 2, 1840. This irregular action was, on application, healed by the General Grand Chapter. Subsequently this body united with two illegal Chapters in the Republic to form a Grand Chapter. This body was declared illegal by the General Grand Chapter, and Masonic intercourse with it prohibited. The Chapter at Galveston submitted to the decree, and the so-called Grand Chapter of Texas was dissolved. Charters were then granted by the General Grand Chapter to seven other Chapters, and in 1850 the Grand Chapter of Texas was duly established.*

The Grand Commandery of Texas was organized January 19, 1855.

T.·.G.·.A.·.O.·.T.·.U.·. The initials of *The Great Architect of the Universe.* Often used in this abbreviated form by Masonic writers.

Thammuz. Spelled also *Tammuz.* A deity worshiped by the apostate Jews in the time of Ezekiel, and supposed by most commentators to be identical with the Syrian god Adonis. (See *Adonis, Mysteries of.*)

Thanks. It is a usage of French Masonry, and in the high degrees of some other Rites, for the candidate, after his initiation and the address of the orator to him, to return thanks to the Lodge for the honor that has been conferred upon him. It is a voluntary and not an obligatory duty, and is not practised in the Lodges of the York and American Rites.

Theism. Theological writers have defined theism as being the belief in the existence of a Deity who, having created the world, directs its government by the constant exercise of his beneficent power, in contradistinction to atheism, which denies the existence of any such creative and superintending being. In this sense, theism is the fundamental religion of Masonry, on which is superimposed the additional and peculiar tenets of each of its disciples.

Theocratic Philosophy of Freemasonry. This is a term invented by Dr. Oliver to indicate that view of Freemasonry which intimately connects its symbols with the teachings of pure religion, and traces them to the primeval revelations of God to man, so that the philosophy of Masonry shall develop the continual government of the Divine Being. Hence he says: "It is the Theocratic Philosophy of Freemasonry that commands our unqualified esteem, and seals in our heart that love for the Institution which will produce an active religious faith and practice, and lead in the end to 'a building not made with hands, eternal in the heavens.'" He has developed this system in one of his works entitled *The Theocratic Philosophy of Freemasonry, in twelve lectures on its Speculative, Operative, and Spurious Branches.* In this work he enters with great minuteness into an examination of the speculative character of the Institution and of its operative division, which he contends had been practised as an exclusively scientific pursuit from the earliest times in every country in the would. Many of the legendary speculations advanced in this work will be rejected at this day as unsound and untenable, but his views of the true philosophy of Freemasonry are worthy of profound study.

Theological Virtues. Under the name of the Cardinal Virtues, because all the other virtues hinged upon them, the ancient Pagans gave the most prominent place in their system of ethics to Temperance, Prudence, Fortitude, and Justice. But the three virtues taught in the theology of St. Paul, Faith, Hope, and Charity, as such were unknown to them. To these, as taking a higher place and being more intimately connected with the relations of man to God, Christian writers have given the name of the Theological Virtues. They have been admitted into the system of Masonry, and are symbolized in the Theological ladder of Jacob.

Theopaschites. Followers of Peter the Fuller, who flourished in the fifth century, and believed in the crucifixion of all three of the Godhead.

Theoricus. The second grade of the "First Order" of the Society of Rosicrucians. (See *Rosicrucianism.*)

Theoricus. The Twelfth Degree of the German Rose Croix.

Theosophists. There were many theosophists—enthusiasts whom Vaughan calls "noble specimens of the mystic"—but those with whom the history of Masonry has most to do were the mystical religious thinkers of the last century, who supposed that they were possessed of a knowledge of the Divinity and his works by supernatural inspiration, or who regarded the foundation of their mystical tenets as resting on a sort of Divine intuition. Such were Swedenborg, who, if not himself a Masonic reformer, has supplied the materials of many degrees; the Moravian brethren, the object of whose association is said to have been originally the propagation of the Gospel under the Masonic veil; St. Martin, the founder of the Philalethans; Pernetty, to whom we owe the Order of Illuminati at Avignon; and Chastanier, who was the inventer of the Rite of Illuminated Theosophists. The object proposed in all these theosophic degrees was the regeneration of man, and his reintegration into the primitive innocence from which he had fallen by original sin. Theosophic Masonry was, in fact, nothing else than an application of the speculative ideas of Jacob Böhme, of Swedenborg,

*The Grand Chapter of Texas has long refused to admit the authority of the General Grand Chapter and takes no part in their proceedings. The Chapters for many years worked the Council degrees in the Chapter, having no separate Council of Royal and Select Masters. The petitions of the Chapter read: "Royal Arch and Appendant Degrees." [E. E. C.]

and other mystical philosophers of the same class. Vaughan, in his *Hours with the Mystics* (ii., 46), thus decribes the earlier theosophists of the fourteenth century: "They believed devoutly in the genuineness of the Kabbala. They were persuaded that, beneath all the floods of change, this oral tradition had perpetuated its life unharmed from the days of Moses downward—even as Jewish fable taught them that the cedars alone, of all trees, had continued to spread the strength of their invulnerable arms below the waters of the deluge. They rejoiced in the hidden lore of that book as in a treasure rich with the germs of all philosophy. They maintained that from its marvelous leaves man might learn the angelic heraldry of the skies, the mysteries of the Divine nature, the means of converse with the potentates of heaven."

Add to this an equal reverence for the unfathomable mysteries contained in the prophecies of Daniel and the vision of the Evangelist, with a proneness to give to everything Divine a symbolic interpretation, and you have the true character of those later theosophists who labored to invent their particular systems of Masonry. For more of this subject, see the article on *Saint Martin*.

Nothing now remains of theosophic Masonry except the few traces left through the influence of Zinnendorf in the Swedish system, and what we find in the Apocalyptic degrees of the Scottish Rite. The systems of Swedenborg, Pernetty, Paschalis, St. Martin, and Chastanier have all become obsolete.

Therapeutæ. An ascetic sect of Jews in the first century after Christ, whom Milman calls the ancestors of the Christian monks and hermits. They resided near Alexandria, in Egypt, and bore a striking resemblance in their doctrines to those of the Essenians. They were, however, much influenced by the mystical school of Alexandria, and, while they borrowed much from the Kabbala, partook also in their speculations of Pythagorean and Orphic ideas. Their system pervades some of the high degrees of Masonry. The best account of them is given by Philo Judæus.

Theriog. The 613 precepts into which the Jews divided the Mosaical law. Thus the Hebrew letters תרי״ג numerically express 613. (See description of *Talith.*)

Theurgy. From the Greek *Theos*, God, and *ergon*, work. The ancients thus called the whole art of magic, because they believed its operations to be the result of an intercourse with the gods. But the moderns have appropriated it to that species of magic which operates by celestial means as opposed to natural magic, which is effected by a knowledge of the occult powers of nature, and necromancy or magic effected by the aid of evil spirits. Attempts have been made by some speculative authors to apply this high magic, as it is also called, to an interpretation of Masonic symbolism. The most notorious and the most prolific writer on this subject is Louis Alphonse Constance, who, under the name of Eliphas Levy, has given to the world numerous works on the dogma and ritual, the history and the interpretation, of this theurgic Masonry.

Third Degree. See *Master Mason.*

Thirteen, The. A Parisian society claiming to exercise an occult influence during the First Empire. A society of growing proportions in the United States, intended to confound and uproot superstition, with an indirect reference to Arthur's Round Table and the Judas of infamy.

Thirty-Second Degree. See *Sublime Prince of the Royal Secret.*

Thirty-Six. In the Pythagorean doctrine of numbers, 36 symbolized the male and female powers of nature united, because it is composed of the sum of the four odd numbers, $1+3+5+7=16$, added to the sum of the four even numbers, $2+4+6+8=20$, for $16+20=36$. It has, however, no place among the sacred numbers of Masonry.

Thirty-Third Degree. See *Sovereign Grand Inspector-General.*

Thokath. תוקת, strength. An expression known to the Brethren of the Scottish Rite in the Twelfth Degree.

Thomists. An ancient Christian church in Malabar, said to have been founded by St. Thomas.

Thor or **Thorr,** contracted from Thonar, and sometimes known as Donar. This deity presided over the mischievous spirits in the elements, and was the son of Odin and Freyia. These three were known in mythology as the triune deity—the Father, Son, and Spirit. Thor's great weapon of destruction or force was the Miolner, the hammer or mallet, which had the marvelous property of invariably returning to its owner after having been launched upon its mission, and having performed its work of destruction.

Thory, Claude Antoine. A distinguished French Masonic writer, who was born at Paris, May 26, 1759. He was by profession an advocate, and held the official position of Registrar of the Criminal Court of the Chatelet, and afterward of first adjunct of the Mayor of Paris. He was a member of several learned societies, and a naturalist of considerable reputation. He devoted his attention more particularly to botany, and published several valuable works on the genus *Rosa*, and also one on strawberries, which was published after his death.

Thory took an important part, both as an actor and a writer, in the Masonic history of France. He was a member of the Lodge "Saint Alexandre d'Ecosse," and of the "Contrat Social," out of whose incorporation into one proceeded the Mother Lodge of the Philosophic Scottish Rite, of which Thory may be justly called the founder. He was at its constitution made the presiding officer, and afterward its treasurer, and keeper of its archives. In this last capacity, he made a collection of rare and valuable manuscripts, books, medals, seals, jewels, bronze figures, and other objects connected with Freemasonry. Under his administration, the library and museum of the Mother Lodge became perhaps the most valuable collection of the kind in France or in any other country. After the Mother Lodge had ceased its labors in 1826, this collection passed by a previous stipulation into the possession of the Lodge of Mont Thabor, which was the oldest of the Rite.

Thory, while making collections for the Lodge, had amassed for himself a fund of the most valuable materials toward the history of Freemasonry, which he used with great effect in his subsequent publications. In 1813 he published the *Annales Originis Magni Galliarum Orientis, ou Histoire de la Fondation du Grand Orient de France*, in 1 vol., 8vo; and in 1815 his *Acta Latomorum, ou Chronologie del 'Histoire de la Franche-Maçonnerie, françaises et étrangère*, in 2 vols., 8vo.

The value of these works, especially of the latter, if not as well-digested histories, certainly as important contributions to Masonic history, cannot be denied. Yet they have been variously appreciated by his contemporaries. Rebold (*Hist. des 3 G. L.*, p. 530) says of the *Annales*, that it is one of the best historical productions that French Masonic literature possesses; while Besuchet (*Précis Historique*, ii., 275) charges that he has attempted to discharge the functions of an historian without exactitude and without impartiality. These discordant views are to be attributed to the active part that Thory took in the contests between the Grand Orient and the Scottish Rite, and the opposition which he offered to the claims of the former to the Supreme Masonic authority. Posterity will form its judgment on the character of Thory as a Masonic historian without reference to the evanescent rivalry of parties. He died in October, 1827

Thoux de Salverte. Founder in 1767, at Warsaw, of the *Academy of Ancients*, which see.

Thread of Life. In the earliest lectures of the last century, we find this Catechism:

"*Q.* Have you the key of the Lodge?

"*A.* Yes, I have.

"*Q.* What is its virtue?

"*A.* To open and shut, and shut and open.

"*Q.* Where do you keep it?

"*A.* In an ivory box, between my tongue and my teeth, or within my heart, where all my secrets are kept.

"*Q.* Have you the chain to the key?

'*A.* Yes, I have.

"*Q.* How long is it?

"*A.* As long as from my tongue to my heart."

In a later lecture, this key is said to "hang by a tow line nine inches or a span." And later still, in the old Prestonian lecture, it is said to hang by "the thread of life, in the passage of entrance, nine inches or a span long, the supposed distance between guttural and pectoral." All of which is intended simply to symbolise the close connection which in every Mason should exist between his tongue and his heart, so that the one may utter nothing that the other does not truly dictate.

Three. Everywhere among the ancients the number three was deemed the most sacred of numbers. A reverence for its mystical virtues is to be found even among the Chinese, who say that numbers begin at one and are made perfect at three, and hence they denote the multiplicity of any object by repeating the character which stands for it three times. In the philosophy of Plato, it was the image of the Supreme Being, because it includes in itself the properties of the two first numbers, and because, as Aristotle says, it contains within itself a beginning, a middle, and an end. The Pythagoreans called it perfect harmony. So sacred was this number deemed by the ancients, that we find it designating some of the attributes of almost all the gods. The thunderbolt of Jove was three-forked; the scepter of Neptune was a trident; Cerberus, the dog of Pluto, was three-headed; there were three Fates and three Furies; the sun had three names, Apollo, Sol, and Liber; and the moon three also, Diana, Luna, and Hecate. In all incantations, three was a favorite number, for, as Virgil says, "numero Deus impari gaudet," God delights in an odd number. A triple cord was used, each cord of three different colors, white, red, and black; and a small image of the subject of the charm was carried thrice around the altar, as we see in Virgil's eighth eclogue (l. 73):

> "Terna tibi hæc primum, triplici diversa colore,
> Licia circumdo, terque hæc altaria circum
> Effigiem duco."

i. e.,

> "First I surround thee with these three pieces of list, and I carry thy image three times round the altars."

The Druids paid no less respect to this sacred number. Throughout their whole system, a reference is constantly made to its influence; and so far did their veneration for it extend, that even their sacred poetry was composed in triads.

In all the mysteries, from Egypt to Scandinavia, we find a sacred regard for the number three. In the Rites of Mithras, the Empyrean was said to be supported by three intelligences, Ormuzd, Mithra, and Mithras. In the Rites of Hindustan, there was the trinity of Brahma, Vishnu, and Siva. It was, in short, a general character of the mysteries to have three principal officers and three grades of initiation.

In Freemasonry, the ternary is the most sacred of all the mystical numbers. Beginning with the old axiom of the Roman Artificers, that *tres faciunt collegium*, or it requires three to make a college, they have established the rule that not less than three shall congregate to form a Lodge. Then in all the Rites, whatever may be the number of superimposed grades, there lie at the basis the three Symbolic degrees. There are in all the degrees three principal officers, three supports, three greater and three lesser lights, three movable and three immovable jewels, three principal tenets, three working-tools of a Fellow-Craft, three principal orders of architecture, three chief human senses, three Ancient Grand Masters. In fact, everywhere in the system the number three is presented as a prominent symbol. So much is this the case, that all the other mystical numbers depend upon it, for each is a multiple of three, its square or its cube, or derived from them. Thus, 9, 27, 81, are formed by the multiplication of three, as $3 \times 3 = 9$, and $3^2 \times 3 = 27$, and $3^2 \times 3^2 = 81$.

But in nothing is the Masonic signification of the ternary made more interesting than in its connection with the sacred delta, the symbol of Deity. (See *Triangle.*)

Three Fires. Guardians of the Sixty-seventh Degree of the Modern Rite of Memphis.

Three-Fold Cord. A triple cord whose strands are of different colors; it is used in several rites as an instructive symbol. (See *Zennaar.*)

Three Globes, Rite of the Grand Lodge of the. On September 13, 1740, the Lodge of the Three Globes, *zu den drei Weltkugeln*, was established in the city of Berlin, Prussia. In 1744 it assumed the rank and title of a Grand Mother Lodge. It is now one of the three Prussian Grand Lodges and has 144 St. John's (or Craft) Lodges and 72 Scottish Lodges under its jurisdiction. At first it worked, like all the other Lodges of Germany, in the English system of three degrees, and adopted the English Book of Constitutions as its law. But it subsequently became infected with the high degrees, which were at one time so popular in Germany, and especially with the Strict Observance system of Von Hund, which it accepted in 1766. At the extinction of that system the Grand Lodge adopted one of its own, in doing which it was assisted by the labors of Dr. I. F. Zöllner, the Grand Master. Its Rite consists of seven high degrees added to the three primitive. The latter are under the control of the Grand Lodge; but the seven higher ones are governed by an Internal Supreme Orient, whose members are, however, elected by the Grand Lodge. The Rite is practised by about two hundred Lodges in Germany.

Three Grand Offerings. See *Ground Floor of the Lodge.*

Three Points. Three points in a triangular form (∴) are placed after letters in a Masonic document to indicate that such letters are the initials of a Masonic title or of a technical word in Masonry, as G∴ M∴ for Grand Master, or G∴ L∴ for Grand Lodge. It is not a symbol, but simply a mark of abbreviation. The attempt, therefore, to trace it to the Hebrew three yods, a Kabbalistic sign of the Tetragrammaton, or any other ancient symbol, is futile. It is an abbreviation, and nothing more; although it is probable that the idea was suggested by the sacred character of the number three as a Masonic number, and these three dots might refer to the position of the three officers in a French Lodge. Ragon says (*Orthod. Maçon.*, p. 71) that the mark was first used by the Grand Orient of France in a circular issued August 12, 1774, in which we read "G∴ O∴ de France." The abbreviation is now constantly used in French documents, and, although not accepted by the English Masons, has been very generally adopted in other countries. In the United States, the use of this abbreviation is gradually extending.

Three Sacred Utensils. These were the vessels of the Tabernacle as to which the Rev. Joseph Barclay, LL.D., makes the following quotation: "Rabbi José, son of Rabbi Judah, said a fiery ark, and a fiery table, and a fiery candlestick descended from heaven. And Moses saw them, and made according to their similitude"; and thus comments: "They also think that the Ark of the Covenant is concealed in a chamber under the Temple Enclosure, and that it and all the holy vessels will be found at the coming of the Messiah." The Apocrypha, however, informs us that Jeremiah laid the Tabernacle, and the Ark, and the Altar of Incense in a "hollow cave, in the mountain, where Moses climbed up and saw the heritage of God. And the place shall be unknown until the time that God gather his people again together, and receive them into Mercy." (2 Mac. ii. 4-7.) The sacred vessels, which were taken to Rome after the destruction of Jerusalem in A.D. 70, and are now seen sculptured on the Arch of Titus, were carried off to Africa by the Vandals under Genseric. Belisarius took them to Constantinople in A.D. 520. They were afterward sent back to Jerusalem, and thence they are supposed to have been carried to Persia, when Chosroes plundered the Holy City, in June, 614.

Three Senses. Of the five human senses, the three which are the most important in Masonic symbolism are Seeing, Hearing, and Feeling, because of their respective reference to certain modes of recognition, and because, by their use, Masons are enabled to practise that universal language the possession of which is the boast of the Order.

Three Steps. See *Steps on the Master's Carpet.*

Threshing-Floor. Among the Hebrews, circular spots of hard ground were used, as now, for the purpose of threshing corn. After they were properly prepared for the purpose, they became permanent possessions. One of these, the property of Ornan the Jebusite, was on Mount Moriah. It was purchased by David, for a place of sacrifice, for six hundred shekels of gold, and on it the Temple was afterward built. Hence it is sometimes used as a symbolic name for the Temple of

Solomon or for a Master's Lodge. Thus it is said in the ritual that the Mason comes "from the lofty tower of Babel, where language was confounded and Masonry lost," and that he is traveling "to the threshing-floor of Ornan the Jebusite, where language was restored and Masonry found." The interpretation of this rather abstruse symbolic expression is that on his initiation the Mason comes out of the profane world, where there is ignorance and darkness and confusion as there was at Babel, and that he is approaching the Masonic world, where, as at the Temple built on Ornan's threshing-floor, there is knowledge and light and order.

Throne. The seat occupied by the Grand Master in the Grand Lodge of England is called the *throne*, in allusion, probably, to the throne of Solomon. In American Grand Lodges it is styled the Oriental Chair of Solomon, a title which is also given to the seat of the Master of a subordinate Lodge.

In ecclesiology, the seat in a cathedral occupied by a bishop is called a throne; and in the Middle Ages, according to Du Cange, the same title was not only applied to the seats of bishops, but often also to those of abbots, or even priests who were in possession of titles or churches.

Thugs. A Hindu association that offered human sacrifices to their divinity Kali. It was dreaded for its violence and the fierceness of its members, who were termed either Stranglers or Aspirants.

Thummim. See *Urim and Thummim*.

Thurible. From Turis, frankincense; Ivos, a sacrifice. A metallic censer for burning incense. It is of various forms, but generally in that of an ornamental cup suspended by chains, whereby the Thurifer keeps the incense burning and diffuses the perfume.

Thurifer. The bearer of the thurible, or censer, prepared with frankincense, and used by the Romish Church at Mass and other ceremonials; as also in the Philosophic Degrees of Masonry.

Thursday. The fifth day of the week. So called from its being originally consecrated to Thor, or the Icelandic Thorr, the god of thunder, answering to the Jove of the Romans.

Tie. The first clause in the covenant of Masonry which refers to the preservation of the secrets is technically called the tie. It is substantially the same in the covenant of each degree, from the lowest to the highest.

Tie, Mystic. See *Mystic Tie*.

Tierce, De la. He was the first translator of Anderson's *Constitutions* into French, the manuscript of which he says that he prepared during his residence in London. He afterward published it at Frankfort, in 1743, with the title of *Histoire, obligations et statuts de la très venerable confraternité des Francs-Maçons, tirez de leur archives et conformés aux traditions les plus anciennes, etc.* His work contains a translation into French of the Old Charges—the General Regulations—and manner of constituting a new Lodge, as given by Anderson in 1723. De la Tierce is said to have been, while in London, an intimate friend of Anderson, the first edition of whose *Constitutions* he used when he compiled his manuscript in 1725. But he improved on Anderson's work by dividing the history in epochs. This course Anderson pursued in his second edition; which circumstance has led Schneider, in the *Neuen Journale zur Freimaurerei*, to suppose that, in writing that second edition, Anderson was aided by the previous labors of De la Tierce, of whose work he was most probably in possession.

Tile. A Lodge is said to be tiled when the necessary precautions have been taken to prevent the approach of unauthorized persons; and it is said to be the first duty of every Mason to see that this is done before the Lodge is opened. The word to tile is sometimes used in the same sense as *to examine*, as when it is said that a visitor has been tiled, that is, has been examined. But the expression is not in general use, and does not seem to be a correct employment of the term.

Tiler. An officer of a Symbolic Lodge, whose duty is to guard the door of the Lodge, and to permit no one to pass in who is not duly qualified, and who has not the permission of the Master.

A necessary qualification of a Tiler is, therefore, that he should be a Master Mason. Although the Lodge may be opened in an inferior degree, no one who has not advanced to the Third Degree can legally discharge the functions of Tiler.

As the Tiler is always compensated for his services, he is considered, in some sense, as the servant of the Lodge. It is, therefore, his duty to prepare the Lodge for its meetings, to arrange the furniture in its proper place, and to make all other arrangements for the convenience of the Lodge.

The Tiler need not be a member of the Lodge which he tiles; and in fact, in large cities, one brother very often performs the duties of Tiler of several Lodges.

This is a very important office, and, like that of the Master and Wardens, owes its existence, not to any conventional regulations, but to the very landmarks of the Order; for, from the peculiar nature of our Institution, it is evident that there never could have been a meeting of Masons for Masonic purposes, unless a Tiler had been present to guard the Lodge from intrusion.

The title is derived from the operative art; for as in Operative Masonry the Tiler, when the edifice is erected, finishes and covers it with the roof (of tiles), so in Speculative Masonry, when the Lodge is duly organized, the Tiler closes the door, and covers the sacred precincts from all intrusion.

Tiler's Oath. See *Oath, Tiler's*.

Tilly de Grasse. See *Grasse, Tilly de*.

Tiluk. The sacred impress made upon the forehead of the Brahman, like unto the Tau to the Hebrew, or the cross to the Christian.

Timbre. The French Masons so call a stamp, consisting of the initials or monogram of the Lodge, which is impressed in black or red ink upon every official document emanating from the Lodge. When such a document has the seal also attached, it is said to be "timbrée et scellée," i. e., stamped and sealed. The timbre, which differs from the seal, is not used in English or American Lodges.

Time. The image of Time, under the conventional figure of a winged old man with the customary scythe and hour-glass, has been adopted as one of the modern symbols in the Third Degree. He is represented as attempting to disentangle the ringlets of a weeping virgin who stands before him. This, which is apparently a never-ending task, but one which Time undertakes to perform, is intended to teach the Mason that time, patience and perseverance will enable him to accomplish the great object of a Mason's labor, and at last to obtain that true Word which is the symbol of Divine Truth. Time, therefore, is in this connection the symbol of well-directed perseverance in the performance of duty.

Time and Circumstances. The answer to the question in the ritual of initiation, "Has he made suitable proficiency?" is sometimes made, "Such as time and circumstances would permit." This is an error, and may be a mischievous one, as leading to a careless preparation of the candidate for qualification to advancement. The true reply is, "He has." (See *Advancement, Hurried.*)

Tirshatha. The title given to the Persian governors of Judea. It was borne by Zerubbabel and Nehemiah. It is supposed to be derived from the Persian *torsch*, austere or severe, and is therefore, says Gesenius, equivalent to "Your Severity." It is in the modern ritual of the Supreme Council for the Southern Jurisdiction of the United States the title of the presiding officer of a Council of Princes of Jerusalem. It is also the title of the presiding officer of the Royal Order of Heredom of Kilwinning.

Tisri. תשרי. The first month of the Hebrew civil year, and corresponding to the months of September and October, beginning with the new moon of the former.

Titan of the Caucasus. The Fifty-third Degree of the Memphis Rite.

Titles. The titles conferred in the rituals of Masonry upon various officers are often apparently grandiloquent, and have given occasion to some, who have not understood their true meaning, to call them absurd and bombastic. On this subject Bro. Albert Pike has, in the following remarks, given a proper significance to Masonic titles:

"Some of these titles we retain; but they have with us meanings entirely consistent with the spirit of equality, which is the foundation and peremptory law of its being, of all Masonry. The *Knight*, with us, is he who devotes his hand, his heart, his brain to the service of Masonry, and professes himself the sworn soldier of truth: the *Prince* is he who aims to be chief [Princeps], first, leader among his equals, in virtue and good deeds: the *Sovereign* is he who, one of an Order whose members are all sovereigns, is supreme only because the law and Constitutions are so which he administers, and by which he, like every other brother, is governed. The titles *Puissant, Potent, Wise*, and *Venerable* indicate that power of virtue, intelligence, and wisdom which those ought to strive to attain who are placed in high offices by the suffrages of their brethren; and all our other titles and designations have an esoteric meaning consistent with modesty and equality, and which those who receive them should fully understand."

Titles of Grand Lodges. The title of the Grand Lodge of England is "The United Grand Lodge of Ancient Free and Accepted Masons." That of Ireland, "The Grand Masonic Lodge." Of Scotland, "The Grand Lodge of the Ancient and Honorable Fraternity of Free and Accepted Masons." That of France is "The Grand Orient." The same title is taken by the Grand Lodges or Supreme Masonic authorities of Portugal, Belgium, Italy, Spain, and Greece, and also by the Grand Lodges of all the South American States. Of the German Grand Lodges, the only three that have distinctive titles are "The Grand National Mother Lodge of the Three Globes," "The Grand National Lodge of Germany," and "The Grand Lodge Royal York of Friendship." In Sweden and Denmark they are simply called "Grand Lodges." In the English possessions of North America they are also called "Grand Lodges." In the United States the title of the Grand Lodge of Maine, of Massachusetts, of Rhode Island, of Alabama, of Illinois, of Iowa, of Wisconsin, of Minnesota, and of Oregon, is the "Most Worshipful Grand Lodge of Ancient Free and Accepted Masons"; of New Hampshire, of Vermont, of New York, of New Jersey, of Pennsylvania, of Arkansas, and of Indiana, it is "The Grand Lodge of the Ancient and Honorable Fraternity of Free and Accepted Masons"; of Maryland, of the District of Columbia, of Florida, of Michigan, of Missouri, and of California, is "Grand Lodge of Free and Accepted Masons"; of South Carolina is "Most Worshipful Grand Lodge of Ancient Freemasons"; of all the other States the title is simply the "Grand Lodge."

Tito. A significant word in the high degrees. The Scottish Rite rituals give the name of Tito, Prince Harodim, to him who they say was the first who was appointed by Solomon a Provost and Judge. This person appears to be altogether mythical; the word is not found in the Hebrew language, nor has any meaning been given to it. He is represented as having been a favorite of the King of Israel. He is said to have presided over the Lodge of Intendants of the Building, and to have been one of the twelve illustrious knights who were set over the twelve tribes, that of Naphtali being placed under his care.

The whole of this legend is, of course, connected with the symbolic signification of those degrees.

Toasts. Anderson says (*Constitutions*, 1738, p. 110) that in 1719 Dr. Desaguliers, having been installed Grand Master, "forthwith revived the old, regular, and peculiar toasts or healths of the Freemasons." If Anderson's statements could be implicitly trusted as historical facts, we should have to conclude that a system of regulated toasts prevailed in the Lodges before the revival. The custom of drinking healths at banquets is a very old one, and can be traced to the days of the ancient Greeks and Romans. From them it was handed down to the moderns, and especially in England we find the "washael" of the Saxons, a term used in drinking, and equivalent to the modern phrase, "Your health." Steele, in the *Tatler*, intimates that the word *toast* began to be applied to the drinking of healths in the early part of the eighteenth century. And although his account of the origin of the word has been contested, it is very evident that the drinking of toasts was a universal custom in the clubs and festive associations which were common in London about the time of the revival of Masonry. It is therefore to be presumed that the Masonic Lodges did not escape the influences of the convivial spirit of that age, and drinking in the Lodge room during the hours of refreshment was a usual custom, but, as Oliver observes, all excess was avoided, and the convivialities of Masonry were regulated by the *Old Charges*, which directed the brethren to enjoy themselves with decent mirth, not forcing any brother to eat or drink beyond his inclination, nor hindering him from going home when he pleased. The drinking was conducted by rule, the Master giving the toast, but first inquiring of the Senior Warden, "Are you charged in the West, Brother Senior?" and of the Junior Warden, "Are you charged in the South, Brother Junior?" to which appropriate replies being made, the toast was drunk with honors peculiar to the Institution. In an old Masonic song, the following stanza occurs:

"'Are you charged in the West? are you charged in the South?'
The Worshipful Master cries.
'We are charged in the West, we are charged in the South,'
Each Warden prompt replies."

One of the catechetical works of the last century thus describes the drinking customs of the Masons of that period: "The table being plentifully supplied with wine and punch, every man has a glass set before him, and fills it with what he chooses. But he must drink his glass in turn, or at least keep the motion with the rest When, therefore, a public health is given, the Master fills first, and desires the brethren to charge their glasses; and when this is supposed to be done, the Master says, *Brethren, are you all charged?* The Senior and Junior Wardens answer, *We are all charged in the South and West.* Then they all stand up, and, observing the Master's motions, (like the soldier his right-hand man,) drink their glasses off." Another work of the same period says that the first toast given was "the King and the Craft." But a still older work gives what it calls "A Free-Mason's Health" in the following words: "Here's a health to our society and to every faithful brother that keeps his oath of secrecy. As we are sworn to love each other, the world no Order knows like this our noble and ancient Fraternity. Let them wonder at the Mystery. Here, Brother, I drink to thee."

In time the toasts improved in their style, and were deemed of so much importance that lists of them, for the benefit of those who were deficient in inventive genius, were published in all the pocketbooks, calendars, and song books of the Order. Thus a large collection is to be found in the *Masonic Miscellanies* of Stephen Jones. A few of them will show their technical character: "To the secret and silent"; "To the memory of the distinguished Three"; "To all that live within compass and square"; "To the memory of the Tyrian artist"; "To him that first the work began," etc.

But there was a regular series of toasts which, besides these voluntary ones, were always given at the refreshments of the brethren. Thus, when the reigning sovereign happened to be a member of the Fraternity, the first toast given was always "The King and the Craft."

In the French Lodges the drinking of toasts was, with the word itself, borrowed from England. It was, however, subjected to strict rules, from which there could be no departure. Seven toasts were called "Santés d'obligation," because drinking them was made obligatory, and could not be omitted at the Lodge banquet. They were as follows: 1. The health of the Sovereign and his family; 2. That of the Grand Master and the chiefs of the Order; 3. That of the Master of the Lodge; 4. That of the Wardens; 5. That of the other officers; 6. That of the visitors; 7. That of all Masons wheresoever spread over the two hemispheres. In 1872, the Grand Orient, after long discussions, reduced the number of *santés d'obligation* from seven to four, and changed their character. They are now: 1. To the Grand Orient of France, the Lodges of its correspondence, and foreign Grand Orients; 2. To the Master of the Lodge; 3. To the Wardens, the officers, affiliated Lodges, and visiting brethren; 4. To all Masons existing on each hemisphere.

The systematized method of drinking toasts, which once prevailed in the Lodges of the English-speaking countries, has been, to a great extent, abandoned; yet a few toasts still remain, which, although not absolutely obligatory, are still never omitted. Thus no Masonic Lodge would neglect at its banquet to offer, as its first toast, a sentiment expressive of respect for the Grand Lodge.

The venerable Oliver was a great admirer of the custom of drinking Masonic toasts, and panegyrises it in his *Book of the Lodge* (p. 147). He says that at the time of refreshment in a Masonic Lodge "the song appeared to have more zest than in a private company; the toast thrilled more vividly upon the recollection; and the small modicum of punch with which it was honored retained a higher flavor than the same potation if produced at a private board." And he adds, as a specimen, the following "characteristic toast," which he says was always received with a "profound expression of pleasure."

"To him that all things understood,
To him that found the stone and wood,
To him that hapless lost his blood,
In doing of his duty,
To that blest age and that blest morn
Whereon those three great men were born,
Our noble science to adorn
With Wisdom, Strength, and Beauty."

It is not surprising that he should afterward pathetically deplore the discontinuance of the custom.

Token. The word *token* is derived from the Anglo-Saxon *tacn*, which means a sign, presage, type, or representation, that which points out something; and this is traced to *tæcan*, to teach, show, or instruct, because by a token we show or instruct others as to what we are. Bailey, whose *Dictionary* was published soon after the revival, defines it as "a sign or mark"; but it is singular that the word is not found in either of the dictionaries of Phillips or Blount, which were the most popular glossaries in the beginning of the last century. The word was, however, well known to the Fraternity, and was in use at the time of the revival with precisely the same meaning that is now given to it as a mode of recognition.

The Hebrew word אות, *ôth*, is frequently used in Scripture to signify a sign or memorial of something past, some covenant made or promise given. Thus God says to Noah, of the rainbow, "it shall be for a *token* of a covenant between me and the earth"; and to Abraham he says of circumcision, "it shall be a *token* of the covenant betwixt me and you." In Masonry, the grip of recognition is called a token, because it is an outward sign of the covenant of friendship and fellowship entered into between the members of the Fraternity, and is to be considered as a memorial of that covenant which was made, when it was first received by the candidate, between him and the Order into which he was then initiated.

Neither the French nor the German Masons have a word precisely equivalent to token. Krause translates it by *merkmale*, a sign or representation, but which has no technical Masonic signification. The French have only *attouchement*, which means the act of touching; and the Germans, *griff*, which is the same as the English *grip*. In the technical use of the word *token*, the English-speaking Masons have an advantage not possessed by those of any other country.

Tolerance Lodge. When the initiation of Jews was forbidden in the Prussian Lodges, two brethren of Berlin, Von Hirschfeld and Catter, induced by a spirit of toleration, organised a Lodge in Berlin for the express purpose of initiating Jews, to which they gave the appropriate name of Tolerance Lodge. This Lodge was not recognised by the Masonic authorities.

Toleration. The grand characteristic of Masonry is its toleration in religion and politics. In respect to the latter, its toleration has no limit. The question of a man's political opinions is not permitted to be broached in the Lodge; in reference to the former, it requires only that, to use the language of the *Old Charge*, Masons shall be of "that religion in which all men agree, leaving their particular opinions to themselves." (*Constitutions*, 1723, p. 50.) The same *Old Charges* say, "No private piques or quarrels must be brought within the door of the Lodge, far less any quarrels about religion, or nations, or state policy, we being only, as Masons, of the Catholic religion above-mentioned; we are also of all nations, tongues, kindreds, and languages, and are resolved against all politics, as what never yet conduced to the welfare of the Lodge, nor ever will." (*Ibid.*, p. 54.)

Tomb of Adoniram. Margoliouth, in his *History of the Jews*, tells the legend that at Saguntum, in Spain, a sepulcher was found four hundred years ago, with the following Hebrew inscription: "This is the grave of Adoniram, the servant of King Solomon, who came to collect the tribute, and died on the day—" Margoliouth, who believes the mythical story, says that the Jesuit Villepandus, being desirous of ascertaining if the statements concerning the tomb were true, directed the Jesuit students who resided at Murviedro, a small village erected upon the ruins of Saguntum, to make diligent search for the tomb and inscription. After a thorough investigation, the Jesuit students were shown a stone on which appeared a Hebrew inscription, much defaced and nearly obliterated, which the natives stated was "*the stone of Solomon's collector.*" Still unsatisfied, they made further search, and discovered a manuscript written in antique Spanish, and carefully preserved in the citadel, in which the following entry was made: "At Saguntum, in the citadel, in the year of our Lord 1480, a little more or less, was discovered a sepulchre of surprising antiquity. It contained an embalmed corpse, not of the usual stature, but taller than is common. It had and still retains on the front two lines in the Hebrew language and characters, the sense of which is: 'The sepulchre of Adoniram, the servant of King Solomon, who came hither to collect tribute.'"

The story has far more the appearance of a Talmudic or a Rosicrucian legend than that of an historical narrative.

Tomb of Hiram Abif. All that is said of it in Masonry is more properly referred to in the article on the *Monument in the Third Degree*. (See *Monument*.)

Tomb of Hiram of Tyre. Five miles to the east of the city of Tyre is an ancient monument, called by the natives Kabr Hairan, or the tomb of Hiram. The tradition that the King of Tyre was there interred rests only on the authority of the natives. It bears about it, however, the unmistakable marks of extreme antiquity, and, as Thompson says (*The Land and The Book*, p. 196), there is nothing in the monument itself inconsistent with the idea that it marks the final resting-place of that friend of Solomon. He thus describes it: "The base consists of two tiers of great stones, each three feet thick, thirteen feet long, and eight feet eight inches broad. Above this is one huge stone, a little more than fifteen feet long, ten broad, and three feet four inches thick. Over this is another, twelve feet three inches long, eight broad, and six high. The top stone is a little smaller every way, and only five feet thick. The entire height is twenty-one feet. There is nothing like it in this country, and it may well have stood, as it now does, ever since the days of Solomon. These large broken sarcophagi scattered around it are assigned by tradition to Hiram's mother, wife, and family."

Dr. Morris, who visited the spot in 1868, gives a different admeasurement, which is probably more accurate than that of Thompson. According to him, the first tier is 14 ft. long, 8 ft. 8 in. broad, 4 ft. thick. Second tier, 14 ft. long, 8 ft. 8 in. broad, 2 ft. 10 in. thick. Third tier, 15 ft. 1 in. long, 9 ft. 11 in. broad, 2 ft. 11 in. thick. Fourth tier, 12 ft. 11 in. long, 7 ft. 8 in. broad, 6 ft. 5 in. thick. Fifth tier, 12 ft. 11 in. long, 7 ft. 8 in. broad, and 3 ft. 6 in. thick. He makes the height of the whole 19 ft. 8 in.

Travelers have been disposed to give more credit to the tradition which makes this monument the tomb of the King of Tyre than to most of the other legends which refer to ancient sepulchers in the Holy Land.

Tongue. In the early rituals of the last century, the tongue is called the key to the secrets of a Mason; and one of the toasts that was given in the Lodge was in these words: "To that excellent key of a Mason's tongue, which ought always to speak as well in the absence of a brother as in his presence; and when that cannot be done with honor, justice, or propriety, that adopts the virtue of a Mason, which is silence."

Tongue of Good Report. Being "under the tongue of good report" is equivalent, in Masonic technical language, to being of good character or reputation. It is required that the candidate for initiation should be one of whom no tongue speaks evil. The phrase is an old one, and is found in the earliest rituals of the last century.

Topaz. In Hebrew, פטדה, *pitdah*. It was the second stone in the first row of the high priest's breastplate, and was referred to Simeon. The ancient topaz, says King (*Antique Gems*, p. 56), was the present chrysolite, which was furnished from an island in the Red Sea. It is of a bright greenish yellow, and the softest of all precious stones.

Topes. Pillars, also signifying towers and tumuli. This is a corruption of the Sanskrit word Stoopa, meaning mounds, heaps, karns. The Topes of the Karli temple, a Buddhist shrine, which may be seen up the Western Ghats from Bombay to Poona, are presumed to be Phallic pillars placed in front, precisely as Solomon placed his Jachin and Boaz. Some travelers state that only one of these pillars stands at present. The pillars were shaft plain, with a capital carrying four lions, representing power and cat-like salaciousness. Between

these pillars may be seen the great window which lights all the Temple, arched in the form of a horseshoe, which is the Isian head-dress and Maiya's holy sign, and after which the Roman Church adopts one of Mary's favorite head-dresses. It is the "crown of Venus Urania."

These pillars are prominent features of Buddhist sacred buildings, and when composed of a single stone are called a Lat. They are frequently ornamented with honeysuckles. The oldest monument hitherto discovered in India is a group of these monoliths set up by Asoka in the middle of the third century B.C. They were all alike in form, inscribed with four short edicts containing the creed and principal doctrines of Buddhism. These pillars stood originally in front of some sacred buildings which have perished; they are polished, 45 feet each in height, and surmounted by lions. The Thuparamya Tope, in Ceylon, has 184 handsome monoliths, 26 feet in height, round the *center holy mound*.

Torch-Bearer. The fifteenth officer in the High Council of the Society of Rosicrucians; also known as an officer in the Appendant Order of the Holy Sepulcher. One who bears a torch.

Torches. The ancients made use of torches both at marriages and funerals. They were also employed in the ceremonies of the Eleusinian mysteries. They have been introduced into the high degrees, especially on the Continent, principally as marks of honor in the reception of distinguished visitors, on which occasion they are technically called "stars." Du Cange mentions their use during the Middle Ages on funeral occasions.

Torgau, Constitutions of. Torgau is a fortified town on the Elbe, in the Prussian Province of Saxony. It was there that Luther and his friends wrote the *Book of Torgau*, which was the foundation of the subsequent Augsburg Confession, and it was there that the

Lutherans concluded a league with the Elector Frederick the Wise. The Stone-Masons, whose seat was there in the fifteenth century, had, with the other Masons of Saxony, accepted the Constitutions enacted in 1459 at Strasburg. But, finding it necessary to make some special regulations for their own internal government, they drew up, in 1462, Constitutions in 112 articles, which are known as the "Torgau Ordinances." A duplicate of these Constitutions was deposited, in 1486, in the Stone-Mason's *hutte* at Rochlitz. An authenticated copy of this document was published by C. L. Stieglitz at Leipsic, in 1829, in a work entitled *Ueber die Kirche der heiligen Kunigunde zu Rochlitz und die Steinmetzhütte daselbst* An abstract of these Ordinances, with critical comparisons with other Constitutions, was published by Kloss in his *Die Freimaurerei in ihrer wahren Bedeutung*. The Torgau Ordinances are important because, with those of Strasburg, they are the only authentic Constitutions of the German Stone-Masons extant except the Brother-Book of 1563.

Torrubia, Joseph. A Franciscan monk, who in 1751 was the censor and reviser of the Inquisition in Spain. Torrubia, that he might be the better enabled to carry into effect a persecution of the Freemasons, obtained under an assumed name, and in the character of a secular priest, initiation into one of the Lodges, having first received from the Grand Penitentiary a dispensation for the act, and an absolution from the oath of secrecy. Having thus acquired an exact list of the Lodges in Spain, and the names of their members, he caused hundreds of Masons to be arrested and punished, and succeeded in having the Order prohibited by a decree of King Ferdinand VI. Torrubia combined in his character the bigotry of the priest and the villainy of the traitor.

Tournon, M. A Frenchman and Freemason, who had been invited into Spain by the government in order to establish a manufactory of brass buttons, and to instruct the Spanish workmen. In 1757 he was arrested by the Inquisition on the charge of being a Freemason, and of having invited his pupils to join the Institution. He was sentenced to imprisonment for one year, after which he was banished from Spain, being conducted under an escort to the frontiers of France. Tournon was indebted for this clemency to his want of firmness and fidelity to the Order—he having solemnly abjured it, and promised never again to attend its assemblies. Llorente, in his *History of the Inquisition*, gives an account of Tournon's trial.

Tow, Cable. See *Cable Tow*.

Tower, Degree of the. (*Grade de la Tour*.) A name sometimes given to the Second Degree of the Royal Order of Scotland.

Tower of Babel. See *Babel*.

Town, Salem. The Rev. Salem Town, LL.D., was born at Belchertown, in the State of Massachusetts, March 5, 1779. He received a classical education, and obtained at college the degree of Master of Arts, and later in life that of Doctor of Laws. For some years he was the Principal of an academy, and his writings give the evidence that he was endowed with more than ordinary abilities. He was ardently attached to Freemasonry, and was for many years Grand Chaplain of the Grand Lodge and Grand Chapter, and Grand Prelate of the Grand Commandery of New York. In 1818 he published a small work, of two hundred and eighty-three pages, entitled *A System of Speculative Masonry*. This work is of course tinged with all the legendary ideas of the origin of the Institution which prevailed at that period, and would not now be accepted as authoritative; but it contains, outside of its historical errors, many valuable and suggestive thoughts. Bro. Town was highly respected for his many virtues, the consistency of his life, and his unwearied devotion to the Masonic Order. He died at Greencastle, Indiana, February 24, 1864, at the ripe age of eighty-nine years.

Townshend, Simeon. The putative author of a book entitled *Observations and Inquiries relating to the Brotherhood of the Free Masons*, which is said to have been printed at London in 1712. Boileau, Levèsque, Thory, Oliver, and Kloss mention it by name. None of them, however, appear to have seen it. Kloss calls it a doubtful book. If such a work is in existence, it will be a valuable and much needed contribution to the condition of Masonry in the south of England just before the revival, and may tend to settle some mooted questions. Levèsque (*Aperçu*, p. 47) says he has consulted it; but his manner of referring to it throws suspicion on the statement, and it is doubtful if he ever saw it.

Tracing-Board. The same as a *Floor-Cloth*, which see.

Trade-Gilds. See *Gilds*.

Tradition. There are two kinds of traditions in Masonry: First, those which detail events, either historically, authentic in part, or in whole, or consisting altogether of arbitrary fiction, and intended simply to convey an allegorical or symbolic meaning; and secondly, of traditions which refer to customs and usages of the Fraternity, especially in matters of ritual observance.

The first class has already been discussed in this work in the article on *Legend*, to which the reader is referred. The second class is now to be considered.

The traditions which control and direct the usages of the Fraternity constitute its unwritten law, and are almost wholly applicable to its ritual, although they are sometimes of use in the interpretation of doubtful points in its written law. Between the written and the unwritten law, the latter is always paramount. This is evident from the definition of a tradition as it is given by the monk Vincent of Lerins: "Quod semper, quod ubique, quod ab omnibus traditum est"; i. e., tradition is that which has been handed down at all times, and in all places, and by all persons. The law which thus has antiquity, universality, and common consent for its support, must override all subsequent laws which are modern, local, and have only partial agreement.

It is then important that those traditions of Masonry which prescribe its ritual observances and its landmarks should be thoroughly understood, because it is only by attention to them that uniformity in the esoteric instruction and work of the Order can be preserved.

Cicero has wisely said that a well-constituted commonwealth must be governed not by the written law alone, but also by the unwritten law or tradition and usage; and this is especially the case, because the written law, however perspicuous it may be, can be diverted into various senses, unless the republic is maintained and preserved by its usages and traditions, which, although mute and as it were dead, yet speak with a living voice, and give the true interpretation of that which is written.

This axiom is not less true in Masonry than it is in a commonwealth. No matter what changes may be made in its statutes and regulations of to-day and its recent customs, there is no danger of losing the identity of its modern with its ancient form and spirit while its traditions are recognized and maintained.

Tramping Masons. Unworthy members of the Order, who, using their privileges for interested purposes, traveling from city to city and from Lodge to Lodge, that they may seek relief by tales of fictitious distress, have been called "tramping Masons." The true brother should ever obtain assistance; the tramper should be driven from the door of every Lodge or the house of every Mason where he seeks to intrude his imposture.

Transfer of Warrant. The English Constitutions (Rule 221) enact that "No warrant can be transferred under any circumstances." Similarly the Scotch Constitution (Rule 148) says "A Charter cannot be transferred under any circumstances."

Transient Brethren. Masons who do not reside in a particular place, but only temporarily visit it, are called "transient brethren." They are, if worthy, to be cordially welcomed, but are never to be admitted into a Lodge until, after the proper precautions, they have been proved to be "true and trusty." This usage of hospitality has the authority of all the Old Constitutions, which are careful to inculcate it. Thus the Lansdowne MS. charges "that every Mason receive or cherish Strange Fellows when they come over the countrey, and sett them on worke if they will worke, as the manner is, (that is to say) if the Mason have any moulde stone in his place, on worke; and if he have none, the Mason shall refresh him with money unto the next Lodge."

Although Speculative Masons no longer visit Lodges for the sake of work or wages, the usage of our Operative predecessors has been spiritualized in our symbolic system. Hence visitors are often invited to take a part in the labors of the Lodge, and receive their portion of the light and truth which constitute the symbolic pay of a Speculative Mason.

Transition Period. Findel calls that period in the history of Masonry, when it was gradually changing its character from that of an Operative to that of a Speculative society, "the Transition Period." It began in 1600, and terminated in 1717 by the establishment of the Grand Lodge of England in London, after which, says Findel (*Hist.*, English translation, p 131), "modern Freemasonry was now to be taught as a spiritualizing art, and the Fraternity of Operative Masons was exalted to a Brotherhood of symbolic builders, who, in the place of visible, perishable temples, are engaged in the erection of that one, invisible, eternal temple of the heart and mind."

Transmission, Charter of. A deed said to have been granted by James de Molay, just before his death, to Mark Larmenius, by which he transmitted to him and to his successors the office of Grand Master of the Templars. It is the foundation-deed of the "Order of the Temple." After having disappeared for many years it was rediscovered and purchased by Bro. F. I. W. Crowe of Chichester, England, who thought it too important and valuable to remain in private hands, and it is now in the possession of the Great Priory of England. It is written in a Latin cipher on a large folio sheet of parchment. The outward appearance of the document is of great antiquity, but it lacks internal evidence of authenticity. It is, therefore, by most authorities, considered a forgery. (See *Temple, Order of the*.)

Trappists, Order of Religious. An order founded by that devotee of secret organizations, Count La Perche, in 1140.

Travel. In the symbolic language of Masonry, a Mason always travels from west to east in search of light—he travels from the lofty tower of Babel, where language was confounded and Masonry lost, to the threshing-floor of Ornan the Jebusite, where language was restored and Masonry found. The Master Mason also travels into foreign countries in search of wages. All this is pure symbolism, unintelligible in any other sense. For its interpretation, see *Foreign Country* and *Threshing-Floor*.

Traveling Masons. There is no portion of the history of the Order so interesting to the Masonic scholar as that which is embraced by the Middle Ages of Christendom, beginning with about the tenth century, when the whole of civilized Europe was perambulated by those associations of workmen, who passed from country to country and from city to city under the name of "Traveling Masons," for the purpose of erecting religious edifices. There is not a country of Europe which does not at this day contain honorable evidences of the skill and industry of our Masonic ancestors. I therefore propose, in the present article, to give a brief sketch of the origin, the progress, and the character of these traveling architects.

Mr. George Godwin, in a lecture published in the *Builder* (vol. ix., p. 463), says: "There are few points in the Middle Ages more pleasing to look back upon than the existence of the associated Masons; they are the bright spot in the general darkness of that period, the patch of verdure when all around is barren."

Clavel, in his *Histoire Pittoresque de la Franc-Maçonnerie*, has traced the organization of these associations to the "collegia artificum," or colleges of artisans, which were instituted at Rome, by Numa, in the year B.C. 714, and whose members were originally Greeks, imported by this lawgiver for the purpose of embellishing the city over which he reigned. They continued to exist as well-established corporations throughout all the succeeding years of the kingdom, the republic, and the empire. (See *Roman Colleges of Artificers*.)

These "sodalitates," or fraternities, began, upon the invasion of the barbarians, to decline in numbers, in respectability, and in power. But on the conversion of the whole empire, they, or others of a similar character, began again to flourish. The priests of the Christian church became their patrons, and under their guidance they devoted themselves to the building of churches and monasteries. In the tenth century, they were established as a free gild or corporation in Lombardy. For when, after the decline and fall of the empire, the city of Rome was abandoned by its sovereigns for other secondary cities of Italy, such as Milan and Ravenna, and new courts and new capitals were formed, the kingdom of Lombardy sprang into existence as the great center of all energy in trade and industry, and of refinement in art and literature. Como was a free republic to which many fled during the invasions of the Vandals and Goths. It was in Lombardy, as a consequence of the great center of life from Rome, and the development not only of commercial business, but of all sorts of trades and handicrafts, that the corporations known as gilds were first organized.

Among the arts practised by the Lombards, that of building held a preeminent rank. And Muratori tells us that the inhabitants of Como, a principal city of Lombardy, Italy, had become so superior as masons, that the appellation of Magistri Comacini, or Masters from Como, had become generic to all of the profession.

Mr. Hope, in his *Historical Essay on Architecture*, has treated this subject almost exhaustively. He says:

"We cannot then wonder that, at a period when artificers and artists of every class, from those of the most mechanical, to those of the most intellectual nature, formed themselves into exclusive corporations, architects—whose art may be said to offer the most exact medium between those of the most urgent necessity, and those of mere ornament, or, indeed, in its wide span to embrace both—should, above all others, have associated themselves into similar bodies, which, in conformity to the general style of such corporations, assumed that of Free and Accepted Masons, and was composed of those members who, after a regular passage through the different fixed stages of apprenticeship, were received as masters, and entitled to exercise the profession on their own account.

"In an age, however, in which lay individuals, from the lowest subject to the sovereign himself, seldom built except for mere shelter and safety—seldom sought, nay, rather avoided, in their dwellings an elegance which might lessen their security; in which even the community collectively, in its public and general capacity, divided into component parts less numerous and less varied, required not those numerous public edifices which we possess either for business or pleasure; thus, when neither domestic nor civic architecture of any sort demanded great ability or afforded great employment, churches and monasteries were the only buildings required to combine extent and elegance, and sacred architecture alone could furnish an extensive field for the exercise of great skill, Lombardy itself, opulent and thriving as it was, compared to other countries, soon became nearly saturated with the requisite edifices, and unable to give these companies of Free and Accepted Masons a longer continuance of sufficient custom, or to render the further maintenance of their exclusive privileges of great benefit to them at home. But if, to the south of the Alps, an earlier civilization had at last caused the number of architects to exceed that of new buildings wanted, it fared otherwise in the north of Europe, where a gradually spreading Christianity began on every side to produce a want of sacred edifices, of churches and monasteries, to design which architects existed not on the spot.

"Those Italian corporations of builders, therefore, whose services ceased to be necessary in the countries where they had arisen, now began to look abroad towards those northern climes for that employment which they no longer found at home: and a certain number united and formed themselves into a single greater association, or fraternity, which proposed to seek for occupation beyond its native land; and in any ruder foreign region, however remote, where new religious edifices and skilful artists to erect them, were wanted to offer their services, and bend their steps to undertake the work."

From Lombardy they passed beyond the Alps into all the countries where Christianity, but recently established, required the erection of churches. A monopoly was granted to them for the erection of all religious edifices; they were declared independent of the sovereigns in whose dominions they might be temporarily residing, and subject only to their own private laws; they were permitted to regulate the amount of their wages; were exempted from all kinds of taxation; and no Mason, not belonging to their association, was permitted to compete with or oppose them in the pursuit of employment.

After filling the Continent with cathedrals, parochial churches, and monasteries, and increasing their own numbers by accessions of new members from all the countries in which they had been laboring, they passed over into England, and there introduced their peculiar style of building. Thence they traveled to

Scotland, and there have rendered their existence ever memorable by establishing, in the parish of Kilwinning, where they were erecting an abbey, the germ of Scottish Freemasonry, which has regularly descended through the Grand Lodge of Scotland to the present day.

Mr. Hope accounts for the introduction of non-working or unprofessional members into these associations by a theory which is confirmed by contemporary history. He says:

"Often obliged, from regions the most distant, singly to seek the common place of rendezvous and departure of the troop, or singly to follow its earlier detachments to places of employment equally distant; and that, at an era when travellers met on the road every obstruction, and no convenience, when no inns existed at which to purchase hospitality, but lords dwelt everywhere, who only prohibited their tenants from waylaying the traveller because they considered this, like killing game, one of their own exclusive privileges; the members of these communities contrived to render their journeys more easy and safe, by engaging with each other, and perhaps even, in many places, with individuals not directly participating in their profession, in compacts of mutual assistance, hospitality and good services, most valuable to men so circumstanced. They endeavored to compensate for the perils which attended their expeditions, by institutions for their needy or disabled brothers; but lest such as belonged not to their communities should benefit surreptitiously by these arrangements for its advantage, they framed signs of mutual recognition, as carefully concealed from the knowledge of the uninitiated, as the mysteries of their art themselves. Thus supplied with whatever could facilitate such distant journeys and labors as they contemplated, the members of these corporations were ready to obey any summons with the utmost alacrity, and they soon received the encouragement they anticipated. The militia of the Church of Rome, which diffused itself all over Europe in the shape of missionaries, to instruct nations, and to establish their allegiance to the Pope, took care not only to make them feel the want of churches and monasteries, but likewise to learn the manner in which the want might be supplied. Indeed, they themselves generally undertook the supply; and it may be asserted, that a new apostle of the Gospel no sooner arrived in the remotest corner of Europe, either to convert the inhabitants to Christianity, or to introduce among them a new religious order, than speedily followed a tribe of itinerant Freemasons to back him, and to provide the inhabitants with the necessary places of worship or reception.

"Thus ushered in, by their interior arrangements assured of assistance and of safety on the road, and, by the bulls of the Pope and the support of his ministers abroad, of every species of immunity and preference at the place of their destination, bodies of Freemasons dispersed themselves in every direction, every day began to advance further, and to proceed from country to country, to the utmost verge of the faithful, in order to answer the increasing demand for them, or to seek more distant custom."

The government of these fraternities, wherever they might be for the time located, was very regular and uniform. When about to commence the erection of a religious edifice, they first built huts, or, as they were termed, lodges, in the vicinity, in which they resided for the sake of economy as well as convenience. It is from these that the present name of our places of meeting is derived. Over every ten men was placed a warden, who paid them wages, and took care that there should be no needless expenditure of materials and no careless loss of implements. Over the whole, a surveyor or master, called in their old documents "magister," presided, and directed the general labor.

The Abbé Grandidier, in a letter at the end of the Marquis Luchet's *Essai sur les Illuminés*, has quoted from the ancient register of the Masons at Strasburg the regulations of the association which built the splendid cathedral of that city. Its great rarity renders it difficult to obtain a sight of the original work, but the *Histoire Pittoresque* of Clavel supplies the most prominent details of all that Grandidier has preserved. The cathedral of Strasburg was commenced in the year 1277, under the direction of Erwin of Steinbach. The Masons who, under his directions, were engaged in the construction of this noblest specimen of the Gothic style of architecture, were divided into the separate ranks of Masters, Craftsmen, and Apprentices. The place where they assembled was called a "hutte," a German word equivalent to our English term lodge. They employed the implements of masonry as emblems, and wore them as insignia. They had certain signs and words of recognition, and received their new members with peculiar and secret ceremonies, admitting, as has already been said, many eminent persons, and especially ecclesiastics, who were not Operative Masons, but who gave to them their patronage and protection.

The fraternity of Strasburg became celebrated throughout Germany, their superiority was acknowledged by the kindred associations, and they in time received the appellation of the "haupt hutte," or Grand Lodge, and exercised supremacy over the *hutten* of Suabia, Hesse, Bavaria, Franconia, Saxony, Thuringia, and the countries bordering on the river Moselle. The Masters of these several Lodges assembled at Ratisbon in 1459, and on the 25th of April contracted an act of union, declaring the chief of the Strasburg Cathedral the only and perpetual Grand Master of the General Fraternity of Freemasons of Germany. This act of union was definitely adopted and promulgated at a meeting held soon afterward at Strasburg.

Similar institutions existed in France and in Switzerland, for wherever Christianity had penetrated, there churches and cathedrals were to be built, and the Traveling Freemasons hastened to undertake the labor.

They entered England and Scotland at an early period. Whatever may be thought of the authenticity of the York and Kilwinning legends, there is ample evidence of the existence of organised associations, gilds, or corporations of Operative Masons at an epoch not long after their departure from Lombardy. From that period, the fraternity, with various intermissions, continued to pursue their labors, and constructed many edifices which still remain as monuments of their skill as workmen and their taste as architects. Kings, in many instances, became their patrons, and their labors were superintended by powerful noblemen and eminent prelates, who, for this purpose, were admitted as members of the fraternity. Many of the old Charges for the better government of their Lodges have been preserved, and are still to be found in our Books of Constitutions, every line of which indicates that they were originally drawn up for associations strictly and exclusively operative in their character.

In glancing over the history of this singular body of architects, we are struck with several important peculiarities.

In the first place, they were strictly ecclesiastical in their constitution. The Pope, the supreme pontiff of the Church, was their patron and protector. They were supported and encouraged by bishops and abbots, and hence their chief employment appears to have been in the construction of religious edifices.

They were originally all operatives. But the artisans of that period were not educated men, and they were compelled to seek among the clergy, the only men of learning, for those whose wisdom might contrive, and whose cultivated taste might adorn, the plans which they, by their practical skill, were to carry into effect. Hence the germ of that Speculative Masonry which, once dividing the character of the fraternity with the Operative, now completely occupies it, to the entire exclusion of the latter.*

But lastly, from the circumstance of their union and concert arose a uniformity of design in all the public buildings of that period—a uniformity so remarkable as to find its explanation only in the fact that their construction was committed throughout the whole of Europe, if not always to the same individuals, at least to members of the same association. The remarks of Mr. Hope on this subject are well worthy of perusal. "The architects of all the sacred edifices of the Latin church, wherever such arose,—north, south, east, or west,—thus derived their science from the same central school; obeyed in their designs the same hierarchy; were directed in their constructions by the same principles of propriety and taste; kept up with each other, in the most distant parts to which they might be sent, the most constant correspondence; and rendered every minute improvement the property of the whole body and a new conquest of the art. The result of this unanimity was, that at each successive period of the monastic dynasty, on whatever point a new church or new monastery might be erected, it resembled all those raised at the same period in every other place, however distant from it, as if both had been built in the same place by the same artist. For instance, we find, at particular epochs, churches as far distant from each other as the north of Scotland and the south of Italy, to be minutely similar in all the essential characteristics."

In conclusion, we may remark, that the world is indebted to this association for the introduction of the Gothic, or, as it has lately been denominated, the pointed style of architecture. This style—so different from the Greek and Roman orders, whose pointed arches and minute tracery distinguish the solemn temples of the olden time, and whose ruins arrest the attention and claim the admiration of the spectator—has been universally acknowledged to be the invention of the Traveling Freemasons of the Middle Ages.

And it is to this association of Operative artists that, by gradual changes into a speculative system, we are to trace the Freemasons of the present day.

Traveling Warrants. Warrants under which military Lodges are organised, and so called because the Lodges which act under them are permitted to travel from place to place with the regiments to which they are attached. (See *Military Lodges.*)

Travenol, Louis. A zealous and devoted French Mason of much ability, who wrote several Masonic works, which were published under the assumed name of Leonard Gabanon. The most valuable of his productions is one entitled *Catechisme des Francs-Maçons, precedé d'un Abrégé de l'Histoire d'Adoram, etc.*, published at Paris in 1743.

Treasure, Incomparable. This was a phrase of mystical import with the alchemists and Hermetic philosophers. Pernetty (*Dictionnaire Mytho-Hermétique*) thus defines it: "The incomparable treasure is the powder of projection, the source of all that is good, since it procures unbounded riches, and a long life, without infirmities, to enjoy them." The "powder of projection" was the instrument by which they expected to attain to the full perfection of their work. What was this incomparable treasure was the great secret of the Hermetic philosophers. They concealed the true object of their art under a symbolic language. "Believest thou, O fool," says Artephius, one of them, "that we plainly teach this secret of secrets, taking our words according to their literal signification?" But we do know that it was not, as the world supposed, the

* There probably never was a time when the Operative Masons did not furnish the architect. When an ecclesiastic performed this function it was an exception, and there were few of them. The profession of the architect seems to have been a distinct profession since Theoderic established himself at Ravenna (493), and appointed an official architect. All through the Lombard period and at all later periods the architect or Master was distinctive.
[E. E. C.]

transmutation of metals, or the discovery of an elixir of life, but the acquisition of Divine truth.

Many of the high degrees which were fabricated in the last century were founded on the Hermetic philosophy; and they, too, borrowed from it the idea of an incomparable treasure. Thus in the ultimate degree of the Council of Emperors of the East and West, which degree became afterward the Sublime Prince of the Royal Secret of the Scottish Rite, we find this very expression. In the old French rituals we meet with this sentence: "Let us now offer to the invincible Xerxes our sacred *incomparable treasure*, and we shall succeed victoriously." And out of the initial letters of the words of this sentence in the original French they fabricated the three most important words of the degree.

This "incomparable treasure" is to the Masons precisely what it was to the Hermetic philosophers—Divine Truth. "As for the Treasure," says one of these books (the *Lumen de Lumine*, cited by Hitchcock), "it is not yet discovered, but it is very near."

Treasurer. An officer, found in all Masonic bodies, whose duty it is to take charge of the funds and pay them out under proper regulations. He is simply the banker of the Lodge or Chapter, and has nothing to do with the collection of money, which should be made by the Secretary. He is an elective officer. The Treasurer's jewel is a key, as a symbol that he controls the chest of the Lodge. His position in the Lodge is on the right of the Worshipful Master, in front.

Treasurer, Grand. See *Grand Treasurer*.

Treasurer, Hermetic. (*Trésorier hermétique*.) A degree in the manuscript collection of Peuvret. This collection contains eight other degrees with a similar title, namely: Illustrious Treasurer, Treasurer of Paracelsus, Treasurer of Solomon, Treasurer of the Masonic Mysteries, Treasurer of the Number 7, Sublime Treasurer, Depositor of the Key of the Grand Work, and, lastly, one with the grandiloquent title of Grand and Sublime Treasurer, or Depositor of the Great Solomon, Faithful Guardian of Jehovah.

Tredic. The king highest in rank in the Scandinavian mysteries.

Tree Alphabet. There are alphabets used among the Persians and Arabs at the present day as secret ciphers, which it can scarcely be doubted were original, and ages ago adopted and recognized as the ordinary business mode of communication among men. Among these the Tree Alphabet is the most common. The Philosopher Dioscorides wrote several works on the subject of trees and herbs, and made prominent the secret characters of this alphabet, which became known by his name, and was adopted and used by others.

The characters were distinguishable by the number of branches on either side of the tree; thus, the TH is recognisable from the SH, notwithstanding each has three limbs on the left hand of the stem or trunk, by the one having six and the other seven branches on the right-hand side.

As an example, here are nine of the mystic characters and their relative values:

The characters in the lower line given above are the relative value, and known as the Alphabet of Hermes or Mercury.

Tree-Worship. The important position which this peculiar faith occupied among the peoples in the earliest ages of the world is apt to be overlooked in the multitude of succeeding beliefs, to which it gave many of its forms and ceremonies, and with which it became materially blended. In fact, Tree and Serpent Worship were combined almost at their inception. So prominent a position does Tree-Worship take in the opinion of Fergusson, in his absorbing work on *Tree and Serpent Worship*, that he designates the Tree as the first of Faiths; and adds that "long before the Theban gods existed, Tree and Serpent Faiths flourished. The Methidy tree was brought into the later religion, to shade with holy reverence the tomb of Osiris; the Sycamore was holy to Netpe, and the Persea to Athor, whilst the Tamarisk played an important part in all the rites and ceremonies of Osiris and Isis; and all who are orthodox will acknowledge that Abram seemed to consider

that he could not worship his Jove till he had planted his grove and digged a well (Gen. xxi. 33). His Oak or 'Terebinth,' or turpentine tree, on the plains of Mamre, was commonly worshiped till the fourth century A. C., and it is revered by Jews to the present hour." And again: "That long ere Buddha or his saints were represented by images and adored, long ere the caves and temples of that faith had sanctuaries for holy relics, *the first actual symbol-worship he can trace is that of the Bo tree*, which he describes as upon a *bas-relief* in a cave called the Jodea-Gopa (Katak, Bengal), proving how early that worship was introduced, and how pre-eminent it was among the Buddhists of those days"; and says J. G. R. Forlong, in his *Rivers of Life, or Faiths of Man*, "*before Vedic days;* and can be found in almost every cave and temple allied to the Phallic faith as certainly as can be found ever standing at the entrance of these 'Houses of God' the Phallic pillar or pillars. It is *the old story* whether we turn to Solomon's temple, 1000 B. C., or to

PALM-TREE WITH CROSS.

the Karli Buddhist temples, which gaze down upon us from Bombay to Poona, and which date from about the Christian era."

The Bael tree, as a representative of the triad and monad, was always offered at Lingam worship, and the god was commonly to be found under an umbrageous Bael.

All nations, Aryans in particular, considered tree-planting a sacred duty. The grand old trees became centers of life and of great traditions, and the character of the foliage had its symbolic meanings.

At the Jewish Feast of Tabernacles, at the autumnal harvest, Jews are ordered to hang boughs of trees, laden with fruit, round the borders of their booths, also boughs of barren trees. The worshipers go to the synagogue carrying in their right hand one palm-branch, three myrtles, and two willows, all tied together; and in the left hand a citron branch with fruit on it. These they make touch each other, and wave to the east, then south, then west, and then north: this is termed Hosana. On the seventh day of the Feast, all save the willow bough must be laid aside.

The Palm, as a tree, yields more to man than any other class of trees. Nineveh shows the Palm surrounded by winged deities holding the pine-cone—symbol of life, which there takes the place of the Crux Ansata. The Phœnix resting on the Palm signifies "Resurrection to eternal life." The four evangelists are depicted in "an evangelum," in the library of the British Museum, as all looking up to the Palm-tree. Christians, for a similar ideal, erected a cross-bar, and placed an Alpha and an Omega on it.

At Najran, in Yemen, Arabia, Sir William Ouseley describes the most perfect tree-worship as still existing close to the city. The tree is the Palm or Sacred date. The Palm has always borne a most important part in all the faiths of the world down to the present day. The Jews gave the Palm a distinguished place in architecture. The tree and its *lotus* top, says Kitto, took the place of the Egyptian column on Solomon's famous phalli, the *Jachin* and *Boaz*.

The two trees in Genesis were those of *Life* and *Knowledge*, and were probably drawn from the Egyptian and Zoroastrian stories. But no further reference is taken in the Bible of the "Tree of Knowledge" after Genesis, but to that of Life, or the "*Tree which gives Life*," as in the Apocalypse ii. 7. This is also the Eastern name and significance of the Lingam or Pillar; and when covered with carved inscriptions, the Toth or Pillar in Egypt became known as the "Tree of Knowledge."

Trestle-Board. The trestle-board is defined to be the board upon which the Master inscribes the designs by which the Craft are to be directed in their labors. The French and German Masons have confounded the *trestle-board* with the tracing-board; and Dr. Oliver (*Landm.*, i., 132) has not avoided the error. The two things are entirely different. The trestle is a framework for a table—in Scotch, *trest;* the *trestle-board* is the board placed for convenience of drawing on that frame. It contains nothing but a few diagrams, usually geometrical figures. The *tracing-board* is a picture formerly drawn on the floor of the Lodge, whence it was called a floor-cloth or carpet. It contains a delineation of the symbols of the degree to which it belongs. The *trestle-board* is to be found only in the Entered Apprentice's Degree. There is a

tracing-board in every degree, from the first to the highest. And, lastly, the *trestle-board* is a symbol; the *tracing-board* is a piece of furniture or picture containing the representation of many symbols.

It is probable that the trestle-board, from

its necessary use in Operative Masonry, was one of the earliest symbols introduced into the Speculative system. It is not, however, mentioned in the *Grand Mystery*, published in 1724. But Prichard, who wrote only six years afterward, describes it, under the corrupted name of *trasel-board*, as one of the immovable jewels of an Apprentice's Lodge. Browne, in 1880, following Preston, fell into the error of calling it a *tracing-board*, and gives from the Prestonian lecture what he terms "a beautiful degree of comparison," in which the Bible is compared to a tracing-board. But the Bible is not a collection of symbols, which a tracing-board is, but a trestle-board that contains the plan for the construction of a spiritual temple. Webb, however, when he arranged his system of lectures, took the proper view, and restored the true word, trestle-board.

Notwithstanding these changes in the name, trestle-board, trasel-board, tracing-board, and trestle-board again, the definition has continued from the earliest part of the last century to the present day the same. It has always been enumerated among the jewels of the Lodge, although the English system says that it is immovable and the American movable; and it has always been defined as "a board for the master workman to draw his designs upon."

In Operative Masonry, the trestle-board is of vast importance. It was on such an implement that the genius of the ancient masters worked out those problems of architecture that have reflected an unfading luster on their skill. The trestle-board was the cradle that nursed the infancy of such mighty monuments as the cathedrals of Strasburg and Cologne; and as they advanced in stature, the trestle-board became the guardian spirit that directed their growth. Often have those old builders pondered by the midnight lamp upon their trestle-board, working out its designs with consummate taste and knowledge—here springing an arch, and turning an angle there, until the embryo edifice stood forth in all the wisdom, strength, and beauty of the Master's art.

What, then, is its true symbolism in Speculative Masonry?

To construct his earthly temple, the Operative Mason followed the architectural designs laid down on the *trestle-board*, or book of plans of the architect. By these he hewed and squared his materials; by these he raised his walls; by these he constructed his arches; and by these strength and durability, combined with grace and beauty, were bestowed upon the edifice which he was constructing.

In the Masonic ritual, the Speculative Mason is reminded that, as the Operative artist erects his temporal building in accordance with the rules and designs laid down on the trestle-board of the master workman, so should he erect that spiritual building, of which the material is a type, in obedience to the rules and designs, the precepts and commands, laid down by the Great Architect of the Universe in those great books of nature and revelation which constitute the spiritual trestle-board of every Freemason.

The trestle-board is then the symbol of the natural and moral law. Like every other symbol of the Order, it is universal and tolerant in its application; and while, as Christian Masons, we cling with unfaltering integrity to the explanation which makes the Scriptures of both dispensations our trestle-board, we permit our Jewish and Mohammedan brethren to content themselves with the books of the Old Testament or Koran. Masonry does not interfere with the peculiar form or development of any one's religious faith. All that it asks is that the interpretation of the symbol shall be according to what each one supposes to be the revealed will of his Creator. But so rigidly exacting is it that the symbol shall be preserved and, in some rational way, interpreted, that it peremptorily excludes the atheist from its communion, because, believing in no Supreme Being—no Divine Architect—he must necessarily be without a spiritual trestle-board on which the designs of that Being may be inscribed for his direction.

Triad. In all the ancient mythologies there were triads, which consisted of a mysterious union of three deities. Each triad was generally explained as consisting of a creator, a preserver, and a destroyer. The principal heathen triads were as follows: the Egyptian, Osiris, Isis, and Horus; the Orphic, Phanes, Uranus, and Kronos; the Zoroastric, Ormuzd, Mithras, and Ahriman; the Indian, Brahma, Vishnu, and Siva; the Cabiric, Axercos, Axiokersa, and Axiokersos; the Phœnician, Ashtaroth, Milcom, and Chemosh; the Tyrian, Belus, Venus, and Thammuz; the Grecian, Zeus, Poseidon, and Hades; the Roman, Jupiter, Neptune, and Pluto; the Eleusinian, Iacchus, Persephone, and Demeter; the Platonic, Tagathon, Nous, and Psyche; the Celtic, Hu, Ceridwen, and Creirwy; the Teutonic, Fenris, Midgard, and Hela; the Gothic, Woden, Friga, and Thor; and the Scandinavians, Odin, Vile, and Ve. Even the Mexicans had their triads, which were Vitzliputzli, Kaloc, and Tescalipuca.

This system of triads has, indeed, been so predominant in all the old religions, as to be invested with a mystical idea; and hence it has become the type in Masonry of the triad of three governing officers, who are to be found in almost every degree. The Master and the two Wardens in the Lodge give rise to the Priest, the King, and the Scribe in the Royal Arch; to the Commander, the Generalissimo, and the Captain-General in Templarism; and in most of the high degrees to a triad who preside under various names.

We must, perhaps, look for the origin of the triads in mythology, as we certainly must in Masonry, to the three positions and functions of the sun. The rising sun or creator of light, the meridian sun or its preserver, and the setting sun or its destroyer.

Triad Society of China. The San Hop Hwai, or Triad Society, is a secret political association in China, which has been mistaken by some writers for a species of Chinese Freemasonry; but it has in reality no connection whatsoever with the Masonic Order. In its principles, which are far from innocent, it is entirely antagonistic to Freemasonry. The Deputy Provincial Grand Master of British Masonry in China made a statement to this effect in 1855, in *Notes and Queries*. (1st ser., vol. xii., p. 233.)

Trials, Masonic. As the only object of a trial should be to seek the truth and fairly to administer justice, in a Masonic trial, especially, no recourse should ever be had to legal technicalities, whose use in ordinary courts appears simply to be to afford a means of escape for the guilty.

Masonic trials are, therefore, to be conducted in the simplest and least technical method, that will preserve at once the rights of the Order and of the accused, and which will enable the Lodge to obtain a thorough knowledge of all the facts in the case. The rules to be observed in conducting such trials have been already laid down by me in my *Text Book of Jurisprudence* (pp. 558–564), and I shall refer to them in the present article. They are as follows:

1. The preliminary step in every trial is the accusation or charge. The charge should always be made in writing, signed by the accuser, delivered to the Secretary, and read by that officer at the next regular communication of the Lodge. The accused should then be furnished with an attested copy of the charge, and be at the same time informed of the time and place appointed by the Lodge for the trial.

Any Master Mason may be the accuser of another, but a profane cannot be permitted to prefer charges against a Mason. Yet, if circumstances are known to a profane upon which charges ought to be predicated, a Master Mason may avail himself of that information, and out of it frame an accusation, to be presented to the Lodge. And such accusation will be received and investigated, although remotely derived from one who is not a member of the Order.

It is not necessary that the accuser should be a member of the same Lodge. It is sufficient if he is an affiliated Mason. I say an affiliated Mason, for it is generally held, and I believe correctly, that an unaffiliated Mason is no more competent to prefer charges than a profane.

2. If the accused is living beyond the geographical jurisdiction of the Lodge, the charges should be communicated to him by means of a letter through the post-office, and a reasonable time should be allowed for his answer, before the Lodge proceeds to trial. But if his residence be unknown, or if it be impossible to hold communication with him, the Lodge may then proceed to trial—care being had that no undue advantage be taken of his absence, and that the investigation be as full and impartial as the nature of the circumstances will permit.

3. The trial must commence at a regular communication, for reasons which have already been stated; but having commenced, it may be continued at special communications, called for that purpose; for, if it was allowed only to be continued at regular meetings, which take place but once a month, the long duration of time occupied would materially tend to defeat the ends of justice.

4. The Lodge must be opened in the highest degree to which the accuser has attained, and the examinations of all witnesses must take place in the presence of the accused and the accuser, if they desire it. It is competent for the accused to employ counsel for the better protection of his interests, provided such counsel is a Master Mason. But if the counsel be a member of the Lodge, he forfeits, by his professional advocacy of the accused, the right to vote at the final decision of the question.

5. The final decision of the charge, and the rendering of the verdict, whatever be the rank of the accused, must always be made in a Lodge opened on the Third Degree; and at the time of such decision, both the accuser and the accused, as well as his counsel, if he have any, should withdraw from the Lodge.

6. It is a general and an excellent rule, that no visitors shall be permitted to be present during a trial.

7. The testimony of Master Masons is usually taken on their honor, as such. That of others should be by affidavit, or in such other manner as both the accuser and accused may agree upon.

8. The testimony of profanes, or of those who are of a lower degree than the accused, is to be taken by a committee and reported to the Lodge, or, if convenient, by the whole Lodge, when closed and sitting as a committee. But both the accused and the accuser have a right to be present on such occasions.

9. When the trial is concluded, the accuser and the accused must retire, and the Master will then put the question of guilty, or not guilty, to the Lodge.

Not less than two-thirds of the votes should be required to declare the accused guilty. A bare majority is hardly sufficient to divest a brother of his good character, and render him subject to what may perhaps be an ignominous punishment. But on this subject the authorities differ.

10. If the verdict is guilty, the Master must then put the question as to the nature

and extent of the punishment to be inflicted, beginning with expulsion and proceeding, if necessary, to indefinite suspension and public and private reprimand. To inflict expulsion or suspension, a vote of two-thirds of those present is required, but for a mere reprimand, a majority will be sufficient. The votes on the nature of the punishment should be *viva voce*, or, rather, according to Masonic usage, by a show of hands.

Trials in a Grand Lodge are to be conducted on the same general principles; but here, in consequence of the largeness of the body, and the inconvenience which would result from holding the examinations in open Lodge, and in the presence of all the members, it is more usual to appoint a committee, before whom the case is tried, and upon whose full report of the testimony the Grand Lodge bases its action. And the forms of trial in such committees must conform, in all respects, to the general usage already detailed.

Triangle. There is no symbol more important in its signification, more various in its application, or more generally diffused throughout the whole system of Freemasonry, than the triangle. An examination of it, therefore, cannot fail to be interesting to the Masonic student.

The *equilateral triangle* appears to have been adopted by nearly all the nations of antiquity as a symbol of the Deity, in some of his forms or emanations, and hence, probably, the prevailing influence of this symbol was carried into the Jewish system, where the yod within the triangle was made to represent the Tetragrammaton, or sacred name of God.

The equilateral triangle, says Bro. D. W. Nash (*Freem. Mag.*, iv., 294), "viewed in the light of the doctrines of those who gave it currency as a divine symbol, represents the Great First Cause, the creator and container of all things, as one and indivisible, manifesting himself in an infinity of forms and attributes in this visible universe."

Among the Egyptians, the darkness through which the candidate for initiation was made to pass was symbolized by the trowel, an important Masonic implement, which in their system of hieroglyphics has the form of a triangle. The equilateral triangle they considered as the most perfect of figures, and a representative of the great principle of animated existence, each of its sides referring to one of the three departments of creation, the animal, vegetable, and mineral

The equilateral triangle is to be found scattered throughout the Masonic system. It forms in the Royal Arch the figure within which the jewels of the officers are suspended. It is in the ineffable degrees the sacred delta, everywhere presenting itself as the symbol of the Grand Architect of the Universe. In Ancient Craft Masonry, it is constantly exhibited as the element of important ceremonies. The seats of the principal officers are arranged in a triangular form, the three lesser lights have the same situation, and the square and compass form, by their union on the greater light, two triangles meeting at their bases. In short, the equilateral triangle may be considered as one of the most constant forms of Masonic symbolism.

The *right-angled triangle* is another form of this figure which is deserving of attention. Among the Egyptians, it was the symbol of universal nature; the base representing Osiris, or the male principle; the perpendicular, Isis, or the female principle; and the hypotenuse, Horus, their son, or the product of the male and female principle.

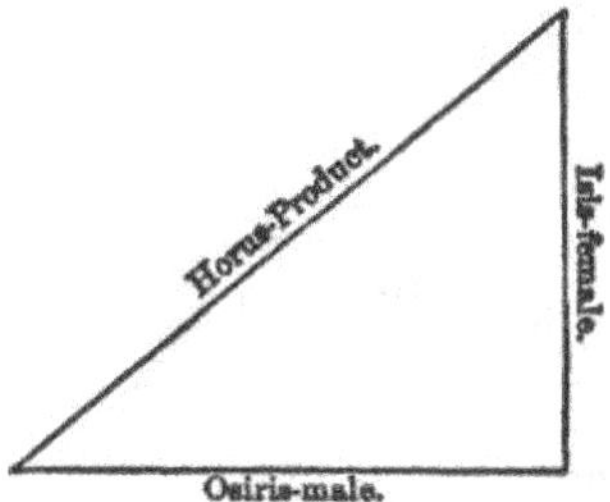

This symbol was received by Pythagoras from the Egyptians during his long sojourn in that country, and with it he also learned the peculiar property it possessed, namely, that the sum of the squares of the two shorter sides is equal to the square of the longest side—symbolically expressed by the formula, that the product of Osiris and Isis is Horus. This figure has been adopted in the Third Degree of Masonry, and will be there recognized as the forty-seventh problem of Euclid.

Triangle and Square. As the Delta was the initial letter of Deity with the ancients, so its synonym is among modern nations. It is a type of the Eternal, the All-Powerful, the Self-Existent.

The material world is typified by the "square" as passive matter, in opposition to force symbolized by the triangle.

The Square is also an emblem of humanity, as the Delta or Triangle typifies Deity.

The Delta, Triangle, and Compasses are essentially the same. The raising one point, and then another, signifies that the Divine or higher portion of our nature should increase in power, and control the baser tendencies. This is the real, the practical "journey toward the East."

2.

The interlacing triangles or deltas symbolize the union of the two principles or forces, the active and passive, male and female, pervading the universe. (1.)

The two triangles, one white and the other black, interlacing, typify the mingling of the two apparent powers in nature, darkness and light, error and truth, ignorance and wisdom, evil and good, throughout human life. (2.)

The triangle and square together form the pyramid (3), as seen in the Entered Apprentice's apron. In this combination the pyramid is the metaphor for unity of matter and force, as well as the oneness of man and God. The numbers 3, 5, 7, 9, have their places in the parts and points of the square and triangle when in pyramidal form, and imply Perfection. (See *Pointed Cubical Stone.*)

3.

Triangle, Double. See *Seal of Solomon* and *Shield of David.*

Triangle of Pythagoras. See *Pentalpha.*

Triangle, Radiated. A triangle placed within and surrounded by a circle of rays. This circle is called, in Christian art, "a glory." When this glory is distinct from the triangle, and surrounds it in the form of a circle, it is then an emblem of God's eternal glory. This is the usual form in religious uses. But when, as is most usual in the Masonic symbol, the rays emanate from the center of the triangle, and, as it were, enshroud it in their brilliancy, it is symbolic of the Divine Light. The perverted ideas of the Pagans referred these rays of light to their sun-god and their Sabian worship.

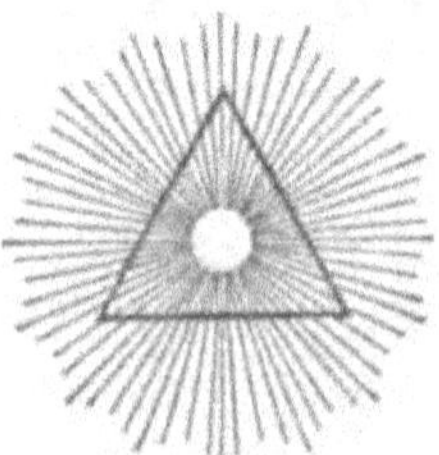

But the true Masonic idea of this glory is, that it symbolizes that Eternal Light of Wisdom which surrounds the Supreme Architect as a sea of glory, and from Him as a common center emanates to the universe of His creation.

Triangle, Triple. The *pentalpha,* or triangle of Pythagoras, is usually called also the triple triangle, because three triangles are formed by the intersection of its sides. But there is another variety of the triple triangle which is more properly entitled to the appellation, and which is made in the annexed form.

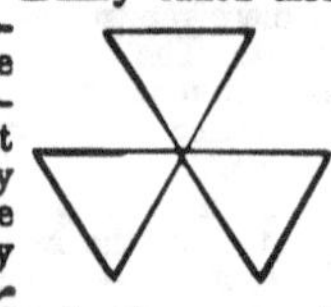

It will be familiar to the Knights Templar as the form of the jewel worn by the Prelate of his Order. Like every modification of the triangle, it is a symbol of the Deity; but as the degree of Knights Templar appertains exclusively to Christian Masonry, the triple triangle there alludes to the mystery of the Trinity. In the Scottish Rite Degree of Knight of the East the symbol is also said to refer to the triple essence of Deity; but the symbolism is made still more mystical by supposing that it represents the sacred number 81, each side of the three triangles being equivalent to 9, which again is the square of 3, the most sacred number in Freemasonry. In the Twentieth Degree of the Ancient and Accepted Scottish Rite, or that of "Grand Master of all Symbolic Lodges," it is said that the number 81 refers to the triple covenant of God, symbolized by a triple triangle said to have been seen by Solomon when he consecrated the Temple. Indeed, throughout the ineffable and the philosophic degrees, the allusions to the triple triangle are much more frequent than they are in Ancient Craft Masonry.

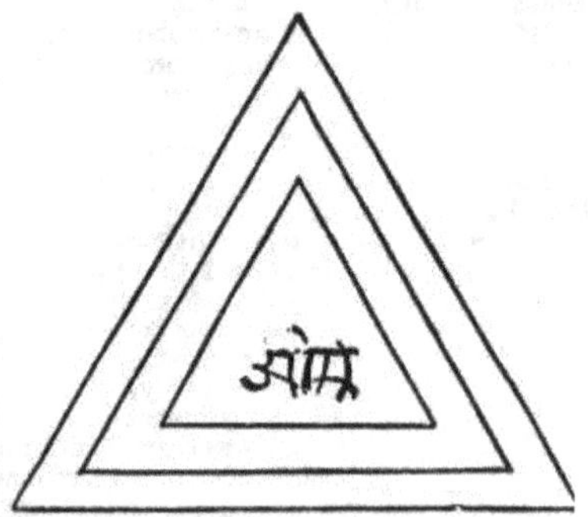

The Indian trimourti, or triple triangle of the Hindus, is of a different form, consisting of three concentric triangles. In the center is the sacred triliteral name, AUM. The interior triangle symbolizes Brahma, Vishnu, and Siva; the middle one, Creation·

Preservation, and Destruction; and the exterior one, Earth, Water, and Air.

Tribe of Judah, Lion of the. The connection of Solomon, as the chief of the tribe of Judah, with the lion, which was the achievement of the tribe, has caused this expression to be referred, in the Third Degree, to Him who brought life and immortality to light. The old Christian interpretation of the Masonic symbols here prevails; and in Ancient Craft Masonry all allusions to the lion, as the *lion's paw*, the *lion's grip*, etc., refer to the doctrine of the resurrection taught by Him who is known as "the lion of the tribe of Judah." The expression is borrowed from the Apocalypse (v. 5): "Behold, the Lion of the tribe of Judah, the Root of David, hath prevailed to open the book, and to loose the seven seals thereof." The lion was also a Medieval symbol of the resurrection, the idea being founded on a legend. The poets of that age were fond of referring to this legendary symbol in connection with the Scriptural idea of the "tribe of Judah." Thus Adam de St. Victor, in his poem *De Resurrectione Domini*, says:

"Sic de Juda Leo fortis,
Fractis portis diræ mortis
Die surgit tertia,
Rugiente voce Patris."

i. e.,

Thus the strong lion of Judah,
The gates of cruel death being broken,
Arose on the third day
At the loud-sounding voice of the Father.

The lion was the symbol of strength and sovereignty, in the human-headed figures of the Nimrod gateway, and in other Babylonish remains. In Egypt, it was worshiped at the city of Leontopolis as typical of Dom, the Egyptian Hercules. Plutarch says that the Egyptians ornamented their temples with gaping lions' mouths, because the Nile began to rise when the sun was in the constellation Leo. Among the Talmudists there was a tradition of the lion, which has been introduced into the higher degrees of Masonry.

But in the symbolism of Ancient Craft Masonry, where the lion is introduced, as in the Third Degree, in connection with the "lion of the tribe of Judah," he becomes simply a symbol of the resurrection; thus restoring the symbology of the Medieval ages, which was founded on a legend that the lion's whelp was born dead, and only brought to life by the roaring of its sire. Philip de Thaun, in his *Bestiary*, written in the twelfth century, gives the legend, which has thus been translated by Mr. Wright from the original old Norman French:

"Know that the lioness, if she bring forth a dead cub, she holds her cub and the lion arrives; he goes about and cries, till it revives on the third day . . . . Know that the lioness signifies St. Mary, and the lion Christ, who gave himself to death for the people; three days he lay in the earth to gain our souls. . . . . By the cry of the lion they understand the power of God, by which Christ was restored to life and robbed hell."

The phrase, "lion of the tribe of Judah," therefore, when used in the Masonic ritual, referred in its original interpretation to Christ, Him who "brought life and immortality to light."

Tribes of Israel. All the twelve tribes of Israel were engaged in the construction of the first Temple. But long before its destruction, ten of them revolted, and formed the nation of Israel; while the remaining two, the tribes of Judah and Benjamin, retained possession of the Temple and of Jerusalem under the name of the kingdom of Judah. To these two tribes alone, after the return from the captivity, was entrusted the building of the second Temple. Hence in the high degrees, which, of course, are connected for the most part with the Temple of Zerubbabel, or with events that occurred subsequent to the destruction of that of Solomon, the tribes of Judah and Benjamin only are referred to. But in the primary degrees, which are based on the first Temple, the Masonic references always are to the twelve tribes. Hence in the old lectures the twelve original points are explained by a reference to the twelve tribes. (See *Twelve Original Points of Masonry*.)

Tribunal. The modern statutes of the Supreme Council of the Ancient and Accepted Scottish Rite for the Southern Jurisdiction of the United States direct trials of Masonic offenses, committed by any brethren of the Rite above the Eighteenth Degree, to be held in a court called a Tribunal of the Thirty-first Degree, to be composed of not less nor more than nine members. An appeal lies from such a Tribunal of Inspectors Inquisitors to the Grand Consistory or the Supreme Council.

Tribunal, Supreme. 1. The Seventy-first Degree of the Rite of Misraim. 2. The meeting of Inquisitors Inspectors of the Thirty-first Degree of the Ancient and Accepted Scottish Rite according to the modern ritual of the Mother Council.

Trifels. The name of the ruined castle, four miles from Madenburg, on a mountain slope, where Sir Richard Cœur de Lion was a prisoner for more than a year, by decree of the Emperor Henry VI., and until his liberation by the faithful Blondel. Naught remains but thirty feet of the tower and some fragments of wall. It is recorded that there may be seen engraved deep in the window-stone of the tower this mark: the passion cross standing upon the square with an apex upward, and having upon it an inverted TAU of proportionate size at an inclination of about forty-nine degrees.

Triliteral Name. The sacred name of God among the Hindus is so called because it consists of the three letters, A U M. (See *Aum*.)

Trilithon. Three stones, two of which are placed parallel on their ends, and crossed by the third at the top.

THE TRILITHON AT ST. MICHAEL'S MOUNT, LAND'S END.

Trinidad. Masonry was introduced into the island of Trinidad by the establishment of a Lodge called "Les Frères Unis," under a Charter from the Grand Lodge of Pennsylvania, in 1797. A Charter had been granted the year before by the Grand Orient of France, but never acted on, in consequence of the suspension of that body by the French Revolution. In 1804, the Grand Lodge of Pennsylvania, in its capitular capacity, granted a Charter for a Royal Arch Chapter, which continued to meet until 1813, when it obtained a new Warrant of Constitution from the Supreme Chapter of Scotland. In 1814, Templar Masonry was established by a Deuchar Warrant from the Grand Conclave of Scotland. In 1819, a Council of Royal and Select Masters was established. Trinidad has at present a Provincial Grand Lodge under the Grand Lodge of Scotland, and there are also three Lodges under the Grand Lodge of England.

Trinitarians, Order of. An androgynous order founded in 1198, in the time of Innocent III., for the purpose of ransoming Christians from the Moors.

Trinity, Religious Fraternity of the Holy. Instituted at Rome by St. Philip Neri in 1548.

Trinosophs. The Lodge of the Trinosophs was instituted at Paris by the celebrated Ragon, October 15, 1816, and installed by the Grand Orient, January 11, 1817. The word *Trinosophs* is derived from the Greek, and signifies *students of three sciences*, in allusion to the three primitive degrees, which were the especial object of study by the members; although they adopted both the French and Scottish Rites, to whose high degrees, however, they gave their own philosophical interpretation. It was before this Lodge that Ragon delivered his *Interpretative and Philosophic Course of Initiations.* The Lodge was composed of some of the most learned Masons of France, and played an important part in Masonic literature. No Lodge in France has obtained so much celebrity as did the Trinosophs. It was connected with a Chapter and Council in which the high degrees were conferred, but the Lodge confined itself to the three symbolic degrees, which it sought to preserve in the utmost purity.

Tripitaka. Tri, three, and Pitaka, basket. The canonical book of the Buddhists, written two hundred years after the third Œcumenical Council, or about 60 B. C. The former Asiatic Indra doctrines having become intolerable, Sakya, a reformer in religion, rejected the god Brahma, and the holy books of the Veda, the sacrifices and other rites, and said: "My law is grace for all." These sacred writings of the Hindus were called the Three Baskets: the basket of Laws, the basket of Discipline, and the basket of Doctrines. The first basket is called "Dharma," and relates to the law for man; the second, "Vinaya," and relates to the discipline of the priests; and the third, "Abhidharma," and pertains to the gods. It is estimated that 350,000,000 people believe in these writings as sacred and canonical.

Triple Alliance. An expression in the high degrees, which, having been translated from the French rituals, should have more properly been the triple covenant. It is represented by the triple triangle, and refers to the covenant of God with his people, that of King Solomon with Hiram of Tyre, and that which binds the fraternity of Masons.

Triple Tau. The tau cross, or cross of St. Anthony, is a cross in the form of a Greek T. The triple tau is a figure formed by three of these crosses meeting in a point, and therefore resembling a letter T resting on the traverse bar of an H. This emblem, placed in the center of a triangle and circle—both emblems of the Deity—constitutes the jewel of the Royal Arch as practised in England, where it is so highly esteemed as to be called the "emblem of all emblems," and "the grand emblem of Royal Arch Masonry." It was adopted in the same form as the Royal Arch badge, by the General Grand Chapter of the United States in 1859; although it had previously been very generally recognized by American Masons. It is also found in the capitular Masonry of Scotland. (See *Royal Arch Badge*.)

The original signification of this emblem has been variously explained. Some suppose it to include the initials of the Temple of Jerusalem, T. H., *Templum Hierosolymæ*; others, that it is a symbol of the mystical union of the Father and Son, H signifying Jehovah, and T, or the cross, the Son. A writer in *Moore's Magazine* ingeniously supposes it to be a representation of three T squares, and that it alludes to the three jewels of the three ancient Grand Masters.

It has also been said that it is the monogram of Hiram of Tyre; and others assert that it is only a modification of the Hebrew letter *shin*, ש, which was one of the Jewish abbreviations of the sacred name. Oliver thinks, from its connection with the circle and triangle in the Royal Arch jewel, that it was intended to typify the sacred name as the author of eternal life. The English Royal Arch lectures say that "by its intersection it forms a given number of angles that may be taken in five several combinations; and, reduced, their amount in right angles will be found equal to the five Platonic bodies which represent the four elements and the sphere of the Universe." Amid so many speculations, I need not hesitate to offer one of my own. The Prophet Ezekiel speaks of the *tau* or tau cross as the mark distinguishing those who were to be saved, on account of their sorrow for their sins, from those who, as idolaters, were to be slain. It was a mark or sign of favorable distinction; and with this allusion we may, therefore, suppose the triple tau to be used in the Royal Arch Degree as a mark designating and separating those who know and worship the true name of God from those who are ignorant of that august mystery.

Trivium. See *Quadrivium*.

Trowel. An implement of Operative Masonry, which has been adopted by Speculative Masons as the peculiar working-tool of the Master's Degree. By this implement, and its use in Operative Masonry to spread the cement which binds all the parts of the building into one common mass, we are taught to spread the cement of affection and kindness, which unites all the members of the Masonic family, wheresoever dispersed over the globe, into one companionship of Brotherly Love.

This implement is considered the appropriate working-tool of a Master Mason, because, in Operative Masonry, while the Apprentice is engaged in preparing the rude materials, which require only the gage and gavel to give them their proper shape, the Fellow-Craft places them in their proper position by means of the plumb, level, and square; but the Master Mason alone, having examined their correctness and proved them true and trusty, secures them permanently in their place by spreading, with the trowel, the cement that irrevocably binds them together.

The trowel has also been adopted as the jewel of the Select Master. But its uses in this degree are not symbolical. They are simply connected with the historical legend of the degree.

Trowel and Sword. When Nehemiah received from Artaxerxes Longimanus the appointment of Governor of Judea, and was permitted to rebuild the walls of Jerusalem, and to restore the city to its former fortified condition, he met with great opposition from the Persian satraps, who were envious of his favor with the king, and from the heathen inhabitants of Samaria, who were unwilling to see the city again assume its pristine importance. The former undertook to injure him with Artaxerxes by false reports of his seditious designs to restore the independent kingdom of Judea. The latter sought to obstruct the workmen of Nehemiah in their labors, and openly attacked them. Nehemiah took the most active measures to refute the insidious accusations of the first, and to repel the more open violence of the latter. Josephus says (*Antiq.*, B. XI., ch. vi., § 8) that he gave orders that the builders should keep their ranks, and have their armor on while they were building; and, accordingly, the mason had his sword on as well as he that brought the materials for building.

Zerubbabel had met with similar opposition from the Samaritans while rebuilding the Temple; and although the events connected with Nehemiah's restoration of the walls occurred long after the completion of the second Temple, yet the Masons have in the high degrees referred them to the time of Zerubbabel. Hence in the Fifteenth Degree of the Scottish Rite, or the Knight of the East, which refers to the building of the Temple of Zerubbabel, we find this combination of the trowel and the sword adopted as a symbol. The old ritual of that degree says that Zerubbabel, being informed of the hostile intentions of the false brethren from Samaria, "ordered that all the workmen should be armed with the trowel in one hand and the sword in the other, that while they worked with the one they might be enabled to defend themselves with the other, and ever repulse the enemy if they should dare to present themselves."

In reference to this idea, but not with chronological accuracy, the trowel and sword have been placed crosswise as symbols on the tracing-board of the English Royal Arch.

Oliver correctly interprets the symbol of the trowel and sword as signifying that, "next to obedience to lawful authority, a manly and determined resistance to lawless violence is an essential part of social duty."

Trowel, Society of the. Vasari, in his *Lives of the Painters and Sculptors* (Life of G. F. Rustici), says that about the year 1512 there was established at Florence an association which counted among its members some of the most distinguished and learned inhabitants of the city. It was the "Società della Cucchiara," or the *Society of the Trowel*. Vasari adds that its symbols were the trowel, the hammer, the square, and the level, and had for its patron St. Andrew, which makes Reghellini think, rather illogically, that it had some relation to the Scottish Rite. Lenning, too, says that this society was the first appearance of Freemasonry in Florence. It is to be regretted that such misstatements of Masonic history should be encouraged by

TRUST
IN
GOD
EUROPE
AFRICA
ASIA
W
S
B

writers of learning and distinction. The perusal of the account of the formation of this society, as given by Vasari, shows that it had not the slightest connection with Freemasonry. It was simply a festive association, or dinner-club of Florentine artists; and it derived its title from the accidental circumstance that certain painters and sculptors, dining together in a garden, found not far from their table a mass of mortar, in which a trowel was sticking. Some rough jokes passed thereupon, in the casting of the mortar on each other, and the calling for the trowel to scrape it off. Whereupon they resolved to form an association to dine together annually, and, in memorial of the ludicrous event that had led to their establishment, they called themselves the Society of the Trowel.

True Light. *Sit lux et lux fuit.* The translation from the Hebrew Bible of this passage, so often quoted in Masonry, is: "And the Lord said, 'Let there be light, and it was light.' And the Lord took care of the light, that it was useful; and He divided the light from the darkness."

True Masons. See *Academy of True Masons.*

Truro Cathedral. A Protestant edifice erected at a seaport of Cornwall, England, standing at the junction of two rivers, the Allen and the Kenwyn. On the 20th of May, 1880, the Grand Master of Masons (Prince of Wales) laid two corner-stones of the cathedral with great pageantry, pomp, and ceremony. This was the first time a Grand Master of Masons in England was known to lay the corner-stone of an ecclesiastical structure; this was, also, the first occasion on which the then Grand Master had performed such a service, in Masonic clothing, surrounded with his staff and officers, in rich robes and in the costume of Masonry.

Trust in God. Every candidate on his initiation is required to declare that his trust is in God. And so he who denies the existence of a Supreme Being is debarred the privilege of initiation, for atheism is a disqualification for Masonry. This pious principle has distinguished the Fraternity from the earliest period; and it is a happy coincidence, that the company of Operative Freemasons instituted in 1477 should have adopted, as their motto, the truly Masonic sentiment, "The Lord is all our Trust."

Truth. The real object of Freemasonry, in a philosophical and religious sense, is the search for truth. This truth is, therefore, symbolized by the WORD. From the first entrance of the Apprentice into the Lodge, until his reception of the highest degree, this search is continued. It is not always found and a substitute must sometimes be provided. Yet whatever be the labors he may perform, whatever the ceremonies through which he may pass, whatever the symbols in which he may be instructed, whatever the reward he may obtain, the true end of all is the attainment of truth. This idea of truth is not the same as that expressed in the lecture of the First Degree, where Brotherly Love, Relief, and Truth are there said to be the "three great tenets of a Mason's profession." In that connection, truth, which is called a "divine attribute, the foundation of every virtue," is synonymous with sincerity, honesty of expression, and plain dealing. The higher idea of truth which pervades the whole Masonic system, and which is symbolized by the WORD, is that which is properly expressed to a knowledge of God.

There was an Egyptian goddess named תם *Thm*, or תמה, *Thme*, *integritas*, Justice and Truth. This one of the three great Masonic principles is represented among the Egyptians by an ostrich feather; and the judicial officer was also thus represented, "because that bird, unlike others, has all its feathers equal." Horapollo. The Hebrew word יען, *ion*, signifies an ostrich, as also a council; and the word רננוה, *Rnne*, is interpreted, poetically, an ostrich, and also *a song of joy*, or *of praise;* hence, "the happy souls thus ornamented, under the inspection of the lords of the *heart's joy*, gathered fruits from celestial trees." In the judgment in Amenti, the soul advances toward the goddess Thme, who wears on her head the ostrich feather. In the scale, Anubis and Horus weigh the actions of the deceased. On one side is the ostrich feather, and on the other the vase containing the heart. Should the weight of the heart be greater than the feather, the soul is entitled to be received into the celestial courts. The forty-two judges, with heads ornamented with ostrich feathers, sit aloft to pronounce judgment. (See *Book of the Dead.*)

Tryonists. Those Pythagoreans who abstained from animal food.

Tsaphiel. צפיאל. Mirans Deus, the angel governing the Moon, in accordance with the Kabbalistical system.

Tschoudy, Louis Theodore. Michaud spells the name *Tschudi*, but Lenning, Thory, Ragon, Oliver, and all other Masonic writers, give the name as Tschoudy, which form, therefore, I adopt as the most usual, if not the most correct, spelling.

The Baron de Tschoudy was born at Metz, in 1720. He was descended from a family originally of the Swiss canton of Glaris, but which had been established in France since the commencement of the sixteenth century. He was a counselor of State and member of the Parliament of Metz; but the most important events of his life are those which connect him with the Masonic institution, of which he was a zealous and learned investigator. He was one of the most active apostles of the school of Ramsay, and adopted his theory of the Templar origin of Masonry. Having obtained permission from the king to travel, he went to Italy, in 1752, under the assumed name of the Chevalier de Lussy. There he excited the anger of the papal court by the publication at The Hague, in the same year, of a book entitled *Etrenne au Pape, ou les Francs-Maçons Vengés;* i. e., "A New Year's Gift for the Pope, or the Free Masons Avenged." This was a caustic commentary on the bull of Benedict XIV. excommunicating the Freemasons. It was followed, in the same year, by another work entitled, *Le Vatican Vengé;* i. e., "The Vatican Avenged"; an ironical apology, intended as a sequence to the former book. These two works subjected him to such persecution by the Church that he was soon compelled to seek safety in flight.

He next repaired to Russia, where his means of living became so much impaired that, Michaud says, he was compelled to enter the company of comedians of the Empress Elizabeth. From this condition he was relieved by Count Ivan Schouwalon, who made him his private secretary. He was also appointed the secretary of the Academy of Moscow, and governor of the pages at the court. But this advancement of his fortunes, and the fact of his being a Frenchman, created for him many enemies, and he was compelled at length to leave Russia and return to France. There, however, the persecutions of his enemies pursued him, and on his arrival at Paris he was sent to the Bastile. But the intercession of his mother with the Empress Elizabeth and with the Grand Duke Peter was successful, and he was speedily restored to liberty. He then retired to Metz, and for the rest of his life devoted himself to the task of Masonic reform and the fabrication of new systems.

In 1762, the Council of Knights of the East was established at Paris. Ragon says (*Orthod. Maçon.*, p. 137) that "its ritual was corrected by the Baron de Tschoudy, the author of the *Blazing Star.*" But this is an error. Tschoudy was then at Metz, and his work and system of the *Blazing Star* did not appear until four years afterward. It is at a later date that Tschoudy became connected with the Council.

In 1766 he published, in connection with Bardon-Duhamel, his most important work, entitled *L'Etoile Flamboyante, ou la Société des Francs-Maçons considerés sous tous les Aspects;* i. e., "The Blazing Star, or the Society of Freemasons considered under Every Point of View."

In the same year he repaired to Paris, with the declared object of extending his Masonic system. He then attached himself to the Council of Knights of the East, which, under the guidance of the tailor Pirlet, had seceded from the Council of Emperors of the East and West. Tschoudy availed himself of the ignorance and of the boldness of Pirlet to put his plan of reform into execution by the creation of new degrees.

In Tschoudy's system, however, as developed in the *L'Etoile Flamboyante*, he does not show himself to be the advocate of the high degrees, which, he says, are "an occasion of expense to their dupes, and an abundant and lucrative resource for those who make a profitable traffic of their pretended instructions." He recognizes the three Symbolic degrees because their gradations are necessary in the Lodge, which he viewed as a school; and to these he adds a superior class, which may be called the architects, or by any other name, provided we attach to it the proper meaning. All the high degrees he calls "Masonic reveries," excepting two, which he regards as containing the secret, the object, and the essence of Masonry, namely, the Scottish Knight of St. Andrew and the Knight of Palestine. The former of these degrees was composed by Tschoudy, and its ritual, which he bequeathed, with other manuscripts, to the Council of Knights of the East and West, was published in 1780, under the title of *Écossais de Saint André, contenant le développement total de l'art royal de la Franche-Maçonnerie.* Subsequently, on the organization of the Ancient and Accepted Scottish Rite, the degree was adopted as the Twenty-ninth of its series, and is considered as one of the most important and philosophic of the Scottish system. Its fabrication is, indeed, an evidence of the intellectual genius of its inventor.

Ragon, in his *Orthodoxie Maçonnique*, attributes to Tschoudy the fabrication of the Rite of Adonhiramite Masonry, and the authorship of the *Recueil Précieux*, which contains the description of the Rite. But the first edition of the *Recueil*, with the acknowledged authorship of Guillemain de St. Victor, appeared in 1781. This is probably about the date of the introduction of the Rite, and is just twelve years after Tschoudy had gone to his eternal rest.

Tschoudy also indulged in light literature, and several romances are attributed to him, the only one of which now known, entitled *Thérèse Philosophe*, does not add to his reputation.

Chemins Despontès (*Encyc. Maçon.*, i., 143) says: "The Baron Tschoudy, whose birth gave him a distinguished rank in society, left behind him the reputation of an excellent man, equally remarkable for his social virtues, his genius, and his military talents." Such appears to have been the general opinion of those who were his contemporaries or his immediate successors. He died at Paris, May 28, 1769.

Tsedakah. צדקה, Justice. The first step of the mystical ladder, known to the Kadosh, Thirtieth Degree A. A. Scottish Rite.

Tsidoni. צידני, Venator. A Seeker or Inquirer. A name used in the Twenty-second Degree of the A. A. Scottish Rite.

Tsoim. צעים. A term used infrequently to designate visitors.

Tuapholl. A term used by the Druids to designate an unhallowed circumambulation around the sacred cairn, or altar; the movement being against the sun, that is, from west to east by the north, the cairn being on the left hand of the circumambulator.

Tubal Cain. Of Tubal Cain, the sacred writings, as well as the Masonic legends, give us but scanty information. All that we hear of him in the Book of Genesis is that he was the son of Lamech and Zillah, and was "an instructor of every artificer in brass and iron." The Hebrew original does not justify the common version, for לטש, *lotesh*, does not mean "an instructor," but "a sharpener"—one who whets or sharpens instruments. Hence Dr. Raphall translates the passage as one "who sharpened various tools in copper and iron." The authorized version has, however, almost indelibly impressed the character of Tubal Cain as the father of artificers; and it is in this sense that he has been introduced from a very early period into the legendary history of Masonry.

The first Masonic reference to Tubal Cain is found in the "Legend of the Craft," where he is called "the founder of smith-craft." I cite this part of the legend from the Dowland MS. simply because of its more modern orthography; but the story is substantially the same in all the old manuscript Constitutions. In that Manuscript we find the following account of Tubal Cain:

"Before Noah's flood there was a man called Lamech, as it is written in the Bible, in the fourth chapter of Genesis; and this Lamech had two wives, the one named Ada and the other named Zilla; by his first wife, Ada, he got two sons, the one Jubal, and the other Jabal: and by the other wife he got a son and a daughter. And these four children founded the beginning of all the sciences in the world. The elder son, Jabal, founded the science of geometry, and he carried flocks of sheep and lambs into the fields, and first built houses of stone and wood, as it is noted in the chapter above named. And his brother Jubal founded the science of music and songs of the tongue, the harp and organ. And the third brother, Tubal Cain, founded smith-craft, of gold, silver, copper, iron, and steel, and the daughter founded the art of weaving. And these children knew well that God would take vengeance for sin, either by fire or water, wherefore they wrote the sciences that they had found, on two pillars that they might be found after Noah's flood. The one pillar was marble, for that would not burn with fire; and the other was clepped laterns, and would not drown in noe water."

Similar to this is an old Rabbinical tradition, which asserts that Jubal, who was the inventor of writing as well as of music, having heard Adam say that the universe would be twice destroyed, once by fire and once by water, inquired which catastrophe would first occur; but Adam refusing to inform him, he inscribed the system of music which he had invented upon two pillars of stone and brick. A more modern Masonic tradition ascribes the construction of these pillars to Enoch.

To this account of Tubal Cain must be added the additional particulars, recorded by Josephus, that he exceeded all men in strength, and was renowned for his warlike achievements.

The only other account of the proto-metallurgist that we meet with in any ancient author is that which is contained in the celebrated fragment of Sanconiatho, who refers to him under the name of Chrysor, which is evidently, as Bochart affirms, a corruption of the Hebrew *chores ur*, a worker in fire, that is, a smith. Sanconiatho was a Phœnician author, who is supposed to have flourished before the Trojan war, probably, as Sir William Drummond suggests, about the time when Gideon was Judge of Israel, and who collected the different accounts and traditions of the origin of the world which were extant at the period in which he lived. A fragment only of this work has been preserved, which, translated into Greek by Philo Byblius, was inserted by Eusebius in his *Præparatio Evangelica*, and has thus been handed down to the present day. That portion of the history by Sanconiatho, which refers to Tubal Cain, is contained in the following words:

"A long time after the generation of Hypsoaranios, the inventors of hunting and fishing, Agreas and Alieas, were born: after whom the people were called hunters and fishers, and from whom sprang two brothers, who discovered iron, and the manner of working it. One of these two, called Chrysor, was skilled in eloquence, and composed verses and prophecies. He was the same with Hephaistos, and invented fishing-hooks, bait for taking fish, cordage and rafts, and was the first of all mankind who had navigated. He was therefore worshiped as a god after his death, and was called Diamichios. It is said that these brothers were the first who contrived partition walls of brick."

Hephaistos, it will be observed, is the Greek of the god who was called by the Romans Vulcan. Hence the remark of Sanconiatho, and the apparent similarity of names as well as occupations, have led some writers of the last, and even of the present, century to derive Vulcan from Tubal Cain by a process not very devious and therefore familiar to etymologists. By the omission in Tubal Cain of the initial T, which is the Phœnician article, and its valueless vowel, we get *Balcan*, which, by the interchangeable nature of B and V, is easily transformed to *Vulcan*.

"That Tubal Cain," says Bishop Stillingfleet (*Orig. Sac.*, p. 292), "gave first occasion to the name and worship of Vulcan, hath been very probably conceived, both from the very great affinity of the names, and that Tubal Cain is expressly mentioned to be an instructor of every artificer in brass and iron, and as near relation as Apollo had to Vulcan, Jubal had to Tubal Cain, who was the inventor of music, or the father of all such as handle the harp and organ, which the Greeks attribute to Apollo."

Vossius, in his treatise *De Idolatria* (lib. i., cap. 36), makes this derivation of Vulcan from Tubal Cain. But Bryant, in his *Analysis of Ancient Mythology* (vol. i., p. 139), denies the etymology and says that among the Egyptians and Babylonians, Vulcan was equivalent to Orus or Osiris, symbols of the sun. He traces the name to the words *Baal Cahen*, Holy Bel, or sacred Lord. Bryant's etymology may be adopted, however, without any interference with the identity of Vulcan and Tubal Cain. He who discovered the uses of fire, may well, in the corruptions of idolatry, have typified the solar orb, the source of all heat. It might seem that Tubal is an attribute compounded of the definite particle T and the word Baal, signifying Lord. Tubal Cain would then signify "the Lord Cain." Again, *dhu* or *du*, in Arabic, signifies Lord; and we trace the same signification of this affix, in its various interchangeable forms of *Du*, *Tu*, and *Di*, in many Semitic words. But the question of the identical origin of Tubal Cain and Vulcan has at length been settled by the researches of comparative philologists. Tubal Cain is Semitic in origin, and Vulcan is Aryan. The latter may be traced to the Sanskrit *ulka*, a firebrand, from which we get also the Latin *fulgur* and *fulmen*, names of the lightning.

From the mention made of Tubal Cain in the "Legend of the Craft," the word was long ago adopted as significant in the primary degrees, and various attempts have been made to give it an interpretation.

Hutchinson, in an article in his *Spirit of Masonry*, devoted to the consideration of the Third Degree, has the following reference to the word (p. 162):

"The Mason advancing to this state of Masonry, pronounces his own sentence, as confessional of the imperfection of the second stage of his profession, and as probationary of the exalted degree to which he aspires, in this Greek distich, Τυμβουχοεω, Struo tumulum: 'I prepare my sepulchre; I make my grave in the pollutions of the earth; I am under the shadow of death.' This distich has been vulgarly corrupted among us, and an expression takes place scarcely similar in sound, and entirely inconsistent with Masonry, and unmeaning in itself."

But however ingenious this interpretation of Hutchinson may be, it is generally admitted that it is incorrect.

The modern English Masons, and through them the French, have derived Tubal Cain from the Hebrew *tebel*, earth, and *kanah*, to acquire possession, and, with little respect for the grammatical rules of the Hebrew language, interpret it as meaning *worldly possessions*.

In the Hemming lectures, now the authorised English system, we find the answer to the question, "What does Tubal Cain denote?" is "Worldly possessions." And Delaunay, in his *Thuilleur* (p. 17), denies the reference to the proto-smith, and says: "If we reflect on the meaning of the two Hebrew words, we will easily recognise in their connection the secret wish of the hierophant, of the Templar, of the Freemason, and of every mystical sect, to govern the world in accordance with its own principles and its own laws." It is fortunate, I think, that the true meaning of the words will authorise no such interpretation. The fact is, that even if Tubal Cain were derived from *tebel* and *kanah*, the precise rules of Hebrew construction would forbid affixing to their union any such meaning as "worldly possessions." Such an interpretation of it in the French and English systems is, therefore, a very forced and inaccurate one.

The use of Tubal Cain as a significant word in the Masonic ritual is derived from the "Legend of the Craft," by which the name was made familiar to the Operative and then to the Speculative Masons; and it refers not symbolically, but historically to his Scriptural and traditional reputation as an artificer. If he symbolized anything, it would be labor; and a Mason's labor is to acquire *truth*, and not *worldly possessions*. The English and French interpretation has fortunately never been introduced into this country.

Tub Baani Amal Abal. Heb. עמל אבל טוב בעני. It is just to reward labor. An expression found in the Thirteenth Degree A. A. Scottish Rite.

Tune, Freemasons'. The air of the song written by Matthew Birkhead, and published in the *Book of Constitutions* of 1723, with the title of "the Entered Prentice's Song," is familiarly and distinctively known as "the Freemasons' Tune." Mr. William Chappell, in a work entitled *Popular Music of the Olden Time*, gives the following interesting account of it:

"This tune was very popular at the time of the ballad operas, and I am informed that the same words are still sung to it at Masonic meetings.

"The air was introduced in *The Village Opera*, *The Chambermaid*, *The Lottery*, *The Grub-Street Opera*, and *The Lover his own Rival*. It is contained in the third volume of *The Dancing Master*, and of Walsh's *New Country Dancing Master*. Words and music are included in Watt's *Musical Miscellany*, iii., 72, and in *British Melody*, or *The Musical Magazine*, fol., 1739. They were also printed on broadsides.

"In the *Gentlemen's Magazine*, for October, 1731, the first stanza is printed as 'A Health, by Mr. Birkhead.' It seems to be there quoted from 'The Constitutions of the Freemasons,' by the Rev. James Anderson, A.M., one of the Worshipful Masters.

"There are several versions of the tune. One in *Pills to Purge Melancholy*, ii., 230 (1719), has a second part; but that being almost a repetition of the first, taken an octave higher, is out of the compass of ordinary voices, and has therefore been generally rejected.

"In *A Complete Collection of Old and New English and Scotch Songs*, ii., 172 (1735), the name is given as 'Ye Commoners and Peers'; but Leveridge composed another tune to these words.

"In *The Musical Mason, or Freemasons' Pocket Companion*, being a collection of songs used in all Lodges, to which are added the 'Freemasons' March and Ode' (8vo, 1791), this is entitled 'The Entered Apprentice's Song.'

"Many stanzas have been added from time to time, and others have been altered."

Turanian. One of the three historical divisions of religion—the other two being the Aryan and the Semitic—and embraces the two sacred codes of China, viz., those of Confucius and Lao-tse.

Turban. The usual head-dress worn in Eastern nations, consisting of a quilted cap, without rim, and a sash or scarf of cotton or linen wound about the cap. In Royal Arch Chapters, the turban, of a purple color, constitutes the head-dress of the Scribe, because that officer represents the Jewish prophet, Haggai.

Turcopolier. The third dignity in the Order of Knights Hospitalers of St. John, or Knights of Malta. It took its name from the Turcopoles, a sort of light horse mentioned in the history of the Christian wars in Palestine. The office of Turcopolier was held by the Conventional Bailiff, or head of the language of England. He had the command of the cavalry of the Order.

Turkey. A writer in the *Freemasons' Quarterly Review* (1844, p. 21) says that there was a Masonic meeting in Constantinople, at which some Turks were initiated, but that the government prohibited the future meetings. This must have been an irregular Lodge, for organized Masonry was not introduced into Turkey until 1838, when the first Lodges were erected by the Grand Lodge of England. They were, however, soon discontinued, in consequence of the opposition of the Mohammedan hierarchy. A more tolerant spirit, however, now exists, and there is a Lodge (No. 687) at Constantinople under the jurisdiction of the Grand Lodge of England. There are also four Lodges at Constantinople, under the Grand Orient of France; four at Smyrna and one at Constantinople, under the Grand Orient of Italy; and one at Constantinople (No. 1049) under the Grand Lodge of Scotland. There are also two Royal Arch Chapters—at Smyrna and Constantinople, chartered by the Supreme Chapter of Scotland. There are also two Rose Croix Chapters—one, from the Supreme Council of England, in Constantinople; and the other, from the Grand Orient of Italy, in Smyrna. In these Lodges many native Mohammedans have been initiated. The Turks, however, have always had secret societies of their own, which has led some writers to suppose, erroneously, that Freemasonry existed long before the date of its actual introduction. Thus, the Begtaschi form a secret society in Turkey, numbering many thousands of Mussulmans in its ranks, and none but a true Moslem can be admitted to the brotherhood. It is a religious Order, and was founded in the year 1328 by the Hadji Begtasch, a famous dervish, from whom it derives its name. The Begtaschi have certain signs and passwords by which they are enabled to recognize the "true brethren," and by which they are protected from vagabond impostors. A writer in *Notes and Queries* says, in allusion to this society, that "One day, during the summer of 1855, an English merchant captain, while walking through the streets of a Turkish quarter of Constantinople, encountered a Turk, who made use of various signs of Freemasonry, some of which, the captain being a Mason, he understood and others he did not." It is, however, probable in this instance, considering the date, that the Turk was really a Mason, and possessed some higher degrees, which had not been attained by the English captain. There is also another equally celebrated Order in Turkey, the Melewi, who have also secret modes of recognition.

Turquoise. Oliver says (*Landm.*, ii., 521) that the first stone in the third row of the high priest's breastplate "was a ligure, hyacinth, or turquoise." The stone was a ligure; but Oliver is incorrect in supposing that it is a synonym of either a hyacinth or a turquoise, which are stones of a very different nature.

Tuscan Order. The simplest of the five orders of architecture, as its columns are never fluted, and it does not allow the introduction of any kind of ornament. It is one of the two modern orders, not being found in any ancient example. Hence it is of no value in Masonic symbolism.

Twelve. Twelve being composed of the mystical numbers 7+5 or of 3×4, the triad multiplied by the quaternion, was a number of considerable value in ancient systems. Thus there were twelve signs of the zodiac, twelve months in the year, twelve tribes of Israel, twelve stones in the pectoral, and twelve oxen supporting the molten sea in the Temple. There were twelve apostles in the new law, and the New Jerusalem has twelve gates, twelve foundations, is twelve thousand furlongs square, and the number of the sealed is twelve times twelve thousand. Even the Pagans respected this number, for there were in their mythology twelve superior and twelve inferior gods.

Twelve Illustrious Knights. The Eleventh Degree of the Ancient and Accepted Scottish Rite; more correctly *Sublime Knight Elected*, which see.

Twelve-Lettered Name. The Jews had among their Divine names, besides the Tetragrammaton, a two-lettered name, which was *Jah*, a twelve-lettered and a forty-two-lettered name. None of these, however, were so sacred and unutterable as the Tetragrammaton. Maimonides says of the twelve-lettered name, that it was formerly used instead of Adonai, as being more emphatic, in place of the Tetragrammaton, whenever they came to that sacred name in reading. It was not, however, like the Tetragrammaton, communicated only to their disciples, but was imparted to any that desired its knowledge. But after the death of Simeon the Just, the Tetragrammaton ceasing to be used at all, the twelve-lettered name was substituted in blessing the people; and then it became a secret name, and was communicated only to the most pious of the priests. What was the twelve-lettered name is uncertain, though all agree that it was not a name, but a sentence composed of twelve letters. Rabbi Bechai says it was formed by a triple combination and permutation of the four letters of the Tetragrammaton; and there are other explanations equally unsatisfactory.

There was also a forty-two-lettered name, composed, says Bechai, of the first forty-two letters of the Book of Genesis. Another and a better explanation has been propounded by Franck, that it is formed out of the names of the ten Sephiroth, which with the ו, vau, or *and*, amount exactly to forty-two letters. There was another name of seventy-two letters, which is still more inexplicable. Of all these names, Maimonides (*More Nev.*, I. lxii.) says that, as they could not possibly constitute one word, they must have been composed of several words, and he adds:

"There is no doubt that these words conveyed certain ideas, which were designed to bring man nearer to the true conception of the Divine essence, through the process we have already described. These words, composed of numerous letters, have been designated as a single name, because, like all accidental proper names, they indicate one single object: and to make the object more intelligible, several words are employed, as many words are sometimes used to express one single thing. This must be well understood, that they taught the ideas indicated by these names, and not the simple pronunciation of the meaningless letters."

Twelve Original Points of Masonry. The old English lectures, which were abrogated by the United Grand Lodge of England in 1813, when it adopted the system of Hemming, contained the following passage:

"There are in Freemasonry twelve original points, which form the basis of the system, and comprehend the whole ceremony of initiation. Without the existence of these points, no man ever was, or can be, legally and essentially received into the Order. Every person who is made a Mason must go through these twelve forms and ceremonies, not only in the first degree, but in every subsequent one."

Hence, it will be seen that our ancient Brethren deemed these "Twelve Original Points of Masonry," as they were called, of the highest importance to the ceremony of initiation, and they consequently took much pains, and exercised much ingenuity, in giving them a symbolical explanation. But as, by the decree of the Grand Lodge, they no longer constitute a part of the English ritual, and were never introduced into this country, where the "Four Perfect Points" constitute an inadequate substitute, there can be no impropriety in presenting a brief explanation of them, for which I shall be indebted to the industry of Oliver, who has treated of them at great length in the eleventh lecture of his *Historical Landmarks*.

The ceremony of initiation, when these points constituted a portion of the ritual, was divided into twelve parts, in allusion to the twelve tribes of Israel, to each of which one of the points was referred, in the following manner:

1. The *opening of the Lodge* was symbolized by the tribe of Reuben, because Reuben was the first-born of his father Jacob, who called him "the beginning of his strength." He was, therefore, appropriately adopted as the emblem of that ceremony which is essentially the beginning of every initiation.

2. The *preparation* of the candidate was symbolized by the tribe of Simeon, because Simeon prepared the instruments for the slaughter of the Shechemites; and that part of the ceremony which relates to offensive weapons, was used as a token of our abhorrence for the cruelty exercised on that occasion.

3. The *report* of the Senior Deacon referred to the tribe of Levi, because, in the slaughter of the Shechemites, Levi was supposed to have made a signal or report to Simeon his brother, with whom he was engaged in attacking these unhappy people while unprepared for defense.

4. The *entrance* of the candidate into the Lodge was symbolized by the tribe of Judah, because they were the first to cross the Jordan and enter the promised land, coming from the darkness and servitude, as it were, of the wilderness into the light and liberty of Canaan.

5. The *prayer* was symbolized by the tribe of Zebulun, because the blessing and prayer of Jacob were given to Zebulun, in preference to his brother Issachar.

6. The *circumambulation* referred to the tribe of Issachar, because, as a thriftless and indolent tribe, they required a leader to advance them to an equal elevation with the other tribes.

7. *Advancing* to the altar was symbolized by the tribe of Dan, to teach us, by contrast, that we should advance to truth and holiness as rapidly as that tribe advanced to idolatry, among whom the golden serpent was first set up to receive adoration.

8. The *obligation* referred to the tribe of Gad, in allusion to the solemn vow which was made by Jephthah, Judge of Israel, who was of that tribe.

9. The *entrusting* of the candidate with the mysteries was symbolized by the tribe of Asher, because he was then presented with the rich fruits of Masonic knowledge, as Asher was said to be the inheritor of fatness and royal dainties.

10. The *investiture* of the lambskin, by

which the candidate is declared free, referred to the tribe of Naphtali, which was invested by Moses with a peculiar freedom, when he said, "O Naphtali, satisfied with favor, and full with the blessing of the Lord, possess thou the West and the South."

11. The *ceremony of the northeast corner of the Lodge* referred to Joseph, because, as this ceremony reminds us of the most superficial part of Masonry, so the two half tribes of Ephraim and Manasseh, of which the tribe of Joseph was composed, were accounted to be more superficial than the rest, as they were descendants of the grandsons only of Jacob.

12. The *closing of the Lodge* was symbolized by the tribe of Benjamin, who was the youngest of the sons of Jacob, and thus closed his father's strength.

Such were the celebrated twelve original points of Freemasonry of the ancient English lectures. They were never introduced into this country, and they are now disused in England. But it will be seen that, while some of the allusions are perhaps abstruse, many of them are ingenious and appropriate. It will not, perhaps, be regretted that they have become obsolete; yet it cannot be denied that they added something to the symbolism and to the religious reference of Freemasonry. At all events, they are matters of Masonic antiquity, and, as such, are not unworthy of attention.

Twenty-Four-Inch Gage. A rule two feet long, which is divided by marks into twenty-four parts, each one inch in length. The Operative Mason uses it to take the necessary dimensions of the stone that he is about to prepare. It has been adopted as one of the working-tools of the Entered Apprentice in Speculative Masonry, where its divisions are supposed to represent hours. Hence its symbolic use is to teach him to measure his time so that, of the twenty-four hours of the day, he may devote eight hours to the service of God and a worthy distressed brother, eight hours to his usual vocation, and eight to refreshment and sleep. In the symbolic language of Masonry, therefore, the twenty-four-inch gage is a symbol of time well employed.

Twenty-One. A number of mystical import, partly because it is the product of 3 and 7, the most sacred of the odd numbers, but especially because it is the sum of the numerical value of the letters of the Divine name, *Eheyeh*, thus:

ה י ה א
$$5 + 10 + 5 + 1 = 21.$$

It is little valued in Masonry, but is deemed of great importance in the Kabbala and in Alchemy; in the latter, because it refers to the twenty-one days of distillation necessary for the conversion of the grosser metals into silver.

Twenty-Seven. Although the number twenty-seven is found in the degree of Select Master and in some of the other high degrees, it can scarcely be called in itself a sacred number. It derives its importance from the fact that it is produced by the multiplication of the square of three by three, thus: $3 \times 3 \times 3 = 27$.

Twenty-Six. This is considered by the Kabbalists as the most sacred of mystical numbers, because it is equal to the numerical value of the letters of the Tetragrammaton, thus:

ה ו ה י
$$5 + 6 + 5 + 10 = 26.$$

Two-Lettered Name. The title given by the Talmudists to the name of God, יה, or *Jah*, which see.

Tyler. *Tyle* and *Tyler* are the old and now obsolete spelling of *Tile* and *Tiler*, which see.

Type. In the science of symbology it is the picture or model of something of which it is considered as a symbol. Hence the word type and symbol are in this sense synonymous. Thus the tabernacle was a type of the Temple, as the Temple is a type of the Lodge.

Typhon. The brother and slayer of Osiris, in the Egyptian mythology. As Osiris was a type or symbol of the sun, Typhon was the symbol of winter, when the vigor, heat, and, as it were, life of the sun are destroyed, and of darkness as opposed to light.

Tyre. An ancient city of Phœnicia, which in the time of King Solomon was celebrated as the residence of King Hiram, to whom that monarch and his father David were indebted for great assistance in the construction of the Temple at Jerusalem. Tyre was distant from Jerusalem about one hundred and twenty miles by sea, and was thirty miles nearer by land. An intercourse between the two cities and their respective monarchs was, therefore, easily cultivated. The inhabitants of Tyre were distinguished for their skill as artificers, especially as workers in brass and other metals; and it is said to have been a principal seat of that skilful body of architects known as the Dionysiac fraternity.

The city of Sidon, which was under the Tyrian government, was but twenty miles from Tyre, and situated in the forest of Lebanon. The Sidonians were, therefore, naturally wood-cutters, and were engaged in felling the trees, which were afterward sent on floats by sea from Tyre to Joppa, and thence carried by land to Jerusalem, to be employed in the Temple building.

Dr. Morris, who visited Tyre in 1868, describes it (*Freemasonry in the Holy Land*, p. 91) as a city under ground, lying, like Jerusalem, twenty to fifty feet beneath a *débris* of many centuries. It consists, to use the language of a writer he has cited, of "prostrate and broken columns, dilapidated temples, and mounds of buried fragments."

Tyre, Quarries of. It is an error of Oliver, and some other writers, to suppose that the stones of the Temple of Jerusalem were furnished from the quarries of Tyre.

If there were such quarries, they were not used for that purpose, as the stones were taken from the immediate vicinity of the edifice. (See *Quarries*.)

Tyrian Freemasons. Those who sustain the hypothesis that Freemasonry originated at the Temple of Solomon have advanced the theory that the Tyrian Freemasons were the members of the Society of Dionysiac Artificers, who at the time of the building of Solomon's Temple flourished at Tyre. Many of them were sent to Jerusalem by Hiram, King of Tyre, to assist King Solomon in the construction of his Temple. There, uniting with the Jews, who had only a knowledge of the speculative principles of Freemasonry, which had been transmitted to them from Noah, through the patriarchs, the Tyrian Freemasons organized that combined system of Operative and Speculative Masonry which continued for many centuries, until the beginning of the eighteenth, to characterize the Institution. This hypothesis is maintained with great ingenuity by Lawrie in his *History of Freemasonry*, or by Dr. Brewster, if he was really the author of that work, and until recently it has been the most popular theory respecting the origin of Masonry. But as it is wanting in the support of historical evidence, it has yielded to the more plausible speculations of recent writers.

U

U. The twenty-first letter of the English alphabet, is a modification of the Greek letter Υ, *upsilon;* it is in the Hebrew עע, or in the Chaldaic and hieroglyphical, the head of an animal with horns, hence its symbolism. U has a close affinity to V, hence they were formerly interchanged in writing and printing.

U.·. D.·. Letters placed after the names of Lodges or Chapters which have not yet received a Warrant of Constitution. They signify *Under Dispensation.*

Uden, Conrad Friederich. A Masonic writer of some celebrity. He was a Doctor of Medicine, and at one time a Professor in Ordinary of the University of Dorpat; afterward an Aulic Counselor and Secretary of the Medical College of St. Petersburg. He was from 1783 to 1785 the editor of the *Archiv für Freimaurerei und Rosenkreuzer*, published during those years at Berlin. This work contains much interesting information concerning Rosicrucianism. He also edited, in 1785 and 1786, at Altona, the *Ephemeriden der gesammten Freimaurerei auf das Logenjahr 1785 und 1786.*

Unaffiliated Mason. A Mason who is not a member of any Lodge. As this class of Masons contribute nothing to the revenues nor to the strength of the Order, while they are always willing to partake of its benefits, they have been considered as an encumbrance upon the Craft, and have received the general condemnation of Grand Lodges.

It is evident that, anterior to the present system of Lodge organization, which dates about the end of the last century, there could have been no unaffiliated Masons. And, accordingly, the first reference that we find to the duty of Lodge membership is in the Charges, published in 1723, in Anderson's *Constitutions*, where it is said, after describing a Lodge, that "every Brother ought to belong to one"; and that "in ancient times, no Master or Fellow could be absent from it, especially when warned to appear at it, without incurring a severe censure, until it appeared to the Master and Wardens that pure necessity hindered him." (*Constitutions*, 1723, p. 51.) In this last clause, Anderson evidently refers to the regulation in the Old Constitutions, that required attendance on the Annual Assembly. For instance, in the oldest of these, the Halliwell or Regius MS., it is said (we modernize the language) "that every Master that is a Mason must be at the General Congregation, if he is told in reasonable time where the Assembly shall be holden; and to that Assembly he must go, unless he have a reasonable excuse." (Ll. 107–112.)

But the "Assembly" was rather in the nature of a Grand Lodge, and neglect to attend its annual meeting would not place the offender in the position of a modern unaffiliated Mason. But after the organization of subordinate Lodges, a permanent membership, which had been before unknown, was then established; and as the revenues of the Lodges, and through them of the Grand Lodge, were to be derived from the contributions of the members, it was found expedient to require every Mason to affiliate with a Lodge, and hence the rule adopted in the Charge already cited. Yet, in Europe, non-affiliation, although deemed to some extent a Masonic offense, has not been visited by any penalty, except that which results from a deprivation of the ordinary advantages of membership in any association.

The modern Constitution of England, however, prescribes that "no brother who has ceased to be a subscribing member of a Lodge shall be permitted to visit any one Lodge more than once until he again becomes a subscribing member of some Lodge." (Rule 152.) He is permitted to visit each Lodge once, because it is supposed that this visit is made for the purpose of enabling him to make a selection of the one in which he may prefer working. But afterward he is excluded, in order to discountenance those brethren who wish to continue members of the Order, and to partake of its benefits, without contributing to its support. The Constitutions of the Grand Lodges of Ireland and Scotland are silent upon the subject, nor is any penalty prescribed for unaffiliation by any of the Grand Lodges of the Continent of Europe.

In America a different view has been taken of the subject, and its Grand Lodges have, with great unanimity, denounced unaffiliated Masons in the strongest terms of condemnation, and visited them with penalties, which vary, however, to some extent in the different jurisdictions. There is, however, no Grand Lodge in the United States that has not concurred in the opinion that the neglect or refusal of a Mason to affiliate with a Lodge is a Masonic offense, to be visited by some penalty and a deprivation of some rights.

The following principles may be laid down as constituting the law in America on the subject of unaffiliated Masons:

1. An unaffiliated Mason is still bound by all those Masonic duties and obligations which refer to the Order in general, but not by those which relate to Lodge organization.

2. He possesses, reciprocally, all those rights which are derived from membership in the Order, but none of those which result from membership in a Lodge.

3. He has a right to assistance when in imminent peril, if he asks for that assistance in the conventional way.

4. He has no right to pecuniary aid from a Lodge.

5. He has no right to visit Lodges, or to walk in Masonic processions.

6. He has no right to Masonic burial.

7. He still remains subject to the government of the Order, and may be tried and punished for any offense by the Lodge within whose geographical jurisdiction he resides.

8. And, lastly, as non-affiliation is a violation of Masonic law, he may, if he refuses to abandon that condition, be tried and punished for it, even by expulsion, if deemed necessary or expedient, by any Grand Lodge within whose jurisdiction he lives.

Unanimous Consent. In the beginning of the eighteenth century, when Masonry was reviving from the condition of decay into which it had fallen, and when the experiment was tried of transforming it from a partly operative to a purely speculative system, the great object was to maintain a membership which, by the virtuous character of those who composed it, should secure the harmony and prosperity of the infant Institution. A safeguard was therefore to be sought in the care with which Masons should be selected from those who were likely to apply for admission. It was the quality, and not the quantity, that was desired. This safeguard could only be found in the unanimity of the ballot. Hence, in the sixth of the General Regulations, adopted in 1721, it is declared that "no man can be entered a Brother in any particular Lodge, or admitted to be a member thereof, without the *unanimous consent* of all the members of that Lodge then present when the candidate is proposed, and their consent is formally asked by the Master." (*Constitutions*, 1723, p. 59.) And to prevent the exercise of any undue influence of a higher power in forcing an unworthy person upon the Order, it is further said in the same article: "Nor is this inherent privilege subject to a dispensation; because the members of a particular Lodge are the best judges of it; and if a fractious member should be imposed on them, it might spoil their harmony, or hinder their freedom; or even break and disperse the Lodge." But a few years after, the Order being now on a firm footing, this prudent fear of "spoiling harmony," or "dispersing the Lodge," seems to have been lost sight of, and the brethren began in many Lodges to desire a release from the restrictions laid upon them by the necessity for unanimous consent. Hence Anderson says in his second edition: "But it was found inconvenient to insist upon unanimity in several cases. And, therefore, the Grand Masters have allowed the Lodges to admit a member if not above three ballots are against him; though some Lodges desire no such allowance." (*Constitutions*, 1738, p. 155.) This rule still prevails in England; and its modern Constitution still permits the admission of a Mason where there are not more than three ballots against him, though it is open to a Lodge to demand unanimity.

In the United States, where Masonry is more popular than in any other country, it was soon seen that the danger of the Institution lay not in the paucity, but in the multitude of its members, and that the only provision for guarding its portals was the most stringent regulation of the ballot. Hence, in almost, if not quite, all jurisdictions of the United States unanimous consent is required. And this rule has been found to work with such advantage to the Order, that the phrase, "the black ball is the bulwark of Masonry," has become a proverb.

Unfavorable Report. Should the committee of investigation on the character of a petitioner for initiation make an unfavorable report, the general usage is (although some Grand Lodges have decided otherwise) to consider the candidate rejected by such report, without proceeding to the formality of a ballot, which is therefore dispensed with. This usage is founded on the principles of common sense; for, as by the ancient Constitutions one black ball is sufficient to reject an application, the unfavorable report of a committee must necessarily, and by consequence, include two unfavorable votes at least. It is therefore unnecessary to go into a ballot after such a report, as it is to be taken for granted that the brethren who reported unfavorably would, on a resort to the ballot, cast their negative votes. Their report is indeed virtually considered as the casting of such votes, and the applicant is therefore at once rejected without a further and unnecessary ballot.

Unhele. To uncover, or reveal. Spenser, in the *Faëry Queen*, says, "Then suddenly both would themselves unhele."

Uniformity of Work. An identity of forms in opening and closing, and in conferring the degrees, constitutes what is technically called uniformity of work. The expression has no reference, in its restricted sense, to the working of the same degrees in different Rites and different countries, but only to a similarity in the ceremonies practised by Lodges in the same Rite, and more especially in the same jurisdiction. This is greatly to be desired, because nothing is more unpleasant to a Mason, accustomed to certain forms and ceremonies in his own Lodge, than on a visit to another to find those forms and ceremonies so varied as to be sometimes scarcely recognizable as parts of the same Institution. So anxious are the dogmatic authorities in Masonry to preserve this uniformity, that in the charge to an Entered Apprentice he is instructed never to "suffer an infringement of our rites, or a deviation from established usages and customs." In the act of union in 1813, of the two Grand Lodges of England, in whose systems of working there were many differences, it was provided that a committee should be appointed to visit the several Lodges, and promulgate and enjoin one system, "that perfect reconciliation, unity of obligation, law, working, language, and dress, might be happily restored to the English Craft." (Article XV.) A few years ago, a writer in *C. W. Moore's Magazine*, proposed the appointment of delegates to visit the Grand Lodges of England, Scotland, and Ireland, that a system of work and lectures might be adopted, which should thereafter be rigidly enforced in both hemispheres. The proposition was not popular, and no delegation was ever appointed. It is well that it was so, for no such attempt could have met with a successful result.

It is a fact, that uniformity of work in Masonry, however much it may be desired, can never be attained. This must be the case in all institutions where the ceremonies, the legends, and the instructions are oral. The treachery of memory, the weakness of judgment, and the fertility of imagination, will lead men to forget, to diminish, or to augment, the parts of any system which are not prescribed within certain limits by a written rule. The Rabbis discovered this when the Oral Law was becoming perverted, and losing its authority as well as its identity by the interpretations that were given to it in the schools of the Scribes and Prophets. And hence, to restore it to its integrity, it was found necessary to divest it of its oral character and give to it a written form. To this are we to attribute the origin of the two Talmuds which now contain the essence of Jewish theology. So, while in Masonry we find the esoteric ritual continually subjected to errors arising mainly from the ignorance or the fancy of Masonic teachers, the monitorial instructions—few in Preston, but greatly enlarged by Webb and Cross—have suffered no change.

It would seem from this that the evil of non-conformity could be removed only by making all the ceremonies monitorial; and so much has this been deemed expedient, that a few years since the subject of a written ritual was seriously discussed in England. But the remedy would be worse than the disease. It is to the oral character of its ritual that Masonry is indebted for its permanence and success as an organization. A written, which would soon become a printed, ritual would divest Symbolic Masonry of its attractions as a secret association, and would cease to offer a reward to the laborious student who sought to master its mystical science. Its philosophy and its symbolism would be the same, but the books containing them would be consigned to the shelves of a Masonic library, their pages to be discussed by the profane as the common property of the antiquary, while the Lodges, having no mystery within their portals, would find but few visitors, and certainly no workers.

It is, therefore, a matter of congratulation that uniformity of work, however desirable and however unattainable, is not so important and essential as many have deemed it. Oliver, for instance, seems to confound in some of his writings the ceremonies of a degree with the landmarks of the Order. But they are very different. The landmarks, because they affect the identity of the Institution, have long since been embodied in its written laws, and unless by a wilful perversion, as in France, where the Grand Mastership has been abolished, can never be changed. But variations in the phraseology of the lectures, or in the forms and ceremonies of initiation, so long as they do not trench upon the foundations of symbolism on which the science and philosophy of Masonry are built, can produce no other effect than a temporary inconvenience. The errors of an ignorant Master will be corrected by his better instructed successor. The variation in the ritual can never be such as to destroy the true identity of the Institution. Its profound dogmas of the unity of God, and the eternal life, and of the universal brotherhood of man, taught in its symbolic method, will forever shine out preeminent above all temporary changes of phraseology. Uniformity of work may not be attained, but uniformity of design and uniformity of character will forever preserve Freemasonry from disintegration.

Union, Grand Masters'. Efforts were made at various times in Germany to organize an association of the Grand Masters of the Grand Lodges of Germany. At length, through the efforts of Bro. Warnatz, the Grand Master of Saxony, the scheme was fully accomplished, and on May 31, 1868, the Grand Masters' Union—*Grossmeistertag*, literally, the diet of Grand Masters—assembled at the city of Berlin, the Grand Masters of seven German Grand Lodges being present. The meetings of this body, which are annual, are entirely unofficial; it claims no legislative powers, and meets only for consultation and advisement on matters connected with the ritual, the history, and the philosophy of Masonry.

Union Master's Degree. An honorary degree, said to have been invented by tho Lodge of Reconciliation in England, in 1813, at the union of the two Grand Lodges, and adopted by the Grand Lodge of New York in 1819, which authorized its Lodges to confer it. It was designed to detect clandestine and irregular Masons, and consisted only of the investiture of the recipient with certain new modes of recognition.

Union of German Masons. (*Verein deutscher Maurer.*) An association of Freemasons of Germany organized at Potsdam, May 19, 1861. The Society meets annually at different places. Its professed object is the cultivation of Masonic science, the advancement of the prosperity and usefulness of the Order, and the closer union of the members in the bonds of brotherly love and affection.

Union of Scientific Freemasons. (*Bund scientifischer Freimaurer.*) An association founded, November 28, 1802, by Fessler, Fischer, Mossdorf, and other learned Masons of Germany. According to their act of union, all the members pledged themselves to investigate the history of Freemasonry, from its origin down to the present time, in all its different parts, with all its systems and retrogressions, in the most complete manner, and then to communicate what they knew to trustworthy brethren.

In the assemblies of the members, there were no rituals, nor ceremonies, nor any special vestments requisite, nor, indeed, any outward distinctions whatever. A common interest and the love of truth, a general aversion of all deception, treachery, and secrecy were the sentiments which bound them together, and made them feel the duties incumbent on them, without binding themselves by any special oath. Consequently, the members of the Scientific Union had all equal rights and obligations; they did not acknowledge a superior, or subordination to any Masonic authority whatever.

Any upright, scientifically cultivated Master Mason, a sincere seeker after truth, might join this Union, no matter to what Rite or Grand Lodge he belonged, if the whole of the votes were given in his favor, and he pledged himself faithfully to carry out the intention of the founders of the Order.

Each circle of scientific Masons was provided with a number of copies of the deed of union, and every new candidate, when he signed it, became a partaker of the privileges shared in by the whole; the Chief Archives and the center of the Confederation were at first to be in Berlin.

But the association, thus inaugurated with the most lofty pretensions and the most sanguine expectations, did not well succeed. "Brethren," says Findel (*Hist.*, English translation, p. 501), "whose co-operation had been reckoned upon, did not join; the active working of others was crippled by all sorts of scruples and hindrances, and Fessler's purchase of Kleinwall drew off his attention wholly from the subject. Differences of opinion, perhaps also too great egotism, caused dissensions between many members of the association and the brethren of the Lodge at Altenburg. Distrust was excited in every man's breast, and, instead of the enthusiasm formerly exhibited, there was only lukewarmness and disgust."

Other schemes, especially that of the establishment of a Saxon Grand Lodge, impaired the efforts of the Scientific Masons. The Union gradually sank out of sight, and finally ceased to exist.

Union of the Twenty-Two. See *German Union of Two and Twenty*.

United Friars, Fraternity of. A society established in 1785, for the "cultivation of a liberal and rational system of good fellowship." The place of meeting was known as the College of St. Luke. The society was a charitable one, giving liberally to the poor. There were a number of Colleges, the "London College languished, and finally died a natural death about 1825." Mackenzie gives the particulars of this Fraternity in the *Royal Masonic Cyclopædia*.

United Grand Lodge of England. The present Grand Lodge of England assumed that title in the year 1813, because it was then formed by the union of the Grand Lodge of the *Ancients*, called the "Grand Lodge of Free and Accepted Masons of England according to the Old Institutions," and the Grand Lodge of *Moderns*, called the "Grand Lodge of Free and Accepted Masons under the Constitution of England." The body thus formed, by which an end was put to the dissensions of the Craft which had existed in England for more than half a century, adopted the title, by which it has ever since been known, of the "United Grand Lodge of Ancient Freemasons of England."

United States of America. The history of the introduction of Freemasonry into the United States of America is discussed in this work under the titles of the different States into which the Union is divided, and to which therefore the reader is referred.

It may, however, be necessary to say, in a general view of the subject, that the first notice we have of Freemasonry in the United States is in 1729, in which year, during the Grand Mastership of the Duke of Norfolk, Mr. Daniel Coxe was appointed Provincial Grand Master for New Jersey. I have not, however, been able to obtain any evidence that he exercised his prerogative by the establishment of Lodges in that province, although it is probable that he did. In the year 1733, the "St. John's Grand Lodge" was opened in Boston, in consequence of a Charter granted, on the application of several brethren residing in that city, by Lord Viscount Montague, Grand Master of England. From that time Masonry was rapidly disseminated throughout the country by the establishment of Provincial Grand Lodges, all of which after the Revolutionary War, which separated the colonies from the mother country, assumed the rank and prerogatives of independent Grand Lodges. The history of these bodies being treated under their respective titles, the remainder of this article may more properly be devoted to the character of the Masonic organization in the United States.

The Rite practised in this country is most correctly called the American Rite. This title, however, has been adopted within only a comparatively recent period. It is still very usual with Masonic writers to call the Rite practised in this country the York Rite. The expression, however, is wholly incorrect. The Masonry of the United States, though founded, like that practised in every other country, upon the three Symbolic degrees which alone constitute the true York Rite, has, by its modifications and its adoption of high degrees, so changed the Rite as to give it an entirely different form from that which properly constitutes the pure York Rite. (See *American Rite.*)

In each State of the Union, and in most of the Territories, there is a Grand Lodge which exercises jurisdiction over the Symbolic degrees. The jurisdiction of the Grand Lodge, however, is exercised to a certain extent over what are called the higher bodies, namely, the Chapters, Councils, and Commanderies. For by the American construction of Masonic law, a Mason expelled by the Grand Lodge forfeits his membership in all of these bodies to which he may be attached. Hence a Knights Templar, or a Royal Arch Mason, becomes *ipso facto* suspended or expelled by his suspension or expulsion by a Symbolic Lodge, the appeal from which action lies only to the Grand Lodge. Thus the Masonic standing and existence of even the Grand Commander of a Grand Commandery is actually in the hands of the Grand Lodge, by whose decree of expulsion his relation with the body over which he presides may be dissevered.

Royal Arch Masonry is controlled in each State by a Grand Chapter. Besides these Grand Chapters, there is a General Grand Chapter of the United States, which, however, exercises only a moral influence over the State Grand Chapters, since it possesses "no power of discipline, admonition, censure, or instruction over the Grand Chapters." In Territories where there are no Grand Chapters, the General Grand Chapter constitutes subordinate Chapters, and over these it exercises plenary jurisdiction.

The next highest branch of the Order is Cryptic Masonry, which, although rapidly growing, is not yet as extensive as Royal Arch Masonry. It consists of two degrees, Royal and Select Master, to which is sometimes added the Superexcellent, which, however, is considered only as an honorary degree. These degrees are conferred in Councils which owe their obedience to Grand Councils. Only one Grand Council can exist in a State or Territory, as is the case with a Grand Lodge, a Grand Chapter, or a Grand Commandery. Grand Councils exist in many of the States, and in any State where no such body exists, the Councils are established by Charters emanating from any one of them. There is no General Grand Council. Efforts have been repeatedly made to establish one, but the proposition has not met with a favorable response from the majority of Grand Councils.

Templarism is governed by a Supreme body, whose style is the Grand Encampment of the United States, and this body, which meets triennially, possesses sovereign power over the whole Templar system in the United States. Its presiding officer is called Grand Master, and this is the highest office known to American Templarism. In most of the States there are Grand Commanderies, which exercise immediate jurisdiction over the Commanderies in the State, subject, however, to the superintending control of the Grand Encampment. Where there are no Grand Commanderies, Charters are issued directly to subordinate Commanderies by the Grand Encampment.

The Ancient and Accepted Scottish Rite is very popular in the United States. There are two Supreme Councils—one for the Southern Jurisdiction, which is the Mother Council of the world. Its nominal Grand East is at Charleston, South Carolina; but its Secretariat has been removed to Washington City since the year 1870. The other Council is for the Northern Jurisdiction. Its Grand East is at Boston, Massachusetts; but its Secretariat is at New York City. The Northern Council has jurisdiction over the States of Maine, Vermont, New Hampshire, Massachusetts, Connecticut, Rhode Island, New York, Pennsylvania, New Jersey, Delaware, Ohio, Indiana, Illinois, and Wisconsin. The Southern Supreme Council exercises jurisdiction over all the other States and Territories of the United States.

Unity of God. In the popular mythology of the ancients there were many gods. It was to correct this false opinion, and to teach a purer theogony, that the initiations were invented. And so, as Warburton says, "the famous secret of the mysteries was the unity of the Godhead." This, too, is the doctrine of Masonic initiation, which is equally distant from the blindness of atheism and the folly of polytheism.

Universality of Masonry. The boast of the Emperor Charles V., that the sun never set on his vast empire, may be applied with equal truth to the Order of Freemasonry. From east to west, and from north to south, over the whole habitable globe, are our Lodges disseminated. Wherever the wandering steps of civilized man have left their footprints, there have our temples been established. The lessons of Masonic love have penetrated into the wilderness of the West, and the red man of our soil has shared with his more enlightened brother the mysteries of our science; while the arid sands of the African desert have more than once been the scene of a Masonic greeting. Masonry is not a fountain, giving health and beauty to some single hamlet, and slaking the thirst of those only who dwell upon its humble banks; but it is a mighty stream, penetrating through every hill and mountain, and gliding through every field and valley of the earth, bearing in its beneficent bosom the abundant waters of love and charity for the poor, the widow, and the orphan of every land.

Universal Aurora, Society of the. Founded at Paris, in 1783, for the practise of mesmerism; Cagliostro, "the Divine Charlatan," taking an active part in its establishment. Very little at this day is known of it.

Universal Language. See *Language, Universal.*

Universal Harmony, Order of. See *Mesmeric Masonry.*

Universalists, Order of. A society of a Masonic bearing, founded by Retif de la Bretonne, in Paris, about 1841, and having but one degree.

Universi Terrarum, etc. Documents emanating from any of the bodies of the Ancient and Accepted Scottish Rite commence with the following epigraph: "Universi Terrarum Orbis Architectonis per Gloriam Ingentis," i. e., "By the Glory of the Great Architect of the Universe." This is the correct form as first published, in 1802, by the Mother Council at Charleston in its Circular of that year, and used in all its Charters and Patents.

Unknown Philosopher. One of the mystical and theosophic works written by Saint Martin, the founder of the Rite of Martinism, was entitled *Le Philosophe Inconnu*, or The Unknown Philosopher, whence the appellation was often given by his disciples to the author. A degree of his Rite also received the same name.

Unknown Superiors. When the Baron Von Hund established his system or Rite of Strict Observance, he declared that the Order was directed by certain Masons of superior rank, whose names as well as their designs were to be kept secret from all the brethren of the lower degrees; although there was an insinuation that they were to be found or to be heard of in Scotland. To these secret dignitaries he gave the title of "Superiores Incogniti," or Unknown Superiors. Many Masonic writers, suspecting that Jesuitism was at the bottom of all the Masonry of that day, asserted that S. I., the initials of Superiores Incogniti, meant really Societas Jesu, i. e., the Society of Jesus or the Jesuits. It is scarcely necessary now to say that the whole story of the Unknown Superiors was a myth.

"Unpublished Records of the Craft." A work thus entitled, edited by the late Bro. Hughan, was published in 1871, forming part of a book called *Masonic Sketches and Reprints* and containing many MSS. of value, theretofore unknown to the general Masonic public. Many others have since been traced, and the work of Masonic progress has a large field in the near future which will be productive of great historic good.

Untempered Mortar. In the lecture used in the United States in the early part of the present century, and in some parts of the country almost as recently as the middle of the century, the apprentices at the Temple were said to wear their aprons in the peculiar manner characteristic of that class that they might preserve their garments from being defiled by "untempered mortar." This is mortar which has not been properly mixed for use, and it thus became a symbol of passions and appetites not duly restrained. Hence the Speculative Apprentice was made to wear his apron in that peculiar manner to teach him that he should not allow his soul to be defiled by the "untempered mortar of unruly passions."

Unutterable Name. The Tetragrammaton, or Divine Name, which is more commonly called the Ineffable Name. The two words are precisely synonymous.

Unworthy Members. That there are men in our Order whose lives and characters reflect no credit on the Institution, whose ears turn coldly from its beautiful lessons of morality, whose hearts are untouched by its soothing influences of brotherly kindness, whose hands are not opened to aid in its deeds of charity, is a fact which we cannot deny, although we may be permitted to express our grief while we acknowledge its truth. But these men, though in the Temple, are not of the Temple; they are among us, but are not with us; they belong to our household, but they are not of our faith; they are of Israel, but they are not Israel. We have sought to teach them, but they would not be instructed; seeing, they have not perceived; and hearing, they have not understood the symbolic language in which our lessons of wisdom are communicated. The fault is not with us, that we have not given, but with them, that they have not received. And, indeed, hard and unjust would it be to censure the Masonic Institution, because, partaking of the infirmity and weakness of human wisdom and human means, it has been unable to give strength and perfection to all who come within its pale. The denial of a Peter, the doubtings of a Thomas, or even the betrayal of a Judas, could cast no reproach on that holy band of apostles of which each formed a constituent part.

"Is Freemasonry answerable," says Dr. Oliver (*Landm.*, i., p. 148), "for the misdeeds of an individual Brother? By no means. He has had the advantage of Masonic instruction, and has failed to profit by it. He has enjoyed Masonic privileges, but has not possessed Masonic virtue." Such a man it is our duty to reform, or to dismiss; but the world should not condemn us, if we fail in our attempt at reformation. God alone can change the heart. Masonry furnishes precepts and obligations of duty which, if obeyed, must make its members wiser, better, happier men; but it claims no power of regeneration. Condemn when our instruction is evil, but not when our pupils are dull, and deaf to our lessons; for, in so doing, you condemn the holy religion which you profess. Masonry prescribes no principles that are opposed to the sacred teachings of the Divine Lawgiver, and sanctions no acts that are not consistent with the sternest morality and the most faithful obedience to government and the laws; and while this continues to be its character, it cannot, without the most atrocious injustice, be made responsible for the acts of its unworthy members.

Of all human societies, Freemasonry is undoubtedly, under all circumstances, the fittest to form the truly good man. But however well conceived may be its laws, they cannot completely change the natural disposition of those who ought to observe them. In truth, they serve as lights and guides; but as they can only direct men by restraining the impetuosity of their passions, these last too often become dominant, and the Institution is forgotten.

Upadevas. Minor works regarded as appendices to the four Canonical Vedas, and comprising the *Ayurveda*, on medicine, the *Dhanurveda*, on archery, the *Gândharvaveda*, on music, and the *Silpasâstra*, or *Arthasastras*, on mechanics and other practical subjects. These were looked upon as inspired works and so classed.

Upanishad. ("Mystic.") A name given to certain Sanskrit works, of which about 150 are known, founded upon the Brahmana portion of the Vedas, and containing the "mysterious doctrine" of the process of creation, the nature of a Supreme Being, and its relation to the human soul. The older Upanishads are placed among the Sruti, or writings supposed to be inspired. (See *Sruti*.)

Upper Chambers. The practise of holding Masonic Lodges in the upper rooms of houses is so universal that, in all my experience, I have no knowledge of a single instance in which a Lodge has been held in a room on the first floor of a building. The most apparent reason for this is, that security from being overseen or overheard may be thus obtained, and hence Dr. Oliver says, in his *Book of the Lodge* (p. 44), that "a Masonic hall should be isolated, and, if possible, surrounded with lofty walls. . . . As, however, such a situation in large towns, where Masonry is usually practised, can seldom be obtained with convenience to the brethren, the Lodge should be formed in an upper story." This, as a practical reason, will be perhaps sufficient to Masons in general. But to those who are more curious, it may be well to say, that for this custom there is also a mystical reason of great antiquity.

Gregory, in his *Notes and Observations on some Passages of Scripture* (1671, p. 17), says: "The upper rooms in Scripture were places in that part of the house which was highest from the ground, set apart by the Jews for their private orisons and devotions, to be addressed towards Solomon's Temple." This room received, in the Hebrew language, the appellation of Alijah, which has been translated by the Greek *huperoon*, and improperly by the Latin *cœnaculum*. The Hebrew and the Greek both have the signification of an upper room, while the Latin appellative would give the idea of a dining-room or place for eating, thus taking away the sacred character of the apartment. The Alijah was really a secret chamber or recess in the upper part of the house, devoted to religious uses. Hence the wise men or Rabbis of Israel are called by the Talmudists beni Alijah, or "the sons of the upper or secret room." And so, in Psalm civ. 2, 3, the Psalmist speaks of God as stretching out the heavens like a curtain, and laying the beams of his chambers in the waters, where, in the original, the word here translated "chambers" is the plural of Alijah, and should more properly be rendered "his secret chambers": an allusion, as Dr. Clarke thinks, to the holy of holies of the tabernacle. Again, in 2 Chronicles ix. 3, 4, it is said that when the Queen of Sheba had seen the wisdom of Solomon and the house that he had built—his provisions, servants, and cup-bearers, "and his *ascent* by which he went up into the house of the Lord—there was no more spirit in her." The word which our translators have rendered "his ascent," is again this word Alijah, and the passage should be rendered "his secret chamber," or "upper room"; the one by which, through a private way, he was enabled to pass into the Temple.

On the advent of Christianity, this Jewish custom of worshiping privately in an upper room was adopted by the apostles and disciples, and the New Testament contains many instances of the practise, the word Alijah being, as I have already remarked, translated by the Greek *huperoon*, which has a similar meaning. Thus in Acts i. 13, we find the apostles praying in an upper room; and again, in the twentieth chapter, the disciples are represented as having met at Ephesus in an upper room, where Peter preached to them. But it is unnecessary to multiply instances of this usage. The evidence is complete that the Jews, and after them the primitive Christians, performed their devotions in upper rooms. And the care with which Alijah, *huperoon*, or *upper chamber*, is always used to designate the place of devotion, abundantly indicates that any other place would have been considered improper.

Hence we may trace the practise of holding Lodges in upper rooms to this ancient custom; and that, again, has perhaps some connection with the sacred character always given by the ancients to "high places," so that it is said, in the Masonic lectures, that our ancient brethren met on high hills and low vales. The reason there assigned by implication is that the meeting may be secret; that is, the lectures place the Lodge on a high hill, a vale, or *other secret place*. And this reason is more definitely stated in the modern lectures, which say that they so met "to observe the approach of cowans and eavesdroppers, and to guard against surprise." Yet it is not improbable that the ancient symbolism of the sanctity of a high place was referred to as well as that more practical idea of secrecy and safety.

"**Upright Man and Mason,**—and given it strictly in charge ever to walk and act as such before God and Man." Admonition in the Apprentice Degree. The definition of *Man* is interwoven with the triangle or pyramid, hence true and upright. In S. P. Andrew's *Radical Etymology*, or the origin of Language and Languages, we find the following: "Throughout the Indo-European family of languages, the syllable *ma* (changeable to *me, mi, mo, mu*) means 'great,' and *na* (changeable to *ne, ni, no, nu*) means 'small,' as their primal sense. Hence mana, mena, menu, etc., mean 'great-small,' and thence 'ratio' or 'proportion,' allied with tapering, the cone, pyramid, or triangle. The Latin *men-sa* is 'a surveyor's triangular measuring-board'; me(n)ta, 'anything conical'; mon-s, 'a mountain'; men-s, 'the mind,' i. e., 'ratio'; Sanskrit, *mā;* Latin, *mensum;* Eng., *measure;* hence, Sansk., *mana, manu*, to think." (Also see *Man*.)

[C. T. McClenachan.]

Upright Posture. The upright posture of the Apprentice in the northeast corner, as a symbol of upright conduct, was introduced into the ritual by Preston, who taught in his lectures that the candidate then represented "a just and upright man and Mason." The same symbolism is referred to by Hutchinson, who says that "as the builder raises his column by the plane and perpendicular, so should the Mason carry himself towards the world." Indeed, the application of the corner-stone, or the square stone, as a symbol of uprightness of conduct, which is precisely the Masonic symbolism of the candidate in the northeast, was familiar to the ancients; for Plato says that he who valiantly sustains the shocks of adverse fortune, demeaning himself uprightly, is truly good and of a square posture.

Ur. (Hebrew, אור, *fire.*) Fire, light, or spirit.

Uriel. Hebrew, אוריאל, meaning the *fire of God*. An archangel, mentioned only in 2 Esdras. Michael Glycas, the Byzantine historian, says that his post is in the sun, and that he came down to Seth and Enoch, and instructed them in the length of the years and the variations of the seasons. The Book of Enoch describes him as the angel of thunder and lightning. In some of the Hermetic degrees of Masonry, the name, as representing the angel of fire, becomes a significant word.

Urim and Thummim. The Hebrew words אורים, *Aurim*, and תמים, *Thummim*, have been variously translated by commentators. The Septuagint translates them, "manifestation and truth"; the Vulgate, "doctrine and truth"; Aquila, "lights and perfections"; Kalisch, "perfect brilliancy"; but the most generally received interpretation is, "light and truth." What the Urim and Thummim were has also been a subject of as much doubt and difference of opinion. Suddenly introduced to notice by Moses in the command (Exod. xxviii. 30) "and thou shalt put in the breastplate of judgment the Urim and the Thummim"—as if they were already familiar to the people—we know only of them from the Scriptural account, that they were sacred lots to be worn concealed in or behind the breastplate, and to be consulted by the high priest alone, for the purpose of obtaining a revelation of the will of God in matters of great moment. Some writers have supposed that the augury consisted in a more splendid appearance of certain letters of the names of the tribes inscribed upon the stones of the breastplate; others, that it was received by voice from two small images which were placed beyond the folds of the breastplate. A variety of other conjectures have been hazarded, but as Godwyn (*Moses and Aaron*, iv., 8) observes, "he spoke best, who ingeniously confessed that he knew not what Urim and Thummim was."

The opinion now almost universally accepted is that the Jewish lawgiver borrowed this, as he did the ark, the brazen serpent, and many other of the symbols of his theocracy, from the usages so familiar to him of the Egyptian priests, with which both he and Aaron were familiar, eliminating, of course, from them their previous heathen allusion and giving to them a purer signification.

In reference to the Urim and Thummim, we know not only from the authority of ancient writers, but also from the confirmatory testimony of more recent monumental explorations, that the judges of Egypt wore golden chains around their necks, to which was suspended a small figure of *Themè*, the

Egyptian goddess of *Justice* and *Truth*. "Some of these breastplates," says Gliddon (*Anc. Egypt.*, p. 32), "are extant in European museums; others are to be seen on the monuments as containing the figures of two deities—*Ra*, the sun, and *Themè*. These represent *Ra*, or the sun, in a double capacity, *physical* and *intellectual* light; and *Themè* in a double capacity, *justice* and *truth*."

Neither in Ancient Craft nor in Royal Arch Masonry have the Urim and Thummim been introduced; although Oliver discusses them, in his *Landmarks*, as a type of Christ, to be Masonically applied in his peculiar system of a Christian interpretation of all the Masonic symbols. But the fact that after the construction of the Temple of Solomon we hear no more of the consultation by the priests of the Urim and Thummim, which seem to have given way to the audible interpretation of the Divine will by the prophets, would necessarily disconnect them with Masonry as a symbol, to be accepted even by those who place the foundation of the Order at the Solomonic era.

Yet they have been introduced as a symbol into some of the continental high degrees. Thus, in the last degree of the Order of Brothers of Asia, the presiding officer wears the Urim and Thummim suspended from a golden chain as the jewel of his office.

Reghellini (*Esprit du dogme*, p. 60) thus gives the continental interpretation of the symbol:

"The folly of Solomon is commemorated in the instructions and ceremonies of a high degree, where the Acolyte is reminded that Solomon, becoming arrogant, was for a time abandoned by the Divinity, and as he was, although the greatest of kings, only a mortal, he was weak enough to sacrifice to idols, and thereby lost the communication which he had previously had through the Urim and Thummim.

"These two words are found in a degree of the *Maître écossais*. The Venerables of the Lodges and the Sublime Masters explain the legend to their recipients of an elevated rank, as intended to teach them that they should always be guided by reason, virtue, and honor, and never abandon themselves to an effeminate life or silly superstition."

It is, I think, undeniable that Urim and Thummim have no legitimate existence as a Masonic symbol, and that they can only be considered such by a forced and modern interpretation.

Uriot, Joseph. The author of a work entitled *Le veritable Portrait d'un Franc-Maçon*, which was published by a Lodge at Frankfort, in 1742. It may be looked upon, says Kloss, as the earliest public exposition of the true principles of Masonry which appeared in Germany. Many editions of it were published. M. Uriot also published at Stoungard, in 1769, a work entitled *Lettres sur la Franche Maçonnerie;* which was, however, only an enlargement of the *Portrait*.

Urn. Among the ancients, cinerary urns were in common use to hold the ashes of the deceased after the body had been subjected to incremation, which was the usual mode of disposing of it. He who would desire to be learned upon this subject should read Sir Thomas Browne's celebrated work entitled *Hydriotaphia, or Urn Burial*, where everything necessary to be known on this topic may be found. In Masonry, the cinerary urn has been introduced as a modern symbol, but always as having reference to the burial of the Temple Builder. In the comparatively recent symbol of the Monument, fabricated by Cross for the degree of Master in the American Rite, the urn is introduced as if to remind the beholder that the ashes of the great artist were there deposited. Cross borrowed, it may be supposed, his idea from an older symbol in the high degrees, where, in the description of the tomb of Hiram Abif, it is said that the heart was enclosed in a golden urn, to the side of which a triangular stone was affixed, inscribed with the letters J. M. B. within a wreath of acacia, and placed on the top of an obelisk.

Uruguay. Freemasonry was introduced into the Republic of Uruguay by the Grand Orient of France, which, in 1827, chartered a Lodge called "the Children of the New World." Up to 1856, other Lodges were established by the G. Bodies of France and Brazil. In that year authority was obtained from the Supreme Council and Grand Orient of Brazil, Valley of Lavradio, to establish a governing Masonic body, and the Supreme Council and Grand Orient of Uruguay was regularly constituted at Montevideo, in the A. A. Scottish Rite.

Usages. The peculiarity of constant intercourse between the kings of Israel and Tyre pending the construction of the Holy House, has been frequently commented upon. That this was so is evident from the old sacred Scriptures, as well as from cumulative history by Josephus and others. This ancient custom of intercommunication would not be so marked, had these two kings ever met, yet during the years of construction, gifts and messages seem to have led to the more intimate custom of propounding problems and difficult questions. Hence the inducement to speculate upon whether there was any secret tie between these two kings or merely friendship and business. The customs, habits, and usages of the ancients are visible in every form and ceremony of Masonic work, as well as in the instruction, except where modern innovators have injured, while endeavoring to improve, the time-worn yet mellowed services of the Brotherhood. One of the most beautiful expressions occurring in the Catechism of Freemasonry is the answer to an interrogatory as to the position of the hand in assuming the vow of the First Degree; to wit, "In accordance with ancient *usages* the right hand has always been deemed the seat of Fidelity." A somewhat similar expression occurs in relation to the casting off of the shoe; answer, "This was in accordance with the *usages* of the ancient Israelites; a man plucked off his shoe and gave it to his neighbor; this was testimony in Israel." The shoe was the symbol of subjection when sent by rulers to princes. (Ruth iv. 7.) It was the symbol of humiliation and surrender with Germans and Israelites. The formal divestiture was surrender of title.

Utah. Freemasonry was introduced into the Territory, October 7, 1867, by the Grand Lodge of Montana, which chartered Wasatch Lodge, No. 8. Mount Moriah Lodge, No. 70, was chartered October 21, 1868, by the Grand Lodge of Kansas, and Argenta Lodge, No. 21, by the Grand Lodge of Colorado, September 26, 1871. All of these Lodges are situated in Salt Lake City. January 16–20, 1872, the representatives of the three Lodges met at Salt Lake City and organized the Grand Lodge of Utah, O. F. Strickland being elected first Grand Master.

V

V. (Heb. ו, *vau.*) The twenty-second letter in the English alphabet; of the Hebrew, numerical value of six. Its definition, a *nail*, which in form it represents, and as a Divine name connected with it is יזו, *Vezio, cum splendore;* the V and O in Hebrew being equal. As a Roman numeral its value is five.

Vacancies in Office. Every Masonic officer is elected and installed to hold his office for the time for which he has been elected, and until his successor shall be installed. This is in the nature of a contract between the officer and the Lodge, Chapter, or other body which has elected him, and to its terms he signifies his assent in the most solemn manner at the time of his installation. It follows from this that to resign the office would be on his part to violate his contract. Vacancies in office, therefore, can only occur by death. Even a removal from the jurisdiction, with the intention of permanent absence, will not vacate a Masonic office, because the person removing might change his intention, and return. For the reasons why neither resignation nor removal can vacate an office, see *Succession to the Chair.*

Vagao or **Bagaos.** Found in the Fourth Degree of the French Rite of Adoption.

Vale or **Valley.** The vale or valley was introduced at an early period into the symbolism of Masonry. A catechism of the beginning of the last century says that "the Lodge stands upon holy ground, or the highest hill or lowest vale, or in the vale of Jehoshaphat, or any other secret place." And Browne, who in the beginning of the present century gave a correct version of the Prestonian lectures, says that "our ancient brethren met on the highest hills, the lowest dales, even in the valley of Jehoshaphat, or some such secret place."

Hutchinson (*Sp. of Mas.*, p. 94) has dilated on this subject, but with a mistaken view of the true import of the symbol. He says: "We place the spiritual Lodge in the vale of Jehoshaphat, implying thereby that the principles of Masonry are derived from the knowledge of God, and are established in the judgment of the Lord." And he adds: "The highest hills and lowest valleys were from the earliest times esteemed sacred, and it was supposed the spirit of God was peculiarly diffusive in those places."

It is true that worship in high places was an ancient idolatrous usage. But there is no evidence that the superstition extended to valleys. Hutchinson's subsequent reference to the Druidical and Oriental worship in groves has no bearing on the subject, for groves are not necessarily valleys. The particular reference to the valley of Jehoshaphat would seem in that case to carry an allusion to the peculiar sanctity of that spot, as meaning, in the original, the valley of the judgment of God. But the fact is that the old Masons did not derive their idea that the Lodge was situated in a valley from any idolatrous practise of the ancients.

Valley, in Masonry, is a symbol of secrecy. And although I am not disposed to believe that the use of the word in this sense was borrowed from any meaning which it had in Hebrew, yet it is a singular coincidence that the Hebrew word for valley, *gnemeth*, signifies also "deep," or, as Bate (*Critica Hebræa*) defines it, "whatever lies remote from sight, as counsels and designs which are deep or close." This very word is used in Job xii. 22, where it is said that God "discovereth *deep things* out of darkness, and bringeth out to light the shadow of death."

The Lodge, therefore, is said to be placed in a valley because, the valley being the symbol of secrecy, it is intended to indicate the secrecy in which the acts of the Lodge should be concealed. And this interpretation agrees precisely with what is said in the passages already cited, where the Lodge is said to stand in the lowest vale "or any secret place." It is supported also by the present lecture in this country, the ideas of which at least Webb derived from Preston. It is there taught that our ancient brethren met on the highest hills and lowest vales, *the better to observe the approach of cowans and eavesdroppers, and to guard against surprise.*

Valhalla. The North German or Scandinavian hall of the gods.

Valley. In the capitular degrees of the French Rite, this word is used instead of Orient, to designate the seat of the Chapter. Thus on such a body a document would be dated from the "Valley of Paris," instead of the "Orient of Paris." The word, says the *Dictionnaire Maçonnique*, is often incorrectly employed to designate the south and north sides of the Lodge, where the expression should be "the column of the south" and "the column of the north." Thus, a Warden will address the *brethren of his valley*, instead of the *brethren of his column*. The valley includes the whole Lodge or Chapter; the columns are its divisions.

Van Rensselaer, Killian Henry. Born 1799, died January 28, 1881. A native of Albany, N. Y. State, and descendant of the well-known old Knickerbocker family, whose name he bore. He had held various positions in Craft Masonry, but in 1824 he became prominent in the A. A. Scottish Rite, to which he devoted himself for the remainder of his life, becoming an Inspector-General on June 17, 1845. Bro. Van Rensselaer commanded the Supreme Council that rebelled against the ruling of Edward A. Raymond, and thus was formed another Supreme Body in the Northern States, whose difficulties were finally overcome, as were all schisms of every nature of the Scottish Rite, on the 17th of May, 1867. "Bro. Van," as he was familiarly termed, resided during the last thirty years of his life in the West, and died in California, an outlying suburb of Cincinnati, Ohio. One more sincerely devoted to the cause of Masonry, and without a day of relenting earnestness, will not in time be found.

Vassal, Pierre Gerard. A French physician and Masonic writer, who was born at Manosques, in France, October 14, 1769. He was intended by his parents for the Church, and entered the Seminary of Marseilles for the purpose of pursuing his ecclesiastical studies. At the commencement of the revolution he left the school and joined the army, where, however, he remained only eighteen months. He then applied himself to the study of medicine, and pursued the practise of the profession during the rest of his life, acquiring an extensive reputation as a physician. He was elected a member of several medical societies, to whose transactions he contributed several valuable essays. He is said to have introduced to the profession the use of the digitalis purpurea as a remedial agent, especially in diseases of the heart. He was initiated into Masonry about the year 1811, and thenceforth took an active part in the Institution. He presided in the Lodge, Chapter, and Areopagus of the Sept Ecossais réunis with great zeal and devotion; was in 1819 elected Secretary-General of the Grand Orient, and in 1827 President of the College of Rites. He attained the Thirty-third Degree of the Ancient and Accepted Rite, and was a warm advocate of Scottish Masonry. But his zeal was tempered by his judgment, and he did not hesitate to denounce the errors that had crept into the system, an impartiality of criticism which greatly surprised Ragon. His principal Masonic works are *Essai historique sur l'institution du Rit Ecossais, etc.*, Paris, 1827, and a valuable historical contribution to Masonry entitled *Cours complet de la Maçonnerie, ou Histoire générale de l'Initiation depuis son Origine jusqu'à sou institution en France*, Paris, 1832. In private life, Vassal was distinguished for his kind heart and benevolent disposition. The Lodge of Sept Ecossais réunis presented him a medal in 1830 as a recognition of his active labors in Masonry. He died May 4, 1840, at Paris.

Vault of Steel. (*Voute d'acier.*) The French Masons so call the *Arch of Steel*, which see.

Vault, Secret. As a symbol, the Secret Vault does not present itself in the primary degrees of Masonry. It is found only in the high degrees, such as the Royal Arch of all the Rites, where it plays an important part. Dr. Oliver, in his *Historical Landmarks* (vol. ii., p. 434), gives, while referring to the building of the second Temple, the following general detail of the Masonic legend of this vault:

"The foundations of the Temple were opened, and cleared from the accumulation of rubbish, that a level might be procured for the commencement of the building. While engaged in excavations for this purpose, three fortunate sojourners are said to have discovered our ancient stone of foundation, which had been deposited in the secret crypt by Wisdom, Strength, and Beauty, to prevent the communication of ineffable secrets to profane or unworthy persons. The discovery having been communicated to the prince, prophet, and priest of the Jews, the stone was adopted as the chief corner-stone of the re-edified building, and thus became, in a new and more expressive sense, the type of a more excellent dispensation. An avenue was also accidentally discovered, supported by seven pairs of pillars, perfect and entire, which, from their situation, had escaped the fury of the flames that had consumed the Temple, and the desolation of war that had destroyed the city. The secret vault, which had been built by Solomon as a secure depository for certain secrets that would inevitably have been lost without some such expedient for their preservation, communicated by a subterranean avenue with the king's palace; but at the destruction of Jerusalem the entrance having been closed by the rubbish of falling buildings, it had been discovered by the appearance of a keystone amongst the foundations of the sanctum sanctorum.

A careful inspection was then made, and the invaluable secrets were placed in safe custody."

To support this legend, there is no historical evidence and no authority except that of the Talmudic writers. It is clearly a mythical symbol, and as such we must accept it. We cannot altogether reject it, because it is so intimately and so extensively connected with the symbolism of the Lost and the Recovered Word, that if we reject the theory of the Secret Vault, we must abandon all of that symbolism, and with it the whole of the science of Masonic symbolism. Fortunately, there is ample evidence in the present appearance of Jerusalem and its subterranean topography, to remove from any tacit and, as it were, conventional assent to the theory, features of absurdity or impossibility.

Considered simply as an historical question, there can be no doubt of the existence of immense vaults beneath the superstructure of the original Temple of Solomon. Prime, Robison, and other writers who in recent times have described the topography of Jerusalem, speak of the existence of these structures, which they visited and, in some instances, carefully examined.

After the destruction of Jerusalem by Titus, the Roman Emperor Hadrian erected on the site of the "House of the Lord" a temple of Venus, which in its turn was destroyed, and the place subsequently became a depository of all manner of filth. But the Calif Omar, after his conquest of Jerusalem, sought out the ancient site, and, having caused it to be cleansed of its impurities, he directed a mosque to be erected on the rock which rises in the center of the mountain. Fifty years afterward the Sultan Abd-el-Meluk displaced the edifice of Omar, and erected that splendid building which remains to this day, and is still incorrectly called by Christians the mosque of Omar, but known to Mussulmans as El-kubbet-es-Sukrah, or the Dome of the Rock. This is supposed to occupy the exact site of the original Solomonic Temple, and is viewed with equal reverence by Jews and Mohammedans, the former of whom, says Mr. Prime (*Tent Life in the Holy Land*, p. 183), "have a faith that the ark is within its bosom now."

Bartlett (*Walks about Jerusalem*, p. 170), in describing a vault beneath this mosque of Omar, says: "Beneath the dome, at the southeast angle of the Temple wall, conspicuous from all points, is a small subterraneous place of prayer, forming the entrance to the extensive vaults which support the level platform of the mosque above."

Dr. Barclay (*City of the Great King*) describes, in many places of his interesting topography of Jerusalem, the vaults and subterranean chambers which are to be found beneath the site of the old Temple.

Conformable with this historical account is the Talmudical legend, in which the Jewish Rabbis state that, in preparing the foundations of the Temple, the workmen discovered a subterranean vault sustained by seven arches, rising from as many pairs of pillars. This vault escaped notice at the destruction of Jerusalem, in consequence of its being filled with rubbish. The legend adds that Josiah, foreseeing the destruction of the Temple, commanded the Levites to deposit the Ark of the Covenant in this vault, where it was found by some of the workmen of Zerubbabel at the building of the second Temple.

In the earliest ages, the cave or vault was deemed sacred. The first worship was in cave temples, which were either natural or formed by art to resemble the excavations of nature. Of such great extent was this practise of subterranean worship by the nations of antiquity, that many of the forms of heathen temples, as well as the naves, aisles, and chancels of churches subsequently built for Christian worship, are said to owe their origin to the religious use of caves.

From this, too, arose the fact, that the initiation into the ancient mysteries was almost always performed in subterranean edifices; and when the place of initiation, as in some of the Egyptian temples, was really above ground, it was so constructed as to give to the neophyte the appearance, in its approaches and its internal structure, of a vault. As the great doctrine taught in the mysteries was the resurrection from the dead—as *to die* and *to be initiated* were synonymous terms—it was deemed proper that there should be some formal resemblance between a descent into the grave and a descent into the place of initiation. "Happy is the man," says the Greek poet Pindar, "who descends beneath the hollow earth having beheld these mysteries, for he knows the end as well as the divine origin of life"; and in a like spirit Sophocles exclaims, "Thrice happy are they who descend to the shades below after having beheld the sacred rites, for they alone have life in Hades, while all others suffer there every kind of evil."

The vault was, therefore, in the ancient mysteries, symbolic of the grave; for initiation was symbolic of death, where alone Divine Truth is to be found. The Masons have adopted the same idea. They teach that death is but the beginning of life; that if the first or evanescent temple of our transitory life be on the surface, we must descend into the *secret vault* of death before we can find that sacred deposit of truth which is to adorn our second temple of eternal life. It is in this sense of an entrance through the grave into eternal life that we are to view the symbolism of the secret vault. Like every other myth and allegory of Masonry, the historical relation may be true or it may be false; it may be founded on fact or be the invention of imagination; the lesson is still there, and the symbolism teaches it exclusive of the history.

V. D. S. A. (*Veut Dieu Saint Amour.*) Four words supposed to be repeated by the fraters of the Temple during certain pauses in the ceremonies. P. D. E. P. refers to the motto "Pro Deo et Patria."

Veadar. (ואדר.) That is, the second Adar. A month intercalated by the Jews every few years between Adar and Nisan, so as to reconcile the computation by solar and lunar time. It commences sometimes in February and sometimes in March.

Vedanga. ("Limb of the Veda.") A collection of Sanskrit works on the grammar, lexicography, chronology, and ritual of the Vedic text. They are older than the Upanishads, and are placed among the Great Shasters, though not among the Sruti.

Vedas. The most ancient of the religious writings of the Indian Aryans, and now constituting the sacred canon of the Hindus, being to them what the Bible is to the Christians, or the Koran to the Mohammedans. The word Veda denotes in Sanskrit, the language in which these books are written, wisdom or knowledge, and comes from the verb *Veda*, which, like the Greek οἶδα, signifies "I know." The German *weiss* and the English *wit* came from the same root. There are four collections, each of which is called a Veda, namely, the Rig-Veda, the Yasur-Veda, the Sama-Veda, and the Atharva-Veda; but the first only is the real Veda, the others being but commentaries on it, as the Talmud is upon the Old Testament.

The Rig-Veda is divided into two parts: the *Mantras* or hymns, which are all metrical, and the *Brahmanes*, which are in prose, and consist of ritualistic directions concerning the employment of the hymns, and the method of sacrifice. The other Vedas consist also of hymns and prayers; but they are borrowed, for the most part, from the Rig-Veda.

The Vedas, then, are the Hindu canon of Scripture—his book of the law; and to the Hindu Mason they are his trestle-board, just as the Bible is to the Christian Mason.

The religion of the Vedas is apparently an adoration of the visible powers of nature, such as the sun, the sky, the dawn, and the fire, and, in general, the eternal powers of light. The supreme divinity was the sky, called *Varuna*, whence the Greeks got their *Ouranas;* and next was the sun, called sometimes *Savitar*, the progenitor, and sometimes *Mitra*, the loving one, whence the Persian *Mithras*. Side by side with these was *Agni*, fire, whence the Latin *ignis*, who was the divinity coming most directly in approximation with man on earth, and soaring upward as the flame to the heavenly gods. But in this nature-worship the Vedas frequently betray an inward spirit groping after the infinite and the eternal, and an anxious search for the Divine name, which was to be reverenced just as the Hebrew aspired after the unutterable Tetragrammaton. Bunsen (*God in History*, b. iii., ch. 7) calls this "the desire—the yearning after the nameless Deity, who nowhere manifests himself in the Indian pantheon of the Vedas—the voice of humanity groping after God." One of the most sublime of the Veda hymns (*Rig-Veda, b. x. hymn* 121) ends each strophe with the solemn question: "Who is the god to whom we shall offer our sacrifice?" This is the question which every religion asks; the search after the All-Father is the labor of all men who are seeking Divine truth and light. The Semitic, like the Aryan poet in the same longing spirit for the knowledge of God, exclaims, "Oh that I knew where I might find him, that I might come even to his seat." It is the great object of all Masonic labor, which thus shows its true religious character and design.

The Vedas have not exercised any direct influence on the symbolism of Freemasonry. But, as the oldest Aryan faith, they became infused into the subsequent religious systems of the race, and through the Zend-Avesta of the Zoroastrians, the mysteries of Mithras, the doctrines of the Neo-platonists, and the school of Pythagoras, mixed with the Semitic doctrines of the Bible and the Talmud, they have cropped out in the mysticism of the Gnostics and the secret societies of the Middle Ages, and have shown some of their spirit in the religious philosophy and the symbolism of Speculative Masonry. To the Masonic scholar, the study of the Vedic hymns is therefore interesting, and not altogether fruitless in its results. The writings of Bunsen, of Muir, of Cox, and especially of Max Müller, will furnish ample materials for the study.

Vehm-gericht. See *Westphalia, Secret Tribunals of.*

Veils, Grand Masters of the. Three officers in a Royal Arch Chapter of the American Rite, whose duty it is to protect and defend the Veils of the Tabernacle, for which purpose they are presented with a sword. The jewel of their office is a sword within a triangle, and they bear each a banner, which is respectively blue, purple, and scarlet. The title of "Grand Master" appears to be a misnomer. It would have been better to have styled them "Masters" or "Guardians." In the English system, the three Sojourners act in this capacity, which is an absurd violation of all the facts of history, and completely changes the symbolism.

Veils, Symbolism of the. Neither the construction nor the symbolism of the veils in the Royal Arch tabernacle is derived from that of the Sinaitic. In the Sinaitic tabernacle there were no veils of separation between the different parts, except the one white one that hung before the most holy place. The decorations of the tabernacle were curtains, like modern tapestry, interwoven with many colors; no curtain being wholly of one color, and not running across the apartment, but covering its sides and roof. The exterior form of the Royal Arch tabernacle was taken from that of Moses, but the interior decoration from a passage of Josephus not properly understood.

Josephus has been greatly used by the fabricators of high degrees of Masonry, not only for their ideas of symbolism, but for the suggestion of their legends. In the Second Book of Chronicles (iii. 14) it is said that Solomon "made the veil of blue, and purple, and crimson, and fine linen, and wrought cherubims thereon." This description evidently alludes to the single veil, which, like that of the Sinaitic tabernacle, was placed before the entrance of the holy of holies. It by no means resembles the four separate and equidistant veils of the Masonic tabernacle.

But Josephus had said (*Antiq.*, l. viii., c. iii., § 3) that the king "also had veils of blue, and purple, and scarlet, and the brightest and softest linen, with the most curious flowers wrought upon them, which were to be drawn before these doors." To this description—which is a very inaccurate one, which refers, too, to the interior of the first Temple, and not to the supposed tabernacle subsequently erected near its ruins, and which, besides, has no Biblical authority for its support—we must trace the ideas, even as to the order of the veils, which the inventors of the Masonic tabernacle adopted in their construction of it. That tabernacle cannot be recognized as historically correct, but must be considered, like the three doors of the Temple in the Symbolic degrees, simply as a symbol. But this does not at all diminish its value.

The symbolism of the veils must be considered in two aspects: first, in reference to the symbolism of the veils as a whole, and next, as to the symbolism of each veil separately.

As a whole, the four veils, constituting four divisions of the tabernacle, present obstacles to the neophyte in his advance to the most holy place where the Grand Council sits. Now he is seeking to advance to that sacred spot that he may there receive his spiritual illumination, and be invested with a knowledge of the true Divine name. But Masonically, this Divine name is itself but a symbol of Truth, the object, as has been often said, of all a Mason's search and labor. The passage through the veils is, therefore, a symbol of the trials and difficulties that are encountered and must be overcome in the search for and the acquisition of Truth.

This is the general symbolism; but we lose sight of it, in a great degree, when we come to the interpretation of the symbolism of each veil independently of the others, for this principally symbolizes the various virtues and affections that should characterize the Mason. Yet the two symbolisms are really connected, for the virtues symbolized are those which should distinguish everyone engaged in the Divine search.

The symbolism, according to the system adopted in the American Rite, refers to the colors of the veils and to the miraculous signs of Moses, which are described in Exodus as having been shown by him to prove his mission as the messenger of Jehovah.

Blue is a symbol of universal friendship and benevolence. It is the appropriate color of the Symbolic degrees, the possession of which is the first step in the progress of the search for truth to be now instituted. The Mosaic sign of the serpent was the symbol among the ancients of resurrection to life, because the serpent, by casting his skin, is supposed continually to renew his youth. It is the symbol here of the loss and the recovery of the Word.

Purple is a symbol here of union, and refers to the intimate connection of Ancient Craft and Royal Arch Masonry. Hence it is the appropriate color of the intermediate degrees, which must be passed through in the prosecution of the search. The Mosaic sign refers to the restoration of the leprous hand to health. Here again, in this representation of a diseased limb restored to health, we have a repetition of the allusion to the loss and the recovery of the Word; the Word itself being but a symbol of Divine truth, the search for which constitutes the whole science of Freemasonry, and the symbolism of which pervades the whole system of initiation from the first to the last degree.

Scarlet is a symbol of fervency and zeal, and is appropriated to the Royal Arch Degree because it is by these qualities that the neophyte, now so far advanced in his progress, must expect to be successful in his search. The Mosaic sign of changing water into blood bears the same symbolic reference to a change for the better—from a lower to a higher state—from the elemental water in which there is no life to the blood which is the life itself—from darkness to light. The progress is still onward to the recovery of that which had been lost, but which is yet to be found.

White is a symbol of purity, and is peculiarly appropriate to remind the neophyte, who is now almost at the close of his search, that it is only by purity of life that he can expect to be found worthy of the reception of Divine truth. "Blessed," says the Great Teacher, "are the pure in heart, for they shall see God." The Mosaic signs now cease, for they have taught their lesson; and the aspirant is invested with the Signet of Truth, to assure him that, having endured all trials and overcome all obstacles, he is at length entitled to receive the reward for which he has been seeking; for the Signet of Zerubbabel is a royal signet, which confers power and authority on him who possesses it.

And so we now see that the Symbolism of the Veils, however viewed, whether collectively or separately, represents the laborious, but at last successful, search for Divine truth.

Venerable. The title of a Worshipful Master in a French Lodge.

Venerable Grand Master of all Symbolic Lodges. The Twentieth Degree of the Ancient and Accepted Scottish Rite. (See *Grand Master of all Symbolic Lodges.*) The *Dictionnaire Maçonnique* says that this degree was formerly conferred on those brethren in France who, in receiving it, obtained the right to organize Lodges, and to act as Masters or Venerables for life, an abuse that was subsequently abolished by the Grand Orient.

Ragon and Vassal both make the same statement. It may be true, but they furnish no documentary evidence of the fact.

Venerable, Perfect. (*Venerable Parfait.*) A degree in the collection of Viany.

Venezuela. Freemasonry first penetrated into Venezuela in the beginning of the present century, when a Lodge was instituted by the Grand Orient of Spain. Several other Lodges were subsequently established by the same authority. In 1825, Cerneau, the head of the irregular Supreme Council at New York, established in Caracas a Grand Lodge and Supreme Council of the Scottish Rite. In 1827, the Liberator, Simon Bolivar, having by his decree prohibited all secret societies, the Masonic Lodges, with the exception of the one at Porto Cabello, suspended their labors. In 1830, Venezuela having become independent by the division of the Colombian Republic, several brethren obtained from some of the dignitaries of the extinct Grand Lodge, in their capacity as Sovereign Inspectors-General of the Thirty-third Degree, a temporary Dispensation to hold a Lodge for one year, in the expectation that they would, in the course of that time, be enabled to obtain a Charter from some foreign Grand Lodge. But their efforts, in consequence of irregularities, were unsuccessful, and the Lodge was suspended. For eight years, Freemasonry in Venezuela was in a dormant condition. But in 1838 the Masonic spirit was revived, the Lodge just referred to renewed its labors, the old Lodges were resuscitated, and the National Grand Lodge of Venezuela was constituted, whether regularly or not, it is impossible at this time, with the insufficient light before us, to determine. It was, however, recognized by several foreign bodies. The Grand Lodge thus established, issued Charters to all the old Lodges, and erected new ones. In conjunction with the Inspectors-General, it established a supreme legislative body, under the name of the Grand Orient, and also constituted a Grand Lodge, which continued to exist, with only a few changes, made in 1852, until the present Grand Lodge and Supreme Council were established, January 12, 1865. There are at present in Venezuela a Grand Lodge, which now has thirty-five Lodges under its obedience, and a Supreme Council of the Scottish Rite.

Vengeance. A word used in the high degrees. Barruel, Robison, and the other detractors of Freemasonry, have sought to find in this word a proof of the vindictive character of the Institution. "In the degree of Kadosh," says Barruel (*Memoires*, ii., 310), "the assassin of Adoniram becomes the king, who must be slain to avenge the Grand Master Molay and the Order of Masons, who are the successors of the Templars."

No calumny was ever fabricated with so little pretension to truth for its foundation. The reference is altogether historical; it is the record of the punishment which followed a crime, not an incentive to revenge.

The word *nekam* is used in Masonry in precisely the same sense in which it is employed by the prophet Jeremiah (50. 15) when he speaks of *nikemat Jehovah*, "the vengeance of the Lord"—the punishment which God will inflict on evil-doers. The word is used symbolically to express the universally recognized doctrine that crime will inevitably be followed by its penal consequences. It is the dogma of all true religions; for if virtue and vice entailed the same result, there would be no incentive to the one and no restraint from the other.

Verger. An officer in a Council of Knights of the Holy Sepulcher, whose duties are similar to those of a Senior Deacon in a Symbolic Lodge.

Veritas. Signifying "truth," a significant word in Templar Masonry. (See *Truth.*)

Vermont. Freemasonry was introduced into the State of Vermont in 1781, in which year the Grand Lodge of Massachusetts granted a Charter for the establishment of a Lodge at Cornish. This town having soon afterward been claimed by New Hampshire, the Lodge removed to Windsor, on the opposite side of the river. In 1785, the Grand Lodge of Massachusetts chartered another Lodge at the town of Manchester. A Grand Lodge was organized October 13, 1794, at Manchester, by a convention of the five Lodges then existing in the State.

In no State of the Union did the anti-Masonic party, as a political power, exercise so much influence as it did in Vermont. The Grand Lodge was, under the pressure of persecution, compelled to suspend its labors in 1833. All the Lodges under its jurisdiction surrendered their Charters, and Masonry for fifteen years had no active existence in that State. The Grand Lodge, however, did not dissolve, but continued its legal life by regular, although private, communications of the officers, and by adjournments, until the year 1846, when it resumed vigor, Bro. Nathan B. Haswell, who was the Grand Master at the time of the suspension, having taken the chair at the resumed communication in January, 1846. The regularity of this resumption, although at first denied by the Grand Lodge of New York, was generally admitted by all the Grand Lodges of the United States, with a welcome to which the devotion and steady perseverance of the Masons of Vermont had justly entitled them.

The Grand Chapter was organized December 20, 1804, Jonathan Wells being elected first Grand High Priest. It shared the destinies of the Grand Lodge during the period of persecution, but was reorganized July 18, 1849, under a commission from Joseph K. Stapleton, Deputy General Grand High Priest of the United States.

The Grand Council of Royal and Select Masters was organized August 19, 1854, by a Convention of four Councils held at Vergennes, and Nathan B. Haswell was elected Grand Master.

The Grand Encampment (now the Grand Commandery) was originally organized in

1825. It subsequently became dormant. In 1850, the Grand Encampment was revived; but it appearing that the revival was attended by irregularities, and in violation of the Grand Constitution of the Grand Encampment of the United States, the members dissolved the body, and the Deputy Grand Master, William H. Ellis, having, in December, 1850, issued a commission to three subordinate Encampments to organize a Grand Encampment, that body was formed January 14, 1852.

Vernhes, J. F. A French litterateur and Masonic writer, who was in 1821 the Venerable of the Lodge la Parfaite Humanité at Montpellier. He wrote an *Essai sur l'Histoire de la Franceh-Maçonnerie, depuis son établissement jusq'à nos jours*, Paris, 1813; and *Le Parfait Maçon ou Repertoire complet de la Maçonnerie Symbolique*. This work was published at Montpellier, in 1820, in six numbers, of which the sixth was republished the next year, with the title of *Apologie des Maçons*. It contained a calm and rational refutation of several works which had been written against Freemasonry. Vernhes became an active disciple of the Rite of Mizraim, and published in 1822, at Paris, a defense of it and an examination of the various Rites then practised in France.

Vertot d'Aubœuf, René-Aubert de. The Abbé Vertot was born at the Chateau de Bennelot, in Normandy, in 1665. In 1715 the Grand Master of the Knights of Malta appointed him the historiographer of that Order, and provided him with the Commandery of Santenay. Vertot discharged the duties of his office by writing his well-known work entitled *History of the Knights Hospitalers of St. John of Jerusalem, afterwards Knights of Rhodes, and now Knights of Malta*, which was published at Paris, in 1726, in four volumes. It has since passed through a great number of editions, and been translated into many languages. Of this work, to which the Abbé principally owes his fame, although he was also the author of many other histories, French critics complain that the style is languishing, and less pure and natural than that of his other writings. Notwithstanding that it has been the basis of almost all subsequent histories of the Order, the judgment of the literary world is, that it needs exactitude in many of its details, and is too much influenced by the personal prejudices of the author. The Abbé Vertot died in 1735.

Vesica Piscis. The fish was among primitive Christians a symbol of Jesus. (See *Fish*.) The *vesica piscis*, signifying literally the air-bladder of a fish, but, as some suppose, being the rough outline of a fish, was adopted as an abbreviated form of that symbol. In some old manuscripts it is used as a representation of the lateral wound of our Lord. As a symbol, it was frequently employed as a church decoration by the Freemasons of the Middle Ages. The seals of all colleges, abbeys, and other religious communities, as well as of ecclesiastical persons, were invariably made of this shape. Hence, in reference to the religious character of the Institution, it has been suggested that the seals of Masonic Lodges should also have that form, instead of the circular one now used.

Vessels of Gold and Silver, for the service of the First Temple, were almost numberless, according to Josephus; thus:

	Gold.	Silver.
Vessels of gold	20,000	40,000
Candlesticks .	4,000	8,000
Wine cups	80,000	......
Goblets	10,000	20,000
Measures	20,000	40,000
Dishes .	80,000	160,000
Censers .	20,000	50,000
	234,000	318,000
Vestments for the priests		21,000
Musical instruments. . .		600,000
Stoles of silver for the Levites .		200,000

The vessels and vestments were always protected by a hierophylax or guardian.

Veterans. Associations of Masons "who, as such, have borne the burden and heat of the day" for at least 21 years' active service —in the State of Connecticut, 30 years. A number of these societies exist in the United States, their objects being largely of a social nature, to set an example to the younger Masons, and to keep a watchful eye on the comfort of those whose years are becoming numbered. The assemblies are stated or casual, but in all cases annual for a Table Lodge. These associations perpetuate friendship, cultivate the social virtues, and collate and preserve the history and biography of their members.

Vexillum Belli. A war-flag. In classical Latin, *Vexillum* meant a flag consisting of a piece of cloth fixed on a frame or cross-tree, as contradistinguished from a *signum*, or standard, which was simply a pole with the image of an eagle, horse, or some other device on the top. Among the pretended relics of the Order of the Temple is one called "le drapeau de guerre, eu laine blanche, à quatre raies noires"; i. e., the standard of war, of white linen, with four black rays; and in the statutes of the Order, the Vexillum Belli is described as being "albo nigroque palatum," or pales of white and black, which is the same thing couched in the technical language of heraldry. This is incorrect. The only war-flag of the ancient Knights Templar was the Beauseant. Addison, on the title-page of his *Temple Church*, gives what he calls "the war-banner of the Order

of the Temple," and which is, as in the margin, the Beauseant, bearing in the center the blood-red Templar cross. Some of the Masonic Templars, those of Scotland, for example, have both a Beaucenifer or Beauseant bearer, and a bearer of the Vexillum Belli. The difference would appear to be that the Beauseant is the plain white and black flag, and the Vexillum Belli is the same flag charged with the red cross.

Viany, Auguste de. A Masonic writer of Tuscany, and one of the founders there of the Philosophic Scottish Rite. He was the author of many discourses, dissertations, and didactic essays on Masonic subjects. He is, however, best known as the collector of a large number of manuscript degrees and cahiers or rituals, several of which have been referred to in this work.

Viceroy Eusebius. The name of the second officer in the Conclave of the Red Cross of Rome and Constantine.

Vielle-Bru, Rite of. In 1748, the year after the alleged creation of the Chapter of Arras by the Young Pretender, Charles Edward, a new Rite, in favor of the cause of the Stuarts, was established at Toulouse by, as it is said, Sir Samuel Lockhart, one of the aides-de-camp of the Prince. It was called the Rite of Vielle-Bru, or Faithful Scottish Masons. It consisted of nine degrees, divided into three chapters as follows: *First Chapter*, 1, 2, 3. The Symbolic degrees; 4. Secret Master. *Second Chapter*, 5, 6, 7, 8. Four *élu* degrees, based on the Templar system. *Third Chapter*, 9. Scientific Masonry. The head of the Rite was a Council of Menatzchim. In 1804 the Rite was refused a recognition by the Grand Orient of France, because it presented no moral or scientific object, and because the Charter which it claimed to have from Prince Charles Edward was not proved to be authentic. It continued to exist in the south of France until the year 1812, when, being again rejected by the Grand Orient, it fell into decay.

Villars, Abbé Montfaucon de. He was born in Languedoc in 1653, and was shot by one of his relatives, on the high road between Lyons and Paris, in 1675. The Abbé Villars is celebrated as the author of *The Count de Gabalis, or Conversations on the Secret Sciences*, published in 2 vols., at Paris, in 1670. In this work the author's design was, under the form of a romance, to unveil some of the Kabbalistic mysteries of Rosicrucianism. It has passed through many editions, and has been translated into English as well as into other languages.

Vincere aut Mori. French, *Vaincre ou Mourir*, to conquer or to die. The motto of the degree of Perfect Elect Mason, the first of the *élus* according to the Clermont or Templar system of Masonry.

Vinton, David. A distinguished lecturer on Masonry, and teacher of the ritual in the first quarter of the present century. His field of labors was principally confined to the Southern States, and he taught his system for some time with great success in North and South Carolina. There were, however, stains upon his character, and he was eventually expelled by the Grand Lodge of the former State. He died at Shakertown, Kentucky, in July, 1833. Vinton published at Dedham, Massachusetts, in 1816, a volume, containing Selections of Masonic, Sentimental, and Humorous songs, under the title of *The Masonic Minstrel.* Of this rather trifling work no less than twelve thousand copies were sold by subscription. To Vinton's poetic genius we are indebted for that beautiful dirge commencing, "Solemn strikes the funeral chime," which has now become in almost all the Lodges of the United States a part of the ritualistic ceremonies of the Third Degree, and has been sung over the graves of thousands of departed brethren. This contribution should preserve the memory of Vinton among the Craft, and in some measure atone for his faults, whatever they may have been.

Violet. This is not a Masonic color, except in some of the high degrees of the Scottish Rite, where it is a symbol of mourning, and thus becomes one of the decorations of a Sorrow Lodge. Portal (*Coleurs Symboliques*, p. 236) says that this color was adopted for mourning by persons of high rank. And Campini (*Vetera Monumenta*) states that violet was the mark of grief, especially among kings and cardinals. In Christian art, the Savior is clothed in a purple robe during his passion; and it is the color appropriated, says Court de Gebelin (*Monde prim.*, viii., 201), to martyrs, because, like their Divine Master, they undergo the punishment of the passion. Prevost (*Hist. des Voyages*, vi., 152) says that in China violet is the color of mourning. Among that people blue is appropriated to the dead and red to the living, because with them red represents the vital heat, and blue, immortality; and hence, says Portal, violet, which is made by an equal admixture of blue and red, is a symbol of the resurrection to eternal life. Such an idea is peculiarly appropriate to the use of violet in the high degrees of Masonry as a symbol of mourning. It would be equally appropriate in the primary degrees, for everywhere in Masonry we are taught to mourn not as those who have no hope. Our grief for the dead is that of those who believe in the immortal life. The red symbol of life is tinged with the blue of immortality, and thus we would wear the violet as our mourning to declare our trust in the resurrection.

Virginia. There is much obscurity about the early history of Freemasonry in this State. The first chartered Lodge appears to have been the "St. John's Lodge" at Norfolk, which received its Warrant in 1741 from the Grand Lodge of Scotland. December 22, 1753, the "Royal Exchange Lodge" at Norfolk was chartered by the Atholl or Ancient York Lodge. But between 1741 and 1758 the Lodge of Fredericksburg had sprung into existence, for its records show that General Washington was there initiated

November 4, 1752. This Lodge was chartered by the Grand Lodge of Massachusetts on July 21, 1758, but had been acting under Dispensation for several years before. In 1777 there were ten Lodges in Virginia, namely, two at Norfolk and one at each of the following places: Port Royal, Fredericksburg, Hampton, Williamsburg, Gloucester, Cabin Point, Petersburg and Yorktown. On the 6th of May in that year, deputies from five of these Lodges met in convention at Williamsburg, "for the purpose of choosing a Grand Master for Virginia." So says the record as contained in Dove's *Text-Book*. The convention, however, adjourned to June 23d, after stating its reasons for the election of such an officer. On that day it met, but again adjourned. Finally, it met on October 13, 1778. The record calls it "a Convention of the Craft"; but it assumed the form of a Lodge, and the Master and Wardens of Williamsburg Lodge presided. Only four Lodges were represented, namely, Williamsburg, Blandford, Botetourt, and Cabin Point. The modern forms of Masonic conventions are not found in the proceedings of this convention. Nothing is said of the formation of a Grand Lodge, but the following resolution was adopted:

"It is the opinion of this Convention, that it is agreeable to the Constitutions of Masonry that all the regular chartered Lodges within this State should be subject to the Grand Master of the said State."

Accordingly, John Blair, Past Master of the Williamsburg Lodge, was nominated and unanimously elected, and on the same day he was installed, by the Master of Williamsburg Lodge, as "Grand Master of Free and Accepted Masons of the State of Virginia." All this was done, if we may trust the record, in Williamsburg Lodge, the Master thereof presiding, who afterward closed the Lodge without any reference to the organization of a Grand Lodge. We may, however, imply that such a body was then formed, for Dove—without, however, giving any account of the proceedings in the interval, when there might or might not have been quarterly or annual communications—says that a Grand Lodge was held in the city of Richmond, October 4, 1784, when Grand Master Blair having resigned the chair, James Mercer was elected Grand Master. Dove dates the organization of the Grand Lodge October 13, 1778.

Royal Arch Masonry was introduced into Virginia, it is said, by Joseph Myers, who was acting under his authority as a Deputy Inspector of the Scottish Rite. The Grand Chapter was organized at Norfolk, May 1, 1808. It has never recognized the authority of the General Grand Chapter.

The Cryptic degrees are conferred in Virginia in the Chapters preparatory to the Royal Arch. There are therefore no Councils of Royal and Select Masters in the State.

The register, or roll published in the *Proceedings of the Grand Encampment of the United States* for 1871 (p. 27), states that the Grand Commandery of Virginia was organized November 27, 1823. But from a report of the committee of the Grand Encampment, made September 17, 1847, we learn the following facts. In 1824 there existed three subordinate Encampments in Virginia, which about the year 1826 formed a Grand Encampment, that was represented that year in the General Grand Encampment. It is supposed that this body ceased to exist soon after its organization, and a Charter was granted, by the General Grand Encampment, for an Encampment to meet at Wheeling. On December 11, 1845, delegates from various Encampments in Virginia met at Richmond and organized a new Grand Encampment which they declared to be independent of the General Grand Encampment. At the session of the latter body in 1847, it declared this new Grand Encampment to be "irregular and unauthorized," and it refused to recognize it or its subordinates. Wheeling Encampment, however, was acknowledged to be a lawful body, as it had not given its adhesion to the irregular Grand Encampment. In January, 1851, the Grand Encampment of Virginia receded from its position of independence, and was recognized by the General Grand Encampment as one of its constituents. It so remained until 1861, when the Grand Commandery (the title which had been adopted in 1859) seceded from the Grand Encampment in consequence of the Civil War. It, however, returned to its allegiance in 1865, and has ever since remained a regular portion of the Templar Order of the United States.

Virgin, Weeping. See *Weeping Virgin.*

"Virtute et Silentio" and "Gloria in Excelsis Deo" are significant mottoes of the Royal Order of Scotland.

Vishnu. See *Puranas.*

Visible Masonry. In a circular published March 18, 1775, by the Grand Orient of France, reference is made to two divisions of the Order, namely, *Visible* and *Invisible Masonry*. Did we not know something of the Masonic contentions then existing in France between the Lodges and the supreme authority, we should hardly comprehend the meaning intended to be conveyed by these words. By "Invisible Masonry" they denoted that body of intelligent and virtuous Masons who, irrespective of any connection with dogmatic authorities, constituted "a Mysterious and Invisible Society of the True Sons of Light," who, scattered over the two hemispheres, were engaged, with one heart and soul, in doing everything for the glory of the Great Architect and the good of their fellow-men. By "Visible Masonry" they meant the congregation of Masons into Lodges, which were often affected by the contagious vices of the age in which they lived. The former is perfect; the latter continually needs purification. The words were originally invented to effect a particular purpose, and to bring the recusant Lodges of France into their obedience.

But they might be advantageously preserved, in the technical language of Masonry, for a more general and permanent object. Invisible Masonry would then indicate the abstract spirit of Masonry as it has always existed, while Visible Masonry would refer to the concrete form which it assumes in Lodge and Chapter organizations, and in different Rites and systems. The latter would be like the material church, or church militant; the former like the spiritual church, or church triumphant. Such terms might be found convenient to Masonic scholars and writers.

Visitation, Grand. The visit of a Grand Master, accompanied by his Grand Officers, to a subordinate Lodge, to inspect its condition, is called a *Grand Visitation.* There is no allusion to anything of the kind in the Old Constitutions, because there was no organization of the Order before the eighteenth century that made such an inspection necessary. But immediately after the revival in 1717, it was found expedient, in consequence of the growth of Lodges in London, to provide for some form of visitation and inspection. So, in the very first of the Thirty-nine General Regulations, adopted in 1721, it is declared that "the Grand Master or his Deputy hath authority and right not only to be present in any true Lodge, but also to preside wherever he is, with the Master of the Lodge on his left hand, and to order his Grand Wardens to attend him, who are not to act in any particular Lodges as Wardens, but in his presence and at his command; because there the Grand Master may command the Wardens of that Lodge, or any other brethren he pleaseth, to attend and act as his Wardens *pro tempore.*" (*Constitutions*, 1723, p. 58.)

In compliance with this old regulation, whenever the Grand Master, accompanied by his Wardens and other officers, visits a Lodge in his jurisdiction, for the purpose of inspecting its condition, the Master and officers of the Lodge thus visited surrender their seats to the Grand Master and the Grand Officers.

Grand Visitations are among the oldest usages of Freemasonry since the revival period. In America they are not now so frequently practised, in consequence of the extensive territory over which the Lodges are scattered, and the difficulty of collecting at one point all the Grand Officers, many of whom generally reside at great distances apart. Still, where it can be done, the practise of Grand Visitations should never be neglected.

The power of visitation for inspection is confined to the Grand and Deputy Grand Master. The Grand Wardens possess no such prerogative. The Master must always tender the gavel and the chair to the Grand or Deputy Grand Master when either of them informally visits a Lodge; for the Grand Master and, in his absence, the Deputy have the right to preside in all Lodges where they may be present. But this privilege does not extend to the Grand Wardens.

Visiting Brethren. Every brother from abroad, or from any other Lodge, when he visits a Lodge, must be received with welcome and treated with hospitality. He must be clothed, that is to say, furnished with an apron, and, if the Lodge uses them (as every Lodge should), with gloves, and, if a Past Master, with the jewel of his rank. He must be directed to a seat, and the utmost courtesy extended to him. If of distinguished rank in the Order, the honors due to that rank must be paid to him.

This hospitable and courteous spirit is derived from the ancient customs of the Craft, and is inculcated in all the Old Constitutions. Thus, in the Lansdowne MS., it is directed "that every Mason receive or cherish strange Fellows when they come over the Countrey, and sett them on worke, if they will worke, as the manner is; (that is to say), if the Mason have any moulde stone in his place on worke; and if he have none, the Mason shall refresh him with money unto the next Lodge." A similar regulation is found in all the other manuscripts of the Operative Masons; and from them the usage has descended to their speculative successors.

At all Lodge banquets it is of obligation that a toast shall be drunk "to the visiting brethren." To neglect this would be a great breach of decorum.

Visit, Right of. Every affiliated Mason in good standing has a right to visit any other Lodge, wherever it may be, as often as it may suit his pleasure or convenience; and this is called, in Masonic law, "the right of visit." It is one of the most important of all Masonic privileges, because it is based on the principle of the identity of the Masonic Institution as one universal family, and is the exponent of that well-known maxim that "in every clime a Mason may find a home, and in every land a brother." It has been so long and so universally admitted, that I have not hesitated to rank it among the landmarks of the Order.

The admitted doctrine on this subject is, that the right of visit is one of the positive rights of every Mason, because Lodges are justly considered as only divisions for convenience of the universal Masonic family. The right may, of course, be lost, or forfeited on special occasions, by various circumstances; but any Master who shall refuse admission to a Mason in good standing, who knocks at the door of his Lodge, is expected to furnish some good and satisfactory reason for his thus violating a Masonic right. If the admission of the applicant, whether a member or visitor, would, in his opinion, be attended with injurious consequences, such, for instance, as impairing the harmony of the Lodge, a Master would then, I presume, be justified in refusing admission. But without the existence of some such good reason, Masonic jurists have always decided that the right of visitation is absolute and positive, and inures to every Mason in his travels throughout the world. See this subject discussed in its fullest extent in the author's *Text Book of Masonic Jurisprudence*, pp. 203–216.

Vitra. The representative deity of darkness in Vedic mythology, and the antagonist of Indra, as the personified light. Vitra also represents ignorance, superstition, fanaticism, and intolerance, the opponents of Masonry.

Vivat. "Vivat! vivat! vivat!" is the acclamation which accompanies the honors in the French Rite. Bazot (*Manuel*, p. 165) says it is "the cry of joy of Freemasons of the French Rite." *Vivat* is a Latin word, and signifies, literally, "May he live"; but it has been domiciliated in French, and Boiste (*Dictionnaire Universel*) defines it as "a cry of applause which expresses the wish for the preservation of any one." The French Masons say, "He was received with the triple vivat," to denote that "He was received with the highest honors of the Lodge."

Vogel, Paul Joachim Sigismund. A distinguished Masonic writer of Germany, who was born in 1753. He was at one time corector of the Sebastian School at Altdorf, and afterward First Professor of Theology and Ecclesiastical Counselor at Erlangen. In 1785 he published at Nuremberg, in three volumes, his *Briefe die Freimaurerei betreffend;* or, "Letters concerning Freemasonry." The first volume treats of the Knights Templar; the second, of the Ancient Mysteries; and the third, of Freemasonry. This was, says Kloss, the first earnest attempt made in Germany to trace Freemasonry to a true, historical origin. Vogel's theory was, that the Speculative Freemasons were derived from the Operative or Stone-Masons of the Middle Ages. The abundant documentary evidence that more recent researches have produced were then wanting, and the views of Vogel did not make that impression to which they were entitled. He has, however, the credit of having opened the way, after the Abbé Grandidier, for those who have followed him in the same field. He also delivered before the Lodges of Nuremberg, several *Discourses on the Design, Character, and Origin of Freemasonry*, which were published in one volume, at Berlin, in 1791.

Voigt, Friederich. A Doctor of Medicine, and Professor and Senator at Dresden. He was a member of the high degrees of the Rite of Strict Observance, where his Order name was *Eques à Falcone*, or Knight of the Falcon. In 1788 he attacked Starck's Rite of the Clerks of Strict Observance, and published an essay on the subject, in the year 1788, in the *Acta Historico-Ecclesiastica* of Weimar. Voigt exposed the Roman Catholic tendencies of the new system, and averred that its object was "to cite and command spirits, to find the philosopher's stone, and to establish the reign of the millennium." His development of the Kabbalistic character of the Rite made a deep impression on the Masonic world, and was one of the most effective attacks upon it made by its antagonists of the old Strict Observance.

Voishnuvus. Those who worship Vishnu, in white garments, and abstain from animal food. Believers in the third member of the Trimurti according to Hindu mythology, in him who was believed to be the preserver of the world, and who had undergone ten Avatars or incarnations, to wit, a bird, tortoise, wild boar, andro-lion, etc., of which the deity Krishna was the eighth incarnation in this line of Vishnu, and in which form he was supposed to be the son of Devanaguy and reared by the shepherd Nanda.

Voltaire. (*François-Marie Arouet.*) One of the most famous of French writers, born at Châtenay, near Sceaux, in 1694. His early life was loose and varied. In 1728 he became infatuated with a Madame du Chatelet. His literary works cover some 90 volumes. In 1743, the French government despatched him on a mission to Frederick the Great, by whom he was held in high favor, and in 1750, at the request of the king, he made his residence in Berlin, but five years later they quarreled, and Voltaire moved to Ferney, Switzerland. His literary talent was most varied, and in invective he had no equal. During his exile in England he imbibed Deistical theories, which marked his life. He was charged with atheism. He was initiated in the Lodge of the Nine Sisters, at Paris, February 7, 1778, in the presence of Benjamin Franklin and others distinguished in Masonry. His death, on May 30, 1778, gave rise to a memorable Lodge of Sorrow, which was held on the succeeding 28th of November.

Voting. Voting in Lodges *viva voce*, or by "aye" and "nay," is a modern innovation in America. During the Grand Mastership of the Earl of Loudoun, on April 6, 1736, the Grand Lodge of England, on the motion of Deputy Grand Master Ward, adopted "a new regulation of ten rules for explaining what concerned the decency of assemblies and communications." The tenth of these rules is in the following words:

"The opinions or votes of the members are always to be signified by each holding up one of his hands; which uplifted hands the Grand Wardens are to count, unless the number of hands be so unequal as to render the counting useless. Nor should any other kind of division be ever admitted among Masons." (*Constitutions*, 1738, p. 178.)

The usual mode of putting the question is for the presiding officer to say: "So many as are in favor will signify the same by the usual sign of the Order," and then, when those votes have been counted, to say: "So many as are of a contrary opinion will signify the same by the same sign." The votes are now counted by the Senior Deacon in a subordinate Lodge, and by the Senior Grand Deacon in a Grand Lodge, it having been found inconvenient for the Grand Wardens to perform that duty. The number of votes on each side is communicated by the Deacon to the presiding officer, who announces the result.

The same method of voting should be observed in all Masonic bodies.

Voting, Right of. Formerly, all members of the Craft, even Entered Apprentices, were permitted to vote. This was distinctly prescribed in the last of the Thirty-nine General Regulations adopted in 1721. (*Constitutions*, 1723, p. 70.) But the numerical strength of the Order, which was then in the First Degree, having now passed over to the Third, the modern rule in America (but not in England) is that the right of voting shall be restricted to Master Masons. A Master Mason may, therefore, speak and vote on all questions, except in trials where he is himself concerned as accuser or defendant. Yet by special regulation of his Lodge he may be prevented from voting on ordinary questions where his dues for a certain period—generally twelve months—have not been paid; and such a regulation exists in almost every Lodge. But no local by-law can deprive a member, who has not been suspended, from voting on the ballot for the admission of candidates, because the sixth regulation of 1721 distinctly requires that each member present on such occasion shall give his consent before the candidate can be admitted. (*Ibid.*, p. 59.) And if a member were deprived by any by-law of the Lodge, in consequence of non-payment of his dues, of the right of expressing his consent or dissent, the ancient regulation would be violated, and a candidate might be admitted without the unanimous consent of all the members present. And this rule is so rigidly enforced, that on a ballot for initiation no member can be excused from voting. He must assume the responsibility of casting his vote, lest it should afterward be said that the candidate was not admitted by unanimous consent.

Vouching. It is a rule in Masonry, that a Lodge may dispense with the examination of a visitor, if any brother present will vouch that he possesses the necessary qualifications. This is an important prerogative that every Mason is entitled to exercise; and yet it is one which may so materially affect the well-being of the whole Fraternity, since, by its injudicious use, impostors might be introduced among the faithful, that it should be controlled by the most stringent regulations.

To vouch for one is to bear witness for him, and in witnessing to truth, every caution should be observed, lest falsehood may cunningly assume its garb. The brother who vouches should know to a certainty that the one for whom he vouches is really what he claims to be. He should know this, not from a casual conversation, nor a loose and careless inquiry, but from "*strict trial, due examination, or lawful information.*" These are the three requisites which the ritual has laid down as essentially necessary to authorize the act of vouching. Let us inquire into the import of each.

1. *Strict Trial.* By this is meant that every question is to be asked, and every answer demanded, which is necessary to convince the examiner that the party examined is acquainted with what he ought to know, to entitle him to the appellation of a brother. Nothing is to be taken for granted—categorical answers must be returned to all that it is deemed important to be asked; no forgetfulness is to be excused; nor is the want of memory to be considered as a valid reason for the want of knowledge. The Mason who is so unmindful of his obligations as to have forgotten the instructions he has received, must pay the penalty of his carelessness, and be deprived of his contemplated visit to that society whose secret modes of recognition he has so little valued as not to have treasured them in his memory. The "strict trial" refers to the matter which is sought to be obtained by inquiry; and while there are some things which may safely be passed over in the investigation of one who confesses himself to be "rusty," because they are details which require much study to acquire and constant practise to retain, there are still other things of great importance which must be rigidly demanded.

2. *Due Examination.* If "strict trial" refers to the *matter*, "due examination" alludes to the *mode* of investigation. This must be conducted with all the necessary forms and antecedent cautions. Inquiries should be made as to the time and place of initiation as a preliminary step, the Tiler's OB. of course never being omitted. Then the good old rule of "commencing at the beginning" should be pursued. Let everything go on in regular course; not is it to be supposed that the information sought was originally received. Whatever be the suspicions of imposture, let no expression of those suspicions be made until the final decree for rejection is uttered. And let that decree be uttered in general terms, such as, "I am not satisfied," or "I do not recognize you," and not in more specific language, such as, "You did not answer this inquiry," or "You are ignorant on that point." The candidate for examination is only entitled to know that he has not complied generally with the requisitions of his examiner. To descend to particulars is always improper, and often dangerous. Above all, never ask what the lawyers call "leading questions," which include in themselves the answer, nor in any way aid the memory, or prompt the forgetfulness of the party examined, by the slightest hints.

3. *Lawful Information.* This authority for vouching is dependent on what has been already described. For no Mason can lawfully give information of another's qualifications unless he has himself actually tested him. But it is not every Mason who is competent to give "lawful information." Ignorant or unskilful brethren cannot do so, because they are incapable of discovering truth or of detecting error. A "rusty Mason" should never attempt to examine a stranger, and certainly, if he does, his opinion as to the result is worth nothing.

if the information given is on the ground that the party who is vouched for has been seen sitting in a Lodge, care must be taken to inquire if it was a "just and legally constituted Lodge of Master Masons." A person may forget from the lapse of time, and vouch for a stranger as a Master Mason, when the Lodge in which he saw him was only opened in the First or Second Degree. Information given by letter, or through a third party, is irregular. The person giving the information, the one receiving it, and the one of whom it is given, should all be present at the time, for otherwise there would be no certainty of identity. The information must be positive, not founded on belief or opinion, but derived from a legitimate source. And, lastly, it must not have been received casually, but for the very purpose of being used for Masonic purposes. For one to say to another, in the course of a desultory conversation, "A. B. is a Mason," is not sufficient. He may not be speaking with due caution, under the expectation that his words will be considered of weight. He must say something to this effect, "I know this man to be a Master Mason, for such or such reasons, and you may safely recognise him as such." This alone will insure the necessary care and proper observance of prudence.

Lastly, never should an unjustifiable delicacy weaken the rigor of these rules. For the wisest and most evident reasons, that merciful maxim of the law, which says that it is better that ninety-nine guilty men should escape than that one innocent man should be punished, is with us reversed; so that in Masonry *it is better that ninety and nine true men should be turned away from the door of a Lodge, than that one cowan should be admitted.*

Voyages. The French Masons thus call some of the proofs and trials to which a candidate is subjected in the course of initiation into any of the degrees. In the French Rite, the voyages in the Symbolic degrees are three in the first, five in the second, and seven in the third. Their symbolic designs are thus briefly explained by Ragon (*Cours des Init.*, pp. 90, 132) and Lenoir (*La Franche-Maçonnerie*, p. 263): The voyages of the Entered Apprentice are now, as they were in the Ancient Mysteries, the symbol of the life of man. Those of the Fellow-Craft are emblematic of labor in search of knowledge. Those of the Master Mason are symbolic of the pursuit of crime, the wandering life of the criminal, and his vain attempts to escape remorse and punishment. It will be evident that the ceremonies in all the Rites of Masonry, although under a different name, lead to the same symbolic results.

W

W. The twenty-third letter of the English alphabet, which originated in the Middle Ages, is a double *v*, and is peculiar to the English, German, and Dutch alphabets.

W.·. An abbreviation of *Worshipful*, of *West*, of *Warden*, and of *Wisdom*.

Waechter, Eberhard, Baron Von. Lord of the Chamber to the King of Denmark, and Danish Ambassador at Ratisbon; was born in 1747. He was at one time a very active member of the Rite of Strict Observance, where he bore the characteristic name of *Eques à ceraso*, and had been appointed Chancellor of the German Priories of the 7th Province. When the spiritual schism of the Order made its vast pretensions to a secret authority derived from unknown superiors, whose names they refused to divulge, Von Waechter was sent to Italy by the old Scottish Lodge of which Duke Ferdinand was Grand Master, that he might obtain some information from the Pretender, and from other sources, as to the true character of the Rite. Von Waechter was unsuccessful, and the intelligence which he brought back to Germany was unfavorable to Von Hund, and increased the embarrassments of the Strict Observance Lodges. But he himself lost reputation. A host of enemies attacked him. Some declared that while in Italy he had made a traffic of Masonry to enrich himself; others that he had learned and was practising magic; and others again that he had secretly attached himself to the Jesuits. Von Waechter stoutly denied these charges; but it is certain that, from being in very moderate circumstances, he had, after his return from Italy, become suddenly and unaccountably rich. Yet Mossdorf says that he discharged his mission with great delicacy and judgment. Thory, quoting the *Beytrag zur neuesten Geschichte* (p. 150), says that in 1782 he proposed to give a new organisation to the Templar system of Masonry, on the ruins, perhaps, of both branches of the Strict Observance, and declared that he possessed the true secrets of the Order. His proposition for a reform was not accepted by the German Masons, because they suspected that he was an agent of the Jesuits. (*Acta Lat.*, i., 152.) Kloss (*Bibliog.*, No. 622b) gives the title of a work published by him in 1822 as *Worte der Wahrheit an die Menschen, meine Brüder*. He died May 25, 1825, one, perhaps, of the last actors in the great Masonic drama of the Strict Observance.

Wages of a Master Mason, Symbolic. See *Foreign Country.*

Wages of Operative Masons. In all the Old Constitutions praise is given to St. Alban because he raised the wages of the Masons. Thus the Edinburgh-Kilwinning MS. says: "St. Albans loved Masons well, and cherished them much, and made their pay right good, standing by as the realme did, for he gave them iis. a week, and 3*d.* to their cheer; for before that time, through all the land, a Mason had but a penny a day and his meat, until St. Alban amended it." We may compare this rate of wages in the third century with that of the fifteenth, and we will be surprised at the little advance that was made. In Grosse and Astle's *Antiquarian Repertory* (iii., p. 58) will be found an extract from the Roles of Parliament, which contains a petition, in the year 1443, to Parliament to regulate the price of labor. In it are the following items: "And y^t^ from the Fest of Ester unto Mighelmasse ye wages of eny free Mason or maister carpenter exceed not by the day iiii*d.*, with mete and drynk, and withoute mete and drink v*d.*, ob.

"A Maister Tyler or Sclatter, rough mason and meen carpenter, and other artificers concernyng beldyng, by the day iii*d.*, with mete and drynk, and withoute mete and drynke, iii*d.*, ob.

"And from the Fest of Mighelmasse unto Ester, a free Mason and a maister carpenter by the day iii*d.*, with mete and drynk, withoute mete and drink, iii*d.*, ob.

"Tyler, meen carpenter, rough mason, and other artificers aforesaid, by the day ii*d.*, ob, with mete and drynk, withoute mete and drynk iiii*d.*, and every other werkeman and laborer by the day i*d.*, ob, with mete and drynk, and withoute mete and drink iii*d.*, and who that lasse deserveth, to take lasse."

Wages of the Workmen at the Temple. Neither the Scriptures, nor Josephus, give us any definite statement of the amount of wages paid, nor the manner in which they were paid, to the workmen who were engaged in the erection of King Solomon's Temple. The cost of its construction, however, must have been immense, since it has been estimated that the edifice alone consumed more gold and silver than at present exists upon the whole earth; so that Josephus very justly says that "Solomon made all these things for the honor of God, with great variety and magnificence, sparing no cost, but using all possible liberality in adorning the Temple." We learn, as one instance of this liberality, from the 2d Book of Chronicles, that Solomon paid annually to the Tyrian Masons, the servants of Hiram, "twenty thousand measures of beaten wheat, and twenty thousand measures of barley, and twenty thousand baths of wine, and twenty thousand baths of oil." The *bath* was a measure equal to seven and a half gallons wine measure; and the *cor* or *chomer*, which we translate by the indefinite word *measure*, contained ten baths; so that the corn, wine, and oil furnished by King Solomon, as wages to the servants of Hiram of Tyre, amounted to one hundred and ninety thousand bushels of the first, and one hundred and fifty thousand gallons each of the second and third. The sacred records do not inform us what further wages they received, but we elsewhere learn that King Solomon gave them as a free gift a sum equal to more than thirty-two millions of dollars. The whole amount of wages paid to the craft is stated to have been about six hundred and seventy-two millions of dollars; but we have no means of knowing how that amount was distributed; though it is natural to suppose that those of the most skill and experience received the highest wages. The Harodim, or chiefs of the workmen, must have been better paid than the Ish Sabal, or mere laborers.

The legend-makers of Masonry have not been idle in their invention of facts and circumstances in relation to this subject, the whole of which have little more for a foundation than the imaginations of the inventors. They form, however, a part of the legendary history of Masonry, and are interesting for their ingenuity, and sometimes even for their absurdity.

Wahabites. A Mohammedan sect, established about 1740, dominant through the greater part of Arabia. Their doctrine was reformatory, to bring back the observances of Islam to the literal precepts of the Koran. Mecca and Medina were conquered by them. The founder was Ibn-abd-ul-Wahab, son of an Arab sheik, born in the latter part of the seventeenth century, and died 1787. Their teachings have been received by the Musulman population of India, and much uneasiness is feared therefrom.

Wales. The earliest Lodges in Wales were two at Chester and one at Congleton, all three established in 1724, and Dr. Anderson records that Grand Master Inchiquin granted a Deputation, May 10, 1727, to Hugh Warburton, Esq., to be Provincial Grand Master of North Wales, and another, June 24th in the same year, to Sir Edward Mansel, to be Provincial Grand Master of South Wales. (*Constitutions,* 1738, p. 191.) Wales forms a part of the Masonic obedience of the Grand Lodge of England, and the Fraternity there are directly governed by four Provincial Grand Lodges, viz., North Wales with 21 Lodges; Shropshire with 13; South Wales (Eastern Division) with 27; and South Wales (Western Division) with 12.

Wallachia, Grand Scottish Degree of. Found in Fustier's lists.

Wands. Oliver, under this title in his *Dictionary*, refers to the three scepters which, in the Royal Arch system of England, are placed in a triangular form beneath the canopy in the East, and which, being surmounted respectively by a crown, an All-seeing eye, and a miter, refer to the regal, the prophetical, and the sacerdotal offices. In his *Landmarks* he calls them *scepters.* But *rod* or *wand* is the better word, because, while the *scepter* is restricted to the insignia of kings, the *rod* or *wand* was and still is used as an indiscriminate mark of authority for all offices.

Wardens. In every Symbolic Lodge, there are three principal officers, namely, a Master, a Senior Warden, and a Junior Warden. This rule has existed ever since the revival, and for some time previous to that event, and is so universal that it has been considered as one of the landmarks. It exists in every country and in every Rite. The titles of the officers may be different in different languages, but their functions, as presiding over the Lodge in a tripartite division of duties, are everywhere the same. The German Masons call the two Wardens *erste* and *zweite Aufseher;* the French, *premier* and *second Surveillant;* the Spanish, *primer* and *segundo Vigilante;* and the Italians, *primo* and *secondo Sorvegliante.*

In different Rites, the positions of these officers vary. In the American Rite, the Senior Warden sits in the West and the Junior in the South. In the French and Scottish Rites, both Wardens are in the West, the Senior in the Northwest and the Junior in the Southwest; but in all, the triangular position of the three officers relatively to each other is preserved; for a triangle being formed within the square of the Lodge, the Master and Wardens will each occupy one of the three points.

The precise time when the presidency of the Lodge was divided between these three officers, or when they were first introduced into Masonry, is unknown. The Lodges of Scotland, during the Operative *régime,* were governed by a Deacon and one Warden. The Earl of Cassilis was Master of Kilwinning in 1670, though only an Apprentice. This seems to have been not unusual, as there were cases of Apprentices presiding over Lodges. The Deacon performed the functions of a Master, and the Warden was the second officer, and took charge of and distributed the funds. In other words, he acted as a Treasurer. This is evident from the minutes of the Edinburgh Lodge, recently published by Bro. Lyon. But the head of the Craft in Scotland at the same time was called the Warden General. This regulation, however, does not appear to have been universal even in Scotland, for in the "Mark Book" of the Aberdeen Lodge, under date of December 27, 1670, which was published by Bro. W. J. Hughan in the *Voice of Masonry* (February, 1872), we find there a Master and Warden recognised as the presiding officers of the Lodge in the following statute: "And lykwayse we all protest, by the oath we have made at our entrie, to own the Warden of our Lodge as the next man in power to the Maister, and in the Maister's absence he is full Maister."

Some of the English manuscript Constitutions recognise the offices of Master and Wardens. Thus the Harleian MS., No. 1942, whose date is supposed to be about 1670, contains the "new articles" said to have been agreed on at a General Assembly held in 1663, in which is the following passage: "That for the future the sayd Society, Company and Fraternity of Free Masons shal bee regulated and governed by one Master & Assembly & Wardens, as ye said Company shall think fit to chose, at every yearely General Assembly."

As the word "Warden" does not appear in the earlier manuscripts, it might be concluded that the office was not introduced into the English Lodges until the latter part of the seventeenth century. Yet this does not absolutely follow. For the office of Warden might have existed, and no statutory provision on the subject have been embraced in the general charges which are contained in those manuscripts, because they relate not to the government of Lodges, but the duties of Masons. This, of course, is conjectural; but the conjecture derives weight from the fact that Wardens were officers of the English gilds as early as the fourteenth century. In the Charters granted by Edward III., in 1354, it is permitted that these companies shall yearly elect for their government "a certain number of Wardens." To a list of the companies of the date of 1377 is affixed what is called the "Oath of the Wardens of Crafts," of which this is the commencement: "Ye shall swere that ye shall wele and treuly oversee the Craft of ——— whereof ye be choosen Wardeyns for the year." It thus appears that the Wardens were at first the presiding officers of the gilds. At a later period, in the reign of Elizabeth, we find that the chief officer began to be called Master; and in the time of James I., between 1603 and 1625, the gilds were generally governed by a Master and Wardens. An ordinance of the Leather-Sellers Company at that time directed that on a certain occasion "the Master and Wardens shall appear in state." It is not, therefore, improbable that the government of Masonic Lodges by a Master and two Wardens was introduced into the regulations of the Order in the seventeenth century, the "new article" of 1663 being a statutory confirmation of a custom which had just begun to prevail.

Senior Warden. He is the second officer in a Symbolic Lodge, and governs the craft in the hours of labor. In the absence of the Master he presides over the Lodge, appointing some brother, not the Junior Warden, to occupy his place in the west. His jewel is a level, a symbol of the equality which exists among the Craft while at labor in the Lodge. His seat is in the west, and he represents the column of Strength. He has placed before him, and carries in all processions, a column, which is the representative of the right-hand pillar that stood at the porch of King Solomon's Temple. The Junior Warden has a similar column, which represents the left-hand pillar. During labor the column of the Senior Warden is erect in the Lodge, while that of the Junior is recumbent. At refreshment, the position of the two columns is reversed.

Junior Warden. The duties of this officer have already been described. (See *Junior Warden.*)

There is also an officer in a Commandery of Knights Templar, the fifth in rank, who is styled "Senior Warden." He takes an important part in the initiation of a candidate. His jewel of office is a triple triangle, the emblem of Deity.

Wardens, Grand. See *Grand Wardens.*

Warder. The literal meaning of Warder is one who keeps watch and ward. In the Middle Ages, the Warder was stationed at the gate or on the battlements of the castle, and with his trumpet sounded alarms and announced the approach of all comers. Hence the Warder in a Commandery of Knights Templar bears a trumpet, and his duties are prescribed to be to announce the approach and departure of the Eminent Commander, to post the sentinels, and see that the Asylum is duly guarded, as well as to announce the approach of visitors. His jewel is a trumpet and crossed swords engraved on a square plate.

Warlike Instrument. In the ancient initiations, the aspirant was never permitted to enter on the threshold of the Temple in which the ceremonies were conducted until, by the most solemn warning, he had been impressed with the necessity of secrecy and caution. The use, for this purpose, of a "warlike instrument" in the First Degree of Masonry, is intended to produce the same effect. A sword has always been employed for that purpose; and the substitute of the point of the compasses, taken from the altar at the time, is an absurd sacrifice of symbolism to the convenience of the Senior Deacon. The compasses are peculiar to the Third Degree. In the earliest rituals of the last century it is said that the entrance is "upon the point of a sword, or spear, or some warlike instrument." Krause (*Kunsturk.*, ii., 142), in commenting on this expression, has completely misinterpreted its signification. He supposes that the sword was intended as a sign of jurisdiction now assumed by the Lodge. But the real object of the ceremony is to teach the neophyte that as the sword or warlike instrument will wound or prick the flesh, so will the betrayal of a trust confided wound or prick the conscience of him who betrays it.

War, Masonry in. The question how Masons should conduct themselves in time of war, when their own country is one of the belligerents, is an important one. Of the political course of a Mason in his individual and private capacity there is no doubt. The Charges declare that he must be "a peaceable subject to the civil powers, and never be concerned in plots and conspiracies against the peace and welfare of the nation." (*Constitutions*, 1723, p. 50.) But so anxious is the Order to be unembarrassed by all political influences, that treason, however discountenanced by the Craft, is not held as a crime which is amenable to Masonic punishment. For the same charge affirms that "if a brother should be a rebel against the State, he is not to be countenanced in his rebellion, however he may be pitied as an unhappy man; and if convicted of no other crime, though the loyal brotherhood must and ought to disown his rebellion and give no umbrage or ground of political jealousy to the government for the time being, they cannot expel him from the Lodge, and his relation to it remains indefeasible."

The Mason, then, like every other citizen, should be a patriot. He should love his country with all his heart; should serve it faithfully and cheerfully; obey its laws in peace; and in war should be ever ready to support its honor and defend it from the attacks of its enemies. But even then the benign principles of the Institution extend their influence, and divest the contest of many of its horrors. The Mason fights, of course, like every other man, for victory; but when the victory is won, he will remember that the conquered foe is still his brother.

On the occasion, many years ago, of a Masonic banquet given immediately after the close of the Mexican War to General Quitman by the Grand Lodge of South Carolina, that distinguished soldier and Mason remarked that, although he had devoted much of his attention to the nature and character of the Masonic institution, and had repeatedly held the highest offices in the gift of his brethren, he had never really known what Masonry was until he had seen its workings on the field of battle.

But as a collective and organized body—in its Lodges and its Grand Lodges—it must have nothing to do with war. It must be silent and neutral. The din of the battle, the cry for vengeance, the shout of victory, must never penetrate its portals. Its dogmas and doctrines all teach love and fraternity; its symbols are symbols of peace; and it has no place in any of its rituals consecrated to the inculcation of human contention.

Bro. C. W. Moore, in his *Biography of Thomas Smith Webb*, the great American ritualist, mentions a circumstance which occurred during the period in which Webb presided over the Grand Lodge of Rhode Island, and to which Moore, I think, inconsiderately has given his hearty commendation.

The United States was at that time engaged in a war with England. The people of Providence having commenced the erection of fortifications, the Grand Lodge volunteered its services; and the members, marching in procession as a Grand Lodge to the southern part of the town, erected a breastwork, to which was given the name of Fort Hiram. (See *Fort Masonic.*) I doubt the propriety of the act. While (to repeat what has been just said) every individual member of the Grand Lodge, as a Mason, was bound by his obligation to be "true to his government," and to defend it from the attacks of its enemies, it was, I think, unseemly, and contrary to the peaceful spirit of the Institution, for any organized body of Masons, organized as such, to engage in a warlike enterprise. But the patriotism, if not the prudence of the Grand Lodge, cannot be denied.

Since writing this paragraph, I have met in Bro. Murray Lyon's *History of the Lodge of Edinburgh* (p. 83) with a record of the Grand Lodge of Scotland, a century ago, which sustains the view that I have taken. In 1777, recruits were being enlisted in Scotland for the British army, which was to fight the Americans in the war of the Revolution, which had just begun. Many of the Scotch Lodges offered, through the newspapers, bounties to all who should enlist. But on February 2, 1778, the Grand Lodge passed a resolution, which was published on the 12th, through the Grand Secretary, in the following circular:

"At a quarterly meeting of the Grand Lodge of Scotland, held here the second instant, I received a charge to acquaint all the Lodges of Scotland holding of the Grand Lodge that the Grand Lodge has seen with concern advertisements in the public newspapers, from different Lodges in Scotland, not only offering a bounty to recruits who may enlist in the new levies, but with the addition that all such recruits shall be admitted to the freedom of Masonry. The first of these they consider as an improper alienation of the funds of the Lodge from the support of their poor and distressed brethren; and the second they regard as a prostitution of our Order, which demands the reprehension of the Grand Lodge. Whatever share the brethren may take as individuals in aiding these levies, out of zeal to serve their private friends or to promote the public service, the Grand Lodge considered it to be repugnant to the spirit of our Craft that any Lodge should take a part in such a business as a collective body. For Masonry is an Order of Peace, and it looks on all mankind to be brethren as Masons, whether they be at peace or at war with each other as subjects of contending countries. The Grand Lodge therefore strongly enjoins that the practice may be forthwith discontinued. By order of the Grand Lodge of Scotland. W. Mason, Gr. Sec."

Of all human institutions, Freemasonry is the greatest and purest Peace Society. And this is because its doctrine of universal peace is founded on the doctrine of a universal brotherhood.

Warrant of Constitution. The document which authorizes or gives a Warrant to certain persons therein named to organize and constitute a Lodge, Chapter, or other Masonic body, and which ends usually with the formula, "for which this shall be your sufficient warrant."

The practise of granting Warrants for the constitution of Lodges, dates only from the period of the revival of Masonry in 1717. Previous to that period "a sufficient number of brethren," says Preston (*Illustrations*, ed. 1792, p. 248), "met together within a certain district, had ample power to make Masons, and discharge every duty of Masonry without a Warrant of Constitution." But in 1717 a regulation was adopted "that the privilege of assembling as Masons, which had been hitherto unlimited, should be vested in certain Lodges or assemblies of Masons convened in certain places; and that every Lodge to be hereafter convened, except the four old Lodges at this time existing, should be legally authorized to act by a Warrant from the Grand Master, for the time being, granted to certain individuals by petition, with the consent and approbation of the Grand Lodge in communication; and that without such Warrant no Lodge should be hereafter deemed regular or constitutional." And consequently, ever since the adoption of that regulation, no Lodge has been regular unless it is working under such an authority. The word Warrant is appropriately used, because in its legal acceptation it means a document giving authority to perform some specified act.

In England, the Warrant of Constitution emanates from the Grand Master; in the United States, from the Grand Lodge. In America, the Grand Master grants only a Dispensation to hold a Lodge, which may be revoked or confirmed by the Grand Lodge; in the latter case, the Warrant will then be issued. The Warrant of Constitution is granted to the Master and Wardens, and to their successors in office; it continues in force only during the pleasure of the Grand Lodge, and may, therefore, at any time be revoked, and the Lodge dissolved by a vote of that body, or it may be temporarily arrested or suspended by an edict of the Grand Master. This will, however, never be done, unless the Lodge has violated the ancient landmarks, or failed to pay due respect and obedience to the Grand Lodge or to the Grand Master. At the formation of the first Lodges in a number of the States in the South and Middle West, the Grand Lodges of other States granted both Dispensation and Charter.

When a Warrant of Constitution is revoked or recalled, the jewels, furniture, and funds of the Lodge revert to the Grand Lodge.

Lastly, as a Lodge holds its communications only under the authority of this Warrant of Constitution, no Lodge can be opened, or proceed to business, unless it be present. If it be mislaid or destroyed, it must be recovered, or another obtained; and until that is done, the communications of the Lodge must be suspended; and if the Warrant of Constitution be taken out of the room during the session of the Lodge, the authority of the Master instantly ceases.

Washing Hands. See *Lustration*.

Washington. Freemasonry in an organized form was introduced into Washington by the Grand Lodge of Oregon, which established four Lodges there previous to the year 1858. These Lodges were Olympia, No. 5; Steilacoom, No. 8; Grand Mound, No. 21, and Washington, No. 22. On December 6–9, 1858, delegates from these four Lodges met in convention at the city of Olympia, and organised the Grand Lodge of Free and Accepted Masons of the Territory of Washington. T. F. McElroy was elected Grand Master, and T. M. Reed, Grand Secretary.

In 1872 the Ancient and Accepted Scottish Rite was introduced by Bro. Edwin A. Sherman, the agent of the Supreme Council of the Southern Jurisdiction, and several bodies of that Rite were organized. The Grand Chapter of Washington was organized in 1884; and the Grand Commandery of Knights Templar in 1887.

Washington, Congress of. A Congress of American Masons was convoked at the city of Washington, in the year 1822, at the call of several Grand Lodges, for the purpose of recommending the establishment of a General Grand Lodge of the United States. The result was an unsuccessful one.

Washington, George. The name of Washington claims a place in Masonic biography, not because of any services he has done to the Institution either as a worker or a writer, but because the fact of his connection with the Craft is a source of pride to every American Mason, at least, who can thus call the "Father of his Country" a brother. There is also another reason. While the friends of the Institution have felt that the adhesion to it of a man so eminent for virtue was a proof of its moral and religious character, the opponents of Masonry, being forced to admit the conclusion, have sought to deny the premises, and, even if compelled to admit the fact of Washington's initiation, have persistently asserted that he never took any interest in it, disapproved of its spirit, and at an early period of his life abandoned it. The truth of history requires that these misstatements should be met by a brief recital of his Masonic career.

Washington was initiated, in 1752, in the Lodge at Fredericksburg, Virginia, and the records of that Lodge, still in existence, present the following entries on the subject. The first entry is thus:

"Nov. 4th, 1752. This evening Mr. George Washington was initiated as an Entered Apprentice"; and the receipt of the entrance fee, amounting to £2 3s., is acknowledged.

On the 3d of March in the following year, "Mr. George Washington" is recorded as having been passed a Fellow-Craft; and on the 4th of the succeeding August, the record of the transactions of the evening states that "Mr. George Washington," and others whose names are mentioned, have been raised to the sublime degree of Master Mason.

For five years after his initiation, he was engaged in active military service, and it is not likely that during that period his attendance on the communications of the Lodge could have been frequent. Some English writers have asserted that he was made a Mason during the old French War, in a military Lodge attached to the 46th Regiment. The Bible on which he is said to have been obligated is still in existence, although the Lodge was many years ago dissolved, at Halifax, Nova Scotia. The records of the Lodge are, or were, not long since, extant, and furnish the evidence that Washington was there, and received some Masonic degree. It is equally clear that he was first initiated in Fredericksburg Lodge, for the record is still in possession of the Lodge.

Three methods have been adopted to reconcile this apparent discrepancy. Bro. Hayden, in his work on *Washington and his Masonic Compeers* (p. 31), suggests that an obligation had been administered to him as a test-oath when visiting the Lodge, or that the Lodge, deeming the authority under which he had been made insufficient, had required him to be healed and reobligated. Neither of these attempts to solve the difficulty appears to have any plausibility.

Bro. C. W. Moore, of Massachusetts, in the *Freemasons' Monthly Magazine* (vol. xi., p. 261), suggests that, as it was then the custom to confer the Mark Degree as a side degree in Masters' Lodges, and as it has been proved that Washington was in possession of that degree, he may have received it in Lodge No. 227, attached to the 46th Regiment. This certainly presents a more satisfactory explanation than either of those offered by Bro. Hayden.

The connection of Washington with the British military Lodge will serve as some confirmation of the tradition that he was attentive to Masonic duties during the five years from 1753 to 1758, when he was engaged in military service.

There is ample evidence that during the Revolutionary War, while he was Commander-in-Chief of the American armies, he was a frequent attendant on the meetings of military Lodges. Some years ago, Captain Hugh Maloy, a revolutionary veteran, then residing in Ohio, declared that on one of these occasions he was initiated in Washington's marquée, the chief himself presiding at the ceremony. Bro. Scott, a Past Grand Master of Virginia, asserted that Washington was in frequent attendance on the communications of the brethren. The proposition made to elect him a Grand Master of the United States, as will be hereafter seen, affords a strong presumption that his name as a Mason had become familiar to the Craft.

In 1777, the Convention of Virginia Lodges recommended Washington as the most proper person to be elected Grand Master of the Independent Grand Lodge of that commonwealth. Dove has given in his *Text-Book* the complete records of the Convention; and there is therefore no doubt that the nomination was made. It was, however, declined by Washington.

Soon after the beginning of the Revolution, a disposition was manifested among American Masons to dissever their connection, as subordinates, with the Masonic authorities of the mother country, and in several of the newly erected States the Provincial

G

Grand Lodges assumed an independent character. The idea of a Grand Master of the whole of the United States had also become popular. On February 7, 1780, a convention of delegates from the military Lodges in the army was held at Morristown, in New Jersey, when an address to the Grand Masters in the various States was adopted, recommending the establishment of "one Grand Lodge in America," and the election of a Grand Master. This address was sent to the Grand Lodges of Massachusetts, Pennsylvania and Virginia; and although the name of Washington is not mentioned in it, those Grand Lodges were notified that he was the first choice of the brethren who had framed it.

While these proceedings were in progress, the Grand Lodge of Pennsylvania had taken action on the same subject. On January 13, 1780, it had held a session, and it was unanimously declared that it was for the benefit of Masonry that "a Grand Master of Masons throughout the United States" should be nominated; whereupon, with equal unanimity, General Washington was elected to the office. It was then ordered that the minutes of the election be transmitted to the different Grand Lodges in the United States, and their concurrence therein be requested. The Grand Lodge of Massachusetts, doubting the expediency of electing a General Grand Master, declined to come to any determination on the question, and so the subject was dropped.

This will correct the error into which many foreign Grand Lodges and Masonic writers have fallen, of supposing that Washington was ever a Grand Master of the United States. The error was strengthened by a medal contained in Mersdorf's *Medals of the Fraternity of Freemasons*, which the editor states was struck by the Lodges of Pennsylvania. This statement is, however, liable to great doubt. The date of the medal is 1797. On the obverse is a likeness of Washington, with the device, "Washington, President, 1797." On the reverse is a tracing-board and the device, "Amor, Honor, et Justitia. G. W., G. G. M." French and German Masonic historians have been deceived by this medal, and refer to it as their authority for asserting that Washington was a Grand Master. Lenning and Thory, for instance, place the date of his election to that office in the year in which the medal was struck. More recent European writers, however, directed by the researches of the American authorities, have discovered and corrected the mistake.

We next hear of Washington's official connection in the year 1788. Lodge No. 39, at Alexandria, which had hitherto been working under the Grand Lodge of Pennsylvania, in 1788 transferred its allegiance to Virginia. On May 29th in that year the Lodge adopted the following resolution:

"The Lodge proceeded to the appointment of Master and Deputy Master to be recommended to the Grand Lodge of Virginia, when George Washington, Esq., was unanimously chosen Master; Robert McCrea, Deputy Master; Wm. Hunter, Jr., Senior Warden; John Allison, Junior Warden."

It was also ordered that a committee should wait on General Washington, "and inquire of him whether it will be agreeable to him to be named in the Charter." What was the result of that interview, we do not positively know. But it is to be presumed that the reply of Washington was a favorable one, for the application for the Charter contained his name, which would hardly have been inserted if it had been repugnant to his wishes. And the Charter or Warrant under which the Lodge is still working is granted to Washington as Master. The appointing clause is in the following words:

"Know ye that we, Edmund Randolph, Esquire, Governor of the Commonwealth aforesaid, and Grand Master of the Most Ancient and Honorable Society of Freemasons within the same, by and with the consent of the Grand Lodge of Virginia, do hereby constitute and appoint our illustrious and well-beloved Brother, George Washington, Esquire, late General and Commander-in-Chief of the forces of the United States of America, and our worthy Brethren Robert McCrea, William Hunter, Jr., and John Allison, Esqs., together with all such other brethren as may be admitted to associate with them, to be a 'first, true, and regular Lodge of Freemasons, by the name, title, and designation of the Alexandria Lodge, No. 22.'" In 1805, the Lodge, which is still in existence, was permitted by the Grand Lodge to change its name to that of "Washington Alexandria," in honor of its first Master.

The evidence, then, is clear that Washington was the Master of a Lodge. Whether he ever assumed the duties of the office, and, if he assumed, how he discharged them, we know only from the testimony of Timothy Bigelow, who, in a Eulogy delivered before the Grand Lodge of Massachusetts, two months after Washington's death, and eleven after his appointment as Master, made the following statement:

"The information received from our brethren who had the happiness to be members of the Lodge over which he presided for many years, and of which he died the Master, furnishes abundant proof of his persevering zeal for the prosperity of the Institution. Constant and punctual in his attendance, scrupulous in his observance of the regulations of the Lodge, and solicitous, at all times, to communicate light and instruction, he discharged the duties of the Chair with uncommon dignity and intelligence in all the mysteries of our art."

There is also a very strong presumption that Washington accepted and discharged the duties of the Chair to the satisfaction of the Lodge. At the first election held after the Charter had been issued, he was elected, or we should rather say reelected, Master. The record of the Lodge, under the date of December 20, 1788, is as follows:

"His Excellency, General Washington, unanimously elected Master; Robert McCrea, Senior Warden; Wm. Hunter, Jr., Junior Warden; Wm. Hodgson, Treasurer; Joseph Greenway, Secretary; Dr. Frederick Spanbergen, Senior Deacon; George Richards, Junior Deacon." The subordinate officers had undergone a change: McCrea, who had been named in the petition as Deputy Master, an officer not recognized in this country, was made Senior Warden; Wm. Hunter, who had been nominated as Senior Warden, was made Junior Warden; and the original Junior Warden, John Allison, was dropped. But there was no change in the office of Master. Washington was again elected. The Lodge would scarcely have been so persistent without his consent; and if his consent was given, we know, from his character, that he would seek to discharge the duties of the office to his best abilities. This circumstance gives, if it be needed, strong confirmation to the statement of Bigelow.

But incidents like these are not all that are left to us to exhibit the attachment of Washington to Masonry. On repeated occasions he has announced, in his letters and addresses to various Masonic bodies, his profound esteem for the character, and his just appreciation of the principles, of that Institution into which, at so early an age, he had been admitted. And during his long and laborious life, no opportunity was presented of which he did not avail himself to evince his esteem for the Institution.

Thus, in the year 1797, in reply to an affectionate address from the Grand Lodge of Massachusetts, he says: "My attachment to the Society of which we are members will dispose me always to contribute my best endeavors to promote the honor and prosperity of the Craft."

Five years before this letter was written, he had, in a communication to the same body, expressed his opinion of the Masonic Institution as one whose liberal principles are founded on the immutable laws of "truth and justice," and whose "grand object is to promote the happiness of the human race."

In answer to an address from the Grand Lodge of South Carolina in 1791, he says: "I recognize with pleasure my relation to the brethren of your Society," and "I shall be happy, on every occasion, to evince my regard for the Fraternity." And in the same letter he takes occasion to allude to the Masonic Institution as "an association whose principles lead to purity of morals, and are beneficial of action."

In writing to the officers and members of St. David's Lodge at Newport (R. I.), in the same year, he uses this language: "Being persuaded that a just application of the principles on which the Masonic fraternity is founded must be promotive of private virtue and public prosperity, I shall always be happy to advance the interests of the Society, and to be considered by them as a deserving brother."

And lastly, for I will not further extend these citations, in a letter addressed in November, 1798, only thirteen months before his death, to the Grand Lodge of Maryland he has made this explicit declaration of his opinion of the Institution:

"So far as I am acquainted with the doctrines and principles of Freemasonry, I conceive them to be founded in benevolence, and to be exercised only for the good of mankind. I cannot, therefore, upon this ground, withdraw my approbation from it."

So much has been said upon the Masonic career and opinions of Washington because American Masons love to dwell on the fact that the distinguished patriot, whose memory is so revered that his unostentatious grave on the banks of the Potomac has become the Mecca of America, was not only a brother of the Craft, but was ever ready to express his good opinion of the Society. They feel that under the panoply of his great name they may defy the malignant charges of their adversaries. They know that no better reply can be given to such charges than to say, in the language of Clinton, "Washington would not have encouraged an Institution hostile to morality, religion, good order, and the public welfare."

Watchwords. Used in the Thirty-second Degree of the Ancient and Accepted Scottish Rite because that degree has a military form, but not found in other degrees of Masonry.

Waterfall. Used in the Fellow-Craft's Degree as a symbol of plenty, for which the word *waterford* is sometimes improperly substituted. (See *Shibboleth*.)

Wayfaring Man. A term used in the legend of the Third Degree to denote the person met near the port of Joppa by certain persons sent out on a search by King Solomon. The part of the legend which introduces the wayfaring man, and his interview with the Fellow-Crafts, was probably introduced into the American system by Webb, or found by him in the older rituals practised in this country. It is not in the old English rituals of the last century, nor is the circumstance detailed in the present English lecture. A wayfaring man is defined by Phillips as "one accustomed to travel on the road." The expression is becoming obsolete in ordinary language, but it is preserved in Scripture—"he saw a wayfaring man in the street of the city" (Judges xix. 17)—and in Masonry, both of which still retain many words long since disused elsewhere.

Weary Sojourners. Spoken of in the American legend of the Royal Arch as three of the captives who had been restored to liberty by Cyrus, and, after sojourning or remaining longer in Babylon than the main body of their brethren, had at length repaired to Jerusalem to assist in rebuilding the Temple.

It was while the workmen were engaged in making the necessary excavations for laying the foundation, and while numbers continued to arrive at Jerusalem from Babylon, that these three worn and weary sojourners, after plodding on foot over the rough and devious roads between the two cities, offered themselves to the Grand Council as willing participants in the labor of erection. Who these sojourners were, we have no historical means of discovering; but there is a Masonic tradition (entitled, perhaps, to but little weight) that they were Hananiah, Mishael, and Azariah, three holy men, who are better known to general readers by their Chaldaic names of Shadrach, Meshech, and Abed-nego, as having been miraculously preserved from the fiery furnace of Nebuchadnezzar.

Their services were accepted, and from their diligent labors resulted that important discovery, the perpetuation and preservation of which constitutes the great end and design of the Royal Arch Degree.

Such is the legend of the American Royal Arch. It has no known foundation in history, and is therefore altogether mythical. But it presents, as a myth, the symbolic idea of arduous and unfaltering search after truth, and the final reward that such devotion receives.

Webb-Preston Work. The title given by Dr. Robert Morris to a system of lectures which he proposed to introduce, in 1859, into the Lodges of the United States, and in which he was partly successful. He gave this name to his system because his theory was that the lectures of Thomas Smith Webb and those of Preston were identical. But this theory is untenable, for it has long since been shown that the lectures of Webb were an abridgment, and a very material modification of those of Preston. In 1863, and for a few years afterward, the question of the introduction of the "Webb-Preston work" was a subject of warm, and sometimes of intemperate, discussion in several of the Western jurisdictions. It has now, however, at least as a subject of controversy, ceased to attract the attention of the Craft. One favorable result was, however, produced by these discussions, and that is, that they led to a more careful investigation and a better understanding of the nature and history of the rituals which have, during the nineteenth century, been practised in America. The bitterness of feeling has passed away, but the knowledge that it elicited remains.

Webb, Thomas Smith. No name in Masonry is more familiar to the American Mason than that of Webb, who was really the inventor and founder of the system of work which, under the appropriate name of the American Rite (although often improperly called the York Rite), is universally practised in the United States. The most exhaustive biography of him that has been written is that of Bro. Cornelius Moore, in his *Leaflets of Masonic Biography*, and from that, with a few additions from other sources, the present sketch is derived.

Thomas Smith Webb, the son of parents who a few years previous to his birth had emigrated from England and settled in Boston, Massachusetts, was born in that city, October 13, 1771. He was educated in one of the public schools, where he acquired such knowledge as was at that time imparted in them, and became proficient in the French and Latin languages.

He selected as a profession either that of a printer or a bookbinder; his biographer is uncertain which, but inclines to think that it was the former. After completing his apprenticeship he removed to Keene, in New Hampshire, where he worked at his trade, and about the year 1792 (for the precise date is unknown) was initiated in Freemasonry in Rising Sun Lodge in that town.

While residing at Keene he married Miss Martha Hopkins, and shortly afterward removed to Albany, New York, where he opened a bookstore. When and where he received the high degrees has not been stated, but we find him, while living at Albany, engaged in the establishment of a Chapter and an Encampment.

It was at this early period of his life that Webb appears to have commenced his labors as a Masonic teacher, an office which he continued to fill with great influence until the close of his life. In 1797 he published at Albany the first edition of his *Freemasons' Monitor; or, Illustrations of Masonry*. It purports to be "by a Royal Arch Mason, K. T., K. M., etc." He did not claim the authorship until the subsequent edition; but his name and that of his partner, Spencer, appear in the imprint as publishers. He acknowledges in the preface his indebtedness to Preston for the observations on the first three degrees. But he states that he has differently arranged Preston's distributions of the sections, because they were "not agreeable to the mode of working in America." This proves that the Prestonian system was not then followed in the United States, and ought to be a sufficient answer to those who at a later period attempted to claim an identity between the lectures of Preston and Webb.

About the year 1801 he removed to Providence, Rhode Island, where he engaged in the manufacture of wall-paper on a rather extensive scale. By this time his reputation as a Masonic teacher had been well established, for a committee was appointed by St. John's Lodge of Providence to wait upon and inform him that this Lodge (for his great exertions in the cause of Masonry) "wish him to become a member of the same." He accepted the invitation, and passing through the various gradations of office was elected, in 1813, Grand Master of the Masons of Rhode Island.

But it is necessary now to recur to preceding events. In 1797, on October 24th, a convention of committees from several Chapters in the Northern States was held in Boston for the purpose of deliberating on the propriety and expediency of establishing a Grand Chapter of Royal Arch Masons for the Northern States. Of this convention

Webb was chosen as the chairman. Previous to this time the Royal Arch degrees had been conferred in Masters' Lodges and under a Lodge Warrant. It is undoubtedly to the influence of Webb that we are to attribute the disseverance of the degree from that jurisdiction and the establishment of independent Chapters. It was one of the first steps that he took in the organization of the American Rite. The circular addressed by the convention to the Chapters of the country was most probably from the pen of Webb.

The Grand Chapter having been organized in January, 1798, Webb was elected Grand Scribe, and reelected in 1799, at which time the body assumed the title of the General Grand Chapter. In 1806 he was promoted to the office of General Grand King, and in 1816 to that of Deputy General Grand High Priest, which he held until his death.

During all this time, Webb, although actively engaged in the labors of Masonic instruction, continued his interest in the manufacture of wall-paper, and in 1817 removed his machinery to the West, Moore thinks, with the intention of making his residence there.

In 1816 he visited the Western States, and remained there two years, during which time he appears to have been actively engaged in the organization of Chapters, Grand Chapters, and Encampments. It was during this visit that he established the Grand Chapters of Ohio and Kentucky, by virtue of his powers as a General Grand Officer.

In August, 1818, he left Ohio and returned to Boston. In the spring of 1819, he again began a visit to the West, but he reached no farther than Cleveland, Ohio, where he died very suddenly, it is supposed in a fit of apoplexy, on July 6, 1819, and was buried the next day with Masonic honors. The body was subsequently disinterred and conveyed to Providence, where, on the 8th of November, it was reinterred by the Grand Lodge of Rhode Island.

Webb's influence over the Masons of the United States, as the founder of a Rite, was altogether personal. In Masonic literature he has made no mark, for his labors as an author are confined to a single work, his *Monitor*, and this is little more than a syllabus of his lectures. Although, if we may judge by the introductory remarks to the various sections of the degrees, and especially to the second one of the Third Degree, Webb was but little acquainted with the true philosophical symbolism of Freemasonry, such as was taught by Hutchinson in England and by his contemporaries in this country, Harris and Town; he was what Carson properly calls him, "the ablest Masonic ritualist of his day—the very prince of Masonic workmen," and this was the instrument with which he worked for the extension of the new Rite which he established. The American Rite would have been more perfect as a system had its founder entertained profounder views of the philosophy and symbolism of Masonry as a science; but as it is, with imperfections which time, it is hoped, will remove, and deficiencies which future researches of the Masonic scholar will supply, it still must ever be a monument of the ritualistic skill, the devotion, and the persevering labor of Thomas Smith Webb.

The few odes and anthems composed by Webb for his rituals possess a high degree of poetic merit, and evince the possession of much genius in their author.

Wedekind, Georg Christian Gottlieb, Baron von. A German physician and Professor of Medicine at Metz, and a medical writer of reputation. He was born at Göttingen, January 8, 1761. As a Mason, he was distinguished as a member of the Eclectic Union, and labored effectually for the restoration of good feeling between it and the Directorial Lodge at Frankfort. His Masonic works, which are numerous, consist principally of addresses, controversial pamphlets, and contributions to the Altenburg *Journal of Freemasonry*. He died in 1831.

Weeping Virgin. The weeping virgin with disheveled hair, in the monument of the Third Degree, used in the American Rite, is interpreted as a symbol of grief for the unfinished state of the Temple. Jeremy Cross, who is said to have fabricated the monumental symbol, was not, we are satisfied, acquainted with Hermetic science. Yet a woman thus portrayed, standing near a tomb, was a very appropriate symbol for the Third Degree, whose dogma is the resurrection. In Hermetic science, according to Nicolas Flammel (*Hieroglyphica*, cap. xxxii.), a woman having her hair disheveled and standing near a tomb is a symbol of the soul.

Weishaupt, Adam. He is celebrated in the history of Masonry as the founder of the Order of Illuminati of Bavaria, among whom he adopted the characteristic or Order name of *Spartacus*. He was born February 6, 1748, at Ingoldstadt, and was educated by the Jesuits, toward whom, however, he afterward exhibited the bitterest enmity, and was equally hated by them in return. In 1772 he became Extraordinary Professor of Law, and in 1775, Professor of Natural and Canon Law, at the University of Ingoldstadt. As the professorship of canon law had been hitherto held only by an ecclesiastic, his appointment gave great offense to the clergy. Weishaupt, whose views were cosmopolitan, and who knew and condemned the bigotry and superstitions of the priests, established an opposing party in the University, consisting principally of young men whose confidence and friendship he had gained. They assembled in a private apartment, and there he discussed with them philosophic subjects, and sought to imbue them with a liberal spirit. This was the beginning of the Order of the Illuminati, or the Enlightened—a name which he bestowed upon his disciples as a token of their advance in intelligence and moral progress.

At first, it was totally unconnected with Masonry, of which Order Weishaupt was not at that time a member. It was not until 1777 that he was initiated in the Lodge Theodore of Good Counsel, at Munich. Thenceforward Weishaupt sought to incorporate his system into that of Masonry, so that the latter might become subservient to his views, and with the assistance of the Baron Knigge, who brought his active energies and genius to the aid of the cause, he succeeded in completing his system of Illuminism. But the clergy, and especially the Jesuits, who, although their Order had been abolished by the government, still secretly possessed great power, redoubled their efforts to destroy their opponent, and they at length succeeded. In 1784, all secret associations were prohibited by a royal decree, and in the following year Weishaupt was deprived of his professorship and banished from the country. He repaired to Gotha, where he was kindly received by Duke Ernest, who made him a counselor and gave him a pension. There he remained until he died in 1811.

During his residence at Gotha he wrote and published many works, some on philosophical subjects and several in explanation and defense of Illuminism. Among the latter were *A Picture of the Illuminati*, 1786; *A Complete History of the Persecutions of the Illuminati in Bavaria*, 1786. Of this work only one volume was published; the second, though promised, never appeared. *An Apology for the Illuminati*, 1786; *An Improved System of the Illuminati*, 1787, and many others.

No man has ever been more abused and villified than Weishaupt by the adversaries of Freemasonry. In such partisan writers as Barruel and Robison we might expect to find libels against a Masonic reformer. But it is passing strange that Dr. Oliver should have permitted such a passage as the following to sully his pages (*Landmarks*, ii., 26):

"Weishaupt was a shameless libertine, who compassed the death of his sister-in-law to conceal his vices from the world and, as he termed it, to preserve his honor."

To charges like these, founded only in the bitterness of his persecutors, Weishaupt has made the following reply:

"The tenor of my life has been the opposite of everything that is vile; and no man can lay any such thing to my charge."

Indeed, his long continuance in an important religious professorship at Ingoldstadt, the warm affections of his pupils, and the patronage and protection, during the closing years of his life, of the virtuous and amiable Duke of Gotha, would seem to give some assurance that Weishaupt could not have been the monster that he has been painted by his adversaries.

Illuminism, it is true, had its abundant errors, and no one will regret its dissolution. But its founder had hoped by it to effect much good: that it was diverted from its original aim was the fault, not of him, but of some of his disciples; and their faults he was not reluctant to condemn in his writings.

His ambition was, I think, a virtuous one; that it failed was his, and perhaps the world's, misfortune. "My general plan," he says, "is good, though in the detail there may be faults. I had myself to create. In another situation, and in an active station in life, I should have been keenly occupied, and the founding of an Order would never have come into my head. But I would have executed much better things, if the government had not always opposed my exertions, and placed others in situations which suited my talents. It was the full conviction of this, and of what could be done, if every man were placed in the office for which he was fitted by nature, and a proper education, which first suggested to me the plan of Illuminism."

What he really wished Illuminism to be, we may judge from the instructions he gave as to the necessary qualifications of a candidate for initiation. They are as follows:

"Whoever does not close his ear to the lamentations of the miserable, nor his heart to gentle pity; whoever is the friend and brother of the unfortunate; whoever has a heart capable of love and friendship; whoever is steadfast in adversity, unwearied in the carrying out of whatever has been once engaged in, undaunted in the overcoming of difficulties; whoever does not mock and despise the weak; whose soul is susceptible of conceiving great designs, desirous of rising superior to all base motives, and of distinguishing itself by deeds of benevolence; whoever shuns idleness; whoever considers no knowledge as unessential which he may have the opportunity of acquiring, regarding the knowledge of mankind as his chief study; whoever, when truth and virtue are in question, despising the approbation of the multitude, is sufficiently courageous to follow the dictates of his own heart,—such a one is a proper candidate."

The Baron von Knigge, who, perhaps, of all men, best knew him, said of him that he was undeniably a man of genius, and a profound thinker; and that he was all the more worthy of admiration because, while subjected to the influences of a bigoted Catholic education, he had formed his mind by his own meditations, and the reading of good books. His heart, adds this companion of his labors and sharer of his secret thoughts, was excited by the most unselfish desire to do something great, and that would be worthy of mankind, and in the accomplishment of this he was deterred by no opposition and discouraged by no embarrassments.

The truth is, I think, that Weishaupt has

been misunderstood by Masonic and slandered by un-Masonic writers. His success in the beginning as a reformer was due to his own honest desire to do good. His failure in the end was attributable to ecclesiastical persecution, and to the faults and follies of his disciples. The master works to elevate human nature; the scholars, to degrade. Weishaupt's place in history should be among the unsuccessful reformers and not among the profligate adventurers.

Welcome. In the American ritual, it is said to be the duty of the Senior Deacon "to welcome and clothe all visiting brethren." That is to say, he is to receive them at the door with all courtesy and kindness, and to furnish them, or see that they are furnished, with the necessary apron and gloves and, if they are Past Masters, with the appropriate collar and jewel of that office, with an extra supply of which all Lodges were in the olden time supplied, but not now. He is to conduct the visitor to a seat, and thus carry out the spirit of the *Old Charges*, which especially inculcate hospitality to strange brethren. These customs are no longer practised and the ritual prescribes other well-known duties.

Well Formed, True, and Trusty. A formula used by the Grand Master at the laying of a corner-stone. Having applied the square, level, and plumb to its different surfaces and angles, he declares it to be "well formed, true, and trusty." Borrowed from the technical language of Operative Masonry, it is symbolically applied in reference to the character which the Entered Apprentice should sustain when, in the course of his initiation, he assumes the place of a typical corner-stone in the Lodge.

Wellington, Duke of. The "Hero of Waterloo," and the renowned, was initiated in Lodge No. 494, about December, 1790.

Wesley, Samuel. At one time the most distinguished organist of England, and called by Mendelssohn "the father of English organ-playing." He was initiated as a Mason December 17, 1788, and in 1812, the office of Grand Organist of the Grand Lodge of England being in that year first instituted, he received the appointment from the Grand Master, the Duke of Sussex, and held it until 1818. He composed the anthem performed at the union of the two Grand Lodges in 1813, and was the composer of many songs, glees, etc., for the use of the Craft. He was the son of the Rev. Charles Wesley, and nephew of the celebrated John Wesley, the founder of Methodism. Born February 24, 1766, at Bristol, England, and died October 11, 1837. He was well entitled to the epithet of the "Great Musician of Masonry."

West. Although the west, as one of the four cardinal points, holds an honorable position as the station of the Senior Warden, and of the pillar of Strength that supports the Lodge, yet, being the place of the sun's setting and opposed to the east, the recognized place of light, it, in Masonic symbolism, represents the place of darkness and ignorance. The old tradition, that in primeval times all human wisdom was confined to the eastern part of the world, and that those who had wandered toward the west were obliged to return to the east in search of the knowledge of their ancestors, is not confined to Masonry. Creuzer (*Symbolik*) speaks of an ancient and highly instructed body of priests in the East, from whom all knowledge, under the veil of symbols, was communicated to the Greeks and other unenlightened nations of the West. And in the "Legend of the Craft," contained in the old Masonic Constitutions, there is always a reference to the emigration of the Masons from Egypt eastward to the "land of behest," or Jerusalem. Hence, in the modern symbolism of Speculative Masonry, it is said that the Mason during his advancement is *traveling from the West to the East in search of light.*

"Westminster and Keystone." The third of the three oldest warranted Lodges in England, having been chartered in 1722. The first is Friendship, No. 6, and the second the British, No. 8. Those assembling *without warrants* are only two, and are numbered two and four, "Antiquity" and "Royal Somerset House and Inverness."

Westphalia, Secret Tribunals of. The Vehmgerichte, or Fehmgerichte, were secret criminal courts of Westphalia in the Middle Ages. The origin of this institution, like that of Masonry, has been involved in uncertainty. The true meaning of the name even is doubtful. *Vaem* is said by Dreyer to signify *holy* in the old Northern languages; and, if this be true, a Fehmgericht would mean a holy court. But it has also been suggested that the word comes from the Latin *fama*, or rumor, and that a Fehmgericht was so called because it proceeded to the trial of persons whose only accuser was common rumor, the maxim of the German law, "no accuser, no judge," being in such a case departed from. They were also called Tribunals of Westphalia, because their jurisdiction and existence were confined to that country.

The Medieval Westphalia was situated within the limits of the country bounded on the west by the Rhine, on the east by the Weser, on the north by Friesland, and on the south by Westerwald. Render (*Tour through Germany*, p. 186) says that the tribunals were only to be found in the duchies of Gueldres, Cleves, and Westphalia, in the principal cities of Corvey and Minden, in the landgravate of Hesse, in the counties of Bentheim, Limburg, Lippe, Mark, Ravensberg, Rechlinghausen, Rietzberg, Sayn, Waldeck, and Steinfort, in some baronies, as Gehmen, Neustadt, and Rheda, and in the free imperial city of Dortmund; but these were all included within the limits of Medieval Westphalia.

It has been supposed that the first secret tribunals were established by the Emperor Charlemagne on the conquest of Saxony. In 803 the Saxons obtained among other privileges that of retaining their national laws, and administering them under imperial judges who had been created Counts of the Empire. Their courts, it is said, were held three times a year in an open field, and their sessions were held in public on ordinary occasions; but in all cases of religious offense, such as apostasy, heresy, or sacrilege, although the trial began in a public session, it always ended in a secret tribunal.

It has been supposed by some writers that these courts of the Counts of the Empire instituted by Charlemagne gave origin to the secret tribunals of Westphalia, which were held in the thirteenth and fourteenth centuries. There is no external evidence of the truth of this hypothesis. It was, however, the current opinion of the time, and all the earlier traditions and documents of the courts themselves trace their origin to Charlemagne. Paul Wigand, the German jurist and historian, who wrote a history of their tribunals (*Fehmgericht Westfälens*, Hamburg, 1826), contends for the truth of these traditions; and Sir Francis Palgrave, in his *Rise and Progress of the English Commonwealth*, says, unhesitatingly, that "the Vehmic tribunals can only be considered as the original jurisdictions of the old Saxons which survived the subjugation of their country." The silence on this subject in the laws and capitularies of Charlemagne has been explained on the ground that these tribunals were not established authoritatively by that monarch, but only permitted by a tacit sanction to exist.

The author of the article on the Secret Societies of the Middle Ages, published in the *Library of Entertaining Knowledge*, who has written somewhat exhaustively on this subject, says that the first writers who have mentioned these tribunals are Henry of Hervorden in the fourteenth, and Æneas Sylvius in the fifteenth century; both of whom, however, trace them to the time of Charlemagne; but Jacob (*Recherches Historiques sur les Croisades et les Templiers*, p. 132) cites a diploma of Count Engelbert de la Mark, of the date of 1267, in which there is an evident allusion to some of their usages. Render says that they are first generally known in the year 1220. But their absolute historical existence is confined to the fourteenth and fifteenth centuries.

The secret Westphalian tribunals were apparently created for the purpose of preserving public morals, of punishing crime, and of protecting the poor and weak from the oppressions of the rich and powerful. They were outside of the regular courts of the country, and in this respect may be compared to the modern "vigilance committees" sometimes instituted in this country for the protection of the well-disposed citizens in newly settled territories from the annoyance of lawless men. But the German tribunals differed from the American committees in this, that they were recognized by the emperors, and that their decisions and executions partook of a judicial character.

The Vehmic tribunals, as they are also called, were governed by a minute system of regulations, the strict observance of which preserved their power and influence for at least two centuries.

At the head of the institution was the Emperor, for in Germany he was recognized as the source of law. His connection with the association was either direct or indirect. If he had been initiated into it, as was usually the case, then his connection was direct and immediate. If, however, he was not an initiate, then his powers were delegated to a lieutenant, who was a member of the tribunal.

Next to the Emperor came the free counts. Free counties were certain districts comprehending several parishes, where the judges and counselors of the secret ban exercised jurisdiction in conformity with the statutes. The free count, who was called *Stuhlherr*, or tribunal lord, presided over this free county and the tribunal held within it. He had also the prerogative of erecting other tribunals within his territorial limits, and if he did not preside in person, he appointed a *Freigraf*, or free judge, to supply his place. No one could be invested with the dignity of a free judge unless he were a Westphalian by birth, born in lawful wedlock of honest parents; of good repute, charged with no crime, and well qualified to preside over the county. They derived their name of free judges from the fact that the tribunals exercised their jurisdiction over only free men, serfs being left to the control of their own lords.

Next in rank to the free judges were the *Schöppen*, as assessors or counselors. They formed the main body of the association, and were nominated by the free judge, with the consent of the stuhlherr, and vouched for by two members of the tribunal. A schöppe was required to be a Christian, a Westphalian of honest birth, neither excommunicated nor outlawed, nor involved in any suit before the Fehmgericht, and not a member of any monastic or ecclesiastical order. There were two classes of these assessors or schöppen: a lower class or grade called the *Ignorant*, who had not been initiated, and were consequently not permitted to be present at the secret session; and a higher grade, called the *Knowing*, who were subjected to a form of initiation.

The ceremonies of initiation of a free judge were very solemn and symbolic. The candidate appeared bareheaded before the tribunal, and answered certain questions respecting his qualifications. Then, kneeling, with the thumb and forefinger of the right hand on a naked sword and halter, he pronounced the following oath: "I swear by the Holy Trinity that I will, from henceforth, aid, keep, and conceal the holy Fehms from wife and child, from father and mother, from sister and brother, from fire and wind, from all that the sun shines on and the rain covers, from all that is between sky and earth, especially from the man who knows the law; and will bring before this free tribunal, under which I am sitting, all that belongs to the secret jurisdiction of the Emperor, whether I know it to be true myself or have heard it from trustworthy men whatever requires correction or punishment whatever is committed within the jurisdiction of the Fehm, that it may be judged, or, with the consent of the accuser, be put off in grace; and will not cease so to do for love or for fear, for gold or for silver, or for precious stones; and will strengthen this tribunal and jurisdiction with all my five senses and power; and that I do not take on me this office for any other cause than for the sake of right and justice. Moreover, that I will ever advance and honor this free tribunal more than any other free tribunals; and what I thus promise will I steadfastly and firmly keep; so help me God and his Holy Gospel."

He further swore in an additional oath that he would, to the best of his ability, enlarge the holy empire, and would undertake nothing with unrighteous hand against the land and people of the *Stuhlherr*, or Lord of the Tribunal. His name was then inserted in the Book of Gold.

The secrets of the tribunal were then communicated to the candidate, and with them the modes of recognition by which he could be enabled to discover his fellow-members. The sign is described as having been made by placing, when at table, the point of their knife pointing to themselves, and the haft away from them. This was also accompanied by the words *Stock Stein, Gras Grein*, the meaning of which phrase is unknown.

The duties of the initiated were to act as assessors or judges at the meetings of the courts, to constitute which at least seven were required to be present; and also to go through the country, serve citations upon the accused, and to execute the sentences of the tribunals upon criminals, as well as to trace out and denounce all evil-doers. The punishment of an initiate who had betrayed any of the secrets of the society was severe. His tongue was torn out by the roots, and he was then hung on a tree seven feet higher than any other felon.

The ceremonies practised when a Fehm court was held were very symbolic in their character. Before the free count stood a table, on which were placed a naked sword and a cord of withe. The sword, which was cross-handled, is explained in their ritual as signifying the cross on which Christ suffered for our sins, and the cord the punishment of the wicked. All had their heads uncovered, to signify that they would proceed openly and fairly, punish in proportion to guilt, and cover no right with a wrong. Their hands also were uncovered, to show that they would do nothing covertly and underhand; and they wore cloaks, to signify their warm love for justice, for as the cloak covers all the other garments and the body, so should their love cover justice. Lastly, they were to wear neither armor nor weapons, that no one might feel fear, and to indicate that they were under the peace of the empire. They were charged to be cool and sober, lest passion or intoxication should lead them to pass an unjust judgment.

Writers of romance have clothed these tribunals with additional mystery. But the stories that they were held at night, and in subterranean places, have no foundation save in the imagination of those who have invented them. They were held, like other German courts, at break of day and in the open air, generally beneath a tree in the forest, or elsewhere. The public tribunals were, of course, open to all. It was the secret ones only that were held in private. But the time and place were made known to the accused in the notification left at his residence, or, if that were unknown, as in the case of a vagabond, at a place where four roads met, being affixed to the ground or to a tree, and the knowledge might be easily communicated by him to his friends.

The Chapter-General met once a year, generally at Dortmund or Arensburg, but always at some place in Westphalia. It consisted of the tribunal lords and free counts, who were convoked by the Emperor or his lieutenant. If the Emperor was an initiate, he might preside in person; if he was not, he was represented by his lieutenant. At these Chapters the proceedings of the various Fehm courts were reviewed, and hence these latter made a return of the names of the persons initiated, the suits they had commenced, the sentences they had passed, and the punishments they had inflicted. The Chapter-General acted also as a court of appeals. In fact, the relation of a Chapter-General to the Fehm courts was precisely the same as that of a Grand Lodge of Masons to its subordinates. The resemblance, too, in the symbolic character of the two institutions was striking. But here the resemblance ended, for it has never been contended that there was or could be any connection whatever between the two institutions. But the coincidences show that peculiar spirit and love of mystery which prevailed in those times, and the influence of which was felt in Masonry as well as in the Westphalian tribunals, and all the other secret societies of the Middle Ages.

The crimes of which the Fehmgericht claimed a jurisdiction were, according to the statutes passed at Arensburg in 1490, of two kinds: those cognisant by the secret tribunal, and those cognizant by the public tribunal. The crimes cognizant by the secret tribunal were, violations of the secrets of Charlemagne and of the Fehmgericht, heresy, apostasy, perjury, and witchcraft or magic. Those cognisant by the public tribunal were, sacrilege, theft, rape, robbery of women in childbirth, treason, highway robbery, murder or manslaughter, and vagrancy. Sometimes the catalogue of crimes was modified and often enlarged. There was one period when all the crimes mentioned in the decalogue were included; and indeed there was no positive restriction of the jurisdiction of the tribunals, which generally were governed in their proceedings by what they deemed expedient for the public peace and safety.

In the early history of the institution, its trials were conducted with impartiality, and its judgments rendered in accordance with justice, being constantly restrained by mercy, so that they were considered by the populace as being of great advantage in those times of lawlessness. But at length the institution became corrupt, and often aided instead of checking oppression, a change which finally led to its decay.

When anyone was accused, he was summoned to appear before the tribunal at a certain specified time and place. If he was an initiate, the summons was repeated three times; but if not, that is, if any other than an inhabitant of Westphalia, the summons was given only once. If he appeared, an opportunity was afforded him of defense. An initiate could purge himself by a simple oath of denial, but any other person was required to adduce sufficient testimony of his innocence. If the accused did not appear, nor render a satisfactory excuse for his absence, the court proceeded to declare him outlawed, and a free judge was delegated to put him to death wherever found. Where three free judges found anyone *flagrante delicto*, or in the very act of committing a crime, or having just perpetrated it, they were authorised to put him to death without the formality of a trial. But if he succeeded in making his escape before the penalty was inflicted, he could not on a subsequent arrest be put to death. His case must then be brought for trial before a tribunal.

The sentence of the court, if capital, was not announced to the criminal, and he learned it only when, in some secret place, the executioners of the decree of the Fehmgericht met him and placed the halter around his neck and suspended him to a neighboring tree. The punishment of death was always by hanging, and from a tree. The fact that a dead body was thus found in the forest, was an intimation to those who found it that the person had died by the judgment of the secret tribunal.

It is very evident that an institution like this could be justified, or even tolerated, only in a country and at a time when the power and vices of the nobles, and the general disorganization of society, had rendered the law itself powerless; and when in the hands of persons of irreproachable character, the weak could only thus be protected from the oppressions of the strong, the virtuous from the aggression of the vicious. It was in its commencement a safeguard for society; and hence it became so popular that its initiates numbered at one time over one hundred thousand, and men of rank and influence sought with avidity admission into its circle.

In time the institution became demoralised. Purity of character was no longer insisted on as a qualification for admission. Its decrees and judgments were no longer marked with unfaltering justice, and, instead of defending the weak any longer from the oppressor, it often became itself the willing instrument of oppression. Efforts were made from time to time to inaugurate reforms, but the prevailing spirit of the age, now beginning to be greatly improved by the introduction of the Roman law and the spread of the Protestant religion, was opposed to the self-constituted authority of the tribunals. They began to dissolve almost insensibly, and after the close of the sixteenth century we hear no more of them, although there never was any positive decree of dissolution enacted or promulgated by the State. They were destroyed, not by any edict of law, but by the progressive spirit of the people.

West Virginia. Originally, all the Lodges in the western part of Virginia were under the jurisdiction of the Grand Lodge of that State. But the new State of West Virginia having been formed in 1863, nine Lodges sent delegates to a convention held at Fairmont, April 12, 1865, which, after some discussion, adjourned to meet again on May 10th of the same year, when the Grand Lodge of West Virginia was organised, and W. J. Bates elected Grand Master.

The Grand Chapter of Royal Arch Masons of West Virginia was organized, November 16, 1871, by a convention of five Chapters. The Grand Chapter of Virginia, under which these Chapters held their Warrants, had previously given its consent to the organization.

Wheat. An emblem of plenty under the name of "Corn." (See *Corn, Wine, and Oil.*)

White. White is one of the most ancient as well as most extensively diffused of the symbolic colors. It is to be found in all the ancient mysteries, where it constituted, as it does in Masonry, the investiture of the candidate. It always, however, and everywhere has borne the same signification as the symbol of purity and innocence.

In the religious observances of the Hebrews, white was the color of one of the curtains of the tabernacle, where, according to Josephus, it was a symbol of the element of earth; and it was employed in the construction of the ephod of the high priest, of his girdle, and of the breastplate. The word לבן, *laban*, which in the Hebrew language signifies "to make white," also denotes "to purify"; and there are to be found throughout the Scriptures many allusions to the color as an emblem of purity. "Though thy sins be as scarlet," says Isaiah, "they shall be as white as snow." Jeremiah, describing the once innocent condition of Zion, says, "her Nazarites were purer than snow, they were whiter than milk." "Many," says Daniel, "shall be purified and made white." In Revelation, a *white stone* was the reward promised by the Spirit to those who overcame; and again, "he that overcometh, the same shall be clothed in white garments"; and in another part of the same book the Apostle is instructed to say that fine linen, clean and white, is the righteousness of the saints. The ancient prophets always imagined the Deity clothed in white, because, says Portal (*Des Couleurs Symboliques*, p. 35), "white is the color of absolute truth, of Him who is; it alone reflects all the luminous rays; it is the unity whence all the primitive colors emanate." Thus Daniel, in one of his prophetic visions, saw the Ancient of days, "whose garment was white as snow, and the hair of his head like pure wool." Here, says Dr. Henry (*Comm. in loco*), the whiteness of the garment "noted the splendor and purity of God in all the administrations of his justice."

Among the Gentile nations, the same reverence was paid to this color. The Egyptians decorated the head of their deity, Osiris, with a white tiara. In the school of Pythagoras, the sacred hymns were chanted in white robes. The Druids clothed their initiates who had arrived at the ultimate degree, or that of perfection, in white vestments. In all the mysteries of other nations of antiquity, the same custom was observed. White was, in general, the garment of the Gentile as well as of the Hebrew priests in the performance of their sacred rites. As the Divine power was supposed to be represented on earth by the priesthood, in all nations the sovereign pontiff was clad in white. Aaron was directed to enter the sanctuary only in white garments; in Persia, the Magi wore white robes, because, as they said, they alone were pleasing to the Deity; and the white tunic of Ormuzd is still the characteristic garment of the modern Parsees.

White, among the ancients, was consecrated to the dead, because it was the symbol of the regeneration of the soul. On the monuments of Thebes the manes or ghosts are represented as clothed in white; the Egyptians wrapped their dead in white linen; Homer (*Iliad*, xviii., 353) refers to the same custom when he makes the attendants cover the dead body of Patroclus, φάρεϊ λευκῷ, with a white pall; and Pausanias tells us that the Messenians practised the same customs, clothing their dead in white, and placing crowns upon their heads, indicating by this double symbolism the triumph of the soul over the empire of death.

The Hebrews had the same usage. St. Matthew (xxvii. 59) tells us that Joseph of Arimathea wrapped the dead body of our Lord "in a clean linen cloth." Adopting this as a suggestion, Christian artists have, in their paintings of the Savior after his resurrection, depicted him in a white robe. And it is with this idea that in the Apocalypse white vestments are said to be the symbols of the regeneration of souls, and the reward of the elect. It is this consecration of white to the dead that caused it to be adopted as the color of mourning among the nations of antiquity. As the victor in the games was clothed in white, so the same color became the symbol of the victory achieved by the departed in the last combat of the soul with death. "The friends of the deceased wore," says Plutarch, "his livery, in commemoration of his triumph." The modern mourning in black is less philosophic and less symbolic than this ancient one in white.

In Speculative Masonry, white is the symbol of purity. This symbolism commences at the earliest point of initiation, when the white apron is presented to the candidate as a symbol of purity of life and rectitude of conduct. Wherever in any of the subsequent initiations this color appears, it is always to be interpreted as symbolizing the same idea. In the Thirty-third Degree of the Ancient and Accepted Scottish Rite, the Sovereign Inspector is invested with a white scarf as inculcating that virtuous deportment above the tongue of all reproach which should distinguish the possessors of that degree, the highest in the Rite.

This symbolism of purity was most probably derived by the Masons from that of the primitive church, where a white garment was placed on the catechumen who was about to be baptized, as a token that he had put off the lusts of the flesh, and, being cleansed from his former sins, had obliged himself to maintain an unspotted life. The ancient symbolism of regeneration which appertained to the ancient idea of the color white has not been adopted in Masonry; and yet it would be highly appropriate in an Institution one of whose chief dogmas is the resurrection.

White Ball. In Freemasonry, equivalent to a favorable or affirmative vote. The custom of using white and black balls seems to have been derived from the Romans, who in the earlier days of the republic used white and black balls in their judicial trials, which were cast into an urn, the former acquitting and the latter condemning the accused.

White Cross Knights. A title sometimes applied to the Knights Hospitalers of St. John, from the color of their cross. Porter (*Hist. Knts. of Malta*, i., 166) says: "Villiers hastily assembled a troop of *White Cross Knights*, and, issuing from the city by a side gate, made a circuit so as, if possible, to fall upon the flank of the foe unperceived."

White Mantle, Order of the. The Teutonic Knights were so denominated in allusion to the color of their cloaks, on which they bore a black cross.

White Masonry. (*Maçonnerie blanche.*) A title given by French writers to Female Masonry, or the Masonry of Adoption.

White Stone. A symbol in the Mark Degree referring to the passage in the Apocalypse (ii. 17): "To him that overcometh will I give to eat of the hidden manna, and will give him a white stone, and in the stone a new name written, which no man knoweth, saving he that receiveth it." In this passage it is supposed that the Evangelist alluded to the stones or tesseræ which, among the ancients and the early Christians, were used as tokens of alliance and friendship. Hence in the Mark Degree, the white stone and the new name inscribed upon it is a symbol of the covenant made between the possessors of the degree, which will in all future time, and under every circumstance of danger or distress, secure the kind and fraternal assistance of all upon whom the same token has been bestowed. In the symbolism of the degree the candidate represents that white stone upon whom the new name as a Mark Master is to be inscribed. (See *Mark* and *Tessera Hospitalis.*)

White, William Henry. Distinguished for his services to the Craft of England, whom he served as Grand Secretary for the long period of forty-seven years. He was the son of William White, who was also Grand Secretary of the Grand Lodge of England for thirty-two years, the office having thus been held by father and son for seventy-nine years. William Henry White was born in 1778. On April 15, 1799, he was initiated in Emulation Lodge, No. 12, now called the Lodge of Emulation, No. 21, having been nominated by his father. December 15, 1800, he was elected Master of the Lodge, and presided until 1809. In 1805 he was appointed a Grand Steward, and in 1810 Grand Secretary, as the assistant of his father. This office was held by them conjointly for three years. In 1813, at the union of the two Grand Lodges, he was appointed, with Edwards Harper, Joint Grand Secretary of the United Grand Lodge of England, and in 1838 sole Grand Secretary. In 1857, after a service of nearly half a century, he retired from the office, the Grand Lodge unanimously voting him a retiring pension equal in amount to his salary. On that occasion the Earl of Zetland, Grand Master, said: "I know of no one, and I believe there never was anyone who has done more, who has rendered more valuable services to Masonry than our worthy Brother White." In view of the great names in Masonic literature and labor which preceded him, the eulogium will be deemed exaggerated; but the devotion of the Grand Secretary to the Order, and his valuable services during his long and active life, cannot be denied. During the latter years of his official term, he was charged with inactivity and neglect of duty, but the fault has been properly attributed to the increasing infirmities of age. A service of plate was presented to him by the Craft, June 20, 1850, as a testimonial of esteem. He died April 5, 1866.

Widow, Sons of the. A society founded in the third century, by a Persian slave, Manes, who had been purchased and adopted by a widow. It consisted of two degrees, Auditor and Elut.

Widow's Son. In Ancient Craft Masonry, the title applied to Hiram, the architect of the Temple, because he is said, in the 1st Book of Kings (vii. 14), to have been "a widow's son of the tribe of Naphtali." The Adonhiramite Masons have a tradition which Chapron gives (*Necessaire Maçonn.*, p. 101) in the following words: "The Masons call themselves the widow's sons, because, after the death of our respectable Master, the Masons took care of his mother, whose children they called themselves, because Adonhiram had always considered them as his brethren. But the French Masons subsequently changed the myth and called themselves 'Sons of the Widow,' and for this reason. 'As the wife of Hiram remained a widow after her husband was murdered, the Masons, who regard themselves as the descendants of Hiram, called themselves *Sons of the Widow*.'" But this myth is a pure invention, and is without the Scriptural foundation of the York myth, which makes Hiram himself the widow's son. But in French Masonry the term "Son of the Widow" is synonymous with "Mason."

The adherents of the exiled house of Stuart, when seeking to organize a system of political Masonry by which they hoped to secure the restoration of the family to the throne of England, transferred to Charles II. the tradition of Hiram Abif betrayed by his followers, and called him "the Widow's Son," because he was the son of Henrietta Maria, the widow of Charles I. For the same reason they subsequently applied the phrase to his brother, James II.

Wife and Daughter, Mason's. See *Mason's Wife and Daughter*.

Wilhelmsbad, Congress of. At Wilhelmsbad, near the city of Hanau in Hesse-Cassel, was held the most important Masonic Congress of the eighteenth century. It was convoked by Ferdinand, Duke of Brunswick, Grand Master of the Order of Strict Observance, and was opened July 16, 1782. Its duration extended to thirty sessions, and in its discussions the most distinguished Masons of Germany were engaged. Neither the Grand Lodge of Germany, nor that of Sweden, was represented; and the Grand Lodge of the Three Globes, at Berlin, sent only a letter: but there were delegates from Upper and Lower Germany, from Holland, Russia, Italy, France, and Austria; and the Order of the Illuminati was represented by the Baron von Knigge. It is not therefore surprising that the most heterogeneous opinions were expressed. Its avowed object was the reform of the Masonic system, and its disentanglement from the confused mass of rites and high degrees with which French and German pretenders or enthusiasts had been for years past overwhelming it. Important topics were proposed, such as the true origin of Speculative Masonry, whether it was merely conventional and the result of modern thought, or whether it was the offspring of a more ancient order, and, if so, what was that order; whether there were any Superiors General then existing, and who these Unknown Superiors were, etc. These and kindred questions were thoroughly discussed, but not defined, and the Congress was eventually closed without coming to any other positive determination than that Freemasonry was not essentially connected with Templarism, and that, contrary to the doctrine of the Rite of Strict Observance, the Freemasons were not the successors of the Knights Templar. The real effect of the Congress of Wilhelmsbad was the abolition of that Rite, which soon after drooped and died.

Will. In some of the continental Rites, and in certain high degrees, it is a custom to require the recipiendary to make, before his initiation, a will and testament, exhibiting what are his desires as to the distribution of his property at his decease. The object seems to be to add solemnity to the ceremony, and to impress the candidate with the thought of death. But it would seem to be a custom which would be "more honored in the breach than the observance." It is not practised in the York and American Rites.

William, Emperor of Germany. An honorary member of the Grand Lodge of Scotland and protector of Freemasonry in Germany, his son, the crown prince, being deputy-protector.

Wilson Manuscript. In the marginal notes to the *Manifesto of the Lodge of Antiquity*, published in 1778, there is reference to an "O. [*old or original*] MS. in the hands of Mr. Wilson of Broomhead, near Sheffield, Yorkshire, written in the reign of King Henry VIII." It seems, from the context, to have been cited as authority for the existence of a General Assembly of the Craft at the city of York. But no part of the MS. has ever been printed or transcribed, and it is now apparently lost.

Winding Stairs. In the 1st Book of Kings (vi. 8) it is said: "The door for the middle chamber was in the right side of the house; and they went up with winding stairs into the middle chamber, and out of the middle into the third." From this passage the Masons of the last century adopted the symbol of the winding stairs, and introduced it into the Fellow-Craft's Degree, where it has ever since remained, in the American Rite. In one of the high degrees of the Scottish Rite the winding stairs are called *cochleus*, which is a corruption of *cochlis*, a spiral staircase. The Hebrew word is *lulim*, from the obsolete root *lul*, to roll or wind. The whole story of the winding stairs in the Second Degree of Masonry is a mere myth, without any other foundation than the slight allusion in the Book of Kings which has been just cited, and it derives its only value from the symbolism taught in its legend. (See *Middle Chamber* and *Winding Stairs, Legend of the*.)

Winding Stairs, Legend of the. I formerly so fully investigated the true meaning of the legend of the winding stairs, as taught in the degree of Fellow-Craft, that I can now find nothing to add to what I have already said in my work on *The Symbolism of Freemasonry*, published in 1869. I might, in writing a new article, change the language, but I could furnish no new idea. I shall not, therefore, hesitate to transfer much of what I have said on this subject in that work to the present article. It is an enlargement and development of the meager explanations given in the ordinary lecture of Webb.

In an investigation of the symbolism of the winding stairs, we shall be directed to the true explanation by a reference to their origin, their number, the objects which they recall, and their termination, but above all by a consideration of the great design which an ascent upon them was intended to accomplish.

The steps of this winding staircase commenced, we are informed, at the porch of the Temple; that is to say, at its very entrance. But nothing is more undoubted in the science of Masonic symbolism than that the Temple was the representative of the world purified by the Shekinah, or the Divine Presence. The world of the profane is without the Temple; the world of the initiated is within its sacred walls. Hence to enter the Temple, to pass within the porch, to be made a Mason, and to be born into the world of Masonic light, are all synonymous and convertible terms. Here, then, the symbolism of the winding stairs begins.

The Apprentice, having entered within the porch of the Temple, has begun his Masonic life. But the First Degree in Masonry, like the lesser mysteries of the ancient systems of initiation, is only a preparation and purification for something higher. The Entered Apprentice is the child in Masonry. The lessons which he receives are simply intended to cleanse the heart and prepare the recipient for that mental illumination which is to be given in the succeeding degrees.

As a Fellow-Craft, he has advanced another step, and as the degree is emblematic of youth, so it is here that the intellectual education of the candidate begins. And therefore, here, at the very spot which separates the porch from the sanctuary, where childhood ends and manhood begins, he finds stretching out before him a winding stair which invites him, as it were, to ascend, and which, as the symbol of discipline and instruction, teaches him that here must commence his Masonic labor—here he must enter upon those glorious though difficult researches the end of which is to be the possession of Divine truth. The winding stairs begin after the candidate has passed within the porch and between the pillars of strength and establishment, as a significant symbol to teach him that as soon as he has passed beyond the years of irrational childhood, and commenced his entrance upon manly life, the laborious task of self-improvement is the first duty that is placed before him. He cannot stand still, if he would be worthy of his vocation; his destiny as an immortal being requires him to ascend, step by step, until he has reached the summit, where the treasures of knowledge await him.

The number of these steps in all the systems has been odd. Vitruvius remarks—and the coincidence is at least curious—that the ancient temples were always ascended by an odd number of steps; and he assigns as the reason, that, commencing with the right foot at the bottom, the worshiper would find the same foot foremost when he entered the Temple, which was considered as a fortunate omen. But the fact is, that the symbolism of numbers was borrowed by the Masons from Pythagoras, in whose system of philosophy it plays an important part, and in which odd numbers were considered as more perfect than even ones. Hence, throughout the Masonic system we find a predominance of odd numbers; and while three, five, seven, nine, fifteen, and twenty-seven, are all-important symbols, we seldom find a reference to two, four, six, eight, or ten. The odd number of the stairs was therefore intended to symbolize the idea of perfection, to which it was the object of the aspirant to attain.

As to the particular number of the stairs, this has varied at different periods. Tracing-boards of the last century have been found, in which only *five* steps are delineated, and others in which they amount to *seven*. The Prestonian lectures, used in England in the beginning of this century, gave the whole number as thirty-eight, dividing them into series of one, three, five, seven, nine, and eleven. The error of making an even number, which was a violation of the Pythagorean principle of odd numbers as the symbol of perfection, was corrected in the Hemming lectures, adopted at the union of the two Grand Lodges of England, by striking out the eleven, which was also objectionable as receiving a sectarian explanation. In this country the number was still further reduced to *fifteen*, divided into three series of *three*, *five*, and *seven*. I shall adopt this American division in explaining the symbolism; although, after all, the particular number of the steps, or the peculiar method of their division into series, will not in any way affect the general symbolism of the whole legend.

The candidate, then, in the Second Degree of Masonry, represents a man starting forth on the journey of life, with the great task before him of self-improvement. For the faithful performance of this task, a reward is promised, which reward consists in the development of all his intellectual faculties, the moral and spiritual elevation of his character, and the acquisition of truth and knowledge. Now, the attainment of this moral and intellectual condition supposes an elevation of character, an ascent from a lower to a higher life, and a passage of toil and difficulty, through rudimentary instruction, to the full fruition of wisdom. This is therefore beautifully symbolised by the winding stairs, at whose foot the aspirant stands ready to climb the toilsome steep, while at its top is placed "that hieroglyphic bright which none but Craftsmen ever saw," as the emblem of Divine truth. And hence a distinguished writer has said that "these steps, like all the Masonic symbols, are illustrative of discipline and doctrine, as well as of natural, mathematical, and metaphysical science, and open to us an extensive range of moral and speculative inquiry."

The candidate, incited by the love of virtue and the desire of knowledge, and withal eager for the reward of truth which is set before him, begins at once the toilsome ascent. At each division he pauses to gather instruction from the symbolism which these divisions present to his attention.

At the first pause which he makes he is instructed in the peculiar organization of the order of which he has become a disciple. But the information here given, if taken in its naked, literal sense, is barren, and unworthy of his labor. The rank of the officers who govern, and the names of the degrees which constitute the Institution, can give him no knowledge which he has not before possessed. We must look therefore to the symbolic meaning of these allusions for any value which may be attached to this part of the ceremony.

The reference to the organization of the Masonic Institution is intended to remind the aspirant of the union of men in society, and the development of the social state out of the state of nature. He is thus reminded, in the very outset of his journey, of the blessings which arise from civilization, and of the fruits of virtue and knowledge which are derived from that condition. Masonry itself is the result of civilization; while, in grateful return, it has been one of the most important means of extending that condition of mankind.

All the monuments of antiquity that the ravages of time have left, combine to prove that man had no sooner emerged from the savage into the social state, than he commenced the organization of religious mysteries, and the separation, by a sort of Divine instinct, of the sacred from the profane. Then came the invention of architecture as a means of providing convenient dwellings and necessary shelter from the inclemencies and vicissitudes of the seasons, with all the mechanical arts connected with it; and lastly, geometry, as a necessary science to enable the cultivators of land to measure and designate the limits of their possessions. All these are claimed as peculiar characteristics of Speculative Masonry, which may be considered as the type of civilization, the former bearing the same relation to the profane world as the latter does to the savage state. Hence we at once see the fitness of the symbolism which commences the aspirant's upward progress in the cultivation of knowledge and the search after truth, by recalling to his mind the condition of civilisation and the social union of mankind as necessary preparations for the attainment of these objects. In the allusions to the officers of a Lodge, and the degrees of Masonry as explanatory of the organisation of our own society, we clothe in our symbolic language the history of the organization of society.

Advancing in his progress, the candidate is invited to contemplate another series of instructions. The human senses, as the appropriate channels through which we receive all our ideas of perception, and which, therefore, constitute the most important sources of our knowledge, are here referred to as a symbol of intellectual cultivation. Architecture, as the most important of the arts which conduce to the comfort of mankind, is also alluded to here, not simply because it is so closely connected with the operative institution of Masonry, but also as the type of all the other useful arts. In his second pause, in the ascent of the winding stairs, the aspirant is therefore reminded of the necessity of cultivating practical knowledge.

So far, then, the instructions he has received relate to his own condition in society as a member of the great social compact, and to his means of becoming, by a knowledge of the arts of practical life, a necessary and useful member of that society.

But his motto will be, "Excelsior." Still must he go onward and forward. The stair is still before him; its summit is not yet reached, and still further treasures of wisdom are to be sought for, or the reward will not be gained, nor the *middle chamber*, the abiding-place of truth, be reached

In his third pause, he therefore arrives at that point in which the whole circle of human science is to be explained. Symbols, we know, are in themselves arbitrary and of conventional signification, and the complete circle of human science might have been as well symbolized by any other sign or series of doctrines as by the seven liberal arts and sciences. But Masonry is an institution of the olden time; and this selection of the liberal arts and sciences as a symbol of the completion of human learning is one of the most pregnant evidences that we have of its antiquity.

In the seventh century, and for a long time afterward, the circle of instruction to which all the learning of the most eminent schools and most distinguished philosophers was confined, was limited to what were then called the liberal arts and sciences, and consisted of two branches, the *trivium* and the *quadrivium*. The *trivium* included grammar, rhetoric, and logic; the *quadrivium* comprehended arithmetic, geometry, music, and astronomy.

"These seven heads," says Enfield, "were supposed to include universal knowledge. He who was master of these was thought to have no need of a preceptor to explain any books or to solve any questions which lay within the compass of human reason, the knowledge of the *trivium* having furnished him with the key to all language, and that of the *quadrivium* having opened to him the secret laws of nature."

At a period, says the same writer, when few were instructed in the *trivium*, and very few studied the *quadrivium*, to be master of both was sufficient to complete the character of a philosopher. The propriety, therefore, of adopting the seven liberal arts and sciences as a symbol of the completion of human learning is apparent. The candidate, having reached this point, is now supposed to have accomplished the task upon which he had entered—he has reached the last step, and is now ready to receive the full fruition of human learning.

So far, then, we are able to comprehend the true symbolism of the winding stairs. They represent the progress of an inquiring mind with the toils and labors of intellectual cultivation and study, and the preparatory acquisition of all human science, as a preliminary step to the attainment of Divine truth, which, it must be remembered, is always symbolized in Masonry by the WORD.

Here let me again allude to the symbolism of numbers, which is for the first time presented to the consideration of the Masonic student in the legend of the winding stairs. The theory of numbers as the symbols of certain qualities was originally borrowed by the Masons from the school of Pythagoras. It will be impossible, however, to develop this doctrine, in its entire extent, in the present article, for the numeral symbolism of Masonry would itself constitute materials for an ample essay. It will be sufficient to advert to the fact, that the total number of the steps, amounting in all to *fifteen* in the American system, is a significant symbol. For *fifteen* was a sacred number among the Orientals, because the letters of the holy name JAH, יה, were, in their numerical value, equivalent to fifteen; and hence a figure in which the nine digits were so disposed as to make fifteen either way when added together perpendicularly, horizontally, or diagonally, constituted one of their most sacred talismans. The fifteen steps in the winding stairs are therefore symbolic of the name of God.

But we are not yet done. It will be remembered that a reward was promised for all this toilsome ascent of the winding stairs. Now, what are the wages of a Speculative Mason? Not money, nor corn, nor wine, nor oil. All these are but symbols. His wages are Truth, or that approximation to it which will be most appropriate to the degree into which he has been initiated. It is one of the most beautiful, but at the same time most abstruse, doctrines of the science of Masonic symbolism that the Mason is ever to be in search of truth, but is never to find it. This Divine truth, the object of all his labors, is symbolized by the Word, for which we all know he can only obtain a *substitute;* and this is intended to teach the humiliating but necessary lesson that the knowledge of the nature of God and of man's relation to him, which knowledge constitutes Divine truth, can never be acquired in this life. It is only when the portals of the grave open to us, and give us an entrance into a more perfect life, that this knowledge is to be attained. "Happy is the man," says the father of lyric poetry, "who descends beneath the hollow earth, having beheld these mysteries: he knows the end, he knows the origin of life."

The middle chamber is therefore symbolic of this life, where the symbol only of the Word can be given, where the truth is to be reached by approximation only, and yet where we are to learn that that truth will consist in a perfect knowledge of the G. A. O. T. U. This is the reward of the inquiring Mason; in this consist the wages of a Fellow-Craft; he is directed to the truth, but must travel farther and ascend still higher to attain it.

It is, then, as a symbol, and a symbol only, that we must study this beautiful legend of the winding stairs. If we attempt to adopt it as an historical fact, the absurdity of its details stares us in the face, and wise men will wonder at our credulity. Its inventors had no desire thus to impose upon our folly; but offering it to us as a great philosophical myth, they did not for a moment suppose that we would pass over its sublime moral teachings to accept the allegory as an historical narrative without meaning, and wholly irreconcilable with the records of Scripture, and opposed by all the principles of probability. To suppose that eighty thousand craftsmen were weekly paid in the narrow precincts of the Temple chambers, is simply to suppose an absurdity. But to believe that all this pictorial repr sentation of an ascent by a winding staircase to the place where the wages of labor were to be received, was an allegory to teach us the ascent of the mind from ignorance, through all the toils of study and the difficulties of obtaining knowledge, receiving here a little and there a little, adding something to the stock of our ideas at each step, until, in the middle chamber of life—in the full fruition of manhood—the reward is attained, and the purified and elevated intellect is invested with the reward in the direction how to seek God and God's truth; to believe this, is to believe and to know the true design of Speculative Masonry, the only design which makes it worthy of a good or a wise man's study.

Its historical details are barren, but its symbols and allegories are fertile with instruction.

Wind, Mason's. Among the Masonic tests of the last century was the question, "How blows a Mason's wind?" and the answer was, "Due east and west." Browne gives the question and answer more *in extenso*, and assigns the explanation as follows:

"How blows the wind in Masonry?

"Favorable due east and west.

"To what purpose?

"To call men to, at, and from their labor.

"What does it further allude to?

"To those miraculous winds which proved so essential in working the happy deliverance of the children of Israel from their Egyptian bondage, and proved the overthrow of Pharaoh and all his host when he attempted to follow them."

Krause very correctly thinks that the fundamental idea of the Masonic wind blowing from the east is to be found in the belief of the Middle Ages that all good things, such as philosophy and religion, came from the East. In the German ritual of *The Three Sts. John's Degrees of the Mother Lodge of the Three Globes*, the idea is expressed a little differently. The Catechism is as follows:

"Whence comes the wind?

"From the east towards the west, and from the south towards the north, and from the north towards the south, the east, and the west.

"What weather brings it?

"Variable, hail and storm, and calm and pleasant weather."

The explanation given is that these changing winds symbolize the changing progress of man's life in his pursuit of knowledge—now clear and full of hope, now dark with storms. Bode's hypothesis that these variable winds of Masonry were intended to refer to the changes of the condition of the Roman Church under English monarchs, from Henry VIII. to James II., and thus to connect the symbolism with the Stuart Masonry, is wholly untenable, as the symbol is not found in any of the high degrees. It is not recognized in the French, and is obsolete in the York Rite.

Window. A piece of furniture in the Mark Degree. It is a mere symbol, having no foundation in truth, as there was no such appendage to the Temple. It is simply intended to represent the place where the workman received his wages, symbolic of the reward earned by labor.

Wine. One of the elements of Masonic consecration, and, as a symbol of the inward refreshment of a good conscience, is intended, under the name of the "wine of refreshment," to remind us of the eternal refreshments which the good are to receive in the future life for the faithful performance of duty in the present.

Wings of the Cherubim, Extended. The candidate in the degree of Royal Master of the American Rite is said to be received "beneath the extended wings of the cherubim." The expression is derived from the passage in the 1st Book of Kings (vi. 27), which describes the setting of "the cherubim within the inner house." Practically, there is an anachronism in the reference to the cherubim in this degree. In the older and purer ritual, the ceremonies are supposed to take place in the council-chamber or private apartment of King Solomon, where, of course, there were no cherubim. And even in some more modern rituals, where a part of the ceremony referred to in the tradition is said to have occurred in the holy of holies, that part of the Temple was at that time unfinished, and the cherubim had not yet been placed there. But symbolically the reference to the cherubim in this degree, which represents a searcher for truth, is not objectionable. For although there is a great diversity of opinion as to their exact signification, yet there is a very general agreement that, under some one manifestation or another, they allude to and symbolize the protecting and overshadowing power of the Deity. When, therefore, the initiate is received *beneath the extended wings of the cherubim*, we are taught by this symbolism how appropriate it is, that he who comes to ask and to seek Truth, symbolised by the True Word, should begin by placing himself under the protection of that Divine Power who alone is Truth, and from whom alone truth can be obtained.

Wisconsin. In January, 1843, Freemasonry was introduced into Wisconsin by the establishment of Mineral Point Lodge at Mineral Point, Melody Lodge at Platteville, and Milwaukee Lodge at Milwaukee, all under the authority of the Grand Lodge of Missouri. December 18, 1843, delegates from these three Lodges assembled in convention at Madison, and organized the Grand Lodge of Wisconsin, Rev. B. T. Kavanaugh, the Master of Melody Lodge, being elected Grand Master.

The Grand Chapter was established February 13, 1850, and Dwight F. Lawton elected Grand High Priest.

The Grand Council of Royal and Select Masters was organized in 1857, and James Collins elected Grand Master.

The Grand Commandery was organized October 20, 1859, and Henry L. Palmer elected Grand Commander.

Wisdom. In Ancient Craft Masonry, wisdom is symbolized by the East, the place of light, being represented by the pillar that there supports the Lodge and by the Worshipful Master. It is also referred to King Solomon, the symbolical founder of the Order. In Masonic architecture the Ionic column, distinguished for the skill in its construction, as it combines the beauty of the Corinthian and the strength of the Doric, is adopted as the representative of wisdom.

King Solomon has been adopted in Speculative Masonry as the type or representative of wisdom, in accordance with the character which has been given to him in the 1st Book of Kings (iv. 30-32): "Solomon's wisdom excelled the wisdom of all the children of the east country, and all the wisdom of Egypt. For he was wiser than all men; than Ethan the Ezrahite, and Heman and Chalcol and Darda, the sons of Mahol; and his fame was in all the nations round about."

In all the Oriental philosophies a conspicuous place has been given to wisdom. In the book called the *Wisdom of Solomon* (vii., 7, 8), but supposed to be the production of a Hellenistic Jew, it is said: "I called upon God, and the spirit of wisdom came to me. I preferred her before sceptres and thrones, and esteemed riches nothing in comparison of her." And farther on in the same book (vii., 25-27) she is described as "the breath of the power of God, and a pure influence [emanation] flowing from the glory of the Almighty, . . . the brightness of the everlasting light, the unspotted mirror of the power of God, and the image of his goodness."

The Kabbalists made *Chochma*, חכמה, or Wisdom, the second of the ten Sephiroth, placing it next to the Crown. They called it a male potency, and the third of the Sephiroth, *Binah*, בינה, or Intelligence, female. These two Sephiroth, with *Keter*, כתר, or the Crown, formed the first triad, and their union produced the *Intellectual World*.

The Gnostics also had their doctrine of Wisdom, whom they called *Achamoth*. They said she was feminine; styled her Mother, and said that she produced all things through the Father.

The Oriental doctrine of Wisdom was, that it is a Divine Power standing between the Creator and the creation, and acting as His agent. "The Lord," says Solomon (proverbs iii. 19), "by wisdom hath founded the earth." Hence wisdom, in this philosophy, answers to the idea of a vivifying spirit brooding over and impregnating the elements of the chaotic world. In short, the world is but the outward manifestation of the spirit of wisdom.

This idea, so universally diffused throughout the East, is said to have been adopted into the secret doctrine of the Templars, who are supposed to have borrowed much from the Basilideans, the Manicheans, and the Gnostics. From them it easily passed over to the high degrees of Masonry, which were founded on the Templar theory. Hence, in the great decoration of the Thirty-third Degree of the Scottish Rite, the points of the triple triangle are inscribed with the letters S.A.P.I.E.N.T.I.A., or Wisdom.

It is not difficult now to see how this word *Wisdom* came to take so prominent a part in the symbolism of Ancient Masonry, and how it was expressly appropriated to King Solomon. As wisdom, in the philosophy of the East, was the creative energy—the architect, so to speak, of the world, as the emanation of the Supreme Architect—so Solomon was the architect of the Temple, the symbol of the world. He was to the typical world or temple what wisdom was to the great world of the creation. Hence wisdom is appropriately referred to him and to the Master of the Lodge, who is the representative of Solomon. Wisdom is always placed in the east of the Lodge, because thence emanate all light, and knowledge, and truth.

Withdrawal of Petition. It is a law of Masonry in America that a petition for initiation having been once presented to a Lodge, cannot be withdrawn. It must be subjected to a ballot. It must be submitted to the action of the Lodge. The rule is founded on prudential reasons. The candidate having submitted his character for inspection, the inspection must be made. It is not for the interests of Masonry (the only thing to be considered) that, on the prospect of an unfavorable judgment, he should be permitted to decline the inspection, and have the opportunity of applying to another Lodge, where carelessness or ignorance might lead to his acceptance. Initiation is not like an article of merchandise sold by rival dealers, and to be purchased, after repeated trials, from the most accommodating seller.

Witnesses. See *Trials*.

Woellner, Johann Christoph Von. A distinguished Prussian statesman, and equally distinguished as one of the leaders of the Rosicrucian Order in Germany, and the Rite of Strict Observance, to whose advancement he lent all the influence of his political position. He was born at Dobritz, May 19, 1732. He studied theology in the orthodox church, and in 1750 was appointed a preacher near Berlin, and afterward a Canon at Halberstadt. In 1786, King William III., of Prussia, appointed him privy councilor of finance, an appointment supposed to have been made as a concession to the Rite of Strict Observance, of which Woellner was a Provincial Grand Master, his Order name being *Eques à cubo*. In 1788 he became Minister of State, and was put at the head of ecclesiastical affairs. No Mason in Germany labored more assiduously in the cause of the Order and in active defense of the Rite of Strict Observance, and hence he had many enemies as well as friends. On the demise of King William, he was dismissed from his political appointments, and retired to his estate at Groesnez, where he died September 11, 1800.

Wolf. In the Egyptian mysteries, the candidate represented a wolf and wore a wolf's skin, because Osiris once assumed the form of that animal in his contests with Typhon. In the Greek mythology, the wolf was consecrated to Apollo, or the sun, because of the connection between *luke*, light, and *lukos*, a wolf. In French, wolf is *louve*, and hence the word *louveteau*, signifying the son of a Mason. (See *Lewis No. 3*.)

Wolfenbüttel, Congress of. A city of Lower Saxony, in the principality of Wolfenbüttel, and formerly a possession of the Duke of Brunswick. In 1778 Ferdinand, Duke of Brunswick, convoked a Masonic Congress there, with a view of reforming the organization of the Order. Its results, after a session of five weeks, were a union of the Swedish and German Masons, which lasted only for a brief period, and the preparation for a future meeting at Wilhelmsbad.

Wolfgang, Albert, Prince of Lippe Schaumberg. Born in 1699, died in 1748. One of the Masonic circle whom Frederick the Great favored and sought at times to meet.

Woman. The law which excludes women from initiation into Masonry is not contained in the precise words in any of the Old Constitutions, although it is continually implied, as when it is said in the Lansdowne MS. (*circa* 1560) that the Apprentice must be "of limbs whole, as a man ought to be," and that be must be "no bondsman." All the regulations also refer to men only, and many of them would be wholly inapplicable to women. But in the Charges compiled by Anderson and Desaguliers, and published in 1723, the word "woman" is for the first time introduced, and the law is made explicit. Thus it is said that "the persons admitted members of a Lodge must be good and true *men*, ... no bondmen, no *women*," etc. (*Constitutions*, 1723, p. 51.)

Perhaps the best reason that can be assigned for the exclusion of women from our Lodges will be found in the character of our organization as a mystic society. Speculative Freemasonry is only an application of the art of Operative Masonry to purposes of morality and science. The Operative branch of our Institution was the forerunner and origin of the Speculative. Now, as we admit of no innovations or changes in our customs, Speculative Masonry retains, and is governed by, all the rules and regulations that existed in and controlled its Operative prototype. Hence, as in this latter art only hale and hearty men, in possession of all their limbs and members, so that they might endure the fatigues of labor, were employed, so in the former the rule still holds, of excluding all who are not in the possession of these prerequisite qualifications. Woman is not permitted to participate in our rites and ceremonies, not because we deem her unworthy or unfaithful, or incapable, as has been foolishly supposed, of keeping a secret, but because, on our entrance into the Order, we found certain regulations which prescribed that only men capable of enduring the labor, or of fulfilling the duties of Operative Masons, could be admitted. These regulations we have solemnly promised never to alter; nor could they be changed, without an entire disorganization of the whole system of Speculative Masonry.

Wood-Cutters, Order of. See *Fendeurs.*

Woodford Manuscript. A manuscript formerly in the possession of one of England's most esteemed Masons, Rev. A. F. A. Woodford, editor of *Kenning's Cyclopædia of Freemasonry*, of 700 pages, London. Bro. Hughan says it is almost a verbatim copy of the Cooke MSS. The indorsement upon it reads, "This is a very ancient record of Masonry, which was copyed for me by Wm. Reid, Secretary to the Grand Lodge, 1728." It formerly belonged to Mr. William Cowper, clerk to the Parliament, and is now in the library of the Quatuor Coronati Lodge, No. 2076, London, England.

Woog, Carl Christian. Born at Dresden in 1713, and died at Leipsic, April 24, 1771. Mossdorf says that he was, in 1740, a resident of London, and that there he was initiated into Ancient Craft Masonry, and also into the Scottish degree of Knight of St. Andrew. In 1749, he published a Latin work entitled *Presbyterorum et Diaconorum Achaiæ de Martyrio Sancti Andreæ Apostoli, Epistola Encyclica*, in which he refers to the Freemasons (p. 32) in the following language: "Unicum adhuc addo, esse inter cæmentarios, seu lapicidas liberos,(qui Franco muratoriorum *Franc-Maçons* nomine communiter insigniuntur quique rotunda quadratis miscere dicuntur,) quosdam qui S. Andreæ memoriam summa veneratione recolant. Ad minimum, si scriptis, quæ detecta eorum mysteria et arcana recensent, fides non est deneganda, certum erit, eos quotunnis diem quoque Andreas, ut Sancti Johannis diem solent, festum agere atque ceremoniosum celebrare, esseque inter eos sectam aliquam, quæ per crucem, quam in pectore gerant, in qua Sanctus Andreas funibus alligatus hæreat, à reliquis se destinguunt"; i. e., "I add only this, that among the Freemasons (commonly called *Franc-Maçons*, who are said to mingle circles with squares,) there are certain ones who cherish the memory of St. Andrew with singular veneration. At all events, if we may credit those writings in which their mysteries and secrets are detected and exposed, it will be evident that they are accustomed to keep annually, with ceremonies, the festival of St. Andrew as well as that of St. John; and that there is a sect among them which distinguish themselves from the others by wearing on their breast the cross on which St. Andrew was fastened by cords." Woog, in a subsequent passage, defends the Freemasons from the charge made by these Expositions that they were irreligious, but declares that *by him their mysteries shall remain buried in profound silence*—"per me vero maneant eorum mysteria alto silentio sepulta." It is, apparently, from these passages that Mossdorf draws his conclusions that Woog was a Freemason, and had received the

Scottish degree of Knight of St. Andrew. They at least prove that he was an early friend of the Institution.

Word. When emphatically used, the expression, "the Word," is in Masonry always referred to the Third Degree, although there must be a word in each degree. In this latter and general sense, the Word is called by French Masons "la parole," and by the Germans "ein Worterzeichen." The use of a Word is of great antiquity. We find it in the ancient mysteries. In those of Egypt it is said to have been the Tetragrammaton. The German Stone-Masons of the Middle Ages had one, which, however, was probably only a password by which the traveling Companion might make himself known in his professional wanderings. Lyon (*Hist. of the L. of Edinb.*, p. 22) shows that it existed, in the sixteenth and subsequent centuries, in the Scotch Lodges, and he says that "the Word is the only secret that is ever alluded to in the minutes of Mary's Chapel, or in those of Kilwinning, Atcheson's Haven, or Dunblane, or any other that we have examined of a date prior to the erection of the Grand Lodge." Indeed, he thinks that the communication of this Word constituted the only ceremony of initiation practised in the Operative Lodges. At that time there was evidently but one Word for all the ranks of Apprentices, Craftsmen, and Masters. He thinks that this communication of the Mason Word to the Apprentices under oath constituted the germ whence has sprung the Symbolical Masonry. But it must be remembered that the learned and laborious investigations of Bro. Lyon refer only to the Lodges of Scotland. There is no sufficient evidence that a more extensive system of initiation did not prevail at the same time, or even earlier, in England and Germany. Indeed, Findel has shown that it did in the latter country; and it is difficult to believe that the system, which we know was in existence in 1717, was a sudden development out of a single Word, for which we are indebted to the inventive genius of those who were engaged in the revival at that period. Be this as it may, the evidence is conclusive that everywhere, and from the earliest times, there was a Word. This at least is no modern usage.

But it must be admitted that this Word, whatever it was, was at first a mere mark of recognition. Yet it may have had, and probably did have, a mythical signification, and had not been altogether arbitrarily adopted. The word given in the Sloane MS., No. 3329, which Bro. Hughan places at a date not posterior to 1700, is undoubtedly a corrupted form of that now in use, and with the signification of which we are well acquainted. Hence we may conclude that the legend, and the symbolism connected with it, also existed at the same time, but only in a nascent and incomplete form.

The modern development of Speculative Masonry into a philosophy has given a perfected form to the symbolism of the Word no longer confined to use as a means of recognition, but elevated, in its connection with the legend of the Third Degree, to the rank of a symbol.

So viewed, and by the scientific Mason it is now only so viewed, the Word becomes the symbol of Divine Truth, the loss of which and the search for it constitute the whole system of Speculative Masonry. So important is this Word, that it lies at the very foundation of the Masonic edifice. The Word might be changed, as might a grip or a sign, if it were possible to obtain the universal consent of the Craft, and Masonry would still remain unimpaired. But were the Word abolished, or released from its intimate connection with the Hiramic legend, and with that of the Royal Arch, the whole symbolism of Speculative Masonry would be obliterated. The Institution might withstand such an innovation, but its history, its character, its design, would belong to a newer and a totally different society. The Word is what Dermott called the Royal Arch, "the marrow of Masonry."

Word, Lost. See *Lost Word.*

Word, Mason. In the minutes and documents of the Lodges of Scotland during the sixteenth, seventeenth, and eighteenth centuries, the expression "Mason word" is constantly used. This continuous use would indicate that but one word was then known. Nicolai, in his *Essay on the Accusations against the Templars*, quotes a "small dictionary published at the beginning of the eighteenth century," in which the "Mason's word" is defined.

Word, Sacred. A term applied to the chief or most prominent word of a degree, to indicate its peculiarly sacred character, in contradistinction to a password, which is simply intended as a mode of recognition. It is sometimes ignorantly corrupted into "secret word." All significant words in Masonry are *secret.* Only certain ones are *sacred.*

Word, Significant. See *Significant Word.*

Word, True. Used in contradistinction to the *Lost Word* and the *Substitute Word.* To find it is the object of all Masonic search and labor. For as the Lost Word is the symbol of death, the True Word is the symbol of life eternal. It indicates the change that is always occurring—truth after error, light after darkness, life after death. Of all the symbolism of Speculative Masonry, that of the True Word is the most philosophic and sublime.

Work. See *Labor.*

Working-Tools. In each of the degrees of Masonry, certain implements of the Operative art are consecrated to the Speculative science, and adopted to teach as symbols lessons of morality. With these the Speculative Mason is taught to erect his spiritual temple, as his Operative predecessors with the same implements constructed their material temples. Hence they are called the working-tools of the degree. They vary but very slightly in the different Rites, but the same symbolism is preserved. The principal working-tools of the Operative art that have been adopted as symbols in the Speculative science, confined, however, to Ancient Craft Masonry, and not used in the higher degrees, are, the twenty-four-inch gage, common gavel, square, level, plumb, skirrit, compasses, pencil, trowel, mallet, pickax, crow, and shovel. (See them under their respective heads.)

Work, Master of the. An architect or superintendent of the building of an edifice. Du Cange (*Glossarium*) thus defines it: "Magister operis vel operarum vulgo, maître de l'œuvre, cui operibus publicis vacare incumbit," i. e., "Master of the work or of the works, commonly, maître de l'œuvre, one whose duty it is to attend to the public works." In the Cooke MS. (line 529) it is said: "And also he that were most of connying [skill] schold be governour of the werke, and scholde be callyd maister." In the old record of the date of Edward III., cited by Anderson in his second edition (p. 71), it is prescribed "that Master Masons, or Masters of Work, shall be examined whether they be able of cunning to serve their respective lords." The word was in common use in the Middle Ages, and applied to the Architect or Master Builder of an edifice. Thus Edwin of Steinbach, the architect of the Cathedral of Strasburg, is called Master of the Work. In the monasteries there was a similar officer, who was, however, more generally called the *Operarius*, but sometimes *Magister operis*.

Workmen at the Temple. We have no historical book, except the meager details in the Books of Kings and Chronicles, of the number or classification of the workmen at the Temple of Solomon. The subject has, however, afforded a fertile theme for the exercise of the inventive genius of the ritualists. Although devoid of interest as an historical study, an acquaintance with these traditions, especially the English and American ones, and a comparison of them with the Scriptural account and with that given by Josephus, are necessary as a part of the education of a Masonic student. I furnish the legends, therefore, simply as a matter of curiosity, without the slightest intention to vouch for their authenticity, at the same time trusting that the good sense and common fairness of the reader will prevent him from including such unauthenticated matter in lectures usually given in the Third Degree and often with much pretense to learning.

In the 2d Book of Chronicles, chap. ii., verses 17 and 18, we read as follows:

"And Solomon numbered all the strangers that were in the land of Israel, after the numbering wherewith David his father had numbered them; and they were found an hundred and fifty thousand and three thousand and six hundred.

"And he set threescore and ten thousand of them to be bearers of burdens, and fourscore thousand to be hewers in the mountain, and three thousand and six hundred overseers to set the people a-work."

The same numerical details are given in the second verse of the same chapter. Again, in the 1st Book of Kings, chap. v., verses 13 and 14, it is said:

"And King Solomon raised a levy out of all Israel; and the levy was thirty thousand men.

"And he sent them to Lebanon, ten thousand a month by courses: a month they were in Lebanon, and two months at home: and Adoniram was over the levy."

The succeeding verses make the same enumeration of workmen as that contained in the Book of Chronicles quoted above, with the exception that, by omitting the three hundred Harodim, or rulers over all, the number of overseers is stated in the Book of Kings to be only three thousand three hundred.

With these authorities, and the assistance of Masonic traditions, Anderson, in the *Book of Constitutions* (2d ed., p. 11), constructs the following table of the Craftsmen at the Temple:

Harodim, Princes, Rulers, or Provosts.		300
Menatzchim, Overseers, or Master Masons		3,300
Ghiblim, Stone-Squarers	All Fellow-Crafts	80,000
Ischotzeb, Hewers		
Benai, Builders		
The levy out of Israel, who were timber-cutters		30,000
All the Freemasons employed in the work of the Temple, exclusive of the two Grand Wardens		113,600

Besides the *Ish Sabal*, or men of burden, the remains of the old Canaanites, amounting to 70,000, who are not numbered among the Masons.

In relation to the classification of these workmen, Anderson says: "Solomon partitioned the Fellow Crafts into certain Lodges, with a Master and Wardens in each, that they might receive commands in a regular manner, might take care of their tools and jewels, might be paid regularly every week, and be duly fed and clothed; and the Fellow Crafts took care of their succession by educating Entered Apprentices."

Josephus makes a different estimate. He includes the 3,300 Overseers in the 80,000 Fellow-Crafts, and makes the number of Masons, exclusive of the 70,000 bearers of burden, amount to only 110,000.

A work published in 1764, entitled *The Masonic Pocket-Book*, gives a still different classification. The number, according to this authority, was as follows:

Harodim	300
Menatschim	3,300
Ghiblim	83,000
Adoniram's men	30,000
Total	116,600

which, together with the 70,000 Ish Sabal, or laborers, will make a grand total of 186,600 workmen.

According to the statement of Webb, which has been generally adopted by the Fraternity in the United States, there were:

Grand Masters	3
Overseers	3,300
Fellow-Crafts	80,000
Entered Apprentices	70,000

This account makes no allusion to the 300 Harodim, nor to the levy of 30,000; it is, therefore, manifestly incorrect. Indeed, no certain authority can be found for the complete classification of the workmen, since neither the Bible nor Josephus gives any account of the number of Tyrians employed. Oliver, however, in his *Historical Landmarks*, has collected from the Masonic traditions an account of the classifications of the workmen, which I shall insert, with a few additional facts taken from other authorities.

According to these traditions, the following was the classification of the Masons who wrought in the quarries of Tyre:

Superexcellent Masons	6
Excellent Masons	48
Grand Architects	8
Architects	16
Master Masons	2,376
Mark Masters	700
Markmen	1,400
Fellow-Crafts	53,900
Total	58,454

These were arranged as follows: The six Superexcellent Masons were divided into two Grand Lodges, with three brethren in each to superintend the work. The Excellent Masons were divided into six Lodges of nine each, including one of the Superexcellent Masons, who presided as Master. The eight Grand Architects constituted one Lodge, and the sixteen Architects another. The Grand Architects were the Masters, and the Architects the Wardens, of the Lodges of Master Masons, which were eight in number, and consisted, with their officers, of three hundred in each. The Mark Masters were divided into fourteen Lodges of fifty in each, and the Markmen into fourteen Lodges also, of one hundred in each. The Mark Masters were the Masters, and the Markmen the Wardens, of the Lodges of Fellow-Crafts, which were seven hundred in number, and with their officers consisted of eighty in each.

The classification of the workmen in the forest of Lebanon was as follows:

Superexcellent Masons	3
Excellent Masons	24
Grand Architects	4
Architects	8
Master Masons	1,188
Mark Masters	300
Markmen	600
Fellow-Crafts	23,100
Entered Apprentices	10,000
Total	35,227

These were arranged as follows: The three Superexcellent Masons formed one Lodge. The Excellent Masons were divided into three Lodges of nine each, including one of the Superexcellent Masons as Master. The four Grand Architects constituted one Lodge, and the eight Architects another, the former acting as Masters and the latter as Wardens of the Lodges of Master Masons, which were four in number, and consisted, with their officers, of three hundred in each. The Mark Masters were divided into six Lodges of fifty in each, and the Markmen into six Lodges also, of one hundred in each. These two classes presided, the former as Masters and the latter as Wardens, over the Lodges of Fellow-Crafts, which were three hundred in number, and were composed of eighty in each, including their officers.

After three years had been occupied in "hewing, squaring, and numbering" the stones, and in "felling and preparing" the timbers, these two bodies of Masons, from the quarries and the forest, united for the purpose of properly arranging and fitting the materials, so that no metallic tool might be required in putting them up, and they were then carried up to Jerusalem. Here the whole body was congregated under the superintending care of Hiram Abif, and to them were added four hundred and twenty Lodges of Tyrian and Sidonian Fellow-Crafts, having eighty in each, and the twenty thousand Entered Apprentices of the levy from Israel, who had heretofore been at rest, and who were added to the Lodges of their degree, making them now consist of three hundred in each, so that the whole number then engaged at Jerusalem amounted to two hundred and seventeen thousand two hundred and eighty-one, who were arranged as follows:

9 Lodges of Excellent Masons, 9 in each, were	81
12 Lodges of Master Masons, 300 in each, were	3,600
1,000 Lodges of Fellow-Crafts, 80 in each, were	80,000
420 Lodges of Tyrian Fellow-Crafts, 80 in each, were	33,600
100 Lodges of Entered Apprentices, 300 in each, were	30,000
70,000 Ish Sabal, or laborers	70,000
Total	217,281

Such is the system adopted by our English brethren. The American ritual has greatly simplified the arrangement. According to the system now generally adopted in this country, the workmen engaged in building King Solomon's Temple are supposed to have been classified as follows:

3 Grand Masters.

300 Harodim, or Chief Superintendents, who were Past Masters.

3,300 Overseers, or Master Masons, divided into Lodges of three in each.

80,000 Fellow-Crafts, divided into Lodges of five in each.

70,000 Entered Apprentices, divided into Lodges of seven in each.

According to this account, there must have been eleven hundred Lodges of Master Masons; sixteen thousand of Fellow-Crafts; and ten thousand of Entered Apprentices. No account is here taken of the levy of thirty thousand who are supposed not to have been Masons, nor of the builders sent by Hiram, King of Tyre, whom the English ritual places at thirty-three thousand six hundred, and most of whom we may suppose to have been members of the Dionysiac Fraternity of Artificers, the institution from which Freemasonry, according to legendary authority, took its origin.

On the whole, the American system seems too defective to meet all the demands of the inquirer into this subject—an objection to which the English is not so obnoxious. But, as I have already observed, the whole account is mythical, and is to be viewed rather as a curiosity than as having any historical value.

Workshop. The French Masons call a Lodge an "*atelier*," literally, a workshop, or, as Boiste defines it, "a place where Craftsmen work under the same Master."

World. The Lodge is said to be a symbol of the world. Its form—an oblong square, whose greatest length is from east to west—represents the shape of the inhabited world according to the theory of the ancients. The "clouded canopy," or the "starry-decked covering" of the Lodge, is referred to the sky. The sun, which enlightens and governs the world at morning, noon, and evening, is represented by the three superior officers. And, lastly, the Craft, laboring in the work of the Lodge, present a similitude to the inhabitants of the world engaged in the toils of life. While the Lodge is adopted as a copy of the Temple, not less universal is that doctrine which makes it a symbol of the world. (See *Form of the Lodge*.)

Worldly Possessions. In the English lectures of Dr. Hemming, the word Tubal Cain is said "to denote worldly possessions," and hence Tubal Cain is adopted in that system as the symbol of worldly possessions. The idea is derived from the derivation of Cain from *kanah*, to acquire, to gain, and from the theory that Tubal Cain, by his inventions, had enabled his pupils to acquire riches. But the derivative meaning of the word has reference to the expression of Eve, that in the birth of her eldest son she had acquired a man by the help of the Lord; and any system which gives importance to mere wealth as a Masonic symbol, is not in accord with the moral and intellectual designs of the Institution, which is thus represented as a mere instrument of Mammon. The symbolism is quite modern, and has not been adopted elsewhere than in English Masonry.

Worldly Wealth. Partial clothing is, in Masonry, a symbol teaching the aspirant that Masonry regards no man on account of his worldly wealth or honors; and that it looks not to his outward clothing, but to his internal qualifications.

Worship. Originally, the term "to worship" meant to pay that honor and reverence which are due to one who is worthy. Thus, where our authorised version translates Matthew xix. 19, "Honour thy father and thy mother," Wycliffe says, "Worschip thi fadir and thi modir." And in the marriage service of the Episcopal Church, the expression is still retained, "with my body I thee worship," that is, honor or reverence thee. Hence the still common use in England of the words *worshipful* and *right worshipful* as titles of honor applied to municipal and judicial officers. Thus the mayors of small towns, and justices of the peace, are styled "Worshipful," while the mayors of large cities, as London, are called "Right Worshipful." The usage was adopted and retained in Masonry. The word *worship*, or its derivatives, is not met with in any of the old manuscripts. In the "Manner of constituting a New Lodge," adopted in 1722, and published by Anderson in 1723, the word "worship" is applied as a title to the Grand Master. (*Constitutions*, 1723, p. 71.) In the seventeenth century, the gilds of London began to call themselves "Worshipful," as, "the Worshipful Company of Grocers," etc.; and it is likely that the Lodges at the revival, and perhaps a few years before, adopted the same style.

Worshipful. A title applied to a symbolic Lodge and to its Master. The Germans sometimes use the title "hochwürdig." The French style the Worshipful Master "Venerable," and the Lodge, "Respectable."

Worshipful Lodge. See *Worshipful*.

Worshipful Master. See *Worshipful*.

Worshipful, Most. The prevailing title of a Grand Master and of a Grand Lodge.

Worshipful, Right. The prevailing title of the elective officers of a Grand Lodge below the Grand Master.

Worshipful, Very. A title used by certain of the Grand Officers of the Grand Lodge of England.

Wound, Mason's. Nicolai, in the appendix to his *Essay on the Accusations against the Templars*, says that in a small dictionary, published at the beginning of the eighteenth century, the following definition is to be found: "*Mason's Wound*. It is an imaginary wound above the elbow, to represent a fracture of the arm occasioned by a fall from an elevated place." The origin and esoteric meaning of the phrase have been lost. It was probably used as a test, or alluded to some legend which has now escaped memory. Also, the Master's penalty in the degree of Perfection.

Wren, Sir Christopher. One of the most distinguished architects of England was the son of Dr. Christopher Wren, Rector of East Knoyle in Wiltshire, and was born there October 20, 1632. He was entered as a gentleman commoner at Wadham College, Oxford, in his fourteenth year, being already distinguished for his mathematical knowledge. He is said to have invented, before this period, several astronomical and mathematical instruments. In 1645, he became a member of a scientific club connected with Gresham College, from which the Royal Society subsequently arose. In 1653, he was elected a Fellow of All Souls' College, and had already become known to the learned men of Europe for his various inventions. In 1657, he removed permanently to London, having been elected Professor of Astronomy at Gresham College.

During the political disturbances which led to the abolition of the monarchy and the establishment of the commonwealth, Wren, devoted to the pursuits of philosophy, appears to have kept away from the contests of party. Soon after the restoration of Charles II., he was appointed Savillian Professor at Oxford, one of the highest distinctions which could then have been conferred on a scientific man. During this time he was distinguished for his numerous contributions to astronomy and mathematics, and invented many curious machines, and discovered many methods for facilitating the calculations of the celestial bodies.

Wren was not professionally educated as an architect, but from his early youth had devoted much time to its theoretic study. In 1665 he went to Paris for the purpose of studying the public buildings in that city, and the various styles which they presented. He was induced to make this visit, and to enter into these investigations, because, in 1660, he had been appointed by King Charles II. one of a commission to superintend the restoration of the Cathedral of St. Paul's, which had been much dilapidated during the times of the commonwealth. But before the designs could be carried into execution, the great fire occurred which laid so great a part of London, including St. Paul's, in ashes.

In 1661, he was appointed assistant to Sir John Denham, the Surveyor-General, and directed his attention to the restoration of the burnt portion of the city. His plans were, unfortunately for the good of London, not adopted, and he confined his attention to the rebuilding of particular edifices. In 1667, he was appointed the successor of Denham as Surveyor-General and Chief Architect. In this capacity he erected a large number of churches, the Royal Exchange, Greenwich Observatory, and many other public edifices. But his crowning work, the masterpiece that has given him his largest reputation, is the Cathedral of St. Paul's, which was commenced in 1675 and finished in 1710. The original plan that was proposed by Wren was rejected through the ignorance of the authorities, and differed greatly from the one on which it has been constructed. Wren, however, superintended the erection as master of the work, and his tomb in the crypt of the Cathedral was appropriately inscribed with the words: "Si monumentum requiris, circumspice"; i. e., "If you seek his monument, look around."

In 1672, Wren was made a Knight, and in 1674 he married a daughter of Sir John Coghill. To a son by this marriage are we indebted for memoirs of the family of his father, published under the title of *Parentalia*. After the death of this wife, he married a daughter of Viscount Fitzwilliam.

In 1680, Wren was elected President of the Royal Society, and continued to a late period his labors on public edifices, building, among others, additions to Hampton Court and to Windsor Castle.

After the death of Queen Anne, who was the last of his royal patrons, Wren was removed from his office of Surveyor-General, which he had held for a period of very nearly half a century. He passed the few remaining years of his life in serene retirement. He was found dead in his chair after dinner, on February 25, 1723, in the ninety-first year of his age.

Notwithstanding that much that has been said by Anderson and other writers of the eighteenth century, concerning Wren's connection with Freemasonry, is without historical confirmation, there can, I think, be no doubt that he took a deep interest in the Speculative as well as in the Operative Order. The Rev. J. W. Laughlin, in a lecture on the life of Wren, delivered in 1857, before the inhabitants of St. Andrew's, Holborn, and briefly reported in the *Freemasons' Magazine*, said that "Wren was for eighteen years a member of the old Lodge of St. Paul's, then held at the Goose and Gridiron, near the Cathedral, now the Lodge of Antiquity; and the records of that Lodge show that the maul and trowel used at the laying of the stone of St. Paul's, together with a pair of carved mahogany candlesticks, were presented by Wren, and are now in possession of that Lodge." By the order of the Duke of Sussex, a plate was placed on the mallet or maul which contained a statement of the fact.

Mr. C. W. King, who is not a Mason, but has derived his statement from a source to which he does not refer (but which was perhaps Nicolai), makes, in his work on the *Gnostics* (p. 176), the following statement, which is here quoted merely to show that the traditionary belief of Wren's connection with Speculative Freemasonry is not confined to the Craft. He says:

"Another and a very important circumstance in this discussion must always be kept in view: our Freemasons (as at present organized in the form of a secret society) derive their title from a mere accidental circumstance connected with their actual establishment. It was in the Common Hall of the London Gild of Freemasons (the trade) that their first meetings were held under Christopher Wren, president, in the time of the Commonwealth. Their real object was political—the restoration of monarchy; hence the necessary exclusion of the public, and the oaths of secrecy enjoined on the members. The pretence of promoting architecture, and the choice of the place where to hold their meetings, suggested by the profession of their president, were no more than blinds to deceive the existing government."

Anderson, in the first edition of the *Constitutions*, makes but a slight reference to Wren, only calling him "the ingenious architect, Sir Christopher Wren." I am almost afraid that this passing notice of him who has been called "the Vitruvius of England" must be attributed to servility. George I. was the stupid monarch who removed Wren from his office of Surveyor-General, and it would not do to be too diffuse with praise of one who had been marked by the disfavor of the king. But in 1727 George I. died, and in his second edition, published in 1738, Anderson gives to Wren all the Masonic honors to which he claims that he was entitled. It is from what Anderson has said in that work, that the Masonic writers of the eighteenth century and the first half of the nineteenth, not requiring the records of authentic history, have drawn their views of the official relations of Wren to the Order. He first introduces Wren (p. 101) as one of the Grand Wardens at the General Assembly held December 27, 1663, when the Earl of St. Albans was Grand Master, and Sir John Denham, Deputy Grand Master. He says that in 1666 Wren was again a Grand Warden, under the Grand Mastership of the Earl of Rivers; but immediately afterward he calls him "Deputy Wren," and continues to give him the title of Deputy Grand Master until 1685, when he says (p. 106) that "the Lodges met, and elected Sir Christopher Wren Grand Master, who appointed Mr. Gabriel Cibber and Mr. Edmund Savage Grand Wardens; and while carrying on St. Paul's, he annually met those brethren who could attend him, to keep up good old usages." Anderson (p. 107) makes the Duke of Richmond and Lennox Grand Master, and reduces Wren to the rank of a Deputy; but he says that in 1698 he was again chosen Grand Master, and as such "celebrated the Cape-stone" of St. Paul's in 1708. "Some few years after this," he says, "Sir Christopher Wren neglected the office of Grand Master." Finally, he says (p. 109) that in 1716 "the Lodges in London finding themselves neglected by Sir Christopher Wren," Masonry was revived under a new Grand Master. Some excuse for the aged architect's neglect might have been found in the fact that he was then eighty-five years of age, and had been long removed from his public office of Surveyor-General.

Noorthouck is more considerate. Speaking of the placing of the last stone on the top of St. Paul's—which, notwithstanding the statement of Anderson, was done, not by Wren, but by his son—he says (*Constitutions*, p. 204), "the age and infirmities of the Grand Master, which prevented his attendance on this solemn occasion, confined him afterwards to great retirement; so that the Lodges suffered from want of his usual presence in visiting and regulating their meetings, and were reduced to a small number."

Noorthouck, however, repeats substantially the statements of Anderson in reference to Wren's Grand Mastership. How much of these statements can be authenticated by history is a question that must be decided only by more extensive investigations of documents not yet in possession of the Craft. Findel says (*Hist.*, p. 127) that Anderson, having been commissioned in 1735 by the Grand Lodge to make a list of the ancient Patrons of the Masons, so as to afford something like an historical basis, "transformed the former Patrons into Grand Masters, and the Masters and Superintendents into Grand Wardens and the like, which were unknown until the year 1717."

Of this there can be no doubt; but there is other evidence that Wren was a Freemason. In Aubrey's *Natural History of Wiltshire* (p. 277), a manuscript in the library of the Royal Society, Halliwell finds and cites, in his *Early History of Freemasonry in England* (p. 46), the following passage:

"This day, May the 18th, being Monday, 1691, after Rogation Sunday, is a great convention at St. Paul's Church of the fraternity of the Adopted Masons, where Sir Christopher Wren is to be adopted a Brother, and Sir Henry Goodric of the Tower, and divers others. There have been kings that have been of this sodality."

If this statement be true—and we have no reason to doubt it, from Aubrey's general antiquarian accuracy—Anderson is incorrect in making him a Grand Master in 1685, six years before he was initiated as a Freemason. The true version of the story probably is this: Wren was a great architect—the greatest at the time in England. As such he received the appointment of Deputy Surveyor-General under Denham, and subsequently, on Denham's death, of Surveyor-General. He thus became invested, by virtue of his office, with the duty of superintending the construction of public buildings. The most important of these was St. Paul's Cathedral, the building of which he directed in person, and with so much energy that the parsimonious Duchess of Marlborough, when contrasting the charges of her own architect with the scanty remuneration of Wren, observed that "he was content to be dragged up in a basket three or four times a week to the top of St. Paul's, and at great hazard, for £200 a year." All this brought him into close connection with the gild of Freemasons, of which he naturally became the patron, and subsequently he was by initiation adopted into the sodality. Wren was, in fact, what the Medieval Masons called *Magister Operis*, or Master of the Work. Anderson, writing for a purpose, naturally transformed this title into that of Grand Master—an office supposed to be unknown until 1717. Aubrey's authority sufficiently establishes the fact that Wren was a Freemason, and the events of his life prove his attachment to the profession.*

Wrestle. A degree sometimes called the "Mark and Link," or Wrestle. It was formerly connected with the Mark Degree in England. Its ceremonies were founded on the passage contained in Genesis xxxii. 24–30.

Writing. The law which forbids a Mason to commit to writing the esoteric parts of the ritual is exemplified in some American Lodges by a peculiar ceremony; but the usage is not universal. The Druids had a similar rule; and we are told that they, in keeping their records, used the letters of the Greek alphabet, so that they might be unintelligible to those who were not authorized to read them.

Wykeham, William of. Bishop of Winchester. Born at Wykeham, in Hampshire, in 1324, and died in 1404. He was eminent both as an ecclesiastic and statesman. In 1359, before he reached the episcopate, Edward III. appointed him surveyor of the works at Windsor, which castle he rebuilt. In his Warrant or Commission, he was invested with power "to appoint all workmen, to provide materials, and to order everything relating to building and repairs." He was, in fact, what the old manuscript Constitutions call "The Lord," under whom were the Master Masons. Anderson says that he was at the head of four hundred Freemasons (*Constitutions*, 1738, p. 70), was Master of Work under Edward III., and Grand Master under Richard II. (*Ibid.*, p.72.) And the *Freemasons' Magazine* (August, 1796) styles him "one of the brightest ornaments that Freemasonry has ever boasted." In this there is, of course, a mixture of myth and history. Wykeham was an architect as well as a bishop, and superintended the building of many public edifices in England in the fourteenth century, being a distinguished example of the connection so common in Medieval times between the ecclesiastics and the Masons.

*R. F. Gould, in his *History of F. M.* (vol. ii., ch. 12) has cast grave doubts upon the alleged fact that Wren was a Freemason.

Wyoming. Cheyenne Lodge, No. 16, at Cheyenne, was chartered by the Grand Lodge of Colorado, October 7, 1868.

Laramie Lodge, No. 18, at Laramie City, received a dispensation from the same Grand Lodge, January 31, 1870, and a Charter, September 28, 1870.

Evanston Lodge, No. 24, at Evanston, received a dispensation from the same Grand Lodge, September 8, 1873, and a Charter, September 30, 1874.

Wyoming Lodge, No. 28, at South Pass City, had a dispensation issued to her by the Grand Lodge of Nebraska, November 20, 1869, and a Charter, June 23, 1870.

The representatives of these four Lodges met in convention December 15, 1874, at Laramie City, and proceeded to organize a Grand Lodge for Wyoming by adopting a constitution, electing and installing their Grand Officers on the 16th. The four Lodges then had a membership of two hundred and fifty.

The first annual communication was held October 12, 1875.

Wyseacre. The Leland MS., referring to Pythagoras, says that "wynnynge entraunce yn al Lodges of Maconnes, he lerned muche, and retournedde and woned yn Grecia Magna wachsynge, and becommynge a mightye wyseacre." The word wiseacre, which now means a dunce or silly person, is a corruption of the German *weissager*, and originally signified a wise sayer or philosopher, in which sense it is used in the passage cited.

X

X. The twenty-fourth letter of the English alphabet and the last letter of the proper Latin alphabet. As a numeral it stands for ten

Xaintrailles, Madame de. A lady who was initiated into Masonry by a French Lodge that did not have the excuse for this violation of law that we must accord to the Irish one in the case of Miss St. Leger. Clavel (*Hist. Pittoresq.*, p. 34) tells the story, but does not give the date, though it must have been about the close of the last century. The law of the Grand Orient of France required each Lodge of Adoption to be connected with and placed under the immediate guardianship of a regular Lodge of Masons. It was in one of these guardian Lodges that the female initiation which we are about to describe took place. The Lodge of "Frères-Artistes," at Paris, over which Bro. Cuvelier de Trie presided as Master, was about to give what is called a Fête of Adoption, that is, to open a Lodge for female Masonry, and initiate candidates into that rite. Previous, however, to the introduction of the female members, the brethren opened a regular Lodge of Ancient Masonry in the First Degree. Among the visitors who waited in the antechamber for admission was a youthful officer in the uniform of a captain of cavalry. His diploma or certificate was requested of him by the member deputed for the examination of the visitors, for the purpose of having it inspected by the Lodge. After some little hesitation, he handed the party asking for it a folded paper, which was immediately carried to the Orator of the Lodge, who, on opening it, discovered that it was the commission of an aide-de-camp, which had been granted by the Directory to the wife of General de Xaintrailles, a lady who, like several others of her sex in those troublous times, had donned the masculine attire and gained military rank at the point of the sword. When the nature of the supposed diploma was made known to the Lodge, it may readily be supposed that the surprise was general. But the members were Frenchmen: they were excitable and they were gallant; and consequently, in a sudden and exalted fit of enthusiasm, which as Masons we cannot excuse, they unanimously determined to confer the First Degree, not of Adoption, but of regular and legitimate Freemasonry, on the brave woman who had so often exhibited every manly virtue, and to whom her country had on more than one occasion committed trusts requiring the greatest discretion and prudence as well as courage. Madame de Xaintrailles was made acquainted with the resolution of the Lodge, and her acquiescence in its wishes requested. To the offer, she replied, "I have been a man for my country, and I will again be a man for my brethren." She was forthwith introduced and initiated as an Entered Apprentice, and repeatedly afterward assisted the Lodge in its labors in the First Degree.

Doubtless the Irish Lodge was, under all the circumstances, excused, if not justified, in the initiation of Miss St. Leger. But for the reception of Madame de Xaintrailles we look in vain for the slightest shadow of an apology. The outrage on their obligations as Masons, by the members of the Parisian Lodge, richly merited the severest punishment, which ought not to have been averted by the plea that the offense was committed in a sudden spirit of enthusiasm and gallantry.

Xavier Mier è Campello, Francisco. He was Bishop of Almeria, and Inquisitor-General of Spain, and an ardent persecutor of the Freemasons. In 1815, Ferdinand VII. having reestablished the Inquisition in Spain and suppressed the Masonic Lodges, Xavier published the bull of Pius VII., against the Order, in an ordinance of his own, in which he denounced the Lodges as "Societies which lead to sedition, to independence, and to all errors and crimes." He threatened the utmost rigors of the civil and canon laws against all who did not, within the space of fifteen days, renounce them; and then instituted a series of persecutions of the most atrocious character. Many of the most distinguished persons of Spain were arrested, and imprisoned in the dungeons of the Inquisition, on the charge of being "suspected of Freemasonry."

Xerophagists. On the 24th of April, 1738, Pope Clement XII. issued his bull forbidding the practise of Freemasonry by the members of the Roman Catholic Church. Many of the Masons of Italy continued, however, to meet; but, for the purpose of escaping the temporal penalties of the bull, which extended, in some cases, to the infliction of capital punishment, they changed their esoteric name, and called themselves *Xerophagists*. This is a compound of two Greek words signifying "eaters of dry food," and by it they alluded to an engagement into which they entered to abstain from the drinking of wine. They were, in fact, the first temperance society on record. Thory says (*Act. Lat.*, i., 346) that a manuscript concerning them was contained in the collection of the Mother Lodge of the Philosophic Scottish Rite.

Xerxes. A significant word in the degree of Sublime Prince of the Royal Secret, the Thirty-second of the Ancient and Accepted Scottish Rite. He is referred to in the old rituals of that degree as represented by Frederick the Great, the supposed founder of the Rite. Probably this is on account of the great military genius of both.

Xinxe. A significant word in the high degrees. Delaunay (*Tuileur*, p. 49) gives it as *Xincheu*, and says that it has been translated as "the seat of the soul." But in either form it has evidently undergone such corruption as to be no longer comprehensible.

Xystus. In ancient architecture a long and open, but sometimes covered, court with porticoes, for athletic exercises.

Xysuthrus. The name of the Babylonish king at the time of the Deluge. According to Berossus, ninth of a race who reigned 432,000 years. Also, Adrahasis of Surippak, son of Ubara-Tutu, the patriarch, to whom, according to the Deluge Tablet, the gods revealed the secret of the impending deluge, and who erected an ark accordingly, whereby he and his family and sevens of all clean beasts were saved. Xysuthrus means "shut up in a box or ark," from the two characters signifying "enclosed," and "box," respectively. In Accadian he is called Tamzi (Tammus), "The sun of life."

Y

Y. The twenty-fifth letter of the English alphabet, derived from the Greek Υ.

One of the symbols of Pythagoras was the Greek letter *Upsilon*, Υ, for which, on account of the similarity of shape, the Romans adopted the letter Y of their own alphabet. Pythagoras said that the two horns of the letter symbolized the two different paths of virtue and vice, the right branch leading to the former and the left to the latter. It was therefore called "Litera Pythagoræ," the letter of Pythagoras. Thus the Roman poet Martial says, in one of his epigrams:

> "Litera Pythagoræ, discrimine secta bicorni,
> Humanæ vitæ speciem præferre videtur."

i. e.,

> "The letter of Pythagoras, parted by its two-branched division, appears to exhibit the image of human life."

Yaksha. The name of a class of demigods in Hindu mythology, whose care is to attend on Kuvera, the god of riches, and see to his garden and treasures.

Yalla. A word said to have been used by the Templars in the adoration of the Baphometus, and derived from the Saracens.

Yama. (Sankr. *Yama*, a twin.) According to the Hindu mythology, the judge and ruler of the departed; the Hindu Pluto, or king of the infernal regions; originally conceived of as one of the first pair from whom the human race is descended, and the beneficent sovereign of his descendants in the abodes of the blest; later, a terrible deity, the tormentor of the wicked. He is represented of a green color, with red garments, having a crown on his head, his eyes inflamed, and sitting on a buffalo, with a club in his hand.

Yates, Giles Fonda. The task of writing a sketch of the life of Giles Fonda Yates is accompanied with a feeling of melancholy, because it brings to my mind the recollections of years, now passed forever, in which I enjoyed the intimate friendship of that amiable man and zealous Mason and scholar. His gentle mien won the love, his virtuous life the esteem, and his profound but unobtrusive scholarship the respect, of all who knew him.

Giles Fonda Yates was born in 1796, in what was then the village of Schenectady, in the State of New York. After acquiring at the ordinary schools of the period a preliminary liberal education, he entered Union College, and graduated with distinction, receiving in due time the degree of Master of Arts.

He subsequently commenced the study of the law, and, having been admitted to the bar, was, while yet young, appointed Judge of Probate in Schenectady, the duties of which office he discharged with great ability and fidelity.

Being blessed with a sufficient competency of the world's goods (although in the latter years of his life he became poor), Bro. Yates did not find it necessary to pursue the practise of the legal profession as a source of livelihood.

At an early period he was attracted, by the bent of his mind, to the study not only of general literature, but especially to that of archeology, philosophy, and the occult sciences, of all of which he became an ardent investigator. These studies led him naturally to the Masonic Institution, into which he was initiated in the year 1817, receiving the degrees of Symbolic Masonry in St. George's Lodge, No. 6, at Schenectady. In 1821 he affiliated with Morton Lodge, No. 87, of the same place, and was shortly afterward elected its Senior Warden. Returning subsequently to the Lodge of his adoption, he was chosen as its Master in 1844. He had in the meantime been admitted into a Chapter of the Royal Arch and an Encampment of Knights Templar; but his predilections being for Scottish Masonry, he paid little attention to these high degrees of the American Rite.

He held several important positions in the A. and A. S. Rite, being elected Sovereign Grand Commander of the Supreme Council in 1851, but soon resigned. He died December 13, 1859.

Yaveron Hamaim. A significant word in the high degrees. The French rituals explain it as meaning "the passage of the river," and refer it to the crossing of the river Euphrates by the liberated Jewish captives on their return from Babylon to Jerusalem to rebuild the Temple. It is in its present form a corruption of the Hebrew sentence, יעברו המים, *yavaru hamaim*, which signifies "they will cross, or pass over, the waters," alluding to the streams lying between Babylon and Jerusalem, of which the Euphrates was the most important.

Year, Hebrew. The same as the *Year of the World*, which see.

Year of Light. *Anno Lucis*, in the year of light, is the epoch used in Masonic documents of the Symbolic degrees. This era is calculated from the creation of the world, and is obtained by adding four thousand to the current year, on the supposition that Christ was born four thousand years after the creation of the world. But the chronology of Archbishop Usher, which has been adopted as the Bible chronology in the authorized version, places the birth of Christ in the year 4004 after the creation. According to this calculation, the Masonic date for the "year of light" is four years short of the true date, and the year of the Lord 1874, which in Masonic documents is 5874, should correctly be 5878. The Ancient and Accepted Masons in the beginning of this century used this correct or Usherian era, and the Supreme Council at Charleston dated their first circular, issued in 1802, as 5806. Dalcho (*Ahim. Res.*, 2d ed., p. 37) says: "If Masons are determined to fix the origin of their Order at the time of the creation, they should agree among themselves at what time before Christ to place that epoch." At that agreement they have now arrived. Whatever differences may have once existed, there is now a general consent to adopt the incorrect theory that the world was created 4000 B.C. The error is too unimportant, and the practise too universal, to expect that it will ever be corrected.

Noorthouck (*Constitutions*, 1784, p. 5), speaking of the necessity of adding the four years to make a correct date, says: "But this being a degree of accuracy that Masons in general do not attend to, we must, after this intimation, still follow the vulgar mode of computation to be intelligible."

As to the meaning of the expression, it is by no means to be supposed that Masons, now, intend by such a date to assume that their Order is as old as the creation. It is simply used as expressive of reverence for that physical light which was created by the fiat of the Grand Architect, and which is adopted as the type of the intellectual light of Masonry. The phrase is altogether symbolic.

Year of Masonry. Sometimes used as synonymous with *Year of Light*. In the eighteenth century, it was in fact the more frequent expression.

Year of the Deposite. An era adopted by Royal and Select Masters, and refers to the time when certain important secrets were deposited in the first Temple. (See *Anno Depositionis*.)

Year of the Discovery. An era adopted by Royal Arch Masons, and refers to the time when certain secrets were made known to the Craft at the building of the second Temple. (See *Anno Inventionis*.)

Year of the Order. The date used in documents connected with Masonic Templarism. It refers to the establishment of the Order of Knights Templar in the year 1118. (See *Anno Ordinis*.)

Year of the World. This is the era adopted by the Ancient and Accepted Scottish Rite and is borrowed from the Jewish computation. The Jews formerly used the era of contracts, dated from the first conquests of Seleucus Nicator in Syria. But since the fifteenth century they have counted from the creation, which they suppose to have taken place in September, 3760 before Christ. (See *Anno Mundi*.)

Yeas and Nays. The rule existing in all parliamentary bodies that a vote may be called for "by yeas and nays," so that the vote of each member may be known and recorded, does not apply to Masonic Lodges. Indeed, such a proceeding would be unnecessary. The vote by yeas and nays in a representative body is taken that the members may be held responsible to their constituents. But in a Lodge, each member is wholly independent of any responsibility, except to his own conscience. To call for the yeas and nays being then repugnant to the principles which govern Lodges, to call for them would be out of order, and such a call could not be entertained by the presiding officer.

But in a Grand Lodge the responsibility of the members to a constituency does exist, and there it is very usual to call for a vote by Lodges, when the vote of every member is recorded. Although the mode of calling for the vote is different, the vote by Lodges is actually the same as a vote by yeas and nays, and may be demanded by any member.

Yeldis. An old Hermetic degree, which Thory says was given in some secret societies in Germany.

Yellow. Of all the colors, yellow seems to be the least important and the least general in Masonic symbolism. In other institutions it would have the same insignificance, were it not that it has been adopted as the representative of the sun, and of the noble metal gold. Thus, in colored blasonry, the small dots, by which the gold in an engraved coat of arms is designated, are replaced by the yellow color. La Colombiere, a French heraldic writer, says (*Science Heroique*, p. 30), in remarking on the connection between gold and yellow, that as yellow, which is derived from the sun, is the most exalted of colors, so gold is the most noble of metals. Portal (*Des Couleurs Symboliques*, p. 64) says that the sun, gold, and yellow are not synonymous, but mark different degrees which it is difficult to define. The natural sun was the symbol of the spiritual sun, gold represented the natural sun, and yellow was the emblem of gold. But it is evident that yellow derives all its significance as a symbolic color from its connection with the hue of the rays of the sun and the metal gold.

Among the ancients, the Divine light or wisdom was represented by yellow, as the Divine heat or power was by red. And this appears to be about the whole of the ancient symbolism of this color.

In the old ritual of the Scottish and Hermetic degree of Knight of the Sun, yellow was the symbol of wisdom darting its rays, like the yellow beams of the morning, to enlighten a waking world. In the Prince of Jerusalem, it was also formerly the characteristic color, perhaps with the same meaning, in reference to the elevated position that that degree occupied in the Rite of Perfection, and afterward in the Ancient and Accepted Rite.

Thirty or forty years ago, yellow was the characteristic color of the Mark Master's Degree, derived, perhaps, from the color of the Princes of Jerusalem, who originally issued charters for Mark Lodges; for it does not seem to have possessed any symbolic meaning.

In fact, as has been already intimated, all the symbolism of yellow must be referred to and explained by the symbolism of gold and of the sun, of which it is simply the representative.

Yellow Caps, Society of. The name of a society said to have been founded by Ling-Ti, in China, in the eleventh century.

Yellow Jacket. Prichard says that in the early part of the last century the following formed a part of the Catechism:

"Have you seen your Master to-day?

"Yes.

"How was he cloathed?

"In a yellow jacket and a blue pair of breeches."

And he explains it by saying that "the yellow jacket is the compasses, and the blue breeches the steel points."

On this Krause (*Kunsturk.*, ii., 78) remarks that this sportive comparison is altogether in the puerile spirit of the peculiar interrogatories which are found among many other crafts, and is without doubt genuine as originating in the working Lodges. Prichard's explanation is natural, and Krause's remark correct. But it is vain to attempt to elevate the idea by attaching to it a symbolism of gold and azure—the blue sky and the meridian sun. No such thought entered into the minds of the illiterate operatives with whom the question and answer originated.

Yevele, Henry. He was one of the Magistri Operis, or Masters of the Work, in the reign of Edward III., for whom he constructed several public edifices. Anderson says that he is called, "in the Old Records, the King's Freemason" (*Constitutions*, 1738, p. 70); but his name does not occur in any of the old manuscript Constitutions that are now extant.

Yezdegerdian. Pertaining to the era of Yezdegerd, the last Sassanian monarch of Persia, who was overthrown by the Mohammedans. The era is still used by the Parsees, and began 16th of June, 632 A.D.

Yezidee. One of a sect bordering on the Euphrates, whose religious worship mixes up the Devil with some of the doctrines of the Magi, Mohammedans, and Christians.

Yggdrasil. The name given in Scandinavian mythology to the greatest and most sacred of all trees, which was conceived as binding together heaven, earth, and hell. It is an ash, whose branches spread over all the world, and reach above the heavens. It sends out three roots in as many different directions: one to the Asa-gods in heaven, another to the Frost-giants, the third to the under-world. Under each root springs a wonderful fountain, endowed with marvelous virtues. From the tree itself springs a honey-dew. The serpent, Nithhöggr, lies at the under-world fountain and gnaws the root of Yggdrasil; the squirrel, Ratatoskr, runs up and down, and tries to breed strife between the serpent and the eagle, which sits aloft. Dr. Oliver (*Signs and Symbols*, p. 155) considers it to have been the Theological Ladder of the Gothic mysteries.

Y-ha-ho. Higgins (*Anacalypsis*, ii., 17) cites the Abbé Bazin as saying that this was the name esteemed most sacred among the ancient Egyptians. Clement of Alexandria asserts, in his *Stromata*, that all those who entered into the temple of Serapis were obliged to wear conspicuously on their persons the name *I-ha-ho*, which he says signifies *the Eternal God*. The resemblance to the Tetragrammaton is apparent.

Yod. The Hebrew letter י, equivalent in sound to I or Y. It is the initial letter of the word יהוה, or Jehovah, the Tetragrammaton, and hence was peculiarly sacred among the Talmudists. Basnage (lib. iii., c. 13), while treating of the mysteries of the name Jehovah among the Jews, says of this letter:

"The *yod* in Jehovah is one of those things which eye hath not seen, but which has been concealed from all mankind. Its essence and matter are incomprehensible; it is not lawful so much as to meditate upon it. Man may lawfully revolve his thoughts from one end of the heavens to the other, but he cannot approach that inaccessible light, that primitive existence, contained in the letter *yod;* and indeed the masters call the letter thought or idea, and prescribe no bounds to its efficacy. It was this letter which, flowing from the primitive light, gave being to emanations. It wearied itself by the way, but assumed a new vigor by the sense of the letter ה, which makes the second letter of the Ineffable Name."

In Symbolic Masonry, the *yod* has been replaced by the letter G. But in the high degrees it is retained, and within a triangle, thus, constitutes the symbol of the Deity.

Yoni. Among the Orientalists, the yoni was the female symbol corresponding to the lingam, or male principle. The lingam and yoni of the East assumed the names of Phallus and Cteis among the Greeks.

York Constitutions. This document, which is also called Krause's MS., purports to be the Constitutions adopted by the General Assembly of Masons that was held at York in 926. (See *York Legend*.) No original manuscript copy of it can be found, but a German translation from a Latin version was published, for the first time, by Krause in *Die drei ältesten Kunsturkunden der Freimaurerbrüderschaft*. It will be found in the third edition of that work (vol. iii., pp. 58–101). Krause's account of it is, that it was translated from the original, which is said, in a certificate dated January 4, 1806, and signed "Stonehouse," to have been written on parchment in the ancient language of the country, and preserved at the city of York, "apud Rev. summam societatem architectonicam," which Woodford translates "an architectural society," but which is evidently meant for the "Grand Lodge." From this Latin translation a German version was made in 1808 by Bro. Schneider of Altenberg, the correctness of which, having been examined by three linguists, is certified by Carl Erdmann Weller, Secretary of the Government Tribunal of Saxony. And it is this certified German translation that has been published by Krause in his *Kunsturkunden*. An English version was inserted by Bro. Hughan in his *Old Charges of British Freemasons*. The document consists, like all the old manuscripts, of an introductory invocation, a history of architecture or the "Legend of the Craft," and the general statutes or charges; but several of the charges differ from those in the other Constitutions. There is, however, a general resemblance sufficient to indicate a common origin. The appearance of this document gave rise in Germany to discussions as to its authenticity. Krause, Schneider, Fessler, and many other distinguished Masons, believed it to be genuine; while Kloss denied it, and contended that the Latin translation which was certified by Stonehouse had been prepared before 1806, and that in preparing it an ancient manuscript had been remodeled on the basis of the 1738 edition of Anderson's *Constitutions*, because the term "Noachida" is employed in both, but is found nowhere else. At length, in 1864, Bro. Findel was sent by the "Society of German Masons" to England to discover the original. His report of his journey was that it was negative in its results; no such document was to be found in the archives of the old Lodge at York, and no such person as Stonehouse was known in that city. These two facts, to which may be added the further arguments that no mention is made of it in the *Fabric Rolls of York Minster*, published by the Surtees Society, nor in the inventory of the Grand Lodge of York which was extant in 1777, nor by Drake in his speech delivered before the Grand Lodge in 1726, and a few other reasons, have led Findel to agree with Kloss that the document is not a genuine York Charter. Such, too, is the general opinion of English Masonic scholars. (See Gould's *Hist. of F. M.*, i., pp. 494–6.) There can be little doubt that the General Assembly at York, in 926, did frame a body of laws or Constitutions; but there is almost as little doubt that they are not represented by the Stonehouse or Krause document.

York, Edward Augustus, Duke of. Initiated a Mason in 1766.

York, Frederick, Duke of. Initiated a Mason in "Britannia Lodge," London, November 21, 1787. A commemorative Masonic token was issued in 1795; the Duke of York having been installed W. M. of the "Prince of Wales Lodge," March 22, 1793.

York Grand Lodge. Bro. Woodford says this is a short title for "The Grand Lodge of all England," held at York, which was formed from an old Lodge, in 1725, at work evidently during the seventeenth century, and probably much earlier. The annual assembly was held in the city of York by the Masons for centuries, and is so acknowledged virtually by all the MSS. from the fourteenth century. A list of Master Masons of the York Minster, during its erection, is preserved, of the fourteenth century; and legend and actual history agree in the fact that York was the home of the Mason-craft until modern times—the "Charter of Prince Edwin" being one of the earliest traditions. The Grand Lodge preserved its position in the north of England until 1792, when it finally died out, it having constituted other Lodges, and a "Grand Lodge, south of the Trent" (at London). All of the "York" Lodges succumbed on the decease of their "Mother Grand Lodge." There has not been a representative of the Ancient York Grand Lodge anywhere whatever throughout this century.

York Legend. The city of York, in the north of England, is celebrated for its traditional connection with Masonry in that kingdom. No topic in the history of Freemasonry has so much engaged the attention of modern Masonic scholars, or given occasion to more discussion, than the alleged facts of the existence of Masonry in the tenth century at the city of York as a prominent point, of the calling of a congregation of the Craft there in the year 926, of the organisation of a General Assembly and the adoption of a Constitution. During the whole of the last and the greater part of the present century, the Fraternity in general have accepted all of these statements as genuine portions of authentic history; and the adversaries of the Order have, with the same want of discrimination, rejected them all as myths; while a few earnest seekers for truth have been at a loss to determine what part was historical and what part legendary. Recently, the discovery of many old manuscripts has directed the labors of such scholars as Hughan, Woodford, Lyon, and others, to the critical examination of the early history of Masonry, and that of York has particularly engaged their attention.

For a thorough comprehension of the true merits of this question, it will be necessary that the student should first acquaint himself with what was, until recently, the recognised theory as to the origin of Masonry at York, and then that he should examine the newer hypotheses advanced by the writers of the present day. In other words, he must read both the tradition and the history.

In pursuance of this plan, I propose to commence with the legends of York Masonry, as found in the old manuscript Constitutions, and then proceed to a review of what has been the result of recent investigations. It may be premised that, of all those who have subjected these legends to the crucible of historical criticism, Bro. William James Hughan of Cornwall, in England, must unhesitatingly be acknowledged as "facile princeps," the ablest, the most laborious, and the most trustworthy investigator. He was the first and the most successful remover of the cloud of tradition which so long had obscured the sunlight of history.

The legend which connects the origin of English Masonry at York in 926 is sometimes called the "York Legend," sometimes the "Athelstane Legend," because the General Assembly, said to have been held there, occurred during the reign of that king; and sometimes the "Edwin Legend," because that prince is supposed to have been at the head of the Craft, and to have convoked them together to form a Constitution.

The earliest extant of the old manuscript Constitutions is the ancient poem commonly known as the Halliwell MS., and the date of which is conjectured (on good grounds) to be about the year 1390. In that work we find the following version of the legend:

"Thys craft com ynto Englond as y yow say,
Yn tyme of good kynge Adelstonus' day;
He made tho bothe halle and eke bowre,
And hye templus of gret honowre,
To sportyn him yn bothe day and nygth,
An to worschepe hys God with alle hys mygth.
Thys goode lorde loved thys craft ful wel,
And purposud to strenthyn hyt every del,
For dyvers defawtys that yn the craft he fonde;
He sende aboute ynto the londe
After alle the masonus of the crafte,
To come to hym ful evene strayfte,
For to amende these defautys alle
By good consel gef hyt mytgth falle.
A semblé thenne he cowthe let make
Of dyvers lordis yn here state
Dukys, erlys, and barnes also,
Knygthys, sqwyers and mony mo,
And the grete burges of that syté,
They were ther alle yn here degré;
These were there uchon algate,
To ordeyne for these masonus astate,
Ther they sowgton by here wytte
How they mygthyn governe hytte:
Fyftene artyculus they there sowgton,
And fyftene poyntys ther they wrogton."

For the benefit of those who are not familiar with this archaic style, the passage is translated into modern English.

"This craft came into England, as I tell you, in the time of good king Athelstan's reign; he made then both hall, and also bower and lofty temples of great honor, to take his recreation in both day and night, and to worship his God with all his might. This good lord loved this craft full well, and purposed to strengthen it in every part on account of various defects that he discovered in the craft. He sent about into all the land, after all the masons of the craft, to come straight to him, to amend all these defects by good counsel, if it might so happen. He then permitted an assembly to be made of divers lords in their rank, dukes, earls, and barons, also knights, squires, and many more, and the great burgesses of that city, they were all there in their degree; these were there, each one in every way to make laws for the estate of these masons. There they sought by their wisdom how they might govern it; there they found out fifteen articles, and there they made fifteen points."

The next old document in which we find this legend recited is that known as the "Cooke MS.," whose date is placed at 1490. The details are here much more full than those contained in the Halliwell MS. The passage referring to the legend is as follows:

"And after that was a worthy kynge in Englond, that was callyd Athelstone, and his yongest son lovyd well the sciens of Gemetry, and he wyst well that hand craft had the practyke of the sciens of Gemetry so well as masons; wherefore he drew him to consell and lernyd [the] practyke of that sciens to his speculatyf. For of speculatyfe he was a master, and he lovyd well masonry and masons. And he bicome a mason hymselfe. And he gaf hem [gave them] charges and names as it is now usyd in Englond and in other countries. And he ordeyned that they schulde have resonabull pay. And purcheesd [obtained] a fre patent of the kyng that they schulde make a sembly when thei sawe resonably tyme a [to] cum togedir to her [their] counsell of the whiche charges, manors & semble as is write and taught in the boke of our charges wherefor I leve hit at this tyme."

Thus much is contained in the MS. from lines 611 to 642. Subsequently, in lines 688–719, which appear to have been taken from what is above called the "Boke of Charges," the legend is repeated in these words:

"In this manner was the forsayde art begunne in the lond of Egypt bi the forsayd maister Euglat [Euclid], & so hit went fro lond to londe and fro kyngdome to kyngdome. After that, many yeris, in the tyme of Kyng Adhelstone, wiche was sum tyme kynge of Englonde, bi his counsell and other gret lordys of the lond bi comin [common] assent for grete defaut y-fennde [found] among masons thei ordeyned a certayne reu'e amongys hem [them]. On [one] tyme of the yere or in iii yere, as nede were to the kyng and gret lordys of the londe and all the comente [community], fro provynce to provynce and fro countre to countre congregacions scholde be made by maisters, of all maisters masons and felaus in the forsayd art. And so at such congregacions they that be made masters schold be examined of the articuls after written, & be ransacked [thoroughly examined] whether thei be abull and kunnyng [able and skilful] to the profyte of the lordys hem to serve [to serve them], and to the honor of the forsayd art."

Seventy years later, in 1560, the Lansdowne MS. was written, and in it we find the legend still further developed, and Prince Edwin for the first time introduced by name. That manuscript reads thus:

"Soone after the Decease of St. Albones, there came Diverse Warrs into England out of Diverse Nations, so that the good rule of Masons was dishired [disturbed] and put down until the tyme of King Adilston. In his tyme there was a worthy King in England, that brought this Land into good rest, and he builded many great workes and buildings, therefore he loved well Masons, for he had a sone called Edwin, the which Loved Masons much more than his Father did, and he was soe practised in Geometry, that he delighted much to come and talke with Masons and to learne of them the Craft. And after, for the love he had to Masons and to the Craft, he was made Mason at Windsor, and he gott of the King, his Father, a Charter and commission once every yeare to have Assembley, within the Realme where they would within England, and to correct within themselves Faults & Trespasses that were done as touching the Craft, and he held them an Assembley, and there he made Masons and gave them Charges, and taught them the Manners and Comands the same to be kept ever afterwards. And tooke them the Charter and commission to keep their Assembly, and Ordained that it should be renewed from King to King, and when the Assembly were gathered togeather he made a Cry, that all old Masons or young, that had any Writeings or Vnderstanding of the Charges and manners that weere made before their Lands, wheresoever they were made Masons, that they should shew them forth, there were found some in French, some in Greek, some in Hebrew, and some in English, and some in other Languages, and when they were read and over seen well the intent of them was vnderstood to be all one, and then he caused a Book to be made thereof how this worthy Craft of Masonrie was first founded, and he himselfe comanded, and also then caused, that it should be read at any tyme when it should happen any Mason or Masons to be made to give him or them their Charges, and from that, until this Day, Manners of Masons have been kept in this Manner and forme, as well as Men might Governe it, and Furthermore at diverse Assemblyes have been put and Ordained diverse Charges by the best advice of Masters and Fellows."

All the subsequent manuscripts contain the legend substantially as it is in the Lansdowne; and most of them appear to be mere copies of it, or, most probably, of some original one of which both they and it are copies.

In 1723 Dr. Anderson published the first edition of the *Book of Constitutions*, in which the history of the Fraternity of Freemasons is, he says, "collected from their general records and their faithful traditions of many ages." He gives the legend taken, as he says, from "a certain record of Freemasons written in the reign of King Edward IV.," which manuscript, Preston asserts, "is said to have been in the possession of the famous Elias Ashmole." As the old manuscripts were generally inaccessible to the Fraternity (and, indeed, until recently but few of them have been discovered), it is to the publication of the legend by Anderson, and subsequently by Preston, that we are to attribute its general adoption by the Craft for more than a century and a half. The form of the legend, as given by Anderson in his first edition, varies slightly from that in his second. In the former, he places the date of the occurrence at 930; in his second, at 926: in the former, he styles the congregation at York a General Lodge; in his second, a Grand Lodge. Now, as the modern and universally accepted form of the legend agrees in both respects with the latter statement, and not with the former, it must be concluded that the second edition, and the subsequent ones by Entick and Noorthouck who only repeat Anderson, furnished the form of the legend as now popular.

In the second edition of the *Constitutions* (p. 63), published in 1738, Anderson gives the legend in the following words:

"In all the Old Constitutions it is written to this purpose, viz.:

"That though the antient records of the Brotherhood in England were most of them destroyd or lost in the war with the Danes, who burnt the Monasteries where the Records were kept; yet King Athelstan, (the Grandson of King Alfred,) the first annointed King of England, who translated the Holy Bible into the Saxon language, when he had brought the land into rest and peace, built many great works, and encouraged many Masons from France and elsewhere, whom he appointed overseers thereof: they brought with them the Charges and Regulations of the foreign Lodges, and prevail'd with the King to increase the wages.

"That Prince Edwin, the King's Brother, being taught Geometry and Masonry, for the love he had to the said Craft, and to the honorable princip es whereon it is grounded, purchased a Free Charter of King Athelstan his Brother, for the Free Masons having among themselves a Connection or a power and freedom to regulate themselves to amend what might happen amiss and to hold an yearly Communication in a General Assembly.

"That accordingly Prince Edwin summon'd all the Free and Accepted Masons in the Realm, to meet him in the Congregation at York, who came and form'd the Grand Lodge under him as their Grand Master, A. D. 926.

"That they brought with them many old Writings and Records of the Craft, some in Greek, some in Latin, some in French, and other languages; and from the contents thereof, they framed the CONSTITUTIONS of the English Lodges, and made a Law for themselves, to preserve and observe the same in all Time coming, etc., etc., etc."

Preston accepted the legend, and gave it in his second edition (p. 198) in the following words:

"Edward died in 924, and was succeeded by Athelstane his son, who appointed his brother Edwin patron of the Masons. This prince procured a Charter from Athelstane, empowering them to meet annually in communication at York. In this city, the first Grand Lodge of England was formed in 926, at which Edwin presided as Grand Master. Here many old writings were produced in Greek, Latin, and other languages, from which it is said the Constitutions of the English Lodge have been extracted."

Such is the "York Legend," as it has been accepted by the Craft, contained in all the old manuscripts from at least the end of the fourteenth century to the present day; officially sanctioned by Anderson, the historiographer of the Grand Lodge in 1723, and repeated by Preston, by Oliver, and by almost all succeeding Masonic writers. Only recently has anyone thought of doubting its authenticity; and now the important question in Masonic literature is whether it is a myth or a history —whether it is all or in any part fiction or truth—and if so, what portion belongs to the former and what to the latter category. In coming to a conclusion on this subject, the question necessarily divides itself into three forms:

1. Was there an Assembly of Masons held in or about the year 926, at York, under the patronage or by the permission of King Athelstan?

There is nothing in the personal character or the political conduct of Athelstan that forbids such a possibility or even probability. He was liberal in his ideas, like his grandfather the great Alfred; he was a promoter of civilization; he patronized learning, built many churches and monasteries, encouraged the translation of the Scriptures, and gave charters to many operative companies. In his reign, the "frith-*gildan*," free gilds or sodalities, were incorporated by law. There is, therefore, nothing improbable in supposing that he extended his protection to the Operative Masons. The uninterrupted existence for several centuries of a tradition that such an Assembly was held, requires that those who deny it should furnish some more satisfactory reason for their opinion than has yet been produced. "Incredulity," says Voltaire, "is the foundation of history." But it must be confessed that, while an excess of credulity often mistakes fable for reality, an obstinacy of incredulity as frequently leads to the rejection of truth as fiction. The Rev. Mr. Woodford, in an essay on *The Connection of York with the History of Freemasonry in England*, inserted in Hughan's *Unpublished Records of the Craft*, has critically discussed this subject, and comes to this conclusion. "I see no reason, therefore, to reject so old a tradition, that under Athelstan the Operative Masons obtained his patronage, and met in General Assembly." To that verdict I subscribe.

2. Was Edwin, the brother of Athelstan, the person who convoked that Assembly? This question has already been discussed in the article *Edwin*, where the suggestion is made that the Edwin alluded to in the legend was not the son or brother of Athelstan, but Edwin, King of Northumbria. Francis Drake, in his speech before the Grand Lodge of York in 1726, was, I think, the first who publicly advanced this opinion; but he does so in a way that shows that the view must have been generally accepted by his auditors, and not advanced by him as something new. He says: "You know we can boast that the first Grand Lodge ever held in England was held in this city, where Edwin, the first Christian king of Northumbria, about the six hundredth year after Christ, and who laid the foundation of our Cathedral, sat as Grand Master."

Edwin, who was born in 586, ascended the throne in 617, and died in 633. He was preeminent, among the Anglo-Saxon kings who were his contemporaries, for military genius and statesmanship. So inflexible was his administration of justice, that it was said that in his reign a woman or child might carry everywhere a purse of gold without danger of robbery—high commendation in those days of almost unbridled rapine. The chief event of the reign of Edwin was the introduction of Christianity into the kingdom of Northumbria. Previous to his reign, the northern metropolis of the Church had been placed at York, and the king patronized Paulinus the bishop, giving him a house and other possessions in that city. The only objection to this theory is its date, which is three hundred years before the reign of Athelstan and the supposed meeting at York in 926.

3. Are the Constitutions which were adopted by that General Assembly now extant? It is not to be doubted, that if a General Assembly was held, it must have adopted Constitutions or regulations for the government of the Craft. Such would mainly be the object of the meeting. But there is no sufficient evidence that the Regulations now called the "York Constitutions," or the "Gothic Constitutions," are those that were adopted in 926. It is more probable that the original document and all genuine copies of it are lost, and that it formed the type from which all the more modern manuscript Constitutions have been formed. There is the strongest internal evidence that all the manuscripts, from the Halliwell to the Papworth, had a common original, from which they were copied with more or less accuracy, or on which they were framed with more or less modification. And this original I suppose to be the Constitutions which must have been adopted at the General Assembly at York.

The theory, then, which I think may safely be advanced on this subject, and which must be maintained until there are better reasons than we now have to reject it, is, that about the year 926 a General Assembly of Masons was held at York, under the patronage of Edwin, brother of Athelstan, at which Assembly a code of laws was adopted, which became the basis on which all subsequent Masonic Constitutions were framed.

York Manuscripts. Originally there were six manuscripts of the *Old Constitutions* bearing this title, because they were deposited in the Archives of the now extinct Grand Lodge of all England, whose seat was at the city of York. But the MS. No. 3 is now missing, although it is mentioned in the inventory made at York in 1779. Nos. 2, 4, and 5 are now in possession of the York Lodge. Recently Bro. Hughan discovered Nos. 2 and 6 in the Archives of the Grand Lodge of England, at London. The dates of these manuscripts, which do not correspond with the number of their titles, are as follows:

No. 1 has the date of 1600.
" 2 " " 1704.
" 3 " " 1630.
" 4 " " 1693.
" 5 is undated, but is supposed to be about 1670.
" 6 also is undated, but is considered to be about 1680.

Of these MSS. all but No. 3 have been published by the late Bro. W. J. Hughan in his *Ancient York Masonic Rolls.* (1894.) Bro. Hughan deems No. 4 of some importance because it contains the following sentence: "The one of the elders takeing the Booke, and that *hee* or *shee* that is to be made mason shall lay their hands thereon, and the charge shall bee given." This, he thinks, affords some presumption that women were admitted as members of the old Masonic gilds, although he admits that we possess no other evidence confirmatory of this theory. The truth is, that the sentence was a translation of the same clause written in other *Old Constitutions* in Latin. In the York MS., No. 1, the sentence is thus: "Tunc unus ex senioribus teneat librum et *ille* vel *illi*," etc., i. e., "*he* or *they*." The writer of No. 4 copied, most probably, from No. 1, and his translation of "*hee* or *shee*" from "*ille* vel *illi*," instead of "*he* or *they*," was either the result of ignorance in mistaking *illi*, they, for *illa*, she, or of carelessness in writing *shee* for *they*. It is evident that the charges thus to be sworn to, and which immediately follow, were of such a nature as made most of them physically impossible for women to perform; nor are females alluded to in any other of the manuscripts. All Masons there are "Fellows," and are so to be addressed.

There are two other York Manuscripts of the Operative Masons, which have been published in the *Fabric Rolls of York Minster*, an invaluable work, edited by the Rev. James Raine, and issued under the patronage and at the expense of the Surtees Society.

York Rite. This is the oldest of all the Rites, and consisted originally of only three degrees: 1. Entered Apprentice; 2. Fellow-Craft; 3. Master Mason. The last included a part which contained the True Word, but which was disrupted from it by Dunckerley in the latter part of the last century, and has never been restored. The Rite in its purity does not now exist anywhere. The nearest approach to it is the St. John's Masonry of Scotland, but the Master's Degree of the Grand Lodge of Scotland is not the Master's Degree of the York Rite. When Dunckerley dismembered the Third Degree, he destroyed the identity of the Rite. In 1813, it was apparently recognized by the United Grand Lodge of England, when it defined "pure Ancient Masonry to consist of three degrees, and no more: viz., those of the Entered Apprentice, the Fellow Craft, and the Master Mason, including the Supreme Order of the Holy Royal Arch." Had the Grand Lodge abolished the Royal Arch Degree, which was then practised as an independent Order in England, and reincorporated its secrets in the degree of Master Mason, the York Rite would have been revived. But by recognizing the Royal Arch as a separate degree, and retaining the Master's Degree in its mutilated form, they repudiated the Rite. In the United States it has been the almost universal usage to call the Masonry there practised the York Rite. But it has no better claim to this designation than it has to be called the Ancient and Accepted Rite, or the French Rite, or the Rite of Schröder. It has no pretensions to the York Rite. Of its first three degrees, the Master's is the mutilated one which took the Masonry of England out of the York Rite, and it has added to these three degrees six others which were never known to the Ancient York Rite, or that which was practised in England, in the earlier half of the eighteenth century, by the legitimate Grand Lodge. In all my writings for years past, I have ventured to distinguish the Masonry practised in the United States, consisting of nine degrees, as the "American Rite," a title to which it is clearly and justly entitled, as the system is peculiar to America, and is practised in no other country.

Bro. Hughan, speaking of the York Rite (*Unpubl. Rec.*, p. 148), says "there is no such Rite, and what it *was* no one *now* knows." I think that this declaration is too sweeping in its language. He is correct in saying that there is at this time no such Rite. I have just described its decadence; but he is wrong in asserting that we are now ignorant of its character. In using the title, there is no reference to the Grand Lodge of all England, which met for some years during the last century, but rather to the York legend, and to the hypothesis that York was the cradle of English Masonry. The York Rite was that Rite which was most probably organized or modified at the revival in 1717, and practised for fifty years by the Constitutional Grand Lodge of England. It consisted of only the three Symbolic degrees, the last one, or the Master's, containing within itself the secrets now transferred to the Royal Arch. This Rite was carried in its purity to France in 1725, and into America at a later period. About the middle of the eighteenth century the continental Masons, and about the end of it the Americans, began to superimpose upon it those high degrees which, with the necessary mutilation of the third, have given rise to numerous other Rites. But the Ancient York Rite, though no longer cultivated, must remain on the records of history as the oldest and purest of all the Rites.

Yug or **Yuga.** One of the ages, according to Hindu mythology, into which the Hindus divide the duration or existence of the world.

Z

Z. (Heb., ז, *Zain.*) Twenty-sixth and last letter of the English alphabet. In Hebrew the numerical value is seven. This letter was added to the Latin from the Greek in the time of Cicero. The Greek letter is *zeta*, ζ.

Zabud. An historical personage at the court of King Solomon, whose name appears in several of the high degrees. In that of Select Master in the American Rite, it has been corrupted into *Izabud.* He is mentioned in 1 Kings iv. 5, where he is described in the authorized version as being "principal officer and the king's friend." The original is *Zabud ben Nathan cohen regneh hahmelek*, which is literally "Zabud, son of Nathan, a priest, the friend of the king." Adam Clarke says he was "the king's chief favorite, his confidant." Smith (*Dict. Bib.*) says: "This position, if it were an official one, was evidently distinct from that of counsellor, occupied by Ahithophel under David, and had more of the character of private friendship about it." Kitto (*Cyclopæd. Bib. Lit.*) says of Zabud and of his brother Azariah, that their advancement in the household of King Solomon "may doubtless be ascribed not only to the young king's respect for the venerable prophet (their father), who had been his instructor, but to the friendship he had contracted with his sons during the course of education. The office, or rather honor, of 'friend of the king,' we find in all the despotic governments of the East. It gives high power, without the public responsibility which the holding of a regular office in the state necessarily imposes. It implies the possession of the utmost confidence of, and familiar intercourse with, the monarch, to whose person 'the friend' at all times has access, and whose influence is therefore often far greater, even in matters of state, than that of the recognized ministers of government."

This has been fully carried out in the legend of the Select Master's Degree.

Zabulon. The Greek form of Zebulun, the tenth son of Jacob. Delaunay (*Thuilleur*, p. 79) says that some ritualists suppose that it is the true form of the word of which *Jabulum* is a corruption. This is incorrect. Jabulum is a corrupt form of *Giblim.* Zabulon has no connection with the high degrees, except that in the Royal Arch he represents one of the stones in the Pectoral.

Zacchai. (Heb., זכי.) A name applied to the Deity.

Zadki-el. The name of one of the angels of the seven planets, according to the Jewish rabbis—the angel of the planet Jupiter.

Zadok. A personage in some of the Ineffable degrees of the Scottish Rite. In Scripture he is recorded as having been one of the two chief priests in the time of David, Abiathar being the other. He subsequently, by order of David, anointed Solomon to be king, by whom he was rewarded with the post of high priest. Josephus (*Ant.*, x., 8, § 6) says that "Sadoc, the high priest, was the first high priest of the Temple which Solomon built." Yet it has been supposed by some authors, in consequence of his name not being mentioned in the detailed account of the dedication, that he had died before the completion of the Temple.

Zaphnath-paaneah. An Egyptian title given to the patriarch Joseph by the Egyptian king under whom he was viceroy. The name has been interpreted "Revealer of secrets," and is a password in the old rituals of the Scottish Rite.

Zarathustra. The name, in the Zend language, of that great reformer in religion more commonly known to Europeans as *Zoroaster*, which see.

Zarriel. The angel that, in accordance with the Kabbalistical system, governs the sun.

Zarthan. The Zarthan of 1 Kings vii. 46 appears to be the same place as the Zeredathah of 2 Chron. iv. 17. In the Masonic ritual, the latter word is always used. (See *Zeredathah.*)

Zarvan-akar-ana. ("Time without limits.") According to the Parsees, the name of a deity or abstract principle which existed even before the birth of Ahriman and Ormudz.

Zeal. Ever since the revival in 1717 (for it is found in the earliest lectures) it was taught that Apprentices served their Masters with "freedom, fervency, and zeal"; and the symbols of the first two of these virtues were chalk and charcoal. In the oldest rituals, *earthen pan* (which see) was designated as the symbol of zeal; but this was changed by Preston to *clay,* and so it still remains. (See *Fervency* and *Freedom.*)

The instruction to the Operative Mason to serve his Master with freedom, fervency, and zeal—to work for his interests willingly, ardently, and zealously—is easily understood. In its application to Speculative Masonry, for the Master of the Work we substitute the Great Architect of the Universe, and then our zeal, like our freedom and our fervency, is directed to a higher end. The zeal of a Speculative Mason is shown by advancing the morality, and by promoting the happiness of his fellow-creatures.

Zebulon. Son of Jacob and Leah; in the exodus his tribe marched next to Judah and Issachar, and received the territory bounded on the east by the south half of the Lake of Galilee, including Rimmon, Nazareth, and the plain of *Buttauf*, where stood Cana of Galilee. Heb. זבלון, Heaven, or the abode of God. (See *Jabulum.*)

Zechariah. "The son of Iddo," born in Babylonia during the captivity, who joined Zerubbabel on his return to Palestine. A leader and a man of influence, being both priest and prophet.

Zedekiah. A personage in some of the high degrees, whose melancholy fate is described in the 2d Book of Kings and in the prophecies of Jeremiah. He was the twentieth and last king of Judah. When Nebuchadnezzar had in his second siege of Jerusalem deposed Jehoiachin, whom he carried as a captive to Babylon, he placed Zedekiah on the throne in his stead. By this act Zedekiah became tributary to the king of the Chaldees, who exacted from him a solemn oath of fidelity and obedience. This oath he observed no longer than till an opportunity occurred of violating it. In the language of the author of the Books of Chronicles, "he rebelled against King Nebuchadnezzar, who had made him swear by God." (2 Chron. xxxvi. 13.)

This course soon brought down upon him the vengeance of the offended monarch, who invaded the land of Judah with an immense army. Remaining himself at Riblah, a town on the northern border of Palestine, he sent the army under his general, Nebuzaradan, to Jerusalem, which was invested by the Babylonian forces. After a siege of about one year, during which the inhabitants endured many hardships, the city was taken by an assault, the Chaldeans entering it through breaches in the northern wall.

It is very natural to suppose, that when the enemy were most pressing in their attack upon the devoted city; when the breach which was to give them entrance had been effected; and when, perhaps, the streets most distant from the Temple were already filled with Chaldean soldiery, a council of his princes and nobles should have been held by Zedekiah in the Temple, to which they had fled for refuge, and that he should ask their advice as to the most feasible method of escape from the impending danger. History, it is true, gives no account of any such assembly; but the written record of these important events which is now extant is very brief, and, as there is every reason to admit the probability of the occurrence, there does not appear to be any historical objection to the introduction of Zedekiah into the legend of the Superexcellent Master's Degree, as having been present and holding a council at the time of the siege. By the advice of this council, Zedekiah attempted to make his escape across the Jordan. But he and his attendants were, says Jeremiah, pursued by the Chaldean army, and overtaken in the plains of Jericho, and carried before Nebuchadnezzar. His sons and his nobles were slain, and, his eyes being put out, he was bound in chains and carried captive to Babylon, where at a later period he died.

Zelator. 1. The First Degree of the German Rose Croix. The title expresses the spirit of emulation which should characterise the neophyte.

2. The First Degree in the First Order of the Rosicrucian Society.

Zemzem. The holy well in Mecca.

Zenana. The inner portion of a gentleman's house in India, devoted to the use of females. In contrast with the front or men's portion, it is devoid of comforts. Each woman has a small cell, on the second or third story, fronting on the inner court of the square structure.

Zendavesta. The scriptures of the Zoroastrian religion containing the doctrines of Zoroaster. *Avesta* means the sacred text, and *Zend* the commentary. The work as we now have it is supposed to have been collected by learned priests of the Sassanian period, who translated it into the Pehlevi, or vernacular language of Persia. The greater part of the work was lost during the persecutions by the Mohammedan conquerors of Persia. One only of the books has been preserved, the Vendidad, comprising twenty-two chapters. The Yasna and the Vispered together constitute the collection of fragments which are termed Vendidad Sadé. There is another fragmentary collection called Yesht Sadé. And these constitute all that remain of the original text. So that, however comprehensive the Zendavesta must have been in its original form, the work as it now exists makes but a comparatively small book.

The ancients, to whom it was familiar, as well as the modern Parsees, attribute its authorship to Zoroaster. But Dr. Haug, rightly conceiving that it was not in the power of any one man to have composed so vast a work as it must have been in its original extent, supposes that it was the joint production of the original Zarathustra Sitama and his successors, the high priests of the religion, who assumed the same name.

The Zendavesta is the scripture of the modern Parsee; and hence for the Parsee Mason, of whom there are not a few, it constitutes the Book of the Law, or Trestle-Board. Unfortunately, however, to the Parsee it is a sealed book, for, being written in the old Zend language, which is now extinct, its contents cannot be understood. But the Parsees recognise the Zendavesta as of Divine authority, and say in the Catechism, or Compendium of Doctrines in use among them: "We consider these books as heavenly books, because God sent the tidings of these books to us through the holy prophet Zurthost."

Zenith. That point in the heavens which is vertical to the spectator, and from which a perpendicular line passing through him and extended would reach the center of the earth. All the old documents of the Ancient and Accepted Scottish Rite are dated "under the Celestial Canopy of the Zenith which answers to ——"; the latitude of the place whence the document is issued being then given. The latitude alone is expressed because it indicates the place of the sun's meridian height. The longitude is always omitted, because every place whence such a document is issued is called the Grand East, the one spot where the sun rises. The theory implied is, that although the south of the Lodge may vary, its chief point must always be in the east, the point of sunrising, where longitude begins.

Zennaar. The sacred cord used in the Hindustanee initiation, which writers on ritualism have compared to the Masonic apron.

Between eight and fifteen years of age, every Hindu boy is imperatively required to receive the investiture of the sennaar. The investiture is accompanied by many solemn ceremonies of prayer and sacrifice. After the investiture, the boy is said to have received his second birth, and from that time a Hindu is called by a name which signifies "twice born."

Coleman (*Mythology of the Hindus*, p. 155) thus describes the sennaar:

"The sacred thread must be made by a Brahman. It consists of three strings, each ninety-six hands (forty-eight yards), which are twisted together: it is then folded into three, and again twisted; these are a second time folded into the same number, and tied at each end in knots. It is worn over the left shoulder (next the skin, extending half-way down the right thigh) by the Brahmans, Ketries, and Vaisya castes. The first are usually invested with it at eight years of age, the second at eleven, and the Vaisya at twelve. The period may, from especial causes, be deferred; but it is indispensable that it should be received, or the parties omitting it become outcasts."

Zeraias. One of the three officers appointed by King Solomon to superintend the hewing of the timbers in the forests of Lebanon.

Zerbal. The name of King Solomon's Captain of the Guards, in the degree of Intimate Secretary. No such person is mentioned in Scripture, and it is therefore an invention of the ritualist who fabricated the degree. If derived from Hebrew, its roots will be found in זר, *zer*, an enemy, and בעל, *baal*, and it would signify "an enemy of Baal."

Zeredathah. The name of the place between which and Succoth are the clay grounds where Hiram Abif is said to have cast the brazen utensils for the use of the Temple. (See *Clay Ground*.)

Zerubbabel. In writing the life of Zerubbabel from a Masonic point of view, it is incumbent that reference should be made to the legends as well as to the more strictly historical details of his eventful career. With the traditions of the Royal Arch, and some other of the high degrees, Zerubbabel is not less intimately connected than is Solomon with those of Symbolic or Ancient Craft Masonry. To understand those traditions properly, they must be placed in their appropriate place in the life of him who plays so important a part in them. Some of these legends have the concurrent support of Scripture, some are related by Josephus, and some appear to have no historical foundation. Without, therefore, vouching for their authenticity, they must be recounted, to make the Masonic life of the builder of the second Temple complete.

Zerubbabel, who, in the Book of Ezra, is called "Sheshbazzar, the prince of Judah," was the grandson of that King Jehoiachin, or Jeconiah, who had been deposed by Nebuchadnezzar and carried as a captive to Babylon. In him, therefore, was vested the regal authority, and on him, as such, the command of the returning captives was bestowed by Cyrus, who on that occasion, according to a Masonic tradition, presented to him the sword which Nebuchadnezzar had received from his grandfather, Jehoiachin.

As soon as the decree of the Persian monarch had been promulgated to his Jewish subjects, the tribes of Judah and Benjamin, with the priests and Levites, assembled at Babylon, and prepared to return to Jerusalem, for the purpose of rebuilding the Temple. Some few from the other tribes, whose love of their country and its ancient worship had not been obliterated by the luxuries of the Babylonian court, united with the followers of Zerubbabel, and accompanied him to Jerusalem. The greater number, however, remained; and even of the priests, who were divided into twenty-four courses, only four courses returned, who, however, divided themselves, each class into six, so as again to make up the old number. Cyrus also restored to the Jews the greater part of the sacred vessels of the Temple which had been carried away by Nebuchadnezzar, and five thousand and four hundred were received by Zerubbabel, the remainder being brought back, many years after, by Ezra. Only forty-two thousand three hundred and sixty Israelites, exclusive of servants and slaves, accompanied Zerubbabel, out of whom he selected seven thousand of the most valiant, whom he placed as an advanced guard at the head of the people. Their progress homeward was not altogether unattended with danger; for tradition informs us that at the river Euphrates they were opposed by the Assyrians, who, incited by the temptation of the vast amount of golden vessels which they were carrying, drew up in hostile array, and, notwithstanding the remonstrances of the Jews, and the edict of Cyrus, disputed their passage. Zerubbabel, however, repulsed the enemy with such ardor as to insure a signal victory, most of the Assyrians having been slain in the battle, or drowned in their attempt to cross the river in their retreat. The rest of the journey was uninterrupted, and, after a march of four months, Zerubbabel arrived at Jerusalem, with his weary followers, at seven o'clock in the morning of the 22d of June, five hundred and thirty-five years before Christ.

During their captivity, the Jews had continued, without intermission, to practise the rights of Freemasonry, and had established at various places regular Lodges in Chaldea. Especially, according to the Rabbinical traditions, had they instituted their mystic fraternity at Naharda, on the Euphrates; and, according to the same authority, we are informed that Zerubbabel carried with him to Jerusalem all the secret knowledge which was the property of that Institution, and established a similar fraternity in Judea. This coincides with, and gives additional strength to, the traditions of the Royal Arch Degree.

As soon as the pious pilgrims had arrived at Jerusalem, and taken a needful rest of seven days, a tabernacle for the temporary purposes of Divine worship was erected near the ruins of the ancient Temple, and a Council was called, in which Zerubbabel presided as King, Jeshua as High Priest, and Haggai as Scribe, or principal officer of State. It was there determined to commence the building of the second Temple upon the same holy spot which had been occupied by the first, and the people liberally contributed sixty-one thousand drachms of gold, and five thousand minas of silver, or nearly a quarter of a million of dollars, toward defraying the expenses; a sum which sinks into utter insignifiance, when compared with the immense amount appropriated by David and Solomon to the construction of their Temple.

The site having been thus determined upon, it was found necessary to begin by removing the rubbish of the old Temple, which still encumbered the earth, and prevented the workmen from making the necessary arrangements for laying the foundation. It was during this operation that an important discovery was made by three sojourners, who had not originally accompanied Zerubbabel, but who, sojourning some time longer at Babylon, followed their countrymen at a later period, and had arrived at Jerusalem just in time to assist in the removal of the rubbish. These three sojourners, whose fortune it was to discover that stone of foundation, so intimately connected with the history of Freemasonry, and to which we have before had repeated occasion to allude, are supposed by a Masonic tradition to have been Esdras, Zachariah, and Nehemiah, the three holy men, who, for refusing to worship the golden image, had been thrown by Nebuchadnezzar into a fiery furnace, from which they emerged uninjured. In the Chaldee language, they were known by the names of Shadrach, Meshach, and Abed-nego. It was in penetrating into some of the subterranean vaults, that the Masonic stone of foundation, with other important mysteries connected with it, were discovered by the three fortunate sojourners, and presented by them to Zerubbabel and his companions Jeshua and Haggai, whose traditionary knowledge of Masonry, which they had received in a direct line from the builders of the first Temple, enabled them at once to appreciate the great importance of these treasures.

As soon as that wonderful discovery was made, on which depends not only the existence of the Royal Arch Degree, but the most important mystery of Freemasonry, the Jews proceeded on a certain day, before the rising of the sun, to lay the foundation-stone of the second Temple; and for that purpose, we are told, Zerubbabel selected that stone of foundation which had been discovered by the three sojourners. On this occasion, we learn that the young rejoiced with shouts and acclamations, but that the ancient people disturbed them with their groans and lamentations, when they reflected on the superb magnificence of the first Temple, and compared it with the expected inferiority of the present structure. As in the building of the first Temple, so in this, the Tyrians and Sidonians were engaged to furnish the timber from the forests of Lebanon, and to conduct it in the same manner on floats by sea to Joppa.

Scarcely had the workmen well commenced their labors, when they were interrupted by the Samaritans, who made application to be permitted to unite with them in the construction of the Temple. But the Jews, who looked upon them as idolaters, refused to accept of their services. The Samaritans in consequence became their bitter enemies, and so prevailed, by misrepresentations, with the ministers of Cyrus, as to cause them to put such obstructions in the way of the construction of the edifice as seriously to impede its progress for several years. With such difficulty and danger were the works conducted during this period, that the workmen were compelled to labor with the trowel in one hand and the sword in the other. To commemorate these worthy craftsmen, who were thus ready, either to fight or to labor in the cause of God, as circumstances might require, the sword and trowel crosswise, or, as the heralds would say, *en saltire*, have been placed upon the Royal Arch Tracing-Board or Carpet of our English brethren. In the American ritual this expressive symbol of valor and piety has been unfortunately omitted.

In the seventh year after the restoration of the Jews, Cyrus, their friend and benefactor, died, and his son Cambyses, in Scripture called Ahasuerus, ascended the throne. The Samaritans and the other enemies of the Jews, now becoming bolder in their designs, succeeded in obtaining from Cambyses a peremptory order for the stoppage of all the works at Jerusalem, and the Temple consequently remained in an unfinished state until the second year of the reign of Darius, the successor of Cambyses.

Darius appears to have had, like Cyrus, a great friendship for the Israelites, and especially for Zerubbabel, with whom he was well acquainted in his youth. We are informed, as an evidence of this, that, when a private man, he made a vow, that if he should ever ascend the throne, he would restore all the vessels of the Temple that had been retained by Cyrus. Zerubbabel, being well aware of the friendly disposition of the king, determined, immediately after his accession to power, to make a personal application to him for his assistance and protection in rebuilding the Temple. Accordingly he departed from Jerusalem, and after a journey full of peril, in which he was continually attacked by parties of his enemies, he was arrested as a spy by the Persian guards in the vicinity of Babylon, and carried in chains before Darius, who, however immediately recognized him as the friend and companion of his youth, and ordering him instantly to be released from his bonds, invited him to be present at a magnificent feast which he was about to give to the Court. It is said that on this occasion, Zerubbabel, having explained to Darius the occasion of his visit, implored the interposition of his authority for the protection of the Israelites engaged in the restoration of the Temple. The king promised to grant all his requests, provided he would reveal to him the secrets of Freemasonry. But this the faithful prince at once refused to do. He declined the favor of the monarch at the price of his infamy, and expressed his willingness rather to meet death or exile, than to violate his sacred obligations as a Mason. This firmness and fidelity only raised his character still higher in the estimation of Darius, who seems, indeed, to have been endowed with many noble qualities both of heart and mind.

It was on this occasion, at the feast given by King Darius, that, agreeably to the custom of Eastern monarchs, he proposed to his courtiers the question whether the power of wine, women, or the king, was the strongest. Answers were made by different persons, assigning to each of these the precedency in power; but when Zerubbabel was called on to assert his opinion, he declared that though the power of wine and of the king might be great, that of women was still greater, but that above all things truth bore the victory. Josephus says that the sentiments of Zerubbabel having been deemed to contain the most wisdom, the king commanded him to ask something over and above what he had promised as the prize of the victor in the philosophic discussion. Zerubbabel then called upon the monarch to fulfil the vow that he had made in his youth, to rebuild the Temple, and restore the vessels that had been taken away by Nebuchadnezzar. The king forthwith granted his request, promised him the most ample protection in the future prosecution of the works, and sent him home to Jerusalem laden with honors, and under the conduct of an escort.

Henceforth, although from time to time annoyed by their adversaries, the builders met with no serious obstruction, and finally, twenty years after its commencement, in the sixth year of the reign of Darius, and on the third day of the month Adar, 515 years B.C., the Temple was completed, the cope-stone celebrated, and the house solemnly dedicated to Jehovah with the greatest joy.

After this we hear nothing further of Zerubbabel, nor is the time or manner of his death either recorded in Scripture or preserved by Masonic tradition. We have, however, reason for believing that he lived to a good old age, since we find no successor of him mentioned until Artaxerxes appointed Ezra as the Governor of Judea, fifty-seven years after the completion of the Temple.

Zetland, Thomas Dundas, Earl of. One of the most noted of the noblemen of England, born in 1795, and initiated in the "Prince of Wales Lodge, No. 259," on June 18, 1830. Appointed J. G. Warden in 1832, Deputy in 1839, Pro. G. M. in 1840. Upon the decease of the Duke of Sussex, in 1843, the Earl became the chief ruler of the Craft, until March, 1844, when he was elected M. W. G. M., which office he held until 1870. He was Prov. G. Master of North and East Yorkshire from 1839 until he died, in 1873.

Zeus. Greatest of the national deities of Greece, son of Chronos and Rhea, brother of Poseidon and Hera, and husband of the latter. Mostly worshiped in Crete, Arcadia, and Dodona. Finally the great Hellenic divinity, identified with Jupiter of the Romans and Amon of the Libyans. Zeus was represented as of majestic form, holding in one hand a scepter, and in the other a thunderbolt, signified by the above symbol.

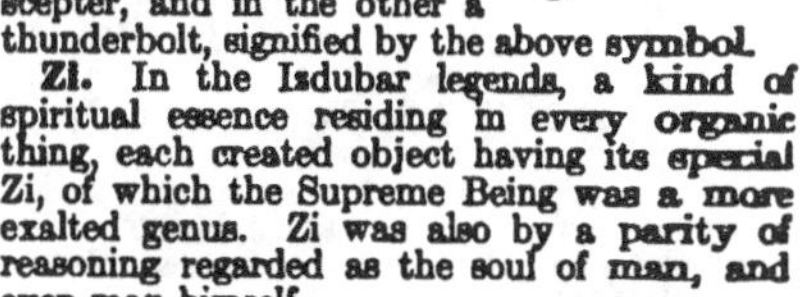

Zi. In the Isdubar legends, a kind of spiritual essence residing in every organic thing, each created object having its special Zi, of which the Supreme Being was a more exalted genus. Zi was also by a parity of reasoning regarded as the soul of man, and even man himself.

Zicu or **Ziggara.** The Accadian name for primeval matter.

Zif. (Iyar) אייר. The eighth month of the civil and the second of the sacred year of the Hebrews, commencing on the first of the new moon in the month of April. The name of this month is mentioned but once in the Scriptures, and then as relating to the date of the commencement of Solomon's Temple. (1 Kings vi. 1.) The month Bul, or Marchesvan, is mentioned as the date of the completion of the Temple. (*Ibid.*, vi., 38.)

Zillah. Wife of Lamech, mother of Tubal Cain and Naamah. One of the few females mentioned as of the antediluvian period.

Zinnendorf, Johann Wilhelm von. Few men made more noise in German Masonry, or had warmer friends or more bitter enemies, than Johann Wilhelm Ellenberger, who, in consequence of his adoption by his mother's brother, took subsequently the title of Von Zinnendorf, by which he is universally known. He was born at Halle, August 10, 1731. He was initiated into Masonry at the place of his birth. He afterward removed to Berlin, where he received the appointment of General Staff Surgeon, and chief of the medical corps of the army. There he joined the Lodge of the Three Globes, and became an ardent disciple of the Rite of Strict Observance, in which he took the Order name of *Eques à lapide nigro*. He was elected Master of the Scottish Lodge. He had the absolute control of the funds of the Order, but refusing to render any account of the disposition which he had made of them, an investigation was commenced. Upon this, Zinnendorf withdrew from the Rite, and sentence of excommunication was immediately afterward pronounced against him.

Zinnendorf in return declared the Strict Observance an imposture, and denounced its theory of the Templar origin of Masonry as false.

In the meantime, he sent his friend Hans Carl Baumann to Stockholm, that he might receive manuscripts of the degrees of the Swedish system which had been promised him by Carl Friederich von Eckleff, Scottish Grand Master of the Chapter in that city. Baumann returned with the manuscripts, which, however, it appears from a subsequent declaration made by the Duke of Sudermania, were very imperfect.

But, imperfect as they were, out of them Zinnendorf constructed a new Rite in opposition to the Strict Observance. Possessed of great talent and energy, and, his enemies said, of but little scrupulousness as to means, he succeeded in attracting to him many friends and followers. In 1766, he established at Potsdam the Lodge "Minerval," and in 1767, at Berlin, the Lodge of the "Three Golden Keys." Masons were found to give him countenance and assistance in other places, so that on June 24, 1770, twelve Lodges of his system were enabled to unite in the formation of a body which they called the Grand Lodge of all the Freemasons of Germany.

The success of this body, under the adverse circumstances by which it was surrounded, can only be attributed to the ability and energy of its founder, as well as to the freedom with which he made use of every means for its advancement without any reference to their want of firmness. Having induced the Prince of Hesse-Darmstadt to accept the Grand Mastership, he succeeded, through his influence, in obtaining the recognition and alliance of the Grand Lodge of England in 1773; but that body seven years after withdrew from the connection. In 1774, Zinnendorf secured the protectorship of the King of Prussia for his Grand Lodge. Thus patronised, the Grand Lodge of Germany rapidly extended its influence and increased in growth, so that in 1778 it had thirty-four Lodges under its immediate jurisdiction, and provincial Lodges were established in Austria, Silesia, Pomerania, Lower Saxony, and Russia. Findel explains this great accession of strength by supposing that it could only have been the consequence of the ardent desire of the German Masons to obtain the promised revelations of the high degrees of the system of Zinnendorf.

In 1774, Zinnendorf had been elected Grand Master, which office he held until his death.

But he had his difficulties to encounter. In the Lodge "Royal York," at Berlin, he found an active and powerful antagonist. The Duke of Sudermania, Grand Master of Sweden, in an official document issued in 1777, declared that the Warrant which had been granted by Eckleff to Zinnendorf, and on the strength of which he had founded his Grand Lodge, was spurious and unauthorized; the Grand Lodge of Sweden pronounced him to be a fomenter of disturbances and an insolent calumniator of the Swedish Grand Master, and in 1780 the Grand Lodge of England withdrew from its alliance.

But Zinnendorf was undismayed. Having quit the service of the government in 1779, he made a journey to Sweden in an unsuccessful effort to secure all the documents connected with the Swedish system. Returning hence, he continued to preside over the Grand Lodge with unabated zeal and undiminished vigor until his death, which took place June 6, 1782.

Von Zinnendorf undoubtedly committed many errors, but we cannot withhold from him the praise of having earnestly sought to introduce into German Masonry a better system than the one which was prevailing in the last quarter of the eighteenth century.

Zinnendorf, Rite of. The Rite invented by Count Von Zinnendorf, and fabricated out of imperfect copies of the Swedish system, with additions from the Illuminism of Avignon and the reveries of Swedenborg. It consisted of seven degrees, divided into three sections as follows:

I. *Blue Masonry.*
   1. Apprentice.
   2. Fellow-Craft.
   3. Master.

II. *Red Masonry.*
   4. Scottish Apprentice and Fellow-Craft.
   5. Scottish Master.

III. *Capitular Masonry.*
   6. Favorite of St. John.
   7. Chapter of the Elect.

It was practised by the Grand Lodge of Germany, which had been established by Zinnendorf, and by the Lodges of its obedience.

Zinzendorf, Count von, Nicolaus Ludwig. Founder of the existing sect of Moravian brethren; also of a religious society which he called the "Order of the Grain of Mustard-Seed." He was ordained bishop of the Moravians in 1737, and at request of King Frederick William I. of Prussia, went to London, and was received by Wesley. In 1741 he proceeded to Bethlehem, in America, and founded the Moravian settlements. The prolific author of a hundred volumes. He was born at Dresden in 1700, and died in 1760.

Zion. Mount Zion was the southwestern of the three hills which constituted the high table-land on which Jerusalem was built. It was the royal residence, and hence it is often called "the city of David." The name is sometimes used as synonymous with Jerusalem.

Zithern. An instrument of music of 28 strings drawn over a shallow box; both hands are employed in playing on it.

Zizon. This is said, in one of the Ineffable degrees of the Scottish Rite, to be the name of the balustrade before the Sanctum Sanctorum. There is no such word in Hebrew.

but it may be a corruption of the Talmudic זיזא, *siza*, which Buxtorf (*Lex. Talm.*) defines as "a beam, a little beam, a small rafter."

Zoan. An Egyptian town, known to the Greeks as Tanais, presumed to have been founded 3700 B.C., and probably the residence of the Pharaohs of the Exodus.

Zodiac. Many of the Egyptian temples contain astronomical representations; notably those of Esneh, Contra Latopolis, and Denderah, which were famous for their zodiacal ceilings. Antiquity was accorded to the records of the Egyptian empire by calculations made from the positions of the stars on the monuments and on these ceilings. Closer criticism now reveals these positions to be fanciful and the data unreliable. The zodiac of Denderah has been removed to Paris, where it forms the chief ornament of the museum of the Louvre. Those remaining in Egypt are suffering from deterioration. Crosses will be found to be a portion of five of the signs of the zodiac.

Zodiac, Masonic. (*Zodiaque Maçonnique.*) A series of twelve degrees, named after the twelve signs of the Zodiac, the first being the Ram. It was in the series of the Metropolitan Chapter of France, and in the manuscript collection of Peuvret.

Zohar. (Heb. זהר, *splendor.*) After the surrender of Jerusalem, through the victory of Vespasian, among the fugitives was Rabbi Simon Ben Jochai, who remained an Anchorite for twelve years, became visionary, and believed he was visited by the prophet Elias. His son, Rabbi Elieser, and his clerk, Rabbi Abba, when visiting him, took down his pronounced Divine precepts, which were in time gathered and formed into the famous Sohar or Zohar. From this work, the *Sepher Jetzirah*, and the *Commentary of the Ten Sephiroth* was formed the Kabbala. The Zohar, its history, and as well that of its author, overflow with beautiful yet ideal mysticism.

Zohariti. ("*The Illuminated.*") A society founded by Jacob Franck at the beginning of the last century.

Zonar. The symbolic girdle of the Christians and Jews worn in the Levant, as a mark of distinction, that they may be known from the Mohammedans.

Zoroaster. More correctly, *Zarathustra.* He was the legislator and prophet of the ancient Bactrians, out of whose doctrines the modern religion of the Parsees has been developed. As to the age in which Zoroaster flourished, there have been the greatest discrepancies among the ancient authorities. The earliest of the Greek writers who mentions his name is Xanthus of Lydia, and he places his era at about 600 years before the Trojan war, which would be about 1800 years before Christ. Aristotle and Eudoxus say that he lived 6,000 years before Plato; while Berosus, the Babylonian historian, makes him a king of Babylon, and the founder of a dynasty which reigned over Babylon between 2200 and 2000 B.C. The Parsees are more moderate in their calculations, and say that their prophet was a contemporary of Hystaspes, the father of Darius, and accordingly place his era at 550 B.C. Haug, however, in his *Essays on the Sacred Language, etc., of the Parsees*, declares that this supposition is utterly groundless. He thinks that we can, under no circumstances, assign him a later date than 1000 B.C., and is not even disinclined to place his era much earlier, and make him a contemporary of Moses.

Bro. Albert Pike, who has devoted much labor to the investigation of this confused subject of the Zoroastrian era, says, in an able article in Mackey's *National Freemason* (vol. iii., No. 3):

"In the year 1903 before Alexander, or 2234 B.C., a Zarathustrian king of Media conquered Babylon. The religion even then had degenerated into Magism, and was of unknown age. The unfortunate theory that Vitaçpa, one of the most efficient allies of Zarathustra, was the father of Darius Hystaspes, has long ago been set at rest. In the Chaldean lists of Berosus, as found in the Armenian edition of Eusebius, the name *Zoroaster* appears as that of the Median conqueror of Babylon; but he can only have received this title from being a follower of Zarathustra and professing his religion. He was preceded by a series of eighty-four Median kings; and the real Zarathustra lived in Bactria long before the tide of emigration had flowed thence into Media. Aristotle and Eudoxus, according to Pliny, place Zarathustra 6000 years before the death of Plato; Hermippus, 5000 years before the Trojan war. Plato died 348 B.C.; so that the two dates substantially agree, making the date of Zarathustra's reign 6300 or 6350 B.C., and I have no doubt that this is not far from the truth."

Bunsen, however (*God in History*, vol. i., b. iii., ch. vi., p. 276), speaks of Zarathustra Spitama as living under the reign of Vistaspa toward the year 3000 B.C., certainly not later than toward 2500 B.C. He calls him "one of the mightiest intellects and one of the greatest men of all time"; and he says of him: "Accounted by his contemporaries a blasphemer, atheist, and firebrand worthy of death; regarded even by his own adherents, after some centuries, as the founder of magic, by others as a sorcerer and deceiver, he was, nevertheless, recognised already by Hippocrates as a great spiritual hero, and esteemed the earliest sage of a primeval epoch —reaching back to 5000 years before their date—by Eudoxus, Plato, and Aristotle."

The name of this great reformer is always spelled in the Zendavesta as *Zarathustra*, with which is often coupled *Spitama*; this, Haug says, was the family name, while the former was his surname, and hence both he and Bunsen designate him as Zarathustra Spitama. The Greeks corrupted Zarathustra into *Zarastrades* and *Zoroastres*, and the Romans into *Zoroaster*, by which name he has always, until recently, been known to

Europeans. His home was in Bactria, an ancient country of Asia between the Oxus River on the north and the Caucasian range of mountains on the south, and in the immediate vicinity, therefore, of the primal seat of the Aryan race, one of whose first emigrations, indeed, was into Bactria.

The religion of Zoroaster finds its origin in a social, political, and religious schism of the Bactrian Iranians from the primitive Aryans. These latter led a nomadic and pastoral life in their native home, and continued the same habits after their emigration. But a portion of these tribes, whom Haug calls "the proper Iranians," becoming weary of these wanderings, after they had reached the highlands of Bactria abandoned the pastoral and wandering life of their ancestors, and directed their attention to agriculture. This political secession was soon followed by wars, principally of a predatory kind, waged, for the purpose of booty, by the nomadic Aryans on the agricultural settlements of the Iranians, whose rich fields were tempting objects to the spoiler.

The political estrangement was speedily and naturally followed by a religious one. It was at this time that Zoroaster appeared, and, denouncing the nature-worship of the old Aryan faith, established his spiritual religion, in which, says Bunsen, "the antagonisms of light and darkness, of sunshine and storm, become transformed into antagonisms of good and evil, of powers exerting a beneficent or corrupting influence on the mind."

The doctrine of pure Zoroastrianism was monotheistic. The Supreme Being was called *Ahuramazda*, and Haug says that Zoroaster's conception of him was perfectly identical with the Jewish notion of Jehovah. He is called "the Creator of the earthly and spiritual life, the Lord of the whole universe, at whose hands are all the creatures." He is wisdom and intellect; the light itself, and the source of light; the rewarder of the virtuous and the punisher of the wicked.

The dualistic doctrine of Ormuzd and Ahrimanes, which has falsely been attributed to Zoroaster, was in reality the development of a later corruption of the Zoroasteric teaching. But the great reformer sought to solve the puzzling question of the origin of evil in the world, by supposing that there existed in Ahuramazda two spirits, inherent in his nature, the one positive and the other negative. All that was good was real, existent; while the absence of that reality was a non-existence or evil. Evil was the absence of good as darkness was the absence of light.

Zoroaster taught the idea of a future life and the immortality of the soul. The doctrine of the resurrection is one of the principal dogmas of the Zendavesta. He also clearly inculcated the belief of a heaven and a hell. The former was called the house of hymns, because the angels were supposed to sing hymns there; the latter the house of destruction, and to it were relentlessly consigned the poets and priests of the old Aryan religion.

The doctrine of sacred names, so familiar to the Hebrews, was also taught by Zoroaster. In one of the Yashts, a portion of the Zendavesta, Ahuramazda tells Zarathustra that the utterance of one of his sacred names, of which he enumerates twenty, is the best protection from evil. Of these names, one is *ahmi*, "I am," and another, *ahmi yat ahmi*, "I am who I am." The reader will be reminded here of the holy name in Exodus, *Ehyeh asher Ehyeh*, or "I am that I am."

The doctrine of Zoroaster was not forever confined to Bactria, but passed over into other countries; nor in the transmission did it fail to suffer some corruption. From its original seat it spread into Media, and under the name of Magism, or the doctrine of the Magavas, i. e., the mighty ones, was incorporated at Babylon with the Chaldean philosophy, whence we find its traces in the Rabbinism and the Kabbalism of the Hebrews. It was carried, too, into Persia, where it has been developed into the modern and still existing sect of the Parsees, of whom we now find two divisions, the conservatives and liberals; the former cultivating the whole modified doctrine of Zoroaster, and the latter retaining much of the doctrine, but rejecting to a very great extent the ceremonial ritual.

Zschokke, J. H. D. One of the most eminent Masons and German authors known to this century. Born at Magdeburg, 1771, died 1848.

Zuni Indians. A tribe inhabiting New Mexico, U. S., whose mystic services have attracted the attention of Masonic scholars in consequence of their similarity to those in vogue by the Masonic Fraternity. These Indians have a formal religious initiation, in which the suppliant kneels at the altar to take his vows, after being received upon the point of an instrument of torture to the flesh. Among their forms and ceremonies are facing the east, circumambulation, tests of endurance, and being peculiarly clothed. Incense is burned, and the sun worshiped at its rising.

Zurthost. The name given by the modern Parsees to Zarathustra or Zoroaster. They call him their prophet, and their religious sect the Zarthosti community.

PRONOUNCING DICTIONARY

FOR USE BY THE

MASONIC FRATERNITY,

Containing over Fourteen Hundred Words liable to Mispronunciation
The Form of Instruction for Pronunciation is the same Defined
in the American Dictionary, by Noah Webster, LL.D.

BY CHARLES T. McCLENACHAN.

KEY TO THE PRONUNCIATION.

VOWELS, REGULAR LONG AND SHORT SOUNDS.

Ā, ā (long), as in *Āle, Fāte.*
Ă, ă (short), as in *Ădd, Făt.*
Ä, ä (Italian), as in *Ärm, Fäther, Fär.*
Ē, ē (long), as in *Ēve, Mēte.*
Ĕ, ĕ (short), as in *Ĕnd, Mĕt.*
Ī, ī (long), as in *Īce, Fīne.*
Ĭ, ĭ (short), as in *Ĭll, Fĭn.*
Ō, ō (long), as in *Ōld, Nōte.*
Ŏ, ŏ (short), as in *Ŏdd, Nŏt.*
Ū, ū (long), as in *Ūse, Hūme.*
Ŭ, ŭ (short), as in *Ŭs, Hŭm.*
Ȳ, ȳ (long), as in *Mȳ, Flȳ.*
Y̆, y̆ (short), as in *Cy̆st, Ny̆mph.*

The above simple process is adopted, omitting instruction relating to diphthongs or tripthongs, occasional sounds, or references to consonants.

ACCENT.—The principal accent is denoted by a heavy mark; the secondary, by a lighter mark, as in *Ab'ra-ca-dab'ra.* In the division of words into syllables, these marks also supply the place of the hyphen.

WORDS OF DOUBTFUL PRONUNCIATION.	PROPER MASONIC PRONUNCIATION.	NOTATIONS.
Ab	Ăb	Heb. Father; 11th Hebraic month.
Abaciscus	Ă'bă-cis'cŭs	Flooring blocks.
Abecus	Ăb'a-cŭs	A drawing-board—a tray.
Abaddon	A-băd'don	The destroyer, or angel of darkness.
Abazar	Ă'bă-zăr	Master of Ceremonies of 6th Degree.
Abchal	Ăb'chăl	
Abda	Ăb'dă	Father of Adoniram.
Abdamon	Ăb'dă'mŏn	To serve.
Abdiel	Ăb'dĭel	Servant of God.
Abditorium	Ăb'dĭ-to'rĭ-ŭm	A secret place for deposit of records.
Abelites	Ā'bel-ītes	A secret order of the 18th century.
Abib	Ăb'ĭb	Seventh Jewish month.

WORDS OF DOUBTFUL PRONUNCIATION.	PROPER MASONIC PRONUNCIATION.	NOTATIONS.
Abibala	Ăb'i-bä-lä	Derived from Hebrew Abi and Balah.
Abibalk	Ăb'ī-bălk	Chief of the three assassins.
Abif	Ăb-īf'	Literally, his father.
Abihael	A-bi'ha-ĕl	Father of Strength.
Abihu	Ăb'i-hū	A son of Aaron.
Abiram	Ăb-ī'răm	Abiram Akisop, traitorous crafts-man.
Ablution	Ăb-lū'shun	Washing, baptizing.
Abrac	Ăb-răc'	Acquiring the science of Abrac.
Abracadabra	Ăb'ră-că-dăb'ră	A term of incantation.
Abraxas	A-brăx'as	A symbol of the year.
Acacia	A-că'ci-ă	Symbolic of the soul's immortality.
Acanthus	A-căn'thus	A part of the Corinthian capital.
Accessory	Ak-ses'so-rī	Private companionship.
Accolade	Ăc'co-lāde'	The welcome into knighthood.
Aceldama	Ă-cĕl'da-mă	Field of blood.
Achad	Ă-chăd	Ă kăd.
Acharon Schilton	Ă'chă-rŏn Schil-tŏn	Ă'kă-rŏn Schil-ton.
Achias	Ă-chī'as	Ă-kē-as.
Achishar	Ăc-hī'shar	One over the household of Solomon.
Achmetha	Ăch'mē-thă	Name of a Hebrew city.
Achtariel	Ăch-tă'rī-el	Kabbalistic name of God.
Acolyte	Ak'ō-līte	Candle bearer. Church servant.
Acousmatici	Ă'coūs-mă-tī'cī	Ă-coos'ma-te'cē.
Adah	Ā'dă	Jephtha's daughter.
Adar	Ā'dar	The twelfth Jewish month.
Adarel	Ă'dă-rĕl	Angel of fire.
Adept	Ă-dept'	An expert.
Adeptus Coronatus	Ăd-ept'us Cōrō-na'tus	Seventh Degree of the Swedish Rite.
Adhere	Ad-hēre'	Cling to.
Adjudicate	Ad-jū'di-kāte	To determine.
Admah	Ăd'mă	A Hebrew city.
Ad Majorum Dei Gloriam	Ăd mă-jō-rum dā-ē glō-ri-ăm	To the greater glory of God.
Adonai	Ă'dō-nă'ī	Ă-dō-năh'e. The Lord.
Adonhiram	Ăd'on-hī'ram	Signifying the master who is exalted.
Adoniram	Ăd'ō-nī'ram	Son of Abda.
Adonis	Ăd-ō'nis	Son of Myrrha and Cinyras.
Adult	Ă-dult'	Of full age.
Ad vitam	Ad vē-tăm	For life.
Adytum	Ăd'y-tum	A retired part of the ancient temples.
Æneid	Æ-nē'id	A creation of Virgil.
Æon	Æ-ŏn	Ē'on. Age or duration of anything.
Affiliate	Af-fil'e-āte	An adopted one.
Agapæ	Ăg'a-pæ	Ag'a-pe. Love feasts.
Agate	Ăg'it	The eighth stone in the breastplate.
Agathopades	Ă'gă-thō-pă'des	Ecclesiastical Order of 16th century.
Age	Āje	Of a given number of years.
Agenda	Ă-jĕn'da	Order of business. Book of precepts.
Agla	Ăg'lă	One of the Kabbalistic names of God.
Agnus Dei	Ăg'nus Dē'ī	Ag'nūs Dā'ē. Lamb of God.

WORDS OF DOUBTFUL PRONUNCIATION.	PROPER MASONIC PRONUNCIATION.	NOTATIONS.
Ahad	Ā'had	A name of God.
Ahabath Olam .	Ā'hă-băth Ō'lăm	Eternal love.
Ahashuerus	A-hăs'-u-ē'rus .	Name of a Persian king.
Ahel .	Ā'hel	A curtain of the Tabernacle.
Ahiah . . .	Ā-hī'ăh	Ā-hē'ā. One of the scribes of Solo-[mon.
Ahilud . . .	Ā-hī'ud	The father of Josaphat.
Ahiman Rezon .	Ā-hī'man Rē-zōn'	The will of selected brethren.
Ahinadab .	A-hĭn'a-dăb .	The son of Jetdo.
Ahisamach	A-hĭs'a-măk	The father of Aholiab.
Ahisar .	A-hī'săr . .	Ā-hī'săr.
Aheshar . .	Ā-hī'shar . .	An officer over Solomon's house-[hold.
Aholiab . .	Ā-hō'li-ăb	A skilful artificer.
Ahriman . .	Āh'rī-man. . . .	Principle of evil in Zoroaster system.
Aichmalotarch	Āich-mal'ō-tarch.	The Prince of Captivity.
Aixlachapelle .	Āks'-lă-shă'pel'	A city of Germany.
Akar . .	Ā'kăr. . . .	Or Achar, a password.
Akirop . .	Ā-kī'rop . .	One of the ruffians of the Third De-[gree
Alapa . .	Ā-lă-pă . . .	A symbol of manumission.
Alchemy	Āl'-ki-my . .	The science of Chemistry.
Aldebaran	Āl-deb'a-ran.	A star of the first magnitude.
Aleppo . .	Ā-lĕp'pō . . .	A town in northern Syria.
Alethophile .	Ā-lē'thō-phile .	Lover of Truth.
Alfader .	Āl-fă'der	Chief God of the Scandinavians.
Algabil . .	Āl'gă-bĭl .	Signifying The Builder.
Allah	Āl'ă . . .	The God of the Moslem.
Allegiance	Āl-lē'jance	Fealty.
Allegory .	Āl'lē-gō-ry	A fable, or figurative expression.
Allelujah .	Āl-le-lū'yă	Praise Jehovah.
Alleviate	Āl-lē've-āte	To relieve.
Allies . .	Al-līz' . . .	Companions in enterprise.
Allocution	Āl-lō-kū'shun	The official opening address.
Almoner	Āl'mō-ner.	Dispenser of alms.
Alms . . .	Āmz . . .	Charitable gifts.
Al-om-Jah	Āl-ōm-jăh.	A name of the Supreme Being.
Alpha . .	Āl'fă . . .	Greek letter A.
Alpina . .	Āl-pī-nă .	Name of Grand Lodge of Switzer-[land.
Als	Ālz.	The All-powerful God.
Al Shaddai	Āl-shăd'dă-e.	The second sanctified name of God.
Al-Sirat . .	Āl' Sī-răt' . .	The path.
Alycuber . .	Āl-e-kū'ber .	Master of the Tribe of Manasseh.
Amal-Sagghi	Āmăl-săg'ghī	Fifth step of Kadosh ladder.
Amar-jah.	Ā'măr-jăh	God spake.
Amboth	Ām'bōth .	A country in Syria.
Amenti .	Ā-men'-tī .	Place of Judgment of the Dead.
Ameth . .	Ā'mĕth . .	See *Emeth*.
Amethyst.	Ām'e-thist	A stone in the breastplate.
Amicists .	Ā'mi-cists. .	Association of students of Germany.
Aminidab.	Ā-mīn'a-dăb.	One of the Chiefs of Israel.
Amis Reunis	Āmīs Re'ūnis	Ā'mē Re'u-nē.
Ammonites .	Ām'mon-īts .	Descendants of Lot.

WORDS OF DOUBTFUL PRONUNCIATION.	PROPER MASONIC PRONUNCIATION.	NOTATIONS.
Amshaspands.	Ăm-shăs'pands.	Principle of good among Persians.
Amulets	Ăm'u-lets .	Mystic gems.
Amun	Ă'mŭn .	The Supreme God of the Egyptians.
Anachronism .	An-a'chrō-nĭsm	An error in computing time.
Anakim.	Ăn'a-kĭm .	Giants.
Ananias	Ăn-a-nī'as	Sapphira's conspirator.
Ancient.	Ăn'shunt .	Indefinite time.
Andre . .	An'drĕ	Christopher Karl André.
Andrea .	An'drĕă.	John Valentine Andreä.
Androgynous	An-drŏg'-ȳnous	An-drŏg-ĕ-nous. Side degrees.
Angel.	Ăn'jel	Messenger.
Angerona.	An'go-rō-nă	A pagan deity of the Romans.
Anima Mundi.	Ăn'ĭ-ma Mŭn'dī .	Soul of the World.
Annihilate	Ăn-nī'he-late	Destroy finally.
Anno Depositionis.	Ăn'nō De'pō-sī'-tio'nĭs	In the year of the Deposite.
Anno Domini	Ăn'nō Dŏm'ĭn-ī .	The year of the Lord.
Anno Hebraico .	Ăn'nō He'bră'ĭ-co	In the Hebrew year.
Anno Inventionis .	Ăn'nō In-ven'she-ō-nĭs	The year of discovery.
Anno Lucis .	Ăn'nō Lū'cis	In the year of light.
Anno Mundi	Ăn'nō Mŭn'dī .	The year of the world.
Anno Ordinis	Ăn'nō Or'di-nis	In the year of the Order.
Annuaire .	Ăn'nū-ăĭre. .	French annual record of proceedings.
Ansyreeh .	Ăn'sȳ-rēĕh	A sect of northern Syria.
Antarctic.	Ănt-ark'tic	Opposite to the northern circle.
Antepenult .	Ăn-tē-pē-nult' .	The last syllable except two.
Antipodeans	Ăn'tĭ-pō-dē'ans	Les Antipodiens.
Antipodes.	Ăn-tip'o-dēz	Opposite sides of the globe.
Anubis or **Anepu**	Ăn-ū-bis or Ăn-ĕ-pū	Egyptian deity. Son of Osiris and [Nephthys.
Apame	Ăp'a-me	Wife of King Darius.
Aphanism	Ăph'an-ism .	Concealing of the body.
Apharsathchites	Ă-phăr'sath-chītes .	A Persian tribe.
Apocalypse .	Ă pŏk'a-lĭps.	Book of Revelation.
Apollo	Ă-pol'o .	A Greek deity.
Aporrheta.	A'pŏrr-hē'tă.	Intelligible to the initiated.
Apostle .	Ă-pŏs'l .	A deputed agent.
Apotheosis	Ăp-ō-the'ō-sis .	Deification.
Apparent .	Ăp-păr'ent	Evident
Apprentice	Ăp-pren'tis	The servitor of a mechanic.
Apron. .	Ă'prun .	Badge of a Mason.
Aquarius .	Ă-quă'ri-us .	Water-bearer. Zodiac.
Arab .	Ăr'ab or Ă'rab.	Inhabitant of Arabia.
Arabici .	Ă'ră-bī'cī	Pertaining to the Wilderness.
Aral	Ă'rĕl	"Lion of God."
Aranyaka .	Ă'ran-yă'kă .	An appendage to the Veda of the [Indians.
Araunah	Ă-rău'năh.	See *Ornan*.
Arbroath .	Ăr-brōath.	Abbey of England, 12th century.
Arcana	Är-kă'na	Secrets, mystery.
Archangel.	Ark-ăn'jel .	An angel of the highest order.
Archbishop .	Arch-bish'op	A church dignitary.
Archetype. .	Är'ke-tīp .	An original model.

WORDS OF DOUBTFUL PRONUNCIATION.	PROPER MASONIC PRONUNCIATION.	NOTATIONS.
Archimagus.	Ăr'chĭ-mă'gŭs . . .	Chief Ruler.
Archipelago.	Är-kĭ-pel'a-go . . .	Group of islands.
Architect . .	Är'kĭ-tect	Skilled in the art of building.
Architectonicus.	Ăr'chi-tĕc-ton'ĭ-cus	Relating to Architecture.
Archives .	Är'kīvz . . .	Place for records.
Archiviste.	Ăr'chi-vīste .	An officer in charge of the archives.
Arctic. .	Ärk'tik . . .	A northern circle of space.
Arduous	Är'dū-us . .	With difficulty.
Area . .	Ā're-a . . .	The given surface.
Arelim	Ăr'ĕ-lim. . .	Literally, valiant, heroic.
Areopagus	Ā're-ŏp'a-gus	A tribunal.
Arianism .	Ā'rĭ-an-ĭsm .	The doctrine of Arius.
Arid . . .	Ăr'id	Exhausted of moisture.
Aries . . .	Ā'ries	The sign Ram in the Zodiac.
Armenbuchse.	Ăr'men-bŭchse.	The poor box.
Armistice.	Är'mis-tis	Temporary truce.
Aroba. .	Ā-rō'bā . .	Pledge, covenant.
Aroma . .	Ā-rō'ma	An agreeable odor.
Arrogant .	Ăr'rō-gant	Overbearing.
Artaban .	Är'ta-băn	A Scribe in the Scottish Rite.
Artaxerxes	Är'-tag-zerk'-zes.	A Persian king.
Artificer	Är-tif'i-cer	Designer of buildings.
Aryan. .	Ā'ry-an . .	One of three historical divisions of religion.
Asarota.	Ā'să-rō'ta .	A variegated pavement.
Asher.	Ăsh'er . .	A tribe of Israel.
Ashlar .	Ăsh'lar . .	Stone as taken from the quarry.
Asia . .	Ā'shĭ-a . .	An Eastern continent.
Asnapper .	As-nap'-per	
Aspirant .	Ăs-pir'ant .	One who aspires.
Associate .	Ăs-so'shĭ-at	Companion with.
Assur. .	Ăs'sur	Assyria.
Astarte .	Ăs-tär'te	Female deity of the Phœnicians.
Astræa .	Ăs'trā-ĕă	The Grand Lodge of Russia.
Asylum .	Ā-sī'lum	Place of retreat.
Atelier .	Ā'tĕl-ier. . .	A workshop where workmen are assembled.
Athenæum .	Ăth-e-ne'um.	A building for philosophic instruction.
Atossa. . . .	Ā-tos'să . .	Daughter of Cyrus.
Attacked . .	Ăt-takt' . .	Assailed, assaulted.
Atthakatha	Ăt'thă-kă'thă	Commentary on Canonical books of Buddhism.
Attouchement	Ā-tou'sh-măn	Ăt-toŭch'emĕnt.
Atys . . .	Ăt'is	The Phrygian god.
Audacious . .	Äw-dā'shus .	Contemning law.
Audience . . .	Äu'dĭ-ence	An assembly of hearers.
Aude, Vide, Tace .	Äu-dĭ, Vī-de, Tă-cē .	Hear, see, and be silent.
Aufseher .	Äŭf'sĕ-her . .	Inspector, overseer.
Auriel	Äu'rĭ-el	Angel of Fire.
Aurim	Äu'rim	Or Urim.
Auserwahlter .	Äŭs'er-wāhl-ter	Chosen, selected.
Aum or Om. .	Äŭm Ŏm. . .	God of the Hindus.

WORDS OF DOUBTFUL PRONUNCIATION.	PROPER MASONIC PRONUNCIATION.	NOTATIONS.
Aut Mori .	Ăut Mō'rī	Either conquer or die.
Aut Vincere.	Aut Vĭn'cĕ-rē	
Avatar	Ă'vă-tăr	The descent of a Hindu deity.
Avis	Ă'vĭs .	
Axiom	Ak'sĭ-um	Self-evident truth.
Aye.	Ā	An affirmative vote.
Aynon	Āy'nŏn .	Agnon, Ajuon.
Azariah .	Ăz-ā-rē'ă	Solomon's Captain of the Guards.
Azazel . .	Ă-ză'zel	"Scapegoat," the demon of dry [places.
Baal	Ba'ăl . .	Ba-a'lim. Master.
Baana	Bă-an'ă . .	Son of grief.
Babylon.	Băb'e-lon .	Gate of Bel. A kingdom.
Bactylea	Băc'tyl-ē'ă	
Baculus.	Bă'cu-lus .	Thepastoralstaff carriedby a bishop.
Bafomet	Ba'fō-mĕt .	See *Baphomet.*
Bagulkal	Ba'gŭl-kăl.	Guardian of the sacred ark.
Baldachin	Băl'dă-chin .	A canopy supported by pillars.
Baldric .	Băl'drik	A ribbon worn from shoulder to hip.
Balm . .	Bām . . .	A medicinal gum.
Balsamo	Băl-sa'mō .	Joseph Balsamo. See *Cagliostro.*
Baluster	Băl'us-ter .	The support of a stair-rail.
Banacas	Băn'a-kăs . .	A Captain of Guards.
Baphomet	Băf'ō-met .	An imaginary idol or symbol.
Barabbas .	Ba-răb'bas	A father's son. Son of Abba or
Barbarous	Băr'bă-rus	Not Băr-ba'ri-ous. [Father.
Barbati Fratres	Băr-bă'tī Fră'tres	Bearded Brothers.
Bar Mitzvah. .	Băr Mĭtz'vah .	Son of Commandment.
Barruel, Abbé	Bar'ruel, Ab'bē.	Augustin Barruel.
Basmoth	Băs'moth .	Fragrant, spicy. [laws.
Basilica	Ba-sil'ĭ-că .	Court-room for administration of
Bath Kol . .	Băth Kōl .	A voice from the Shekinah.
Bea Macheh	Bē-ă Măk'-ă.	To be with God.
Beauceniler.	Beau-cĕn'ĭ-fer .	To carry.
Beauchaine	Beau-chaine	Bō-shă'ne.
Beauseant	Beau'se-ănt	A war banner
Begone .	Be-gon' . . .	Not Be-gawn'.
Bel . . .	Bĕl.	A contraction of Baal.
Belenus.	Bĕ-le'nus . .	The Baal of Scripture.
Belshazzar	Bel-shăz'zar	King of Babylon.
Belus .	Bē'lus	Corruption of Baal. Lord. A temple.
Benac.	Bē'năc . .	See *Macbenac.*
Benai. . .	Be-nă'ī .	The Intelligent God.
Bendekar .	Ben'dĕ-kăr	One of the Princes of Solomon.
Benjamin.	Ben'ja-min	Youngest son of Jacob.
Benkhurim .	Ben-ku'rim	Free since birth.
Benyah .	Ben'yăh	The son of Jah.
Bereth . .	Bĕ-rith .	Alliance.
Beryl . . .	Bĕr'il.	Chrysolite, topas.
Bethlehem	Bĕth'le-em	Literally, Place of food. Of Judah.

WORDS OF DOUBTFUL PRONUNCIATION.	PROPER MASONIC PRONUNCIATION.	NOTATIONS.
Beyerle .	Bey'er-le .	François Louis de Beyerle.
Beyond .	Be-yond' .	Not Be-yund'.
Bezaleel.	Be-zăl'e-el	A builder of the Ark of the Covenant.
Biennial	Bī-en'ni-al.	Not Bī-en'yal.
Binah.	Bī'na.	The mother of understanding.
Blatant .	Blā'tant	Not Blăt'ant.
Blessed .	Bless-ed	Not Blest.
Boaz	Bo'ăz.	Literally, fleetness, strength.
Boehim	Bō'chīm	Bō'kim. The weepers.
Boeber .	Bō-e'ber	Johann Boeber.
Boehmen .	Bōeh'men .	Jacob Boehmen.
Bonaim.	Bō-nā'im .	Bō-nah'im.
Bone .	Bōne'.	Boneh, a builder.
Bosonian	Bō-sō'nī-an	Fourth Degree of African Architects.
Bourn	Bōurn	Bound, limit.
Bramin.	Brā'min	Corruption of Brahman.
Brethren .	Breth'ren .	Not Breth'er-en.
Buddha	Bŭ'dă	A Hindu god.
Buh	Bŭh	A corruption of the word Bel.
Buhle	Bŭhle	Johann Gottlieb Buhle.
Bul.	Bŭl. .	The rain-god.
Buri or **Bure**	Bŭ'ri or Bŭ're .	The first god of Norse mythology.
Byblos	Byb'los .	An ancient city of Phœnicia.
Byzantine	Biz'an-tin	An art from the days of Constantine.
Caaba or **Kaaba**	Că-ă'bă or Kă-ă'bă.	Square building or temple in Mecca.
Cabala .	Că-bă'lă	Kabbala. Mystical philosophy or theosophy of Jews.
Cabiric	Că'bir-ic	Dry, sandy.
Cable-tow	Kā'ble-tō .	A man's reasonable ability.
Cabul.	Că'bul	A district containing twenty cities.
Caduceus .	Că'dŭ'ce-us .	Peace, power, wisdom.
Cæmentarius	Ca'ē-men-ta'ri-us	A builder of walls.
Cagliostro.	Căg'li-os'tro	A Masonic charlatan.
Cahier	Căh'ier .	Sheets of paper or parchment fastened together.
Cairns	Cāirns	Heaps of stones of a conical form.
Calatrava .	Căl'ă-tră'vă.	Military Order, instituted 1158.
Calid . .	Căl'īd. .	A sultan of Egypt about 1110.
Callimachus	Căl-lim'ă-chŭs	Noted Grecian artist.
Calm .	Käm .	Tranquil, serene.
Cama.	Kā'mā .	A Hindu god.
Canaanite	Kā'năn-īte	Descendants of Canaan.
Candelabra	Kăn-del-ā'bră	A branched candlestick.
Cantilever	Căn'ti-lĕv'er	A projecting block or bracket.
Capitular . .	Kă-pĭt'u-lar .	Pertaining to a Chapter.
Capella .	Kă-pĕl'la .	The name of a star.
Capricornus	Kăp-ri-korn'us .	A Zodiacal sign, the Goat.
Capuchin .	Că-pŭ'chin	A monk of the Order of St. Francis.
Caravan. .	Kăr'a-van . .	Not Kăr-a-van'. Company of merchants
Carbonarism	Căr'bō-nar-ism.	A secret society of Italy.

WORDS OF DOUBTFUL PRONUNCIATION.	PROPER MASONIC PRONUNCIATION.	NOTATIONS.
Carbuncle	Kär′bun-kĕl . .	A stone in the breastplate.
Carmel . .	Kär′mel	Literally, a fruitful place.
Caryatides	Căr′y-ăt′i-dēs .	The women of Caryæ.
Casmaran.	Căs′mă-răn . .	The angel of air.
Catacombs .	Kat′a-kōmbs .	A cave for the burial of the dead.
Catechumen	Căt′ē-chū′men .	A novice in religious rites. [tury.
Cathari .	Căth′ăr-ī	Italian heretical society, 12th cen-
Cement	Sem′ent or Sē-ment′	The noun. The bond of union.
Cement	Se-ment′ . . .	The verb. To bind together.
Cemetery .	Sem′e-tĕr-ĭ . .	A place of burial. [ments.
Cenephorus	Cĕn′ē-phō′rus	Officer in charge of sacred imple-
Centaine	Cĕn′tāine . .	A mystical society of 19th century.
Centenary	Sen′te-na-rĭ	Not Sen-ten′a-rĭ. A century.
Censer .	Sĕn′ser . .	An incense cup or vase.
Cephas . .	Sē′fas. . .	A Syrian name. Literally, a stone.
Ceres . . .	Sē′rēs. . .	The goddess of corn.
Ceridwen .	Cē-rid′wen	The Isis of the Druids.
Cerneau	Cĕr′neau .	Cĕr′no.
Cerulean	Sē-ru′le-an	The color of the sky.
Chaldea. .	Chăl-dē′ă .	A country along the Euphrates and
Chalice . .	Chăl′is . .	A cup or bowl. [Tigris rivers.
Chamber .	Chăm′ber .	An enclosed place.
Chaos. . .	Ka′os . . .	Not Ka′us. A confused mass.
Chapeau .	Chăp′eau . .	Shăpo′.
Chapiters.	Chăp′e-tĕrs	The capital of a column.
Chasidim .	Chă′sĭd-im. .	A sect in the time of the Maccabees.
Chasm . .	Kazm . . .	Not Kaz′um. A void space.
Chastanier	Chăs′tan-ĭ′er	Benedict Chastanier.
Chasuble .	Chăs′ū-ble .	An outer dress in imitation of the
Chef-d'œuvre	Chef-d'œuvre′ .	She-deū′vr. [Roman toga.
Cherubim	Chĕr′u-bim	Literally, those held fast.
Chesed .	Chĕ′sĕd. .	Signifying mercy.
Chesvan .	Chĕs′van .	Name of the second Jewish month.
Cheth . .	Chĕth . .	A city of Palestine.
Chibbelum .	Chĭb′bē-lum.	A worthy Mason. [carpenter.
Chisel. . .	Chiz′el . .	An instrument used by a mason or
Chivalric .	Shiv-ăl′rik	Pertaining to chivalry.
Chochmah	Chŏk′măh.	Heb., Wisdom.
Chrisna. .	Krish′nă	The Hindu God.
Chrysolite	Kris′o-līte. .	A stone in the breastplate.
Clandestine.	Klăn-des′tĭn.	Illegal.
Cleche . . .	Klēēch . . .	A cross charged with another cross.
Clothed. . .	Klōthd . . .	Invested with raiment.
Cœur de Lion.	Kūr de Lī′on	Surname of Richard I. of England.
Cochleus	Cŏch′lē-us	A winding staircase.
Coetus .	Cō′e-tŭs .	An assembly.
Coexist . .	Ko-egz-ist′	Living at the same time.
Coffin. . .	Kŏf′in . .	Not Kawf′in. Casket for the dead.
Cognizant	Kon′ĭ-zant .	Within the knowledge.
Collation .	Kol-la′shun .	Not Co-la′shun. Luncheon.

WORDS OF DOUBTFUL PRONUNCIATION.	PROPER MASONIC PRONUNCIATION.	NOTATIONS.
Collocatio	Cŏl'lō-că'ti-o	Cŏl-lo-că'sheo.
Column.	Kŏl'um.	Not Kol'yoŏm. A pillar.
Comment.	Kom'ment	To explain, to expound.
Commiserate.	Kom-miz'er-āt.	Compassion for, to pity.
Compagnon.	Cŏm-păn'ion	A French term for Fellow-Craft.
Composite	Kom-pŏs'ĭt.	An order of Architecture.
Conclave.	Kŏn'klāve. .	An assemblage of Templars.
Condemner.	Kon-dem'ner	Not Kon-dem'er. One who censures.
Condolence	Kon-do'lence	Not Kon'do-lence. Sympathy.
Confidant.	Kon-fĭ-dant'.	Not Kon'fĭ-dant. A bosom friend.
Consistory	Kon-sis'to-ry	An assemblage of brethren of the R. Secret.
Consummatum.	Cŏn'sum-mă'tum.	It is finished.
Conspiracy.	Kon-spĭr'a-sĭ.	A combination for evil purpose.
Constans.	Kŏn'stăns. .	Unwavering, constant.
Contemplating	Con'-tem-pla-ting	Looking around carefully on all sides.
Convocation	Kŏn'vo-kă'shun.	An assemblage of Royal Arch Masons.
Corde Gladio Potens.	Kŏr'dă glă'dĭ-o pŏ'tĕnz	Powerful in heart and with the sword.
Cordon.	Kŏr'don.	A ribbon of honor.
Corinthian	Kŏr-in'thi-an	An order in Architecture.
Corybantes	Cŏr'y-ban'tes	Rites in honor of Atys.
Costume	Kos'tūm	A manner of dress.
Cottyto	Cŏ-tȳt'ŏ	Mysteries of. Rites of the Bona Dea.
Coustos.	Coūs'tos	John Coustos.
Couvreur.	Coū'vrier.	Kū'vrir.
Covenant.	Kŭv'e-nant.	An agreement, a contract.
Cowans. .	Kŏw'ans	Pretenders, dry dikers, intruders.
Cowls.	Kowls	The hood of the mantle.
Crata Repoa	Cră'tă Re-pŏ'ă	An Egyptian rite of seven degrees.
Credence.	Krē'dence.	Not Krĕd'ence. Reliance on evidence.
Cresset.	Crĕs'set.	Symbol of Light and Truth, open lamp.
Crete. .	Krēte.	An island in the Mediterranean.
Cromlech.	Crŏm'lĕch.	A large stone resting on two or more stones.
Crosier	Krō'zher	The staff of the Prelate.
Crotona.	Crō-tō'nă	A city of Greek colonists in Italy.
Cryptic.	Krĭp'tic.	Pertaining to Royal and Select Masonry.
Crux Ansata	Crŭx-ăn-să'tă	The cross with a handle.
Cum Civi.	Kūm Sĭvĭ.	Arise and kneel.
Cupola.	Kū'pō-la.	Not Kū'pa-lo. A surmounting dome.
Curetes. .	Cū-rē'tēs.	Priests of ancient Crete.
Custos Arcani.	Kŭs'tŏs Ar-că'ni	The guardian of the treasury.
Cynocephalus.	Cyn'ō-cĕph'a-lŭs.	Figure of a man with head of a dog.
Cynosure.	Sĭn'ō-shōōr	The center of attraction.
Cyrene.	Cy-rē'nĕ. .	Ancient city of North Africa.
Cyrus.	Si'rŭs. .	A King of Persia.
Dabir.	Dă-bēr'.	Most sacred.
Dactyli.	Dăc'ty-li	Priests of Cybele.
Daduchos.	Dă'dū-chŏs	A torch-bearer.

WORDS OF DOUBTFUL PRONUNCIATION.	PROPER MASONIC PRONUNCIATION.	NOTATIONS.
Dædalus	Dæd'a-lus	A famous artist and mechanician.
Dais.	Dā'is	A canopy.
Dambool	Dăm-bool	Rock temple of Buddhists of Ceylon.
Dao	Dā'ō	From Daer, to shine.
Darakiel	Dā-rā-kiel'	By direction of God.
Darius	Dā-rī'us.	A King of Persia.
Dathan	Dă'than	A Reubenite who revolted against [Moses.
Dazard	Dă'zard	Michel François Dazard.
Decrepit	De-crep'ĭt	Wasted by age.
Deiseil	Dē-is'ēil	Southward, following the course of [the sun.
Delalande.	Dĕ-lă-lan'de	Joseph Jérôme François.
Delaunay	Dĕ-lāu'nāy	François H. Stanislaus Delaunay.
Delineated	De-lin'e-ā-ted	Marked, described.
Delta	Dĕl'tā	Fourth letter of Greek alphabet.
Demeter	Dĕ-me'ter	Greek name of Ceres.
Demit	De-mĭt'	Release.
Denderah	Dĕn-dĕ'rāh	A ruined town of Upper Egypt.
Depths	Depths	Not Deps nor Debths. Profundity.
Derogate	Dĕr'-o-gāte	Degrade.
Desaguliers	Dĕ-sā-gū'liērs	John Theophilus Desaguliers.
Design	De-sīn'	A preliminary sketch.
Dessert	Dez-zert'	The last course of a feast.
Deuchar Charters	Deū-chăr' Chārters.	Working warrants.
Deus Meumque Jus	Dĕ'us Mē-ŭm'que Jus	God and my right.
Devoir	Dĕ'voir	Dĕ'vōa.
Dew	Dū	Atmospheric moisture.
Dieseal	Dī-es-ē'al	A Druidic term.
Dieu et mon Droit	Dieu ĕt mŏn Droit	Dieū ā mon droa.
Dieu le Veut	Dieu lĕ Veūt	Dieū lĕ Veu-t.
Different	Dif'fer-ent	Not Dif'rent. Distinct, separate.
Dionysian.	Dī'o-nys'ĭan.	Celebrations by which the years were numbered.
Dionysus	Dī'o-nys'us	Greek name of Bacchus.
Diploma	Dī-plo'ma	Not Dī-plo-ma. A sealed writing.
Dislodge	Dis-lŏdge'	To drive from a place of rest.
Disloyal.	Dis-loy'al	Faithless.
Dissolve.	Diz-zolv'	Separation into component parts.
District	Dis'trikt	A portion of territory.
Diu	Dī'ū	The "Shining Light of Heaven."
Divest	Dī-vest'.	Deprive of, remove.
Divulge	Dī-vulj'	To make publicly known.
Domino Deus Meus	Dŏm'i-nĕ Dā'us Mā'us	O Lord, my God.
Domitian	Do-mĭsh'i-an	A Roman Emperor.
Donats	Dō'nāts	Wearers of the demi-cross.
Doric	Dŏr'ik	An order in Architecture.
Doth	Duth	Not Dŏth. Third person of do.
Drachma	Drăk'mā	A coin, a weight.
Dræseke	Drā'e-sēke.	Johann Heinrich Bernhardt Dræseke
Druid.	Drōō'id	A Celtic priest.
Druses	Drū'sēs	A sect of religionists in Syria.

WORDS OF DOUBTFUL PRONUNCIATION.	PROPER MASONIC PRONUNCIATION.	NOTATIONS.
Duad	Dū'ad . .	Number two in Pythagorean system.
Due Guard .	Dū' Gärd .	Mode of recognition.
Dupaty . .	Du'pă-ty	Louis Emanuel Charles M. Dupaty.
Dyaus. . .	Dy'aus . .	Sanskrit for sky. Bright, exalted.
Dyena Sore .	Dy'ē-nă So-ré .	A Masonic romance by Van Meyern.
Eastward . .	East'ward . . .	Not East'ard. Direction of the East.
Ebal.	Ē'băl	Literally, bare. Son of Shobal.
Eban Bohan	Ē'băn Bō'hăn .	A witness stone set up by Bohan.
Eblis . . .	Ĕb'lis	Arabic for Prince of Apostate Angels.
Echatana .	Ĕc-băt'ă-nă	Capital of Media.
Ecossais. .	Ē'cōe-săis . .	Ā'cōe-sais.
Ecossism .	Ē'cōe-sism. .	
Edicts . .	Ē'dikts . . .	Decrees by an authority.
Eheyeh . .	Ē-hĕ'yĕh	I am that I am.
Elai beni almanah.	Ē'lă-ī bĕn-i ăl-mă'năh	Third Degree A. A. Scottish Rite.
Elchanan .	Ĕl-chăn'ăn . .	Āl-kănă'n.
Eleazar	Ĕl-e-ā'zar . . .	Son of Aaron.
Electa.	E-lĕk'tă. . . .	An eminent woman of Judea.
Eleemosynary.	El-e-moz'ĭ-na-rĭ	Relating to charity.
Eleham . .	Ĕl'ē-ham . .	See *Elchanan*.
Elephanta	Ĕl-ĕ-phăn'ta .	Ancient temple in Gulf of Bombay.
Eleusinian	Ē'leū-sin'ī-an	Mysteries of ancient Athenian religion.
Eleusis . .	E-lū'sis . . .	An ancient Grecian city.
Eliasaph .	E-lī'a-saf . .	A Levite.
Elihoreph.	Ĕl'ī-hō'rĕph .	One of Solomon's secretaries.
Elohim . .	Ĕl-ō'hīm . .	The Creator.
El Shaddai	El Shăd'dă-ē	The second name of God in the Bible.
Elu .	Ĕl'u . . .	See *Elus*.
Elul . .	Ĕl'ūl . . .	Twelfth civil month of Jewish year.
Elus . .	Ĕl'ūs . . .	Elected.
Elysium	E-lish'ī-um	A place of happiness.
Emeritus .	Ē-mĕr'ī-tūs	One who has served out his time.
Emeth . .	Ē'mĕth . .	Integrity, fidelity, firmness.
Emir . . .	A'mīr . . .	An Arabic counselor.
Emounah.	Ē-mou'năh .	Fidelity, truth.
Empyrean	Em-pī'rē-an .	The highest Heaven.
Emunah .	Ē-mū'năh . .	Fidelity to one's promises.
Encyclical	Ĕn-cy'clī-cal .	Circular, sent to many places and persons.
En famille	Ĕn fă-mīlle' .	En fă-meēl.
Enochian .	Ē-nō'chi-an	Ē-nō'kee-an, relating to Enoch.
En Soph	Ĕn' Sŏph .	
Ephod .	Ē'phŏd .	Sacred vestment of the high priest.
Eons . .	E'ŏns .	Divine spirits in intermediate state.
Eostre	E-os'tre	Easter.
Ephesus	Ĕf'ē-sus	An ancient city of Asia.
Ephraim	Ē'fra-im	A tribe of Israel.
Epistle .	Ē-pis'l . .	A letter, a missive.
Epitome	Ē-pĭt'o-me	A summary.

WORDS OF DOUBTFUL PRONUNCIATION.	PROPER MASONIC PRONUNCIATION.	NOTATIONS.
Epopt	E'pŏpt .	An eye-witness.
Eques	É'quĕs .	Signifying knight.
Equitas .	Ĕk'wī-tăs	Equity.
Eranoi	E'ră-nŏ'ī	Friendly societies among the Greeks.
Erica .	E-rī'că .	A sacred plant amongtheEgyptians.
Erosch	A-rŏsh' .	The Celestial Raven.
Errand .	Ĕr'rand	A commission.
Erratum	Ĕr-ra'tum	An error in writing.
Esar Haddon	Ē-sar Hăd'don	A king of Assyria.
Esoteric	Ĕs'o-tĕr'ic	That which is taught to a select few.
Esperance.	Ĕs'pĕ-rănce	Ĕs'pĕ-rănse.
Esquire .	Es-kwīr'	An armor-bearer.
Esrim	Ĕz'rim .	The Hebrew number twenty.
Essenes	Ĕs'sĕn-ĕs	Es'sen-ēes. A Jewish sect.
Esther	Ĕs'ter	Wife of King Ahasuerus.
Ethanim or **Tishri**.	Ĕth'a-nīm	The seventh Hebrew month.
Eumolpus	Eū-mŏl'pūs	A king of Eleusis.
Eunuch	Eū'nūch	Prohibited candidates.
Eureka .	Ū-rē'ka	I have found it.
European .	Ū-rō-pe'an	Relating to Europe.
Evates. .	Ē-vă'tes	2d Degree in the Druidical system.
Eveilles, Secte des	Ē-vĕil-lĕs, Sĕct-e dĕs	Ē-vă-ēā. Bright, enlightened.
Evergeten Bundder	Ē'vĕr-gē'ten Būnd'dĕr	Secretordersimilartothe *Illuminati*.
Evora.	Ē-vŏ-ră .	Knights of. A military order.
Exalt	Egz-awlt .	To elevate.
Examine	Egz-am'īn	To scrutinize.
Example	Egz-am'pl	To be imitated.
Excalibar .	Ex-căl'i-băr	King Arthur's famous sword.
Excellent .	Eks-sel-lent	Admirable.
Executive .	Egz-ek'ū-tiv	An executor of the laws.
Exempt	Egz-emt' .	Not subject.
Exist	Egz-ist'	The state of being.
Exordium.	Egz-or'dī-um	The introduction.
Exoteric	Ĕx'o-tĕr'ic	Public, not secret.
Expert	Eks'pert	An experienced person.
Expiration	Eks-pī-ră'shun .	A breathing out.
Extempore	Eks-tem'pŏ-re	Without previous study.
Ezekiel	Ē-zē'ki-el	A Hebrew prophet.
Ezel	Ē'zĕl	Division, separation.
Familien Logen	Fă-mil'ī-en Lŏgen	A family lodge, private.
Fanor.	Făn'or .	Name given to the Syrian Mason.
Fasces	Făs'cēs	Speeches or records done up in a roll.
Fealty	Fē'al-ty . .	Loyalty.
February .	Feb'rōō-a-rī	Second month in the Calendar.
Feix-Feax .	Fe-īx'-Fe-ăx'	Signifying School of Thought.
Fendeurs .	Fĕn-deūrs.	Făn-deūr.
Fervency	Fŭr'ven-cy	Devotion.
Feuillants	Feu-īl-lănts	Feu-iăn-ts.
Fiat Lux	Fē'at Lux .	Let there be light.

WORDS OF DOUBTFUL PRONUNCIATION.	PROPER MASONIC PRONUNCIATION.	NOTATIONS.
Fiat Justitia . . . Ruat Cœlum .	Fē'at Jūs-tĭ-shĭ-a rū'ăt sē-lŭm	Let justice be done though the heavens fall.
Fidelity .	Fĭ-del'ĭ-tĭ .	Faithfulness.
Fides . .	Fĭ'dēs . .	A Roman goddess. Faith.
Fiducial	Fĭ-dū'cĭ-al	Confiding trust.
Fillet . .	Fĭl'let .	Head-band.
Finance.	Fĭ-nănce'	Revenue of a person or state.
Forehead .	Fŏr'ed	The front of the skull.
Forest . .	Fŏr'est	Not For'ist. A large tract of wood.
Frankincense	Frănk'in-sĕnse .	An odorous resin.
Frater	Fră'ter	Latin for Brother.
Freimaurer . .	Freĭ-maur'ĕr .	Fri-mou'rer. A builder of walls.
Frères Pontives .	Frĕres Pŏn-tives .	Frâres Pŏn-tives.
Friendship	Frend'ship	Personal attachment.
Frieze.	Frees. .	The entablature, between architrave and cornice.
Fylfot .	Fȳl'fŏt	An ancient symbol.
Gabaon.	Gă'bă-ŏn	A high place.
Gabor	Gă'bor .	Strong.
Gabriel .	Ga'bri-el .	An anchangel.
Gaedicke .	Găed'ĭcke .	Johann Christian Gădicke.
Galahad	Gă'lă-hăd .	A corruption of Gilead.
G. A. O. T. U..	G. A. O. T. U. .	Great Architect of the Universe.
Gareb. . .	Gă'reb . .	A Hebrew engraver.
Garimout.	Găr'i-mŏut	Corruption of Garimond or Garimund.
Garinus	Gă'rĭ-nus .	A standard-bearer.
Gavel. . .	Găv'el . .	A working tool of an Entered Apprentice.
Gebal. . .	Gĕ'băl . .	A city of Phœnicia. Border, hilly.
Gedaliah	Gĕ-dal'iăh .	Son of Pashur.
Gemara. .	Gĕ-mă'ră	See *Talmud.*
Generalissimo.	Gen-ĕr-al-ĭs'si-mŏ	Second officer in command of K. T.
Geometry. .	Je-om'ĕ-trĕ . . .	A science of magnitudes.
Gethsemane	Geth-sem'a-nĕ . .	A garden near Jerusalem.
Gershon . .	Gŭr'shon	A son of Levi.
Ghemoul . .	Gē'mul	A step of the Kadosh ladder.
Ghemoul Binah Thebounah .	Ghe'moul Bĭ'nah Thĕ-boū'nah	Prudence in the midst of vicissitude.
Gibeah .	Gĭb'e-ah	Literally, height.
Giblim .	Gib'lim .	Stonesquarer.
Gilead .	Gĭl'e-ad	The Syrian mountains.
Gnostics	Gnŏs'tics	Nŏs'tiks. Superior or celestial knowledge.
God . .	God	Not Gawd.
Godfrey de St. Aldemar	God'fry de San Aldemar . .	One of the founders of ancient Knights Templarism.
Goethe . .	Gŏe'thĕ . . .	John Wolfgang von Goethe.
Goetia . .	Gŏ-e'tiă. . .	Go-ĕ'sha.
Golgotha .	Gol'go-tha	Name given to Calvary by the Jews.
Gomel . .	Gŏ'mĕl . . .	Reward.
Gormogons .	Gŏr'mŏ-gons	A society opposing Freemasonry.
Gomorrah	Gom-ŏr'ra	Name of a Hebrew city.

WORDS OF DOUBTFUL PRONUNCIATION.	PROPER MASONIC PRONUNCIATION.	NOTATIONS.
Gonfalon .	Gŏn′făl-ŏn′	Ecclesiastical banner.
Gordian .	Gor′dĭ-an .	Not Gord′yan.
Gorgeous .	Gor′jus . .	Magnificent.
Gothic . .	Gŏth′ic . .	A style of Architecture.
Gravelot .	Grăv′ĕ-lot .	One of the three ruffians.
Gugomos .	Gū′gō-mŏs	Baron von Gugomos.
Guibs. . .	Gibz	A ruffian in the Scottish Rite.
Guillemain .	Guil′lĕ-māin.	Gĕ′ye-māin.
Guttural . .	Gŭt′tŭr-ăl .	Pertaining to the throat.
Gymnosophists	Gўm-nŏs′ŏ-phists	Signifying "naked sages."
Habakkuk	Hăb′ak-kŭk .	Love's embrace. A Jewish prophet.
Habin. . .	Hăb′ĭn . . .	Initiate of 4th Degree, Mod. Fr. R.
Habramah	Hăb′ră-măh .	Used only in France. [med.
Hadeases .	Hă-dēes′ĕs	Traditions handed down by Moham-
Hafedha	Hăf′ĕd-hă .	Second of four gods of Arab tribe
Haggai .	Hăg′gā-ī	A Hebrew prophet. [of Ad.
Hah	Hăh′ .	Hebrew definite article "the."
Hail . .	Hāil . .	Whence do you hail?
Hale . .	Hāle′. . . .	To hide.
Hallelujah	Hăl-le-lū′yă .	Praise ye Jehovah.
Hamaliel .	Hăm-ā′lī-el .	The angel of Venus.
Haphtziel	Hăpht′zī-el .	Hăf-zi-el.
Harnouester	Hărn-ouest-er	Harn-west-er.
Harodim . .	Har′ŏ-dĭm . .	Princes in Masonry.
Haruspices .	Hă′rŭs-pī′cĕs	Implying a soothsayer or aruspice.
Haupt-Hutte .	Hăupt-Hŭtte .	Hoŭt-hŭte.
Hautes Grades	Hăutes Grades	Hō-grā-d.
Heal . . .	Hēal′	To make legal.
Heaven . .	Hĕv′n . .	The abode of bliss.
Hecatomb	Hĕc′ă-tŭm	A sacrifice of a hundred oxen.
Heptagon	Hĕp′ta-gŏn	A plane figure of seven equal sides.
Hermaimes .	Hĕr-māimes	A corruption of Hermes.
Hermandad.	Hĕr-măn-dăd	"Spanish Brotherhood."
Hermes	Hĕr′mēz .	The Greek God, Mercury.
Herodoin . .	Hĕr′ŏ-dŏin	Mythical mountain in Scotland.
Hesed. . . .	He′sĕd	Literally, kindness.
Hibbut-Hakkeber	Hĭb′bŭt Hăk′kĕ-ber	Beating of the sepulcher.
Hieronymites	Hī′e-rŏn′y-mites .	Hermit Order of the 14th century.
Hierophylax.	Hī′ĕ-ro-phy′lăx	Guardian of the holy vessels and
Hindu . . .	Hĭn′du	A native of Hindustan. [vestments.
Hiram Abba	Hī′ram Ab′bă .	Not Abi. Hiram the Master, Father.
Hiram-Abif	Hiram-ăb-īf′.	A widow's son of the tribe of Naph-
Ho La Tai	Hō lă tā-e	He has suffered. [tali.
Homage	Hŏm′āj . .	Reverential worship.
Hor . .	Hŏr . . .	The mountain on which Aaron died
Horeb .	Hō′rĕb . .	The Mount Sinai range. [earth.
Horizon	Hō-ri′zun .	Not Hor′i-zŏn. Visible boundary of
Hoschea	Hŏs-chē-a . .	A corruption of the word huzza.
Hospitalers	Hŏs′pī-tal-ers	A branch of the Templar Knighthood.

WORDS OF DOUBTFUL PRONUNCIATION.	PROPER MASONIC PRONUNCIATION.	NOTATIONS.
Humble . .	Hum'bl . . .	Lowly of mind.
Huzza . . .	Hŭz-zä' . . .	Acclamation.
Hypotenuse	Hi-pot'e-nūs.	The longest side of a right angle triangle.
Hystaspes	His-täs'pēz	Father of the Persian King, Darius.
Hyssop . . .	Hĭs'up . . .	A species of caper.
Iatric	Ī-ăt'ric . . .	Searchers after universal medicine.
I-Colm-Kill.	Ic'ōlm-Kill' .	Ik'ŏm-kil'.
Iconoclasts	Ī-cŏn'ō-clăsts	Image-breakers.
Iconology	Ī'con-ŏl'o-gy	Teaching the doctrine of images.
Iesus Hominum Salvator . . .	Yā'sūs Hom'e-nūm Săl-vā'tor . . .	Jesus, savior of men.
Iesus Nazerenus Rex Judæorum .	Yā'sūs Nā-zā-rā-nūs Răx jū-dē-ō-rūm	Jesus of Nazareth, King of the Jews.
Ih-Ho . .	Īh-hō	See *Ho-hi*.
Ijar . . .	Ī-jär	Eighth month of the Hebrew year.
Illuminati	Īl-lū'mi-nā'tī	Immaculate.
Immanuel	Im-man'-u-el	God with us.
Imaum	Īm'aum . .	Im'ŏm.
Immortality	Im-mor-tal'ĭ-tĭ	Unending existence.
Impious . .	Im'pĭ-us . . .	Profane, wicked.
Impostor . .	Im-pŏs'tor . .	Not Im-paw'stor. A deceiver.
Incomparable	In-kŏm'pa-ra-bl	Transcendent, peerless.
Indian . . .	In'dĭ-an . . .	Pertaining to the Indies.
Ineffable . .	In-ĕf'fā-bl . .	Unutterable.
Inexplicable .	In-eks'plĭ-ka-bl . . .	Without explanation.
In Hoc Signo Vinces	In Hŏk Sĭg'nō Vĭn'sēz	By this sign thou shalt conquer.
Initiate .	In-ĭ'shē-ăt .	Performing the first rite.
Inquiry . .	In-kwī'rĭ . .	Search for information.
Institute . .	In'stĭ-tūt . .	Erect, establish.
Interesting	Ĭn'ter-ĕst-ing	Engaging the attention or curiosity.
Ionic	Ī-on'ic . . .	A style of Architecture.
Irrevocable	Ir-rev'ō-ca-bl	Incapable of being recalled.
Ischngi . . .	Īsch'n-gī .	One of the five masters of Solomon.
Ish Chotzeb	Īsh-chŏtzĕb	Literally, hewers.
Ishmael	Īsh-ma'ĕl . .	God is hearing.
Ish Sabal	Īsh-sā'băl . .	Men of burden.
Ish Sodi	Īsh-sŏ'dĭ . . .	A select master.
Isiac Tables	Īs'ĭ-ăc Tā'bles	A flat rectangular bronze plate.
Islamism .	Īz'lam-ĭzm	The Moslem faith.
Isolate	Īz'ō-lăte	Place by itself.
Israfeel .	Īs'rā-fēĕl .	Trumpeting Angel of Resurrection.
Isis . . .	Ī-sis . . .	Sister of Osiris. Beneficent Goddess of Egypt.
Ithamar	Īth'ā-mār	Youngest son of Aaron.
Itratics .	Ī-trā'tics	A society of adepts.
Izads . .	Īz'ăds . .	The twenty-eight creations of Ormuds
Jaaborou Hammain	Jā-āb'ō-rōuHăm-mā'ĭn	A word of covered significance
Jabesh . .	Jā'băsh	Dry place.
Jabescheh	Jā-bĕs'chĕh	The dry soil.

WORDS OF DOUBTFUL PRONUNCIATION.	PROPER MASONIC PRONUNCIATION.	NOTATIONS.
Jabulum .	Jă'bū-lŭm	Corruption of Jū-bē-lŭm'. [temple.
Jachin .	Jă'kĭn . .	To establish. A pillar in Solomon's
Jachinai .	Jă'chĭn-āī .	Jă'kin-āhī. Corruption of Shekinah.
Jacinth .	Jă'sinth	A mineral gem of value.
Jacques de Molay	Shăk' dă Mō-lāy'	Past Grand Master of the Templars.
Jafuhar . .	Jă'fū-hăr . .	Synonym for Thor.
Jah	Jāh	Triliteral name of God.
Jamblichus . .	Jăm'blĭ-chus . .	A Neoplatonic philosopher.
James de Molay	James dē Mōlāy .	Last Grand Master of ancient K. T.
Jaina	Jă-ī'nă . .	A cross adopted by the Jainas.
Jared	Jă'red . . .	Descendant of Seth. Lived 962
Jasher	Jă'sher . . .	Upright. [years.
Jasper	Jăs'per . . .	Fourth stone in the breastplate.
Jebusites .	Jeb'ū-sites .	Natives of Jebus (afterward Jerusa-
Jehoshaphat	Jē-hŏsh'a-făt	A valley east of Jerusalem. [lem).
Jeksan . . .	Jĕk'săn	Son of Abraham and Keturah.
Jeroboam	Jĕr-o-bō'am . . .	First king of the ten tribes.
Jetzirah Sepher	Jĕt-zī'rah Sē'pher	A traditional document.
Jeva. Jova. Jua	Jă'vă. Jō'vă. Jū-ă	Abbreviations and corruptions of
Jezeeds .	Jĕz'ēēds .	Jah is honor. [Jehovah.
Joabert .	Jō-ă'bert	The chief favorite of Solomon.
Joah . .	Jō'ah . .	Jah is brother.
Jobel . .	Jō'bĕl . .	A name of God.
Jochebed .	Jō-che'bĕd	Jō-kē'bĕd. Jah is honor.
Jod he vau he	Yŏd hă vau hē	Hebrew letters spelling Jehovah.
Joha . . .	Jō'ha . .	Jah is living.
Jo-ha-ben	Yō-hă'ben	A mystical word.
Jokshan	Jŏk'shăn .	Fowler. Second son of Abraham.
Joppa .	Jŏp'pa . .	Seacoast city, 37 miles from Jerusa-
Jordan .	Jŏr'dan .	A tortuous river of Palestine. [lem.
Josedech	Jō'sē-dek .	Jah is righteous. Father of Jeshua.
Joshua .	Josh'-u-a .	High priest who rebuilt the temple.
Jua . .	Jū'a . . .	Corrupted form of Tetragrammaton.
Jubal .	Jū'bal . .	Shout, blow. Son of Adah.
Jubalcain	Jū'bal-cāĭn . .	Founder of the science of music.
Jubela-o-m .	Jū-bē-lă'-ō'm' .	Assassins.
Jubala	Jū-bē-lă' .	First ruffian.
Jubalo	Jū-bē-lō' .	Second ruffian.
Jubelum	Jū-bē-lŭm	Third ruffian.
Kaaba	Kă-ă'bă	Kă-ăr'bar. Holy temple of Mecca.
Kabbala	Kăb'bă-lă'	A mystical philosophy of the Jews.
Kabbalistic .	Kab'bal-is-tic	Pertaining to the mysteries.
Kadosh	Kă'dosh . .	Holy. Same as *Kedesh*.
Kadiri . . .	Kă'dĭ-rĭ . .	An Arabian secret society.
Kamea . . .	Kă'mē-ă . .	An amulet.
Karmatians	Kăr-mă'tiăns	A Mohammedan sect.
Kasideans	Kă'sĭ-dē'ans	Latinized spelling of Chasidim.
Katharsis .	Kă-thăr'sis	Ceremony of purification.
Khem . .	Khĕm . . .	The Egyptian deity, Amon.

WORDS OF DOUBTFUL PRONUNCIATION.	PROPER MASONIC PRONUNCIATION.	NOTATIONS.
Khepra	Khĕ'pră	An Egyptian deity.
Kher-heb .	Khĕr'hĕb .	Master of Ceremonies.
Khesvan .	Khĕs'văn	Second month of Jewish civil year.
Khetem el Nabiim	Khĕ'tĕm el Năb-ĭim	Kĕ'tĕm el Nahb-ĭim.
Khon	Khŏn	The dead. Subject to examination.
Khotbah	Khŏt'băh .	Mohammedan Confession of Faith.
Khurum-Abba	Khū-rŭm-Ăb'bă .	Hiram Abba.
Ki	[illegible] .	In old Ritual of A. A. Scottish Rite.
Kidron .	Kĭd'ron	Turbid water. A brook near Mount of Olives.
Kislev	Kĭs'lev .	The third Hebrew month.
Knewt-neb-s	Knewt'nĕb-s	Nūte'nĕbs.
Kohath	Kō'hăth	Assembly. Ancestor of Moses.
Kojiki	Kō'jĭ'ki	The ancient religion of Japan.
Konx Ompax .	Kŏnx Ŏm'păx	Definition uncertain.
Korah	Kō'răh	Baldness. A son of Esau.
Koran	Kō'răn	The reading. The Moslem Bible.
Krishna	Krĭsh'nă	A Trimurti in Hindu religious system.
Kulma .	Kŭl'mă	Hindustani Confession of Faith.
Kum Kivi	Kŭm Kĭ-vĭ	Arise! and kneel!
Kun	Kūn	The creative fiat of God.
Laanah .	Lă'a-năh .	Wormwood.
Labarum .	Lă'bă-rum	Monogram of Christ.
Laborare est orare	Lă'-bō-ră're est ō-ră'rē	To labor is to pray.
Lacorne	Lă-corne' .	Lă'kor'nă'.
Lakak Deror Pessah	Lă'kăk Dĕr'or Pĕs'săh	Liberty of passage and thought.
Lalande	Lă'lănde'	See *Delalande.*
Lamaism .	Lă'mă-ism	Religion of Tibet and Mongolia.
Lamma Sabactani	Lăm'mă Să'băc-tă'nĭ .	Used in French Rite of Adoption.
Lanturelus .	Lăn'tū-rē'lŭs	Instituted in 1771.
Lapicida	Lă'pĭ-cĭ'dă	A stone-cutter.
Larudan, Abbé .	Lă'rū-dan, Ăb'bē	Author of a libellous work.
Latomia	Lă'tō-mē'ă	A stone quarry.
Latres	Lă-três' .	A brick.
Laus Deo .	Lăw-ŭs Dē'ō	God be praised.
Laurel	Lŏr'el	An evergreen shrub.
Lebanon	Lĕb'a-non	The forest mountains in Syria.
Lechangeur .	Lē-chăn'geur	
Lefranc	Lē-frănc'	A bitter enemy of Freemasonry.
Legate .	Lĕg'ate .	An embassador.
Legend .	Lĕj'end .	A fable.
Lehrling	Lēhr'ling .	German for Entered Apprentice.
Lemanceau .	Lē-man-ceău'	Lă-man-so'.
Leontica	Lē-on'tĭ-că	Ancient sacrifices in honor of the sun.
Lepage .	Lē-păge'	Lē-pa'j.
Leucht .	Leūcht	A Masonic charlatan.
Level .	Lĕv'el	An instrument to find a horizontal line.
Levitikon .	Lē-vit'ĭ-kŏn .	The spurious Gospel of St. John.
Libanus	Lĭ-bă'nus .	The Latin for Lebanon.

WORDS OF DOUBTFUL PRONUNCIATION.	PROPER MASONIC PRONUNCIATION.	NOTATIONS.
Libation .	Lī-bā'shun	A pouring out of liquor.
Liber . . .	Lī'bĕr . .	The Book.
Libertas	Lib-er-tas'	Liberty.
Libertine .	Lib'er-tīn	A dissolute, licentious person.
Licht	Licht . . .	Light.
Lichtseher	Licht'sē-bĕr	A mystical sect of the 16th century.
Linear Triad	Lin'ē-ăr Trī'ad	A figure in some old floor cloths.
Listen	Lis'n	To attend and hear.
Livre d'Architecture	Lī'vre d'Ăr'chi-tec-tur	Lī'vr d'Ar'she-tek-tū-r.
Livre d'Or. .	Lī'vre d'Or .	Lē'vr-d'or. The Book of Gold.
Lodge . .	Lŏdg	A place of shelter.
Logos . .	Lŏg'ŏs . . .	The word.
Loki . . .	Lō'kī . . .	
Lotos . .	Lō'tus . . .	An Egyptian aquatic plant.
Louveteau	Loū-vē-teāu'	Loū-v-to'.
Loyal . .	Loi-al . . .	Devoted, faithful.
Lubec . .	Lū'bĕk	A town in Germany.
Lumiere la Grande .	Lū'miere lă Grăndē	The Grand Light.
Lux e tenebris . . .	Lŭx ē ten'ē-bris . .	Light out of darkness.
Lux Fiat et Lux Fit	Lŭx Fī'at ĕt Lŭx Fit	Let there be light, and there was light.
Lux . . .	Lŭs	Literally, bending, curve.
Maacha	Mā-ā-chā	Mā-ăr'kā.
Macbenac	Măc-bē-năc	See *Mac*.
Maccabees	Măc'că-bēēs	A heroic Jewish family.
Maçonniere Rouge	Mă-çŏn'nē-rie Rouge	Mă-sŏn-nē-rē Rūge.
Macconnieke Societeiten .	Mă-çon'niē-ke Sō-ci'e-teī'ten . .	Dutch Masonic clubs.
Macerio . .	Mă'ce-rī'ō	This word is now obsolete.
Macio . . .	Mă'ci-o . .	Mă'she-o.
Maconetus .	Mă'cŏn-ē'tŭs	Mă'-son-e-tus.
Maçonne . .	Mă'çon-ne . .	Ma-son-e.
Macrocosm .	Măc'ro-cŏsm .	Ma'cro-cŏsm. Creating the universe.
Maczo . . .	Măc'zō	A mason, a constructor of walls.
Magi	Mă'gī	Mă'ji. Wise Men of Persia.
Magna est veritas et prævalebit	Măg'nă ĕst vĕr'e-tas ĕt prē'vă-lā-bĭt	Truth is mighty and will prevail.
Magus	Mă'gŭs	Mā-gŭs.
Mah	Māh	Hebrew pronoun what.
Mahabharata	Mă'hă-bhă'ră-tă . .	A Sanskrit poem.
Mahadeva . .	Mă'hă-dē'vă . . .	"The Great God."
Mahakasyapa	Mă'hă-kă'sy-ă-pă' . .	Disciple of Buddha Sakyamuni.
Maher - Shalal - Hash-Bas	Mă'hĕr Shă-lăl Hăsh-Bas	Make haste to the prey, fall upon the spoil.
Mahomet	Mă-hŏm'et . . .	The Moslem prophet.
Mah Shim	Mă'shēm	A standard-bearer.
Maitre Maçon . . .	Māī'trĕ Mă-çŏn'.	Mē'tr Mă-sŏn'.
Maitresse Agissante.	Māī'trĕsse	Acting mistress.
Maitrise	Māī'trise	Without an English equivalent.
Malach .	Mă-lăch'	An angel.

WORDS OF DOUBTFUL PRONUNCIATION.	PROPER MASONIC PRONUNCIATION.	NOTATIONS.
Malachi	Măl-ā′chī	Messenger of Job.
Malakoth	Măl′a-kŏth	The angelic messenger. [of Faith.
Malek Adhel Sayfeddin	Mă′lek′ăd-ĕlSăf-ĕd-dīn	The just king who holds the Sword
Malta . . .	Măl′tă	An island in the Mediterranean Sea.
Manasseh	Ma-năs′să . .	A tribe of Israel.
Manes . . .	Mă′nēs	Souls of the dead.
Manichæans	Măn′i-chē′ans .	Also termed Gnostics.
Manu . . .	Măn′ū	Corresponding to the word West.
Marchesvan	Măr-kesh′van .	The second Jewish month.
Marduk . .	Măr′duk . . .	A victorious warrior-god.
Masora . . .	Măs-ō′ră	A Hebrew work on the Bible.
Masoretic Points	Mă′sō-rĕt′ic points .	Vowel signs.
Massonus .	Măs-sō′nŭs . .	Mason.
Master . . .	Măs-ter . . .	Lord, Chief, Prince.
Mathoc . .	Mă′thŏc . . .	Amiability.
Mausoleum	Mau-sō-lē′ŭm .	A stately sepulcher.
Maut	Măut . . .	Mort.
Megacosm	Mĕg′a-cŏsm . .	An intermediate world.
Mehen .	Mĕ′hĕn . . .	Or, May-hĕn.
Mehour .	Mĕ′hoūr . . .	Or, May-hūre.
Meister . .	Meist′ĕr . . .	German for master.
Melchizedek	Mĕl-chĭz′ĕ-dĕk	King of Salem.
Melech . . .	Mĕ′lĕck . . .	Mă′lak.
Melesino, Rite of	Mĕl′es-ī′-nō . .	Scarcely known out of Russia.
Melita	Mĕl-ī′tă	Ancient name of island of Malta.
Memento Mori	Mē-mĕn′tō Mō-re	Remember death. [duce thoughts.
Memory . .	Mem′ō-re	NotMem′ry. Mentalpowertorepro-
Menatzchim	Mĕ-năt′chim . .	Expert Master Masons.
Menu . .	Mĕ′nū	Son of Brahma.
Merari . . .	Mē-ră′re	Heb., Bitter. Youngest son of Levi.
Mer-Sker . .	Mĕr′ Skĕr	Space in which the sun moves.
Meshia Meshiane .	Mĕsh′ī-a Mĕsh′ī-āne	Corresponding to Adam and Eve.
Mesopolyte .	Mĕs′ō-pō-ly′te	4thDegreeofGermanUnionofXXII.
Mesouraneo	Mĕ′sōu-ră-nē′ō	I am the center of heaven.
Metusael .	Mĕ-tu′să-el .	Heb. quarryman,oneoftheassassins.
Mezuza	Mĕz′ū-ză . .	Third principle of Judaism.
Microcosm	Mī-crō-cosm	See *Man*.
Minos . .	Mī′nos .	The lawgiver of Crete.
Mistletoe .	Mĭz′l-tō .	An evergreen plant.
Mithras	Mĭth′răs .	The principal deity of the Persians.
Miter	Mī′ter . .	The covering of a bishop's head.
Mizeph .	Mĭz′pĕ . .	A city in Gilead.
Mizraim	Mĭz′raim .	Rite of, originated at Milan in 1805.
Moabon	Mō-ā′bŏn .	Mō-ah′bŏn.
Moloch .	Mŏl′ok	The deity of the Ammonites.
Montfauçon, Prior of	Mont′fău-çon′, Prior of	One of the two traitors.
Monument .	Mon′ū-ment	A memorial.
Mopses .	Mŏp′sēs	A pretended name for Masonry.
Moriah .	Mō-rī-ă . .	The hill on which the Temple was
Mortal .	Mor′tal . .	Subject to death. [built.

WORDS OF DOUBTFUL PRONUNCIATION.	PROPER MASONIC PRONUNCIATION.	NOTATIONS.
Mosaic	Mō-sā-Ic	Variegated, tessellated.
Moslem	Mŏz'lem	Mohammedan.
Mot de Semestre	Mŏt' dě Se-mes'tre	Mō' de se-mest-r.
Murderer . .	Mur'der-er . .	Not Murd'rer. Assassin.
Mystagogue	Mўs'tā-gŏgue'	One who makes or conducts an initiate.
Mystes . .	Mys'tēs . .	To shut the eyes.
Mythology	MI-thol'ō-jī .	The science of myths.
Naamah	Nā-ā'māh	The daughter of Lamech.
Nabaim	Nā'bā-im .	See *Schools of the Prophets.*
Nadab .	Nā'dăb . .	High priest of the Persians.
Naked	Nā'kĕd . .	Unclothed, defenseless.
Naphthali	Năf'ta-lī	One of Jacob's sons.
Narbonne	Năr-bonne . .	
Naymus Grecus.	Nāy'mŭs Grē'cŭs	Possible corruption of Magna Græcia.
Nazarene	Năz'ā-rene	An inhabitant of Nazareth.
Nebuchadnezzar	Nĕb-uk-ăd-nĕz'zar .	A King of Babylon.
Nebuzaradan . .	Nĕb-ū-zăr'ā-dăn . .	An officer under Nebuchadnezzar
Necum	Nē'kōōm	Vengeance.
Nec proditur, nec proditur, innocens ferat	Nĕkprŏ'dī-tor,nĕkprŏ'-dī-torIn-nō-sĕnz fē-răt	Not the traitor, not the traitor, let the innocent bear it.
Neder	Nā'dĕr . .	Promise.
Neith . .	Nēith . . .	Egyptiansynonym forGreekAthenē.
Nekam . .	Nĕ'kăm . . .	Signifying vengeance.
Nekamah	Nĕ'kā-māh . .	Same as Nekam.
Neocorus .	Nē'ō-cō'rŭs . .	The Guardian of the Temple.
Ne plus ultra	Nā plus ŭl'trā .	Nothing beyond.
Ne varietur .	Nā vā-rī-e'tŭr .	Unless changed.
Nicotiates . .	Nĕ-cō'tī-a'tes .	Nē-cō'tī-ah'tes.
Nihongi . . .	Nī-hon'gī . . .	Chronicles of Nihon.
Nil nisi clavis	Nīl nisī clāvis .	Nothing but the key is wanting.
Nisan . .	Nī'san . . .	First month of Jewish year.
Noachidæ.	Nō-ach'ī-dæ .	Descendants of Noah.
Noffodei .	Nŏf'fō-dĕī' . .	An apostate Templar.
Nonage . .	Nŏn'aj	Under lawful age.
Nonesynches	Nŏnē-sўn-chēs	A corruption of Noonshun (luncheon).
Nonis . . .	Nō'nīs	A mystic word.
Non nobis, Domine, non nobis, sed nomini tuo da gloriam	Nŏn nō-bis, Dŏm-ī-nē, nŏn nōbis, sĕd nōm-in-ē tū-ō dā glō-rī-ăm	Not to us, O Lord! not to us, but to Thy name give the glory.
Nornæ	Nŏr'nae	Signifying Past, Present and Future.
Notuma	Nō-tūm	Anagram of Aumont.
Novice Maconne	Nŏvice Ma-çon'ne .	Novice Má-sŏn-né.
Novitiate .	Nō-vish'e-āte	A person under probation.
Nuk-pe-nuk	Nŭk'pē-nŭk . .	"I am that I am."
Nyaya . . .	Nў-ā'yā . . .	A system of ancient Hindu philosophy.
Nyctazontes	Nўc'tā-zōn'tes	An ancient sect.

WORDS OF DOUBTFUL PRONUNCIATION.	PROPER MASONIC PRONUNCIATION.	NOTATIONS.
Oannes	Ō-ăn'nes . . .	
Oath . .	Ōth	Solemn affirmation.
Obligatory	Ob'lĭgā-to-rȳ. .	Binding in law or conscience.
Obsequies	Ob'sē-kwis	Funeral rites or solemnities.
Occult .	Ok-kult'	Secret, unknown.
Odious .	O'di-us .	Deserving hatred.
Off . . .	Off . . .	Not Awf. Away from.
Offer	Of'fer	Not Aw'fer. Present for acceptance.
Office	Of'fis	Not Aw'fis. Assumed duties or business.
Officiate	Of-fish'ĭ-āt	To act as an officer.
Often	Of'n	Not of'ten. Frequent.
Oheb Eloah	Ō-hĕb E-lō'ā	Love of God.
Oheb Karobo	Ō-hĕb kā-rō'bō	Love of neighbor.
Olibanum	Ol-ĭ-bă'num . .	An aromatic sap, frankincense
Omega . .	Ō-mē'gā	Last letter of Greek alphabet.
Omer	Ō'mĕr	A Hebrew measure.
Omnia Tempus Alit	Ŏm'nĭ-ă tĕm'pŭs ă'lĭt	Time heals all things.
On . . .	Ŏn' . .	A name for Jehovah among Egyptians.
Onech	Ō'nĕch	After Enoch or Phenoch (the Phœnix).
Onyx	Ō'nix . . .	A stone of the breastplate.
Ophites . .	Ō'phītes	Brotherhood of the Serpent.
Oral	Ō'ral	Verbal, by word of mouth.
Ordo ab Chao.	Ŏr'dō ăb chā'o	Order out of chaos.
Oriflamme .	Ō'rĭ-flamme .	Ancient banner of the Counts of Vexin.
Orion	O-rĭ'un	One of the constellation of stars.
Ormuzd and Ahriman	Ŏrmŭdsand Āh-rĭ-măn	Good and evil. Darkness and light.
Ornan	Ŏr'nan	Strong. Whose threshing floor became David's altar.
Osiris	Ō-sī'ris . .	Chief god of old Egyptian mythology.
Oterfut.	Ō'ter-fŭt .	The assassin at the west gate.
Otreb	Ō'trĕb . .	Pseudonym of Rosicrucian Michel Mayer.
Ouriel	Ou'rĭ-ĕl	
Overseer	O-ver-sēr .	Nutsach. One who inspects.
Ozee . .	Ō'zēē	Acclamation.
Oziah	O'zi-āh . .	A Prince of Judah.
Pachacamac	Păch'ā-cā'măc	Peruvian for Creator of the Universe.
Paganis, Hugo de	Pā-gā'nĭs, Hŭgō de	Latinized name of Hugh de Payens.
Palestine .	Pal-es'tine	Commonly called The Holy Land.
Palladium	Pal-lā'di-um . . .	That which is an effectual defense.
Paracelsus	Pā-rā-cĕl'sŭs . . .	Degree in MSS. collections of Peuvret.
Parent	Păr'ent	One who begets offspring.
Parian . .	Pā'ri-an	A fine quality of marble.
Parikchai Agrouchada	Pa'rĭk-chā'ī A'groū-chā'dā	An occult scientific work of Brahmans.
Parlirer	Păr'lĭr-er . .	Spokesmen.
Parsees . . .	Păr'sēs .	Followers of Zoroaster.
Pas perdus	Pás' pĕr-dŭs'	French name for room for visitors.
Pastophori	Păs'tō-phō'rĭ	Couch or shrine bearers.
Pastos . . .	Păs'tos . . .	Greek for couch.

WORDS OF DOUBTFUL PRONUNCIATION.	PROPER MASONIC PRONUNCIATION.	NOTATIONS.
Patent	Pat'ent	A letter securing certain rights.
Pax vobiscum	Pax vō-bes'cūm	Peace be with you.
Pectoral	Pĕk'tō-ral . .	Pertaining to the breast.
Pedal	Pē'dal	Pēdes, the feet.
Pedum	Pē'dūm. . . .	Literally, a shepherd's crook.
Peetash . . .	Peēt'ăsh . . .	The Demon of Calumny.
Peleg or **Phaleg** .	Pē'leg or Fā'leg	Division. A son of Eber.
Penance . .	Pen'ance . . .	Suffering as evidence of repentance.
Pentacle . .	Pĕn'tă-kl . . .	Two intersecting triangles.
Pentateuch .	Pĕn'tă-tūk . .	The five books of Moses.
Perambulate	Per-ăm'bu-lāte	To walk over.
Periclyte	Pĕr'ĭ-clȳte	
Perignan . .	Pĕr'ig-năn . .	See *Elect of Perignan.*
Persian . . .	Per'shan . . .	A country in Western Asia.
Pestle . . .	Pes'tl	An instrument for pounding.
Phaal Chol .	Fā'ăl Kōl . . .	Separated, driven apart.
Phainoteletian Society	Phāi'nō-tē-le'tian	Founded at Paris in 1840.
Pharaxal . .	Phā'răx-ăl	Division and subsequent reunion.
Pharaoh . .	Fā'ra-ō	A king, a sovereign.
Pharaoschol	Fā-rā-ōs'kōl . . .	Congregated, reassembled.
Philalethes .	Phĭ'lă-lē'thēs . .	Literally, Friends of Truth.
Philistine	Fĭ-lis'tĭn	An inhabitant of Philistia.
Philocoreites, Order of	Phĭ'lō-cō-re'ĭ-tes .	Established in French army in Spain [in 1808.
Phylacteries	Phȳ-lac'ter-ies	Ornaments.
Picart's Ceremonies	Pĭ'cart . .	By Bernard Picart.
Pilaster	Pĭ-las'ter	A partly projecting column.
Pilier . .	Pĭl'iĕr	A pillar or support of an edifice.
Pinceau	Pĭn'ceău	Pin-so. To act as secretary.
Pirlet	Pĭr'let	Organiser of Council of Knights of the East.
Pitaka	Pĭt'a-ka	The Bible of Buddhism.
Pitris	Pĭt'rĭs	Spirits.
Planche Tracee	Plan'che Tră-cēe	Designation for minutes in French [Lodges.
Pleiades . . .	Pley'a-dēs . .	A group of seven stars.
Polkal	Pōl'kăl	Altogether separated.
Polycronicon	Pōlȳ-crŏn'i-cŏn	Latin Chronicle by Ranulf Higden.
Pomegranate	Pōme'gran-ate	Adopted as the symbol of plenty.
Pomme Verte	Pōmme Vĕrtĕ .	Pō-m Vĕr-t.
Poniard	Pŏn'yard . . .	A small dagger.
Pontifes Frères .	Pŏn'ti-fēs Frĕres	Pon'te-fēes Frāres.
Pontiff . .	Pŏn'tiff .	A high priest.
Porch . .	Porch . .	Not Pawrch. A gate or entrance.
Position	Po-sish'un	Situation, station.
Postulant	Pŏs'tū-lănt	From Latin postulans—asking for.
Potens . .	Pō'tĕns	Powerful.
Potentate	Pō'tan-tăt .	One of high authority.
Poursuivant	Pour-su'ĭ-vănt	Poor-su'e-van.
Praxeans . .	Prăx'ō-ĕans	Followers of Praxeas.
Prelate .	Prĕl'ate . . .	A dignitary of the church.
Precept . . .	Pre'sept . . .	An injunction, mandate.

WORDS OF DOUBTFUL PRONUNCIATION.	PROPER MASONIC PRONUNCIATION.	NOTATIONS.
Presentation	Prĕz-en-ta'shun	Setting forth, a gift.
Princeps . .	Prĭn'cēps . . .	Chief.
Progress . .	Prog'res . . .	Advancement.
Proponenda	Prō'pō-nen'dă .	Subjects to be proposed.
Propylæum .	Prŏp'y-lae'um .	Court or vestibule in front of an edifice.
Pro tempore	Prō tĕm'pō-rē	For the present time.
Protean	Pro'tē-an .	Assuming different shapes.
Protocol	Prō'tō-kŏl .	The original writing.
Provost	Prŏv'ust . .	A presiding officer.
Prudence .	Prū'dence .	Wisdom applied to practice.
Psalms . .	Sāms . . .	A sacred song.
Psaterians	Psăt-ē'rians .	A sect of Arians.
Pseudonym .	Pseū-dō-nym	Sū'do-nim. False or fictitious name.
Puissant . .	Pū-is'sant	Powerful.
Pulsanti Operietur	Pul-san'ti Ŏpē-rĭ-ē-tur	To him who knocks it shall be opened.
Punjaub	Pun-jaub'. .	Pun-jawb.
Puranas	Pū-rā'nas . .	Text-books of worshipers of Vishnu.
Pursuivant .	Pŭr'sui-vant.	Per'swē-vant, messenger.
Pythagoras .	Py-thag'o-ras	School of, supposed model of Masonry.
Quadrivium and Trivium . .	Quăd-rĭv'i-um .	Trĭv'ĭ-um.
Quaternion . .	Quă-ter'nĭ-ŏn .	The number four.
Quetzalcoatl	Quet'zi-ăl'coatl	Kĕt'ze-al'cotl.
Rabbanaim	Răb'bă-nā'ĭm	Chief of the architects.
Rabbi . .	Răb'bē . . .	An eminent teacher.
Rabbinism	Răb'bĭn-ism	A Jewish system of philosophy.
Rabboni	Răb-bō'nī	My Rabbi. A most excellent Master.
Ragon . .	Ră'gŏn . . .	A noted Masonic writer of France.
Rahab . .	Ră'ab . . .	A name of Egypt.
Ramayana	Rā'ma-yā'na	The great epic of ancient India.
Raphodom	Răf'ō-dŏm .	A mystic word.
Ratisbon .	Răt'is-bon . .	A city of Bavaria.
Razahbelsijah	Ră-zăbĕl-sī'yă .	A mystic word.
Recognize	Rĕk'ŏg-nīz	To know again.
Recovery .	Rē-kuv'er-ĭ	Restoration.
Rectitude	Rek'tĭ-tūd	Straightness, justice.
Recusant .	Rē-cū'sant	Insubordinate.
Rehoboam	Rē-hō-bō'am	Son and successor of Solomon.
Rehum . .	Rē-hūm . .	A Persian officer.
Rendezvous	Ren'de-vōō .	An appointed place.
Requiem . .	Re'kwī-em	A hymn for the dead.
Research . .	Re-serch' . . .	Investigation, examination.
Resplendens	Rē-splen'dans . . .	Resplendent.
Restoravit pacem patri	Re-stō-răv'it pā-sĕm pătrī . . .	He restored peace to his country.
Reverent	Rev'er-ent.	Expressing veneration.
Revestiary	Re-vĕst'ĭ-a-ry . . .	Wardrobe, place for sacred vestments.

WORDS OF DOUBTFUL PRONUNCIATION.	PROPER MASONIC PRONUNCIATION.	NOTATIONS.
Rex regum dominus dominorum	Rex regum dŏm-ĭ-nŭs dominōrum	King of King and Lord of Lords.
Robelot	Rō'bē-lŏt . . .	A distinguished French Mason.
Rose Croix	Rōse Croix . .	Roz-crwa. Literally, Rose Cross.
Rosenkreuz, Christian	Rō'sen-kreuz .	See *Rosicrucianism*.
Rosicrucians	Rōs'ĭ-crū'cians	A Brotherhood of the 14th century.
Route .	Root . . .	The course or way.
Ruchiel .	Rŭch'ĭ-el .	Rōōch'e-el.
Saadh	Sā'ădh . .	Literally, hosts.
Sabaism	Săb'a-ism	Worship of the sun, moon, and stars.
Sabaoth	Să-bā'ōth .	Jehovah of Hosts.
Sabbal	Săb-bal' .	Mystic word, Scottish Rite.
Sabianism	Săb'ĭ-an-ism	Same as *Sabaism*.
Sacellum .	Să-cĕl'lum	A walled enclosure without roof.
Sacerdotal	Sas-er-dō'tal	Pertaining to the order of priests.
Sacrifice	Săk'rĭ-fīz . .	An offering. [cestor of Jesus.
Sadoc .	Să'dok . . .	Heb., just. Father of Achim, an-
Sadonias	Sa-dō'ne-as .	Significant word in the higher de-
Sagitta .	Să-git'ta	The keystone of an arch. [grees.
Saint Adhabell	Saint Ad'hă-bell . .	Evidently meaning St. Amphibalus.
Saint Amphibalus	Saint Am'phĭ-bal'us	
Saint Nicaise .	Saint Nĭ-caise	Title of a sensational Masonic work.
Sakinat . .	Să'kĭ-năt	The Divine presence.
Sakti	Săk'tĭ	The female energy of Siva.
Salah-eddin	Să-lăh-ed-deen' . .	King of Kings.
Salix . . .	Săl'ĭx	Initials forming part of a sentence.
Salle des Pas Perdus	Săllè des Păs' Per-dūs'	The Hall of the Last Steps.
Salsette	Săl-sĕtte'	An island in the Bay of Bombay.
Salute . .	Sa-lūt'	To greet, to hail.
Salutem .	Sal-ū'tĕm	Health, a Roman greeting.
Samaritan	Sa-măr'ĭ-tan.	Of the principal city of the Ten
Samothracian	Să-mō-thră'cĭ-an . . .	See *Mysteries of Cabiri*. [Tribes.
Sanctum Sanctorum	Sănk'tŭm Sănk-tō-rūm	Holy of Holies.
San Graal	Săn Grăăl .	An emerald dish.
Sanhedrim .	Săn-he-drĭm	Highest judicial tribunal of the Jews.
Sapicole	Să'pĭ-cōle .	Cited in the nomenclature of Fustier.
Saracens	Săr'a-cens	Arabic followers of Mohammed.
Sardius .	Săr'de-us .	A precious stone of the breastplate.
Sarsena	Sar-sē'nă . .	Pretended exposition of Freema-
Sat B'hai .	Săt B'hăi' . . .	Sot-b-hoi'. [sonry.
Satrap . .	Săt'rap or Sa'trap	A local Eastern ruler.
Scarabæus	Skăr'ă-bē-us	An insect with wings cased.
Schism . .	Sizm	Division, separation.
Schismatic .	Schis-măt'ic . . .	Insubordinate Masons.
Schor-Laban	Schor-Lăban' . .	White Ox, or Innocence.
Secretary . .	Sek're-tă-rĭ	A superintending officer of records.
Sefidd Schamagan	Sē-fĭdd Schă'mă-gan	A secret Moslem society.
Sejjin	Sĕj'jin	Arabic register of all the wicked.
Selah	Sē'lăh	A pause or musical note.

WORDS OF DOUBTFUL PRONUNCIATION.	PROPER MASONIC PRONUNCIATION.	NOTATIONS.
Selamu Aleikum .	Sĕ-la′mū Ă′lĕi-kūm	Se-lä′moo A′li-koom.
Semester .	Sĕ-mĕs′ter .	Semi-annual word used only in France.
Seneschal	Sĕn′e-shal .	A steward.
Seniority	Seen-yŏr′ĭ-ty	Priority, or superiority in rank.
Sephiroth	Sĕph′i-rŏth .	From Saphiri—splendid.
Seraphim	Sĕr′ă-fim . .	An angel of the highest order.
Serai . . .	Se-ră′e . . .	A rest house.
Serapis . .	Se-ră′pis . .	An Egyptian deity.
Seah Bazzar	Sĕsh bas-zăr′	A name of Zerubbabel.
Sethos . . .	Sĕ′thŏs . . .	A popular work published in 1731.
Shaddai . .	Shăd-dă-ī	One of the names of God.
Shalal Shalom Aba .	Shăl′ăl Shăl′ŏm Ăb′ba	He restored peace to his father.
Shalash esrim	Shăl′ăsh ĕs-rem	Twenty-third.
Shamir . .	Shăm′ĭr	The worm used for building the Temple.
Shastras	Shăs′trăs	The sacred book of the Hindus.
Shaveh . .	Shă′vă . .	A valley in Palestine.
Shealtiel	Shē-ăl′te-el	Father of Zerubbabel, who led back the Jews from Babylon.
Shebat . .	Shē-băt . .	Fifth month of Hebrew civil year.
Shekel . .	Shĕk′l . .	A Jewish coin. Value about 62 cents.
Shekinah .	Shē-kī-năh .	To dwell.
Shelomoth .	She′lŏ-mŏth .	Peacefulness.
Shelum lecka	Shē-lūm leck′ă . .	Password of the Order of Felicity.
Shem Ham Phorash	Shem hăm fŏ′răsh .	The unsolved mystery. The name.
Shemitic . . .	Shĕm-it′ic . . .	An historical religious division.
Shesha	Shē′shă	Free, noble.
Shetharbosnai	Shē-thar-bŏs′nă-ī	See *Tatnai*. A Persian officer.
Shibboleth .	Shĭb-bŏ′leth	An ear of corn. Stream of water.
Shimshai	Shims-shaī	
Shinar . .	Shī′năr . .	Babylonia in its fullest extent.
Shoulkain	Shŏul′kain	Stolkin, mentioned in A. A. S. R.
Shrine . .	Shrīn. . .	A hallowed place.
Shrub . .	Shrub. . .	Not Srub. A dwarf tree.
Shushan	Shū′shan .	The ancient capital of Persia.
Sic transit gloria mundi	Sĭk trăns′ĭt glŏr′ia mŭndī. . . .	Thus passes the glory of the world.
Sijel Al	Sĭg′el Ăl	Recording Angel in Islam.
Simeon .	Sĭm′e-on .	One of the tribes of Israel.
Simorgh	Sĭm′orgh .	Guardian of the Persian mysteries.
Sinai . .	Sī′năī	A mountain of Arabia.
Sirat . .	Sī′răt. . .	
Siroc . .	Sī′rŏc . .	Signifies a shoe-latchet.
Sivan . .	Sĭv′ăn . . .	The ninth Hebrew month.
Smaragdine	Sma-răg′dīne	Foundation of Hermetic knowledge.
Socius .	Sŏ′cī-ūs	6th Deg. of Order of Strict Observance.
Sofism . .	Sŏ′fism . .	A mystical religious sect of Persia.
Sojourn	Sŏ′jurn . .	Temporary residence.
Solemn . .	Sŏl′em . .	Reverential, devout.
Solomon .	Sŏl′ŏ-mon	King of Israel.

WORDS OF DOUBTFUL PRONUNCIATION.	PROPER MASONIC PRONUNCIATION.	NOTATIONS.
Solstice .	Sŏl'stis . .	The apparent stoppage of the sun.
Solus . . .	So'lus . .	Latin, alone.
Sorbonne .	Sŏr'bonne .	College of theological professors in Paris.
Southerly	Sŭth'er-le	Toward the South.
Spes mea in Deo est	Spĕs me'a in Deo' ĕst	My hope is in God.
Squarmen	Squăr'men	Companies of wrights, slaters, in Scotland.
Sruti . .	Srū'tī . . .	Revelation.
Stauros . .	Stou'rus . .	A stake. Cross.
Stibium	Stĭb'i-um . .	Antimony.
Steinmetz	Stĕin'mĕtz	German for stonemason.
St. Jean d'Acre	Shăn dă'ker .	The city Acca, taken by Richard I. in 1191 and given the new name.
Stolkin . .	Stŏl'kin .	Inspector of the Tribe of Benjamin.
Strength .	Strength	Not Strenth. Force, vigor.
Succoth	Suc-kōth' .	Heb., Booths. A place east of Jordan.
Sultan . .	Sŭl'tan . .	A Turkish sovereign.
Superficies	Sū'per-fĭsh-ēs	The surface, the face of a thing.
Summoned .	Sŭm'mund	Not Sum'mansd. Commanded.
Sword . .	Sŏrd . . .	Not Sword. Military officer's weapon.
Symbolic .	Sim-bŏl-ik	Relating to symbols.
Synagogue	Sĭn'a-gŏg	Place of Jewish worship.
Synod	Syn'od	A meeting, convention or council.
Syria . .	Sĭr'i-ă . .	Heb., Aram. East of the Mediterranean.
Systyle .	Sȳs'tȳle	An arrangement of columns.
Tabaor .	Tă'bă-or .	A name of Edom.
Tabernacle .	Tab'er-nă-kl	A temporary habitation.
Tableau .	Tab'lō . .	A vivid representation.
Tadmor	Tăd'mŏr .	City of Palms.
Talisman .	Tăl'iz-man	Magical charm.
Talith . .	Tăl'ĭth . .	An oblong shawl.
Taljahad	Tăl-jăh'ad	Angel of water.
Talmud .	Tăl'mud	The Hebrew laws and traditions.
Tamuz . .	Tă'mŭz	The tenth Jewish month.
Tapestry	Tap'es-trē	Woven hangings.
Tarshatha	Tăr-shă'thă .	See *Tirshatha*.
Tassel	Tăs'sĕl . . .	A pendant ornament.
Tatnai . .	Tăt'nă-ī . .	A Persian officer.
Tau . . .	Tău	The last letter of Hebrew alphabet.
Taurus . .	Tău'rŭs . .	Bull. A sign of the Zodiac.
Tchandalas .	Tchăn'dăl-as	A class of pariahs.
Tebet . . .	Ta'bet . . .	The fourth Jewish month.
Tebeth . . .	Te'bĕth.	Literally, winter.
Templum Hierosolymæ	Tĕm'plum Hī'ĕ-rō-sŏl'y-mæ	Latin for Temple of Jerusalem.
Tenets	Tĕn'-ets	Dogmas, doctrines and principles.
Tengu	Tĕn-gū	Initials of a sentence.
Tenzio-Dai-Sin .	Ten'zī-o-Daī'-Sin	A deity held in adoration by Japanese.
Teraphim	Tĕr'ă-fim	Household deities.
Tessellated . . .	Tĕs'se-lā-ted . .	Ornament of a lodge.

WORDS OF DOUBTFUL PRONUNCIATION.	PROPER MASONIC PRONUNCIATION.	NOTATIONS.
Tessera .	Tĕs′sĕ-rā . .	Tessera Hospitalis, token of the guest.
Tetractys .	Tē-trăc′tȳs .	The number four.
Tetradites	Tĕt′rā-dītes .	Believers in a Godhead of four persons.
Tetragram	Tĕt′ra-grăm . . .	A four-letter word.
Tetragrammaton	Tet′ra-gram-ma-ton	Signifies a word of four letters.
Teutonic	Tū-ton′ĭk . .	Relating to the ancient Germans.
Thammuz	Thăm′mūz . .	Syrian god Adonis.
Thebet .	Thā′bet	Same as *Tebet*, above.
Thebounah .	The-bū′nā	A mystic word in Kadosh.
Theopaschites	Thē′o-pas′chītes	Followers of Peter the Fuller.
Theoricus	Thē-or′ī-cūs	12th Degree of German Rose Croix.
Therapeutæ	Thĕr′a-peū′tæ	Ascetic sect of Jews in first A. D.
Theriog . .	Thē′rī-ŏg .	
Theurgy	Thē-ŭr′gy	Magic operated by celestial means.
Thokath	Thō′kăth .	Strength.
Thummim	Thum′mim	See *Urim and Thummim*. Truth.
Tiara	Te-ā′rā .	A crown. The Pope's triple crown.
Tiberius	Tī-be′re-ŭs	A city of Palestine.
Tiluk	Tī′lūk . .	Impress upon forehead of Brahman.
Timbre .	Tĭm′brē	Name given in France to a stamp.
Tirshatha	Tĭr-shā′thā	Title of Persian governors of Judea.
Tisri .	Tĭs′rī . .	The first Hebrew month.
Tito	Tī-tō	A favorite of the King of Israel.
Torgau .	Tŏr-gău	A fortified town on the Elbe.
Tortuous .	Tŏrt′ū-us .	Deviating from rectitude.
Traveler	Trăv′el-er	One who journeys.
Tredic	Trĕd′ic	The ranking king in Scan. Mysteries.
Trestle	Trĕs′sel	The designing board.
Triad .	Trī′ăd	The union of three objects.
Tribute	Trĭb′ūte	A subsidy or tax.
Triglyphs .	Trī′glifs	An ornament in the Doric Order.
Triliteral .	Trī-lit′e-ral	Sacred name of God among Hindus.
Trimurti	Trī-mūr′tē	The Hindu Trinity.
Trinosophs .	Trī′nō-sophs	A lodge instituted at Paris in 1816.
Tripitaka .	Trī-pit′ā-kā .	Canonical book of the Buddhists.
Triune	Trī′ūn . .	Three in one.
Tsaphiel	Tsā′phī-el	Sā′fē-ēl. The Luna angel.
Tsedakah .	Tse-dā-kāh	First step of the mystical ladder.
Tsidoni .	Tsī-dō-ni	An enquirer.
Tsoim	Tsō′ĭm	Sō-ĭm.
Tuapholl .	Tū-ā-pholl	A term used by the Druids.
Tubal Cain .	Tū-băl Că′ĭn	Son of Lamech and Zillah.
Tunic	Tū′nĭk . .	The long undergarment of the clergy.
Turcopolier	Tŭr′cō-pō-li′er	Commander of cavalry.
Turquoise	Tŭr-quōīse	Tur-koā-z. A stone in breastplate.
Tuscan .	Tŭs′căn	An order of Architecture.
Typhon	Tȳ′fōn . .	The Egyptian evil deity.
Tyrian .	Tĭr′e-an	Relating to Tyre.

PRONOUNCING DICTIONARY

WORDS OF DOUBTFUL PRONUNCIATION.	PROPER MASONIC PRONUNCIATION.	NOTATIONS.
Unaffiliated.	Ŭn-af-fil'ē-ā-ted	Not a member.
Unhele .	Ŭn-hele'	To uncover or reveal.
Unison .	Yū'ne-sun	Harmony, concord.
Upadevas .	Ū'pă-de'văs .	
Upanishad	Ū'păn-ĭsh-ăd	Name for certain Sanskrit works.
Ur .	Ūr	Fire, light, or spirit.
Uri .	Ū'rī	Heb., Enlightened. Son of Hur.
Uriel	Ū'ri-el	God is light.
Urim .	Ū'rim	Lights.
Usage	Yū'zij	Custom, use, habit.
Utopia	Ū-tō'pe-a .	Ideal perfection.
Usurp	Ū-zŭrp'.	Seize and hold possession.
Vagao	Vă'gă-ō	Found in French Rite of Adoption.
Valorous	Văl'or-ŏŭs	Brave, courageous.
Vase	Văs	An ornamental vessel.
Vashti	Văsh'tē .	Wife of Ahasuerus.
Veadar .	Vē'ă-dar	That is, the second Adar.
Vedas	Vē'dăs	Sacred canon of the Hindus.
Vehm-gericht.	Vĕhm'-gĕr-ĭcht'	See *Secret Tribunal of Westphalia.*
Verger	Vĕr'jer	An attendant upon a dignitary.
Veritas .	Ver'i-tas	Truth.
Vesica Pisces	Vĕs'ĭ-ca Pis-cis	The air-bladder of a fish.
Vespasian	Ves-pa'sian	
Vexillum Belli	Vĕx-il'lum Bellī	A war flag. [other.
Vicegerent	Vis'gē-rent	An officer authorized to act for an-
Vielle-Bru	Vī'elle Brū	V-ie-l Brū, Rite of, established 1748.
Vincere aut Mori	Vin'cē-rē ăut Mori .	To conquer or to die.
Vineyards	Vin'yărds .	A plantation of vines.
Vitra .	Vī'tră	A Mohammedan sect, established
Viva voce	Vē'vă vō'să .	By word of mouth. [1740.
Vivat .	Vī'văt	Vivat! vivat! vivat! Acclamation.
Voishnuvus .	Vō-ĭsh'nū-vŭs	
Volutes .	Vō'lūts .	A spiral ornament in Architecture.
Vouch	Vouch	To attest or bear witness.
Wahabites	Wă'hă-bītes .	Represents the opponents of Ma-
Warrant	Wŏr'rant	Commission, authority. [sonry.
Westward	West'ward	Not West'urd. Toward the West.
Wilhelmsbad	Wil'helms-băd .	A city of Germany.
Wolfenbuttel	Wŏl-fen-bŭttel	A city of Lower Saxony.
Worship	Wŭr'ship .	Title of honor. To adore.
Worthy .	Wŭr'the	Estimable, possessing merit.
Xerophagists	Xē'ro-pha'gists	Eaters of dry food.
Xinxe	Xin'xe .	The seat of the soul.
Xysuthrus	Xys'ū-thrŭs	Zis'ū-thrŭs.
Yah, Yeva, Yod	Yă, Yăvă, Yŏd	Corrupt names of the Deity.
Yaksha .	Yăk'shă	Hindu deity.

WORDS OF DOUBTFUL PRONUNCIATION.	PROPER MASONIC PRONUNCIATION.	NOTATIONS.
Yaveron Hamaim	Yă've-rŏn Hă'măim	The passage of the river.
Yezdegerdian	Yĕz'dĕ-gĕr'dian	Pertaining to the era of Yezdegerd.
Yezidee .	Yĕz'i-dēe	A sect bordering on the Euphrates
Yggdrasil .	Ygg-dră'sil	Sacred tree, Scandinavian mythology.
Y-ha-ho	Y-hă'hō	Signifying the Eternal God.
Yod	Yŏd . . .	A Hebrew letter.
Yoni . .	Yō'nĭ . .	A female symbol of the Orientalists.
Zabud	Ză-bŭd . .	An historical personage at Solomon's court.
Zabulon	Ză'bū-lŏn .	Tenth son of Jacob.
Zadok .	Ză'dŏk . .	Righteous. Son of Ahitub, a priest.
Zadki-el	Zăd'kĭ-el	Angel of the planet Jupiter.
Zaherlaherbon	Ză-her'lă-her-bon' . .	
Zaphnath-paaneah	Zăph-năth-paa'ne'ăh .	Savior of the world.
Zarathustra	Ză'ra-thŭs-tră . .	Name of Zoroaster in Zend language.
Zarriel . .	Zăr'rĭ-el	The angel that governs the sun.
Zarthan . .	Zăr'thăn	See *Zeredatha.*
Zebedee . .	Zĕb'e-dē Zeb-ē'de .	Jah is gift. Husband of Salome.
Zedekiah . .	Zĕd'e-kī'ă . .	Jah is might. A false prophet.
Zend-Avesta	Zĕnd Ă-vĕs'tă	Persian Bible in Zend language.
Zennaar .	Zĕn'năăr . . .	Sacred cord used in Hindustanee initiation.
Zeraias . . .	Zē-răi'ăs . . .	
Zerbal . . .	Zĕr'băl	King Solomon's Captain of Guards.
Zeredatha	Ze-rĕd'ă-tha .	See *Clay Ground.*
Zerubbabel .	Zē-rŭb-ba'bel	A prince of the House of Judah.
Zeus . . .	Zē'ūs . . .	The chief deity of the Greeks.
Zicu . . .	Zĭ'cū . . .	
Zif	Zĭf	Blossom. The second Jewish month.
Zipporah .	Zĭp-pō'ră	Little bird. Wife of Moses.
Zithern	Zĭth'ern .	A musical instrument of 28 strings.
Zizon	Ze'zōn . .	Balustrade.
Zodiac . .	Zō'de-ak .	An imaginary belt in the heavens.
Zohar . .	Zō'hăr . .	Distinction, nobility.
Zohariti	Zō'ha-rī'tī .	Nobility.
Zoroaster .	Zō-rō-as'ter	Founder of the Parsee religion.
Zschokke .	Zschŏk'kē	An eminent German Masonic author.
Zuni . . .	Zū'nĭ . .	Indian tribe of New Mexico.
Zurthost .	Zŭr-thōst .	Modern Parsee name for Zoroaster.
Zuzim . .	Zū'zim . .	Strong. A primitive race.

ORDER OF THE EASTERN STAR

By Robert I. Clegg

Degrees for women, under the title of the "Masonry of Adoption", were as long ago as 1765 in vogue on the continent of Europe. These were administered under the patronage of the ruling Masonic body and especially flourished in the palmy days of the Empire in France, the Empress Josephine being at the head of the Order and many women of the highest standing were active members.

The term "Adoption", so it is said, was given to the organization because the Freemasons formally adopted the ladies to whom the mysteries of the several degrees were imparted.

Albert Pike, who took great interest in this "Masonry of Adoption" and made a translation of the ritual into English with some elaboration dictated by his profound knowledge of symbolism and philosophy, points out the reason that in his judgment existed for the conferring of degrees upon the women of a Mason's family. He says in the preface to his ritual of the Masonry of Adoption, "Our mothers, sisters, wives and daughters cannot, it is true, be admitted to share with us the grand mysteries of Freemasonry, but there is no reason why there should not be also a Masonry for them, which may not merely enable them to make themselves known to Masons, and so to obtain assistance and protection; but by means of which, acting in concert through the tie of association and mutual obligation, they may cooperate in the great labors of Masonry by assisting in and, in some respects, directing their charities, and toiling in the cause of human progress. The object of 'la Maçonnerie des Dames' is, therefore, very inadequately expressed, when it is said to be the improvement and purification of the sentiments."

The Order of the Eastern Star has become just such an organization, strong enough to take an active and powerful cooperative concern in the beneficent labors of Masons for the care of the indigent and the afflicted. While entirely different and distinct from the Masonry of Adoption, being indeed of American and not French development, all the expectations so ably expressed by Brother Pike have in no other fraternal association been so admirably fulfilled as in the Order of the Eastern Star.

Some mystery involves the origin of the Order. In this respect the Order of the Eastern Star is closely akin to the various branches of the Masonic brotherhood. To unravel the truth from the entanglement of myth is, with many of these knotty problems, a troublesome and perhaps a never wholly satisfactory task. Evidence having few and incomplete records, dependent rather upon memory than in documents of authority is the usual subject-matter of discussion when laboring at the historic past of human institutions.

First of all let us take the testimony of Brother Rob Morris, than whom no one person has, it is conceded, given more freely of his service in the early development of the Order. None ought to know of the Eastern Star's inception story more than he, the acknowledged pioneer propagandist during its tender infancy and struggling youth.

During the latter part of 1884 Brother Rob Morris gave an account of the origination of the Eastern Star, which is in part as follows:

"In the winter of 1850 I was a resident of Jackson, Mississippi. For some time previous I had contemplated, as hinted above, the preparation of a Ritual of Adoptive Masonry, the degrees then in vogue appearing to me poorly conceived, weakly wrought out, unimpressive and particularly defective in point of motive. I allude especially to those degrees styled the Mason's Daughter, and the Heroines of Jericho. But I do expressly except from this criticism, the Good Samaritan, which in my judgment possesses dramatic elements and machinery equal to those that are in the Templar's Orders, the High Priesthood, the Cryptic Rite, and other organizations of Thomas Smith Webb. I have always recommended the Good Samaritan, and a thousand times conferred it in various parts of the world.

"About the first of February, 1850, I was laid up for two weeks with a sharp attack of rheumatism, and it was this period which I gave to the work in hand. By the aid of my papers and the memory of Mrs. Morris, I recall even the trivial occurrences connected with the work, how I hesitated for a theme, how I dallied over a name, how I wrought face to face with the clock that I might keep my drama within due limits of time, etc. The name was first settled upon—The Eastern Star. Next the number of points, five, to correspond with the emblem on the Master's carpet. This is the pentagon, 'The signet of King Solomon,' and eminently proper to Adoptive Masonry.

"From the Holy Writings I culled four biographical sketches to correspond with my first four points, viz., Jephthah's Daughter (named 'Adah' for want of a better), Ruth, Esther, and Martha. These were illustrations of four great congeries of womanly virtues, and their selection has proved highly popular. The fifth point introduced me to the early history of the Christian Church, where, amidst a noble army of martyrs, I found many whose lives and death overflowed the cup of martyrdom with a glory not surpassed by any of those named in Holy Writ. This gave me Electa, the 'Elect Lady', friend of St. John the Christian woman whose venerable years were crowned with the utmost splendor of the crucifixion.

"The colors, the emblems, the floral wreaths, the esotery proper to these five heroines, were easy of invention. They seemed to fall ready-made into my hands. The only piece of mechanism difficult to fit into the construction was the cabalistic motto, but this occurred to me in ample time for use.

"The compositions of the lectures was but a recreation. Familiar from childhood as I had been with the Holy Scriptures, I scarcely needed to look up my proof texts, so tamely did they come to my call. A number of odes were also composed at that time, but the greater part of the threescore odes and poems of the Eastern Star that I have written were the work of subsequent years. The first Ode of the series of 1850 was one commencing 'Light from the East, 'tis gilded with hope.'

"The theory of the whole subject is succinctly stated in my 'Rosary of the Eastern Star,' published in 1865: To take from the ancient writings five prominent female characters, illustrating as many Masonic virtues, and to adopt them into the fold of Masonry. The selections were: I. Jephthah's Daughter, as illustrating respect to the binding force of a vow; II. Ruth, as illustrating devotion to religious principles; III. Esther, as illustrating fidelity to kindred and friends; IV. Martha, as illustrating undeviating faith in the hour of trial; and V. Electa, as illustrating patience and submission under wrong. These are all Masonic virtues, and they have nowhere in history more brilliant exemplars than in the five characters presented in the lectures of the Eastern Star. It is a fitting comment upon these statements that in all the changes that the Eastern Star has experienced at so many hands for thirty-four years, no change in the names, histories or essential lessons has been proposed.

"So my Ritual was complete, and after touching and retouching the manuscript, as professional authors love to do, I invited a neighboring Mason and his wife to join with my own, and to them, in my own parlor, communicated the Degrees. They were the first recipients—the first of twice fifty thousand who have seen the signs, heard the words, exchanged the touch, and joined in the music of the Eastern Star. When I take a retrospect of that evening—but thirty-four years ago—and consider the abounding four hundred Eastern Star Chapters at work today, my heart swells with gratitude to God, who guided my hand during that period of convalescence to prepare a work, of all the work of my life the most successful.

"Being at that time, and until a very recent period, an active traveler, visiting all countries where lodges exist—a nervous, wiry, elastic man, unwearying in work—caring little for refreshments or sleep, I spread abroad the knowledge of the Eastern Star wherever I went. Equally in border communities, where ladies came in homespun, as in cities, where ladies came in satins, the new degree was received with ardor, and eulogized in strongest terms, so that every induction led to the call for more. Ladies and gentlemen are yet living who met that immense assemblage at Newark, New Jersey, in 1853 and the still greater one in Spring Street Hall, New York City, a little earlier, where I stood up for two hours or three, before a breathless and gratified audience, and brought to bear all that I could draw from the Holy Scriptures, the Talmud, and the writings of Josephus, concerning the five 'Heroines of the Eastern Star.'

"Not that my work met no opposition. Quite the reverse. It was not long until editors, report writers, newspaper critics and my own private correspondents, began to see the evil of it. The cry of 'Innovation' went up to heaven. Ridicule lent its aid to a grand assault upon my poor little figment. Ingenious changes were rung upon the idea of 'petticoat Masonry.' More than one writer in Masonic journals (men of an evil class—we had them; men who knew the secrets, but have never applied the principles of Masonry), more than one such expressed in language indecent and shocking, his opposition to the Eastern Star and to me. Letters were written me, some signed, some anonymous, warning me that I was periling my own Masonic connections in the advocacy of this scheme. In New York City the opponents of the Eastern Star even started a rival project to break it down. They employed a literary person, a poet of eminence, a gentleman of social merit, to prepare rituals under an ingenious form, and much time and money were spent in the effort to popularize it, but it survived only a short year and is already forgotten.

"But the Eastern Star glittered steadily in the ascendant. In 1855 I arranged the system of 'Constellations of the Eastern Star,' of which the 'Mosaic Book' was the index, and established more than one hundred of these bodies. Looking over that book, one of the most original and brilliant works to which I ever put my hand, I have wondered that the system did not succeed. It must be because the times were not ripe for it. The opposition to 'Ladies' Masonry' was too bitter. The advocates of the plan were not sufficiently influential. At any rate it fell through.

"Four years later I prepared an easier plan, styled 'Families of the Eastern Star', intended, in its simplicity and the readiness by which it could be worked, to avoid the complexity of the 'Constellations.' This ran well enough until the war broke out, when all Masonic systems fell together with a crash.

"This ended my work in systematizing the Eastern Star, and I should never have done more with it, save confer it in an informal manner as at first, but for Brother Robert Macoy of New York, who in 1868, when I had publicly announced my intentions of confining my labors during the remainder of my life to Holy Land investigations, proposed the plan of Eastern Star Chapters now in vogue. He had my full consent and endorsement, and thus became the instigator of a third and more successful system. The history of this organization, which is now disseminated in more than four hundred chapters, extending to thirty-three states and territories, I need not detail. The annual proceedings of Grand Chapters, the indefatigable labors of the Rev. Willis D. Engle, Grand Secretary of the General Grand Chapter, the liberal manner in which the Masonic journals have opened their columns to the proceedings of the Adoptive Order, the annual festivals, the sociables, concerts, picnics, etc., which keep the name of the Society before the public, make a history of their own better than I can write."

In another statement under date of 1884, Brother Morris further informs us: "Some writers have fallen into the error of placing the introduction of the Eastern Star as far back as 1775, and this they gather from my work, 'Lights and Shadows of Freemasonry,' published in 1852. What I intended to say in that book was that the French officers introduced Adoptive Masonry into the Colonies in 1775, but nothing like the degree called the Eastern Star, which is strictly my own origination."

The statements of Brother Morris are deserving of the utmost consideration and confidence. His devotion to Masonic service was long and honorable, freely acknowledged by his brethren with promotions to places of the highest prominence within their gift. We can thus approach his assertions confident of their accuracy so far as the intent of Brother Morris is concerned. Candor, nevertheless, compels the conclusion that our excellent brother did not in his various and valuable contributions to the history of the Eastern Star, and the related bodies, always clearly define his positions, and the studious reader is therefore somewhat in doubt whether on all occasions the meaning is unmistakable. For example, the foregoing references are in themselves very clear that Brother Morris was the originator of the Eastern Star. It is substantially shown in detail how the several items of consequence were actually put into practice by him.

Let us now briefly mention what may be set forth on the other side. The "Mosaic Book," by Brother Rob Morris, and published in 1857, says in Chapter II, Section 2: "In selecting some Androgynous Degree, extensively known, ancient in date, and ample in scope, for the basis of this Rite, the choice falls, without controversy, upon the 'Eastern Star.' For this is a degree familiar to thousands of the most enlightened York Masons and their female relations—established in this country at least before 1778—and one which popularly bears the palm in point of doctrine and elegance over all others. Its scope, by the addition of a ceremonial and a few links in the chain of recognition, was broad enough to constitute a graceful and consistent system, worthy, it is believed, of the best intellect of either sex."

Brother Willis D. Engle, the first R. W. Grand Secretary of the General Grand Chapter of the Order, says on page 12 of his History that "The fact is that Brother Morris received the Eastern Star degree at the hands of Giles M. Hillyer, of Vicksburg, Mississippi, about 1849."

Puzzling as is this mixture of statements, there is the one possible explanation that in speaking of the Order, Brother Morris had two quite different things in mind and that he may have inadvertently caused some to understand him to be speaking of the one when he referred to the other, or to both, as the case might be. We know that he had received Adoptive degrees and we are well aware that he had prepared more than one arrangement of Eastern Star degrees or of allied ceremonies. What more likely that in speaking of the one his thoughts should dwell upon the other; the one, Adoptive Masonry, being as we might say the subject in general; the other, the Eastern Star, being the particular topic. He could very properly think of the degree as an old idea, the Masonry of Adoption, and he could also consider it as being of novelty in the form of the Eastern Star; in the one case thinking of it as given him, and in the second instance thinking of it as it left his hands.

In any event, the well-known sincerity and high repute of Brother Morris absolve him from any stigma of wilful misrepresentation.

Certainly it is due his memory that the various conflicting assertions be given a sympathetic study and as friendly and harmonious a construction as is made at all possible by their terms.

Another curious angle of the situation develops in "The Thesauros of the Ancient and Honorable Order of the Eastern Star as collected and arranged by the committee, and adopted by the Supreme Council in convocation, assembled May, 1793." A copy of this eighteen-page pamphlet is in possession of Brother Alonzo J. Burton, Past Grand Lecturer, New York. This book of monitorial instruction has been reprinted and does afford a most interesting claim for the existence of an Eastern Star organization as early as the eighteenth century.

A Supreme Constellation was organized by Brother Rob Morris in 1855 with the following principal officers: Most Enlightened Grand Luminary, Rob Morris; Right Enlightened Deputy Grand Luminary and Grand Lecturer, Joel M. Spiller, Delphi, Ind.; Very Enlightened Grand Treasurer, Jonathan R. Neill, New York, and Very Enlightened Grand Secretary, John W. Leonard, New York. Deputies were appointed for several States and by the end of 1855 seventy-five charters for subordinate Constellations had been granted. These Constellations were made up of five or more persons of each sex, with a limit of no more than twenty-five of the one sex, and several Constellations might be associated with a single lodge.

There subsequently arose a second governing body of which James B. Taylor of New York became Grand Secretary. This organization was known as the "Supreme Council of the Ancient Rite of Adoptive Masonry for North America." How much of a real existence was lived by this body is now difficult of determination because of the secrecy with which its operations were conducted. Early in the seventies it expired after a discouraging struggle for life.

Brother Morris was not a partner in the above enterprise and had in 1860 begun the organizing of "Families" of the Eastern Star. To use his own expression, "The two systems of 'Constellations' and 'Families' are identical in spirit, the latter having taken the place of the former." A further statement by Brother Morris was to the effect that the ladies who were introduced to the advantages of Adoptive Masonry under the former system retained their privileges under the latter. During the next eight years more than a hundred "Families" were organized.

Brother Robert Macoy of New York had in 1866 prepared a manual of the Eastern Star. In this work he mentions himself as "National Grand Secretary." He also maintained the semblance of a Supreme Grand Chapter of the Adoptive Rite. Brother Morris decided in 1868 to devote his life to Masonic exploration in Palestine. His Eastern Star powers were transferred to Brother Macoy, as has been claimed. The latter in later years described himself as "Supreme Grand Patron."

Still another attempt at the formal organization of a governing body occurred in 1873 at New York, when the following provisional officers of a "Supreme Grand Council of the World, Adoptive Rite," were selected: Supreme Grand Patron, Robert Macoy, of New York; Supreme Grand Matron, Frances E. Johnson, of New York; Associate Supreme Grand Patron, Andres Cassard, of New York; Deputy Supreme Grand Patron, John L. Power, of Mississippi; Deputy Supreme Grand Matron, Laura L. Burton, of Mississippi; Supreme Treasurer, W. A. Prall, of Missouri; Supreme Recorder, Rob Morris, of Kentucky; Supreme Inspector, P. M. Savery, of Mississippi. But nothing further came of this organisation except that when later on measures were taken to make a really effective controlling body, the old organisation had claimants in the field urging its prior rights, though to all intents and purposes its never more than feeble breath of life had then utterly failed.

The various bodies of the Order under this fugitive guidance became ill-assorted of method. Laws were curiously conflicting. A constitution governing a State Grand Chapter had in one section the requirement that "Every member present must vote" on petitions; which another section of the same constitution forbade Master Masons "when admitted to membership" from balloting for candidates or on membership. There was equal or even greater inconsistency between the laws of one State and another. Serious defects had been discovered in the ritual. Some resentment had been aroused over the methods employed in the propaganda of the Order. The time was ripe for a radical change.

Rev. Willis D. Engle, in 1874, publicly proposed a Supreme Grand Chapter of Representatives from the several Grand Chapters and "a revision and general boiling down and finishing up of the ritual which is now defective both in style and language."

Not content with saying this was a proper thing to do, Brother Engle vigorously started to work to bring about the conditions he believed to be most desirable. Delegates from the Grand Chapters of California, Illinois, Indiana, Missouri, and New Jersey, met in Indianapolis, November 15-16, 1876, on the invitation of the Grand Chapter of Indiana.

Grand Patron, James S. Nutt, of Indiana, welcomed the visitors and opened the meeting. Brother John M. Mayhew, of New Jersey, was elected President, and Brother John R. Parson, of Missouri, Secretary. A Constitution was adopted, a committee appointed on revision of the ritual, and a General Grand Chapter duly organised.

The second session of the General Grand Chapter was held in Chicago, May 8-10, 1878, and the name of the organisation became officially "the General Grand Chapter of the Order of the Eastern Star." The Most Worthy Grand Patron was then the executive head, though in later years this was decided to be the proper province of the Most Worthy Grand Matron. In 1880 Mrs. Lorraine J. Pitkin, of Chicago, became the Most Worthy Grand Matron, and afterwards the Grand Secretary, being elected in 1883. She joined the Order in 1866.

The Grand Chapters with their dates of organisation are as follows:

Alabama	March 6, 1901
Alberta	July 20, 1912
Arizona	November 15, 1900
Arkansas	October 2, 1876
British Columbia	July 21, 1912
California	May 8, 1873
Colorado	June 6, 1892
Connecticut	August 11, 1874
District of Columbia	April 30, 1896
Florida	June 7, 1904
Georgia	February 21, 1901
Idaho	April 17, 1902
Illinois	November 6, 1875
Indiana	May 6, 1874
Iowa	July 30, 1878
Kansas	October 18, 1878
Kentucky	June 10, 1903
Louisiana	October 4, 1900
Maine	August 24, 1892
Maryland	December 23, 1898
Massachusetts	December 11, 1876
Michigan	October 31, 1867
Minnesota	October 18, 1878
Mississippi	May 29, 1906
Montana	September 25, 1890
Missouri	October 13, 1875
Nebraska	June 22, 1875
Nevada	September 19, 1905
New Hampshire	May 12, 1891
New Jersey	July 18, 1870
New York	November 31, 1870
New Mexico	April 11, 1902
North Carolina	May 20, 1905

North Dakota................June 14, 1894
Ohio.........................July 28, 1889
Oklahoma..............February 14, 1902
Ontario......................April 27, 1915
Oregon....................October 3, 1889
Pennsylvania............November 21, 1894
Porto Rico..............February 17, 1914
Rhode Island..............August 22, 1895
Saskatchewan................May 16, 1916
Scotland..................August 20, 1904
South Carolina...............June 1, 1907
South Dakota................July 10, 1889
Tennessee ....October 18, 1900
Texas........................May 5, 1884
Utah................September 20, 1905
Vermont..............November 12, 1873
Virginia....................June 22, 1904
Washington..................June 12, 1889
West Virginia...............June 28, 1904
Wisconsin..............February 19, 1891
Wyoming.............September 14, 1908

Of the above Grand Chapters there are three not constituent members of the General Grand Chapter. These independent bodies are New Jersey, New York, and Scotland.

Chapters of the Eastern Star are also to be found in Alaska, the Canal Zone at Panama, the Hawaiian Islands, the Philippine Islands, Manitoba, New Brunswick, Quebec, Cuba, Delaware, India, Mexico, and in the Yukon.

A Concordat or treaty agreement adopted by the General Chapter on September 20, 1904, and by a convention of Scottish Chapters of the Eastern Star held at Glasgow on August 20, 1904, was to the following effect:

"The Grand Chapter of Scotland shall have supreme and exclusive jurisdiction over Great Britain, Ireland, and the whole British dominions (excepting only those upon the Continent of America), and that a Supreme or General Grand Chapter of the British Empire shall be formed as soon as Chapters are instituted therein and it seems expedient to do so."

According to the terms of this agreement the territory in the East Indies wherein Chapters were already instituted, as at Benares and Calcutta, was ceded to the Grand Chapter of Scotland, which retains control. The other Chapters not so released are still under the jurisdiction of the General Grand Chapter.

The Most Worthy Grand Matrons of the General Grand Chapter of the Eastern Star have been the following:

Mrs. Elizabeth Butler, Chicago, Ill......1876
Mrs. Elmira Foley, Hannibal, Mo.......1878
Mrs. Lorraine J. Pitkin, Chicago, Ill....1880
Mrs. Jennie E. Mathews, Rockford, Ia...1883
Mrs. Mary A. Flint, San Juan, Calif.....1886
Mrs. Nettie Ransford, Indianapolis, Ind..1889
Mrs. Mary C. Snedden, Wichita, Kans...1892
Mrs. Mary E. Partridge, Oakland, Calif..1895
Mrs. Hattie E. Ewing, Orange, Mass....1898
Mrs. Laura B. Hart, San Antonio, Tex...1901
Mrs. Madeline B. Conkling, Checotah, Oklahoma..........................1904
Mrs. Ella S. Washburn, Racine, Wis.....1907
Mrs. M. Alice Miller, E. Reno, Okla......1910
Mrs. Rata A. Mills, Duke Center, Pa....1913
Mrs. Emma C. Ocobock, Hartford, Michigan..........................1916
Mrs. Ellie Lines Chapin, Pine Meadow, Conn..............................1919

Most Worthy Grand Patrons of the General Grand Chapter of the Eastern Star have been:

Rev. John D. Vincil, St. Louis, Mo......1876
Thomas M. Lamb, Worcester, Mass.....1878
Willis Brown, Seneca, Kansas..........1880
Rollin C. Gaskill, Oakland, Calif........1883
Jefferson S. Conover, Coldwater, Mich...1886
Benjamin Lynds, St. Louis, Mo.........1889
James R. Donnell, Conway, Ark.........1892
H. Harrison Hinds, Stanton, Mich......1895
Nathaniel A. Gearhart, Duluth, Minn...1898
L. Cabel Williamson, Washington, D. C..1901
William F. Kuhn, Kansas City, Mo.....1904
William H. Norris, Manchester, Ia......1907
Rev. Willis D. Engle, Indianapolis, Ind..1910
George A. Pettigrew, Sioux Falls, S. Dak...........................1913
George M. Hyland, Portland, Ore.......1916
Alfred G. McDaniel, San Antonio, Texas..........................1919

From 1876 to 1889 Rev. Willis D. Engle of Indianapolis was the Right Worthy Grand Secretary and he was succeeded by Mrs. Lorraine J. Pitkin, of Chicago.

www.ingramcontent.com/pod-product-compliance
Lightning Source LLC
Chambersburg PA
CBHW050548270326
41926CB00012B/1970

* 9 7 8 1 6 3 9 2 3 2 3 7 6 *